Sri Ramakrishna
and His Divine Play

SRI RAMAKRISHNA
and His Divine Play

Originally written in five volumes in Bengali
as *Sri Sri Ramakrishna Lilaprasanga* by
Swami Saradananda
a direct disciple of Sri Ramakrishna

Translated by
Swami Chetanananda

Vedanta Society of St. Louis

Library of Congress Cataloging-in-Publication Data

Saradananda, Swami, 1865-1927.
  [Sri Sri Rāmakrsna Līlāprasanga. English.]
  Sri Ramakrishna and his divine play / Swami Saradananda, Swami
Chetanananda.— 1st ed.
      p. cm.
Includes index.
In English translated from Bengali.
  ISBN 0-916356-81-7 (hard)
  1. Ramakrishna, 1836-1886. 2. Ramakrishna Mission—Biography. 3.
Hindus—India—Biography. I. Chetanananda, Swami. II. Title.
  BL1280.292.R36S266 2003
  294.5′55′092—dc22

2003021062

10 9 8 7 6 5 4 3 2 1

FIRST EDITION

Cover design by Diane Marshall
Printed in Canada

*Those who wish to learn in greater detail about the
teachings contained in this book may write to:*
Vedanta Society of St. Louis
205 S. Skinker Blvd.
St. Louis, MO 63105, U.S.A.

www.vedantastl.org

Translator's Note

Sri Ramakrishna and His Divine Play is a new translation of *Sri Sri Ramakrishna Lilaprasanga*, which was written in Bengali by Swami Saradananda, a monastic disciple of Sri Ramakrishna. This is the authentic, factual, descriptive, interpretive, and comprehensive biography of Sri Ramakrishna, the spiritual phenomenon of our age.

Sri Ramakrishna was born on 18 February 1836 and passed away on 16 August 1886. He enacted his divine play in three parts. First, he spent his early life (1836 to 1852) in the rural atmosphere of his native village, Kamarpukur. Second, he spent his adult life (1852 to 1885) in Calcutta and nearby Dakshineswar. He stayed in Calcutta with his brother for a couple of years, and then moved to the temple garden of Dakshineswar, where he lived for the next thirty years. It was in Dakshineswar that he practised various sadhanas, attained illumination, and began to promulgate his divine mission. Third, he spent the last year of his life (September 1885 to August 1886) in Calcutta and in the Cossipore garden house, where he brought his divine drama to its close by forming the future Ramakrishna Order.

Swami Saradananda wrote his magnum opus in five volumes, beginning with volumes three and four, then completing two, one, and five. He explained why he did not follow a chronological sequence as he worked: "Unless people understand how the Master remained in *bhavamukha* (an exalted state between the Absolute and the Relative) and how the mood of a guru was natural to him, they will not be able to comprehend the Master's wonderful character, unprecedented mental state, and extraordinary activities. That is why we tried to make the reader understand this subject at the outset." He published serially some parts of *Lilaprasanga* in the magazine *Udbodhan*, beginning in 1909 and continuing until 1919. He later said that it was because he was not inspired from within that he did not complete the last part of the Master's life with details about the daily events in Cossipore and an account of the Master's death.

It is amazing that Swami Saradananda was able to collect all of the important details about the Master's life even though he started writing this biography twenty-three years after the Master passed away. I have had the privilege of seeing the notebook in which he jotted down brief descriptions of incidents along with his sources of information. Swami Saradananda painstakingly gathered stories of the Master's early life from the villagers of Kamarpukur, and collected accounts of the Master's sadhana from the Master himself and also from his nephew and attendant Hriday. The Master's wife Sarada Devi, his relatives, his men and women devotees, and his disciples contributed many stories and eyewitness accounts. Swami Saradananda wrote in the preface to his fifth volume: "When we first started writing about the Master's divine play, we never imagined that we would proceed so far. It was possible only by his inconceivable grace." This detailed biography of Sri Ramakrishna is unique in spiritual literature; we can find no similar detailed accounts for Krishna, Buddha, or Christ.

The swami wrote in his preface to the third volume: "The Master told us explicitly again and again: 'He who was born as Rama and as Krishna in previous ages is now in this sheath' (*as he pointed to his own body*). 'The spiritual experiences of this place (*meaning himself*) have surpassed even the Vedas and Vedanta.' While recounting as impartially as possible the biography of Sri Ramakrishna, who was established in bhavamukha, we were forced to admit that such an extraordinary life had never before been seen in the spiritual world."

I humbly ask the reader to approach this book with an open mind. Sri Ramakrishna experimented with and verified the Truth, or God, like a scientist. He never taught anything that he had not experienced himself. Later, when Swami Vivekananda asked the Master, "Sir, have you seen God?" he replied without a moment's hesitation: "Yes, I have seen God. I see Him as I see you here, only more clearly. God can be seen. One can talk to Him." Thus, Sri Ramakrishna met the challenges raised by some of his English-educated disciples and dispelled their doubts. Even agnostics and atheists were dumbfounded when they saw the Master in samadhi. He never said anything that was contrary to reason, and he always encouraged his disciples to test his words before accepting them. His life is a glowing beacon in an age that is trying to recover its bearings in a turbulent sea of opinions about religion.

In addition to an account of the god-intoxicated life of Sri Ramakrishna, the reader will find in this book glimpses of mysticism, discussions of various religious and philosophical traditions of India, accounts of different religious leaders, and descriptions of the social customs, the educational system, and the socio-religious movements of nineteenth-century India. It is really astounding how Sri Ramakrishna, who had no formal education, overwhelmed the great savants and religious leaders of India with his spiritual power. In this book the reader will see how Sri Ramakrishna, the avatar of our modern age, lived and behaved, how he practised sadhana and taught spirituality, how he evaluated and trained his disciples by observing their physical characteristics and reading their minds as one would a book, how he used parables and folktales in his teachings, how he laughed and cried, sang and danced, made jokes like an ordinary human being, and at the same time frequently experienced spiritual visions and samadhi. It is important to see how Sri Ramakrishna's divine life reflected his phenomenal renunciation, passion for truth, childlike simplicity, complete lack of egotism, longing for God, and love for humanity.

This book bears witness to Sri Ramakrishna's testimony that all religions are equally valid. He found a place for each one in his own life. He first realized God by following Hindu practices, and then by following the Christian and Muslim paths. Such a journey is unique in the religious history of the world. He afterwards proclaimed, "As many faiths, so many paths," thus establishing an ideal harmony of religions for our present age, in which religions are in conflict and hatred and violence are rampant. He taught a religion so badly needed today, a religion that is constructive and not destructive, scientific and not fanatical, practical and not theoretical, rational and not superstitious, universal and not parochial. Truly, Sri Ramakrishna worked to create unity in our time and he repeatedly stated that the goal of human life is to realize God.

In Sri Ramakrishna's life can be found a synthesis of four yogas: karma, jnana, bhakti, and raja. And the philosophies of the three main schools of Vedanta — dualism, qualified nondualism, and nondualism — were blended in his teachings. He lived his life at the crossroads where many religious sects of India met. He never spoke a harsh word against anyone's faith. He was so all-embracing that members of every sect thought that he was one of them. His all-encompassing love and compassion transcended all sectarian narrowness and bigotry.

Truly, Sri Ramakrishna's life is a bridge between the ancient and the modern, between the East and the West. Five of his monastic disciples came to the West carrying the universal message of Sri Ramakrishna and Vedanta. Swami Vivekananda, the Master's foremost disciple, said: "This is the message of Sri Ramakrishna to the modern world: 'Do not care for doctrines; do not care for dogmas, or sects, or churches, or temples. They count for little compared with the essence of existence in each man, which is spirituality; and the more this is developed in a man, the more powerful is he for good. Earn that first, acquire that, and criticize no one, for all doctrines and creeds have some good in them. Show by your lives that religion does not mean words, or names, or sects, but that it means spiritual realization.'"

It is Sri Ramakrishna's infinite grace that he made me an instrument to translate the *Lilaprasanga*. It took me five years to complete this herculean task. It is the most difficult work I have ever done: First, translating the *Lilaprasanga* is difficult because its language is elegant and formal, and the sentences are long and full of clauses. Second, the *Lilaprasanga* contains many Sanskrit terms and Bengali colloquialisms, as well as technical and philosophical terms that are not so easy to translate into English. So I have tried to help the reader by supplying translations in parentheses or brackets, adding explanations in footnotes, and compiling a glossary. Third, Sri Ramakrishna's words and colloquial expressions have both extraordinary charm and profound meaning; it requires tremendous effort and skill to express them in English without losing their essence. Fourth, Sri Ramakrishna's life was his message: His biography is therefore an extremely important piece of literature, and the philosophy of the Ramakrishna Movement is based upon it. Much rests on the accuracy of this translation. I meditated on each word and each idea presented in *Sri Ramakrishna and His Divine Play* and tried my utmost to express this massive classic in the English language as perfectly as I could. As I worked, I imagined that each sentence was a flower offering to Sri Ramakrishna. May the Master forgive me if there is any mistake on my part.

Many swamis of the Ramakrishna Order, as well as many Western devotees, encouraged me in this endeavour and helped me to undertake this project. Swami Bhuteshananda, the 12th president of the Ramakrishna Order and a disciple of Swami Saradananda, deserves special mention: He answered many of my questions pertaining to the *Lilaprasanga* and approved the English title, *Sri Ramakrishna and His Divine Play*.

Swami Saradananda himself began to translate into English the first volume of the *Lilaprasanga*. This was published in *Prabuddha Bharata*, in the April, May, June, August, September, October, and December issues of 1915 and the April issue of 1916. (I saw his hand-written English manuscript.) He was unable to finish his translation of the first volume. Swami Sharvananda later completed this volume and published it in 1920 as *Sri Ramakrishna, the Great Master*. Swami Saradananda wrote to him: "I am glad you have taken up the translation of the Bengali life of the Master to satisfy the eagerness of the English-knowing general public, [who want] to learn all that is possible of that towering personality. And I wish you every success in your undertaking. I wish I could do it myself but I have not yet been permitted — and who knows whether I shall ever be in a position to do so or not?" In 1921, Swami Sharvananda translated part of the second volume. In 1952, Swami Jagadananda translated the entire *Lilaprasanga*; Ramakrishna Math, Chennai, published this version. I must express my indebtedness to those translators because I had the opportunity to compare my translation with theirs.

I worked directly from the most recently published *Lilaprasanga*, 22nd edition (1996). Swami Saradananda wrote his masterpiece in classical Bengali. I tried to translate his words as literally as possible, and at the same time I made a sincere effort to make the translation readable and understandable, faithful and beautiful. Of course, no translation can do full justice to the original. I followed the original format of the Bengali *Lilaprasanga*, wherein the author listed the contents in detail and used them as subtitles in boxes in the body of the book. If any reader finds flaws in my translation, I shall be glad to make corrections in the next edition. I have included photographs of Sri Ramakrishna as well as of persons and places connected with him so that the reader can visualize and experience the Master's divine play. At the end of my translation I have added a short biography of its great author, Swami Saradananda, who said, "Nothing beyond my spiritual experience has been recorded in this book." In fact, the swami was an excellent writer, a great historian, a profound philosopher, an ideal monk, and a genuine mystic. I humbly pray to the Master that this new translation of *Sri Sri Ramakrishna Lilaprasanga* may receive his blessing and satisfy the spiritual hunger of humanity.

Every biographer of Sri Ramakrishna, the Holy Mother, and the Master's disciples is indebted to Swami Saradananda's *Lilaprasanga* because it is the source book for the Master's life and message. Many writers have drawn on this source book, and the following works deserve special mention: *Life of Sri Ramakrishna*, published by Advaita Ashrama; *The Life of Ramakrishna* by Romain Rolland; *Ramakrishna and His Disciples* by Christopher Isherwood; and *The Life of Swami Vivekananda* by His Eastern and Western Disciples. I must express my gratitude to these authors for the help I received from their writings, but I always compared my translation with the original Bengali. In *Sri Ramakrishna and His Divine Play*, I used Swami Nikhilananda's translation of a few songs in *The Gospel of Sri Ramakrishna* and some verses from the Bhagavad Gita. I am grateful to the publishers of these books for granting me permission to do this.

Truly, I have no words to express my gratitude to my editors, proofreaders, typesetter, designer, and those who corrected the manuscript on the computer. It was teamwork, but I shall feel guilty if I do not acknowledge my editors: Kim Saccio-Kent (a freelance editor in San Francisco) edited my first draft with her professional skill; Linda Prugh (an English teacher in Kansas City) edited the manuscript, and prepared the glossary and chronology; Susan Menne (a former professor of journalism at California State University, Fullerton) edited the manuscript and created the index. Janice Thorup (a former adjunct professor of writing at Washington University, St. Louis), and Chris Lovato (an associate professor at the University of British Columbia, Vancouver) also edited the manuscript. Father Francis X. Clooney, S.J. (professor of theology at Boston College) read the manuscript and gave many valuable suggestions.

Romain Rolland wrote in *The Life of Ramakrishna*: "I am bringing to Europe, as yet unaware of it, the fruit of a new autumn, a new message of the Soul, the symphony of India, bearing the name of Ramakrishna. The man whose image I here evoke was the consummation of two thousand years of the spiritual life of three hundred million people. . . . In the life of Ramakrishna, the Man-God, I am about to relate the life of this Jacob's ladder, whereon the twofold unbroken line of the Divine in man ascends and descends between heaven and earth."

On 1 January 1886, Sri Ramakrishna blessed the assembled devotees at the Cossipore garden house, saying, "Be illumined." May the Master's blessing continue to grace humanity forever.

5 March 2003   Chetanananda
Sri Ramakrishna's birthday   St. Louis, U. S. A.

Contents

Detailed Chapter Contents

VOLUME ONE

INTRODUCTION AND EARLY LIFE

Introduction

1. The Need of the Age

2. Kamarpukur and Sri Ramakrishna's Ancestry

3. The Pious Family of Kamarpukur

4. Various Experiences of Chandradevi

5. The Birth of a Great Soul

6. Gadadhar's Childhood and the Death of His Father

7. Gadadhar's Boyhood

8. At the Threshold of Youth

VOLUME TWO

SRI RAMAKRISHNA AS A SPIRITUAL ASPIRANT

Introduction: The Necessity of Discussing Spiritual Practice

1. The Spiritual Aspirant and Spiritual Discipline

2. The Avatar as a Spiritual Aspirant

3. The First Manifestation as a Spiritual Aspirant

6. His Longing and First Vision

7. Sadhana and Ecstasy

8. Story of the First Four Years of Sadhana

12. Jatadhari and the Master's Sadhana of Vatsalya Bhava

13. The Quintessence of Madhura Bhava

14. The Master's Practice of Madhura Bhava

19. Death of the Master's Relatives

20. The Worship of Shodashi

21. Epilogue to the Master's Sadhana

VOLUME THREE

SRI RAMAKRISHNA AS A GURU — PART 1

2. A Discourse on Bhava, Samadhi, and Darshana

3. Sri Ramakrishna as a Guru

4. Early Manifestations of His Power as a Guru

5. As a Guru in His Youth

6. As a Guru, His Attitude Towards Mathur

7. As a Guru, the Master Bestows Grace on Mathur

8. As a Guru, the Master's Relationship with His Own Gurus

VOLUME FOUR

SRI RAMAKRISHNA AS A GURU — PART 2

2. Sri Ramakrishna as a Guru, and Sadhus of Various Orders

3. Pilgrimage of the Master as a Guru and
His Association with Holy Men

4. The Master as a Guru: Conclusion

5. Sri Ramakrishna in the Company of Devotees: The Nine-Day Festival in 1885

6. Sri Ramakrishna in the Company of Devotees: The Story of Gopal-ma, First Part

7. Sri Ramakrishna in the Company of Devotees: The Return Chariot Festival in 1885 and the Story of Gopal-ma, Last Part

Appendix: The Human Aspect of the Master

VOLUME FIVE

THE MASTER'S DIVINE MOOD
AND NARENDRANATH

3. Narendra's Early Life and His First Visit to Dakshineswar

4. Narendra's Second and Third Visits to the Master

5. The Master's Selfless Love and Narendra

6.1 The Master and Narendra's Divine Relationship

6.2 The Master and Narendra's Divine Relationship

7. The Master's Methods of Testing, and Narendra

8.1 Narendra's Education in the World and from the Master

8.2 Narendra's Education in the World and from the Master

10. The Great Festival at Panihati

11. The Master Moves to Calcutta

12.1 The Master's Stay at Shyampukur

12.2 The Master's Stay at Shyampukur

12.3 The Master's Stay at Shyampukur

13.1 The Cossipore Garden House

13.2 The Vow of Service to the Master at Cossipore

13.3 The Master Bestows Fearlessness through Self-Revelation

Illustrations

Volume Five: The Master's Divine Mood and Narendranath

Swami Saradananda: A Brief Biography

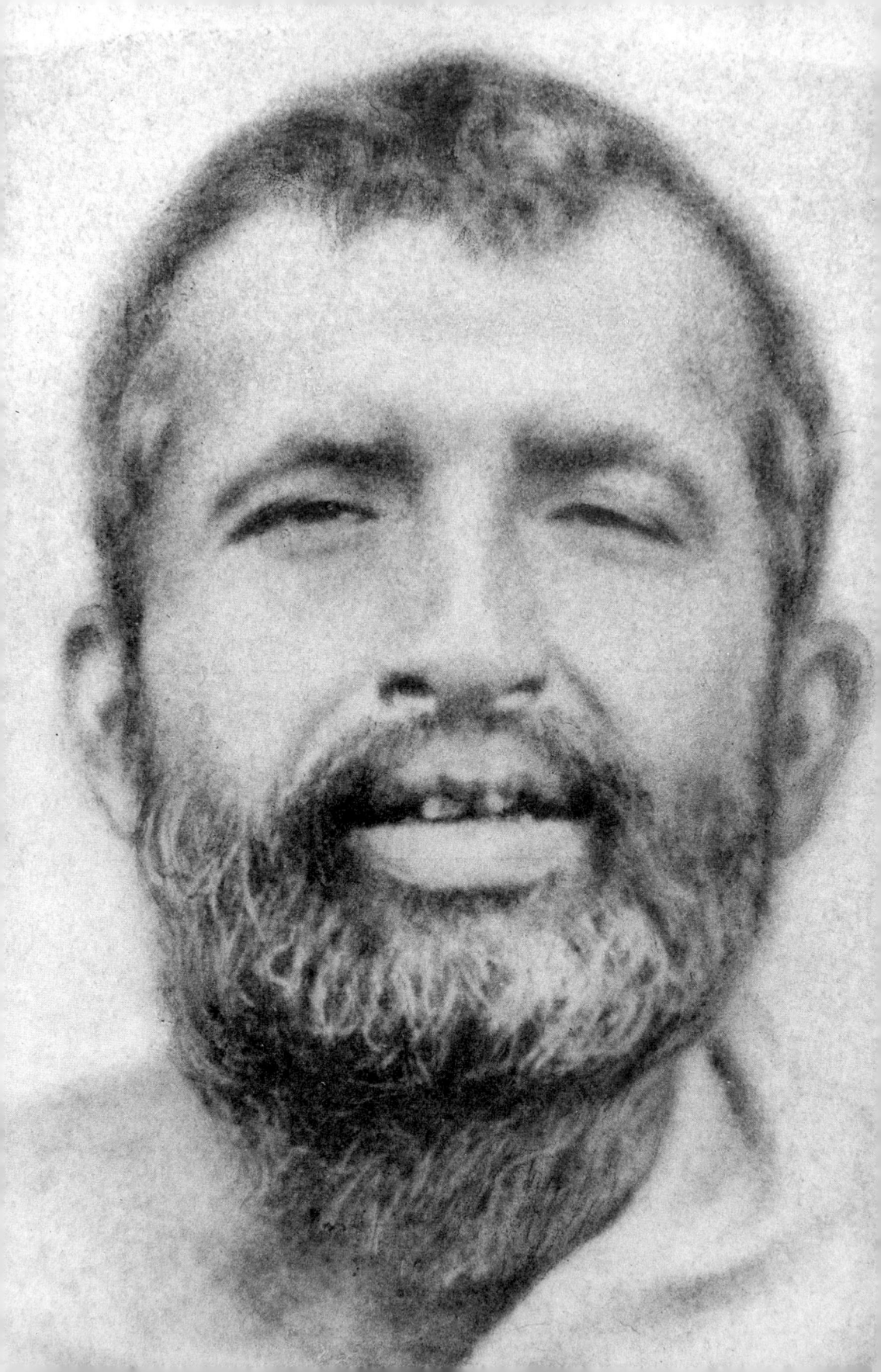

INTRODUCTION AND
EARLY LIFE

VOLUME ONE

Preface to Volume One

By God's grace a detailed account of Sri Ramakrishna's early life is now published. This account includes an introduction and an account of the purpose of his advent. We have tried to present for the reader the mental picture that we formed as we listened to various people narrate unconnected events that occurred early in his life. Sri Ramakrishna's nephews, Hridayram Mukhopadhyay and Ramlal Chattopadhyay, as well as other sources, helped us as best they could to ascertain the dates of some events, but some discrepancies still remain. They could not show us the astrological charts for Sri Ramakrishna's father, his elder brothers, or other close relatives, so they supplied us with dates by reasoning in this manner: "When Sri Ramakrishna was born, his father was sixty-one or sixty-two years old"; "Ramkumar, his elder brother, was thirty-one or thirty-two years old," and so on.

At any rate, there is no possibility of error regarding the date and year of Sri Ramakrishna's birth that we have recorded in this volume, as the reader will be convinced while reading the fifth chapter, "The Birth of a Great Soul." We were able to determine the date of the Master's birth from his own words, so he deserves our gratitude. Many incidents in this book were told to us by the Master himself. When we began writing of Sri Ramakrishna's divine play, we could not have believed that we would be able to record the events of his childhood and youth in such a detailed and connected way. But by the grace of the Lord — who makes the dumb eloquent and the lame scale mountains — we were able to do so. We bow down to Him again and again. If one reads volumes two, three, and four, after finishing this first volume, one will find the history of Sri Ramakrishna's life recorded chronologically from his birth to the year 1881.

The Author [Swami Saradananda]
Phalgun 1321 B.E. [mid-February to mid-March 1914]

Introduction

SIGNIFICANT DIFFERENCES EXIST BETWEEN THE SPIRITUAL ideals and religious

1. Religion is the soul of Indian life.	

beliefs of India and those of other countries. From time immemorial it has been apparent that India has truly and firmly committed itself to achieving the experience of transcendental realities such as God, the Atman, and the hereafter, and has concluded that the direct experience of these realities is the ultimate goal of both the individual and the collective national life. As a result, much of India's efforts and activities throughout the ages have been infused with an intense spirituality.

When one attempts to trace the reason for India's acquisition of such

2. Its cause is the regular reappearance of great souls.	

intense passion for transcendental realities, one finds that the only cause is the repeated appearance of illu-mined souls in India. Through observing and studying those mystics' visions and supernatural powers, the Indian people have developed a firm faith and deep interest in spiritual matters. Thus, from ancient times India's national life has been firmly based on spirituality, and this has created a unique society with social customs aimed at the direct real-ization of Truth. India's social rules and customs were formulated so that the nation and its inhabitants could gradually make progress by performing their daily duties in accordance with their temperaments, and finally attain spirituality or God-realization. Because the Indian people have followed these social rules from one generation to the next, the spiritual values of India have remained alive. Even today the Indian people strongly believe that each individual can experience God and attain union with Him by prac-tising austerities, self-control, and intense spiritual longing.

We can easily deduce that India's religion is based on the direct experience

3. Its proof: India's religion is based on the direct experience of God.	

of God when we evaluate the meaning of the words *rishi* [a seer of truth], *apta* [a realized soul], *adhikari* [a teacher with authority], or *prakriti-lina purusha* [a free soul absorbed in *prakriti*, primordial nature], and so on. Beginning in the

69

Vedic Age, these terms were used to describe the teachers who established religion. Undoubtedly such names were ascribed to these ancient seers because, after realizing transcendental reality, they demonstrated extraordinary powers. This can be said about all exalted persons from the rishis of the Vedic period to the avatars [divine incarnations] of the Puranic [Epic] period.

One sees that in the course of time the rishis of the Vedic period came to be regarded, in the Puranic Age, as divine incarnations. People in the Vedic period recognized some individuals as having had the experience of transcendental reality, but they could not differentiate between the degrees of these seers' powers and so were content to classify all of them as rishis. As people developed intellectually and their powers of discrimination increased, they realized that not all rishis were endowed with equal powers. Some rishis shed light on the spiritual world like a blazing sun, others like the moon, others like a bright star, and some like a firefly. In the age of classical Indian philosophy [from the sixth or seventh century onward] people began to classify the rishis. They concluded that while some rishis were capable of manifesting their special spiritual powers, others possessed them in a latent form. Some rishis were called *adhikari purushas*, or persons with special authority. Even Kapila, the founder of Sankhya philosophy, who did not believe in the existence of God, acknowledged the existence of those advanced rishis. Who can doubt a thing that is seen directly? The adhikari purushas were therefore referred to as *prakriti-lina* in the Sankhya scriptures that were written by Kapila and his followers. To ascertain the origin of these extraordinarily powerful beings, the Sankhya philosophers said:

> Endowed with purity, self-control, and other divine qualities, and capable of attaining full illumination, those great souls keep in their minds an intense desire to benefit humanity. For this reason they cannot, even for a moment, merge into the infinite, glorious Self. But, by the power of that desire, they become united with the all-powerful Prakriti and experience Her powers as theirs. Thus, equipped with six divine powers [knowledge, strength, lordship, power, virility, and splendour] they do good for humanity in various ways for a cycle and finally merge into the Self.

Again, according to their different degrees of power, the Sankhya teachers classified the prakriti-lina purushas into two groups: *kalpa-niyamaka ishwara* [the ruler of a cycle] and *ishwarakoti* [a godlike soul].

By the end of the Age of Philosophy, an era of *bhakti* [devotion] was highly developed in India. Through the profound message of Vedanta, Indians came to believe in a cosmic Personal God, the sum total of all beings. They also acquired the faith that by worshipping God with one-pointed devotion they could

4. Cause and concept of the evolution of the avatar in India. "Ruler of a cycle" according to Sankhya philosophy.

5. The Personal God during the era of *bhakti*.

achieve knowledge and reach the culmination of yoga. In Sankhya philosophy, the "ruler of a cycle" was transformed partly or fully into a cosmic Personal God, who is by nature eternally pure, illumined, and free. Thus, it is assumed that faith in avatars originated in the Puranic Age, and belief in the transformation of the great rishis into divine incarnations developed in the Vedic Age. It is clear that by observing the advent of extraordinary spiritual persons, Indians gradually developed faith in the incarnations of God. Based on the transcendental visions and experiences of those great souls, the unshakable edifice of Indian religion slowly rose to the sky, like the snowclad Himalayas. Because those great souls attained the highest goal of human life, the Indians called them *apta*; and their words became the Vedas, which are the culmination of knowledge.

Another reason that some prominent rishis became accepted as divine

6. Worship of the guru — another cause of people's faith in avatars.

incarnations was the practice of guru worship in India. From the period of the Vedas and Upanishads, the men and women of India worshipped their gurus, the givers of knowledge, with great reverence. In the course of time, that worship, in conjunction with meditation, convinced them that a person could not occupy the position of a guru unless he or she had been endowed with divine power. In comparing the selfish behaviour of ordinary people with the unconditional, compassionate service to humanity of real gurus, people for the first time began to worship gurus as superhuman beings. The more that worshippers became endowed with faith, reverence, and devotion, the more they witnessed the manifestation of the transcendental power of real gurus, and the more they were convinced of the gurus' divinity. For a long time ordinary people had prayed to the compassionate Lord to release them from bondage: "O Rudra, may Thy benign face protect us forever." Eventually, they grew convinced that their prayers came to fruition through their gurus, and that the compassion of the Lord was manifested through the power of the guru.

Once the human mind became thus advanced in the worship of the guru,

7. The doctrine of the avatar is supported by the Vedas and the experience of samadhi.

it did not take long to identify the guru, through whom the divine power became manifest, with the enlightening, benign form of God. Thus, it seems that guru worship eventually helped to shape the doctrine of the avatar in India. Although the doctrine of the avatar clearly flourished in the Puranic Age, its roots extended deep into the Vedic Age. During the periods of the Vedas, the Upanishads, and of classical Indian philosophy, people learned about the attributes, actions, and nature of God. Gradually, in the Puranic Age, these ideas took a definite shape and developed into belief in an avatar. It may also be that during the Upanishadic period, the rishis followed the path of *neti neti* [not this, not this] through self-control and austerity. They succeeded in the meditation on *Nirguna Brahman*; then, upon descending from samadhi through the reverse process, they perceived the world as a manifestation of Brahman. Endowed with love and devotion, they began to worship *Saguna Brahman*, or God with attributes. They then reached a firm conclusion regarding His attributes, actions, and nature, and believed that God incarnates as an avatar.

It has been said that belief in the avatar spread widely during the Puranic Age. Although there were many obstacles to the development of spirituality, the greatness of that age is that the glory of the avatars became manifest. By adopting faith in the avatar, people developed the capacity to understand the eternal play of Saguna Brahman. Consequently, they realized that God, the Cause of the universe, was their only guide in the spiritual world; and they became convinced that the infinite compassion of the Lord would not allow them to be eternally doomed. Rather, He would incarnate in every age, discover a new spiritual path suitable to human nature, and make God-realization easier.

8. The doctrine of the avatar spread during the Puranic Age as a result of people's experience of God's compassion.

It will not be out of place here to mention the gist of the *Smriti* and *Purana* scriptures regarding the divine birth and activities of avatars, who are endowed with illimitable virtues. These scriptures say that an avatar, like God, is by nature eternally pure, illumined, and free. Unlike a *jiva* [individual being], an avatar is never entangled by his actions. From his very birth the avatar is self-contented, so he does not pursue worldly enjoyments as do self-motivated jivas. The life of an avatar is solely dedicated to doing good for others. Being always free from the meshes of maya, the avatar never forgets his previous births.

9. The gist of the scriptures about the divine nature of an avatar.

It may be asked: Does that unbroken memory exist in the avatar from his very childhood? The authors of the Puranas reply: Although it is always latent within the avatar, it does not always manifest itself in childhood. However, as the avatar's body-mind organism becomes mature, his memory awakens with little or no effort. This is to be understood regarding every one of the avatar's actions. Since the avatar assumes a human body, he behaves in all respects like a human being.

10. Unbroken memory of an avatar.

As soon as the body and mind are completely developed, an avatar becomes fully aware of the goal of his present life. The avatar then realizes that the purpose of his birth is to reestablish religion. Again, whatever is necessary to fulfill that goal comes spontaneously to the avatar. The path that is perpetually dark to ordinary souls is luminous to the avatar. The avatar boldly advances and, after reaching the goal, inspires people to follow. Thus, the avatar discovers new paths to the realization of Brahman, or God, again and again in every age.

11. An avatar establishes a new religious path.

The authors of the Puranas not only noted the attributes, actions, and

12. Scriptural forecasts concerning the advent of an avatar.

nature of an avatar, but they also clearly ascertained the exact time of his advent. They said that the eternal, universal religion declines with the passage of time. Infatuated by the inscrutable power of maya, people lead their lives in the belief that this world and its mundane enjoyments are their all in all; they consider the Atman, God, liberation, and other eternal transcendental realities to be a poet's fancy — an illusory dream. They achieve wealth and worldly pleasures one way or another, but still they cannot satisfy their hearts' desires. Carried away by a dark, endless, terrible current of despair, they cry out in agony and seek deliverance. Under such circumstances, the all-powerful God makes the eternal religion luminous, like the moon when it has emerged from an eclipse. Out of compassion for human weakness, He takes a human form and again puts humanity on the spiritual path. As there cannot be an effect without a cause, so God in His *lila* [divine play] never assumes a human body without the purpose of removing the sufferings of humanity. When such suffering affects every part of society, God's infinite mercy crystallizes and induces Him to appear as a world teacher. The authors of the Puranas came to this conclusion upon observing the repeated appearance of divine incarnations, or avatars.

It follows therefore that the omniscient avatar, who is a world teacher and

13. Advent of the avatar in the modern age.

discoverer of the new religious path, appears in order to fulfill the need of the age. India, a land of spirituality, has been sanctified by the footprints of avatars many times throughout the ages. Even now, when the need arises, avatars, endowed with illimitable virtues, are born in India. It is well known that a little over 400 years ago, Bhagavan Sri Chaitanya overwhelmed the people, arousing their passion for God by chanting the name of Hari [God]. Has such a time recurred? To satisfy the need of this present age, has God's overwhelming compassion compelled Him to again incarnate in India, a country that is viewed as poor, inglorious, and contemptible by many foreigners? This has actually happened, as will be understood by studying the life story of an extremely virtuous and great soul that has been recorded in this book. Once again, India has been blessed to witness the advent of the Supreme One to fulfill the need of the age. He who was born long ago as Ramachandra and as Krishna has come again to reestablish the eternal religion.

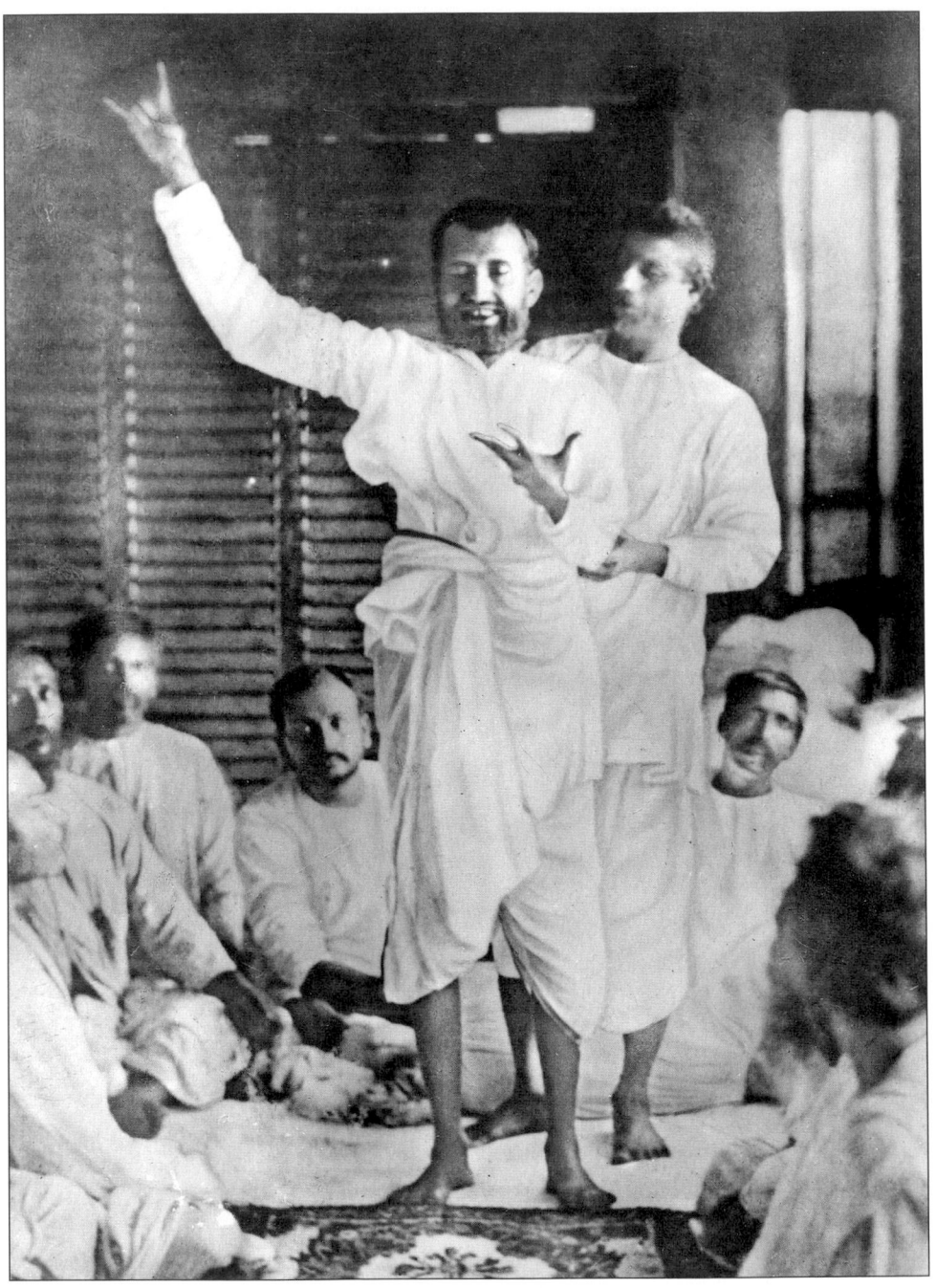

Ramakrishna in Samadhi during a kirtan at Keshab Sen's house in Calcutta,
21 September 1879. His nephew, Hriday, holds him.
Brahmo devotees sit on the carpet.

Chapter 1

The *N*eed of the Age

IN THE PRESENT AGE, IT IS EASY FOR EVEN AN ORDINARY person to see the extent

| 1. Humanity's progress and power in the present age. |

to which human beings are making progress all over the world through knowledge, wealth, and self-effort. It seems that in every area of life, people do not want to be confined to a limited sphere. Dissatisfied with travelling on land and water, they have invented the aeroplane. They have satisfied their curiosity by diving to the bottom of the sea and by exploring erupting volcanoes. They have unveiled nature's mysteries by climbing to the peaks of perpetually snowclad mountains and by crossing the oceans. They have discovered signs of life similar to their own in creepers, trees, and other plants; and they have gained knowledge of the animal kingdom through observation and experimentation. Achieving control over the five elements — earth, water, fire, air, and ether — they have amassed considerable knowledge of almost everything about this inanimate world. Still unsatisfied, they are anxious to explore far-off planets and stars, and they have already succeeded in this quest to some extent.

In addition, humans do not lack the zeal to explore the internal world. Every day people are making new findings in that field through broad experimentation and research. By studying the mystery of life, they have come to understand the evolution of one species into another. By reflecting on the nature of the body and the mind, they have ascertained that the mind consists of subtle matter, which has a beginning and an end. They are aware that every event in the microcosm, like that of the macrocosm, is regulated by an inviolable law; and they have perceived an invisible chain of cause and effect associated with suicide and other mental disorders. Although humans have no definite proof of the eternal existence of an individual life, the study of history has confirmed the continuity of nations. Thus, finding individual fulfillment within the collective national life, they have waged an incessant war against ignorance with the help of science and have unified their efforts to achieve success on this front. They have launched themselves on a current of countless desires, imagining that endless struggle will bring infinite progress and that they will succeed in reaching the hidden regions of both the internal and external worlds.

Although the expansion of materialism originated primarily in the West,

2. Materialistic progress originated in the West and spread to the East.

its influence is abundantly visible in India and other Eastern countries. As the power of science daily brings the East and West closer to each other, the ancient Eastern outlook on life is becoming more and more similar to the Western pattern. This becomes evident when one studies the present condition of Persia [Iran], China, Japan, and India, among others. Whatever may be the future outcome, there is no doubt that the West has influenced the East; it seems inevitable that in the course of time the whole world will be Westernized.

To determine the long-term effects of Western influence, we must concen-

3. The future effect of that progress can be determined by observing Western life.

trate our analysis on the West and analyze the lives of its people. What is the source of the West's materialistic progress? What is its nature? And how has its influence affected the early ideas of the West and brought progress or deterioration? In relation to the past, in what proportion has it influenced the happiness and misery of Westerners? If the effect of this materialism on the lives of individuals and of nations in the West can be determined, it will not be at all difficult to extrapolate the same results elsewhere in the course of time.

Historical records clearly indicate that from ancient times the severity of

4. The origin and history of progress in the West.

cold climates firmly instilled body-consciousness in the Western mind. On one hand, this body-consciousness made Westerners selfish; on the other, it led them to pursue their self-interest through collective effort, which developed their nationalism. This combination of selfishness and nationalism eventually motivated them to vigorously amass wealth by defeating other nations. When they had satisfied their material needs, they gradually became introspective and engaged themselves in learning and acquiring virtues. When the struggle for existence was no longer paramount and they were able to focus on the pursuit of higher things, they perceived bigoted religious beliefs and the supreme authority of the priesthood to be obstacles to their goals. Not only did the priests say that the pursuit of materialistic science would displease God and doom its practitioners to eternal hell, but they also firmly resolved not to allow people to progress further. But Western people forcefully set aside the priesthood and moved forward with their studies of science and philosophy. Disregarding the priests, as well as the scriptures and religious belief, Westerners set their lives upon a new path. Their guiding principle became the following: Do not believe or accept anything without definite evidence from the five senses.

The truth regarding a particular object was henceforth to be based on direct sense perception and ascertained through reasoning and inference. Holding this view, Westerners grew to adore the objective world of matter. Considering the subjective realm, which is perceived as "I-consciousness," to be a kind of matter, Western scientists began to explore the nature of that consciousness from their materialistic point of view. Thus, over a period of 400 years, Western peoples learned to accept the reality of each individual being and material object through examination based on the five senses. Within that period, physical science freed itself from the sluggishness and helplessness of its infancy and reached its youth invigorated with strength, zeal, hope, and joy.

Although this made possible great progress in the physical sciences, the

| 5. Western materialistic progress precludes knowledge of the Self; this leads to restlessness. | method of direct examination via the senses could not reveal the path of Self-knowledge to the West. The only way to attain Self-realization is through self-control, selflessness, and introspection; and the only |

procedure for achieving this is to gain absolute control over the thought waves of the mind. It is no wonder that most Westerners, being extroverted, missed the path to Self-knowledge and became materialists, identifying themselves with the body.

For this reason, they now consider worldly enjoyment to be the main goal of life and dedicate themselves to achieving it. Their knowledge of material objects acquired through science has been applied primarily to that purpose. Because of this, over time they have become proud and greedy. We therefore now find in the West a caste system based on wealth. We see terrible cannons, bombs, guns, and weapons of mass destruction. Relentless misery born of poverty exists side by side with the enjoyment of immense wealth. Because of this unquenchable thirst for wealth, the occupation and domination of other countries is rampant.

One can see that in spite of reaching the acme of enjoyment, the souls of men and women in the West are not satisfied; they are not content with the theory that although they may die, the nation will live on and benefit from their self-sacrifice. After careful examination, some Westerners have realized that they cannot discover the Reality beyond space and time through the limited knowledge grasped through their five senses. Science may present to them a momentary glimpse of that transcendental reality, but it cannot go further because it is incapable of reaching or comprehending that realm. Science, like a god, made Westerners powerful; it offered enjoyment, prosperity, and wealth. Now, because that science has been discovered to be inadequate, there is a void in the hearts of Westerners that is increasing day by day, and they feel utterly helpless.

When studying the history of the West, one observes that the expansion of its civilization was based on the drive for enjoy-

| 6. To make progress like that of the West, one must be selfish and have a drive for enjoyment. |

ment, on selfishness, and on a lack of faith in religion. Whoever wants to achieve the results that the West enjoys must somehow establish their personal or national lives on Western materialistic values. One can see that Japan and some other Asian countries have built their national lives according to the Western pattern. As a result, along with their nationalism, they are developing the attendant problems of materialistic civilization. This terrible drawback to Westernization can be clearly understood by studying the present condition of India's national life following its contact with the West.

Now the question arises: Was there any national life in India before it came in contact with the West? The answer is that undoubt-

| 7. The basis of the national life in ancient India. |

edly it did exist in practice, but was not articulated. Even in those days all Indians were devoted to their gurus, the Ganges, the Gayatri mantra, and the Gita. Cows were revered all over India [because of their usefulness in agriculture and because they provided milk and other products]. The spiritual ideas of the Ramayana, the Mahabharata, and other scriptures inspired and guided the life of every man, woman, and child. And pandits from different parts of India communicated their ideas with one another in Sanskrit, the language of the gods. Thus, various unifying links [among the different regions] can be observed. Without doubt, religious ideas and practices constituted the main basis of that unity.

Because India's national life was based on religion, its civilization was constituted in a unique way. To put it briefly, self-control

| 8. With religion as its basis, Indian society never struggled for sense pleasure. |

was the life force of this civilization. India taught each individual and race to regulate their respective lives with self-control. Mottos such as "the purpose of enjoyment is to renounce it ultimately," and "the lessons in this life are preparations for the next," have always reminded Indians of the highest ideal and guided them towards that end in every stage of their individual lives and collective national lives. That is why the caste or class system had not yet created any class conflict or terrible discontent amongst them. Irrespective of higher or lower birth, if a person completed his or her caste duties without selfish motives, that person would achieve knowledge and liberation, the main goal of human life. Where then was the possibility for discontent? Disparity of material enjoyment between the classes caused conflict in Western society, but in ancient times such conflict did not occur in Indian society because each individual had an equal right to the highest goal of life — liberation. Having reviewed the characteristics of ancient India's national life, let us now review the changes that emerged after coming in contact with the West.

After the Western conquest of India, it was natural and inevitable that remarkable changes should take place in the distri-

9. The Western conquest of India and its result.

bution of the country's wealth. But the West did not stop with changing only that aspect of India's national life. The West brought about a radical change by influencing the fundamental ideals that had guided the individual and national lives of India from time immemorial. Westerners taught that the concept that "the purpose of enjoyment is to renounce it ultimately" was invented by priests to advance their own self-interests, that belief in an afterlife and the existence of the Atman were a kind of poetic fancy, and that the caste rule that a person must remain in whatever stratum of society he or she is born into was unjust and irrational.

Indians gradually became convinced that Western ideas were valid. Relinquishing their previous life goals, which had been based on renunciation and self-control, they became eager for more material pleasures. Their ancient system of education and training disappeared, and they became atheistic, fond of imitating the West, and lacking in self-confidence. As a result, they became as weak as worms. Indians came to believe that the long-cherished beliefs they had held and practised were completely wrong. They believed it was true that their traditions were primitive and semicivilized because Western science had proved them to be so. Infatuated by earthly pleasures, the Indian people forgot their ancient history and glory. This failure of memory led to the ruin of discrimination, and thus India's national identity was at stake. Realizing that they had to depend on other nations even for worldly enjoyment, the Indian people became completely frustrated. The paths of both *yoga* [spirituality] and of *bhoga* [enjoyment] were lost to them. Imitating others and buffeted by waves of worldly desires, India began to drift aimlessly like a boat without anyone to steer it.

Gradually a clamour arose all around that India had never had a national

10. The effort to revitalize India with Western ideas and its result.

life and that, by the grace of the West, the country was now developing one national life. But there were many obstacles to its full manifestation. India's irresistible religious tradition had ruined its national life. India could not make progress because of idolatry, its practice of worshipping innumerable gods and goddesses. Destroy idolatry, uproot that tradition! Only then will the men and women of India be rejuvenated.

Foreign missionaries began to preach Christianity and the doctrine of monotheism. Organizations were formed according to the Western fashion; they infused moribund India with the utility of politics, sociology, widow remarriage, women's emancipation, and so on. But the people's feelings of emptiness and frustration did not diminish; rather they increased daily. Railways, telegraphs, and other apparatus of Western civilization were brought to India; but all efforts to revitalize the nation were in vain. These Western methods did not attempt to search for or to reestablish the inspiring traditional ideas that had sustained India. How can one expect a disease to be cured if the medicine is not properly applied? How can India, whose soul is religion, survive if her religion is not restored to life? How is it possible for the atheistic West to eradicate the religious degradation that resulted from its own materialism? Being themselves imperfect, how can Western countries make others perfect?

It cannot be said that India's national life was free from defects before

| 11. Virtues and disadvantages of the ancient national life of India. | the conquest of the West. But the nation was then vigorous and full of life, so its people constantly strove to rectify those defects. As we observe a certain lack of effort on the part of the nation and society |

today, we understand that the application of medicine in the form of materialistic Western ideas is about to kill the patient along with the disease.

It is now evident that the degradation of religion in the West has also

| 12. The spread of Western ideas caused a decline in religion in modern India. | affected India. In fact, it is striking to see how far that degradation has spread all over the world in this present age. If there is any truth in religion, and if by God's grace one can attain that truth, then undoubt- |

edly the present hedonistic age has deviated far from it. Modern science has improved the condition of human life by providing people with various objects of enjoyment, but it has failed to bring them peace. Who will now set it right? Who will be so moved by the constant restlessness and agony of the world's people as to relinquish personal enjoyment and find a new religious path suitable for the present age? Who will halt the degradation of religion in the East and the West and teach people to follow the new path of peace?

Lord Krishna has promised in the Gita that whenever there is a decline in

| 13. God reincarnates to avert the decline of religion. | religion, he embraces his own maya in order to become incarnate, to restore religion and help people to regain peace. Will not the need of the age intensely |

arouse his compassion? Will not humankind's emptiness and anxiety induce God to assume a body?

O reader, the need of the age has accomplished that task! The Lord has truly reappeared as a world teacher. Listen with faith to His blessed messages: "As many faiths, so many paths"; "You will realize God through any spiritual discipline if you practise it wholeheartedly." Reflect intensely upon the superhuman renunciation and austerities Sri Ramakrishna practised to revive the Supreme Knowledge! Come, let us purify ourselves by studying and meditating on his pure, divine life.

Chapter 2

$\mathcal{K}$amarpukur and Sri Ramakrishna's Ancestry

OF THOSE GREAT SOULS WHO ARE STILL WORSHIPPED as incarnations of God, all

1. Why a divine incarnation is born into a poor family.

except Sri Ramachandra and Lord Buddha began their lives in sorrow, poverty, and hardship. Here are some examples: Although Sri Krishna belonged to a royal dynasty, he was born in a prison and spent his early life in a community of poor cowherds, separated from his relatives. Lord Jesus was born in the stable of an inn, glorifying his poor parents. Sri Shankara was born after his father's death, the son of a poor widow. Sri Chaitanya's parents were most ordinary people. Finally, the prophet Muhammad, the founder of Islam, also came from a poor family. All of these great souls were born in families where there was contentment amidst suffering and poverty; where there were self-lessness and love in the midst of hardship; and where the hearts of their poor parents were filled with a blend of renunciation, purity, steadfast humane-ness, compassion, charity, and other noble qualities.

Through careful reflection one can see a subtle connection between the avatars' births in poverty and the future courses of their lives. If they had no previous awareness of and sympathy for the condition of the poor, how could they in later life accomplish their mission to give solace and peace to society's afflicted, poor, and persecuted? However, this is not the sole purpose for their advent. We have previously discussed the fact that avatars come to halt the decline of religion. To fulfill that mission, they first become intimately familiar with the traditional religious laws; after reflecting upon the causes of religion's present degradation, the avatars discover a new dispensation according to that particular time and place in order to revive those ancient laws. The huts of the poor, not the palaces of the rich, offer the opportunity to become intimate with religious traditions. It is the poor person, deprived of worldly enjoyment, who always holds fast to God and His dispensation. Therefore, in spite of widespread religious degradation, a glimpse of the ancient religion keeps the poor person's hut luminous. That is why, it seems, the great teachers of the world are attracted to birth in poor families. The same situation occurred in the life of Sri Ramakrishna, whose story we are about to relate.

About sixty miles northwest of Calcutta, in the northwestern part of

2. Kamarpukur: Ramakrishna's birthplace.

Hooghly District, very close to the borders of Bankura and Midnapore districts, there is a cluster of three villages forming a triangle. Although these three villages are known to the villagers distinctly as Sripur, Kamarpukur, and Mukundapur, they are so close that they appear to travellers as different sections of the same village. That is why the three together are known as Kamarpukur to people in the surrounding villages. Kamarpukur was prominent in the early nineteenth century because the local landlords had lived there for many generations. At that time, Kamarpukur was a tax-free estate belonging to the family of the guru of the Maharaja of Burdwan. The descendants of that family, Gopilal Goswami, Sukhlal Goswami, and others,[1] were living there.

The town of Burdwan is situated thirty-two miles north of Kamarpukur. A paved road begins at Burdwan and encircles half of Kamarpukur Village, then turns southwest to Puri. Many poor pilgrims and monks travel along this path to visit Lord Jagannath [Krishna] at Puri.

There is a famous Tarakeswar Shiva temple about twenty miles east of Kamarpukur. From Tarakeswar there is a path to Kamarpukur via Jahanabad or Arambagh, which is situated on the bank of the Dwarakeswar River. Additionally, there are two more roads to reach Kamarpukur: one from Ghatal, eighteen miles south, and the other from Vana-Vishnupur, twenty-six miles west.

Words cannot express the serene atmosphere that pervaded the agricul-

3. The past glory and present condition of Kamarpukur.

tural villages of Bengal before the malaria epidemic of 1867. In the midst of expansive paddy fields, these small hamlets of Hooghly District looked like islands floating in a vast green ocean. The villagers were healthy and strong, happy and contented. They had an abundance of food from the fertile land, and the

---

1. Hridayram Mukhopadhyay mentioned the name of Anup Goswami in place of Sukhlal, but his statement cannot be verified. We have heard from the Lahas, the present landlords of the village, that the name of that person was Sukhlal Goswami. They bought most of the land of Kamarpukur about fifty-five years ago from his son Krishnalal Goswami. It is said that Gopilal Goswami installed the large image of Gopeswar Shiva, so it can be guessed that Gopilal Goswami was an ancestor of Sukhlal, or it may be that Gopilal was another name of Sukhlal.

Kamarpukur village, Ramakrishna's birthplace.

unpolluted air refreshed their hard-working bodies. Apart from agriculture, the people of those populous villages engaged in various small industries. Kamarpukur is still known locally for various kinds of sweets, such as *jilipi*, *nabat*, and other delicacies; to this day people make a decent living by manufacturing tobacco pipes from ebony and exporting them to Calcutta. Once Kamarpukur was well known for manufacturing yarn, towels, and cloth, and for other handicrafts. Vishnu Chapari and other famous cloth merchants lived in this village and conducted a prosperous business with Calcutta. Even today the village market is held every Tuesday and Saturday. People from Tarahat, Badanganj, Sihar, Deshra, and other surrounding villages come to Kamarpukur on market day with their merchandise, such as yarn, cloth, towels, earthen pots and pitchers, winnowing fans, baskets, fine and coarse mats, and other commodities for daily use, as well as agricultural produce. They buy each other's products and sell their own.

To this day, there is no want of festivities in the village. During mid-March to mid-April, Kamarpukur reverberates with devotional songs and worship of the Goddess Manasa and Lord Shiva; and beginning on the eleventh day after the full or new moon in May or June, people dance and sing of the glory of Krishna continuously for three days. In addition, different religious festivals are traditionally held all year round in the house of the landlord; and daily worship and other rituals are performed in all of the village temples. Of course, at present the grinding poverty of the village has put a stop to many of those religious observances.

At one time Dharma, one of the gems of the Buddhist Trinity, was worshipped in the Kamarpukur area with great éclat;

4. Worship of Dharma.

but this practice has passed into oblivion. At present the same Dharma has been transformed into Kurma [the Tortoise, the second of the ten incarnations of Vishnu] and is worshipped nominally in surrounding villages. Sometimes even brahmins are seen worshipping the image of that deity. One hears different names of the same Dharma in different villages. For example, the name of the Lord Dharma in Kamarpukur is "Rajadhiroy Dharma"; in Sripur, "Yatrasiddhiroy Dharma"; and in Madhubati Village near Mukundapur, He is known as "Sannyasiroy Dharma." At one time the chariot festival of Dharma was celebrated at Kamarpukur with pomp and grandeur. One could see the tall chariot with nine pinnacles next to the Dharma temple; but after the chariot broke down, it was never rebuilt. As the Dharma temple fell to pieces for want of repair, the priest Yajneshwar moved the deity to his own house.

In Kamarpukur live people of all castes, such as brahmins, kshatriyas, weavers, milkmen, blacksmiths, potters, fishermen, and undertakers, among others. There are three or four big ponds in the village; Haldar Pond is the largest among them. There also are many small

5. Haldar Pond, Bhuti's Canal, the mango orchard, and other places.

Haldar Pond in Kamarpukur, where Ramakrishna bathed and swam.

ponds; some of them are adorned with hundred-petalled lotuses and white water lilies. There is no dearth of brick buildings and tombs in the village; previously there were many more. The ruins of Ramananda Sankhari's temple, Fakir Datta's dilapidated *rasa-mancha* [a stage for Krishna's festival], heaps of bricks covered with jungle foliage, and many deserted temples in various places indicate the former prosperity of the village. There are two cremation grounds in the village, at Budhui Moral in the northwest and at Bhuti's Canal in the northeast. To the west of Bhuti's Canal there is a grazing field, Manikraja's public mango orchard, and the Amodar River. Not far from the village, Bhuti's Canal flows south and joins the Amodar River.

A mile north of Kamarpukur is Bhursubo Village. Manikchandra Bandyo-

6. Manikraja of Bhursubo Village.	padhyay, an extremely wealthy man, lived there. He was known as "Manikraja" to the people of surrounding villages.

Besides owning the mango orchard, he is well known for constructing some lakes such as Sukhasayar and Hatisayar. It is said that on many occasions, 100,000 brahmins were invited to his house and fed.

To the southeast of Kamarpukur is Mandaran Village. At one time there

7. Gara Mandaran [Fort Mandaran].	had been an impregnable fort to protect the surrounding villages from enemy attack. A moat was constructed around the fort by carefully diverting the

course of the nearby Amodar River.

The ruins of the broken gate, the mound, and the moat of Fort Mandaran

8. Uchalan Lake and the Mogul's battlefield.	and its nearby Shaileswar Shiva temple exist even today. They indicate the importance of these places during the period of Pathan rule [from the twelfth to

fifteenth century]. The highway leading to Burdwan passes near Fort Mandaran. On both sides of this highway there are many lakes; the largest one is in Uchalan, eighteen miles north of the fort. One can also see a dilapidated elephant stable along this highway. Observing all these remains, it can be surmised that the highway was built for the purpose of war. The existence of the famous battlefield of Mogulmari near this highway bears witness to that assumption.

A couple of miles west of Kamarpukur there are three villages — Satbere,

9. The story of Ramananda Roy, the landlord of Dere Village.	Narayanpur, and Dere [Derepur] — located side by side. At one time these villages were prosperous; this can be inferred by observing the lake, the nearby

temple of Dere Village, and other remains. At the time of which we are speaking, these three villages were under separate landlords. Ramananda Roy, the landlord of Dere, lived in Satbere. Although he was not very wealthy, he was a tyrant towards his tenants. If he was annoyed with someone for any reason, he would not hesitate to deprive that person of everything. None of his children survived him, and after his death his wealth and property fell into the hands of others. It is said that his dynasty was destroyed because of his sins of oppression.

Nearly 150 years ago, a middle-class, pious, brahmin family lived in Dere Village. They were of noble descent and virtuous conduct, and were worshippers of Ramachandra. They are still commemorated by their Shiva temple and the adjacent pond, known as Chatujye Pond. Manikram Chattopadhyay belonged to that family. He had three sons and one daughter: Kshudiram, the eldest son, was probably born in 1775; then came a daughter, Ramshila, and two sons, Nidhiram and Kanairam.

10. Manikram Chattopadhyay of Dere Village.

It is not known whether Kshudiram learned any practical, money-earning trade as he grew up. But God blessed him with truthfulness, contentment, forgiveness, renunciation, and other noble qualities that are considered by the scriptures to be characteristics of a good brahmin. He was tall and strong, but not bulky; he was handsome, with a fair complexion. Following the family tradition, he had an intense devotion to Ramachandra. After finishing his daily spiritual disciplines, he would pick flowers and worship Raghuvir [Ramachandra]; only then would he eat. He was so rigid about adhering to his brahminical rules that he would not accept any gifts from *shudras* [the labouring caste] nor would he accept an invitation from a brahmin who performed rituals for them. He would not even drink water from the hands of brahmins who gave away their daughters in exchange for a dowry. Because of his steadfast devotion and good conduct, the villagers loved and respected him greatly.

11. His son Kshudiram Chattopadhyay.

After his father's death, Kshudiram took over the management of his ancestral property and performed the household duties the best he could while remaining steadfast on his religious path. He married, but his wife died young. When he was about twenty-five, he remarried. His second wife's name was Chandramani, but her family called her "Chandra." Her father's house was in the village of Saratimayapur. Chandra was beautiful, simple, and devoted to God and holy people. But her most remarkable qualities were her deep faith and her loving and affectionate nature; that is why she was dear to all. Chandramani was likely born in 1791; she would have been eight at the time of her marriage in 1799. Her first son, Ramkumar, was probably born in 1805. Five years later, her daughter, Katyayani, was born. Then in 1826, she rejoiced in the birth of her second son, Rameswar.

12. Kshudiram's wife Chandramani.

It did not take long for Kshudiram to realize how difficult it was to manage a household while following the path of righteousness. Shortly after his daughter's birth, Kshudiram fell into a terrible predicament. We have already described the oppressive nature of Ramananda Roy,

13. Kshudiram loses everything because of a dispute with the landlord.

the landlord of the village. Ramananda became annoyed with someone at Derepur and instigated a false lawsuit against him. As the landlord needed a trustworthy witness, he requested Kshudiram to testify in his favour. The religiously minded Kshudiram always dreaded legal affairs and courts, and he never resorted to them against anyone, even for a just cause. Ramananda's request made him extremely anxious: If Kshudiram did not bear false witness, he would incur the landlord's rage. Although he fully realized this, he did not agree to testify. As a result, events unfolded as they had been preordained. The landlord accused Kshudiram falsely and filed a lawsuit against him; after winning the litigation, he obtained Kshudiram's paternal property through an auction. There was not even a little plot of land for Kshudiram in Derepur. Although the villagers were genuinely sympathetic to Kshudiram's predicament, their fear of the landlord prevented them from helping him.

Thus, at the age of forty, Kshudiram became completely destitute. The property[2] he had inherited and everything he had acquired from his own effort — it all disappeared like a cloud blown apart by a gust of wind. But this predicament did not disturb his righteous conduct even slightly. He took refuge solely in Raghuvir and then calmly reflected on his duty. He left his parental homestead and village for good with a view to ridding himself of the villainous landlord.

| 14. Kshudiram leaves Dere Village. |

We have already mentioned Sukhlal Goswami of Kamarpukur. He and Kshudiram were longstanding close friends because of their similar dispositions. Sukhlal was extremely disturbed when he heard of his friend's predicament; he invited Kshudiram to settle in Kamarpukur permanently, and offered him a few thatched huts on his own homestead. Kshudiram thus found a haven. Realizing that the invitation had come by the inconceivable grace of the Lord, Kshudiram accepted it with gratitude and moved to Kamarpukur permanently. The well-wisher, Sukhlal, was very happy about this move; he made a permanent gift of a rice field nearly half an acre in size to the righteous Kshudiram for the maintenance of his family.

| 15. Kshudiram moves to Kamarpukur at the invitation of Sukhlal Goswami. |

⚜

---

2. We have heard from Hridayram Mukhopadhyay that Kshudiram had about 150 bighas [nearly 50 acres] of land in Derepur.

Ramakrishna's temple under construction in Dere Village, where Kshudiram had his original home.

Ramakrishna's family home in Kamarpukur.

Chapter 3

The Pious *F*amily of Kamarpukur

IT IS HARD TO DESCRIBE KSHUDIRAM'S AND CHANDRA'S state of mind the day they

| 1. The reason for Kshudiram's reclusive life at Kamarpukur. |

moved into the thatched hut in Kamarpukur with their ten-year-old son, Ramkumar, and four-year-old daughter, Katyayani. The world appeared to be filled with jealousy and hatred and seemed like a dark and horrible cremation ground. Love, affection, compassion, righteousness, and other noble qualities shed a dim light occasionally, raising hope and happiness in the heart. But the next moment, that light disappears and the darkness appears even darker. One can imagine the couple thinking along these lines when comparing their past condition with their present. People truly realize the worthlessness and impermanence of this world when they encounter trials and tribulations. It is therefore no wonder that Kshudiram now harboured renunciation in his heart. His righteous mind was filled with devotion and reliance on God as he reflected on how he had received this new haven, unasked for and unexpected. It is not surprising that Kshudiram now surrendered himself fully to Raghuvir, remaining indifferent to worldly prospects and passing his days in service and worship of the Lord. Although he was a householder, from that point on he led his life like a *vanaprasthi* [a forest-dweller] of ancient times.

An incident that occurred during this period further intensified Kshu-

| 2. Kshudiram obtains a stone image of Raghuvir under mysterious circumstances. |

diram's faith in God. One day, Kshudiram travelled to another village on an errand. On his way home he became exhausted, so he rested awhile under a tree by the side of the road. The vast empty meadow

90

brought peace to his weary mind, and a pure, gentle breeze soothed his tired body. He felt an urge to lie down, and as soon as he did so, he fell asleep. After a while, he began to dream: His Chosen Deity, Ramachandra, appeared before him as a divine boy with a complexion like that of a blade of young grass. Pointing to a particular spot, Ramachandra said: "Unnoticed and uncared for, I have been starving here for many days. Take me to your home. I am eager to accept your service." Overwhelmed with joy, Kshudiram humbly replied: "My Lord, I am devoid of devotion and extremely poor. It is not possible to serve you properly in my hut. Moreover, if I cannot serve you well, I shall incur sin and go to hell. So why are you making such a difficult request?" Pleased, the boy Ramachandra reassured him: "Do not be afraid. I shall be satisfied with your service even if it is imperfect. Take me with you." Unable to control his emotion over this unsolicited blessing from God, Kshudiram burst into tears and his dream ended.

When he awoke, Kshudiram reflected deeply on his wonderful dream and thought. Alas, could it be true that such good fortune would come to him? At that moment his eyes fell on a nearby rice field, and he immediately recognized it as the place in his dream. Curious, he arose and approached the field. As soon as he drew near, he saw a beautiful *shalagrama* [a stone emblem of Vishnu] sheltered under the hood of a venomous cobra. He felt he must possess the stone image and hastened to the spot. The cobra disappeared, and the shalagrama lay at the entrance to the snake's hole. Knowing that his dream had come true, Kshudiram's heart was filled with joy. Realizing that he had received a divine command, he cast aside his fear of being bitten. Kshudiram shouted "Victory to Raghuvir!" and took the stone before the cobra's den. As Kshudiram was well versed in the scriptures, he examined the marks on the stone and concluded that it was truly an image of Raghuvir. Overwhelmed with joy and wonder, he returned home. After performing the sacrament of purification as enjoined by the scriptures, he installed the shalagrama as his family deity and began to worship it daily. Before acquiring the image of Raghuvir in this mysterious way, Kshudiram had been performing daily worship of his Chosen Deity, Ramachandra, and also the goddess Shitala by invoking Her presence in a consecrated water-vessel.

Difficult days passed one after another, yet Kshudiram remained aloof

3. Despite their poverty, Kshudiram is steadfast and dependent on God.

from all sorrow and suffering. He passed the time cheerfully, holding fast to the Lord. On some days there was no food in their home. The devoted Chandra would anxiously inform her husband but Kshudiram remained unperturbed. He would console her, saying: "Don't worry. If Raghuvir fasts, we shall fast with him." Under such circumstances, the simple-hearted Chandra followed her husband's example and continued her household duties, depending completely on Raghuvir. Somehow they always obtained enough food for the day.

Kshudiram did not suffer from scarcity of food for very long. As

4. The rice field of
Lakshmijala.

mentioned earlier, his friend Sukhlal Goswami had given him a half-acre rice field located in Lakshmijala. By the grace of Raghuvir, the land was soon producing so much rice that it became more than sufficient for the little family. The surplus was given to guests and visitors. Kshudiram hired farmers to plough the field; when the seedlings were ready, he would transplant a few bunches while taking the name of Raghuvir and then ask the farmers to finish the job.

Thus time passed and two or three years went by. Although Kshudiram

5. Kshudiram's
exuberant devotion and
divine vision; the
neighbours' respect for
him.

depended solely on Raghuvir and lived on what chance might bring, his family never lacked plain food and clothing. Those two or three years of hardship gave Kshudiram the peace, contentment, and reliance on God that are experienced by only a fortunate few. His mind became naturally indrawn; consequently, he occasionally experienced divine visions. During his morning and evening prayers he would repeat the meditation mantra of the goddess Gayatri and become absorbed in Her. His chest would turn crimson and tears of love would flow continuously. In the morning, with basket in hand, he would pick flowers for worship and would see his family deity, the goddess Shitala, as an eight-year-old girl dressed in a red sari and bedecked with various ornaments. With a smile on Her face She would accompany him and help him pick flowers by bending the branches of the trees. These divine visions filled his heart with bliss. His firm faith and devotion were reflected on his face and kept him always in an ecstatic mood. Seeing his serene and dignified demeanour, the villagers realized his greatness and gradually began to love and honour him as a *rishi* [sage]. Upon seeing him approach, they would stop their idle chatter and stand up to greet him respectfully. When he was bathing, the villagers hesitated to enter the pond and waited in deference till he had finished. Having complete faith in him, they came to him for his blessings during times of joy and of sorrow.

Chandradevi was an embodiment of love and simplicity. She captivated

6. How the neighbours
regarded Chandradevi.

the villagers through her love and compassion. She truly became like their own mother; during times of happiness and misery no one else had such heartfelt sympathy for them. The poor knew that whenever they went to Chandradevi not only would they be given food, but also such love and care as would thoroughly gratify their hearts. Mendicants knew that her door was always open for alms. The neighbourhood children knew that whatever they asked from her, they would receive. Thus, all the neighbours, young and old, would come to Kshudiram's cottage at any time; and in spite of his suffering and poverty, his home was an abode of peace and joy.

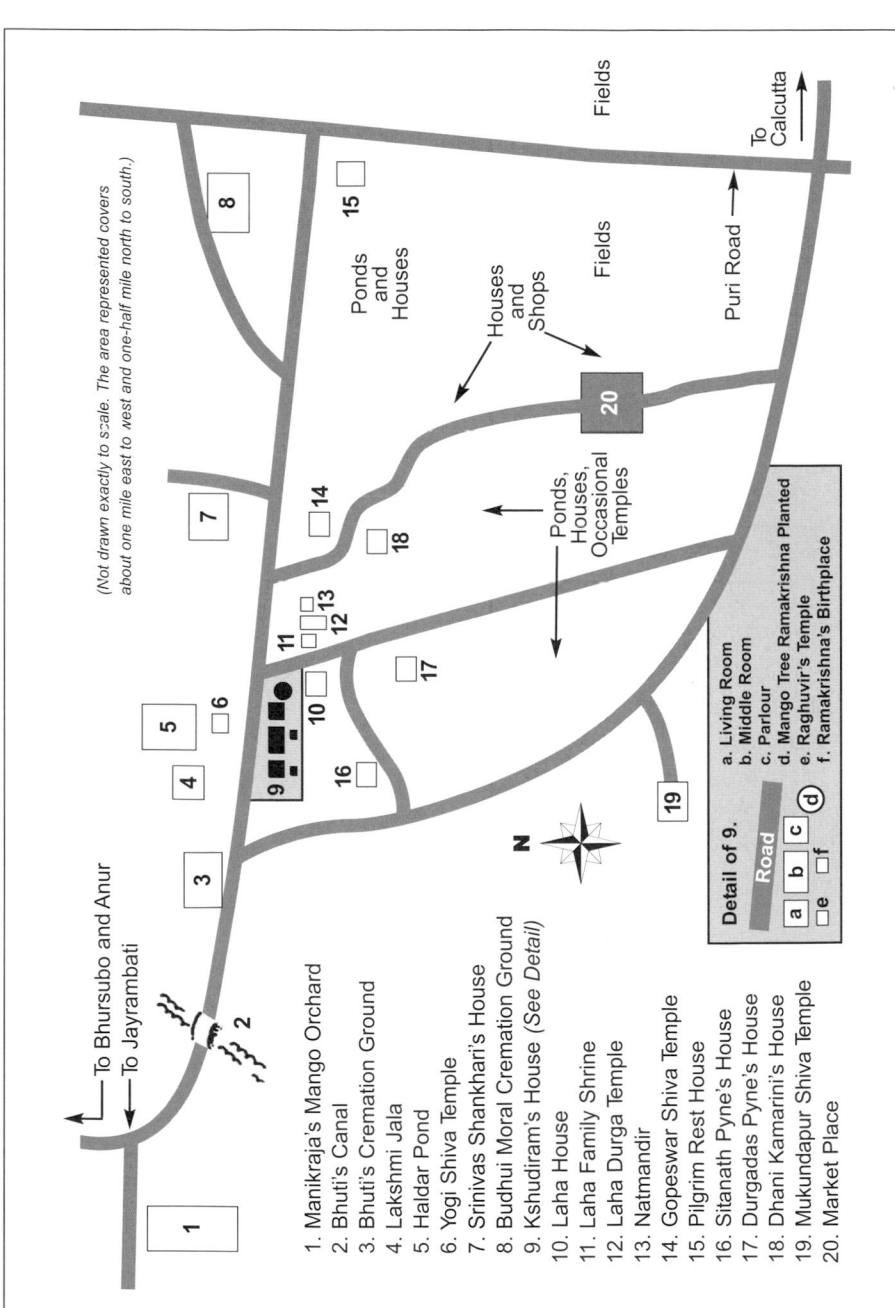

(Not drawn exactly to scale. The area represented covers about one mile east to west and one-half mile north to south.)

To Bhursubo and Anur
To Jayrambati

To Calcutta
To
Calcutta

Fields

Fields

Puri Road

Ponds
and
Houses

Houses
and
Shops

Ponds,
Houses,
Occasional
Temples

N

1. Manikraja's Mango Orchard
2. Bhuti's Canal
3. Bhuti's Cremation Ground
4. Lakshmi Jala
5. Haldar Pond
6. Yogi Shiva Temple
7. Srinivas Shankhari's House
8. Budhui Moral Cremation Ground
9. Kshudiram's House (See Detail)
10. Laha House
11. Laha Family Shrine
12. Laha Durga Temple
13. Natmandir
14. Gopeswar Shiva Temple
15. Pilgrim Rest House
16. Sitanath Pyne's House
17. Durgadas Pyne's House
18. Dhani Kamarini's House
19. Mukundapur Shiva Temple
20. Market Place

Detail of 9.

Road

a. Living Room
b. Middle Room
c. Parlour
d. Mango Tree Ramakrishna Planted
e. Raghuvir's Temple
f. Ramakrishna's Birthplace

Map of Kamarpukur and the places connected with Ramakrishna, as they were during his lifetime.

As has already been mentioned, Kshudiram had a sister named Ram-

7. Kshudiram's sister, Ramshila.

shila, and two younger brothers, Nidhiram and Kanairam (who was also called Ramkanai). When Kshudiram lost everything during his conflict with the landlord of Derepur, his sister was about thirty-five years old and his brothers thirty and twenty-five, respectively. All three of his siblings were married and had families. Ramshila was married to Bhagavat Bandyopadhyay of Chilimpur, a village twelve miles west of Kamarpukur. She had a son, Ramchand, and a daughter, Hemangini. During Kshudiram's crisis, Ramchand was twenty-one and Hemangini, sixteen. Ramchand was then practising law in Midnapore. Hemangini was born at her maternal uncles' house at Derepur, and was her uncles' favourite. Kshudiram raised her like his own daughter and gave her in marriage to Krishnachandra Mukhopadhyay of Sihar, a village five miles northwest of Kamarpukur. In the course of time Hemangini had four sons: Raghav, Ramratan, Hridayram, and Rajaram.

It is not known whether Kshudiram's brother Nidhiram had any chil-

8. Kshudiram's two brothers.

dren; but his youngest brother, Kanairam, had two sons: Ramtarak (also called Haladhari) and Kalidas. Kanairam was devout and contemplative. Once he went to a *yatra* [folk play] that dramatically depicted the banishment of Ramachandra to the forest. He became so absorbed in the performance that when Kaikeyi [Rama's stepmother] was plotting to send Ramachandra to the forest, he imagined it was real and nearly struck the actor. Nidhiram and Kanairam left Dere after losing their ancestral property and likely took shelter in the homes of their fathers-in-law.

It has been mentioned that Ramshila's son Ramchand Bandyopadhyay

9. Kshudiram's nephew, Ramchand.

practised law in Midnapore. He gradually began earning a good income there. Because he was aware of his maternal uncles' distress, he began to give fifteen rupees per month to Kshudiram and ten rupees per month each to Nidhiram and Kanairam. If Kshudiram did not receive news of his nephew for some time, he would become anxious and visit Midnapore. After staying a few days, he would return home to Kamarpukur. We have heard about a remarkable incident that occurred during one of his visits to Midnapore. We relate it here as an example of Kshudiram's sincere devotion to God.

Midnapore is situated about forty miles southwest of Kamarpukur. One

10. An incident illustrating Kshudiram's devotion to God.

day, following a long period without any news of Ramchand and his family, a worried Kshudiram left for Midnapore. It must have been sometime in February or March. At that time, the bel trees were shedding their leaves. Until the new leaves grew it was difficult to worship Shiva without this essential item. This lack had been a problem for Kshudiram for some time.

Early that morning Kshudiram left home for Midnapore, walking steadily till 10:00 a.m. He reached a village and was overjoyed to find that the bel trees there were decked with new leaves. He completely forgot about his journey to Midnapore. He bought a new basket and a towel from the village and washed them both thoroughly in a nearby pond. He then filled the basket with fresh bel leaves, covered them with the wet towel, and returned to Kamarpukur at about 3:00 in the afternoon. Immediately after his bath, he joyfully worshipped Shiva and Shitala for a long time and then ate some food. Afterwards, Chandradevi casually asked why he had not gone to Midnapore. She was extremely surprised when she heard the whole story of how he had walked such a distance just to worship the Lord with new bel leaves. The next morning Kshudiram again started for Midnapore.

Thus Kshudiram passed six years in Kamarpukur. Now his son Ram-

| 11. Ramkumar's and Katyayani's marriages. |

kumar was sixteen years old, and his daughter, Katyayani, was eleven. He began to search for a bridegroom for his daughter, as she was of marriage-able age. He gave his daughter in marriage to Kenaram Bandyopadhyay of Anur, a village two miles northwest of Kamarpukur. At the same time he arranged for Ramkumar to wed Kenaram's sister. Ramkumar had finished his courses in grammar and literature and was studying Smriti [Hindu law] at the time of his marriage.

Another three or four years passed. By Raghuvir's grace Kshudiram's

| 12. Sukhlal Goswami's death. |

financial condition was much improved, and he continued his spiritual disciplines without worry. Ramkumar finished his study of Hindu law and began doing his best to help the family financially. At this time Kshudiram's closest friend, Sukhlal Goswami, died. Kshudiram was greatly saddened by Sukhlal's death.

Seeing that Ramkumar had matured and assumed family responsibilities,

| 13. Kshudiram's pilgrimage to Rameswaram and the birth of his son Rameswar. |

Kshudiram felt relieved. He now had the opportunity to concentrate on other things, and he became eager to visit holy places. It was probably in 1824 that he left for Rameswaram on foot; he returned home after a year of visiting holy places in South India. He brought a *banalingam* [a stone image of Shiva] to Kamarpukur from Rameswaram and began worshipping it daily. Even today in the Kamarpukur shrine one can see that very banalingam, which is named Rameswar, adjacent to the stone image of Raghuvir and the consecrated water pot of Shitala.

In 1826, long after the birth of her second child, Chandradevi again became pregnant. She gave birth to a son that year. Kshudiram named him Rameswar, as he received the child after returning from Rameswaram.

The life of this poor Kamarpukur family continued almost unchanged for

14. Ramkumar's supernatural power.

another eight years. Ramkumar was now making a living by interpreting the code of Hindu law and performing rituals for the purpose of obtaining peace and overcoming obstacles. The family therefore did not suffer from financial hardship as they had earlier. Ramkumar became expert in performing these rituals. It is said that he acquired supernatural powers to that effect. As a result of studying the scriptures, he had become very drawn to the worship of the Divine Mother; and now he was initiated into a *Shakti* mantra by an adept guru. One day while worshipping the Goddess, his Chosen Deity, Ramkumar had a wonderful vision. With Her finger, the Goddess wrote on his tongue a mantra for the attainment of perfection in astrology. After that, whenever he saw someone who was ill, he could tell whether that person would be cured. Because of that power, whatever he predicted came true and he became a well-known soothsayer. It is said that when he saw a critically ill person, he would begin performing a propitiatory rite for the patient's recovery. Then he would say emphatically, "As soon as the grains that I am scattering on the altar sprout, this person will recover." His words always came true. As an example of this power, his nephew Shivaram Chattopadhyay told us the following story.

Ramkumar went to Calcutta on business. One day he was bathing in the

15. An example of Ramkumar's power.

Ganges when a rich man and his wife came there to bathe. The young wife was seated in a palanquin that was carried into the Ganges so she could bathe inside of it. Being from a village, Ramkumar had never seen a woman protecting her modesty while bathing in this manner. While watching this in wonder, he momentarily saw the face of the woman within the palanquin. Through his supernatural power, he foresaw her death and lamented: "Alas! The person who is having her bath today with such decorum will tomorrow be thrown into the Ganges in front of all." The woman's husband overheard the remark, and in order to test its validity, he cordially invited Ramkumar to his home. He intended to humiliate Ramkumar if his prediction proved to be false. The young woman was in perfect health and there was no sign that such a mishap could occur. But in fact what Ramkumar had predicted came to pass; and the man respectfully allowed him to leave.

Regarding his own wife's future, Ramkumar once made a sad prediction

16. Another example of Ramkumar's power, pertaining to his wife.

that eventually came true. We have heard that his wife was blessed with auspicious signs. It was probably 1820 when Ramkumar married; his wife was seven years old at the time. The very day she came to Kamarpukur, Ramkumar's fortune turned towards prosperity. His father's poor condition also began to improve, because at that time Kshudiram's nephew in Midnapore began to send him an allowance each month.

Understandably, Hindus always love and respect someone whose very entrance into the family brings good fortune. Moreover, Ramkumar's little wife was then the only daughter-in-law in that poor family. It is no wonder that everyone became very fond of her. We have heard that because she was indulged with so much love and care she became very sensitive and arrogant despite having good qualities. Everyone noticed her shortcomings, but none dared to say anything or correct her because they believed that, in spite of her minor defects, she brought prosperity to the family. When she became an adult, however, Ramkumar predicted: "Although she has auspicious marks, she will die if she ever becomes pregnant." When she did not conceive after some years, Ramkumar was relieved, thinking her to be barren. But in 1848 at the age of thirty-five, she became pregnant. The following year, she died after giving birth to a handsome son. The child was named Akshay. Although this incident took place much later, we have narrated it here for the sake of convenience.

Every member of Kshudiram's family was endowed with a special char-

17. A characteristic of Kshudiram's family.

acteristic. If you examine this, you will see that each person's subtle powers originated from the spiritual realm. It seems that Kshudiram and his wife were endowed with unique divine qualities and their children inherited these traits. In this respect, we have already related some stories about Kshudiram; it will not be out of place to mention a similar story about Chandramani that shows that she also had divine visions from time to time. The following incident took place sometime before Ramkumar's marriage. The fifteen-year-old Ramkumar was then studying at a Sanskrit school and contributing to the household by performing rituals in various homes.

It was the full-moon night of *Ashwin* [mid-September to mid-October].

18. Chandradevi's divine vision.

Ramkumar had gone to perform worship of Lakshmi, the goddess of fortune, at a house in Bhursubo, a nearby village. As midnight passed and her son did not return, Chandradevi became extremely anxious; she went outside and waited, gazing up the road. After some time she saw someone coming from Bhursubo towards Kamarpukur across the rice field. Thinking that her son was coming, she joyfully walked a short distance and waited for him. When that person came close, she realized it was not Ramkumar but a beautiful woman, adorned with various ornaments, walking alone towards her. However, Chandradevi was so apprehensive that evil had befallen her son, she was not surprised when she saw this aristocratic young woman walking alone so late at night. Chandradevi came to her and asked simply, "My child, where are you coming from?" The woman replied, "From Bhursubo." Chandra then asked anxiously: "Did you see my son Ramkumar? Is he coming back?" It did not occur to her for a moment to ask herself how a strange woman could possibly know her son. But consoling Chandra, the woman replied:

"Yes, I am coming from the same house where your son went to perform worship. Don't worry. Your son will be back soon." Chandra was relieved and began to notice other things. Observing the woman's extraordinary beauty, expensive clothing, and unusual jewellery, and listening to her sweet voice, Chandra asked: "My child, you are very young. Where are you going this late at night, wearing so many ornaments? What kind of earrings are those?" Smiling, the woman replied: "They are called *kundala*. I still have a long distance to go." Thinking her to be helpless, Chandradevi said affectionately, "My child, please rest at our house tonight and go to your destination tomorrow." The woman said: "No, Mother, I have to go right now. I shall visit your home another time."

Then the woman took leave of her and walked in the direction of the Laha's granaries, close to Chandradevi's house. Surprised to see her going towards the Lahas instead of following the road, Chandradevi thought that the woman had lost her way. Chandradevi immediately rushed after her. She looked all around but could not find the woman. Recalling their conversation, a thought suddenly flashed in Chandra's mind: She might have seen the goddess Lakshmi! Excited, Chandra rushed to her husband and told him the whole incident in detail. After listening to the entire story, Kshudiram assured her, saying, "Goddess Lakshmi has graciously revealed Herself to you." After a while Ramkumar returned home. He was amazed when he heard the story from his mother.

It was 1835. At this time a significant event took place in Kshudiram's life.

| 19. Kshudiram's pilgrimage to Gaya. | He once again felt the urge to go on a pilgrimage. He decided to go to Gaya, the abode of Vishnu, to perform rites for the redemption of his departed |

ancestors. Although he was then sixty years old, he had no hesitation about going to Gaya on foot [a distance of nearly 300 miles]. Hriday, the son of Kshudiram's niece Hemangini, told us an amazing story about the trip that Kshudiram made to Gaya.

During this time, Kshudiram went to Anur to visit his daughter, Katya-

| 20. Hriday's story about Kshudiram's Gaya visit. | yani, after receiving news that she was seriously ill. She was then about twenty-five years old. Observing her demeanour and manner of conversation, Kshu- |

diram became firmly convinced that a spirit had possessed her. After concentrating deeply on God, he addressed the spirit in his daughter's body: "Whatever you may be — a god or a demigod — why are you tormenting my daughter this way? Leave her at once and go somewhere else." At this the spirit became frightened and timidly answered through Katyayani: "If you promise to perform rites and offer a *pinda* [obsequial cake] at Gaya to release me from this present suffering, I promise to leave your daughter right now. I assure you that the moment you leave this house for this purpose, your daughter will be cured."

Vishnu temple at Gaya, which Kshudiram visited in March 1835.

Vishnu's footprint in the
inner shrine at Gaya.

Moved by the spirit's suffering, Kshudiram replied: "As soon as possible I shall go to Gaya and fulfill your wish. But I shall be happy if you will show me a sign that you are definitely released after the pinda has been offered." The spirit replied, "I assure you that, as definite proof of my deliverance, I shall break the big branch of yonder margosa tree as I leave." Hriday said that this incident made Kshudiram determined to go to Gaya. After some time the branch of that tree suddenly snapped, and all were convinced that the spirit had been released. From that moment on Katyayani was fully cured. We do not know the validity of Hriday's story, but there is no doubt that during this time Kshudiram visited Gaya.

Sometime during the winter of 1835, Kshudiram went to Varanasi[1] and Gaya. He first visited Lord Vishwanath at Varanasi and then in *Chaitra* [mid-March to mid-April] he went to Gaya. It seems he went to Gaya during that auspicious month because he knew that his departed ancestors would obtain boundless satisfaction if the rites were performed at that time. While staying there for a month, he performed all necessary rites according to the scriptures and at last he offered a pinda at the feet of Lord Gadadhar [Vishnu]. The devout Kshudiram experienced untold satisfaction and peace as he performed the prescribed obsequial rites for his ancestors. He was relieved from all anxiety as he fulfilled his obligations to them to the best of his ability. Reflecting on how God had endowed an unworthy person like himself with the strength to complete that task, his grateful heart was filled with humility and love. Peace and joy were with him, not only during the day, but also at night as he slept.

21. Kshudiram's divine dream at Gaya.

One night as he fell asleep he started dreaming: He saw himself again offering pindas to his ancestors at the holy feet of Lord Gadadhar in the temple. He also saw his ancestors in their luminous celestial forms joyfully accepting the offerings and blessing him. After gazing at them for a long time, he could not control himself. Overwhelmed with devotion, he began to weep and bowed down to them, touching their feet. In the next moment the temple was filled with a divine effulgence. He saw his ancestors standing on both sides of the shrine in a reverential attitude with folded hands, praying to a luminous Person seated graciously on a beautiful throne. He saw that the complexion of this Effulgent One was as green as a blade of new grass, and that he was looking at Kshudiram affectionately. Smiling, the Effulgent One beckoned Kshudiram to draw near. Like an automaton, he walked towards the Effulgent One, prostrated before Him with overwhelming

1. Some say that long before this Kshudiram had left Derepur for a pilgrimage to Vrindaban, Ayodhya, and Varanasi. Afterwards, his son and daughter were born; remembering his pilgrimage, he named them Ramkumar and Katyayani. During this last pilgrimage, he visited Gaya only.

devotion, and began to praise Him with various hymns. The Effulgent One was pleased and spoke the following words to him in a sweet, melodious voice: "Kshudiram, I am very pleased with your sincere devotion. I shall incarnate Myself as your son and accept the loving service you offer Me in your cottage."

Listening to these amazing words, Kshudiram's joy knew no bounds. But in the very next moment he wondered how such a poor man as himself could feed and shelter such an Exalted Being. Filled with sadness, Kshudiram sobbed: "No, no, my Lord, I am not deserving of this favour. It is more than enough that You have blessed me by graciously revealing Yourself and wishing to be born as my son. If You truly would be my son, how could I, a poor man, be able to serve You?" The Divine Being was even more pleased upon hearing Kshudiram's plaintive words, and said: "Don't be afraid, Kshudiram. Whatever you offer, I shall accept with satisfaction. Don't raise any objections to the fulfillment of My wish." At this Kshudiram was speechless. Conflicting emotions of joy and sorrow flowed with such force that he was left stupefied and senseless. At that moment his sleep broke.

For a long time after he awoke, Kshudiram did not recognize where

22. Kshudiram's return to Kamarpukur.

he was. The reality of his dream had completely overwhelmed him. When he finally regained consciousness of the external world, he arose from his bed and carefully recalled every detail of that wonderful dream, considering it from various perspectives. Finally, his devoted heart was convinced that because a divine dream is never false, a great soul would definitely be born into his home. Although he was advanced in age, he was destined to again see the face of a newborn son. He decided not to disclose the wonderful dream to anyone until it proved to be true. A few days later he left Gaya, returning to Kamarpukur in April of 1835.

Chapter 4

Various Experiences of Chandradevi

THE RELIGIOUS BOOKS OF ALL PEOPLES RECORD THAT when the great saviours of

1. Scriptural testimony regarding the parents' spiritual experiences during the advent of an avatar.

the world are born, their parents experience extraordinary spiritual fervour and visions. This fact has been proven in the scriptures regarding the parents of Ramachandra, Krishna, Buddha, Jesus, Shankara, Chaitanya, and other great religious personalities who are still worshipped with love and reverence. To illustrate this truth it will be sufficient to recall the following instances.

It is recorded in the Ramayana that the mothers of Ramachandra and his three half-brothers conceived them by eating rice pudding left over from a sacrifice. Moreover, the women realized many times, both before and after the births of their sons, that the children manifested divine powers and aspects of Vishnu, the Lord of the Universe.

The parents of Krishna had a vision of God endowed with six powers at the time of conception as well as immediately after his birth. In addition, it is recorded in the Bhagavata and other Puranas that Krishna's parents had various wonderful visions after his birth.

When Buddha was conceived, his mother, Mayadevi, saw a Supreme Being enter her womb in the form of a luminous white elephant, while Indra and other gods paid homage to her for her good fortune.

Before Jesus was born his mother Mary felt that she had become pregnant, even though her marriage to Joseph had not been consummated. As her pregnancy became evident, she was overwhelmed with spiritual emotions.

Shankara's mother realized that she had conceived when the great god Shiva appeared to her and granted her a boon.

Chaitanya's mother Shachidevi had similar spiritual experiences, which are recorded in *Sri Chaitanya Charitamrita* and other books.

Hinduism, Buddhism, Christianity, and other religions have shown that devoutly worshipping God is the easiest way to attain liberation. As they all hold the same premise, a question spontaneously arises in the mind of an impartial investigator as to whether there is any truth underlying this assertion, and if there is, how much of the life stories of those great teachers is to be accepted or rejected.

2. The reason for that scriptural testimony.	Reason implies that there may be some truth in the nativity stories of the great souls. Modern science concedes that highly evolved parents are capable of begetting children of noble character.

It is therefore to be admitted that the parents of great souls like Krishna, Buddha, and Jesus were endowed with divine qualities. Moreover, it is clear that when these great souls were born, the minds of their parents dwelt in exalted planes of consciousness that ordinary minds cannot reach. As a result, they had wonderful visions and spiritual experiences.

3. Though difficult to believe, scriptural testimony cannot be dismissed as false.	The Puranas mention many wonderful stories regarding the great teachers. Although those stories are supported by reason, the human mind still does not believe them completely. The human mind relies above all on its own experience, so without direct experience it cannot unequivocally

believe in the reality of the Atman, God, liberation, the afterlife, and so on. Although this is true, a person with an impartial and discriminating intellect does not reject anything simply because it is uncommon or supernatural. Rather, such a person acts as a witness and calmly collects all data for and against a particular subject. At the right time, the subject is either rejected as false or accepted as true.

We have learned from reliable sources that at the time of Sri Ramakrishna's birth his parents had various divine visions and spiritual experiences. We have no alternative than to record the facts. In the previous chapter we have mentioned some incidents concerning Kshudiram, and now in this chapter we will relate some stories about Chandradevi.

4. Returning from Gaya, Kshudiram sees a change in Chandradevi's mood.	We have already mentioned that Kshudiram had a wonderful dream in Gaya. After returning home he did not tell anyone about it, but he silently observed its effect. First of all, he noticed that a wonderful change had come over

Chandradevi. He saw that Chandra had indeed been elevated from the human level to the rank of a goddess. An all-embracing love occupied her heart and raised her to a lofty plane above the bustle of worldly desires. At that time Chandra was more concerned about their needy neighbours than about her own household. In between her household duties, she would often visit her neighbours and attend to their needs. If she found that they needed food or anything else, she would secretly take these things from her own household and give them to the neighbours. After completing the service of Raghuvir, she would serve food to her husband and children without eating any herself. Then, although it was late, she would go to her neighbours to inquire whether they had eaten their meals. If someone was without food, she would immediately bring that person home and give the guest her own food. Then she would joyfully take a little refreshment. In this way she passed her days.

Chandra had always loved the neighbours' children as her own. Now

5. Chandradevi's motherly affection increases.

Kshudiram observed that her motherly affection had been extended to the deities as well. She actually looked upon the family deity, Raghuvir, as one of her own sons, and in her heart she had the same feeling for the other deities, the goddess Shitala and Rameswar Shiva. Previously, her heart had been filled with awe during the service and worship of these deities, but love vanquished that fear. Now she had no hesitation about approaching the deities; she had nothing to hide from them and nothing to ask of them. She considered those deities to be her very own self; she wished to surrender herself completely to make them happy; and she was overwhelmed with joy because of her eternal relationship with them.

Kshudiram realized that her unreserved devotion to God and joyful self-

6. Kshudiram's concern for her.

surrender were making the simple-hearted Chandra more liberal and guileless than ever. As a result, she could not mistrust anyone or consider anyone a stranger. But would worldly people, selfish by nature, properly appreciate her wonderful guilelessness? Of course not. People would call her dull-witted or crazy, or she might be harshly criticized. Therefore, Kshudiram looked for an opportunity to caution her.

That opportunity soon arrived. The simple-hearted Chandra could not

7. Chandradevi's divine dream.

hide her thoughts from her husband. She often confided in her friends; how could she withhold anything from someone who was, by divine providence, closer to her than anyone else in this world? When Kshudiram returned home from Gaya, Chandradevi took every opportunity to relate to him her visions and experiences, and whatever else had happened during his absence. One day she told him: "Listen, when you went to Gaya, one night I had a wonderful dream. I saw a luminous being lying on my bed. First I thought it was you. Then I realized that no human could have that kind of beauty. When I awoke, however, I felt that the being was still in the bed. The next moment I thought, 'Does a god appear to a human like this?' Then it occurred to me that perhaps a wicked person had entered the room with evil intent, and the sound of his footsteps had caused my dream. The very thought frightened me. I immediately got up and lit the oil lamp; but I found no one in the room and the door was bolted as before. Nevertheless, I passed the night sleepless and in fear. I thought that perhaps someone had entered the room by carefully opening the bolt, and then, seeing me awake, ran away again, bolting the door as before. At daybreak I sent for Dhani and Prasanna. After telling them the whole story, I asked: 'What do you think about it? Did anyone truly enter my room? I have no enemies in the village, but the other day I had a little quarrel with Madhu Yugi over a trifling matter. Is it possible that he entered my room secretly that way?' Then both of them laughed and scolded me, saying: 'You silly woman, have you become senile? Why are you behaving strangely because of a dream? Think of what other people will say when they hear this story. They will spread rumours about you. If you divulge this to anyone else, we will teach you a lesson.' Listening to them, I thought perhaps it really was a dream. I decided not to mention it to anybody except you when you came back.

"Another day, I was standing in front of the Yogi Shiva temple and talking with Dhani. Suddenly I saw a divine light emanating from the image of Shiva. It filled the temple and rushed towards me like a wave. Overwhelmed, I was about to tell Dhani about it, but suddenly the light engulfed me and entered my body. Stupefied with fear and wonder, I fell unconscious. Later, when I regained consciousness with Dhani's help, I told her my experience. At first she was amazed; but then she said, 'You had an epileptic fit.' From then on I have had the feeling that the light is still in my womb and that I am pregnant. When I mentioned this to Dhani and Prasanna, they scolded me and called me foolish, mad, and so on. They explained to me that the feeling that I was pregnant was either coming from a delusion or hypochondria, and they forbade me to disclose it to others. Well, what do you think about it? Did I have that vision by God's grace or was it hypochondria? Even now I feel that I am with child."

8. Her divine vision and experience in the Shiva temple.

Recalling his own dream at Gaya, Kshudiram listened to Chandra's experiences and assured her that they were not the products of a disease. He then said: "Henceforth, do not speak about your visions or experiences to anyone except me. Do not worry. Know for certain that whatever Raghuvir shows you out of his mercy, is for your good. While I was in Gaya, in a miraculous way Gadadhar revealed to me that we would have another son." Chandra was heartened by the assurances of her godlike husband and did as he advised, depending fully on Raghuvir. Three or four months after this conversation between Kshudiram and Chandra it became apparent to all that, at the age of forty-five, Chandra had become pregnant again. When a woman becomes pregnant, invariably her beauty and grace increase; this

9. Kshudiram cautions her not to disclose it to anyone.

Yogi Shiva temple next to Ramakrishna's
family cottage in Kamarpukur.

Interior of Yogi Shiva
temple showing the
image of Shiva.

happened to Chandra also. Dhani and the other village women remarked that this pregnancy made her more beautiful and graceful than had her previous ones. Observing Chandra's charm, some of the women gossiped and speculated: "Look, this woman looks so beautiful after conceiving at such an advanced age! This time she may die during delivery."

During her pregnancy, Chandra's divine visions and spiritual experiences increased. It is said that during this time she would see gods and goddesses daily; sometimes she would smell a divine fragrance that emanated from their bodies and filled the room. Sometimes she would hear divine voices. It is also said that at this time her motherly affection overflowed towards all gods and goddesses. Almost every day she would confide her visions and experiences to her husband and ask him why she was having them. Kshudiram would reassure her in many ways and advise her not to be afraid. We shall relate an incident that took place during this period as we have heard it.

> 10. Chandradevi's visions during pregnancy.

One day the awestruck Chandra told her husband the following: "Listen, my dear, since I had the vision of light in front of the Shiva temple, I have been having innumerable visions of different gods and goddesses. I have never seen some of their forms, even in pictures. Today a god appeared riding on a swan. At first I was frightened; then my heart melted as I saw that his face had been scorched red by the sun. I called to him and said: 'O my little god mounted on the swan, your face has become burnt by the sun. In my house there is some cool soaked rice. Please have some to cool yourself before you leave.' Hearing my words, he smiled and vanished into air. I couldn't see him anymore. Likewise, I see so many forms. I see those divine forms not only during worship or meditation, but frequently in my normal state. Sometimes I see them coming in human form and then disappearing. Can you tell me why I see these forms? Is it some kind of disease? Sometimes I wonder whether I am possessed by the spirit of Gosain."[1]

Kshudiram reminded her again about his own dream at Gaya and explained that this time, as a result of great good fortune, the Supreme Being had been conceived in her womb. It was because of His holy contact that she was having these visions. Chandra had absolute faith in her husband, so his comforting words filled her heart with supreme devotion. Strengthening herself with new vigour, she became free from anxiety.

Time passed. Surrendering solely to Raghuvir, Kshudiram and his noble wife spent their time in expectation of the great soul who was to be their son, whose advent filled their lives with heavenly devotion.

---

1. After the death of Sukhlal Goswami, some unforeseen calamities took place that convinced the villagers that Goswami or someone in his family had become a ghost and was living in the bakul tree in front of his house. Under the influence of that belief, if anyone had a divine vision, people would say, "That person is possessed by Gosain (Goswami)." That is why the simple-hearted Chandra made this remark.

Chapter 5

The *B*irth of a Great Soul

SPRING, THE KING OF SEASONS, HAD ARRIVED AFTER fall and winter. The weather was neither cold nor hot, and all of creation pulsated with new life. It was the sixth day of the pleasant month of Phalgun [mid-February to mid-March]. An upsurge of zeal, joy, and love was visible among the people. The scriptures say that people are blissful because they have a particle of the bliss of Brahman inside. Does spring, having a little more of that divine bliss, bring so much joy everywhere in this world?

One spring day Chandra was cooking food for Raghuvir. She was nearing the end of her pregnancy, and although she was experiencing celestial bliss in her heart, physically she was extremely exhausted. Suddenly she realized that her physical condition was unpredictable. If the labour pains were to start right then, there would be no one at home who could prepare the Lord's offerings. What could be done? Alarmed, Chandra expressed her concerns to her husband. Kshudiram assured her, saying: "Don't fear. He who is in your womb would never enter our home at a time when the worship of Raghuvir would be disturbed. This is my firm conviction. Therefore, don't worry. Today you will certainly be able to manage the service of the Lord, and beginning tomorrow I have already made different arrangements. I have asked Dhani to begin sleeping here tonight." At this Chandra felt new energy in her body and cheerfully continued her household duties. Everything happened as it had been predicted. The noon and evening food offerings of Raghuvir were performed without disturbance. After supper, Kshudiram and Ramkumar slept in one room; Dhani came and lay in another room with Chandra. Apart from the shrine of Raghuvir, the household consisted of two huts and a kitchen. In another small thatched

> 1. Chandradevi's apprehension is removed by her husband's assurance.

108

shed there was a husking machine on one side and a wood-burning stove for boiling rice on the other. Because there was no other place available, this shed was reserved as the delivery room.

About twelve minutes before dawn, Chandradevi felt the first labour pain.

2. Birth of Gadadhar [Sri Ramakrishna].

Dhani immediately escorted her to the shed; and as soon as she lay down, she gave birth to a male child. After providing Chandra with the necessary help, Dhani turned her attention to the baby. But he had disappeared from where she had put him. Alarmed, Dhani turned up the flame of the oil lamp and searched the hut. She found that the baby, who was covered with blood and fluid, had slid over the floor and was lying in the wood-burning stove, besmeared with ashes. Nevertheless, the baby did not cry. Dhani then carefully lifted him up, washed him, and saw in the light of the lamp a wonderfully handsome child who looked as if he were six months old. In the meantime, a few of Chandra's friends including Prasanna and some women of the Laha family, had been summoned. When they arrived, Dhani told them the good news. At the auspicious and solemn moment before sunrise, Kshudiram's humble, holy cottage reverberated with the sound of conch shells proclaiming to the world the advent of a great soul.

Being well versed in the scriptures, Kshudiram checked the astrological

3. Astrological signs at Gadadhar's time of birth.

signs of the newborn child and found that he had come into the world at a very auspicious moment. It was Wednesday, 6 *Phalgun* 1242 in the Bengali era, or 1757 in the Saka era, or Thursday, 18 February 1836 A.D. The child was born twelve minutes before sunrise.[1] The auspicious second lunar day of the bright fortnight and *Purvabhadrapada* [the twenty-fifth of the lunar constellations] had joined at the time of his birth, which created *siddhiyoga*, a fortunate astrological conjunction. The Sun, Moon, and Mercury had come together as the astrological sign under which the child was born. Moreover, Venus, Mars, and Saturn were in the highest ascension; this indicated that the child would have an extraordinary life. Again, the sage Parashara's astrological chart showed that the planets *Rahu* [ascending node] and *Ketu* [descending node] were at the highest point during the child's birth. Finally, Jupiter, which was then in an ascending mode, exerted a strong and auspicious influence on the child's destiny.

Later, some distinguished astrologers studied the time of his birth and said

4. Gadadhar's name, according to his natal sign.

to Kshudiram that the child had been born during an auspicious arrangement of the planets. Astrological science decisively concludes: "Such a person will be profoundly religious, highly respected, and will be always engaged in virtuous deeds. He will live in a temple surrounded by many disciples. He

1. According to the Hindu calendar the day begins at sunrise, whereas according to the Gregorian calendar it begins at midnight.

Site of the threshing shed where Ramakrishna was born on 18 February 1836.

will establish a new religious order. He will be renowned all over the world as a great soul and will be worshipped by the people as a part of Narayana."

Kshudiram's mind was filled with wonder. He realized with gratitude that the divine dream he had experienced in Gaya had actually come true. After performing the proper birth rites, Kshudiram named the child Shambhuchandra according to his natal sign. But to commemorate his wonderful dream in Gaya, he decided to publicly call him Gadadhar.

Here we present a portion of Gadadhar's horoscope. Those who are

5. Gadadhar's horoscope. | experts in astrological science will understand that it is similar to those of Ramachandra, Krishna, Shankara, Chaitanya, and other avatars.

Gadadhar's (Sri Ramakrishna's) Horoscope
by Narayan Chandra Jyotirbhushana

शुभमस्तु । शकनरपतेरतीताब्दादय: १७५७।१०।५।५९।२८।२९। सन १२४२ साल । एतच्छकीय-सौर-फाल्गुनस्य षष्ठदिवसे, बुधवासरे, शुक्लपक्षीयद्वितीयायां तिथौ, पूर्वभाद्रपदनक्षत्रस्य प्रथम चरणे, सिद्धियोगे, वालवकरणे एवं पञ्चाङ्गसंशुद्धौ, रात्रि चतुर्दशविपलाधिकैक त्रिंशद्दण्डसमये अयनांशोद्धव-शुभ-कुम्भलग्ने (लग्नस्फुटराश्यादि १०।३।१९'।५३"।२०"') शनैश्वरस्य क्षेत्रे, सूर्यस्य होरायां सूर्यसुतस्य द्रेक्काणे, शुक्रस्य नवांशे, बृहस्पतेर्द्वादशांशे, कुजस्य त्रिंशांशे एवं षड्वर्ग परिशोधिते पूर्वभाद्रपद-नक्षत्राश्रितकुम्भराशिस्थिते चन्द्रे बुधस्य यामार्धे जीवस्य दण्डे, कोणस्थे गुरौ केन्द्रस्थे बुधे चन्द्रे च लग्नस्थे चन्द्रे, त्रिग्रहयोगे, धर्मकर्माधिपयो: शुक्रभौमयो: तुंगस्थितयो:, वर्गोत्तमस्थे लग्नाधिपे शनौ च तुंगे, पराशरमतेन तु राहुकेत्वोस्तुंगस्थयो: (यत: उक्तं, ''राहोस्तु वृषभं केतोर्वृश्चिकं तुंगसंगितम्'' इत्यादिप्रमाणात) अतएव उच्चस्थे ग्रहपञ्चके, असाधारण पुण्यभाग्ययोगे, शुक्लपक्षे निशि-जन्महेतो: विंशोत्तरीदशाधिकारे जन्म, एतेन बृहस्पतेर्दशायां, तथा देशभेदेन दशाधिकारनियमाच्च अष्टोत्तरीय-राहोर्दशायां, अशेषगुणालंकृत स्वधर्मनिष्ठ-क्षुदिरामचट्टोपाध्याय-महोदयस्य (सहधर्मिणी-दयावती-चन्द्रमणिदेवी-महोदयाया: गर्भे) शुभ: तृतीयपुत्र: समजनि ।

तस्य राश्याश्रितं नाम शम्भुराम देवशर्मा । प्रसिद्ध नाम गदाधर चट्टोपाध्याय: । साधनासिद्धिप्राप्त-जगद्विख्यातनाम श्रीरामकृष्णपरमहंसदेव महोदय: ।।

जन्मकुण्डली—

दिवा — २८ । २८ । १५		
४	२४	२०
१	५१	४९
४६	२६	५९
४४	किं	६

जाताः

दिवा — २८ । ३१		
५	२५	२१
२	५१	४१
४५	४१	४८
१६	२	७

पराहः

चान्द्रफाल्गुनस्य शुक्लपक्षीयद्वितीया जन्मतिथिः ।

पूर्वभाद्रपदनक्षत्रमानं	६०	१५	०
तस्य भोगदण्डादिः	५२	१२	३१
भुक्तदण्डादिः	८	२	२९

जन्मकोष्ठीफलम् —

धर्मस्थानाधिपे तुंगे धर्मस्थे तुंगखेचरे । गुरुणा दृष्टिसंयोगे लग्नेशे धर्मसंस्थिते ॥
केन्द्रस्थानगते सौम्ये गुरौ चैव तु कोणभे । स्थिरलग्ने यदा जन्म सम्प्रदायप्रभुर्हि सः ॥
धर्मविन्माननीयस्तु पुण्यकर्मरतः सदा । देवमन्दिरवासी च बहुशिष्यसमन्वितः ॥
महापुरुषसंज्ञोऽयं नारायणांशसम्भवः । सर्वत्र जनपूज्यश्च भविष्यति न संशयः ॥
इति भृगुसंहितायां सम्प्रदायप्रभुयोग: तत्फलं च ॥

[Sri Ramakrishna was born in the year A.D. 1836 on the 2nd day of the bright fortnight of the month when the sun was in the zodiac of Aquarius (*Kumbha* — 18 February), early in the morning at about 5:00 a.m. His birth took place when it was *siddhiyoga* owing to the auspicious union of *Shukla Dwitiya* with *Purvabhadrapada Naksatra*. His natal star was *Purvabhadrapada* (Pegasi), the twenty-fifth lunar mansion. In his *Janmalagna*, that is, in the zodiac at the time of his birth, there was the conjunction of three planets, namely, the Sun, Moon and Mercury (*Surya, Candra,* and *Budha*) and three other planets, namely, Venus, Mars and Saturn (*Shukra, Mangala,* and *Shani*) were in exaltation in the 12th, 10th, and 7th houses respectively. And again, according to the sage Parasara, the planets *Rahu* and *Ketu* (two other ascending and descending nodes of the moon) also occupied the highest positions as they were in the 2nd and 8th houses respectively; Jupiter (*Brihashpati*) occupied the 3rd house and so it had a tendency towards ascendancy (*Tungavilasi*). The result of this natal arrangement of the planets is, according to *Bhrigu Samhita*, that the man becomes the head of a religious movement; he is virtuous, highly honoured, and always engaged in doing virtuous deeds; he lives in a temple and gets a large following of disciples; he is called a great man by all, and is born of the spirit of Lord Narayana; he is worshipped by all.]

Looking at the face of their beautiful child and hearing of his unique destiny, Kshudiram and Chandra considered themselves blessed. At the proper time they performed the ceremonies of naming the child and of taking him out for the first time. Thereafter, they concentrated on raising the child with special care.

Ramakrishna's marble image in the Kamarpukur temple.

Temple dedicated to Ramakrishna in 1951 on the spot where he was born.

Chapter 6

Gadadhar's Childhood and the Death of His Father

IN THE SCRIPTURES IT HAS BEEN RECORDED THAT before and after their children's

1. Ramchand's gift of a cow.

birth, the parents of Rama, Krishna, and other divine incarnations had various spiritual visions. However, although they well knew that their sons were protected by Providence, parental affection caused them to forget this, and they worried about their children's care and upbringing. The same happened to Kshudiram and his wife, Chandradevi. When they saw Gadadhar's beautiful face, the divine dream at Gaya and the vision in front of the Shiva temple at Kamarpukur were nearly forgotten, and they began to make various plans for the child's proper care. News of Gadadhar's birth was sent to the prosperous nephew Ramchand in Midnapore. Realizing that there would not be sufficient milk in his uncle's poor family, Ramchand sent a dairy cow to Kshudiram and relieved him of that particular worry. Thus, the newborn child's needs were fulfilled unexpectedly from various sources. Still there was no end to Kshudiram's and Chandra's anxiety. Thus time rolled on.

Day by day the newborn child's influence increased, first working on his

2. Gadadhar's charm.

parents, then slowly captivating the hearts of the village women. Every day during their leisure hours, the village women would visit Chandra. When asked the reason for their visits, they replied: "We love to see your son; that is why we come. What else can we do?" Women relatives in neighbouring villages frequently visited Kshudiram's humble cottage for this same reason. Thus the new child was raised with the loving care of all. When he was five months old, the time came for his rice-feeding ceremony.

At first Kshudiram planned to arrange the rice-feeding ceremony according to his means. He thought that after performing the scriptural rites, he would finish the ceremony by feeding his son a little bit of food consecrated to Raghuvir. He planned to invite a few close relatives for the occasion. But the event took a different turn. Dharmadas Laha, the village landlord and Kshudiram's great friend, secretly prompted the leading brahmins to visit Kshudiram. The brahmins joyfully insisted that Kshudiram feed them all on that auspicious occasion [the rice-feeding ceremony]. Their request put Kshudiram in an awkward position. As he was loved and respected by all the villagers, he could not decide whom to invite and whom to leave out. But how could he afford to entertain everyone? "Let Raghuvir's will be done," said Kshudiram. He surrendered himself to the Lord, then consulted with Dharmadas about the ceremony. Upon learning of his friend's good intentions, Kshudiram handed over responsibility for the function to Dharmadas and returned home. Dharmadas cheerfully arranged the ceremony, spending his own money for most of it. The event went off smoothly. We heard that during Gadadhar's rice-feeding ceremony, village people of all castes joyfully partook of Raghuvir's prasad at Kshudiram's cottage. Many beggars also enjoyed the food on that occasion, and they left praying for Gadadhar's long life and for his welfare.

> 3. Dharmadas Laha's help during Gadadhar's rice-feeding ceremony.

As the days went by, every little act of Gadadhar appeared even sweeter to Chandradevi, filling her heart with joy and awe. Prior to Gadadhar's birth she had not been eager to ask any favour from the gods; but now she prayed for her son's welfare innumerable times, both consciously and unconsciously. Still her motherly heart was not free from anxiety. It is easy to understand that Chandra's mind was fully preoccupied with her son's care and well-being, and those concerns eclipsed the power of her divine visions. Yet from time to time that divine power would display itself to a slight degree, and her mind would become filled with awe and sometimes with an apprehension that unseen evil might befall her son. In this connection we have heard an incident from a reliable source that we shall relate to our readers.

> 4. Manifestation of Chandradevi's divine visions.

One morning when Gadadhar was seven or eight months old he fell asleep while Chandra was breast-feeding him. Seeing that her son was asleep, Chandra put him to bed, dropping the mosquito curtain to protect him. She then left the room and began her housework. Shortly afterwards, she returned to the room for something and found a tall, strange man lying in place of her child, covering the whole bed. She cried out in panic and hurriedly left the room, calling for her husband. When Kshudiram arrived, Chandra told him what had happened. They entered the room, but found no stranger; the child was sleeping as before. Even then, Chandra's fear did not subside. She said

> 5. An incident: Gadadhar looks unusually large.

repeatedly: "An evil spirit must have possessed him. I clearly saw a large person lying in place of my son. In no way was it a delusion — there is no possibility that it was. Please bring an experienced exorcist to examine the child soon; otherwise who knows what harm will befall him."

Kshudiram reassured her, saying, "We were blessed with divine visions before the birth of our son. It is no wonder that you have seen that person. Please don't harbour the notion that the child is possessed by an evil spirit. As Raghuvir himself dwells in our house, no spirit can come here to do any harm to the child. Therefore, rest assured and do not divulge this to anyone. Know for certain that Raghuvir is always protecting the child." Chandra was temporarily pacified by her husband's words, but her mind was not fully relieved from fear for her son. That day she fervently prayed to the family deity, Raghuvir, for a long time, thereby relieving the agony of her heart.

Thus, the parents of Gadadhar passed their days in joy and excitement, fervour and anxiety. From the very beginning the little child exerted his sweet and loving influence on his parents as well as others, and this influence increased and became more established day by day. Four or five years elapsed. During this period [in 1839] Kshudiram's youngest daughter, Sarvamangala, was born.

6. Gadadhar's younger sister, Sarvamangala.

As his son grew, Kshudiram observed with awe and joy the manifestation of Gadadhar's extraordinary memory and talents. Taking the lively boy on his lap, Kshudiram would repeat the names of his ancestors, short hymns and salutation mantras for different gods and goddesses, and various stories from the Ramayana and the Mahabharata. When he tested the boy, Kshudiram noticed that he had learned most of them after hearing them only once. When the boy was asked to repeat those hymns and stories after many days, he could do so without faltering. At the same time Kshudiram discovered that although the boy eagerly learned and absorbed some subjects, he remained indifferent to others and nothing could rouse his interest in them. Kshudiram discovered this while teaching Gadadhar the multiplication table, but he felt it unnecessary to force the little boy to learn that subject at such an early age. Observing that the boy was becoming extremely restless, Kshudiram sent him to school at the age of five, after performing the ceremony for the commencement of studies. Gadadhar was happy to become acquainted with other children, and his loving nature made him popular with his friends and his teacher.

7. Gadadhar's initiation into student life.

The primary school was held in the spacious theatre hall in front of the house of the Lahas, the village landlords. A teacher was appointed, mostly at the landlords' expense, to teach their children and those of their neighbours. In fact, the Lahas established the school for the good of the village children. The

8. The Lahas' primary school.

Lahas' school in Kamarpukur, which Ramakrishna attended.

In the centre, a page from The Tales of Subahu, a long poem Ramakrishna copied by hand, with his signature below.

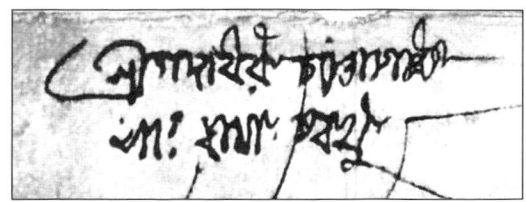

school was very close to Kshudiram's house. It was open every day in the mornings and afternoons. The students would arrive in the morning and study two or three hours, then go back home to bathe and eat. They returned at 3:00 or 4:00 p.m., and went home before sunset. Of course, young students like Gadadhar did not have to study for such long periods, but they did have to remain at school. After finishing their lessons during the study period, they would either sit in their places or play nearby with their friends. The older students would coach the newer ones and check to see whether they had learned their lessons.

Although there was only one teacher, the activities of the school proceeded smoothly. When Gadadhar was first admitted, Jadunath Sarkar was the teacher. Shortly thereafter he retired for various reasons, and Rajendranath Sarkar took charge.

The wonderful dreams and visions that Kshudiram had experienced before Gadadhar's birth, as a sign of his great life to come, left a permanent impression on his mind. Consequently, whenever he saw Gadadhar display childlike and naughty behaviour, he disciplined him mildly rather than chastising him harshly. Either because the boy enjoyed too much attention from everyone, or because of his inherent nature, Kshudiram occasionally observed signs of willfulness in his son. Kshudiram noticed that the self-willed boy would sometimes go with his friends to play outside the village rather than going to school, or he would attend an open-air dramatic performance nearby without first asking permission. But Kshudiram did not scold the boy as other parents would have; he thought that the boy's willfulness would improve his life in the future. There was sufficient reason for him to think this: Whenever Gadadhar began anything, he could not stop till it was finished; he never tried to conceal his actions by lying; and his loving heart never induced him to harm anyone.

9. Kshudiram's experience regarding Gadadhar's amazing character.

Despite all these good qualities, Kshudiram was concerned by one thing: When the boy was forbidden to do something he would disobey, unless he was given convincing reasons for the instruction. Gadadhar's nature compelled him to inquire about the reason for everything. Kshudiram was concerned that people would not tolerate this kind of behaviour or take the time to fulfill the boy's curiosity by explaining the reason for everything. So it was possible that occasionally the boy might not follow conventional rules of good conduct. About this time an incident raised these thoughts in Kshudiram's mind concerning the boy. Once he understood the boy's nature, Kshudiram began to guide him carefully.

There is a big pond known as Haldar Pond near Kshudiram's house. The villagers used its clean and pure water for drinking, cooking, and bathing. It had two bathing ghats, one for men and the other for women. Young boys like

10. An incident in this respect.

Gadadhar sometimes went to the women's ghat to bathe. One day Gadadhar went to the women's ghat with some of his friends and created a disturbance by swimming, jumping, and splashing water. The women found it very difficult to have their bath. According to custom, some elderly women engaged in prayer after their bath, and they were distracted by the boys' splashing. They told the boys to stop, but could not quiet them. Then one of the women angrily scolded them, saying: "Why do you come to this ghat? Can't you go to the men's ghat? Here women wash their clothes after bathing. Don't you know it is bad for you if you watch when women change their clothes?" Gadadhar asked her, "Why?" But she continued to scold him instead of explaining the reason so that he could understand. Seeing that the women were irritated and fearing that they might complain to their parents, the boys settled down.

But Gadadhar resolved to try an experiment. For two or three days he hid himself behind a tree near the pond and watched the women while they were bathing. Afterwards, he told that elderly woman who had scolded him: "The day before yesterday I saw four women bathing, yesterday six, and today eight. But nothing bad has happened to me." The woman then went to Chandradevi and laughingly told her what Gadadhar had said. Later, while they were resting, Chandra told Gadadhar gently in a convincing way: "My son, it is true that nothing bad will happen to you if you watch the women bathing, but they will feel humiliated. They are like me. If you dishonour them, it is the same as dishonouring me. So in the future don't be disrespectful towards them. Is it good to hurt them as well as me?" Gadadhar understood, and never did that again.

Gadadhar made fair progress in school. Within a short period he was able

| 11. The progress and range of Gadadhar's education. | to read and write, but his aversion for arithmetic remained. Day by day his ability to imitate others and his ingenuity extended to many new areas. |

Gadadhar began to visit the village sculptors and watch them make images of gods and goddesses. He learned their art of moulding and started to practise it at home; this became one of his hobbies. Similarly, he met painters, and he began to paint pictures like they did. Whenever there was any exposition of the Puranas or a *yatra* [performance] in the village, he attended and learned the myths of the Puranas. He also carefully observed the type of presentation that most appealed to the audience. His extraordinary memory and intelligence helped him in these pursuits.

On one hand, from an early age the ever-cheerful Gadadhar developed a sense of humour and fantastic skills of imitation, and he began to mimic the peculiar gestures of both men and women. On the other, his natural simplicity and devotion to God, and the ideal examples of his parents' day-to-day activities, helped him to make rapid progress in life. Even in his later years, Sri Ramakrishna always remembered and acknowledged his indebtedness to his parents with gratitude. The reader will understand this from the following account that he gave us at Dakshineswar: "My mother was an embodiment of simplicity. She was not worldly-wise at all; she did not even know how to count money. She was not clever enough to keep confidences when necessary. She would divulge whatever was in her mind to everyone. That is why people called her 'loose-lipped.' She was fond of feeding people. My father never accepted gifts from a *shudra* [the labouring caste]. He spent most of his day in worship, japa, and meditation. While practising his daily spiritual disciplines, when he would recite the invocation of the Gayatri mantra, 'Do Thou reveal to me, O Goddess Gayatri, the giver of boons,' and so on, his chest would swell and turn crimson. Tears flowed from his eyes. When he was not engaged in worship, he would spend his time making flower garlands with needle and thread to decorate Raghuvir. He left his parental home because he refused to give false testimony. The villagers loved and respected him as a rishi."

Gadadhar's indomitable courage manifested itself day by day. The boy

12. His courage.

would fearlessly go to places that older people avoided out of fear of ghosts and goblins. His aunt, Ramshila, was sometimes possessed by the goddess Shitala. During those times she seemed to become a different person. Once while visiting her brother at Kamarpukur she suddenly experienced that divine mood, creating awe and devotion in the minds of family members. Gadadhar observed his aunt's state with reverence, but he was not afraid. He stayed near her and carefully observed the change that had come over her. Later, he remarked, "It would be wonderful if the Being who possessed my aunt would possess me."

The reader has already been told about Manikraja, the generous and

13. His ability to make friends.

devout landlord of Bhursubo Village, which was situated a mile north of Kamarpukur. Attracted by Kshudiram's pious nature, Manikraja established a friendly relationship with him. One day Gadadhar, who was then six years old, went with his father to Manikraja's house. He behaved in such a sweet, natural, and intimate way that from then on he was dear to all of them. On that day Ramjay Bandyopadhyay, Manikraja's brother, was so impressed with Gadadhar that he said to Kshudiram: "Friend, your son is not an ordinary child; he seems to be greatly endowed with divine qualities. Whenever you come here, please bring your son with you. Seeing him brings me real joy." For several days, Kshudiram could not visit Manikraja for various reasons. Then Manikraja sent one of the women in his family to inquire about Gadadhar, and if possible to bring him to Bhursubo for a short visit. At his father's command Gadadhar went with the woman, staying the whole day and returning before evening with presents of jewellery and sweets. Gradually, Gadadhar became so favoured in that brahmin family that if

Kshudiram was delayed in visiting Bhursubo, they would send someone to fetch the boy.

Time passed and Gadadhar reached the age of seven. The child's sweet-

14. The result of Gadadhar's extraordinary imagination.

ness made him dear to all. Whenever the village women cooked any delicacies at home, they would think of feeding Gadadhar the first portion. His friends were extremely happy to share their food with him. The neighbours were so moved by his sweet talk, singing, and behaviour that they cheerfully put up with his childish pranks.

At this time an incident made his parents and friends very concerned about him. By God's grace Gadadhar was born with a healthy and strong body, and until this time had not had any particular illness. Consequently, Gadadhar enjoyed his life with freedom and contentment like a bird on the wing. Well-known physicians have said that a lack of body-consciousness is the sign of perfect health. For that reason, from his very birth Gadadhar experienced the joy of good health. However, when his naturally one-pointed mind was absorbed in a particular object, he would become completely identified with it, almost losing body-consciousness altogether. The enchanting scenery of a vast green field undulating in the gentle breeze, the incessant flow of the river, the melodious songs of the birds, and above all the magical kingdom of ever-changing clouds in the blue sky attracted his mind. Its mystical glory became manifest to the boy, and he would become instantly immersed in that inner realm, forgetting himself. The following incident arose from his overflowing spiritual emotion. The Master himself told us this incident (see II.2.19).

Once while roaming through a field, Gadadhar saw a beautiful black cloud heavy with rain; against it flew a flock of cranes, rhythmically spreading their white wings. He was so captivated by this sight that he completely lost awareness of his body and the objects of the world and fell unconscious on a ridge in the field. His friends were frightened and helpless when they found him in that condition. They informed his parents, and his body was carried home. Sometime after regaining outer consciousness, Gadadhar felt normal again. Kshudiram and Chandra were naturally very concerned by this incident, and they devised various means to ensure that it would not happen again. They thought it was a symptom of epilepsy and used medicines and performed religious ceremonies for his recovery from this illness.

Gadadhar repeatedly told his parents that this incident was the result of his mind becoming merged in a new and amazing feeling; contrary to outward appearance, he had indeed been conscious and had experienced wonderful bliss. Because the incident did not recur and Gadadhar seemed to be physically well, Kshudiram thought that he had an epileptic fit. However, Chandra was convinced that an evil spirit had cast a spell on him. Because of

that incident, they kept Gadadhar out of school for a time. Carefree, Gadadhar began to visit the neighbours, roam around the village, and devote
himself to more fun and play.

During the autumn worship of Durga in 1843, Gadadhar was seven

| 15. Durga worship at Ramchand's house. |

and a half years old. We have already mentioned
Kshudiram's successful nephew, Ramchand Bandyopadhyay. Although Ramchand spent most of his
time in Midnapore, where he worked, his parental home was in the village of
Selampur, where his family lived. Every year Ramchand spent a great deal
of money on the occasion of Durga Puja [worship]. We have heard from
Hriday that during worship Ramchand's Selampur house would rever-
berate with music and song for eight days, and a current of bliss would
flow continually. On this particular occasion Ramchand fed the brahmins
and the poor, gave clothes to the needy, and offered gifts to the pandits.
During this festive event, Ramchand would invite his respected uncle to
stay with him for a few happy days. This year also Kshudiram and his
family were cordially invited.

Kshudiram had now almost completed his sixty-eighth year. For some

| 16. Kshudiram and Ramkumar visit Ramchand's house. |

time he had suffered occasionally from dyspepsia
and dysentery, and his strong body had weakened.
So in spite of his willingness to visit Ramchand's
home, he was hesitant to accept the loving invitation. He felt an inexplicable
but strong disinclination to leave his modest cottage, his family, and especially Gadadhar, even for a few days. Again, he thought that since his body
was becoming weaker every day, who could say whether he would be able
to go to Ramchand's home again? He thought he would go and take Gadadhar along, but he reconsidered because it would make Chandra anxious.
He finally decided to go with his eldest son, Ramkumar, and spend a few days
of worship with Ramchand. He bowed to Raghuvir, bade good-bye to all,
kissed Gadadhar, and left for Selampur a few days before the worship began.
Ramchand was delighted to have his respected uncle and cousin Ramkumar.

Upon arriving at Selampur, Kshudiram had another attack of dysentery;

| 17. Kshudiram's illness and death. |

he was immediately placed under treatment. The
first three days of Durga Puja [shashthi, saptami, and
ashtami] went off with great joy; but on the fourth day
[navami] Kshudiram's disease took a serious turn, interrupting the mart of
joy. Ramchand brought in expert doctors and nursed his uncle with the help
of his sister Hemangini and cousin Ramkumar. But there was no sign of
improvement. Somehow the fourth day passed. The fifth day [vijaya
dashami], the auspicious day of reunion, arrived. On that day Kshudiram
was so weak that it was difficult for him to speak.

In the afternoon [of the fifth day], after the Durga image was ceremoni-
ously immersed, Ramchand rushed to his uncle to find that his last moment

was imminent. He was informed that Kshudiram had been unconscious for some time. Tearfully, Ramchand addressed him: "Uncle, you always repeated the name of Raghuvir. Why don't you do so now?" Upon hearing the name of Raghuvir, Kshudiram suddenly regained consciousness. Slowly he asked in a quivering voice: "Is it Ramchand? Have you come back after immersing the image? Please help me to sit up." Then Ramchand, Hemangini, and Ramkumar sat him up on the bed and held him carefully. Kshudiram immediately chanted thrice the name of Raghuvir in a solemn voice, then passed away. Thus, a drop of water mingled with the ocean: Lord Raghuvir absorbed the individual life of his devotee into his infinite life, making him immortal and giving him eternal peace. During the late hours of the night the whole village reverberated with *kirtan* [devotional singing] as Kshudiram's body was carried to the bank of the river and cremated. The sad news reached Kamarpukur the next day, plunging the once joyful family into grief. When the mourning period was over, Ramkumar performed the *shrāddha* [obsequial] ceremony for his departed father, as enjoined by the scriptures, and fed many brahmins. It is said that Ramchand provided 500 rupees for his uncle's shrāddha ceremony.

Chapter 7

Gadadhar's *B*oyhood

KSHUDIRAM'S DEATH BROUGHT A GREAT CHANGE to his family. By Providence

| 1. The impact of Kshudiram's death on his family. |

Chandra had him as her companion in happiness and misery for forty-four years. She now naturally found the world to be empty without him and felt his absence at every moment. As she was accustomed to taking refuge in Raghuvir, her mind was now continually diverted from her family affairs to focus on Him. Although her mind was ready for renunciation, the time was not ripe. Her concern for her seven-year-old son, Gadadhar, and five-year-old daughter, Sarvamangala, gradually drew her back to family responsibilities and to the joys and sorrows of daily life. Grief-stricken, Chandra passed her days serving Raghuvir and raising her youngest son and daughter.

The entire financial responsibility of the household now fell on the devoted Ramkumar, who thus did not have the leisure to grieve. His thoughts and actions were focussed on looking after his bereaved mother and little brother and sister so that they might not lack for anything. He helped his eighteen-year-old brother Rameswar finish his study of Smriti [Hindu law] and astrology so that he could contribute to the family's support. Ramkumar himself also tried to earn more money to improve the family's condition. His efficient wife, finding that Chandradevi was unable to cope with all the household work, took on most of the responsibility for cooking and other duties.

Wise people have said that nothing makes a man's life so empty as the loss

| 2. Its effect on Gadadhar's mental condition. |

of his mother in childhood, the loss of his father in boyhood, or the loss of his wife in youth. The mother's love and care are the mainstay of childhood, so if the father dies when the child is an infant, he or she does not feel the loss. But as the intellect develops and adolescence begins, the same child becomes aware of the father's precious love. A boy is then naturally drawn towards his father, who fulfills some of those needs that the affectionate mother cannot provide. If the boy loses his father during this period, he feels a terrible emptiness. This happened to Gadadhar when he lost his father. Every day, various small things would remind Gadadhar of his father's absence, making his heart heavy with sorrow. Because his heart and intellect were more developed than those of other boys, in consideration for his mother, he did not express his grief. Everyone believed that Gadadhar was happy as usual and passing his days in fun and laughter. However, sometimes he was seen wandering alone in the cremation ground at Bhuti's Canal, the mango orchard of Manikraja, and other solitary places around the village; but no one thought it was due to anything more than his natural boyish restlessness. From this point, Gadadhar became reflective and began to love solitude, and he also began to study the lives and behaviour of the people around him.

In this world two people become close to one another when they have

3. Gadadhar's behaviour towards his mother.

suffered the same loss. Perhaps that is why Gadadhar felt especially drawn to his mother. He now spent more time with his mother than before and enjoyed doing his best to serve the family deities and to help his mother with household work. In no time, he noticed that his mother almost forgot her emptiness when he was with her. Now his behaviour towards his mother took a different turn. Following his father's death, Gadadhar did not make any demands on his mother. He knew that if his mother was unable to fulfill his childish requests, her pent-up grief would be rekindled and she would be miserable. In fact, after his father's death, Gadadhar had a heartfelt urge to protect his mother.

Gadadhar resumed his studies in school as before. But his favourite activi-

4. Gadadhar's activities and his love of holy company.

ties were listening to the recital of the Puranas, attending dramatic performances, and sculpting clay images of gods and goddesses. Perhaps those activities helped him to forget the loss of his father. At this time, Gadadhar's extraordinary nature took a new turn. The wealthy Laha family had built a resthouse for pilgrims at the southeast corner of the village, adjacent to the road to Puri. Monks and ascetics sometimes stopped there on their way to and from visiting Lord Jagannath of Puri. During their stay they would collect alms from the villagers. Gadadhar had already heard about the transitoriness of the world, and now with his father's death he experienced it directly. He had learned from the Puranas that monks renounce the impermanent world to spend their time seeking God-realization. He had also learned that holy company bestows eternal peace. He therefore began to frequent the resthouse to meet the monks.

During his leisure, Gadadhar began to observe how the monks ignited the *dhuni* [sacred fire] in the morning and evening and sat around it, absorbed in meditation; how they offered to their Chosen Deities the simple food they had obtained by begging and joyfully partook of the *prasad*; how they endured severe illness without a murmur, solely depending on God; and how they were reluctant to disturb anyone even for their pressing needs. He also noticed how some hypocrites in monastic garb enjoyed selfish pleasures, disregarding all decency. Gradually he began to associate with the genuine monks and to help them by providing small services such as collecting wood for cooking, fetching drinking water, and so on. The monks were pleased with the behaviour of the handsome boy. They taught him prayers and devotional songs, gave him spiritual instructions, and enjoyed sharing with him the food they had collected as alms. Of course, Gadadhar had the opportunity to be closely associated with only those monks who stayed in the resthouse for longer periods of time for one reason or another.

When Gadadhar was eight years old, some monks stayed at the Lahas'

5. Chandradevi's fear regarding her son's friendship with monks, and how it is overcome.

resthouse for an unusually long period, either to recuperate from the fatigue of their journey or for some other reason. As usual, Gadadhar mixed with them and soon became their favourite. In the beginning, no one in his family knew about his association with the monks, but as he became closer and began to spend long periods of time with them, it became known to all. Some days he ate so much with them that he skipped his meal at home. When Chandradevi asked for an explanation, he told her everything. At first Chandra did not worry about it; she considered the monks' graciousness to be a blessing for her son, and she began to send various dishes to the monks through Gadadhar. But one day later on Gadadhar appeared before his mother with his body besmeared with ashes; another day he appeared with a mark on his forehead. Once he tore his own cloth into pieces and made a *kaupin* [loincloth], then wore it like a monk. Upon returning home he said, "Look, Mother, how the monks have dressed me." Chandra became alarmed at this. She thought that one day the mendicants might persuade her son to follow them. She expressed her concern to Gadadhar and began to weep. Gadadhar made every effort to pacify her but failed. Then he made a promise that he would not go to visit the monks anymore, thus reassuring his mother. However, before carrying out his resolution, he went to say good-bye to the monks. When the monks asked him the reason, he told them that his mother was apprehensive. They then accompanied Gadadhar home to visit Chandra and assured her that they had absolutely no intention of luring her son away. Moreover, they said that taking a young boy away without his parents' permission would be considered stealing, a terrible crime unworthy of a monk. This assurance removed

Chandra's misgivings, and at the monks' request she gave Gadadhar permission to continue visiting them as before.

At this time another occurrence made Chandra extremely anxious about

| 6. Gadadhar's second bhava samadhi. |

her son. Although everyone thought that this event happened suddenly, actually it was brought on gradually by Gadadhar's increasing spiritual mood and profound introspection. One day he left home to visit the famous goddess Vishalakshi at Anur, a village a couple of miles north of Kamarpukur. On the way he fell to the ground, unconscious. One of his companions, Prasannamayi, the pious daughter of Dharmadas Laha, realized that Gadadhar had lost external consciousness due to spiritual ecstasy. But when Chandra was told what had happened, the anxious mother did not believe Prasanna; she thought he had had an epileptic seizure or some other attack (see II.2.20). This time, as before, Gadadhar said that he had become unconscious because his mind had merged in the goddess as he was contemplating Her.

Thus, two years passed. Gradually Gadadhar almost forgot the loss of

| 7. Gadadhar's friend, Gayavishnu. |

his father as he adjusted to the ups and downs of daily life. We have already mentioned Dharmadas Laha, Kshudiram's intimate friend. At this time his son Gayavishnu became Gadadhar's close friend. They studied, played, and spent time together; and they even began to address each other as *sengat* [pal]. Whenever the village women invited Gadadhar to their homes to eat, he always brought his friend along with him. Whenever his elderly nurse, Dhani, presented him with fancy homemade sweets, he never ate any without sharing them with his friend Gayavishnu. Dharmadas and Gadadhar's guardians were happy to see this friendship between the two boys.

When Gadadhar was about to complete his ninth year, Ramkumar began

| 8. The story of Gadadhar's sacred thread ceremony. |

to arrange his *upanayana* [sacred thread ceremony]. Long before this time, Dhani had implored Gadadhar to accept his first alms from her and to address her as "mother" during his sacred thread ceremony. Overwhelmed by her genuine affection, Gadadhar promised to fulfill her wish. Counting on his word, the poor woman saved a little money according to her means and eagerly awaited the auspicious event. Just before the ceremony Gadadhar mentioned his promise to his eldest brother. Ramkumar objected because this went against their family tradition. [A brahmin does not accept first alms from a nonbrahmin.] Remembering his promise, Gadadhar was adamant on this matter. He told his brother that if he did not keep his word, he would be guilty of breaking his promise — and that an untruthful person is unworthy of wearing the sacred thread.

As the time for the sacred thread ceremony drew closer, all the arrangements were made; but the ceremony was in danger of being cancelled because of Gadadhar's unyielding stand. When the news reached Dharmadas Laha, he came forward to solve the dispute. He told Ramkumar that although there was no such precedent in their family, such things had happened in other good brahmin families. Thus, he reasoned, it would not bring any criticism upon them; moreover, it would give Gadadhar peace and satisfaction. Listening to the advice of their father's old friend, Ramkumar and the others did not raise any further objections. Following the brahminical tradition Gadadhar was invested with a sacred thread and he joyfully began to practise spiritual disciplines and perform worship like a brahmin. Dhani considered her life blessed because she had become Gadadhar's godmother. Soon after this event, Gadadhar reached his tenth year.

Sometime after the sacred thread ceremony, an incident occurred that

9. He solves a theological dispute at a scholars' conference.

revealed Gadadhar's extraordinary divine talent and struck the villagers with wonder (see III.4.3). A very large meeting of scholars was convened at the house of the wealthy Laha family during a shrāddha ceremony. The pandits debated on a complicated theological question but could not reach any suitable conclusion. Gadadhar was present, and after listening to their debate, he solved the disputed point. The pandits were amazed, and they praised and blessed him heartily.

Following the sacred thread ceremony, Gadadhar was happy as his

10. The result of Gadadhar's religious inclination, and his third bhava samadhi.

devotion-prone mind found the opportunity to do something that was suitable to his nature. Gadadhar had heard how the Lord Raghuvir had appeared to his father in a dream and was installed in their house by him, and how, upon His arrival, the family's small plot of land at Lakshmijala began to yield an abundance of rice. The yield was sufficient to supply their family, and the compassionate Chandradevi used the surplus to entertain guests and poor visitors. Knowing this, Gadadhar developed special reverence and devotion for the family deity Raghuvir. After his investiture with the sacred thread, he was permitted to touch the image of Raghuvir and to perform worship, which filled his heart anew with ardent devotion. Every day after finishing his regular spiritual disciplines, Gadadhar began to spend long periods of time in worship and meditation. He served Raghuvir with deep love and sincerity so that the Lord might bestow His grace and at times give him visions and guidance as He had done for his father. Gadadhar also worshipped and served Rameswar Shiva and the goddess Shitala. It did not take long for the result of his worship to manifest itself. Gadadhar's pure heart became so absorbed in worship that he experienced *bhava samadhi* or *savikalpa samadhi* and sometimes had various spiritual visions. He first encountered samadhi and experienced a spiritual vision during Shiva-ratri [the festival of Shiva] that year (see II.2.20-21).

Kshudiram's family shrine at left, with the veranda of
Ramakrishna's bedroom at right.

Family deities
worshipped by
Kshudiram: from
left to right, Shitala,
Rameswar Shiva, and
Raghuvir Ramachandra.

Gadadhar fasted that day and worshipped the Lord Shiva with unwavering devotion. His friend Gayavishnu and some other boys were also fasting on that auspicious occasion. They planned to observe the nightlong vigil by attending a drama based on the glory of Shiva at the house of their neighbour Sitanath Pyne. After completing the first three-hour period of worship, Gadadhar was absorbed in contemplation. Suddenly his friends came to inform him that he would have to perform the role of Shiva because the boy who was to play that part had become sick. Gadadhar declined at first, saying that it would interrupt his worship, but they persuaded him. They reasoned that if he played the role of Shiva, he would think of Him all the time. It would be in no way inferior to worship. Moreover, he should consider the many people in the audience who would be deprived of spiritual joy. They were also fasting and had decided to keep their vow of nightlong vigil by watching the play. Having no alternative, Gadadhar agreed. He appeared on stage in the role of Shiva; but in his costume of matted hair, rudraksha rosary, and ashes, he became so absorbed in the thought of Shiva that he lost outer consciousness. Even after a long while, he did not regain his external consciousness. The play was halted.

From then on Gadadhar occasionally experienced samadhi. During meditation or while listening to songs in praise of gods and goddesses, his mind would become so concentrated that it would withdraw for a period of

11. His repeated bhava samadhi.

time, becoming oblivious to external objects. When his absorption was profound, he would completely lose outer consciousness and become like a lifeless statue. If questioned after returning from that state, he would say that he had been blessed with a rapturous vision of the deity whom he had been meditating upon or whose praises he had heard being sung. At this Chandradevi and others in the family became extremely alarmed for several days, but their fear gradually disappeared when they found that Gadadhar's health did not deteriorate and that he was active and cheerful. As Gadadhar experienced samadhi again and again, it became natural to him and subject to his own will. As a result, he began to understand subtle spiritual matters and realize various aspects of gods and goddesses. These experiences of samadhi made him full of joy rather than fearful. From this period on, Gadadhar's religious inclination increased immensely; he began to join heartily in all the religious functions of the village, no matter whether they were connected with Hari, Shiva, Manasa, or Dharma. Gadadhar's catholic and religious nature made him free of malice towards the devotees of different gods and goddesses, and he established friendships with all kinds of devotees. Undoubtedly, the traditional customs of the village helped him in this respect: The followers of Vishnu, Shiva, and Dharma, and other sects, lived in Kamarpukur harmoniously and in amity, without the ill will common in some other villages.

Gadadhar had a highly developed interest in religion, but he did not have much use for book learning. Observing that pandits and teachers with advanced degrees had cravings for money and worldly enjoyments, he did not see any value in having an education like theirs. Gadadhar came to this conclusion by using his keen insight first to ascertain the motive behind people's actions, and then to evaluate their behaviour against the standard of his father's renunciation, devotion, truthfulness, ethical conduct, and righteousness. Thus judging the values that people lived by, Gadadhar was amazed at seeing how almost everyone in the world had different motives. Moreover, he was saddened when he saw people constantly suffering because they accepted the unreal world as real. It is no wonder that, after observing the miseries of worldly life, he resolved to conduct his own life differently. At this, the reader may ask if it is possible for a boy of eleven or twelve to have such subtle insight and power of discrimination. The answer is that although this may not be true in the case of ordinary boys, Gadadhar was not ordinary. He was born with extraordinary talents, a retentive memory, and spiritual tendencies. Although he was young, it is not surprising that he developed such attributes. Regardless of what people may think about it, in the interest of truth we must narrate all the facts that we have gathered in our investigation.

12. The reason for Gadadhar's indifference to education.

Although Gadadhar was gradually losing interest in traditional education, he went to school regularly and became adept in writing and in reading books written in Bengali, his mother tongue. When he read the Ramayana, the Mahabharata, and other scriptures, his devotion and his melodious voice would hold the audience spellbound. The simple, uneducated villagers were eager to hear him recite those religious stories, and Gadadhar was always willing to make them happy. Sitanath Pyne, Madhu Yugi, and others would invite Gadadhar to their houses; and men and women would listen with devotion as he recited the stories of Prahlada, Dhruva, and other epic tales from the Ramayana and Mahabharata. In the Kamarpukur area, in addition to the Ramayana and Mahabharata, one also finds lively stories of local gods and goddesses written by village poets in simple verse. Occasionally Gadadhar heard the story of how Tarakeswar Shiva revealed Himself, or a musical narrative describing the Divine Mother Yogodya, or the story of Madanmohan [Krishna] of Vana-Vishnupur, or many other stories of gods and goddesses and how they revealed themselves to monks and devotees. With the help of his prodigious memory, Gadadhar memorized these stories and musical compositions after hearing them only once; sometimes he copied them if they were available in manuscript or printed form. While investigating the Kamarpukur house we came across Gadadhar's handwritten manuscript of *Ramakrishnayana* and musical compositions on Yogodya and Subahu. Undoubtedly, whenever requested, Gadadhar would

13. His educational progress.

read or recite these stories from memory many times for the simple villagers.

Gadadhar's indifference to arithmetic has already been mentioned. But in school he did make some progress in that subject. We have heard that he advanced as far as the table of land-measurement from the Book of Tables, and from addition to simple multiplication and division. When Gadadhar occasionally experienced samadhi at the age of ten, some people, including his elder brother Ramkumar, thought that he had epilepsy. They therefore permitted him to go to school whenever he wanted to, and to learn whatever he wished. Gadadhar's teacher also did not press him when the boy did not progress in his studies. It is evident that henceforth Gadadhar's formal education did not advance any further.

Thus two years passed and Gadadhar reached his twelfth year. His

| 14. The marriages of Rameswar and Sarvamangala. |

second elder brother, Rameswar, was twenty-two and his youngest sister Sarvamangala, was nine. Since Rameswar had reached marriageable age, Ramkumar arranged his marriage to the sister of Ramsaday Bandyopadhyay of Gaurhati, a village near Kamarpukur; and at the same time he betrothed his sister Sarvamangala to Ramsaday. Due to this exchange, Ramkumar was not obliged to provide a dowry for Sarvamangala.

At this time, another important event took place in Ramkumar's family. When his wife had not conceived towards the end of her youth, everyone believed her to be barren. When she now became pregnant, the family members were simultaneously happy and fearful. Some had heard previously from Ramkumar that she would die if she ever conceived.

After his wife conceived, a significant change came over Ramkumar's

| 15. The nature of changes in Ramkumar's wife during pregnancy. |

fortune. To that point he had been earning money by various means, but now his income dwindled. In addition, his health deteriorated and he was not able to be as active as before. His wife's behaviour also altered; it became strange. From his father's time there had been an established rule in the family that no one should eat or even drink anything before the worship of Raghuvir; the only exceptions were uninitiated children or sick people. Now his wife broke that rule. Sensing an evil omen, everyone protested her actions but she did not listen to them. She also began to quarrel with family members over trifling matters, straining the relationships. Chandradevi and Ramkumar cautioned her, but could not stop her hostile behaviour. Thinking that these changes in her nature were due to her pregnancy, they left her alone. But from time to time a storm of disharmony blew through the pious household of Kamarpukur, shattering the peace.

Ramkumar's second brother, Rameswar, although well educated, was

| 16. The change in Ramkumar's financial condition. |

not capable of earning sufficient money. The family became insolvent because its income did not increase in proportion to the family's growth. Worried, Ramkumar attempted various means to solve their financial problems, but failed. It was as if an unseen power made all his efforts fruitless. Thus, a succession of misfortunes made Ramkumar's life burdensome. As the days and months passed and the time of his wife's delivery approached, he became increasingly sad, remembering his previous reading of her fate.

At last the time arrived. Sometime in 1849, Ramkumar's wife gave birth to a beautiful boy. But after seeing the child, she passed away in the delivery room. A pall of grief again fell over Ramkumar's poor family.

17. Ramkumar's wife dies during childbirth.

Chapter 8

At the *T*hreshold of Youth

AFTER RAMKUMAR'S WIFE DIED, HIS MISERY AND MISFORTUNE continued unabated.

| 1. Ramkumar opens a Sanskrit school in Calcutta. | His income, composed of gifts and collections for performing rituals, dwindled; day by day his financial condition worsened. Although there was sufficient |

rice from the land at Lakshmijala, the family suffered from a shortage of clothes and other everyday necessities. Moreover, his elderly mother and his motherless child Akshay needed milk on a daily basis. He met these expenses by borrowing money, and his debt increased day by day. Ramkumar made various attempts to solve his problem but failed. Ramkumar's friends suggested that he might earn more if he moved elsewhere, so he began to prepare himself. His grief-stricken mind gladly welcomed this decision. Memories of his wife, his companion for thirty years, permeated the house. He thought that he might have some peace if he left Kamarpukur. So a discussion ensued as to whether Calcutta or Burdwan would be a better place to earn more money. Finally his friends suggested that he go to Calcutta because Mahesh Chandra Chattopadhyay of Sihar, Ramdhan Ghosh of Deshra, and other acquaintances were making good money there and had improved their financial conditions. Ramkumar's friends also reminded him that those people were his inferiors in terms of learning, intelligence, and quality of character. Consequently, soon after his wife's death Ramkumar handed over responsibility for the family to Rameswar and left for Calcutta. He opened a *tol* [a Sanskrit school] in the Jhamapukur area and began to teach a few students.

After the death of Ramkumar's wife, many changes took place in the

| 2. How the death of Ramkumar's wife affected the family. | Kamarpukur family. Chandradevi had to resume responsibility for all the household work, including bringing up Ramkumar's son, Akshay. Rameswar's |

wife assisted her as much as possible, but she was then quite young and so was unable to be of much assistance. Chandradevi did everything almost single-handedly — serving Raghuvir, caring for Akshay, cooking, and doing other household work. She was forced to spend her entire day performing her duties and had not a moment's rest. It was not easy to carry such a heavy load at the age of fifty-eight,[1] but accepting it as the will of Raghuvir, Chandradevi carried on without complaint.

Now as the financial responsibility for the family fell on Rameswar, he had

3. The story of Rameswar.

to seriously consider how to earn money and make the family happy. Although he was well educated, he never earned much money. Whenever he met itinerant monks or spiritual aspirants, he would spend a long time with them and never hesitated to spend money in fulfilling their needs. Although he was earning a little more than he had been, it was not sufficient to pay off the family debt nor to meet their daily needs. He was not a frugal householder, and sometimes he spent more than he earned. He led a carefree life, holding on to the idea that Raghuvir would somehow provide everything.

Rameswar dearly loved his younger brother, but he did not pay attention

4. Rameswar's anxiety about Gadadhar.

to how Gadadhar progressed in his studies, because Rameswar had a different kind of temperament and moreover he was busy attempting to earn money. He had neither the inclination nor the time to supervise his brother's education. Observing Gadadhar's wonderful spiritual development at such an early age, Rameswar was convinced that his inherent nature would always lead him to the path of good rather than of bad. He developed this firm conviction by observing how the men and women of the village deeply trusted Gadadhar and loved him as their very own. Rameswar knew that if a man's character was not pure and noble, he would not be praised by all people, nor would he attract their hearts. Rameswar's heart was therefore joyful when he imagined Gadadhar's bright future and he had no misgivings at all. When Ramkumar left for Calcutta, Gadadhar was thirteen. From that point forward he was practically without a guardian and he was free to move in whatever direction his divine nature led him.

As has been mentioned, from his early youth Gadadhar's keen insight

5. Gadadhar's mental condition and activities at this time.

revealed to him a person's character and the motive behind his or her actions. So it did not take him long to understand that people seek a formal education and advanced degrees in order to make money. He also noticed that although people might enjoy worldly pleasures with their hard-earned money, they were not necessarily endowed with truthfulness, strength of

---

1. Chandradevi was born in 1791 and died in 1876 at the age of eighty-five. It is said that she passed away on Sri Ramakrishna's birthday.

character, and righteousness as his father had been. Blinded by selfishness, some members of a village family quarreled and entered into a legal battle over property; they divided their home and land with a measuring tape, saying, "This side is mine and the other side is his." But they had scarcely enjoyed their shares for a few days when death snatched them away. As Gadadhar witnessed these events, he clearly realized that money and the desire for enjoyment create suffering in human life. So it is no wonder that Gadadhar became indifferent to a mere money-making education. He decided to be content with "plain food and clothing" as his father had been; he realized that the prime goal of human life is to attain love for God. However, Gadadhar did attend school nearly every day because he enjoyed the company of his friends. But he spent more time in worship of Raghuvir and in assisting his mother with the housework to relieve her burden. He stayed at home the greater part of the day, engaged in these activities.

As Gadadhar spent much of his time at home, the village women had

| 6. Gadadhar sings and reads to the village women. |

many opportunities to be with him. After finishing their housework, some of the women would visit Chandra; seeing Gadadhar there, they would invariably ask him to sing or read religious stories to them. He tried his utmost to fulfill their requests. If they found him busy helping his mother, they would all rush to finish Chandra's work for her and thus make time to hear Gadadhar recite stories from the Puranas and sing the songs. This became part of his daily routine. The women enjoyed it so much that they would quickly finish their own household chores and rush to Chandra's house so that they could listen to Gadadhar as long as possible.

Besides reading stories from the Puranas, Gadadhar entertained the women in various ways. In Kamarpukur at that time there were three *yatra* [theatrical] groups, one *baul* [minstrel] party, and a couple of *kavis* [versifiers who compete in tournaments]. Furthermore, many Vaishnavas lived there, and they would read the Bhagavata and sing kirtan in their homes every evening. From his childhood Gadadhar had heard the operas, songs, and kirtans of these groups and had committed everything to memory. To entertain the women, one day he would recite dialogues from a drama, another day he would sing baul songs, and other days he would recite the compositions of the kavis or sing kirtan. While enacting a play, he alone would act out all the roles, changing his voice to suit each character. If he noticed that his mother, or any other woman, was depressed, he would portray the role of a clown from a play or mimic the particular manner and gestures of someone well known in the village, making them burst into laughter.

Gadadhar gradually exerted an immense influence over the village women.

| 7. Their love for and faith in Gadadhar. |

They had already heard about the wonderful dreams and visions his parents had before he was born. On occasion they also witnessed a transformation came over Gadadhar when he was in divine ecstasy. It is no wonder that his palpable devotion to God, his passionate readings from the Puranas, his sweet singing, and his simple, loving behaviour towards these women aroused unique devotion and affection in their hearts. We have heard that Dharmadas Laha's daughter, Prasannamayi, and other elderly women experienced the manifestation of the child Gopala [Krishna] in Gadadhar and loved him more than they did their own sons. The younger women believed that Gadadhar was a part of Krishna and so looked upon him as their friend. Most of these women had been born in Vaishnava families; a simple, imaginative faith was the mainstay of their religion. It is therefore no wonder that they believed that the handsome Gadadhar, who was endowed with divine qualities, was God Himself. On the basis of this faith they freely mixed with Gadadhar, confiding all their thoughts to him. They often asked for his advice, and tried to follow it. For his part, Gadadhar behaved with them as though he were one of them (see II.14.8).

Gadadhar [who was then thirteen or fourteen] would sometimes put on

| 8. Gadadhar in the guise of a woman. | women's clothing and jewellery and perform important dramatic roles for the village women. It was at their request that he dressed like a woman while acting in |

the role of Radha or her main female confidante, Vrinda. When he was portraying these roles his gestures, posture, conversation, and movements were exactly like those of a woman. When they saw him in women's clothing, the village women would say that no one could tell that it was Gadadhar. This indicates how minutely he had observed the various ways of women. When disguised as a woman, the fun-loving Gadadhar would walk to Haldar Pond to fetch water carrying a pitcher on his waist, and no man on the street would recognize him.

We have already mentioned Sitanath Pyne, a rich merchant in Kamar-

| 9. Gadadhar's intimacy with Sitanath Pyne's family. | pukur. He had seven sons and eight daughters. His daughters lived with their father in the joint household even after their marriages. It is said that the |

family needed such a large volume of spices in their cooking that they had to use ten stone slabs and pestles to grind them. In addition, many of Sitanath's distant relatives lived near his house. The Pyne family's part of Kamar-pukur was known as the Merchant Quarter. As this area was adjacent to Kshudiram's house, many women from these merchant families, including Sitanath's wife and daughters, would often visit Chandradevi. Thus, they became acquainted with Gadadhar. Sometimes Sitanath's wife and daughters would take Gadadhar to their home and ask him to put on women's clothing and perform a dramatic role. It seems that they invited Gadadhar to their house because some of their women relatives were prohibited from visiting any house other than Sitanath's [because of the *purdah* system]. They therefore had no opportunity to hear Gadadhar's reading and singing.

Whenever they heard that Gadadhar was at Sitanath's, they would go there and enjoy his performances. This is how some of the women of the Merchant Quarter who could not visit Chandra became Gadadhar's devotees.

Sitanath, the head of the household, was very fond of Gadadhar. Other men of the Merchant Quarter were also aware of his noble qualities. Therefore, they did not object to their womenfolk listening to Gadadhar's kirtan. Only Durgadas Pyne of the Merchant Quarter raised an objection. Although he was devoted to Gadadhar, he would not relax the purdah system that the women of his household were bound to. Sometimes he boasted to Sitanath and other relatives that no outsiders had ever seen the women of his household, nor could others possibly know anything about them. Durgadas looked down upon Sitanath and the others because they were not in favour of the strict observance of purdah, as he was.

One day when Gadadhar happened to be present, Durgadas was bragging to a relative about his enforcement of purdah. Gadadhar said to Durgadas: "Can women be protected by purdah? They can be protected only through moral education and devotion to God. If I wish, I can visit the women of your household and learn everything about them." Durgadas arrogantly challenged him, saying, "Let me see how you can do that." "All right, you will see," replied Gadadhar, who then left.

10. Durgadas Pyne's ego is crushed.

One afternoon some time later, without telling anyone Gadadhar dressed himself like a poor weaver woman, putting on a dirty sari, silver bracelets, and other jewellery. Just before dusk he walked to Durgadas's house from the direction of the market, with a basket on his waist and a veil covering his face. Durgadas was with his friends in the parlour. Thus disguised, Gadadhar introduced himself as a helpless weaver woman who had come from a distant village to sell yarn in the market but had unfortunately been left behind by her companions. He begged to be given shelter for the night. Durgadas asked a few questions and was satisfied with the answers. He then said, "All right, go in and ask the women to find a room for you."

Gadadhar bowed down to him in gratitude and entered the women's quarters. He introduced himself to them as a weaver woman and charmed them with his manner and conversation. Pleased with their young guest's sweet words, the women arranged a room for him and served some refreshments with puffed rice and sweets. As he was eating, he minutely observed the rooms and the women, and took note of their conversation. He also talked to them and asked some questions. Thus the whole evening passed.

When it grew late and Gadadhar had not returned home, Chandra sent Rameswar to look for him in the Merchant Quarter, knowing that he typically went there. Rameswar first went to Sitanath's house and learned that he was not there. As he passed Durgadas's house, he shouted Gadadhar's name loudly. Upon hearing his brother's voice, Gadadhar realized it was late. He shouted back from the inner apartment, "Brother, I am coming," and rushed to his brother. Durgadas realized that Gadadhar had outwitted him and his family. At first he was a little embarrassed and angry, but later he laughed in appreciation of Gadadhar's wonderful mimicry. When Sitanath and other relatives of Durgadas heard the whole story the next day, they were delighted that Gadadhar had crushed his pride. From then on, whenever Gadadhar visited Sitanath's house, the women of Durgadas's family also came to see him.

The women of Sitanath's family and of the Merchant Quarter became so

11. The Pyne women's love for and faith in Gadadhar.

devoted to Gadadhar that if he did not visit them for a few days they would send for him. While reading and singing to the women at Sitanath's, Gadadhar sometimes went into ecstasy, which increased the women's devotion for him. We have heard that when Gadadhar was in bhava samadhi, some of the women worshipped him as an embodiment of Gauranga or Krishna. They even had a gold flute and various costumes of male and female characters made for him to use when he performed for them.

Occasionally we had the opportunity to hear from some of these women about Gadadhar's virtuous nature, sharp intellect, presence of mind, affectionate and simple behaviour, and his influence on them. In April 1892 Swami Ramakrishnananda and some of us went to visit Kamarpukur. There we met Rukmini, one of Sitanath Pyne's daughters. She was then sixty years old. The reader will have a clear picture if we include here what she told us about Gadadhar.

Rukmini said: "You can see our house to the north. It is now dilapidated

12. Rukmini's story about Gadadhar.

and most of the family members are gone. But when I was seventeen or eighteen, it was the home of a prosperous family. My father's name was Sitanath Pyne. There were seventeen or eighteen girls in our family, including the cousins. Although our ages varied a few years from one to the other, we were all adults at that time. Gadadhar had played with us since his childhood, so we were fond of him. As an older boy he used to visit our home, even when we were no longer children. He had free access to our inner apartments. My father loved him deeply. He looked upon him as his Chosen Deity and had devotion and respect for him. Some neighbours told him: 'You have so many young girls at home. Why do you allow young Gadadhar inside the house?' My father replied: 'Don't worry. I know Gadadhar very well.' They did not dare say anything more. When he visited our inner apartment, Gadadhar would tell us many stories from the Puranas and entertain us with jokes. Almost every day we did our housework joyfully while listening to him. I can't express how happy we were when he was with us. If he did not come one day, we became worried thinking that he was not well. We had no peace until one of us would go to Chandradevi on the pretext of bringing water or something else and get news of Gadadhar from her. Every word of his was like nectar to us. When he did not visit our house, we spent our time talking about him."

Gadadhar was not only popular with the women, but his all-round

13. All the villagers were devoted to Gadadhar.

creativity and affectionate ways also brought him close to everyone in the village. Every evening he visited the places where both old and young enjoyed readings from the Bhagavata and kirtan singing. Joy overflowed wherever and whenever Gadadhar was present. No one else could read and expound the mysteries of religion with such passion. During devotional singing, no one had such ecstasy or such improvisational ability to supplement the lyrics with significant words. His sweet voice was unique, as was his delightful dancing. During celebrations he surpassed everyone in performing comic characters and mimicking the various affectations of both men and women. No one else was as capable of entertaining people by inventing new stories and singing songs befitting an occasion. Both young and old were very fond of him and eagerly awaited him every evening. Gadadhar was also delighted to meet and entertain the villagers on different days at various locations.

In spite of his youth, he was as mature as an adult, so some villagers would ask his advice in solving their worldly problems. Virtuous people were attracted by his pure character, and after witnessing his ecstasy while chanting and singing God's name, they sought instruction for their spiritual journeys.[2] Only hypocrites and cheats did not like him; his keen insight pierced their façades and unearthed their secret motives. As he was truthful and outspoken, he would sometimes expose them publicly and humiliate them. In addition to that, the fun-loving Gadadhar would on occasion publicly imitate their hypocritical actions. Although this irritated them, they were helpless to retaliate against the fearless Gadadhar because he was dear to all. Most of the time they would escape censure by surrendering themselves to his mercy, because he was very compassionate towards those who were humble.

As mentioned before, Gadadhar went to school every day because of his love

14. The reason for Gadadhar's indifference to a money-making education.

for his friends. However, when he reached the age of fourteen, the intensity of his devotion and his spiritual moods had increased to such an extent that he became convinced that the money-making education offered by the school was completely unnecessary. From that time on, he felt that his life was meant for a specific purpose. He would have to focus all his energy on the realization of God. Occasionally a vague picture of that goal would appear in his mind, but he could not yet grasp it. Whenever he considered his future, his

2. It is said that from then on Srinivas Sankhari and some young men loved and worshipped Gadadhar as God.

discriminating mind would always turn towards complete dependence on God, and a bright picture of monastic life — wearing the ochre cloth, meditating before a sacred fire, living on alms, and roaming independently — would appear in his mind. But in the next moment his affectionate heart would remind him of his mother and brothers, and the family's condition, making him forsake his dream of treading the monastic path. Instead, he felt an urge to help them as best as he could while living in the world and depending on God, as his father had. Since his head and heart were pointing in opposite directions, he waited for a command from God; his loving heart took complete refuge in their family deity. He consoled himself by thinking, "Let Raghuvir guide me and solve my problem." Whenever there was any conflict between his head and heart, his pure heart always won. From then on, it influenced his every action.

At this time Gadadhar occasionally experienced an extraordinary feeling

15. What he felt in his heart.

in his pure heart. Previously this feeling had brought him close to the villagers when he sang and read from the Puranas, and now he felt their happiness and misery as his own. Therefore, whenever his discriminating mind urged him to renounce the world, his heart would remind him of the simple villagers' love for and faith in him. He felt a calling to lead his life as a role model so that they could follow his example to achieve the highest ideal and transform their ordinary human relationship with him into a deep, spiritual, eternal one. Gadadhar's unselfish mind distinctly prompted him thus: "It is sheer selfishness to renounce the world for one's own liberation. Do something that may benefit others."

Both Gadadhar's head and heart were fully convinced that it would be

16. Gadadhar leaves school and performs dramas with his friends.

useless to continue studying at the village school and later to enter the Sanskrit school. But he was reluctant to stop going to school because he knew his friends would miss him. Gayavishnu and the others loved him deeply and had made him their leader because of his extraordinary intelligence and indomitable courage. During this time Gadadhar was given an opportunity to leave school. Observing Gadadhar's acting talent, one day some of his friends proposed that they form a yatra group and asked him to train them. Gadadhar agreed. However, the boys knew that their guardians would object, so they were worried about finding a secluded place in which to rehearse. The quick-witted Gadadhar suggested the secluded mango orchard of Manikraja, and they decided that every day at a particular time they would slip away from school and meet there.

The plan was soon carried out. Under Gadadhar's direction the boys quickly learned their roles and memorized the songs of the dramas based on the lives of Ramachandra and Krishna, and their performance resounded throughout the mango orchard. Of course, Gadadhar had to draw upon his creativity to direct every aspect of those performances, as well as to perform the main roles. The boys were very happy when they found their little group was working well together. It is said that while performing in the mango orchard, Gadadhar would experience bhava samadhi.

Since Gadadhar spent most of his time singing and acting, his painting skill did not improve considerably. It is said that during this time Gadadhar once went to visit his youngest sister Sarvamangala at the village of Gaurhati, and upon entering the house, saw her cheerfully serving her husband. Some days later he painted a portrait of this scene. We heard that members of the family were surprised to see how accurate the portrait was.

17. His faculty for painting and sculpting.

Gadadhar also became expert in making clay images of gods and goddesses. His religious nature induced him to make those images and with his friends to worship them according to tradition.

After quitting school, Gadadhar continued his usual activities as prompted by his heart and helped his mother in her household work. He was also very fond of his little nephew Akshay. It became a part of his daily routine to care for the child, freeing Chandradevi for her household work.

Thus three years passed, and Gadadhar became seventeen. During that period Ramkumar worked hard, increasing the number of students in his Calcutta school and also his income.

Although Ramkumar spent most of his time in Calcutta, he came to Kamarpukur once a year for a few weeks to look after his mother and brothers. He was concerned when he saw Gadadhar's indifference to studying and asked how Gadadhar was spending his time. After consulting with his mother and Rameswar, he decided to take Gadadhar back with him to Calcutta. As the number of his students had increased, so had his school's office work; he felt in need of an assistant. It was therefore decided that Gadadhar would help him a little and at the same time study along with the other students. When Gadadhar was informed of this proposal and he realized that his eldest brother, whom he respected like his father, needed his help, he made no objection to the plan. On an auspicious day Ramkumar and Gadadhar bowed to Raghuvir and, taking their mother's blessings, left for Calcutta. The mart of joy at Kamarpukur came to an end. Chandra and the people devoted to Gadadhar would now have to live on their sweet memories and thoughts of his bright future.

18. Ramkumar's concern for Gadadhar; he takes Gadadhar to Calcutta.

Sri Ramakrishna As a Spiritual Aspirant

Volume Two

Preface to Volume Two

By God's grace, the unique spiritual practices of Sri Ramakrishna have been recorded in this volume. We have tried not only to communicate his unprecedented passion for these spiritual practices and the philosophical truths of sadhana, but also to chronologically narrate the main events of his life from his seventeenth to his fortieth year. This volume may be regarded as a history of the Master's life as a spiritual aspirant until the time just before the arrival of Swami Vivekananda and the other disciples.

While writing this volume, we doubted whether we could determine the dates of all the important events in the Master's life. The Master told many of us the stories of his life as a spiritual aspirant, but he never narrated them chronologically. For that reason, the events of this period of his life seemed mysterious and complicated. But after thorough investigation, by his grace we have been able to determine the correct dates of many events.

Until now the date and year of the Master's birth was controversial because, as he himself told us, his original horoscope had been lost and a later one was full of errors. However, we have been able to settle the problem by consulting several almanacs more than a hundred years old, which helped us to easily ascertain the dates of many events in the Master's life. For a long time, people did not know the facts concerning the Master's Shodashi worship. This volume clarifies that event for the reader.

Finally, we humbly pray to the Master that this book may receive his blessing and do good to humanity.

The Author [Swami Saradananda]
15 Phalgun 1320 B.E. [March 1913]

Introduction

The *N*ecessity of Discussing Spiritual Practice

WITH THE EXCEPTION OF BUDDHA AND CHAITANYA, there are no detailed accounts of

1. Details of the spiritual practices of the great teachers are not available.

the avatars' spiritual practices in the religious history of the world. In all their life stories we cannot find any detailed descriptions of their exuberant passion, or of the zeal with which they must have struggled to attain

the Truth, or of how they were carried away in their spiritual journeys by hope and hopelessness, fear and awe, and joy and longing. Surely they were sometimes elated and other times depressed, but they never let their focus waver from the goal. In addition, it is difficult to trace the natural cause-and-effect relationship between the amazing actions performed in the latter part of their lives and the education, enthusiasm, and actions of their earlier years. For example, it is not clear how Krishna, the darling of the gopis of Vrindaban, was transformed into the Krishna of Dwaraka, the reviver of religion. Moreover, only a few episodes are known about the great life of Jesus before he reached the age of thirty; and only the stories of Shankara's conquest of other philosophical schools are recorded in detail. So it is with all the other avatars.

The reason for this pattern is difficult to trace. Perhaps those details about

2. Devotees do not like to think that those teachers are ever imperfect.

the avatars were not recorded because of excessive devotion. Devotees may have been hesitant to attribute human imperfections to a divine character. Perhaps they considered it justifiable to conceal any

perceived imperfections from the public gaze. Or it may be that devotees felt that humanity would benefit more by embracing the highest ideals embodied by the beautiful, perfect characters of great souls than by knowing how they arrived at those ideals through superhuman efforts. Thus, devotees may have considered it unnecessary to record avatars' spiritual practices.

Devotees always want to see their masters as perfect. Even though their masters have assumed human bodies, devotees do not like to admit that they have ever experienced any human weakness or lack of insight or power. Devotees are always eager to hear of something miraculous, such as [Yashoda's] beholding the universe in the mouth of baby Krishna. They not only expect to find mature intelligence and vast experience in their masters' irrelevant childhood activities, but they are also eager to see them as perfect embodiments of omniscience, omnipotence, universal love, and kindness. It is therefore no wonder that devotees conclude that avatars do not like to reveal their divine natures to the masses, and that mental efforts such as spiritual practices, as well as physical activities such as eating and sleeping, and conditions such as fatigue, disease, and death, are all mere show. Even during our own lifetime we have witnessed how some prominent devotees of Sri Ramakrishna were convinced that his physical disease [cancer] was feigned.

Devotees arrive at such conclusions because of their own weaknesses.

3. It is untenable that such thoughts should diminish one's devotion.

Perhaps they do not like to attribute human struggles and motives to avatars because such an adverse view might diminish their own devotion. We have nothing to say in criticism of them. When devotion is at an immature stage, such weakness is observed in a devotee. At the early stage of devotion, a devotee cannot imagine God as being devoid of power. In the course of time, devotion deepens and love for God is established. Thinking of God as all-powerful then becomes an obstacle in the path of devotion; the mature devotee shuns that attitude. All devotional scriptures declare this repeatedly. It is well known that Yashoda, the foster mother of Krishna, experienced various divine manifestations of Gopala [child Krishna] every day, and yet she nurtured and disciplined him as her own son. The gopis [cowherd girls] knew that Krishna was the creator of the universe, yet they could think of him only as their beloved. There are many such instances in the scriptures.

When devotees fervently asked the Master [Sri Ramakrishna] to grant

4. Sri Ramakrishna's advice: The experience of God's splendour destroys an intimate, loving relationship with Him. Never disrupt anyone's spiritual attitude.

them the vision of a particular manifestation of God's majesty power, he would tell them: "Look, it is not good to ask for that kind of vision. You will be terrified when you see His power. Serving Him food, dressing Him with clothes, and the loving 'You and I' relationship with Him will all cease." Alas, many times we sadly thought that the Master refused our request because he did not wish us to have visions. Sometimes a bold devotee would beseech him passionately, saying: "Sir, your grace can make the impossible possible. Please be merciful and grant me the vision of God." At this the Master would say tenderly: "My child, can I bring about anything? What the Divine

Mother wills, happens." If the devotee would insist, saying, "Whatever you wish shall be the Mother's will," the Master's usual reply was: "My child, I do wish that all of you would have all kinds of spiritual states and visions. But does that happen?" If that devotee still insisted with dogged faith, the Master would express his love for that devotee with an affectionate look and a sweet smile. Then he would either remain silent or say: "My child, what more shall I say? Let the Mother's will be done." Even when pressed with great insistence, the Master never disturbed a devotee's spiritual attitude by destroying his erroneous but firm faith. Quite often we saw the Master respond in that manner and heard him say repeatedly, "My child, never destroy another's spiritual attitude."

Although the following incident has no direct connection with this intro-

| 5. An example of how one's spiritual mood can be disturbed: the story of Shiva-ratri at the Cossipore garden. |

ductory chapter, it will serve as an illustration of the topic. Only a few spiritual aspirants achieve the power to transmit spirituality to others through mere thought or touch. The Master told us repeatedly that, in the course of time, Swami Vivekananda would be endowed with that power and would use it to do much good for people. A competent aspirant like Swami Vivekananda is indeed rare in this world. Knowing this fully from the very beginning, the Master began to mould Vivekananda's character and spiritual life through the teachings of nondualistic Vedanta in particular. Swamiji [Vivekananda] was accustomed to worshipping God according to the dualistic mode of the Brahmo Samaj, so the nondualistic mode of "I am Brahman" was blasphemy to him. Nonetheless, the Master tried in various ways to make him practise nondualism. Swamiji once recalled: "As soon as I arrived at Dakshineswar, the Master asked me to read certain books that he forbade others to read. Among other books in his room, there was a copy of *Ashtavakra Samhita*. If the Master found someone reading that book, he would forbid him to do so and would ask him to read instead such books as *Mukti O Tahar Sadhan*, the Bhagavad Gita, or any of the Puranas. But whenever I visited him, he would ask me to read either *Ashtavakra Samhita* or a section of *Adhaytma Ramayana*, which were both full of nondualistic ideas. I would say: 'What is the use of reading this book? It is a sin even to think, "I am God." Such blasphemous terms are in this book. It would be better to burn it.' Then the Master would laugh and say: 'Am I asking you to read it for yourself? I am asking you to read to me. Please just read a little. You will not have to think that you are God.' So I had to read a little to him at his request."

Although the Master trained Swamiji in this manner, he guided other young men in spiritual life in other ways: some through the worship of God with form, some through the worship of the formless God with attributes, some through the path of pure devotion, some through devotion mingled with knowledge, and so on. Thus, Swami Vivekananda and other boy devotees lived with the Master at Dakshineswar, practising spirituality under his guidance, but the Master trained them individually, according to their respective aptitudes and tendencies.

The following incident occurred in March 1886 at the Cossipore garden house. Day by day the Master was growing weaker due to cancer. Despite his illness, he was concentrating more vigorously than ever on moulding the devotees' spiritual lives, especially Swami Vivekananda's. The Master did not confine himself to giving Swamiji spiritual advice and helping him to practise it. Every evening the Master would ask everyone to leave his room and then would call Swamiji to his side. Over the course of two or three hours, the Master would talk with him and teach him how to guide and keep the young devotees together so that they might not return to their homes. Observing the Master's behaviour, most of the devotees believed that he was feigning cancer in order to firmly establish his Order, and that when this had been accomplished, he would recover. Only Swami Vivekananda whole-heartedly understood that the Master was making his last arrangements and preparing to take leave of the devotees. It is doubtful, however, that even Swamiji was able to hold onto that idea all of the time.

By practising spiritual disciplines, Swamiji had by this time developed some limited ability to transmit spirituality to others by touch. Sometimes he distinctly felt the awakening of that power within, but he had not yet tested its validity on others. Because of various recent experiences, he now believed in the truth of nondualistic Vedanta, and he tried to introduce it to the young men and householder devotees through reasoning. This created a tremendous commotion among the devotees, and sometimes they argued over it. It was Swamiji's nature that when he considered something to be true, he talked about it to others and tried to use logical arguments to convince them. At that time the young Swamiji did not realize that in the practical world truth assumes various forms according to the different conditions and capabilities of aspirants.

It was Shiva-ratri, the night of the spring festival of the Lord Shiva. Three or four boy devotees were fasting with Swamiji. They wished to pass the auspicious night worshipping and keeping vigil. So that the noise would not disturb the Master's rest, the worship had been set up in a newly built kitchen a little to the east of the main building. That evening there was a heavy shower, and the devotees were delighted to see on the newly formed clouds occasional flashes of lightning that looked like Lord Shiva's matted hair.

At 10:00 p.m., after finishing the first quarter of the night's worship, chanting, and meditation, Swamiji remained seated, relaxing and conversing with others. One of his companions left the room to prepare a smoke for him, and another went to the main building to finish a particular chore. Swamiji suddenly felt that divine power awaken within him. Intending to put it into effect and test its results, he said to Swami Abhedananda, who was seated facing him, "Please touch me for a while." After a little while, the boy who had gone to prepare the tobacco returned. He saw Swamiji meditating, sitting motionless, while Abhedananda sat close by, his right hand touching Swamiji's right knee. Abhedananda's hand was trembling rapidly, and his eyes were closed. After a few minutes Swamiji opened his eyes and said: "That is enough. How did you feel?"

Abhedananda replied, "As one feels a shock wave while touching an electric battery, and one's hand trembles, so I felt when touching you."

The boy asked Abhedananda, "Was your hand trembling of itself as you touched Swamiji?"

Abhedananda responded: "Yes. I could not keep it steady, though I tried."

There was no further discussion of the incident. Swamiji smoked his tobacco. Afterwards all were involved in the second quarter of worship and meditation. Abhedananda then went into deep meditation. We had never seen him so absorbed. His whole body became stiff, his neck and head were bent, and for a time he completely lost consciousness of the outer world. Everyone present thought he had that deep meditation as a result of having touched Swamiji shortly before. Swamiji also noticed his condition and silently pointed it out to a companion.

At 4:00 a.m. when the worship of the fourth quarter was over, Swami Ramakrishnananda came to the worship room and told Swamiji, "The Master is calling for you." Swamiji immediately went to the second floor of the main building, where the Master was staying. Ramakrishnananda also followed him because he was serving the Master.

Seeing Swamiji, the Master said: "Hello! You are frittering away your power before you have accumulated enough of it. First gather it deep within yourself, and then you will understand where and how you should use it. Mother will let you know. Don't you see what great harm you have done to that boy by infusing your ideas into him? He had been following a specific practice for a long time, and now all is spoilt like a miscarriage in the sixth month of pregnancy. Well, what was supposed to happen has happened. From now on don't do such a thing rashly. The boy is lucky that greater harm did not befall him."

Swamiji said later: "I was completely dumbfounded. The Master had come to know whatever we did during worship! What could I do? I remained silent as he scolded me."

Because of this incident, the spiritual attitude that Abhedananda had previously cultivated was completely annihilated. Furthermore, because it takes a long time to completely grasp nondualistic Vedanta, Abhedananda began to behave inappropriately, according to his mistaken idea of nondualism. From that point on the Master began guiding him along the nondualistic path, affectionately correcting the mistakes he made. But it was not until long after the Master's passing away that Abhedananda was able to fully incorporate nondualistic ideas into his daily activities.

To those devotees who think that the efforts of an avatar to attain truth

6. When God incarnates, all of his actions become like those of a human being.

and manifest it fully in his life are mere pretense, our response is that we never heard the Master express such a view. Rather, we heard him say many times: "When God incarnates, all of His actions become like those of ordinary humans. He assumes a human body and attains perfection through zeal, self-effort, and austerity like other human beings." The history of world religions testifies to this; and reason dictates that if this were not so, there would be no point in God's assuming a human body out of compassion for human beings.

The Master's teachings to his devotees can be classified into two categories:

7. The Master's views regarding divine grace and self-effort.

divine grace and self-effort. The reader will understand the distinction between them by considering the following sayings of the Master. On one hand he said to devotees: "I have cooked the food, you need only enjoy the meal"; "I cast the mould, you put your mind into it and shape yourselves accordingly"; and "If you can't do anything, give me your power of attorney." But on the other hand, he also said: "Give up all desires one by one, only then will you succeed"; "Be like a cast-off leaf before a gale"; "Renounce lust and gold, and call on God"; and "I have done sixteen parts, you do one-sixteenth of that." It seems that because we often do not understand the Master's two types of teachings — divine grace or self-effort, self-surrender or spiritual practice — we fail to determine which one we should follow in our lives.

One day in Dakshineswar we had a long discussion with Swami Niranjanananda, a friend of ours, about whether human beings have free will; then we went to the Master for the definitive answer. The Master listened to us debate for a while and was amused. He then said seriously: "Is there any free will for anyone? Everything is happening and will happen eternally by God's will. People understand this eventually. Let me give you an example: Here is a cow tied to a post with a long tether. She can walk one cubit from the post or up to the whole length of the tether. A person ties a cow with the intention of allowing her to lie down, stand, or move around as she likes within that area. Man's free will is also like that. God has given some power to human beings and has also given them the freedom to use it as they wish. That is why people think they are free. But the rope is still fastened to the post. Let me tell you, if anyone intently prays to God, He can move that person to another place with the same stake, or extend the rope's length, or even take the tether away completely."

At this, we asked: "Sir, is it not then in human hands to practise spiritual disciplines? A person might simply say, 'Whatever I do is according to God's will.'"

The Master replied: "What good does it do to say that? One may say, 'There is no thorn, no pricking; but one still cries out when one's hand is pricked by a thorn. If practising spiritual disciplines were at one's discretion, everyone would practise them. Why don't they do it? If you don't properly use the power God has given to you, He won't give you more. That is why one needs self-effort or perseverance. Look, everyone has to make some effort. Only then can one attain God's grace. When one makes the effort, by God's grace ten lifetimes of suffering are finished in one lifetime. But one must make some effort, even while depending on Him.

"Listen to a story: Once Vishnu, who lives in heaven, cursed Narada that

8. An example: a dialogue between Vishnu and Narada.

he would have to suffer in hell, for some reason. Narada was worried. He praised the Lord with hymns to please Him, then said: 'Lord, please be gracious enough to tell me where hell is. What is it like? How many types of hell exist? I am curious to know.' Vishnu then drew heaven, earth, and hell on the ground with a piece of chalk and said, 'Here is heaven and here is hell.' Narada said: 'Is that so? In that case then my suffering in hell is now over.' While saying this he rolled over the chalk mark representing hell and bowed down to the Lord. Vishnu said with a smile: 'What? How could you suffer in hell?' Narada replied: 'Why not, Lord? You have created heaven and hell. When as You drew You said 'This is hell,' that spot truly became hell. As I rolled over it, my suffering was completed.' Narada uttered these words with wholehearted faith. Then Vishnu said, 'So be it.' Having genuine faith in Him, Narada had only to roll over that mark representing hell. That small effort ended his suffering."

Sometimes with the help of this story the Master explained to us that in the domain of grace there is room for both enthusiasm and self-effort.

Assuming human bodies and living like human beings, avatars to a great

9. By taking on human imperfections, avatars discover paths to liberation.

extent experience our shortsightedness and limited knowledge. Like us, they must struggle to discover a path to liberation from all those limitations. Until that path is discovered, the awareness of their divine nature sometimes manifests itself within, but only momentarily — a veil then covers it up. Thus, for the good of many they accept the veil of maya and, like us, grope along the path in this realm of light and darkness. Because they do not have a trace of selfish desire, they see more light during their spiritual journey than we see in ours. They focus all of their energy in one direction and quickly solve life's problems. Afterwards they devote themselves to doing good to humanity.

The godman Sri Ramakrishna actually admitted his human imperfec-

10. Without regarding an avatar as human, one cannot make any sense of his life and actions.

tions, so we shall benefit greatly by discussing his human aspect. That is why we request the reader to study the Master's divine aspect while always keeping in mind his human characteristics. If we do not think of him as one of us, we shall not be able to find meaning in the superhuman enthusiasm and effort he made at the time of his *sadhana* [spiritual disciplines]. We may think: Why would he, who is eternally perfect, need to try to attain the Truth? Again we may think: His lifelong effort was nothing but a matter of show. That is not all: His effort, steadfastness, and renunciation, which he applied in his life for God-realization, may cause terrible apathy in our hearts instead of encouraging us to emulate them, and in this life we will not then be able to break free from inertia.

Although we long for the Master's grace, we nonetheless must also accept

11. An ignorant person sees him only as a human being.

him as a person endowed with human feelings like ours. Because he is sympathetic to our misery, the Master has to come forward to mitigate our suffering. Therefore, from whatever angle we look at it, we have no option but to think of him as a human being. In fact, until we become free from all forms of bondage and have established ourselves in that attributeless divine nature, we must think of and accept God and each of the divine incarnations as a person. "Becoming God, one should worship Him" — this saying is indeed true. Only when you have reached the *nirvikalpa* [absolute or transcendental] plane through samadhi will you experience and understand the true nature of God and be able to worship Him properly. Until you have achieved that state, your worship is simply an incomplete attempt to ascend to that divine plane. You will naturally consider God, the creator of the universe, to be a person endowed with extraordinary powers.

Rare is the person who is established in the Divine and can perform true

12. God assumes a human form out of compassion. It is therefore beneficial to study an avatar's life.

worship of God, whose real form is beyond maya. Weak aspirants like ourselves are still far from that state. That is why, out of compassion for ordinary people like us and to accept our heartfelt worship, God descends to the human plane and assumes a human body and human feelings. We have a greater opportunity to discuss the history of Sri Ramakrishna's sadhana than that of earlier avatars. From time to time the Master himself told us detailed stories of his life during sadhana, deeply imprinting those vivid pictures in our minds. Again, shortly before we came to him, various events of his life as an aspirant had been observed by the people associated with the Kali temple of Dakshineswar. Many of them were still present when we arrived there. We therefore had the opportunity to hear some of those stories directly from them. However, before we narrate these stories, it is important to describe in a general way the basic principles of sadhana. We shall now briefly discuss that topic.

Chapter 1

The Spiritual Aspirant and Spiritual Discipline

IF WE WANT TO UNDERSTAND SRI RAMAKRISHNA as a spiritual aspirant, we must first understand what sadhana [spiritual discipline] is. Some readers may comment that the people of India are always practising sadhana in some form or other. Why then are we making this book longer by raising this topic? From time immemorial Indians have spent most of their energy [in the quest] for the direct experience of spiritual truths. Is there any other country that can make this claim? Is there any other country in which so many avatars and knowers of Brahman have been born? Since we are so familiar with the topic of sadhana, it should be unnecessary to recapitulate here the basic principles of the subject.

Although what has been said above is true, it is still necessary to discuss

| 1. Erroneous conceptions about sadhana. |

sadhana because many people have strange ideas about it. Losing sight of the goal of sadhana, some people consider it to be mere physical mortification, or the performance of rituals that require one to collect rare objects in a particular place, or control of the breath, or even the strange activities of deranged minds. In fact, great teachers sometimes advise disturbed people who are obsessed with evil impressions and habits to perform special practices to make them calm and normal so they can follow a spiritual path. Some people consider those prescribed disciplines to be sadhana and claim that they are suitable for every aspirant to practise. In addition, some people who are attached to transient sensual objects of the world make vain efforts under the erroneous notion that God can be controlled by means of mantras or particular rituals, like a snake charmed by a spell. So it will not be out of context to briefly discuss the truths of sadhana that were

153

discovered by Indian sages through millennia of persistent effort.

The Master used to say, "Seeing Brahman, or God, in all beings is the last word of sadhana." At the culmination of sadhana, one reaches that plane. The Vedas and Upanishads, the most authoritative Hindu scriptures, support this statement. The scriptures say that whatever you see in the world is truly one nondual Brahman, be it gross or subtle, sentient or insentient, bricks, wood, clay, stone, trees, plants, human beings, animals, gods, or demigods. You are seeing, hearing, touching, smelling, and tasting the same Brahman in various forms and in different states. Although you accomplish all of your daily activities with Brahman's help, you are unaware of It: you believe you are dealing with a multiplicity of objects and persons. When we hear statements such as these, doubts may arise in our minds. This topic will be easy for the reader to understand if we set forth, in question and answer form, certain doubts that arise and how the scriptures satisfy them.

> 2. Sadhana's ultimate result is the experience of Brahman in all beings.

Question: Why do we not perceive that all is Brahman?

Answer: You are deluded. Until your delusion is dispelled, how can you detect it? We recognize our delusions only by comparing our perceptions with real objects or states. You need to have a basis for comparison in order to discover that delusion.

Question: What is the cause of that delusion? When did it come to us?

Answer: The cause of this delusion is ignorance, just as it is in all other situations. How can you know when that ignorance first appeared? As long as you remain in ignorance, all of your efforts to realize this will be futile. As long as one is dreaming, the dream appears to be reality. When one awakens, the dream is compared with the waking state and is recognized as unreal. You may say that sometimes while dreaming one may realize it is a dream. But in such a situation that knowledge appears in the mind from the memory of the waking state. Similarly, while perceiving the world in the waking state, some people have the memory of nondual Brahman.

> 3. Truth is not revealed when delusion or ignorance is present. The cause of ignorance cannot be understood while one is ignorant.

Question: What is the way out then?

Answer: One must eradicate ignorance. I can definitely assure you that delusion and ignorance can be removed. The sages of the past were able to rid themselves of ignorance and have left us instructions for doing the same.

Question: Before we learn the means, we want to ask a few more questions. You assert that what so many ordinary people see and experience is unreal, and that what only a few sages have experienced is real. Could it be that their perceptions are wrong?

> 4. Only the sages' perception of this world is true: the reason.

Answer: There is no rule that what most people believe is always true. We know that the sages' direct experiences are true because, with the knowledge they gained, they became free from misery and attained complete fearlessness and eternal peace. Moreover, they discovered the ultimate purpose of all actions and efforts of human life, which inevitably ends in death. In addition, this true knowledge manifests itself as forbearance, contentment, compassion, humility, and other noble qualities. It also makes a person's outlook amazingly catholic. In the scriptures we find evidence of these extraordinary qualities and powers in the lives of the sages; and even now we find the same in those who have attained perfection by following in their footsteps.

Question: Well, how is it that all of us experience the same delusion? What I recognize as an animal, you also see as an animal — not as a man. It is the same for all external objects. It is amazing that so many people have the same delusion at the same time, regarding all objects. Everywhere it

> 5. Though the same delusion may be seen by many, that does not make it true.

can be seen that although some people have a false impression of a certain thing, others correctly perceive the same object. But here we find an exception to that rule; your position seems to be indefensible.

Answer: You find here an exception to that rule, because you are not including those few sages among the people. If you do include them, you will see that the answer was given in response to your previous question. You ask how all people can be under the same delusion. The scriptures say in reply: The universe has arisen by way of ideation in the limitless, infinite Cosmic

> 6. The imaginary world exists in the Cosmic Mind, so all beings have the same delusion. But the Cosmic Mind is not deluded because of this.

Mind. We all experience the same mental images because the individual minds of yours, mine, and all people are parts of and included in the Cosmic Mind. That is why we cannot see an animal in any way we like, nor can we perceive it to be other than an animal. Similarly, one among us may attain true knowledge and become free from all delusion, while others remain under its spell. Although the world arises in the Cosmic Mind of the Divine Being by ideation, He is not affected by the bond of ignorance as we are. Because He is omniscient, He sees that the nondual Brahman thoroughly pervades this world, which originated from ignorance. Because we are incapable of this perception, our case is different. The Master used to say: "There is poison in the fangs of the snake. The snake eats its food daily with those fangs and is not at all affected. But a person bitten by a snake dies instantly."

From the standpoint of the scriptures it can be seen that the world, which is only an idea in the Cosmic Mind, is in a way imagined by our minds as well. Our limited individual minds have an eternal and inseparable relationship with the collective Cosmic Mind, like one's limbs

> 7. The world is beyond space and time. Prakriti [Nature] is without beginning.

with the rest of one's body. Again, one cannot say that at an earlier time the idea of the world did not exist in the Cosmic Mind, and that it later arose.

This is not possible because name and form, or space and time — without which there cannot be any diversity in creation — are included in the idea of the world; they are eternally inseparable from that idea. With a little calm reflection, the reader will understand this and will realize why the Vedic scriptures have taught that prakriti, or maya — the basic cause of creative power — is without beginning and is beyond time. If the world is an idea of the mind, and if the beginning of that idea is not within what we know as "time," then it must be that the idea of time and the idea of the world exist simultaneously in the Cosmic Mind, the source of all ideas. Because our limited individual minds have been experiencing this idea [i.e., the world] for a very long time, we are firmly convinced that the world is real. We cannot detect our own delusion because we have completely forgotten that the world is imaginary, and for a long time we have been deprived of the direct experience of nondual Brahman, who is beyond the imaginary world. As we have said earlier, we are able to recognize deluded ideas or perceptions only by comparing them with the real things and states.

Now it is clear that our conceptions about and experiences of the world have taken their present form as a result of habits accumulated over a very long period of time. If we want to have the right knowledge about the world, we shall have to realize that truth which is beyond name and form, space and time, mind and intellect, and other attributes of the world. The effort to know that truth has been called *sadhana* by the Vedas and other scriptures. This effort exists, knowingly and unknowingly, in men and women who in India are called sadhakas, or spiritual aspirants.

8. Sadhana is the effort to know the cause of the world, which is beyond space and time.

Generally speaking, this effort to know the truth that transcends the world has developed along two main paths: the negative and the positive. The first is described by the scriptures as *neti, neti* [not this, not this], the path of knowledge; the second as *iti, iti* [this, this], the path of devotion. The aspirant who follows the path of knowledge understands the ultimate goal from the very beginning; remembering the goal, the aspirant consciously moves forward towards it every day. Followers of the path of devotion, however, are not fully aware of their ultimate goal. They move forward by adopting higher and higher ideals one after another, until they finally have direct experience of the nondual Reality beyond the world. The followers of both paths must renounce the idea about the reality of the world that is held by ordinary people. The *jnani* [follower of the path of knowledge] tries to renounce this idea completely from the beginning. The devotee begins sadhana by partly renouncing the world and partly holding onto it, but eventually reaches the truth, "One without a second," and renounces everything, as does the jnani. Giving up the ordinary, selfish, sense-pleasure-oriented idea about the world is called *vairagya* [renunciation] by the scriptures.

9. Two paths of sadhana: *neti, neti* and *iti, iti*.

Because human life is ever-changing and subject to inevitable death, the knowledge that the world is impermanent comes naturally. For that reason it seems that in ancient times people first renounced the ordinary conception of the world and then began to search for the cause of the world by following the path of *neti, neti*. Although the paths of devotion and knowledge were both in practice during the same period, it is seen in the Upanishads that the path of knowledge was fully developed before every aspect of the path of devotion reached completion.

The Upanishads bear witness to the fact that people who followed the

| 10. The goal of the path called *neti, neti* is to know "What am I?"

path of *neti, neti* quickly became introspective: Brahman, the cause of the world, is "not this, not that." These spiritual aspirants understood that it was better to explore their own bodies and minds, which were directly connected with the world, rather than other external objects. It would therefore be quicker to discover the cause of the world if they proceeded through the body and mind. As one can press one grain of rice to see if the entire pot of rice is well cooked, so if one finds Brahman within oneself, one can see It in all animate and inanimate objects. This is why the inquiry "What am I?" becomes the only goal of the jnani.

We have mentioned before that those who follow the path of knowledge,

| 11. Nirvikalpa samadhi.

as well as those who follow the path of devotion, have to give up the common conception of the world [that it is real]. The complete eradication of that idea frees the human mind from thought waves and leads it to samadhi. This particular state is called by the scriptures *nirvikalpa samadhi*. We shall tell the reader in a different place (see III.2.32-34) how the follower of the path of knowledge proceeds with the inquiry of "What am I?" and how he attains nirvikalpa samadhi; then we will describe the experience he has at that time. But now it is necessary to briefly tell the reader how one who follows the path of devotion attains the experience of nirvikalpa samadhi.

We have described the path of devotion as the path of *iti, iti*. Although the devotee experiences the impermanence of the world, he or she believes in God, the creator of the world; and he or she also believes that His creation exists and is real. Devotees look upon the world — and all beings and objects in it — as related to God, so they consider everything to be their very own. They shun whatever they believe to be an obstacle on the path leading to the experience of that relationship. The pressing goal of a devotee is to love and be absorbed in meditation on a particular form of God[1] and to perform every action for His delight.

---

1. We consider the worship of the Brahmo Samaj as meditation on a form of God: When a person meditates on a Personality endowed with noble qualities but without form, he is bound to think of something like space, water, air, fire, and so on.

We shall now discuss how a person can forget the existence of the world

12. The attainment of nirvikalpa samadhi is reached by following the path of *iti, iti*.

through deep meditation on the form of God and then reach the transcendental state. We have mentioned earlier that a devotee accepts a certain form of God as his or her own Chosen Deity, and contemplates and meditates on that deity. In the early stages of meditation, the devotee cannot visualize the entire form of the Chosen Deity. Sometimes the hands or feet, or only the face, appear in the mind. As soon as those are visualized, they disappear; the images do not remain constant. As meditation gradually deepens, that form begins to remain steady in front of the devotee, until the mind becomes restless. Later, as meditation becomes still deeper, the devotee sees that divine form move and smile, hears the deity speak, and ultimately even feels the touch of that divine form. The devotee then perceives that form as alive in all respects. Whether the devotee meditates with eyes open or closed, he or she can see the deity's graceful movements. Later still, as a result of the devotee's faith that the Chosen Deity can assume various forms at will, the devout aspirant attains the vision of various divine forms emanating from the form of the Chosen Deity. The Master used to say that a person who has vividly seen one divine form in this manner can easily have visions of other divine forms.

We can understand one thing from what has been said so far: An aspirant who has been graced with the vision of those living divine forms feels that those forms seen in the realm of ideas during meditation are as real as objects seen in the waking state. The more the devotee feels that the external world and the realm of ideas are both real, the more deeply he or she realizes that the external world is the projection of the mind. During deep meditation, the devotee so intensely experiences the realm of ideas that he or she does not have the slightest knowledge of the external world. The scriptures call this state *savikalpa samadhi*. Although during this samadhi concentration has banished the external world from the devotee's mind, the realm of ideas remains. As we experience happiness and misery every day when dealing with people and objects in the external world, so the devotee experiences the same emotions when interacting with the Chosen Deity. Any thoughts, desires, and doubts that arise in the devotee's mind all relate to the Chosen Deity. Because the series of thoughts that arise at that time in the devotee's mind focus on one object only, the scriptures call this state *savikalpa*, or samadhi with mental modifications.

When the devotee is thus absorbed in one particular object in the spiritual realm, the gross external world disappears from his or her mind; when one idea becomes predominant, all other ideas cease to exist. For the devout aspirant who has proceeded this far, the attainment of nirvikalpa samadhi is not too remote. One who has been able to eradicate his or her lifelong belief about the reality of the world has developed an extremely powerful and steadfast mind. A devotee who can make the mind completely free from modifications can more deeply enjoy the relationship with God. When the devotee realizes this, his or her whole mind runs enthusiastically in that direction. The devotee soon ascends to the highest plane of consciousness by the grace of the guru and of God, and attains eternal peace by becoming established in nondual knowledge. Alternatively, it can be said that passionate love for the Chosen Deity shows the devotee that highest plane and helps him or her to experience oneness with God, as did the gopis of Vrindaban.

These are the ways, described in the scriptures, by which aspirants who follow the paths of knowledge and of devotion can reach the ultimate goal. But because both divine and human characteristics always coexist in the lives of the avatars, even during their sadhana they sometimes appear to be perfect and powerful. This may happen because they have the power to move on both divine and human planes naturally; or perhaps because their divine nature is innate and spontaneous, it sometimes pierces the external veil of their human nature and manifests itself. Whatever the explanation is, such stories [of superhuman perfection early on] have made the lives of avatars difficult to comprehend and mysterious to the human intellect. It seems that this intricate mystery will never be solved completely. It is a gospel truth that people will benefit immensely if they study the lives of the avatars with reverence. During the ancient Puranic [Epic] Age, the avatars' human characteristics were kept hidden and only their divine aspects were discussed. In our sceptical modern age, however, the human aspects of the avatars have been stressed and their divine natures have been completely disregarded. In this present context, while discussing the avatars' lives we shall try to explain to the reader how both aspects exist simultaneously in them. It is no exaggeration to say that we would never be able to understand the life of an avatar in that way if we had not seen the godman Sri Ramakrishna.

> 13. Avatars are both divine and human, so they seem to be perfect even during their sadhana. It is necessary to study their lives in both aspects.

Chapter 2

The *A*vatar as a Spiritual Aspirant

BLESSED BY THE GRACIOUS COMPANY OF THE HOLY MASTER, we contemplate his life and

1. The coexistence of divine and human aspects in the Master.

character. The more we do so, the more we are overwhelmed by the wonderful coexistence of divine and human characteristics in him. Without seeing him, we could never have understood how it was possible for such contrary aspects to coexist harmoniously in one person. But because we have seen him, we are convinced that he was a godman: His divine qualities and powers were fully manifested through the veil of a human body and human nature. Because we lived with him, we realized that he never feigned any of these aspects. He truly took on a human nature in order to do good to humanity; he showed us the path leading from the human plane to the divine. Because we observed him closely, we understood that avatars of past ages had also displayed such wonderful manifestations of divine and human aspects.

We shall see the same truth if we reverently study the life story of any

2. It is the same with all avatars.

avatar. We will find that sometimes avatars live on the same plane with us and deal with the objects and persons of the world as we do. But sometimes they travel on the highest spiritual plane and bring to us news of a realm of ideas and power that is unknown to us. Although they have no desires, they perform actions in accordance with an unseen power that has ordered their lives from their very childhood. Sometimes during childhood they are aware of that power; but many times they do not know that it is their own, that it dwells within themselves. When they use that power to ascend to the highest spiritual plane, they may not be able to see everything and

160

every being in the world in the light of divine consciousness or behave with them accordingly. As they repeatedly experience the existence of that power, a keen desire arises in their minds to become fully acquainted with it. It is this desire that creates intense passion and induces them to undertake sadhana.

Avatars do not have even the slightest trace of selfish desire. They have no

| 3. Avatars have no desire for selfish enjoyment. |

wish to enjoy sensual pleasures here or hereafter, nor any intention of enjoying infinite bliss by liberating themselves while disregarding the fate of others in the world. The primary object of their [spiritual] quest is to investigate the unknown divine power that has helped them from their birth. Does that power — by which they experience unique ecstasies and perceive divine forms in the realm of ideas to be as real as anything in the gross world — truly exist? Or is it a mere fabrication of their own imaginations? By comparing their knowledge and experiences with those of ordinary people, they soon realize that others do not perceive the world as they do. Other people are almost completely without the ability to see the world from a higher plane of consciousness.

When avatars compare themselves with ordinary people, they realize that

| 4. They practise sadhana for others out of compassion. |

seemingly sweet, yet fleeting, sense objects cannot tempt them as they do others in this transient life. This is because avatars see the world from both the human and divine planes of consciousness. The thick clouds of despondency and unrest that arise under different circumstances in this ever-changing world cannot cover their minds. Their compassionate minds are therefore solely absorbed in the question of how they can gain full control over that divine power, ascend to higher and higher planes of consciousness at will and stay there as long as they want, and then teach that technique to all people so that they too can attain peace. For this reason, the two powerful currents of sadhana and compassion are seen constantly flowing side by side in their lives. The avatars' compassion may increase a hundredfold when they compare their condition with that of ordinary people, but one cannot say that it originates from that act. They are endowed with that compassion when they are born in this world. Let us refer to an illustration from the Master on that subject.

"Once three friends went for a walk through a field. In the middle of the

| 5. An example: the Master's story, "Three Friends Visit the Blissful Grove." |

field they found a place enclosed by high walls. Sweet sounds of music came from inside. They wanted to see what was happening there. They looked around but found no entrance. What could they do? One of them procured a ladder and climbed up while the other two stood below. Upon reaching the top, the first friend looked down into the enclosure and burst into loud joyful laughter when he saw the festivities within. He jumped right into the enclosure; he couldn't wait even for a moment to tell his two friends below what he had seen. They thought: 'Aha! What a wonderful friend! He didn't care to tell us what he saw. However, we shall find out for ourselves.' Then the second friend climbed to the top of the wall. Like the first person, he also burst into loud laughter and jumped into the enclosure. The third friend finally climbed up that ladder and saw the mart of joy within. At first he had a strong desire to jump inside and join the others. But then he thought: 'If I join the festivities now, then other people outside won't know that there is a place where one can enjoy such divine bliss. Shall I enjoy this bliss without sharing it?' With these thoughts, he forcefully turned his mind away and descended the ladder. Then he went about, proclaiming to whomever he met: 'Hello! There is a mart of bliss inside this place. Please come and let us enjoy it together.' Thus, he brought many people to share the bliss." Now you see, just as we cannot discover the cause of the third friend's wish to share bliss with others, so we cannot ascertain why the desire to do good to humanity exists from childhood in the minds of the avatars.

Based on previous statements, some readers may conclude that avatars never have to struggle against the turbulent senses, as we do. Some may assume that the senses always remain under the avatars' control from their very birth, like calm and well-behaved children; and that avatars can therefore easily lead their minds away from the sense objects of the world and towards the highest spiritual ideals. We say in reply: This is not so. In that respect also, avatars act like human beings. They fight against the senses and move towards the goal after becoming victorious.

6. Avatars practise self-control like other human beings.

Anyone who has tried to learn even a little about the nature of the human mind must have observed that it contains infinite layers of desires, ranging from gross to subtle, subtler, and the subtlest. If you are somehow able to overcome one desire, another one will come forward to obstruct your path. When you conquer that one, the next one will appear. Thus, when you defeat a gross desire, a subtle one will arise; and when that one is defeated, a series of more subtle desires will challenge you. For example, if you renounce sex, the desire for money will arise. When you refrain from indulging in lust and gold[1] in a gross way, desires for beauty, name and fame, power and position, and so on will emerge. Or you may carefully rid yourself of worldly attachments, but then laziness — or a spell of infatuation in the guise of compassion — will occupy your mind.

7. Innumerable desires in the mind.

1. The term *kamini-kanchana* has been translated in this book as "lust and gold," which take the mind away from God. It has other connotations, such as, woman and gold, lust and greed, sex and money. The root of the word *kamini* is *kama*, which means lust or desire; and *kanchana* means gold or money. — *Translator*

The Master described the inscrutable nature of the human mind. He

| 8. The Master's advice on how to shun desires. | always cautioned us to avoid the traps set by desires. In order to convince us in this regard, he would sometimes cite as examples how he had thought and acted |

during events in his own life (see III.1.24-29,2.22-23). He gave the same advice to women devotees as he did to men, and enkindled love for God in their hearts as well. The reader will understand if we narrate an incident that illustrates the Master's behaviour.

Whoever went to the Master, whether male or female, was deeply attracted

| 9. Advice to women devotees in this respect. | by his amiability, courteous behaviour, and wonderful, unselfish, pure love. They were anxious to see him again whenever there was an opportunity. Not |

only did they themselves visit the Master frequently, but they would also make special efforts to bring their acquaintances to him, so that they also could enjoy pure bliss in his company.

One afternoon, one of the women devotees we knew went to visit the Master at Dakshineswar with her stepsister and that woman's sister-in-law. After bowing down, they took their seats. The Master then inquired about their welfare and began to talk about the goal of human life: to love God.

"Is it so easy to take refuge in God? Inscrutable are the workings of Mahamaya, the great enchantress! Does She free anyone so easily? A person who has no relatives, She entangles in this world with a pet cat. That poor person collects fish and milk from here and there and says: 'What can I do? The cat won't eat anything but fish and milk.'

"Take for an example an aristocratic family in which the women have lost their husbands and children. All are gone except a few widows, who live on as if they had cheated death. One part of their old house has collapsed; another part is falling to ruin. Banyan saplings and some spinach have grown on the roof. The widows cook curry with that spinach and continue their household life. What for? Why do they not call on God? It is indeed the time for them to take refuge in Him, but they won't do it.

"Again, perhaps a woman has lost her husband shortly after the wedding ceremony. She is now a young widow; let her call on God. But she will not do it. She becomes the caretaker of her brother's household. Her hair is braided and secured in a bun on the top of her head, and a bunch of keys hangs from a corner of the cloth thrown over her shoulder. She carries herself with arrogance and commands everyone. All the neighbors are frightened at the very sight of that monstrous woman. She tells everyone, 'My brother can't even have a meal if I am not present.' What a wretched woman! Why don't you see what has happened to you?"

What a mysterious coincidence! The sister-in-law of that devotee's stepsister, who had met the Master for the first time on that day, was indeed such a caretaker in her brother's household. Nobody had told the Master about this beforehand. But in the course of conversation, the Master referred to that example in order to explain the powerful influence of desire, and to describe the infinite layers of desire in the human mind. Those words of the Master penetrated deeply into that woman's mind. Listening to those examples, the stepsister nudged the devotee and whispered: "Sister, how strange! Why has the Master spoken those words today? How will my sister-in-law react?" Our acquaintance replied: "What can we do? It is the Master's will. No one has prompted him."

When one studies human nature, it becomes obvious that the higher a

| 10. Avatars fight with subtle desires. | person's mind rises, the more intense is the pain caused by subtle desires. A person who has committed theft, deceit, or adultery many times can |

repeat those acts without suffering any pangs of guilt. But a noble and high-minded person feels terribly guilty and suffers from great distress when merely thinking of those heinous acts. Although throughout their lives avatars refuse to indulge in the enjoyment of gross sensual objects, they fight against subtle desires the same as the rest of us. Those horrible images of desire that arise in their minds cause them distress a thousand times greater than that which we suffer; this they frankly admit. Therefore, how can we say that their struggles to withdraw the senses from sense objects are mere feigning?

A reader who is well versed in the scriptures may object in the following

| 11. The human aspect of an avatar: objection and answer. | manner. "How can I accept your statement? In the introduction to his commentary on the Gita, Shankara — the paragon of nondualism — states in connection |

with Krishna's human birth: 'God is in reality unborn, unchanging, the Lord of all created beings, and by nature eternal, pure, illumined, and free. But He is seen as though born, as though endowed with a body through his own maya power, for the benefit of humanity.' When the great Shankara himself says this, how can your statement hold true?"

We say that what Shankara has said is true, but we still have sufficient support for our position. In order to understand Shankara, we must remember that just as he considers God to only *seem* to be endowed with name and form, so he regards as equally false that you, I, and every object and every being in the world are endowed with name and form. He considers the whole world to be an illusory superimposition on Brahman, and he does not accept its existence as real. Therefore, we can understand Shankara's conclusion only if we accept both his statements together. It is not his intention to say that an avatar's incarnation and his experience of pleasure and pain are unreal, even though those sensations are real to us. If we accept our perceptions and feelings as real, we must also accept those of avatars as real. So our previous statement still stands.

This topic will be clear if we discuss the subject from another standpoint.

12. This topic from another angle. The scriptures say that two types of ideas about the world appear before us — one from the nondualistic plane and the other from the ordinary or dualistic plane. When we try to examine the reality of the world by looking at it from a nondualistic perspective, we immediately realize that it does not exist and has never existed at any time. "Brahman is one without a second." Nothing else exists except Brahman. Again, when we view the world and its aggregate of various names and forms from the dualistic perspective, as do all ordinary people, we feel they are real and have always existed. Avatars and *jivanmuktas* [those who are liberated in this life] have bodies but lack body-consciousness. Because they spend most of their time in the nondualistic plane, when they come down to the dualistic plane, they feel that the world is as unreal as a dream. When it is compared to the waking state, a dream appears to be unreal; but while one is dreaming, one does not understand that the dream is completely unreal. Similarly, the perception of the world in the minds of avatars and illumined souls cannot be regarded as absolutely unreal.

Just as one can see the world in two different ways from the nondualistic **13. The world is experienced differently when one attains a higher spiritual state.** and the dualistic perspectives, so can one see a particular individual from two planes of consciousness. When a man is viewed from the dualistic plane, he appears to be a bound soul; but when seen from the nondualistic plane, he appears to be Brahman, ever pure and ever free. The absolute nondualistic plane is the highest region in the realm of ideas. The mind passes through higher and higher planes of consciousness before it reaches its goal, the nondualistic plane. As an aspirant's mind ascends through planes of consciousness, and the world and its individual beings appear in various forms, the aspirant's conceptions about them change accordingly. For example, at that time he or she feels the world is made of ideas and an individual being is separate from the body and endowed with extraordinary powers, or is manifest as a subtle form or as a luminous divine form.

If an ordinary person approaches the avatars with faith and devotion, that **14. When human beings are raised to a higher plane by the power of avatars, they see avatars as devoid of their human nature.** person ascends unconsciously to higher and higher planes of consciousness, as mentioned earlier. By their wonderful power avatars grant that person the ability to make this ascension. When the devout aspirant reaches the highest plane, he or she sees the avatars and recognizes their true nature to be divine.

He or she sees that they are endowed with various powers and that their human aspect, which ordinary people see, is mere show. As devotion deepens, the aspirant's idea of divinity expands to include first God's devotees and then God's creation.

It has already been mentioned that from their childhood avatars at times

15. The gradual evolution of the avatar's mind: jivas [individual souls] and avatars differ only in degree of power.

perceive objects in the realm of ideas with the same intensity and vividness as they see the objects and persons of the world. As they experience spiritual visions with increasing frequency, they come to understand that the spiritual realm is more real than the gross physical world. They finally ascend to the nondualistic plane and attain perfection by discovering that the world of name and form originates from Brahman, One without a second.

The same thing happens to jivanmuktas, those who have attained liberation while living. The difference is that jivanmuktas need to put forth a lifelong effort to realize the truth, whereas avatars take but a very short time. Alternatively, jivanmuktas may quickly ascend to the nondualistic plane, but compared to avatars they manifest very little power to help others reach that plane. Please remember the teaching of the Master in this respect: "The difference between an individual soul and an avatar is a difference in manifestation of power only."

After staying for some time on the nondualistic plane and enjoying the

16. An avatar is a godman, omniscient.

direct experience of Brahman, the cause of the world, avatars return to the lower plane. They may still look like human beings, but in fact they have become divine. After directly experiencing both the world and Brahman, and comparing the two, they perceive the whole world to be but a shadow. The highest divine powers then spontaneously manifest through their minds, in order to do good to humanity. They attain omniscience, becoming fully aware of the origin, middle, and end of all objects of the world. When we observe their divine lives and actions, ordinary people like ourselves take refuge in them. It is by their grace that we realize that it is not possible to attain the supreme truth, or peace, or to investigate the cause of the world by using our external senses to study the objects and beings of the world.

The reader well-versed in Western thought may make the following

17. It is impossible to understand the hidden cause of the universe by studying material science with an extroverted mind.

comment on our previous statement: "Well, one cannot make such a statement who has seen how much human knowledge has grown and is progressing daily, based on investigation of the external world." To this we reply: It is true that human beings have widened their knowledge by developing material science, but that definitely will not help in attaining the ultimate truth. Science teaches that the cause of the world [Brahman] is insentient, or that it is an insignificant entity that is inferior to us. By developing that science, we gradually become extroverted and convince ourselves that the only goal of our lives is to enjoy more sense objects. Therefore, if at any time a machine proves that all worldly things have originated from matter only, the truths of the inner or subjective realm will remain unproven, eternally hidden under a veil of darkness. Until we realize that liberation can be reached only by renouncing our desire for sensual pleasures and by turning our minds inward, true peace, the realization of the indivisible truth beyond time and space, will remain beyond our grasp.

It is common knowledge that all avatars are sometimes absorbed in spiri-

18. Avatars are absorbed in divine moods from childhood onward.

tual visions during their childhoods. When he was a boy, Krishna revealed his divinity to his parents and friends many times. While walking in a garden, the child Buddha went into samadhi under a rose-apple tree and attracted the attention of both gods and human beings. In his childhood, Jesus attracted the birds of the forest with his love, and he fed them with his own hands. As a boy, Shankara overwhelmed his mother with his divine power and then renounced the world. In addition, during his boyhood, Chaitanya demonstrated through his ecstatic life that a lover of God sees the manifestation of God in everything, good and bad. Sri Ramakrishna's life is filled with incidents such as these. We shall present a few of them here as examples for the reader. When we heard these incidents directly from the Master, we understood that he had been absorbed in the spiritual realm even in his very early life.

The Master said: "In that part of the country [Kamarpukur] children are

19. The Master's first ecstasy at the age of six.

given puffed rice to eat from small baskets. Those who are poor and have no baskets eat from the corner of a cloth. Boys go out to play on the roads or in the fields carrying puffed rice either in a basket or in the corner of a cloth. It was June or July. I was then six or seven years old. One morning I took some puffed rice in a small basket and was eating it as I walked along the narrow ridges of the rice fields. In one part of the sky a beautiful black cloud appeared, heavy with rain. I was watching it and eating the puffed rice. Very soon the cloud covered almost the whole sky. Then a flock of cranes came flying, white as milk against the black cloud. It was so beautiful that I became absorbed in the sight; I lost consciousness of everything outside of myself. I fell down, and the puffed rice was scattered over the ground. I cannot say how long I was in that state. Some people saw this and carried me home. That was the first time I lost external consciousness due to ecstasy."

The village of Anur is located a few miles north of Kamarpukur, the birth-

20. The story of the Master's second ecstasy, on his way to visit the goddess Vishalakshi.

place of Sri Ramakrishna. The goddess Vishalakshi [literally, the One with large eyes] of Anur is a living deity. People of surrounding villages, far and near, vow to offer worship to the goddess if their various desires are fulfilled. When their wishes are granted, they come to offer their worship and sacrifices. Most of the pilgrims are women, and the majority of them go to Anur with votive offerings for recovery from diseases. Even now groups of village women from noble families walk fearlessly through the fields to visit the goddess. During their journey they talk and sing about how She first appeared and revealed Herself. During the Master's childhood, Kamarpukur and the neighbouring villages were more populated and prosperous than they are now. This can be inferred from the deserted and dilapidated brick buildings covered with jungle foliage, the broken-down temples, and the ruined platforms that were once used for religious festivals. So the number of pilgrims to the goddess of Anur must have been many at one time.

The shrine of the goddess is in the middle of a field under the open sky. Every year the farmers build a simple canopy of leaves to protect Her from rain and sun. The nearby heap of ruins indicates that there was once a brick temple there. If the villagers are asked about the temple, they will tell you that the goddess Herself willfully brought it down.

The villagers explain: "The cowherd boys are the favourite companions of the goddess. They come there in the morning and let the cows loose to graze. Sitting in the temple, they tell stories, sing songs, and play games. They decorate the goddess with wildflowers, enjoy sweets, and pick up coins offered by pilgrims and travellers. This pleases and amuses the goddess. A rich villager once built a temple on that spot and installed the deity in gratitude for the fulfillment of a desire. The priest would come daily in the mornings and evenings, and would leave after performing worship, closing the temple door behind him. The visitors who came between worship times would throw the coins they offered through the grill of the door. The cowherd boys could therefore no longer collect the coins to buy sweets and offer them to the deity, then make merry as they had before. With sorrowful hearts the boys implored: 'Mother, you have deprived us of entering the temple and enjoying our food. By your grace we used to eat various sweets every day, and now who will give us those things?' The goddess heard their complaint, and that very night a huge crack developed in the temple. The next day the priest brought the image out and placed it in the open lest it be buried under the debris of the temple when it fell. Since that incident the goddess has appeared to anyone who tries to rebuild the temple. Either in a dream or in some other way, She informs that person that She does not approve." The villagers also say: "Mother even frightened some people and stopped them from building a temple. She told them, 'I am happy in this open field with the cowherd boys. If you confine Me inside a temple, I will destroy you. I will not keep any of your dynasty alive.'"

At the time of the following incident, Gadadhar was eight years old and had not yet been invested with the sacred thread. One day a group of respectable village women crossed through the field to perform their promised offerings to the goddess Vishalakshi. Prasanna, the widowed daughter of Dharmadas Laha, and one or two women of the Master's own family were included in the group.

In later life, the Master thought highly of Prasanna's simplicity, spirituality, purity, and amiability. Many times the Master told his wife, Sarada Devi, to follow her advice in all matters, and sometimes talked about her to his women devotees. Prasanna also had genuine affection for the Master from his childhood, and many times considered him to be the real Gadadhar [Lord Vishnu]. The simple-hearted Prasanna was captivated when she heard him recount the sacred stories of gods and goddesses and sing devotional songs. She often asked him: "Look, Gadai [his nickname], why is it that you sometimes seem to me to be God? Yes, I truly feel that you are God." At this the boy would smile sweetly and make no reply; or he would change the subject. Not deterred by his words, Prasanna would nod and say gravely, "Whatever you may say, you're not an ordinary human being."

Prasanna had a temple built and installed the images of Radha and Krishna, and she arranged everything for the daily worship service herself. Dramatic performances with song and music were held in the temple on festive occasions, but Prasanna seldom listened to them. When asked why, she would say, "After hearing Gadai's singing, no other singing sounds sweet to me. Gadai has spoiled my ears." Of course, these events took place at a much later time than our current story.

When Gadadhar saw the women on their way to Anur, he insisted upon going with them. Although they tried to discourage him, thinking it would be hard for him to walk such a distance, the boy followed them without paying any attention to their words. Of course, the women were delighted rather than irritated. Who would not be captivated by a boy who is always cheerful and humourous? More important, even at this young age Gadadhar had learned by heart many songs about gods and goddesses, and folk rhymes as well. During their journey they knew he would certainly sing a few songs at their request. It would be no problem if he felt hungry during the return trip, for then the offered food and milk would be available. So how could there be any objection to Gadadhar accompanying them? Thus the women pondered, and finally started their journey with Gadai. While joyfully walking with them, the boy told stories and sang songs about gods and goddesses as they had expected.

But as Gadadhar was crossing the field, singing of the glory of the goddess Vishalakshi, an extraordinary incident took place. Suddenly he appeared to be stricken dumb. His body stiffened and became numb. Tears poured from his eyes. He did not respond when the women asked if he felt ill. As they knew the boy was unaccustomed to making such a journey, the women were alarmed at the thought that he might have sunstroke. They brought water from a nearby pond and splashed it over his head and eyes. But Gadadhar did not regain consciousness. Then those helpless women began to worry:

"What is the way out of this predicament? How can we offer our promised worship to the goddess? How can we take Gadai, another's darling, home safely? There is no one here to help us. What do we do now?" The women were terribly worried and forgot all about gods and goddesses. They encircled the boy and fanned him, splashed water on him, and called his name repeatedly.

After a short while, the thought occurred to Prasanna that perhaps the goddess Vishalakshi had possessed the simple, trusting boy. She told her companions, "I have heard that the gods and goddesses possess simple and pure children, men, and women." She then suggested, "Instead of calling 'Gadai,' let us call 'Mother Vishalakshi' wholeheartedly." The women had deep respect for Prasanna because of her noble character, so they readily accepted her advice and began to address Gadai as though he were indeed the goddess: "O Mother Vishalakshi, be pleased with us. Protect us. Look upon us with compassion. Mother, save us from this great danger."

Wonder of wonders! No sooner had the women called upon the goddess a few times than Gadadhar's face glowed with a sweet smile, and slight signs of consciousness became visible. They were now convinced that the goddess truly had possessed the boy. They bowed down to him again and again; and addressing him as Mother, they prayed to him.[2]

Gadadhar gradually returned to normal consciousness. Amazingly, he showed no sign of fatigue or weakness from his ecstasy. Overwhelmed with devotion, the women went to the shrine of the goddess with Gadadhar and duly worshipped Her. Upon returning home, they reported the entire incident to the boy's mother. Chandramani was alarmed by their report. That day she offered special worship to the family deity Raghuvir for Gadadhar's welfare, and repeatedly expressed her gratitude to Mother Vishalakshi, promising to make a special offering to Her as well.

Another incident from Sri Ramakrishna's early life clearly shows that he would often ascend to a higher plane of consciousness during his childhood.

A goldsmith family lived in Kamarpukur, southwest of the Master's ancestral home. The Pyne family was very wealthy at that time, which is evident even now from their brick Shiva temple decorated with beautiful artistry. One or two people from this family are still alive, but their house is in ruins. The villagers say that the Pynes were very prosperous at that time and that their house was full of people. They were rich farmers with vast agricultural lands and a large number of cattle and ploughs. They also enjoyed a good income from their jewellery business. But they were not as wealthy as the landlords of the village; they belonged to the upper middle class of society.

2. Some say that out of exuberant devotion the women served the boy with the food they carried for the goddess.

The head of the Pyne family, Sitanath, was a very religious man. Although he had the means to convert his house into a brick building, he always lived in a two-storeyed house made of bamboo, wood, straw, and earth. For the family temple, however, he arranged for brick to be manufactured, engaged the best mason, and had the structure built beautifully. Sitanath had seven sons and eight daughters. Although all those daughters were married, they lived in their father's home. We have heard that the youngest of the daughters reached her youth when Gadadhar was ten or twelve years old. All the daughters were beautiful and devoted to gods and brahmins, and were affectionate towards little Gadai. During his boyhood, the Master spent some time with this holy family. Even today one can hear from the villagers many stories about the boy's divine play at the Pyne household. But we heard the following incident from the Master himself.

It seems that in Kamarpukur the devotees of Vishnu and Shiva lived side by side without harbouring any ill feeling towards each other. Even now both the *gajan* [festival] of Shiva and the annual Vishnu festival, in which the glorious name of Vishnu is sung for seventy-two hours, are observed. But in Kamarpukur there are more temples to Shiva than to Vishnu. In general, most of the people in the goldsmith community are orthodox Vaishnavas. The Vaishnava faith greatly prevailed in that community after Nityananda [a disciple of Chaitanya] initiated Uddharan Datta and saved him from worldly life. The Pynes of Kamarpukur, however, were devotees of both Shiva and Vishnu. The elderly Sitanath would chant Hari's [Vishnu's] name three times a day, but he also installed the image of Shiva in the temple and observed Shiva-ratri [the spring festival of Shiva] every year. During the festival a dramatic performance was held in the Pyne's courtyard to help devotees keep the nightlong vigil.

Once during Shiva-ratri a dramatic performance had been arranged at the Pyne's. A troupe from the neighbouring village was to perform a religious drama based on the glory of Shiva. The performance was to begin about half an hour after dusk. That evening, news reached the village that the boy who was to play Shiva had become seriously ill and that the director could not find a substitute. Disappointed, the director sent an apologetic message that the performance must be postponed. What could be done? How could the nightlong vigil be kept? The elders assembled to discuss the matter. They sent word to the director asking whether he could conduct the drama that night if they found someone to act in the role of Shiva. He responded in the affirmative. The village council met again to select someone who could play the part, and they decided on Gadadhar. Although he was young, his looks were right for the part and he knew many songs of Shiva. The director himsel f could tactfully manage the few spoken lines required for the role.

21. The Master's third ecstasy, while acting as Shiva during Shiva-ratri.

Gadadhar was approached. Seeing the eagerness of all, he agreed. The performance began on schedule, half an hour after dusk.

Dharmadas Laha, the landlord of the village, was a close friend of the Master's father. So his eldest son, Gayavishnu Laha, and the Master had become close friends. When Gayavishnu learned that his friend would play the role of Shiva, he and his companions helped him with make-up for the part. Once he was in costume, Gadadhar sat in the dressing room and thought of Shiva. When he was called to appear on the stage, one of his friends led him there. He mounted the stage at his friend's request. Absent-mindedly, without looking in any direction, he slowly walked to the middle of the stage and stood there motionless. The audience was overwhelmed with joy and awe upon seeing Gadadhar in that costume, with matted hair, bedecked with rosaries, and smeared with ashes. He entered with slow and steady footsteps, and then stood motionless, with a heavenly, indrawn, unblinking gaze, and a sweet smile on the corners of his lips. According to village custom, the audience suddenly cried out, chanting the name of Hari. Some women made auspicious sounds and some blew conches. To calm the audience during the pandemonium, the director began to sing a hymn of Shiva. At this the audience quieted slightly. But beckoning and nudging one another, they began to comment in hushed voices: "Bravo, Bravo!" "How beautiful Gadai looks!" "We never thought the boy could act in the role of Shiva so wonderfully!" "If we somehow secure this boy, we can form a yatra party of our own."

Gadadhar remained standing there all the while; moreover, tears continually trickled down onto his chest. Thus some time passed, and Gadadhar neither changed his position nor said anything. Then the director and a few elderly villagers went over to Gadadhar and found that his hands and feet were numb and that he seemed to have lost all external consciousness. At this point the commotion in the audience increased terribly. Some shouted, "Water! Splash water on his eyes and face!" Some said, "Fan him!" Some called out, "Lord Shiva has possessed him. Chant Shiva's name!" Again some grumbled, "This boy has spoiled everything. Now they will have to stop the play!" After a long while, when all efforts had failed to bring him back to normal consciousness, the audience dispersed. Some men carried Gadadhar home on their shoulders. We have heard that his family wept because despite all their efforts Gadadhar could not be roused from his ecstatic state that night. He became normal again after sunrise the next day.[3]

---

3. Some say that he remained outwardly unconscious for three whole days.

Chapter 3

The First *M*anifestation as a Spiritual Aspirant

IN ADDITION TO THE AFORESAID EVENTS REGARDING Sri Ramakrishna's spiritual ecsta-

> 1. Other examples of the Master's childhood spiritual moods.

sies, many more stories of his childhood are known. The nature of his concentrated mind was revealed through many small incidents.

First example: While the village sculptor was making images of Shiva, Durga, and other deities, Gadadhar happened to pass by with his friends. When he saw the images he said suddenly to the sculptor: "What is this? Do divine eyes look like this? They should be drawn this way." He then explained how to draw the lines of the eyes so that they manifested superhuman power, compassion, inwardness, and bliss, thus making the images living and godlike. People wondered how, without any training in art, the boy Gadadhar could understand these matters and was also able to make others understand them.

Second example: Sometimes when he was in a playful mood Gadadhar would decide to worship a particular deity with his friends. He would then make an image or paint a portrait of that deity in such a beautiful way that people thought it was the work of an expert sculptor or painter.

Third example: Sometimes Gadadhar would unexpectedly tell a man something that removed a longstanding doubt from his mind and gave him direction and strength to regulate his future life. That astonished person would think that his Chosen Deity had compassionately shown him the way by means of the young Gadadhar.

Fourth example: Gadadhar amazed others when he answered in one sentence a complicated theological problem that pandits well versed in the scriptures had not been able to solve (see III.4.3).

Not all of the remarkable events in the Master's early life that we have

2. Other events in the Master's life can be classified into six types.

heard are the expressions of his divine power emanating from a higher plane of consciousness. Although some of them were of a divine nature, others sprang from the Master's unique characteristics: his powerful memory, strong power of judgement, extreme steadfastness and firm resolution, indomitable courage, joyful sense of humour, and immense love and compassion. The Master's extraordinary faith, purity, and selflessness were constant throughout his life. It is quite evident that faith, purity, and selflessness were the natural components of his mind, and the actions and reactions of the world created various waves in that mind in the form of memory, intelligence, resolution, courage, humour, love, and compassion. The reader will thoroughly understand all of this from the following examples.

In the village once there was a dramatic performance based on the life of

3. An example of his fantastic memory.

either Rama or Krishna. The boy Gadadhar attended it along with other villagers. The next day the villagers were involved with their own activities, having forgotten those sacred stories and songs. But in Gadadhar's mind the holy words flowed uninterruptedly. He repeated the entire play to his friends, and for fun assembled them in the nearby mango grove. He helped them to learn by heart as well as possible the parts of the different characters of the play. He took the main role himself. The boys enacted the entire drama. While ploughing the nearby field, simple-hearted farmers watched the play acted out by the boys. They wondered how these boys had learned almost all of the dialogue and songs of the play after hearing them only once!

During his sacred thread ceremony Gadadhar went against family and

4. An example of his firm determination.

social customs and insisted upon accepting his first ceremonial alms from Dhani, a woman of the blacksmith caste (see I.7.8). Impressed with Dhani's love and affection, and knowing her inmost wish, the boy brushed aside social restrictions and ate food cooked by this low-caste woman. Fearful, Dhani earnestly tried but failed to stop the boy from eating her food.

Children in both towns and villages are always frightened when they see

5. An example of his indomitable courage.

naga monks with their matted hair and naked bodies smeared with ashes. It is rumored in Bengal that naga monks recruit young boys in various ways, or if the opportunity arises, they kidnap boys and take them to distant places just to increase the population of their community.

There is a road leading to Puri at the southern periphery of Kamarpukur. When the Master was young, many naga monks and Vaishnava mendicants would use that road to travel back and forth to Puri every day. Sometimes those travellers would enter the village to beg for food, rest a few days, and then continue on to their next destination. Because they believed the stories that were told about naga monks, Gadadhar's friends would stay away from them. But Gadadhar was not at all afraid. He mixed freely with those monks, talked to them, and pleased them with his service. He spent a great deal of time with them in order to observe their conduct. On some days he would eat the food that they had offered to God. Upon returning home, he would report everything to his mother. One day he wanted to look like a monk, so he put holy marks all over his body; then he tore his own new cloth into pieces to make a loin cloth, which he wore like a monk. In this garb he presented himself to his mother.

Many uneducated people of the village were unable to read the Rama-

6. An example of his wonderful sense of humour.

yana and the Mahabharata. In order to hear the epics they would invite to their homes a brahmin or an educated man of their community who could read and explain the texts to them. When the reader arrived, people would wash his feet, offer him tobacco in a new hubble-bubble [water pipe], and give him a good seat or a new mat to sit on for the reading. Thus honoured, it would sometimes happen that the reader became puffed up with pride. The sharp-witted Gadadhar observed how the reader would haughtily occupy an elevated platform in front of the audience and express his own superiority by reciting the verses, using an affected tone and making various odd gestures. Later, the fun-loving Gadadhar would amuse people by mimicking that egotistical reader amidst their peals of laughter.

By studying stories of the Master's early life we understand the kind of

7. The natural characteristics of the Master's mind.

mind he had when he began his spiritual disciplines. He accomplished whatever he set out to do; he never forgot anything he heard; he shunned forcefully and immediately any obstacle that prevented him from reaching his goal. We see that he performed all actions in this world by placing his firm faith in God, in himself, and in the innate divine nature of all people. He could not accept any idea tinged with even the slightest narrowness, nor could he bear any low, impure thoughts. Purity, love, and compassion guided him always in every respect. We realize that this aspirant's mind could not be deceived by its own thoughts, nor could it be deceived by others. Keeping before us the characteristics of the Master's mind, we shall be able to comprehend the uniqueness of his life as a spiritual aspirant.

We see the first clear manifestation of the Master as a spiritual aspirant

8. The first manifestation as a spiritual aspirant: "I will not pursue a bread-winning education; rather I will pursue that education which produces right knowledge."

when he was at his brother's Sanskrit school in Calcutta. The day his elder brother, Ramkumar, admonished him to concentrate on his studies, Gada-dhar emphatically replied: "I do not want to pursue a bread-winning education. I want an education that helps one manifest right knowledge and find true fulfillment in life." The Master was then seventeen

years old. Knowing that there was very little opportunity for further education in the village school, his guardians had sent him to Calcutta.

Ramkumar was righteous and well versed in astrology and Hindu law.
He had his school near the house of Digambar Mitra

9. The Master's
activities at Jhamapukur,
Calcutta.

in Jhamapukur, Calcutta. He also performed daily
worship services for the Mitra family and for a few
other wealthy families in that area. After performing his religious duties, he
spent most of his time teaching students. Soon it became very difficult for
him to conduct worship services properly twice a day in different homes.
Nevertheless, he could not give it up: His income from the school, in the
form of gifts and collections, was not adequate; it was dwindling day by day.
Under such circumstances, how could he manage his household without the
additional income from worship services? He finally brought Gadadhar to
Calcutta, handed over the worship services to him, and concentrated on
teaching.

After arriving in Calcutta Gadadhar happily performed his duties, which
suited him very well. He also served his elder brother and received some
lessons from him. In a short time the noble and handsome Gadadhar became
a favourite of the families for whom he worked. As in Kamarpukur, the
respectable women of those families in Calcutta were impressed by his
skillful actions, simple behaviour, sweet conversation, and devotion to God.
The cloistered ladies freely associated with him, asked him to do some small
errands for them, and eagerly requested him to sing his sweet devotional
songs. Thus here also, without any effort on his part, a group of devotees
formed around him, as it had in Kamarpukur. During moments of leisure
Gadadhar spent time with these devoted men and women and passed his
days joyfully. However, it became quite evident that after coming to Calcutta
he was still making no progress in his studies.

Although Ramkumar observed Gadadhar's way of life, he did not say
anything to his brother right away. He realized that he had deprived his
mother's dearest and youngest son of maternal affection, and had brought
him far away for his own convenience. Moreover, people were attracted by
his brother's noble qualities and were inviting him to their homes. Would it
now be proper to restrict his movements and ruin his joyful life? If
Ramkumar intervened, his brother's stay in Calcutta would be as unbearable as banishment to the forest. If his family had not been in such
difficulties, it would not have been necessary to bring Gadadhar away from
his mother; he could easily have sent the boy to a Sanskrit scholar in a village
near Kamarpukur. Gadadhar could have then continued his studies while
still living with his mother. Ramkumar thought about these issues for a few
months but remained silent. Finally, impelled by a sense of duty, Ramkumar
mildly admonished Gadadhar to apply his mind to his studies. Someday his
simple-hearted and self-forgetful brother would have to begin leading a

family life. If he did not start learning how to improve his worldly affairs and guide himself in that direction now, how could he manage in the future? Both brotherly affection and worldly wisdom therefore induced Ramkumar to scold his brother.

Although the affectionate Ramkumar had learned some hard lessons

| 10. Ramkumar's lack of awareness of his brother's mental disposition. | from the selfish and cruel ways of the world, he was unaware of his youngest brother's unique mental disposition. He had no concept of how his brother at such a young age had understood the motive behind |

the lifelong efforts and goals of worldly people, and had determined a different goal for human life that shunned ephemeral sense enjoyments as well as name and fame. So when the simple Gadadhar, unperturbed by the scolding, opened his heart and explained that he did not care for a bread-winning education, Ramkumar was unable to understand him. Ramkumar reasoned that because Gadadhar had been very dear to his parents, and because this was the first time he had been scolded, he made that reply because his feelings were wounded. On that day the sincere Gadadhar tried his utmost to make Ramkumar understand that he had no inclination to acquire a money-making education. But who would listen to the words of a boy? A boy is after all only a boy! In addition, whenever we find an adult who has relinquished self-interest, we conclude that he or she has become insane.

Ramkumar did not understand his young brother's statement that day. For a while after that encounter, Ramkumar behaved carefully with Gadadhar. After scolding a loved one, we tend to become repentant and try to regain peace of mind by bestowing a hundredfold more love and care than before. Nonetheless, we find clear evidence from his later actions that the boy Gadadhar was seeking an opportunity to fulfill the desires of his heart.

In the next two years after this event the life current of Gadadhar and his

| 11. The condition of Ramkumar's family. | brother changed rapidly. Ramkumar's financial condition worsened day by day, and in spite of his best efforts he could not improve it. A crisis was |

growing in his mind: Should he close the school and look for other employment? He was unable to make any decision. He was convinced, however, that if he continued to spend his days in this way, without finding any alternative means of earning money, he would soon end up heavily in debt and face other difficulties. But what could he do? He learned no other trade than teaching, performing sacrifices, and officiating as a priest. And at this time in his life he did not have the energy to learn a more lucrative trade. And if he now switched to a new occupation, it might be very difficult for him to find time to practise his own spiritual disciplines and perform worship. Ramkumar had a holy nature. He was content with little and had hardly any desire for worldly prosperity. He replaced his worries with "Let Raghuvir's will be done," and with a broken heart he continued his day-to-day life as before. By the will of God an incident soon occurred that showed Ramkumar a way out of his difficulties and reassured him amidst all uncertainties.

Chapter 4

The Kali Temple at Dakshineswar

RAMKUMAR WAS PROBABLY FORTY-FIVE WHEN HE OPENED his Sanskrit school in Calcutta

| 1. When and why Ramkumar opened a Sanskrit school in Calcutta. |

in 1850. The Master was then fourteen years old. Before Ramkumar went to Calcutta, he was oppressed by family problems: His wife had died immediately after giving birth to his only son, Akshay. It is said that the evolved soul Ramkumar had a premonition about this and told some members of the family that she would not survive the birth. When Ramkumar came to Calcutta he was perhaps thinking along these lines: Calcutta was a prosperous city filled with upper- and middle-class people. If he could provide these families with services, such as performing rituals for obtaining peace and overcoming obstacles, and writing opinions concerning religious matters, he would no longer have to worry about his family's finances. He could even earn a reputation as a scholar by making the students of his school proficient in learning. Another possible reason for his starting a school in Calcutta was that Ramkumar must have felt a great emptiness after his wife's death. He may have thought that if he could keep himself occupied in a distant place, this would relieve his sorrow.

We have already explained why Ramkumar brought his brother Gadadhar to Calcutta in 1852, a few years after establishing the school at Jhamapukur, and how the Master spent three years there. If we want to learn about the subsequent events of Sri Ramakrishna's life, we must turn our attention elsewhere. The Master's elder brother joined Chatu Babu's group in order to increase his income through gifts and collections, and he was also trying to improve his school. At that time, by the will of God, a series of

179

events took place in a well-known family in another area of Calcutta. Now the reader must focus on them.

At that time a highly respected woman named Rani[1] Rasmani lived at Janbazar in central Calcutta. The mother of four daughters, she had been widowed at forty-four, inheriting an enormous fortune from her husband, Rajchandra Das. From then on she managed an immense property herself and expanded it greatly, quickly becoming well known in Calcutta. She did not become famous only because she managed the estate skillfully, but also because of her faith in God, courage,[2] boundless sympathy for the poor,[3] extensive charities, lavish distribution of food among the hungry, and other philanthropic activities that made her popular with all. This woman, through her noble qualities and actions, justified the name "Rani" and commanded love and

2. Rani Rasmani.

---

1. Rani means "queen." This was a nickname her mother had given her in childhood. When she grew up, people continued to call her Rani in recognition of her royally benevolent and commanding nature. — *Translator*

2. It is said that there were barracks for British soldiers near the Janbazar house of Rani Rasmani. One day some drunken and rowdy soldiers forcefully subdued the Rani's guards, entered her house, and began looting. Rani's son-in-law, Mathur, and other male family members were then out on business. When the soldiers were about to enter the inner apartment, unobstructed, the Rani armed herself and prepared to oppose them. In the meantime Mathur arrived and realizing the situation, he rushed to the barracks and complained to the commanding officer. Immediately the officer sounded a bugle, and the soldiers returned to the barracks. Rasmani then hired twelve trustworthy British soldiers to protect her palace and collected compensation from the British Government for the damage to her property. — *This footnote has been slightly elaborated by the Translator.*

3. On one occasion the British Government imposed a tax on fishing in the Ganges. Many of the fishermen lived on the Rani's estate. Impoverished by this tax, they complained to the Rani about their predicament. She told them not to worry. She immediately obtained a lease on the fishing rights for the Ganges, paying a large sum of money to the government. The government thought the Rani planned to open a fishery. But no sooner had she obtained the rights than she had chains hung across the Ganges in several places, keeping British ships from entering the river. When the British protested, she replied: "I bought these fishing rights from you at great expense, and my action is completely justified. If ships pass up and down the river continually, the fish will be frightened away, and I shall lose a lot of money. How can I unchain the river? However, if you agree to abolish your new tax, I will agree to give up my rights. If you won't, I will sue you in the courts, and you will have to pay damages to me." It is said that the government accepted the Rani's reasonable argument and knew that she was acting in this manner in order to protect the poor fishermen. So the tax was abolished immediately and the fishermen were able to catch fish as before, blessing the Rani.

Rani Rasmani always showed a great interest in philanthropic activities: "She constructed market buildings in Sonai, Beleghata, and Bhawnipur; built a ghat and a hospice for dying people at Kalighat, and another ghat on the bank of the Ganges at Halisahar; and constructed a portion of the road that went to Puri from the other bank of the Subarnarekha River. Rasmani went on pilgrimage to Gangasagar, Triveni, Navadwip, Agradwip, and Puri, and donated large sums for the worship services of the deities." In addition, she protected her tenants on the Makimpur estate from being persecuted by British indigo planters. She spent 10,000 rupees to construct a canal at Tona that connected the Madhumati River with the Navaganga River. Thus, she performed many philanthropic activities.

respect in every way from people, irrespective of caste. At that time three of the Rani's daughters were married and had children. Her third daughter died, leaving a son. Concerned that her handsome third son-in-law, Mathur Mohan (Mathuranath Biswas), might become dissociated from the family, Rani Rasmani married her fourth daughter, Jagadamba, to him and made him her own again. The descendants of the Rani's four daughters are still alive.[4]

The virtuous Rani Rasmani had a constant and genuine devotion to the

| 3. Rasmani's devotion to the Divine Mother. |

goddess Kali. To stamp the official documents of her estate, she had a seal made with this inscription: "Srimati Rasmani Dasi, desirous of the feet of Kali." We have heard from the Master that the glorious Rani's devotion to the goddess was manifest in her actions and conduct.

For a long time the Rani had an intense desire to go to Varanasi and

| 4. Rasmani receives a divine command while preparing to visit Varanasi. |

perform a special worship ceremony for Vishweswar Shiva and goddess Annapurna. It is said that for this pilgrimage she had saved a large sum of money. But she could not fulfill her wish, because her husband died suddenly and the responsibility for managing the estate fell on her shoulders. By 1847, however, her sons-in-law had been trained to help run the estate — especially the youngest one, Mathur, who became her right-hand man — so the Rani decided to visit Varanasi. The night before the journey, when all arrangements were complete, the Rani had a vision of the goddess and received this command: "You need not go to Varanasi. Install My image in a beautiful spot on the bank of the Ganges and arrange for daily worship and food offerings to Me. I will manifest Myself within that image

4. For the information of the reader we present here a brief genealogical table of Rani Rasmani, from the booklet *Sri Dakshineswar*.

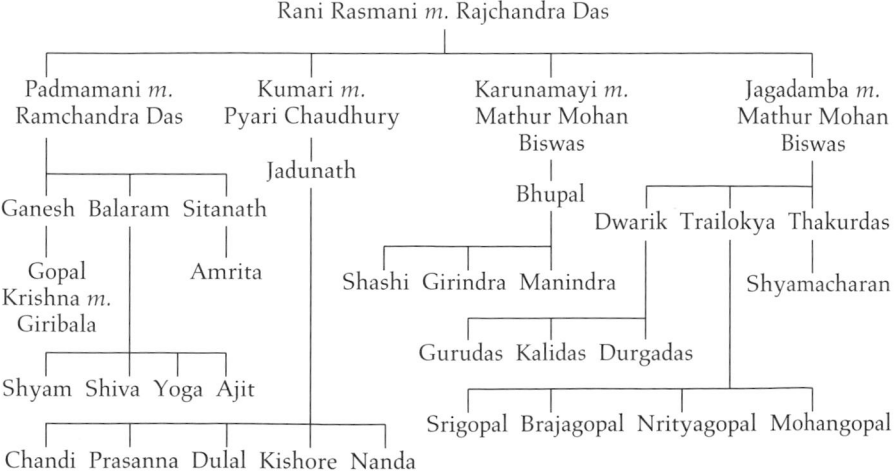

Rani Rasmani (1793-1861), wealthy widow of Rajchandra Das, built the Kali temple at Dakshineswar in 1855.

Mathur Mohan Biswas (1817-1871), a son-in-law of Rani Rasmani, who managed her extensive estate.

and accept your worship every day."[5] The devout Rani was delighted when she received this command. She cancelled her pilgrimage to Varanasi and resolved to build the temple with the money she had accumulated.

Now the Rani's long-cherished devotion took a visible form. She bought a

| 5. Rasmani builds the Mother's temple. |

large plot of land[6] on the bank of the Ganges and began to build a huge temple with nine spires, a temple complex, and a garden, spending money lavishly. The construction continued for seven or eight years, but by 1855 the temple complex was still not complete. The Rani thought to herself that life is uncertain: If she waited a long time until the temple construction was completed before installing the image of the Divine Mother, her resolve might not be fulfilled during her lifetime. With this in mind, the Rani had the installation ceremony performed on 31 May 1855, the auspicious day of *Snanayatra* [the bathing festival of Jagannath, or Krishna]. The reader should be aware of a few events that took place prior to the inauguration ceremony.

Devotees love to serve their Chosen Deity as they themselves want to be

| 6. Rasmani's desire to offer cooked food to the goddess. |

served. So, prompted either by a divine command or by the natural passion of her heart, the Rani was eager to offer cooked food to the Divine Mother. The Rani reflected: "The temple complex is being built according to my liking. I have given sufficient money for the maintenance of the service. If in spite of that I cannot offer cooked food to the Divine Mother every day to my heart's content, everything will be in vain. But nonetheless, people will say: 'What a glorious achievement of Rani Rasmani! She left this gorgeous temple as a legacy.' Who cares for such praise? O Divine Mother, please don't deny my heart's desire by giving me worthless fame. Always reveal Yourself here and graciously fulfill my prayer."

The Rani observed that the main obstacle to her offering cooked food to

| 7. Scriptural injunctions she obtains from the pandits become obstacles to the fulfillment of her wish. |

the deity was her own low caste status and the prevailing social system. She never felt that the Divine Mother would not accept cooked food if it were offered. In fact, the thought of offering cooked food to the deity made her heart joyful, and she had no misgivings at all. Why had such an adverse system prevailed in society? Were the authors of the scriptures heartless? Or were they prompted by self-interest to reserve the right to serve God as an exclusive privilege of the highest caste? If she followed the dictates of her pure heart and acted against the prevailing custom, devotees, brahmins, and holy people would not eat

---

5. Some say the Rani started her journey by boat. On the first night she halted near Dakshineswar, north of Calcutta; there she received that divine command in a dream.

6. According to the deed of endowment, the area of the Dakshineswar Kali temple grounds is 20 acres. On 6 September 1847 this land was bought from Mr. Hastie, an English attorney of the Calcutta Supreme Court. It took ten years to construct the entire temple complex.

184

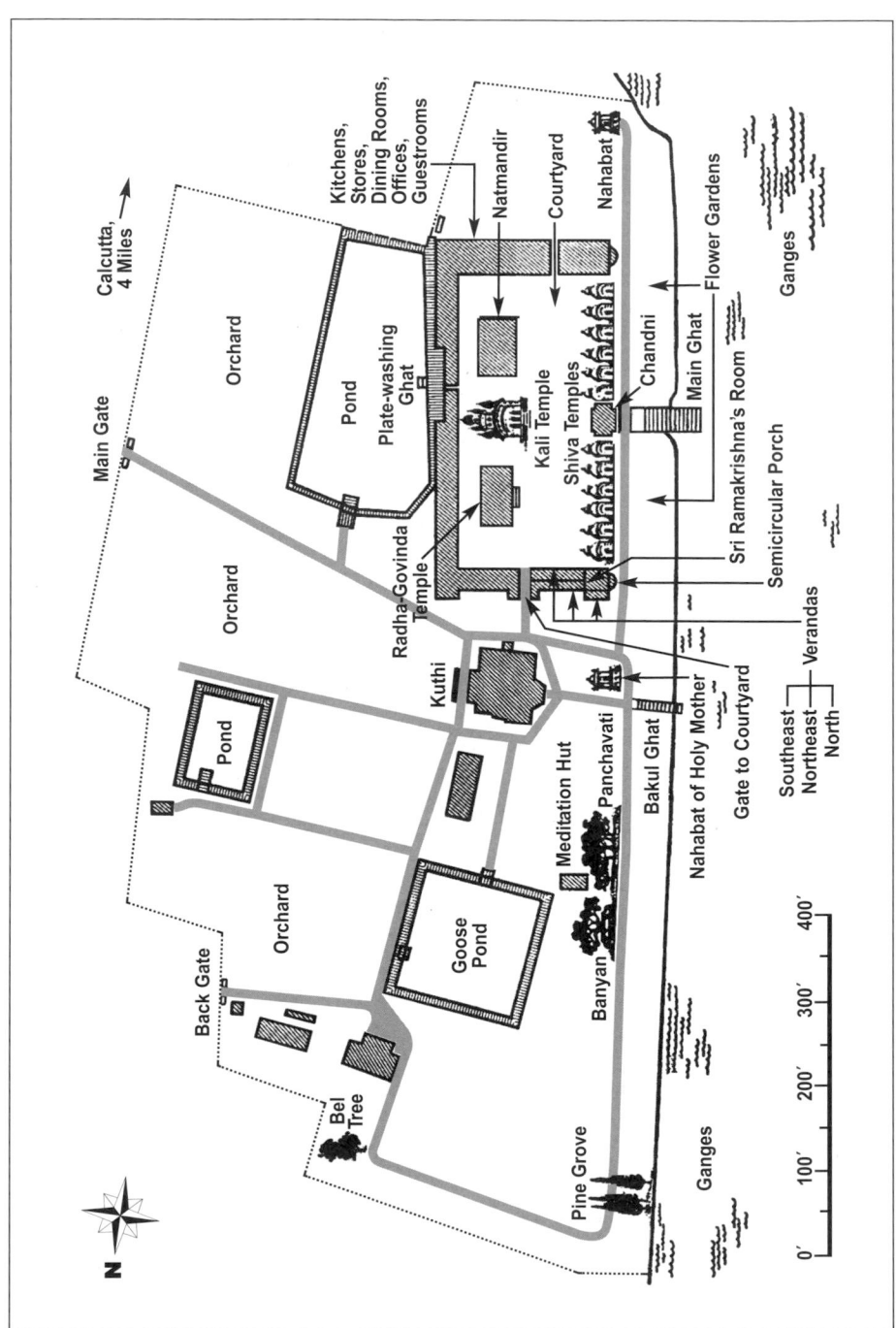

Map of the Dakshineswar temple garden.

Temple garden of Dakshineswar facing the Ganges.
From left to right: nahabat, Ramakrishna's room, twelve Shiva temples, office building, nahabat.

the food offered in the temple. What, then, was the way around this proscription? The Rani began to collect written opinions on the subject from many different pandits who were well versed in the scriptures. But none encouraged her in her desire.

Although construction of the Kali temple was complete and the image

| 8. Ramkumar gives a favourable interpretation. |

was ready, there was no sign that the Rani's wish would be fulfilled. One day, when her hope had been almost destroyed by the pandits' repeated rejections, a written opinion came from Ramkumar: "If the Rani were to donate the property to a brahmin before the dedication ceremony, and if that brahmin were to install the goddess in the temple and arrange for the cooked food offering, there would be no violation of the scriptural injunctions. Brahmins and people of other high castes would not incur any demerit if they took prasad in the temple."

The Rani's hope was enkindled by that interpretation of the scriptures.

| 9. Rasmani's resolution regarding the temple dedication. |

She decided to consecrate the temple in the name of her guru. Then, with his permission, she would assume the position of an officer to supervise the temple services on his behalf. The pandits learned that the Rani had decided to act according to Ramkumar's opinion. Although they did not dare to say that it was contrary to the scriptures, they criticized it [Ramkumar's advice] indirectly by commenting: "This action is against the prevailing custom of society." "If it is followed, brahmins and holy people will not eat prasad in the Dakshineswar temple."

We can assume that after this event the Rani's attention was greatly drawn

| 10. Ramkumar's catholicity. |

towards Ramkumar. At that time it was not insignificant for Ramkumar to issue such liberal declarations. In those days the minds of the brahmin pandits, the leaders of society, were bound by narrow confines. Very few among them could go beyond the limitations of those confines to embrace a liberal interpretation of scriptural law and grant written declarations accordingly. As a result, people were often inclined to violate the pandits' injunctions.

The connection between the Rani and Ramkumar did not end there.

| 11. Rasmani's search for a competent priest. |

Although the intelligent Rani paid the appropriate respect to the descendants of her guru, she knew they were completely lacking in knowledge of the scriptures and unfit to perform worship in the proper manner. So she decided to pay them their rightful income and gifts as usual, but to hand over the worship service of the new temple to brahmins of good conduct who were well versed in the scriptures. Here again the prevailing social custom stood in her way. In those days high-class brahmins did not even pay obeisance to the deities installed by people of lower castes, let alone worship them. And these brahmins thought that "degraded brahmins," such as the family of the

Rani's guru, had lost their caste status. Therefore, no orthodox brahmin who was able to perform rituals and officiate as a priest was willing to accept the position at the Rani's temple. Not giving in to disappointment, the Rani increased the salary and gifts and continued to search in various places for a priest.

Hemangini, a cousin of Sri Ramakrishna, lived in the village of Sihar, not far from Kamarpukur. Sihar was home to many brahmins. Mahesh Chandra Chattopadhyay of Sihar was then working on the Rani's estate. To make a little more money, he undertook the task of recruiting brahmins for the Rani's temple to work as priests or cooks or to perform other duties. He went to his village and told the poor brahmins there that it would not be degrading to work in the Rani's temple. In order to convince them, he selected his elder brother, Kshetranath, to be a priest of the Radha-Govinda [Krishna] temple at Dakshineswar. After appointing one of his own family to a post in the Rani's temple complex, it was easier for him to attract other workers. But he became anxious when even after much effort he could not find an appropriate priest for the Kali temple.

> 12. Mahesh Chandra Chattopadhyay of Sihar, an office worker for Rani Rasmani, takes responsibility for providing a priest.

Mahesh had been acquainted with Ramkumar for a long time. It seems they had a friendly relationship as neighbouring villagers. Mahesh knew that Ramkumar was a devout spiritual aspirant and had been initiated into a Shakti mantra. He was also aware that Ramkumar's family was in financial distress. When it came time to select the priest for Mother Kali, his attention was drawn to Ramkumar. But the next moment he reconsidered. It was known that Ramkumar did not perform rituals for people of lower castes. He did perform worship for Digambar Mitra's family and a few households in Calcutta, but Mahesh doubted that Ramkumar would accept the position as a priest in the temple of the Rani, because she belonged to the *kaivarta* [fisherman] caste.

> 13. Rasmani requests Ramkumar to officiate.

The day of the installation ceremony was nearing and a qualified priest for the Kali temple had not been found. Mahesh reviewed the situation and finally decided to try for Ramkumar. But instead of approaching him directly, he explained everything to the Rani and asked her to invite Ramkumar to perform worship on the day of the installation ceremony. The Rani already had a high opinion of Ramkumar's competence, since she had received the favourable written opinion from him. Now she was delighted by the possibility of his officiating as priest. She sent the following humble invitation to Ramkumar: "Based on your scriptural interpretation, I have proceeded to install the Divine Mother in the temple and have arranged everything for performing the ceremony on the coming auspicious day of Snanayatra. We have found a priest for Radha-Govinda, but no competent brahmin has come forward to officiate as the priest for Mother Kali and to help me in the installation ceremony. Therefore, please arrange something soon in this respect and save me from this predicament. You are a great scholar and well versed in the scriptures, so you know that not just anyone can be appointed to officiate as the priest."

Mahesh took the Rani's letter to Ramkumar himself. He explained the whole situation and persuaded Ramkumar to accept the position of priest until a competent replacement could be found. Not motivated by greed, the devout Ramkumar, went to Dakshineswar[7] on the appointed day to ensure that the Divine Mother's installation would proceed unimpeded. Later, when it became apparent that no other suitable priest could be found, the Rani and Mathur humbly requested that he stay on. Ramkumar served as priest there till the end of his life. Everything in this world, small or great, happens by the will of the Divine Mother. Perhaps Ramkumar, the Mother's devotee, accepted that post because he knew that it was Her will.

Thus, in an unexpected way Rani Rasmani hired Ramkumar to officiate as

14. Rasmani installs the Divine Mother.

priest. She installed the Divine Mother Kali in the new temple with great éclat on Thursday, 31 May 1855, the auspicious day of Snanayatra. On that occasion the temple compound resounded day and night with the bustle of feasts and festivities. The Rani spent money lavishly to entertain her guests and other visitors and tried her best to make them as happy as she was. On this occasion many scholars of the scriptures and brahmin pandits came from various distant centres of learning such as Kanyakubja, Varanasi, Sylhet, Chittagong, Orissa, Navadwip, and other places. Each of them received a silk cloth, a shawl, and a gold coin as a farewell gift. It is said that the Rani spent 900,000 rupees for the construction of the temples and for the

7. We heard the above description of Ramkumar's arrival at Dakshineswar Kali temple from Hriday, the Master's nephew. But Ramlal, another nephew of the Master, gave us a different account: "Ramdhan Ghosh of Deshra Village, near Kamarpukur, worked for Rani Rasmani. Because of his efficiency, he won the Rani's favour and later became the temple manager. As he knew Ramkumar, he invited him to come to his office and to receive a gift in return for performing the consecration ceremony of the Kali temple. Ramkumar went to the Rani's Janbazar house and said to Ramdhan: 'The Rani belongs to the kaivarta caste. If we accepted her invitation and gift, we would be cast out of society.' At this Ramdhan showed him the office register and said, 'Why would you be an outcast? See how many brahmins have been invited. They will all eat and accept the Rani's gifts.' Then Ramkumar agreed to accept the gift. He arrived at Dakshineswar with Sri Ramakrishna the day before the consecration. On that day festivities reverberated throughout the temple compound — dramatic performances, devotional songs to Kali, and readings from the Bhagavata and the Ramayana. That current of bliss continued throughout the night. The temples were illumined with innumerable lights so that every corner was as bright as day. The Master used to say: 'Seeing those temples at that time I felt as if the Rani had uprooted a silver mountain and placed it in Dakshineswar.' Ramkumar arrived at the Kali temple on the day before the installation to see these festivities."

installation ceremony. In addition, she bought from Trailokya Nath Thakur the Shalbari estate, in the Thakurgaon subdivision in Dinajpur, and executed a deed of gift to finance the continuing service of the deities.

Some say that on the day of the installation Ramkumar took uncooked

| 15. The Master's response on the installation day. |

food from the temple store, cooked it on the bank of the Ganges, and ate it after offering it to his Chosen Deity. But this seems improbable because it was Ramkumar, the Mother's devotee, who himself had given the scriptural interpretation and arranged the offering of cooked food to the goddess. It would be illogical if he were to refuse that food and go against his own opinion and the direction of the devotional scriptures. We did not hear such a thing from the Master. Therefore, we believe that after performing the worship, Ramkumar joyfully ate the food offered to the Divine Mother. But although the Master wholeheartedly joined that joyful festival, he followed strict caste rules regarding food. In the evening he bought one pice worth of puffed rice from a nearby market and ate it. That night he walked back to the Jhamapukur school to rest.

Regarding Rani Rasmani's dedication ceremony of the Kali temple, the

| 16. What the Master says about the dedication ceremony of the Kali temple. |

Master later told us many things on different occasions. Once he said the following: "The Rani set a date and made all the arrangements for her journey to Varanasi. Nearly one hundred boats of different sizes were ready at the ghat, loaded with various objects. In a dream on the night before her departure, she received the divine command of the goddess. The Rani cancelled her pilgrimage and began to search for a suitable place to establish the temple.

"There is a saying, 'The western bank of the Ganges is as holy as Varanasi.' With this in mind the Rani first tried to find land in the villages of Bally and Uttarpara on the west side of the Ganges, but she failed.[8] The Rani offered enormous amounts of money, but out of petty jealousy the famous landlords of those places refused to sell land to her. Moreover, they even said that they would not bathe at a ghat on the Ganges if it was built by anyone else in their jurisdiction. So the Rani finally bought this place at Dakshineswar on the eastern bank of the Ganges.

"Part of the land at Dakshineswar selected by the Rani had belonged to an Englishman; the other part was an abandoned Muslim graveyard where a Muslim holy man had been buried. The plot was in the shape of a tortoise shell, high in the centre and low around the edges. Such a burial ground, according to the Tantras, is a favourable site on which to establish Mother's temple and perform sadhana. As if guided by Providence the Rani selected this place."

---

8. Even now the old people of those villages corroborate this statement.

Image of Bhavatarini Kali at Dakshineswar that Ramakrishna worshipped.

The Rani dedicated the Divine Mother's temple on the day of Snanayatra, the bathing festival of Vishnu [Jagannath], instead of on a day deemed by the scriptures to be auspicious for the installation of Shakti. The Master told us the reason for this: "From the day the making of the image of Kali was begun, the Rani practised severe austerities in accordance with the scriptures. She bathed three times a day, ate plain rice with clarified butter, slept on the floor, repeated a mantra, and performed worship according to her capacity. When the temple was completed and the image was ready, the Rani carefully considered an auspicious day for installation. The image was kept packed in a box lest it be broken. Over time, the image began to perspire. The Rani received a command in a dream: 'How long will you keep me confined in this way? I am suffering terribly. Install me as soon as possible.' As soon as she received this command, the Rani anxiously consulted the almanac to set an auspicious day for installing the deity. As there was no auspicious date before the Snanayatra, she decided to perform the ceremony on that day."

We heard from the Master many other stories on this topic, including the Rani's dedication of the temple in the name of her guru so that cooked food could be offered to the goddess. We heard two episodes from Hriday, the Master's nephew. First, Ramkumar granted the Rani a written scriptural interpretation so she could consecrate the temple. Second, Ramkumar had to consult *dharmapatra*, "the leaf of impartiality"[9] to convince the Master that it would be appropriate for him to accept the office of priest.

We understand from the Master's conduct at this time that Ramkumar at first had no intention of permanently accepting the office of priest at the Dakshineswar Kali temple. When we reflect upon this issue, it seems the simple-hearted Ramkumar did not fully understand the situation. He thought that he had sanctioned the cooked food offering to the deity and that on the consecration day he would perform that service himself, then return

9. There is a village custom that when reasonable discussion can offer no solution to a particular problem, people resort to Providence. To know God's will on the subject, they consult *dharmapatra*, the leaf of impartiality. They then act accordingly without further argument. The leaf of impartiality is used in the following manner:

One writes "yes" and "no" on some pieces of paper or bel leaves and puts them in an empty water pot. Then a child is asked to pick out one piece of paper. If the scrap reads "yes," the performer understands that God approves his action, and vice versa. Sometimes the leaf of impartiality is used to divide property. For example, four brothers decide to go their separate ways and to divide the joint property. Failing to settle the matter, they request some unselfish and pious men of the village to solve their problem. Then they divide the entire estate, including movable and immovable properties, into four parts and decide which part will go to a particular brother by means of the leaf of impartiality. The same method is followed in this case. The names of the brothers are written on small pieces of paper and folded so that none can see the names. They are placed in a small empty water pot. The four parts of the estate are indicated by A, B, C, and D on small pieces of paper put in another water pot. Then two children are asked to each pick up a paper from those water pots separately. The judges read each corresponding set of papers, and each brother is to accept the portion corresponding to his name.

to Jhamapukur. In addition, from his dealings with his younger brother at this time we believe that Ramkumar was not at all hesitant while offering cooked food to the deity on that day; he did not think that his actions were in any way contrary to the scriptures.

Early the next morning after the consecration, the Master returned to Dakshineswar to inquire about his elder brother. He was also curious about the activities that would take place after the dedication ceremony. He stayed at the temple compound for some time before he realized that there was no possibility of his elder brother's returning to Jhamapukur that day. Although Ramkumar asked him to remain in Dakshineswar, he did not obey; instead he returned to Jhamapukur for his meal. The Master did not return to Dakshineswar for nearly a week. He stayed at Jhamapukur, thinking that his elder brother would come back when it was appropriate after finishing his responsibilities at Dakshineswar. But when Ramkumar did not come home even after a week, the Master grew anxious and returned to Dakshineswar to find out what had happened to his brother. He learned that, at the Rani's fervent request, Ramkumar had agreed to be the permanent priest of the Divine Mother. At this news the Master's mind whirled with thoughts. He tried to dissuade Ramkumar from his commitment by reminding him that their father had never officiated for lower castes, nor had he accepted gifts indiscriminately. It is said that Ramkumar explained his decision to the Master in various ways, using scripture and reasoning, but when nothing touched his brother's heart, he finally adopted the simple method of using dharmapatra, the leaf of impartiality. It is said that the following was inscribed on the dharmapatra: "Ramkumar's acceptance of the office of priest cannot be condemned. It will be beneficial to all."

Although the verdict of the dharmapatra relieved the Master's anxiety, another thought now occupied his mind. With the school now closed, what was he going to do?

17. The Master's observances regarding food.

Absorbed in that thought, he did not return to Jhamapukur that day. Ramkumar asked him to take prasad from the temple, but he refused. Ramkumar tried to persuade him in various ways, saying: "This is a temple, and the food has been cooked with Ganges water. Moreover, it has been offered to the Divine Mother. It won't do you any harm to eat it." But these arguments did not convince the Master. Then Ramkumar said: "Well, you can take uncooked provisions from the temple stores and cook your meal on the bank of the Ganges under the Panchavati. Don't you agree that everything is pure on the bank of the Ganges?" The Master's deep devotion to the Ganges defeated his strict observance regarding food. His faith accomplished what Ramkumar, well versed in the scriptures, could not do through reasoning. The Master agreed to that proposal and remained in Dakshineswar, living on food he cooked himself.

We ourselves actually observed the Master's lifelong deep devotion to the Ganges. He used to say: "The ever-pure Brahman has been transformed into the Ganges to purify all beings. So the Ganges is truly Brahman in the form of water. The minds of all who live on the bank of the Ganges become divine, and the spiritual inclinations of these people manifest spontaneously. The air filled with the moisture of the Ganges purifies the land as far as it blows. The people who live in that area are endowed with good conduct, devotion to God, steadfastness, generosity, and austerity by the grace of the Ganges, the daughter of the great Himalayas." If anybody had talked for a long time about worldly things or had associated with worldly people, the Master would say, "Go and drink a little Ganges water." If a godless, worldly man polluted any spot of the temple complex by thinking of mundane things, the Master would sprinkle Ganges water there. He was distressed if anyone washed himself with Ganges water after answering the call of nature.

18. The Master's devotion to the Ganges.

The environment of the temple garden of Dakshineswar brought about a change in the Master's mind: He saw the panoramic garden on the bank of the Ganges, with the Panch-avati grove that resounded with the songs of birds. He observed the worship services expertly performed in the vast temples by devout priests. He received genuine affection from his virtuous, father-like elder brother and also love and respect from the devoted and pious Rani Rasmani and her son-in-law Mathur. Soon the Master came to regard the temple garden of Dakshineswar as fondly as his home in Kamarpukur. Although for some time he cooked his own meals while he lived there, he was happy and able to set aside his indecision regarding the future.

19. The Master moves to Dakshineswar and cooks his own food.

Learning of the Master's rigid observance regarding food, some may comment: "That kind of narrow orthodoxy is common among ordinary human beings like our-selves. In reference to the Master's life, however, do you mean to imply that one cannot attain the highest spirituality without becoming similarly conservative?" We say in reply: "Narrow orthodoxy and steadfastness in religion are not the same thing. The first trait originates from ego. When it prevails, people consider whatever they know and do to be the best, and thus hold themselves aloof from others, circumscribing their activities. The second trait originates from faith in the scriptures and in the teachings of great souls. When it prevails, a person curbs his ego, makes progress in spiritual life, and gradually realizes the supreme truth. In the beginning, such a person may appear to be too conser-vative; but this orthodoxy helps that person to gradually reach higher and higher planes in his spiritual journey, so that the limitations of orthodoxy drop off automatically. Steadfastness in the spiritual path is therefore abso-lutely necessary. As we observed this evolutionary process in the Master's

20. The difference between narrow-mindedness and steadfast devotion.

life, we learned that we must proceed through experiences of spiritual truths by strictly following the injunctions of the scriptures. Only then will we be endowed with true catholicity and attain supreme peace in the course of time. As the Master used to say: 'If a thorn gets stuck in your foot, you use another thorn to pry it out.' In order to reach the catholicity of truth, we must be firm in religious steadfastness. We have to follow the disciplines and rules in order to reach the state beyond disciplines and rules."

Observing that kind of imperfection in the early life of the Master, some may comment: "Why then do you call him an incarnation of God, rather than a man? If you want to make him a God, it is better to conceal those imperfections or your purpose won't be easily served." We say: "Brother, there was a time when we couldn't believe even in our dreams that it would be possible for God to come down to this earth and assume a human body. When the Master, out of his unbounded grace, made us understand that this was possible, we realized that since he had assumed a human body he had to accept the imperfections of the mind as well as of the body. The Master used to say: 'If you don't mix gold with an alloy, you can't shape it into an ornament. Likewise, it is impossible to form the body and mind without mixing the impurities of rajas and tamas with pure sattva.' He never hesitated to describe his imperfections to us, yet he told us clearly over and over again: 'He who was born as Rama and Krishna in past ages has now come into this case (*pointing to his own body*). But this time He has come in disguise, as the king visits the capital incognito. It is like that.'" Therefore, we shall try to record everything we know about the Master. O reader, accept whatever you consider believable and reasonable, and if you censure us for the rest we shall not mind.

Chapter 5

The *M*aster Accepts the Office of Priest

THE MASTER'S HANDSOME APPEARANCE, GENTLE NATURE, devout personality, and youth attracted the notice of Mathur, a son-in-law of Rani Rasmani, within a few weeks of the temple dedication. The first time people meet someone with whom they will form an intimate and lasting relationship, they often feel an immediate attraction in their hearts. The scriptures say that this feeling arises from the impressions made by relationships in our past lives. When Mathur first met the Master, that kind of indefinable attraction arose in his mind. This we presume by observing the strong and loving relationship that later developed between them.

> 1. Mathur is attracted to the Master at first sight.

A month passed after the dedication and still the Master could not decide what to do. While he was staying at Dakshineswar at the request of his elder brother, Mathur resolved to appoint him to be a dresser of the goddess Kali. When Mathur discussed the matter with Ramkumar, however, he was informed in detail of Ramakrishna's reservations and was discouraged from proceeding further on that matter. But Mathur was not one to give up easily. Although he was deterred, he waited for an opportunity to carry out his resolution.

During this period another person arrived at Dakshineswar who was closely connected with the Master's life. Some months before the Master came to Dakshineswar, Hridayram Mukhopadhyay, a sixteen-year-old son of the Master's cousin Hemangini, went to Burdwan in search of a job. Hriday stayed there with some people of his own village but could not find

> 2. Hriday, the Master's nephew.

195

work. When he heard that his maternal uncles were well established in the new temple of Rani Rasmani, he thought that he might find work if he went there. Without further delay Hriday went to the Dakshineswar temple, where he lived happily with his uncle, Sri Ramakrishna,[1] who was almost his contemporary, and whom he had known since childhood.

Hriday was tall and handsome. His body was as strong and stout as his mind was energetic and fearless. Hriday was a hard worker. He exercised good judgement appropriate to the circumstance. His resourcefulness enabled him to come up with effective ways of surmounting adverse situations. Moreover, his love for his young uncle was genuine, and he never hesitated to undergo any physical suffering to make the Master happy.

Hriday was constantly active, and was not at all emotional. But like a worldly person, his mind was never completely free from selfish desires. The more we discuss the Master's relationship with Hriday in the early days, the more we shall see that whatever devotion and unselfishness Hriday achieved in his later life came from his constant association with the Master, whom he sometimes tried to imitate. The help of a person like Hriday, who was faithful, courageous, and a zealous worker, was necessary during the spiritual journey of the Master, who was indifferent to food, rest, and other physical needs, and was contemplative and devoid of self-interest. Was this why the Divine Mother engaged a person like Hriday to serve the Master during his sadhana? The Master repeatedly told us that without Hriday it would have been impossible for him to preserve his body during that long period. It is for this reason that Hriday's name is eternally connected with the

1. Here we present a genealogical table of Sri Ramakrishna for the convenience of the readers.

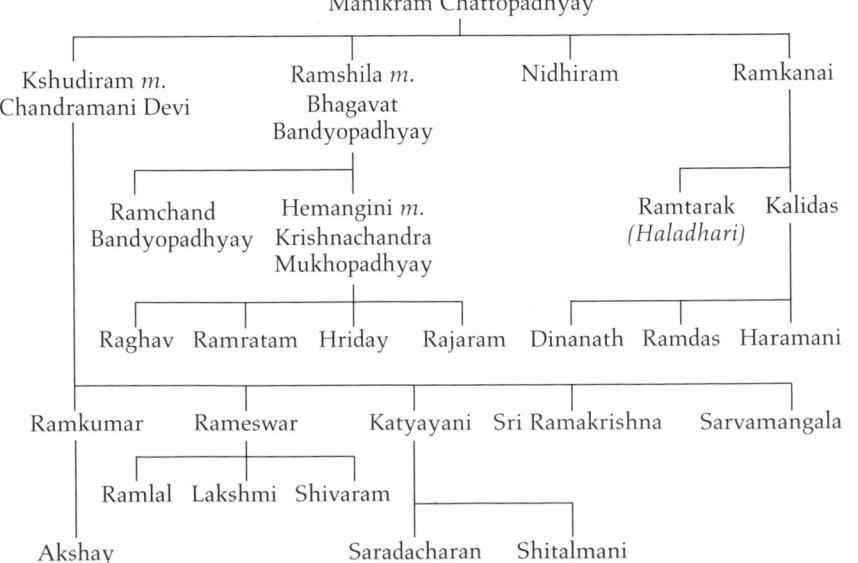

The kuthi at Dakshineswar temple garden where Rasmani and Mathur stayed during their visits and where Ramakrishna lived for sixteen years.

On the right, Hridayram Mukhopadhyay, son of Hemangini Devi and Ramakrishna's nephew.

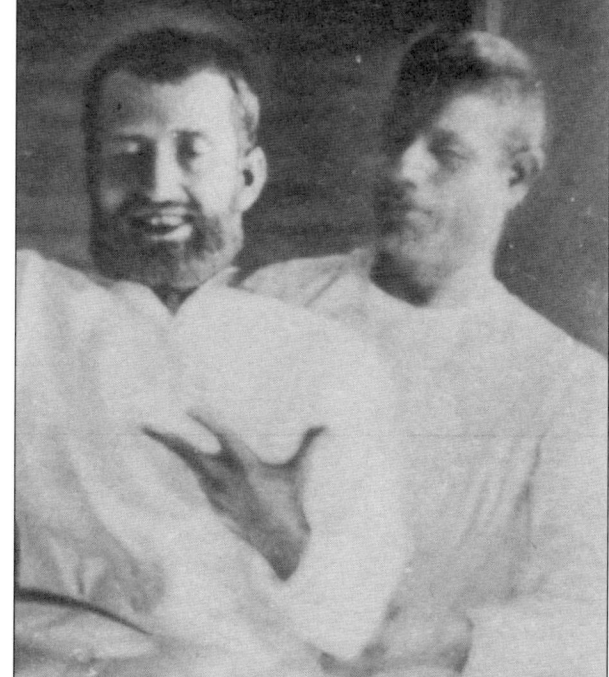

life of Sri Ramakrishna, and for which he forever deserves our heartfelt love and respect.

The Master was a few months past his twentieth [nineteenth] birthday when Hriday came to Dakshineswar. We can presume that the Master's life in Dakshineswar became much smoother after he had Hriday as a companion. From then on they did everything together. Because of his childlike nature, some of Sri Ramakrishna's activities appeared to be purposeless; but Hriday approved of them wholeheartedly, without protest. Thus, his sympathetic attitude made him dear to the Master.

3. Hriday becomes his companion.

Hriday himself told us: "From the very beginning I felt an indescribable attraction towards the Master and followed him like a shadow. It was painful for me to be separated from him even for a moment. We carried out all our activities together. We had to part for a while only during the lunch hours, when the Master would take provisions from the temple store, cook them himself in the Panchavati, and eat there, while I took prasad in the temple. However, I arranged everything for his preparations and also ate with him sometimes. He was so strict in observing caste rules regarding his food that he had no peace even eating the food he had cooked himself. Although at noon he cooked for himself, at night he would eat the *luchi* [fried bread] offered to the Divine Mother, as we did. On many days I saw him eating luchis while tearfully lamenting to the Divine Mother, 'Mother, You make me eat the food of the kaivarta caste!'"

4. Hriday's love for the Master.

Sometimes the Master himself talked to us about what happened during that period. Once he said: "I was greatly pained because I had to eat the food of a kaivarta. Even many poor beggars would not come to eat at the Kali temple of Rani Rasmani for that very reason. Because there were not enough people accepting that food, some days they fed cows the offered food and threw the rest into the Ganges." However, we heard from Hriday and the Master that he did not have to cook his own food for long. We assume that he followed that routine until he became the priest of the Kali temple, which happened two or three months after the temple was dedicated.

Hriday knew that the Master loved him dearly. But he could not understand one thing in particular about him. The Master would disappear for a while when Hriday went to help his elder uncle, Ramkumar, or during his nap after lunch, or in the evenings when he attended the vesper service in the temple. After a couple of hours Ramakrishna would return. If he were asked his whereabouts, he would say only that he had been nearby. While looking for him on some days Hriday would find him coming from the direction of the Panchavati. He thought that perhaps the Master had gone to answer the call of nature and did not ask him anything more.

5. Hriday's inability to understand the Master's behaviour.

Hriday told us, "One day during this time the Master had a desire to make

6. Mathur praises the image of Shiva made by the Master.

an image of Shiva for worship." We mentioned earlier that during his boyhood days at Kamarpukur the Master would perform worship in that way. As soon as that desire arose in his mind, he gathered some clay from the bed of the Ganges and made an image of Shiva with His bull, His drum, and His trident. While he was worshipping that image, Mathur happened near in the course of his walk. Curious about what the Master was worshipping so intently, he drew closer and found an image that was small but beautiful. Mathur was amazed, and realized that such a divine image was not available in the market. Curious, he asked Hriday where he got the image and who made it. Mathur was astonished to hear that the Master knew how to make the images of gods and goddesses and also how to repair broken images. He asked Hriday to give him the image after the worship. Hriday agreed, and with the Master's permission brought it to Mathur when the worship was over. Mathur scrutinized the image closely and was extremely impressed by what he saw. He then sent the image to the Rani for her to see it. She praised the maker of the image and, like Mathur, was amazed when she was told the Master had made it.[2] Prior to this incident Mathur had wished to appoint the Master to the temple service; that desire became stronger with the knowledge of his artistic skill. The Master had already heard of Mathur's intention from his elder brother, but he paid it no heed. From his childhood he had firmly resolved that he would not serve anyone but God.

Many times we heard the Master express this opinion about accepting

7. The Master's opinion about accepting employment.

employment: He did not think highly of anyone who willingly accepted employment if they were not in dire need. Once when he learned that one of his boy devotees[3] had taken a job, we heard him say sadly, "I wouldn't have felt more pain hearing news of his death than I felt on hearing that he had accepted a job." Later, when the Master saw him again and heard that he had accepted the position only to care for his helpless elderly mother, he was pleased. Affectionately caressing his head and body, the Master said: "There is no harm in that. No blemish will touch you because you are working for your mother. But if you were working for your own sake rather than for your mother, I wouldn't be able to touch you. So I say that there is no *anjan* [blemish] in my Niranjan. Why should he degrade himself?"

All the newcomers were surprised when they heard the Master's words to Niranjan. Someone asked, "Sir, you are condemning work, but without it

2. Some say that this incident took place when the Master assumed the office of the priest; and Mathur remarked, showing the image to the Rani, "As we have such a wonderful priest, the goddess will be awakened soon."
3. Swami Niranjanananda.

how shall we maintain our families?" The Master replied: "Let him work who wants to. I am not forbidding everybody from taking a job. I am saying this to these boys (*pointing to Niranjan and other boy devotees*). Their case is different." The Master was shaping the lives of his young devotees in a particular way. He made that remark because he believed that full-fledged spirituality and holding a job were incompatible.

After learning of Mathur's intention from his elder brother, the Master

| 8. The Master is hesitant to meet Mathur, lest the latter ask him to take a job. |

began avoiding Mathur and tried to stay out of his sight. Although he was uncompromisingly truthful in his dealings with people, with more concern for righteousness than for others' feelings, he was always reluctant to hurt people unnecessarily. However, it was natural for the Master to appreciate the qualities of a noble person, and to humbly respect an honourable person without any expectation of reward. Therefore, if Mathur were to ask him to accept the office of temple priest before he himself had arrived at a conclusion on the matter, he would have to cause Mathur pain by rejecting his offer. We understand clearly that such apprehension motivated the Master's conduct in avoiding Mathur. The Master was then an insignificant young man, and Mathur, Rani Rasmani's right-hand man, was an important and powerful person. Under such circumstances it would have been considered childish on his part to reject Mathur's request. But as the days went by, the Master found life in the Dakshineswar temple garden growing ever more delightful. He now had no objection to living in Dakshineswar, provided he would not have to accept any heavy responsibility. Moreover, we understand from subsequent events that he was no longer anxious to return to Kamarpukur, his birthplace.

What the Master had feared came to pass. Mathur came to visit the Kali

| 9. The Master accepts the office of priest. |

temple and sent for the Master upon seeing him at a distance. The Master had been walking with Hriday and tried to move in another direction when he saw Mathur from afar. In the meantime, Mathur's servant came and informed him, "Sir, Mathur Babu is calling for you." Observing that the Master was hesitant to go to Mathur, Hriday asked why. He replied, "If I go he will ask me to stay here and take a job." Hriday said: "What is wrong with that? It is truly good to live in this holy place and work under a noble man. Why are you hesitant?"

The Master replied: "I have no desire to be tied down to a job for life. In particular, if I agree to perform worship here, I'll be put in charge of the goddess's ornaments. This worries me. It is not possible for me to accept that responsibility. However, if you were to take responsibility for the ornaments, I would then have no objection to performing the worship."

Because Hriday had come to Dakshineswar looking for work, he gladly agreed to the Master's proposal. The Master then went to Mathur, who asked him to accept service in the temple. Mathur agreed to his conditions and on that day appointed the Master to be a dresser of Kali, with Hriday assisting him and Ramkumar. Ramkumar was relieved when informed that Mathur had engaged his brother to serve in the temple.

The incidents just narrated took place during July through August of 1855, within three months of the temple dedication. The *Janmashtami* festival [the birthday of Krishna] had been performed; the next day was *Nandotsava* [the birthday festival of Krishna arranged by his foster father, Nanda]. By noon that day the special worship of Radha-Govinda had been performed, and the food offerings were finished. As was customary, the priest, Kshetranath Chattopadhyay, carried the image of Radha to the adjacent room and put the deity on her bed to rest. While carrying the image of Govinda to his bed, the priest tripped, dropping the image and breaking one of its legs. This mishap created a large commotion in the temple, and various pandits were solicited for opinions about what should be done. Because he had seen the Master in divine ecstasy and had heard that he received divine commands, Mathur was eager to have the Master's opinion on whether the broken image should be replaced. According to the Master's advice, the broken part of the image was repaired, and the worship of the deity resumed as usual (see III.6.22-23). Hriday said later that the Master had been in an ecstatic mood before he answered Mathur's question about the broken image. After he came down from that state he said that replacing the image was not necessary. Mathur was aware that the Master had the skill needed to repair the image, so he asked him to do so. The Master accordingly glued the broken part of the right foot back onto the image. He repaired it so skillfully that even now it is hard to believe that the image had ever been broken, even if one examines it carefully.

After Krishna's image was damaged, some people remarked that worshipping a broken image would not produce any result. But Rani Rasmani and Mathur had deep faith in the Master's rational advice, so they ignored what other people were saying. However, the priest Kshetranath lost his job because of his clumsiness, and from that point on the responsibility of worshipping Radha-Govinda fell on the Master. Hriday continued to assist Ramkumar and in addition began to dress the image of Mother Kali during the time of worship.

Hriday once told us another story regarding the broken image. Ratan Roy, a famous landlord of Naral, has a ghat near Baranagore Kutighat, a few miles north of Calcutta. Near that ghat is a temple with ten forms of the Divine Mother installed in it. In the past there had always been fine arrangements for worship, but by the time of the Master's sadhana in Dakshineswar, the temple had become badly run down. One day, after

10. The image of Govinda [Krishna] breaks.

11. The Master's remark to Jaynarayan regarding the worship of a broken image.

Image of Govinda (Krishna) in Dakshineswar.

Detail of Krishna's broken foot, which Ramakrishna repaired.

Mathur had become extremely devoted to the Master, he and the Master went to visit the temple. Seeing its poor condition, the Master asked Mathur to donate two rupees and 164 pounds of rice as food offerings for that temple every month. Mathur agreed to do this. From then on the Master often visited the ten forms of the Divine Mother there.

Once while returning to Dakshineswar after a visit to the temple, the Master saw the local landlord, Jaynarayan Bandyopadhyay, standing on his ghat with some people. As they knew each other, the Master walked over to greet him. Jaynarayan saluted him and cordially introduced him to his companions. In the course of conversation he raised the topic of Rani Rasmani's Kali temple and asked, "Sir, is the Lord Govinda in the Dakshineswar temple broken?" The Master replied: "Ah, how shallow is your intelligence! Can One who is an indivisible Whole be broken?" To avoid becoming entangled in idle chatter about the image, the Master then changed the topic. He told Jaynarayan to accept only what is essential and to give up everything that is nonessential. The intelligent Jaynarayan took the Master's advice and refrained from asking such questions anymore.

We heard from Hriday that the Master's method of worship was

12. The Master's musical talent.

something special to see. Whoever saw it was overwhelmed. How sweetly the Master sang, and how passionate was his heart! Whoever heard those songs even once could never forget them. There was no pretence in his singing, no attempt to parade his skill as do some classical musicians. He would fully absorb the theme of the song and then express it with his impressive, yet sweet, voice, using the correct musical tempo and cadence. Whoever heard the Master's songs realized that emotion is the very life of music. When the Master's singing was compared with that of others, it became clear that mood cannot express itself if the tempo and the cadence are not perfect. Whenever Rani Rasmani came to Dakshineswar, she sent for the Master to listen to him sing. This song was her favourite:

> Where is Your consideration, O Mother, when You stand
> With Your feet on Hara's bosom?
> Willfully You have stuck out Your tongue,
> As if You are a naïve girl!
> O Mother Tara, I have known Your play;
> Is this the way You play with all?
> Did Your mother stand on Your
> Father's bosom in this way?

There was another reason why the Master's songs sounded so sweet. As he sang, he would become so absorbed in the mood of the song that he would completely forget that he was singing to please anyone else. We have never in our lives seen any other person who would fully forget himself while singing in ecstasy, as the Master did. Even devotional singers expect some appreciation from their audience. But as for the Master, we noticed that when someone praised his singing, he truly believed that the praise was due to the emotion of the song and not to himself at all.

Hriday said that while the Master sang, tears would pour profusely from his eyes and flow down his chest. As he performed worship, the Master would become so absorbed that if anyone came near or talked to him, he could not hear them at all. The Master mentioned that while performing rituals such as *anganyasa* and *karanyasa* he actually saw the words of those mantras written on his body in bright colours. In addition, he watched as the *kundalini* power in his own body rose like a snake through the *sushumna* channel to the *sahasrara* (see III.2.30-34). Those parts of his body that were left behind by that power as it ascended immediately became motionless, insensible, and nearly dead. When according to the prescribed method of worship he uttered the mantra *"rang,"* sprinkled water around himself, and imagined that the place of worship was encircled by a wall of fire, he actually saw an impassable wall of fire with hundreds of flames on all sides, protecting the place of worship. Hriday said that when the other temple brahmins saw the Master's luminous body and absorbed mood, they would say to one another, "It seems Narayana Himself has assumed a human body and has sat for worship!"

13. The Master's visions during worship.

Although after coming to Dakshineswar the devout Ramkumar was to some extent free from anxiety regarding the mainte-nance of his family, he sometimes worried about another matter. He observed his young brother's fondness for solitude and his indifference towards worldly affairs. His brother's actions revealed a lack of interest in their household's financial well-being. In the mornings and evenings he saw his brother walking alone on the bank of the Ganges, away from the temple, or sitting motionless under the Panchavati, or entering the jungle around the Panchavati and not emerging for a long time. At first Ramkumar thought that perhaps Gadadhar was anxious to return to Kamarpukur to see his mother and was thinking of her. Days passed, but Gadadhar never expressed any longing to return home. From time to time Ramkumar would ask him about this and was always assured that he had no such desire. Ramkumar therefore gave up the idea of sending him home. Furthermore, he thought: "I am growing older and my health is failing day by day. Who knows how long I will live? Under such circumstances, and without further delay, it is my duty to train Gadadhar in such a way so that when I am gone he will be able to make a living and maintain the family on his own." So Ramkumar was very pleased when Mathur asked him about appointing Gadadhar to temple service. Later he was greatly relieved when, at Mathur's request, Gadadhar first

14. Ramkumar trains the Master to be an expert worshipper.

became the dresser of the goddess Kali and afterwards accepted the office of priest, competently performing those duties. At that point Ramkumar began teaching his brother how to chant the Chandi and how to worship Kali and other gods and goddesses. The Master soon learned to perform various modes of worship as did the traditional brahmin priests. Moreover, because he knew that it is not proper to perform worship of the goddess without being initiated in a Shakti mantra, he resolved to take initiation.

Kenaram Bhattacharya, a proficient Shakti worshipper, lived at Baithak-

15. The Master takes initiation in a Shakti mantra from Kenaram Bhattacharya.

khana Bazar in Calcutta. He frequented the temple of Rani Rasmani in Dakshineswar, and was probably acquainted with Mathur and others. We heard from Hriday that those who knew him had a high regard for him as a devout spiritual aspirant. He had also been well known to Ramkumar for some time. The Master decided to take initiation from him. We have heard that as soon as the Master was initiated he went into ecstasy and that Kenaram was amazed by his extraordinary devotion. He blessed the Master wholeheartedly that he might realize his Chosen Deity.

From then on, either because he was no longer physically capable or

16. Ramkumar's death.

because he wanted to make the Master become accustomed to performing temple work, Ramkumar began to engage him in worshipping Mother Kali, taking for himself the less strenuous worship service of Radha-Govinda. Mathur approved of this arrangement. He also learned that the Master had become adept in Mother worship, so he asked Ramkumar to perform the worship of Radha-Govinda in the Vishnu temple permanently. From that point on, the Master remained priest of the Kali temple. Mathur made these changes because he realized that Ramkumar was growing old and was physically unable to perform the more demanding duties required in the Kali temple. Ramkumar was happy with this arrangement. He taught his younger brother how to properly perform the worship and other services of the Mother, and thus he was relieved of his worries. Shortly afterwards, he consulted with Mathur and engaged Hriday as a priest of Radha-Govinda. Then he prepared himself for an extended visit home. But Ramkumar was never to return home again. While he was making arrangements for his trip, he had to go to Shyamnagar-Mulajor, north of Calcutta, to settle some business. There he suddenly died.

Following the dedication of Rani Rasmani's temple, Ramkumar had lived at Dakshineswar and worshipped the Divine Mother for one year. It was probably the middle of 1856 when he died.

Chapter 6

His Longing and First Vision

SRI RAMAKRISHNA WAS QUITE YOUNG WHEN HIS father died, and he was raised under

1. The Master's behaviour at this time.

the loving care of his mother, Chandramani, and his elder brother, Ramkumar. Ramkumar was thirty-one years older than the Master. So it seems that much of the devotion the Master had felt for his father was shifted to Ramkumar. Therefore, he was extremely sad when his elder brother suddenly died. Who can say how much this mishap contributed to his conviction about the transitoriness of the world and enkindled the fire of renunciation in his pure mind? But it is known that from that point on he concentrated more on the worship service of the Divine Mother and longed to know whether a person could truly see Her. After the worship was completed, he would sit near the image of the Mother in an absorbed mood. When he sang the devotional songs of Ramprasad, Kamalakanta, and other mystics he would lose himself in overwhelming love. He did not spend a single moment in idle talk. When the door of the temple was closed at night, he would abandon all company and enter the jungle near the Panchavati to meditate on the Divine Mother.

Hriday did not like the Master's strange behaviour. But what could he

2. Hriday's observation and anxiety.

do? Hriday was fully aware that from his childhood the Master had always accomplished whatever he undertook, and that no one could prevent him from doing so. It would therefore be of no use to protest his behaviour or oppose him. As the days went by Hriday observed his extreme behaviour and could not help but express his concern. He was extremely anxious when he found that the Master was going to the Panchavati at night instead of sleeping. The Master had to work hard in the temple, and in addition he was not eating as well as before. Under such circumstances, his health might break down if he did not sleep at night. Hriday decided to investigate the situation and do what he could.

The land around the Panchavati was not as level as it is now. It was a low

3. The condition of the Panchavati.

land full of pits and ditches, covered with dense foliage. This area had been a burial ground and was thickly overgrown, so people seldom went to the Panchavati even in the daytime. If someone did go there, he would not enter the jungle surrounding it. Especially at night no one would venture in that direction for fear of ghosts. Among the wild trees and plants in the Panchavati there was an *amalaki* tree. Hriday told us that in the early days that tree had been in a low place; anyone sitting under it could not be seen from the higher ground outside the jungle. At night the Master would meditate under that tree.

One night when the Master was going to that place, Hriday followed him

4. Hriday asks the Master what he does in the jungle at night.

surreptitiously. He saw him entering the jungle but did not follow him farther because he knew the Master would be annoyed. In order to frighten him, however, he threw some stones in that direction for some time. This did not bring the Master back, so Hriday returned to his room. When the Master was resting the next day, Hriday asked him, "What do you do at night in the jungle?" The Master replied: "I meditate under an amalaki tree there. The scriptures say that if a person meditates under an amalaki tree, whatever he desires is fulfilled."

For the next few nights, Hriday continued throwing stones and creating

5. Hriday tries to frighten the Master.

all sorts of disturbances while the Master was sitting for meditation under the amalaki tree. The Master realized this was Hriday's mischief and did not say anything to him. When he realized that the Master could not be frightened away, Hriday could restrain himself no longer. One evening after the Master had gone to that spot, Hriday silently entered the jungle and saw from a distance that the Master had discarded his clothes and sacred thread and was immersed in meditation. Immediately he thought: "Has my uncle gone mad? Only a crazy person behaves like this. It is all right if he meditates, but why does he sit naked?"

Pondering thus Hriday appeared before the Master suddenly and asked:

6. The Master tells Hriday: "One should meditate while free from ties."

"What is this? Why are you sitting naked, having discarded your cloth and sacred thread?" After being addressed several times, the Master slowly regained his normal consciousness. Then he listened to Hriday's question and replied: "What do you know? One should meditate by becoming free from all ties. From their very birth human beings are tied with eight fetters: hatred, shame, family status, good conduct, fear, fame,

208

Panchavati at Dakshineswar where Ramakrishna practised sadhana. Photo taken c.1900.

pride of caste, and ego. This sacred thread is a fetter because it signifies vain-glory: 'I am a brahmin and superior to all.' One should call on Mother with a one-pointed mind, shunning all bondage. That is why I took off those things. When I return after meditation I shall put them on again." Hriday was dumbfounded; he had never before heard such words. Unable to say anything in reply, Hriday left the place. Previously he had thought he could scold his uncle and make him see his mistake. Now he realized he could do nothing.

It is appropriate to mention something here in connection with the

| 7. The Master's efforts to destroy pride of lineage; to look on a clod of earth, a stone, and gold as of equal worth; and to experience God in all beings. | previous event. If we know this, it will be easier for us to understand some subsequent events in the Master's life. To be free of the eight fetters, we saw that the Master not only renounced them mentally but also physically, as far as possible. We saw him behave in a similar manner in all other matters in his |

later life.

For example, in order to destroy his pride of lineage and to instill true humility in his mind, the Master cleaned the latrine carefully and with his own hands, an action that is generally shunned by people as unclean.

Also, the Master heard that the mind of a spiritual aspirant should consider "a clod, a precious stone, and a piece of gold as being of equal worth." Without disregarding precious things as one would a clod of dirt, one cannot transcend desires for physical enjoyment, focus the mind fully on God, and be established in yoga. So the Master took some coins and clods of dirt in his hands and threw them one after another into the Ganges, saying repeatedly, "rupee is clay; clay is rupee."

In order to make firm his knowledge that God dwells in all beings,

| 8. The sequence of the Master's renunciation. | Ramakrishna ate as prasad the leftovers from beggars who had been fed at the Kali temple. He then carried their leaf-plates on his head and discarded |

them on the bank of the Ganges. Afterwards, he swept clean the place where the beggars had eaten. He considered himself blessed by serving those living gods with his mortal body.

Many such events in the Master's life can be cited. It is seen in every case that he was not satisfied by merely renouncing mentally whatever obstructed his path to God-realization. First he gave up those gross objects, keeping himself as far away from them as possible. Then he forced his body and senses to act contrary to basic human instincts. Such actions wiped his mind clean of past impressions, allowing new ideas to take root in such a way that no other thoughts could enter. He would not believe that past impressions had been completely replaced by new ideas until he had been able to put the new ideas into practice with his body and senses and had complete control over them.

We are reluctant to give up our own past impressions, so we like to think

9. His method of
sadhana was due to his
own eccentricity:
objection and answer.

that the Master did not need to perform such practices. While discussing the Master's actions, someone remarked: "The incidents such as cleaning a dirty, abominable place [the latrine] and throwing the clods and coins into the Ganges, saying, 'rupee is clay; clay is rupee' seem to be but his own whims. One can attain control over the mind quickly and easily without the extraordinary means that he adopted."[1]

In reply we say: Very well! Thus far how many people have been able to concentrate their minds on God, completely renouncing sense objects, by adopting your so-called simple means of renouncing mentally, without performing external disciplines? This cannot be done. When the mind thinks one thing and moves in that direction, and the body moves in another direction — nothing great can be achieved, not to speak of God-realization! But a person hankering after sense objects does not understand this fact. Dominated by past impressions, he makes no effort to give up sense objects, even though he realizes it would be good to renounce them. And he thinks: "Let the body do as it likes; I am thinking higher thoughts." Thus, he is deceived into thinking that both yoga [spirituality] and bhoga [worldly enjoyment] can be achieved. As light and darkness never appear together, so yoga and bhoga cannot coexist. No one has ever yet discovered an easy path that allows one to serve simultaneously God and the world of lust and gold.[2] So the scriptures repeatedly teach us: "Whatever one should renounce or accept, one should do it with body, mind, and speech equally. Only then will a spiritual aspirant be worthy of God-realization." That is why the sages stated that a person cannot realize the Atman through excessive emotion without knowledge accompanied by renunciation.[3] By means of reasoning, the human mind proceeds gradually from the gross plane to the subtle and from the subtle to the causal plane. "There is no other way to reach the Supreme Goal."[4]

We have already mentioned that after Ramkumar's death the Master

10. The Master's mode
of worship.

concentrated more intensely on the worship service of the Divine Mother. Whatever he considered necessary for attaining Her vision, he performed with eagerness and wholehearted faith. We heard from the Master that after the regular service was completed he would continue his worship of Her by singing devotional songs of Ramprasad and other mystics. His heart filled with emotion as he sang those songs with exuberant devotion. He thought:

1. Adapted from Shivanath Shastri's "Personal Reminiscences of Ramakrishna Parama-hamsa." See *Modern Review,* November 1910.
2. Ye cannot serve God and Mammon together. — Matthew 6:24
3. Mundaka Upanishad 3:2:4
4. Shvetashvatara Upanishad 6:15

"Ramprasad and other devotees had the vision of the Divine Mother. One can definitely see Her. Why can't I?" He would often exclaim piteously: "Mother, You showed Yourself to Ramprasad. Why won't You show Yourself to me? I don't want wealth, friends and family, or objects of enjoyment. Please reveal Yourself to me." Thus he would pray, as tears streamed from his eyes and flooded his chest. This would somewhat lighten the burden of his heart. Then prompted by burning faith and heartened with hope, he would again try to please the goddess with songs. Thus the Master spent his days in worship, meditation, and devotional singing; and day by day his love and longing increased.

From that point on he began spending more time performing worship and serving the goddess than was regularly allotted. While performing worship, he sometimes placed a flower on his head, according to the prescribed rule, and then he would meditate for two hours, sitting still as a log. After offering food to the goddess, he might spend a long time thinking that the Mother was eating the food. On some mornings he would spend several hours picking flowers, making garlands, and decorating the goddess. Or for a long period he would remain engaged in performing the vesper service with exuberant devotion. Sometimes in the afternoon he would sing for the Divine Mother and become so absorbed and overwhelmed with devotion that he would be unaware that the time for the vesper service had passed. Although he was reminded again and again, no one could induce him to conduct the vesper service. Thus, the worship continued for some time.

It is clear that the Master's steadfastness, devotion, and longing attracted the attention of others in the temple compound.

11. Mathur's and others' concerns about the Master's worship service.

People at first ridicule a person who leaves the usual path trod by the masses and does something new. The more that person moves forward steadfastly towards his goal, however, the more people's attitudes become transformed into reverence. This actually happened in the case of the Master's activities at that time. When he continued his novel method of worship, he became an object of derision to some people of the temple; but later others became very respectful towards him. It is said that when he had observed the Master performing worship, Mathur joyfully told Rani Rasmani: "We have got a wonderful worshipper. It seems the goddess will be awakened very soon." In spite of people's criticism, the Master never deviated from his spiritual journey. As the river always flows towards the ocean, so from this point on the Master's mind continued to move towards the Divine Mother.

As the days went by, the Master's love and longing continued to increase.

12. Intense longing for God causes changes in the Master's body.

Because of his uninterrupted current of thought towards the Divine Mother, some external signs manifested in his body. His appetite and need for sleep diminished. As blood flowed continually to his chest and head, his chest turned crimson and his eyes were often drenched with tears. He constantly and intensely desired to see the Divine Mother, and repeatedly asked himself, "What shall I do? How can I see Her?" Signs of anxiety and restlessness were therefore always visible in his body except when he meditated and performed worship.

We heard from the Master that one day at that time he was singing to the Divine Mother and praying and crying bitterly. He implored piteously: "Mother, I have been praying to You so long! Why don't You listen to me? You showed Yourself to Ramprasad. Why won't You show Yourself to me?"

The Master described what happened then: "There was an unbearable pain in my heart because I could not have a vision of Mother. Just as a man wrings out a towel with all his strength to get the water out of it, so I felt as if my heart were being wrung out. I began to think I should never see Mother. I was dying of despair. In my agony, I asked myself: 'What's the use of living this life?' Suddenly my eyes fell on the sword that hangs in the Mother's shrine. I decided to end my life then and there. Like a madman, I ran to the sword and seized it. Then I had a marvellous vision of the Mother and fell down unconscious. Afterwards what happened in the external world, or how that day and the next passed, I don't know. But within me there was a steady flow of undiluted bliss that I had never before experienced, and I felt the immediate presence of the Divine Mother."

13. The Master's longing and his first vision of the Divine Mother.

On another occasion, the Master narrated to us in detail the same wonderful vision: "It was as if the room, doors, temple, and everything else vanished altogether; as if there were nothing anywhere! And what I saw was an infinite shoreless ocean of light; that ocean was consciousness. However far and in whatever direction I looked, I saw shining waves, one after another, coming towards me to swallow me up. They were madly rushing towards me from all sides, with a terrific noise. Very soon they were upon me, and they pushed me down into unknown depths. I panted and struggled and lost consciousness." Thus, the Master told us that during his first vision he saw a shining ocean of consciousness. But was this pure consciousness the Divine Mother Kali, bestowing boons and fearlessness? Did the Master see Her in that ocean of light? It seems that he did. We heard that when he partially regained his consciousness after the first vision, he uttered plaintively, "Mother, Mother!"

When this vision ended, an incessant and violent urge for a constant, uninterrupted vision of the Divine Mother's luminous form arose in the Master's heart. Although this longing did not always manifest itself externally through signs such as weeping, it remained in his heart all the time. Sometimes it would increase to such a point that he could not contain it anymore. Restlessly rolling on the ground with agony, he would pray:

"Mother, be gracious unto me. Reveal Yourself to me." He would cry so bitterly that people would gather around him to watch. He was completely unconcerned about what people might say when they saw him in that condition. He later said: "I scarcely realized the presence of people around me. They looked more like shadows or painted pictures than real objects, and so I did not feel any shame or embarrassment at all. Sometimes I would lose outer consciousness from that unbearable agony. Immediately after that I would see the Mother's luminous form bestowing boons and fearlessness! I used to see Her smiling, talking, consoling, or teaching me in various ways."

Chapter 7

Sadhana and Ecstasy

AFTER HIS FIRST VISION OF THE DIVINE MOTHER, the Master was so absorbed in bliss

1. The Master's condition after his first vision.

that he was incapable of doing any work. It became impossible for him to conduct worship in the temple on a regular basis. Hriday managed it somehow with the help of another brahmin priest. He also arranged for treatment of his uncle, thinking that he was suffering from a neurosis. Sometime earlier Hriday had become acquainted with an excellent physician who cared for the royal family of Bhukailas, Calcutta. Now he engaged that doctor for the Master's treatment. Finding no possibility of a quick recovery, Hriday sent word to Kamarpukur.

On the days when the Master was not uncontrollably restless for God-

2. The Master's physical state and mental perceptions and visions.

vision or did not lose consciousness, he attempted to perform worship as usual. Later, he told us some of the thoughts and experiences that he had in those days during worship and meditation: "There is an image of Bhairava [a form of Shiva] in meditation on the parapet of the natmandir in front of the Kali temple. While going to the temple to meditate, I would point to that image and tell my mind, 'You must meditate on the Mother like that motionless statue.' No sooner did I sit down to meditate than I would hear clattering sounds in all of my joints, beginning in my legs. It was as if someone inside me were turning keys to lock me up, joint by joint. I was powerless to move my body or change my posture, even slightly. I couldn't stop meditating, or leave the temple, or do anything else I wanted. I was forced to sit in that posture until my joints began clattering again and were unlocked, this time beginning at my neck and ending in my legs.

"When I sat to meditate, at first I would see particles of light like swarms of fireflies. Sometimes I would see masses of light on all sides, covering everything like a mist; at other times I would see that everything was pervaded by bright waves of light like molten silver. I would see those things sometimes with eyes closed and sometimes with eyes open. I didn't understand what I saw, nor did I know if it was good or bad to be having such visions. So I prayed anxiously to Mother: 'I don't understand what's happening to me. I don't know any mantras and incantations to call You. Please teach me how to know You. Mother, if You won't teach me, who will? I have no refuge or guide except You.' Thus I used to pray with a one-pointed mind and cry profusely with a longing heart."

During this period the Master's method of worship and meditation

3. The change in the Master's behaviour and attitude after his first vision.

underwent phenomenal changes. It is hard to explain his wonderful ecstatic mood, his simple and childlike reliance upon the Divine Mother, and the beauty of his self-surrender. In his behaviour there was no hint of an adult's seriousness, nor any effort to follow the customary rules of appropriate behaviour, nor any attempt to consider the future and conduct his activities accordingly. The Master wholeheartedly adopted this attitude: "Mother, I have taken refuge in You. I am Your child. Teach me what to do and say." Thus, he plunged his little ego into the will of the Divine Mother and performed all of his actions as Her instrument. His conduct therefore became significantly different from that of other people. Public opinion began to turn against him as people criticized his behaviour, at first in whispers, then openly. But what could they do? The child of the Divine Mother was carrying out Her wishes, and the vain clamour of the perplexed world did not reach his ears at all. The Master was then in the world but not of it. The external world now appeared to be a dream. He could not make it appear real as it had seemed before, despite his efforts to do so. The conscious and blissful form of the Divine Mother was his only reality.

Previously, during worship and meditation the Master would see the

4. The difference between his earlier and later modes of worship and visions.

Mother's hands, or Her shining delicate feet, or Her beautiful, loving, and smiling face. But now — even when it was not the time for worship and meditation — the Master would see the complete form of the luminous Divine Mother smiling, talking, accompanying him, and guiding him by saying, "Do this; don't do that."

Earlier in his sadhana, while offering food to the Mother, the Master would see a flashing ray of light emanate from the Mother's eyes, touch the offered food articles, gather their essence, and then withdraw back into Her eyes. But now as soon as he offered food, and sometimes even before that, he would see the Mother Herself seated to eat the food, the luster of Her body pervading the whole temple. Hriday told us that one day he went to the shrine and watched as the Master took a hibiscus flower and a bel leaf in his hand to offer at the feet of the Mother. He held them and meditated, but then he suddenly cried out: "Wait, wait! Let me say the mantra first, and then You can eat." He then offered food to the Mother before finishing the ritual.

During worship and meditation the Master used to see the living presence of the Mother in the temple's stone image of Her; now he could not see that stone image at all. In its place was the living Mother, the embodiment of consciousness, Her hands bestowing boons and fearlessness. Later, he described what happened: "I put my hand near the Mother's nostrils and felt that She was actually breathing. At night I watched carefully, but in the lamplight I could never see Her shadow on the temple wall. From my room I would hear Mother running upstairs, as merry as a little girl, with Her anklets jingling. I would rush outside to see if this was true. And there She would be standing on the veranda of the second floor of the temple, with Her hair blowing in the breeze. Sometimes She would look towards Calcutta and sometimes towards the Ganges."

Hriday recalled: "When one entered the Kali temple in those days one

5. Hriday's testimony about the Master's worship.

could perceive an ineffable divine presence and feel an eerie sensation, even when Uncle wasn't there — and much more so when he was. I couldn't resist the temptation of seeing how he acted when he was performing the worship. As long as I was actually watching him, my heart was full of reverence and devotion. But when I left the temple, I would begin to have doubts and ask myself: 'Has Uncle really gone mad? Why else would he do such strange things?' I was afraid of what the Rani and Mathur Babu would say when they came to hear of it. But Uncle was unconcerned and paid no heed to my warnings. I didn't venture to speak to him much any longer; my mouth was closed by a fear I can't describe. I felt that there was some kind of barrier between us. So I just looked after him in silence, as best I could. But I was afraid he'd make a scene someday."

Sometimes Hriday would visit the temple during worship. Upon seeing the Master's actions, he immediately felt awe, fear, and devotion. Later, he narrated the following to us:

"I saw Uncle taking hibiscus flowers and bel leaves in his hand, touching first his head, then his chest, then all over his body and even his feet, and finally offering those at the feet of the Divine Mother.

"I saw Uncle's chest and eyes become red, like those of a drunkard. He'd get up reeling from the worshipper's seat, climb onto the altar, and caress the Divine Mother, chucking Her affectionately under the chin. He'd sing, laugh, joke, and talk with Her. Sometimes he'd catch hold of Her hands and dance!

"I saw how when he was offering cooked food to the Divine Mother he'd suddenly get up, take a morsel of rice and curry from the plate in his hand, touch the Mother's mouth with it, and say: 'Eat it, Mother. Do eat it!' Then maybe he'd say: 'You want me to eat it, and then You'll eat some afterwards? All right, I'm eating it now.' Then he'd take some of it himself and put the rest to Her lips again, saying: 'I've had some. Now You eat.'

"One day Uncle saw a cat at the time of the food offering. It had come into the temple, mewing. He fed it with the food that was to be offered to the Divine Mother. 'Will You take it, Mother?' he said to the cat.

"Some nights I saw that when Uncle put the Divine Mother to bed he would sometimes ask: 'Mother, do You want me to lie down next to You? All right, I'm lying down.' Saying so, he would lie down for some time on the Divine Mother's silver bedstead.

"Again I saw that while Uncle performed worship he was so deeply absorbed in meditation that he had not the slightest outer consciousness for a long time.

"Every morning when he arose, Uncle would pick flowers to make garlands for the Divine Mother. At those times I noticed him talking with someone unseen, laughing, coaxing, and joking.

"I further saw that at night Uncle did not sleep at all. Whenever I awoke I found him in an exalted mood, talking, singing, or immersed in meditation in the Panchavati."

Hriday said that although the Master's strange behaviour made him

6. Observing the Master's ecstatic worship, the temple manager and workers decide to notify Mathur.

apprehensive, he could not express his fears to others and seek their advice. He feared that others might report the news to the high officials of the temple, who would harm his uncle by notifying Mathur. But how could one keep the situation a secret when such things were happening every day? Like Hriday, some people visited the temple during the worship service and saw the Master's unusual behaviour. They complained to the temple officials, who rushed to the Kali temple and saw everything. But when confronted by the Master's god-intoxicated form, familiar behaviour with the deity, and fearless composure, they were stupefied with fright. They could neither say anything to him nor put a stop to his worship. The officials returned to their office and after discussion they concluded that Ramakrishna had either become mad or had been possessed by a ghost. No normal person would behave in such an unscriptural, wayward manner during worship. In fact, the worship service and food offering to Kali were not being performed properly: Ramakrishna had ruined everything. The officials determined that a message should be sent to Mathur immediately.

When their complaint reached Mathur at Calcutta, he replied that he would visit Dakshineswar very soon and take whatever actions were necessary. Until he did so, however, Ramakrishna was to be allowed to continue the worship in his own way, and none should oppose him. The officials waited anxiously for Mathur, and began to gossip: "Now Ramakrishna will be fired. Mathur will throw him out. He has committed a sin against Kali. How long will She put up with him?"

One day Mathur came to Dakshineswar unannounced. He entered the

| 7. Mathur arrives to watch the Master's worship: his impression. |

Kali temple during the worship service and watched the Master's activities for a long time. Being overwhelmed with devotion, the Master did not notice Mathur at all. Every day during worship he was absorbed in Mother; he did not notice who was moving in or out of the temple. Mathur realized this immediately. He further understood that the Master's childlike, importunate demands on the Divine Mother originated from his sincere devotion. Mathur asked himself, if the Mother could not be seen with such unostentatious faith and devotion, then how else could She be realized? Mathur's heart was filled with a wonderful joy when he saw how tears trickled down the Master's face during worship, and how sometimes he was filled with unbounded joy and sometimes was unconscious like an inanimate object, unperturbed and completely oblivious of external objects. Mathur experienced a tangible divine presence in the temple and became convinced that Sri Ramakrishna had been blessed by the Divine Mother. He then bowed down to the Mother and Her wonderful worshipper with heartfelt devotion and tearful eyes, saying: "Now the purpose of the goddess's installation has been fulfilled. The Mother has truly appeared here, and Her worship has been performed properly." He returned to his Calcutta home without saying anything to the temple officials. The next day he sent an order to the temple manager: "Let Ramakrishna perform the worship in any way he chooses; please don't obstruct him" (see III.6.6,10).

With knowledge of these events, a reader well versed in the scriptures

| 8. The Master attains supreme devotion through intense love for God: its effect. |

will easily understand that during this period the Master's mind had transcended the limited bounds of *vaidhi bhakti* [preparatory devotion] and was moving fast towards the higher realm of *raga bhakti* [supreme devotion]. This happened in such a simple, natural way that he himself could not comprehend it, much less others! This much he realized: Compelled by his exuberant love for the Divine Mother, he could not desist from acting as he did. It was as if someone were forcing him to do so. That is why it was seen that sometimes he questioned himself: "What is happening to me? Am I on the right track?" He supplicated the Divine Mother with a longing heart: "Mother, I don't understand. Why am I in this situation? Please make me do what I am supposed to do and teach me what I am supposed to learn. Hold me close to You all the time." Thus he prayed to the Mother from deep within his heart, withdrawing his mind from desire for sex, money, name, fame, and other worldly enjoyments. For Her part, the Divine Mother held him, protected him under all circumstances, and fulfilled his prayers.

At the proper times She brought to him unasked whatever objects and persons were necessary for the development and perfection of his spiritual life, and made him reach the culmination of pure knowledge and pure devotion easily and naturally. In the Bhagavad Gita (9:22), Krishna promises his devotees: "Those persons who worship Me, meditating on their identity with Me and ever devoted to Me, to them I carry what they lack and for them I preserve what they already have."

The more we study the Master's life, the more we shall be amazed and astounded by learning how that promise of the Gita was literally fulfilled in his life. It was necessary to again prove the truth of the Lord's promise in this selfish present age, in which the goal is to enjoy lust and gold. There is a Hindi saying, "Renounce all [worldly things], receive All [God]." In every age spiritual teachers have taught people that if they give up everything for God, they will not suffer for lack of life's necessities. Weak-hearted worldly people listened to that advice but could not trust it until it was clearly demonstrated in this present age. So in order to show the validity of that scriptural message, the Divine Mother enacted a wonderful drama with the Master, who completely surrendered to Her. O reader, listen to this story with a pure heart and proceed along the path of renunciation according to your capacity.

The Master used to say that when the tidal wave of the spirit unexpect-

9. The Master's remark: Only the body and mind of an avatar can withstand the full impact of supreme devotion.

edly appears in human life, one cannot suppress it even with great effort. The physical body of an ordinary human being is incapable of withstanding that spiritual force, and as a result it breaks down completely. In this manner many spiritual aspirants have died. A suitably strong body is necessary in order to absorb the overpowering energy that results from the intensity of complete knowledge or devotion. So far it has been seen that the bodies of great souls, like those of avatars, continue to survive in this world while bearing the force of spirituality. That is why the devotional scriptures repeatedly state that avatars embody pure sattva. Because they are born in this world with bodies that are made of pure sattva, they are capable of withstanding the full spiritual force. But in spite of having this kind of special body, they — especially avatars of the devotional path — are sometimes extremely affected by that spiritual force. Scriptural records indicate that because of this intense surge of spiritual energy , the joints of Jesus and of Chaitanya became very flexible and drops of blood oozed like perspiration from every pore. Although those physical changes are very painful, they help the body to become accustomed to the extraordinary emotional upsurges that arise from devotion. Later, as the body gradually gets used to absorbing that force, those physical changes become less visible.

From now on a series of unusual physical changes came over the Master's body because of his exuberant love and devotion. We have already mentioned that from the beginning of his sadhana he felt a burning sensation. On many occasions the Master himself pointed out its cause: "When I performed spiritual disciplines and worship according to scriptural directions, I used to think that the *papa-purusha* [evil spirit] within me had been burnt. Who knew then that a papa-purusha dwells in every human body, and that it could be truly burnt and destroyed? In the beginning of sadhana I felt a burning sensation in my body. I thought, 'What kind of disease is this?' Gradually it increased in severity until it became unbearable. I applied various medicated oils, but to no avail. Later on, I was seated in the Panchavati one day when suddenly I saw a terrible-looking, red-eyed man of black complexion come out of this body (*pointing to himself*) and begin to stumble about in front of me like a drunkard. The next moment I saw a handsome person emerge from this body, wearing an ochre cloth and holding a trident in his hand. He vehemently attacked the terrible person and killed him, and from that point on the burning sensation diminished. Prior to this I had suffered from that burning continually for six months."

> 10. The Master's body changes due to that devotion, resulting in a painful burning sensation: first, when the *papa-purusha* is burnt; second, during the pang of separation from God after the first vision; third, during the sadhana of *madhura bhava*.

We heard from the Master that after the destruction of the papa-purusha his burning sensation halted temporarily, but then it started again. He had then crossed the boundaries of vaidhi bhakti and he now began to perform the worship of the Divine Mother with raga bhakti. Gradually his pain increased so much that he had to immerse himself in the Ganges for three to four hours at a time, keeping a wet towel on his head. But even this could give him no relief. We have described elsewhere in detail (see IV.1.10) how later the Brahmani easily removed that burning sensation, explaining that his pain had originated from the pangs of separation from God and the longing for His vision. Later on, while he was practising *madhura bhava* [lover-beloved attitude], the Master again suffered from that burning sensation. Hriday said: "The Master then suffered from an unbearable heat and pain similar to what a person would feel if a potful of live embers were placed inside his chest. This pain continued for a long while and occasionally became even more acute. A few years after the Master's sadhana, he became acquainted with Ramkanai Ghoshal, a lawyer of Barasat and an advanced aspirant of the Shakti tradition. Listening to the Master's description of his burning sensation, Ramkanai advised him to wear the amulet of his Chosen Deity. Once the Master put on the amulet, he never again suffered from that burning sensation."

After observing the Master's wonderful method of worship, Mathur

11. Rasmani thinks about a lawsuit during worship; the Master chastises her.

returned to Janbazar in Calcutta and reported everything to Rani Rasmani. The devout Rani was delighted to hear the news. She had already developed an affection for Ramakrishna as she listened to his devotional songs, and when Krishna's leg was broken she had marvelled at the Master's ecstatic demeanor and devout intelligence (see III.6.22-23). It did not take long for her to realize that it was possible that the pure-hearted Master had received the grace of the Divine Mother. But shortly afterwards an incident took place that put the Rani's and Mathur's confidence in Ramakrishna to a severe test.

One day while she was in the temple performing worship of the Divine Mother, the Rani became absent-minded. She was deeply thinking about the possible result of a pending lawsuit. The Master was singing a song for her. While in ecstasy, the Master saw what was in her mind and exclaimed indignantly: "Shame on you to think such thoughts even here!" Then he slapped her to teach her not to think of those worldly things in the temple. Because the Rani was a spiritual aspirant blessed by the Divine Mother, she realized her mental weakness and became repentant. This incident enhanced her devotion to the Master. We have described this occurrence in detail elsewhere (see III.5.8-9).

Shortly after this event, the Master's ecstatic delight with the Divine

12. As his devotion deepens, the Master gives up external worship; his condition at that time.

Mother increased to such an extent that it became impossible for him to conduct the daily worship as well as the occasional special services to the goddess. The Master thus illustrated how one's obligations naturally fall away with spiritual progress. He used to say: "Until the daughter-in-law conceives, the mother-in-law allows her to eat all kinds of food and do all sorts of work. But as soon as she's with child, the mother-in-law becomes very careful about the kind of food and work she is given; later, when her pregnancy is far advanced, her work is strictly limited so that the child will not be harmed. When the baby is born at last, she has nothing to do but play with it."

Likewise, the Master's inability to perform external worship and service to the Divine Mother developed naturally. He could no longer follow any regular timetable for worship services. Continually absorbed in ecstasy, he served the Divine Mother whenever and however he pleased. For example, sometimes he offered food to the deity without performing the worship. Or when he was absorbed in meditation he would forget his separate existence from the Mother and decorate his own body with the flowers and sandal paste that were intended for the worship of the goddess. On many occasions we heard from the Master that he acted that way because of his constant vision of the Divine Mother within and outside himself. He said further that if that ecstasy diminished even a little and his divine vision were interrupted for even a moment, his agony would become so intense that he would throw himself down, rub his face against the earth, and cry aloud, gasping and struggling for his life. He would be unaware that his body was bleeding and bruised. Sometimes he would not notice if he fell into water or fire. The next moment he would have the vision of the Divine Mother and his anguish would disappear. His face would beam with joy, and he would become a different person altogether.

Mathur somehow managed the worship service utilizing the Master until

13. Hriday's story of how the Master gave up the worship services; Mathur's doubt.

he was absorbed in the ecstatic state. But now Mathur decided to make separate arrangements for worship, as the Master was no longer capable of handling it. Hriday said: "There was another reason Mathur made that decision. One day the intoxicated Master suddenly got up from the worshipper's seat and saw Mathur and myself in the temple. He took my hand and made me sit on that seat, then told Mathur: 'From today Hriday will perform the worship. Mother says that She will accept his worship as She would my own.' The devout Mathur accepted the Master's words as a command from the Mother." We do not know how true Hriday's words are, but we do know that Mathur completely understood that under such conditions it was impossible for the Master to conduct the daily worship.

We have already mentioned that Mathur was drawn to the Master from his first sight of him. From that point on he made all efforts to keep the Master in Dakshineswar, removing all his difficulties. As time passed, the more he became acquainted with the Master's wonderful qualities, the more he was charmed by them; and he served him according to his needs and protected him from the oppression of others. For example: Mathur arranged a daily drink of rock-candy syrup for the Master, knowing his system had an excess humour of wind. When under the influence of supreme devotion the Master became involved in an unusual method of worship, Mathur protected him from criticism and persecution. We have mentioned some similar incidents elsewhere (see III.6.6,10).

However, we presume that on the day the Master struck Rani Rasmani in

14. The Master is put under the treatment of Kaviraj Gangaprasad Sen.

order to instruct her, Mathur began doubting him and concluded that he had become insane. It seems that the incident made Mathur suspect that there was a combination of spirituality and insanity in the Master, because at that time he arranged for the Master to be treated by Kaviraj Gangaprasad Sen, a prominent Calcutta physician.

Not only did Mathur arrange for the Master's treatment, he also tried his utmost to use reasoning to convince the Master to control his mind and then proceed with his spiritual practices. He admitted complete defeat when the

Master showed him a white hibiscus on the branch of a red hibiscus tree. We have related this incident elsewhere (see III.6.8,IV.4.14).

We have already mentioned that Mathur realized it was not possible for the Master to continue the daily worship of the goddess, so he made a separate arrangement. During this time Ramtarak Chattopadhyay, a cousin of the Master's, arrived at Dakshineswar temple in search of work. Mathur engaged him to perform worship of Kali until the Master recovered. This happened in 1858.

The Master used to call Ramtarak by the nickname "Haladhari." We have

15. Haladhari's arrival at Dakshineswar.

heard many stories about him from the Master. Haladhari was a great scholar as well as a strict and devout aspirant. Every day he would study the Bhagavata, the Adhyatma Ramayana, and other scriptures. Haladhari was drawn to Lord Vishnu, but he had no aversion to the Divine Mother. So although he was a devotee of Vishnu, at Mathur's request he took over the worship service of the Divine Mother. With Mathur's consent, Haladhari took groceries from the temple store and cooked his own meals every day. Mathur objected at first, asking: "Why do you want to cook for yourself? Your cousin Ramakrishna and nephew Hriday eat prasad from the temple." The intelligent Haladhari replied: "My cousin is in an exalted spiritual state; he can do as he likes. But I have not reached that state and I must obey my caste rules." Mathur was pleased by this response. From then on Haladhari took groceries and cooked his own food under the Panchavati.

Although Haladhari was not against Mother worship, he did not approve of making any animal sacrifices to the goddess. As it was customary in the Dakshineswar temple to offer animal sacrifices to the Divine Mother during festivals, he could not perform the service with enthusiasm on those days. It is said that Haladhari continued the worship service for a month, but with resentment. Then one evening while he was meditating, the goddess appeared to him in Her terrible form and said: "Do not worship Me anymore; if you do, your son will die because of your lack of reverence." At first he thought his mind had played a trick on him, so he paid no heed to that command. But shortly afterwards Haladhari received news of his son's death. He then told the Master the whole story and stopped worshipping Kali. It was then arranged that Hriday would perform the Divine Mother's worship and that Haladhari would worship Radha-Govinda. This story we heard from Rajaram, Hriday's brother.

Chapter 8

Story of the First Four Years of Sadhana

IF WE WANT TO STUDY THE PERIOD OF SRI RAMAKRISHNA'S sadhana, we must first remember what he told us about it himself. Then it will not be difficult to determine the chronology of events. We have already mentioned that the Master had told us that for twelve years he was absorbed continuously in the sadhana of various faiths. According to the deed of gift for Rani Rasmani's temple endowment, the Dakshineswar Kali temple was consecrated on Thursday, 31 May 1855. A few months after that the Master assumed the office of priest. So it is certain that his sadhana was performed from 1856 to 1867. However, although those twelve years have been determined to be the period of his sadhana, we see that he practised some spiritual disciplines even afterwards when he visited holy places and when he returned to Dakshineswar.

1. Chronology of the Master's sadhana.

We shall divide those twelve years into three parts and discuss each part separately. We have already discussed the main events that occurred during the first four years, from 1856 to 1859. The second four-year span was from 1860 to 1863. During the last two years of this period, the Master practised spiritual disciplines under the guidance of Bhairavi Brahmani, from *Gokul-vrata* to sixty-four main Tantric disciplines that are prevalent in Bengal. The third four-year period covers 1864 to 1867. During this period, the Master was initiated into the Ram mantra by Jatadhari, a Ramait monk, and received the image of Ramlala. He wore women's clothes for six months in order to attain perfection in madhura bhava in accordance with Vaishnava

2. The three main divisions of this period.

Tantra. He also received monastic vows from Tota Puri and attained nirvikalpa samadhi. Finally, he received instruction in Islam from Govinda.

During the twelve years of his sadhana, the Master also became acquainted with the *sakhya bhava* [friendly attitude] according to the Vaishnava Tantra and the disciplines of Kartabhaja, Navarasik, and other subsidiary Vaishnava sects. The Master was quite familiar with various denominations of Vaishnavism, as is clear from the fact that Vaishnavcharan Goswami and other aspirants of those sects came to him for spiritual guidance. When we divide the period of the Master's sadhana into three parts, we see precisely that each period is distinguished by a particular form of spiritual discipline that he practised.

We have seen that the only external help he had in the beginning of his

| 3. A summary of the Master's state of mind and his visions during his first four years of sadhana. | sadhana was the initiation he received from Kenaram Bhattacharya. His inmost longing for God-realization was his mainstay during this period. Soon that longing grew more intense and greatly affected his body |

and mind. This longing brought immense love for his Chosen Deity, and gradually it led him along the path of raga bhakti, transcending the regulations of vaidhi bhakti. That longing allowed him to finally have the direct vision of the Divine Mother and endowed him with yogic powers.

The reader may ask: "At that time the Master had already realized God

| 4. Why did the Master practise sadhana after his vision of the Divine Mother? He attains peace only after realizing that his own experiences agree with the teachings of the guru and of the scriptures. | and become perfect in yoga. What else was left? Why did he continue to practise sadhana?" Our answer is that this is true in one sense, but it was still necessary for him to continue his sadhana. The Master used to say: "According to the general law of nature, trees and creepers first bloom and then bear fruit. But there are some that grow fruit first, then flowers." The spiritual evolution of the Master's |

mind was exceptional in that way. So in one sense we admit that the reader's question is reasonable. But although in the beginning of his sadhana the Master had wonderful visions of the Divine Mother, he was not firmly convinced of their authenticity, nor was he certain that he had reached the ultimate goal. He needed to compare his experiences with those of illumined souls, as they are recorded in the scriptures. The experiences that he had achieved by means of his inmost longing needed to be verified by following the paths and methods prescribed in the scriptures. The scriptures say that a spiritual aspirant cannot be completely certain about his own visions and mystical experiences until they have been compared with the truth taught by the guru and with the experiences of the past seers of truth that are recorded in the scriptures. When the aspirant finds that these three — the words of the guru, the testimony of the scriptures, and his or her own experience — are identical, he or she becomes free from doubt and attains perfect peace.

To illustrate this point we can refer to the life story of Shukadeva, son of

5. The same thing happens to Shuka, the son of the sage Vyasa.

Vyasa. Shuka was free from maya; from his very birth he had divine visions and other extraordinary experiences. But he did not understand that this happened because he had attained supreme knowledge. One day, after his father had taught him the Vedas and other scriptures, Shuka said to Vyasa: "From my birth I have been experiencing the spiritual states recorded in the scriptures, but I am still not certain whether I have experienced the highest truth of the spiritual realm. Please tell me what you know about this." Vyasa thought to himself: "I have been continually teaching Shuka about the goal of spiritual life and the ultimate truth, but still his mind is not free from doubt. Perhaps he thinks that if he becomes illumined he will renounce the world, and for that reason I have not taught him everything because of my attachment for him, or for some other reason. It will therefore be beneficial for him to hear about this from another sage." Reflecting thus, Vyasa then told Shuka: "I am unable to remove your doubt. You are aware that Janaka, the king of Mithila, is truly a man of knowledge. Go to him and have all of your questions answered." At his father's behest, Shuka immediately went to Mithila, where he learned from Janaka about the experiences of the knowers of Brahman. Shuka attained peace after realizing that the instruction of the guru and the words of the scriptures were identical with his own experience.

There were many other reasons for the Master's practising sadhana after he had already attained the goal. We shall refer here to some of them.

The aim of the Master's sadhana was not to attain peace for himself.

6. Another reason why the Master performs sadhana: His spiritual disciplines are not for himself but for others.

The Divine Mother made him assume a body for the good of the world. That is why he practised contending religious paths and evaluated the validity of each. It can be said that he had to acquaint himself with the ultimate goal of those religious practices so that he could teach the entire spiritual world. But that is not all. The Divine Mother revealed the truths of the scriptures in the Master. Because he was unlettered, his life proved that it was possible to reach the goal of each path through practice alone. And thus through the Master She reestablished the truths of the Vedas, the Bible, the Puranas, the Koran, and other scriptures in this present age. For that reason, his sadhana continued even after he had attained peace. The Divine Mother brought illumined teachers and scholars of each religious path to Dakshineswar so that the Master could learn the spiritual practices recorded in their scriptures and verify his own experiences. This point shall become clearer as we continue to study his wonderful life.

We have already explained that during the first four years of the Master's

7. True longing leads to God-realization. The intensity of the Master's longing.

sadhana, intense longing for God-realization was his main support. At that time no capable teacher came to guide him in his spiritual journey along the path enjoined by the scriptures. So he needed to rely on his own intense longing, the common factor of all sadhanas. The Master attained the vision of the Divine Mother by virtue of his longing alone, proving that in the same way an aspirant can realize God without any external help. But if we want to attain perfection through longing alone, we must keep in mind how intense our desire must be. This becomes clear to us when we study the Master's life during this period. We have observed that his intense longing pushed aside eating and sleeping, as well as his feelings of shame and fear, and other physical and mental habits and impressions. He was totally indifferent to his own life, much less to maintaining his physical health.

The Master used to say: "Because at that time I paid no attention whatsoever to taking care of my body, my hair grew long and became matted with dirt. During meditation my body would become stiff and motionless as a log because of my intense concentration. Thinking it to be an inert object, birds would perch freely on my head and peck at the dust of my matted hair seeking particles of grain. Again sometimes the pain of my separation from God would make me rub my face desperately on the ground until it was cut and bleeding in some places. I was completely oblivious to how the entire day would slip away in meditation, devotional practices, prayer, and self-surrender. At the advent of evening when the temple garden reverberated with the sound of conch shells and bells, I would be reminded: 'Another day is gone in vain; still I have not seen the Mother.' Then such a frenzy of despair would seize my soul that I could bear no more. I would throw myself down and shout, 'Mother, still You haven't revealed Yourself to me.' I would cry bitterly, tormented with pain. People would say, 'He is suffering from colic; that is why he is crying so terribly.'"

When we visited the Master, he would sometimes refer to his condition during his years of sadhana to make us understand the intensity of the longing that is needed for God-realization. He further lamented: "People shed a jugful of tears at the death of a wife and children or at the loss of property. But tell me, who weeps for God? Yet they say, 'We called on Him so much and still He did not reveal Himself!' Let them cry for God with that kind of intense longing. Then let me see how He can withhold Himself from them!" The Master's words would penetrate deep into our hearts. It seemed to us that he had truly experienced this in his own life and could therefore speak with such conviction.

During the first four years of his sadhana, the Master was not satisfied

8. The Master's practice of *dasya bhava* following the path of Mahavir Hanuman.

with merely having visions of the Divine Mother. After experiencing the Mother in *bhavamukha* [an exalted state between the Absolute and the Relative], his mind became attracted to his family deity, Raghuvir [Ramachandra]. He knew that if one has the one-pointed attention that Hanuman had, it is possible to have the vision of Rama. The Master therefore set out to immerse himself in the attitude of Hanuman, that of a servant, in every respect and began his sadhana to attain perfection in *dasya bhava* [servant attitude]. During this period, he constantly focussed his mind on Hanuman and was so absorbed in that ideal that he completely forgot his separate existence and individuality. He later recalled: "I had to eat and walk like Hanuman, and perform every action as he would have done it. I didn't do this of my own accord; it happened of itself. I tied my *dhoti* around my waist to make it look like a tail, and I moved about by jumping. I ate nothing but fruit and roots, and I didn't like them when they were skinned or peeled. I spent a lot of my time in trees, and I kept crying out 'Rama!' in a deep voice. My eyes took on a restless look, like the eyes of a monkey. And the most marvellous thing was that the lower end of my spine [the coccyx] lengthened nearly an inch!" Upon hearing this, we inquired, "Sir, do you still have the same growth there?" The Master replied: "No. When I later withdrew my mind from that kind of devotion, it [the coccyx] gradually went back to its normal size."

It was during this period that the Master had an unprecedented

9. A description of his vision of Sita during his practice of dasya bhava.

vision. This spiritual experience was so different from his previous ones that it became deeply imprinted in his mind and forever remained vivid in his memory. He described the event as follows: "One day at that time I was seated under the Panchavati. I was in a state of ordinary consciousness, well aware of my surroundings. All of a sudden, a luminous female figure of exquisite grace appeared before me. Her radiance lit up everything around her. I could see her, and at the same time I could see the trees and plants of the Panchavati, the Ganges, everything. I saw that she was human, for she had no marks of a divine being upon her, such as a third eye. But the sublime qualities reflected in her face —love, sorrow, compassion, and fortitude — are seldom to be seen even among goddesses. Slowly she advanced towards me, from the direction of the north, all the while looking at me with gracious eyes. I was amazed. I was wondering who she might be when suddenly a monkey uttered a cry, fell at her feet, and rolled on the ground. Then it came to me in a flash that this must be Sita, the daughter of King Janaka, who had suffered so greatly all her life, and whose whole life had been devoted to her husband, Rama. Overcome by emotion, I cried out 'Mother' and was about to fall at her feet when she instantly passed into my body and became merged in it. Overwhelmed with joy and wonder, I fell unconscious on the ground. This was the first vision I ever had with my eyes wide open, and when I wasn't meditating. It seems that it is because my first such vision was of Sita in her sorrowful aspect that I've had so much suffering in my life."[1]

During this period the Master felt the need for a sacred place where he

| 10. The Master plants the Panchavati himself. |

could practise austerities, so he told Hriday that he wanted a new Panchavati to be planted.[2] Hriday later told us: "The small goose pond near the Panchavati had been reexcavated at that time and the low land near the old Panchavati had been filled up with that mud and levelled. The amalaki tree under which the Master used to meditate was destroyed." To the west of the present *sadhan-kutir* [meditation hut], the Master planted the *ashwatha* tree himself and asked Hriday to plant the banyan, *ashoka*, *vilva*, and *amalaki* saplings; then the entire place was surrounded by a hedge of *tulsi* plants and *aparajita* vines. We have mentioned elsewhere (see III.2.45) how the Master set up a fence around that place with the help of Bhartabhari, a temple gardener, to protect those saplings from cattle and goats. Under the Master's care the tulsi plants and aparajita vines soon grew so dense and tall that no one could see the Master when he sat inside to meditate.

When the consecration of the Dakshineswar temple had become widely

| 11. The Master practises *hatha yoga*. |

known, itinerant monks on their way to Gangasagar [the confluence of the Ganges and the Bay of Bengal] and the holy shrine of Lord Jagannath at Puri began to halt for a few days at Dakshineswar and receive the generous hospitality of the devout Rani Rasmani (see IV.2). The Master said that many spiritual aspirants and illumined souls thus visited the temple. During this period, it seems that some of them instructed the Master in *pranayama* and other disciplines of hatha yoga. The Master indicated this one day as he narrated the following story regarding Haladhari. The Master himself had practised the techniques of hatha yoga and knew their results. He later told us not to practise them. If anyone asked for advice regarding hatha yoga, he would reply: "Those practices are not meant for this age. In this Kaliyuga people are short-lived and their existence depends on food alone. Where is the time now to make the body strong by practising hatha yoga, and then to call on God through raja yoga? If one wants to practise the techniques of hatha yoga, he should stay constantly with a perfect guru and follow strict rules

---

1. Swami Saradananda, the author, recalled: "The Master also said that Sita had made a gift of her sweet smile to him during that vision. So those who saw the Master smile knew how she smiled." — *Swami Saradanander Jivani* by Akshay Chaitanya, p.152; and *Sri Rama-krishna the Great Master* (1978), tr. by Swami Jagadananda, p. 183. — *Translator*
2. A Panchavati is a grove of five sacred trees, designed as a place for practising austerity and meditation. These trees include the ashwatha, vilva, amalaki, banyan, and ashoka. They must be planted according to a certain arrangement: the ashwatha to the east, the vilva to the north, the banyan to the west, the amalaki to the south, and the ashoka to the southeast. A beautiful altar of two square yards in size must be placed in the middle of the circle. — *Skanda Purana*

regarding food and other activities, according to the guru's instructions. Even the slightest deviation from those requirements causes serious health problems, and sometimes the aspirant can die. So it is not necessary to practise hatha yoga. Moreover, it is for the sake of controlling the mind that one controls the breath by practising pranayama and *kumbhaka*. One can have automatic control over the mind and breath through meditation on God and devotion. In this Kaliyuga human beings are short-lived and weak, so out of compassion God made their path for Self-realization easy. A person feels anguish and emptiness at the death of a spouse or child; if one has that kind of longing for God for twenty-four hours continuously, God will definitely reveal Himself."

We have mentioned elsewhere in this book (see IV.1.27) that some devout

12. Haladhari's curse.

present-day male aspirants very often practise the disciplines of left-handed Tantra while following the code of the Smritis. These Vaishnava aspirants usually pursue the sadhana of *parakiya-prema* [having another's wife or a mistress as a means of intensifying devotion for God]. As Haladhari was devoted to the Vaishnava doctrine, he secretly began to practise parakiya-prema while he was a priest of the Radha-Govinda temple. People began to gossip when they knew of Haladhari's practices with women. But they did not dare to say anything openly or to criticize him lest he should curse them; many people believed that his curses always took effect. However, as soon as the Master heard these rumours, he went straight to Haladhari and told him frankly how people were criticizing him behind his back. Misunderstanding the Master's motives, Haladhari flew into a rage at once, and cried: "You're my cousin and my junior. How dare you criticize me! Blood will come out of your mouth!" The Master tried to pacify him, saying that he had only wished to warn him, but Haladhari would not listen to him anymore.

One night shortly after that incident, at 8:00 or 9:00, the Master felt an

13. Its effect.

itching sensation in his palate and blood suddenly began to gush from his mouth. The Master later described the event: "The colour of that blood was like the dark juice of kidney-bean leaves. A little of it fell on the ground; it was so thick that the rest clotted and hung down from my lip like the roots of a banyan tree. I tried to stop the bleeding by pressing a piece of cloth against my palate, but I couldn't stop it. I was scared. When the news spread, many people ran in and gathered round me. Haladhari was then finishing his worship in the temple, and he also hurried to me. I said to him: 'See, Brother, what you have done to me with your curse!' Seeing my pitiable condition he began to weep.

"Luckily, earlier that day a wise old monk had arrived at the Kali temple. When he heard the uproar that night he came to see me. He examined the colour of my blood and the part of my mouth that it was coming from. He said to me: 'Don't be afraid. It is very good that you are bleeding like this. I see you have been practising hatha yoga. The practice of hatha yoga leads ultimately to *jada samadhi* [another name for nirvikalpa samadhi according to the yoga scriptures], and you were about to attain that state. Your sushumna channel had been opened, so the blood was flowing into your head. Fortunately, this blood has made a passage for itself through your palate; otherwise you would have entered jada samadhi and never come back to ordinary consciousness. The Divine Mother must have some special purpose She wants to accomplish through you, so She protected your body in this way.' When I heard the words of this monk, I was reassured and at peace." Thus, Haladhari's curse unexpectedly turned into a blessing.

Haladhari had an interesting and stormy relationship with the Master. We have already mentioned that Haladhari was an older cousin of the Master's. It was probably in 1858 that he came to Dakshineswar and became priest of the Radha-Govinda temple; he continued conducting the worship service until sometime in 1865. He therefore had an excellent opportunity to watch the Master closely during six years of his sadhana at Dakshineswar. Nonetheless, he could not come to a clear understanding of the Master. Haladhari himself adhered very strictly to his brahminical rules, so he disliked it when during ecstasy the Master would throw off his wearing cloth and sacred thread. He thought that his younger cousin was either mad or wayward. Hriday later said: "Haladhari would sometimes tell me: 'Hriday, it is not proper for Ramakrishna to discard his cloth and sacred thread. A person is born as a brahmin due to the accumulated virtues of many past lives. Ramakrishna now shuns that prestigious brahminhood as insignificant. What sort of exalted state has he attained that causes him to do all these strange things? Hriday, Ramakrishna listens to you. You should therefore keep an eye on him to ensure that he does not behave inappropriately. It is your duty to stop his nonbrahminical behaviour, even if you need to tie him up.'"

14. The story of Haladhari's repeated change of opinion regarding the Master.

But when he saw the Master performing worship in the temple, Haladhari was overwhelmed by his tears of devotion, his exuberant joy when he listened to the glory of God's name, and his extraordinary longing for God-realization. Haladhari thought that divine ecstasy was causing his cousin to have those experiences; such states are not usually seen in ordinary human beings. Sometimes he would say to Hriday: "Hriday, you must have seen some divine presence in Ramakrishna; you would not serve him so faithfully otherwise."

Haladhari's mind was constantly clouded by doubt, so he could not reach any definite conclusion about the true condition of the Master. The Master said later: "Many times Haladhari would be charmed by my devout worship in the temple, and he'd say to me, 'Ramakrishna, now I know what your real nature is!' So I'd tell him jokingly, 'Then don't get mixed up again!'

Then he'd say, 'You can't deceive me again. The Lord is definitely within you. This time I'm quite certain.' So I'd reply, 'All right. Let me see how long your conviction lasts.' Then after finishing the temple service, he would take some snuff and begin to give a discourse on the Bhagavata, the Gita, the Adhyatma Ramayana, and other scriptures. He would then become puffed up with egotism and become quite a different person. Sometimes I would attend his discourses and would say to him, 'I've realized all those spiritual states you've been reading about; I can understand everything that's in the scriptures.' Immediately he would say indignantly: 'You idiot! You think you can understand the scriptures!' 'Believe me,' I'd say, 'the One who is within this body of mine teaches me everything. A little while ago you said that there was a divine presence in me. He tells me everything.' Then he'd become frantic with rage and tell me: 'Get out of here, you crazy fool! Are you claiming to be an incarnation of God? The scriptures say there'll be only one avatar in this age — Kalki. You must be out of your mind to think such things!' So I would laugh and ask, 'Didn't you tell me you'd never get mixed up about me again?' But of course he wouldn't listen to me when he was in that mood. We had the same scene over and over. One day he saw me in an ecstatic mood sitting naked on a branch of the banyan tree in the Panchavati and passing water like a boy. From that day on he was thoroughly convinced that I had been possessed by a ghost."

We have already mentioned Haladhari's terrifying vision in the Kali temple and the subsequent death of his son. From that day on he considered Kali to be the embodiment of tamas and believed that She manifested in the aspect of the Destroyer only. One day he even questioned the Master: "Can a person make any spiritual progress worshipping Kali, the embodiment of tamas? Why do you worship that goddess?" The Master did not answer him, but he was deeply hurt by hearing the slander against his Chosen Deity. He hurried into the Kali temple and said with tearful eyes: "Mother! Haladhari, a great scholar who knows the scriptures, says You're nothing but wrath and destruction. Is that really true?" At once he was reassured: The complete nature of Mother Kali was revealed to him. Wild with joy and relief, the Master ran to the Radha-Govinda temple, where Haladhari was seated at worship, and jumped on his shoulders. Excited, he told Haladhari again and again: "How dare you say that Mother is wrathful and full of tamas. She is everything. She is the embodiment of the three gunas and again She is pure love and goodness." The Master's words and divine touch illumined Haladhari's heart. As he sat there on the worshipper's seat he wholeheartedly accepted the Master's words. He saw the manifestation of the Divine Mother within the Master; filled with devotion, he offered flowers and sandal paste at his feet. Hriday soon came to Haladhari and asked him: "Uncle, you have said that Ramakrishna is

15. The Master admonishes Haladhari when the latter describes Kali as full of tamas.

possessed by a ghost. What made you worship him?" Haladhari replied: "I don't know. When he came in from the Kali temple, he simply overwhelmed me. I forgot everything. I clearly saw the Divine manifest Itself in him. He affects me like that whenever I am with him in the Kali temple. It is amazing! I don't understand it at all."

Although on many occasions Haladhari saw the Divine manifest Itself in the Master, whenever he discussed the scriptures and took snuff he would become puffed up with pride in his own scholarship and revert to his former self. Haladhari's conduct confirms that when a person is still attached to lust and gold he does not benefit

16. Haladhari scolds the Master when he sees him eating leftovers from beggars' plates: the Master's answer.

much from external purity, observance of rules, and knowledge of the scriptures; the ultimate truth will not be revealed to such a person. We have mentioned earlier that the Master once ate food left over by beggars at the temple because he considered them to be divine. Because the Master was breaking caste rules by doing this and thus defiling himself, Haladhari said to him angrily: "I shall see what brahmin will ever marry any of your children now!" Immediately the Master replied sharply to Haladhari, who was proud of his knowledge of the Vedas: "You hypocrite! You keep quoting from the scriptures that the world is nothing but illusion and that one should look upon all beings as Brahman. Do you think that like you I shall preach that the world is unreal, and then start begetting children? Fie upon your knowledge of the scriptures!"

Confused by Haladhari's scholarly arguments, the childlike Master would sometimes rush to the Divine Mother for guidance about what he should do. We heard that Haladhari once raised a terrible doubt in the Master's mind: He tried to prove as false the Master's experiences of God that occurred during ecstasy by pointing out

17. Haladhari's scholarship raises doubts in the Master's mind; another vision of the Divine Mother and Her command: "Remain in *bhavamukha.*"

with the help of the scriptures that God is beyond existence and nonexistence. The Master said later: "I thought that the divine visions I had had during ecstasy and the commands I had received were all false. The Mother must have cheated me! I was extremely upset. Piqued, I cried to the Mother: 'Mother, I am unlettered and ignorant. Why have You cheated me in this way?' I couldn't control myself, and kept crying. I was in a room of the *kuthi* [bungalow]. After a while a smoke-like mist arose from the floor and covered some space before me. Then I saw within it a golden-complexioned, living, calm face with long flowing beard. That figure looked at me intently and said in a deep voice: 'My child, you remain in bhavamukha. You remain in bhavamukha. You remain in bhavamukha!' After repeating this three times, the form slowly dissolved into the mist, then that mist also disappeared. This vision reassured me." Much later, the Master himself related this incident to Swami Premananda. On another occasion the Master said: "Haladhari's words raised doubt in my mind at another time. So while performing worship in the temple, I cried and pressed the Mother to solve that matter. At that time the Mother, in the guise of a woman known as 'Rati's mother,' appeared beside the consecrated pitcher [installed in front of the image] and told me: 'You remain in bhavamukha!'" Later, when the itinerant monk Tota Puri left Dakshineswar after teaching Vedanta to the Master, Sri Ramakrishna remained continuously in the nirvikalpa state for six months. Towards the end of that period, he heard the Divine Mother's voice again commanding: "You remain in bhavamukha!"

Haladhari lived at the temple for about seven years. He therefore met the

18. The length of Haladhari's stay in Dakshineswar.

following people, who visited Dakshineswar one after another: an unconventional, illumined monk; Bhairavi Brahmani; Jatadhari, a monk of the Ramait Order; and Tota Puri. We heard from the Master that Haladhari sometimes studied the Adhyatma Ramayana with Tota Puri. The incidents we have narrated that were connected with Haladhari took place at different times during those seven years, but we have placed them all here for the convenience of the reader.

Without doubt, as we have seen from our discussion of the Master's sadhana

19. A discussion about the Master's divine madness.

thus far, it is clear that although others might have considered him to be slightly mad, in fact he did not suffer from any derangement of the brain or mental illness. At that time he could not control himself because an intense longing for God-realization possessed his mind. That longing, like a blazing fire, constantly consumed his heart; he was incapable of functioning like an ordinary person. People therefore called him mad. Who could behave properly when one's mind is in such a state? When the intense anguish of the heart transcends one's normal powers of endurance, it is impossible to get along with others by thinking one thing and saying something else. One may say that the limits of endurance are different for everyone: Some are disturbed by a little happiness or misery; and again some remain unaffected like the ocean, absorbing the intensity of both. How can we judge the Master's power of endurance? If we study other events of his life, it will be evident that his forbearance was phenomenal: He spent twelve long years sometimes without food, or with very little food, and without sleep. Immense wealth was offered to him many times, but he always rejected it as an obstacle to God-realization. We can cite many examples illustrating these points. Is it necessary to say anything more about his physical and mental powers of endurance?

As we study the events of this period we find that people who were attached

20. Ignorant people, not spiritual aspirants, considered his state a disease.

to lust and gold considered the Master's ecstatic state to be a mental illness. It seems that, except for Mathur, no one present in the Dakshineswar temple at that time could even partially understand the Master's mental state, even with the help of imagination and reasoning. We do not know where Kenaram Bhattacharya went after initiating the Master; we heard nothing further about him either from Hriday or anyone else. And the testimony given by the ignorant and greedy temple officials about the Master's activities and mental states during that period cannot be accepted as valid. Therefore, the only reliable evidence about the Master's condition at that time can be the remarks of perfected souls and holy people who came to Dakshineswar. From what we have heard from the Master and others, it is evident that those great ones always held him in high esteem rather than considering him to be mad.

As we study subsequent events, we shall see that the Master willingly followed others' advice for the good of his health, until his intense longing for God-realization caused him to lose consciousness of his body. When someone suggested that he should have medical treatment, he agreed; that he should be sent to his mother at Kamarpukur, he did not object; that he should marry, he did not protest. Under such circumstances, how can one discern the difference between his behaviour and actions and those of a madman?

21. Observing the Master's behaviour, one could not say that he was sick.

Moreover, from the time his god-intoxicated state began, the Master always tried to avoid worldly people and mundane matters; but he was extremely eager to join others when they were performing worship or singing devotional songs. This is evident from his visits to Dashamahavidya [a temple devoted to ten forms of the Divine Mother] at Baranagore and to Mother Kali at Kalighat in Calcutta, and from his participation in the annual festival at Panihati. In those places he met and talked with spiritual aspirants who were well versed in the scriptures. From what little we have learned of these occasions, it is apparent that those spiritual leaders had great veneration for him.

As an example of that respect, we can mention the Master's visit to the great festival at Panihati in 1858. On that day he first met Vaishnavcharan, the son of Utsavananda Goswami. Some of us have heard from Hriday as well as from the Master that he went to Panihati and rested awhile there in the parlour of Mani Sen's temple, where Vaishnavcharan came to see him. Upon meeting him, Vaishnavcharan was firmly convinced that the Master was a unique, spiritually evolved great soul. On that day Vaishnavcharan spent most of his time with the Master on the festival grounds. He bought flattened rice, puffed rice, mango, curd, and sweets, then mixed them together to make a special offering to the Lord, which he then joyfully shared with the Master. Furthermore, after the festival, when he was on his way back to Calcutta, he stopped

22. Vaishnavcharan meets the Master for the first time at the Panihati Festival in 1858: his impression.

at the temple garden of Rani Rasmani to see the Master once more; but he left disappointed when he learned that the Master had not yet returned from the festival. We have elaborately described elsewhere (see IV.1) how Vaishnavcharan met the Master again three or four years later and developed a close relationship with him.

During the first four-year period of his sadhana, the Master practised

23. The Master's other sadhanas during this period: "rupee is clay; clay is rupee"; cleaning the privy; considering excrement and sandal paste to be the same.

discrimination between the real and the unreal by taking both coins and lumps of clay in his hands in order to completely remove the attachment for money from his mind. He came to the conclusion that a person who has made God-realization the only goal of his life knows that neither money nor clay can be of use in attaining that end; clay and money are therefore of equal value to such a person. In order to become established in this conviction, the Master repeatedly said, "rupee is clay; clay is rupee"; and then threw both clay and coins into the Ganges, along with the desire for money.

Moreover, in order to realize that everything and all beings — from Brahma down to a blade of grass — are manifestations and parts of the Divine Mother, he ate the beggars' leftover food and cleaned their dining place. He felt that he was no better than even the lowliest sweeper who cleans privies; so in order to eradicate conceit and ego from his mind, he cleaned the privy. He knew that all objects — from sandal paste to excrement — are composed of the five elements, so in order to transcend all concepts regarding likes and dislikes, he calmly touched others' excrement with his tongue. All of these remarkable, unheard-of stories of the Master's sadhana took place during the first four-year period [1856–1859]. When we reflect upon the Master's practices and visions during those first four years, we understand clearly the phenomenal longing for God-realization that dominated his mind at that time and also understand how his superhuman faith helped him to proceed in the realm of sadhana. Furthermore, it is evident that within that period he succeeded in having the blessed vision of the Divine Mother by virtue of his longing alone, without any help from others. Only after he had achieved the final results of his sadhana did he proceed to compare the words of the guru and the scriptures with his own extraordinary experiences.

A spiritual aspirant becomes pure by controlling the mind completely

24. The aspirant's own mind ultimately becomes his guru. Examples of the Master's mind acting as a guru: (1) Experiencing the joy of kirtan through his subtle body.

through constant practice of detachment and self-control. The Master used to say that one's very mind then becomes one's guru. Whatever thought waves arise in a pure mind lead the aspirant quickly to the goal rather than leading him or her astray. It is therefore to be understood that within the first four years of his sadhana, the Master's ever-pure mind acted as his guru to guide him and help him to realize God. We have heard from the Master that at that time his mind not only taught him what to do and what not to do, but at times it would also manifest itself as a separate person who would emerge from his own body and appear before him. That person would encourage him to practise sadhana and threaten him with punishment if he did not dive deep into meditation. That person would also explain to him why he should practise a particular ritual, and would tell him what the result would be. During meditation he would see a young monk holding a sharp trident emerge from his body and say to him, "If you do not meditate on your Chosen Deity, shunning other thoughts, I will pierce your chest with this trident!" On another occasion he saw that young monk emerge to kill the pleasure-loving papa-purusha when it emerged from his body. Whenever the Master wished to make a long journey to see the images of deities or to hear devotional songs, the same monk would come out of his body. He would then travel to that place through a luminous path, enjoy divine bliss for a while, and then again enter the Master's body treading the same luminous path. The Master told us of many such visions.

From almost the outset of his sadhana, the Master often saw that young monk within himself, like his own form reflected in a mirror. He would follow the monk's advice to solve all his problems. One day while he was telling us about the experiences and visions he had had during sadhana, the Master said: "A young monk exactly resembling me would come out of my body and instruct me in all matters. Sometimes when he would emerge from me I would have a little outer consciousness; at other times I would lose it altogether and become inert. I would watch his movements and listen to him speak. The Brahmani and Tota Puri only reiterated the spiritual teachings that I had heard from him. They taught me what I had already learned. It seems that they came into my life as gurus in order that respect for the injunctions of the scriptures would be maintained. No other purpose can be found for my acceptance of Tota Puri and others as gurus."

(2) His internal vision of the young monk; the advice he received.

Towards the end of the first four years, the Master had a similar wonderful vision when he was living at Kamarpukur. One day the Master was travelling by palanquin from Kamarpukur to Hriday's house at Sihar. During that journey the Master enjoyed seeing the vast fields under the blue sky, the green rice fields, the rows of banyan trees providing cool shade along the path, the creepers bedecked with sweet fragrant blossoms, and hearing the melodious singing of birds. Suddenly two beautiful adolescent boys emerged from his body. They wandered far into the field searching for wildflowers and then came back near the palanquin, laughing, joking, and talking playfully. Thus, they proceeded joyfully for a long time and then reentered the Master's body.

(3) His vision on the way to Sihar, and the Bhairavi Brahmani's explanation.

Nearly a year and a half after this vision, Bhairavi Brahmani arrived at Dakshineswar. One day in the course of conversation, the Master described this vision to her. She responded: "My child, your vision was true. This time Chaitanya has been manifested in Nityananda's body. Both Chaitanya and Nityananda have come and are dwelling inside you now. That is why you had that vision." When Hriday later described that conversation to us, he mentioned that the Brahmani then recited the following two verses from the *Chaitanya Bhagavata*: "Putting his arms around the neck of Advaitacharya, Chaitanya said repeatedly: 'I shall enact my wonderful divine play once more. My form will be manifested as bliss during kirtan.' Gaur [another name for Chaitanya] is still enacting his divine play; only a fortunate few can see it."

Once when we asked the Master about this vision, he replied: "I truly did have that vision, and the Brahmani did make that remark when she heard of it. But how can I tell you what it really meant?" However, after hearing about those visions, it seems to us that from then on he was aware that a Being, well known to the world from time immemorial, was living within his body and mind in order to fulfill a specific purpose. The extraordinary insights about his personality that he was experiencing at that time eventually convinced him that the One who was born as Ramachandra in Ayodhya and then as Krishna in Vrindaban, to establish religion in previous ages, had been reborn in a new body as Ramakrishna to demonstrate a new religion to India and to the world. We heard him say again and again: "He who came as Rama and as Krishna has come now in this body (*pointing to himself*). As the king sometimes disguises himself to visit the capital, so this time He has come secretly to the world."

25. What one can surmise from those visions.

If we want to verify the authenticity of the vision just discussed, there are no means other than believing what the Master said about himself to his close devotees. However, we can confirm the authenticity of other visions that he experienced during our time. Such visions occurred daily in the Master's life, and his sceptical English-educated disciples had to admit defeat when they tested the visions' reality. They were dumbfounded. Although many such examples have been mentioned elsewhere in this book (see IV.4.18-25), we shall narrate one here for the satisfaction of the reader.

26. The Master's visions never prove false.

It was the autumn of 1885 and everyone in Calcutta was charged with enthusiasm during the festivities surrounding the annual Durga Puja. The Master's devotees felt a joyful current in their hearts, but a great obstacle prevented them from expressing it. Their fountainhead of joy, the Master, was suffering from cancer and was seriously ill. Nearly a month earlier the devotees had rented a

27. An example: the Master's vision during Durga Puja at Surendra Nath Mitra's house in 1885.

two-storeyed house at Shyampukur in Calcutta and had moved the Master there. Mahendralal Sarkar, a well-known physician, was trying his utmost to cure the Master with appropriate medicine and a proper diet. But so far the disease had not abated, but rather was getting worse. Householder devotees were coming to Shyampukur every morning and evening to make all the arrangements necessary for the Master's care. Many of the young students engaged in serving the Master went home only for meals; some stayed with the Master twenty-four hours a day.

If the Master talked too much or went into samadhi frequently, his blood would flow upwards and aggravate the disease by constantly irritating the wound in his throat. So the doctor advised him to control himself in both respects. The Master tried to follow his doctor's instructions, but would frequently violate them unintentionally. Because he had neglected his body for most of his life, considering it to be a "cage of flesh and bone" and with-drawing his mind from it, he was now incapable of regarding it as a precious thing as ordinary people would. Whenever there was any spiritual discussion, he would join in, then go into samadhi as before — forgetting his body and the doctor's instructions. In addition, people who had never seen him before began to visit him. When he saw their sincere longing, he could not restrain himself; he would give them spiritual instruction in a feeble voice. Observing the Master's zeal and joy in this respect, some devotees were relieved and began to consider his disease to be ordinary and easily curable. Some even tried to console others, saying that the Master had temporarily assumed this disease in order to bestow grace on newcomers and to spread spirituality amongst many people.

Dr. Sarkar would visit the Master daily in the morning or in the afternoon to examine him and prescribe proper medicine and diet. Afterwards he would become so overwhelmed as he listened to the spiritual conversation of the Master that he could not leave even after two or three hours. Sometimes he would ask question after question of the Master, then listen to his wonderful responses. After passing a long time in this manner, he would say regretfully: "Today I have made you talk for a long time. That was wrong on my part. However, if you talk to no one else today, no harm will come to you. You see, there is so much charm in your words that I spend two or three hours with you, neglecting my profession. I don't know how the time flies! Again I caution you, please don't talk to anyone else for a long time. Only when I come you may talk; that will not do any harm." The doctor and the devotees laughed.

Surendra Nath Mitra, whom the Master sometimes called Suresh Mitra, arranged Durga Puja that year in his residence at Simla. Previously his family had celebrated this worship every year, but it had been discontinued after an unfortunate incident occurred. After that mishap no brother of the household dared to perform the worship; if anyone tried, the others would dissuade him. But because Surendra was a staunch devotee who drew strength from his faith in the Master, he was not afraid of any misfortune. And once he resolved to do something, he paid no heed to anyone's pleas or objections. That year all the members of the household tried in many ways to stop him from performing the worship, but failed. Surendra received the Master's approval, bought an image of Mother Durga, and arranged for Her worship at his own expense. On this joyful occasion, however, Surendra was sad because the Master's illness prevented him from attending the celebration. A few days before the worship, a couple of Surendra's relatives fell ill and Surendra was held responsible. The whole family was displeased with him. Unperturbed, Surendra began the worship of the Divine Mother with great devotion and invited all his brother disciples.

The first day of worship, the *saptami* puja,[3] had passed. On *ashtami*, the auspicious second day of worship, many devotees gathered around the Master at the Shyampukur house and were enjoying spiritual conversation and devotional singing. Dr. Sarkar arrived at 4:00 p.m., and after a while Narendra (Swami Vivekananda) began to sing devotional songs. All were enchanted as they listened to his sweet, heavenly voice. In a low voice, the Master explained the import of the song to the doctor seated nearby, and sometimes he went into ecstasy for short periods. The spiritual atmosphere caused some devotees to lose outer consciousness.

The whole room was vibrating with an intense current of bliss. It was 7:30 p.m. when the doctor at last realized the lateness of the hour. He embraced Narendra like an affectionate father, then stood to take leave of the Master. The Master also got up, smiling, and suddenly went into deep samadhi. The devotees began whispering: "This is the auspicious time of *sandhi-puja*.[4] That is why the Master has gone into samadhi. It is amazing that the Master has become absorbed in divine ecstasy at this auspicious moment, without knowing the time of sandhi-puja!" About half an hour later the Master's samadhi ended, and the doctor left.

The Master then told the devotees what he had seen in samadhi: "A luminous path opened from this place to Surendra's house. I saw the presence of the Divine Mother in the image; She had been evoked by Surendra's devotion. A ray of light beamed forth from Her third eye! Rows of lamps were lit before the goddess in the worship hall. In the courtyard Surendra was crying piteously 'Mother, Mother!' All of you, go to his house right now. When he sees you he will regain his peace of mind."

3. The preliminary ritual and invocation of Durga Puja starts on the sixth day of the bright lunar fortnight in the autumn and continues for four days. Saptami puja is the first main worship, held on the seventh day of the bright fortnight. Then come the ashtami, navami, and dashami pujas. — *Translator*
4. A special worship that takes place between the second (ashtami) and third (navami) day of worship. — *Translator*

Narendra and some others bowed down to the Master, then left for Surendra's house. When they asked him, they learned that rows of lamps had in fact been lit in the worship hall as described by the Master. And when the Master had been in samadhi, Surendra was indeed seated in the courtyard facing the image, loudly crying "Mother, Mother," like a boy, for about an hour. The amazed devotees were thrilled with joy when they found that the Master's vision during samadhi was consistent with external events.

Sometime during the first four years of the Master's sadhana, Rasmani and Mathur thought he had developed a mental disorder due to his unbroken celibacy. They also believed that this was the cause of his spiritual unrest. Because they thought that the Master would regain his health if his chastity were broken, they engaged Lakshmi Bai and some other beautiful prostitutes to seduce him, first at Dakshineswar and then in a house at Mechuabazar in Calcutta. The Master told us that when he saw those women he saw only the Divine Mother; saying "Mother, Mother," he lost outer consciousness. As a tortoise draws its limbs inside its shell, so the Master's sex organ shrank inside his body. Witnessing this amazing phenomenon, and charmed by his childlike nature, those young women felt maternal affection in their hearts. They felt guilty for attempting to break his continence and with tearful eyes begged his forgiveness. Afraid that they had committed a grave sin by trying to tempt him, they bowed down to him again and again, and left.

28. Rasmani and Mathur test the Master because they misunderstand him.

Chapter 9

$\mathcal{M}$arriage and Return to Dakshineswar

IN KAMARPUKUR THE MASTER'S MOTHER AND BROTHER were extremely worried when

1. The Master at Kamarpukur.

they heard that he had given up his priestly duties. Scarcely two years had elapsed since Ramkumar's death when Chandramani and Rameswar, to their deep distress, received news of Gadadhar's insanity. It is said that misfortune never comes alone. Misfortunes of all sorts come from all directions, one after another, covering human life with deep darkness. This is exactly what happened in the lives of Chandramani and Rameswar. Chandra had borne her youngest son when she was advanced in years, so he was very dear to her. Overwhelmed with grief and anguish, she had Gadadhar brought back home. She grieved when she saw her son's indifference to worldly matters and his restlessness for God, and heard him crying piteously "Mother, Mother." She tried various remedies, from regular medicines, to rites performed to propitiate gods, to charms and incantations to exorcise evil spirits. These events took place towards the end of 1858.

After the Master returned home he generally behaved normally. Some-

2. The Master's relatives believe that a spirit possesses him.

times, however, he would cry out for the Divine Mother, and sometimes he would go into ecstasy and lose outer consciousness. His deportment and behaviour were sometimes like those of ordinary people and at other times were quite unusual. On one hand, he exhibited truthfulness, simplicity, devotion to God and to his mother, and love for his friends. On the other hand, he also showed a complete indifference to all worldly affairs; a longing for something unseen; an absence of shame, hatred, and fear; and an intense effort to reach his desired goal. This strange behaviour confused people, and they concluded that a ghost had possessed him.

This thought had also occurred to the simple-hearted Chandradevi. Now,

3. An exorcist invokes a spirit.

when she heard the opinions of others, she decided to engage an exorcist for the welfare of her son. The Master later told us: "One day an exorcist came. He burned a lampwick that had been sanctified by a special mantra, and then made me smell it. He said, 'If you're possessed by a ghost, this will make it run away.' But nothing happened. Later, one night some prominent exorcists performed worship and called down a spirit through a medium. The spirit accepted their worship and offerings and was pleased. Through the medium it said to the exorcists, 'He hasn't been possessed by a ghost, and he isn't suffering from any disease.' Then it spoke to me in front of all: 'Gadai, if you want to be a holy man, why do you chew so many betel nuts? Don't you know that betel nuts make people lustful?' It was true that I liked betel nuts very much and used to chew them now and then. But I gave them up as the spirit advised me to."

The Master was then about to complete his twenty-third year. After he

4. The Master's relatives narrate the stories of his becoming normal.

had been in Kamarpukur a few months, he became normal to a great extent. Now he was pacified by having repeated visions of the Divine Mother. We got this impression from what his relatives told us about what happened at that time. We shall now narrate their accounts.

The Master spent a good part of his time, day and night, in Bhuti's Canal and Budhui Moral — two cremation grounds situated at the west and northeast borders of Kamarpukur, respectively. At that time his relatives learned that an extraordinary power was manifesting in him. We heard from them that often he would offer some food to the jackals and demigods who lived in those cremation grounds. As soon as he brought a new earthen pot filled with sweets and other food for the jackals, they would come from all directions and eat the offerings; and when he would offer another pot to the demigods, it would disappear into the air. Sometimes he would see those demigods.

When Rameswar found that his younger brother had not returned home even after midnight, he would go near the cremation grounds and call for him. Hearing his name, the Master would answer in a loud voice: "All right, Brother, I'm coming. But don't come any nearer — the spirits might harm you." During this time the Master planted a bel tree seedling in the cremation grounds of Bhuti's Canal. He would spend a long time practising japa and meditation there under an old peepul tree. It is clear from the testimonies of his relatives that the terrible emptiness he had been experiencing as he pined for the vision of the Divine Mother was now relieved by some wonderful visions and spiritual experiences. As we study this period of his life, it seems clear that he was having almost constant visions of the Divine Mother: Her gracious form, consisting of consciousness, held a sword and a severed head in Her two left hands and bestowed blessings and fearlessness with Her two right hands. Whenever the Master asked Her a question, he received an answer, and he moulded his life accordingly. It seems that from now on he was fully convinced that he would be blessed with the uninterrupted vision of the Divine Mother.

We find that during this period that the Master developed the ability to see the future. Hriday and many people of Kamarpukur and Jayrambati have testified to this, and the Master also discussed it with us. The following examples will make this clear to the reader.

5. The Master's yogic powers.

Observing the Master's behaviour, his mother and some other family members realized that by God's grace his insanity had abated to a great degree. They noticed that he no longer cried piteously, that he was eating at appropriate times, and that in many respects he was behaving like everyone else. However, he was still preoccupied with divine beings, continued to visit the cremation grounds, and still took off his clothes when he practised meditation or performed worship. If anyone tried to stop this behaviour, he would disregard them. But the Master had been acting in this odd manner for years, so his family did not regard this behaviour as a sign of insanity. Still, they were concerned about his complete indifference to domestic affairs and his constant contemplative mood. They were anxious because they thought his insanity would return unless his mind calmed down and settled into worldly affairs. To protect him from such a relapse, his loving mother and brother planned his marriage to a suitable girl. They reasoned that if he were in love with a beautiful, good-natured girl from a noble family, his mind would not be absorbed in spiritual matters; rather, it would become engaged in improving his family's financial condition.

6. The Master's relatives see that he has become normal, so they decide to arrange for his marriage.

Lest Gadadhar protest his marriage, his mother and brother consulted secretly. But it was not long before the intelligent Gadadhar discovered their plan. He accepted the idea without the least objection, behaving like a child who makes merry when there is any festive occasion in the family. Did the Master express his joy in the planned marriage because he had the Divine Mother's approval? Or was it due to his boyish lack of foresight and his thoughtlessness? We have discussed this subject in detail elsewhere (see III.4.8-25).

7. Why the Master consents to marry.

People were sent to surrounding villages to search for a suitable bride, but none could be found. The parents of the few available girls demanded large dowries that Rameswar could not afford. When a bride had not been found even

8. The Master selects his bride.

after intense searching, Chandradevi and Rameswar became frustrated and anxious. Then one day Gadadhar, in an ecstatic mood, told them: "It is useless to search here and there. You must go to the family of Ramchandra Mukhopadhyay in the village of Jayrambati. Fate has marked my bride with a straw."[1]

Without putting much faith in Gadadhar's words, his mother and brother

| 9. The marriage. |

sent someone to Jayrambati to make an inquiry. Their representative returned with the news that the girl was not suitable. Apart from other considerations, she was too young — barely five years old. But as this girl had been discovered in an unexpected way, Chandradevi agreed to marry Gadadhar to her. The negotiations were settled in a few days. Then on an auspicious day and at an auspicious time, Rameswar accompanied his younger brother to Jayrambati, four miles from Kamarpukur. The marriage ceremony of Gadadhar and Sarada, the five-year-old daughter of Ramchandra Mukhopadhyay, was performed. Rameswar paid a dowry of three hundred rupees for this marriage. It was May 1859, and the Master had reached his twenty-fourth year.

Chandramani was much relieved after Gadadhar's wedding. When she

| 10. What Chandramani and the Master did after the wedding. |

found that her son had obeyed her order to marry, she thought that Providence had been kind to her. She also felt the grace of God: Her eccentric son had returned home, a bride of noble descent had graced the family, and the financial problem had been solved temporarily in a surprising way. The simple-hearted, virtuous Chandradevi was happy to some extent. In order to satisfy Sarada's parents and to maintain appearances, Chandra had borrowed some jewellery from the wealthy Laha family for the bride to wear during the wedding ceremony. Chandradevi was extremely anxious when the time came to return those ornaments to their owners. She had lovingly made the new bride her own by showing her affection. Now she would have to take the jewellery away from Sarada. This thought filled the old woman's eyes with tears. Although she did not express her agony to anyone, it did not take long for Gadadhar to perceive it. He consoled his mother, and then while Sarada was sleeping he took the jewellery away so deftly that she was unaware of it. Those were immediately sent to the Lahas. But when the intelligent girl awoke, she asked, "Where is my jewellery?" Chandradevi took Sarada on her lap and consoled her with tears, saying, "My darling, later Gadadhar will give you better ornaments than those." The matter did not end there. Sarada's uncle came to see her that day. When he learned of this incident he was offended and took her home at once. Chandradevi was terribly hurt. To ease her pain Gadadhar said playfully, "Whatever they say or do, they can't annul the marriage now!"

1. The expression "marked with a straw" refers to a Bengal village custom. If a farmer has a particularly fine fruit or vegetable that he wishes to offer to the Lord when it is fully ripe, he twists a straw around it so that no one will pluck it to sell.

Sarada Mukhopadhyay (1853-1920). Photo taken in 1898.

After his wedding Gadadhar remained in Kamarpukur about one year and seven months. It seems that Chandradevi did not allow him to return to Calcutta because she feared that he would have a relapse of his insanity if

11. The Master returns to Calcutta.

he was not fully cured. In December 1860 the bride reached her seventh year. According to traditional Hindu custom, a married couple should leave together a second time from the bride's home. So Gadadhar went to Jayrambati for a few days and then on an auspicious day returned to Kamarpukur with his wife. Shortly after this ceremony he decided to return to Calcutta. Although his mother and brother asked him to stay a little longer, he was aware of his family's financial difficulties. So against their wishes, he returned to Dakshineswar and resumed his service of the Divine Mother.

He had performed worship for only a few days when he became so absorbed in it that his mother, his brother, his wife,

12. The Master's second episode of divine madness.

the poverty of his family, and everything about Kamarpukur disappeared from his mind. The only thought that occupied him now was how he could see the Divine Mother in all beings at all times. His chest again turned crimson because of his constant recollectedness of God and his reflection, japa, and meditation. Worldly affairs and mundane talk appeared to him as deadly poison. The terrible burning sensation in his body reappeared, and sleep vanished altogether. But as he had previously experienced such physical and mental conditions, he was not overwhelmed by them as he had been before.

We heard from Hriday that Mathur called for Gangaprasad Sen, the famous Ayurvedic physician of Calcutta, who prescribed various medicines and oils to cure the Master's flatulence, his insomnia, and the burning sensation in his body. Although the treatment had no immediate result, Hriday did not give up hope. He would occasionally take the Master to the doctor's Calcutta residence for further treatment. The Master said: "One day while we were at Gangaprasad's house, he was concerned because the treatment was not having the expected result. He examined me carefully and prescribed new medicines. A physician from East Bengal was also present. Hearing of the symptoms of the disease, he remarked: 'It seems to me the patient's condition is due to divine ecstasy. It is a yogic condition and is not curable by medicine.'[2] This physician was the first person who was able to diagnose the real cause of my physical problems, which appeared as a disease. But no one believed his words then." Mathur and other well-wishers of the Master grew anxious and arranged for various treatments of his uncommon disease. But instead of abating, the symptoms grew worse.

2. Some say that it was Durgaprasad, a brother of Gangaprasad, who made this remark.

Eventually the news reached Kamarpukur. Seeing no alternative,

13. Chandramani
undertakes a fast to
death for a divine
favour.

Chandradevi decided to undertake a vow of fasting and prayer before Shiva for her son's welfare. Knowing the ancient Shiva of Kamarpukur was an awakened deity, she went to His temple and began a fast called *prayopavesana*.[3] Here she received this instruction: "Your desire will be fulfilled if you undertake the vow of fasting and prayer to the Shiva of Mukundapur." So she went there and recommenced her fast. No one had ever before undertaken such a fast before the Shiva of Mukundapur in order to fulfill a desire. Chandra knew this, but still went there as she had been instructed. After two or three days she dreamt that the silver-white form of Lord Shiva — bedecked with shining, matted hair and wearing a tiger skin — appeared before her and consoled her, saying: "Don't be afraid; your son is not mad. He is in this state because he is so powerfully possessed by God." Thus reassured by the word of God, the pious old woman offered worship to the Lord Shiva and returned home. In order that her son might have mental peace, she continued her devoted service to the family deities Ramachandra and Shitala. We heard that from then on many people have undertaken the fasting vow before the Shiva of Mukundapur and have had their desires fulfilled.

Recalling his divine ecstasy of this period, the Master used to tell us: "An

14. The Master's
condition.

ordinary man could not have borne a quarter of that tremendous spiritual fervour; it would have burnt him up. I could forget my indescribable pangs only by seeing the Mother in some form or other for the greater part of the day and night. Otherwise this body could not have survived. I had no sleep at all for six long years. My eyes lost the ability to blink. Despite repeated efforts, I could not close my eyelids. I had no idea of time. I almost forgot that I needed to maintain my body. When at rare intervals my attention would fall on the body a little, I was frightened by its condition. I thought, 'Am I on the verge of insanity?' Standing in front of a mirror, I tried to close my eyelids with my fingers — and I couldn't! I became frightened and tearfully said to the Mother: 'Mother, is this the result of praying and wholly surrendering myself to You? Now You have given me this terrible disease!' But the next moment I would say: 'Let it be as You wish. Let this body go to pieces, but don't leave me. Reveal Yourself to me; bestow Your mercy on me. I have taken refuge at Your lotus feet alone. I have none else but You.' I would shed tears, then suddenly be filled with ecstasy. I would feel my body to be a trifling thing. I was comforted when I saw the Mother and heard Her reassuring voice."

---

3. A devotee throws himself or herself down before the deity in the shrine and remains there until the prayer is granted or that person dies of starvation. — *Translator*

One day during this period Mathur was overwhelmed by unexpectedly

15. Mathur sees Shiva and Kali in the Master.

seeing in the Master a wonderful manifestation of the Divine, by Mother's grace. We have described elsewhere (see III.6.12-13) how Mathur saw Shiva and Kali in the Master on that day and then worshipped him as a living God. From that point on, a divine power forced Mathur to see the Master from a different perspective and to look after him with faith and devotion. It is evident from this unexpected incident that the Divine Mother had bound them together with a cord of love, because henceforth the Master needed Mathur's assistance and service to continue his spiritual journey. We become awestruck when in events like these we find proof of the great care and wonderful means the Divine Mother employed to strengthen the Master's body and mind so they could serve as instruments of living spirituality to counteract the agnosticism, materialism, and atheism of the present age.

Chapter 10

Arrival of the
*B*hairavi Brahmani

IN 1861, AFTER HE RETURNED TO DAKSHINESWAR FROM Kamarpukur, two important
events took place in the Master's life. Because they
changed his life greatly, it is necessary to discuss them
in detail. In the beginning of 1861, Rani Rasmani
became gravely ill with dysentery. The Master told us that one day the Rani
had a sudden fall, which led to fever, bodyaches, dyspepsia, and other
complications that gradually developed into dysentery. Within a short time
the disease took a serious turn.

1. Rani Rasmani's
serious illness.

We have already mentioned that Rani Rasmani dedicated the Kali temple
of Dakshineswar on Thursday, 31 May 1855. During
the same year, to maintain the temple complex she
purchased three estates in the Dinajpur District (now
in Bangladesh) for 226,000 rupees.[1] Although she had resolved to make an
endowment of the property to defray the expenses of the Dakshineswar
temple complex, the deed of endowment had never been formally executed.
When she realized that her end was approaching, she became anxious to
settle the matter. Two of her four daughters, Kumari and Karunamayi (the
second and the third) had died before the consecration of the Kali temple.

2. Rasmani endows her
Dinajpur property to the
temple, then dies.

1. Plaint in High Court Suit No. 308 of 1872, Puddomoni Dasee vs. Jagadamba Dasee, recites
the following from the Deed of Endowment executed by Rani Rasmani: "According to my
late husband's desire . . . I on 18th Jaistha, 1262 B.S. (31st May 1855) established and consecrated the *Thakurs* . . . and for purpose of carrying on the *Sheba* purchased three lots of
Zemindaris in District Dinajpur on 14th Bhadra 1262 B.S. (29th August 1855) for Rs.
226,000."

The eldest, Padmamani, and the youngest, Jagadamba, were present at the Rani's deathbed. When the draft of the deed of endowment had been drawn up according to her wish, she asked her two daughters to give their assent to the terms of the deed and to sign a separate bond waiving their claims to the temple property, so that there would be no conflict in the future. Jagadamba signed the bond, but Padmamani refused, despite Rani's repeated requests. Therefore, the Rani had no peace even on her deathbed. Finding no alternative, the Rani surrendered herself to the will of the Divine Mother and signed the deed of endowment[2] on 18 February 1861. The next night, 19 February 1861, she entered *Deviloka*, the Divine Mother's abode.

The Master told us that a few days before she passed away, Rani Rasmani

3. Rasmani's vision at the time of her death.

was taken to her residence at Kalighat on the bank of the Adi-Ganga, a small channel of the main river. Shortly before her death she was brought to the Adi-Ganga. It is auspicious to die while touching the water of the holy river Ganges. Seeing that lamps had been lighted around her, she suddenly exclaimed: "Remove those lamps. I don't care for that artificial illumination anymore. Now my Divine Mother is coming and the lustre of Her body illumines everything!" After a slight pause she said: "Mother, You have come! Padma has not signed. What's going to happen, Mother?" At that very moment a pack of jackals, Mother's companions, began to howl from all directions, as if answering the Rani's question. After uttering those words the virtuous Rani quietly passed away. It was midnight.

After her death the grandchildren of Rani Rasmani began to quarrel

4. What Rasmani foresaw before her death actually came to pass.

amongst themselves and file lawsuits to win ownership of the property at Dakshineswar. This justifies the farsighted Rani's apprehension about the future disturbance of the temple service, and explains why at the time of her death she suffered more terribly from that anxiety than from the pain of her disease. The court documents show that the temple property was mortgaged for nearly 100,000 rupees to defray the heavy expenses of litigation.[3] Who can say whether Rani Rasmani's unique divine glory [the Dakshineswar temple] will exist only in name or become extinct in the future because of this quarrel?

2. The Deed of Endowment dated 18th February 1861 was executed by Rani Rasmani; she acknowledged her execution of the same before J. F. Watkins, Solicitor, Calcutta. This dedication was accepted as valid by all parties in Alipore Suit No. 47 of 1867, Jadu Nath Chowdhury vs. Puddomoni and in the High Court Suit No. 308 of 1872, Puddomoni vs. Jagadamba and also when that Suit (No. 308) was revived after contest on 19th July 1888.
3. Debt due on mortgage by the Estate is Rs. 50,000; interest payable quarterly is Rs. 876-0-0; cost of the Referee already stated amount to Rs. 20,000, as yet untaxed.

Mathur Mohan Biswas, the Rani's youngest son-in-law, had become her

5. Mathur's prosperity and his temple management.

right-hand man in managing the estates. From the day of the founding of the Kali temple, Mathur had been looking after the financial aspects of the temple property and managing the temple according to the direction of the Rani. After her death, therefore, he continued to supervise the temple services. As the holy influence of Sri Ramakrishna had infused Mathur's mind with deep devotion, the service of the Mother at Dakshineswar was not disturbed at all following the Rani's death.

We have already discussed in many places the wonderful relationship

6. Mathur's wealth and his power to help the Master.

between the Master and Mathur. One thing we must mention here is that Rani Rasmani passed away before the Master began his Tantric sadhanas and that Mathur had full control over temple affairs; so he was able to assist the Master in his Tantric disciplines, which extended over a long period. It seems that Mathur had attained that authority of temple management in order to help the Master, because from that point on his main focus in life was to serve the Master as a divine being. Only God's grace allows a person to maintain steadfast faith in one object for a long time to spend his life holding fast to a high ideal. Therefore, it seems to have been Mathur's great fortune that he did not go astray, even after gaining full control over the Rani's immense wealth. His faith in the Master grew day by day, and from this point on he served him without fail for eleven long years.

Only spiritual aspirants understood the Master's extraordinary, divine,

7. How Mathur and others understood the Master.

ecstatic state. Ordinary people considered him to be mad because they saw that he had no interest at all in worldly enjoyments, that he was in an intoxicated mood beyond their comprehension, and that he spent his days calling out various names — sometimes "Hari," sometimes "Rama," and sometimes "Kali, Kali." So many people who had the favour of the Rani and Mathur became wealthy by taking advantage of their influence; but although the Master was their favourite, he did not try to become prosperous through them. As he had no sense of what was good or bad for him, people thought he must be mad. But this they all understood: Although the Master was incompetent in worldly affairs, his bright eyes, pleasant behaviour, sweet voice, fascinating conversation, and wonderful presence of mind were tremendously attractive powers, and made him dear to wealthy patrons and distinguished pandits. He could move among them without any hesitation, whereas others would not venture to approach them. This was the opinion of the public and the temple officials, but Mathur had a different view. He said, "He is intoxicated because the Divine Mother shines Her grace on him."

Shortly after Rani Rasmani's death, another important event took place in the Master's life. There was a beautiful flower garden located to the west of the temple complex on the spacious embankment of the Ganges. The garden was meticulously maintained, and trees and creepers enhanced its beauty with their various flowers, spreading sweet fragrance all around. Although the Master was not performing the worship of the Mother at that time, he would go to that garden every day to pick flowers and make garlands to decorate Her. In the middle of that garden there was a wide flight of steps leading from the Ganges to the temple through a beautiful open portico called the *Chandni*. At the northern end of the embankment there still exists a brick bathing ghat for the women, and the nahabat (concert tower). Because there is a large bakul tree adjacent to the ghat, people call it the Bakul ghat.

8. Arrival of the Bhairavi Brahmani.

One morning while Sri Ramakrishna was picking flowers, a boat anchored at the Bakul ghat. A beautiful woman with long dishevelled hair, clad in the ochre robes of a bhairavi, landed there and walked towards the Chandni. Although she was past her youth, she looked much younger than her age. We heard from the Master that the Bhairavi was then nearly forty. As a person feels an affinity when seeing a close relative, so the Master immediately felt drawn to the Bhairavi. He returned to his room and asked his nephew Hriday to bring her to him. Hriday hesitated, saying: "The woman is a stranger. Why should she come?" The Master replied, "If you ask her in my name, she will come." Hriday later said that he was surprised to see his uncle's eagerness to speak to that unknown sannyasini. He had never before seen him act like that.

Hriday did not dare to disobey his mad uncle, so he went to the Chandni and found the Bhairavi seated there. He approached her and said that his devout uncle wished to meet her. Hriday was even more amazed when he saw the Bhairavi rise to accompany him without any question.

When the Bhairavi entered the Master's room and her eyes first fell on him, she was overwhelmed with joy and surprise. She said tearfully: "My son, you are here! I knew that you lived somewhere along the banks of the Ganges. I have been searching for you so long. Now I have found you." The Master asked, "Mother, how could you know about me?" The Bhairavi replied: "Through the grace of the Divine Mother I came to know that I was to meet three of you. Two I have met already in East Bengal, and today I have found you."

9. The Bhairavi's remark to the Master at their first meeting.

As a boy joyfully opens his heart to his mother, so the Master sat near the Bhairavi and related his daily spiritual experiences, such as his divine visions, his loss of outer consciousness while talking about God, the burning sensation in his body, his sleeplessness, and other physical symptoms. He asked repeatedly: "Mother, what are these things that keep happening to me? Am I

10. Their first conversation.

mad, really? Have I truly developed this terrible disease by wholeheartedly calling on the Divine Mother?" While listening to the Master, the Bhairavi sometimes became excited, and sometimes elated. Like a compassionate mother, she reassured him repeatedly: "Who calls you mad, my son? This is not insanity. You have achieved *mahabhava*, and that is why you are having all these experiences. How can ordinary people understand your condition? They cannot — so they call you mad. Sri Radha experienced this state and so did Sri Chaitanya. All this is recorded in the bhakti scriptures. I have all these books with me. I will read them to you and prove that whoever has sincerely yearned for God has experienced these states, and everyone doing so must pass through them." Hriday was amazed at seeing his uncle and the Bhairavi Brahmani[4] talking together like close relatives.

Finding that the day was advancing, the Master offered Mother's prasad — fruits, sweets, butter, and sugar candy — to the Brahmani for her breakfast. Before he did so, he ate a little himself: He realized that she had a maternal attitude toward him and would not accept the prasad unless he partook of it first. After she had her breakfast and visited the temple deities, the Brahmani collected rice, flour, and other food from the temple store. She then began cooking in the Panchavati, preparing her offering to a stone image of Raghuvir that she carried about with her which hung around her neck.

When she had finished cooking, she placed the food before Raghuvir, closed her eyes, and began to think of her Chosen Deity. Soon she entered deep meditation and had a wonderful vision. Plunged in samadhi, she lost outer consciousness, and tears of joy trickled down her cheeks. At that moment the Master was in an ecstatic mood and felt an urge to go to the Panchavati. He went there, and possessed by a divine power, began to eat the food that had been offered by the Brahmani. After a while the Brahmani regained outer consciousness and saw the Master there, in an ecstatic mood. Finding this scene to be similar to her vision, she was filled with delight, and her hair stood on end. When the Master returned to the normal plane he felt ashamed of what he had done. He apologized, saying, "Who knows, Mother, why I lose control over myself and do such things?" The Brahmani lovingly reassured him: "You did well, my son. It is not really you who has done this, but He who dwells within you. In my meditation I clearly realized Who did it and why. I have come to understand that I do not need to perform formal worship anymore: My worship has borne fruit at last." Then the Brahmani unhesitatingly took the Master's leftover food as prasad. She saw that her beloved Raghuvir was living in Sri Ramakrishna, and she was overwhelmed with happiness. With tears of joy, she consigned to the Ganges the stone image that she had so lovingly worshipped for many years.

> 11. The Bhairavi's wonderful vision at the Panchavati.

4. The Bhairavi is sometimes referred to by the author as the Bhairavi Brahmani, or simply as Brahmani. Her actual name was Yogeswari. — *Translator*

Following their first meeting, the mutual affection and affinity between

12. Scriptural discussion at the Panchavati.

the Master and the Brahmani deepened day by day. The sannyasini's motherly affection for the Master kept her at Dakshineswar. They both lost track of time as they were immersed in spiritual conversation. Without any hesitation the Master told the Brahmani about his visions and states. Every day he would ask various questions about his experiences, and she would answer them by quoting from the Tantric scriptures. She also removed his doubts by reading from devotional scriptures that recorded the avatars' similar physical and mental conditions when they were overwhelmed by the powerful surge of divine love. Thus, a current of divine bliss flowed in the Panchavati for some days.

After six or seven days the Master realized that it would not be proper for

13. Why the Bhairavi stays at the Devamandal ghat.

the Brahmani to stay in the temple compound. Worldly people might misunderstand his close association with her and slander her pure character. When the Master told the Brahmani about his concern, she understood the situation. She left the Kali temple and decided to stay nearby in the village. From there she could easily visit the Master daily for short periods.

The Brahmani began to live in a room at the Devamandal ghat in the village of Dakshineswar, on the bank of the Ganges to the north of the Kali temple.[5] She soon became acquainted with the village women, and her noble qualities gained their respect. Therefore, she had no inconvenience about her room and board, and she was able to visit the Master freely every day without fear of public criticism. She went to the Kali temple daily and talked with the Master. Occasionally, she collected food from the village women, cooked various dishes herself, and brought them to the Master (see III.8.5).

Judging from what Sri Ramakrishna had told her, the Brahmani

14. How the Bhairavi concludes that the Master is an avatar.

concluded that his divine visions and states were caused by his extreme love of God. She observed that while talking about God, the Master frequently went into bhava samadhi and lost outer consciousness, and that during kirtan he went into ecstasy. These characteristics convinced her that the Master was not an ordinary spiritual aspirant. In the *Chaitanya Charitamrita*, *Chaitanya Bhagavata*, and other Vaishnava scriptures there are some intimations that Chaitanya would incarnate again to redeem human beings from misery. This thought repeatedly arose in her mind when she saw the Master. The learned Brahmani compared the Master's behaviour and divine visions with

5. Hriday later told us that it was the Master who suggested that the Brahmani live at the Devamandal ghat and that he sent her to the Mandal's house. There she was received by the virtuous widow of Navin Chandra Neogi. She gave permission to the Brahmani to live in a room of the ghat as long as she liked and also gave her a bedstead, rice, lentils, ghee, and other groceries.

those of Chaitanya recorded in those books and found striking similarities. She saw in the Master, as in Chaitanya, the power of enkindling spirituality in others by a touch while in ecstasy. It is recorded that Chaitanya had a burning sensation in his body due to the pain of separation from God; it subsided when he wore a garland, sandal paste, and other things. She saw the same effect when she used those items to stop the burning sensation in the Master's body (see IV.1.10). So she became convinced that both Chaitanya and Nityananda had reincarnated as Sri Ramakrishna to redeem humanity. We have described elsewhere in detail (see II.8.24) about how two young boys emerged from the Master's body while he was going to Sihar. When she heard of that vision from the Master, the Brahmani became firmly convinced of her own opinion regarding Sri Ramakrishna. She remarked, "This time Chaitanya has been manifested in Nityananda's body."[6]

Because the Brahmani was a nun, she did not expect favours from anyone, nor was she concerned about criticism or ridicule when she expressed what she felt to be true. So she did not hesitate to proclaim to all her own conclusions about Sri Ramakrishna. We heard that one day during this period the Master and Mathur were at the Panchavati, and Hriday was also present. In the course of conversation the Master told Mathur the Brahmani's findings about him. He said: "She says that all the signs of the avatars are in this body and mind (*pointing to himself*). She is well versed in the scriptures and she has many books with her." Mathur replied with a laugh: "Father, whatever she may say, according to the scriptures there are no more than ten avatars. So how can her words be true? But it is true that Mother Kali has bestowed Her grace on you."

While they were talking, Mathur saw a sannyasini approaching them. He

15. The Bhairavi declares her conclusions in front of Mathur.

asked the Master, "Is this the woman?" "Yes," replied the Master. They saw the Brahmani carrying a plate of sweets and walking towards them in an abstracted mood, as mother Yashoda would carry food to feed her beloved Gopala in Vrindaban. Coming near the Panchavati she saw Mathur, and then carefully restraining herself she handed the plate to Hriday to feed the Master. Pointing to Mathur the Master told the Brahmani: "Mother, I was just telling him what you say about me. But he says that the scriptures mention only ten avatars and no more than that." Mathur saluted the Brahmani and admitted that he had raised that objection. She immediately replied: "Bhagavan Vyasa mentioned twenty-four avatars in the Bhagavata and then indicated an infinite number of them. Moreover, the Vaishnava scriptures clearly state that

---

6. This statement can be interpreted in this way: Chaitanya was absorbed in God-consciousness most of the time, so he could not preach to the people very often. He asked his main disciple, Nityananda, to carry God's name from door to door and to teach the religion of love. But Ramakrishna, like Chaitanya, was absorbed in God-consciousness and also, like Nityananda, was a teacher. — *Translator*

Chaitanya would be incarnated again. In addition, there is a striking resemblance in many characteristics between him and Sri Ramakrishna." After defending her view, the Brahmani said that the scholars of the Bhagavata and Vaishnava literature of Bengal would have to admit her statement to be true. She was prepared to defend her view to them. Unable to respond to the Brahmani, Mathur remained silent.

Gradually the Brahmani's view concerning the Master became known to the people of the Kali temple. This created a terrible commotion. We have recorded the results elsewhere in detail (see IV.1.6-7,10-11). Although the Brahmani honoured the Master as God in front of all, he was not at all affected. Regarding the Brahmani's conclusions, the Master was curious to know the opinions of the scholars who were well versed in the scriptures. Like a boy, he asked Mathur to arrange a meeting. As a result of this request Vaishnavcharan and other pandits came to the Dakshineswar Kali temple. We have described elsewhere how the Brahmani defended her view to them (see IV.1.19-20).

16. Why Pandit Vaishnavcharan came to Dakshineswar.

Chapter 11

The Master's
*T*antra Sadhana

THE BRAHMANI'S CONVICTION THAT THE MASTER WAS an avatar was not based

| 1. The divine insight she gains from her own sadhana helps the Brahmani to correctly understand the Master's condition. |

upon reasoning alone. The reader may remember that during her first meeting with Sri Ramakrishna, the Brahmani had told him that she had been destined to help him and two others with their spiritual awakening. She had received that command from the Divine Mother long before she met the Master. So it is clear that the divine insight that came from her sadhana brought her to Dakshineswar and helped her to understand the Master so deeply after having only one brief interview. Again, the more time she spent in close association with the Master, the more the manner and extent of her role in helping him became evident to her. Therefore, she lost no time in removing the erroneous ideas the people surrounding him had, and she also made sure that the Master could practise sadhanas according to the scriptures and, by the Divine Mother's grace, become firmly established in the divine plane.

It was not long before the Brahmani, a highly adept aspirant, realized that

| 2. Why the Brahmani advised the Master to practise Tantra. |

the Master could not understand his high spiritual state because he had achieved the vision of God by virtue of his intense longing only, not by following one of the traditional paths enjoined by the gurus and the scriptures. The Master was often tormented by doubt: He thought that his wonderful spiritual experiences could be caused by insanity and that his physical symptoms could be signs of a disease. To free him from this doubt, the Brahmani encouraged him to practise the disciplines of Tantra. She knew that he would find in the Tantra scriptures descriptions of how a spiritual aspirant attains a particular result by practising a particular rite, and that he himself would achieve the same result by following the same steps. Then he would become firmly convinced that the more a person ascends to higher and higher states of the inner realm by practising spiritual disciplines, the more he will experience unique physical and mental conditions. As a consequence, the Master would understand that whatever uncommon experiences he might have in the future would be authentic and infallible. He would thus continue moving towards the goal without any worry. The Brahmani knew that it was for this very reason that the scriptures advise aspirants to compare their experiences with the words of the guru and the scriptures in order to verify them as true.

One may ask: If the Brahmani recognized the Master to be an avatar, why then did she engage him in practising sadhana? We know that an avatar is endowed with divine powers and is perfect, so any effort in practising spiritual disciplines would seem to be unnecessary. In response we say that if the Brahmani had always been aware of

> 3. Why the Brahmani helped the Master in his sadhana even though she knew he was an avatar.

the Master's greatness and divine power, perhaps she would have had this attitude. But this was not the case. We have already mentioned that from their first meeting the Brahmani loved the Master as she would her own son. In this world only love drives one to do whatever is necessary for the good of the beloved and makes one oblivious to that person's greatness. Therefore, we can presume that out of pure love she persuaded the Master to practise spiritual disciplines. This we find in the lives of all the avatars. We notice that those who are close to the avatars may from time to time be overwhelmed by their divine power, but they forget it the next moment. Again, captivated by the avatars' love, they try to do what is best for them, considering them to be as imperfect as other ordinary human beings. Sometimes the Brahmani was awestruck as she witnessed the Master's extraordinary ecstasy and manifestations of power, but soon his pure love, faith, and reliance on her would call forth the motherly affection in her tender heart. She then seemed unaware of his powers and wished only to make him happy and to help him in every respect.

When an opportunity comes to teach a qualified disciple, great joy and satisfaction arise in the guru's heart. The Brahmani's heart was therefore filled with joy at the chance to teach someone as supremely competent as the Master. In addition, her affection for him was abso-

> 4. The Brahmani's eagerness to transmit all the results of her austerities to the Master.

lutely pure. It is no wonder that the Brahmani was eager to help the Master quickly experience the fruits of her lifelong studies and austerities.

At times the Master told us that before he began practising Tantric disci-

5. The Master practises Tantra at the command of the Divine Mother. The magnitude of his intense sadhana.

plines he asked the Divine Mother whether they were appropriate. He then practised them with Her permission. Therefore it was not only the Brahmani's eagerness and enthusiasm that induced him to engage in this sadhana; he now also realized whole-heartedly, through his highly-developed spiritual insight, that the time had come for him to experience the Divine Mother by following methods enjoined by the scriptures. Thus, the Master's one-pointed mind quickly and enthusiastically moved along the spiritual path directed by the Brahmani. It is not possible for us to comprehend the magnitude and intensity of his earnestness. Our minds are scattered among mundane things; we don't possess that kind of self-restraint and single-mindedness. Do we have that indomitable courage to renounce everything and dive deep into the inner ocean of consciousness, instead of floating on its surface and being buffeted by wanton waves? The Master would inspire us again and again, saying, "Dive deep completely"; "Dive deep within yourself." Are we able to dive into the inner sanctum of spirituality, relinquishing our attachment for worldly objects and for our own bodies? Day after day, tormented by the anguish of his heart, the Master would rub his face on the bank of the Ganges near the Panchavati, saying, "Mother, reveal Yourself to me." When we hear these words, they merely enter our ears: They rouse no corresponding thrill in our hearts at all. Why should this be? The Divine Mother truly exists. We can see Her by renouncing everything and calling on Her with a longing heart. Do we have this simple faith of the Master?

One day while living at Cossipore the Master astounded us when he told us a little about the magnitude and intensity of longing he had experienced during his sadhana. We do not know how much we will be able to make the reader understand what we then felt; however, we shall try.

At the Cossipore garden house we witnessed Swami Vivekananda's

6. At the Cossipore garden house, the Master talks about the intensity of his sadhana.

intense longing for God-realization. He had gone to deposit the fee for his final law examination, but then suddenly felt an awakening of consciousness. He was so inspired that he restlessly ran barefoot through the streets of Calcutta like a mad person, wearing only a single piece of cloth. He reached his guru, Sri Ramakrishna, at Cossipore and, intoxicated, he expressed his mental anguish to the Master and received his grace. For some time he forgot to eat or sleep, and was absorbed day and night in japa, meditation, devotional singing, and spiritual discussion. His intense passion for sadhana made his tender heart extremely firm: He became completely indifferent to the suffering of his mother, sisters, and brothers. Steadfastly following his guru's instructions, he had divine visions one after another. At the end of three or four months he experienced the bliss of nirvikalpa samadhi for the first time. These incidents all took place before our eyes. We were amazed. Every day the Master would joyfully praise Swamiji's intense devotion, longing, and zeal for spiritual practices. Then one day, the Master, comparing his love and longing for sadhana with that of Swamiji's, remarked: "Narendra's love and zeal are really outstanding. But during my sadhana the volume of intensity that came here (*pointing to himself*), compared to that, it [Narendra's sadhana] is very little — not even a quarter." Can you imagine, O reader, what we felt when we heard these words from the Master?

Under the direction of the Divine Mother, the Master now became

| 7. Construction of the *panchamundi* seat, and practice of sixty-four disciplines of Tantra. |

absorbed in Tantra sadhana, forgetting everything else. The wise and skillful Brahmani collected all the ingredients necessary for Tantric rituals and carefully instructed the Master in their use during sadhana. The skulls[1] of men and of four other animals were carefully brought from a place far from the Ganges. And two altars[2] propitious for Tantra sadhana were built — one under the bel tree at the northern border of the temple garden and the other under the Panchavati planted by the Master himself. The Master would sit on either one of those skull seats to practise japa, *purashcharana* [a prescribed number of japa], and meditation. This wonderful aspirant and his guide were oblivious to the days and nights that slipped by over a period of some months.

The Master said[3]: "During the day the Brahmani would travel to various places far away from the temple and collect rare articles prescribed by Tantra. At nightfall she would set up the ritual either under the bel tree or under the Panchavati, then call me to worship the Divine Mother with those articles, advising me to be absorbed in japa and meditation. But I could seldom do japa after worship because my mind was so absorbed that I would merge into samadhi while turning the rosary. I would truly

1. In the fifth chapter of the *Yogini Tantra* (51-56), Shiva tells his wife, Parvati: "Now listen, O Goddess, about the sadhana of skulls, which helps an aspirant to reach the supreme goal, the vision of the Divine Mother. O beautiful Devi, one can make an altar on the skulls of a man, a buffalo, and a cat; or on three human skulls; or on the skulls of a jackal, a snake, a dog, and a bull with that of a man in the centre; or on five, or one hundred, or one thousand, or one million human skulls."

2. Generally aspirants set up an altar on five skulls and practise japa and meditation on it. But the Master told us of two skull seats: Three human skulls were buried under the altar of the bel tree, and the skulls of five beings were placed under the altar of the Panchavati. Shortly after he attained perfection in his sadhana, he threw all the skulls into the Ganges and broke the altars. Two seats were made either because the seat of three skulls was more favourable for sadhana, or because the spot under the bel tree at that time was very solitary and more convenient for performing special rites. Or it may be that it was difficult to kindle a fire for *homa* ceremonies under the bel tree because of its proximity to the British Government's powder magazine.

3. We heard all this from the Master at different times, and present it here in a connected way.

Bel tala or panchamundi at
Dakshineswar,
site of Ramakrishna's
Tantric sadhana.

Sadhan-kutir at Dakshineswar, site of Ramakrishna's Vedantic sadhana.

experience the result of that rite, as described by the scriptures. Thus I had vision after vision and innumerable wonderful spiritual experiences. The Brahmani made me practise all the sixty-four sadhanas prescribed in the *Vishnukranta*[4] section of the Tantra, one after the other. Those were difficult practices; most aspirants fall while practising them. But I got through them successfully by the Mother's grace.

"One night the Brahmani brought a beautiful young woman from some-

8. He realizes the goddess in all female forms.

where and arranged the worship. She put the woman on the Devi's seat, then instructed me, 'My child, worship her as the goddess.' When the worship was over, she said to me: 'My child, think of her as the veritable Divine Mother. Sit on her lap and practise japa wholeheartedly.' I was seized with fear, wept piteously, and said to the Divine Mother: 'Mother, why do You give this command to one who has taken refuge in You? Does Your weak child have the power to withstand such a severe trial?' As soon as I said that, my heart was filled with divine strength. Like a hypnotized person, not knowing what I was doing, I repeated the mantra, sat on the woman's lap, and immediately went into samadhi. When I regained outer consciousness, the Brahmani said: 'You have completed the rite, my child. Under such circumstances, others restrain themselves with great difficulty and finish by repeating the mantra for a very short time. But you entered samadhi, losing body-consciousness completely!' When I heard this I was reassured. With a grateful heart I bowed down to the Divine Mother again and again for enabling me to withstand the ordeal.

"One day I saw the Brahmani cook fish in a human skull and offer it to the

9. Giving up aversion.

Divine Mother. She made me do the same and asked me to eat that fish. At her command I did so, and I had no aversion in my mind.

"But on another day she brought a piece of rotten human flesh, offered it to the Mother, and asked me to touch it with my tongue. I was horrified with disgust and protested, 'How can I do that?' She replied: 'What do you say, my child? Look, I am doing it.' Saying so, she put a little into her mouth. Saying 'Please shun aversion,' she placed a portion of it in front of me. As soon as I saw that, the Divine Mother's terrible form of Chandika arose in my mind; then repeating 'Mother, Mother,' I went into ecstasy. I then felt no aversion when the Brahmani put a bit of the flesh into my mouth.

---

4. According to the Tantric tradition, there are three geographical regions, called *Vishnu-kranta*, *Rathakranta*, and *Ashvakranta*, and different Tantras are assigned to each one of them. According to the *Shaktimangala Tantra*, Vishnukranta extends from the Vindhya Mountain to Chittagong, thus including Bengal; Rathakranta from the same mountain to China, including Nepal; and Ashvakranta from the same mountain to the great ocean, apparently including the rest of India. A list of the Tantras under the Vishnukranta has been mentioned in *Principles of Tantra* by Arthur Avalon (Introduction, lxv). — *Translator*

"Having thus initiated me into *Purnabhisheka* [full initiation into Tantric rites], the Brahmani made me perform innumerable rites. I don't recall all the details now. But I do remember the day I witnessed the union of a man and a woman: I perceived only the divine sport of Shiva and Shakti, and went into samadhi. When I regained outer consciousness, the Brahmani told me: 'My child, you have attained perfection in an extremely difficult esoteric sadhana and are established in the divine mode. This is the last sadhana of the heroic mode of worship.' Shortly afterwards, with the help of another Bhairavi who came to Dakshineswar, I performed the worship of the female figure in accordance with Tantric rites. This ritual was performed in the daytime in view of all, in the open natmandir of the Kali temple. I gave her one and a quarter rupees as an offering. Thus, I completed the sadhana of the heroic mode. Throughout the long period of the Tantric sadhana, I always maintained my attitude towards all women as mother, and I also could not touch even a drop of *karana* [meaning *wine*, but also *cause*]. Whenever I heard the word *karana* or smelled wine, I would realize the Cause of the universe, God, and lose outer consciousness. I would likewise go into samadhi as soon as I heard the word *yoni*, [meaning *female organ*, but also *source*], thinking of the Source of the world, God."

10. The Master attains perfection in some difficult Tantric sadhanas: his conduct at that time.	

Once while living at Dakshineswar the Master told us a Puranic story that illustrated his filial attitude towards all women. This story explains how a firm knowledge of the motherhood of all women became established in the heart of Ganesha, chief among the illumined ones. Previously we did not have much devotion to or reverence for this pot-bellied, elephant-headed God with sweat dripping from his temples. But the following story told by the Master convinced us that Ganesha is truly fit to be worshipped before all the gods.

11. The Master's story about Ganesha's filial attitude towards all women.	

One day when Ganesha was a child, He saw a cat while He was playing. Out of boyish playfulness He wounded it by torturing it in various ways and beating it. The cat somehow escaped with its life. When Ganesha calmed down and went to His mother, the goddess Parvati, He saw bruises all over Her body. Seeing His mother's pitiable condition He was pained and asked Her how this happened. Parvati sullenly replied, "You Yourself are responsible for My misery." At this, the devoted Ganesha was very much surprised and saddened. He asked with tearful eyes: "What do You mean, Mother! When did I strike You? Although I am an imprudent son, I don't remember having done something so wrong that others would inflict such humiliation on You."

The all-pervading Mother Parvati said, "Try to recall: Have You beaten any creature today?" Ganesha replied: "Yes, I have. I struck a cat a short while ago." Ganesha then began to weep, thinking that the cat's owner had attacked His mother. Embracing Her repentant son, Parvati said: "It is not so, My child. No one has struck My body. But I dwell in the cat, as in all beings of the world. That is why You see on My body the marks of the beating You gave that cat. You have done this without knowing it, so do not grieve. But from now on You must keep firmly in mind that all female beings have originated from Myself and all male beings from Your Father. Nothing exists in the world apart from Shiva and Shakti." Ganesha accepted His mother's words completely and kept them in His heart forever. He refused to marry when He was of the appropriate age, lest He have to wed His mother. Thus, Ganesha remained a *brahmachari* forever. He became foremost among the illumined ones because He constantly experienced the truth that the universe is pervaded by Shiva and Shakti.

After telling this story the Master narrated the following to illustrate the

12. The story of Ganesha and Kartika's circumambulation of the universe.

supreme wisdom of Ganesha: Once Parvati showed Her precious necklace of gems to Ganesha and Kartika and said, "I will present this necklace to the one who is the first to circumambulate the universe of fourteen worlds." Kartika smiled derisively, thinking of His elder brother's pot-bellied and bulky body, and comparing His slow carrier mouse to His own speedy peacock. Certain that the necklace was as good as His already, Kartika got on His peacock and set out on His journey around the universe. Long after Kartika had left, Ganesha arose from His seat and through His eye of wisdom saw the universe, consisting of Shiva and Shakti, within the bodies of Hara and Parvati. He then slowly walked around Them and, after prostrating at Their feet, sat quietly. When Kartika returned, Parvati announced that Ganesha had truly earned the necklace and affectionately put it around His neck.

Thus citing the greatness of Ganesha's wisdom and His filial attitude towards all women, the Master said: "I have the same attitude towards all women. That is why, after vividly seeing the form of the Divine Mother in my wife, I worshipped her and bowed down at her feet."

We have never heard of any male aspirant in any age who practised the

13. The uniqueness of the Master's Tantra sadhana.

heroic mode of sadhana prescribed by Tantra while maintaining a completely filial attitude towards all women. Till now, male followers of this heroic mode have taken women companions during sadhana. That is why aspirants who follow this heroic mode are firmly convinced that unless one has a woman companion one cannot attain perfection or obtain the grace of the Divine Mother. Possessed of this idea and desiring to gratify their bestial propensities, some aspirants do not hesitate to use mistresses on occasion. For this reason, people criticize the heroic mode prescribed by Tantra.

The incomparable Master, the avatar of this age, repeatedly told us that throughout his life he never had a sexual relationship with any woman, even in a dream. It was the hidden intention of the Divine Mother to engage the Master, who looked upon all women as mother from his very birth, in practising the sadhanas of the heroic mode.

14. The Master's uniqueness was the will of the Divine Mother.

The Master told us that it took him no more than three days to attain success in each particular discipline. He said, "Whenever I took up a new sadhana, I earnestly prayed to the Divine Mother to show me its result, and She granted success within three days." The Master practised the heroic mode of Tantra without a woman companion and attained success quickly. This proves clearly that the five articles [wine, meat, fish, cereal, and woman] are not absolutely necessary for the performance of Tantric rites. Because of his weak nature, the unrestrained aspirant becomes involved with women. In spite of that, the Tantra scriptures reassure such a male aspirant, advising him to continue practices with a woman companion, until eventually he is established in the divine mood. This concession reveals the infinite compassion of the Tantra scriptures for the weakness of human beings, helping them to transcend their animal nature.

15. The Master's success proves that perfection is possible in Tantra sadhana without having a woman companion.

Lured by sense objects, human beings undergo repeated births and deaths and are unable to attain God or Self-knowledge. Therefore, it seems that the goal of Tantric rites is to make the aspirant practise self-control by continual zeal and effort and to understand that all sense objects are various forms of God. Evaluating the differing degrees of aspirants' self-control and their conception of God in all beings, the Tantra scriptures prescribe three modes of worship — *pashu* [animal], *vira* [heroic], and *divya* [divine][5] — and advise aspirants to worship God in any one of those modes according to their abilities. In the course of time, people almost forgot that Tantric disciplines bear visible results only if they are practised with strict self-control, but otherwise do not. The general public has blamed the Tantra scriptures

16. The goal of Tantric rituals.

---

5. The Tantra scriptures classify human beings into three types according to their temperament: (1) *Divya*. A person with divya, or divine disposition, is endowed mainly with sattva. According to the *Kamakhya Tantra*, such a person is sparing in his speech, quiet, steady, sagacious, and attentive to all. He is always contented and devoted to his guru. He is fearless, never swerves from the path of truth, and avoids all that is evil. He is good in every way and is Shiva's very self. (2) *Vira*. A person with vira, or heroic disposition, is endowed mainly with rajas. He is gentle in his speech and is always mindful of the five elements. He is physically strong, courageous, intelligent, and enterprising. He is humble in his ways and cherishes the good. (3) *Pashu*. A person with pashu, or animal disposition, is endowed mainly with tamas. He is a slave to the six enemies: lust, anger, greed, pride, delusion, and envy. The Tantra scriptures made room for lower to higher human beings to practise spiritual disciplines according to their temperaments, so that eventually all can reach God. — *Translator*

for those who indulge in sensual acts in the guise of sadhana, and criticize Tantra vehemently. The Master attained success in all Tantric rites while maintaining his filial relationship with all women: From his example sincere aspirants have learned how they can best reach their goal and benefit greatly. At the same time the validity of the Tantra scriptures has been well established and glorified.

Although the Master practised the mystical Tantric sadhanas continually

17. Another reason for the Master's Tantra sadhana.

over a period of two years, he may never have given any of us an account of his entire sadhana. But sometimes he would tell us some stories to encourage us on the spiritual path. On rare occasions, he would make someone practise particular rites according to that individual's personal need. It is clear that the Divine Mother made the Master fully acquainted with the Tantric path. If he had not had the extraordinary experiences resulting from Tantric rites, he would not have been able later to assist the various devotees who came to him, ascertaining their mental states and leading them easily on their chosen paths. We have mentioned briefly elsewhere (see III.1.23-30,2.47-71) the many ways in which the Master guided those who surrendered to him. When the reader studies that section he will easily understand that what we have said above is quite reasonable.

In addition to describing some Tantric rites to us, the Master sometimes

18. The Master's visions and experiences during this time.

mentioned the visions and experiences he had during his Tantra sadhana. We shall now narrate a few of them.

The Master said that while practising Tantra his nature was radically

19. He eats defiled food left by jackals and dogs.

changed. When he heard that the Divine Mother sometimes assumes the form of a jackal, and that the dog is the carrier of Bhairava, he would take the food they had defiled as sacred prasad without the slightest hesitation.

20. He sees himself pervaded by the fire of knowledge.

When he offered his body, mind, and senses as oblations to the lotus feet of the Divine Mother, he saw the fire of knowledge pervading his whole being.

During this time the Master saw the awakened kundalini rising from the

21. He sees the awakening of kundalini.

muladhara to the sahasrara; the lotus of each centre was turned upward and in full bloom. As soon as the lotus of each centre had blossomed in succession, the Master had extraordinary spiritual experiences (see III.2.31-34). He saw a luminous Divine Being passing through the sushumna channel, making each lotus bloom by touching it with His tongue.

At one time when Swami Vivekananda would sit for meditation, a large,

22. His vision of *Brahmayoni*.

luminous, multicoloured triangle would spontaneously appear before him. This triangle appeared to be living. One day he went to Dakshineswar and told the Master about it. The latter said: "Very good! You have seen the *Brahmayoni* [the source of creation]. During my sadhana under the bel tree, I also saw this. It was bringing forth innumerable worlds at every moment."

At that time the Master heard the long sound, *Pranava* [OM], that

| 23. He hears the *anahata dhvani,* the music of the spheres. |

combines all the individual sounds of the world, arising spontaneously and unceasingly everywhere in the universe. Some of us heard about this from the Master. He also said later that at that time he could understand the meanings of the voices of beasts, birds, and other creatures.

While practising Tantra the Master saw the Divine Mother vividly in the

| 24. He sees the Divine Mother in the female body and views occult power as filth. |

female body. Towards the end of this period he experienced within himself the manifestation of *anima* and other occult powers. One day, at the request of his nephew Hriday, he went to the Divine Mother in the temple and asked whether it was appropriate to use these powers. She showed him that those powers are as disgusting as the filth of a prostitute and should be shunned completely. He said that from that point on he had a terrible aversion to occult powers.

We remember an incident in connection with the Master's experience of

| 25. The Master and Swami Vivekananda discuss the eight occult powers. |

the eight occult powers. One day he called Swami Vivekananda to come to the Panchavati alone and told him: "Look, I possess the eight main occult powers. But I decided long ago that I would never use them, and I find no need for them. But you will have to preach religion and do many other things. I have decided to give those powers to you. Please accept them." Swamiji asked in reply, "Sir, will they help me to realize God?" When he understood from the Master's reply that they might help to some extent in preaching religion, but would not help him to see God, he declined those powers. Swamiji later said that the Master was extremely pleased by his refusal.

During this period the Master wished to see the bewitching form of the

| 26. His vision of the Divine Mother's bewitching maya. |

Divine Mother's maya. He therefore saw an exquisitely beautiful female form arise from the Ganges and slowly walk to the Panchavati. Gradually that woman became fully pregnant. She gave birth to a beautiful boy in front of him and affectionately nursed the baby. But the next moment that woman became cruel and frightful; she ate the child and then again entered the Ganges.

During this period the Master had innumerable visions of various

| 27. The beauty of the goddess Shodashi. |

goddesses, who had from two hands to as many as ten. Some of those goddesses gave him instructions. We heard from the Master that those forms were extremely lovely, but their beauty could not be compared with that of the form of Sri Rajrajeswari, or Shodashi. He said, "I saw charm and beauty melting from Shodashi's body, spreading out and radiating in all directions." In addition, the Master had the vision of Bhairava and other divine beings.

During the time of his Tantra sadhana the Master had so many divine visions and spiritual experiences every day that it is beyond human capacity to describe all of them here.

We heard from the Master that from the time of his Tantra sadhana, the gate of his sushumna channel was fully opened. As a result his nature became that of a boy. Towards the end of this period he could not keep his cloth or sacred thread on his body, despite some effort to do so. He was unaware of when and where they would fall off. Undoubtedly, this was because his mind was constantly absorbed in the Divine Mother and he therefore lacked body-consciousness. We heard from him many times that he did not discard his clothes intentionally: He did not remain naked to follow the example of ordinary *paramahamsas*. The Master said that at the end of those disciplines his nondualistic attitude towards every object developed so much that the things he had considered despicable and trivial since his childhood now appeared to him to be the purest objects. He remarked: "I came to feel that the leaves of the holy tulsi [basil] and the ordinary *sajina* [drumstick] are equally sacred."

> 28. Succeeding in Tantra sadhana, the Master transcends body-consciousness and attains a childlike nature.

Beginning from this period, and continuing for some years, the Master's physical splendour increased so much that he attracted the attention of all eyes. This created so much disgust in his humble heart that he prayed many times to the Divine Mother to rid him of this celestial beauty, saying: "Mother, I don't need this external beauty at all. Please take it away and grant me in exchange inner spiritual beauty." We have told the reader elsewhere (see III.7.2-4) that this prayer of his was later fulfilled.

> 29. The physical splendour of the Master during his Tantra sadhana.

As the Brahmani helped the Master in Tantra sadhana, so the Master later helped the Brahmani to fulfill her spiritual life. If he had not done that, the Brahmani could not have become established in the divine mood — this we have described elsewhere (see III.8.18-22). The Brahmani's name was Yogeswari, and the Master indicated that she was a part of Yogamaya, the goddess Durga.

> 30. The Bhairavi Brahmani was a part of Yogamaya.

As a result of his Tantra sadhana the Master attained divine powers that brought an important revelation to him: By the grace of the Divine Mother he came to know that in the future many people would come to him for spirituality and would be gratified. He mentioned this to Hriday and the devoted Mathur. At this, Mathur said: "It will be wonderful, Father! Together we shall all enjoy the bliss of your company."

Chapter 12

*J*atadhari and the Master's Sadhana of Vatsalya Bhava

In 1861, AFTER RANI RASMANI PASSED AWAY, Bhairavi Yogeswari arrived at the

Dakshineswar Kali temple. From the end of 1861 to the end of 1863 the Master practised the disciplines of Tantra. Beginning in 1861 Mathur was blessed with the opportunity to serve the Master. Prior to that year, Mathur had tested the Master many times, and he became convinced that Sri Ramakrishna's unique passion for God, his self-control, and his renunciation were genuine. But Mathur could not come to any firm conclusion about whether the Master's spirituality had any connection with his apparent mental illness. However, he was freed of that doubt during the Master's period of practising Tantra. Seeing the repeated manifestation of extraordinary powers in the Master, Mathur became convinced that his Chosen Deity, the Divine Mother, was pleased with him and had therefore taken the form of Sri Ramakrishna to accept his service. Moreover, She was always with him, protecting him. She allowed him to maintain his power and authority over the estate and bestowed increasing honour and glory on him as time went on. He enjoyed success in whatever he undertook. With the Master's grace, he felt protected by divine power. So it was no wonder that during this time Mathur spent money lavishly, acquiring whatever articles the Master needed for his sadhana, serving the deities, and performing charitable works.

At the same time as the Master's spiritual power gradually became manifest through sadhana, his devoted Mathur correspondingly developed enthusiasm, courage, and strength. Depending fully on God, a devotee attains grace and divine protection, and feels indomitable zeal and strength.

Mathur experienced all of this at that time. But the worldly and active Mathur was satisfied with serving the Master and doing virtuous deeds; he was not eager to explore the inner realm and experience spiritual mysteries. Nonetheless, Mathur was fully convinced that the Master was the source of his strength and intelligence, his only hope, his sole recourse in this life and the next, and the true cause of his worldly prosperity and powerful status.

Mathur's activities during this time prove that he felt himself to be exalted

| 2. Mathur's performance of *annameru-vrata*. | by the Master's grace. We find in *Rani Rasmanir Jivan-vrittanta* [the life story of Rani Rasmani] that in 1864 he performed the very expensive *annameru-vrata* [a |

mountain of food distributed among the needy]. Hriday said that during this religious rite, apart from a huge quantity of gold and silver, 1,000 maunds [82,000 pounds] of rice and 1,000 maunds of sesame seeds were distributed amongst the brahmin pandits. Sahachari, a famous performer, sang kirtan, and Rajnarayan sang songs from the Chandi. These and other entertainers made the Dakshineswar temple garden a festival ground for some time. The Master went into ecstasy repeatedly as he listened to the devotional songs. Mathur observed the level of the Master's satisfaction with each singer. Using this as an indication of those performers' skills, he rewarded them accordingly with expensive shawls, silk cloths, and large sums of money.

Sometime before the religious function just described, the Master went to

| 3. The Master meets the Vedic Pandit Padmalochan. | visit Padmalochan, the chief court pandit of the Maharaja of Burdwan. He was attracted by Padma-lochan's vast erudition and humility. The Master |

later told us that Mathur was anxious to bring Padmalochan to the meeting of the pandits that was convened during the annameru-vrata and to offer him gifts. Knowing that Padmalochan had great devotion for the Master, Mathur sent Hriday to him with an invitation. However, for various reasons Padmalochan was unable to accept Mathur's invitation at that time. We have narrated the story of Padmalochan in detail elsewhere (see IV.2.44-52).

After practising the Tantric sadhanas, a desire arose in the Master's mind

| 4. Why the Master undertook Vaishnava sadhanas. | to perform disciplines according to the Vaishnava scriptures.[1] As to the reasons for that attraction, we can identify a few obvious points: First, the devoted |

Bhairavi Brahmani was adept in the disciplines of the five kinds of relationships with God according to the Vaishnava Tantra, and would remain absorbed for long periods of time in one or the other of them. We have already mentioned that when she was absorbed in the mood of Yashoda [Krishna's foster mother], she considered the Master to be Gopala [child

---

1. This was the second time that the Master practised Vaishnava disciplines, but the first time he had the instruction of a guru. Previously he had practised the servant attitude towards God out of his own inner inspiration and attained perfection in that sadhana.

Krishna], and fed him accordingly. So it is no wonder that she encouraged the Master to practise Vaishnavism. Second, the Master was born in a Vaishnava family, so he had a natural inclination for that type of sadhana. And because Vaishnavism was prevalent in the Kamarpukur area, during his childhood the Master had many opportunities to cultivate respect for its sadhanas. The third and most important reason, however, was that throughout his life the Master manifested a wonderful union of both masculine and feminine natures. Under the influence of his masculine nature, he appeared to be as fearless as a lion, powerful, and possessed of an inquisitive intellect and a strong personality. Again, under the influence of his feminine nature, he was endowed with the tender yet firm qualities of a woman, and would perceive and evaluate all things and all beings of the world accordingly. When his feminine nature predominated, he would have deep attachment for some things and intense detachment from others. When overpowered by emotion, he could bear endless pain joyfully. But unlike ordinary people he could do nothing if his heart did not respond.

During the first four years of his sadhana the Master practised different

5. The feminine mood arises in the Master before he practises vatsalya bhava and madhura bhava.

attitudes towards God according to the Vaishnava Tantra, such as the attitude of serenity [*shanta*], of a servant [*dasya*], and sometimes of a friend [*sakhya*] like Krishna's companions Sudama and the other boys of Vrindaban. Although he did all these on his own, he attained success in each attitude. We have already mentioned that the Master practised the attitude of a servant [*dasya-bhakti*] (see II.8.8-9) for a while, following the ideal of Mahavir, the great devotee of Ramachandra, and had a vision of the all-suffering Sita. He now concentrated on practising the attitude of a mother for her child [*vatsalya*] and that of a lover for her or his beloved [*madhura*], two important sadhanas of Vaishnava Tantra. During this period he considered himself to be a female companion of the Divine Mother, and he fanned Her with a *chamara*. Once at the time of Durga Puja, he went to Mathur's Calcutta residence, dressed in women's clothing and surrounded by women to visit the image of the goddess Durga. Under the influence of the feminine mood, he often forgot that he had a male body (see III.7.2). When we began to visit the Master at Dakshineswar, we sometimes noticed the feminine mood in him, but it did not last as long as it had during that earlier period. And there was no need for it to do so, because by the grace of the Divine Mother it had become easy for him to stay in any mood at will — masculine, feminine, or nondual. He assumed any one of those moods as needed for the good of each new devotee.

To understand the greatness of the Master's sadhana, the reader must

6. A discussion on the Master's frame of mind.

reflect upon the extraordinary type of mind that he had from his very birth, how it functioned in day-to-day life, and how it reacted to the spiritual tempest that faced him during the last eight years of his sadhana. We heard from him that upon his arrival at Dakshineswar in 1855 and even for some time afterwards, he believed that he would simply lead a virtuous house-holder's life as his forefathers had. Because he was devoid of ego from his very birth, it never crossed his mind that he was superior to others or endowed with noble qualities. But when he entered the field of action, his extraordinary qualities began to manifest with every step. It was as if an unseen divine power were guiding him at every moment, placing before him in bright colours the transitoriness and worthlessness of all worldly sense objects, and driving him in the opposite direction. Soon the selfless and truth-loving Master became accustomed to moving according to the prompting of that power. So it would have been extremely difficult for him to exert himself even if he had had a strong desire to achieve any worldly object of enjoyment.

This statement will be clear if the reader reflects upon the Master's life-

7. His mind is almost free from past impressions.

long conduct in all matters. As a young man he discontinued his studies when he realized that the goal of a regular education was to make money. He accepted the job of priest in order to help his family financially, but he soon understood that the purpose of worship was quite different — that is to see and serve God — and he became desperate for God-realization. Knowing that complete self-control would be indispensable for God-realization, when he later married he had no physical relationship with his wife. Knowing that someone who saved money could not fully rely on God, he completely uprooted from his mind the idea of saving even trifling things, not to speak of hoarding gold or money. We can make many such points about the Master. Reflecting upon these instances, one can understand how from his childhood the delusions that ordinary people have had little effect on his mind. Moreover, his intellect was so powerful that no adverse tendencies could cause him to deviate from his goal.

In addition, we know that from his childhood the Master was capable of

8. How his mind was endowed with noble qualities before sadhana.

remembering whatever he heard, a capability called *shrutidhar*. Anything he heard, even only once, he could repeat verbatim and retain in his memory forever. The reader already knows that once the Master had heard the stories of the Ramayana, Mahabharata, the Puranas, as well as other songs and dramas, he would rehearse them with his friends in the grazing field of Kamarpukur. So we find that the Master began his life as a spiritual aspirant endowed with a tremendous passion for truth, a fantastic memory, complete concentration, and other divine characteristics. It is hard for ordinary aspirants to acquire those qualities even through lifelong effort. It is therefore no wonder that the Master quickly attained success in his spiritual life. We were dumbfounded when we first heard that he had achieved the goal of each sadhana within three days, because at that time we were completely unaware of his extraordinary mental constitution.

The reader will better understand our statements if we give as examples a

9. A discussion on and examples of the Master's extraordinary mental capacities.

few events of the Master's life. In the beginning of his sadhana the Master discriminated between the real and the unreal, then he threw some coins and lumps of clay into the Ganges, saying "rupee is clay; clay is rupee." Immediately, the attachment to money, which is so deeply ingrained in the human mind, was completely uprooted from his mind forever. When most people encounter a dirty, abominable place, they do not feel clean again until they have bathed; but the Master cleaned such a place [a privy] with his own hands. Instantly, any pride he had in his brahminical caste disappeared from his mind and he became convinced forever that he was not superior to those whom society considered untouchable.

As soon as he was certain that he was a child of the Divine Mother and came to understand that "all women in the world are parts of Her," he could not look at women as objects of enjoyment, nor could he have a physical relationship with his wife. When one reflects upon all these points, it becomes clear that the Master could not have achieved those results if he did not have that extraordinary power of comprehension. When we hear these stories of the Master we are in awe and do not easily believe them. This is so because when we look in our own hearts, we find that our attachment for money would not leave us even if we were to throw money and clay into the water a thousand times. Furthermore, our pride would not be washed away even if we cleaned a filthy latrine a thousand times. And we would not look upon all women as the Divine Mother even if throughout our lives we heard that She dwells in all women. Because our power of understanding is so strongly confined by the chains of past karma, we cannot obtain the same results as the Master despite our best efforts. We attempt to realize God with minds that are devoid of self-control and the power of comprehension and are full of worldly impressions; so it is not possible to succeed as he did.

It is doubtful whether a person endowed with an extraordinary and powerful mind like the Master's comes to this world more than once in the course of four or five hundred years. His mind was fully controlled, concentrated, and free of worldly impressions, and it was motivated by such an intense longing for the Divine Mother that he almost forgot to eat and sleep for eight years. It is impossible for us to imagine the extent to which his mind became so powerful and his keen insight helped him achieve spiritual visions.

We have already mentioned that the service of the Divine Mother in

10. Mathur's service to holy people at the Master's direction.

Dakshineswar did not suffer after Rani Rasmani passed away. The devoted Mathur spent not only the budgeted amount for temple services, but also on many occasions he spent money lavishly for that purpose at the Master's request. In addition to performing the service of gods and goddesses, he was fond of serving holy people. As a devotee of the Master, Mathur learned to look on holy people as representatives of God. During this period, the Master asked him to make arrangements for giving clothes, blankets, water pots and other daily necessities to holy people, in addition to food. Mathur accordingly bought those articles in large quantities and stored them in a room of the temple complex. He ordered the temple officials to distribute them according to the Master's directions. Shortly afterwards, Mathur learned that the Master desired to serve monks of all denominations by providing them with articles necessary for their spiritual practices, so he immediately arranged for this too (see IV.2). It was most likely in 1862 or 1863 when Mathur served monks who visited the temple according to the Master's wishes. As a result, the news spread everywhere of the wonderful hospitality to be found at Rani Rasmani's Kali temple. Although during Rani Rasmani's lifetime, the Kali temple was regarded by itinerant monks as a brief resting place on their way to holy places, its reputation now spread in all directions, and monks of every denomination began coming to Dakshineswar. Pleased with the hospitality there, they would bless the host and leave for their next destination. We have recorded elsewhere what we heard from the Master about those distinguished monks (see IV.2.6-11, 16-17). We relate here the story of Jatadhari, a Ramait monk who initiated the Master in the mantra of Rama and gave him the image of Ramlala [the child Rama]. It was probably in 1864 when he came to Dakshineswar and met the Master.

On many occasions the Master told us about Jatadhari's wonderful love

| 11. Arrival of Jatadhari. |

and devotion for Ramachandra. Jatadhari was very fond of the image of Ramlala. Because he had served that image for a long time, his mind was extremely contemplative and established in an ecstatic state. Before he came to the Master at Dakshineswar, he would actually see the luminous form of Ramlala appearing before him and receiving his loving service. At first he would occasionally have that vision only for a moment, and then be overwhelmed with bliss. In the course of time, as he progressed in his sadhana, that vision became more intense and lasted for longer periods of time. Eventually, the vision became a daily occurrence and Ramlala was his constant companion. This image of Ramlala thus brought a great blessing to his life. Engaging himself in the daily service of Ramlala, Jatadhari travelled freely to various holy places in India and at last arrived at the Dakshineswar Kali temple.

Jatadhari never divulged to anyone that while serving his image of

| 12. The close relationship between the Master and Jatadhari. |

Ramlala he always saw the living form of the child Rama. People knew only that he always served the metal image of Ramlala with steadfast devotion. But at their very first meeting, the Master, a unique spiritual teacher, was able to see behind the façade that Jatadhari showed to the world, revealing the mystery that he kept hidden. That is why the Master showed such respect for Jatadhari from the very beginning of their relationship and gladly supplied all the articles he needed for the service of Ramlala. Moreover, the Master began to stay with Jatadhari for long periods every day and would devoutly observe his service to Ramlala. We have also mentioned elsewhere that the Master behaved that way because Jatadhari used to have the vision of the divine, living form of Ramachandra (see IV.2.11). Thus, the Master's relationship with Jatadhari gradually became intimate and respectful.

We have mentioned earlier that, as part of his sadhana, during this

| 13. At the onset of the feminine mood, the Master begins to practise vatsalya bhava. |

period the Master spent some time in the attitude of a woman. Inspired from within, he dressed in women's clothing and considered himself to be a constant companion of the Divine Mother. He would make garlands and bedeck Her with flowers, and during the summer he would spend long periods of time fanning Her. At his request Mathur procured some new ornaments with which to decorate Her. The Master also spent many hours entertaining the Divine Mother with singing and dancing. After meeting Jatadhari, the Master's love and devotion for Ramachandra were enkindled, and he had the vision of Ramlala's luminous form. As the feminine mood surged, his heart became filled with affection. He felt the same love and attraction for Ramlala that a mother feels for her child. This loving attraction made him sit beside the image of Ramlala, unaware of how time was slipping away. We heard from the Master that the luminous divine child would try to keep him near by means of sweet, childish pranks. Ramlala would wait anxiously for the Master's return when he was away and try to follow him everywhere, despite being forbidden to do so.

The Master's energetic mind could not leave any work half done. This

| 14. When any mood arose, the Master would strive to realize it fully: its pros and cons. |

characteristic of his was as manifest in the subtle realm of the spirit as it was in the gross material realm. Because of this natural proclivity, if his mind became filled with an idea, he could not rest until he had explored it to its ultimate limit. Studying this aspect of his nature some readers may ask: "But is this good? Is it beneficial for a person to pursue any idea that arises at any time and become its puppet?" Although the Master's nature did not lead him astray, his behaviour in this respect should not be followed by most people. Positive and negative thoughts constantly arise in weak human minds. It is not prudent for ordinary people to have such faith in themselves so as to believe that only good thoughts will arise in their minds. Therefore, it should be everyone's duty to harness powerful ideas with the rein of self-control.

Undoubtedly the above view is reasonable, but we must respond none-

<table>
<tr><td>15. For an established aspirant like the Master, the practice of self-control is unnecessary: the reason.</td><td>theless. In no way do we deny that it is unwise for a person to have such self-confidence when that person's mind is attached to lust and gold and is full of greed. It is possible for a shortsighted person to</td></tr>
</table>

raise doubts about the necessity of self-control for ordinary human beings. But it is stated in the Vedas and other scriptures that, by the grace of God, some rare aspirants find self-control to be as easy and as normal as breathing. Their minds become completely free from the attraction of lust and gold, and they harbour only good thoughts. The Master said that when a person completely surrenders to the Divine Mother, Her grace permits no evil thought to rise and capture the mind. "The Divine Mother does not allow that person to take a false step." When a person has reached that state, there is no harm in trusting every thought; rather, those thoughts become beneficial to others.

We become selfish when we are propelled by the little "I" identified with the body, and we would not be satisfied even if we enjoyed all the pleasures of the world. When an individual's little "I" merges forever with God's "Cosmic I," it becomes almost impossible for that person to seek his or her own self-interest. Then the all-benevolent will of the Cosmic God manifests in his or her mind, and various promptings to do good for others arise. This spiritual aspirant then also becomes deeply convinced: "I am the instrument and You are the operator." That person realizes that all desires originate from God's will, so there is no need to hesitate about acting on those desires. It is evident that the actions of such a person benefit others greatly. Such a state occurs early in the lives of all superhuman beings such as the Master. That is why we find in their biographies that they have full faith in their inclinations, and they act accordingly without thinking their actions through. Identifying their small individual wills with the Cosmic Willpower, these beings are capable of detecting and understanding things that are beyond the comprehension of ordinary human minds because those things exist in the Cosmic Mind as subtle ideas.

Again, because they are always completely dependent on the Cosmic

<table>
<tr><td>16. Such aspirants remain unperturbed even when they know of their impending death: some examples.</td><td>Will, these aspirants become so selfless and fearless that despite the fact that they know about their preordained death — and who will bring this about, and in what manner — they never become angry or take any precautionary measures. Instead, they joyfully</td></tr>
</table>

help the perpetrators to fulfill their tasks. The reader will understand if we cite some examples. Ramachandra had a premonition about his destiny, so he banished his wife Sita to the forest even though he knew full well that she was innocent. Rama also forsook his dearest brother, Lakshmana, knowing that doing so would inevitably bring to an end his own divine play in this world.

Knowing beforehand that his Yadu dynasty would be destroyed, Krishna did not make any effort to prevent this destruction, but rather acted in such a way that it might take place at the proper time. In addition, he knew that he would be killed by a hunter, so when the time arrived, he hid his body behind the leaves of a tree and kept his two reddish feet dangling in such a way that when the hunter saw them he would mistake them for a bird and shoot a sharp arrow at him. Krishna blessed and consoled the repentant hunter, then left his body through the power of yoga.

The great Buddha knew that if he accepted the hospitality of the *chandala* he would attain *parinirvana* [the cessation of individual existence], yet he accepted it. He blessed and consoled him, protecting him from others' contempt and reproach. He then became established in Buddhahood. Again, he was aware that his religion would be degraded if women were permitted to join his order as nuns; still he permitted his venerable aunt, Gautami, to take the vows of sannyasa.

Lord Jesus knew that his disciple Judas would accept payment to betray him to his enemies, thus putting an end to his life, yet still his love for Judas remained constant, and he tried to do good to him.

In addition to the examples of avatars, we find many similar events in the lives of persons who were perfected and liberated in life. In order to reconcile the avatars' extraordinary self-effort and complete self-surrender to God's will,

17. No selfish desire arises in such an aspirant's mind.

we must conclude that their self-effort is exercised with the authority of God's will. It is therefore clear that those who are completely guided by God's will have absolutely no selfish desires whatsoever. Their minds reach a high spiritual plane where only unselfish, pure desires can arise. Such aspirants can safely and completely trust their desires and do not incur any blame when acting under their impulses. Some of the sadhanas that the Master practised might not be appropriate for ordinary people to undertake, but extraordinary aspirants would undoubtedly find that these practices enlighten their lives significantly and help to guide them. Their impulses to eat and sleep, and other desires necessary to maintain the body, have been compared by the scriptures with roasted seeds. As seeds of trees and creepers lose their vitality when roasted and can no longer germinate, so the worldly desires of illumined souls are burnt by the fire of self-control and knowledge of the Self and cannot allow them to be attracted by enjoyment and led astray. The Master explained this concept to us in this way: When an iron sword touches the philosopher's stone and turns into gold, it cannot be used to injure anyone even though it retains its original dangerous form.

The sages of the Upanishads say that the thoughts of illumined souls are true. In other words, any ideas that arise in their minds are found to be objectively factual and not otherwise. We could never have believed these words had we not seen through repeated tests how the exalted

18. Such an aspirant's thoughts come true: some examples in the Master's life.

Master's wishes became reality. We have seen that if the Master hesitated to accept a particular food, it would invariably be found upon inquiry to have been polluted. If he suddenly became unable to speak while talking to a person about God, it would later be confirmed that the listener was in fact unfit for such knowledge. If the Master felt either that a person would not experience the truth in this life or that he would make little progress, that would actually prove to be so. If he saw a person and any particular mood or the thought of a particular deity arose in his mind, it would later become known that the individual was a devoted aspirant of that mood or that deity. If he suddenly became inspired to say something to an individual, that person received special insight from his words, and his life was completely changed. Many incidents of this kind can be cited about the Master.

We have mentioned that when Jatadhari came to Dakshineswar the

| 19. The Master is initiated by Jatadhari, practises vatsalya bhava, and attains perfection. | Master, prompted by his inner devotional mood, was practising sadhana in the attitude of a woman. He adopted vatsalya bhava in order to attain the vision of Ramachandra as a sweet child. Long before this he |

had been initiated into the Rama mantra in order to perform worship and to serve Raghuvir, the family deity, but at that time he had practised the attitude of a servant towards his master. He now felt a new affection for Ramachandra, so he wanted to be initiated by a guru in a mantra befitting that mode of sadhana, according to the scriptures. He was anxious to realize the ultimate goal of that sadhana. Jatadhari was an adept in the mantra of Ramlala, and knowing the Master's eagerness in this regard, he gladly initiated him into the mantra of his Chosen Deity. With that mantra and Jatadhari's instruction, the Master became absorbed in sadhana, and within a few days had the uninterrupted vision of Ramlala. Adopting vatsalya bhava, he became absorbed in the meditation of that divine form and soon he saw that: *Yo Ram Dasharathka beta, Ohi Ram ghat-ghatme leta; Ohi Ram jagat pasera, Ohi Ram sabse neyara.* [Rama, who is a son of Dasharatha, is in every being; the same Rama is immanent in the universe and yet transcends it.]

The meaning of this couplet is that Ramachandra is not only Dasharatha's son but also exists as the individual soul in each body. Although He has entered the universe and has become all things, He is distinct from everything in this universe, completely free of maya, and ever-present in His attributeless nature. On many occasions we heard the Master reciting this Hindi couplet.

In addition to giving the Master initiation, Jatadhari, before leaving

| 20. Jatadhari presents the image of Ramlala to the Master. | Dakshineswar, presented him with the image of Ramlala that he had served with steadfast devotion for such a long time, because that living image had |

expressed his wish to live henceforth with the Master. We have described in detail elsewhere the wonderful divine play of that image with both Jatadhari and the Master, so it is unnecessary to recount that here (see IV.2.11-12,16-17).

We have mentioned that the Bhairavi Brahmani was at Dakshineswar

21. The Master receives help from the Bhairavi Brahmani during his Vaishnava sadhana.

when the Master focussed his efforts on achieving perfection in the affectionate attitude and realizing its ultimate goal. We heard from the Master that the Brahmani was adept in the sadhana of the five moods according to the Vaishnava Tantra. The Master did not tell us clearly whether he received any help from her while he was practising vatsalya bhava and madhura bhava. We did hear from the Master and Hriday that the Brahmani, under the influence of vatsalya bhava, would sometimes serve the Master as Gopala. Therefore, it can be inferred that the Master must have received some help from her when he adopted this attitude towards Gopala and achieved its ultimate goal, and while he was practising madhura bhava. It can also be admitted that the Master saw the Brahmani practising those modes of sadhana and heard them eulogized. Thus, he developed a strong desire in his mind to practise those sadhanas, though he may not have received any direct help from her.

Chapter 13

The Quintessence of
$\mathcal{M}$adhura Bhava

It is extremely difficult for one who is not a spiritual aspirant to understand the

| 1. An aspirant's intense inner struggle and goal. |

life story of a spiritual aspirant, because only sadhana can unveil the mystery of the subtle spiritual realm. In that spiritual realm the alluring sense objects of the world cannot be perceived; and time itself — which pertains to the external objects and events in human life — ceases to exist. In that place there is none of the frantic effort we see among worldly people: Driven by their desires, they trample upon others in the struggle to acquire more sense pleasures, and other deluded people even praise their actions as heroic and great. In the spiritual realm, an aspirant can witness his or her mind and view within it the endless current of impressions gathered there from past lives. Tormented by the conflicts of worldly life, the aspirant becomes attracted to spiritual ideals and seeks a higher goal. That person then focuses on proceeding towards the goal, resolving to fight constantly against all adverse impressions from the past. Gradually the aspirant withdraws from all external sense objects and becomes completely absorbed within his or her own self. Diving deep into the mind's inner recesses, the aspirant experiences mental states that become ever more subtle, finally reaching the innermost Self — from which all ideas and I-consciousness originate, and in which they remain. The aspirant then realizes the Reality that is "soundless, intangible, formless, incorruptible, and one without a second," remaining identified with It. This is the state of samadhi. As long as the mind is not free of all impressions, it continues to function: The aspirant comes down from samadhi to experience the external world again, reversing the process

281

through which he or she ascended to nondual Reality. Thus, the mind of an aspirant continually moves from the absolute to the relative and back again.

From ancient times to the present day, the spiritual history of the world has recorded a few individuals whose natural abode was the state of samadhi. However, for the good of humanity they forced themselves to remain confined for some time to the plane of the external world. The more we study the history of Sri Ramakrishna's sadhana, the better we will understand that he belongs in that category. If the reader does not have that impression while reading this book, the author is at fault. The Master told us repeatedly: "I force myself to hold on to one or two trivial desires in order to keep my mind in this world for your sake. Otherwise, its natural tendency is to remain united to and identified with the indivisible One."

2. The natural inclination of extraordinary aspirants such as Sri Ramakrishna is to remain in nirvikalpa samadhi.

Some ancient sages described the indivisible, nondual Reality experienced during samadhi as being the extinction of everything, or "void" (sunya); others explained it as the meeting ground of everything, or "full" (purna). But in truth, both were describing the same experience. All the sages indicate It as being the source as well as the dissolution of everything. Buddha described Reality as void, the extinction of everything, whereas Shankara taught that the same thing is full, the unity of everything. We come to this conclusion if we study the philosophies of Buddha and Shankara, disregarding the views of later Buddhist teachers.

3. Reality can be described as being either "void" or "full."

The plane of nondual consciousness, described as either void or full, has been explained in the Upanishads or Vedanta as being beyond thought. When an aspirant is fully established in that state, his mind transcends the entire realm of God's creation, preservation, and dissolution and becomes absorbed in blissful existence. Entering the spiritual realm, an aspirant establishes a permanent relationship with God through shanta, dasya, and other attitudes. Nondual knowledge itself, however, is transcendental and therefore distinct from the five spiritual moods. People experience nondual knowledge when they become completely indifferent to all enjoyments of this world and the next, surpassing even the gods in purity. Aspirants achieve the goal by realizing Nirguna Brahman, which is the substratum of the entire universe — including Ishwara, the creator, preserver, and destroyer of the world.

4. The nature of nonduality.

In addition to nondual knowledge and its goal of Nirguna Brahman, we find in the dualistic spiritual world five kinds of attitudes, or moods: shanta [peace and serenity], dasya [attitude of the servant towards the master], sakhya [attitude of friendship], vatsalya [attitude of a parent towards a child], and madhura [attitude of a lover

5. God-realization through the five attitudes: shanta, dasya, sakhya, vatsalya, and madhura.

towards the beloved]. The goal attainable through each attitude is Ishwara, or Saguna Brahman. A spiritual aspirant adopts one of these five moods in order to experience God, who is all-powerful and all-controlling, and who is by nature eternal, pure, illumined, and free. God, who is all-knowing and the repository of all attitudes, sees the aspirant's sincerity and one-pointed devotion. To nourish the aspirant's devotion, God assumes a form appropriate to the aspirant's devotional mood and becomes manifest. Thus, in different ages God assumes various luminous forms according to the devotees' temperaments, and even incarnates to fulfill their desires. We learn this from the scriptures.

Having been born in this world, human beings are connected to one

6. The nature of the five attitudes and how they help spiritual aspirants.

another through their relationships; the five attitudes, such as shanta, dasya, and so on, are the subtle and pure forms of those earthly relations. In this world a person experiences particular relationships with father, mother, husband, wife, male friend, female friend, master, servant, son, daughter, king, subject, guru, disciple, and so on. It is considered a duty to behave with all except enemies in a gentle and respectful manner. Teachers of the bhakti path classified these relations into the five attitudes mentioned above and advised people to adopt one of them according to their aptitude, then to focus on God. Because people are already familiar with the five basic relationships, it becomes easy for them to try to know God by adopting one of them. But that is not all. Before aspirants set out on the spiritual path, those five attitudes are associated with worldly relationships and will raise various thoughts of attachment and aversion in their minds, causing them to behave badly. But as those attitudes [and the emotions that arise from them] are related to God, they will drive aspirants forcibly towards the goal of God-realization. Take for example, lust, a mental disease and the cause of great misery: It will now keep them engaged in desiring the vision of God. As for anger, it will be directed against those objects and persons who stand in the way of that goal. Aspirants will madly crave God's wonderful love and beauty and be enchanted by them. They will be anxious to achieve the spiritual splendour of those blessed souls who have attained the vision of God.

People did not learn to apply those five attitudes to their relationship with

7. Love is the means of these five sadhanas, and the personal form of God is the goal.

God at any particular time or from any particular person. In every age many great teachers have been born who engaged themselves in realizing God by practising one, two, or more moods. They loved God in order to make Him their own, and taught others to do the same. It is evident from studying the extraordinary lives of great teachers that the practice of these spiritual attitudes is founded on love alone, and this love has always been focussed on some personal form of God. Until an aspirant can experience nondual Reality, he or she must conceive of or experience some limited form of the Personal God.

It becomes clear when we consider the nature of love that it gradually oblit-

8. Love brings an end to the awareness of power, and that is the test of all five attitudes.

erates the feeling of difference that can be created by an inequality in power between two lovers. Love also removes by degrees the awareness of God's limitless powers from the mind of an aspirant who is engaged in practising those moods, and accordingly teaches that aspirant to regard God as being simply his or her own beloved. So the aspirant who treads this path makes God entirely his or her own through love, and then does not hesitate to issue demands, to importune, and even to scold Him, or to complain that his or her feelings have been wounded. That particular attitude which makes the aspirant forget God's powers and makes him or her experience only God's love and sweetness is considered to be the highest. Based on this criterion, the teachers of bhakti, having compared the characteristics of the five moods, declared madhura bhava to be the highest. However, these teachers unanimously admitted that every spiritual attitude is capable of leading the aspirant to the realization of God.

A study of the history of religions shows that in the final stage of each of

9. Both devotional scriptures and Sri Ramakrishna's life testify to the fact that each attitude ultimately leads to the experience of nondual Reality.

the five attitudes, an aspirant forgets himself or herself and becomes happy when the Beloved is pleased. Moreover, when the aspirant is separated from the Beloved, he or she remains absorbed in the thought of God and sometimes even loses the awareness of his or her own existence. It is seen in the Bhagavata and other devotional scriptures that the gopis of Vrindaban would not only forget their own existence but also from time to time would become completely identified with their beloved Krishna. It is well known that the devotional books of Christianity[1] record that while absorbed in meditation on the Passion of Christ some mystics developed stigmata, that is, blood appearing from the parts of their bodies where Christ had been wounded. So it is evident that at the culmination of each attitude, the aspirant becomes completely immersed in the thought of the Beloved. United then with God out of intense love, the aspirant finally realizes nondual Reality. Sri Ramakrishna's unique life of sadhana has shed wonderful light on this matter. After practising each spiritual mood he attained its goal and became identified with the Beloved. Totally forgetting his own existence, he then realized nondual Reality.

One may question how practising these spiritual attitudes can help the human mind realize nondual Reality, which is beyond all thought. No spiritual attitude can arise, exist, or develop without the awareness of at least two persons.

1. See the lives of St. Francis of Assisi and of St. Catherine of Sienna.

This point is valid. But the more a spiritual mood develops, the more it

10. The attainment of nonduality by means of the five moods: objection and response.

spreads its influence over the aspirant's mind and gradually erases all contrary thoughts. When a particular mood is fully developed, the aspirant's concentrated mind during meditation sometimes forgets "You" (God, the Master) and "I" (the servant), and also the relationship between the two. Then the mind becomes identified through love with the Master, who is denoted by the word "You." The great teachers of India have said that the human mind cannot simultaneously experience both "You" and "I" and the relationship between them. The mind experiences in one moment the entity denoted by "You" and in the next the entity denoted by "I." As it continually travels rapidly back and forth between those entities, the idea of a relationship develops. Then it seems that the mind simultaneously experiences both entities and the relation between them. When a spiritual attitude has matured and become predominant in an aspirant's mind, the mind's restlessness is subdued and it gradually grasps what has been stated above. As the mind becomes free from thought waves during meditation, it gradually comprehends that it saw nondual Reality from two angles and mistook It as two entities, "You" and "I."

It is amazing how much time aspirants spent in making tremendous

11. The predominance of different modes of sadhana in different eras.

efforts to develop each spiritual attitude and thereby experience nondual Reality. When we study the history of religions as it is recorded in the scriptures in any particular age, we see that aspirants predominantly practised an attitude that was specific to that period; by means of that spiritual mood prominent aspirants experienced God, and rare ones realized the indivisible nondual Brahman. We find that shanta bhava prevailed during the Vedic and Buddhist periods. In the Upanishadic Age, shanta bhava evolved into nonduality, its culmination; and the *dasya* and *apatya*[2] (God as Father) moods were developed. In the Epic Age of the Ramayana and the Mahabharata, the shanta and dasya moods became combined with motiveless action and evolved to a great extent. In the Tantric Age, the apatya mood (God as Mother) and a form of madhura bhava were prevalent; and in the Vaishnava Age, sakhya, vatsalya, and madhura bhava spread widely.

In the religious history of India, it is seen that all five spiritual attitudes

12. The full development of the five bhavas in India and abroad.

developed fully and flourished along with the nondual attitude; but we find in the religious communities of other countries that only the shanta, dasya, and apatya (God as Father) moods flourished. Although the songs of Solomon, the royal sage, are endowed with sakhya bhava and madhura bhava, the Jewish, Christian, and Muslim communities misunderstand them

---

2. *Apatya* means *child*. Apatya bhava is looking upon God as Father or Mother.

and attribute different meanings to them. The sakhya and madhura moods are practised to a great extent among members of the Sufi sect within Islam, but Muslims in general consider such devotion to God as being contrary to the Koran. Among Christians, followers of the Catholic religion venerate the image of Mother Mary, but this practice is not explicitly connected with the motherhood of God. It has therefore not been as effective as the worship of the Divine Mother in India, and has not enabled aspirants to realize the indivisible Satchidananda and to see every woman as a manifestation of the Divine. So the Catholic's idea of the Motherhood of God has disappeared midway, like the subterranean river Phalgu.

We mentioned earlier that when an aspirant is attracted to God and 13. The signs of an aspirant's depth of mood. adopts a particular spiritual mood, he gradually becomes absorbed in it. The aspirant then withdraws from the external world and merges within his own Self. While an aspirant merges into samadhi, past impressions in the mind stand in the way, push him or her back towards the surface plane, and try to keep the mind focussed outward. Therefore, an ordinary person who carries past impressions cannot become absorbed in even one spiritual mood, though he or she may struggle a whole lifetime to do so. An aspirant in that situation first becomes discouraged, then depressed, and finally loses faith in God. He or she then comes to regard worldly sense enjoyments as being of primary importance and again pursues them. Aversion for external objects, absorption in meditation on a Chosen Deity, and ecstasy arising from a spiritual mood are therefore considered to be the criteria by which an aspirant's progress towards the goal is measured.

It is not possible to understand the enormity of the battle that takes place 14. The Master's success in all spiritual attitudes was unique. within an aspirant's mind unless one has experienced the tremendous resistance that rises up from deep-rooted past impressions. That resistance begins when progress is being made in the absorption of a spiritual mood. Anyone who has faced this knows how difficult it is to become established in a spiritual mood. It is therefore amazing to learn that in a short time Sri Ramakrishna became completely established in each and every spiritual mood, one after another, a feat that seems to be beyond human capacity.

Because ordinary people could not understand the subtle truths of the 15. A discussion on the fact that the great teachers' spiritual practices have not been recorded. spiritual realm, they did not record completely the history of the spiritual practices of many renowned religious leaders, known as avatars. As we study their life stories, we find elaborate descriptions of how they renounced all worldly things at the threshold of sadhana, and how after attaining perfection they manifested their wonderful spiritual powers in order to benefit others who were still attached to the world. We find only hints about how during their sadhana they continued their intense inner struggles to uproot and destroy all past impressions from their minds, and how they finally achieved complete mastery over themselves. Whenever those struggles were described, so many allegorical expressions and exaggerations were used that it is extremely difficult for us to determine the truth in the various records. The reader will understand what we mean from the following examples.

We find in the scriptures that many times Krishna practised austerities to (1) Krishna | achieve specific powers to use for the well-being of humanity. But there is no description of his inner struggle to be free from adverse thoughts except that for some time he remained standing on one leg, living on water or air, in order to attain perfection in that respect.

We find an exhaustive account of Buddha's renunciation, his departure (2) Buddha | from family and kingdom, and later the establishment of the wheel of dharma; however, details regarding his sadhana are not available. But at least some of his spiritual moods are recorded. This information is not available for other religious heroes. According to the records, when Buddha resolved to attain perfection, he practised moderation in eating and in performing austerities, and meditated for six long years without leaving his seat. Then, controlling the inner breath, he practised *asphanaka* meditation and attained samadhi. However, when Buddha's biographer described his mental struggle to uproot past impressions from his mind, he introduced the story of his fight with Mara [the Evil One], relating the struggle as though it were an external event.

The history of Jesus' sadhana is nearly unrecorded. His biographers document (3) Jesus | only a few incidents of his life up to the age of twelve, then record how at the age of thirty he was baptized by John, a holy man. They describe how he then entered a desert alone and practised austerity and meditation for forty days, during which time he was tempted by Satan but emerged victorious. It is said that after returning from the desert he engaged himself in doing good for the well-being of humanity. Afterwards, he lived in his body for only three years. There is no record of what he did from his twelfth to his thirtieth year.

Although the chronological events of Shankara's life are available to a (4) Shankara | great extent, one must infer the story of his inner attitude.

Many events of Chaitanya's sadhana have been recorded, but ordinary (5) Chaitanya. Sri Ramakrishna on the ultimate truth of madhura bhava. | people cannot properly understand the story of his unworldly and exalted love of God, because it has been described metaphorically as the amorous sport of Radha and Krishna. Of course it must be admitted that Chaitanya and his main followers recorded in minute detail, though in metaphorical language, the states that gradually appear in an aspirant's mind from the beginning to almost the final unfolding of each attitude, in particular sakhya, vatsalya, and madhura. But those who chronicled these experiences did not express this supreme truth: By adopting any of those three moods, the aspirant's mind ultimately becomes united with the beloved Lord and then merges into nondual Reality. If they mention this at all, they merely hint at the truth and caution spiritual aspirants against it by referring to it as a lower state. In the present age, Sri Ramakrishna's unique life and the history of his unprecedented sadhana clearly teaches us the ultimate truth and enables us to comprehend that all spiritual traditions of all religious communities worldwide lead the minds of their aspirants to the same goal. Apart from many other things to be learnt from his life, we have realized the aforesaid truth by his grace. This has made our religious outlook broad and given us a hint of religious harmony; for that reason we are undoubtedly and eternally indebted to him.

Madhura bhava is the main gift of Chaitanya and the Vaishnava teachers
16. Madhura bhava and Vaishnava teachers.
to the spiritual world. If they had not demonstrated this path, so many people would not have been able to adopt it as a means of God-realization; consequently, they could not have achieved peace and bliss. The Vaishnavas first understood that Krishna's play in Vrindaban with the *gopas* [cowherds] and gopis was not meaningless; they then tried to help others understand this. If Chaitanya had not been born, Vrindaban would be regarded today as an ordinary forest.

Following the Western method of recording external events only, modern
17. Regarding the historicity of Krishna's play in Vrindaban: objection and response.
historians may say: "There is no proof that Krishna's play in Vrindaban actually took place as you say. Therefore, all of your expressions of emotion, your laughter and your tears, as well as your ecstasy and mahabhava — that intense love of God — are founded on nothing at all." The Vaishnava teachers reply: "Do you have any infallible evidence that what was described in the Puranas was never enacted? Until we find certain proof that your historical methods have brought to light the events that took place at this ancient time, we shall say your doubt is unfounded. Moreover, if you ever were to succeed in proving your case, that would not damage our faith at all. It would not have any effect on the eternal play of God in the eternal Vrindaban. That mystical, divine play of God will remain forever in the spiritual realm. If you want to see that wonderful, divine romance between Radha and Krishna in the abode of your consciousness, you must first make your body, mind, and speech free from lust, then learn to perform selfless service by following the example of any one of Radha's companions. Then you will realize that Vrindaban, the playground of Krishna, is ever established in your heart and that divine play is continually enacted there."

After experiencing the reality of the spiritual realm, if one has not learned

18. To understand Krishna's play in Vrindaban, one must first understand the mystery of devotional moods: the Master's comment.

to disregard external events, and has not studied the history of devotional moods, one will not be able to appreciate the authenticity and enjoy the sweetness of Krishna's play in Vrindaban. When Sri Rama-krishna spoke enthusiastically about the divine play of Krishna, he would notice that his young English-educated disciples did not appreciate his words. He would then say to them: "Look, why don't you accept the attraction of Radha for Krishna in that divine drama? One attains God when one develops that kind of desire for God. Don't you see how the gopis became impassioned for Krishna? They set aside their husbands, children, and families, gave up any consideration for their reputations, honour and dishonour, shame and hatred, and set aside all concern for public opinion and social propriety! This is the way one attains God." The Master also said: "Unless one is free of lust, one cannot understand Radha, the embodiment of mahabhava. When the gopis saw Satchidananda Krishna, they would lose body-consciousness as they experienced bliss a million times more intense than sexual union. Could the thought of trivial sensual pleasure arise then in their minds? The divine lustre of Krishna's body would touch them, making them experience more ecstasy in every pore of their bodies than sexual pleasure could ever give them!"

Once Swami Vivekananda raised an objection before the Master regarding the historical authenticity of the play of Radha and Krishna in Vrindaban, attempting to prove that it had not actually occurred. The Master said in reply: "Well, take it for granted that there never was any such person as Radha, and that a loving spiritual aspirant invented that character. Will you not grant that when that aspirant imagined Radha's character, he became completely absorbed in the mood of Radha? At that time the aspirant became Radha, forgetting himself, and thus the play of Vrindaban was truly enacted on the external plane."

In fact, although innumerable objections regarding Krishna's play of love at Vrindaban may be raised, the madhura bhava that Chaitanya and other Vaishnava teachers first discovered and then demonstrated through their pure lives will nonetheless remain forever. The true aspirant who embraces this attitude, that of the lover towards the beloved, will always consider himself or herself to be the wife and God to be the husband, and will be blessed with His vision. At the culmination of this spiritual attitude, the aspirant becomes established in the pure nondual Brahman.

Although it is natural and easy for women to practise a sadhana that

19. Why Chaitanya encouraged men to practise madhura bhava.

requires one to relate to God as husband, it seems to be unnatural for men. The question naturally arises in one's mind: Why did Chaitanya introduce such an unusual sadhana to the world? In reply, we say that whatever act the avatar

of an age performs is for the good of humanity; Chaitanya therefore introduced this mode of sadhana in order to benefit the whole world. During
Chaitanya's time, spiritual aspirants were eager to experience God as their
Beloved. Keeping that in mind, Chaitanya guided them along the path of
madhura bhava. It cannot be possible that the ever-free Chaitanya, an incarnation of God, practised that attitude for his own good and then introduced
it as a perfect ideal for society. Sri Ramakrishna said: "As the elephant's
external teeth [tusks] are for attacking enemies and its internal ones are for
chewing food to get physical nourishment, so Chaitanya had two kinds of
moods: one external and the other internal. Externally, he did good for
human beings with the help of madhura bhava; and internally he had
reached the culmination of his love for God and was established in nondual
Brahman, enjoying infinite bliss."

Historians say that towards the end of the Buddhistic period the Vajra-

20. The spiritual
condition of India at that
time, and how
Chaitanya elevated it.

yana school prevailed in India. The teachers of this
Buddhist school preached the following doctrine:
When aspirants strive for nirvana, after becoming
free from desires, and move towards merging into
the great Void through meditation, the goddess Niratma appears before
them and keeps them united with Her own body, preventing them from
proceeding further. At that time a man may have no sensation in his gross
body, but Niratma makes him enjoy the essence of all sense pleasures
through his subtle body. It is no wonder that this doctrine — that one must
shun physical pleasure in order to enjoy subtle sense pleasures uninterruptedly in the realm of ideas — was distorted in the course of time. People
understood the goal of religious practice to be the enjoyment of uninterrupted gross sense pleasures; as a result, adultery spread throughout the
country.

When Chaitanya appeared, uneducated people in India were following
various distorted doctrines of Buddhism and were divided into many sects.
Most of society's upper classes were attempting to achieve occult powers
and sensual enjoyment by means of a specific form of meditation on and
worship of the Divine Mother that evolved from a distorted form of the
Vamachara path of Tantra. Nonetheless, there were sincere aspirants who
were eager to attain uninterrupted bliss by following the spiritual moods,
but they had no one to guide them. Chaitanya, who had practised various
devotional attitudes in his life, placed in front of these sincere aspirants the
ideals of extraordinary renunciation and purity. Furthermore, he demonstrated that if one becomes pure and holy and worships God as husband,
thinking of oneself as wife, one will certainly achieve uninterrupted divine
bliss in the subtle spiritual realm. Chaitanya also preached the glory of God's
name to ordinary people and encouraged them to practise japa and sing
kirtan. Thus, by his grace many confused and aimless followers of some of

the Buddhist sects that had become distorted again made progress in a true spiritual path. Although at first many followers of the corrupt Vamachara sect openly opposed him, they were later attracted by his wonderful, ideal life. They began to practise detachment and tried to attain the vision of the Divine Mother through motiveless worship. While chronicling the divine life of Chaitanya, some biographers have specifically mentioned that even the nihilist Buddhists rejoiced at his birth.[3]

Satchidananda Krishna is the Supreme Self and the sole Purusha, or the

21. The main significance of madhura bhava.

male principle. Because all gross objects and all subtle objects of the world and all beings (jivas) originate from His all-powerful Prakriti, or the female principle, they can be considered His wives. When jivas become pure and holy, and wholeheartedly worship God as their husband, by His grace they attain liberation and uninterrupted bliss. This is the sum and substance of madhura bhava as preached by Chaitanya. All of the devotional moods come together in mahabhava, the most intense ecstatic love of God. Radha, the foremost gopi, is the embodiment of mahabhava; and each gopi is endowed with one, two, or more moods within mahabhava. Therefore, an aspirant who masters those spiritual moods by practising sadhana in the manner of the gopis of Vrindaban finally becomes blessed with a glimpse of the great bliss that originates from mahabhava. The ultimate goal of madhura bhava is to practise the mood of Radha, the embodiment of mahabhava,[4] to completely shun any desire for personal happiness, and to take joy in all respects at the happiness of Krishna.

According to the rules of society, a married couple is regulated by caste

22. One should adopt the same all-devouring love for God that a lover has for a paramour.

and family lineage and by rules of appropriate conduct and concern for social propriety and public opinion. Living within the bounds of these rules, a married couple follows the norms of propriety, and each partner makes a determined effort to sacrifice self-interest for the other's happiness. While observing the rigid rules of society, a married woman does not hesitate on many occasions to set aside or limit her display of affection towards her husband. But the loving behaviour of a paramour is different. Quite often, out of exuberant love, that woman disregards all social

---

3. See *Chaitanya-mangala*.
4. The state in which a lover is extremely anxious and fearful that Krishna may become ill, even when he is well, is called the *rudha* stage of mahabhava. At that time all *sattvic* feelings are as consuming as a raging fire. In the *adhirudha* stage of mahabhava, there is no raging fire but an indescribable feeling that mixes bliss with pain, which arises respectively from union with or separation from Krishna. The lover feels that, compared to union with Krishna, the joy of millions of universes is negligible; compared to separation from Krishna, the pain of all snake bites and the stings of scorpions is insignificant. The adhirudha state manifests in two ways: *Modana,* or gladness, and *madana,* or intoxication. — *Bhakti Granthavali* by Vishwanath Chakrabarty

conventions and does not hesitate to unite with her beloved, risking the loss of everything offered by society. The Vaishnava teachers have advised aspirants to adopt that all-devouring, loving relationship with God. The scriptures describe Radha of Vrindaban as the wife of Ayan Ghosh who renounced everything for her love of Krishna.

The Vaishnava teachers have described madhura bhava as the combined essences of the four other moods, plus something more. The female lover serves her beloved as if she were a maidservant. She always gives him good counsel and becomes an equal partner of his joy and

> 23. Madhura bhava is the sum total of all other moods, plus something more.

misery, like a friend. She nourishes his body and mind and invariably thinks of his welfare as would a mother. Thus, forgetting herself, she loves and entertains her beloved, filling his heart with joy and peace. The woman who forgets herself out of love and focuses completely on the welfare and happiness of her beloved has the highest kind of love. She has been described by the devotional scriptures as *samartha*, the excellent lover. All other types of love are tinged with selfishness and fall into one of two classes: *samanjasa*, the balanced, and *sadharani*, the ordinary. The woman of the former class equally desires her own happiness and that of her beloved; the woman of the latter class considers her beloved dear only for the sake of her own happiness.

Chaitanya taught spiritual aspirants to shun sense enjoyments as they would avoid deadly poison and to love God in the manner of the beloved of Krishna. He also preached the glory of God's name, thus attempting to put an

> 24. How Chaitanya did good to humanity through madhura bhava.

end to adultery and do good for the country. Consequently, at that time his philosophy and teachings showed the true path to those who were lost, brought the outcast into a newly formed society, and incorporated those who were outside the castes [non-Hindus] into a new caste, that of the devotees of God. His message set before all religious communities the high ideals of purity and detachment and brought immense benefit to society.

As the love and union of a man and a woman generate physical and mental changes in them, so "eight sattvic modifications"[5] actually become manifest in a pure aspirant who thinks of and meditates intensely on the Lord of the Universe. This fact was clearly proven in Chaitanya's divine life. His teachings on madhura bhava incorporated the science of rhetoric (*alankara shastra*) into spiritual scriptures and gave spiritual colouring to the sensual language of literature, making it enjoyable to aspirants and also

---

5. When spiritual emotion agitates the body and the mind, eight sattvic modifications manifest: stupor, perspiration, horripilation, choking of voice, trembling, paleness of complexion, tears, and loss of consciousness. On the basis of the gradation of happiness, they are subdivided into five: smouldering, flaming, burning, glowing, and incandescent.

beneficial for their spiritual progress. A person who practises shanta bhava must give up lust, anger, and other lower thoughts, but with madhura bhava aspirants can divert those impulses towards God to make Him their own, thus making their spiritual journey easier.

To the Westernized young generation, madhura bhava appears to be

> 25. A Vedantin adopts the sadhana of madhura bhava because it is beneficial to an aspirant.

unnatural and unbecoming for those who have male bodies, but a Vedantin can quickly ascertain its proper value. The Vedantin knows that because of deeply ingrained habits practised over a very long time, all thoughts become *samskaras* [deep impressions] in the human mind. It is due to these accumulated impressions, many carried over from past lives, that people perceive the universe of diversity instead of the one nondual Brahman. If by God's grace a person becomes fully convinced even for a moment that the world does not exist, it will instantly disappear from his or her sense perception. The world exists because people think it does. I think of myself as a man, so I remain a man; and another person thinks of herself as a woman, so she remains a woman. Again it is evident that when an idea becomes predominant in the human mind, it eclipses contrary ideas and gradually destroys them. Similarly, a spiritual aspirant superimposes madhura bhava on God and this overwhelming mood covers other moods and gradually wipes them out. This method, according to a Vedantin, is like using one thorn to remove another thorn from one's foot. Based on the sum total of impressions in the mind, one feels "I am embodied." The most powerful impression that arises from the body-idea is: "I am a man," or "I am a woman." But when a male aspirant takes God to be his husband and constantly thinks of himself as wife, that aspirant becomes capable of forgetting his male nature. He can then easily discard the idea "I am a wife" and reach that state which is beyond all moods. So it is evident to a Vedanta philosopher that if an aspirant is perfect in madhura bhava, that person comes very close to that transcendental state.

One may ask: Is it the goal of an aspirant to attain the mahabhava of

> 26. The ultimate aim of practising madhura bhava is to attain the mood of Radha.

Radha? The present Vaishnava teachers do not advocate it. They say that it is possible for an aspirant to attain the attitude of a friend, like the gopis, but not the mahabhava of Radha. However, it seems that mahabhava is actually the aspirant's goal; the difference between the mahabhava of Radha and that of the gopis is one of degree, not of kind. The gopis, like Radha, also worshipped Satchidananda Krishna as their husband. Seeing Krishna's supreme happiness while with Radha, they were always eager to arrange their union in order to make their Beloved happy. In addition, although Rupa, Sanatana, Jiva, and other early Vaishnava teachers spent their lives in serving different images of Krishna in Vrindaban in order to achieve fulfillment in madhura bhava, they never installed Radha's image next to Krishna. It seems that they considered themselves to be Radha, so they did not need an image of her.

Aspirants who want to study in detail the madhura bhava of Vaishnava Tantra should review the works of Rupa, Sanatana, Jiva, and other earlier Vaishnava teachers, and also the songs on *purvaraga, dana, mana,* and *mathura*[6] by Vidyapati, Chandidas, and other Vaishnava poets. We have briefly discussed the essence of madhura bhava so that the reader can more easily understand how the Master achieved the highest excellence in practising this mood.

6. *Purvaraga* is the stage of courting, or when an attraction is felt even before acquaintance with the lover. *Dana* is offering gifts to the beloved. *Mana* is an essential ingredient in lovemaking, and marks the stage when the course of progressive intimacy is jolted by a misunderstanding. This can be removed by sweet words, presents, or praise. *Mathura* is a cycle of songs expressing the pangs of separation and sorrow that the gopis felt when Krishna left Vrindaban and went to Mathura. — *Translator*

Chapter 14

The *M*aster's Practice of
Madhura Bhava

WHENEVER A SPIRITUAL MOOD AROSE IN THE MASTER'S one-pointed mind, he would

1. From childhood, the nature of the Master's mind was to be absorbed in spiritual moods.

become absorbed in it for some time. That mood would fully occupy his mind, eradicating all else and transforming his body into a suitable instrument for its manifestation. We heard that he possessed this nature from childhood; while we were visiting Dakshineswar regularly we also witnessed this phenomenon. We observed that when his mind was absorbed in a particular mood — which arose from listening to a song or in some other manner — he felt an excruciating pain if someone sang a different song or spoke in a different mood. Evidently he experienced pain because his thought waves were suddenly obstructed from flowing towards that particular goal. When a current of thought flows forcefully toward a particular object, the great sage Patanjali called that mental state *savikalpa samadhi*; the devotional scriptures describe it as *bhava samadhi*. From childhood, the Master's mind was accustomed to remaining in that type of samadhi.

The nature of the Master's absorbed mind took a new turn when he

2. How his nature changed during sadhana.

began his sadhana. His mind no longer shifted from one mood to another at short intervals. Rather, when his mind became absorbed in a particular mood, it would remain there until he reached the culmination of that mood and caught a glimpse of nondual Reality. For example, until he had reached the acme of the dasya bhava, he did not start to practise the sadhana of God as Mother prescribed by Tantra; again, without attaining the highest experience of Tantra sadhana, he did not begin to practise vatsalya bhava. This pattern is evident when we study the chronology of his sadhana.

During the Brahmani's visit, the Master's mind was absorbed in medita-

3. Previously the Master was not fond of madhura bhava.

tion on God as Mother. At that time he saw the veritable manifestation of the Divine Mother in all objects and beings of the world, especially in women. Therefore it is clear why he addressed the Brahmani as "Mother" when he first met her, and why he sometimes sat on her lap like a child and ate food from her hand. Hriday told us that sometimes when the Brahmani was in the mood of the gopis and would sing songs based on a loving relationship with Krishna, the Master would tell her that he did not relish that mood and would ask her to sing about the Divine Mother instead. Realizing the Master's mental condition, the Brahmani would immediately begin singing songs in the attitude of a maidservant to the Divine Mother, or songs expressing the overwhelming affection of Yashoda for her Gopala. Of course, these incidents took place long before the Master started to practise madhura bhava. It is therefore evident that there was not an iota of "theft in the chamber of his heart" [hypocrisy] at any time.

We have already mentioned how a few years later the Master's mind changed and he practised vatsalya bhava (see II.12.13). Now we shall describe the disciplines that the Master undertook while practising madhura bhava.

As we study the Master's life, we find that although from the ordinary

4. The Master's sadhanas never contradicted the scriptures, but rather verified their words.

point of view he was almost illiterate, he observed the rules of the scriptures throughout his life. Without the guidance of a guru, he practised various sadhanas, prompted by inner inspiration; however, his practices never contradicted the scriptures but rather adhered to them. It is evident that such a thing happens when a man of pure mind longs to attain God, for there is no theft in the chamber of his heart. This should not be wondered at: One can easily understand this when one considers that long ago the efforts of the great souls to realize the truth and their spiritual experiences were recorded and later took the form of the scriptures. Indeed, the authenticity of the scriptures is verified by the fact that the uneducated Master's experiences are in accordance with the scriptures. In reference to this, Swami Vivekananda remarked: "The reason the Master incarnated as an unlettered person this time is to prove that the scriptures are true."

To illustrate his instinctive adherence to the scriptural injunctions, we can

5. Examples of his respect for the scriptures: assuming appropriate religious marks and attire.

mention that the Master assumed various kinds of dress when under the influence of each mood. The sages of the Upanishads have said that one cannot attain perfection "through austerity unassociated with renunciation."[1] We find in the Master's life that whenever he practised

---

1. *Tapaso vapyolingat* — "The Atman cannot be attained through intellectual knowledge without putting on the signs of sannyasa (i.e., ochre cloth, etc.)." — Mundaka Upanishad 3:2:4

a particular sadhana, he was inspired to first put on the dress and external marks conducive to that mood. For example, while practising the sadhana of God as Mother according to Tantra, he wore a red cloth and rudraksha beads, and adorned himself with ashes and vermilion. When he practised the moods of Vaishnava Tantra, he donned a white cloth and tulsi beads and applied white sandal paste, the well-known traditional garb of Vaishnava ascetics. When he desired to realize the nondual Reality of Vedanta, he gave up his tuft of hair and sacred thread and wore an ochre cloth. Again, as he donned men's clothing while practising masculine moods, he did not hesitate to wear women's clothing and jewellery while practising feminine moods. The Master taught us repeatedly that one cannot attain God without relinquishing the eight fetters: shame, hatred, fear, pride of caste, hesitation, secretiveness, appropriate conduct, and grief. How he practised this teaching physically, mentally, and verbally can be clearly understood if one studies everything he did, including the kinds of clothing he wore during sadhana.

When the Master started to practise madhura bhava, he was eager to wear

6. The Master wears women's clothing during his madhura bhava.

women's clothing and ornaments. Knowing the Master's desire, the devoted Mathur provided him with a beautiful and expensive sari from Varanasi, a skirt, a bodice, and a scarf. To complete the transformation, Mathur brought him a wig with curly hair and a set of gold jewellery. We heard from a reliable source that Mathur's gifts provided an opportunity for evil-minded gossipers to spread scandalous rumours disputing the Master's strict renunciation. But he and Mathur did not pay attention to that talk. At the satisfaction of the "Father," Mathur was extremely delighted and believed that the Master was acting this way for a specific reason. Adorned with women's clothes and ornaments, the Master gradually became so absorbed in the mood of Krishna's lovelorn gopis of Vrindaban that his masculine consciousness completely vanished. His thoughts, speech, and gestures were transformed into those of a woman. The Master told us that he wore women's attire for six months while practising madhura bhava.

We have mentioned elsewhere (see III.1.22,35) that there was a wonderful

7. The Master manifests feminine traits.

coexistence of male and female temperaments in the Master. It is no wonder that under the influence of women's attire his feminine traits were aroused. But no one could have ever imagined that while submerged in that mood his movement, speech, smile, glance, gestures, and other actions, as well as his thoughts, would become completely feminine. We heard from the Master and Hriday many times that this transformation, however impossible it may seem, actually happened. During our visits to Dakshineswar we occasionally saw the Master mimicking women's roles. His mimicries were so natural and perfect that even the women were amazed at seeing them.

During this time the Master sometimes went to Rani Rasmani's Janbazar

8. The Master acts as a female confidante to the women of Mathur's family.

residence and lived as a woman with the ladies of Mathur's family. The ladies already knew the Master's stainless, pure character and adored him as a god. Now they were charmed by his womanly conduct and behaviour, and his natural affection and service. They were so convinced by his behaviour that they considered him to be one of themselves and abandoned their bashfulness and hesitation in front of him (see III.7.1-8). The Master told us that when the husband of any of Mathur's daughters visited the house, the Master would adorn the girl with ornaments and arrange her hair with his own hands. Behaving as though he were an older and more experienced woman friend, he would show her how she should conduct herself and how to entertain her husband. Then, taking her by the hand, he would lead her to meet her husband. He later told us, "At that time they considered me a female confidante of theirs and did not feel at all uncomfortable."

Hriday said: "When the Master was thus surrounded by ladies, it was hard

9. It is difficult to recognize the Master as a man in women's clothes.

for even his closest relatives to recognize him at once. One day during that time Mathur took me to the women's quarters and said, 'Can you tell me which of them is your uncle?' And although I had been living with him for so long and serving him daily, I did not recognize him at first. During that period at Dakshineswar, every morning Uncle would take a basket and pick flowers from the garden. As we watched him, we noticed that he always stepped out with his left foot first, as a woman does. The Brahmani said, 'When I saw him picking flowers I often mistook him for Radha.' Every day after collecting flowers, he would make beautiful garlands and decorate the images of Radha and of Krishna. Sometimes he adorned the image of the Divine Mother and prayed piteously to Her, as did the gopis to the goddess Katyayani, begging Her to give him Krishna as his spiritual husband."

After he had performed worship and service of the Divine Mother, the

10. Changes in the Master's behaviour and body while engaged in the practice of madhura bhava.

Master would visit the Krishna temple. He then wholeheartedly served Radha and Krishna and prayed intensely to have Krishna as his beloved. That fervent prayer in his heart never ceased at any time — either day or night. Thus days and months passed, but neither despondency nor scepticism could disturb his heartfelt expectation. Gradually his prayer became bitter wailing and his eager desire turned into a mad frenzy and restlessness; as a result he forgot to eat or sleep. How great was his pain of separation! When a lover cherishes a boundless desire to be always united with his or her beloved, and this desire is obstructed from all directions, that lover's heart is crushed and the body is broken. Such was the Master's condition. Not only did the pang of separation manifest as painful mental agony, but the terrible burning sensation that he had experienced all over his body in the earlier stage of sadhana reappeared. The Master told us that sometimes drops of blood oozed from the pores of his body because of this fierce pain of separation from Krishna. At times the joints of his body seemed to become loose or almost dislocated. Owing to the intensity of his anguish, his senses sometimes stopped functioning and he looked like a corpse.

As ordinary human beings we are always conscious of our bodies, so we

| 11. The Master's transcendental love compared to our concept of it. |

understand love to mean the attraction of one body for another. Or, if with strenuous effort we raise our consciousness a little from the gross physical plane and consider love as the attraction for the combination of noble qualities residing in a body, we call it "transcendental love" and we eulogize it. But we can quickly understand that our so-called transcendental love, which is praised by poets, is not free from the gross body idea or subtle sensual desires. Oh, how worthless, trivial, and hollow that love appears in contrast with the true transcendental love manifested in the Master's life!

According to the devotional scriptures, Radha, the goddess of Vrindaban,

| 12. What devotional scriptures say about Radha's love. |

alone experienced the culmination of true transcendental love and left its perfect ideal to this world. She shunned shame, hatred, fear, public opinion, and social criticism; she forgot pride of caste, family ties, appropriate conduct, personal dignity, and her own comfort and enjoyment in order to take joy in Krishna's happiness alone. There is not another example like hers in any of the devotional scriptures. So the Vaishnava scriptures say that without Radha's grace it is impossible for anyone in this world to have the vision of Krishna: The Satchidananda Krishna is eternally and completely captivated by the love of Radha, and he fulfills the wishes of devotees at her intercession. The intention of the Vaishnava scriptures is to teach that until one attains the same kind of pure, lust-free love that Radha had, one cannot achieve God as husband and experience the full sweetness of madhura bhava.

Although the ever-free paramahamsa Shukadeva and other illumined

| 13. Gauranga came to demonstrate Radha's transcendental love. |

sages eulogized the divine glory of Radha's love, for a long time the ordinary people of India did not understand how to experience it in their own lives. The Vaishnava teachers of Bengal say that in order to demonstrate this phenomenon, God had to reincarnate and unite Himself with Radha in one body. That unique form of God was manifested internally as Krishna and externally as Gauranga [Chaitanya]; it was Gauranga who established in this life Radha's ideal love of madhura bhava. The same signs that manifested in Radha's body and mind as a result of her love for Krishna were all revealed in Gauranga, due to his exuberant love for God, despite having a male body. Observing this, his followers recognized him as Radha. Thus, Gauranga is the second example of that ideal transcendental love.

Knowing that the vision of Krishna is not possible without Radha's grace,

14. The Master's meditation on Radha, and his vision.

the Master began to worship her with his one-pointed mind. He remained absorbed in meditation on her loving form and prayed to her unceasingly with a longing heart. As a result he was soon blessed with the vision of Radha. Her form merged into him like the forms of other gods and goddesses whose visions he had previously realized. He said: "It is impossible to describe the incomparable, pure, heavenly beauty and sweetness of Radha, who renounced everything out of her passionate love for Krishna. Her complexion was light yellow like the stamens of the *nagakeshara* [*mesua ferra*] flower."

For some time following that vision, the Master felt that he was Radha.

15. Why the Master felt himself to be Radha.

This happened as a result of deep meditation on Radha's form and character. He also completely lost his sense of individuality. So it is evident that his love for God as husband became as profound as Radha's. After that vision all signs of mahabhava that resulted from the culmination of the madhura bhava manifested in him as they had in Radha and Gauranga. The descriptions of the physical signs that manifest themselves during mahabhava are recorded in the books of the Vaishnava teachers. The Bhairavi Brahmani, and later Vaishnavcharan and other religious leaders, who were all well versed in the Vaishnava scriptures, were astonished at seeing those signs of mahabhava in the Master's body and they offered him their love and respect. Referring to mahabhava, the Master told us many times: "The devotional scriptures say that when nineteen kinds of bhava[2] [emotion or mood] for God manifest

2. Jiva Goswami and other Vaishnava teachers divide Ragatmika Bhakti in two ways:

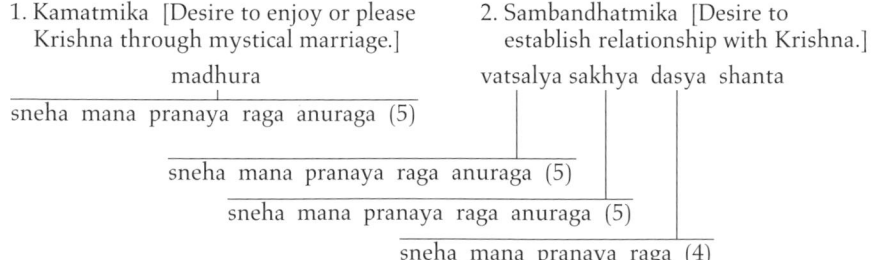

1. Kamatmika [Desire to enjoy or please Krishna through mystical marriage.]

madhura

sneha mana pranaya raga anuraga (5)

2. Sambandhatmika [Desire to establish relationship with Krishna.]

vatsalya sakhya dasya shanta

sneha mana pranaya raga anuraga (5)

sneha mana pranaya raga anuraga (5)

sneha mana pranaya raga (4)

The aforesaid nineteen emotions [excluding shanta] of both the kamatmika and the samban-dhatmika devotions manifest during mahabhava. The Master indicated that here.

[According to the Vaishnava tradition, *prema* or love for God increases from a lower state to a higher one and culminates in mahabhava. Each bhava (emotion) has a special meaning: 1. Sneha (affection) manifests when intense love melts the heart and flows towards the Beloved, Krishna. 2. Mana (pique) develops when the lover's genuine love seems to be rejected or not reciprocated; the Beloved feels guilty and tries to please the lover. 3. Pranaya (friendship) creates the feeling of oneness; the lover feels the Beloved's pain. 4. Raga (intense love) is a tremendous passion for the Beloved that brings forgetfulness of one's body and transforms pain into joy. 5. Anuraga (a constant feeling of fresh love) removes a monotonous state of the mind and generates unceasing waves of love for the Beloved. — *Translator*]

together in one person, it is called mahabhava. An ordinary man takes a whole lifetime to practise one bhava before he achieves perfection in it. All nineteen spiritual emotions are fully manifested here (*pointing to his own body*)."

We have mentioned previously that so great was the pain of the Master's

| 16. Unusual changes in the Master's body during madhura bhava. | separation from Krishna that blood oozed from every pore of the Master's body. This phenomenon came about with the culmination of the mahabhava. |

He was so absorbed in thinking of himself as a woman that he could not think of himself as a man even in dreams. His body and senses functioned naturally like those of a woman. We heard from the Master that during this time, every month drops of blood would ooze from the pores near his *swadhisthana chakra* for three days, like a woman's monthly cycle. Hriday told us that he saw this himself and noticed that the Master wore a *kaupin* [loincloth] to avoid soiling his clothes.

Vedanta teaches that the mind creates the body. Our minds give the present

| 17. Intense emotion changed his body, proving that "the mind creates the body." | shape to our bodies. Our intense will and desires recast our bodies every moment of our lives, giving them new forms. We are unable to fully comprehend that the mind has such mastery over the body. But this |

occurs because when a fierce desire arises the mind becomes centred on that particular object and withdraws itself from others, thus creating tremendous power. However, we do not feel that kind of strong desire for any object. The fact that the Master's body was quickly transformed in a short time, out of an intense desire to experience a particular object, supports the aforesaid statement of Vedanta. Padmalochan and other famous pandits heard of the Master's spiritual experiences. While comparing them with those of the ancient illumined sages, they remarked, "Your experiences have surpassed even the Vedas and the Puranas." Studying the Master's physical changes, which were caused by an upsurge of emotions, one may remark with amazement that his bodily changes went beyond the findings of modern physiology and indicated a new dimension to it.

When the Master's love for God as beloved was purified and intensified,

| 18. The Master's vision of Krishna. | he experienced the grace of Radha, the goddess of Vrindaban, and shortly afterwards had the vision of Satchidananda Krishna. The form of Krishna merged |

into his body, as the other deities had done before.

Two or three months after this vision, Paramahamsa Tota Puri initiated the Master into the disciplines of nondualistic Vedanta. So it seems that after attaining perfection in madhura bhava, the Master spent some time in divine communion through that mood. The Master told us that he was then so absorbed in the thought of Krishna that he forgot his own identity. Sometimes he regarded himself as Krishna, and sometimes he saw Krishna in all beings, from Brahma down to a blade of grass. When we were visiting the Master at Dakshineswar one day, he picked a blue grass-flower from the garden and came to us joyfully. He said, "When I was practising madhura bhava I used to see Krishna, whose complexion was like this flower."

At the threshold of his youth a kind of fancy arose in the Master's mind, prompted by the influence of his inner feminine nature. Because they were born as women, the gopis of Vrindaban attained Satchidananda Krishna through love. This led him to think that if he were born as a woman, he could worship and attain Krishna like the gopis. Thus, viewing the male body as an obstacle to attaining Krishna, he imagined that if he were to be born again he would be a beautiful young widow with long hair, born in a brahmin family, knowing none other than Krishna as husband. There would be provision for plain food and clothes and a small plot of land next to his hut, where he would grow a few kinds of vegetables. There would be an elderly woman with him who served as a guardian, a cow that he would milk himself, and a spinning wheel. His boyish imagination went further. After finishing the household work for the day, he would sing songs about Krishna while spinning the cotton. Then in the evening he would make sweets from the milk of that cow and cry piteously to feed the sweets to Krishna with his own hands. Pleased, Krishna would suddenly appear as a cowherd boy and eat them; thus he would visit daily without anyone knowing. Although the Master's fantasy was not fulfilled in that particular manner, it was accomplished in a modified form when he practised madhura bhava.

19. When he was young, the Master had wanted to be born as a woman.

We shall conclude the present topic by describing another of the Master's visions that took place when he was in madhura bhava. One day while he was listening to the reading of the Bhagavata in the front hall of the Vishnu temple, he went into ecstasy and saw the resplendent form of Krishna. Next, a beam of light, like a cord, came forth from Krishna's feet and first touched the Bhagavata and then the Master's chest, connecting all three for some time.

20. The Master's vision: "Bhagavata [the scriptures], Bhakta [the devotees], and Bhagavan [the Lord] — these three are one, and the One manifests as three."

After this vision the Master was firmly convinced that God, His devotee, and the scriptures that are His words, are in reality one and the same, though they appear to be distinct entities. The Master used to say, "The Bhagavata, the devotee, and God — these three are one and the One manifests as three."

Chapter 15

The Master's *Vedanta* Sadhana

WHEN THE MASTER ATTAINED PERFECTION IN madhura bhava, he reached the culmi-

1. The Master's mental state during this period: (1) He was firmly established in renunciation of lust and gold.

nation of devotional disciplines. It is important to discuss his mental condition during this period before we record the history of the next wonderful sadhana he embarked upon.

We know that if an aspirant wants to succeed in any one of the devotional moods, that person must shun all sensual objects of enjoyment in order to practise that sadhana. What the great saint Tulasidas said is true: "Where Rama is, there can be no selfish action."[1] The unprecedented history of the Master's sadhana testifies to this. Once he had established a firm foundation of renunciation of lust and gold, he began to practise the devotional moods; thereafter, he never deviated from his resolve. That is why, when he undertook the practice of any spiritual attitude, he mastered it within a short time. It is evident that his mind constantly dwelt in a higher realm, far beyond the allure of lust and gold.

Because for nine years he had shunned all desire for worldly enjoyment

(2) He attained discrimination between the real and the unreal, as well as dispassion for worldly and heavenly enjoyments.

and struggled constantly to realize God, his mind had now reached such a state that any thought other than that of God was like deadly poison to him. Because he was wholeheartedly convinced that God is the essence of all essences and the Supreme Reality,

his mind was completely indifferent to anything in this world or the next, and he had no worldly ambitions.

---

1. "Where Rama is, there can be no selfish action; and where selfish action is, there can be no Rama. Like the sun and the night, the two do not coexist." — Tulasidas

His mind became accustomed to one-pointed meditation on his Chosen

| (3) He acquired the six spiritual treasures (*shama, dama, uparati, titiksha, samadhana,* and *shraddha) and a burning desire for liberation.* | Deity, forgetting sense objects and physical pain and pleasure. Because of this he could easily withdraw his mind from external objects, become absorbed in concentration on that deity, and enjoy divine bliss. Days, months, and years rolled by, yet that joy never subsided. The thought never arose in his mind even |

for a moment that there was anything desirable in this world other than God.

The Master's mind ultimately developed unlimited love for God, devout

| (4) Divine visions awakened his dependence on God and his fearlessness. | faith, and dependence on the Creator of the universe as "the Goal, the Support, the Lord, the Witness, the Abode, the Refuge, and the Friend" (Gita 9:18). Because of this he established a loving relationship |

with the Divine Mother and felt Her presence always. Furthermore, he had proof that a true aspirant experiences God's constant presence through childlike dependence on the mother. That blessed one always hears God's sweet message and always travels fearlessly in this world protected by His powerful hands. Now the Master's mind became fully accustomed to performing all actions, big or small, at the command or prompting of the Divine Mother.

One may ask: Why did the Master continue practising sadhana even after

| 2. What the Master says about his practising sadhana even after God-realization. | attaining the constant presence of the Divine Mother, the Cause of the Universe? An aspirant practises meditation and austerities in order to realize God, but what is the need for sadhana if one looks upon |

Him as a close relative? Previously we answered this question from one point of view; now we shall address it in a different way. As we listened to the Master's story of his sadhana, the same question arose in our minds. We did not hesitate to ask him about it. The Master said in reply: "One who lives near the sea sometimes has a desire to find out how many pearls are hidden in the ocean depths. Similarly, after realizing the Divine Mother and being constantly near Her, I thought that I should see Her multiple forms. If I had a desire to see Her in a particular way, I would importune Her with a longing heart. Then the gracious Mother would supply whatever was necessary to experience that form, make me practise that sadhana, and reveal Herself to me accordingly. Thus, I practised sadhanas belonging to various paths."

As we have said before, after he had attained perfection in madhura bhava the Master reached the culmination of devotional disciplines. He then felt a great urge to practise the nondualism of Vedanta, which is beyond all devotional moods. Now we shall tell the reader how that inspiration came to his life by the grace of the Divine Mother and how he experienced Her formless, attributeless, and absolute transcendental nature.

When the Master began his nondualistic sadhana, his aged mother was

| 3. The Master's mother decides to live near the Ganges and comes to Dakshineswar. |

living at the Dakshineswar Kali temple. After the death of her eldest son, Ramkumar, the bereaved woman found herself depending on her two remaining sons. But soon people began to spread rumours that her youngest son, Gadadhar, had become insane, and her sorrow knew no bounds. She had Gadadhar brought to Kamarpukur, and when his condition improved by means of various treatments and propitiatory rites, she arranged his marriage with great hope. But when Gadadhar returned to Dakshineswar after the wedding, and his former condition reemerged, his mother could no longer control herself. She went to the temple and took a vow to fast until her son recovered. Lord Shiva revealed that her son was affected by divine inebriation, and she was reassured a little. But shortly afterwards she lost all interest in the world, went to her son at Dakshineswar, and decided to spend the rest of her life on the bank of the Ganges. She had asked herself: What was the use of her being involved in the world in her old age when her children, for whom she had committed herself to the world, were leaving home one after another? We have already mentioned the festival of annameru that Mathur had arranged (see II.12.2). At that time [1864], the Master's mother was in Dakshineswar; from then on, for the next twelve years until her death [1876], she never returned to Kamarpukur. Therefore, it was undoubtedly during his mother's stay in Dakshineswar that the Master was initiated into the Rama mantra by Jatadhari and practised madhura bhava and nondualistic Vedanta.

We want to relate an event that took place shortly after the arrival of the

| 4. The Master's mother is completely free from greed. |

Master's mother at Dakshineswar that illustrates her lack of covetousness. As we have previously mentioned, at that time Mathur had full control of the temple management, and he was spending money lavishly on the completion of many religious functions and the distribution of food. Because he had tremendous love and devotion for the Master, he was constantly trying secretly to arrange everything so that the Master's physical needs would always be met. But he had observed the Master's unflinching renunciation, so did not dare to speak to him about this. Earlier he had caused trouble with the Master when he consulted with Hriday about transferring an estate to the Master's name. They were within hearing distance of the Master, and as soon as he realized what they were discussing, he became angry and chased Mathur, trying to hit him, saying, "Rascal, you want to make me a worldly man!" Although Mathur wished to ensure the Master's security, he had been unable to find any opportunity to do that.

When the Master's mother arrived at Dakshineswar, Mathur found an opportunity to fulfill his wish. He addressed the elderly Chandradevi as "Granny." He visited her every day and talked with her about various things. Thus he gradually became her favourite. Then one day he found his opportunity and implored her: "Granny, you have never accepted any service from me. If you truly look upon me as your own, please ask me for whatever you want." The simple-hearted woman was in a dilemma, because after a good deal of thought she could not come up with anything she needed. In such a predicament, she said at last: "My child, due to your benevolence, I lack nothing at present. If I need anything, I shall ask you for it." With this, the elderly woman opened her trunk and said to Mathur: "Look, I have so many clothes! Moreover, due to your loving care there is no lack of food here. You have arranged everything. So, tell me, what else could I want?" But Mathur was adamant. He entreated her repeatedly, "Please, ask for anything." Then she remembered what she needed. With a smile she said: "If you really want to give me something, please buy an anna worth of tobacco leaf; I need tobacco powder for my teeth." At this request the worldly Mathur shed tears. He bowed down to her and remarked, "Only a mother such as yourself could have such an all-renouncing son!" He then got some tobacco leaves for her.

When the Master began to practise Vedantic disciplines, his cousin Hala-

| 5. Haladhari resigns from worship service; Akshay arrives. |

dhari was the priest of the Radha-Govinda temple at Dakshineswar. He was older than the Master and had some knowledge of the Bhagavata and other scriptures. Maddened by pride, he would sometimes ridicule the Master and tell him that his spiritual visions and states were due to a disorder of the brain. We have already mentioned how the Master was so hurt by this that he prayed to the Divine Mother, and She reassured him again and again. Once one of Haladhari's harsh insinuations made the Master very sad. He then went into ecstasy and had a vision of a beautiful divine form who commanded him to remain in bhavamukha. This vision probably took place shortly before the Master practised Vedanta, while he was practising madhura bhava. Seeing him wearing women's clothes, Haladhari scolded him and called him an idiot.

When Paramahamsa Tota Puri, an itinerant monk, came to Dakshineswar and stayed, Haladhari was also there. We heard from the Master that sometimes Haladhari and Tota would discuss the scriptures. One day when they were discussing the Adhyatma Ramayana, the Master had a vision of Rama-chandra with Sita and Lakshmana. It was probably near the end of 1864 when Tota arrived at Dakshineswar. A few months later, Haladhari's health forced him to retire from the temple service, and Akshay, one of the Master's nephews, was appointed in his place.

It is not in the nature of a devotee to strive for identification with God or to

| 6. Why the Master begins practising nondual Vedanta, though established in bhava samadhi. |

seek nirvana. A devotee always endeavours to enjoy God's glory and the sweetness of God's love. "I don't want to *become* sugar, Mother; I want to *taste* sugar" — this well-known saying of the mystic Ramprasad is a natural outburst from a devotee's heart. Some may therefore consider the Master's effort to attain the nondual state to be irrelevant after he had achieved the culmination of devotional moods. But before passing judgement we must remember that from that point on he was incapable of performing any action of his own volition. As a child of the Divine Mother, the Master depended on Her completely; in whatever direction She led him, he followed with delight. For Her part, the Divine Mother took all of his responsibilities upon Herself and, without his knowledge, shaped his life in a new and unique way so that he could fulfill Her special mission. At the end of all sadhanas the Master came to understand the will of the Divine Mother. United with Her in love, he felt Her great responsibility for doing good to humanity to be his own, and he joyfully carried that responsibility for the rest of his life.

The reason for practising nondualism after attaining madhura bhava can

7. Justification for attaining the nondual experience as a consummation of devotional sadhana.

be understood from another perspective. The transcendental realm and the realm of devotional moods are interrelated as cause and effect: The infinite bliss of the nondual realm takes on limitations and manifests itself as the enjoyment of the bliss of sight, touch, and so on in the realm of devotional moods. Therefore, after reaching the culmination of madhura bhava, the final stage of devotional moods, the Master's mind moved towards the absolute nondual state. Where else could it go?

The following event makes it clear that the Master began his nondualistic sadhana under the direction of the Divine Mother.

Roaming at will, Tota Puri came to Bengal from Central India. He was on

8. Arrival of Tota Puri.

his way to bathe in the holy confluence of the Ganges and the Bay of Bengal [Gangasagar] and also to visit Lord Jagannath at Puri. He had been absorbed in solitary spiritual disciplines for a long time on the bank of the sacred river Narmada, and had realized Brahman through nirvikalpa samadhi. Even now the old monks in that area testify to this. After becoming a knower of Brahman, a desire arose in his mind to travel freely for a period of time; under this impulse he went to the eastern part of India and visited one holy place after another. When knowers of Brahman are not in samadhi, they perceive the external world but experience it to be Brahman. As they visit shrines, sacred places, and holy people, they experience the manifestation of Brahman to varying degrees in all beings, places, and things of the world created by maya. So it was not unusual for the illumined Tota to go on a pilgrimage. After visiting Gangasagar and Puri, he stopped at Dakshineswar on his way to northwestern India. It was his custom to remain in one place for no more than three days, so he resolved to stay in the Kali temple only for a short time. He did not realize that the Divine Mother had brought him there in order to complete his own knowledge and to induce Her son to practise Vedantic disciplines through him.

When Tota Puri arrived at the Kali temple, he first went to the main porch of

9. The first conversation between the Master and Tota Puri; the Master receives a divine command to practise Vedanta.

the ghat. The Master was seated there in an abstracted mood. As soon as Tota saw the Master's face, radiant with austerity and shining with devotion, he was attracted to him. He felt strongly that this person was not ordinary and that such a student, so fit to practise

Vedanta, is seldom to be found. Tota Puri was amazed when he realized that such a qualified aspirant of Vedanta existed in Bengal, where Tantra is predominant. He carefully examined the Master and then asked him: "It seems you are an excellent spiritual aspirant. Would you like to practise Vedanta?"

The Master replied to the tall, naked monk with matted hair: "I don't know what to do or not to do. My Mother knows everything. If She commands it, then I will undertake the practice."

Tota responded: "All right, go and ask your mother. But I shall not be here long."

Without another word, the Master walked slowly to the Kali temple, then went into ecstasy. He received the Divine Mother's command: "Go and learn. It is to teach you that the monk has come here."

The intoxicated Master returned to Tota Puri with a smiling face and

10. Tota's conception of the Divine Mother.

informed him of the Mother's command. Understanding now that by "Mother" the Master was referring to the goddess in the temple, Tota was

charmed by his childlike simplicity, but he believed his conduct was caused by ignorance and superstition. We can easily guess that such a conclusion raised a little smile of pity and disdain on Tota's lips. Endowed with a sharp intellect, Tota did not care to bow down to any deity except for Ishwara [God], who, according to Vedanta, dispenses the results of actions. The self-controlled Tota would meditate on Brahman, and he had faith in the existence of God, but he did not believe there was any need to worship and practise devotion to God to achieve grace. Tota believed that the Divine Mother is maya, the power of Brahman, and consists of the three gunas. Because he considered Her to be a delusion, Tota did not feel any need to accept Her personality or to propitiate Her through worship. He wholeheartedly believed that an aspirant should become free from the bondage of ignorance through self-effort rather than by praying to a deity for help. In fact, he considered those who prayed in that manner to be superstitious.

However, Tota thought that the Master's superstition would disappear

11. Why the Master receives initiation into sannyasa secretly.

quickly if he were initiated and began to practise the path of knowledge. At this time, he said nothing about this to the Master. He changed the topic, telling him

he would have to take formal monastic vows and give up the sacred thread and tuft of hair before he could be instructed and begin to practise Vedanta. The Master hesitated a little and then said that he had no objection to receiving sannyasa if it could be arranged in secret. It would not be possible for him to perform the ceremony publicly, because that would give a terrible blow to the heart of his elderly, grief-stricken mother. Tota understood the Master's intent and agreed to initiate him secretly at an auspicious time. Then Tota went to the Panchavati, spread out his seat, and decided to stay there.

When the auspicious day arrived, Tota asked the Master to perform the

12. The performance of preliminary rites before sannyasa.

shrāddha and other rites to propitiate his departed ancestors. Then he instructed his disciple to offer pindas [rice balls] for the satisfaction of his own soul, according to tradition. From the moment of initiation into sannyasa, an aspirant completely renounces the desire for and right to attain all worlds, such as *bhuh* [earth], *bhuvah* [ethereal region], *svah* [heaven], and so on. That is why the scriptures require an aspirant to offer pinda to his own spirit before undertaking sannyasa.

Whenever the Master accepted anyone as his guru, he unhesitatingly surrendered to that person and followed with absolute faith the instructions he was given. Whatever Tota now instructed him to do, he carried out exactly as he was told. After performing the shrāddha and preliminary rites, he observed a fast. Then at his guru's direction he collected the articles for the ceremony and put them in his own sadhan-kutir [meditation hut] near the Panchavati and waited joyfully for the auspicious moment.

At the end of the night the auspicious *brahma muhurta* [48 minutes before sunrise] arrived. Guru and disciple entered the hut. After they completed the preliminary rituals, they ignited the *homa* fire. The Panchavati and the surrounding groves reverberated with the holy and profound sound of the mantras chanted prior to the monastic vows. From ancient times these vows to renounce everything for God have been passed along in succession from guru to disciple, making India a land of knowers of Brahman. When that sweet sound touched the gentle undulating surface of the holy river Ganges, it seemed that She came to life. She flowed joyfully with a sweet murmuring sound as if carrying this message in all directions: After a long time, here in this age an extraordinary aspirant is taking the all-renouncing monastic vows for the good of all people in the world.

The guru was prepared to recite the mantras; he instructed the disciple to follow them attentively and repeat them while pouring oblations into the homa fire. The prayer mantras were uttered first.

"May the truth of Supreme Brahman be revealed unto me. May the

13. Prayers before sannyasa.

blissful Reality be realized by me. May the indivisible blissful Brahman become manifest in me. O Supreme Self, You eternally coexist with Your Power to reveal the knowledge of Brahman! Among Your children — gods, humans, and other beings — I am Your child and servant, a special object of compassion. O Supreme Lord, destroyer of the dreary dreams of the world, please destroy all my painful dreams and the perception of duality. O Supreme Self, I offer my vital forces as oblations to You, and controlling my senses I focus my mind on You alone. O Shining One, creator and director of all beings, do remove from me all the impurities that obstruct true knowledge, and bestow upon me Self-knowledge free from doubt and error. At Your command may the sun, the wind, the pure water of the rivers, plants and trees, grains such as rice, wheat, barley, and everything in this world be favourable to me and help me to attain the knowledge of Reality. O Brahman, You become manifest in various forms in this world through Your special power. I offer my oblations to You in this fire so that I may become fit to retain knowledge of the Self by purifying the body and the mind. Be gracious unto me."[2]

Then the *viraja homa* began: "May this oblation purify the five elements I am made of: earth, water, fire, air, and ether. Freed from impurities and ignorance, may I become the self-luminous Brahman. Swaha!

14. The purport of a few *viraja homa* mantras.

"May this oblation purify my five vital forces: *prana, apana, vyana, udana,* and *samana.* Freed from impurities and ignorance, may I become the self-luminous Brahman. Swaha!

"May this oblation purify the five sheaths: *annamaya, pranamaya, manomaya, vijnanamaya,* and *anandamaya.* Freed from impurities and ignorance, may I become the self-luminous Brahman. Swaha!

"May this oblation purify the five objects of my senses: sound, touch, form, taste, and smell. Freed from impurities and ignorance, may I become the selfluminous Brahman. Swaha!

"May this oblation purify my mind, speech, body, and actions. Freed from impurities and ignorance, may I become the self-luminous Brahman. Swaha!

"Awake, O red-eyed Divine Being dwelling in the fire. You are expert in removing the obstacles to knowledge. O fulfiller of desires, please destroy whatever impediments lie in the path of Self-knowledge and purify completely all the impressions of my mind, so that the knowledge imparted by my guru may be manifest in my heart. May this oblation make me free from impurities and ignorance, so that I become the self-luminous Brahman. Swaha!

"I am identified with the consciousness of Brahman. I offer all my desires for sex, progeny, wealth, honour, physical beauty, and so on in the fire as oblations. I renounce everything completely. Swaha!"

Thus, many oblations were offered into the fire. Finally the homa ceremony was concluded with these vows: "At this moment I give up the desire for earth, heaven, and other worlds. I promise all beings of the world that they have nothing to fear from me." He then offered

15. The Master takes the vow of sannyasa, renouncing his tuft of hair and sacred thread.

2. The gist of the *Trisuparna-mantra.*

his tuft of hair and sacred thread into the fire as oblations, according to scriptural injunctions. The Master received a loincloth, an ochre robe, and a name[3] from his guru, in accordance with the tradition followed by generations of aspirants since ancient times. He then approached Tota for instructions.

Tota, a knower of Brahman, now encouraged the Master to become established in Brahman by following the famous Vedantic method of neti, neti, or "not this, not this." He said:

16. Tota instructs the Master to become absorbed in Brahman.

"Brahman by nature is ever-pure, ever-illumined, ever-free, beyond the limits of space, time, and causation. It is the only absolute Reality. Though apparently divided into names and forms by the inscrutable agency of maya, that enchantress who makes the impossible possible, Brahman is in truth one and undivided. During samadhi one does not experience space and time or name and form, which are the products of maya. Whatever exists within the domain of name and form cannot be absolutely real — so give it up. Break this strong cage of name and form and rush out of it like a lion! Dive deep in the search for the Atman within yourself and become firmly established in It through samadhi. Then the world of name and form will vanish into nothingness; this little I-consciousness will merge into Cosmic Consciousness and cease to function; and you will experience the indivisible Satchidananda as your own Self. The knowledge with which one sees, hears, or knows another is little or finite. What is finite is worthless and can never give supreme bliss. But that knowledge with which one does not see, hear, or know another is vast and infinite, and it helps a person to attain supreme bliss. How can the mind and senses grasp that nondual Brahman, which is not an object, that shines in the heart of all as the eternal Knower?[4]"

Tota tried to make the Master attain samadhi on that day with the help of various arguments and quotations from the scriptures. We heard from the Master that Tota was determined to transmit his whole life's spiritual experiences to him, so that he could be rapidly absorbed into the nondual state. The Master said:

17. When the Master fails to remove all thoughts from his mind, Tota helps him to attain nirvikalpa samadhi.

---

3. Some of us say that during the sannyasa ceremony Tota Puri gave the name "Ramakrishna" to the Master. Others say that the great devotee Mathur gave that name to the Master. The first opinion seems to us to be reasonable.

[Later some researchers found that the name "Ramakrishna" was given by his father, as he was a devotee of Ramachandra. He gave similar names to his two other sons, Ramkumar and Rameswar. A deed of document executed by Rani Rasmani on 18 February 1861 shows that in 1858: "Sri Sri Radhakantaji — Sri Ramakrishna Bhattacharya: Rupees 5/-, 3 pairs of cloths, plus Rs. 4.50." — see *Sri Sri Ramakrishna Kathamrita* — Part 2, by M. It proves that in 1858 the Master was the priest of the Radha-Govinda temple and his monthly salary was five rupees, whereas Tota Puri arrived at Dakshineswar in 1864. It seems Tota Puri gave the same family name to the Master. — *Translator*]

4. Chandogya Upanishad 7:24:1, and Brihadaranyaka Upanishad 2:4:14

"After initiating me into sannyasa, the Naked One[5] began to teach me various established truths of Vedanta and asked me to withdraw my mind from all objects and dive into the Atman. But despite all my attempts, during meditation I could not cross the realm of name and form and bring my mind to the unconditioned state. I had no difficulty in withdrawing my mind from all objects except one: the all-too-familiar form of the Blissful Mother, radiant with Pure Consciousness, that appeared before me as a living reality and prevented me from passing beyond the realm of name and form. For more than three days this happened again and again when I tried to meditate according to the instructions of Vedanta. I almost lost hope of reaching nirvikalpa samadhi. I opened my eyes and told the Naked One: 'No, it can't be done. I cannot raise my mind to the unconditioned state and force it to be absorbed in the Atman.' Irritated, the Naked One said sharply: 'What do you mean — can't be done? It must be done!' Then he looked around the hut and found a bit of broken glass. He picked it up and stuck its needle-sharp point between my eyebrows and said, 'Fix the mind here.' I sat down to meditate again, firmly determined. As soon as the form of the Divine Mother appeared in my mind, I used my discrimination as a sword of knowledge and with it mentally cut that form in two. Then all distinctions disappeared from my mind, and it swiftly soared beyond the realm of name and form. I lost myself in samadhi."

When the Master went into samadhi, Tota remained seated near him for a long time. He then silently left the hut and locked the door behind him lest anybody should intrude and disturb the Master. He took his seat near the hut in the Panchavati and waited for the Master to call for the door to be opened.

18. Tota verifies the Master's nirvikalpa samadhi and is amazed.

The day passed and night came. Thus three days passed. Still the Master did not call for Tota. With amazement and curiosity, Tota left his seat and unlocked the door to check his disciple's condition. He found the Master sitting exactly as he had been left: His body showed no sign of life, but his face was calm, serene, and radiant. Tota realized that his disciple was totally unaware of the external world and that his mind was absorbed in Brahman, like an unflickering lamp in a windless place.

An expert in samadhi, Tota marvelled: "Is what I see really true? Is it possible that this great soul has realized in three days what I could accomplish only after forty years of strenuous sadhana?" Driven by doubt, Tota began a careful examination and scrutinized the signs manifested in his disciple's body. He checked thoroughly to determine whether there was any heartbeat or even the slightest trace of respiration. He repeatedly touched the disciple's motionless body, seated like a piece of dead wood, and found

5. This was the appellation that Sri Ramakrishna, out of respect, invariably used for his guru, who was a Naga sannyasin and generally went naked. — *Translator*

no response, no change, or any sign of outer consciousness. Overwhelmed with joy and wonder, Tota cried out: "Ah! What a display of divine maya! This is real samadhi — nirvikalpa samadhi — the ultimate result of the path of knowledge according to Vedanta. He has achieved it in three days! How miraculous is God's power!"

Tota then took steps to bring the Master's mind down to the phenomenal

| 19. Tota's efforts to interrupt the Master's samadhi. | world. He began to chant the mantra *Hari Om*. That solemn sound reverberated all around the Panchavati. |

We have described elsewhere (see III.8.26,39-40) how, charmed by his disciple's love and desiring to establish him firmly in the nirvikalpa plane, Tota spent day after day and month after month in Dakshineswar. We have also mentioned how he made his own spiritual life perfect with the Master's help.

Tota left for northwest India after living in Dakshineswar for eleven months. Immediately thereafter, the Master firmly resolved that from then on he would remain continually in nirvikalpa samadhi, the nondual plane of consciousness. We have told the reader elsewhere (see III.2.12-13,19-20) how the Master translated that resolve into action. For six months without interruption he was able to stay in that absolute nondual state. Not even highly qualified aspirants akin to the avatar could stay in that state for that period of time, not to speak of ordinary aspirants! At that time a holy man came to the Kali temple and became aware that in the future the Master would accomplish a great mission that would benefit humanity. He therefore remained in Dakshineswar for six months to care for the Master, protecting the Master's body by various means.

We shall conclude this chapter by referring to an extraordinary event that took place in Mathur's life with the help of the Master.

Because he had seen the Master manifest various divine powers, Mathur's

| 20. The Master cures Jagadamba of a fatal disease. | love for and faith in him were already great. About this time an incident occurred in his family that made Mathur's love even more firm and led him to take |

refuge in the Master for the rest of his life.

Jagadamba, Mathur's second wife, had an attack of dysentery during this time. Gradually the disease worsened to the point that famous physicians of Calcutta first doubted whether she could survive, then lost all hope.

We heard from the Master that Mathur was very handsome, but had been born of a poor family. Charmed by his beauty, Rasmani had arranged his first marriage with her third daughter, Karunamayi. When the latter died, she arranged his second marriage with her youngest daughter, Jagadamba. After his marriage with Jagadamba, Mathur's situation changed. Due to his intelligence and efficiency, he gradually became indispensable to his mother-in-law. We have already mentioned how, after Rani Rasmani's death, he achieved almost sole authority in the management of her vast estate.

Jagadamba was in critical condition. Mathur was now not only going to be deprived of his beloved wife, he was also about to lose control over his mother-in-law's estate. So it is needless to say more about his state of mind.

When the doctors left, declaring the case to be hopeless, Mathur rushed to the Kali temple in Dakshineswar with an afflicted heart. After bowing down to the Divine Mother, he went to the Panchavati in search of the Master. Seeing Mathur in a frantic state, the Master made him sit by his side and tenderly inquired into the cause of his grief. Mathur fell at the Master's feet and in a choked voice, tearfully reported everything. He humbly said again and again: "Father, not only am I threatened with a terrible personal loss, but also, if the management of the estate passes into other hands, I will be deprived of the privilege of serving you."

Seeing Mathur's miserable plight, the Master's heart was filled with compassion. In an ecstatic mood he said to Mathur: "Don't be afraid. Your wife will recover." The devout Mathur considered the Master to be none other than God; so his reassuring words brought hope to Mathur and he left for home. When he returned to Janbazar, Mathur found that Jagadamba's disease had suddenly taken a turn for the better. When he later referred to this incident, the Master said: "From that day on Jagadamba slowly began to recover, but the suffering caused by her disease was transferred to this body (*pointing to himself*). After curing her, I suffered for six months from dysentery and other complaints."

One day while talking about the wonderful and loving service that Mathur had tendered him, the Master told us, referring to this incident: "Was it for nothing that Mathur served me faithfully for fourteen years? The Divine Mother showed him various supernatural things through this body (*pointing to himself*). For that reason he served me with such devotion."

Chapter 16

Epilogue to Vedanta Sadhana and the Practice of *J*slam

THE MASTER WAS AFFLICTED WITH ILLNESS FOR SOME MONTHS, and his strong body

| 1. The Master's serious illness and his unusual behaviour. |

broke down, either because he had cured Jagadamba's critical illness, as mentioned before, or because of his superhuman effort to remain in the nondualistic plane of consciousness for six months continuously. He told us that he suffered a severe attack of dysentery at that time. His nephew Hriday served him steadfastly. Mathur engaged the famous physician Gangaprasad Sen to treat him, and also arranged a special diet. Although the Master was afflicted by disease, his mind dwelt in a wonderful calm and blissful state without interruption, because it was devoid of body-consciousness. At the slightest spiritual prompting (see III.2.12,20-21), his mind would transcend the body-idea, his illness, and all objects of the world, and instantly reach the highest transcendental plane. Whenever he remembered Brahman, Atman, or God, he became absorbed for some time, forgetting everything — even his own individual existence. Therefore, it is understood that despite the terrible physical pain caused by the violent outbreak of disease, he actually felt very little of it. However, he told us that sometimes the excruciating pain of that disease would bring his mind from the highest spiritual plane down to his body. The Master said that during this period some great paramahamsas who followed Vedanta came to Dakshineswar. His room continually reverberated with discussions on the great truths of Vedanta, such as, "Not this, not this," "Existence-Consciousness-Bliss," "This Atman is Brahman," and so on (see IV.2.5-6). When they could not arrive at the correct conclusion to a particular subject as they discussed those profound truths, the Master would act as mediator and settle the matter. If the Master had been disturbed by the violent outbreak of disease, as would an ordinary person, it would not have been possible for him to participate regularly in those complex philosophical discussions.

We have mentioned earlier (see II.8.17, III.3.11) that the Master had a
wonderful experience towards the end of his constant dwelling in the transcendental plane. For a third time he was commanded to remain in bhavamukha. Although we described this experience as a

2. The Master's experience after being established in the nondual state: its results.

vision, the reader should understand that he realized this profoundly. This time the Master did not hear that voice coming from a visible form, as he had on the previous two occasions. When his mind was separated a little from the transcendental nondual Brahman and experienced itself as part of the personal God with attributes rather than being fully identified with Brahman, his mind directly realized any idea or wish that appeared in the Cosmic Mind of the omnipresent Brahman (see III.3.12-14). The purpose of his future life was thus completely revealed to him. Although he had no desire to preserve his body, he was repeatedly commanded by the Divine Mother to remain in bhavamukha. The Master realized that although he had no need of his body, it should be protected for the purpose of the divine play. Moreover, he received that command because if he were to be absorbed in Brahman eternally, his body would not last long. Based on the memory of his past lives, the Master then fully realized that he was an avatar, by nature eternally pure, awakened, and free. He had assumed a body and performed austerities in order to do good to humanity by eradicating the corruption of religion in this present age. Furthermore, he felt deeply that it was for a special purpose that the Divine Mother had brought him to earth this time as the son of a poor brahmin, unlettered, and devoid of all grandeur of external powers. Although this divine mystery would be understood by few during his lifetime, the spiritual current that would be manifest to the world through his body and mind would never fail and would continue to do good to humanity for a long time.

We must recall some passages from the scriptures if we want to understand how the Master achieved those extraordinary spiritual experiences. The scriptures say that aspirants attain the memory of past lives before they become fully established in pure consciousness by way of the nondual attitude.[1] Or, at the culmination

3. What the scriptures say about attaining the power to remember past lives before realizing Brahman.

of that attitude, the aspirant's memory reaches such an advanced state that the aspirant remembers how, where, and how many times he was born, and also everything he did in every previous incarnation, whether good or bad.

---

1. Through the perception of past impressions comes the knowledge of past lives. — *Yoga Aphorisms* of Patanjali 3:18

Consequently, the aspirant fully realizes the impermanence of all worldly objects and the futility of being born again and again to chase sense objects for enjoyment. An intense detachment then arises in the aspirant's mind, which makes that person free from all desires forever.

The Upanishad says that whatever a knower of the Self resolves always

4. What the scriptures say about attaining yogic powers and the state when all desires come true after realizing Brahman.

comes to pass. If such a person desires to perceive the abode of the gods or of the ancestors, or any other world, that person's mind can see those abodes instantly through samadhi. In reference to this, the great sage Patanjali mentioned in his *Yoga Sutras* that all of the supernatural yogic powers appear spontaneously to such a person. Reconciling their desirelessness on one hand and their attainment of yogic powers on the other, the author of *Panchadashi* says that these aspirants may attain those wonderful powers, but they do not use them because their hearts are free of desire. In whatever condition such an aspirant attains the knowledge of Brahman, that person continues to live in that manner even after becoming illumined. As the person's mind is completely desireless, he or she feels no need to change that condition, even though that person is capable of doing so. Depending solely on God's will, from time to time the great souls use that power in order to benefit humanity.

If we study the Master's life at this time in light of the scriptures we just

5. The causes of the Master's unique experiences can be understood by studying his life in the light of these scriptures.

discussed, we shall understand to a great extent, if not fully, the wonderful experiences he had during this period. We understand that he became completely desireless by offering everything wholeheartedly to God, and that he therefore was able to quickly reach the transcendental plane and become firmly established in it. We understand that after he attained knowledge of his past lives, he realized that He who had appeared as Rama and as Krishna in previous ages for the good of humanity had come again in this age, assuming a body as Ramakrishna. We understand why we did not see him using those divine powers for his personal joy and comfort, although we saw the manifestation of those wonderful powers in him every day. We understand how he was able by a mere wish to awaken in others the power to realize spiritual truths, and why his divine influence is even now spreading all over the world day by day.

When the Master descended to the realm of ideas after having become

6. Why those experiences did not occur simultaneously.

firmly established in the nondual state, he fully experienced his past and his future. It does not seem that those experiences came to him suddenly, or in one day. We guess that he came to understand those things within a year after he had descended into the realm of ideas. During this time, the Divine Mother made him clearly comprehend events yet to come by removing veil after veil from before his eyes. If someone were to ask why those experiences did not arise in his mind all at once, we would reply that he was then dwelling in the nondual plane uninterruptedly and enjoying the bliss of Brahman deeply. As long as his mind was not turned outward, he had neither time nor inclination to experience those things. At the beginning of his sadhana, the Master had prayed to the Divine Mother, "Mother, I don't know what I should do. Whatever you will teach me, I shall learn." Thus, his prayer was fulfilled during this period.

Established in the nondual state, the Master experienced another truth

7. The Master realized that the goal of all disciplines is to attain the nondual state.

also. He discovered that the ultimate goal of all spiritual disciplines is to become firmly established in nonduality. After performing sadhana according to the main religious denominations prevalent in India, he observed that each one of them led the aspirant towards the nondual plane. When we asked about the nondual state, he told us repeatedly: "It is the finale, my child, the culmination of sadhana. At the ultimate development of love for God, this nondual experience manifests spontaneously in the life of all aspirants. Know it to be the goal of all faiths; and as many faiths, so many paths."

After having this nondual experience, the Master's mind achieved an

8. No one had ever experienced this completely before the Master.

unbounded catholicity. He had then a tremendous sympathy for religious communities that taught that the goal of human life is the realization of God. But in the beginning he did not know that such catholicity and sympathy were his personal achievements alone, and that no other great teachers of past ages had been able to realize these as completely as he had. He understood this gradually when he became acquainted with the elderly leaders of different religious organizations in Dakshineswar and other holy places. From then on, he would be terribly hurt if he met anyone who held an exclusive view of religion, and he would try his utmost to remove that narrow-mindedness.

An event that occurred during this time illustrates clearly how liberal the

9. The Master was endowed with nondual knowledge. An example of his catholicity of mind: He practises Islam.

Master's mind became after he had attained nondual knowledge. We have already mentioned that the Master was ill for a few months after he had become perfect in the nondual sadhana. The following event took place after he had recovered from that disease.

About this time a man named Govinda Roy was seeking God. He was kshatriya by caste, according to Hriday. He was probably proficient in Persian and Arabic languages. He had studied various schools of religion, associated with different religious organizations, and finally he became attracted by the liberal doctrine of Islam and took formal initiation into that religion. Although the sincere seeker Govinda accepted Islam, we cannot say how far he followed its social rules and customs. But this we have heard: After being initiated, he read the Koran devotedly and sincerely practised the disciplines prescribed by it. Govinda was a true lover of God. It seems that his heart was drawn to the religious practices, teachings, and spiritual attitude of the Sufis, a sect of Islam. At that time he was absorbed day and night in practising the devotional moods of the Dervishes, devotees of that sect.

Somehow or other Govinda came to the Kali temple of Dakshineswar and lived for a while in the peaceful atmosphere of the Panchavati, considering it to be a favourable place for sadhana. Muslim fakirs were as welcome as Hindu monks in Rani Rasmani's Kali temple, and hospitality was accorded equally to all mendicants, irrespective of caste and religion. Therefore, Govinda did not have to go out and beg for food while staying there, so he spent his time joyfully thinking of his beloved Allah.

10. Arrival of the Sufi Govinda Roy.

The Master was attracted to the devout Govinda, and after talking to him was impressed by his sincere faith and his love for God. Thus the Master's mind was drawn to Islam. He thought: "It too is a path to attain God. The infinitely sportive Divine Mother has shown Herself to many people through this sadhana too. I must see how She fulfills the aspirations of the followers of this path. I shall take initiation from Govinda and practise this path of Islam."

11. The Master's resolve after talking to Govinda.

This thought was immediately followed by action. The Master expressed his wish to Govinda, received initiation from him, and then began to practise Islam according to its tradition. The Master said: "I then devoutly repeated the holy name of Allah dressed like the Muslims, and said their prayers several times a day. Because the Hindu feeling had disappeared from my mind altogether, I felt disinclined to visit the Hindu deities, much less to bow down to them. I spent three days in that mood, and I had the full realization of the sadhana of their faith." While practising Islam, the Master at first had a vision of a radiant Being who looked grave and had a long beard; then he experienced the cosmic Saguna Brahman; and finally his mind merged into absolute Nirguna Brahman.

12. Initiated by Govinda, the Master succeeds in his Islamic sadhana.

Hriday said that while the Master practised Islam he wanted to eat all the favourite foods of the Muslim, including beef. It was only Mathur's earnest entreaty that kept him from doing so. Knowing the Master's childlike nature, and that he would not give up until at least a part of his wish was fulfilled, Mathur hired a Muslim cook. Under that cook's direction a brahmin cook prepared Muslim dishes and that food was given to the Master. During the time he practised Islam, the Master never stepped inside the courtyard of the Kali temple; instead he lived in Mathur's bungalow.

13. The Master's behaviour while practising Islam.

It is understood from the aforesaid event how the Master's mind became

14. The Master's practice of Islam indicates that in the future Hindus and Muslims in India will be united as brothers.

sympathetic towards other religious communities after he had become perfect in the Vedantic sadhana. This indicates that only through the Vedantic knowledge of oneness can the Hindus and Muslims of India become sympathetic towards one another and feel as though they are one family. As the Master used to say: "There exists, as it were, a mountain of a barrier between Hindus and Muslims. Their modes of thinking, religious faith, actions, and behaviour have remained incomprehensible to each other despite their living together for such a long period." Does the Master's Islamic sadhana indicate that one day that mountain-high barrier will disappear and Hindus and Muslims will embrace each other in love?

As a result of being established in the transcendental plane, when the

15. Later, the Master had an intense memory of nonduality.

Master saw objects and persons within the bounds of the dualistic plane, quite often his memory of nonduality would suddenly arise and his mind would merge into the Absolute. We saw him go into that state at the slightest prompting, without prior intent. Therefore, from now on he was capable of ascending to that state even by a mere thought. This proves clearly how dear this nondual attitude was to him. Readers will understand if we mention some incidents that illustrate how deeply that attitude was rooted in his heart and how it spread widely.

During the rainy season, the spacious garden of Dakshineswar would

16. Some examples: (1) An old grasscutter.

become covered with grass and it was difficult for the gardeners to sow the seeds for vegetables. For that reason, grasscutters were permitted to cut the grass and take it away. One day an old man was given permission to take as much grass as he wanted. Joyfully he spent most of the day cutting grass, then in the afternoon he bundled it and was getting ready to take all of it to the market to sell. The Master saw that the greedy man had cut so much grass that it was beyond his physical strength to carry the heavy load. Without comprehending this simple fact, the poor grasscutter tried repeatedly in different ways to lift his large bundle onto his head, but failed. Observing this scene, the Master went into ecstasy. He reflected: "The Atman, the embodiment of infinite knowledge, exists within, whereas there is so much foolishness and ignorance without!" He exclaimed, "O Rama, how inscrutable is your play!" and then went into samadhi.

One day the Master saw a butterfly flying towards him with a tiny stick

(2) A wounded butterfly.

stuck in its tail. At first he was pained by the thought that some naughty boy had done this. But in the next moment he said in ecstasy, "O Rama, you have created your own distress," and then burst into laughter.

A certain area of the temple garden was covered with fresh durva grass; it was a beautiful sight. As the Master looked at it, he became so absorbed in ecstasy that he felt completely that the area was part of his own body. Suddenly a man walked across that field. This caused the Master unbearable pain and he became terribly restless. When he later referred to this incident, he told us: "At that time I felt that kind of sharp pain that would be felt if someone trampled on one's chest. This kind of ecstasy is extremely painful. I had it for six hours only, but still that pain was too much for me."

(3) The green durva grass trampled under foot.

One day the Master was in an ecstatic mood as he stood on the spacious ghat of the main porch watching the Ganges. Two boats were anchored there, and the boatmen were quarreling with each other. Gradually the quarrel grew intense, and the stronger man slapped the weaker one sharply on the back. At this, the Master cried out loudly in pain. The sound of his distressed cry reached Hriday inside the Kali temple. He hurriedly came to the ghat and saw that the Master's back was red and swollen. Impatient with anger, Hriday asked repeatedly: "Uncle, show me the person who hit you. I will chop off his head." When the Master regained his composure, he told Hriday what had happened. Hriday was dumbfounded by this and asked himself, "How is this possible?" Girish Chandra Ghosh heard of this incident from the Master and later told us about it. Many such events can be related concerning the Master.

(4) The fighting boatmen's blows felt by the Master on his own body.

Chapter 17

A Visit to His *B*irthplace

AFTER THE MASTER HAD SUFFERED FOR SIX MONTHS, his body finally became free of

1. The Master's visit to Kamarpukur with the Bhairavi Brahmani and Hriday.

disease, and his mind became accustomed to remaining in bhavamukha, on the border between the Absolute and the Relative. Still his body was not as healthy and strong as before, and there was some concern that his dysentery might return for lack of pure drinking water when the Ganges water became salty during the rainy season. So Mathur and others decided that it would be better for the Master to go for a few months to Kamarpukur, his birthplace. This happened during *Jaishtha* 1274 [mid-May to mid-June 1867]. The devout Jagadamba, Mathur's wife, knew that the Master's household in Kamarpukur was as poor as that of Lord Shiva. She carefully arranged all the things "Father" would need and sent them with him so that he might not be inconvenienced (see IV.1.14). Then at an auspicious time the Master left for Kamarpukur, accompanied by Hriday and the Bhairavi Brahmani. His elderly mother had previously resolved to remain on the bank of the Ganges, so she stayed in Dakshineswar.

The Master had not visited Kamarpukur for eight years, and his relatives

2. What the Master's friends and relatives thought of him.

and friends were eager to see him. There was another reason to want him at home. They had heard all sorts of rumours about his strange behaviour: that he would sometimes wear women's clothes and chant "Hari, Hari"; that he had become a sannyasin; and that he repeated "Allah, Allah" at times. But when the Master arrived in their midst and they saw him themselves, they became free of any doubts caused by what they had heard.

They found him just as he was before. They saw in him in full measure the same amiability, the same loving merriment and jests, the same strict adherence to truthfulness, the same passion for God, and the same overwhelming

Ramakrishna's family cottages in Kamarpukur, opposite to Yogi Shiva temple. The mango tree at left, planted by Ramakrishna, still stands.

devotion to the name of Hari. But there was something more. They found that such a novel, indescribable divine atmosphere always surrounded him that they felt hesitant to enter his presence suddenly, or to discuss small family matters with him unless he himself raised the topic. In addition, they observed another thing: When they were with him, all their worries and anxieties disappeared and a steady current of peace and bliss flowed in their hearts. When they were away, they felt a strong and mysterious attraction to return to him. Having him back after such a long time, his poor family was filled with merriment. To make the family's happiness complete, the women sent a messenger to the village of Jayrambati to bring his wife, Sarada, to Kamarpukur. When he learned of this, the Master expressed neither approval nor disapproval.

Sarada had seen her husband only once after their wedding. During

3. Arrival of the Holy Mother [Sarada Devi] at Kamarpukur.

Sarada's seventh year, the Master was taken to Jayrambati according to the family custom. Since she was then a little girl, the only thing she remembered in connection with her husband's visit was that when he arrived with Hriday, she tried to hide herself in a secluded part of the house. But Hriday sought her out and worshipped her feet with some lotuses as she shrank into herself out of bashfulness and fear. Six years later, when she was thirteen, she was taken to Kamarpukur. On that occasion she stayed there for a month. But she did not have the opportunity to see the Master and his mother, as both of them were then at Dakshineswar. Six months later she returned to her father-in-law's house. She stayed for a month and a half but could not see her husband or her mother-in-law for the same reason. Three or four months after her return to Jayrambati, news of the Master's arrival came and she was asked to go back to Kamarpukur. She was then fourteen. So this was in fact her first meeting with her husband after the marriage ceremony.

This time the Master stayed at Kamarpukur for six or seven months. His

4. The Master's behaviour with his relatives and boyhood friends.

boyhood friends and the men and women of the village who knew him mixed with him as before and tried to make him happy. The Master was delighted to see them after such a long time. As wise men, after retiring from a hard-working life, enjoy the carefree play and activities of children, the Master felt a similar joy participating in the domestic lives of the Kamarpukur villagers. Undoubtedly he guided them so that they could realize the transitoriness of this life and slowly learn self-control while living in the world and depending on God in all matters. We infer this from seeing the way he constantly taught us through play and jest, mirth and merriment.

The Master was overwhelmed by the inscrutable glory of God when he

5. The Master's remarks about the spiritual progress of some villagers.

found that some villagers had made unexpected progress in spiritual life while living in their small households. To illustrate this he repeatedly mentioned one incident to us: One day he was resting in his room after lunch. Some neighbour women came to see him, and sitting near him they began discussing spiritual matters. All of a sudden he went into ecstasy. In that state he felt that he was joyfully swimming like a fish in the ocean of Satchidananda — sometimes sinking and sometimes floating. The Master would quite often go into ecstasy like this while talking with others; so without paying much attention to it, the women were noisily expressing their own opinions about his condition. Then one of them asked the others to keep quiet until the Master's ecstasy came to an end. She said: "He is now swimming in the ocean of Satchidananda like a fish. If you make noise, that will interrupt his bliss." Although many of them did not believe her, they became silent. Later, when the Master came down to the normal plane and heard what the woman had said about his experience, he remarked: "She is right. It is really amazing. How could she know?"

It is understood that to a great extent the daily life of the people of

6. The reason for the Master's new outlook towards the villagers.

Kamarpukur appeared to the Master as new. As a person who returns home from a far-off land after a long time sees his native people and things anew, so now the Master felt the same way. Although he had been away from his birthplace for only eight years, during that period a great tempest of sadhana had blown in his heart, bringing a radical transformation in it. During that time, he had forgotten himself, forgotten the world, and gone far beyond the boundaries of space and time. When he returned to the phenomenal universe he was endowed with the experience of seeing Brahman in every being, so his perception of all people and all objects was completely changed. It is an established philosophic principle that we experience time and its duration through the succession of our thoughts. Therefore, if many thoughts appear and disappear in the mind within a short period, it seems to us that a long time has passed. The tremendous volume of thought waves that passed through the Master's mind during those eight years is incredible. It is no wonder that he felt that period to be like an age.

It is remarkable how the Master had bound himself to the people of

7. The Master's constant loving relationship with the people of his birthplace.

Kamarpukur with a wonderful cord of love. He was tied with a loving and reverential relationship to all the neighbourhood men and women, from the wealthy Lahas to the brahmins, blacksmiths, carpenters, gold merchants, and others. We were moved when the Master at different times told us with delight about the love and devotion of the simple-hearted and devout Prasanna, the widowed daughter of Dharmadas Laha; the Master's childhood friend Gayavishnu Laha, the son of Dharmadas; the sincere faith of Srinivas Sankhari; the devout women of the Pyne family; the blacksmith woman Dhani, his godmother; and others. They remained with him most of the time during his stay in Kamarpukur. Those who could not do so because of household duties or other business would visit when they had free time in the morning, at noon, or in the evening. The women were delighted to feed the Master, so they would come carrying various kinds of sweets and delicacies. We have mentioned elsewhere (see IV.1.14) how the Master was always in a god-intoxicated mood when surrounded by his relatives and enjoying the loving care of the villagers.

During this visit to Kamarpukur the Master earnestly attended to a noble

8. The Master begins his duty to his wife.

duty. Although he was initially indifferent to his wife's coming to Kamarpukur, when she arrived to serve him, he began to educate and train her for her well being. Knowing that the Master was married, Tota Puri had once said to him: "What does it matter? He alone is firmly established in the knowledge of Brahman who can keep intact his renunciation, detachment, discrimination, and self-awareness even while living with his wife. He alone has attained supreme illumination who can always look upon man and woman alike as the Atman and deal with them accordingly. A person who is aware of the differences between the sexes may be a good aspirant, but that person is still far from having the knowledge of Brahman." Remembering Tota Puri's words, the Master now began to test the Self-knowledge that he had achieved after his long sadhana and to train his wife for her own spiritual development.

The Master could not neglect any action or leave it half-finished if he

9. How far the Master succeeds in this respect.

considered it to be his duty. The same applied to the present situation. The Master came forward to thoroughly train his adolescent wife, who solely depended on him in every respect relating to both secular and spiritual matters. He taught her how to serve God, the guru, and the guest; how to perform household work skillfully and spend money discreetly; and most important, how to surrender everything to God and become expert in dealing with people according to place, time, and circumstance (see III.2.68 and III.4.20-21). We have hinted elsewhere how far-reaching was the result of the teaching that the Master imparted to her by setting the example of his ideal life endowed with unbroken chastity. It is enough to say that Sarada was fully satisfied with the Master's chaste and pure love. Throughout her life she worshipped the Master as her Chosen Deity and built her own life by following his example.

The Bhairavi Brahmani quite often misunderstood the Master when he

10. The Brahmani's apprehension and change of mood on observing the Master's behaviour with his wife.

became engaged in training his wife. Previously the Brahmani had tried to prevent the Master from taking the vows of sannyasa when he came in contact with Tota Puri (see III.2.11). She thought that the Master's love of God would completely disappear from his heart if he became a sannyasin and practised nondualism. Some such fear might now have taken possession of her mind. She probably thought that if the Master became too close to his wife, his celibacy would be compromised. But the Master did not listen to the Brahmani's advice in either case. Consequently, it is understood that the Brahmani was extremely hurt. But the matter did not end there. This incident gradually turned her wounded feeling into egotism and for some time she became disrespectful towards the Master. We heard from Hriday that sometimes she was openly impolite. For example, if someone asked her a spiritual question and then said that he was going to Sri Ramakrishna to get his opinion about it, the Brahmani would angrily respond: "What will he say? It is I who opened his eyes." Or sometimes she would rebuke the women of the family over some trivial matter, or for no reason at all. But the Master remained calm and maintained his love and respect for her despite her insulting remarks and outrageous behaviour. As instructed by the Master, Sarada looked upon the Brahmani as her own mother-in-law, always served her carefully, and never protested against any of her remarks or actions.

When pride and ego swell, even an intelligent person loses good judge-

11. Pride and ego ruin the Brahmani's power of discrimination.

ment. But when such people see that their egos are crushed at every step and realize the inevitable harmful effect of egotism, they then begin to shun their egos and strive to improve themselves. Now the learned Brahmani was in this situation. One day her pride kept her from acting appropriately in a particular circumstance, and as a result she created an awkward situation.

We have already mentioned the name of Srinivas Sankhari. Although he was not born of a high-caste family, he surpassed many brahmins in his

12. The incident pertaining to this.

devotion to God. One day he came to visit the Master and to partake of the prasad of Raghuvir. The Master and other members of the family were extremely pleased to see Srinivas. Even the devout Brahmani was very impressed with his faith and devotion. Till noon they discussed various devotional topics, and when the worship and food offering to Raghuvir were over, Srinivas sat down to partake of the prasad. After lunch when Srinivas was about to clean his place, following the prevalent custom, the Brahmani forbade him, saying, "We will do it later." When the Brahmani said this repeatedly, Srinivas had no alternative but to give up and leave for his home.

Generally caste rules are strictly observed in villages. If anybody violates

13. The quarrel between the Brahmani and Hriday.

those rules, it creates friction and dissension. Now such a thing was about to happen. When the brahmin Bhairavi was trying to clean up the leavings of the lower-caste Srinivas, the brahmin women of the village who came to visit the Master objected. But the Bhairavi Brahmani did not agree with their objections. Gradually the quarrel spread, and Hriday heard about it. Recognizing the possibility of a terrible fight over this petty matter, Hriday asked her to stop what she was doing, but she refused. A bitter argument broke out between Hriday and the Brahmani. Enraged, Hriday said, "If you violate the caste rule, we won't let you stay in this house." The Brahmani was not a person to yield easily. She replied: "It does not matter. Manasa[1] will now sleep in Shitala's room."[2] The members of the family mediated, persuading the Brahmani to stop cleaning up the leavings, and thus the quarrel ended.

Although she yielded on that day, the Brahmani's feelings were terribly

14. Realizing her mistake, the Brahmani repents; begging forgiveness from the Master, she leaves for Varanasi.

wounded. But when her anger subsided and she calmly thought about the matter, she understood her mistake. She realized that it would be better not to stay there after making such an error in judgement. When a discriminating and conscientious spiritual aspirant examines his or her own mind, no impure thought can hide itself. Now that happened to the Brahmani. Pondering the change in her attitude towards the Master, she recognized her own shortcomings and became extremely repentant. A few days passed. Then one day she adorned the Master beautifully as Gauranga with garlands of various flowers and sandal paste and wholeheartedly begged his forgiveness. After composing herself, she offered herself completely to God and departed for Varanasi, leaving Kamarpukur behind. The Brahmani took leave of the Master after living near him continually for about six years.

The Master lived in Kamarpukur joyfully with his friends and relatives

15. The Master returns to Dakshineswar.

and then returned to Dakshineswar, most likely in November 1867. He had regained his former health and felt strong. Shortly after his return, a significant event took place in his life, which we shall now relate to the reader.

---

1. Manasa is the goddess of snakes. The Brahmani thus compared herself to an angry snake.
2. The temple of Shitala, a goddess.

Chapter 18

Pilgrimage and a
Story Concerning *H*riday

MATHUR PLANNED TO VISIT SOME IMPORTANT HOLY places in northwestern India. It

1. The plan for the Master's pilgrimage.	was decided that he would be accompanied by his family members, the son of his guru, and others.

Mathur and his wife earnestly entreated the Master to
go with them. He agreed to accompany them with his aged mother[1] and Hriday.

Mathur started his journey with the Master and others on an auspicious

2. The date of the journey.	day, 27 January 1868. We have described the Master's pilgrimage in detail elsewhere (see IV.3.15-23,30-32), so we shall narrate here what we have heard from

Hriday.

Hriday told us that Mathur took more than a hundred people on the

3. Arrangements for the journey.	pilgrimage. He reserved one second-class car and three third-class cars from the Railway Company, and it was arranged that at some point between Calcutta

and Varanasi he could disconnect those four cars and take a separate trip.

Mathur stopped at Deoghar, in Bihar, and stayed a few days to visit and

4. The visit to Vaidyanath and Mathur's service to the poor.	worship the Lord Vaidyanath [Shiva]. An important incident took place there. The Master's heart was moved with compassion upon seeing the miserable

plight of the poor men and women in a nearby village. He asked Mathur to
feed them for one day and give a piece of cloth to each person (see III.7.38),
which Mathur did.

1. Some say that the Master's mother did not go on the pilgrimage, but Hriday told us that she did.

329

Vaidyanath Shiva temple in Deoghar where Ramakrishna demanded
that Mathur feed the poor.

Varanasi viewed from the Ganges. Ramakrishna visited sacred sites here in 1868.

From Deoghar, Mathur went directly to Varanasi. On the way nothing

5. An incident on the way.

noteworthy happened, except that at a station near Varanasi the Master and Hriday got off the train for some purpose and it moved on before they could reboard. When the train reached Varanasi, the anxious Mathur hurriedly sent a cable to the stationmaster asking that the Master and Hriday be sent on the next train. But fortunately they did not have to wait that long. In a short time Rajendralal Bandyopadhyay, a distinguished officer of the Railway Company, arrived at their station in a special train on inspection duty, and seeing their predicament, took the Master and Hriday in his train to Varanasi. Rajendralal was a resident of Baghbazar, Calcutta.

When they arrived in Varanasi, Mathur rented two adjacent houses at

6. Their residence at Kedarghat and visit to Vishwanath Shiva.

Kedarghat. Here Mathur spent money lavishly on worship and charity (see III.7.37). Whenever he went out to visit any place, some guards would hold a silver umbrella over his head, and others would walk in front and in back of him bearing silver staffs. For that reason people considered Mathur to be of royalty.

While staying in Varanasi, Sri Ramakrishna went by palanquin almost daily to visit the Lord Vishwanath, with Hriday accompanying him. Considering that merely travelling to the temple put the Master into ecstasy, what can we say of his visit to the deity. Although he went into ecstasy in all temples, he experienced it most deeply in Kedarnath.

In addition to visiting the temples, the Master went to see the prominent

7. The Master and Trailanga Swami.

holy men of Varanasi. Hriday always accompanied him. The Master went several times to see Trailanga Swami, a leading paramahamsa. The swami was then observing a vow of silence and staying at Manikarnika ghat. During the first visit he received the Master with respect and offered him snuff from his own box. Observing his eyes, ears, other sense organs, and the formation of his limbs, the Master said to Hriday: "All the signs of a real paramahamsa exist in him. He is the veritable Vishwanath." At that time the swami had resolved to have another ghat built near Manikarnika. At the Master's request Hriday put a few shovels of earth there to help with the project. One day later on the Master went to see the swami and fed him rice pudding with his own hands (see IV.3.20).

The Master stayed in Varanasi for a week and then went to Prayag

8. The Master at Prayag.

[Allahabad]. He bathed in the confluence of the holy rivers, the Ganges and the Yamuna, and stayed there for three nights. Following the injunctions of the scriptures, Mathur and other men shaved their heads, but the Master did not do so. He said, "It is not necessary for me to perform this rite." From Prayag Mathur and his party returned to Varanasi, stayed there for two weeks, and then moved on to Vrindaban.

In Vrindaban Mathur stayed in a house near Nidhuban. As he was in
Varanasi, Mathur was generous in his gifts to the
needy. When he and his wife visited the temples,
Mathur offered a few gold coins to the deity of each

9. The Master visits
Nidhuban and other
places in Vrindaban.

sacred place. In addition to Nidhuban, the Master visited Radhakunda,
Shyamkunda, and Govardhan Hill. In ecstasy, the Master climbed to the top
of this hill. The Master visited the prominent holy people of Vrindaban and
was delighted to meet the saintly woman Gangamata in Nidhuban. Indicating her physical characteristics, the Master told Hriday, "This woman has
achieved a very high state of spirituality."

Mathur and his party remained in Vrindaban for about two weeks and then
returned to Varanasi. They stayed there until *Vaishakh*
1275 [mid-April to mid-May 1868] in order to attend the

10. Return to Varanasi.

festival when Lord Vishwanath was adorned with special clothing and ornaments. During this period the Master also saw the golden image of Annapurna.

While in Varanasi the Master again saw Yogeswari, the Bhairavi Brahmani. On several occasions he visited her residence at
Chaushatti-Yogini, where she was living with a
woman named Mokshada. The Master was very
pleased with Mokshada's faith and devotion. The
Brahmani accompanied the Master to Vrindaban,

11. The Master's
meeting with the
Brahmani in Varanasi:
the last story about the
Brahmani.

and he advised her to live there permanently. Hriday told us that she died in
Vrindaban shortly after the Master returned to Varanasi.

In Vrindaban the Master expressed a desire to listen to the vina, but this
desire was not fulfilled because no player was avail-
able at that time. When he returned to Varanasi that
desire again arose in his mind. Accompanied by

12. The Master visits
Mahesh, a famous vina
player.

Hriday, the Master went to the house of Mahesh Chandra Sarkar, an expert
vina player, and asked him to play. Mahesh lived in the Madanpura area of
Varanasi. On that day he gladly played the vina for a long time at the
Master's request. As soon as the Master heard the sweet jingling sound of the
vina, he went into ecstasy. When he was in a semiconscious state, he prayed
to the Divine Mother, "Please keep me in the conscious plane, O Mother, so I
can listen to the music." After this, he was able to remain externally conscious. He listened to the vina with delight and from time to time sang along
with it. He thus enjoyed the music from 5:00 to 8:00 p.m., accepted a little
refreshment at Mahesh's request, and then returned to Mathur. From then
on Mahesh visited the Master every day. The Master remarked of him,
"When Mahesh plays, he loses himself completely."

Mathur expressed a desire to leave Varanasi and visit Gaya, but the Master
strongly objected to this (see IV.3.25). So Mathur
abandoned that idea and they all returned to Calcutta. Hriday said that after visiting those important

13. The Master's return
to Dakshineswar.

holy places for four months, the Master returned to Dakshineswar in the last part of May 1868. The Master had taken some holy dust from Radhakunda and Shyamkunda in Vrindaban, and he now scattered some of it around the Panchavati in Dakshineswar. Burying some in his sadhan-kutir [meditation hut], he said, "From today this place is as sacred as Vrindaban." Hriday also mentioned that shortly after this the Master asked Mathur to invite Vaishnava teachers and devotees and arrange a big festival in the Panchavati. The festival was held, and as a token of respect Mathur gave sixteen rupees to each of those teachers and one rupee to each devotee as they left.

Shortly after Hriday returned from the pilgrimage, his wife died. For a while his mind was filled with dispassion for the world. We have mentioned previously that Hriday was not contemplative. He was a pragmatic person whose ambition was to improve the financial condition of his little family and enjoy a comfortable worldly life. Constant association with the Master sometimes created a spiritual mood in his mind, but it never lasted long. Whenever there was any opportunity to satisfy his desire for enjoyment, Hriday would forget everything to pursue it, and until his desire was fulfilled, he could think of nothing else. Although the Master's entire sadhana was performed during Hriday's stay at Dakshineswar, Hriday saw very little of it and understood even less. Nonetheless, Hriday sincerely loved his uncle and never failed to render any service he needed at any time. Because of this, Hriday developed courage, intelligence, and practical wisdom. As he heard of the superhuman nature of his uncle from famous religious leaders, and observed the manifestation of the Master's divine power, Hriday felt a special strength within. He thought that because his uncle was his very own and he was blessed by serving him, he therefore in some way shared in the spiritual results his uncle had achieved. He believed that if he ever had any desire for spiritual experiences, his uncle would make him attain them through his divine power. So he had never felt any need to think of the hereafter. He had planned to apply his mind to spiritual matters after he had enjoyed the world for a while. But now, grief-stricken at the death of his wife, Hriday felt that the right time had arrived. He concentrated more steadfastly than before on the worship of the Divine Mother, and at times removed his cloth and sacred thread to meditate. Hriday also importuned the Master, asking for spiritual realizations like those he had experienced. The Master tried to convince him that such experiences were not necessary, and that he would get all the results by merely serving him. Moreover, the Master reminded him, if both Hriday and he were absorbed in God-consciousness day and night, forgetting food and sleep, who would look after them? But Hriday would not listen. The Master at last said: "All right, let the Mother's will be done. Does anything happen by my will? It

14. Death of Hriday's wife and his dispassion.

was the Mother who created a revolution in my mind and made me pass through all those stages of realization. If She wills, you will also have them."

A few days after this conversation, Hriday began to have visions of lumi-

15. Hriday's ecstasy.

nous deities and experienced a touch of ecstasy during worship and meditation. One day after seeing Hriday in an ecstatic mood, Mathur asked the Master, "Father, what has happened to Hriday?" The Master explained: "Hriday is not feigning these states. He earnestly prayed to the Mother to have some visions, and this is the result. The Mother will calm him down again after giving him a taste of it." Mathur said: "Father, this is your play. You have brought about this state in Hriday. Now make him normal. Both of us should be with you like Nandi and Bhringi [attendants of Shiva] and serve you. These spiritual states are not meant for us."

One night shortly after this conversation, Hriday saw the Master going

16. Hriday's wonderful vision.

towards the Panchavati. Thinking that he might need his water pot and towel, Hriday obtained them and followed. While walking, Hriday had an extraordinary vision. He saw that the Master was not a human being made of flesh and blood. Light was emanating from his body and illumining the entire Panchavati. As he walked, his luminous feet moved through the air without touching the ground. Hriday repeatedly rubbed his eyes, thinking this must be an optical illusion. He looked at the other objects around him and then back at the luminous form of the Master. Although he perceived the trees, creepers, Ganges, hut, and so on as before, he saw the Master's shining form again and again. Amazed, Hriday thought, "Is there any change in me that I am seeing the Master this way?" Then he looked at himself and saw that his own body was also luminous. He felt that he was a veritable attendant of God, living with Him and serving Him eternally. He felt as if he were a part of that luminous form of God and had assumed a separate form in order to serve Him. With this vision Hriday realized the mystery of his own life, and a current of bliss flowed in his heart. He then forgot himself, forgot the world, and forgot to consider whether others would call him mad. In ecstasy, he shouted frantically again and again: "O Ramakrishna, O Ramakrishna, we are not human beings. Why are we here? Come, let us go from place to place and save human souls. You and I are the same."

The Master said later: "Hearing his loud cry, I said: 'Ah! Keep quiet, keep

17. Hriday's mind becomes dull.

quiet. Why are you shouting like that? People will rush here thinking some calamity has happened.' But he paid no heed to my words. Then I hurried to him and said, touching his chest, 'Mother, make this rascal dull and stupid again.'"

Hriday said that as soon as the Master uttered those words, the vision and his bliss vanished and he became the same as before. The sudden fall from that unique blissful state filled his mind with sorrow. Sobbing, he asked:

"Uncle, why did you do that to me? Why did you say that I should be dull? Now I will not have that blissful vision again." The Master consoled him, saying: "I do not mean for you to be dull forever. I only wanted to calm you down. I had to say that because you were making such a commotion over that little vision of yours. I experience many divine visions in a day, but do I raise such a racket? You are not yet ready for visions. Keep quiet now; you will have many more experiences when the right time comes."

The Master's words quieted Hriday, but he was terribly hurt. Later, out of egotism, he resolved to somehow attain that kind of vision again. He increased the frequency of his meditation and japa, and decided that at night he would go to the Panchavati, where the Master had formerly practised sadhana, and pray to the Divine Mother. Very late one night he left his bed, went to the Panchavati, and sat to meditate on the Master's seat. After a while the Master also felt an impulse to go to the Panchavati, so he walked in that direction. On his way he heard Hriday calling him piteously: "O Uncle, save me! I'm being burned to death!" The Master hurried to him, asking, "Tell me, what happened?" Tormented with pain, Hriday replied: "Uncle, no sooner had I sat down on this spot for meditation than I felt as if someone had thrown a plate of live embers right over me. I feel an unbearable burning sensation!" The Master stroked his body gently and said: "Don't worry, now you will feel cool. Tell me, why do you do such things? Haven't I told you that you'll gain everything just by serving me?" Hriday said later that upon the Master's touch his pain instantly disappeared. After this incident, he never again went to the Panchavati for meditation. He was now convinced that if he did not follow his uncle's advice, things would go badly for him.

18. Obstacle to Hriday's sadhana.

Hriday's faith in the Master's words gave him some peace; but the daily duties of the temple were becoming distasteful to him. His mind began to look for new undertakings that would bring him fresh excitement. In the autumn of 1868, Hriday decided to perform Durga Puja at his country home in Sihar. Ganganarayan, Hriday's elder stepbrother, had then passed away; and Raghav, his own elder brother, was making good money as a tax collector for Mathur's estate. As the family's financial condition was now improved, a new worship hall had been built. Ganganarayan had expressed a desire to celebrate Durga Puja there, but never had the opportunity to do so. Remembering his late stepbrother's wish, Hriday now made an effort to fulfill it. The Master agreed to this plan, thinking that the restless Hriday would find some peace by worshipping the Divine Mother. Mathur made a financial contribution to Hriday's celebration, but he wanted the Master to be at his Calcutta residence during Durga Puja instead of going to Hriday's worship. Heavy hearted, Hriday then prepared to go home alone to perform the worship. Seeing him sad as he departed, the Master consoled him, saying: "Why are

19. Hriday celebrates the worship of Durga.

you grieving? I shall go to your place every day in a subtle body and watch your worship, and no one will be able to see me except you. Arrange for a brahmin to read the mantras to you, and perform the worship in your own way. Don't fast altogether, but at noon take milk, Ganges water, and rock candy syrup. If you proceed in this way, the Divine Mother will definitely accept your worship." The Master also gave him specific instructions as to who should make the image, who should prompt the mantras, and how all other things should be done. Now filled with joy, Hriday left for home to perform the worship.

Hriday reached his home and arranged everything according to the Master's instructions. In accordance with tradition, he invoked the goddess on the sixth day of the bright fortnight and performed the preliminary rituals pertaining to the consecration of the image. The next day he completed the saptami puja and, while waving the lighted lamp during the vesper service, he saw the Master's luminous form standing in ecstasy beside the image. Hriday told us that he was overjoyed when he saw the Master next to the image every day during vespers, and also during the sandhi-puja. Shortly after the Durga Puja, Hriday returned to Dakshineswar and told the Master what had happened. The Master responded: "It is true that I felt an intense longing to see your worship during vespers and the sandhi-puja. While in ecstasy I felt that in a shining body I moved along a luminous path and entered your worship hall."

20. Hriday sees the Master during the worship.

Hriday told us that once the Master said to him in an ecstatic mood, "You will perform worship for three years only." Events happened as he foretold. In the fourth year Hriday, disregarding the Master's words, tried to arrange the worship service, but a series of misfortunes occurred and he was finally compelled to stop.

21. The story of Hriday's last Durga festival.

Shortly after the first year's celebration, Hriday married for the second time and began to devote himself to the worship of Kali at Dakshineswar and the service of the Master as before.

Chapter 19

*D*eath of the Master's Relatives

WE HAVE ALREADY BRIEFLY MENTIONED AKSHAY, the son of the Master's eldest

1. The story of Akshay, Ramkumar's son.

brother, Ramkumar. In 1865, shortly after Tota Puri's arrival, Akshay came to Dakshineswar and became the priest of the Vishnu [Radha-Govinda] temple. He was then seventeen years old. It is necessary to say a few things about him here.

Because Akshay's mother died when he was born, he became especially

2. Akshay's beauty.

dear to his relatives. Akshay was three or four years old when the Master went to Calcutta in 1852. Before he left Kamarpukur, the Master would carry Akshay in his arms and always took care of him lovingly. But Ramkumar never held the child. When asked the reason, he replied: "It is unnecessary to increase maya. This child will not live long." Later, the Master became absorbed in sadhana, forgetting the world and himself. Beyond his gaze this beautiful child gradually passed through boyhood and became a handsome youth. The Master and his relatives told us that Akshay was strikingly good-looking. They said that his complexion was fair and the limbs of his body were well formed and delicately soft. He looked like a living image of Shiva.

From his childhood Akshay was very devoted to the family deity Rama-

3. Akshay's devotion to Ramachandra and love of sadhana.

chandra and would spend a long time in worship. So the position he received when he came to Dakshineswar was very much to his liking. The Master said: "While worshipping Radha-Govinda, Akshay would become so absorbed in meditation that he would be unaware of the large crowd in the temple. After he had remained in that condition for a couple of hours, he

337

would regain his normal consciousness." Hriday told us that after Akshay had performed the daily worship in the temple, he would go to the Panchavati and worship Shiva there for a long time. Then he would cook his own food, and after lunch he would read the Bhagavata attentively. In addition, his passion for God-realization led him to practise nyasa and pranayama so excessively that his throat and palate would swell and sometimes bleed. His sincere faith and devotion endeared him to the Master.

Years passed one after another. It was the early part of 1869. When

| 4. Akshay's marriage.

Akshay's uncle Rameswar realized that he had reached marriageable age, he began to search for a bride. He found a suitable girl in the village of Kuchekol near Kamarpukur, and then went to Dakshineswar to bring Akshay home. It was the Bengali month of *Chaitra* [mid-March to mid-April]. When the objection was raised that the month of Chaitra was inauspicious for a journey, Rameswar disregarded it. He said that it was not necessary to observe the prohibition of the almanac when one was returning home from temporary residence in a distant place. Shortly after they returned to Kamarpukur, Akshay's marriage ceremony was held in Vaishakh 1276 [mid-April to mid-May 1869].

A few months after his wedding, Akshay went to his father-in-law's

| 5. Akshay's serious illness after the wedding; his return to Dakshineswar.

house, where he became seriously ill. When he heard the news, Rameswar brought Akshay back to Kamarpukur and arranged for his treatment. When he was cured, Rameswar sent him to Dakshineswar. On his return he looked well, and his health seemed to be gradually improving, but one day he had a sudden attack of fever. The physicians said that it was a simple fever and he would recover soon.

Hriday later said that when the Master heard that Akshay had become

| 6. Akshay's relapse; the Master's premonition of his death.

sick at his father-in-law's house, he remarked: "Hriday, the omen is very bad. He was married to a girl of *rakshasa-gana* [an ungodly nature]. This boy will die." When Akshay's fever had not abated even after three or four days, the Master said to Hriday: "Look, the doctors cannot diagnose the disease. Akshay has contracted typhoid fever. Consult good physicians and treat him to your satisfaction, but the boy will not survive."

Hriday said: "When I heard the Master say this, I protested: 'God forbid,

| 7. Hearing of Akshay's imminent death, Hriday's apprehension.

Uncle. How can you utter such ominous words?' He then replied: 'Did I say that of my own accord? I say things involuntarily, as the Divine Mother makes me know and speak. Do I wish that Akshay should die?'"

Hriday became extremely anxious upon hearing those words of the Master.

| 8. Akshay's death and the Master's reaction.

He called in good doctors and tried his utmost in various ways to cure Akshay's disease. But the illness gradually became worse, and Akshay suffered for a month. When the Master saw that Akshay's last moment had arrived, he went to his bedside and told him: "Akshay, say, 'Ganga, Narayana, Om Rama.'" Akshay repeated that mantra three times, then passed away. Hriday told us that the more he cried at Akshay's death, the more the Master laughed in ecstasy.

When the Master was in an exalted state he laughed at the death of his

| 9. The Master's grief for Akshay. | handsome nephew Akshay. But Akshay had been like a son to him, and he grieved terribly. When he referred to this incident many years later, the Master |

sometimes told us that when he was in ecstasy he saw death as merely a change of state, but when he came down to the normal plane he felt a great void at Akshay's passing (see III.1.24). Because Akshay had died at the owner's bungalow, the Master could not live there anymore.

After Akshay's death, Rameswar became the priest of the Radha-Govinda

| 10. The Master's brother Rameswar becomes a priest. | temple in Dakshineswar. But because the management of the entire family in Kamarpukar was entrusted to him, he could not stay in Dakshineswar |

all the time. Sometimes he would hand over his temple duties to a reliable person, then go to Kamarpukar and stay there. We heard that Ramchandra Chattopadhyay and a man named Dinanath would conduct the worship service during Rameswar's absences.

Shortly after Akshay's death, Mathur visited his estate and his guru's

| 11. The Master goes to Ranaghat with Mathur and advises him to serve the poor. | house, with the Master accompanying him. Perhaps he made this arrangement in order to relieve the Master's grief over Akshay's death. On one hand, the devout Mathur followed the Master's spiritual |

advice in every respect, considering him to be God; on the other, with respect to worldly affairs he thought of the Master as a naïve boy who needed Mathur to protect him.

While visiting a village in Mathur's estate, the Master was deeply grieved upon seeing the people's misery and poverty. He asked Mathur to give each of them enough oil to bathe with, a new cloth to wear, and some food. Mathur fulfilled the Master's wishes. Hriday told us that this event took place at Kalaighat near Ranaghat in the Nadia district, when Mathur, accompanied by the Master, was taking a boat trip in the Churni Canal.

We heard from Hriday that Mathur's ancestral home was in the village of

| 12. The Master's visit to Mathur's ancestral home and his guru's home. | Sonabere at Satkshira in the Khulna district. All of the villages adjacent to Sonabere were in Mathur's estate, and he took the Master there. Mathur's guru's home was not far from this place. At that time the descen- |

dants of his guru were quarrelling over the division of their property in the village of Talamagro, and they invited Mathur to settle the dispute. For the journey to the village, Mathur gave his elephant to the Master and Hriday to

ride and he went by palanquin.[1] The Master spent a few weeks under the
loving care of Mathur's guru's sons and then returned to Dakshineswar.

Shortly after returning from Mathur's home and his guru's dwelling, an
important event connected with the Master took
place at Coolootola in Calcutta. The regular meeting of
the Coolootola Harisabha was then being held at the
house of Kalinath Datta (also known as Kalinath
Dhar). The Master was invited to that meeting, and
while he was in ecstasy he sat on the seat reserved for Lord Chaitanya. Elsewhere we have provided for the reader a detailed description of this incident
(see IV.3.38). Soon after this event, the Master wished to visit Navadwip, the
birthplace of Chaitanya, so Mathur took him to Kalna, Navadwip, and other
places. Elsewhere we have told the reader (see IV.3.33-34) how in Kalna the
Master met Bhagavandas Babaji, an illumined Vaishnava devotee, and how
he had a wonderful vision in Navadwip. It was probably in 1870 that the
Master visited those holy places. In Navadwip the Master was not very
inspired, but he did experience deep ecstasy in the boat as it was passing near
the silted riverbed of the Ganges in the area of Navadwip. When Mathur
asked the reason for this, the Master replied that the ancient Navadwip,
where Chaitanya's divine play took place, was deep below the Ganges in
that area. Those holy spots were now in this silted riverbed. For that reason,
he experienced deep ecstasy when they came near that place.

13. The Master sits on
Sri Chaitanya's Seat at
the Harisabha in
Coolootola; his visit to
Kalna and Navadwip.

Mathur served the Master wholeheartedly for fourteen years continually,
and as a result his mind developed selfless devotion.
It will not be out of place to present here an incident,
related by Hriday, that illustrates this.

14. An example of
Mathur's unselfish love.

Mathur was once bedridden because of an abscess in one of his joints, and
he was extremely eager to see the Master. Hriday notified the Master, but he
said: "What good would it do if I visited? Do I have the power to cure an
abscess?" The Master did not go. Mathur then sent messenger after messenger
imploring him to come to his Calcutta residence. At last the Master yielded
to his earnest entreaties. When the Master arrived, Mathur's joy knew no
bounds. With great difficulty he got up, sat reclining against a bolster, and
said, "Father, give me a little dust of your feet."

The Master said: "What good would it do to have the dust of my feet? Will
it cure your abscess?"

Mathur replied: "Father, am I so mean? Do you think I want the dust of
your feet to cure my abscess? I have doctors for that purpose. I want the dust
of your feet so that I may cross the ocean of worldly maya."

---

1. Hriday said that while going to that village the road was rough, so he gave the palanquin
to the Master, and he himself rode on the elephant. After reaching the village he sometimes
let the Master ride on the elephant to satisfy the Master's curiosity.

As soon as the Master heard this, he went into ecstasy. Mathur laid his head on the Master's feet and felt blessed, and tears of joy trickled from his eyes.

Both the Master and Hriday told us many stories of Mathur's love for and

| 15. The intense, loving relationship between the Master and Mathur. |

faith in the Master. Mathur was firmly convinced that the Master was his only refuge in this life and the next. Correspondingly, the Master's compassion for him was boundless. Sometimes the independent-minded Master would be annoyed by some of Mathur's actions, but he would forget his annoyance immediately and fulfill Mathur's requests, trying to do what was good for him in this world and the next. From the following incidents one can understand how deep, loving, and inseparable was the relationship that existed between the Master and Mathur.

Once when he was in an ecstatic mood the Master said to Mathur, "As

| 16. First example. |

long as you are alive, I shall be in Dakshineswar." This startled Mathur and made him apprehensive because he knew that the Divine Mother was protecting him and his family through the Master. So when he heard the Master's words, he thought that the Master would forsake his family after his death. He then said to the Master humbly: "What are you saying, Father? My wife and son Dwaraka are very much devoted to you." Observing Mathur's distress, the Master replied, "All right, I shall remain as long as your wife and Dwaraka live." It indeed came to pass that the Master left Dakshineswar for good shortly after the death of Jagadamba and Dwaraka. Jagadamba died in 1881;[2] after this the Master remained in Dakshineswar a little more than three years. [He actually left Dakshineswar in September 1885.]

On another day Mathur said to the Master, "Father, once you said that

| 17. Second example. |

your devotees would come, but they have not yet arrived." The Master replied: "Well, I don't know when the Mother will bring them. But the Mother Herself made known to me that they would come. Whatever She has shown me always comes true. I don't know why this has not yet come to pass." Depressed, the Master wondered, "Is this particular vision then false?" Seeing the Master sad, Mathur felt remorseful and thought that he should not have raised that point. Then he consoled the childlike Master, saying: "Father, it does not matter whether they come or not. I am your ever-obedient devotee. So how can one say that your vision has not come true? I alone am equivalent to one hundred devotees. That must be why the Mother told you that many devotees would come." The Master said: "Well, who knows? Perhaps what you

---

2. "Jagadamba died on or about 1ˢᵗ January, 1881, intestate, leaving defendant Trayluksha, then the only son of Mathura, her surviving." [sic] Quoted from Plaintiff's statement in High Court, Suit No. 203 of 1889.

say is true." Without proceeding further on this subject, Mathur raised another topic to divert the Master's mind.

Elsewhere we have described for the reader (see III.6.7) the great change

| 18. It is no wonder that Mathur had such selfless devotion: scriptural testimony about this. | that took place in Mathur's mind because of his constant association with the Master. The scriptures say that those who serve free souls receive the results of their good deeds. Therefore, it is no wonder that |

the attendants of an avatar also attain various divine qualities.

The incessant flow of time with its waves of prosperity and adversity,

| 19. Mathur's death. | happiness and misery, union and separation, life and death ultimately brought the year 1871. The |

relationship between the Master and Mathur had gradually deepened, and reached its fifteenth year. May and June of 1871 passed. In the early part of July Mathur became bedridden with fever, which gradually worsened. Within seven or eight days it developed into typhoid, and Mathur lost his ability to speak. The Master knew beforehand that Mathur's vow of devoted service had now come to its end and that the Divine Mother would soon take Her devotee into Her bosom. Therefore he sent Hriday to Mathur's Calcutta residence to make inquiries every day, but he did not go to see him even once. At last the fateful moment arrived, and Mathur was taken to Kalighat in South Calcutta. On that day the Master did not send Hriday. In the afternoon, the Master stayed in his room, absorbed in ecstasy for two or three hours. Then he went forth in the subtle body along a luminous path and came to the side of the devoted Mathur. He blessed him and guided him to reach the holy sphere that one achieves through many virtuous deeds.

At 5:00 p.m., the Master came out of ecstasy and informed Hriday: "The companions of the Divine Mother carefully and lovingly took Mathur into their celestial chariot. His soul has ascended to the Deviloka [the sphere of the Mother]." Late that night the officials of the Kali temple returned to Dakshineswar and informed Hriday that Mathur had passed away at 5:00 p.m.[3] Although the great devotee Mathur attained the holy sphere after death, because his desire for enjoyment had not yet been exhausted he would have to come back to this world. This we heard from the Master on a different occasion and we have mentioned it elsewhere (see III.7.39).

3. "Mathura Mohan Biswas died in July, 1871, intestate, leaving his surviving Jagadamba, sole widow, Bhupal since deceased, a son by his another [i.e., first] wife who had predeceased him — and Dwaraka Nath Biswas since deceased, defendant Trayluksha Nath and Thakurdas alias Dhurmadas, three sons by the said Jagadamba." [sic]

Chapter 20

The Worship of Shodashi

MATHUR PASSED AWAY, BUT THE CURRENT OF LIFE at the Kali temple in Dakshineswar flowed as it always had. Time went by and gradually six months passed. In Phalgun 1278 [mid-February to mid-March 1872] a significant event in the Master's life took place. In order to understand it completely, we must focus our attention on the Master's father-in-law's house in Jayrambati.

We mentioned earlier that in 1867 the Master visited his native village of

1. Sarada is very young when she first sees the Master after their marriage ceremony.

Kamarpukur with the Bhairavi Brahmani and Hriday, and the women of his family had his wife brought there. That was Sarada's first real meeting with her husband after the marriage ceremony.

Whoever has had the opportunity to compare the girls of Calcutta with

2. The natural development of village girls.

those of Kamarpukur Village will notice that the bodies and minds of city girls mature earlier than do those of village girls. In the country, girls of four-teen and sometimes even fifteen or sixteen years of age are not fully developed. Like their bodies, their minds also develop later. The reason for this seems to be that the village girls enjoy pure air, move around freely, and lead a natural life, rather than living like caged birds in a small room in a city.

When Sarada visited the Master at the age of fourteen, she was quite

3. Sarada's impression at her first meeting with the Master.

naïve. She was just beginning to develop the ability to understand the purpose and responsibility of married life. The pure-hearted girl enjoyed un-speakable bliss when she experienced the holy association and selfless love and care of the Master, who was devoid of body-consciousness. Later, she described this joy to some of the Master's women devotees:

"At that time I constantly felt as if a pitcher full of bliss were placed in my heart. I can't describe how my heart was filled with that serene divine bliss."

A few months later, when the Master left Kamarpukur for Calcutta,

4. Sarada lives at Jayrambati in a blissful mood.

Sarada was endowed with an infinite wealth of joy that she carried back to Jayrambati with her. We can easily guess that this blissful experience had effected a transformation in all her movements, speech, and conduct, and in how she worked. But it is doubtful whether ordinary people noticed this. She was now gentle and not fickle, thoughtful and not impertinent, and her love was not blinded by selfishness. Moreover, her experience had eradicated all types of worldly desire from her heart, made her infinitely sympathetic to the pain and suffering of others, and gradually transformed her into an embodiment of compassion. Due to the influence of this inner bliss, she felt no physical suffering, and she was not disappointed if the loving care she gave to her relatives was not reciprocated. Content in every respect and absorbed within herself, she passed her days at her father's house. Although her body was in Jayrambati, her mind was with the Master at Dakshineswar. At times she felt an intense desire to see the Master and be with him, but she carefully controlled herself and waited patiently. She believed that since the Master had graciously loved her so much at their first meeting, he would not forget her. When the right time arrived, he would call her to him. Thus, days passed one after another as she waited for that auspicious day, all the while holding to her firm faith within.

Four long years passed. The strong current of hope and expectation kept

5. The reason for Sarada's anxiety and her desire to visit Dakshineswar.

flowing uniformly in Sarada's mind. But her body did not remain unchanged. By December 1872, time had slowly changed her into a young woman of eighteen years. The blissful memory of her first meeting with her godlike husband kept her above the happiness and misery of daily life. But is uninterrupted bliss possible in this world? She heard the idle gossip of the villagers: Some men would say that Sarada's husband was mad and that he would discard his clothes and roam about, chanting "Hari, Hari." The women her age considered her to be the wife of a madman, and showed either pity or indifference to her. She said nothing, but she was terribly hurt. She would think anxiously: "Is he no longer the same person that I saw before? People are saying he has become mad. Is this true? If this has indeed happened by the decree of Providence, I should not stay here. I must go there and take care of him." After long deliberation she decided to go to Dakshineswar and see for herself, so she might be freed from doubt about what she had heard. Then she would do whatever was necessary, according to the circumstances.

Jayrambati, the birthplace of
Sarada Devi,
as it was in the 1920s.

Temple in Jayrambati
dedicated to Sarada Devi
in 1923.

Chaitanya was born on the full moon day[1] in the month of Phalgun,

6. Her plan to fulfill that desire.

which is Dol-yatra, the swing festival of Krishna. On that auspicious day many people go from remote parts of Bengal to Calcutta to bathe in the holy river Ganges. Some of Sarada's distant women relatives had been planning to go to Calcutta for this purpose, so she told them she wished to accompany them to take the holy bath in the Ganges. The ladies thought that it would not be proper to take her with them without her father's permission, so they asked Ramchandra Mukhopadhyay. Her insightful father was quick to understand why his daughter wanted to go to Calcutta and made arrangements to take her there himself.

Because of the railways, distant Varanasi and Vrindaban now seem very

7. Sarada journeys on foot with her father to bathe in the Ganges; her fever along the way.

close to Calcutta, but Kamarpukur and Jayrambati are still far away because there is no speedy transport system. If those places are remote even now [in the 1910s] — what can we say about those days [1870s]![2] At that time the railroad had not yet been constructed from Calcutta to Vishnupur or Tarakeswar, and Ghatal was not connected by steamer either. Thus, there was no way for villagers to travel to Calcutta other than to go by palanquin or on foot. And everyone, except for wealthy landlords, were forced to resort to the latter. So Ramchandra started the long journey on foot, accompanied by his daughter and other companions. They passed through the panoramic scenery of the vast paddy fields with beautiful lotus ponds between them, and sometimes they rested under the shade of the peepul and banyan trees along the road. Thus they walked happily for two or three days. But that joy ended before they reached their destination. Unaccustomed to such a wearisome journey, Sarada developed a high fever on the way, which greatly worried her father. Finding it was not possible to continue travelling with his sick daughter, he took shelter in a wayside inn.

Sarada felt terrible anguish that she had fallen ill. But at that time she had

8. Sarada's wonderful vision during her illness.

a wonderful vision that greatly reassured her. Later she described that vision to women devotees, saying: "I was lying almost unconscious with fever, without even any sense of decorum. Just then I saw a girl come and sit down beside me. She was black in complexion. I had never seen such beauty before. She began passing her hand over my head and body; it was so soft and cool that the burning sensation of my body began to subside. I asked, 'Where do you come from?' She replied, 'I come from Dakshineswar.' Amazed, I said: 'From

---

1. It fell on 25 March 1872. — *Translator*
2. Of course, now one can go to Kamarpukur and Jayrambati by train from Howrah to Vishnupur or Tarakeswar and then by bus; or one can travel by bus or car directly from Calcutta. — *Translator*

Dakshineswar! That's where I long to be — to see my husband and to look after him. But now I have this fever, and perhaps I shall never see him again.' 'What are you saying?' said the girl. 'Of course you'll get to Dakshineswar. As soon as you're better, you shall go to him. I've been taking care of him there for your sake.' I said, 'How good you are! Tell me — are you one of our relatives?' 'I am your sister,' she told me. I said, 'Ah — so that's why you've come to me!' I then fell asleep."

The next morning Ramchandra found that his daughter's fever had

9. Sarada reaches Dakshineswar at night with a fever; the Master's concern.

broken. He thought that it would be better to continue on slowly rather than to stay helplessly in the inn. Encouraged by her vision of the previous night, Sarada eagerly agreed with his idea. Luckily, after walking a short distance, they found a palanquin for her. She had a relapse of the fever, but it was not as severe as on the previous day. As a result she was not incapacitated and said nothing about it. Finally, the journey ended and Sarada reached the Master at Dakshineswar at 9:00 p.m.

The Master was extremely concerned when he saw that Sarada was

10. The Master's loving concern makes her stay joyful.

feverish when she arrived. He arranged a separate bed for her in his room lest the cold increase her fever. He repeatedly said with regret, "Ah, you have come too late — my Mathur is no longer here to look after you!" With good treatment and a special diet, Sarada recovered within three or four days. All that time the Master himself supervised her medicine and diet and then arranged for her to live with his mother in the nahabat [music tower].

Sarada was now entirely reassured. The cloud of doubt that had arisen from the villagers' gossip and had almost obscured her faith was now scattered and blown away by the force of the Master's loving care. She felt with her whole heart that the Master was the same as before and that worldly people had spread those rumours in ignorance. Her godlike husband had not forgotten her, and he was as gracious to her as before. She immediately decided what her duty was: She would live in the nahabat and joyfully serve the Master and his mother. Her father was pleased at seeing his daughter happy, and joyfully returned home after staying in Dakshineswar for a few days.

We have already described to the reader the sequence of thoughts that

11. The Master tests his knowledge of Brahman and educates his wife.

arose in the Master's mind when Sarada came to see him at Kamarpukur in 1867. Remembering Tota Puri's remarks regarding the establishment of the knowledge of Brahman, the Master had begun to test the Self-knowledge that he had achieved after long sadhana, and also to perform his duty towards his wife. He had just begun these endeavours when he had to return to Calcutta, leaving them unfinished. Now having Sarada with him, he again concentrated on those two objectives.

One may ask: Why did he not bring his wife to Dakshineswar earlier to

12. Why the Master did not test himself earlier.

test his Self-knowledge? The answer is that undoubt-edly an ordinary person would have done that, but the Master was not such a person — so he did not behave in that manner. Those who are accustomed to performing every action while depending solely on God at every moment of their lives do not make any plans. For the good of themselves and others, they depend on the assistance of God's cosmic intelligence and wait for a signal rather than resorting to their own limited, puny intellects as we do. For that reason, they are always reluctant to undergo any test of their own accord. But if any chal-lenge appears to them spontaneously, they gladly come forward to face it, guided by the Divine Will. The Master did not voluntarily proceed to test the depth of his Self-knowledge. But he had found that his wife had come to him at Kamarpukur, and if he was to carry out his duty towards her, he would have to pass through a test; only then did he engage himself in that task. Again, when the situation changed by God's will and he had to return to Calcutta and live apart from his wife, he did not act on his own to regain that opportunity. Until Sarada came of her own accord, he did not make any attempt to bring her to Dakshineswar. Thus by means of our ordinary intel-lect we can determine the Master's propriety of conduct; in addition, we can say that the Master knew through his yogic vision that this was the will of God.

Seeing that the opportunity had arrived to put himself to the test by

13. How the Master trained and guided Sarada.

fulfilling his duties to his wife, the Master now gladly came forward to meet this challenge. He began to teach Sarada the goal of human life, as well as how to perform all household duties. It is said that at this time he told Sarada: "As Uncle Moon is the dear uncle of all children, so God is dear to all beings. Everyone has a right to call on God. Out of grace He reveals Him-self to all who call upon Him. You, too, will see Him if you but call upon Him." The Master's method of teaching was not limited to verbal instruc-tion only. He would keep his disciple near him and through his love completely make that person his very own. After giving the first instruc-tion, he kept a keen eye on how the disciple was translating it into action; and if the disciple inadvertently acted contrary to his instruction, he corrected that person with an explanation. It seems he adopted the same method with respect to Sarada. It is evident how much the Master loved her from the first day and made her his very own. As soon as she arrived he kept her in his room, and later when she recovered from her illness he permitted her to sleep in his bed every night. We have told the reader else-where (see III.4.20-25) about the Master's pure and godly behaviour towards Sarada at that time, so we shall not repeat it. We shall mention here only a few things left unsaid.

One day while Sarada was massaging the Master's feet, she asked him,

14. How the Master looked upon Sarada.

"How do you look upon me?" The Master replied: "The same Mother who is in the temple, the same Mother who gave birth to this body and is now living in the nahabat, that same Mother is now rubbing my feet. Truly, I always see you as a form of the blissful Divine Mother."

One night as he watched Sarada lying asleep beside him, the Master

15. The Master tests his self-control.

began to discriminate, addressing his own mind: "O my mind, this is the body of a woman. Men look on it as an object of great enjoyment and they always lust after it. But if one possesses this body, one must remain confined within the flesh; one can't realize God. O my mind, let there be no theft [hypocrisy] in your inner chamber. Don't be thinking one thing inwardly and pretending another outwardly! Be honest — do you want this woman's body, or do you want God? If you want the body, here it is in front of you. Enjoy it." Discriminating in this way, the Master was about to touch Sarada's body when his mind suddenly recoiled and lost itself so deeply in samadhi that he did not regain normal consciousness all night. The next morning after considerable difficulty he was brought back to the conscious plane when the Lord's name was repeated in his ear.

The Master told us many such stories of the transcendental relationship

16. No avatar had ever treated his wife the way the Master did: its result.

that he and Sarada shared when they were in the prime of their youth. Such events are unheard of in the lives of any other great teachers in the religious history of the world. Charmed by the exalted lives of this couple, people naturally believe in their divinity and feel an urge to offer them love and respect. During this time the Master would pass almost entire nights in samadhi, and when he descended from it to the earthly plane, his mind would dwell in such a high state that not even for a moment did he feel any body-consciousness, as ordinary human beings would.

Days and months passed. They lived together more than a year, but the

17. The Master's remark regarding Sarada's superhuman nature.

self-control of the wonderful Master and Sarada remained intact. Not even for a moment did their minds inadvertently covet physical union, imagining it to be joyful. Recalling the events of this time, the Master would sometimes tell us: "If she hadn't been so pure, and if she had lost her self-control and made demands on me — who knows? Perhaps my own self-control would have given way. Perhaps I would have come down to the physical plane. After I married, I implored the Divine Mother, 'O Mother, eradicate lust completely from my wife's mind.' While living with her at that time I realized that the Mother had truly granted my prayer."

After a year no sexual thought had even momentarily arisen in the Master's mind. Sometimes he saw Sarada as a part of the Divine Mother, sometimes as Atman or Brahman; no other attitude arose in his mind. Then the Master realized that the Divine Mother had graciously enabled him to pass the test and that his mind was now established in the divine plane in a natural way. By the grace of the Divine Mother he deeply experienced that his sadhana had been completed, and that his mind was now so absorbed in the Divine Mother that neither knowingly nor unknowingly could any desire contrary to the Mother's wishes arise in it. As commanded by the Divine Mother, a novel desire now arose in his heart, and without the least hesitation he translated it into action. We heard about this important episode from the Master and Sarada Devi at different times; we shall describe it to the reader in a continuous narrative.

18. The Master's resolve after passing the test.

A little more than half of the Bengali month of Jaishtha 1280 [mid-May to mid-June 1873] had passed.[3] It was the new moon night, an auspicious occasion for Phalaharini Kali Puja. This special festival is also observed in the Kali temple of Dakshineswar. The Master made a special arrangement for privately worshipping the Divine Mother as Shodashi[4] in his room rather than performing it in the temple. At the right side of the worshipper's seat, a low wooden seat, beautifully painted with rice powder pigment, was placed for the goddess to sit on during worship. The sun had set and the new moon night arrived in a veil of deep darkness. Hriday was performing the worship in the Kali temple that night, so he helped with the preparations for the Master's worship as much as possible and then left for the temple. After the priest Dinu had finished the evening worship service in the Radha-Govinda temple, he came to help the Master prepare for the worship, and then he left. It was 9:00 in the evening when the preparations for the mystical worship were complete. The Master had sent a message to Sarada beforehand to be present during the worship, and now she arrived in the Master's room. The Master sat for worship.

19. The preparations for the Shodashi worship.

The Master finished the preliminaries and sanctified the articles of worship by repeating the mantras. He then beckoned for Sarada to sit on the decorated wooden seat. While she was watching the worship, Sarada had already

20. Sprinkling consecrated water, the Master worships Sarada.

3. Regarding the exact date of this event there are two versions: (1) According to *Sri Sri Ramakrishna Lilaprasanga* by Swami Saradananda, the date of Shodashi Puja, which was held on the Phalaharini Kali Puja night, was 25 May 1873. (2) According to *Sri Sri Mayer Katha*: II.130, published by Udbodhan Office (1965), the date was 5 June 1872. In that book Sarada Devi is reported to have said that it took place about a month and a half after her arrival at Dakshineswar. — *Translator*
4. The term refers to the worship of the Divine Mother in one of Her ten aspects, namely Shodashi, a woman as beautiful as an immaculate sixteen-year-old girl. — *Translator*

Sri Sarada Devi, the Holy Mother, in 1898.

entered a semiconscious spiritual state. So without fully knowing what she was doing, she moved like one who is spellbound and sat facing north on the right side of the Master, who was seated facing east. According to the scriptural injunctions, he repeatedly sprinkled sanctified water on her from the pitcher placed in front of him. He then uttered mantras and invoked the deity with the following prayer:

"O Divine Mother Tripura-sundari! O Eternal Virgin, possessor of all power! Please open the gate of perfection. Purify her body and mind, and manifest Yourself through her for the welfare of all."

He then performed the ceremony of *nyasa*[5] in accordance with the injunction of the scriptures, and worshipped Sarada with sixteen items as a veritable manifestation of the Devi. After offering food, he took some of it and put it in her mouth. Sarada lost outer consciousness and went into samadhi. While uttering mantras in a semiconscious state, the Master also went into deep samadhi.

21. The Master goes into samadhi at the end of the worship and offers the results of his japa and worship at the feet of the goddess.

Thus, the worshipper and the worshipped became fully united and unified in the Atman, the Existence-Knowledge-Bliss Absolute.

Some time passed in this way. It was long after midnight when the Master gradually regained partial consciousness of the world. In that semiconscious state he offered himself to the Devi manifest in the person of Sarada, and then forever surrendered at her feet himself, the result of his sadhana, his rosary, and everything else. He then bowed down to her with this prayer:

"O Consort of Shiva, the most auspicious of all auspicious beings! O Doer of all actions! O Refuge of all! O three-eyed[6] goddess of golden complexion! O Power of Narayana, I salute You again and again."

The worship was completed. The Master's sadhana culminated in this worship of the Divine Mother in the body of a woman who was an embodiment of spiritual wisdom. Both his divine and human aspects had achieved ultimate perfection.

After the Shodashi Puja the Holy Mother[7] lived with the Master for about five more months. During that period she spent her days in the nahabat and served the Master and his mother, and at night she shared his bed. Day and night the Master was almost incessantly in bhava samadhi. Sometimes his mind would suddenly vanish into nirvikalpa samadhi and signs of death would manifest themselves in his body. The Holy Mother could not sleep at

22. Disturbance of Sarada's sleep due to the Master's constant samadhi: she moves to the nahabat and later returns to Kamarpukur.

5. Nyasa consists of touching the different parts of the body with appropriate mantras and mentally identifying them with the different parts of the deity. — *Translator*
6. The third eye, placed on the forehead between the eyebrows, denotes the eye of wisdom. — *Translator*
7. The name by which Sarada Devi is known among devotees. — *Translator*

Nahabat or concert tower at left, where Sarada Devi lived on the ground floor, and her mother-in-law, Chandramani Devi, lived upstairs. The semicircular porch of Ramakrishna's room is at the right.

night because the Master's nirvikalpa samadhi made her apprehensive. One night when she found that the Master had not returned from samadhi to the conscious plane for a long time, she became scared and anxious. She then awoke Hriday and others from their sleep. Hriday came and for a long time repeated the Lord's name into the Master's ear, and finally he returned to the normal plane. When the Master was told what had happened, he realized that the Holy Mother's sleep was being disturbed every night. He then made arrangements for her to sleep in his mother's room at the nahabat. Thus, she lived with the Master at Dakshineswar for approximately one year and four months [actually a total of eight months] and then returned to Kamarpukur, most likely in October 1873.

Chapter 21

Epilogue to the Master's Sadhana

THE MASTER'S JOURNEY OF SADHANA REACHED ITS END with the worship of Shodashi.

> 1. After the Shodashi Puja the Master's desire for sadhana ceased.

The holy fire of passion for God had remained ablaze in his heart for twelve long years without interruption, forcing him to perform various spiritual practices and never allowing him to rest completely, even after the completion of a particular sadhana. Now, after he had offered the final oblation at the end of the Shodashi Puja, his mind became calm. What else could it do? Was there anything left of his own that he had not already sacrificed? Long ago the Master had renounced wealth, prestige, name, fame, and other desirable things of this world. He had offered his heart, senses, mind, intellect, *chitta* [mind-stuff], ego, and everything else as oblations into that all-devouring fire. At that point, there was only one desire left, and that was to see the Divine Mother in Her myriad forms; and now he had also offered that into the fire. So his mind had nothing left to do but to remain silent.

Seeing the Master's intense longing, the Divine Mother had first blessed

> 2. Nothing is left for him to do after finishing the sadhanas of all paths.

him by revealing Herself. She had then given him the opportunity to validate his experience by introducing him to extraordinary spiritual teachers who substantiated it from various scriptural points of view. What else could he now ask of Her? He had practised the sixty-four disciplines of Tantra one after another; he had duly performed all sadhanas connected with the five moods of the Vaishnava Tantra prevalent in India; he had followed the traditional Vedic path by taking monastic vows and experiencing the formless, attributeless aspect of the Divine Mother. And it was

355

due to the inscrutable play of the Divine Mother that he had realized the goal of Islamic sadhana, which had originated outside India. What else could he now expect Her to show or to teach him?

A year after the worship of Shodashi, the Master's mind was eager to see the Divine Mother by means of another religious path. At that time he was acquainted with Shambhu Charan Mallick, who would read the Bible to him. Thus, he became aware of the pure life of Jesus and of the Christian faith. As soon as the desire to practise Christianity arose in his mind, the Divine Mother fulfilled it in a miraculous way; he did not have to make any special effort. The event took place as follows.

3. The Master attains perfection in Christianity in a marvellous way.

Jadulal Mallick's garden house is situated at the south side of the Dakshineswar Kali temple. The Master occasionally went there for a walk. From their first meeting, Jadulal and his mother loved and respected the Master greatly. If they were away when the Master went to Jadu's garden for his walk, the caretakers would open the parlour for him and ask him to sit and rest awhile. There were some magnificent pictures hanging on the walls of that room, and one of them depicted the child Jesus on his mother's lap. The Master said that one day he sat in that room and intently studied that image, thinking of the wonderful life of Jesus. Just then he saw the picture become animate and luminous. Rays of light emanated from the bodies of Mother Mary and the child Jesus, entering the Master's heart and revolutionizing his mental attitudes. When he observed that his inborn Hindu impressions were vanishing from his mind and that different ones were arising, he tried to control himself by resisting them in various ways. He entreated the Divine Mother, saying, "Mother, what are You doing to me?" But the onslaught continued. The waves of those impressions rose forcefully and completely submerged the Hindu bent of his mind. The Master's love and devotion for Hindu gods and goddesses disappeared and his heart was filled with faith in and reverence for Jesus and his religion. He then had a vision of Christian clergymen offering incense and lights in front of the image of Jesus in a church, expressing their inner longing through prayer.

After he returned to the Dakshineswar temple garden, the Master remained uninterruptedly absorbed in meditation on those experiences pertaining to Jesus. He completely forgot to visit the Divine Mother in the temple. The waves of Christian faith that swayed him lasted for three days. When the Master was walking in the Panchavati at the end of the third day, he saw a beautiful but unfamiliar godman with a fair complexion advancing towards him, gazing at him steadily. The Master immediately realized that he was a foreigner, and that he belonged to a different race. He saw that his eyes were large and beautiful, and though his nose was a little flat at the tip, it in no way marred the handsomeness of his face. The Master was charmed by the unique divine expression on his serene face and wondered who he could

Painting of the Madonna and Child in Jadu Mallick's parlour that prompted Ramakrishna's vision of Jesus.

Jadu Mallick's garden house at Dakshineswar where Ramakrishna had a vision of Christ.

be. Very soon after that the figure drew near, and a voice from within told him, "This is Jesus Christ, the great yogi, the loving Son of God who is one with his Father, who shed his heart's blood and suffered torture for the salvation of humanity." Then the godman Jesus embraced the Master and merged into him. In ecstasy, the Master lost external consciousness and his mind remained united with Saguna Brahman for some time. With this vision, the Master became convinced that Jesus was truly a divine incarnation.

One day when we visited the Master, long after his vision of Christ, he

| 4. How the Master's vision of Jesus proved to be accurate. | raised the topic of Jesus and asked us: "Well, you have read the Bible. What does it say about the features of Christ? What did he look like?" We replied: "Sir, we |

have not seen this particularly mentioned anywhere in the Bible. But Jesus was born a Jew, so he must have been fair, with large eyes and an aquiline nose." The Master then said: "But I saw that his nose was slightly flattened at the tip. Who knows why I saw him this way?" Although we did not respond further at that time, we wondered how the image seen by him in ecstasy could resemble the actual form of Jesus. Like all Jewish men, he must have had an aquiline nose. Sometime after the Master passed away, we learned that there were three recorded versions regarding the features of Jesus, and that one of them mentioned that the tip of his nose was a little flat.

Knowing that the Master attained perfection in the major religions of the

| 5. The Master's remarks on Buddha as an avatar and on his religion. | world, a question might arise in the reader's mind regarding the Master's view about Buddha. Therefore, it is good to record here what we know about |

this. In regard to Buddha the Master shared the same belief as all Hindus: He always offered loving worship and reverence to Buddha as a divine incarnation, and he believed that Buddha still manifests in the holy triad in the temple at Puri, as Jagannath, Subhadra, and Balarama. When the Master heard about the glory of the holy shrine of Jagannath and that His prasad removes all distinctions of high and low status, as well as of caste, he was eager to visit Puri. But he gave up the idea when he learned that if he went there he might die; he realized through his yogic insight that the Divine Mother had different plans for him (see IV.3.25).

We have already mentioned that the Master firmly believed that the water of the Ganges is supremely purifying, and that he considered it to be *Brahma-vari*, a liquid form of Brahman. Similarly, he strongly believed that partaking of the rice prasad of Jagannath caused the impure minds of worldly people instantly to become pure and capable of grasping spiritual ideas. If he had to spend some time with worldly people, he would immediately afterwards take a little Ganges water and some dry rice prasad of Jagannath, and he would ask his disciples to do the same. In addition to what has been mentioned earlier about the Master's belief that Buddha was a divine incarnation, we heard him make another remark. Girish Chandra

Ghosh, a great poet and a devoted disciple of the Master, wrote a drama based on the divine life of Buddha. After seeing that play, the Master said: "Buddha was definitely an incarnation of God. There is no difference between his religion and the Vedic path of knowledge." We believe that the Master came to realize this through his yogic insight.

In the later part of his life, the Master heard from some Jains about the

6. The Master's love for and faith in the Jaina and Sikh religions.

Tirthankaras, the founders of Jainism, and from some Sikhs about the ten gurus from Nanak to Govinda, the founders of Sikhism. Consequently he developed love and respect for the founders of those religions. In his room beside the pictures of Hindu gods and goddesses there was a stone image of Mahavir Tirthankar and a picture of Jesus. Every morning and evening the Master would wave incense before all the deities, including these last two. Although he showed his love and respect for all, we never heard him speak of the Tirthankaras of the Jains or the gurus of the Sikhs as avatars. The Master said about the ten gurus of the Sikhs: "They are all incarnations of the sage Janaka. I heard from some Sikhs that the royal sage Janaka had a desire to do good to humanity before he attained liberation. That is why he was born ten times as ten gurus from Nanak to Govinda, established religion among the Sikhs, and then merged forever into the Supreme Brahman. There is no reason to disbelieve this statement of the Sikhs."

After he had attained perfection in various sadhanas, the Master had

7. After attaining perfection in various religious paths, the Master sums up his extraordinary experiences.

many unique intuitive perceptions. Some of them were related to the Master himself and others to spirituality in general. Although we have told the reader about some of these earlier in this book, we present the most important ones here. We think that the Master realized the true meaning of those experiences when he was in bhava-mukha at the end of his sadhana, united with the Divine Mother. Although these revelations resulted from his yogic insight, we will try to express them in terms of human reasoning.

First, the Master realized that he was an incarnation of God, a person

(1) He is an incarnation of God.

commissioned by God to do good to the world, and that the sadhanas he undertook were practised for the sake of others. When he compared his spiritual life with the lives of other aspirants, he realized that there was a significant difference between them from a general point of view. He observed that an ordinary aspirant attains peace by realizing God through lifelong practice of a single spiritual discipline; whereas he himself could not rest until he had practised the sadhanas of all paths. Moreover, it took very little time for him to attain perfection in each sadhana. There cannot be an effect without a cause: His sincere search to discover why that was so led him to deep meditation and revealed the cause to him. This inquiry revealed that such things happened to him because he was by nature pure, awakened, and free, and a special incarnation of Almighty God. He also understood that his extraordinary sadhanas would shed new light in the realm of spirituality and that they had been undertaken for the good of humanity, rather than to remove any personal deficiency of his own.

Second, the Master realized that he would not attain liberation like other beings [jivas]. It does not take long to understand this

> (2) There is no liberation for him.

through ordinary reasoning: He who is always inseparable from God and is indeed a part of God, who is by nature pure, awakened, and free at all times, and who has no deficiency or any limitation — how can the question of liberation arise for such a person? As long as God continues to redeem all human beings, He will have to accomplish this by becoming incarnate in every age. So how could the Master have liberation? As the Master used to say, "An officer of the landlord must run to any part of the estate where there is trouble." He not only knew this about himself through his yogic insight, but he also told us many times, pointing to the northwest, that the next time he would reincarnate there. Some of us[1] said that the Master even told them the time of his advent, stating: "I shall have to be born in that direction after two hundred years. Then many will be liberated, and those who fail at that time will have to wait a long time for liberation."

Third, absorbed in yoga, the Master knew the time of his death long before it occurred. At Dakshineswar he once told the

> (3) He knew the time of his death.

Holy Mother, in an ecstatic mood: "When you find me accepting food from anyone and everyone, spending nights in Calcutta, and feeding a portion of food first to someone else, then eating what is left — then know that the day I will leave this body is near." These words of the Master were literally fulfilled.

On another occasion at Dakshineswar, when he was in an exalted mood, the Master told the Holy Mother, "Towards the end I shall eat rice pudding only and nothing else." We have mentioned elsewhere how the Master's prediction came true (see III.2.15-16).

Now we shall describe a second group of realizations, pertaining to spiritual matters in general.

First, after attaining perfection through different religious paths, the Master was firmly convinced: "All religions are true.

> (4) All religions are true: "As many faiths, so many paths."

As many faiths, so many paths." It can be said that the Master understood this both intuitively and intellectually. After he had practised the disciplines of different faiths, the Master realized the ultimate goal of each one of them. It does not take long to understand that the purpose of the Master's advent in this present age was to stop

---

1. Girish Chandra Ghosh and others.

religious conflict and degradation in this world by propagating the aforesaid truth. No other divine incarnation has fully realized this universality of truth through sadhana and has taught it to the world. If the greatness of an avatar is to be determined on the basis of the catholicity of his spiritual views, undoubtedly the foremost place should be accorded to the Master for preaching this.

Second, the ideas of dualism, qualified nondualism, and nondualism —

| (5) Human beings adopt dualism, qualified nondualism, and nondualism according to their temperaments. |

known as *dvaita*, *vishishtadvaita*, and *advaita* — emerge spontaneously according to one's spiritual growth. The Master said that they were not contradictory but depended on the stages of one's spiritual progress. One can quickly understand how the Master's experiences are helpful in comprehending the voluminous scriptures. The sages recorded those three philosophical views in the Vedas, Upanishads, and other scriptures; consequently those ideas created unending confusion and made spiritual paths complicated. Unable to find any harmony in the experiences and statements of the sages, each philosophical school tortured the texts and tried to interpret them from its own point of view. As a result of the commentators' dogmatic ideas, people have come to view philosophical discussions with apprehension. This fear has engendered disbelief in the scriptures, which has led to the religious degradation of India. So the Master, the avatar of this age, experienced for himself those three philosophical paths as different stages of the same truth and propagated their wonderful harmony. The only way to enter into the study of the scriptures is to always remember this conclusion of the Master. We present here a few of his statements in this respect:

"Know that nonduality is the last word in realization. It is beyond the mind and speech, and a matter of experience."

"Only the states up to qualified nondualism can be understood through the mind and intellect and expressed in words. There the Absolute and the Relative both are equally real. The Lord Himself, His name, and His abode — all are pure consciousness."

"Duality is meant for ordinary human beings who are attached to sense objects. An excellent practice for them is to chant the Lord's name loudly according to the *Narada Pancharatra*."

The Master indicated the limits of action when he said: "The action of a

| (6) Ordinary people will progress through karma yoga. |

sattvic person drops off automatically. He cannot work even if he tries to; the Lord does not allow him to work. It is just as when a young wife advances in pregnancy. She is given less and less work to do; and when the child is born, she gives up household work altogether and is busied exclusively with the infant. But an ordinary person must try to do his duties with detachment, depending on the Lord, like the maidservant who does everything for her master, knowing in her heart that her home is elsewhere. This is known as karma yoga. As far as possible one should take the name of the Lord and meditate on Him while discharging one's everyday duties in an unattached way."

Third, the Master realized that as an instrument of the Divine Mother, he
would have to establish a new religious order based on the universal truths revealed in his life. The Master first saw this through a vision he had during Mathur's lifetime. He then told Mathur that the Divine Mother had revealed to him that many devotees would come to him to attain spirituality. Later, this literally came true. At the Cossipore garden house the Master looked at his own photograph [seated in meditation] and told us: "This represents a high yogic state. This image will be worshipped in many homes as time goes on."

(7) A religious organization based on this catholic attitude should be founded.

Because he realized this through his yogic insight, the Master was firmly convinced that those who are in their last life would come to him for spirituality. We have recorded elsewhere our opinion about this (see IV.4.48-50).

(8) Those who are in their last life will accept his gospel.

During three important periods of the Master's sadhana, three eminent spiritual pandits who were well versed in the scriptures came to him, observed his spiritual condition, and had the opportunity to discuss their impressions. Pandit Padmalochan met the Master when he had become perfected in the Tantra sadhana; Pandit Vaishnavcharan met him when he had attained success in the Vaishnava Tantra; and Pandit Gauri was blessed to see the Master endowed with divine splendour at the completion of all his sadhanas. When Padmalochan saw the Master, he said, "I see God's presence and divine power in you." Vaishnavcharan, in ecstasy, composed a hymn to the Master in Sanskrit and sang it to him, declaring him to be an avatar. When Gauri met the Master, he concluded: "I see that everything I have read in the scriptures concerning high spiritual states is manifest in you. In addition, I see other exalted states that are not recorded in the scriptures. You have reached a spiritual plane that surpasses anything described in the Vedas, Vedanta, or other scriptures. You are not human. Ishwara, the source of all avatars, dwells in you." When we study the Master's unique life and his wonderful spiritual experiences, we clearly understand that these spiritual pandits did not make their remarks out of mere flattery. We ascertain the time those pandits arrived in Dakshineswar by the following means.

8. Remarks of three eminent spiritual pandits who met the Master at different times.

The Holy Mother saw Pandit Gauri during her first visit to Dakshineswar. Again, the Master told us that Gauri had come to Dakshineswar during Mathur's lifetime. Therefore, it seems that Gauri arrived in Dakshineswar sometime in 1871 and stayed with the Master until 1873. The Master was eager to meet those spiritual pandits who had not only acquired scriptural

9. The time of their arrival.

knowledge but also tried to practise it in their lives. Gaurikanta Tarkabhusan [the full name of Pandit Gauri] belonged to that group, so the Master had a desire to see him. He invited Gauri through Mathur and had him brought to Dakshineswar. Gauri's home was in Indesh Village, not far from the Master's birthplace. Ramratan, Hriday's brother, carried Mathur's letter of invitation to Gauri and brought him to the Kali temple of Dakshineswar. We have told the reader elsewhere (see IV.1.31,33) about Gauri's wonderful occult power that had originated from his sadhana, and how, after coming in contact with the Master in Dakshineswar, he gradually developed intense detachment and renounced the world.

It is mentioned in *Rani Rasmanir Jivanvrittanta* [The Life Story of Rani Rasmani] that in 1864 Mathur performed the annameru-vrata. The Master told us that at Mathur's request he invited Pandit Padmalochan to accept a gift on that occasion. So it can be said that Padmalochan Tarkalankar, the Vedantic scholar, came to the Master in 1864.

The arrival date of Vaishnavcharan, the son of Utsavananda Goswami, is easily ascertained. The Master told us that Vaishnavcharan discussed the Master's uniqueness with Bhairavi Brahmani Yogeswari and later with Gaurikanta Tarkabhusan at the Dakshineswar temple. Like the Brahmani, Vaishnavcharan also saw in the Master the signs of mahabhava as mentioned in the Vaishnava scriptures. He was amazed. Concurring with the Brahmani, he declared that Gauranga had reincarnated as Sri Ramakrishna. It seems from the Master's statements that Vaishnavcharan came to him in 1865, after he had become perfect in madhura bhava, and then visited him occasionally in Dakshineswar till 1873.

After he had attained all the spiritual experiences described earlier, divine

10. The Master's desire to see his disciples and devotees: his call to them.

inspiration prompted a new desire to arise intensely in the Master's mind. He became extremely anxious to meet the devotees he had seen previously in spiritual visions and to transmit his spiritual power into their hearts. The Master said: "In those days there was no limit to my yearning. During the daytime I could just manage to keep it under control. Severely tormented by the worthless, mundane talk of worldly people, I would wistfully anticipate the day when my beloved companions would arrive. I hoped to find solace in conversing with them about God and to lighten my heart by relating to them my own spiritual experiences. Every little incident would remind me of them, and thoughts of them completely engrossed me. I kept planning what I should say to this one and what I should give to that one, and so forth. When evening came, I couldn't control my feelings any longer. I was tortured by the thought that another day had passed and they still hadn't arrived! When the vesper service started, and the temples resounded with the ringing of bells and the blowing of conch shells, I would climb up to the roof of the kuthi [bungalow] and cry out at the top of my voice, with the anguish of my heart: 'Come to me, my children! Where are you? I can't bear to live without you!' A mother never longed so for the sight of her child, or a friend for a friend, or a lover for his sweetheart, as I did for them. Oh, it was beyond all describing! And soon after this, they did at last begin to come."

Some important events took place before the devotees arrived in Dakshineswar at the passionate call of the Master. As they are not directly connected with this part of the book, we will record them in the appendix to this section.

Appendix

Major Events of the Master's Life from after the Shodashi Puja to the Coming of His Chosen Devotees

WE HAVE TOLD THE READER THAT THE Holy Mother returned to Kamarpukur in

1. Death of Rameswar.

September 1873, after the Shodashi Puja. Rameswar, the Master's second elder brother, died of typhoid shortly after her return. Every man and woman of the Master's paternal lineage was very spiritual. We shall mention here what we have heard about Rameswar in this respect.

Rameswar was generous by nature. Whenever wandering monks came to

2. Rameswar's generous nature.

his door, he would give them anything they asked for if it was in the house. His relatives told us that when mendicants would ask for a cooking pot or a water pot or a blanket, Rameswar would immediately take those items from the household and give them away. If anyone raised an objection, he would gently respond: "Let them have these. Don't say anything. We shall get more of them somehow. Why worry about it?" Rameswar also had some knowledge of astrology.

When Rameswar was about to return home from Dakshineswar for the

3. The Master's premonition about Rameswar's death and his warning to him.

last time, the Master knew that he would never come back. He told him: "So you're going home? All right — but don't share your bed with your wife. If you do, you won't live much longer." One of us[1] heard this from the Master later on.

1. Swami Premananda

365

Rameswar fell sick soon after he reached home. When the Master heard

4. Knowing that the news of Rameswar's death would endanger his mother's life, the Master prays to the Divine Mother: the result.

the news, he said to Hriday: "So he didn't listen to the warning; now I'm afraid they won't be able to save his life." After five or six days the news came from Kamarpukur that Rameswar had passed away. The Master was deeply concerned by the thought that Rameswar's death would be a terrible shock to their mother. He then went to the temple and implored the Divine Mother to protect his mother from grief.

The Master told us that after he left the temple he went to the nahabat with tearful eyes to break the sad news to his mother and to console her. The Master later said: "I was afraid that my mother would collapse when she heard of Rameswar's death and that it would be difficult to save her life. But, in fact, the opposite happened. When mother heard the news she expressed some grief — but then she started to console me, saying: 'This world is transitory. Everyone must die someday, so what is the use of grieving?' and so forth. It seemed to me that the Divine Mother had tuned mother to a high pitch, like a stringed instrument keyed up to a very high note. That was why worldly grief and sorrow couldn't touch her. When I saw this, I repeatedly bowed down to the Divine Mother and I wasn't anxious about mother any longer."

Rameswar himself foresaw the time of his death five or six days before it

5. Rameswar's behaviour when he knows death is approaching.

took place. He warned his relatives about it, and he personally made arrangements for his own funeral and shrāddha ceremony. Seeing that a mango tree in front of the house was being cut down, he remarked, "That's fortunate — it will provide the wood for my pyre." During his last hours, he continued to chant the name of Rama until he lost consciousness. He died shortly afterwards, in the middle of the night. Before his death, Rameswar asked his relatives not to cremate his body in the cremation ground but on the road that ran alongside it. When asked why he wanted this done, he replied: "If I am cremated on the road, the feet of many holy people will pass over the spot. I shall have the dust of their feet and be greatly blessed."

Gopal of Kamarpukur was a longtime friend of Rameswar. Gopal said

6. After death, Rameswar speaks to his friend Gopal.

that at the exact time Rameswar died, he heard a tap on his door. Immediately he asked, "Who is there?" And he heard the answer: "I am Rameswar. I am going for a bath in the Ganges. Lord Raghuvir is at home. Please see that His service should not be disturbed." When Gopal was about to open the door to see his friend, he again heard: "I have no body. Even if you open the door you will not see me." Nevertheless, Gopal opened the door. When he found no one there, he went to Rameswar's house to verify what he had heard. Then he learned that Rameswar had indeed passed away.

Ramlal Chattopadhyay, Rameswar's
eldest son.

Lakshmi Chattopadhyay,
Rameswar's daughter.

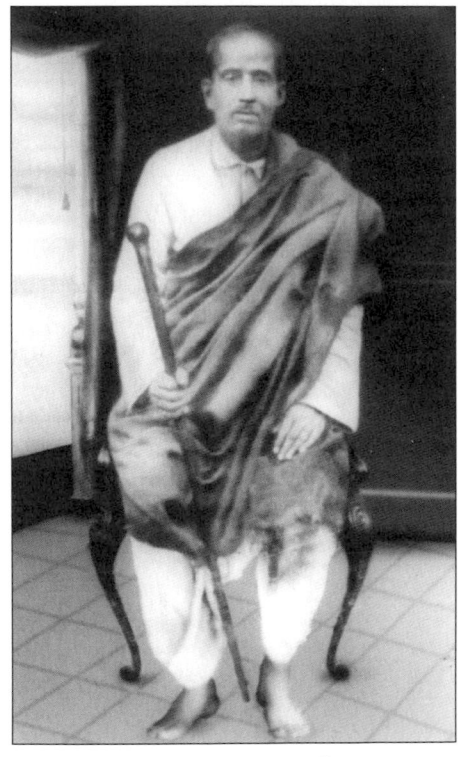

Shivaram Chattopadhyay,
Rameswar's youngest son.

Ramlal Chattopadhyay, the eldest son of Rameswar, said that his father

7. The Master's nephew Ramlal arrives at Dakshineswar and becomes a priest; the Annapurna temple at Barrackpore.

died in December 1873 [27 Agrahayan 1280] and was about forty-eight years old at the time. Ramlal collected his father's remains and immersed them in the Ganges at Vaidyabati, some miles from Calcutta. From there he crossed the Ganges by boat to visit the Master at Dakshineswar. While crossing the river he saw that the construction of the Annapurna temple at Barrackpore was half-way complete. This temple was dedicated on 12 April 1875 by Jagadamba Dasi, the wife of Mathur. After Rameswar's death, Ramlal became a priest of the Dakshineswar temple.

After Mathur's death Shambhu Charan Mallick of Sinduriapati in Cal-

8. The story of Shambhu Charan Mallick, the second supplier who meets the Master's needs.

cutta became acquainted with the Master and developed a great love and reverence for him.[2] Previously, Shambhu had been very devoted to the Brahmo faith and was well known to the Calcutta people for his innumerable charitable deeds. Gradually, Shambhu's love and devotion for the Master grew deeper and he was blessed by serving him for some years. Whatever the Master and the Holy Mother needed, Shambhu gladly supplied. Shambhu used to call the Master "Guruji." Sometimes the Master became annoyed and would say: "Who is whose guru? You are my guru!" However, that did not keep Shambhu from addressing the Master in that manner for the rest of his life. His respectful way of addressing the Master indicates that the Master's holy association and its influence on his life had enlightened his spiritual journey, helping him to achieve success and fulfillment in his spiritual life. Shambhu's wife also loved the Master as God; and whenever the Holy Mother was at Dakshineswar, she would invite the Holy Mother into her house on Tuesdays [an auspicious day for Mother worship] and worship her with sixteen items.

It was probably in 1874 that the Holy Mother came to Dakshineswar for

9. Shambhu builds a cottage [outside the temple garden] for the Holy Mother; Captain Vishwanath Upadhyay helps; the Master spends one night there.

the second time. She lived with the Master's mother in the nahabat as before. Shambhu felt that the tiny room was inconvenient for the Holy Mother to live in, so he acquired on lease a piece of land near the Dakshineswar temple for 250 rupees and decided to build a spacious thatched cottage for her there. Captain Vishwanath Upadhyay, an officer of the

---

2. Some of the Master's devotees told us they heard him say that after Mathur's death, Manimohan Sen of Panihati took on the responsibility of supplying the Master's needs. Manimohan was then very respectful to the Master and visited him frequently. Afterwards, Shambhu took over the Master's service. Because the Master himself mentioned that Shambhu was his second supplier, we think that although Manimohan took on the duty of serving the Master, he did not continue it for long.

Nepalese government, was then visiting the Master and became devoted to him. When Vishwanath heard about Shambhu's building project, he promised to supply all of the timber needed. As the sal wood industry of the Nepal government was under his control, it was not expensive for him to secure the timber. When the construction started, Vishwanath sent three big logs of sal wood from the warehouse located in Belur Village across the Ganges. But that night a strong high tide carried away one of the logs. Believing it to be a bad omen, Hriday was annoyed and remarked that the Holy Mother was unlucky. When the Captain heard this, he sent another log and the cottage was completed. The Holy Mother lived there for nearly a year. A woman was then appointed to be with her and to help her with the household work. Every day the Holy Mother cooked various dishes for the Master in that cottage, carried them to the Dakshineswar temple, and returned to her cottage after he had finished his meal. Sometimes during the day the Master would visit the cottage to care for her and make sure she was happy. He would stay with her for a while and then he would return to the temple. There was only one exception to this routine: One afternoon as soon as the Master arrived at the Holy Mother's cottage, a heavy rain started falling. It continued until midnight, making it impossible for him to return to the temple. He was compelled to stay there overnight, and the Holy Mother cooked rice and soup to serve him.

After living in that cottage for a year, the Holy Mother had a severe attack of dysentery. Shambhu took special care for her recovery and arranged for Dr. Prasad to treat her. When she recovered a little, she left for her native village of Jayrambati, probably in September 1875.

> 10. Holy Mother became seriously ill while staying there and left for Jayrambati.

Shortly after her arrival there, she had a severe relapse and was bedridden. Gradually, the disease worsened so much that her condition became critical. The Holy Mother's father had passed away by then, so her mother and brothers served her the best they could. We heard that when the Master was told of her severe illness, he said to Hriday: "Well, Hriday, just think — if she should die now, her coming into the world would have been in vain. She would have failed to achieve the main purpose of human life."

The disease had not abated at all, so the Holy Mother resolved to fast in front of the Simhavahini temple to cure her disease. Thinking that her mother and brothers might keep her from going if they knew her intention, she went without their knowledge to the temple of the village goddess Simhavahini and lay there, intending to fast until death. Within a few hours the goddess became gracious and prescribed the medicine for her cure.

> 11. The Holy Mother's vow of fasting in front of the Simhavahini temple for a divine favour; she receives medicine.

When the Holy Mother took that medicine, she recovered from her disease and gradually regained her health. Because the Holy Mother had received the medicine through a vow of fasting, Mother Simhavahini became well known among the surrounding villages as a living goddess.

Shambhu served the Master and the Holy Mother for about four years

12. Shambhu's fearlessness at the time of death.

before he fell ill. One day the Master went to see him on his sickbed. Upon his return he remarked, "There is no oil left in Shambhu's lamp." His prediction soon proved true. Shambhu died of diabetes with other complications. Shambhu was liberal-minded, courageous, and a wonderful devotee of God. During his illness he never lost his cheerfulness even for a day. A few days before his death, he joyfully said to Hriday: "I have no anxiety about death. I've packed my baggage and I'm ready for the journey." Long before he had met Shambhu, the Master's yogic insight revealed that the Divine Mother had chosen Shambu to be his second supplier, and he recognized him as such at their first meeting.

A few months after the Holy Mother's illness and departure for Jayram-

13. The last days of Chandramani, and her death.

bati, an important event took place in the Master's life. In 1876, Chandramani Devi passed away at the age of eighty-five; it is said that this happened on Sri Ramakrishna's birthday. Due to old age, she had become somewhat senile towards the end and suffered from physical problems. We record here the account of her death that we heard from Hriday.

Four days before Chandradevi died, Hriday was due to go to his native village for a few days' vacation. Before his departure he felt a vague foreboding and was reluctant to leave the Master alone. When he mentioned this to the Master, the latter replied, "Then you had better stay here." Three days passed without incident.

Every day the Master would spend time with his mother and give her some personal service, and Hriday also used to care for her. In addition, a woman known as Kali's Mother, a maidservant, stayed with her for most of the day. At that time Chandradevi had taken a dislike to Hriday. Since Akshay's death, she had the strange notion that Hriday had killed Akshay and was trying to murder the Master and his wife. So she sometimes warned the Master, "Never do anything Hriday says." Her senility, which was due to infirmity and old age, manifested itself in various ways. For example, the Alambazar jute mill was situated near the Dakshineswar garden. The millworkers had a midday break for half an hour and were called back to work by a steam whistle. Chandradevi somehow came to believe that the sound of this whistle was the blowing of the conch shell of Vaikuntha, or heaven [calling the Lord Vishnu to eat His meal]. If she did not hear that whistle, she would not eat her meal. If someone asked her to eat, she would reply: "How can I have my meal? Food has not yet been offered to Lakshmi and Narayana. The conch shell has not yet been blown in Vaikuntha. It is impious to begin eating before the gods have begun." On holidays, when the

Keshab Chandra Sen
(1838-1884), charismatic
leader of the Brahmo
Samaj.

Shambu Mallick (d. 1877),
who read to Ramakrishna
from the Bible in 1874.

mill was closed and the whistle silent, it was extremely difficult to get Chandradevi to eat at all. The Master and Hriday had to coax her in various ways.

The fourth day arrived, and Chandradevi's health appeared to be normal. The Master spent the evening with her, talking of his childhood and telling stories that filled the elderly woman with delight. After seeing her to bed at midnight, the Master returned to his room.

At 8:00 the next morning Chandradevi did not open her door and come out, as she usually did. Kali's mother went upstairs to the door of the nahabat room and called her. There was no answer. She put her ear to the door and heard harsh and laboured breathing. Alarmed, she ran and called the Master and Hriday. Hriday skillfully unbarred the door from the outside and opened it, to find Chandramani unconscious. He brought some ayurvedic medicine and put it on her tongue, and at frequent intervals he fed her milk and Ganges water drop by drop. She thus was kept alive in that manner for three days. When she was at the point of death, she was carried to the bank of the Ganges. The Master made an offering of flowers with sandal paste and tulsi leaves at her feet as she quietly passed away. Because he was a sannyasin, the Master could not perform his mother's funeral rites, so he appointed his nephew Ramlal to complete that duty. Later, when the mourning period was over, Ramlal was deputed by the Master to perform the traditional shrāddha ceremony for his mother.

According to the scriptural injunctions, a sannyasin does not have the right to perform funeral rites of any kind; so the Master respectfully followed the monastic tradition when his mother died. One day he began to think that he had not done his proper duty as a son, so he tried to perform *tarpana*, an offering of water to his departed mother. But as soon as he lifted water in his cupped hands, he entered into ecstasy: His fingers became numb and opened of their own accord, letting the water run through them. He tried again and again without success. Then he tearfully begged his mother's spirit to forgive him for his failure. Later a pandit told him that such a thing happens to a person who has reached a certain state when all actions drop off. Due to spiritual development that person's activities cease naturally. If a man cannot then perform duties enjoined by the scriptures, he incurs no sin.

14. The Master was unable to perform the rite for his departed mother: for one like him, such actions come to an end.

A year before his mother's death, a significant event took place in the Master's life by the will of the Divine Mother. In March 1875, the Master had a desire to visit Keshab Chandra Sen, the leader of the Brahmo Samaj of India; while he was in ecstasy the Divine Mother had prompted him to do so. The Master heard that at that time Keshab was practising spiritual disciplines with his disciples in the garden house of Jaygopal Sen at Belgharia, a

15. The Master's visit to Keshab Chandra Sen.

few miles north of Calcutta. The Master went there with Hriday, who told us that they arrived at about 1:00 p.m. in a carriage belonging to Captain Vishwanath Upadhyay. On this occasion the Master wore a *dhoti* [cloth] with a red border, one end of which was thrown over his shoulder.

Hriday got out of the carriage first and saw Keshab and his disciples seated on the brick ghat of a pond in the garden. Hriday went to Keshab and told him: "My uncle loves to hear discussions and songs about the Lord. When he hears them, he goes into samadhi. He has heard that you are a great devotee, and he has come to listen to you talk about God and His glories. With your kind permission, I'll bring him to you." Keshab of course agreed, and Hriday helped the Master out of the carriage and led him over to them. Keshab and the others had been awaiting him with keen curiosity, but after seeing him they concluded that he was merely an ordinary man.

16. Keshab at the Belgharia retreat.

The Master said to Keshab: "Is it true that you gentlemen have had a vision of God? I want so much to know what it's like. That's why I've come to see you." We do not know what Keshab said in reply, but the Master then sang to them a well-known song of Ramprasad's: "Who knows what Kali is? The six philosophies cannot explain Her." Immediately after singing, he went into samadhi. This we heard from Hriday. But even when they saw the Master in ecstasy, Keshab and the others did not consider it to be a high spiritual state. They took it to be some kind of mental illness or a trick played to impress them. To bring the Master back to his senses, Hriday began to chant "Om" in his ear, and gradually the Master's face beamed with a sweet smile. When the Master had thus regained partial consciousness, he began explaining profound spiritual topics in such simple language and by citing such common examples that all present gazed at him. Enthralled, they were unaware that the time for bathing and eating had long since passed and that the time for the next prayer was nearly upon them. Observing them spellbound, the Master said: "If any other kind of animal comes to a herd of cattle, they'll turn on it and gore it with their horns. But if a cow joins the herd, they'll lick its body and welcome it as one of themselves. That's what has happened to us here today."

17. The Master's first conversation with Keshab.

Then addressing Keshab, the Master added, "Your tail has dropped off." That odd remark seemed to startle and displease Keshab's disciples. Realizing that they had not understood him, the Master went on to explain: "As long as a tadpole has its tail, it can live only in the water; it can't come on land. But when its tail drops off, it can live on land or in the water. Similarly, as long as a man wears the tail of ignorance, he can only live in the world; but when the tail drops off, he can live either in Satchidananda or in the world, whichever he pleases. Your mind, Keshab, has reached that state now. You can live in the world and still be aware of God." All were overwhelmed. That day the Master discussed various topics, spent some delightful hours with them, and then returned to Dakshineswar.

After this first meeting Keshab was so attracted to the Master that he often visited him at Dakshineswar, and sometimes he invited the Master to his Calcutta residence, Kamal Kutir [Lily Cottage], to enjoy his holy company. Gradually, the relationship between the Master and Keshab became so deep that they missed each other if they were away from one another even for a few days. Then either the Master would go to see Keshab or he would come to Dakshineswar. In addition, Keshab considered it to be part of the annual festival of the Brahmo Samaj to visit the Master at Dakshineswar or to invite him to his Calcutta residence and spend the day in spiritual conversation. A few times Keshab and his followers came to Dakshineswar in a steamer, singing devotional songs, and took the Master for a cruise on the Ganges, all the while enjoying his divine discourses.

18. The close relationship between the Master and Keshab.

Remembering scriptural traditions, Keshab never visited Dakshineswar empty-handed: He always carried some fruits and sweets and presented them to the Master. Then, like a devoted disciple, he would sit at the Master's feet and talk to him. Once the Master said to him playfully, "Keshab, you delight so many people with your lectures — please expound something to me, too!" To which Keshab humbly replied: "Sir, am I to sell needles in a blacksmith's shop?[3] Please talk and let me listen. People are delighted whenever I tell them anything you have told me."

19. Keshab at Dakshineswar.

Once in Dakshineswar the Master explained to Keshab that if one admits the existence of Brahman, one must also necessarily admit the existence of Brahman's power, since Brahman and Its power are eternally one and the same. To this Keshab agreed. Then the Master said to him that, like the relation between Brahman and Its power, the scriptures, devotees, and God are the same substance and eternally connected. These three are one, and the One manifests as three. Keshab understood this and also agreed. The Master next told him, "Now I shall explain to you that the Guru, Krishna [God], and Vaishnava [the devotee] are one, and this One manifests as three." Keshab reflected awhile. We do not know what went through his mind, but he humbly said: "Sir, just now I can't accept anything more. Please, let us not speak of this for the present." "Very well," said the Master. "Then we'll stop there." Although Keshab was greatly influenced by Western culture, the holy company of the Master brought new light to his life. Keshab gradually grasped more and more of the deeper truths of Vedic religion and became

20. The Master explains to Keshab: "Brahman and Its power are identical"; and "The scriptures, the devotees, and God — these three are one, and the One manifests as three."

---

3. The Indian proverbial equivalent of "carrying coal to Newcastle." — *Translator*

absorbed in practising them. It is evident that Keshab's religious views gradually went through a change after he became acquainted with the Master.

Without experiencing pain, the human mind does not want to detach

| 21. On 6 March 1878, the Maharaja of Coochbehar marries Keshab's daughter. Hurt by the repercussions, Keshab advances spiritually: the Master's remark regarding that marriage. |

itself from the world, and therefore cannot make God its own. Three years after he met the Master, Keshab married his daughter to the Maharaja of Coochbehar and was terribly hurt.[4] This marriage created a great conflict in the Brahmo Samaj of India and split it into two factions. The opposition party separated itself from Keshab and founded a new organization called the Sadharan Brahmo Samaj. The Master was very distressed when he heard of this petty schism. When he heard of the rule for the marriageable age of girls in the Brahmo Samaj, the Master said: "Birth, death, and marriage are all subject to the will of God. They can't be made to obey hard-and-fast rules. Why does Keshab try to make such rules?" If anybody spoke of the Coochbehar marriage in the Master's presence and blamed Keshab, the Master would defend him, saying: "How is Keshab to blame? He's a family man. Why shouldn't he do what he thinks best for his sons and daughters? He wasn't acting contrary to religion or morality. He has only done his duty as a father." From the standpoint of family duty, the Master supported Keshab's action as blameless. But after receiving the terrific blow of the reaction to the Coochbehar marriage, Keshab became more indrawn and undoubtedly made tremendous progress on his spiritual path.

Keshab received the Master's sincere love and had many opportunities to

| 22. Keshab cannot fully grasp the Master's ideology: his two attitudes towards the Master. |

see him closely, but it was doubtful whether he understood the Master completely, because he had been indoctrinated with Western ideas. On one hand, he considered the Master to be a living embodiment of spirituality. He personally took the Master to his home and requested him to bless his bedroom, dining room, living room, and office, so that wherever he might be, his mind would think of God and forget the world. Finally, he took the Master to his meditation room and offered flowers at his feet.[5] Many of us saw Keshab bowing down to the Master at Dakshineswar, exclaiming, "Victory to the New Dispensation!"

But on the other hand, Keshab could not fully accept the Master's position

| 23. The New Dispensation and the Master's views. |

when he declared: "All religions are true. As many faiths, so many paths." Keshab took the essentials of all religions according to his own understanding, rejecting what he considered to be unnecessary, and then tried to establish a

---

4. The girl was not yet fourteen years old. Keshab acted against one of his own public declarations that the minimum age of marriage for girls should be fourteen and for boys eighteen. — *Translator*

5. We heard this story from Vijay Krishna Goswami.

new creed that he called *Navavidhan*, "The New Dispensation." As this creed came into existence shortly after his acquaintance with the Master, it seems that Keshab to some extent preached the Master's final conclusion about all religions: All paths are true and lead to the same goal.

Huge waves of Western education and civilization began to radically change ancient India's spiritual education, social customs, and ways of living. The great thinkers of India tried their utmost to bring harmony between the education, religion, and culture of the East and those of the West. In Bengal, Rammohan Roy, Devendra Nath Tagore, Keshab Chandra Sen, and others devoted their lives to harmonizing the East and the West in this respect. Similarly, many great thinkers tried to do the same in other parts of India. But before the Master's advent, no one could solve that national problem completely. In his life the Master duly practised each main religious path of India, and after attaining success in each one of them, he realized that the cause of India's degradation was not religion; it must be sought somewhere else. He pointed out that India's society, manners, customs, culture, and civilization were based on religion, which had brought glory and prosperity to India in ancient times. He realized that that living force still existed in religion, and that we would succeed in every respect only if we exerted ourselves by sincerely treading the path of religion. The Master was the first to demonstrate in his life the extent to which religion can make a person free from narrowness. Then he transmitted the power of that liberal religion to his Westernized disciples, especially to Swami Vivekananda, and taught them how to perform all their activities with the help of religion, thus providing a wonderful solution to the aforesaid national problem of India. Having succeeded in practising all the major religions, the Master devised a method for eradicating the religious conflicts of the world. Similarly, he attained success in practising the various religious paths of India, and then he harmonized their differences. He pointed out what the true basis of our nationality has been in the past and what it will be in the future.

24. The Master solves India's national problem.

How much love the Master had for Keshab, we clearly understood from the Master's behaviour when Keshab died in January 1884. The Master later told us: "When I heard of Keshab's death, I remained in bed for three days. I felt as if part of my body had been paralyzed."

25. The Master's reaction to Keshab's death.

We shall conclude this chapter by describing another event of the Master's life that occurred after he met Keshab. During that period the Master had a desire to witness the ecstatic *nagar-kirtan*[6] of Chaitanya. The Divine Mother fulfilled his wish in this manner: As he stood outside his room, the

26. The Master's vision of Gauranga during sankirtan.

6. The act of singing religious songs while in procession through a city.

Master saw wonderful waves of sankirtan coming towards him from the Panchavati. The crowd then flowed towards the main gate, finally vanishing behind the trees. In that crowd he saw Gauranga of Navadwip, absorbed in divine love. Accompanied by Nityananda and Advaita, Chaitanya walked slowly in the midst of a great multitude of people. Everyone around him was intoxicated by his love, some expressing their inner joy by losing control of themselves and some by dancing wildly. The crowd was so vast that it seemed there was no end to the flow of humanity. A few faces in that wonderful kirtan party were clearly imprinted on the Master's mind. When the Master's own devotees began to arrive shortly after this vision, he recognized them and concluded that they had been Chaitanya's companions in their previous births.

Sometime after that vision, the Master visited Kamarpukur and Sihar,

27. The Master's visit to Phului-Shyambazar and his experience during kirtan: the date of that event.

Hriday's birthplace. Phului-Shyambazar Village is situated a few miles from Sihar. The Master heard that in that place are many Vaishnavas who create a blissful atmosphere in their village by singing kirtan daily. So he had a desire to go there and listen to their kirtan. The village of Belte is next to Shyambazar. Natavar Goswami of Belte had met the Master previously and invited him to sanctify his house with the dust of his feet. Accompanied by Hriday, the Master then went to Natavar's house, stayed seven days, and enjoyed kirtan with the Vaishnavas of Shyambazar. Ishan Chandra Mallick of Shyambazar became acquainted with the Master and invited him to his house to attend the kirtan. When they saw the Master's wonderful ecstasy during the kirtan, the Vaishnavas felt a special attraction towards him. Gradually, the news of the Master's ecstasy spread not only throughout Shyambazar but also to Ramjivanpur, Krishnaganj, and other villages far and near. The kirtan parties of those villages came to enjoy divine bliss with him. Thus Shyambazar became overcrowded and kirtan continued day and night. Then a rumour spread that a devotee of God had arrived who dies one moment and revives the next. Forgetting food and sleep, people anxiously climbed up into the trees and onto the rooftops to have a glimpse of the Master. Thus, a current of bliss flowed there for seven days and nights. People became so frantic to see the Master and to touch his feet that he seldom had any time to bathe or eat.

The mart of joy finally came to an end when Hriday and the Master secretly fled to Sihar. Ishan Chaudhury, Natavar Goswami, Ishan Mallick, Srinath Mallick, and others of Shyambazar and their descendants talk about that event even now and cherish a special love and respect for the Master. Raicharan Das, the famous drum player of Krishnaganj, became acquainted with the Master. When he heard Raicharan play his drum, the Master would go into ecstasy. The description of this event we heard partly from the Master and partly from Hriday. We have been able to ascertain when it occurred in the following way: Dr. Mahendra Nath Pal of Baranagore-Alambazar [who previously lived in Sinthi] first saw the Master after Keshab had met him in 1875. Mahendra was a great devotee of the Master. He told us that when he first went to see the Master, he had just returned from Sihar. And on that day the Master told him the story of Phului-Shyambazar.

The Master's chosen devotees began to come to him in 1879, except for Swami Yogananda whose home was near the Dakshineswar temple and might have met him earlier. Swami Vivekananda met the Master in 1881. Jaga-damba Dasi died on 1 January 1881. About six months after Jagadamba's death, Hriday foolishly worshipped Mathur's young granddaughter. The girl's father was apprehensive that evil might befall his child, so he was furious and immediately dismissed Hriday from the temple forever. So the event of Phului-Shyambazar must have taken place sometime between 1879 and 1881.

SRI RAMAKRISHNA AS A GURU
PART 1

VOLUME THREE

Preface to Volume Three

The third volume "Sri Ramakrishna as a Guru — Part 1" of *Sri Ramakrishna and His Divine Play* is now published. It contains most of the events of the Master's life from the period after his sadhana to the time he became well known to the public. We have recorded not only those events and the Master's activities during that time, but we have also discussed, when possible, the moods that prompted him and the purpose that guided him in performing those actions. Human beings are composed of bodies and minds, so a life history cannot be obtained by studying the material body and its activities. In the materialistic West, a biography or a history shows a skill in collecting facts and figures, but the spiritualistic Hindus focus their efforts on describing thoughts and feelings in an orderly way. We think that a true biography or history can be produced only by combining those two approaches, and that one should record the activities of the material body while keeping the history of the mind in the forefront.

In many places in this volume we have discussed Sri Ramakrishna's divine life in light of the scriptures. We have also done a study of his unique mental states, experiences, and activities, comparing them with those of other great souls, such as Krishna, Buddha, Shankara, and Chaitanya of India, and Jesus and others in other countries. The Master told us explicitly again and again: "He who was born as Rama and as Krishna in previous ages is now in this sheath," as he pointed to his own body. "The spiritual experiences of this place (*meaning himself*) have surpassed even the Vedas and Vedanta." In fact, while discussing as impartially as possible the biography of Sri Ramakrishna, who was established in bhavamukha, we were forced to admit that such an extraordinary life had never before been seen in the spiritual world.

Sri Ramakrishna followed the teachings of all previous avatars and quickly attained perfection in various religious paths. He discovered a new truth — "As many faiths, so many paths" — which he declared for the good of humanity. When we studied this, we came to a complete understanding that he was a new manifestation, the embodiment of all past avatars. The more we studied the unprecedented and holy life of Sri Ramakrishna, the more we became convinced that he was the first fruit of the universal, eternal, spiritual tree of the Vedic religion — the very quintessence of it.

When Swami Vivekananda, the foremost disciple of Sri Ramakrishna, came to the West to preach religion, people became eager to know more about the Master's life. As a result, many people have written many things about the Master. But until now no one has clearly indicated that his extraordinary life was deeply connected to the eternal Hindu, or Vedic, religion. While reading those other books one might come to the opposite conclusion, that Sri Ramakrishna was an individual who had separated from the eternal Hindu religion, and who had created a particular religious sect. Many stories of the Master's life in those books contain errors, and some fail to mention the significance of the events they describe and have errors of consistency and chronology. In this volume we have tried to present to the public an accurate picture of the Master's great life as it was revealed to us. Moreover, we have followed the lead of Swami Vivekananda and have recorded those important ideas of the Master that inspired us as well as Swami Vivekananda to dedicate our lives to him.

Let us remind the reader that if we have correctly portrayed the Master's divine life to even a small extent, it is due to his grace; and if there are any imperfections and distortions in this book, they are due to our own lack of proper understanding and faulty powers of exposition. We cherish a desire that in the future we shall present to the reader the first and the last parts of the Master's precious life.[1] Before we begin this volume, we shall present an article by Swami Vivekananda, a collection of aphorisms that discusses the deep connection between the eternal Vedic religion and the incomprehensible life of Sri Ramakrishna, who was established in bhavamukha.

The Author [Swami Saradananda]
Shravan 1318 B.E. [mid-July to mid-August 1911]

---

1. The author first wrote volume three of *Sri Ramakrishna and His Divine Play* and then volumes four, two, one, and five. — *Translator*

Hinduism and
Sri Ramakrishna

The Supreme One was born as Rama, the beloved of Sita —
Ah, his stream of love flowed unobstructedly even to the pariah;
Although superhuman, he never gave up doing good to people;
His glory was unparalleled in the three worlds;
He was the embodiment of knowledge, sheathed in devotion.
Again, the Supreme One was born as Krishna —
He subdued the terrible war cry of destruction;
He destroyed [Arjuna's] inherent, deep darkness of ignorance;
He heroically proclaimed the serene and sweet message of the Gita.
That celebrated Supreme One is now born as Ramakrishna.[1]

THE WORD *SHASTRA* DENOTES THE VEDAS, which are without beginning or end. The Vedas alone are capable of teaching religion.

The Puranas and all other religious scriptures are denoted by the word *Smriti*; their authority is undisputed so far as they follow the Vedas and do not contradict them.

Truth is of two kinds: (1) that which is perceivable by the five human senses and is deducible based upon them; and (2) that which is perceivable by the subtle yogic power, which is beyond the senses.

Knowledge acquired by the first means is called *science*; that acquired by the second means is called the *Vedas*.

The beginningless and endless mass of transcendent truths called the Vedas is eternal. With its help the Creator Himself creates, preserves, and destroys this universe.

The person in whom this supersensory power is manifested is called a rishi or a saint, and the transcendent truths he realizes by this power are called the Vedas.

This rishihood, this realization of the Vedic truths, is true religion. Until

1. This is the translation of a Sanskrit hymn to Sri Ramakrishna composed by Swami Vivekananda. — *Translator*

this experience dawns in an aspirant, religion is merely an empty word; know for certain that such a person has not yet taken even the first step in the realm of religion.

The authority of the Vedas extends to all places, times, and persons; in other words, their application is not confined to any particular place or time or person. The Vedas are the only expounder of the universal religion.

Although some transcendent truth is found in the Puranas, in histories, in other books of our country, and also in the scriptures of other countries, still the fourfold scriptures known among the Aryan race as the Vedas hold the first, the most complete, and the most undistorted collection of transcendent knowledge. So the Vedas deserve to occupy the highest place among all scriptures, to command the respect of all the world's people, and to furnish the proof of truth for all other scriptures.

Regarding the collection of truths discovered by the Aryan race, known as the Vedas, it is to be understood that the portions that refer to secular matters, eulogy, and tradition, are not the Vedas.

The Vedas are divided into two parts: *jnana-kanda* [the knowledge portion] and *karma-kanda* [the ritual portion]. The rituals and the results achieved by practising them, as described in the karma-kanda, remain in the domain of maya. They therefore have been changed, are changing, and will change according to the law of change that operates through space, time, and personality. And because social manners and customs are based on the karma-kanda, they also have changed and will continue to change with the course of time. Popular customs and practices that do not contradict the scriptures or run counter to virtuous practices have been accepted in the past and will also be in the future. One of the main causes of the downfall of the Aryans is that they blindly followed prevailing social customs that are forbidden by the scriptures and antithetical to good conduct.

The jnana-kanda, or Vedanta, is eternally bestowing liberation and leading people beyond maya with the help of four yogas: karma, jnana, bhakti, and raja. As the authority of Vedanta is in all respects unaffected by any limitations imposed by place, time, or person, it is the sole preceptor of the universal and eternal religion for all humankind.

The laws of Manu and of other sages, based on the teachings of the karma-kanda, have ordained rules of conduct conducive to social welfare that are appropriate to place, time, and person. The Purana scriptures have taken the truths that lie within Vedanta and explained them in detail by describing the exalted lives and deeds of avatars and saints. In addition, the Puranas have taught by emphasizing some aspects of the infinitely multifaceted Divine Lord.

Over the course of time, however, the descendants of the Aryans deviated from proper conduct; they lost their spirit of renunciation and their sharp intelligence and became deeply attached to popular customs. They even failed to understand the import of the Puranas, thinking them contradictory to one another because each one taught by emphasizing only a particular aspect of the spiritual ideal and because each taught people of ordinary intelligence the abstruse truths of Vedanta by using concrete imagery and elaborate language. They divided the whole of the *Sanatana Dharma* [eternal religion] — the sum total of all religious ideals — into many sects. They enkindled the fire of sectarian jealousy and anger and tried to throw each other into it. When the degraded Aryans had almost turned India, the land of religion, into a hell, Bhagavan Sri Ramakrishna incarnated himself to demonstrate the true religion of the Aryan race. He made visible the unity among the innumerable sects and denominations of the Hindu religion that had cropped up throughout the country over a vast period of time. At that time the Hindu religion had been devastated by continuous sectarian fights, and was seemingly divided into many sects. Its various sects were overrun by hideous customs, and Hinduism had become confusing to Indians and an object of contempt to foreigners. Over time, this eternal religion had been debased, but Sri Ramakrishna incorporated its universal and eternal aspects in his own life to become a living example of the eternal religion, which he lived before all for the good of humanity.

God creates, preserves, and destroys with the help of the eternal Vedic scriptures, which reveal themselves spontaneously within the pure heart of a rishi. If this scripture is proven by this revelation, the eternal religion will be restored, reestablished, and disseminated again. To demonstrate this truth, in His new incarnation the Divine Lord, the embodiment of the Vedas, almost entirely neglected external education.

It is said in the Smriti scriptures that God incarnates again and again to preserve the Vedas, the true religion, and brahminhood, the ministry of that religion.

As a stream falling over a precipice gains tremendous speed, as a wave swells higher after a big hollow, so after every downfall Aryan society sheds its stagnation by the merciful dispensation of God and becomes more glorious and vigorous. History testifies to this fact.

After every downfall, our revived society manifests more of its inherent and eternal perfection, and so also does the omnipresent Lord reveal Himself to a greater and greater degree in successive incarnations.

India has lost her life-force again and again, so the Divine Lord has repeatedly revived her by manifesting Himself. Before this present degeneration, no veil of darkness had ever enveloped the holy land of India so deeply as this last dismal night, which is now merely a remnant — it is almost gone. And compared to the depth of this last fall, all previous collapses seem like the little hoof-marks of a cow.

Therefore, before the effulgence of this new awakening, the glory of all past revivals of Aryan society will pale like stars before the rising sun. And compared to the reawakening of this great divine power, the manifestation of powers in past ages will appear as child's play.

During the recent downfall, the ideals of the eternal religion were scattered for want of competent people to preserve them. As a result many small sects were formed. Some preserved a part of the spirit of the eternal religion and some lost it completely.

During this current spiritual renaissance, the new avatar of the age, endowed with tremendous divine power, will gather together the divided and scattered religious ideals, practise and realize them in his own life, and rediscover the knowledge that was lost. To bring this about, the all-merciful God has therefore incarnated Himself as an avatar in this present age, one who is exceedingly perfect, more so than those who came before him. He is the embodiment of all religious ideals and the support of all branches of learning.

So at the dawn of this momentous epoch, the message of the harmony of religions has been proclaimed. This boundless and all-embracing idea, which has been hidden in the Vedic scriptures and religion, has been rediscovered and declared to humanity with a clarion call.

This new religion of the age will benefit the whole world, but most especially India. Bhagavan Sri Ramakrishna, the founder of this new religion, is the reconstructed manifestation of the earlier founders of religions. O human beings, have faith in this and realize it.

O human beings, the dead never return; a night past does not reappear; a passionate emotion never takes the same form again; and a jiva does not assume the same body twice. So from the worship of the dead past, O human beings, we invite you to the worship of the living present; from the regretful brooding over bygones, we invite you to the activities of the present day; from wasted energy spent retracing lost pathways, we call you to tread the wide new highway close at hand. O wise one, try to understand what we mean.

The mere opening of this divine power is echoing throughout the world; just feel through your imagination its fully developed state. Shun the useless misgivings, weakness, jealousy, and malice that are characteristic of an enslaved people, and help to turn the mighty wheel of the new dispensation.

We are the servants of the Lord, His children, and helpers in His divine play: Have this faith firmly in your heart and plunge into the field of action.

— *Vivekananda*

Ramakrishna in Samadhi. This photo was taken on 10 December 1881, at the studio of Bengal Photographers, Calcutta.

Chapter 1

Sri Ramakrishna in *B*havamukha

And whatever things there be — of the nature of sattva, rajas, and tamas — know they are all from Me alone. I am not, however, in them; they are in Me. Deluded by these threefold gunas constituting Nature, this whole world fails to recognize Me, who am above the gunas and immutable. — GITA 7:12-13

WHEN AFTER TWELVE YEARS THE MASTER HAD completed his unprecedented, super-human austerities, the Divine Mother told him, "Now you remain in bhavamukha."[1] Many people now know that the Master followed the Mother's command. But bhavamukha is extremely difficult to understand. It is also difficult to explain the inner meaning of bhavamukha and how anyone could remain in such a state. Twenty-eight years ago[2] Swami Vivekananda said to a friend (Haramohan Mitra), "One can write shelves of philosophical books based on a single teaching of Sri Ramakrishna." Surprised, the friend replied: "Is that so? But we don't find any such profundity in his teachings. Could you explain one of his sayings in that manner?"

Swamiji: "Do you have the brains to understand the Master? Well, pick any saying of his, and I shall explain it to you."

1. The profundity of the Master's words.

1. Bhavamukha — Literally, *bhava* means ideas or thoughts, and *mukha* means source. It is an exalted state of spiritual experience in which the aspirant keeps his mind on the border-line between the Absolute and the Relative. From this position he can contemplate the ineffable and attributeless Brahman and also participate in the activities of the relative world, seeing in it the manifestation of God alone. — *Translator*
2. Probably in 1883 or 1884, as the first edition of *Sri Sri Ramakrishna Lilaprasanga*, volume 3, was published in 1911. — *Translator*

The friend: "All right. Please explain the story of the elephant-god and the mahout-god that the Master used to illustrate his instruction to see God in all beings."

At once Swamiji launched into a discussion of the controversial doctrines of free will versus predestination and self-effort versus the will of God, which are perpetually unresolved conflicts among scholars of both the East and the West. For three days continually Swamiji explained to his friend in simple language that the Master's story was a solution to those age-old controversies.

Indeed, anyone who reflects deeply on the Master's ordinary everyday

2. The mode of teaching of all avatars is the same.

conduct and on his teachings would be amazed to discover profound meanings in them. This is true of each avatar, and it is evident when one studies the stories of their lives. However, Shankara and a few other great teachers had to establish their religious views by shattering their opponents' fallacies. Apart from these exceptions, the great teachers communicated their teachings through simple language, using short parables, similes, and allegories. They avoided bombastic words, rhetoric, or complicated language in their teachings. Their simple language and short similes contain so much wisdom and have so much power to elevate ordinary human beings to the highest ideal that we have not been able to fathom their depths over thousands of years. The more we study their teachings, the deeper are the meanings we find. The more we meditate on them, the higher our minds soar, leaving the impermanent and inauspicious world. All the great teachers reached the same ultimate truth, but they expressed it in different terms: "attainment of the supreme goal," "establishment in Brahman," "liberation," or "vision of God." The more an aspirant moves forward, the more he or she realizes the depth of those simple teachings.

This is the law. We cannot find any exception to this in the words and

3. An example: Girish gave his power of attorney to the Master.

conduct of the Master. Previously we had a limited understanding of his sayings, but now we find such profound meaning in those same sayings! It will suffice to cite one example. After he had visited the Master a few times, Girish Chandra Ghosh completely surrendered to him one day and asked, "Sir, what shall I do from now on?"

The Master: "Do just what you are doing now. Hold on to God with one hand and to the world with the other. Eventually, when one side [the world] falls to pieces, whatever is ordained to happen will happen. At a minimum, think of God in the morning and evening." After saying this the Master looked at Girish as if waiting for his reply.

Girish thought sadly: "The type of work I do does not allow me to keep

4. Girish's mental condition.

fixed hours for bathing, eating, or sleeping. I shall surely forget to remember God in the morning and evening. This is a difficult situation. If I disobey my

Girish Chandra Ghosh (1844-1912), actor and playwright.

guru's order, I will incur sin — which will cause me harm. So how can I make that promise? It is definitely wrong to fail to keep one's promise to a person in this world. How much worse it will be if I cannot keep my promise to a person whom I have accepted as my spiritual guide."

Girish was hesitant to express these thoughts. Again he reflected: "The Master did not ask me to do a very difficult task. If he had asked someone else to do this, that person would have gladly agreed to it right away." What could Girish do? As he reflected on his own outgoing tendencies, he realized that it was beyond his capacity to practise even that little spiritual discipline daily. Again, as he examined his own nature, he felt suffocated at the mere thought of being bound forever to a particular vow or to a rule; he knew he would have no peace of mind until that rule was broken. This had happened all through his life. He had no problem doing good or bad according to his will, but the moment he felt that he was under any sort of compulsion to do any work, his mind would rebel and turn away from doing it. Realizing his own powerless and helpless condition, he humbly kept quiet, unable to say either "I shall do so," or "I cannot." How could he shamelessly declare that he would not be able to perform such an easy task? And if he did admit this, how would the Master and others react? They probably wouldn't understand his utterly helpless condition, and might think, without expressing it, that his silence was mere pretension.

Finding Girish silent, the Master read his mind and said, "Well, if you cannot do that, then remember God before you eat and before you sleep."

But Girish remained silent. He wondered how he could do even that. Some days he ate lunch at 10:00 a.m. and some days at 5:00 p.m., and the same irregularity continued with his dinner. Again, sometimes he was troubled with litigation. On those days he would not realize that he was eating at all. He would then be anxiously thinking: "I have not received confirmation that the fee I sent to the barrister reached him on time. If he cannot appear in court as scheduled, it will be a disaster," and so on. In truth, if such an occasion occurred — and it was not impossible — then on that day he would certainly forget to think of God.

Alas, the Master was asking him to do such a simple thing and he was unable to agree to do it. Girish was in an embarrassing situation, but he remained calm and silent even though a tempest of anxiety, fear, and despondency was blowing in his mind. The Master looked at Girish again and said to him with a smile: "So you are unwilling to agree even to this. All right. Give me your power of attorney."[3] Immediately the Master went into ecstasy!

---

3. This means to surrender responsibility for one's own welfare. When a person transfers the power or right to manage his or her worldly affairs to another, the latter makes all business transactions, gives receipts, writes letters, and signs all documents on that person's behalf.

This was to Girish's liking and he felt greatly relieved. In addition, thinking

| 5. Girish's mental state after giving the power of attorney. |

of the Master's infinite compassion, his heart swelled with overwhelming love and faith in him. Girish thought: "What a relief! I will not be trapped by the bondage of rules, which are like dreadful tigers to me. Now whatever I do, I shall have firm faith that the Master will save me somehow or other through his infinite divine power." This was the way Girish at that time understood the power of attorney, which meant surrendering all of his responsibility to the Master. He thought that he would not have to make any effort to give up anything or to practise spiritual disciplines; rather, the Master would use his own power to remove all worldly thoughts from his mind.

At that time Girish did not realize that he had willingly put a noose of love

| 6. The power of attorney turned into a bond of love. |

around his own neck that was a hundred times stronger than the bondage of rules, which he considered unbearable. Neither did he understand completely, nor did he have the power to foresee, that no matter what came into his life — good or bad, praise or blame, joy or suffering — he would be able to do nothing but silently bear it. All other thoughts disappeared from his mind, and he felt only the infinite grace of Sri Ramakrishna. And his ego swelled a hundredfold because of this relationship with Sri Ramakrishna. He thought: "Let people say whatever they like about me; let them look down upon me; the Master is mine always and in all circumstances. What else is needed? Of whom should I be afraid?" He did not know then that according to the devotional scripture[4] such an ego is a kind of spiritual practice that comes to a person as a result of great fortune. However, Girish was now reassured. While he was eating, lying, or sitting, he had only one thought: "Sri Ramakrishna has taken full responsibility for me." He could not realize that this thought was constantly making his mind meditate on Sri Ramakrishna and putting the Master's impression on every one of his actions and thoughts, changing him radically. He was very happy, because he knew that Sri Ramakrishna loved him and that he was more than his own.

The Master always taught, "Never disturb another's faith," and he would

| 7. Girish's insight afterwards. |

behave with each devotee accordingly. Knowing of Girish's new attitude of self-surrender, the Master began to train him with this in mind. One day while in the Master's presence, Girish said "I shall do this," regarding a trifling matter. Immediately the Master said: "What is this? You must not talk in that dogmatic way. Suppose you fail to do it! Say 'I shall do this if God wills.'" Girish understood: "That's right. When I have given all of my responsibilities to God and He has accepted them, I shall be able to do that work if He thinks that I should and that it is good for me." Henceforward, he began to shun the

4. The *Bhakti Sutras* of Narada.

idea of ego and such expressions as "I shall do," "I shall go," and so on.

Thus the days rolled on. The Master passed away. Girish faced grief and

8. Girish understood the hidden meaning of the power of attorney.

pain as he also lost his wife and son. But at every point his mind reminded him as before: "Sri Ramakrishna has allowed these things to happen because they are good for you. You gave your responsibility to him and he accepted it. He did not give you any written assurance regarding the path on which he would lead you. Now he is leading you along this path, considering it to be easy for you. You have no reason to refuse it nor any right to complain. Did you make an empty promise when you gave him the power of attorney and transferred your responsibility to him?" Thus as time passed, Girish began to understand more and more the hidden meaning of the power of attorney. Did he now comprehend its whole meaning? When asked about this, Girish replied: "There is still much to understand! Did I realize then that there was so much mystery in the power of attorney? Now I see that there is a limit to the time one must spend practising meditation, japa, and austerities, but the work of a person who has given the power of attorney is unending. Now he has to watch every step and with every breath determine whether he is depending on God and performing those actions by His power or by the power of his own rascal ego!"

Various thoughts arise in our minds in the context of the power of

9. Only avatars can accept the power of attorney.

attorney. We find in the religious history of the world that some great teachers like Jesus and Chaitanya sometimes gave assurances of this kind to a few people. Ordinary gurus do not have the ability to accept that responsibility, nor do they have the right to do so. Ordinary teachers or monks can at best instruct others by giving them a mantra or a specific spiritual practice, which can help them to make spiritual progress. Or by leading a pure life they can inspire others to become more pure. When a person who is entangled in worldly bondage and is completely helpless is instructed to do a certain thing, that person says in despair: "How can I do that? If you give me the power, I can try." It is beyond the capacity of an ordinary guru to help such a person. It is impossible for one person to say to another, "I am taking on responsibility for your bad karma, and I shall accept its consequences on your behalf." When spirituality declines in human hearts, God incarnates out of compassion, suffers on behalf of the people, and redeems them from the whirlpool of maya. Although He does that, He does not completely absolve humanity. He makes individuals put forth some self-effort so that they may learn. As the Master used to say: "By the grace of the avatars, a person finishes the sufferings of ten lives in one."

This is as true for an individual as it is for a nation. This truth has been

10. Examples.

expressed by various means. In the Gita Arjuna attained divine sight, which allowed him to see God's cosmic form. In the Puranas it is called the attainment of the grace of God. In the Vaishnava scriptures it is described as the redemption of Jagai and Madhai [two ruffians], or the repression of the wicked. And Christianity speaks of vicarious atonement: Jesus took on himself the punishment for others' sin. We could not have understood the validity of these examples if we had not seen them verified in Sri Ramakrishna's life.

One day when the Master was being treated [for throat cancer] at

| 11. The Master's vision regarding his acceptance of the power of attorney. | Shyampukur in Calcutta, he saw that his subtle body had left his gross body and was moving around. The Master said: "I saw some wounds on the back of its |

[his gross body's] throat. I wondered why this had happened. The Divine Mother then showed me: People commit all kinds of sins and then touch this body. And out of compassion for their misery, I take on the results of their evil deeds. That is why I have this (*pointing to his throat*). Otherwise, why should this body suffer from disease? It has never done anything wrong." We were dumbfounded. We wondered at the fact that one could make a person advance in spiritual life by accepting the results of that person's bad karma! Hearing the Master's words, some thought out of love for him: "Alas! Why have we touched the Master after committing all sorts of sinful acts such as lying, cheating, and so on? He is suffering so much from this cancer and undergoing this excruciating pain because of us! We will never again touch the Master's divine body."

In this connection we remember another incident in the Master's life.

| 12. The Master cured a man of leucoderma. | Once a man suffering from leucoderma came and plaintively implored the Master to pass his hand over his leucoderma and thus cure his disease. The Master |

said compassionately: "Well, I don't know anything; but because you ask me I will pass my hand over you. If the Divine Mother wills it, you will be cured." He then passed his hand over the man's skin. For the rest of that day the Master's hand hurt so terribly that he restlessly prayed to the Divine Mother, "I will never do such a thing again, Mother." Later the Master told us, "That man's disease was cured, but his suffering had passed over to it (*pointing to his own body*)." These events in the Master's life tell us that in this age, the Vedas, the Bible, the Koran, the Tantra, the Mantra, and other scriptures can be clearly understood if studied in the light of Sri Ramakrishna's life. The Master told us: "Look, the currency during the reign of a *Nawab* [a Muslim governor] cannot be the legal tender during the reign of a *Badsha* [a Muslim emperor]."

It seems as though it would be easy to give the power of attorney, as if

| 13. The difficulty in giving the power of attorney. | one were handing an object over to another. Human beings are slaves to their passions, so they seek opportunities to satisfy themselves even while prac- |

tising religion. Constantly they look for ways in which they may have both worldly pleasures and divine bliss. They consider sense enjoyments to be sweet, like nectar. If they even consider having to give them up, they see emptiness all around. They wonder how they can live without them. So they get excited when they hear that one can give the power of attorney in the spiritual world, and they think of this as a wonderful thing. They say: "Let us enjoy worldly pleasures to our heart's content by any means — such as stealing, cheating, or robbing — and let Chaitanya, Jesus, or Sri Ramakrishna look after our happiness in the hereafter. Someday we shall die." They do not understand that such a thought is nothing but the deception of a wicked mind. They do not realize that in this way they are continually deceiving themselves. They are just rushing headlong towards destruction, putting blinders over their eyes so that they will not have to see the terrible forms of their own wicked deeds. They cannot envision the day when someone will remove those blinders and force them to understand that they are in great danger. Ultimately they will realize that nobody accepts the power of attorney for hypocrites. Ah, human beings! How many ways you deceive yourselves and think that you have won! And hail Mahamaya, the great enchantress! What an illusion You have created in human minds! Indeed what Ramprasad says in his song to You is true:

> Bravo, O Mother Dakshina Kali!
> You have created delusion in the world.
> You put Your feet, the dice of delusion,
> on the body of Lord Shiva.
> You are such a juggler's daughter that You have kept
> Father Shiva in the guise of a madman.
> Endowed with the gunas, You have become Purusha and Prakriti.
> I wonder, those feet cannot be attained even by Shiva —
> O Ramprasad, how can you hope to attain them?
> Will you also be crazy?

Is the power of attorney so easily given? The condition of giving the power of attorney arises as a result of zeal and perseverance; only then does a person give it. At that time God accepts responsibility for him or her. Only after people have run around seeking happiness in this world, only to find that they have been clutching at shadows; only after they have practised meditation, japa, and austerities, only to realize deep within themselves that the Infinite God cannot be bought by means of those spiritual disciplines; only after they have resolved to make a path through a mountain by indomitable self-effort, only to feel utterly helpless — only then do they cry piteously: "Where are you, Lord? Please protect us." And only then does God accept their power of attorney.

14. A requisite condition for giving the power of attorney.

Otherwise I do not like to practise spiritual disciplines or pray to God; I love to follow my wanton impulses. And if anybody protests against this, I say: "What is wrong? I have given the power of attorney to God. He is making me act that way — what can I do? Why does He not change my mind?" This kind of attitude towards the power of attorney just deceives others as well as oneself. It leads a person to lose both here and hereafter.

15. Beware of the mind's deception.

This subject can be understood better if it is discussed from another standpoint: All right, we understand that you have given the power of attorney and have no need to practise spiritual disciplines or to pray to God. But if you truly give the power of attorney, the feeling of God's infinite compassion will constantly rise within the deepest recesses of your heart. You will feel as if you had been drowning in the ocean of worldliness, and that now God in His mercy has rescued you. When you experience that, just imagine how much your love and devotion for Him will flow. Your heart will be filled with love and gratitude; you will constantly think of Him and repeat His name. And you will not need anybody to remind you to do so. Even a vicious creature like a snake becomes a pet to the one who gives it shelter, and it will not bite anyone in that household. Is your heart worse than a snake that it still has not been filled with gratitude and love for Him who has accepted responsibility for you here and hereafter? Therefore, after giving the power of attorney, if you find that you do not like to call on God, you have not truly given the power of attorney and He has not taken responsibility for you either. Do not deceive yourself by saying, "I have given the power of attorney" and then imposing the sins of your wrong-doings on the sinless, immaculate God. Such a harmful attitude would be very detrimental to you. Please remember the Master's story of the brahmin who killed a cow.

16. Concluding discussion on the power of attorney.

With great effort and care, a brahmin created a beautiful garden. He planted various kinds of flowering plants and fruit trees, and his joy knew no bounds when he saw their luxuriant growth. One day, finding the gate open, a cow entered the garden and began to eat the plants. The brahmin was away on business. When he returned, he saw that the cow was eating his plants. In a rage he attacked the cow with a staff and hit her on a vital spot, killing her instantly. Now the brahmin became afraid: He had just killed a cow, which to a Hindu is the gravest of all sins. The brahmin had studied a little Vedanta, and he had learned that each of the human senses performs its respective functions by means of the power of a particular deity. For example, the eyes see with the power of the sun god, the ears hear with the power of the wind god, the hands work with the power of Indra [the king of gods], and so on. Remembering this, the brahmin thought: "Then I

17. The Master's story of a brahmin killing a cow.

am not the one who killed the cow. My hands move by the power of Indra, so it is Indra who has killed the cow." Thus firmly convinced, the brahmin was reassured.

Now the sin of cow-killing came to enter the brahmin's body, but his mind drove the sin away, saying: "Get away, you have no place here. Indra has killed the cow, so go to Him." The sin then went to seize Indra. Indra told the sin: "Please wait awhile. Let Me go and talk to the brahmin a little; then you can take Me." Indra then assumed a human form and entered the brahmin's garden. He saw the man nearby tending to his trees and plants. As Indra walked slowly towards the brahmin, He began to praise the beauty of the garden so that the brahmin could hear. Indra said: "Ah! What a beautiful garden! These trees are planted with great taste! Each one is in its proper place." As He thus talked about the garden, Indra reached the brahmin and asked: "Sir, do you know whose garden this is? Who has planted these trees so neatly and artistically?" Listening to this praise of his garden, the brahmin replied joyfully: "Sir, this is my garden. I have planted all these trees. Please come, let me show you around." He showed Indra his garden in detail and told Him many stories about the plants. Then inadvertently they came to the spot where the dead cow was. Startled, Indra exclaimed: "O God! Who has killed this cow?" So far the brahmin had said about his garden, "I have done this; I have done that." And now when he was asked who had killed the cow, he was terribly embarrassed and kept quiet. Then Indra reassumed His real form and said to the brahmin: "You hypocrite! You have done what is best in the garden, yet it is I who have killed the cow! Is that so? Now accept the sin of your cow-killing." With that Indra disappeared and the sin seized the brahmin's body.

We have said enough about the power of attorney. Let us now return to our

| 18. The inner meaning of the Master's words becomes apparent as an aspirant's mind develops. | previous topic. When asked, every one of the Master's devotees would openly acknowledge that they previously had understood the teachings of the Master in one way, and now with the passage of time they were |

finding deeper and deeper meaning in them by the Master's grace. Again, at one time we could not understand many words and actions of the Master; we only listened to him or watched his behaviour in bewilderment. Now we are amazed as we comprehend their wonderful inner meanings and the ideas they contain.

The Master used to say: "Look, my children! You will succeed in the course of

| 19. "Understanding comes at the right time." | time and understand at the proper time. Can you get a fruit as soon as you sow a seed? First the seed germinates into a sprout, then it becomes a sapling, then a big |

tree; afterwards it blooms and yields fruits. It is just like that. But one should persevere and never give up the struggle. Listen to this song." After speaking thus, the Master began to sing in his melodious voice:

Brother, joyfully cling to God;
Thus striving, someday you may attain Him.
Your misfortune will turn into fortune.
Poor devotees like Anka and Banka were saved,
And so also the butcher Sujan.
Teaching the parrot to repeat God's name,
A prostitute was saved; and so was the queen Mira Bai.
Despite having all the wealth and treasures of the world,
The trader still drives the bullock cart.
And when death strikes him
All his wealth is left behind.
Give up all hypocrisy and crookedness,
Have deep devotion in your heart.
The Lord Rama will be easily attained
Through service, worship, and humility.

After singing this song, the Master said: "Serve and worship God, surrender and be humble to Him. Only when you practise these disciplines with faith and perseverance will you succeed. You will definitely have His vision.

20. The necessity of perseverance in sadhana.

If you discontinue your sadhana, your progress will stop. A man used to work hard and save money little by little. Once he counted his money and found that he had one thousand rupees. Overwhelmed with joy, he thought: 'Why should I work anymore? I have one thousand rupees. That is enough.' So he gave up his job. This insignificant man had very little ambition. He became puffed up because of that small amount of money and cared for no one. But how long does it take to spend one thousand rupees? The entire amount was gone within a few days. Afflicted, he began to search desperately for another job, going from office to office. A person who behaves like this will never succeed in spiritual life. One must wait patiently at the door of God, then only will one see Him."

Again sometimes the Master would quote the second line of the song "Thus striving, someday you may attain Him." In other words, one can attain God by practising devotion. While singing that line he would suddenly

21. One must give up lukewarm devotion.

exclaim: "Fie on you, rascal! What is this 'someday you may attain Him?' One should not have that kind of lukewarm devotion. Have self-confidence and cultivate this attitude: 'I shall realize God *right now*; I shall see Him *at this moment*.' Can anyone attain God through lukewarm devotion?"

When we saw the Master we felt that he was truly the embodiment of living spirituality. When we looked at his form, it was as if we were seeing the accumulation of his spiritual ideas made concrete. We glibly discuss how changes in the mind can affect the body, but seldom do we actually experience this

22. The Master's body changed with the change of his moods.

phenomenon. We never imagined, even in a dream, that thoughts could have such an effect on a human body as we saw happen in the Master. When his I-consciousness had completely dissolved during nirvikalpa samadhi, his pulse and heartbeat would also disappear. Dr. Mahendralal Sarkar and other physicians examined the Master with their instruments but found no evidence that his heart was functioning.[5] Another doctor (Dr. Sarkar's friend) was not satisfied, so he touched the Master's eye with his finger and found that it did not react: It was like the eye of a dead person. When the Master was practising *sakhi bhava*, he was so absorbed in the thought of himself as a maidservant of Krishna that his body spontaneously manifested feminine behaviour and he performed all actions — sitting, standing, walking, talking, and so on — in the way a woman would. On many occasions during that time, Mathur and others who were his constant companions mistook him for a visiting woman. The Master has told us so much, and we ourselves have seen so many events of this kind, that we believe the mundane theories of modern psychology and physiology should be reconsidered. But would people believe those stories if we told them?

The most amazing thing we observed in the Master was his ability to

23. The Master's ability to perceive everyone's state of mind.

travel freely in the realm of ideas. He could understand all ideas, great or small. He knew what was in the mind of a child, a youth, or an elderly person. He could grasp the thoughts of the worldly and of the holy, of the followers of knowledge and of devotion, of men and of women. He could see how far they had advanced in spiritual life and what methods they had used to do so, as well as the kind of spiritual disciplines they needed at present to make further progress along the path they had adopted. He guided each person in a way that was appropriate for his or her condition. It seemed to us that the Master had experienced in his life the entire range of mental states of the past, present, and future; and he remembered precisely what had happened when each one of those states appeared and disappeared in his mind. So when a person described his or her own thoughts to the Master, he could understand them by comparing them with his own experiences; and he would then instruct that person accordingly. This happened in every case. When people would humbly approach the Master, having been unable to find their way out from the meshes of maya and from worldly sufferings, or desiring to learn how to practise the path of renunciation, and so on, he would invariably give them proper direction, and most of the time he would also share with them his own experiences under similar circumstances. The Master would say, "Look, at that time this happened to me and I adopted such a measure," and so on. This would stir hope in the inquirer's mind, and

5. The examination took place in our presence when the Master was staying at Shyampukur House in Calcutta for cancer treatment.

that person would move forward with great faith and zeal along the path directed by the Master. Not only that, but when the Master would tell the story of his own life, the aspirant would feel the Master's great love. Such an aspirant would even wonder if the Master was confiding his heart's secret! A few examples will make this clear.

A worthy son of Manimohan Mallick of Sinduriapati, Calcutta, passed away. Immediately after cremating his son, Mani-mohan came to the Master. After saluting the Master he sat mournfully in a corner of the room. He saw that many men and women devotees were seated in the room, and the Master was talking to them about spiritual life. Soon the Master's eyes fell on him, and with a nod of his head, he asked, "Hello, why do you look so pale today?"

> 24. First example: the story of Manimohan's grief for his dead son.

Manimohan answered, choking back tears, "My son died today."

Everyone in the room was stunned and speechless as they saw old Mani-mohan in disheveled clothing and heard his grief-stricken voice. They all realized that no words of consolation could heal that old man's deep mental affliction and overwhelming grief. Nevertheless, touched by his sorrow, they began to console him with soothing words such as these: "Such is the way of the world; everyone will die someday. Whatever has happened cannot be changed by shedding a thousand tears. Therefore, renounce grief and forbear." From the beginning of creation, people have consoled their grief-stricken friends with similar words. But alas! How many people are pacified by such consolation? Is it so easy to calm bereaved hearts? Only when the focus of the mind, speech, and action is in unison can our words touch others' hearts and raise similar waves of feeling in them. We are almost completely bereft of this harmony. We may say the world is impermanent, but our thoughts and deeds reveal that we believe differently. We advise others to consider the world to be as unreal as a dream, but we ourselves are deeply convinced that it is real, and we make arrangements to remain here permanently. So how can our words generate the power to convince others?

Although everyone said consoling words to Manimohan, the Master kept quiet for a while and listened to his outburst of grief. Observing the Master's indifference, some wondered how he could be so hard-hearted and devoid of compassion.

While listening to the laments of the old man, the Master entered into a semiecstatic state. Suddenly he stood up and energetically slapped the upper part of his left arm like a wrestler, then began to vigorously sing the following song, pointing to Manimohan.

> To arms! To arms, O Man!
> Look, death storms your house in battle array!
> Mount the chariot of virtue,
> Yoke to it the two horses of devotion and meditation,

> Pull the bow of your knowledge,
> And set the arrow of divine love.
> Listen, here is a ruse for the fray:
> You need no chariot or charioteer to kill all your foes
> If Dasharathi[6] fights from the bank of the Ganges.

The song's heroic theme and the appropriate gesture united with the Master's spirit of renunciation and strength to create a wonderful current of hope and enthusiasm in the hearts of all. The onlookers' minds then transcended the realm of grief and delusion and were filled with pure divine bliss, beyond the senses and the world. Manimohan also felt this deeply in his heart; forgetting his grief, he became still, calm, and reflective.

The song ended. But the spiritual current generated by the Master with the help of the song's few phrases pulsated throughout the room for a long time. Awestruck, all remained motionless and reflected: "God is our very own. We offer ourselves to Him. May He bestow grace on us. May He reveal Himself to us." After a while the Master came down from samadhi. Sitting near Manimohan, he said: "Ah! Is there any pain in this world worse than the grief caused by the death of a son? The son is born from the seed of the father's body. This relation is physical, so it lasts as long as the body lasts."

The Master then began to describe his nephew Akshay's death, as an example. He spoke in such a serious and solemn way that it seemed as if he were experiencing his relative's death again. He said: "Akshay died before my very eyes, and I felt nothing at the time. I stood there and watched how a man dies. It was as if there were a sword in a sheath, and the sword was suddenly drawn out of the sheath. The sword remained the same as before. Nothing had happened to it. And the sheath lay there, empty. When I saw that, I felt great joy. I laughed and sang and danced. They took Akshay's body away and burned it and came back. But the next day as I stood there (*pointing to the southeastern veranda of his room*), I felt as though a wet towel were being wrung inside my heart. That was how I suffered for Akshay. 'O Mother,' I thought, 'this body of mine has no relation even to the cloth that enfolds it; how can it feel so much for a nephew? And if I feel so much pain, what agony must householders suffer! Is that what You are teaching me, Mother?'"

After a while the Master continued: "But, you know, those who hold on to the Lord do not lose themselves in grief. After experiencing a few blows, they soon regain control over themselves. But people of poor calibre become very restless and are completely lost. Have you not seen the plight of small fishing boats when steamers pass through the Ganges? It seems as if they are about to sink and cannot survive. A boat may even turn upside down. But

---

6. The composer. Customarily, some mystics address themselves when composing their spiritual songs. — *Translator*

the large thousand-ton barges soon regain their balance after having a few jolts. Similarly, everyone will have to encounter a few jolts in this life."

Again the Master solemnly paused for a while and then said: "The relationship with children lasts for only a few days in this world! Expecting happiness, people get involved in the world: They get married; then children are born; they grow up; and the parents marry them off. Thus, days go by smoothly. But the parents are perturbed with worries and anxieties when they see one child is sick, another dies, and still another goes astray. The more the parents become frustrated, the louder they lament. Have you not seen how raw *sundri* wood burns in the big wooden stove of a confectioner? It burns well at first; but as it continues to burn, all of its sap begins to ooze out through its rear part. The froth rises in bubbles and makes various noises, such as *chu-cha, phus-phas*. Likewise, when people burn with misery, they cry." Thus the Master consoled Manimohan and reminded him of the transitoriness and worthlessness of this world, and that real happiness lies in taking refuge in God. When he had collected himself, Manimohan said: "That is why I rushed to you [from the cremation ground]. I knew that no one except you could quench the burning fire of my grief."

We were amazed as we observed these wonderful actions of the Master and reflected that a little while earlier we had considered him to be hardhearted and indifferent. A person who is truly great does not perform even small actions like ordinary people. Such a person's greatness manifests in every action, be it important or trivial. Is he the same Master whose heartbeat stopped a little while earlier when he was in samadhi, united with God? Is he the same person who has truly become like an ordinary human being out of sympathy for Manimohan's condition? He could have easily discarded the old man's lamentation with a short statement, "It is maya!" Not that he did not have the ability to do that — but if he had shown his greatness in that manner, we would have thought that although he might be a great teacher, or something else, he could not be a teacher of humankind — not a world teacher. We would have believed that he was not able to understand the feelings of ordinary people. And we would have asked ourselves: "If he once fell into the helpless condition we are in, weak with our attachment to wife and children, would he still remain indifferent to the play of maya?"

The next moment a young man might come and sadly ask the Master:

25. Second example: the Master's advice on how to overcome lust.

"Sir, how can I get rid of lust? I strive so hard, still I suffer from restlessness due to passion and bad thoughts."

The Master: "Look, lust doesn't completely go away even when one realizes God. As long as the body lasts, a little lust remains even after God-vision — but it can't raise its head. Do you think I am free from it? At one time I believed that I had conquered lust. Then one day when I was seated in the Panchavati, I suddenly had such an onrush of lust that it was hard for me to maintain control! Immediately I began crying, rubbing my face in the dust, and saying to the Divine Mother: 'I have made a big mistake, Mother. I shall never again think that I have conquered lust.' Only then did it subside. Do you know, you boys are now passing through a flood tide of adolescence? You can't stop it. Can an embankment or a breakwater stop a tidal wave? The overflowing water breaks through and rushes forward, and then the water stands as high as a bamboo over the paddy fields. There is a saying, 'Mental sin is not considered to be a sin in this Kaliyuga.' If a bad thought happens to arise once or twice in the mind, why should you go on brooding about it? Sometimes those feelings come and go. They are natural to the body; consider them to be physical functions like the call of nature. Do people worry when they have an urge for the call of nature? Similarly, consider those feelings to be insignificant, trifling, and worthless, and don't think of them anymore. Pray to God intensely, chant His name, and meditate on Him. Don't pay any heed to whether those feelings come or go. Gradually, they will come under control." It was as if the Master had become a youth while talking to that young man.

In this connection we mention a story concerning Swami Yogananda. He was one of those rare persons who had complete self-control. One day at Dakshineswar he asked the Master the same question, how to conquer lust. He was then young, about fourteen or fifteen years old, and had been visiting the Master for a short while. At that time, Narayana, a hatha yogi, lived in the hut of the Panchavati at Dakshineswar and was attracting some people by performing *neti-dhauti*.[7] Swami Yogananda said that he had been among those visitors. As he observed those performances, he thought that perhaps unless one practised these disciplines one could not overcome lust and see God. So after asking that question, he expected the Master to prescribe for him a particular yogic posture, or advise him to eat a *myrobalan* or some other thing, or to teach him a pranayama technique.

26. Third example: advice to Yogananda in this respect.

Yogananda later said: "In answer to my question the Master said, 'Go on repeating the name of Hari, then lust will go away.' This answer was not at all to my liking. I thought: 'He does not know any technique so he just said something to pacify me. Does lust go away by chanting the name of Hari? So many people do that. Are they free from lust?' Then one day I came to the temple garden and instead of going to the Master I went to the Panchavati and eagerly began to listen to the hatha yogi talk. In the meantime,

---

7. *Neti* is to gradually swallow a piece of wet cloth ten or fifteen cubits long and an inch wide and then to pull it out from the stomach. *Dhauti* is to drink two or three seers [one seer equals about two cups] of water and then expel it. Sucking water through the anus and forcing it back out is called *dhauti*. Hatha yogis thus clean out all mucus, phlegmatic humours, and other such substances from the body. They say these techniques prevent disease and make the body strong.

the Master arrived there. As soon as he saw me, he called me over and took my hand. While we were walking towards his room, he said: 'Why did you go there? Don't go there anymore. If you learn and practise those techniques of hatha yoga, your mind will dwell on the body and will never turn towards God.' At this, I thought: 'He is telling me this lest I stop visiting him.' I always considered myself to be highly intelligent, so my inflated intellect made me think that. It did not occur to me even once that it mattered very little to the Master whether I visited him or not. What a mean and doubtful mind I had! There was no limit to the Master's grace. In spite of my harbouring such erroneous notions in my mind, he gave me shelter. Then I thought: 'Why don't I do what he told me and see what happens?' So resolved, I took the name of Hari with a concentrated mind. And as a matter of fact, within a few days I began to experience the tangible result that the Master had referred to."

Many such examples can be cited about the Master's ability to grasp the

27. Fourth example: the story of Manimohan's relative.

thoughts and conditions of all people. We have already mentioned Manimohan of Sinduriapati. A woman devotee from his family used to visit the Master. One day she informed the Master plaintively that when she sat for meditation her mind was very much disturbed with worldly thoughts, including the thought of someone, or another's face, and so on. Immediately the Master understood what was in her mind. He knew that when she had thoughts about someone she loved, that person's face would appear in her mind. He asked affectionately: "Well, whose face comes to your mind? Whom do you love in this world?" She replied that she loved one of her young nephews, whom she was raising. The Master said: "All right. Whenever you do anything for him, such as feeding, dressing, and so on, think that you are serving Gopala. Develop the attitude that God in the form of Gopala dwells in your nephew and that you are feeding, dressing, and serving Him. Why should you think that you are doing this for a human being? As you think, so you receive." We heard that when the woman followed the Master's instruction she made significant spiritual progress and even attained bhava samadhi.

It is quite understandable that the Master could comprehend men's

28. The Master's ability to understand women's mental states.

mental states because he had a male body. But it was amazing how he correctly grasped all the moods of women, upon whom God has bestowed the extra faculty of tenderness and affection towards children. The Master's female devotees later said: "Many times we did not feel that the Master was a man; we considered him to be one of us. For that reason, we did not feel the slightest shyness or hesitation in his presence, as we normally do in the presence of men. Even if such a feeling came on rare occasions, we forgot it immediately and expressed our thoughts to him without any reservation."

The Master had been absorbed for a long time in the thought that he was a
female confidante or a maidservant of Krishna, and so
he had completely forgotten that he was a man. In the
Yoga Aphorisms (2:35) Patanjali says: "If the idea of injuring others is completely
erased from your mind, no being in the world, not even tigers and snakes, will
injure you. When they see you, the very tendency to violence will not rise in
their minds at all." This must be understood to be equally true of all other feelings, such as lust and anger, as well as violence.

29. The reason for this.

Many examples of this can be found in the Puranas, but it will be enough
if we mention one. The ever-pure young Shuka, who was constantly immersed
in God-consciousness, left home. As he was walking away, his elderly father
Vyasa, blinded by affection, ran after him, crying: "Where are you going, my
son? Where are you going?" They passed a lake where celestial maidens
were bathing, having left their clothes on the shore. When they saw Shuka
walking by, they felt no shyness or hesitation and continued bathing as
usual. But as soon as elderly Vyasa arrived, they hurriedly covered their
bodies. Vyasa thought: "This is strange. My young son passed by and they
did not move but when they see me, an old man, they are so bashful!" When
they were asked the reason, the girls replied: "Shuka is so pure that he
constantly thinks one thought only, 'I am the Atman.' He is not at all aware
whether he is a man or a woman. So when we saw him we did not feel
bashful in the least. But you are an old man who is familiar with the gestures,
deportment, and gazes of women, and you have described extensively their
physical beauty and charms. Unlike Shuka, you do not look upon men and
women as the Atman, nor will you ever achieve that state. So when we saw
you the thought of men arose in our minds and then simultaneously came
the feeling of shyness."

We think of the Master in the same way. He had vivid, direct knowledge
of the Atman, and he would see It in men, women,
and all other beings. As long as we lived with him,
our minds soared so high that most of the time we
did not have such thoughts as "I am a man," and "She is a woman." So
women, like men, also felt free with him. Moreover, when they were in the
Master's company at that time their spiritual knowledge was so deeply
rooted that at his request they could perform actions that they considered to
be very daring and would not have done if anyone else had asked them. At
the Master's command some aristocratic women, who did not travel
anywhere without a carriage or a palanquin, walked through the main street
to the bank of the Ganges in the daytime and went with him to the Dakshineswar Kali temple by boat. Moreover, after they arrived, at the Master's
request they went to the market nearby and bought groceries, then returned
to their Calcutta residence on foot in the evening. This subject will be clearer
if we cite two examples.

30. Why women felt
free with the Master.

It was sometime in August or September of 1884. The Holy Mother was

31. First example. | then at her father's house in Jayrambati. Balaram had gone with his father to Vrindaban along with Rakhal (Swami Brahmananda), Gopal (Swami Advaitananda), and some men and women devotees. A woman from a respectable family of Baghbazar, who had heard about the Master but had never met him, had a keen desire to see him. She told this to a woman friend who had been visiting the Master for two years. Accordingly they planned to visit him. The next day they took a boat to Dakshineswar, arriving in the afternoon. The Master's door was closed. There were two holes in the northern wall, so they peeped through them and saw the Master resting. They then went to the nahabat where the Holy Mother lived and waited for him. Soon the Master got up and opened the north door. When he saw them sitting on the upper veranda of the nahabat he called to them, "Hello, please come here." When the women had come and sat on the carpet, the Master got down from his wooden cot and sat near the woman devotee whom he knew. When the bashful woman tried to move away a little, the Master said: "Why are you so shy? One will not succeed as long as one has these three: shame, hatred, and fear. Basically you and I are the same *(indicating her and himself)*, but you feel shy because of this *(pointing to his beard)*. Is that not so?"

He then talked about God and gave them some spiritual instruction. Forgetting the distinction between men and women, they freely asked questions of the Master and listened to his answers. When after a long conversation they took their leave, the Master said: "Come here once a week. In the beginning one should visit frequently." Knowing that they belonged to respectable families but were not wealthy, the Master again said: "Form a group of three or four and then come to Dakshineswar by boat; and while returning home, walk up to Baranagore and then share a carriage." From then on the women devotees acted accordingly.

Once another woman devotee [Golap-ma] told us: "As we knew that the

32. Second example. | Master liked *sar* [a sweet made from thick boiled milk], one day we bought a large piece for him from the shop of Bhola, a famous confectioner in Calcutta. Five of us together then hired a boat and went to Dakshineswar. Ah, when we heard that the Master had gone to Calcutta, we were brokenhearted. Now what should we do? Ramlal was there. When he was asked where in Calcutta the Master had gone, he said, 'To M.'s[8] house in Kambuliatola.' To this, A's mother said: 'I know that house. It is near my father's. Will you go? Come, let us go.' All agreed. We handed the sweet to Ramlal and left, saying, 'Please give it to the Master when he returns.'

---

8. M. was the pen name of Mahendra Nath Gupta, a great devotee of the Master. He recorded and published *Sri Sri Ramakrishna Kathamrita* [*The Gospel of Sri Ramakrishna*].

"We had already sent the boat away, so we started out on foot. But such was the Master's grace that we had hardly covered the short distance to Alambazar when an empty carriage returning to Calcutta became available. We hired the carriage and soon reached Shyampukur. Again we faced trouble: A.'s mother could not find the house. After searching for some time, she finally stopped the carriage in front of her father's place and called for a servant. He came with us and pointed out the house. And how could we blame A.'s mother? She was three or four years younger than we were, about twenty-six or twenty-seven. A mere daughter-in-law, she had never come out on a road by herself. Moreover, the house was located in a narrow lane. How could she recognize it?

"Finally, with great difficulty, we reached the house. We were not then acquainted with M.'s family. When we entered, we saw the Master sitting on a wooden cot in a small room; no one was near him. As soon as he saw us he smiled and said affectionately, 'Ah, how could you come here?' We bowed down to him and told him the whole story. He was very happy. Then he asked us to sit and began to talk on various subjects. Nowadays, many people say he did not allow women to touch him or even to go near him. At this we laugh and think, 'We are not dead yet!' Who can comprehend how compassionate he was! He had the same feeling towards men and women. It is true that if women stayed near him long he would say, 'Please go now and pay reverence to the deities in the temples.' But we have also heard him ask men to do the same.

"Anyway, we were sitting on the floor and talking to him. The two of us who were most senior sat very near the door, and the other three sat in a corner of the room. In the meantime, Prankrishna Mukhopadhyay, whom the Master called 'the fat brahmin,' arrived. There was no way to get out of that small room.[9] Moreover, where could we go? There was a window near the door where the two oldest ones hid; the remaining three of us crawled under the cot on which the Master was seated and lay down there. Our bodies swelled from mosquito bites. But what could we do? We lay there without moving. The fat brahmin talked to the Master for about an hour and then left. At last we came out and we all laughed.

"The Master was then taken to the inner apartment for refreshment and we accompanied him. After some time the Master got into a carriage to return to Dakshineswar, and we walked back home. It was about 9:00 p.m.

"The next day we went to Dakshineswar again. As soon as we arrived,

33. The Master bestows grace equally on men and women devotees.

the Master came to us and said: 'Ah, I ate almost all of the sweet you gave me; only a little was left over. It did not make me sick. My stomach was just a little

9. At that time young Indian women were shy. They wore veils over their faces or hid themselves from men they did not know. — *Translator*

heavy.' I was surprised to hear that he had eaten a whole piece of sar, because his delicate stomach could not handle such rich food. Then I heard that he had eaten it while in an ecstatic mood. He had taken his food at M.'s house and returned to Dakshineswar at 10:30 p.m. Shortly after his arrival he went into ecstasy and told Ramlal: 'I am very hungry. Give me whatever there is in the room.' Immediately, Ramlal served that sar to the Master, and he had eaten almost the whole piece. Then I remembered what I had heard from the Holy Mother and Lakshmi about how sometimes when he was in ecstasy he would eat an abnormal quantity of food and digest it. Ah, he bestowed so much grace on us! We cannot express in words what that compassion was like. And how attracted we were to him! Even we ourselves do not understand how we used to go to him and do all those things. Alas! We can no longer go on foot to strangers' homes without telling anyone in order to see a holy man or listen to spiritual talks. The power we had to do all those things vanished with the one who was its source. We do not know why we have lived so long after losing the Master!"

We can cite many such examples. Women who never went out of the house alone were made by the Master to buy groceries from the market and beg from door to door like ordinary beggars in order to remove their ego and pride of lineage. He even took them to attend the public religious festival of Panihati, and without any hesitation they joyfully did what the Master asked them to do. In fact, when we think deeply on this we see it is no small matter. The indecisiveness that originates from the perception of duality was temporarily removed by the current of the Master's spiritual wisdom. They felt blessed as they saw their own spiritual ideals made perfect in the Master, who was the living embodiment of spirituality. Men bowed down their heads seeing the full manifestation of manliness in him; and women, finding all their feminine traits in him, unhesitatingly considered him to be their very own.

The Master would sometimes imitate women's gestures and manners in

34. The Master mimicked feminine gestures and manners.

front of us. As we watched we were amazed by the exactitude of his mimicry. Regarding this, once a woman devotee told us: "One day in our presence the Master began to demonstrate the gestures women make when they see men — that pulling of the veil, removing of the tresses near the ear, pulling of the cloth over the breast, and babbling of various things. His imitation was perfect. We all laughed, but we were embarrassed and hurt, thinking that the Master was looking down upon women. We thought, 'Are all women like that?' We were women after all; we were naturally hurt to see women caricatured like that. Ah, the Master immediately understood our thoughts and said affectionately: 'Well, I don't mean *you*. You are not of a worldly nature. Only women of that nature behave that way.'"

Every one of the Master's devotees has seen to greater or lesser degrees

35. Male and female moods coexisted in the Master.

the coexistence of masculine and feminine moods in him. Once Girish experienced this and boldly asked, "Sir, are you a man or a woman?" The Master replied with a smile, "I don't know." Who will now decide what the Master meant when he made that remark? Was he saying this from the point of view of one who has realized the sexless Atman, who experiences "I am neither a man nor a woman," or was he acknowledging the coexistence of both male and female characteristics within himself?

Dwelling in the state of bhavamukha, the Master, who was the embodi-

36. Dwelling in the state of bhavamukha, the Master was able to understand the thoughts of others.

ment of all moods, would act as a woman with women and a man with men and could correctly grasp each one of their thoughts. He himself expressed this to some of us. A woman devotee[10] told us that the Master once said to her: "I can determine the nature of a person with just a look. I know who is good and who is bad, who is of noble descent and who is not, who is a man of knowledge and who is one of devotion, who will realize God and who will not. All these things I know, but I do not express them lest people should feel pained." Because he dwelt in bhavamukha, the whole world always appeared to him to be made of ideas. He felt as though every animate and inanimate object — men and women, cows and horses, wood and earth — was rising and floating in the Cosmic Mind as different aggregates of ideas. The infinite, indivisible Brahman was manifest within those ideas in varying degrees — in some places more, some less, and in other places It did not appear to be present because It was hidden behind thick veils. Sri Ramakrishna, the pure and spiritual son of the blissful Divine Mother, voluntarily offered everything to Her, his body, mind, and heart's desires. He then attained the incorporeal, blissful Brahman through samadhi and was about to merge with It forever, but when he reached that point he became aware that the Divine Mother had a different plan for him. At Her command he humbly forced his mind, which was absorbed in the indescribable state beyond duality and nonduality, to be covered with a veil of *vidya-maya*.[11] He then carried out Her behest unceasingly. The omniscient Divine Mother was pleased with the Master, so She kept him as an embodied being and at the same time kept his mind constantly attuned to the highest realm of Oneness. As a result, he would experience any thoughts that arose in the vast Cosmic Mind as his own. And he was so identified with them that one felt the Mother was the Son and the Son was

---

10. Matangini Ghosh, the mother of Swami Premananda.
11. Maya has two aspects: *avidya-maya*, or the maya of ignorance and *vidya-maya*, or the maya of knowledge. Vidya-maya, consisting of kindness, purity, renunciation, unselfishness, and so on, leads one to liberation. Both belong to the relative world. — *Translator*

the Mother: "The abode is Consciousness, the name is Consciousness, and God is Consciousness."

We have said as much as we can. O reader, now you decide who this omniscient Ramakrishna is.

Chapter 2

A *D*iscourse on Bhava, Samadhi, and Darshana

(Divine Ecstasy, Samadhi, and Visions)

Again listen to My supreme word, the profoundest of all. You are well beloved of Me; therefore I will tell you what is for your good. — GITA 18:64

IT WOULD NOT BE AN EXAGGERATION TO SAY that before the Master became well known, the people of Calcutta, both educated and uneducated, were completely ignorant about bhava samadhi or the extraordinary visions of the spiritual realm. Uneducated people had strange ideas originating from fear and awe about these subjects. And at that time the modern, educated community was completely carried away by the current of foreign education, which was not based on religion, and considered visions, ecstasy, and so on, as either impossibilities or signs of mental illness. Physical changes caused by spiritual ecstasy were considered by them to be epilepsy or some sort of physical disease. Nowadays that situation has changed considerably, but still very few people are capable of properly understanding divine ecstasy and the mystery of samadhi. One should have a fair knowledge of samadhi if one wants to have even a little understanding of Sri Ramakrishna's state of bhavamukha. Therefore, we shall now try to explain this subject to the reader, as far as possible.

Whatever most people do not experience is usually considered abnormal.

1. Samadhi is not mental illness.

The subtle experiences of the spiritual world can never be understood by the ordinary human mind. One needs instruction, training, and constant practice to achieve those experiences. Those spiritual visions and experiences make an aspirant more pure day by day and fill his or her heart with new strength and insight, and gradually that aspirant attains eternal peace. Therefore, is it reasonable to say that those visions and experiences are abnormal? Everyone must admit that disorders make one's body and mind weak. Because spiritual visions and experiences have a completely opposite effect, one must admit that their causes must also be opposite. Therefore, it cannot be said that those visions and experiences are caused by mental illness or disease.

All through the ages divine visions and experiences have led to spiritual realization. But one cannot attain eternal peace until one reaches the nirvikalpa state by controlling all thought waves and becoming established in nonduality. As Sri Ramakrishna used to say, "If a thorn is stuck in your foot, get another thorn and take out the first with its help; then throw away the second thorn also." Because we have forgotten God, this world appears to us in a perverse form. Visions and experiences of the spiritual world counteract these corrupted experiences of sight, taste, and so on, ultimately leading a person to attain nondual knowledge. Then that aspirant becomes blessed, realizing the dictum of the sage, "Brahman is truly the source of bliss" (Taittiriya Upanishad 2:7). This is the process; all doctrines, visions, and experiences of the spiritual world lead human beings to that goal [Brahman]. Swami Vivekananda said that those visions and experiences are an aspirant's "milestones on the way to progress" towards the goal. So the reader should not think that a person has reached the culmination of realization when he or she has had a couple of visions of a divine form during meditation, or when a particular spiritual mood has become intense. That person would be terribly mistaken. Some spiritual aspirants fall into this kind of error and miss the goal, becoming narrow-minded and harbouring hatred and animosity towards one another. When a person is trapped in that error while practising devotion to God, he or she becomes bigoted and monotonous. This defect is a stumbling block on the path of devotion, and it originates from narrow-mindedness.

2. True spirituality and eternal peace can be attained only through samadhi.

Some people attribute too much importance to this kind of momentary vision or experience and conclude that those who do not have such experiences are not spiritual. Spirituality and aimless miracle-mongering appear to such people to be the same thing. Hankering after miracles cannot make people spiritual; rather it makes them weaker day by day in every respect. That which does not promote a steadfast intellect and strong character, teach people to establish themselves on the firm ground of purity and shun the whole world to seek Truth, and make people free instead of entangling them with worldly desires — that is not in the realm of

3. Having visions of divine forms is not the only criterion for spiritual progress.

spirituality. If the visions and experiences you are encountering do not produce those results, know for certain that you are not yet within the realm of spirituality: Your visions and experiences are due to mental illness and therefore have no value. And if you have not had any visions, but feel inner spiritual strength, know for certain that you are on the right track and will eventually have authentic visions.

One of our friends[1] was very upset when he heard that many of the Master's devotees were experiencing ecstasy, whereas he had been visiting the Master for a long time and had had no such experience. He went to Sri Ramakrishna and tearfully expressed the anguish of his heart. The Master consoled him, saying: "Don't be silly, my boy. Do you think that everything has been achieved when one has had a little ecstasy? Is ecstasy the highest experience? Know for certain that true renunciation and faith are far more important than that. Narendra (Swami Vivekananda) does not generally experience ecstasy, but see how great are his renunciation, faith, mental strength, and steadfastness!"

| 4. Signs of true spirituality are renunciation, faith, and strength of character. |

When an aspirant's desires come to an end with the help of a one-pointed intellect, firm faith, and single-minded devotion, that aspirant is about to be united with God. But at that time, due to innate instincts, pure desires arise in the minds of some aspirants, such as: "I will do good to humanity. I will work for the happiness of many." Under the influence of such desires they cannot remain completely in the nondual state. They descend a little from that high spiritual plane and again enter the domain of "I and mine." But that "I" is now constantly connected with God, as in "I am a servant of God. I am a child of God. I am a part of God." One cannot enjoy lust and gold day and night with that "I." That "I" knows that God is one's all in all and never covets the sense enjoyments of the world. Whatever sense objects are necessary and helpful for reaching the goal, such aspirants accept as much as they wish of them and no more.

| 5. "Ripe ego" and pure desire: jivanmukta, adhikarika purusha, ishwarakoti, and jivakoti. |

Those who were previously bound, who later attain illumination by practising spiritual disciplines and pass the rest of their lives in a divine mood — they are called *jivanmukta*, or the liberated-in-life. Those who are born endowed with a special relationship with God and never become entangled with maya as ordinary human beings do are called by the scriptures *adhikarika purushas* [persons commissioned by God], *ishwarakotis* [godlike souls], or *nityamukta* [ever-free souls]. There is yet another group of aspirants who, after achieving the nondual experience, do not return to do good to humanity either in this life or the next — they are *jivakotis* [ordinary liberated

1. Gopal Chandra Ghosh.

souls]. We have heard from the Master that most liberated beings belong to this last group.

Even among those who, after attaining nondual realization, have returned

6. Differences in nondual experience.

from samadhi in order to do good to humanity, there is a difference in degree of the unity they have experienced with the indivisible Brahman. Some have only seen the Ocean of Consciousness from a distance; some have gone near and touched It; and some have drunk a little of Its water. As Sri Ramakrishna used to say: "The sage Narada returned after seeing that Ocean of Consciousness from a distance; Shukadeva touched It three times; and Lord Shiva drank three handfuls of Its water and then collapsed, completely devoid of external consciousness." Becoming absorbed in nondual consciousness, for even a short time, is called *nirvikalpa samadhi*.

As there are degrees of nondual experience, so there are differences in the

7. The deepening of devotional moods leads to savikalpa samadhi.

experience of dualistic moods such as shanta, dasya, sakhya, vatsalya, and madhura, which lead an aspirant to the nondualistic plane. Some aspirants are blessed with the full realization of one of these states, and some get only a glimpse. The complete realization of any one of these dualistic moods is called *savikalpa samadhi* in the yoga scriptures.

Unusual physical changes and wonderful visions occur in aspirants in

8. Mental and spiritual states inevitably affect the body.

each spiritual state, whether it is the higher nondualistic state or a lower dualistic state. Those physical changes and visions manifest in different ways among aspirants: These signs may be seen clearly in some who have little experience; and again they may be only slightly visible in others who have had profound experiences. As Sri Ramakrishna used to say: "If a couple of elephants enter a small pool with shallow water, there is tremendous agitation and splashing of water on all sides. But even if scores of elephants plunge into a big lake, the water remains calm." Therefore, it cannot be said that physical changes and visions are accurate signs of spiritual depth.

If spiritual depth needs to be measured, then as said before, it is to be done

9. How to determine higher or lower samadhi.

by observing the aspirant's degree of steadfastness, renunciation, strength of character, and lessening of worldly desires. The genuineness of samadhi can be tested by these touchstones only and nothing else. So it is clear that only in aspirants who have become pure, awakened, and free by shunning desires for sense objects can one see a complete picture of any of the spiritual moods — shanta, dasya, sakhya, vatsalya, and madhura — and not in people who are entangled in lust and gold. A lustful person understands the attraction for objects of desire. How can such a person comprehend the spiritual longing of a person who is completely free of lust?

We attempt here to briefly describe the philosophical aspect of samadhi that the Master explained to us. But first we must say a few things more to give the reader a clear understanding. As we mentioned earlier, different degrees are visible in the experience of nondualistic as well as shanta, dasya and other dualistic moods. However

> 10. Only avatars are able to experience all spiritual moods fully: an example is the Master's samadhi.

one should not think that avatars are confined to any one of those spiritual moods. They can fully demonstrate at will shanta, dasya, or any other mood at any time in their lives. Again, they can assume a nondualistic attitude to proceed in the experience of oneness with God to an extent that is beyond the capacity of any other individual, such as a jivanmukta, nityamukta, or ishwarakoti. It is not possible for an individual being to be united with the blissful Brahman to such a great extent and then to separate from It and return to the realm of "I and mine." This is possible only for the avatars. The records of their extraordinary experiences in the spiritual realm evolved into the Vedas and other scriptures. It is therefore not surprising that the avatars' spiritual experiences will in many instances surpass the records of the Vedas and other scriptures. As Sri Ramakrishna used to say, "The condition of this place (*my experience*) has gone far beyond what is recorded in the Vedas and Vedanta." Sri Ramakrishna was the foremost amongst that group of avatars because he was able to return to the realm of "I and mine" for the good of many and for teaching others, even after being completely absorbed in the nondualistic state for six months continuously. This is a wonderful story. It will not be out of place here to say a few things about it to the reader.

On the third day after Tota Puri had given him initiation into sannyasa, the Master experienced complete oneness with God, or nirvikalpa samadhi as described in Vedanta. At that time the Master had completed his Tantra sadhana,

> 11. The Brahmani forbade the Master to practise Vedanta.

and the learned Bhairavi (whom the Master called "Bamni"), who had provided all the articles necessary for that sadhana and had taught him their use, was then living in Dakshineswar. We heard from the Master that the Bhairavi now forbade him to associate with Tota Puri, saying: "My son, don't mix with him too much. Such people have a very dry attitude. If you associate with him closely, your love and devotion will disappear." But the Master paid no heed to her warning and remained absorbed day and night in discussions of Vedanta and the experiences connected with it.

Tota Puri left Dakshineswar after he had spent eleven months there. The Master then decided that he would remain united with God, dwelling in the nondual state rather than living in the realm of "I and mine." He began to act accordingly. This is an amazing story. At that time he was not

> 12. The Master's resolve to remain in nirvikalpa samadhi: the nature of this state.

at all aware that he had a body. Even thoughts of maintaining the body by eating, sleeping, bathing and so forth did not arise in his mind — not to speak of any wish to talk with others! In that state there is no idea of "I and mine" and "you and yours." Nor is there any idea of "two" or "one" since the idea of "one" arises when there is the memory of "two." In that state all of the mind's thoughts become still and calm. There "the illumined person realizes within himself, through samadhi, the infinite and indescribable Brahman, which is the nature of eternal knowledge and absolute bliss, without equal in the world of relative experience. It transcends all limitations and is ever free and actionless, like the boundless sky, indivisible and absolute. It is completely free from the concept of cause and effect. It is Reality, beyond imagination."[2]

In nirvikalpa samadhi there is only bliss and more bliss! There is no direction, no extension, no object, no form, and no name. In that state the disembodied Atman is absorbed within Its own inexplicable bliss and abides in an incomprehensible state that is beyond all ideas of the mind and of the intellect. About this state the scriptures say, "The Atman delights with the Atman." For six months the Master constantly experienced this indescribable state.

The Master said that no worldly object or relationship obstructed his

| 13. The wonderful constitution of the Master's mind. |

journey to the experience of nirvikalpa samadhi according to Vedanta. At the outset of his spiritual quest he had renounced all desire for enjoyment in exchange for the vision of the Divine Mother. He prayed: "Mother, here is Thy knowledge and here is Thy ignorance; here is Thy righteousness and here is Thy unrighteousness; here is Thy good and here is Thy evil; here is Thy virtue and here is Thy vice; here is Thy fame and here is Thy infamy. Grant me only pure love for Thee. Do Thou reveal Thyself to me." With this, he sincerely renounced all desires within his mind because of his pure love for the Mother. Ah, can we experience — or even imagine — that kind of one-pointed love? Sometimes we say to God, "Lord, I offer everything to You"; in the next moment in everyday life we take possession of everything and reject God, and calculate our own profit and loss. We consider public opinion before we perform any action. We run around restlessly. As we dream about the future we sometimes sink in boundless misery and the next moment float in excitement. And we are convinced that although we may not be able to overturn the whole world ourselves, at least we can have some effect on it. However, the Master's mind was not deceptive, as is ours. When he said, "Mother, please take back the things You gave me," his mind immediately stopped casting covetous looks at them. From that point on, even such thoughts as these did not arise in his mind at all: "Alas, I have said this. What can I do now? It would be better if I did not say so." So we see the Master could never claim anything as his own once he had offered everything to the Divine Mother.

2. *Vivekachudamani* 408-409

Here we would like to mention another thing in connection with this.

14. The Master's adherence to truth.

Even though the Master offered the Divine Mother righteousness-unrighteousness, virtue-vice, good-evil, fame-infamy, and everything else pertaining to the body and mind, he could not say, "Mother, take Your truth and take Your untruth." The Master himself once told us the reason for this. He said that if he renounced truthfulness in that way, how could he hold onto the truth that he had offered everything to the Divine Mother? What steadfast love for truth did we witness in the Master, even though he had offered everything to the Mother! When he said that he would go to a place on a particular day, invariably he went there at the proper time. If he said that he would accept something from a certain person, he could not take that thing from anyone else. When he said that he would not eat a particular thing or do a certain action anymore, he could not eat that food or do that thing from that day on. The Master used to say: "One who has steadfast love for truth attains the God of truth. The Divine Mother never allows the words of one who adheres to truth to become untrue." We have witnessed many illustrations of these axioms in the Master's life. We must mention a few here.

One day in Dakshineswar Gopal-ma, a great woman devotee, cooked rice

15. First example.

for the Master. When the food was ready, the Master sat down to eat his meal. He found the rice hard; it had not been boiled properly. The Master was a little irritated and said: "How can I eat this rice? I will never again eat rice she has cooked." When those words left his mouth, everyone thought that he was only warning Gopal-ma to be more careful in the future. How could it be possible for him to refuse rice from her, whom he loved so much? Perhaps he would forgive her after a while and the matter would end there. But the situation took a different turn. Shortly after this incident the Master developed throat cancer. Gradually the disease became grave and he could no longer eat solid food. Thus his casual remark came true and he never again ate rice that Gopal-ma had cooked.

Once in Dakshineswar the Master said, in an ecstatic mood, "Henceforth I

16. Second example.

shall eat nothing but rice pudding." The Holy Mother overheard this as she was carrying a tray of food to him. She knew that the words that came from the Master's lips were never false. Alarmed, she asked: "Why only rice pudding? I shall cook rice and fish soup for you." The Master exclaimed in the same mood, "No, only rice pudding." Shortly after that the Master developed throat cancer and could no longer eat spicy food. In fact, he lived on rice pudding, milk and barley, and other soft foods.

The Master designated Shambhu Charan Mallick, a well-known, wealthy

17. Third example.

and generous devotee of Calcutta, as the second of four suppliers of his provisions. Shambu had a garden

Golapsundari Devi (d. 1924), known as Golap-ma.

Yogindra Mohini Biswas (1851-1924), known as Yogin-ma.

house near Rani Rasmani's Kali temple, where he used to spend time with the Master in spiritual conversation. He had a charitable dispensary in that garden. Sri Ramakrishna quite often suffered from stomach trouble, and one day Shambhu came to know about it. He suggested that the Master take a little opium as a remedy and asked that he get it from him before he returned to Rasmani's garden. The Master agreed to do so. In the course of conversation, however, both forgot about this.

The Master took his leave of Shambhu and was starting down the road

| 18. The Divine Mother does not allow him to take a wrong step. |

when he remembered the opium. But when he returned to pick it up, he found that Shambhu had retired to his inner apartment. So without disturbing him any further, the Master went to the dispensary supervisor and got some opium from him. The Master left for the temple garden, but as soon as he came near the road he became dizzy and could not find his way. He felt as if someone were pulling his legs towards the ditch beside the road. He said to himself: "What is this? This is not the road!" At the same time he could not find the road. Thinking that he had made a wrong turn, he looked back to Shambhu's garden and clearly saw the road in that direction. After further deliberation he returned to the gate of Shambhu's garden, checked his bearings, and again carefully resumed his journey towards Rasmani's garden. But after a few steps he experienced the same problem — he could not find the road. He felt as if someone were pulling his legs in the opposite direction. When this had happened a few times, it struck him: "Oh, Shambhu told me, 'Please take the opium from me.' But instead I took it from his supervisor without telling him; for that reason the Mother is not allowing me to move on. The supervisor had no right to give it to me without Shambhu's permission, and I should have taken it from Shambhu as he suggested. My action was wrong on two counts, falsehood and theft. Because of that the Mother is turning me around and keeping me from returning to the temple." With that thought he went to Shambhu's dispensary but could not find the supervisor, who had gone to eat. So the Master threw the opium packet through a window, calling loudly, "Hello, here I am returning your opium." Then he started towards Rasmani's garden. This time he did not have any dizzy spells; he saw the road clearly and reached the temple garden.

The Master said: "I have completely surrendered myself to the Mother, so She is holding my hand all the time. She never allows me to take a false step." We have heard so many wonderful stories about the Master in this regard! Could we ever imagine such steadfastness in truth and such total reliance on God? It is that kind of reliance that the Master described repeatedly with this parable: "In that part of the country (Kamarpukur) there are narrow ridges in the rice fields, and people go from one village to another along them. Because the ridges are very narrow, a father carries his youngest son in his arms lest he may fall. The oldest son holds his father's hand as they walk along. While they are walking like this one day, the children see a white kite, or something like that, and begin to clap with joy. The child in his father's arms knows that he is safe, so he goes on clapping merrily. But as soon as the elder one lets go of his father's hand and begins to clap, forgetting the narrow ridge, he falls off and cries. Similarly, one who is held by the Mother has nothing to fear; but one who clasps the Mother's hand has reason to be anxious: That person will fall the moment he lets go."

No worldly desires blocked the Master's way to attaining nirvikalpa samadhi, because his passion for God was so intense that no worldly person or object could attract him or hold him back. The obstacle in his path was the form of the Divine Mother — "charming, more charming than all charming things, and exceedingly beautiful" — whom the Master had loved and worshipped for such a long time and considered to be the Supreme Being. The Master said: "As soon as I gathered my mind and made it one-pointed, the Mother immediately appeared before me. I then had no inclination to push beyond that form. As many times as I tried to make the mind empty by driving everything away, so many times did that form appear. After long deliberation I at last strengthened my mind, envisioned knowledge to be a sword, and mentally cut that form in two. Then the mind became completely empty, and it speedily reached the nirvikalpa state." These words seem meaningless to us because we have never tried to make any form of the Divine Mother our own, nor have we become established in any loving attitude towards Her. We have never even learned to love another person wholeheartedly. All of our deep love is concentrated on the ego and on the body, a lump of flesh. Because of that we are frightened when we face death or find any sudden radical change in our minds. The Master did not have that problem. He knew that the Divine Mother was his heart's only desire, and he spent his time meditating on Her form and serving Her day and night. So when he somehow removed that form from his mind, what else could his mind hold on to? His mind became completely objectless and free from thought waves and finally reached the nirvikalpa state. O reader, if you cannot understand this phenomenon, please at least try to imagine it. Then you may understand the extent to which Sri Ramakrishna made the Divine Mother his own and how he loved Her with "one hundred twenty-five percent" of his mind.

19. The Master's obstacle to attaining the nirvikalpa state.

For six months the Master dwelt in the nirvikalpa state almost uninterruptedly. He later said: "For six months I was in that state from which ordinary mortals never return. Ordinarily, the body can live only for twenty-one days in that state; then it falls like a dry leaf from a tree. There is no consciousness of time, the coming of

20. He remains in the nirvikalpa state for six months; usually in that state the body dies within twenty-one days.

day or the passing of night. Flies would enter my mouth and nostrils just as they do a dead body, but I did not feel them. My hair became matted with dust. Sometimes I did not know when the call of nature was answered. Could this body survive? It should have died at that time. But luckily a monk then arrived at Dakshineswar. He held a small stick, like a ruler. As soon as he saw me, he recognized my state. He understood that much of Divine Mother's work was yet to be done through this body, and many people would benefit if it were preserved. So at mealtimes he would bring some food and strike my body with his stick again and again to bring it back to consciousness. The moment he saw signs that I was becoming conscious, he would thrust some food into my mouth. Some days a little food found its way into my stomach; on other days none did. Six months passed in this way. At last I received the Mother's command: 'Stay in bhavamukha! Remain on the threshold of relative consciousness for the sake of humanity.' Then I got a horrible disease — blood dysentery. I had terrible spasms and excruciating pain in the abdomen. After suffering from that pain for six months, my mind came down to the physical plane little by little. I regained my normal consciousness like other people. But at times the mind would frequently rush towards the nirvikalpa state and merge in it."

Those who were fortunate to meet the Master ten or twelve years before

| 21. Captain Vishwanath Upadhyay's remark about the Master's samadhi. |

he passed away told us that even then they rarely heard him speak. He was in ecstasy almost twenty-four hours at a time. Who could utter any words under those circumstances? Captain Vishwanath Upadhyay, an official of the Government of Nepal, told us that he saw the Master immersed in samadhi continually for three days and three nights. He further said that when the Master was in samadhi for such a long period, one had to occasionally rub *ghee* [clarified butter] on his body in a downward direction — from his neck to the bottom of his backbone and from his knee to his foot. This helped him to come down from the high state of samadhi to the realm of "I and mine."

The Master himself told us many times: "The natural tendency of this [*his*

| 22. What the Master himself said about it. |

own] mind is upward (*towards the nirvikalpa plane*). When it is in samadhi, it does not want to come down. I force it down for all of you. If I don't hold a petty desire, I don't feel any urge to come down. So I create some trifling desires in the mind: 'I shall smoke tobacco'; 'I shall drink water'; 'I shall eat bitter squash curry'; 'I shall meet this person'; 'I shall talk to that person.' After I repeat a particular desire again and again, the mind gradually returns to the physical plane. Later, while coming down, it may again shoot upward. When that happens, I have to trap the mind again with a desire and bring it back down." What a wonderful phenomenon! When we heard this, we were dumbfounded. If this is the meaning of his saying, "Tie the knowledge of nonduality in a corner of your cloth and then do as you please," then is there any hope of realizing it in our lives? We find that the only course for us is to take refuge in God. But when we try to practise this, we face severe problems within a few days. While treading that path, the roguish mind sometimes thinks: Why does the Master not love me more than others? Why does he not love me as much as he loves Narendra? In what respect am I inferior to Narendra? and so on. So far we have discussed the Master's frame of mind; now we shall return to the main topic (see III.2.8).

We shall now tell the reader what we have learned from the Master about the exalted spiritual state and the nature of samadhi and then try to explain the state of bhava-mukha. As we have said earlier, some physical changes are inevitable as higher and lower thoughts arise in the mind. This needs no explanation; it is self-evident. It is easily

| 23. Views of the East and the West regarding physical changes caused by the mind. |

understood by observing the ordinary moods experienced in daily life; for example, one kind of change takes place under the influence of anger, another under the influence of love. Again, if a person harbours an excess of either good or bad thoughts, his body changes accordingly and one can easily detect that person's nature. This is evident from these common expressions: "That person seems to be angry; that one is lustful; that one is holy." Many of us may have noticed that both the appearance and the character of a demoniacal, perverted, monstrous-looking man become gentle and simple if for some reason or other he spends six months continually thinking good thoughts and leading a spiritual life. A Western physiologist says that every thought that arises in your mind leaves a permanent impression in your brain. Thus your character is formed more or less by the sum total of those good or bad impressions, and you are considered to be a good or a bad person accordingly.

The yogis and sages of the East, especially of India, say that good and bad thoughts do not merely leave their marks on the brain: They become transformed into an impelling subtle force that engages you in good or bad actions in the future. This force remains eternally at the base of the tailbone, the basic centre of kundalini, which is

| 24. Kundalini, the repository of accumulated past impressions; how these impressions are wiped out. |

called *muladhara*. This is the dwelling place of the motivating powers that accumulate birth after birth, which are called *samskaras*, or past impressions. Samskaras can be destroyed only through the realization of God or the achievement of nirvikalpa samadhi. Otherwise, when an individual soul moves from one body to another, it carries that bundle of impressions as "the wind carries scents from place to place."[3]

---

3. Gita 15:8

The relationship between the body and the mind exists before nondual

25. The relationship between the body and the mind.

knowledge or God-realization has been attained. If anything happens to the body, it affects the mind; and again events in the mind affect the body. This relationship between the body and the mind is as true in individuals as it is in the aggregate: The actions and responses of your body and mind affect my body and mind as well as those of others. Thus the external and internal, the gross and subtle worlds, are eternally interdependent, constantly acting on and reacting to each other. So you experience grief where all are grief-stricken, and in the company of devotees you feel devotion in your heart without any effort. This is true in every circumstance.

It is evident that mental illness and spiritual moods are as contagious as

26. Because feelings are contagious, one should keep holy company.

bodily disease and good health. Spiritual moods also influence other people according to their receptivity. That is why the scriptures so greatly emphasize the importance of holy company for enkindling love of God. For that reason the Master used to say to newcomers: "Come here now and then. In the beginning one should visit frequently."

Like ordinary emotions, the spiritual moods that arise from one-pointed,

27. A one-pointed mind affects the body.

intense love of God cause extraordinary physical changes. For example, when an exuberant divine love is manifest, aspirants feel less attracted to sense objects. They eat and sleep less; they develop a taste for particular foods and lose interest in others; they try to avoid attachment to relatives like poison because it turns them away from God. As the Master said: "I could not then bear the presence of worldly people, and the company of relatives would make me feel suffocated, as if my life-force were leaving my body." He further said, "In those who sincerely call on God, the *mahavayu* [life-force] of their bodies rushes rapidly to the head."

So it is clear that any changes that occur in the mind because of love for

28. The harmony between the paths of devotion and of yoga.

God have corresponding effects on the body. The Vaishnava scriptures categorize these mental changes into five moods, or bhavas: shanta, dasya, sakhya, vatsalya, and madhura. And in connection with the physical effects caused by those moods, the Yoga scriptures describe kundalini and its six centres in the spine and the brain.

We have already briefly described kundalini. Any mental modifications

29. What is kundalini? Its active and dormant states.

or moods that have arisen and are emerging in an individual, in this life and in past lives, remain in a subtle form and manifest in a great vigorous motivating power that is called *kundalini* according to Patanjali and other sages. The yogis say that in bound souls it remains almost completely dormant, or unmanifest. Even when kundalini is dormant, memory, imagination, and other thoughts arise in a person's mind. If it somehow becomes awakened, it can move a spiritual aspirant to attain Self-knowledge, or God-realization. One may question how memory and imagination can arise from the sleeping state of kundalini. The answer is that even when it is asleep, sense objects are still perceived, which constantly vibrate the brain and raise a little momentary consciousness. For example, if a mosquito bites a sleeping man, his hand automatically slaps it or scratches his body.

The yogis say that the *Paramatman* [indivisible existence-knowledge-bliss Absolute], or God, dwells as consciousness in the *brahmarandhra*, the aperture in the crown of the head. The kundalini power that is in the base of the spine has tremendous affinity for the Supreme Self; in other words, God attracts it constantly. When the kundalini is sleeping, it does not feel that attraction. But as soon as it is awake, it is drawn to God and moves towards Him. The path that the kundalini takes to reach God exists within each one of us. Starting from the brain, this path extends through the spine down to the muladhara, the lowest centre, located at the base of the spine. According to the Yoga scriptures, this path is called the sushumna channel. Western physiologists have described it as the canal centralis, but so far they have not discovered its purpose. It is by this path that the kundalini, once separated from the Supreme Self, has descended from the brain to the muladhara. The kundalini ultimately goes back upward to the brain through the same path by passing through six centres that exist one above the other [in the sushumna channel] inside the spine.[4] As the awakened kundalini advances from one centre to the next, the aspirant has different kinds of novel experiences. When the kundalini reaches the brain, the aspirant attains the ultimate experience of spirituality, which is the nondual knowledge that unites the aspirant with the Supreme Self, the Cause of causes. At that time the aspirant also reaches the culmination of the devotional mood that he or she has been following — the ultimate source of all ideas that arise in human minds — and remains absorbed in the realm beyond all ideas.

30. Movement of the awakened kundalini as it penetrates the six centres, and samadhi.

Ah, how simple was the language that the Master would use to explain the intricate subject of yoga! He said: "Look, something moves upward from the feet to the head, creeping along with a tingling sensation. As long as it does not reach the brain, I remain conscious; but the moment it does, I

31. The Master's experience in this respect.

---

4. The yoga scriptures name the six centres of kundalini and describe their respective locations: 1. *muladhara,* between the base of the sexual organ and the anus; 2. *swadhisthana,* at the base of the sexual organ; 3. *manipura,* at the navel; 4. *anahata,* at the heart; 5. *vishuddha,* at the lower end of the throat; 6. *ajna,* between the eyebrows. Of course it is to be understood that all these centres are situated in the sushumna channel within the spine, and the words *heart, throat,* and so on indicate the corresponding regions in the body.

completely forget myself. Even the eyes and the ears cease to function, and speech is out of the question. Who can speak? The very distinction of 'I' and 'you' vanishes. Sometimes I think I shall tell you everything about what I see and feel when that mysterious power rises up through the spinal column. When it comes up to this, or even this (*pointing to the heart, then the throat*), it is possible to speak, which I do. But the moment it has gone above this (*pointing to the throat*), it is as if someone were pressing my mouth closed, and I lose all external awareness. I don't have any control. I make up my mind to relate to you what I feel when kundalini goes beyond the throat, but as I consider this, the mind leaps upward and speaking then becomes impossible."

Ah, how often the Master made great efforts to control himself, yet failed to describe to us the visions and experiences he had when his mind reached the centre above the throat!

32. The Master's efforts to describe the experience of nirvikalpa samadhi.

One of our friends told us: "One day the Master said emphatically, 'Today I'll tell you everything; I'll keep nothing secret.' He described clearly the centres and the corresponding experiences up to the heart and throat, and then, pointing to the sixth centre between the eyebrows, he said: 'When the mind reaches this point one gets the vision of the Paramatman [Supreme Self] and enters samadhi. Only a thin transparent veil intervenes between the individual self and the Supreme Self. One then sees —,' and as he attempted to provide details about the vision of the Paramatman, he went into samadhi. When his mind came down a little, he tried again, and again became immersed in samadhi. After repeated, fruitless attempts he said tearfully: 'Look, I sincerely wish to tell you everything, without hiding anything whatsoever, but the Mother won't let me do so. She keeps closing my mouth!' Dumbfounded, we thought: What is this? We see he is trying his utmost to tell us his experience, and moreover he is in pain because he is unable to express himself. The Mother is really a mischievous woman! He wants to tell us something good — about God-realization. So why is She holding his mouth closed? At that time we did not understand that the mind and the intellect, through which one must speak, are very limited. And unless one goes beyond their range, one cannot have complete realization of the Supreme Self. Did we then understand that the Master was trying to make the impossible possible because of his love for us?"

The Master described to us the experiences he had when kundalini rose through the sushumna channel: "Look," he would say, "that which rises to the brain with a tingling sensation does not always move in the same way.

33. The five ways that kundalini moves towards samadhi.

The scriptures speak of its five kinds of motion. First, it moves like an ant: One feels a slow creeping sensation from the feet upwards, like a row of ants crawling along with food in their mouths. When it reaches the brain, the aspirant merges into samadhi. Second, it moves like a frog: Just as a frog makes two or three short jumps in quick succession, stops for a while, then proceeds again in the same way, so something is felt advancing from the feet to the brain. When it reaches the brain, the aspirant goes into samadhi. Third, it moves like a serpent: As a snake lies quietly, straight or coiled up, but moves in a zigzag motion when it sees prey or is frightened, so does the kundalini move upward to the head. When it reaches the brain, the aspirant goes into samadhi. Fourth, it moves like a bird: Birds in their flight from one place to another sometimes fly a little high and sometimes low, but never stop till they reach their destination. Likewise, something is felt moving towards the head; when it reaches the brain, samadhi ensues. Fifth, it moves like a monkey: As a monkey goes from one tree to another, leaping from branch to branch and clearing the distance in two or three bounds, so the yogi feels the kundalini power go to the brain, and samadhi follows."

Regarding the visions that occur in each centre as kundalini rises through the sushumna channel, the Master said: "Vedanta speaks of seven planes, in each of which the aspirant has a particular kind of vision. The human mind has a natural tendency to confine its activities to the three lower centres — the regions of the anus, the genitals, and the navel — and therefore is content with the satisfaction of eating, dressing, coition, and so forth. If the mind transcends those three centres and reaches the fourth, the one near the heart, the aspirant sees a divine light. The mind may sometimes reach the heart centre but then descend to the three lower centres. However, when the mind comes to the fifth centre, near the throat, the aspirant cannot speak of mundane things: He or she talks about God only. While I was in this state, if anybody spoke of worldly things before me I would feel as though I were being struck violently on the head. I would run away to the Panchavati, just to avoid hearing secular talk. I would hide fearfully at the sight of worldly-minded people. Relatives appeared to me to be on the edge of a yawning chasm, trying to push me down into it, and there would be no escape if I once fell. In their presence I felt suffocated— almost to the point of death — and found relief only when I fled from them. Even from this throat centre a person may slip down to the three lower centres; so one should remain vigilant.

34. Seven planes of Vedanta: the Master's description of his experience in each plane.

"But if one's mind reaches the sixth centre, between the eyebrows, there is no more fear of falling. The aspirant then attains the vision of the Paramatman, the Supreme Self, and remains always in samadhi. There is only a thin veil, as transparent as glass, between this centre and the *sahasrara*, the thousand-petalled lotus at the crown of the head. The Supreme Self is then so close that one can imagine oneself merged in It. But that is not the case. From this state the mind can come down to the fifth, or at the most to the fourth centre, but not below that. However, ordinary aspirants, classed as jivas, cannot return from this state. After remaining constantly in samadhi for twenty-one days, they break that thin veil and become one with Brahman forever. This eternal union of the jiva and Brahman in the sahasrara is known as reaching the seventh plane."

Sometimes as we listened to the Master discuss the Vedas, Vedanta, and

35. The Master's extraordinary memory.

the science of yoga, some of us would ask him: "Sir, you have never cared for reading books. How do you know all these things?" This strange question did not disturb the wonderful Master. He would reply with a smile: "It is true that I have not read them myself. But I have heard a lot, and I remember everything. I have heard the Vedas, Vedanta, Puranas, and philosophy from good and scholarly pandits. After hearing them and learning all they contained, I made a garland of the scriptures, put it around my neck, and offered it to the Divine Mother, saying, 'Please take Your scriptures and Puranas; grant me pure devotion.'"

Regarding the nondual state described in Vedanta, that which is beyond

36. His simple explanation of nondualism.

all ideas, the Master said: "That is the last word in spiritual attainment. Do you know what it is like? Here is an old servant who has worked for a long time. His employer is pleased with the servant's good qualities, so he trusts his words and consults with him in every respect. One day, out of delight, the employer takes his servant's hand and tries to make him sit on his own seat. The embarrassed servant exclaims, 'Sir, what are you doing?' But the employer forces the servant to sit on his own seat and says: 'Ah, sit down. You and I are one.' It is just like that."

Once one of our friends [Harinath, later Swami Turiyananda] was

37. An example: Swami Turiyananda.

extremely busy studying Vedanta. The Master loved him dearly for his devotion and steadfastness and the fact that he had practised brahmacharya from his childhood onward. Because he was deeply preoccupied in his study of Vedanta and his meditation, Harinath could not visit the Master frequently for some time, as he had before. This absence did not escape the Master's keen observation. When he saw one of Harinath's companions, who used to come with him, alone in Dakshineswar, the Master asked: "Hello, I see you are alone today? Has your friend not come?" The boy replied: "Sir, nowadays he is absorbed in studying Vedanta. He spends day and night in study, discussion, and reasoning. He probably did not come because he considers it to be a waste of time." At this the Master said nothing more.

A few days later Harinath came to see the Master at Dakshineswar. The

38. What is Vedanta? Realizing Brahman as real and the world as unreal.

Master told him: "Hello, I hear that nowadays you are studying and discussing Vedanta philosophy. That is good, of course. But tell me, what does Vedanta teach? Is it not that Brahman alone is real and the

Harinath Chattopadhyay (1863-1922), later Swami Turiyananda. At right,
Baburam Ghosh (1861-1918), later Swami Premananda.

world unreal? Isn't that its substance? Or does it say something else?"
Harinath: "That is correct, sir. What else?"

Harinath later said that on that day the Master had truly opened his eyes
to the meaning of Vedanta with those few words. Listening to the words of
the Master, he thought to himself: "It is true, indeed! The whole of Vedanta is
understood if one realizes those few words."

The Master continued: "Hearing, reflecting, and meditating are the three
main disciplines of Vedanta. At first you hear that Brahman alone is real
and the world unreal. Then you reflect upon this idea and become
convinced of it through reasoning and discrimination. And finally you
meditate on Brahman, the Absolute Reality, relinquishing the unreal
world. That is all. Otherwise, what does it avail if you hear and understand
the teachings of Vedanta but do not try to renounce what is unreal? That is
like the knowledge of worldly people. This kind of knowledge cannot help
you to attain Reality. You need conviction and renunciation — only then
can you succeed. Otherwise, you are saying, 'There is no thorn, no pricking'; but the moment you touch a thorny plant, those thorns get into your
hands, and you cry out with pain. You are saying: 'The world does not
exist. It is unreal. Brahman alone exists,' and so on, but the moment you
come in touch with the sense objects of the world, you immediately
consider them to be real and get attached to them. Once a monk came to
live in the Panchavati of Dakshineswar. He would talk about Vedanta
extensively with people. Then one day I heard that he was having an illicit
love affair with a woman. I went in that direction to answer the call of
nature and found him seated in the Panchavati. I said to him, 'You talk so
much about Vedanta — now, what is this?' He replied: 'What does it
matter? Let me explain to you that I have done nothing wrong. When
everything in this world is unreal in the past, present, and future, how can
my slips of character be real? They are also unreal.' Disgusted, I said to him,
'I spit upon such Vedantic knowledge as yours!' Worldly people have that
kind of knowledge about Vedanta. That knowledge is no knowledge at
all."

Harinath said that there the conversation ended. On that day the Master
told him all this while he was walking with him in the Panchavati. Previously Harinath believed that Vedanta could not be understood, that
liberation would be remote if he did not study the Upanishads, *Panchadashi*,
and other serious books on Vedanta and have a clear understanding of
Sankhya, Nyaya, and other philosophical systems. On that day he learned
from the Master that the main purpose of all Vedantic discussions was to
become convinced of the idea that "Brahman alone is real and the world is
unreal." Otherwise, if one studied volumes of philosophy and logic but had
no conviction about the aforesaid idea, it would make no difference whether
one studied those books or not. Harinath then took leave of the Master.

While returning to Calcutta he thought that from then on he would concentrate more on spiritual disciplines than on studying books. He resolved to realize God through spiritual disciplines and began to apply himself accordingly.

If the Master went to Calcutta and visited any devotee's house, the news of his arrival quickly spread amongst those who were close to him. It was not that some took the responsibility to inform others, but that the devotees were always eager to see the Master. If their work kept them from visiting the Master in Dakshineswar, they would often meet at someone's house and take joy in talking about him. If any one of them knew about the Master's coming to Calcutta, immediately that news would spread effortlessly by word of mouth. It is difficult to make the reader understand how the Master's power tied the devotees to one another with an indescribable cord of love. Most of the Master's devotees lived in the Baghbazar, Simla, and Ahiritola areas of Calcutta, so he visited those three places, but among them he went most frequently to Baghbazar.

One day sometime after the aforesaid incident with Harinath, the Master went to Balaram Basu's house in Baghbazar. Many of the devotees in Baghbazar got news of this and came to see him. Harinath's house was very close to Balaram's. The Master inquired about him, so a young man who was his neighbour immediately brought him there. Harinath entered the spacious parlour on the second floor and saw the Master surrounded by devotees. He bowed down to the Master and sat near him. The Master greeted him with a smile, briefly inquired about his welfare, and then resumed the topic he had been discussing.

When Harinath had heard a few sentences, he understood that the Master was explaining to the devotees that without God's grace one cannot attain knowledge, devotion, or spiritual visions. It struck him that the Master had raised that topic in order to remove any misconceptions from his mind. He felt that whatever the Master was saying in that context was directed towards him.

Harinath heard the Master say: "Well, is it an easy matter to realize that
39. God-realization is not possible without God's grace.
lust and gold are truly unreal and to have the firm conviction that the world does not exist, and has never existed? Is it possible to achieve this without God's compassion? This [realization] happens only if God graciously bestows that conviction on a person. Otherwise, can anyone achieve this through self-effort? A human being is after all a tiny creature with very limited powers. How much effort can an individual exert with such meagre strength?" While thus discussing God's grace, the Master went into ecstasy. After a while he returned to a semiconscious state and said, "A man cannot practise one path properly, yet he wants to try another." The Master then began to sing, in ecstasy:

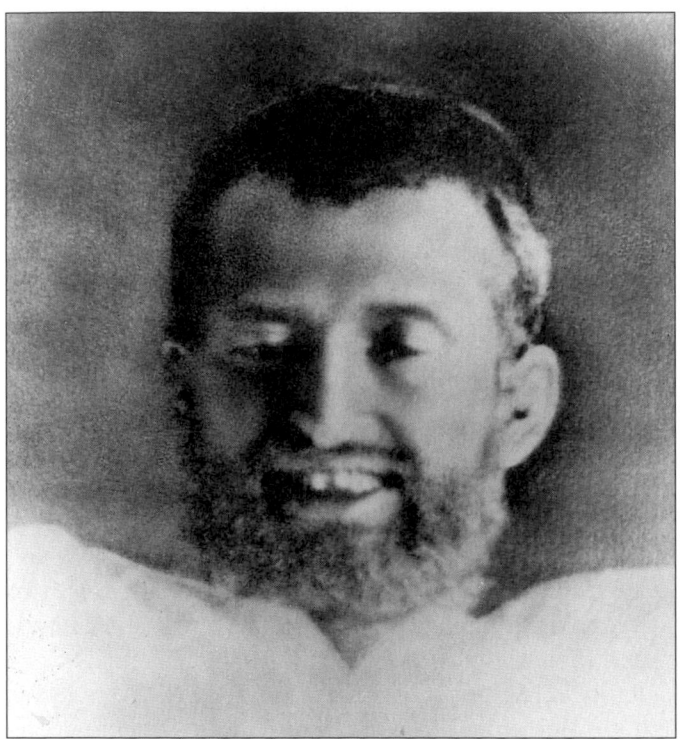

Ramakrishna's face in
samadhi cropped from
the photo taken on
21 September 1879.

Pandit Shashadhar Tarkachudamani
(1850-1928).

> O Kusa and Lava, why are you so proud?
> If I had not let myself be captured,
> Could you have captured me?[5]

While the Master was singing, tears began rolling down his face, dampening part of the bed sheet. Harinath also shed tears profusely, touched by that wonderful teaching. After a while both returned to a normal state. Harinath said later: "That teaching was permanently imprinted on my mind. From that very day I understood that nothing could be achieved without God's grace."

We cannot resist relating another event regarding the depth of the Master's

| 40. Pandit Shashadhar asks the Master to cure his own disease through yogic power: his response. |

nondual knowledge. At this time the Master was in the Cossipore garden house, critically ill. When they heard of this, Pandit Shashadhar Tarkachudamani and a few others came to see the Master. In the course of conversation, the pandit told him: "Sir, we have read in the scriptures that a great soul like yourself can cure his own physical illness by mere willpower. If you but concentrate your mind on the affected part of the body for a while with the resolve that it be healed, you will be cured. Why don't you try it, sir?"

The Master replied: "As a pandit, how can you make such a suggestion? This mind has been given up to God once and for all. How can I withdraw it from Him and make it dwell on this cage of flesh and bone?"

Pandit Shashadhar was silenced. But Swami Vivekananda and other devo-

| 41. Swami Vivekananda and other devotees make similar requests: the Master's reply. |

tees did not remain quiet. As soon as the pandit left, Swamiji fervently begged the Master to follow the pandit's advice. He said, "Sir, you must cure yourself, at least for our sake."

The Master: "Do you think I'm suffering like this because I want to? Of course I want to get better, but does that desire cure my disease? It all depends on Mother."

Swamiji: "Then please pray to Her for your recovery. She will definitely listen to you."

The Master: "It is easy for you to say that, but I could never utter such words."

Swamiji: "No, sir, that won't do. You must tell the Mother about it, at least for our sake."

The Master: "All right, let me see if I can ask Her."

After a few hours Swamiji returned to the Master and asked: "Sir, did you ask the Mother? What did She say?"

The Master: "I said to the Mother, 'I can't eat anything because of this pain (*pointing to the sore in the throat*) — please let me eat a little.' But She pointed to

---

5. This is what Hanuman, a devotee of Rama, said to Rama's two sons. — *Translator*

all of you and said: 'Why? You are eating through so many mouths already!'
I then felt ashamed and couldn't utter another word."

What a wonderful example of the Master's lack of body-consciousness
and how established he was in the knowledge of

42. The depth of the
Master's experience of
nonduality.

and how established he was in the knowledge of
nonduality! For more than six months at that time his
daily diet was about a half pound of boiled barley.
When the Divine Mother told him on that occasion, "You are eating through
so many mouths," he immediately thought: "What a sinful act I have
committed! I have called this little body 'I'!" He became silent and hung his
head with shame. O reader, can you imagine this exalted state of the Master?

What great fortune we had to meet such a wonderful Master! We
witnessed in him an unprecedented synthesis of

43. The Master passed
all tests.

witnessed in him an unprecedented synthesis of
knowledge and devotion, yoga and karma, both
ancient and modern, and of all religious beliefs. The
sages of the Upanishads say that "a real knower of Brahman becomes omniscient and his thoughts come true." All beings and objects in the external
world implicitly obey that person's wishes and change according to them. So
it is no wonder that the body and mind of an illumined soul act in the same
way! It is impossible for an ordinary person to test the validity of that statement in the Upanishads. But we can definitely say that at every available
opportunity we tested the Master thoroughly as far as our limited abilities
allowed. Each time the Master passed the test effortlessly and then with a
smile would tell us playfully: "Still you doubt! Have firm faith and strong
conviction. He who in the past was born as Rama and Krishna is now living in
this very body (*pointing to himself*). But this time his advent is very secret, like
a king who visits his own kingdom incognito! As soon as people recognize
him and whisper, he immediately departs from that place. It is just like that."

Many events in the Master's life reveal the aforesaid Upanishadic truth to
us. Generally, whatever ideas arise in an individual's

44. Things the Master
saw while in ecstasy
corresponded to things
in the external world.

us. Generally, whatever ideas arise in an individual's
mind are truly known only to that person; in other
words, that person alone knows the exact magnitude
and intensity of those ideas. Others can only observe
the external effects and make inferences. Therefore, the subjective nature of
spiritual ecstasy is evident to all. Everyone knows that spiritual moods, like
other thoughts, are mere modifications of the mind or manifestations of
mental powers. They appear and disappear in the mind. It is impossible to
see the mental picture or a similar image in the external world or to show it.
But on the contrary, we find that some of the Master's thoughts actually did
take form in the external world.

For example, when the Master saw that goats and cattle were eating the
saplings of the Panchavati that he had planted

45. Some examples: the
fence in the Panchavati,
and so on.

saplings of the Panchavati that he had planted
during his sadhana, he wished to build a fence
around it. Shortly the high tide of the Ganges brought

near that spot the materials needed for making a fence: some wooden posts, split bamboo, rope, and even a machete. He then built a fence with the help of Bhartabhari, a gardener of the Kali temple.

Another example: Once in the course of conversation the Master said to Mathur, a son-in-law of Rani Rasmani: "Anything may happen by the will of God. Even a white flower may bloom in a red hibiscus tree." Mathur disagreed. The next day the Master saw in the garden two flowers, one white and the other red, on one branch of a red hibiscus tree. He broke off that branch with the flowers and presented it to Mathur.

Another example: Whenever the Master wished to practise the sadhanas of Tantra, Vedanta, Vaishnavism, Islam, and so on, teachers who had become perfect in those disciplines arrived at the Dakshineswar Kali temple and initiated him in their respective faiths.

Another example: The Master longed to meet his close devotees, whom he had seen only in a vision. When they later came to him, he recognized each one.

We could mention many such examples. When we reflect on these events, we can see that many of the Master's ideas did not remain as mere thoughts like those of ordinary human beings. According to a mysterious law unknown to us, his thoughts produced corresponding changes in the events of the external world. We leave the matter here after simply relating the truth; let the reader reflect upon and discuss those facts and draw his or her own conclusions.

We mentioned earlier that the Master always remained in bhavamukha
| 46. The Master's unique relationship with each devotee. | except when he was in nirvikalpa samadhi. That is why he established a unique relationship with each devotee and maintained it steadfastly, as we noticed. |

It is now well known that the Master had a lifelong relationship with all women as mother, recognizing them as veritable manifestations of the Divine Mother's blissful and creative aspects. But it seems people do not know that he also had particular relationships with individual male devotees. So it will not be out of place here to say something in that connection. Generally, the Master classified his devotees into two categories: those who originated as aspects of Shiva and those who were aspects of Vishnu. He said that there were differences between those two groups of devotees in terms of nature, conduct and behaviour, and aptitude for spiritual practices. The Master understood this very well, but it is beyond our capability to explain exactly what the difference is.

Briefly, the reader should know these differences: The characters of Shiva
| 47. Two classes of devotees. | and Vishnu can be understood as two types of moulds or models; the mental make-up of each devotee is cast in one of those moulds. The Master |

had all kinds of relationships — shanta, dasya, sakhya, vatsalya, and so on —

with his devotees. He had a unique relationship with each individual. For example, he used to say about Narendra (later, Swami Vivekananda): "Narendra is like my father-in-law's house, that is, the realm of the Indivisible Brahman. The principle that resides within this (*pointing to himself*) is female [Prakriti], and that which is within him (*pointing to Narendra*) is male [Purusha]." He considered Rakhal (later, Swami Brahmananda) to be his own son. Likewise, he had a special relationship with each intimate monastic and householder devotee. Moreover, he maintained shanta bhava [a calm attitude] in his relationships with all ordinary devotees, as he considered them to be Narayana Himself.

The Master established a particular spiritual relationship with each

48. The Master established relationships with devotees according to their natures.

devotee based on that person's inner nature. He used to say, "I see vividly what is inside human beings, as one sees the items in a glass case." A person can never act contrary to his or her nature, so the devotees were incapable of acting in a way inconsistent with the relationship adopted by the Master. If a man imitated another person, going against his own nature by doing so, the Master would be displeased and would point out that man's mistake. For example, he used to call Girish "Bhairava" [a form of Shiva]. One day at Dakshineswar Kali temple when he was in ecstasy, he saw Girish in that form. He put up with Girish's importunities and harsh words because he could see the wonderful tenderness and complete dependence hidden under the veil of his rough mannerisms. Once another devotee of the Master used that kind of rude language towards him, imitating Girish. The Master was very displeased and later pointed out his error.

Established in bhavamukha, the Master had full knowledge of the

49. The Master guided devotees individually along their respective spiritual paths.

innate spiritual mood of each man and woman devotee and established a permanent loving relationship with each of them accordingly. We shall complete this chapter by presenting to the reader a few of the various methods that the Master adopted to guide each devotee to realize God, in accordance with his or her respective spiritual mood. After the Master had descended from the nondual plane, he practised the sakhya, vatsalya, and madhura attitudes in order to enjoy the essence of each of them. He reached the culmination of each one. Long after this, while the Master was in an ecstatic mood one day, he had the desire that the devotees who had come to him should also have samadhi. He prayed to the Divine Mother for this, and some devotees began to experience ecstasy from time to time. When this ecstatic mood was upon them, their awareness of the external world, as well as of their bodies, would decrease significantly, and a spiritual current would make them see vividly a divine form as if the deity were laughing and speaking to them. They would generally have this experience while listening to devotional songs.

The Master had another group of devotees who would see divine forms during meditation instead of when they were listening to devotional songs. At first they would see the form only, but then as meditation deepened they would see the deity move and would hear His or Her voice. Again, some had various visions in the beginning, and when their meditation deepened they did not see any forms. But it is amazing that when he listened to their visions and experiences, Sri Ramakrishna knew who belonged to which class, what that person needed, and what each would later see.

50. Devotees' visions of gods and goddesses.

Let us mention the story of one of our friends (Kali, later Swami Abhedananda) as an example. He began to practise meditation as instructed by Sri Ramakrishna. In the beginning he saw his Chosen Deity in various ways during meditation. Quite often he would go to Dakshineswar and report his experiences to the Master. The Master would respond, "Very well," or "Do this thing next," and so on. Later, during meditation one day, our friend saw all forms of gods and goddesses merge into a particular divine form. When he informed the Master of this, the latter said: "Ah, you have seen *Vaikuntha* [the abode of Vishnu]! Henceforth, you won't have any other visions." Abhedananda said later: "In fact, this proved to be true. I did not see any more divine forms during meditation. My mind was then occupied with lofty ideas, such as the all-pervasiveness of God. I was happy to have the visions of the divine forms and I tried to have them again, but despite all my efforts I could not see any form."

51. A devotee's vision of Vaikuntha.

The Master said to the devotees of God with form: "During meditation, think that your mind has been tied to the feet of your Chosen Deity with a silk thread, so that He cannot run away. Why do I say a silk thread? Because those feet are extremely soft and delicate. It would hurt the deity if a different type of string were used." Again, he said: "Should one think of the Chosen Deity during meditation only and then forget Him? Always try to keep part of your mind towards the deity. You have seen how a vigil lamp is kept burning during Durga Puja. One should always keep a lamp near the deity; it should not be allowed to go out. It is inauspicious if a householder's lamp goes out. Likewise, after placing the Chosen Deity in the lotus of the heart, one's meditation should be like the flame of a vigil lamp. While performing household duties one should look inside from time to time to see if the lamp is still burning."

52. The Master's advice to the devotees of God with form: silk thread and the vigil lamp.

Sri Ramakrishna once said: "During my sadhana, before starting meditation on the Chosen Deity I would first imagine that I was washing the mind thoroughly. You see, there are various kinds of dirt and dross (bad

53. Cleansing the mind before meditation.

thoughts and desires) in the mind. I would imagine that I was flushing out all impurities and placing the Chosen Deity there. Adopt this method."

Once the Master told us about meditation on God with form and without

54. Which is higher —
God with form or God
without form?

form. He said, "Some reach the formless God by worshipping God with form, and again some attain God with form by adopting the sadhana of formless God." At Girish's house one day, one of our friends (Devendra Nath Basu) asked the Master, "Sir, which aspect of God is higher — that with form or without?" The Master replied: "The formless aspect is of two kinds: mature and immature. The mature one is very high indeed and must be reached through God with form. The immature one, as professed by the Brahmos,[6] is like darkness perceived merely by closing the eyes."

The Master had a group of devotees who followed the "immature" form-

55. Harmony between
the two aspects of God.

less aspect as a result of their Western education. The Master forbade this group to act like the Christian missionaries and criticize those who think of God with form or to hate those who worship God in the images and call them "idolaters," "blind believers," and so on. He said: "Look, God is with form and again formless. Who knows what else He is besides these? Do you know what God with form is like? It is like water and ice. When water freezes, it becomes ice — which inside and outside is water only. Ice is nothing but water. But look, water does not have any particular form, whereas ice does. Similarly, through the cooling influence of the devotee's love the ocean of the indivisible Satchidananda freezes and takes various forms, as does ice." The Master's explanation gave peace to the minds of so many people by convincing them that it is possible for both form and formless aspects of God to exist at the same time.

We cannot but help relating another story here. Swami Vivekananda was

56. Swami Vivekananda
and blind faith.

the foremost among the followers of the "immature" formless aspect of God. The Master placed him not only as the foremost of that group but also of all classes of devotees. Under the influence of Western education and of the Brahmo Samaj, Vivekananda would sometimes make caustic remarks about the followers of God with form, especially during an argument. Sometimes the Master would set up a lively debate between him and some devotees of God with form, and then enjoy the fun. On these occasions almost no one could withstand Vivekananda's fluent argumentation. His keen intellect

6. For the sake of truth we have mentioned this, but let no one think that the Master ever criticized the modern Brahmo Samaj or the Brahmos. After the kirtan when the Master would bow down to all devotees of all religious denominations, we heard him say many times, "Salutations to the followers of the modern Brahmo Samaj." It is known to all that it was Keshab Chandra Sen, the famous leader of the Brahmo Samaj, who first made Sri Rama-krishna known to the Calcutta public. Some monastic disciples of the Master, including Swami Vivekananda, unhesitatingly admit their indebtedness to the Brahmo Samaj.

and sharp reasoning left his opponents speechless, and some of them also felt hurt when this happened. Sometimes the Master would joyfully mention this to others: "The other day Narendra cut the arguments of so-and-so into pieces! What an outstanding intellect!"

But one day Swamiji was silenced while arguing with Girish, a follower of God with form. On that occasion we felt that the Master took Girish's side in order to strengthen and nourish his faith. On another day, while talking with the Master, Swami Vivekananda referred to the belief of the devotees of God with form as "blind faith." The Master replied: "Well, can you explain what you mean by 'blind faith?' Faith is always blind. Has faith eyes? Either simply say 'faith,' or say 'knowledge.' What do you mean by classifying faith — one kind having eyes, the other being blind?" Swami Vivekananda said later: "In fact I was embarrassed when explaining the meaning of blind faith to the Master that day. I could not find any meaning in that expression. After understanding that the Master's words were true, I never again used that phrase."

The Master looked equally upon the devotees of God with form and those who followed the "immature" doctrine of the form-

> **57. Advice to the devotees of formless God.**

less God. He also told them what kind of meditation would be helpful. He said: "Look, during my sadhana I used to look upon God as if He had completely covered the universe like the water of the ocean, and like a fish I was diving, floating, and swimming in that ocean of Satchidananda. Again, sometimes I considered myself to be a pitcher immersed in the water of that indivisible Satchidananda, which pervaded me through and through."

He also said: "Look, before you begin meditating, think of this (*pointing to himself*) for a while. Do you know why I say this?

> **58. The Master's advice to meditate on his form.**

Because you have faith in this place (*me*). If you think of this place, that will remind you of God. It is like when one sees a herd of cows, one remembers a cowherd; seeing a son, the father; seeing a lawyer, the court. Do you understand? Look, your mind is scattered among various places. If you think of this (*me*), it will be gathered in one spot. And if you think of God with that concentrated mind you will truly get deep meditation. That is why I am telling you all this."

The Master continued: "Whatever form of God or spiritual mood you like, hold onto that firmly; only then will you get

> **59. "Unripe ego and ripe ego." By intensifying any relationship with God, one can force demands on Him.**

steadfast devotion. 'God can be reached through devotion. Can anyone attain Him without that?' One needs bhava [spiritual mood]. One should adopt a particular attitude and call on Him. 'As is a man's meditation, so is his feeling of love. As is a man's feeling of love, so is his gain; and faith is the root of all.' One should cultivate a spiritual attitude and faith, and hold onto Him firmly. Only then can one succeed. Do you know what *bhava* means? It is to establish a relationship with God and then to remember it all the time: for example, I am a servant of God; I am a child of God; I am a part of God. This is the ripe ego, the ego of Knowledge. Always remember this — even while you are eating, sitting, and resting. Again, I am a brahmin, I am a kshatriya, I am the son of so-and-so, I am the father of so-and-so — these are all examples of the unripe ego, the ego of Ignorance. One should shun this because it increases vanity and pride and brings bondage. One should practise the constant recollectedness of God. Part of the mind should be directed towards Him always. Only then will you succeed. Establish a particular spiritual relationship with God and make Him your own. Only then can you force your demands on Him. Look at human relationships: In the beginning of intimacy, one addresses the other, *apani*; as it deepens, *tumi*; and when it reaches the final state, *tui*.[7] One should make God one's very own. Only then will you succeed.

"Take for example an adulterous woman. When she first begins to love

| 60. Example of an adulterous woman. |

her paramour, there is so much secrecy, fear, and bashfulness! Then as intimacy deepens, all emotional barriers disappear. She leaves her family and appears in front of everyone holding her lover's hand. If at that time the man does not take care of her or wants to leave her, she throws a cloth around his neck and pulls him, saying: 'You wretch, I have left everything and everybody for you, and now you want to drop me on the street! Tell me — will you maintain me or not?' Likewise, a man who has renounced everything for God and made Him his very own forces his demands on Him and says: 'I have renounced everything for You. Now tell me — will You reveal Yourself to me or not?'"

If the Master noticed that a devotee's love for God had waned, he would

| 61. One should have a firm resolve to realize God in this life. |

say: "Why do you say, 'I shall realize God in the next life, if not in this?' You should not have that kind of lukewarm devotion. 'By His grace I will realize Him in this life and right now' — one should maintain such determination and faith. How can it be possible otherwise? In Kamarpukur when the peasants go to market to buy bullocks for their ploughs they first grab the animals' tails. Some bullocks do not react and meekly lie down on the ground. The peasants recognize that these are without mettle and no good. They select only those bullocks that show spirit and frisk about when their tails are grabbed. Lukewarm devotion is no good. Strengthen your determination and say with conviction, 'I must realize God right now.' Only then will you succeed."

---

7. In the Bengali language there are three forms of the second personal pronoun. When addressing a stranger or a respected elder person, *apani* is used; to a known person of equal rank, *tumi*; and to an extremely familiar or a socially inferior person, *tui*. — *Translator*

Again, the Master said: "Only when you renounce worldly desires one

62. Desires must be given up one after another.

after another will you see God. You are supposed to give up those desires one by one, but instead you are increasing them. So how can you expect to succeed?"

When the devotees were despondent because their japa, prayer, and

63. One must have perseverance like an angler who waits after casting the bait.

meditation seemed to have no results, the Master would encourage them by saying: "If you want to catch fish, first throw some spiced bait into the water. You may sit there for a long time holding a line and a

rod without any sign of fish. You may think perhaps there are no fish in the pond. Then perhaps one day you may see a big fish jumping with a splash, and immediately you know there are fish in the pond. Another day perhaps the float on the line moves, and you believe a fish has come near the hook. Some days later when the float sinks, you lift the line and find the fish has eaten the bait and fled. Again you put bait on the hook and watch carefully after dropping the line. Then one day when the fish swallows the bait, you pull the line and the fish is landed."

Sometimes the Master would say: "God is quick of hearing. He listens to

64. God is "quick of hearing": He listens to everything.

everything. He has heard everything you have prayed for. Someday He will certainly reveal Himself to you — at least at the time of death." He told someone: "If

you cannot ascertain whether God has form or is formless, pray in this way: 'O Lord, I don't know whether You are with form or formless. Whatever You may be, please bestow grace on me and reveal Yourself to me.'" Again he said to some others: "Truly one can see God. As we are sitting here together and talking, so one can see God and talk to Him. I am speaking the truth — I swear to you."

If a person remains in the state of bhavamukha for twenty-four hours a

65. Although absorbed in deep ecstatic moods, the Master had his eye on everything.

day, that person's ecstasy increases to such an extent that he or she can no longer perform household work and cannot keep any small details in mind. This is what we see everywhere. Examples of this are found

not only among spiritual people but also in the lives of great individuals in the fields of science, politics, and so on. Perhaps they cannot keep themselves clean and tidy, or keep items they use daily in their proper places. But we found in the Master's life that in spite of his overwhelming ecstasy, he was fully aware of even ordinary things. When he was in samadhi, he had no awareness of his own body, or any person or objects of the world. But when he was in the normal state he was careful about everything. Is this not a matter of wonder? We shall cite a few examples here.

One morning the Master took a carriage to Balaram's house with Ramlal

66. First example.

and Jogin [later, Swami Yogananada]. When the carriage reached the gate of Dakshineswar, the Master asked Jogin, "Did you bring my cloth and bath towel?" He replied: "I have your towel, but I forgot to bring the cloth. Anyhow, Balaram will be happy to give you a new piece of cloth." The Master said indignantly: "Nonsense! People will say, 'What a hapless fellow has come!' It will cause them trouble and they will be embarrassed. Stop the carriage. Go back and get the cloth." When Jogin obeyed, the Master commented: "There is an abundance of everything when a good and fortunate person comes as a guest. But when a wretched and unfortunate fellow comes, the host finds great difficulty in accommodating him, particularly if he arrives on a day when there just happens to be a lack of necessities in the household."

Pratap Hazra, a self-styled holy man, lived with the Master at Dakshi-

67. Second example.

neswar for a long time. We used to call him "Hazra Mahashay." Sometimes he accompanied the Master when the latter visited devotees in Calcutta. Once while returning from Calcutta Hazra forgot his towel. When the Master learned about it after they had arrived at Dakshineswar, he said to Hazra: "While chanting God's name I lose control of my body, but I have never left my towel and spice bag in Calcutta even for a day. And you are so forgetful after practising a little japa!"

The Master taught the Holy Mother: "When you travel by carriage or boat,

68. Third example: advice to the Holy Mother.

get into it first; and while leaving it, get out last after checking thoroughly to see whether any luggage has been left behind." The Master had such keen observation regarding even small matters.

Although he constantly dwelt in the state of bhavamukha, the Master was

69. Conclusion of this topic.

careful about his necessities. He always kept things in their proper places. He kept track of his own clothes, his spice bag, and other articles of daily use. While going to and returning from a place, he would ask whether anything had been left behind. And as he oversaw the devotees' spiritual problems in detail, he also inquired about their household situations. He guided their external activities so that their environment was favorable for their spiritual journey.

When one reflects on the life and teachings of the Master, one understands

70. The Master was a veritable king in the realm of spirituality.

that he was the embodiment of all spiritual moods. Such a great king in the realm of spirituality had never been seen before. Dwelling in the state of bhavamukha, the Master fully demonstrated in his life the immense range of spiritual states, from the nondual nirvikalpa to the spiritual moods of savikalpa. Then he guided different types of devotees along different paths according to their goals and brought them to the light of knowledge from the darkness of ignorance, to unprecedented hope from despair, and to incomparable peace amidst worldly tribulations. Words are not adequate to explain how the Master was the repository of hope for all. It is impossible for us to express the indomitable power that he had in the entire realm of the mind.

Swami Vivekananda said: "It is no great matter to control external mate-

71. The Master's wonderful power over human minds: Swami Vivekananda's remark in that respect.

rial powers by some means and to perform miracles. But I have never seen a greater miracle than the way that 'mad brahmin'[8] would handle human minds like a lump of clay. He would pound those minds, beat them into shape, develop them, and then with a mere touch he would cast them into a new mould, with new thoughts."

8. Thus Swami Vivekananda endearingly referred to Sri Ramakrishna. — *Translator*

Chapter 3

Sri *R*amakrishna as a Guru

Some look on the Self as a wonder; some speak of It as a wonder; some hear of It as a wonder; still others, though hearing, do not understand It at all. — GITA 2:29

THOSE WHO HAD SEEN THE MASTER A FEW TIMES, or who were not closely acquainted with him and knew him superficially, are amazed when someone tells them about the Master's divine play as a guru with his devotees. They think: "This person must be lying." Again when they find that many people speak in the same vein, they think: "These people have formed a group with the purpose of making Sri Ramakrishna a god. They are trying to add one more to the existing 333 million deities. What is this? Are they not satisfied with such a large number of deities? They can choose whomever, as many as they like, from among them. Why increase their number by one more? It is strange that these fellows do not realize that people will lose respect for this holy man if their false claims are exposed. We have seen Sri Ramakrishna — how humble he was with everyone, how meek, how patient like the earth, how devoid of egotism, lower than the lowliest! Moreover, you say and we have also seen that he could not bear it if anyone called him 'guru,' or 'baba' [father], or 'karta' [master]. He always said: 'God is the only guru, father, and master. I am the lowliest of the lowly, a servant of servants. I am equal to a tiny hair of your body — not even a big hair.' So saying, he would take the dust of a person's feet and put it on his own head. Has anyone witnessed such humility? And now his followers are calling him 'guru,' 'god,' and whatnot! They are absurd!"

> 1. The Master was irritated when addressed as guru, baba, or karta: How then was it possible for him to be a guru?

To prevent the continuation of such mistaken attitudes, we feel we should

> 2. The Master adopted the servant attitude because he saw God in all.

say something about what we have seen and heard about the Master as a guru. It is true that when the Master was in a normal state, he maintained the conviction that all beings from the lowest to the highest are God; moreover, he had the attitude that he was a servant to all beings. Truly, at that time he considered himself to be lower than the lowliest, humbler than the humblest, and he would take the dust of the feet of all. Then indeed he could not bear being addressed as "guru," "father," or "master." But even though he behaved that way when he was in a normal state, how can we deny the unique divine play of the Master as a guru?

When he was under the influence of an extraordinary divine power and

> 3. During ecstasy the play of the power as a guru manifested in him every day: How the devotees responded.

had become its instrument, the Master by a mere touch could put someone into samadhi, or into deep meditation, or make a person intoxicated[1] with divine bliss. By means of a mysterious spiritual power, he could remove the impurities from a person's mind so completely that the latter would immediately achieve deep concentration, purity, and bliss to an extent that he or she had not experienced before. Such a devotee would then consider himself or herself to be blessed and would surrender to the Master forever. When we saw the Master at such a time, we felt that he was no longer the lowliest of the lowly but that he had been possessed by a divine power that willfully or playfully manifested itself within him and made him perform those actions. He was then indeed a guru, a saviour, and a guide to the path of God for those helpless human beings who were blinded by ignorance, afflicted by miseries, and sickened by worldly disease. When they observed this aspect of the Master, the devotees called him "guru," "the merciful one," "the Lord," and so on. Although it may appear to be contradictory, in this age we have actually seen within Sri Ramakrishna the coexistence of two moods: the humble mood of a true devotee and the divine mood of a true spiritual teacher.

Because we have witnessed that, we now attempt to show the reader,

> 4. Limitless moods of the Master.

according to our understanding, how those two can coexist in one mind. But despite our efforts, we are not sure whether we are capable of explaining what little we have grasped. It is beyond the capability of the author to make this understood, and beyond the reader to understand it. Because the Master remained in bhavamukha, there was no limit to his spiritual moods. The

---

1. In fact, at that time one feels oneself to be heavily intoxicated, as if one had drunk an overdose of pulped marijuana. We even saw some devotees staggering. Of course, the Master's condition was beyond description. Under the influence of that divine inebriation, he staggered so much that he could move only when holding onto one of us. People thought that he was dead drunk.

Master used to say, "God is limitless." Similarly we have witnessed that the spiritual moods of this extraordinary person were also without limit.

Usually when people hear that the Master dwelt in bhavamukha, they

5. Ordinary people thought the Master followed the path of devotion, not of knowledge. One cannot say that if one understands the significance of bhavamukha.

immediately conclude that he was not a jnani, a follower of the path of knowledge: They believe that he always lived in a state of devotion and experienced happiness when united with God and pain when separated from God. But we shall understand this subject if we can properly grasp what it is to remain in bhavamukha and the conditions that make this possible. Therefore, let us once more briefly discuss the state of remaining in bhavamukha (see III.1.1) from a different angle. First, remember that the Master attained nirvikalpa samadhi after practising sadhana for only three days.

Question: What is nirvikalpa samadhi?

6. Thought waves arise from I-consciousness. The partial disappearance of I-consciousness leads to savikalpa samadhi; its full disappearance leads to nirvikalpa samadhi. How to differentiate samadhi, fainting, and deep sleep.

Answer: To bring the mind to a state where there are absolutely no desires or doubts (*samkalpa-vikalpa*).
Question: What do you mean by "desires and doubts?"
Answer: These include all of the mind's thought waves, such as the knowledge of sense objects in the external world; the experience of happiness and misery; imagination, discrimination, inference, and other mental acts, and various desires such as "I shall do this," "I shall understand that," "I shall enjoy this," "I shall renounce that," and so on.

Question: What supports the rising thought waves?

Answer: The awareness of "I." If this I-consciousness disappears or is interrupted for a time, no thought waves can affect or control the mind at that time.

Question: This I-consciousness does not exist when one faints or falls into a deep sleep. Is nirvikalpa samadhi then something like that?

Answer: No, this I-consciousness remains within during fainting and deep sleep, but the instrument called the brain, through which the mind manifests I-consciousness, becomes inert or functionless for some time. But thoughts still continue to babble inside the mind. As the Master used to say: "Pigeons eat dried peas and keep them in their crops. They then coo through their inflated throats. You may think that a pigeon's throat is empty, but if you touch it, you can feel those peas rattling around in there."

Question: How shall I know that the I-consciousness remains that way

7. The results of samadhi — knowledge, enhancement of bliss, and God-vision.

when one has fainted or is in deep sleep?
Answer: You can know by observing the results. For example, when one has fainted or is in deep sleep, the heartbeat, pulse, circulation, and so on, do not pause.

The performance of all these physical functions depends on the I-consciousness. Moreover, although the external signs of fainting or deep sleep are somewhat similar to those of samadhi, when a person returns to the ordinary waking state, that person's knowledge and joyfulness remain the same as they were before. They neither increase nor decrease: the lust of the lustful remains the same, as does the anger of the angry, the greed of the greedy, and so on. But when people attain nirvikalpa samadhi, those worldly thoughts can no longer raise their heads. Such people achieve extraordinary knowledge and infinite bliss. Because they have had the direct experience of God, they no longer doubt that there is a hereafter or that God exists.

Question: All right. In nirvikalpa samadhi the Master's I-consciousness dissolved for some time. What happened next?

Answer: After his I-consciousness dissolved, he had the vision of the Divine for a short time. But not satisfied with that, he tried to remain in that state constantly.

Question: How was his mind affected by that effort, and what signs were manifested in his body?

8. The Master's visions and experiences during his six months in the nirvikalpa state.

Answer: Sometimes the I-consciousness was fully dissolved and signs of death appeared in his body, but he had an unobstructed vision of the Divine Mother within. Again, sometimes a little I-consciousness would appear, and some signs of life would return. At that time he would see the Divine Mother through the thin veil of his pure, clean, and transparent mind, which was like that due to a preponderance of sattva quality. Thus, sometimes I-consciousness dissolved entirely, as did the mind's thought waves, and the Divine Mother was completely visible. Again, sometimes I-consciousness would manifest to some extent, so minor modifications of the mind remained, and the Divine Mother was visible, although slightly obstructed. This happened again and again.

Question: How long did he struggle like this?

Answer: Over a period of six months.

Question: What do you mean? How did he survive? A human body cannot last for six months without food. Moreover, you say that although his I-consciousness did return from time to time during that period, the Master still did not have the amount of body-consciousness necessary in order to eat.

9. How his body survived when his I-consciousness had fully dissolved.

Answer: It is true that the Master's body should not have lasted, and moreover at that time he did not have even the slightest desire to maintain it. But his body survived because the Divine Mother wanted to do good to humanity by using it to manifest Her extraordinary spiritual power.

Question: Well, did the Divine Mother assume a form and force the Master to eat during those six months?

10. A yogi arrived who understood the Master's condition and fed him by force.

Answer: Yes, it was somewhat like that. At that time a monk came to Dakshineswar of his own accord. He completely understood that the Master's deathlike condition was due to his yogic sadhana and his experience of being united with God. This monk stayed at the Kali temple for six months. Every day he tried to bring the Master back to a little consciousness, even by striking his body with a stick. Whenever the monk saw that a little consciousness seemed to be returning, he would thrust a few morsels of food into the Master's mouth. We do not know why that monk was so eager to maintain the life of a complete stranger who was motionless and seemed to be dying, but we consider incidents such as this to be God's will. What else can we say? By the will and power of the Divine Mother the impossible became possible, and the Master's body was preserved.

Question: Well, what happened next?

11. The Divine Mother's command: "Remain in bhavamukha."

Answer: Then the Divine Mother — God, the Cosmic Consciousness Whose power manifests Itself as the universe, pervades all sentient and insentient beings, and appears as diverse names and forms — commanded the Master, "Remain in bhavamukha."

Question: What is bhavamukha?

12. Both Nirguna and Saguna aspects of God exist simultaneously in nondual Reality, along with the all-pervading Cosmic I-ness. This Cosmic I-ness is God, or the Divine Mother, and all the activities of the world are executed by It.

Answer: We shall explain it. To comprehend the state of bhavamukha, it is necessary to use one's imagination regarding the condition of the Master during that period. As we said earlier, at that time the Master's I-consciousness would sometimes disappear and then again manifest itself slightly. When his I-consciousness returned a little, the world did not appear to him as we see it. To him it was as if innumerable waves of ideas were rising, floating, playing, and dissolving within the Cosmic Mind. He felt that his own body, mind, and I-consciousness — as well as those of other beings — formed waves in that Cosmic Mind. The materialistic, learned fools of the West tried to use their intellects and scientific instruments to measure Cosmic Consciousness and Power, and concluded, "It is One, but it is insentient matter." But when the Master reached that state, he saw Its true nature and experienced It as the living, conscious, One without a second, the source of all will and action, and the infinite, gracious Divine Mother. He further observed that the same "One without a second" is divided within Itself as Nirguna [attributeless] and Saguna [with attributes]. For that reason the scriptures call it *svagata-bheda* [difference-in-itself], and a Cosmic I-ness, pervading everything from Brahma down to the lowest created being, is manifest within It.

Not only that, the Master saw innumerable waves of ideas arising in the Cosmic Mind because of that Cosmic I. And because ordinary people see the waves of ideas more or less in parts, their individual little "I's" perceive It to be the external world and its various objects, and thus they speak, move, and function in this world. The Master saw that the individual little "I's" exist and function by the power of the Cosmic I. Unable to see and comprehend the Cosmic I, the little "I's" are deluded and consider themselves to be endowed with free will and the power to act on their own. The scriptures call this spiritual blindness *avidya* [ignorance].

The Cosmic I-ness that exists between the Nirguna and the Saguna aspects of Brahman is called *bhavamukha*, and because of it, innumerable ideas arise in the Cosmic Mind. This Cosmic I is the "I" of God, or the Divine Mother. To describe this Cosmic I, the Vaishnava teachers of Bengal call It "Bhagavan Krishna, the embodiment of Pure Consciousness, where diversity and oneness coexist (*achintya-bheda-abheda*)."

> 13. This Cosmic I-ness is called *bhavamukha*, because all ideas in the world constantly arise from it.

When the Master's I-consciousness was completely dissolved, he dwelt in the Nirguna aspect of the Divine Mother that is beyond the limit of the Cosmic I. At that time he had no experience of that Cosmic I and Its innumerable waves of ideas, which we call the world. And when the Master's I-consciousness became slightly manifest, he saw the Saguna Cosmic I and Its waves of ideas to be connected with the Divine Mother's Nirguna aspect. Put another way, as soon as the Master ascended to the Nirguna state, his experience of the difference-in-itself (svagata-bheda) dissolved in the One without a second. And when he experienced the Saguna Cosmic I, he saw that what is Brahman is Shakti; what is the Nirguna is the Saguna; what is the Purusha is the Prakriti. The same snake is both motionless and moving. What is truly Nirguna is Saguna in play (*lila*). After he had experienced the full vision of Divine Mother, with Her Nirguna and Saguna aspects, he received the command: "Remain in bhavamukha." That is, "Do not dwell in the Nirguna state with I-consciousness dissolved completely. You are that Cosmic I from which all the ideas of the world continually evolve. Now that you can maintain direct awareness that God's will is your will and His action is your action, you must live in this world, doing good to humanity."

> 14. The Master's experience in the nirvikalpa state and his vision in the savikalpa, or bhavamukha, state.

Therefore, the meaning of remaining in bhavamukha is to see and experience completely, all the time, and in every condition: I am that Cosmic I, the "ripe I." When one reaches this state of bhavamukha, all such ideas as "I am the son of so-and-so," "I am the father of so-and-so," "I am a brahmin," or "I am a shudra," completely disappear from the mind, and one constantly realizes, "I am that all-pervading I." That is why the Master repeatedly told us: "Look, all these I's — 'I am the son of so-and-so; I am the father of so-and-so; I am a brahmin; I am a shudra; I am a pandit; I am rich; and so on — are unripe I's; they create bondage. You should shun those ideas and think: 'I am God's servant; I am His devotee; I am His child; I am a part of God.' Hold

> 15. The meaning of the command "Remain in bhavamukha."

these ideas firmly in your mind." Or he would say, "Tie the knowledge of nonduality in a corner of your cloth and then do as you please."

The reader may ask: "Then was the Master not a true nondualist? The

16. As an aspirant progresses spiritually, dualism, qualified nondualism, and nondualism appear one after another.

Master saw both the Nirguna and Saguna aspects of the Divine Mother, and he maintained that She encompassed these differences within Herself. It therefore seems that he did not accept Shankara's nondualism, in which the existence of the world is denied." No, it is not like that. The Master accepted all three philosophical systems: nondualism (advaita), qualified nondualism (vishishtadvaita), and dualism (dvaita). But he said that those three beliefs appear one after another, according to the evolutionary progress of the human mind. When at a certain stage the dualistic mood prevails, one feels that the other two philosophical beliefs are wrong. After one ascends to a higher stage of spiritual progress and reaches the state of qualified nondualism, one realizes that the eternal, attributeless Brahman has in play become manifest with attributes. Then not only does dualism become unreal, but one also does not believe nondualism to be true either. And when one reaches the culmination of spiritual progress through sadhana, one experiences only the Nirguna aspect of the Divine Mother and dwells in the nondualistic state. Then everything becomes One — I and you, jiva and the world, devotion and liberation, virtue and vice, merit and demerit.

In this context the Master referred to the realization of the wise Hanuman,

17. The wise Hanuman's testimony.

who was a glowing example of dasya bhava [the attitude of a devoted servant]. The Master said: "Once Ramachandra asked his devoted servant Hanuman: 'How do you look on Me? How do you think of and worship Me?' Hanuman replied: 'O Rama, while I identify myself with the body, I see that You are the Master and I am Your servant; You are to be served and I am Your attendant; You are to be worshipped and I am the worshipper. When I consider myself to be an individual self, consisting of the mind, the intellect, and the soul, I see that You are the Whole and I am a part. And when during samadhi I become one with the pure Atman devoid of attributes, I experience that You are I and I am You. You and I are the same; there is no difference.'"

The Master used to say: "One who is a true nondualist becomes silent.

18. The nondual state is beyond speech, thought, and imagination. As long as the body and mind function, one must accept both the *nitya* and the *lila* aspects of God.

Nonduality is not a subject for discussion. As soon as a person tries to talk about it or explain it, the knowledge of duality creeps in. When there is thought or imagination, there is duality within the mind, and one has not yet attained nondual knowledge. In this world only Brahman, or the Nirguna aspect of the Divine Mother, has not been defiled [like food that has been touched by the tongue]." In other words, no one has ever been able to say what Brahman is. Human language is inadequate for expressing It: Nirguna Brahman is beyond the mind and the intellect. How can It be spoken of or explained in words? When he referred to the nondual Truth, the Master said repeatedly, "Look, that is the last word in spiritual attainment." It is clear that, as the Master said: "As long as there are the ideas of 'I and you,' 'speaking and listening,' and other activities, one must accept in practice both aspects of Brahman — Nirguna and Saguna, nitya [the Absolute] and lila [the Relative]. You are thus for all practical purposes a qualified nondualist, although you may talk about nondualism." In this context the Master gave many examples.

He often said: "Take for example the ascending and descending order of the musical scale. You raise the pitch of your voice, following the notes of the scale, sa-re-ga-ma-pa-dha-ni-sa, and then lower it in descending order, sa-ni-dha-pa-ma-ga-re-sa. Similarly, after experiencing the nondual consciousness in samadhi, you descend to the lower plane and live with I-consciousness.

> 19. Some examples given by the Master: the ascending and descending notes of the musical scale, the bel fruit, the pith of a plantain tree, the layers of an onion.

"Again, take a bel fruit in your hand and decide which part — the shell, flesh, or seeds — is the bel. At first you discard the shell, considering it to be unimportant and so the seeds; then taking only the flesh, you say, 'This is the essence of the fruit, the real bel.' But you conclude: 'The flesh belongs to the bel, as do the shell and seeds. The shell, seeds, and flesh — all three parts together form the bel.' Likewise, after realizing God one concludes that the Absolute has become the phenomenal world and its living beings.

"Removing the outer sheaths of the plantain tree, you reach the inner pith and consider it to be the essence. Then you realize that the sheaths go with the pith, and the pith goes with the sheaths, and both together form the stem.

"It is like taking off the layers of an onion one by one; at last nothing is left. Similarly, while exploring the nature of 'I,' one finds that this is not the body, mind, or intellect. And one finds that finally there is no such thing as 'I'; everything is He, He, He — God only. It is like putting a fence around a section of the Ganges and saying, 'This is my Ganges.'"

Let us resume the main topic. When the Master dwelt in the state of bhavamukha, experiencing all-pervading I-ness, he saw the One manifesting Itself as many. Descending a few steps from the Nirguna aspect of the Divine Mother, he moved around in the realm of *vidya-maya* [the maya of knowledge]. But even in that state, the manifestation and realization of the One was so intense that the Master truly felt that he himself was

> 20. Although the bhavamukha state is a few steps below Nirguna Brahman, the experience of that nonduality persists. How one feels in that state: the Master's example.

doing, thinking, or saying whatever anyone else in this world was doing, thinking, or saying. Even a glimpse of that state is wonderful! One day at Cossipore when a man walked on some grass, the Master told us he was feeling a terrible pain, as if someone were walking on his chest. In fact, some bruises actually appeared on the Master's chest and he was restless with pain.

Coming down further from that state, when the Master dwelt in the realm of maya, he always maintained this attitude: "I am a servant of the Divine Mother; I am Her devotee; I am Her child; I am part of Her." Still further down is the realm of *avidya-maya* [the maya of ignorance] where lust, anger, greed, delusion, and so on are rampant.

21. Descending further from the realm of *vidya-maya*, one experiences "I am a servant, devotee, child, or part of God."

With great endeavour and constant practice the Master renounced this realm, and as a result his mind never again descended to that plane; the Divine Mother would not allow it. As the Master used to say, "One who depends solely on the Mother is not allowed to take a false step."

It is evident that after he attained nirvikalpa samadhi, the Master's little I, or unripe I, completely disappeared. And whatever I-ness was left saw itself as ever connected with the Cosmic I, or ripe I. Sometimes it would feel itself to be a limb or a part of the Cosmic I, and sometimes it would ascend gradually to the level of the Cosmic I and merge in It. The Master could therefore grasp all ideas within all minds, because all ideas of all minds in the world spring from that Cosmic I. Because the Master was always identified

22. After eradicating the "unripe I" the Master lived in the Cosmic "ripe I." In this state, his mood as a guru would become manifest. It is possible for the mood of a guru and the mood of humility to coexist in different states within the same person.

with that all-pervading I, he was able to know and understand any ideas that arose in the Cosmic Mind. In that exalted state, the Master's feeling "I am a part of God" would gradually vanish and the Cosmic I or the Divine Mother's "I" would become manifest through him, and he would act as a guru, possessing the power of bestowing grace and inflicting punishment. At that time the Master would not appear to be humbler than the humblest: His demeanour, behaviour with others, and other actions took a different form. Becoming like the mythical wish-fulfilling tree, he would ask a devotee, "What do you want?" as if he was ready to use his superhuman power to fulfill the devotee's desire immediately. Almost daily in Dakshineswar we witnessed the Master, endowed with that divine mood, bestowing his grace on special devotees. We saw this happen on 1 January 1886. Endowed with that mood, the Master touched the devotees present on that day and transmitted spiritual power to them or awakened their own dormant spirituality. It will not be out of place to narrate that wonderful story here.

It was 1 January 1886. It had been a little over two weeks since the devotees

23. The Master's power to awaken spirituality in others by a mere wish or touch: an example is the event of 1 January 1886.

brought the Master to a garden house in Cossipore (a suburb to the north of Calcutta) on the advice of Dr. Mahendralal Sarkar. The house belonged to Gopal Babu, the son-in-law of Rani Katyayani. Dr. Sarkar said that the air of an open garden area was purer than that of Calcutta and that the Master's throat cancer might abate if he could live in a place that had pure air. A few days after the Master arrived at the Cossipore garden, Dr. Rajendralal Datta came to visit him and prescribed Lycopodium 200, a homeopathic medicine that gave him a little relief. But since his arrival the Master had not descended even once from the upper floor to the ground floor, nor had he walked in the garden. But on that first day of January, he felt much better and in the afternoon expressed a desire to take a walk. So the devotees were excited.

At that time Swami Vivekananda was undergoing intense renunciation. He had given up worldly prosperity and was living with the Master, striving for God-realization by practising various kinds of sadhana according to his instructions. Vivekananda would kindle a sacred fire under a tree and spend nights in meditation, japa, devotional singing, and study. Junior Gopal, Kali, and some other devotees would help him in his sadhana by bringing the articles he needed; they also practised spiritual disciplines to the best of their abilities. Because the householder devotees were busy with their worldly affairs, they could not always stay with the Master. They would visit him at their convenience, and they made arrangements for food and other necessities for those who were continually engaged in the Master's personal service. Sometimes these householder devotees would stay at the Cossipore garden house for a day or so. As it was New Year's Day, a holiday, many devotees had come there.

At 3:00 p.m. the Master put on a red-bordered cloth, a shirt, a thick, red-bordered wrapper, a cap covering his ears, and a pair of slippers, and then descended the stairs slowly with Swami Adbhutananda. He closely examined the main hall, went out through the western door, and began to walk along the garden path. Seeing the Master walking, some householder devotees followed him joyfully. Vivekananda and other young disciples had observed a vigil the night before, so they were asleep in the small room next to the main hall on the ground floor. When Adbhutananda saw that the devotees were accompanying the Master to the south side of the pond in front of the hall, he thought it unnecessary to go further. He returned to the house and called for another young disciple.[2] Both then busied themselves in sweeping and cleaning the Master's room upstairs and in airing his bedding and clothing in the sunshine.

---

2. The author, Swami Saradananda. — *Translator*

Among the householder devotees, Girish had the most intense love for God. Once the Master highly praised his overwhelming faith and told the other devotees: "Girish has one hundred and twenty-five percent faith! Hereafter, people will be amazed by seeing his transformation." Driven by faith and devotion, Girish looked on the Master veritably as God, who had graciously become incarnate to release human beings from bondage. Although the Master had forbidden him to do so, he publicly expressed his belief to all. On that day Girish was present in the garden, talking to Ram and other devotees under a mango tree.

The Master, accompanied by devotees, walked along the broad garden path and then slowly moved towards the gate. When he was halfway along the path, he noticed Ram and Girish sitting in the shade of the mango tree. Addressing Girish, the Master said, "Girish, what have you found (in me) that makes you say all these things (I am an avatar, and so on) to everyone, wherever you go?"

Girish's faith remained unshaken although he had been asked this question so abruptly. Hurriedly he got up, went to the path, and knelt down at the feet of the Master. Saluting him with folded hands, Girish responded in a voice choking with emotion: "What more can I say of Him? Even the sages Vyasa and Valmiki could find no words to measure His glory!"

As the Master listened to those wonderful words of faith, the hairs on his body stood on end, his mind ascended to a higher plane, and he went into samadhi. Seeing the Master's face radiant with divine ecstasy, Girish joyfully shouted, "Jai Ramakrishna! Jai Ramakrishna!" [Victory to Ramakrishna!] and took the dust of his feet again and again.

Meanwhile, the Master came down to a semiecstatic state, looked at the assembled devotees with a smile, and said: "What more need I tell you? May you all be illumined!" When they heard that benediction, the devotees were possessed with an overwhelming fervour and they cried repeatedly, "Jai Ramakrishna!" Then some bowed down to him, some showered him with flowers, and some touched his feet. As soon as the first person stood up after touching his feet, the Master, still in that semiecstatic state, touched the devotee's chest and passing his hand upward, said, "Be illumined!" When the second person bowed down and stood up, he did the same thing, and so he did to the third and the fourth. Thus, he touched nearly all the assembled devotees one after another.

The Master's wonderful divine touch generated an incredible spiritual mood in the mind of each devotee. Some began to laugh, some to weep, some to meditate, and some out of overflowing joy began to loudly call for others to come and receive the unbounded grace of the merciful Master. Hearing the commotion and ecstatic shouting, some of the Master's young disciples arose from sleep and others threw aside their work. Rushing to the spot, they saw devotees behaving like madmen, encircling the Master on the garden path. Immediately they realized that the Master was bestowing grace on all, enacting the same divine play that he had performed in Dakshineswar, when out of ecstasy he had blessed a few special devotees. But as soon as those young disciples arrived, the Master's ecstatic mood disappeared, and he returned to a normal state.

Some of the householder devotees were later interviewed about their experiences at that time. One person became as intoxicated and joyful as if he had drunk *bhang* [a beverage of pulped marijuana]. Another man had a vivid vision: When he closed his eyes, he saw the divine

> 24. At the Master's divine touch, devotees had visions and realizations.

form upon which he had previously meditated daily, but that he had never been able to visualize. Yet another devotee felt a mysterious substance or force creeping upward within his body, filling him with bliss. When another person closed his eyes, he saw a light that he had never seen before and felt tremendous bliss. It was evident that each person's vision or experience was different, but the feeling of being flooded with an extraordinary divine bliss was common to all. Moreover, each of them believed that the Master's superhuman power, transmitted through touch, had caused that wonderful realization and transformation.

There were only two of the assembled devotees whom the Master did not touch, saying to them, "Not now." On that blissful occasion they considered themselves unfortunate and felt dejected.[3] There was never any certainty as to

> 25. No one knew when or whom the Master would graciously touch.

when that divine power would manifest itself through the Master and upon whom it would bestow grace. It is doubtful whether the Master himself knew or understood this when he was in his normal state.

So it is evident that the Master became a great instrument of the Cosmic I, or the Divine Mother, only because he could completely shun the unripe I, or limited I. And it is because he totally renounced that unripe I and became truly humbler than the humblest that the guru or the world

> 26. The scriptures testify that power of the guru manifests itself after the raw ego ceases to exist.

teacher aspect of the Divine Mother was manifest wonderfully through him. The religious history of the world bears eternal witness to the fact that it is by dissolving the limited I-ness that the divine mood or power of the guru is manifest in the lives of all avatars in all religions.

From time immemorial we have heard that one cannot have a true spiritual experience or God-realization if one considers the guru to be human. With or without faith we recite this hymn to the guru who gives initiation with a mantra: "The guru is Brahma; the guru is Vishnu; the guru is Shiva." But under the spell of foreign

> 27. The power of the guru is not human: It is the Divine Mother's power possessing one's body and mind.

---

3. Later, one day the Master also blessed those two with his touch.

education, many [Indians] have given up their traditional education and religious culture. They consider it to be a great sin to repeat that hymn, and they argue in defense of their views. For who can understand that although the power of the guru manifests itself through certain personalities, it is not within the realm of human knowledge. Who can then comprehend that just as the Divine Mother provides air, water, food, and other necessities to maintain the bodies of all beings, so She fully manifests Her power in a pure, illumined, and egoless human being in order to bestow peace and remove the sufferings of humans who are tormented by the terrible bonds of maya? Who can then realize that a person becomes an instrument to manifest that power in so far as that person is able to renounce the ego or the unripe I? Because that divine power manifests itself to a very negligible extent in ordinary human minds, we cannot recognize or understand much of it. Fortunately, when a person witnesses the wonderful play of that divine power in Krishna, Buddha, Chaitanya, Shankara, Jesus, and other avatars of the past, and Ramakrishna in the present age, he or she realizes wholeheartedly that the manifestation of that divine power belongs not to a human being but to God alone. Only then do the delusions and impurities of a bound, lost seeker cease to exist, and that person bursts forth declaring, "O guru, you are not a human being — you are He!"

The exalted power by which the Divine Mother removes ignorance and delusion from human minds is called *guru-bhava* or *guru-shakti*, the nature or power of the guru. The scriptures declare this divine power to be the guru and advise human beings to have faith in it and to offer wholehearted reverence and devotion to it. But a worldly-minded person who has just started to learn to practise devotion and respect cannot comprehend or love an incorporeal power; so the scriptures advise paying respect to the human guru who gives initiation in spiritual life. There are those who say that they are ready to love and respect the power itself but question why they should love and respect the human being through whom that power is manifest. That power does not belong to him or her.

28. The compassionate Lord removes ignorance and delusion from human minds through the divine power of the guru; this is why devotion to the guru and to God are the same.

Our answer to such people is: "Brothers, it is fine if you can respect that divine power. But be careful that you are not being cheated by your deceptive mind. Actually, you have never seen that power and a person endowed with that power existing separately. It is like fire: Fire and its power to burn cannot be separated. Therefore, we do not know how you can accept one and pay love and respect to it but reject the other!" When a person loves someone, an ordinary thing that the beloved has used becomes precious to the lover. Even used clothing or a flower touched by the beloved become sacred to the lover. The very ground on which the beloved treads is extremely precious and dear to the lover. Is it then necessary to explain why a devotee should love and respect the human guru? It is God who dwells in the guru's body, accepts a devotee's worship, and bestows grace on that devotee. Only those who do not understand this mystery of the guru can speak in that way. Those who have true devotion to the power of the guru will definitely develop love and respect for the guru's human form, which is the vessel for that divine power.

The Master explained this subject by telling us the following example of

| 29. The Master's advice on devotion to the guru: the story of Vibhishana. |

Vibhishana's devotion: "Once, long after Rama-chandra passed away, a man's boat sank into the ocean and the big waves tossed him onto the coast of Sri Lanka. The immortal Vibhishana rules eternally in Sri Lanka. When news of the castaway reached his court, the mouths of many rakshashas [demonic beings] began to water as they heard of the arrival of a dainty morsel — a human body. But this news brought about a wonderful mood in the mind of King Vibhishana. With tearful eyes and his voice choking with emotion, he said repeatedly, 'What great fortune!' The rakshashas were amazed — they could not understand his devotion. Then Vibhishana explained to them: 'My Lord Ramachandra came to Sri Lanka as a human being and blessed me. What great fortune that today, after such a long time, I shall see another human form! It seems to me that Ramachandra himself has returned.' Speaking thus, King Vibhishana went to the coast, accompanied by his court-iers and friends, and with great love and reverence brought that man to the palace. He placed the man on his throne, and he and his family served and worshipped him like devoted servants. Vibhishana kept him in Sri Lanka for some time, presented him with money and various jewels, and then sent him back home with attendants, seeing him off with tearful eyes."

After telling this story, the Master continued: "This happens at the onset of

| 30. True devotion causes even trifling things to stir divine impulses. Saying, "Drums are made from this clay!" Chaitanya went into ecstasy. |

true devotion. Even from a trifling thing a person feels a divine impulse and becomes absorbed in ecstasy. Have you not heard that Chaitanya went into ecstasy, saying, 'Drums are made from this clay?' Once, while passing through a village, he heard that its people maintained themselves by making and selling the earthen drums that were played during kirtan. At this, he exclaimed, 'Drums are made from this clay!' As he said that he went into ecstasy and lost outer consciousness. Inspiration arose from this chain of association: 'Drums are made from this clay. Hari's name is sung when these drums are played. That Hari is the Life in all — more beautiful than the most beautiful.' Recollecting all these thoughts, Chaitanya's mind became absorbed in Hari. When a man has this kind of devotion to his guru, he is inspired by seeing the relatives of the guru. Out of excitement he even bows down to the people of the guru's native village, takes the dust of their feet, and serves them food. When one reaches this state one never finds any shortcoming in the guru. Only then can one say, 'Though my guru visits the tavern, still to me he is the holy Nityananda.'[4] Every human being has good and bad qualities. But when a man has this kind of exuberant devotion, he does not see human beings as human, but as God. It is like a person with jaundice who sees everything with a yellow hue. The devotee's intense devotion then reveals that God is everything — He has become the guru, father, mother, man, cow, and sentient and insentient objects."

Once in Dakshineswar a proud, yet sincere, young devotee[5] was raising

| 31. The story of Arjuna's devotion to his guru. |

objections to what the Master was telling him. The Master told him three or four times, but still he continued arguing. The Master then gave him a sweet scolding, saying: "What sort of man are you? I am telling you, yet you do not accept my words!" Immediately the young man was touched by the Master's love. He said: "Of course, I accept whatever you say. It was for the sake of argument that I spoke that way."

Delighted, the Master said with a smile: "Do you know what true devotion to the guru is? Whatever the guru says, the disciple perceives. Arjuna had this kind of devotion. Once while they were riding in a chariot, Krishna said to Arjuna, 'Look, friend, what a beautiful flock of pigeons is flying!' Seeing it Arjuna immediately said, 'Yes, friend, those pigeons are beautiful!' The next moment Krishna looked again and said, 'No, friend, they are not pigeons.' Arjuna also looked and said, 'That is correct, friend, they are not pigeons.' Now try to understand this: Arjuna was intensely devoted to truth. He did not say that just to flatter Krishna or to please him. But he had so much faith in and respect for the words of Krishna that he actually saw whatever Krishna described."

According to the scriptures, a true guru is one who is capable of removing

| 32. As manifestations of God's power, all gurus are the same. But one should have love, faith, and steadfast devotion for one's own guru: Hanuman's remark. |

the darkness of ignorance. We have ascertained that the guru is endowed with this special divine power. Now it must be admitted that gurus are not many but one. Although the power of God is manifest in different vessels, or bodies, your guru and my guru are not different — the power they share is the same. The story of Ekalavya from the Mahabharata illustrates this: When Drona refused to accept him as his disciple, Ekalavya practised archery before the clay image of Drona, whom he regarded as his teacher, and became an expert archer. Although this fact seems reasonable, one must undertake spiritual practices in order to fully comprehend it. One may understand it, but as long as one's body-consciousness remains, one has no alternative other than to worship the human guru through whose body the divine power is

4. God, the embodiment of eternal bliss.
5. Vaikuntha Nath Sanyal.

bestowing grace. To illustrate this, the Master placed before us the glowing example of Hanuman's steadfast devotion.

He said: "Once during the war in Sri Lanka, Ramachandra and Lakshmana were bound by the great hero Meghanad with a noose made of serpents. To free himself and his brother, Ramachandra summoned Garuda, the eternal enemy of snakes. As soon as the snakes saw Garuda, they were frightened and fled in all directions. Pleased with his devotee, Ramachandra appeared before Garuda in the form of Vishnu, Garuda's beloved Chosen Deity, and thus convinced him that Vishnu had truly incarnated as Rama. But Hanuman did not like seeing Ramachandra in the form of Vishnu; he could only think of how soon Ramachandra would resume his own form. Ramachandra immediately understood Hanuman's feeling. After seeing Garuda off, he again assumed the form of Rama and asked Hanuman: 'My child, why did your mood change upon seeing me in the form of Vishnu? You are endowed with supreme knowledge. You know very well that He who is Rama is also Vishnu.' To this, Hanuman humbly replied: 'It is true that the same supreme Self has assumed both forms and therefore there is no difference between Vishnu and Rama. But nonetheless I always want to see the lotus-eyed Rama, as he is my all in all. It is through that form that I was blessed with the vision of God.'"

The power of the guru is a special power of the Divine Mother; this power

33. This power of the guru is dormant in all human beings.

is either dormant or manifest in each human mind. A spiritual aspirant who is devoted to the guru can therefore reach such a high state that this power manifests within him or her also and begins to explain many hidden truths of spirituality. At that time the aspirant no longer needs anyone else to resolve doubts and problems regarding spiritual matters. Krishna said to Arjuna in the Gita (2:52): "When your mind has crossed the slough of delusion, you will achieve indifference regarding things already heard and things yet to be heard." The aspirant ultimately attains this state.

Referring to this state, the Master said: "Finally, the mind becomes the

34. The Master said: "Finally, the mind becomes the guru."

guru or acts as a guru. The human guru imparts the mantra to the ear, and the divine guru transmits the mantra to the soul." But there is a gulf of difference between that exalted mind and this ordinary mind. In that state the mind is pure and endowed with sattva quality; it has now become an instrument for manifesting God's divine power. But when the mind is turned away from God, it longs to be engrossed in lust, greed, anger, and so on.

The Master used to say: "The guru is like a female companion to Radha.

35. "The guru is like a female companion."

As there is no end to her love-errands until her friend Radha is united with Krishna, so there is no rest for the guru until the spiritual aspirant is united with God. Thus the great guru accompanies the sincere devotee to higher and higher realms of spirituality and finally presents the devotee to the Chosen Deity, saying, 'My child, look there!' then immediately disappears."

One day when a devotee heard the Master saying this, he realized that someday separation from the guru would be inevitable. So with a sorrowful heart, he asked, "Sir, where does the guru go then?" The Master replied: "The guru merges into the *Ishta* [Chosen Deity]. The guru, Krishna, and the devotee — these three are one, and the One is manifest as three."

36. "Finally, the guru merges into the Ishta: the guru, Krishna, and the devotee — these three are one, and the One manifests as three."

Chapter 4

Early *M*anifestations of His Power as a Guru

Fools disregard Me when I assume a human form; for they are unaware of My higher nature as the Supreme Lord of all beings. — GITA 9:11

ONE CAN SEE THE MANIFESTATION OF THE POWER as a guru in the Master's life from

| 1. The Master's power as a guru becomes manifest in childhood. |

his very childhood, but it became fully developed in his youth after he attained nirvikalpa samadhi. Let no one think that we are exaggerating in order to glorify Sri Ramakrishna when we say that his power as a guru became apparent during his childhood. No one who impartially studies the Master's life will have any need to exaggerate. Those people who critically analyze the events of the Master's wonderfully unique life will ultimately find their power of judgement baffled, stupefied, and spellbound. We also had no lack of doubts, and we think that at present no one would dare to test and investigate the Master as we did. It often happened that many of us who doubted the Master and challenged him were defeated, and we had to hang our heads in shame. We have already narrated some examples earlier in this book (see III.2.43,56), and we will provide more later. The reader will then be able to understand this better.

In connection with the lives of the ever-free ishwarakotis, the Master

| 2. "First fruit and then flower" — all avatars share this special trait. |

always used this expression: "They are like gourds and pumpkins, which grow fruits first and then flowers." By this he meant that whatever spiritual disciplines those great souls practise for perfection, they do so to make aspirants understand that they must put forth similar efforts in order to achieve the same

459

results. When one studies the lives of those great ones, it becomes evident that although they appear to exert intense efforts to achieve supreme knowledge, their actions show that they are endowed with that knowledge throughout their lives. From their childhood onward these ishwarakotis behave like illumined souls in every respect. It is as if they acquired the result of that knowledge at their very births. When this is true regarding ever-free souls, what can we say of avatars or divine incarnations?

The fact that such knowledge is manifest throughout the lives of avatars is recorded in the scriptures in every age and in all countries. The avatars of different ages behave in similar ways. For example, we find in the lives of Jesus, Chaitanya, and Ramakrishna that they transmitted spirituality to others with a touch. We come across many similar stories in their lives. For example, some virtuous persons were aware of their advent in a supernatural way; their power as a guru was manifest in them during their childhood; they knew from their early life onward that out of compassion they had taken a human form to demonstrate a particular path to uplift ordinary people. It is therefore not surprising to hear that the power of the guru appeared in the Master's life during his childhood. It is a mistake to think that because such a thing is impossible for ordinary people, it is not possible for avatars either. Avatars are simply in a class by themselves.

The first vivid display of the Master's power as a guru occurred in his birthplace at Kamarpukur after he had been invested with the sacred thread. He would have been nine or ten years old at the time. The celebrated pandits in that part of the country were invited to a shrāddha ceremony at the home of the Lahas, the village landlords. As is usual when many pandits gather in one place, they started debating vociferously. When after prolonged discussion the pandits could not come to a conclusion on a particular scriptural point, the boy Gadadhar asked a pandit whom he knew, "Can't the problem be solved in this way?" Then he stated a solution.

3. The first manifestation of the power as a guru in the Master's life: he discusses the scriptures during a gathering of pandits at the Lahas' house in Kamarpukur.

Driven by curiosity, many village boys attended the meeting, but they hardly understood any of the pandits' noisy and animated debate. Some boys giggled, considering it to be a joke; some were disgusted and loudly mimicked the excited gestures of the pandits; and some remained indifferent and busied themselves in their play. So at first this pandit was amazed when he realized that this wonderful boy had patiently listened to the various arguments, had understood everything, and had now reached a sensible conclusion. Then he told his friends what Gadadhar had said, and they all agreed it was the only solution to the dispute. They inquired whose keen intellect had first discovered such a wonderful solution. When they learned that it was the boy Gadadhar, some looked at him in awe and considered him to be endowed with divine powers; others joyously took him on their laps and blessed him.

This subject must be elaborated upon. A similar incident, concerning

| 4. A similar event happened in Jesus' life at Jehovah's temple in Jerusalem. |

Jesus Christ, is recorded in the Bible.[1] This divine incarnation was then twelve years old. At that time he was taken by his poor and pious parents, Joseph and Mary, on a pilgrimage with others from their native village of Nazareth to the province of Galilee to offer worship at the famous temple of Jehovah in Jerusalem. This holy place of the Jews was like any of the pilgrim centres of the Hindus. Devout aspirants considered themselves blessed to see the holy presence of Jehovah in a golden casket and to worship the deity with light and incense on an altar, by offering flowers, fruits, and sweets and by sacrificing animals and birds, such as sheep and pigeons. Even today pigeons and other birds are sacrificed to Hindu deities in holy places such as Kamakhya and Vindhyachal.

Joseph and Mary completed their visit, worship, and sacrifice as was

| 5. Jewish pilgrimage in those days. |

customary and then started on the return journey to their village with their companions. At that time the condition of the pilgrims who came from different countries to visit Jerusalem was to some extent similar to those who visited Puri and other holy places on foot before the railways were laid in India. The [Jewish] pilgrims would walk along the same kind of long road, which was sparsely shaded by beautiful trees and had wells and ponds by the roadside. On the way there were rest houses, inns, and plenty of guesthouses for the pilgrims. During this exhausting journey a priest would act as leader and guide. The pilgrims would buy rice, lentils, flour, and other necessities from roadside grocery shops. The road was dusty and swarms of mosquitoes rendered a friendly service by keeping them from rest and sleep so they might not forget their spiritual fervour. In certain notorious areas the pilgrims travelled in groups to protect themselves from thieves and robbers. And finally, the pilgrims depended on God alone and had deep devotion.

While they were on their way home, Joseph and Mary could not find Jesus

| 6. Jesus explains the scriptures in Jehovah's temple. |

in their group. At first they thought he was perhaps following the party with other pilgrim boys. But when they could not find Jesus after proceeding quite a distance, they became worried. They looked everywhere but could not locate him. Anxious, they returned to Jerusalem and searched in various places but still could not find him. Finally they entered the Jehovah temple and found the boy Jesus discussing scriptures with scholars, enchanting them all by elucidating complicated scriptural questions that had confounded those pandits.

---

1. Luke 2:42

Professor Max Müller has cast doubt upon the authenticity of the previ-

7. Max Müller's opinion is refuted.

ously mentioned incident that occurred in the early life of Ramakrishna. In his book, *Ramakrishna: His Life and Sayings*, he compared it to the event in Jesus' life described above. Not only that, he even made the uncharitable remark that those disciples of Sri Ramakrishna who knew English intentionally incorporated Jesus' boyhood story into their Master's biography in order to glorify their guru. With all due respect to Professor Müller's keen intelligence, we must vigorously disagree with him. Some elderly villagers of Kamarpukur told us about the incident that occurred in the Master's boyhood, and the Master himself narrated it to some of us from time to time. It is best that we leave the matter here.

While studying the life of the Master, one may ask why he married. He

8. Why did the Master marry? Was it at the request of his relatives? No.

had no intention of having any physical relationship with his wife, so why then did he marry? It is in fact difficult to ascertain the reason. If one believes that his relatives forced him to marry in his youth, when thoughts of God were almost driving him mad, we reply that it is nonsense to entertain such an idea. From his childhood onward no one could force him to do even a small thing against his will. Moreover, once he resolved to do anything, he accomplished it by some means or other. For instance, during his sacred thread ceremony, he first took alms from Dhani, a woman of the low-status blacksmith caste because he had promised her previously that he would do so (see I.7.8). The social rules and customs of Kamarpukur Village were not as loose as they were in Calcutta, where one could do as one liked. The Master's parents were extremely orthodox and family tradition dictated that one must first receive alms from a brahmin woman. The entire family was against Gadadhar's intention to accept alms from a blacksmith woman instead of a brahmin. In spite of all that, Gadadhar insisted that Dhani be his first alms-giver. This is not a matter of small surprise. Every event of his life demonstrates that the Master's wishes and words prevailed over the wills and desires of others. How then can anyone think that such an important event of his life, his marriage, took place at the desire and request of his relatives?

Again, one may ask why it is necessary to believe that from his very child-

9. Was his marriage for enjoyment? No.

hood Sri Ramakrishna had planned to renounce everything for love of God. One could say instead that in the beginning he had a desire for worldly enjoyment through marriage like ordinary human beings, but as soon as he reached youth, the course of his mind suddenly underwent a radical change. Intense renunciation of the world and a violent tempest of longing for God overwhelmed him in such a way that his old desires disappeared forever. If his marriage had taken place before that storm of renunciation and longing, then there would be no further argument.

Our answer is this: Although this opposite view seems reasonable, there are some irrefutable objections. First, when the Master married he was twenty-four years old, and a violent storm of renunciation was already raging within him. And because throughout his life he was reluctant to cause trouble to anybody, it cannot be true that he entered into wedlock without consid-

> 10. To those who were searching for his bride, the Master said: "Go and see. The bride is marked with a straw." His marriage was thus voluntary.

ering the consequences, knowing very well that it would bring lifelong misery to someone's daughter. Second, the more we analyze it, the more we understand that no event in the Master's life was performed without a purpose. Third, it is definite that the Master married voluntarily. He told Hriday and other family members who were searching for a bride that it was preordained that he would marry the daughter of Ramchandra Mukhopadhyay of Jayrambati. The reader may wonder at this, or disbelieve it and remark: "These are all incredible, fanciful stories! Can anyone accept them in this twentieth century?" We must reply: "Whether you believe it or not, it actually happened. Many are still alive [in 1911] who can testify to these facts. Why don't you find out for yourself?" When his relatives could not find a suitable bride after much searching, the Master told them to go to a particular village [Jayrambati] and see that a certain person's [Ramchandra's] "daughter is marked with a straw."[2] So it is clear that the Master knew he would be married, where the ceremony would take place, and whose daughter would become his bride. He never objected. Of course, he became aware of all these details while in ecstasy.

What then was the purpose of the Master's marriage? A scholarly reader, perhaps irritated, might say: "How silly you are! Why do you make such a big fuss about this simple thing? One should study the scriptures before

> 11. Did the Master marry because of his *prarabdha karma*? No.

venturing to write the life stories of great souls. The scriptures say that when a person experiences God or attains full knowledge of Brahman, his *sanchita karma* [actions accumulated in the past] and *agami karma* [actions acquired in this life that will have results in the future] are all wiped out. But even after attaining this knowledge, such a person must experience the results of *prarabdha karma* [actions already bearing results] in this life. Suppose there are some arrows in a quiver tied to the back of a hunter. He has shot one arrow at a bird in a tree, has taken another in his hand, and is ready to release it. Just then intense renunciation dawns in his mind, and he resolves to forswear violence. He throws away the arrow in his hand and

---

2. It is customary in the villages of Bengal for a farmer to offer to God his best fruit or cucumber, and so on. He marks it by twisting a straw around its stem so that no one will pluck it by mistake. The Master made that remark with this custom in mind. He meant that it was predetermined that he should marry such a person's daughter: That girl had been reserved by Providence to be his bride.

those in the quiver on his back. But can he bring back the arrow that has already been shot at the bird? The arrows on his back are like the actions accumulated in his past lives (sanchita), and the arrow in his hand represents future actions, whose results are yet to come (agami). Knowledge of Brahman destroys both those types of actions. The arrow that has already been released is like his prarabdha karma: He will have to experience its results. It is inevitable that even great souls like Sri Ramakrishna must experience the results of prarabdha karma. They know and understand the kinds of events that will happen according to their prarabdha karma. So it is no wonder that Sri Ramakrishna indicated who would be his bride and where his marriage would take place."

We say in reply: Well, we may not be very proficient in knowledge of the

12. An illumined soul is free to experience prarabdha karma or not.

scriptures, but as far as we know, a true jnani (knower of Brahman) is not forced to experience the results of prarabdha karma. Such a person has forever dedicated his or her mind, which experiences happiness and misery, to God. So how could such a mind experience happiness and misery anymore? If you contend that such a person's body experiences the results of prarabdha karma, how could this be possible? Only when that person wishes to keep a little ego-consciousness for a specific purpose, such as doing good to others, does he or she become conscious of the body and mind. At the same time he or she experiences the results of prarabdha karma. Therefore, illumined souls attain the power to experience or renounce prarabdha karma at will. That is why they are called "conquerors of the world," "conquerors of death," "omniscient," and so on.

Moreover, if we accept Sri Ramakrishna's own experience, we cannot call

13. What can be said of the Master? He himself said: "He who was Rama and Krishna is now Ramakrishna."

him a jnani or classify him in that group. We have heard him say again and again, "He who was Rama and Krishna is verily now Ramakrishna." In other words, He who was born previously as Rama and then as Krishna is present in the form of Sri Ramakrishna and is manifesting his divine play. If one believes the Master's words, one must admit that he was an incarnation of God, by nature ever-pure, ever-illumined, and ever-free. And if this is admitted, one cannot maintain that he was under the control of prarabdha or of any other kind of karma. So we come to a different logical conclusion about the Master's marriage, which we shall narrate here.

The Master would sometimes joke when the topic of his marriage was

14. The Master jokes about his marriage.

raised. It was so sweet! In Dakshineswar one day while the Master was having lunch, Balaram Basu and some other devotees present were discussing various subjects with him. On that day the Holy Mother had left for Kamarpukur for a few months to attend Ramlal's marriage ceremony.

The Master (*pointing to Balaram*): "Well, can you tell me why I married? What is the purpose of having a wife? I cannot even take care of the cloth on my body — it just drops off. Why then do I have a wife?"

Balaram smiled and kept quiet.

The Master: "Oh, I understand (*taking a little curry from the plate and showing it to Balaram*) — for this reason I married. Otherwise, who else would cook for me with such care? (*Balaram and the other devotees laughed.*) Truly speaking, who else would look after my food? They all left today — (*seeing that the devotees did not understand who had left*) along with Ramlal's aunt. Ramlal is going to be married, so everyone left for Kamarpukur today. I watched her departure impassively. It was truly as if someone else had left. Then I grew anxious when I thought about who would cook for me. You see, some kinds of food do not agree with my stomach, nor am I always conscious enough to eat. She (*the Holy Mother*) knows what kind of food suits me and makes various preparations accordingly. So I asked myself, who will cook for me?"

Once in Dakshineswar, when the Master raised the topic of his marriage,

15. Ordinary teachers marry to fulfill ten kinds of sacraments. Did the Master marry for that reason? No.

he said: "Do you know why one should be married? There are ten kinds of sacraments for a brahmin's body; marriage is one of them. Only after undergoing those ten kinds of sacraments can one become a religious teacher." Again sometimes he would say: "One who aspires to become a paramahamsa, or a knower of Brahman, must go through all the experiences of life from those of scavengers and sweepers to those of kings and emperors. Otherwise, how can a person develop true renunciation? Whatever you have not seen or enjoyed, your mind will hanker after and be restless. Do you understand? Have you not seen how the players move their checkers all over the squares of the checkerboard till they reach home? It is similar to that."

Although the Master thus indicated the reason why ordinary teachers of

16. The purpose of a Hindu marriage is to attain renunciation through enjoyment, following scriptural laws.

religion marry, we shall now explain our understanding of the special purpose of his marriage. The scriptures teach us at every step that wedlock is not meant for enjoyment only. We are constantly reminded that Hindu marriage has as its goal following the edict to maintain God's creation and begetting virtuous children, thereby benefiting society. Do the Hindu scriptures then maintain that there should be no self-interest in marriage? No, they say no such absurd thing. By observing the weakness of human nature, the authors of the Hindu scriptures understood that ordinary people care for nothing but themselves and undertake nothing without calculating their own profit and loss. Even though the ancient sages understood this completely, they boldly stated the goal of marriage. They realized that if peoples' self-interests were strongly tied to a high ideal, this would be beneficial to them. Otherwise they would suffer endlessly, entangled in the bondage of repeated birth and death.

Forgetting their ever-free divine nature, human beings run after external

17. Enjoyment through discrimination eventually brings the knowledge that "pleasure comes wearing a crown of thorns."

sense objects, considering them to be sweet and delightful! How many people are capable of understanding that every pleasure in this world is eternally connected with pain, and that if one wants to enjoy pleasure, one must also accept pain? Swami Vivekananda used to say, "Pleasure comes to people wearing a crown of thorns on its head." When people become busy with pleasant things, they have no time to consider that they are wearing a crown of thorns on their heads and that if they embrace pleasure, eventually they will have to endure pain. So the scriptures remind them, saying: "Listen, why do you think that attaining pleasure is the goal of your life? You cannot have pleasure without accepting pain. Why not strive to reach a higher plane, considering both pleasure and pain to be your teachers? The goal of your life is to be free from both of them forever." So it is clear that the authors of the scriptures meant to teach married people to enjoy through discrimination. Moreover, after experiencing the inevitable pleasures and pains of life and developing dispassion for the apparent momentary pleasures of the world, such people should wholeheartedly love God and move forward earnestly to have His vision, knowing Him to be their all in all.

If the mind considers the positives and negatives of a particular sense

18. The Master's advice on shunning sense pleasures through discrimination.

object before enjoying it, the mind will definitely give it up. That is why the Master said: "Listen, one should discriminate between the real and the unreal. Always endowed with discrimination, one should talk to one's mind in this manner: 'You, mind, are eager to enjoy various objects — to eat this thing, to put on that thing, and so on. You see, potatoes, vegetables, rice, lentils, and so on are produced from five elements,[3] and again sandesh, rasagolla, and other delicious sweets are made from the same. The same five elements that made a beautiful female body, consisting of bones, flesh, blood, and marrow, made your body as well — and also all bodies of men, cows, goats, sheep, and so on. Why do you crave such things and even die for them? They cannot help you to attain God.' If the mind is still not convinced, enjoy something a couple of times with discrimination, and then renounce it. For example, your mind is inordinately desirous of eating rasagolla, and you are helpless to bring it under control. All your powers of discrimination are ineffective. So buy some rasagollas, put them into your mouth, and tell your mind while you are chewing them: 'Mind, this is called "rasagolla." It consists of modifications of the five elements, the

3. Ether, air, fire, water, and earth. — *Translator*

same as potatoes and vegetables. When it is eaten, the body transforms it into blood, flesh, faeces, and urine. It is sweet as long as it is in the mouth, but after it goes down the throat, you won't remember its taste. And if you eat too much, you will be sick. Still you are so greedy for it! Shame on you! Fie on you! Now you have eaten rasagolla; don't hanker after it anymore.' (*Pointing to the would-be monastics*:) One should use this process of discrimination when enjoying ordinary things, and then renounce them. But this method does not apply to serious things; one becomes entangled as soon as one indulges in them. That is why one should drive serious worldly desires away from the mind by using discrimination and seeing the fault in them."

Although the scriptures have described the high ideal of marriage, how

19. The present national degeneration of India is due to not observing the rule of continence in married life.

many people remember or follow it at present? How many married people make themselves and society blessed by sincerely practising continence? How many wives inspire their husbands to dedicate themselves to the well being of all, let alone to realize God? How many husbands teach their wives that "renunciation is the goal of human life" after realizing this themselves? O India! Just try to reflect upon this and see how hedonistic Western materialism has slowly penetrated into your bone and marrow and made you a spineless animal! That is why Sri Ramakrishna, pointing to the defects in modern married life, said to his would-be monastic disciples: "Look, if it is wrong to make enjoyment the all in all or the goal of life, then do you think that simply offering a few flowers during the marriage ceremony will make it pure or remove all blemishes from it?" In fact, it is doubtful that the indulgence of sensual appetites in married life was ever so excessive in India as it is now. Nowadays we have almost forgotten that apart from sense gratification there is a very sacred and lofty purpose to marriage. That is why, day by day, we are reduced to a state worse than that of animals! Sri Ramakrishna married in order to eradicate the bestial nature of the modern men and women of India. Like all other activities of his life, the act of marriage was performed to benefit humanity.

The Master used to say: "Whatever is done here (*meaning by him*) is meant

20. The Master married to revive ideal marriage by demonstrating it himself.

for you all. Look, if I do sixteen parts, you may possibly do one-sixteenth." For this reason alone the Master took on his own shoulders the responsibility of married life and demonstrated its highest ideal by practising it in front of all. If the Master had not been married, householder devotees could have said: "He is not married, so he talks glibly about continence. He has never made a wife his own and lived with her, and he is giving long sermons to us." But the Master did not marry in order to silence that kind of criticism.

After having the ultimate vision of the Divine Mother, his divine ecstatic state became normal to him, and he brought his young wife to Dakshineswar. He saw in his wife the veritable manifestation of the Divine Mother and worshipped her as the goddess Shodashi, one of the ten forms of the Mahavidya, offering himself to her. He lived with her continuously for eight months and even shared a bed with her. Afterwards, he went to Kamarpukur and sometimes to Jayrambati and lived there for a month or two to teach his wife and bring peace and happiness to her mind.

When the Holy Mother later reminisced about the period when the

21. The Master's unprecedented spiritual, loving relationship with his wife: the Holy Mother's testimony.

Master lived with her in Dakshineswar, she would tell the women devotees: "It is impossible to describe his spiritual moods in those days. In a god-intoxicated state he would sometimes say things that were incomprehensible to me, sometimes laugh, sometimes weep, and sometimes remain motionless in samadhi, like a corpse. The whole night would pass that way. What a divine presence! My body trembled in fear and I eagerly awaited the break of day. At that time I knew almost nothing about samadhi. One night his mind did not come down to the ordinary plane of consciousness for a long time. Afraid, I cried and sent for Hriday. He came and repeated the Lord's name into the Master's ear for a while. Only then did the Master regain a normal state of mind. When he came to know of my fear and anxiety, the Master taught me various mantras and told me how to use them for different kinds of samadhi. Thus, I slowly got rid of my fear, and also became successful in bringing his mind down from samadhi. But as I never knew when he would go into samadhi, I would stay awake all night. Several days passed in this manner. When he realized my plight, he asked me to sleep in the nahabat." The Holy Mother said that the Master trained her in all domestic matters, such as how to place a wick in a lamp and how to recognize the nature of family members and deal with them appropriately. He also taught her various spiritual disciplines, kirtan, meditation, samadhi, and even the knowledge of Brahman.

O married men, how many of you teach your wives in this way? If this

22. The Master enacted that play of love to teach householders.

trivial, momentary physical relationship comes to an end for some reason, how many of you can offer respect, devotion, and unselfish love to your wives all throughout your lives in this way? So we say that it was only for you that this wonderful avatar of the age was married. Without having any physical relationship with his wife even for a day, he maintained an unprecedented sweet and loving attitude towards her. He married so that you might learn that there is a great purpose to marriage apart from sensual pleasure, and that both of you — husband and wife — might practise continence in married life, as far as you are able, and fix your sights on this high ideal. Thus being blessed, you can produce intelligent, heroic, and virtuous children and benefit Indian society, which at present is weak, devoid of prosperity and power. In previous ages there was no need for Ramachandra, Krishna, Buddha, Jesus, Shankara, Chaitanya, and other great teachers to demonstrate the ideal of marriage because it was prevalent in society. But in this present age Sri Ramakrishna has demonstrated that ideal for your benefit. This is the first time in the world a unique, pure "mould" of marriage has been made by lifelong severe austerity and sadhana. As the Master used to say, "Cast your life in that ideal mould and shape it accordingly."

"But —! " says the married householder. Oh yes, we understand your

| 23. One should build one's married life following the Master's ideal, and at least partially observe continence: it will benefit all. | problem. In answer to your "but," we must tell you what Swami Vivekananda remarked about our spiritual practices. He said: "Do you think that each one of you will be a Ramakrishna Paramahamsa? That will never be. 'Neither will nine maunds[4] of oil burn nor will Radha dance.'[5] A Ramakrishna Paramahamsa is |

born once in the world. Only one lion rules in a forest." O married men, we reply to your "but" in a similar vein: The Master was fully aware that it is beyond your capacity to follow his example and observe absolute unbroken continence while living with your wife. Still he demonstrated this discipline so that you might be inspired to practise at least one-sixteenth of it. But remember, if you follow that high ideal but cannot see all women as the veritable manifestation of the Divine Mother and offer them your unselfish pure love, and if you instead always look upon them as dependent slaves and objects of lust, then there is no hope for you. Your doom is inevitable and near at hand. Remember what happened to the race of Jadu who ignored the advice of Krishna, and also the tribulation of the Jewish people who disregarded the precepts of Jesus.[6] Ignoring the message of the avatar has always brought destruction to nations.

As we answer another question here, we shall conclude the wonderful

| 24. Although married, the Master had no physical relationship with his wife: some objections and responses. | manifestation of the Master's power as a guru through his marriage and then elaborate on this topic. The minds of ordinary human beings are slaves to sense objects and are focussed on external things. Most people invariably think that because the Master was married, it would have been better if he |

had fathered at least one child before giving up a physical relationship with his wife. If he had done that, perhaps he could have demonstrated that it was the duty of human beings to maintain God's creation. At the same time the injunction of the scriptures would have been observed: The scriptures say that a married man should have at least one child; it releases him from the debt to his forefathers.

4. One maund is equal to 82 pounds. — *Translator*
5. This is a Bengali proverb indicating impossibility, such as "If the sky falls, we shall catch larks." — *Translator*
6. This is the author's personal opinion, written in 1911, long before the Jewish state came into existence. — *Translator*

To this we reply: Is creation really limited to what we see, hear, think, or imagine? Diversity is the law of creation. It would not take long for creation to be destroyed if from this moment we all started to think and act alike. Let us ask you: "Do you know all of the laws governing creation? Is it to perpetuate God's creation that you have now exhausted your virility?" Please answer with utmost honesty. "Let there be no theft in the chamber of your heart," as the Master said. Well, take it for granted that you are observing that law of perpetuating creation. What right do you have to ask others to do the same? It is also one of the laws of creation that one should not fritter away energy in indulgence that could be used for brahmacharya or exercising higher mental powers. If everyone is as busy as you are in displaying power on the sensual plane, who will manifest power on the higher spiritual plane? Spiritual power will no longer be manifested.

Furthermore, it is our nature to choose passages of the scriptures that are to our liking. Thus to justify one's actions one quotes the injunction about begetting offspring. But the scriptures offer different instructions to qualified aspirants, such as *Yadahareva virajet tadahareva pravrajet* [As soon as your intense love of God leads to detachment, renounce the world immediately]. If the Master had subscribed to your view, who would then abide by this scriptural injunction? This is also applicable to paying off debts to the forefathers. The scriptures say that a true sannyasin liberates the seven generations that preceded him and the seven generations of his family that follow him by the merits of his virtue. So there is no need for us to worry that the Master's debt to his ancestors was not paid.

It is now clear that the Master's marriage took place only to teach us the lofty and pure ideal of married life. We understand this a little by seeing how the Holy Mother throughout her life worshipped the Master as a veritable manifestation of the Divine Mother. It is true that a man can hide weaknesses from others but never from his wife. On this point the Master sometimes told us: "You see, the bigwigs — babus, judges, magistrates, and so on — may brag or talk big outside, but they are like earthworms and slaves to their wives. If an order, however unjustifiable, comes from the inner apartment [*meaning from the wife*], he has no power to overrule it." Therefore, if a wife sees her husband's pure and ideal life and worships him as God all her life with sincere, wholehearted devotion, it definitely proves that there is no falseness in the ideal that he teaches. We can say this about the Master more emphatically than we can about anyone else. But this is not the place to discuss the Master's wonderful, spiritual marriage, although we have much to say about it. We stop here after giving just a glimpse of the way in which the Master manifested his extraordinary power as a guru within his marriage.

25. Inspired by the divine mood, the Master married: This is substantiated by the Holy Mother's worship of the Master as the Divine Mother.

Chapter 5

As a Guru in His Youth

Veiled by My maya born of the gunas, I am not revealed to all. This deluded world knows Me not as the unborn and eternal. — GITA 7:25

WHEN THE MASTER MOVED TO DAKSHINESWAR and became a priest of the Divine Mother, his power as a guru became manifest within him to a great extent. His sadhana had begun, and he was intoxicated with the love of God. Regardless, a guru is always a guru, and a leader is always a leader from childhood onward. It is not that people form a committee and consult with one another to appoint an individual to be a guru or a leader. As soon as a true leader appears before the public, the minds of others become filled with devotion for that person. They humbly take lessons from such a leader and obey that person's commands. This is the law. Swami Vivekananda used to say, "A leader is always born and never created." People do not create a guru or a leader: Those who become gurus or leaders were born with that authority. That is why it is seen that society becomes angry and punishes an ordinary man when he does a particular act, but when the same action is performed by a world teacher, people accept that person's direction without resentment. Krishna said in the Gita (3:21): "Whatever a great man does, that others follow; whatever he sets up as a standard, that the world follows." This may sound strange, but it has always happened that way and will continue to do so.

> 1. To become a guru or a leader is not subject to human will.

Krishna said, "Let the worship of Indra be stopped from today, and let Mount Govardhan[1] be adored." And people began to do that. Buddha said,

---

1. This is a story from the Bhagavata. To put Krishna's power to the test, Indra poured rain onto Vrindaban continually for seven days and nights, flooding the entire area. People came to Krishna for shelter. He told them to go to Mount Govardhan, then he lifted that hill himself, thwarting Indra's effort. That is why Krishna is called "the upholder of Govardhan." — *Translator*

ɔm today let there be no more sacrificing of animals," and immediately ɔciety revoked the injunction *Yajnarthe pashavah srishtah*. [Animals are created to be killed for sacrifices.] Jesus gave his disciples permission to eat on the Sabbath,[2] and it became law. Muhammad had many wives, yet people still respect and obey him as a selfless religious leader. In all matters, great or small, whatever great teachers say and do becomes the standard of good conduct.

We have already mentioned (see III.3.2,15) this phenomenon: The selfish

2. Cosmic I-consciousness appears spontaneously in the great teachers of the world but not in ordinary people.

"I" of the great teachers of the world is completely eradicated forever, and in its place the Cosmic I manifests itself, impregnated with ideas. The nature of this "I" is to seek the good of all. When flowers bloom, bees come of their own accord to gather honey, even though the flowers do not invite them. Similarly, as soon as the Cosmic I manifests itself in a person, afflicted people somehow know about it immediately and flock to that person for peace and bliss.

A tiny drop of that Cosmic I appears in ordinary beings after they have gone through tremendous hardship and austerities to attain it. But in the lives of the great world teachers, we see that it starts to manifest in their childhood, becomes more apparent in youth, and finally becomes fully manifest during their mature years. When that happens we are amazed to see their divine play and we consider them to be one with God. That superhuman condition becomes so natural to them that it is easily manifest in every action and movement of their daily lives. What can ordinary people do? They see that their puny, selfish minds cannot measure the divine nature of those teachers. Dumbfounded, they love and respect the great teachers as God and take refuge in them.

As we study the Master's life, we find that in his youth, from the beginning

3. When did the power of the guru manifest fully and become natural in the Master's life?

of his sadhana, his power as a guru unfolded gradually day by day. At the end of his austere twelve-year sadhana, this power was completely manifested and became natural to him. When the Master reached that point, most of the time ordinary people could not ascertain from moment to moment whether he was in a state of I-consciousness or in the mood of a guru and identified with the Cosmic I. But when this power as a guru became fully developed is a different story that we shall

2. Jews were not forbidden from eating on the Sabbath, but from working. The disciples of Jesus picked corn from the fields and ate it on the Sabbath, which is unlawful under Jewish custom. Jesus defended their actions, saying: "Have you never read what David did that time when he and his men were hungry? He went into the house of God, and he and his men ate the bread offered to God, even though it was against the Law for them to eat it — only the priests were allowed to eat that bread. . . . The Sabbath was made for the good of man; man was not made for the Sabbath. So the Son of Man is Lord even of the Sabbath." Matthew 12:3-5 and Mark 2:27-28. — *Translator*

narrate later in the proper place. Now it is necessary to tell the reader some-thing about the times in his youth when during his sadhana he was overwhelmed by that power, and how he behaved.

We find that the first manifestations of the Master's power as a guru in his

| 4. The power as a guru during his sadhana: his behaviour with Rani Rasmani and Mathur. |

youth were connected with Rani Rasmani and Mathur, whom we did not have the good fortune to see. But it is clear from what the Master told us that they felt a sincere love for him upon their first meeting, and gradually this regard profoundly deepened. To many of us, it may seem like a fairy tale rather than fact that one can love and trust another to such a great extent! From an ordinary point of view, the Master was then merely an insig-nificant brahmin priest, whereas, although they were of a low caste, Rani Rasmani and Mathur were at the pinnacle of society in terms of wealth, posi-tion, learning, and intelligence.

From his childhood onward, the Master had a very mysterious nature. A

| 5. The Master's wonderful nature. |

person is generally considered great based on such things as wealth, position, learning, intelligence, or fancy titles. But in the Master's eyes, those things were not worthy of consideration. He used to say, "When one reaches the top of the monument,[3] one sees that three-storeyed buildings, four-storeyed buildings, tall trees, grass on the ground — all are alike." We noticed that, from his childhood onward, the Master's mind always dwelt in a high state because of his passion for truth and for God. From that summit he could see no differences between people in wealth, position, or learning. In contrast, we ourselves become puffed up with those things, and out of pride we disre-gard everything but ourselves. Again, before the Master undertook any action, he would use his discrimination to determine how he should proceed, by considering the following: Why should he undertake that action? What would be the result of establishing a relationship with a partic-ular person? Other people have been in the same circumstances: What is their condition now? There was no way that anything or anyone could deceive him by hiding behind false appearances or playing tricks on him even for a short while.

The reader may say: "Well, if a man has this kind of discriminating intel-lect, he will see the defects in everything immediately and that will remove his incentive to do anything at all." This is true. If the mind is not desireless and pure beforehand, and if its goal is not based on God-realization, then in fact that discriminating intellect will confound a person and make him or her apathetic or sometimes even wild and wayward. On the other hand, if the mind is attuned to purity and focussed on a high ideal, then the penetrating intellect finds fault in sense objects and helps a person to more quickly

3. The Ochterloney Monument of Calcutta. — *Translator*

ance towards God. That is why in the Gita (13:9) Krishna advised spiritual seekers to practise renunciation by cultivating "perception of the evil of
birth, death, old age, sickness, and pain."

It is apparent that the Master's power of discrimination was so well developed from his childhood that it found worldly things to be insignificant.
People generally go to school in order to achieve name and fame by earning
titles such as "Tarkalankar" and "Vidyavagish." But such titles held no
attraction for the Master as he saw those "Tarkavagish," "Nyayachanchus,"
and others reciting grandiloquent words from Nyaya and Vedanta to
wealthy people and flattering them in order to earn a livelihood. People
generally marry because they are attracted by worldly pleasures and amusement. But the Master saw how marriage was a permanent noose around the
neck for a few days of pleasure and how it led to running after money for the
fulfillment of various desires. How uncertain and momentary those pleasures are! Although most people believe that one should strive to earn
money, because in this world one can do everything through money, the
Master saw that money could provide rice, lentils, clothes, or a house made
of brick, clay, and wood — but not God. In this world people try to become
famous through charity to the poor and other philanthropic activities. But
the Master saw that even after a lifetime of effort one can establish only a
couple of free schools, free dispensaries, or guesthouses for pilgrims. Then
that person dies, and the wants of the world remain the same. Thus the
Master's discriminating intellect considered all aspects of life.

It has always been extremely difficult for ordinary people, especially

6. Why wealthy people
and pandits found it
difficult to recognize the
Master.

those who are proud of their learning and their
wealth, to properly understand the Master, who had
such an enigmatic nature. The wealthy are accustomed to hearing only flattery from others, not
outspoken remarks, and they lose the ability to hear the plain truth because
they are blinded by the vanity of wealth and honour. So it is no wonder that
these people did not understand the Master and considered him to be rustic,
mad, or egotistic. It is therefore surprising that Rani Rasmani and Mathur
had so much love for and devotion to the Master. It seems that by the grace of
God, they had not only the great fortune to maintain their love for the Master
uninterruptedly, but also to witness his divine power as a guru day by day.
They fully offered themselves at his feet. If they had done otherwise, it
would not have been easy for Rasmani and Mathur to renounce their vanity
of wealth and honour and maintain that loving attitude towards the Master
from the beginning, despite his unusual behaviour. For example, when his
brother officiated as priest during the dedication ceremony of the Kali
temple, the Master would not partake of the Divine Mother's prasad,
thinking that this cooked food belonged to people of low caste; he lived on
his own cooking for some time on the bank of the Ganges. Again, although

Mathur repeatedly called to the Master, he was reluctant to respond because Mathur was a worldly person. Later, the Master repeatedly rejected Mathur's earnest request to accept the position of priest in the Kali temple.

At this time the Master was married and in the prime of his youth.

7. The Master's condition after his marriage; Mathur gradually becomes attracted to him; others' opinions about him.	When he returned to Dakshineswar from Kamarpukur, he resumed performing the worship service in the Kali temple. Immediately after that he again became mad for God. Deprived of the vision of God, he would rub his face on the ground and cry, "Mother, Mother." People would gather round him and

murmur sympathetically: "Ah! This poor man must have some serious disease. Only terrible colic makes a person so restless." Sometimes during worship he would put all the flowers on his head and remain motionless, and sometimes he would excitedly sing the devotional songs of the mystics for a long time. But when he was in a somewhat normal state, he would behave as usual with people and show proper respect for others. However, when he was in ecstasy while meditating on the Divine Mother — and that ecstasy would occur intensely many times a day — then he was completely oblivious to his surroundings. He neither heard nor responded to anybody. Even at such times, however, one could find glimpses of the sweet and gentle aspects of his divine character. For example, if at that time someone asked him to sing a couple of devotional songs to the Mother, he immediately would begin to sing with his sweet voice to please that person, and while singing would lose himself in that mood.

The low-minded officials and the temple manager had previously complained to Rani Rasmani and Mathur about the Master's improper and unconventional activities, telling them: "The junior priest[4] is ruining this place. The Mother's ritual worship and food offerings are being performed improperly. Can the Mother accept worship and food that are offered in this bizarre way?" Nonetheless, they were not successful in carrying out their intention to get rid of the Master. Mathur himself began visiting the temple without any warning. Concealing himself, he observed the Master's overwhelming devotion during worship, his childlike behaviour, and his importunate demands on and requests to the Divine Mother. After seeing all this, with tearful eyes Mathur told the temple officials: "Do not obstruct the junior priest, no matter how he performs his worship. Don't say anything to him. Report to me first, then do as I say."

Occasionally, Rani Rasmani also visited the Kali temple and was moved when she saw how the Mother was decorated with flowers and when she heard the Master sing songs to Her in his sweet voice. Whenever Rani Rasmani

---

4. The Master's elder brother was called the senior priest, so the Master was referred to as the junior priest.

came to the Kali temple, she called to the junior priest and asked him to sing a few devotional songs. While he was singing, the Master would forget that he was singing for another person. Absorbed in ecstasy, he felt as if he were singing before the Divine Mother Herself.

Thus the days rolled on. As in the big household of the world, the people of the Kali temple's small household were busy with their respective duties. Whatever time was left after doing their work and looking after their self-interests, they used to indulge in gossipping and in criticizing others, thus relieving the dull monotony of their lives. Who cared about the changes that were taking place in the junior priest, caused by his love of God? Sometimes the temple officials commented about the Master: "That fellow is mad. He has somehow won the favour of Mathur Babu; that is why he still has the job. But how long can he keep it? Someday he will do something horrible and will be thrown out. Is there any security in the whims of rich people? This moment they are pleased and the next moment displeased." In the meantime, the Master's nephew Hriday had joined him there as his attendant.

One day Rani Rasmani went to the temple. The temple officials were very

8. The Master, as a guru, punishes Rani Rasmani.

busy. Even those who usually evaded their work were wholeheartedly carrying out their respective duties. After bathing in the Ganges, the Rani entered the Kali temple. The worship and the decoration of Kali were finished. She bowed down to the Divine Mother and sat on a seat near the image to perform her daily worship. Seeing the Master nearby, she asked him to sing a few songs in praise of the Mother. The Master sat near the Rani and with overwhelming devotion began to sing the songs of Ramprasad, Kamalakanta, and other mystics. As the Rani listened, she performed worship and japa. But after a while the Master became irritated and stopped singing. He exclaimed indignantly, "Shame on you — to think such thoughts even here!" With that, he suddenly slapped the Rani. The Master was then like an angry father who punishes a misbehaving child. But who could understand this?

The temple staff and the Rani's female servants began screaming for help,

9. Its result.

and the gatekeepers rushed in to seize the Master. The office workers heard the commotion and were curious, so they quickly ran to the temple. But those who were responsible for the commotion — the Master and Rani Rasmani — remained calm and unperturbed. Paying no attention to the hue and cry of the temple staff, the Master remained aloof and composed, with a sweet smile on his lips. As for the Rani, instead of meditating on the Divine Mother, she had been thinking about the result of a lawsuit. As she reflected on this and realized her fault, she became embarrassed and pensive. At the same time she was surprised that the Master had known what was in her mind. When the noise around her suddenly brought her back to her senses, she realized the gravity of the

Kali temple of Dakshineswar flanked by
Radha-Govinda temple on the left and Natmandir on the right.

situation and became apprehensive that the small-minded temple staff might persecute the innocent Master. She gravely ordered them: "The junior priest is not to blame. Don't say anything to him. Leave him alone." When Mathur later heard the whole story from his mother-in-law, he repeated the same order to the temple staff. Some of them were very disappointed, but what could they do? They kept quiet, thinking, "These aristocrats have their own ways of life!"

In the context of this incident, a reader may ask: What sort of guru is this? Is assaulting others an example of manifesting the power as a guru? Our answer is that if you study the religious history of the world, you will find such incidents recorded in the lives of all the great teachers. Remember how Chaitanya subdued the Muslim judges? And how, overwhelmed with the power as a guru, he struck Advaita Acharya and imparted devotion to him?

10. Similar incidents occurred in the lives of Chaitanya and Jesus.

There is no paucity of such incidents in the life of Jesus. For example, once Jesus went with his disciples to worship in Jehovah's temple at Jerusalem. Just as Hindus feel wonderful love and devotion when they visit the deities in Varanasi, Vrindaban, and other holy places, so do Jews feel in visiting the temple of Jerusalem. Moreover, Jesus was in an ecstatic mood, and when he saw the temple from a distance, he rushed forward to enter the holy presence. At the temple, various worldly people were busy making money in different ways at the entrance, in the courtyard, and outside. Priest-cum-guides were running around extracting fees from pilgrims without caring whether they visited the shrine. And shopkeepers and peddlers were concerned with making the most profit by selling animals, flowers, and other articles of worship. They were close to the temple of God, but who cared to think of Him? As the god-intoxicated Jesus entered the temple, however, he did not see these things. He went straight inside and was delighted to be in the presence of the Lord. He was overwhelmed as he experienced the Lord within as the Life of life and the indwelling Self. He felt every thing and every being inside and outside of the temple to be his very own, as in coming here he had experienced his beloved Lord.

Later, when his mind came down to the normal plane and he tried to see spirituality manifest within the people and things outside, he saw everything to be perverse. No one was engaged in the service of God; everyone was too busy enjoying sensual objects and money. His heart was filled with despair and sorrow. He thought: "What is this? You do whatever you like in the world outside. But why have you brought worldly affairs to this holy place, where God is especially manifested? When you come here you are supposed to think of Him and find relief from the burning of worldly life. Instead, you have filled up this place with worldliness!" Thinking thus, he was seized with anger. Assuming a terrible form, he took a cane in hand and forcefully drove the shopkeepers and peddlers away from the temple. As he did so, for a moment they saw the wisdom of his words. Realizing that they were doing wrong, they slowly left the temple without offering resistance. Bound souls who were not enlightened by his words were awakened by his lashes and went out. But none dared to persecute him in anger.

We find similar events in Krishna's life. For example, once some villains attacked Krishna. But when he struck them, they realized his divine nature and praised him as God. Again, some earthbound souls tried to harm Krishna, but were stunned and nonplussed by his smile and words. But let us no longer continue relating Puranic stories.

This incident, in which the Master chastised Rani Rasmani, shows vividly

| 11. Inspired by divine power, the Master taught in an amazing way; Rani Rasmani was fortunate. | how he taught others and behaved with them when he was overwhelmed by the power of a guru. If we carefully examine this event, we shall find it was not a negligible matter. Here is an ordinary salaried |

brahmin priest, quite insignificant, and there is Rani Rasmani, whose wealth, status, intelligence, fortitude, courage, and power astounded Calcutta's élite. It should be understood that such a poor brahmin had little chance of even going near her. Or, if he found a way, he would seek an opportunity to please her with flattery or some other means and feel himself blessed. But in this case just the opposite happened. Instead of merely protesting the Rani's misconduct, the Master physically punished her. From the standpoint of the Master, it was a matter of no little surprise; but on the Rani's part, it was truly remarkable that such ill treatment did not awaken anger, egotism, vengeance, or the like in her mind. As we mentioned earlier, when the selfless Cosmic I causes the power of the guru to arise in the minds of great teachers, ordinary people who encounter them must humble themselves before these great teachers, even against their will. What can be said of Rani Rasmani, who was endowed with devotion and a sattvic nature? Blessed by the grace and power of the great teachers, selfish, ordinary people automatically understand that whatever they are asked to do is for their own good, so they have no option but to obey.

Again, as the Master used to say: "Unless one has a special power of God inside, one can never become great in any respect, nor be capable of absorbing fame, power, or position." Because of her sattvic nature, the Rani was endowed with this divine power. She was therefore able to accept the guru's grace through the Master, even though it was manifested harshly. The Master would say: "Rani Rasmani was one of the eight *nayikas* [companion goddesses] of the Divine Mother. She came down to the world to spread the worship of the Divine Mother. Her official seal was engraved with these words: 'Kalipada-abhilashi, Srimati Rasmani Dasi' [Srimati Rasmani Dasi, who wishes to attain the feet of Kali]. Thus, the Rani's unflinching devotion for the Divine Mother was visible in every action."

The scriptures discuss how one dwells in this world when one's mind is fully absorbed in God. Shankara has described it beautifully in his book *Vivekachudamani* (540): "Established in the eternal plane of Absolute Knowledge, an illumined soul wanders in the world naked, or wraps himself in cloths or animal skins. Sometimes he behaves like a madman, sometimes like a child, and at other times like a ghoul."

12. The signs of a god-intoxicated mind according to the scriptures.

To ordinary people, these illumined souls look strange because they remain identified with the Cosmic I for long periods of time. But God's power as a guru is manifest through them specifically in order to remove the darkness of ignorance from human beings. As we said earlier, when the small, selfish "I" is destroyed, the Cosmic I and its power as a guru appear in order to benefit humanity.

13. Why it is so difficult to understand the actions of the great teachers, especially those of Sri Ramakrishna.

Again, among illumined souls, some act in the role of gurus or rishis by God's will. To teach others, they demonstrate noble qualities (passion for truth, dispassion for untruth, good conduct, steadfastness, observance of rules, discrimination, scriptural knowledge, erudition, and so on) as circumstances dictate, like ordinary people. We have used the word *demonstrate* because, although these illumined souls are endowed with full knowledge of the absolute, nondual Brahman — in which there is no good and bad, virtue and vice, piety and sin, and the other objects and ideas that exist in the realm of maya — they remain on the dualistic plane to show people how to transcend the realm of maya. If ordinary gurus and rishis spend time working for the good of humanity, what can we say of the avatars or the great teachers of the world? It is therefore difficult for ordinary people to comprehend what such great ones do and how they behave, especially in the case of Sri Ramakrishna, the avatar of this age. The avatars' displays of splendour, vigour, and supernatural power are recorded in the scriptures, but these were so hidden in the Master that no one could discern a hint of them by seeing him superficially a few times. Only true spiritual seekers who received his grace and had a close relationship with him understood him.

Ask yourself: What external quality of his would make him attractive to you? His learning? He was practically illiterate. How could you know that due to his prodigious memory he had complete mastery over the Vedas, Vedanta, and other scriptures after hearing them only once? Do you intend to understand him by measuring his intellect? He always said: "I am nobody. I know nothing. My Mother knows everything." What counsel can you seek from such a person? If you insisted upon his guidance, he would respond: "Ask Mother. She will tell you." Could you then trust his words and act accordingly? You may think: "Ah, what advice he has given me! We have been hearing such things since we read children's books like *Kathamala* and *Bodhodaya*: God is omniscient, omnipotent, formless, and the embodiment of consciousness. If He wills, He can make us know and understand every-thing. But can we function according to this proposition?" Do you intend to evaluate the Master by means of wealth, name and fame? Good gracious! He had very little of those things. Yet he would advise us to renounce all of them at the outset. Such was the case with every aspect of his life. The only way to comprehend him is to be drawn by his purity, his love of God, and his devotion. It is well and good if these attract you; otherwise, it will be impossible for you to understand him or know him. So we say that it was no small fortune for Rani Rasmani that she realized the import of the harsh manifestation of the Master's power as a guru and was blessed by accepting his teaching in her heart instead of rejecting it because of egotism and vanity.

Chapter 6

As a Guru, His *A*ttitude Towards Mathur

I will tell you now of My divine attributes, O best of the Kurus — only of those that are preeminent; for there is no limit to My extent. — GITA 10:19

WE MENTIONED EARLIER THAT THE GRADUAL manifestation of the Master's power as

> 1. "It takes a long time for a large flower to bloom."

a guru revealed itself to a great extent in the presence of Rani Rasmani and Mathur. Regarding the highest spiritual manifestation, the Master would say: "It takes a long time for a large flower to bloom. And a pithy tree takes longer to grow." In the Master's life it took twelve years of continuous austere sadhana to develop his unprecedented power as a guru. This is not the place to describe his sadhana. Here we shall talk only about the power of the guru that, like a beautiful flower, blossomed fully in the rays of Cosmic Consciousness. But while narrating the story of that power from beginning to the end, some other topics will crop up incidentally. Some stories of the devotees who were connected with the unfolding of the Master's power as a guru will inevitably arise.

The Master's relationship with Mathur was wonderful. Mathur was

> 2. The wonderful relationship between Mathur and the Master: Mathur's nature.

wealthy and at the same time largehearted; a man of the world, yet a devotee; he was rash, but intelligent; hot-tempered, but patient. Mathur was both strong and resolute. He was well versed in English and skilled in logic, yet he was quite open to correction if someone could convince him he was wrong. He believed in God and was a devotee, but he was not the kind of person to blindly accept anything about religion without exercising his reason, whether it came from the Master, or his guru, or someone else. Mathur was openhearted and simple, but he was not a man to be cheated like a fool in worldly affairs. Rather, he sometimes used unscrupulous means to expand his estate and property, as did other shrewd and worldly landlords. Rani Rasmani had no son, and Mathur, her youngest son-in-law, was her right-hand man in managing her vast estate, even though her other sons-in-law were still living. It was due to the combined talents of mother- and son-in-law that Rani Rasmani's name became very well known.

The reader may ask: "Why this 'song of Shiva while husking paddy?'[1] Why do you bring in Mathur while talking about the Master?" As one can observe a colourful butterfly slowly evolve within its cocoon, then begin to emerge, so Mathur caught a little glimpse of the future unfolding of the Master's wonderful power as a guru. He then became his main protector and helper. Inspired by a noble and sacred purpose, Rani Rasmani built a sanctuary where this unique character could unfold and expand, and under the same impulse Mathur supplied whatever was needed when that divine life was developing. Of course, we understood this only after a long time. Although the Rani and Mathur sometimes saw some glimpses of this, it seems they could not fully realize why they were doing those things.

3. Unconsciously, Rani Rasmani and Mathur helped in manifesting the Master's power as a guru. A group of people, acting as friends or enemies, help to manifest the avatar's power.

The same circumstances are found while studying the lives of great teachers in every age. It is evident that an Unknown Power imperceptibly clears their paths by removing all obstructions, protects them completely — always and under all circumstances — and subdues others who have rebellious natures and brings them under their control. At the same time these people do not know that what they are doing for those great souls, out of their own will or impelled by love or hatred, is for the avatars' benefit, to help their mission and unveil their inner power by removing the obstacles to their goal. When after many years they realize this, people become amazed. Consider the result of Kaikeyi's sending Ramachandra to the forest; consider Kamsa's lifelong effort to keep Vasudeva and Devaki in prison; and remember what happened when King Suddhodana built a pleasure garden to prevent Siddhartha from renouncing the world. Consider the consequence of the cruel Buddhist Kapalika's effort to kill Shankara by black magic; consider the outcome of the opposition and enmity of government officials to Chaitanya's preaching the religion of love; and consider the effect of those who killed Jesus on a false charge. The

---

1. A Bengali proverb equivalent to "beating around the bush." — *Translator*

results in all these events turned out to be the opposite of what had been intended, as in the story, "Rama misunderstood the prayer."[2]

The powerful, intelligent enemies and loving friends of those great teachers always "misunderstood" them and acted from their own motives, using their diplomacy and worldly wisdom. As it happened in the past, so it will be in the future. The Bhagavata and other scriptures say that one who acts as an enemy remains completely ignorant about the aims and activities of that divine power. A devotee, however, follows that divine power with faith and devotion and sometimes understands it a little. Gradually, the devotee becomes free from desire with the help of that knowledge and attains liberation and permanent peace. Mathur's conduct towards the Master belonged to this latter category.

It is not that the play of the Divine Power is seen in the lives of the avatars only; it is just that its vivid play in their lives is more conspicuous, and we marvel at seeing it. That is all. When we study our own daily lives and the practical affairs of the world, we see that power manifesting itself to a lesser degree. Despite the vast experience of human beings and their eventful lives, it is evident that they are always puppets controlled by that Divine Power. It is therefore not surprising that there is a similarity between the unique life of an avatar and that of an ordinary human being, since the latter is modelled on the former. Ordinary human beings try to mould their lives according to the ideals of the avatars, and they will continue to do so eternally. See how Rama, Krishna, Chaitanya, and a few other great souls have such a hold on the lives of vast India, the common ground of many races and cultures! In the present age the ideal of Ramakrishna, a unique mould newly formed by a combination of the ideals of previous avatars, is spreading rapidly and captivating the Indian people within such a short time! O reader, guess, if you wish, how far his influence will spread in the course of time; we are totally incapable of understanding or saying anything about that subject.

4. The same thing happens in ordinary human life; there is a great similarity between ordinary human life and an avatar's life.

2. *Ulta bujhilu Rama*: This Hindi proverb originated from the following story. A Vaishnava monk travelled from one holy place to another for many years. He carried a bundle consisting of necessary articles such as cooking utensils, a water pot, and so on. One day he thought that if he had a horse, he would no longer have to carry the heavy bundle. Then he began to pray loudly, "O Rama, please give me a horse," so that people might know his need. At that time the king's army was passing nearby. An army officer was riding a mare that had brought forth a foal. The rider thought: "What can I do? Now the army will march to another place. The mare will be able to walk, but how can I take this newborn with me?" Thinking awhile he looked for a man to carry the foal and saw that monk who was crying for a horse. Finding the monk to be strong, the officer forced him to carry the foal, without any consideration. Trapped in a difficult situation, the monk said repeatedly, "O Rama, you have misunderstood my prayer." The horse was supposed to carry him and his bundle, whereas he now had to carry a foal.

When we heard that Mathur loved the Master wholeheartedly and had

| 5. Though Mathur was a devotee, he was not foolish. |

one hundred and twenty-five percent faith in him, our doubtful minds immediately thought: "Perhaps Mathur was like a foolish monkey. How could one person offer so much love and reverence to another? Had we been in his position, we would have found out how Ramakrishna could instill that much devotion and faith in our minds by the power of his character." As if to have heartfelt devotion and faith deserves censure! But we must make the reader understand here that whatever we have heard and understood about Mathur from the Master, Mathur was not a fool. He was no less intelligent or critical than the rest of us. He also doubted the Master's extraordinary character and activities and did not spare him from testing at every step in the beginning. But to what avail? How long could Mathur's gigantic doubt-elephant withstand scientific reasoning and the loving, powerful, and forceful spiritual current of the Master, which had never before been witnessed in any age? Within a short time Mathur's doubt was weakened, crushed, vanquished, and destroyed, and it finally disappeared forever. When Mathur was thus completely defeated, what could he do? He wholeheartedly took refuge at the Master's feet. Therefore, it is quite understandable that as we speak about Mathur, we are glorifying the Master's power as a guru.

Mathur was attracted to the Master at first sight because of his childlike

| 6. The cause of Mathur's initial attraction to the Master and its gradual development. |

simplicity, sweet nature, and handsome appearance. Later, during the first stage of his sadhana, the Master began to experience divine madness. Sometimes he lost control of himself while worshipping the Divine Mother, and sometimes he worshipped himself, seeing Her within. When out of exuberant devotion he transcended the boundary of vaidhi bhakti [preparatory devotion] and began doing things in a way that was contrary to the scriptures, his actions became reprehensible to others, even though they were motivated by devotion. When the Master thus became an object of suspicion and public criticism, the worldly Mathur pondered with his sharp intellect and sense of justice: "From the very first, I saw the Master as a wonderful, simple-natured person. I shall not believe any report against him without seeing what is happening with my own eyes."

Mathur secretly began to visit the Dakshineswar Kali temple and to closely observe the Master's activities. He came to this conclusion: "Young Gadadhar is a living embodiment of devotion and simplicity. He behaves in that unusual manner out of exuberant love and devotion." So the intelligent man of the world tried to convince the Master: "It is good to act according to one's means or capacity. It is a blessing to have faith and devotion. But is it proper to be beside oneself? You will definitely become an object of public criticism. Moreover, if you continue to act as you please without listening to others, there is a chance that you will lose your discrimination and become mad."

Although Mathur attempted to persuade him in this way, sometimes the holy association with the Master would awaken Mathur's sleeping devotion. He would then wonder: "It is known that Ramprasad and other spiritual aspirants in the past appeared to be mad because of devotion. It may be that Gadadhar's conduct and condition are similar to that." Therefore, instead of obstructing the Master's activities, Mathur decided to wait and see how far he would go, and then take necessary steps at the proper time. The fact that a wealthy employer had such consideration for and patience with an ordinary employee is not insignificant.

Devotion is contagious. Every day we see that moods, like physical states,

| 7. Mathur is changed by the contagious power of devotion. | are transmitted from one person to another. The gross and subtle universes are composed entirely of modifications of the same substance and governed |

by the same natural law. This truth no longer needs to be validated by the experience of Vedic rishis; modern science is coming close to proving it. So it is no wonder that one person's awakened devotional mood will call forth a similar mood lying dormant in another. That is why the scriptures emphatically insist that holy company is extremely helpful in enkindling spirituality. We can presume that such a thing happened to Mathur. The more he observed the Master's actions and conduct day after day, the more his inner devotion began to awaken without his knowledge. We find clear indications of this in his subsequent activities. As faith and devotion ebb and flow in the mind of a worldly person, so Mathur's mind oscillated between belief and doubt for a long time. It is clear that ultimately the Master became firmly established in Mathur's heart. We see that in the beginning the Master's intense longing and unusual conduct appeared to Mathur as an excess of devotion. As love and longing increased in the Master day after day, Mathur became concerned and wondered, "Is he going out of his mind?" But Mathur's suspicion turned into compassion, and he focussed his thoughts on improving the Master's physical health and halting his mental aberration by engaging a good physician.

Mathur had a fair knowledge of English. When Western thought and

| 8. Western-educated Mathur debates with the Master. Any change in natural law is subject to God's will. The white flower on a red hibiscus tree. | culture enter the mind through English education, a person develops self-esteem and feels equal to all. Mathur had this kind of independent attitude. That is why we find him trying to use reasoning to dissuade the Master from losing control in ecstatic love of God. |

As an example we will describe here the conversation between the Master and Mathur on whether God is bound to abide by His own laws regarding worldly matters. The Master said: "Mathur told me: 'Even God has to obey His own laws. Once God establishes a law, not even He can overrule it.' I said: 'What do you mean? He who makes a law can unmake it if he so desires, or he can replace it with another law.' Mathur refused to accept this view. He said: 'It is God who made the law that a red flower tree will produce only red flowers and never white ones. Let me see if He can produce a white blossom on a red flowering tree.' I replied: 'If He wills, He can do everything — even that.' Still he refused to accept my words.

"The next day when I went towards the pine grove to answer the call of nature, I saw two flowers on the same branch of a red hibiscus tree, one red and the other dazzling white without any red stain. I broke off the branch, took it to Mathur, and said, 'Look.' Mathur then said, 'Yes, Father, I am defeated!'" Sometimes Mathur believed that a physical illness was responsible for the Master's mental state and was manifesting itself as excessive devotion. Mathur would therefore try to dispel that mood by arguing with him.

The worldly-minded Mathur began to spend long periods of time with the Master, partly out of curiosity, partly out of compassion, because he considered the Master's overwhelming devotion to be caused by some sort of physical ailment. But sometimes he was filled with wonder and devotion at the thought that the Master's condition was the result of genuine devotion to God. Thus Mathur reflected a great deal and discussed the Master's condition with him. How could Mathur refrain from worrying? Every day the Master did all sorts of strange things, impelled by his intense passion for God. One day while he was worshipping in the shrine, he saw the Divine Mother within his own body and offered all the worship articles to himself. The previous day he had conducted the vesper service for three hours, irritating the temple officials. The day before that, he had rolled on the ground, rubbed his face into it, and cried so piteously because he had not had the vision of God that people gathered around him. The Master told us many stories of daily occurrences such as these.

9. Mathur is concerned about the Master's state of mind.

One day the Master entered one of the Shiva temples of Dakshineswar and began to recite the *Shiva-mahimnah*, a hymn in praise of the Deity. He was beside himself in ecstasy as he recited the following verse: "O Lord, if the blue mountain be the ink, the ocean the ink pot, the biggest branch of the celestial tree the pen, and the earth the writing-leaf, and if by taking this, the goddess of Learning writes forever, even then the limit of Your glory can never be reached."

10. Reciting the hymn of *Shiva-mahimnah,* the Master goes into samadhi: Mathur's reaction.

While the Master was reciting the above verse, he intensely felt the glory of Shiva in his heart and he lost himself. He forgot the hymn, the Sanskrit language of the hymn, the order of the verses, and so on, and repeatedly cried aloud, "O Lord, how can I express Your infinite glory?" Tears poured down his cheeks, chest, and clothes, finally dampening the floor. The temple servants and officials rushed in, drawn by his loud cries, his indistinct anguished words like those of a madman, and his bizarre behaviour. When they encountered him in that ecstatic condition, some were amazed and

Twelve Shiva temples of Dakshineswar and the Chandni ghat where Ramakrishna bathed.

Image of Shiva at Dakshineswar.

waited to see what would happen next. Some remarked: "It is all the young priest's craziness! He's even crazier than usual today." Others mocked: "Is he going to ride on Shiva's shoulders? There is still time to pull him out of the temple." Thus, they made fun of him.

The Master was not at all conscious of his surroundings. Absorbed in the thought of Shiva's greatness, his mind had transcended the external world and soared to a higher realm where mundane thoughts and words could never reach. So he was completely unaware of the opinions, remarks, and ridicule of these people.

Mathur was in the Kali temple that day. Hearing the commotion, he immediately went to the Shiva temple. The officials hurriedly made way for him. Mathur was moved when he saw the Master in that condition. At that time one official in all seriousness suggested that Ramakrishna be forcibly removed from the shrine because he was very close to the Deity. "Touch him only if you don't value your head!" rejoined Mathur furiously. Frightened, the officials did not dare to say or do anything. After a short time the Master regained consciousness of the outer world. Seeing Mathur and the temple officials standing around him, he asked, like a fearful child, "Did I do anything wrong when I was unconscious?" Bowing down to the Master, Mathur said: "Oh no, Father, you were just reciting a hymn. I came here to make sure that no one disturbed you."

Recalling his condition during his sadhana, the Master once told us: "At that time anyone who came here would quickly be spiritually awakened when they associated with this place [*meaning himself*]. Two young men used to come from Baranagore. They belonged to a lower caste, either *kaivarta* or *tamli*. They were good and had love for and faith in me. They came quite often. One day I was seated with them in the Panchavati, and one of them had a spiritual experience. I saw his chest turn crimson, his eyes become deep red, and tears trickle down his cheeks continually. He could neither talk nor stand. It was as if he had drunk two bottles of wine! There was no sign that his ecstasy would come to an end. Frightened, I said to the Mother: 'What have You done to him, Mother? People will say that I have cast a spell on him. His parents are at home and he must return there now.' I passed my hand over his chest and continued to pray to the Mother. After a while he somehow calmed down and returned home."

11. An example of others' quick spiritual awakening in the Master's company.

The Master told us that Mathur had similar spiritual experiences because he was in contact with his tangible spiritual life. These experiences increased Mathur's love and devotion a thousandfold. One day the Master was pacing back and forth on the northeastern veranda of his room, which extended east to west. He was in a spiritual mood, completely oblivious of his surroundings. Mathur was then seated alone in a room in his bungalow, which was situated

12. Mathur's vision of Shiva and Kali in the Master.

490

Northeastern veranda of Ramakrishna's room at Dakshineswar.
Mathur had the vision of Shiva and Kali in Ramakrishna's body while he was walking here.

between the temple complex and the Panchavati. It was not far from Mathur's room to the veranda where the Master was pacing, so Mathur could see him through a window. Sometimes he thought of the Master as he watched him walking in what was obviously an indrawn mood, and again he thought about various worldly affairs and made plans for his own future. The Master was not at all aware that Mathur was watching him from time to time as he sat in his parlour. But what would it have mattered if he had been aware of it? The disparity between their social, domestic, and other conditions was so great that there was no need for them to be concerned about one another. If the Master had not been preoccupied with and absorbed in a divine mood, it would have been reasonable for him to feel slightly discomfited and to move away from that place when he knew that Mathur could see him.

Mathur was a wealthy, respected, learned, and intelligent aristocrat and could be regarded as the sole proprietor of the Kali temple and the Rani's estate. And it was because the Master had won the favour of Mathur that he was not thrown out of the temple. The Master was an ordinary, insignificant, poor brahmin priest whom people considered to be stupid, mad, and unconventional. They even ridiculed him. In this perspective the Master should have been a little timid and humble in front of Mathur. But an unexpected and inconceivable event happened. All of a sudden Mathur hurriedly ran out of his bungalow, threw himself down at Sri Ramakrishna's feet, and began to cry profusely.

The Master later narrated: "I asked Mathur: 'What are you doing? You are an aristocrat and Rani Rasmani's son-in-law. What will people say if they see you behaving like this? Calm yourself. Please, get up!' But who would listen to this? Gradually, Mathur got control of himself and described his wonderful vision. He said: 'Father, I was watching you just now as you walked back and forth. I saw it distinctly: As you walked towards me, you were no longer yourself. You were the Divine Mother Kali from the temple! Then, as you turned around and walked in the opposite direction, you became Lord Shiva! At first I thought it was some kind of optical illusion. I rubbed my eyes and looked again, but I saw the same thing. As often as I looked I saw it!' He said this again and again, crying. I said, 'But I know nothing about this.' He ignored me. I became very nervous. I thought that if someone reported this to Rani Rasmani, she might misunderstand and think that I had put a spell on Mathur. I consoled him in various ways and finally calmed him down. Was it for nothing that Mathur served me and loved me so much? The Divine Mother granted him various visions and experiences on many occasions. It was written in Mathur's horoscope that his Ishta [Chosen Deity] would always be gracious to him — nay, would even accompany him wherever he went and assume a human form to protect him."

This event firmly established Mathur's faith. This was the first time he
13. Its effect on Mathur. | truly realized that the Master was no ordinary
human being, even though he had been attracted to
the Master from their first meeting and had glimpses of the truth behind
the Master's extraordinary conduct, even though some people criticized
the Master without understanding him. From this point on, Mathur
believed that the Divine Mother resided in the Master's body, bestowing
Her grace on him. Mathur felt that Mother Kali within the stone image had
assumed a human form and accompanied him, just as his horoscope had
predicted. The Master's intimacy with Mathur increased significantly from
then on.

Great fortune had truly dawned in Mathur's life. The scriptures say that
14. Scriptural evidence | a person must experience both good and bad karma
regarding Mathur's | as long as the body remains. This holds true not only
good fortune. | for ordinary human beings but also for liberated
souls. Ordinary people experience the results of what they have done in the
past, good and bad. Now, who experiences the results of good and bad
actions performed by a liberated person? A liberated being cannot experience the results of karma: The ego itself experiences happiness and misery,
and in the case of the illumined ones, that very ego has been burnt away by
knowledge. Who can then experience the results of virtue and vice of such
a one? Someone must, because the results of karma are inevitable. As long
as the bodies of the liberated ones do not fall like dry leaves, they must
perform actions, both good and bad. In this respect the scriptures say that
the people who serve and love the liberated ones enjoy the results of their
good actions, and those who hate them suffer by taking the results of their
bad actions.[3] If one can have such benefits by serving an ordinary liberated
soul, then who can say how much good one can reap by serving an avatar
with love and devotion?

As the days passed, Mathur witnessed ever more manifestations of the
15. The continual | Master's power as a guru, and his devotion became
manifestation of the | more established. In the meantime, many events were
Master's power as a | taking place. The Master experienced a terrible
guru: Mathur is | burning sensation caused by the pain of his separa-
convinced after testing | tion from God and was treated for it. Bhairavi
him. | Brahmani arrived at Dakshineswar and established
that the Master was an avatar by quoting passages from the Vaishnava
scriptures to a group of pandits whom Mathur had invited. The great

---

3. According to the reading of the Satyayani recension: "His [a liberated one's] sons inherit
his properties, friends, his virtuous deeds, and enemies, his vicious deeds." Similarly in the
text of the Kaushitakins: "He [an illumined soul when dead] shakes off both virtues and
vices by that [power of his Self-knowledge]; his dear relatives get his virtues and his haters
his vices." — See Shankara's commentary on the Brahma Sutras 3:3:26.

Vedantin Tota Puri arrived and initiated the Master into sannyasa. The Master's aged mother came to Dakshineswar to live. Many other events occurred.

After the wonderful vision we have described, Mathur became involved in almost every event in the Master's daily life. Mathur engaged Ganga-prasad Sen and Mahendralal Sarkar, two physicians famous in Calcutta, to care for the Master. When the Master wished to adorn the Divine Mother with anklets like those worn by the women of Western India, Mathur had them made immediately. While the Master was practising sadhana as a female confidante of Krishna, according to Vaishnava Tantra, he wanted to wear women's clothing. Accordingly, Mathur supplied a set of diamond jewellery, a Varanasi sari, a scarf, and other items. When he learned that the Master wanted to attend the Vaishnava festival at Panihati, he not only arranged his trip, but also secretly went with his bodyguards to protect the Master from the crowd.

In addition to the many stories about Mathur's wonderful service of the Master, we have also heard many other tales from the Master. To test the Master's purity of heart, Mathur engaged some immoral women to tempt him. When Mathur proposed in writing to transfer to the Master all of the temple's property held in trust, the latter blurted out in an ecstatic mood: "What? Do you want to make me a worldly person?" Then he became very angry with Mathur and rushed to hit him. Once Mathur was involved in a brutal rivalry in connection with his estate, and a person of an opposing party was killed on his orders. Frightened that he would be severely punished by the court, he confessed his guilt to the Master, thereby escaping the consequences of his actions by surrendering to him.

We understand from these events that Mathur's devotion to the Master was gradually becoming steady and unwavering. But how could it be otherwise? The Master's wonderful, rare, superhuman character became more luminous daily as he passed all of Mathur's tests. And the Master's limitless, selfless love captured Mathur's heart. Mathur observed that he could not affect the Master's ideal of renunciation by offering him property worth millions of rupees. He could not create any lust in the Master's mind by hiring beautiful women. The highest respect one person can offer to another is to worship that individual as God. But although he offered that worship to the Master, he could not disturb the Master's evenness of mind or cause him to become egotistic, because the Master sought no worldly object, respect, or fame. The Master did not look down upon Mathur even though he knew all of his character weaknesses. Rather, the Master continued to love Mathur as his very own, saved him repeatedly from all dangers, and looked after his welfare in all respects. Mathur wondered how this could be. He realized that although the Master was an embodied being, he was a person of "that realm where there is no night." The

Master's renunciation was wonderful; his self-control, knowledge, and devotion, and all of his actions were wonderful; and above all, his love and his compassion for a weak and egotistic person like Mathur himself were wonderful!

At the same time Mathur felt another thing deeply: the sweetness and beauty of the Master's remarkable character! Regardless of the superhuman power that manifested itself within him, the Master remained the same simple boy. It was truly amazing that there was not the slightest hint of ego in him. Whatever thought arose in his mind, he expressed it; like a five-year old boy, he could hide nothing. All of his feelings, whether expressed or hidden, were in harmony. He frankly expressed in his words and actions whatever was in his mind. But he never said anything that could harm others, even if he had to undergo physical pain. Is it possible for an ordinary human being to behave in this manner?

[Chandra] Haldar of Kalighat, Mathur's family priest, burned with jealousy upon seeing Mathur's unwavering devotion to the Master. He thought: "This fellow [the Master] has somehow cast a spell over Mathur Babu and hypnotized him. My long struggle to bring Mathur Babu under my control is undone because of this fellow. He pretends to be a simple boy. If he is so simple, let him tell me how he enchanted Mathur Babu. Applying all my art and magic, I was slowly bringing Mathur Babu under my control. In the meanwhile this rogue arrived from somewhere."

16. The priest Haldar's reaction to Mathur's deep devotion to the Master.

As his faith and devotion increased, Mathur was considering how he could stay with the Master all the time and serve him more and more. For that reason he sometimes importuned the Master and brought him to his residence at Janbazar in Calcutta. In the afternoon he would accompany the Master in his carriage and take him to the Esplanade and to other places of interest in Calcutta. "Is it proper to serve the Father food on ordinary plates and saucers?" he wondered. Thinking thus, Mathur had a new set of gold and silver vessels made and used them for serving the Master. He dressed the Master in elegant clothes and told him: "Father, you are the owner of everything, including the estate. I am nothing but your steward. Look, you have just finished your meal from a gold plate and have drunk from a silver glass, and then you have left without giving them a backward glance. Now it is my duty to have them cleaned and put in a safe place so that you may use them again. I must also take care of them and make sure they are not stolen or damaged."

The Master told us the story of the pitiful condition that a Varanasi shawl (which Mathur bought for a thousand rupees) fell into. To whom but the Master should he present such a beautiful gift? Thinking thus, Mathur joyfully wrapped it around the Master's body. That shawl was very expensive. Its

17. The pitiful condition of the Master's Varanasi shawl.

price was high at that time [1860s] and perhaps now that kind of thing might not be available at all. At first the Master wore the shawl and walked around the temple garden like a jubilant boy. He admired it again and again and showed it off to people, telling them that Mathur had spent a huge amount for it. But soon the Master had a different mood, like a boy. He considered: "What is there in this shawl? Nothing but sheep's wool. Like everything else it is a modification of the five elements. It protects one from cold, no doubt, but that can be done with a blanket or a quilt just as well. And like other material things it does not help one to realize God. Rather, it makes the owner assume an air of superiority and enhances his vanity and egotism. So it takes a man away from God. Such are its defects!" With that thought he threw the shawl on the ground, exclaiming: "This cannot help one to realize God!" He began to spit on it and trample it into the dusty ground. Then he got a match and tried to burn it, but someone grabbed it away from him. When he heard of the shawl's sad fate, Mathur was not at all offended. He just remarked: "Father did the right thing!"

The above incidents show clearly that although Mathur tried to keep the

18. The Master's nonattachment.

Master in comfort and enjoyment, his mind dwelt constantly in a higher realm. Wherever he lived, he remained absorbed within himself. Where ordinary people would see darkness piled upon darkness, the Master would see only a Light that casts no shadow and neither waxes nor wanes. The luminosity of the sun, moon, and stars, a flash of lightning, and even fire are all dim, almost dark, in the presence of this Light. The Master's mind dwelt constantly in this realm. Out of compassion, his mind for a short time visited this mundane world filled with malice, hatred, and hypocrisy, the permanent abode of lust and anger. Therefore, although the Master was staying at Mathur's luxurious Janbazar house, which was full of amenities, he remained the same Master — unattached, devoid of egoism, and enraptured day and night in his own divine mood.

Early one evening the Master was lying on the floor in ecstasy at the

19. The last story concerning the priest Haldar.

Janbazar house. No one else was in the room. The Master was coming down from samadhi and slowly becoming aware of the external world. At that time Chandra Haldar, the family priest, arrived. Seeing the Master alone in that condition, he thought his time had come. He approached him, looked around, and shaking the Master's body several times, demanded: "Hey, tell me how you captured Mathur Babu? Don't pretend you can't talk! How did you hypnotize him? Speak up!" Despite this kind of repeated insistence, the Master did not say anything because at that moment he had no power to speak. This made Chandra extremely angry. "So you won't tell me, you scoundrel!" he cried. He kicked the Master violently and left the room in disgust. The humble Master said nothing of this incident, knowing that if

Rani Rasmani's house, Jan Bazar, Calcutta. Ramakrishna visited this house many times and attended Durga Puja here.

Mathur learned of it he would be furious and might punish the brahmin priest severely. Soon after this, Chandra incurred Mathur's anger by committing an offence and was dismissed. Then one day in the course of conversation the Master told Mathur what had happened. To this, Mathur said in anger and agony, "Father, if I had known that then, he would have been killed."

Mathur and his wife felt wholeheartedly the Master's infinite grace as a guru towards them. They considered him to be God and surrendered themselves to him. We find clear proof that they did not hide anything in their minds from him. Both of them would say: "Father is not a human being. Of what avail would it be to hide anything from him? He is omniscient and knows the inmost secrets in every human mind." These were not mere words; they behaved according to this understanding. They lived, ate, and travelled with the Father. What did it matter if the Father freely visited the private rooms of their household? Even without going to the inner apartment, he knew the secret thoughts of each man and woman of the household. They had seen evidence of this many times. The main danger of free mixing between men and women is the impure feeling that might arise in the mind; in that respect the Father could be considered to be a wall or some other insentient object. The women of the household felt no shyness or hesitation with the Father as they did in the presence of other men. It was as if the Father were one of them, or a five-year-old boy! Once when he was in Janbazar during Durga Puja, he was in the mood of a female companion of the Divine Mother; he dressed like a woman, accompanied the ladies of Mathur's family to visit the Deity, and fanned Her. Sometimes when the husband of a young bride of Mathur's family arrived, he would adorn her with beautiful clothes and jewellery, teach her how to talk to her new husband, and send her to him. We heard many such stories from the Master and marvelled when we considered the devotion that those women had for the Master! Because the Master was endowed with the power of the guru, those women firmly believed that he was God. They also experienced the Master's unselfish, pure love for them and saw him as their very own. It is hard for us to imagine how they lived with him and behaved freely with him!

On one hand, we find the manifestation of superhuman, pure, unselfish love for the women of Mathur's family and his behaviour with them as a female companion; on the other, we see the Master in the midst of men and pandits, behaving towards them with incomparable intelligence and divine wisdom. We wonder how it was possible for the Master to manifest such different aspects. Who was this Master who assumed different forms?

20. The devotion of Mathur and his wife, Jagadamba, to the Master; his relationship with their family.

21. Contrary moods coexisted in the Master.

In the Dakshineswar Radha-Govinda temple in those days, the images of

22. A meeting of pandits was convened to hear their opinions regarding the broken Krishna image at Dakshineswar.

the deities were brought from the adjacent bedroom to the altar every morning, and after midday worship and the food offering, they were returned to that room for rest. After 4:00 p.m. they were again placed on the altar, and at night after vespers and the food offering, they were taken back to the bedroom. One day someone spilled water on the marble floor of the temple. The priest slipped on the slick floor while carrying the image of Govinda to the bedroom, injuring himself badly and breaking a leg off the image. This accident caused commotion, and the priest trembled with fear. The news reached the temple owners. What could be done? One cannot worship a broken image. What was the solution? Rani Rasmani and Mathur invited prominent pandits of Calcutta for a meeting to decide the issue. They also gathered opinions from pandits who could not attend the meeting. What a great uproar, and what a huge waste of money to pay the pandits' honoraria! The pandits opened their books and notes, took snuff again and again to stimulate their intellects, and finally gave the verdict: "Let the broken image be immersed into the Ganges and a new one be installed in its place." Accordingly an image was ordered from a sculptor.

When the meeting was over, Mathur said to the Rani: "We have not asked

23. The Master's solution to the problem; the end of the subject.

the opinion of the junior priest on this matter. Let me see what he says." So he asked the Master's opinion.

The Master replied, in an ecstatic mood: "If any one of the Rani's sons-in-law were to break a leg, would she forsake him and put someone else in his place? Wouldn't she rather have him treated by a doctor? Let it be the same in this case. Mend the image and worship it as before. Why should the image be discarded?"

All were dumbfounded by this solution. Ah, this simple and logical answer had not occurred to anyone else! The image is living because of the divine manifestation of Govinda, which is called forth by a devotee's deep heartfelt love and devotion. If a devotee has faith, love, and devotion, why would it not be possible for that divine manifestation to exist in the broken image, out of God's grace and compassion? The merit or demerit of a broken image could by no means affect that divine manifestation. Moreover, as long as this image has been worshipped with love as God, can the love of a true devotee be destroyed as soon as one of its limbs is broken? The Vaishnava teachers advise devotees to serve God as they serve themselves. Those teachers believe that whatever service one offers to the Lord with love, He accepts with love: One should develop this attitude. From this point of view also, the decree to discard the image is improper. Therefore, the injunction found in the Smriti scriptures that says one should not use a broken image to offer worship to a deity must have been meant for a novice who has not yet developed love for God and has just entered the path of devotion.

However, some egotistic pandits differed with the Master's opinion, and some did not clearly express their views lest they get less of an honorarium. But those who had attained a little genuine knowledge and devotion through learning highly admired the Master's solution. Later, the Master himself skillfully mended the image, and the worship of Govinda continued as usual. When the sculptor brought the new image, it was kept in a corner of the Govinda temple and was not installed. After Rani Rasmani and Mathur had both passed away, some of their descendants from time to time tried to make arrangements to install that new image. But on every occasion they were forced to postpone it because of some mishap in their families. So even now the new image of Govinda is kept in the same way.[4]

4. Later, the new image was installed on the main altar, and the broken image was placed in the room at the left corner of the Radha-Govinda temple. — *Translator*

Chapter 7

As a Guru, the Master Bestows
*G*race on Mathur

I am the Self, O Gudakesha, seated in the hearts of all creatures. I am the beginning, the middle, and the end of all beings. — GITA 10:20

THAT YEAR [1869] THERE WAS GREAT REJOICING ON THE occasion of Durga Puja at

1. The story of the Durga Puja with the Master at Mathur's Janbazar house in Calcutta.

Mathur's Janbazar house. Although every year all those present experienced indescribable joy during the worship of the Divine Mother, this year the Master enhanced that joy a thousandfold with his holy presence. So their happiness knew no bounds. As a young boy, out of exuberant joy, freely makes demands on his mother and entertains her with laughter and dance without any motive, so the childlike Father behaved with the Divine Mother when in ecstasy he saw Her palpable presence in the image. And in fact it appeared that the image was living, luminous, and smiling. The appearance of the Divine Mother in the image as well as in the Master's divine body and mind joined together, filling the atmosphere of the worship hall with an indescribable and indefinable divine presence that was felt even by worldly-minded people. The hall glowed with light and radiant splendour. This wonderful divine presence pervaded the entire house, lending it an enchanting beauty.

It was natural that Mathur's house would vibrate with spiritual beauty. Rajas characterized the wealthy Mathur's devotion, and he did not fail to decorate the image with beautiful clothes and ornaments, to arrange the worship so there would be an abundance of flowers, fruits, sweets, and other articles, and to provide the ceremony with sweet music from the concert tower. At the same time it seemed that the divinity of the unique Master was touching those external material objects and infusing its life into everything. The beauty of serenity shown by ochre-clad monks in groves of evergreen deodar trees in the snow-capped Himalayas; the beauty of compassion manifested by a handsome baby nursing in the lap of a beautiful and loving mother; the beauty of a pure mind revealed in a comely face — all of these beauties were combined and manifested at Mathur's house, to his good fortune. And although Mathur and his wife were constantly busy making the proper arrangements for worship and other activities, their hearts were filled with the unspeakable bliss of that spiritual atmosphere.

The day's worship was over. Mathur and his wife took a little time to joyfully offer flowers at the feet of the Divine Mother and the Father.

It was evening, and the vesper service of the Divine Mother was about to begin. The Father was then in the inner apartment, having in his ecstasy completely forgotten his male body. His words and behaviour expressed that he

2. The Master's ecstasy and physical beauty.

was a maid or female confidante of the Divine Mother and had been so birth after birth in every age. The Divine Mother was his heart and soul, his all in all. He had been born to serve Her. His face radiated love and emotion, and the sweet smile on his lips, the gaze of his eyes, the movement of his limbs, and even his gestures were like those of a woman. The Master was wearing a silk cloth that Mathur had given him, and he had wrapped it like a sari. Who could say then that he was a man! The Master's complexion was so bright that it seemed his beauty would burst forth. When he was in ecstasy, his complexion would become brighter, and a light seemed to emanate from his body. When people saw his beauty, they could not turn their eyes away, and they looked at him in wonder.

The Holy Mother told us that the Master's complexion blended with the colour of the gold amulet that he used to wear at all times, which contained a mystical mantra. We also heard from the Master: "At that time my beauty became manifest in such a way that people would stare at me. My face and chest were always crimson, and a lustre would emanate from my body. Because people stared at me, I would cover myself with a thick *chadar* [shawl]. I would pray to the Divine Mother, 'Take away my external beauty, O Mother, and give me inner beauty.' I used to pass my hand over the body and slap it again and again, saying, 'Go within, go within.' After some days my skin turned pale, as you see it now."

We recall another incident of the Master's life in connection with his phys-

3. The Master's physical beauty and noble qualities attract many people in Kamarpukur.

ical beauty. At that time the Master used to stay in Kamarpukur every year for three or four months during the rainy season. While in Kamarpukur, the Master would sometimes visit Hriday's home in

Sihar. The road to Sihar goes through Jayrambati, near his father-in-law's house. So at the request of the Holy Mother's family and the villagers, he would spend a few days with them also. Hriday, the Master's devoted attendant, was always with him and served him in every possible way.

Whenever the Master was in Kamarpukur, the villagers would crowd his home from morning to evening to see him and to hear a few words from his lips. In the morning the neighbourhood women would finish cleaning and sweeping their houses and come to Haldar Pond for their bath. They would first stop at the Master's house, leaving at the ghat the pitchers they had brought for carrying water home. They would spend an hour or so talking with the Master and the women of his family and then go for their baths. This happened every day. If someone had made any fancy sweet the night before, she would save the first portion for the Master and bring it to him the next morning. Seeing those women arriving at dawn, the fun-loving Master sometimes jokingly said to them: "In Vrindaban the gopis would meet Krishna at different times in different ways: The 'pasture meeting' took place when the gopis went to the Jamuna to get water; the 'twilight meeting' occurred when Krishna returned home after grazing the cows; the 'rasa meeting' came about at night when the gopis would dance in a circle around Krishna, and so on. So may I ask you if this is your 'bath-time meeting?'" The women would roll with laughter at this. When the women left to cook lunch and perform other household tasks, the men would come to the Master and talk to him as long as they could. The women would return in the afternoon, then the men would come again in the evening. Men and women who came from distant places would generally arrive in the afternoon and leave before evening. Thus the Master's house was full of people throughout the day, as crowded as the Chariot Festival or the Swing Festival.

Once while the Master was in Kamarpukur, arrangements were made for

4. An incident regarding the Master's beauty and his humility.

his visits to Jayrambati and Sihar. Because the Master was constantly in bhava samadhi, his limbs were as delicate as those of a boy or a woman. He could not walk even a short distance and needed a palanquin or a carriage to convey him. A palanquin had been brought for the trip to Sihar via Jayrambati. Hriday was also ready to go. After lunch the Master put on a scarlet silk cloth and fastened his gold amulet around his arm. His lips were crimson from chewing betel. As he was about to get into the palanquin, he noticed that a large crowd had gathered on the street nearby. Seeing so many men and women around, the Master asked Hriday in wonder, "Hriday, what is the reason for this crowd?"

Hriday: "For what else? You are going away, and they (*pointing to the crowd*) won't see you for some days. So they have come to have a parting look at you."

Hriday's house at Sihar c.1930. Ramakrishna visited this house many times.

The Master: "But they see me every day. What new feature has attracted them in such large numbers today?"

Hriday: "You look so handsome in that silken cloth, and your lips shine with crimson colour. That is why they want to see you."

As soon as the Master heard that those people were attracted to his physical beauty, an unusual mood filled his mind. He thought: "Alas! These people are preoccupied by this external, ephemeral, physical beauty. No one wants to see God, who is within."

He had abhorred physical beauty beforehand, but this incident increased that aversion a thousandfold. "What!" he exclaimed. "People are gathering just to look at a man! I won't go. Wherever I go, people will crowd about like this!" In utter disgust the Master returned to his room and took off the silk cloth. Filled with humility, the Master did not go to Jayrambati and Sihar that day. In spite of the entreaties of Hriday and others, he did not go out at all. Just imagine, O reader, how this unique person was repelled by his body and felt it to be insignificant. And then consider ourselves: How crazy we are for physical beauty! How busy we are in meticulously grooming and dressing the body! What an abundance of cosmetics and other accessories we use: mirrors, combs, razors, soaps, powders, creams, perfumes, pomades, and so on! Imitating the West, we rush headlong every day to ruin ourselves by lavishing more indulgence on this "cage of flesh and bones," thus increasing our delusion. O reader, one is physically neat and clean and mentally pure, and the other is obsessed with the body and its beauty — are they the same? However, let us return to our story of the Master in Janbazar.

The vesper service of the Divine Mother was about to begin, but the
Master's ecstatic mood did not cease. Jagadamba thought that she should somehow try to bring the Master down to a normal state, then go to attend vespers with other women of the family. But when she saw that his samadhi would not end, she felt that it would not be proper to leave him alone. She was at a loss. She pondered: "What shall I do? If I go and leave someone else to look after the Father, that person will run to the worship hall as soon as the music for vespers begins. But the Father is totally incapable of caring for himself when he is in samadhi. Once he fell onto a pan of burning charcoal while in this ecstatic state and was not conscious of it; that wound healed only after a long time, with various treatments. If I leave him alone and another such mishap occurs on this festive occasion, how would I face it? And what would my husband think?" Thus ruminating, a solution suddenly arose in her mind. She hurriedly brought her precious jewellery and, while adorning the Father with it, she repeatedly said into his ears: "Father, let us go. It's time to wave the lights. Won't you come and fan Mother Durga?"

5. Jagadamba's technique for interrupting the Master's samadhi.

We have observed that when the Master went into deep samadhi while thinking of a particular deity or while in a particular spiritual mood, he would lose all outer consciousness, and his mind would be far away from persons, objects, and ideas that were not related to the deity.

6. The method of the Master's descending from samadhi to the normal plane is verified by the scriptures.

But if someone repeated into his ears the name of that deity or words pertaining to the glorious nature of that deity, immediately his mind would be attracted to that sound and would return to the normal conscious plane. That the concentrated mind functions in this manner has been recorded briefly, if not in detail, in the yoga scriptures by Patanjali and others. It will not take long for a reader who is well versed in the scriptures to understand that characteristic of the Master's mind. Those whose virtue has allowed them to experience a little concentration of the mind will easily understand this phenomenon. Let us therefore continue our main story.

The words of Jagadamba reached the Master's ears. Immediately he came to his senses to some extent, and then, in a semiconscious state, joyfully walked with her. As soon as they reached the worship hall, the vesper service started.

7. In the mood of a female confidante, the Master fans the goddess Durga with a chamara.

Surrounded by women, the Master used a chamara to fan the image of the Mother.

Women stood on one side of the hall; the men, including Mathur, stood on the other. All were watching the vespers. Suddenly, Mathur's eyes fell on the women, and he saw a stranger, adorned with gorgeous clothes and ornaments, standing next to his wife, fanning the Divine Mother. Despite looking again and again, he could not recognize her. He thought that she might be a friend of his wife, or the wife of a wealthy man who had perhaps come at her invitation.

Vespers was over. After bowing down to the Divine Mother, the women returned to their living quarters and began their household duties. Because the Master was still in a semiconscious state, he returned with Jagadamba to the inner apartment. Gradually, he became completely normal and removed all the jewellery. He went to the parlour to sit with the men, where he discussed religious topics and charmed them with his clear explanations and apt illustrations.

After a while, Mathur went to the inner apartment and by the by asked his wife, "During vespers, who was standing next to you, fanning the Deity?" Jagadamba replied with a smile: "What! You did not recognize him? It was the

8. Unable to recognize the Master in that state, Mathur is curious.

Father, in an ecstatic mood, who was fanning. It is quite understandable that you did not recognize him — when the Father is dressed like a woman, it is hard to recognize him as a man." Dumbfounded, Mathur said: "This is why I say that even in trifling matters no one can know the Father if he doesn't allow himself to be known. Look, I live with the Father twenty-four hours a day, and still I did not recognize him!"

Three days of Durga Puja (saptami, ashtami, and navami) passed joyfully.

9. *Vijaya*, the last day of Durga Puja.

It was the morning of vijaya dashami, the last day of worship. The priest was hurriedly finishing the short ritual pertaining to the immersion ceremony, which needed to be performed within a certain period of time prescribed by the almanac. The image was to be immersed into the Ganges that evening. A shadow of sadness dominated the minds of everyone in Mathur's family, and there was indescribable apprehension due to the inevitable and imminent separation from the blissful image of the Deity. Sorrow always casts a long shadow over the purest joys of this world. According to this natural law, it seems that even a great lover of God must sometimes experience an unbearable pang of separation from God. Even we stonehearted people shed warm tears while immersing the Mother's image on the day of vijaya. And what of Jagadamba? Since morning she had been soaking the corner of her cloth with tears as she worked.

Mathur was in the parlour, unaware of the immersion ceremony that was

10. The blissful Mathur is oblivious to it.

near at hand. He was in a festive mood as usual, absorbed in overwhelming joy because he had brought the Divine Mother to his home and was also enjoying the rare company and inconceivable grace of the Father. Who cared what was going to happen in the world? Why would one need to think about it? Thus, his days passed in the company of the Divine Mother and the Father. Meanwhile, a message came from the priest: The immersion ceremony was about to be performed; please ask Mathur Babu to come downstairs to the worship hall, bow down, and say his final prayer to the Mother before the worship ends.

At first Mathur could not understand the message. When he finally

11. Mathur decides not to immerse the Mother's image in the Ganges.

understood, he came to his senses and realized that it was vijaya dashami, the last day of worship. He was terribly shocked. Grief-stricken, he pondered: "Why should I immerse the Mother today? By the grace of the Divine Mother and the Father, there is no want in my home. Any lack of joy I had has been remedied by the advent of the Mother in my home. Why should I invite misery into my life by immersing the Mother into the Ganges? No, I can't destroy this market of bliss. My heart aches when I think of the Mother being immersed." Mathur shed tears as his thoughts ran along these lines.

Meanwhile, the prescribed time for concluding the ceremony was almost up. The priest sent messenger after messenger, saying, "Let Mathur Babu come for a minute, and the immersion ceremony will be over." Irritated, Mathur sent back the message: "I won't allow anyone to immerse the image of the Mother. Let Her worship be continued. If anyone immerses the image against my will, it will lead to a terrible disaster — even bloodshed!" With that, Mathur remained seated in a pensive mood. Seeing his master in that strange mood, Mathur's frightened servant left for the worship hall and reported everything to the priest. All were dumbfounded.

The priest and others consulted and sent to Mathur those members of his

| 12. Mathur's response to others' persuasion. |

family whom he respected. These relatives tried to persuade him to proceed with the immersion, but they failed to change his mind. Refusing to listen to them, he said: "I shall worship the Mother every day. Since by the grace of the Mother I have the means to do this, why should I then immerse Her?" What else could anyone do? Dejected, they concluded that Mathur had lost his mind. What was the way out of this problem? Everyone in the household knew Mathur's hotheaded nature. When he became angry, he lost all sense of right and wrong. Who would be willing to incur his anger by giving orders to immerse the image of the Mother without his approval? No one came forward to save the situation. The news, greatly magnified, at last reached his wife. Frightened, Jagadamba asked the Master to persuade her husband. Who else, except the Father, could save them from danger? She was deeply concerned that her husband had truly lost his mental balance.

The Master found Mathur pacing back and forth in an abstracted mood,

| 13. The Master persuades Mathur. |

his face grave and his eyes red. Seeing the Master, Mathur came near and said: "Father, whatever others may say, I won't allow the Mother to be immersed into the Ganges. I have ordered the worship to be continued daily. How can I survive in this world without the Mother?"

The Master stroked Mathur's chest and said: "Oh, is this what makes you afraid? Who has told you that you will have to live without the Mother? And where will She go even if you immerse Her image in the Ganges? Can the Mother stay away from Her son? For the last three days She has accepted your worship in the worship hall, but from today She will accept your worship constantly, sitting in your heart."

It is difficult to describe the wonderfully enchanting power of the

| 14. The tremendous power of the Master's words and touch. |

Master's touch and his words. We have seen that sometimes a man who held an opposite view would argue with him and refuse to accept his conclusion. The Master would somehow tactfully touch that man's body, and immediately his thought current would change. He would accept the Master's words and cease to argue. Regarding this, the Master told some of us: "Do you know why I touch a person while talking to him? My touch reduces the power of his obstinacy, and he understands the truth correctly." We have seen and heard many instances of how the Master, with a mere touch, would draw within himself the powers that kept others from realizing the truth, thereby reducing their intensity or permanently destroying them. We have also seen it happen that someone would say something but not create any impression on others, whereas the Master would say the same thing and it would penetrate the listeners' hearts in such a way that from that point on the current of their lives was changed. We shall try to tell the reader about this in detail some other time. Let us now continue the story of Mathur.

Gradually, the Master's words and touch restored Mathur to his normal state. We do not know for certain whether Mathur had any vision or experience at that time, but he probably did. It seems that he saw the luminous form of the Divine Mother living in his heart, and that increased his bliss a hundredfold. His intense desire to save the image was greatly reduced. Thus, a true guru draws the disciple's mind towards the splendour of a lofty and luminous ideal, and lower spiritual moods drop off automatically.

15. How Mathur regains his normal state.

Although Mathur's faith and devotion might appear to us to be remarkable, they undoubtedly arose as a result of testing the Master in various ways. He tested the Master in every possible manner: For example, he offered him money, engaged beautiful women to tempt him, turned over to him complete control of himself and his entire household, and spent money lavishly on Hriday and other relations of the Master. Finally, Mathur realized that, unlike ordinary people, the Master was above all temptation. He also noticed that when faced with the Master's keen insight, insincerity could not remain hidden behind its façade. If a person, after committing any sinful act — even murder — frankly and sincerely took refuge in the Master, he lovingly accepted that person and forgave all misdeeds. He endowed that person with the power to recognize and realize the higher ideal. The impossible became possible by virtue of the mysterious power that worked through the Master.

16. As a result of testing the Master, Mathur develops unflinching love for and faith in him.

Living in the company of the Master and watching his experience of immense bliss in bhava samadhi, the worldly-minded Mathur wanted to know more about this mysterious phenomenon. He was then fully convinced: "The Father has the power to transmit samadhi to others by a mere wish. Because he himself is Shiva, Kali, Krishna, Rama, and all forms of God, it is easy for him. It is not surprising that out of mercy he can show any one of his forms to anybody." Those who came in close contact with the Master developed this conviction after their first meeting: They believed that the impossible could be made possible by his will and that by a mere wish he could make anyone realize the truths of the spiritual realm. It is extremely difficult to use the power of one's own spiritual strength and pure character to transmit

17. Mathur's desire to attain bhava samadhi.

spirituality to a single person, not to speak of doing so to many. This is only possible for an avatar. In fact, the ability to do this is one of the main characteristics of an avatar. Knowing that in this world of falsehood, fraud, and hypocrisy many people deceive others in the name of the avatars, Jesus publicly proclaimed: "When I depart from this world, many hypocrites will appear before you and say, 'I am the Messiah; I am the refuge and saviour of weak human beings.' Beware of those false prophets. Take heed that no man deceives you."[1]

As soon as Mathur felt the desire to experience ecstasy, he went to the

18. Mathur prays to the Master for it.

Master and demanded: "Father, you must do something so that I may have bhava samadhi." We can presume that the Master responded to him as he always did to others on similar occasions, saying: "Look, it will come at the right time. Does a seed sprout into a tree as soon as it is sown and bear fruit to be eaten immediately? Why are you asking for samadhi? You are all right; you are enjoying both secular and spiritual joy. If you attain samadhi, your mind will be completely withdrawn from the world. Who will protect your wealth and property then? Everything you own will be looted indiscriminately. What will you do then?"

But who would listen to those words? Mathur was inexorable. He insisted

19. The Master dissuades Mathur, citing the example of Uddhava and the gopis.

that the Father must give him bhava samadhi. When the Master found that his arguments were having no effect, he raised the theme to a higher scale. He said: "Look, do devotees want to see the Cosmic God? They want only to serve Him. If a man experiences the cosmic power of God, he becomes afraid and his love for God is suppressed. When Krishna went to Mathura, the gopis were extremely distressed by pangs of separation. Knowing their sad condition, Krishna sent Uddhava to console them. Uddhava was a jnani, a man of nondual knowledge. He could not understand the loving attitude of the gopis of Vrindaban, who had fed and dressed Krishna, played with him, and cried for him. He considered the pure love of the gopis to be something inferior that was based on maya. So Krishna sent Uddhava to the gopis for another reason as well, so that he could learn something by seeing them.

"Uddhava went and began to console the gopis, asking: 'Why are you so upset and crying for Krishna? You know that he is God and omnipresent. It can't be that he is in Mathura but not in Vrindaban. Instead of lamenting in this way, if you close your eyes you will see your beloved One — with blue complexion, wearing a garland of wild flowers, and playing a flute — dwelling always in your hearts.' To this, the gopis replied: 'Uddhava, you are Krishna's friend and also a jnani. How can you talk like this? Have we

---

1. Adapted from Matthew 24:4,5,11,23-26.

experienced Krishna through meditation, or knowledge, or through japa, or austerities, like the sages and hermits? We fed him, dressed him, adorned him, and made him beautiful. How can we do those things through meditation? Is it possible for us to act that way? If we had the type of mind that is needed for japa and meditation, we could do those things. But long ago we offered our minds completely at the lotus feet of Krishna. Do we own anything — such as a body, senses, or a mind — which we could connect to our I-consciousness and perform japa?' Uddhava was dumbfounded at this. He then realized how deep and unique was the gopis' love for Krishna. He bowed down to them as he would to a guru and returned to Mathura. Look, do true devotees want to see God? They get joy only by serving Him. Beyond that they do not care for visions or any other experiences. Such things ruin their spiritual mood."

But Mathur was not convinced, so the Master said: "Very well, I'll ask Mother about it. She will do as She thinks best."

A few days later Mathur experienced bhava samadhi. The Master told us later: "Mathur sent for me. When I went to his place, I found him altogether changed. He wasn't the same man. While talking about God, he shed floods of tears. His eyes were red from weeping, and his heart was pounding. When he saw me, he fell down and clasped my feet. 'Father,' he said, 'I admit it — I am beaten! I've been in this state for the past three days. I can't apply my mind to worldly affairs, however hard I try. Everything is going wrong. Please take back the ecstasy you gave me. I don't want it.' 'But you begged me for ecstasy,' I said. He then said: 'I know I did. And it is indeed a blissful state — but what is the use of bliss when all my worldly affairs are going to pieces? This ecstasy of yours, Father, suits only you. The rest of us don't really want it. Please take it back.' Then I laughed and said, 'That's what I told you all along.' 'I know you did, Father,' replied Mathur. 'But what I didn't understand was that this thing would possess me like a spirit, and that I'd have to take every step and do everything exactly as it told me to, twenty-four hours a day!' Then I rubbed Mathur's chest, and he was himself again."

20. Mathur's samadhi and subsequent prayer.

In truth, it is not enough to achieve a spiritual mood or samadhi. How many people can bear its force and retain it? It is impossible to stay in that state as long as one has a little desire. For that reason the scriptures have suggested that seekers of God be free from desires at the outset: "Immortality can be attained through renunciation only."[2] Momentary outbursts of emotion can bring on a lower form of samadhi, but it does not last long if that person's mind is crowded with desires for money, name and fame, and so

21. Samadhi cannot be retained without renunciation.

2. Kaivalya Upanishad 1:2; Narayana Upanishad 11:3.

on. As Shankara said in the *Vivekachudamani* (79): "So-called seekers for liberation, who lack the true spirit of renunciation, try nevertheless to cross the ocean of this world. The shark of craving catches them by the throat, drags them violently from their course, and drowns them midway."

While we were with the Master, we witnessed many such instances. Here is one example: The Master was then staying in the Cossipore garden house. One day some Vaishnava devotees came, bringing with them an agitated young man. We had never seen him before. The reason for their visit was to introduce the young man to the Master and to ask his opinion regarding a spiritual state that had suddenly come upon this man. The Master was told of this group's arrival.

> 22. An example: the story of a young devotee at Cossipore garden.

When we saw the young man, his chest and face were flushed. He was humbly taking the dust of everyone's feet while chanting God's name. He was shivering with delight, and goose bumps covered his body. His eyes were red and swollen with the tears that flowed continuously. His complexion was dark blue. He was neither fat nor thin. His face and limbs were handsome and well formed, and he had a tuft of hair on his head. He was clothed in a dirty white dhoti and had neither shoes nor a chadar to cover his upper body. He was completely indifferent to his body and was not concerned about keeping it clean or protecting it. We were told that this ecstatic state had suddenly come on him while he was singing of the glory of Hari. From that point on, he had virtually stopped eating and could not sleep. Day and night he cried and rolled on the ground because he could not attain God. He had been in that state for a few days.

We have seen in no one except the Master such power to grasp and recognize the changes in the human body that can be caused by an exuberance of spiritual emotions. The guru has been described in the Guru-Gita and other scriptures as "the physician of worldly disease." Before we met the Master, we did not understand the profound meaning of this. In truth, the guru is the physician of mental disease, and he can also diagnose at first sight the changes produced in the mind by various spiritual emotions. If these changes are favourable, he directs the aspirant so that this mood becomes natural and helps that person to ascend to higher planes of spirituality. If the changes are unfavourable, he prescribes specific means to make the mood disappear without harming the aspirant. We had not heard of such things before. But as we observed the Master guiding aspirants in this manner every day, we became convinced of this point.

> 23. The Master had the power to recognize changes caused by excessive spiritual emotion. The guru is truly a physician of worldly disease.

When Swami Vivekananda first attained nirvikalpa samadhi, we saw the Master prescribe the following: "Now for a few days, don't eat food cooked by others. Cook your own meals. In this state one can eat food cooked at most by one's mother, but this ecstatic mood will disappear if one takes food touched by others. This will no longer be a concern when samadhi becomes natural to you." And when he saw that Gopal-ma had physical pain due to the humour of wind, the Master said: "It is caused by your *Hari-bai*, an excess of spiritual energy. How will you pass your time if it goes away? Let it be with you. When you feel too much pain, please eat something." When he noticed that a devotee could not forget the body and fully concentrate his mind on God because of his obsession regarding external cleanliness, the Master told him privately, "Put a mark on your forehead with the clay of that place where people answer the call of nature and then call on God."

When he observed that someone's spiritual progress was being obstructed by his uncontrollable agitation during sankirtan, the Master scolded him: "You rascal! You have come to display ecstasy to me! Does real ecstasy create such a physical convulsion? On the contrary, at that time one becomes motionless, absorbed in God. What is this? Be still and calm. (*To the others*:) Do you know what kind of ecstasy this is? It is like an ounce of milk boiling in a cauldron over the fire. One thinks it is a huge quantity of milk — a cauldronful. When you take the cauldron from the fire, you see no milk, and whatever milk may be left is stuck inside the cauldron." Watching the worldly tendency of another person, the Master said: "You rascal! Eat well, dress well, and enjoy the world to your heart's content, but don't think that you are doing all these things as religious duties." We can cite many such examples.

When the Master saw that young man, he remarked: "I see a preliminary

| 24. The Master's conclusion regarding that young man's condition. | sign of madhura bhava.[3] But this state will not last; he will not be able to hold it. It is extremely difficult to retain this state. As soon as he touches a woman with desire in his mind, this ecstasy will vanish. It will be |

utterly destroyed." The visiting devotees were relieved to some extent, understanding from the Master's remark that the young man's brain was not deranged, and they all left. After some time we heard that the Master's prediction had come true; the young man's fate betrayed him. He had the fortune to ascend to a higher plane by the momentary excitement of the sankirtan, but alas, he descended to a very low plane when his emotional side was exhausted. To avoid this predicament, Swami Vivekananda always advocated devotion tempered with knowledge, and he taught people to practise this.

3. Radha of Vrindaban had so much intense love for Krishna that it would manifest in her body with nineteen modifications, classified in eight groups known as "eight sattvic modifications," such as laughing, weeping, tears, tremor, horripilation, sweating, fainting, and so on. According to the Vaishnava scriptures, this state is called madhura bhava, and its culmination is mahabhava. During mahabhava nineteen physical modifications appear out of exuberant love for God. It is said that it is impossible for an ordinary being to achieve all aspects.

As Mathur had nothing to hide from the Father, so the Father had nothing

25. The childlike Master would speak frankly with Mathur and seek his opinion.

to hide from Mathur. As a boy behaves with his mother and a friend with his friend, similarly the Master, except when he was in samadhi, would talk frankly and freely to Mathur, cordially ask his opinion, accept his advice, and seek his loving care. We have already shared with the reader the scriptural statement that when a person reaches the highest plane of supreme knowledge, in the eyes of ordinary people he or she appears to be a lunatic, or a ghoul, or a child. Moreover, Shankara wrote explicitly that such illumined souls remain unperturbed whether they enjoy royal riches or live on alms and wear a loincloth, and whether they are in a state of happiness or misery according to public estimation. Dwelling always in the bliss of the Atman, they are immersed within themselves. Shankara said in the *Vivekachudamani* (542): "Sometimes he appears to be a fool, sometimes a sage, sometimes possessed of regal splendour. Sometimes he wanders, and sometimes behaves like a motionless python that waits for its food to come to it. Sometimes he is honoured, sometimes insulted, and sometimes unknown. Thus lives an illumined soul, always absorbed in supreme bliss." When this is true in the case of an ordinary liberated person, it is no wonder that the great avatars behave like children and remain unperturbed under all circumstances. So it is not at all surprising that the Master behaved with Mathur in that manner. Again, it was no small fortune for Mathur to live in such close contact with the Master for such a long time.

What a wonderful relationship the Master had with Mathur! During the

26. The Master was deeply concerned for Mathur's welfare.

time of his sadhana and afterwards, if the Master needed anything, he would ask Mathur for it. If he had any vision or spiritual experience during samadhi or at other times, he would ask Mathur: "Can you tell me why such a thing happened? Tell me what you think of that?" and so on. The Master kept an eye on Mathur's welfare to ensure that he would attain virtue by using his money properly — meaning that the money meant for the service of each deity was spent for that purpose and that it was used to help support the guests, beggars, and holy people who visited the temple. We heard many stories in this respect. We often witnessed such conduct of the Master when we visited him long after Rani Rasmani and Mathur had passed away. It will not be out of place here to give one example.

From Mathur's time onward, it was arranged that every day after food

27. An example: The Master demands his share of the Divine Mother's prasad.

was offered to Mother Kali and Radha-Govinda, a big plateful of cooked food and one of sweets and fruits should be sent to the Master's room. The Master and those who were with him would partake of that prasad. In addition, on festival occasions when there were special food offerings to Kali and Radha-Govinda, part of that prasad was also sent to the Master.

It was during the rainy season, and the day for worshipping Mother Pha-laharini Kali. The temple celebrated this festival on a small scale with a special worship to Mother Kali and offerings of sweets and fruits. The worship was going on, and the music flowed from the nahabat. Jogin (Swami Yogananda) and some other devotees were with the Master on that day.

On each festival day a particular divine mood would manifest itself in the Master. On the day of a Vaishnava festival, the mood of Vishnu would be manifest in him, and on a Shakta festival day, the mood of Shakti. During Durga Puja, especially at the time of sandhi-puja or Kali Puja, the Master would become absorbed and motionless in the thought of the Divine Mother. His hands would even assume the gestures of Kali — offering a boon with one hand and bestowing fearlessness with the other. Similarly, on the festive occasion of Janmashtami [Krishna's birthday], he was absorbed in the mood of Radha and Krishna, and the eight sattvic modifications (such as shivering, horripilation, and so on) would appear in his body. That ecstasy would come upon him in such a natural way that it seemed he made no effort at all to attain it. Sometimes we have seen that on a particular festival occasion the Master would be focussed on discussing various topics and apparently had forgotten the special manifestation of that particular deity on that day. But suddenly his mind would be withdrawn from those topics and become absorbed in the mood of that one deity, as if someone had forced him to focus on that deity. We witnessed many such instances while the Master was staying in Shyampukur. One time the Master was talking to Dr. Mahendralal Sarkar and many others in his room when all of a sudden he went into ecstasy. It was the time for sandhi-puja (a special worship of the goddess Durga). As we gazed on his luminous face beaming with a smile, who could then think that he had any disease or even that he was the same pale-faced, ill person seen just moments before?

28. The Master had different kinds of samadhi appropriate to specific holy days.

On the day of the Phalaharini Kali Puja, the Master experienced ecstasy intermittently. Like a five-year-old boy, the Master was singing the Mother's name and dancing with joy. Overwhelmed, people gazed at his wonderful face. They experienced various spiritual moods by virtue of the holy company of this godman. The night was almost over when the Mother's worship was finished, and no one had had much rest. Morning arrived.

At 8:00 or 9:00 a.m., the Master realized that his allotted portion of the special food offering had not arrived. He asked his nephew Ramlal, the priest of the Kali temple, why he had not received the prasad. Ramlal did not have an answer, but he reported: "All of the prasad has been sent as usual to the temple manager. It is being distributed from his office according to each person's allotted share. I don't know why your share has not yet been sent." At this the Master became impatient and anxious. He asked several persons, "Why has prasad not yet come from the office?" and went on talking about it. After he had waited for a while and the prasad had still not arrived, he put on his slippers and went to the manager. The Master asked the manager: "Hello, why has the allotted prasad for that room (*pointing to his room*) not been sent? Is it a mistake? This is a long-standing arrangement. It would be wrong to stop it now, even by mistake." Embarrassed, the manager said: "Has prasad not yet been sent to you? That is a bad mistake. I will send it immediately."

Jogin [later, Swami Yogananda] was then a boy. He was a little proud

| 29. Observing the Master's demand of prasad, Swami Yogananda is puzzled. |

because he had been born into the noble and aristocratic Savarna Chaudhury family. He considered the manager, other officials, and priests of the temple to be worthless. But the Master's unselfish love and unconditional grace forced Jogin to completely surrender at his holy feet. Because his home was very near Rasmani's temple garden, he had the great advantage of being able to visit the Master every day. But what else could he do? The Master's strong attraction pulled him to the temple regularly. Although he respected the Master, he had always kept his distance from the temple staff. Therefore, when he saw that the Master was anxious because he had not received his share of the prasad, he said: "Sir, it matters little if it does not come. This is a negligible thing! Moreover, the food does not suit your stomach, and you do not eat it either. Let them not send it." When the Master ignored him and after a while went to the manager to inquire of the matter, Jogin pondered: "How strange! Why is he so anxious today for some ordinary fruits and sweets? I have never known him to be perturbed in any matter. Then why is he in such a mood?" Finding no reason after long deliberation, he concluded: "Now I understand! The Master may be a great spiritual teacher, but he is tied to his family tradition. He was born into a brahmin family. These hereditary priests are attached to petty things like rice and plantains; he is supposed to have a little quality of his lineage. That's it. Important matters do not concern him, but he is so restless for this trifling thing! He does not eat those things, and he cannot use them himself, so why is he so anxious for them? It is nothing but hereditary habit!"

After reaching this conclusion, Jogin waited in the Master's room. Mean-

| 30. The Master explains his action. |

while, the Master returned and said to him: "Look here. Rani Rasmani has bequeathed her large estate to the service of this temple so that the offerings may be distributed among devotees and sadhus. The part of the offerings that comes to this room is taken only by devotees who come here with yearning for God, so the gift of Rani Rasmani is put to good use. But what use is made of the other portion that goes to the temple priests? They sell the offered rice in the market, and some even feed their mistresses with the prasad! I fight with the temple officials for the share that comes here so that Rasmani's objective may be at least partially fulfilled." Jogin was dumbfounded and realized that every one of the Master's acts, no matter how trivial it might appear, had deep significance.

What a wonderful relationship the Master had established with Mathur!

31. The wonderful relationship between Mathur and the Master.

It is clear that the Master's unlimited grace intensified Mathur's love until finally the Father became the life of his life. The Master's childlike nature also attracted Mathur tremendously. Is there anyone in this world who is not attracted to an innocent, naïve boy? Is there anyone who will not keep a concerned eye on his sweet, carefree activities and rush to protect him lest he be harmed in the excitement of play? Moreover, there was not an iota of artificiality or pretense in the Master's boyish nature. When he was in that mood, it seemed then that he was truly a boy incapable of protecting himself. So it was no wonder that the strong and intelligent Mathur would spontaneously wish to protect him in every respect. On one hand Mathur depended on the Master's divine power, but on the other he was always ready to protect him, knowing him to be a naïve boy. As Mathur observed the striking combination of all-knowing guru-nature and little-knowing boy-nature in the Father, Mathur perhaps decided that he needed to protect him regarding worldly matters, including his personal safety, and the Father would protect him in matters pertaining to the subtle spiritual realm beyond human sight and power. We clearly understand that Mathur's love for the Master took a form that is difficult to understand, because he saw in the mysterious Master a wonderful meeting of very complicated and contrary attributes: the divine and the human; omniscience and limited knowledge.

Although Mathur's Chosen Deity was the Father, who was established in

32. Mathur consoles the childlike Master, mentioning the lust-producing worm.

bhavamukha and identified with Kali, sometimes he had to console the Father in various ways because he was an embodiment of childlike simplicity and dependence. Mathur's genuine love gave him the ingenuity to answer all sorts of questions. One day while talking with Mathur, the Father suddenly left. He returned with a sad face and asked Mathur: "Can you tell me what kind of disease this is? I saw a worm coming out of my body with the urine. I have never heard that such a worm dwells in the human body. Now what has happened to me?" Shortly before, this very Father had been charming everyone by explaining hidden spiritual truths in simple language, and now the same Father was extremely anxious, like a boy considering the unknown, and he was depending on Mathur's intelligence and consolation. Mathur quickly reassured the Master: "It is good, Father, that it happened. Everyone has a worm in his body that generates lust. It is this lust-worm that creates various bad thoughts in the mind and forces one to commit evil. It is the grace of the Mother that the lust-worm has left your body. Why are you so worried about it?" The Father was greatly relieved by this and said: "You are right. It is fortunate that I asked you about it." He was then as joyful as a child.

One day the Father said to Mathur: "You see, the Divine Mother has shown

33. The Master tells Mathur about forthcoming devotees.

me many times that this place (*himself*) has an inner circle of devotees and that they will come. They will know and hear about God from this place. These devotees will also attain love and devotion and direct experience of God. (*Pointing to his own body*) The Mother will play with this body in many ways and do good to many people. That is why She has not yet destroyed this body, but has saved it. What do you say? Can you tell me whether these are hallucinations or true visions?"

Mathur replied: "Why should they be hallucinations, Father? The Mother has never before shown you anything false, so how can this not be true? This also will come to pass. But why are those devotees so late in coming? Let them come soon, and we shall be happy in their company."

The Father was also convinced that what the Mother had shown was true. He said: "Well, I don't know when they will come. But the Mother told me about it and showed it to me in a vision. Everything happens by Mother's will."

Rani Rasmani had four daughters, but no sons. Mathur married the third

34. An example of the Master's childlike nature: the incident of picking watercress.

daughter, and when she died, the youngest one. During her lifetime, the intelligent Rani carefully distributed the shares of her estate among her sons-in-law, so that later on there would be no dispute among them on that account. One day after the distribution of the estate, Jagadamba went to bathe in a pond that belonged to her sister. There she found a fine bed of watercress and plucked some to take back with her. The Master, who happened to be passing, saw her do this. Immediately there was a great commotion in his mind: "It is very wrong for Jagadamba to take something that belongs to another in this way. Does she not know that taking something without asking first is theft? Why does she crave what belongs to another?" As he was thinking in this way, he saw the daughter who owned that pond. The Master immediately reported everything to her. Listening to the story and seeing the Master's serious mood because of Jagadamba's "heinous" act, she could hardly control her laughter. However, she pretended indignation and exclaimed, "That was very wrong of her, Father!" Meanwhile, Jagadamba arrived. When she learned why her elder sister was merry, Jagadamba jokingly reproached him: "Father, is it proper for you to expose me in this way? I took that watercress secretly so that she might not see it. And now you have embarrassed me by reporting my theft to her." Then the sisters could no longer control themselves and began to laugh. "I don't know your worldly ways," the Master told Jagadamba. "But when property has been divided, it is not good to take anything without the owner's knowledge. So I informed your sister. Now let her decide." Both sisters continued laughing, thinking how simple and naïve the Father was.

On one hand the Father had such a childlike nature, and on the other he

| 35. During times of danger Mathur took refuge in the Master. |

acted like a chastising father to Mathur. Once there was a quarrel between Mathur and another landlord. Mathur ordered his guards to take part in a brutal gang fight with the guards of the rival party, and one of them was killed. Finding himself in danger of prosecution, Mathur rushed to the Father and implored, "Father, save me." Annoyed, the Father scolded him, saying: "Rascal, you will create a row every day and come and cry, 'Save me!' What can I do? Go and suffer the consequences." But at last, seeing Mathur's deep anguish, the Master said, "Well, it will be as Mother wills." In fact Mathur escaped the calamity.

We can cite many similar examples that illustrate the Master's paradox-

| 36. An example of how the miserly Mathur lavishly spent money for the Master. |

ical nature. As he witnessed these events, Mathur was firmly convinced that his own wealth, prestige, power, and everything else were due to the grace of the wonderful Father. So it was not strange that Mathur would pay obeisance to the Father as an incarnation of God and that he would maintain unwavering devotion and faith in him. The extent of a worldly man's devotion can be measured by the money he spends on that which he adores. Like many shrewd and wealthy people, Mathur was a little miserly. But he spent money freely to please the Master, proving that he indeed had sincere love for and faith in the Master. Mathur once dressed the Father in beautiful clothing and then took him to watch a yatra performance. He placed one hundred rupees or more, arranged in stacks of ten, in front of the Father so that he could reward the various actors. But the Master was in an exalted mood, and while listening to a song or speech that appealed to him, he immediately pushed all of the money to that particular actor as a reward. Mathur expressed his joy without the least irritation, saying, "The Father's generosity befits his royal mood!" Mathur again arranged stacks of money in front of him. But how long could any money last with the Father, who was established in bhavamukha and completely free from greed? He had renounced money by saying, "Rupee is clay, clay is rupee." Again, beside himself in ecstasy, he gave all of the money to another actor. Then, wishing to reward a third actor and finding no money laid out for him, he took off his own expensive clothes and shawl and gave them to the actor and then remained motionless in samadhi. Mathur was delighted with the thought that his money had been properly used and began to fan the Father.

There are many such examples of how the miserly Mathur spent gener-

| 37. Other examples. |

ously to please the Master. Mathur accompanied the Father on a pilgrimage to Varanasi, Vrindaban, and other places. At Varanasi, according to the Father's wishes he dispensed charity like a wish-fulfilling tree; he gave people whatever articles they needed. He then asked the Father to request something for himself, but the latter could not find anything he lacked. At last he said, "Give me a water pot." Mathur's eyes filled with tears at this spirit of renunciation.

On the way to Varanasi and Vrindaban, the party stopped for a few days at Deoghar to visit the famous temple of Vaidyanath Shiva. The Master was overcome with compassion when he saw the miserable condition of the poverty-stricken people in a nearby village. He said to Mathur: "You are a steward of Mother's estate. Give each of these poor people one piece of cloth, and one good meal, and also some oil for their heads." At first Mathur was reluctant. He said: "Father, this pilgrimage is going to cost a great deal, and there are many people here. If I give them what you ask, I may find myself short of money later. What do you think I ought to do?" The Father paid no heed to that excuse. Overwhelmed with compassion, he shed tears at the sight of the villagers' abject misery and cried in anguish: "You wretch! I'm not going to Varanasi. I'm staying here with these people. They have no one to care for them. I won't leave them." Like an obstinate child, he left Mathur's company and sat with the poor villagers. Seeing such compassion in the Father, Mathur had cloth brought from Calcutta and fulfilled his other requests as well. The Father was pleased by the villagers' happiness. He then took leave of them and joyfully left for Varanasi with Mathur. We heard that at another time the Master went with Mathur to a village near Ranaghat, in his estate, where he had similar feelings of compassion for the pitiable condition of those villagers and made Mathur do what he had done near Deoghar.

> 38. At the Master's command Mathur served the poor in Vaidyanath.

As a guru, the Master had bound Mathur with love forever. Once when the Master was in an ecstatic mood during his period of sadhana, he prayed to the Divine Mother: "Mother, don't make me a dry monk. Let me have fun and merriment in my life." As a result of this prayer, the Master enjoyed a wonderful relationship with Mathur. The Divine Mother showed him that four suppliers of provisions had been sent to the world to take care of his needs and that Mathur was the first and foremost of them. Could this relation have continued uninterruptedly for such a long time had it not been determined by Providence? Alas! Has the world ever witnessed such a pure spiritual relationship?

O worldly desire, how strongly you have bound human beings! Although we have seen this wonderful Master and established our relationship with him, who is by nature pure, illumined, free, and an embodiment of selfless love, our minds are still attached to worldly objects! One day a friend of ours, while listening to the Master tell the marvellous story of Mathur, and thinking of his

> 39. The Master's relationship with Mathur was predestined: the Master's remark on Mathur's rebirth, as the latter still had a desire for enjoyment.

great fortune, asked him: "Sir, what became of Mathur after his death? Surely, he won't have to be born again, will he?" The Master replied: "Perhaps he has been born as a king somewhere. He still had a desire for enjoyment." Then he changed the subject.

Chapter 8

As a Guru, the Master's
*R*elationship with His Own
Gurus

I am seated in the hearts of all; from Me are memory and knowledge, and their loss as well. It is I alone who am to be known through all the Vedas; I am indeed the Author of Vedanta and the Knower of the Vedas. — GITA 15:15

WE HAVE ALREADY SAID THAT IN ONE WHO IS BORN TO be a guru, indications of this

1. The power of a guru is inherent in all avatars.

destiny are visible in that person's life from childhood onward (see III.5.3,5). This is also evident in the lives of avatars. And among those who have been born to establish a particular ideal in society, one can see that ideal manifest in them from childhood. The maturity of their bodies and minds, as well as a favourable time and place, and other circumstances, may help to develop the ideal fully in their lives, but those factors do not create that ideal in them and make them gurus. It is seen that the ideal is their own property and has been so since the beginning of their lives, and that all efforts to trace its source are futile. We find a similar situation while studying the Master's life to determine the origin of his power as a guru. It is amazing how this power manifested itself to greater or lesser degrees in his boyhood, youth, during his sadhana, and at other times. One cannot successfully use reason to determine how this power first originated in the Master's life. We don't intend to increase the length of this volume by narrating here the events of his early life. But we think it is not out of place to present to the reader some previously unrelated events regarding the manifestation of the Master's power as a guru, from his youth and the period of his sadhana to his association with Mathur.

The Master used to refer to the story of the Avadhuta from the Bhagavata

2. The Master takes initiation from several gurus.

to explain to us that an aspirant must have only one mantra-guru [who gives initiation into a mantra] but can have many subsidiary teachers or preceptors. The Bhagavata describes how the Avadhuta gradually attained perfection after receiving special instructions from each of twenty-four upa-gurus [subsidiary gurus], one after another. Similarly, various gurus taught the Master how to practise different sadhanas and ultimately experience the truth inherent in each one of them. Of these teachers, the Master most often mentioned the Bhairavi Brahmani, the naked Tota Puri, and the Muslim Govinda. Although he learned the sadhanas of other Hindu traditions from different gurus, he seldom mentioned their names. He said only that he learned different methods of sadhana from various gurus and attained perfection within three days of beginning to practise each sadhana. It is now difficult to say whether the Master had forgotten their names or whether he did not consider them to be worth mentioning. It seems that they had contact with the Master for a short while only, so they do not need special mention.

Of the Master's teachers the Bhairavi Brahmani stayed with him for the

3. The Bhairavi Brahmani.

longest period, but it is hard to determine exactly how long. Sometime before we went to the Master, she left Dakshineswar permanently. Later, the Master located her once when she was living in Varanasi.

The Master told us that the Bhairavi Brahmani spent a long time at the

4. The Brahmani helps the Master.

Dakshineswar Kali temple and other places nearby, such as the Devamandal ghat on the bank of the Ganges. The Brahmani made the Master practise the main disciplines of sixty-four Tantras, one after another. She was well versed in Vaishnava Tantra, but it is not clear if she helped the Master when he was practising *sakhi bhava* and other devotional moods. We heard that after helping the Master during the period of his sadhana, she remained in Dakshineswar for almost six more years and was respected by all. During that period she also went to Kamarpukur with the Master and Hriday and stayed with the Master's relatives. The Holy Mother respected the Brahmani as her mother-in-law and addressed her as "Mother."

Following Vaishnava sadhanas, the Brahmani had some periods of bliss

5. The Brahmani's experience in Vaishnava Tantra.

arising from the sakhya and vatsalya attitudes. While she was staying at the Devamandal ghat in Dakshineswar, she would become absorbed in the vatsalya mood. Shedding tears for the Master, she would hold butter in her hand and loudly call for him, "Gopala, Gopala." Meanwhile, at Dakshineswar the Master was extremely anxious to see the Brahmani. Like a boy pining for his mother, the Master would run a mile to see her, sit near her, and eat the butter. The Brahmani would sometimes dress herself in a red silk

Varanasi sari and jewellery borrowed from some neighbours and visit the Master accompanied by some village women. She would bring various delicacies to him and sing songs about Gopala on her way and after feeding the Master would return. The Master told us that when the Brahmani was in that state — with dishevelled hair and overwhelmed by her spiritual mood — it seemed that she was Nanda's queen Yashoda [the foster mother of Krishna] grieving because of separation from Gopala.

The Brahmani possessed extraordinary beauty along with her noble qualities. The Master told us that Mathur at first doubted her character upon seeing her grace and beauty and hearing that she travelled freely without companions. One day Mathur sarcastically remarked, "O Bhairavi, where is your Bhairava?"[1] The Brahmani was then leaving the Kali temple after saluting the deity. She was neither embarrassed nor angered by this rude question. She calmly looked at Mathur and pointed to the image of Shiva in the shrine, lying prostrate beneath the feet of Kali. The worldly, suspicious Mathur would not let this go so easily. He said, "But that Bhairava is motionless." The Bhairavi then gravely replied, "Why should I have become a Bhairavi if I could not move the immovable?" Hearing this answer and noting the Brahmani's calm and majestic demeanour, Mathur remained speechless, ashamed and embarrassed. Later, when day by day Mathur became aware of her noble nature and many good qualities, his suspicions slowly disappeared.

6. Mathur's misgivings upon observing the Brahmani's beauty and noble qualities.

The Master told us that the Brahmani had been born somewhere in East Bengal. Upon seeing her, one would undoubtedly guess that she came from a respectable family. She did indeed. But the Master never told us where she was from, which family she had been born into, whether she had ever married, why she had renounced her home, or why she had become a nun and travelled from place to place. Nor do we know where she acquired such vast learning or where and when she had made such tremendous progress in sadhana.

7. The Brahmani's early life.

It need hardly be mentioned that the Brahmani was extremely advanced in sadhana. This is evident because she was selected by Providence to be a guru to the Master. Again, the Master told us that before she came to him, the Brahmani's yogic power had revealed to her that during her lifetime she would have to give spiritual help to three men, including the Master. And as soon as she met these individuals, in different places at different times, she immediately recognized them and helped them in their sadhana. This proves that she was undoubtedly a spiritual aspirant of a high order.

8. The Brahmani was a spiritual aspirant of high degree.

1. *Bhairava* is the masculine form of *Bhairavi,* a Tantric nun. Mathur's insinuation was that Bhairavi must have a lover somewhere in the neighbourhood. — *Translator*

During their first meeting the Brahmani told the Master about Chandra

9. The Brahmani's yogic vision.

and Girija. "My son," she said, "I have already found those two disciples. Today I have found you, after searching all these years. I shall introduce you to the others later." She did in fact bring Chandra and Girija to Dakshineswar and introduced them to the Master. We have heard from the Master that they were highly developed aspirants. But although they were far advanced on the path of sadhana, they could not succeed in realizing God: They had achieved some occult powers and had been diverted from the right path.

The Master mentioned that Chandra had a contemplative nature and was

10. The story of Chandra, a disciple of the Brahmani.

a lover of God. He achieved an occult power called *gutika-siddhi*. After sanctifying a *gutika* [a tiny ball] with a mantra and fastening it onto his arm, he could make himself invisible and thus gain access to even closely guarded places. If a person achieves occult powers before realizing God, he or she becomes egotistic. This enhancement of the ego traps the aspirant in a net of desires, preventing any further movement towards a higher spiritual ideal. It finally becomes the cause of his or her downfall.

Ah, in how many ways did the Master explain to us: "As the ego grows, so does sin; when the ego shrinks, one attains virtue. The increase of egotism destroys spirituality, but by annihilating the ego one becomes spiritual. Selfishness is sin; selflessness is virtue. All troubles cease when the 'I' dies." He said further: "Look, the scriptures describe the ego as *chit-jada-granthi* [a knot of consciousness and unconsciousness]. *Chit* means the Atman, which is consciousness itself; *jada* means matter, such as the body, the senses, and so on. Tying these two together, this ego has created firm delusion in the human mind: 'I am a jiva endowed with a body, senses, an intellect, and so on.' One cannot make any progress without cutting this terrible knot. One must give up the ego. The Divine Mother has shown me that occult powers are to be shunned like excrement. One should pay no attention to them. Sometimes they arise of themselves when you practise sadhana. But if you take notice of them, you'll be caught. You won't be able to reach God."

The main focus of Swami Vivekananda's life was meditation. While

11. An occult power causes one to fall from yoga.

eating, resting, or performing other activities, he always kept part of his mind focussed on the thought of God. The Master would say, "He is perfect in meditation." One day during meditation Vivekananda suddenly developed powers of clairvoyance and clairaudience. As soon as he became absorbed in deep meditation, his mind would rise to such a high plane that from that vantage point he could see people in a discussion at someone's house. He would want to immediately verify whether this experience was real. He would abandon his meditation to go to that place, where he would discover that what he had seen during meditation was indeed true. After experiencing this a few times, he reported it to the Master. The latter said: "Those powers are obstacles to the path of God-realization. Don't meditate now for a few days."

Chandra's ego became inflated after he achieved gutika-siddhi. The

| 12. Chandra fell because of his occult power. | Master told us that Chandra gradually became very attached to lust and gold. He became infatuated with the daughter of a respected and wealthy man and |

began to visit her using his miraculous power of invisibility. As his egotism and selfishness increased, Chandra lost his occult power and was humiliated.

The Master also told us about Girija's amazing occult power. One day the

| 13. The story of Girija, another disciple of the Brahmani. | Master walked with Girija to Shambhu Mallick's garden house near the Dakshineswar Kali temple. Shambhu loved the Master sincerely and considered |

himself blessed if he could serve the Master in any way. He leased some land near the Dakshineswar temple for 250 rupees and built a cottage for the Holy Mother. The Holy Mother lived there in those days. Every day she would take her bath in the Ganges and then visit the Master. Once the Holy Mother had a severe attack of dysentery while staying at that cottage, and Shambhu arranged for her treatment and a special diet. His devout wife also adored the Master and the Holy Mother, regarding them as divine beings. If the Holy Mother was at Dakshineswar, Shambu's wife would invite her to her house on Tuesdays, which are auspicious, and worship her as a goddess. Shambhu would pay the carriage fare when the Master went to Calcutta and also provide him with food and other necessities. Of course, this privilege of serving the Master came to him after Mathur passed away. The Master described Shambhu as his "second supplier of provisions." Quite often he would walk to his garden and spend a few hours discussing spiritual matters with him.

On one occasion the Master went with Girija to take a walk in Shambhu's

| 14. Girija's occult power. | garden, where they spent a long time discussing spiritual matters. The Master used to say: "The nature of |

a devotee is like that of a hemp smoker. A hemp smoker pulls deeply on the pipe, then hands it over to another smoker and slowly releases the smoke. He does not find any joy in smoking alone. Similarly, when devotees get together, one of them becomes overwhelmed when talking about God and then remains in blissful silence. The devotee then allows others to talk about Him and enjoys listening to them." On that day Shambhu, Girija, and the Master were so absorbed in their spiritual discussion that they took no notice of time passing and the evening deepened into night. Suddenly, the Master came to his senses and took his leave of Shambhu. He started down the road, heading in the direction of the Kali temple. But it was too dark, and he was unable to see anything on the road. He stumbled at every step and lost his way. Because he had left Shambu's garden in a god-intoxicated mood, he had not noticed the darkness and had not borrowed a lantern. Now where was the way? He moved forward with great difficulty, holding Girija's hand. When Girija noticed this, he stopped and said, "Wait a bit, brother, I will give you light." He then turned around and projected a beam of light from his back, illuminating the road. The Master told us, "With that light I clearly saw the way up to the gate of the Kali temple and reached it without difficulty."

The Master then smiled and concluded his narration: "But they did not retain those occult abilities. While they lived with me, their powers disappeared." When we asked the reason for this, he said: "The Divine Mother withdrew their powers into this (*pointing to his body*) for their own good.

15. Acting as a guru, the Master destroyed Chandra's and Girija's occult powers.

Afterwards, they gave up supernatural practices and resumed their progress along the path towards God."

The Master continued: "What is there in occult powers? When one's mind is entangled with them, one moves away from Sat-chidananda. Listen to this story. A man had two sons. The elder left home while he was still young and became a monk. Meanwhile, the younger one got his education and became learned and virtuous. He married and settled down to fulfill his duties as a householder.

16. Occult powers are obstacles to God-realization: the Master's parable about walking on the river.

"According to tradition, after twelve years a monk can visit his birthplace if he wishes. So this monk went to visit his birthplace after being gone for twelve years. He saw his younger brother's farm, his crops, and his wealth. When he reached the door, he called out his brother's name. Hearing his name, the younger brother came out to greet his elder brother. He was overwhelmed with happiness at seeing him after such a long time. He bowed to him, brought him inside the house, and began to serve him. After sharing a meal, they began to talk about various things. The younger brother asked the elder: 'Brother, you have given up worldly pleasures and wandered as a monk for many years. Please tell me what you have gained by this.' The elder brother said: 'You want to see what I've achieved? Come with me.' So he took his brother to the bank of a nearby river and said, 'Watch!' He then crossed the river, walking on the water. Reaching the other bank, he called back, 'Did you see that?' The younger brother paid half a penny to the ferryman, crossed the river by boat, went up to his brother and said, 'What have I seen?' The elder brother said, 'Did you not see me cross the river on foot?' Smiling, the younger brother replied: 'Didn't you see me pay half a penny to cross that river? Is that all you gained by performing austerities for twelve years? Your power is worth only half a penny.' As the monk listened to his brother's words, he was awakened and focussed his mind on God-realization."

Thus conversing with us, the Master explained in many ways that in

<table>
<tr><td>17. Occult powers inflate the ego: the Master's parable of killing and reviving the elephant.</td><td>spiritual life the attainment of such powers is trifling, worthless, and contemptible. We cannot resist mentioning another of the Master's stories on this</td></tr>
</table>

subject. He said: "By performing yogic practices a yogi achieved a state in which everything he said was infallible. Whatever he told anyone came to pass. If he said to a man 'die,' that man died immediately; if the yogi said 'live,' he came back to life at once. One day while he was on a journey, the yogi met a devout holy man who was practising meditation and repeating God's name. He heard that the holy man had been performing austerities for many years. So the vain and arrogant yogi said condescendingly to the holy man: 'Well, you've been repeating the name of God all this time. Tell me, what have you gained from it?' The holy man answered humbly: 'What should I gain? I don't want anything. I want only to realize Him — and that's only possible through His grace. So what can I do but call upon Him and hope that He will have mercy on me, even though He considers me to be poor and lowly.' 'All that effort for nothing!' said the yogi. 'You ought to try to get something.' The holy man remained silent. After a while he asked, 'And you, sir, what have you achieved?' 'Watch this,' said the yogi. He turned to an elephant that was tied to a tree close by and said, 'Elephant, die!' At once the elephant dropped dead. The yogi proudly said: 'Did you see? Now watch again.' He then commanded the dead elephant, 'Elephant, live!' And at once the elephant came to life, shook the dust off its body, and stood under the tree as before. 'Well,' said the yogi triumphantly, 'now you've seen for yourself!' All this while, the holy man had been silent, but now he said: 'I've seen an elephant die and come back to life again. But what have you gained by having this power? Has it freed you from the wheel of death and rebirth? Will it save you from sickness and old age? Can it help you to realize God?' The yogi was speechless and his understanding awakened."

With the Bhairavi Brahmani's help, Chandra[2] and Girija had made great progress in the path of God, but they had not attained perfection. When they became associated with the Master, his divine power destroyed their occult

---

2. In June 1899, Swami Vivekananda went to England and America for the second time. Shortly after this, a man who introduced himself as Chandra came to Belur Math and lived there for about a month. Swami Brahmananda was then living in the monastery, and we saw him talking to Chandra privately. We heard that he asked repeatedly of Swami Brahmananda, "Do you feel the living presence of the Master here?"

He told us that whatever the Master had said about him had come to pass. Only one prediction remained to be fulfilled, and that was the Master's promise to appear before him at his death. He used to spend long hours in japa and meditation in the shrine, with tears running down his face. If anyone asked him about the Master, he would joyfully relate whatever he knew. He appeared to us to be a quiet man. Seeing him remaining silently seated with closed eyes, someone asked him derisively, "Sir, do you take opium?" He humbly replied, "What offence have I committed that you are saying this to me?" When he went to the shrine for the first time, he bowed down and addressed the Master's *(continued)*

abilities and their deep-rooted egos. Thus, their understanding was awakened, and they moved forward along their spiritual paths with renewed energy.

We have clear evidence that although the Bhairavi Brahmani made great

18. Proof that the Brahmani had not attained nirvikalpa samadhi.

progress in her sadhana, she did not achieve full realization of the indivisible Satchidananda. The Master perfected the disciplines of Tantra with the help of the Brahmani before Tota Puri came to Dakshineswar Kali temple. This naked itinerant monk had attained nirvikalpa samadhi, the culmination of Vedantic experience. When Tota Puri saw the Master, he recognized him to be a competent aspirant of Vedanta. After he initiated the Master into sannyasa, Tota instructed him in the sadhana of nirvikalpa samadhi. The Brahmani tried her utmost to dissuade the Master from continuing along that path. She said: "My son, don't visit him often. Don't mix with him too much. His path is the path of dry knowledge. If you associate with him too closely, your love and devotion for God will disappear."

It is evident from this that although the learned Brahmani was endowed with extraordinary devotion to God, she had no knowledge of — nor could she even imagine — the fact that the nirvikalpa state of Vedanta, which she considered to be a "dry" path, is in fact the first step to attaining supreme devotion. She did not know that only those who are pure, illumined, and content in the Atman can love God without motive. As the Master used to say, "Pure devotion and pure knowledge are one and the same." We suppose that the Brahmani was not able to understand this. For this reason, when the Master shaved his head, put on an ochre cloth, and practised nirvikalpa samadhi after being initiated into sannyasa by Tota Puri, he kept it secret from his own mother as well as from the Bhairavi Brahmani. We heard that the Master's aged mother was then living in the upper floor of the northern nahabat of Dakshineswar. The Master confined himself to the hut near the Panchavati for three days to practise the sadhana of Vedanta beyond the range of public view. At that time only Tota Puri occasionally visited him. The Master had paid no heed to the Brahmani's words.

From what the Master told us, it seems that the Brahmani was an aspirant

19. Description of the bestial, heroic, and divine modes of Tantra.

of the heroic mode of Tantra. Three modes of sadhana are described in the Tantra: bestial, heroic, and divine. Lust, anger, and other animal propensities

---

(2. continued) picture as "elder brother" and then profusely shed tears of love and devotion. He looked like an ordinary man and wore no ochre cloth, nor did he display any religious marks on his body. He wore a dhoti and scarf and carried an umbrella and a canvas bag. In this bag he had another dhoti, a towel, and probably a water pot. He said that he often travelled to various holy places in that way. Swami Brahmananda showed him particular love and respect and asked him to live in Belur Math permanently. Chandra agreed and said, "I shall come and live here after making some arrangements regarding the landed property at home." But he never returned. This man was probably the "Chandra" referred to above.

Panchavati at Dakshineswar c.1930, where Ramakrishna had many visions.

are predominant in the aspirant of the bestial mode. An aspirant of this type should avoid all objects of temptation, carefully maintain external purity and conduct, and engage in japa and *purashcharana* [repeated recitation of a mantra for perfection]. In the heroic aspirant, passion for God prevails over animal propensities. The attraction of lust and gold and other sense objects only intensifies this aspirant's love and longing for God. So this type of aspirant should remain unperturbed while living amidst the temptations of lust and gold and try to devote his or her whole mind to God. As for the aspirant of the divine mode, the mind of such a one is free from lust and anger and has been carried away forever by the current of divine love. For that person, the practice of forgiveness, sincerity, kindness, contentment, truthfulness, and other virtues has become as natural as breathing. In short, it can be said about these three modes of sadhana that the best, the second best, and the inferior aspirants mentioned in Vedanta are correspondingly the followers of the divine, heroic, and bestial modes described in Tantra.

Although the Brahmani was foremost amongst heroic aspirants, she had

20. A heroic aspirant, the Brahmani had not yet attained the divine mode.

not achieved the divine mode. As she observed the living example of the divine mode in the Master and benefited from his support, the Brahmani gradually developed a desire to achieve that state. The Brahmani saw that as soon as the Master heard the word siddhi [marijuana] or karana [wine], he became overwhelmed with the consciousness of God, the cause of the universe. Whenever he saw a woman, whether chaste or unchaste, he remembered the Divine Mother's powers of creation and of bestowing joy and felt himself to be Her child. His hands and limbs recoiled from the very touch of gold and other metals even while he was asleep! Living near such a spiritual dynamo, what person would not have the passion for God enkindled? What person would not become disgusted with ephemeral wealth and power and desire to establish a personal relationship with God? We heard that this is why the Brahmani decided to practise severe austerities for the rest of her life.

The Master told us that the Brahmani would become jealous if he associated

21. Proof of this.

with other devotees or paid great respect to any saintly person. We understand that her attitude towards the Master was that of a grandmother or an elderly woman relative who feels distressed on finding a boy she had raised begin to show affection for others in the household as he grows older. As a highly advanced aspirant, the Brahmani should not have had that feeling. She had the opportunity to observe the Master's life day and night over a long period, so she ought to have known that the Master's love and respect were not transient as is often the case with other people. She should have realized that the affection and respect that he rendered to her were permanent, without ebb or flow. O worldly love, you constantly attempt to possess your beloved forever, allowing no freedom from your bonds of love. You think that if your beloved were given liberty, he or she would leave you and find someone else to care for more. You do not understand that it is your own mental weakness that prompts you to feel this way. You do not understand that love often vanishes quickly if the beloved is not allowed freedom and if the lover does not learn to take pleasure in whatever makes the beloved happy, forgetting him- or herself completely. Know for certain that if you wholeheartedly love your beloved, that person will always be yours. And that pure, selfless love will in the end bring to both of you the vision of God and liberation from all bondage.

It seems surprising that although the Brahmani was a highly advanced aspirant and a great devotee, she did not recognize her own weakness or was incapable of accepting it despite an intellectual understanding. In fact, she lacked the awareness of selfless love. On the contrary, because she had the great fortune to become a guru to Sri Ramakrishna, she slowly came to believe that she was superior to everyone else and that others should follow her advice or they would come to harm. We have heard that she was even jealous when the Master gave instruction to the Holy Mother. We have also heard that the Holy Mother was fearful and meek when she had to face the Brahmani's horrible attitude. Finally, by the grace of the Master the Brahmani came to realize this weakness of her mind. She understood that under such circumstances she could overcome this mental imperfection only by staying away from the Master. She felt that her attraction for the Master was like being bound with a golden chain and that she needed to cut it in order to move forward towards her cherished goal. There is a saying among itinerant monks, "A monk is pure who goes, and the water is pure that flows."[3] The Brahmani therefore gave up the Master's company and left Dakshineswar to spend her days travelling to various holy places and practising austerities. However, it was through the Master's help as a guru that the Brahmani reached that understanding.

22. By the Master's grace, the Brahmani realizes her inadequacy in spirituality and leaves to practise austerities.

Tota Puri was a tall and robust man. After concentration and meditation in solitude for forty years, his mind had become free from thought waves and he had attained nirvikalpa samadhi. Yet he continued to practise meditation and spent some time in samadhi every day. As a monk of the Naga sect, Tota remained naked like a young boy, so the Master would call him *Nangta*, meaning the Naked One. He may have called him that because it is disrespectful to mention one's guru's name frequently or to address one's guru by name. The Master said that the Naked One never stayed indoors and always kept a sacred fire burning, as is customary in the Naga sect. Naga monks

23. The story of Tota Puri.

3. Its meaning is that the mind of a wandering monk does not get attached to any object or person.

regard fire as very sacred. Wherever they happen to be, they collect firewood and keep a fire lit. Such a fire is called a *dhuni*.

Naga monks worship the dhuni in the morning and evening. They offer their food, obtained from begging, to Agni [the Fire God] in the form of the dhuni and then partake of it. During his stay in Dakshineswar, the Naked One made his living place in the Panchavati and kept a dhuni burning near him regardless of the weather. He would eat and rest next to the dhuni. In the dead of night when everyone else was asleep — forgetting their worries and anxieties like children in their mothers' laps — the Naked One would get up to feed the flames of his dhuni. He would then sit as motionless as a mountain and immerse himself in samadhi like the unflickering flame of a lamp in a windless place. Sometimes during the day he would meditate in such a way that nobody realized he was doing so. Quite often he was seen lying like a corpse next to the dhuni, his entire body covered by a chadar. People thought he was sleeping.

Tota's only possessions were a water pot, a pair of long tongs, an animal skin for his seat, and a thick chadar to cover his body. Every day he polished his water pot and tongs until they glittered. Observing his regular habit of meditation, the Master once asked him: "You have realized Brahman and have become perfect. Why then do you meditate every day?" Tota looked at the Master calmly and pointed to the water pot. "See how bright it is," he said. "But will it not lose its lustre if I don't polish it regularly? The mind is like that. It gets tarnished if it isn't kept clean with daily meditation." The keen-sighted Master admitted the truth of this statement but remarked: "Suppose the water pot were made of gold. It wouldn't get tarnished even if it was not polished every day." "Yes, that is true," Tota admitted with a smile. All his life the Master remembered Tota's words regarding the importance of daily meditation and would often mention that teaching to us. We presume that the Master's statement — "a golden water pot never becomes tarnished" — was also permanently imprinted in Tota's mind. Tota realized that the Master's mind was indeed as bright as a golden water pot. From the very beginning the guru and disciple had many such intellectual exchanges.

24. The exchange of ideas between the Master and Tota Puri.

According to Vedanta scriptures, a person becomes completely fearless after attaining the knowledge of Brahman. Indeed, it is the only way to become free from fear. A person who has realized that he or she is the indivisible Satchidananda, by nature ever-pure, ever-illumined, all-pervading, ageless, deathless Atman — how can such a one fear any thing or any person? A person who truly perceives and experiences in his or her heart that there is no second thing or person in the world except that One — how can such a one fear anybody? That person always feels that he or she is the indivisible Satchidananda in all

25. The scriptures describe the fearlessness and freedom from bondage of a knower of Brahman.

circumstances, whether eating, lying down, sitting, sleeping, or waking. Such a person experiences the truth that he or she is all-pervading — existing at all times in every place and in every being. One who has achieved this state does not eat, walk, sleep, or awaken. Such a person does not experience any want, laziness, misery, happiness, birth, death, past, or future. In fact, that person does not even possess the five senses, mind, and intellect through which ordinary human beings see, hear, think, and imagine. The experience of such a person has been described by the scriptures as the culmination of the discriminating process of *neti, neti* [not this, not this]. After this, one directly experiences the Atman and becomes fully established in It. To constantly experience the Atman means to become one with Pure Consciousness, which leads to liberation from all bondage.

The Master used to say: "When a man is fully established in this nondual consciousness his body lasts only twenty-one days. It drops off like a dry leaf — in other words, it is destroyed. And that man never comes back to the world with I-consciousness. A jivanmukta occasionally identifies with this Pure Consciousness for a short while. While experiencing the Atman in this way, such a one ultimately becomes fully established in It. And the ever-free ishwarakotis, who have been born to benefit humanity by establishing a particular truth, occasionally experience being one with Pure Consciousness for brief periods from their childhood onward. When they have accomplished the missions for which they were born, they again merge back into Pure Consciousness. But avatars are extraordinarily powerful human beings: In them God has taken human form to benefit humanity, and no one in this world can comprehend their superhuman spiritual power. Only avatars, from their childhood onward, can reach that nondual Consciousness at will and stay as long as they like. In order to serve humanity they force themselves to return to this world, the meeting ground of birth, old age, misery, happiness, and so on."

Tota Puri, who initiated the Master into Vedanta, attained the state of jivanmukti by practising severe austerities for forty years. This is why his actions — eating, resting, sleeping, wandering, and so on — were not like those

26. The exalted state of Tota Puri.

of ordinary human beings. Like the ever-free air, he roamed freely from place to place; like the air, he was untouched by the good and evil of this world; and like the air, he was not confined to one place. The Master told us that Tota would not remain in one location for more than three days. But his attraction for the Master kept him in Dakshineswar for eleven months. Ah, what enchanting power the Master had!

The Master told us many stories about Tota's fearlessness, one about an event involving a spirit. It was very late at night. Tota had built up the dhuni in the Panchavati and was preparing to meditate. The deep silence around was

27. Tota remains fearless when seeing a Bhairava.

broken only by the chirping of crickets and occasional hooting of owls on the pinnacles of the temples. The air was still. Suddenly the branches of the tree under which Tota was standing began to shake, and a tall man descended from it. Looking steadfastly at him, the figure slowly advanced and sat down near the dhuni. Tota was surprised to see that the man was naked like himself and asked, "Who are you?" "I am a demigod, a Bhairava," he replied. "I dwell in the tree to protect this holy place." Tota was not in the least afraid. "Good," he said. "You and I are the same, just two manifestations of the same Brahman. Let us meditate together." But the apparition laughed loudly and vanished, dissolving into the air. Tota then sat down to meditate as though nothing had happened. The next morning he described this encounter to the Master. "Yes, it's true he lives there," the Master answered. "I've seen him many times. Sometimes he foretells events. Once the English government tried to acquire the entire area of the Panchavati on which to build their gunpowder magazine. I was worried because I thought I would no longer be able to sit in this solitary place and call on the Divine Mother far away from the uproar of the world. But to stop the English from acquiring the land, Mathur filed a lawsuit against them on the Rani's behalf. One day during that time, I saw the Bhairava seated in the tree. He motioned to me and said, 'The English will lose the lawsuit; they will not get the land.' And that's how it actually turned out."

The Master did not tell us anything about the area in the northwest where

| 28. The story of Tota Puri's guru. |

Tota had been born. Perhaps, the Master had not felt it necessary to ask Tota about this. Monks generally do not answer if asked about their pre-monastic name, birthplace, family, and so on. The scriptures say that it is forbidden to ask such questions of monks, as well as for monks to answer them. This may be the reason why the Master did not ask those questions of Tota. After the Master passed away, some of his monastic disciples travelled through the northwestern part of India. They inquired of some old monks and came to know that Tota Puri had been born somewhere in Punjab. His guru's Ashrama was at Ludhiana near Kurukshetra.[4] His guru had been a famous

4. Swami Alokananda, a monk of the Ramakrishna Order, visited Tota Puri's monastery on 31 August 1962 and wrote an article that was published in the *Prabuddha Bharata,* November 1977. The following facts are gleaned from his research: Tota Puri's monastery was at Ladhana in the Karnal District of the present Haryana state, not in Ludhiana near Kurukshetra in Punjab. The monastery is 56 miles from Ambala. Previously it was prosperous, but as of 1962 had become dilapidated. There are only three monks who take care of the place, and the present head is Badri Puri, who is 70 years old. There are five temples in the compound — one for the dhuni, where the sacred fire is kept burning 24 hours a day, others built on the tombs of different gurus, and one belonging to Tota Puri. There are 30 to 35 tombs in the compound, and no one could ascertain which one was for Tota's guru. A list of gurus is given here in descending order: Bhagwan Puri (the founder-guru of this sect), Jagmohan Puri, Janged Puri, Hardwar Puri, Mansa Puri, Saraswati Puri, Raj Puri, Siddha Puri, Bhandar Puri, Dalel Puri, Aan Puri, Tota Puri, Chaitanya Puri, Hazari Puri, Gopal Puri, Kedar Puri, and Badri Puri. — *Translator*

yogi who presided over a monastery there, but it is not clear whether he himself or one of his predecessors established it. The old monks told one of the Master's disciples that Tota's guru had been the head of the monastery and that every year people from the neighbouring villages arrange a fair there in his memory. As he used to smoke tobacco, even now during the fair the villagers present tobacco to his monastic community. After his guru's death, Tota Puri became the head of that monastery.

Tota's own words indicate that his guru had been the head of the monastic

29. Tota Puri describes his guru's monastery and the community. | community and that he received instructions in Vedanta from him during his boyhood. He lived with his guru for a long time, studied Vedanta, and learned the mystery of sadhana. He told the Master that there were seven hundred monks in his community who meditated upon the truths of Vedanta every day under the guidance of their guru. He said further that their monastery had an excellent method of training monks to meditate. The Master told us many times what he had heard from Tota on this subject: "The Naked One mentioned that there were seven hundred Naga monks in their monastery. The beginners were taught to meditate while sitting on thick cushions, for a hard seat would be uncomfortable and the pain would divert their minds from God to the body. As they progressed in meditation, they were given less and less comfortable seats, and finally only an animal skin or the bare ground sufficed. In food and other matters also the same gradation was observed. In dress, for instance, they were trained by degrees to go without clothes. People from their very birth are fettered with the eightfold ties of shame, hatred, fear, pride of caste, good conduct, honour, and so on, so these monks were taught to renounce them one by one. After they were well-grounded in meditation, they were asked to roam from one holy place to another, first in the company of other monks and subsequently alone. Such was the method of training among the Nagas."

Regarding the election of the head of the monastery, the Master told us the following account that he heard from his guru: "Whenever there was a vacancy, they used to elect for the office one from among themselves whom they found to be a real paramahamsa. Otherwise, there was danger of going astray in handling money or in being the recipient of honour and power. So the one whom they found to be truly above the temptation of money was raised to this position. Such a monk would spend the funds at his disposal in the service of God and the monastic members of the Order."

We infer from Tota's account that he was brought up under the affec-

30. The early life of Tota Puri. | tionate care of his guru in a heavenly atmosphere, far removed from worldly attachments, delusion, jealousy, hatred, and so on. In the northwestern part of India, it is customary for childless couples to go to a temple and pray for a child whom they will offer to the Lord as a monk. They keep their promise.

Who knows, perhaps Tota was offered to his guru in that way? It seems to be so, because he never told the Master about his parents, brothers, sisters, or any other family members.

As a result of the impressions from his virtuous deeds done in past lives, Tota's mind was endowed with simplicity, sincerity, and faith. Shankara wrote in the beginning of *Vive-kachudamani* (3): "Only through God's grace can one obtain these three rare things: human birth, the longing for liberation, and the company of an illumined teacher." Not only had Tota been fortunate to achieve these three things, but he also used them properly and attained liberation, the goal of human life. He absorbed the instructions of his guru and translated them into action. It seems that he did not suffer like other people from a deceptive and hypocritical mind. There is a saying among Vaishnavas: "One may receive the grace of the guru, God, and the devotees, but without the grace of one's own mind, one will perish." We believe that Tota was not tormented by a roguish mind. His pure intellect sincerely believed in God, followed the instructions of his guru, and steadily moved forward, never casting a covetous glance towards the alluring and lust-producing objects of the world. So he knew that his own enthusiasm, self-effort, self-reliance, and self-confidence were enough to achieve the goal.

31. The state of Tota's mind.

But Tota did not realize that when the mind is not cooperative, self-effort can be carried away like a bunch of straw in a swift current, and self-reliance and self-confidence can be pushed aside by terrible doubts in one's own abilities, making one feel weaker than a worm. Observing the success of his own life, Tota could not imagine that if, by God's grace, a person did not enjoy favourable conditions in the external world, intense spiritual effort would not bear fruit. Rather, the unfavourable conditions would bind that person more and more. He never dreamt of such a difficulty because all through his life he had accomplished whatever he set out to do, and whatever he considered good for human beings, he had been able to accomplish in his own life. It is doubtful whether it ever occurred to Tota that a person could be in a situation where "the mind understands, but the heart does not respond," or that failing "to unite the mind and the speech" a person would constantly feel the painful stings of a hundred scorpions. Nor had he encountered the distracting and painful situation in which various manifestations of ego and all sense organs act independently according to their respective whims without coordinating with one another, thus driving a person into terrible despondency. He might have known this, but learning something by hearing of it or seeing it is quite different from experiencing it for oneself.

So there was a huge gap between how Tota might have imagined human suffering and the state of mind of a person who was actually suffering. Tota was completely ignorant of the overwhelming influence of beginningless maya, the power of Brahman. For that reason, it is doubtful whether he had any compassion for human weaknesses; rather, he had a disdainful outlook. But when Tota encountered the Master's power as a guru, this deficiency of his was removed. He ultimately admitted the power of maya, realized that Brahman and the power of Brahman are identical, and left the Kali temple of Dakshineswar with humility and devotion in his heart. We shall now describe the events.

Tota was an austere monk and had been celibate from his childhood, so in fact he did believe that the path of devotion was strange, as the Brahmani had told the Master. Tota did not understand that love and devotion could teach a spiritual aspirant to slowly renounce everything in this world for the beloved — even self-complacency — and could ultimately lead to God-realization. Nor was he aware that at the culmination of devotion, a true devotee experiences pure nondual knowledge, and that because of this, japa, kirtan, singing, and other spiritual practices cannot be discounted. This ignorance sometimes led Tota to ridicule devotees who gave free rein to their overwhelming devotion. But the reader should not consider Tota to be an atheist who had no love for God. Tota had developed a calm nature by practising control of the mind and the senses. He was a follower of the shanta attitude towards God, and he could understand this kind of devotional attitude in others. It did not enter his mind, however, that an aspirant could worship the Supreme God by imagining a relationship with Him as friend, son, wife, or husband, and thereby progress rapidly towards Him. Instead, he regarded as delirium and fancy a devotee's importunate demands upon God as well as the pain of separation, the longing, pique, egoism, and unrestrained laughing, crying, and dancing caused by exuberant emotion focussed on God. He could not even imagine that such devotional practices might help an aspirant to attain the cherished result quickly. Because of all this Tota and the Master quite often engaged in lively debates on topics such as heartfelt devotion to the Divine Mother, the Power of Brahman, and devotional practices.

32. Tota was ignorant of the path of devotion.

From his childhood, the Master had a custom of chanting God's name in the morning and evening. He would clap his hands and sometimes dance in ecstasy, loudly repeating: "Hari bol, Hari bol!" "Hari is guru, guru is Hari!" "Hari is my heart, Govinda is my life!" "Krishna is mind! Krishna is life! Krishna is knowledge! Krishna is meditation! Krishna is consciousness! Krishna is intellect!" "You are the world and the world is in You!" "I am the instrument and You are the operator!" and so on. The Master practised this discipline every day, even after he had attained nirvikalpa samadhi, the nondual knowledge of Vedanta. One afternoon, the Master was engaged in a spiritual discussion with Tota in the Panchavati. When evening fell, the Master stopped talking and began to chant God's names as usual, clapping his hands. Amazed, Tota pondered: "Ramakrishna is a

33. Its proof: "What! Are you making chapatis by clapping your hands?"

competent master of Vedanta and attained nirvikalpa samadhi in three days. Why then does he act like a beginner?" Tota then sarcastically remarked: "What? Are you clapping your hands to make chapatis?"[5] The Master laughingly replied: "Nonsense! I am taking the name of God, and you say I am making chapatis!" The Master's childlike answer made Tota laugh also. He understood that the Master's kind of devotional practice was not meaningless. He recognized there might be some deeper significance that he could not grasp because of his distaste for it, so it was better not to protest further.

On another evening the Master was seated with Tota near his sacred

34. The story of how Tota gave up anger.

dhuni. Both of their minds were almost completely absorbed in nondual knowledge as they talked about God. The Atman, as if dwelling in the flames of the dhuni, was experiencing oneness with them, smiling joyfully, and expressing that oneness through hundreds of leaping tongues of fire! Meanwhile, a servant of the garden wished to smoke, and he made his pipe ready with tobacco. Spotting the fire, he came over and began to take a piece of hot charcoal to light his pipe. Tota was so absorbed in discussion with the Master and in the nondual bliss of Brahman within that he did not notice that a man had come and was about to take charcoal from the dhuni. But when he saw the intruder, he flew into a rage and began to scold him, threatening him with his tongs. As we mentioned earlier, Naga monks worshipped and respected Agni [the Fire God] in the form of the dhuni.

Witnessing this display of Tota's anger, the Master laughed in ecstasy until he rolled on the ground, crying, "Oh, for shame!" Surprised, Tota asked: "What are you laughing about? The man is insolent!" Still laughing, the Master answered: "Oh yes, he is insolent. But I am also observing the depth of your knowledge of Brahman! Just now you were telling me that Brahman alone exists, and all objects and beings in the universe are Its manifestation. Yet in the next moment you forget all that and are ready to beat that poor man! I laugh to see the irresistible power of maya!" Tota became very serious and was silent for some time. Then he said: "You are quite right. I did indeed forget everything under the influence of anger. Anger is a deadly thing! I shall never again be angry; I give it up this very moment." And it is said that Tota never was angry again.

The Master used to say: "Brahman weeps when ensnared in the meshes of

35. People cannot realize God unless the Divine Mother graciously allows them to.

maya. You may close your eyes and reason, 'There is no thorn, nothing to prick'; but you cry out in pain as soon as your hand is pricked by a thorn. Similarly, you may reason that there is no such thing as birth or death, virtue or vice, pain or misery, hunger or thirst — that you are the

5. The allusion is to the practice among the people of northwestern India who sometimes make chapatis, a thin pancakelike bread, by clapping the dough between the palms instead of using rolling pin and board.

eternal Brahman, the Existence-Knowledge-Bliss Absolute. But the moment your body succumbs to illness, or your mind is overcome by temptation, or you commit a transgression distracted by the seemingly sweet enjoyment of lust and gold, you forget your high philosophy and are overwhelmed by delusion and its painful consequences. Therefore, know for certain that no one can attain Self-knowledge and become free from misery without God's grace and the Divine Mother's unlocking the door. Have you not read in the *Chandi,* 'When the Divine Mother is pleased, She bestows the boon of liberation upon human beings?'

"Rama, Sita, and Lakshmana were walking through the forest on a narrow path where only one at a time could go. Rama led the way, bow and arrow in hand. Sita followed him, and behind her was Lakshmana with his bow and arrow.

36. An example: the story of Rama, Sita, and Lakshmana walking in the forest.

Lakshmana was so intensely devoted to Rama that he wanted to see his beautiful form at all times. But Sita was obstructing his view, so he became anxious. The intelligent Sita understood this and was sympathetic. She stepped aside now and then, saying, 'Look!' Only then could Lakshmana see his beloved Lord Rama. Similarly, between the jiva and God there is maya in the form of the Divine Mother, here represented by Sita. Know for certain that unless She is moved by sympathy and steps aside, the jiva (Lakshmana) cannot see God. The moment She bestows Her grace, the jiva sees Narayana (Rama) and escapes all misery. Otherwise you may use your discrimination a thousand times, but it will be of no avail. It is said that one grain of *joan* [ptychotis or caraway seed] digests one hundred grains of rice, but when there is stomach trouble, one hundred grains of joan cannot digest even one grain of rice."

Swami Tota Puri did not realize that he had received the Divine Mother's grace from his very birth. From his childhood onward he had enjoyed good tendencies, a pure mind, a strong and healthy body, and the company of a great yogi.

37. Tota was unaware that his exalted state was due to the grace of the Divine Mother.

The Divine Maya never showed him Her terrible, frightening, all-devouring form, like Death itself, nor had She entrapped him with Her bewitching form of avidya [ignorance]. So it was easy for Tota to attain nirvikalpa samadhi and Self-knowledge and to have the vision of God through self-effort and perseverance. How could he know that the Divine Mother Herself had removed every obstacle in his spiritual journey? Now after a long time the Divine Mother wished to make Tota understand Her grace, thereby providing him with the opportunity to realize his own limitations.

Tota's constitution had always been strong. He had had little experience with stomach trouble or any other physical ailment.

38. Tota's illness.

His digestion was good, and he always enjoyed sound sleep. A current of peace and bliss constantly flowed into his mind — the result of his vision of and experience of God. Attracted by the Master's love and respect, when Tota had stayed for just a few months in Dakshineswar, his strong body sickened because of the polluted water and the hot, humid climate of Bengal. He had a severe attack of blood dysentery. Day and night he suffered spasms and throbbing pains in his stomach, diverting his calm and steady mind from absorption in Brahman to the troubles of the body. Brahman had been "ensnared in the meshes of maya." Where did freedom lie except in the grace of the Divine Mother, the ruler of all?

Sometime before he fell sick, his alert, illumined mind had made it known

| 39. Tota disregards a warning from his mind. |

to him that he should not remain in Dakshineswar because his body was not doing well there. But how could he give up the wonderful company of the Master for the sake of his body? After all, the body is a cage of flesh and bone filled with blood, filth, and other disagreeable materials. According to Vedanta scriptures, its very existence is illusory. How could he suddenly forsake the blissful company of this godman because of his attachment to his body? Moreover, he could contract diseases wherever he might go. Why should he be afraid of falling ill? Why should he care for the body, the very nature of which was to suffer, decay, and ultimately die? Had he not realized that he was the independent, immutable Atman and not connected with the body? Why then should he fear death? Tota silenced his mind with thoughts such as these.

As the symptoms of Tota's disease multiplied and the pain increased, his

| 40. Tota is unable to take leave of the Master, and his illness worsens. |

desire to leave Dakshineswar gradually became stronger. Occasionally he went to the Master to take leave of him but would become engrossed in discussing spiritual matters and forget to bring it up. And when he did remember to say good-bye to the Master, he always felt as if someone inside of him was restraining him. Thus prevented, Tota thought: "Let it go today; I shall tell him tomorrow." The next day, however, he would spend some time with the Master discussing Vedanta, then return to his place in the Panchavati. Thus the days went by. Tota's body slowly weakened and the disease became more serious. The Master noticed that Tota was more emaciated every day, so he arranged a special diet and medicine for him — but they were of no use. Regardless, he continued to serve Tota to the best of his ability and asked Mathur to continue providing the best diet and medical treatment available. Up to this point Tota had been experiencing physical pain, but his mind was still disciplined enough to enter into samadhi at will and avoid all discomfort.

One particular night Tota's pain became excruciating and he could find no

| 41. Unable to control his mind, Tota walks into the Ganges to give up his body; his vision of the Cosmic Divine Mother. |

relief. He was restless and would try to lie down only to get up again. Then he decided to put the mind into deep meditation and not to think about the body. As he was trying to withdraw his mind from the body and make it calm, it rushed towards the stomach pain instead. Again he made an effort but met with the same result. Before his mind could rise to the level of samadhi where body-consciousness would disappear, it slipped back to his physical pain. He tried again and again but failed every time. He was then filled with disgust for his body and thought: "My mind is beyond control today because of this wretched body. I must get rid of this nuisance. I know positively that I am not the body. Why should I suffer pain by associating with this rotten body? What is the use of dragging it about? In this dead of night I'll commit it to the Ganges and put an end to all troubles."

With this determination Tota fixed his mind on Brahman and waded out into the great river, advancing farther and farther. But what was this? Was the Ganges really dry tonight, or was this an external projection of his imagination? Who could say? Tota had crossed almost to the other side, yet he could not reach sufficiently deep water to drown himself. When the trees and houses of the opposite bank became visible in the darkness, Tota was amazed and thought: "What is this divine maya! There is not water enough in the river tonight to drown me! What a mysterious play of the Lord!" Immediately it was as if someone within him lifted a veil covering his mind. He had a dazzling sense of enlightenment and was struck with this realization: "The omnipresent Divine Mother, Cosmic Mother, Omnipotent Mother! Mother is in the water and land; Mother is the body and the mind; Mother is illness and healthiness; Mother is knowledge and ignorance; Mother is life and death. Whatever I see, hear, think, and imagine is Mother! She turns yes into no and no into yes. No embodied being can go beyond Her jurisdiction unless She is pleased to release him. And no one has even the power to die. Again, the same Mother is beyond the body, mind, and intellect — transcendent and devoid of attributes." All his life, Tota had been worshipping this same Mother as Brahman, offering his heartfelt love and devotion. Shiva and Shakti are one, existing in the form of Hara and Gauri. Brahman and the Power of Brahman are identical.

Late that night Tota saw the Divine Mother's inconceivable, indescrib-

42. Tota gives up his desire for death.

able, cosmic form. His heart was flooded with devotion, and the area around him resounded with his solemn voice chanting the Mother's name. He then surrendered completely at the feet of the Divine Mother and waded back the way he had come. Although his body was still in pain, he was oblivious to it. His heart was filled with the joyous and exhilarating memory of his revelation. He slowly returned to the Panchavati and sat beside the dhuni, where he spent what was left of the night chanting the Divine Mother's name and meditating on Her.

When the Master came to inquire about Tota's health the next morning, he

43. His illness causes Tota to realize that Brahman and Its power are identical.

found him an altogether different man. Bliss radiated from his face, and his body seemed to be free of illness. He motioned to the Master to sit beside him and slowly related what had happened during the night. He said: "The disease has acted like a friend to me. Last night I was blessed with the vision of the Divine Mother and through Her grace have been freed from disease. Ah, how ignorant I have been all these years! Now please ask your Mother to let me leave this place. I now understand that She has kept me here so long to teach me this lesson. Many times I thought of leaving and actually went to you to bid you good-bye. But every time I tried to speak of this to you, it was as if someone distracted me by introducing other topics and prevented me from taking my leave." Smiling, the Master said: "Ah, at that time you refused to believe in my Mother! You argued with me, saying that Shakti is not real. Now you have seen for yourself that She exists. She taught me long ago that 'Brahman and Shakti are identical, like fire and its power to burn.'"

When the morning music began to flow from the nahabat, reverberating throughout the temple garden, the two great souls, bound together as guru and disciple like Shiva and Rama,[6] arose from their seats to go to the temple of the Divine Mother. Upon entering the temple, they bowed down to the Divine Mother. Both felt deeply that the Mother was pleased and that She graciously assented to Tota's departure. A few days later Tota took leave of the Master and started on his homeward journey. This was his only visit to the Dakshineswar Kali temple; he never returned.

44. Tota leaves after accepting the Divine Mother.

If we raise one last topic, we shall consider that we have shared with the reader everything the Master told us about Tota Puri. Tota believed in alchemy. Not only did he believe in it, but he also told the Master that by means of that knowledge he had converted copper and other metals into gold on many occasions. He said that the old paramahamsas of his community possessed this knowledge and that he had learned it from his guru. He continued: "It is strictly forbidden to use this power for self-interest or enjoyment of luxury; the penalty for doing so is incurring the curse of one's guru. There are many monks in the community, and sometimes the head of the community has to travel with them from one place of pilgrimage to another. He also has to arrange for their food and other necessities. It is the command of the guru: 'If there is any shortage of money at such a time, the head monk can use the knowledge of alchemy to serve the monks.'"

45. Tota's knowledge of alchemy.

Thus assisted by the Master's power as a guru, the Bhairavi Brahmani and Tota Puri were blessed, attaining the culmination of their respective paths. We can easily infer that the Master's other teachers must have also achieved spiritual broad-mindedness with his help.

46. Conclusion.

---

6. According to the Hindu tradition, Rama's guru was Shiva, and Shiva's guru was Rama.
— *Translator*

Sri Ramakrishna As a Guru
Part 2

Volume Four

Preface to Volume Four

The fourth volume "Sri Ramakrishna as a Guru — Part 2" of *Sri Ramakrishna and His Divine Play* is now published. After reading the middle part of Sri Ramakrishna's life in this volume, the reader may ask: "Why did you adopt this unchronological method [see the translator's note]? Why are you describing the Master's perfected state before recording his life story from his birth to his sadhana?" We reply:

First, we did not start writing the life of this extraordinary man with a plan in mind. We never dared to cherish the ambition that it would ever be possible for insignificant persons such as ourselves to properly write the story of his great life. It so happened that we undertook this project to inform *Udbodhan* [magazine] readers about some events in Sri Ramakrishna's life. We did not then know that we would come so far. Under such circumstances, it is not surprising that some later events [of the Master's life] have been described before earlier ones.

Second, some before us tried to write about the miraculous events in Sri Ramakrishna's life and about his unprecedented sadhana. Although there were some errors in those accounts, people did learn about many aspects of the Master's life from them. So, instead of wasting our energy by recording the same events over again, we considered it reasonable to properly explain to readers the Master's extraordinary ideas, which no one had done so far. Unless people understand how the Master remained in bhavamukha and how the mood of a guru was natural to him, they will not be able to comprehend the Master's wonderful character, unprecedented mental state, and extraordinary activities. That is why we tried to make the reader understand this subject at the outset.

Some may object: "But while explaining the Master's unique actions and mental states in various places in this book, you have described them to the reader as you have understood them. As a result, you have made your own intellect and discretion the criterion by which the Master's inconceivable character and mental states are to be measured. Moreover, you have claimed indirectly, if not directly, that your intellect and discretion are capable of comprehending the Master. Have you not thus belittled the Master? Would it not have been better if you had limited yourself to accurately recording the facts? That would not belittle the Master, and readers would be free to interpret his ideas according to their understanding."

The above statement may seem reasonable, but a little thinking reveals its insubstantiality. Human beings have always used the senses, the mind, and the intellect to perceive and comprehend things and will continue to do so in the future. They have no alternative. But it does not follow that their minds and intellects are greater than the objects they try to understand. People know that space, time, the universe, the Self, God, and other infinite beings are beyond the mind and the intellect, yet they still try to perceive and comprehend them through those faculties. We do not say that their efforts to understand those infinite beings limit them; nor do we consider their attempts to be reprehensible. Rather, we think that their efforts will eventually bring them good by expanding their minds and intellects.

Therefore, if we reflect upon the extraordinary lives and actions of great souls, this benefits us, and our reflection does not limit their infinite nature. People are capable of understanding or helping others to understand the divine ideas and actions of great souls to greater or lesser degrees according to the purity and subtlety of their own minds and intellects, as formed by their sadhana. A person endowed with a greater spirituality than ours will understand the life of Sri Ramakrishna better than we do, so it is not wrong for us to apply our minds and intellects to understanding the divine life of the Master. It is sufficient if we bear in mind that we have not understood the entire character of Sri Ramakrishna. If we can firmly hold this attitude in our minds, there will be no possibility of any unnecessary misgivings.

The Author [Swami Saradananda]
Ashwin 1318 B.E. [mid-September to mid-October 1911]

Ramakrishna, photographed while in Samadhi at Dakshineswar in October 1883.

Chapter 1

The Story of *Vaishnavcharan and Gauri*

Those who, full of faith, ever follow this teaching of Mine and do not reproach Me —
they too are released from the bonds of actions. — GITA 3:31

THE PEOPLE OF CALCUTTA HAD THE IMPRESSION THAT Sri Ramakrishna transmitted

> 1. People of Calcutta were ignorant of the Master's relationship as a guru with the monks and spiritual aspirants who visited Dakshineswar.

spirituality to, or enhanced the existing spiritual fervour of, Keshab Chandra Sen and some other modern Hindus who were educated in English and infused with Western concepts and ideals. But most people in Calcutta were unaware that long before they had learned of the Master's presence in Dakshineswar, many prominent monks, spiritual aspirants, and pandits well versed in the scriptures had come to the Master from Bengal and the northern states of India. The Master's power as a guru and the blazing spiritual ideal that his life exemplified revitalized their lethargic spiritual lives. Afterwards, they left to share this divine power and new spiritual ideal with many others.

The Master used to say: "When flowers bloom, bees come of their own

> 2. "When flowers bloom, bees come of their own accord." Preaching is meaningless without the ability to impart religion.

accord. They do not need to be invited. It is an inexplicable spiritual law that if love and devotion for God are truly manifest within you, then those who have dedicated their lives to searching for God and experiencing the Truth, or have resolved to do so, will definitely come to you." The Master believed that God-realization must come first. You must see God and receive His grace in order to become endowed with the ability to help people appropriately. You must try to obtain His command before you begin to preach religion or work for the good of humanity. Otherwise, as the Master would say: "Who will believe you? Why should they listen to you or do as you bid them?"

Inflated with pride in our learning, we may consider ourselves to be supe-

| 3. Most people are blind in spiritual matters. | rior to others. But in fact we are all in the same condition in this world of birth, disease, and death, |

which is full of misery, poverty, and ignorance. In the inscrutable domain of maya, we may make some progress in material science and technology, manufacturing many goods in our factories, but still our misery remains constant. Although we want to use our five senses, the mind, and the intellect to experience Truth, we are deceived and misguided by sensual desires, lust, greed, and the constant fear of death. And we are completely ignorant regarding the important questions of life: Who am I? Why am I in this world? Where will I go after death? What is the goal of this life? How can I be free from this play of maya?

In this world everyone needs true knowledge to become free from misery. But who can teach them? If in fact someone does have knowledge to give, let that person give as much as he or she can. But deluded by manifold ignorance, people do not realize their inadequacy. Without having any wisdom themselves, they try to impart it to others, or pretend to do so, to acquire name and fame or to satisfy some other selfish motive. Thus, as the blind led by the blind, the teacher and the taught fall into the same predicament. Soon both repent, lamenting bitterly.

The Master followed a path diametrically opposite to that of others. He

| 4. How the Master taught religion. | practised selflessness, renunciation, and self-control to the fullest degree, thereby making himself a true instrument in the hands of the Divine Mother. After |

realizing the Truth, he became calm and free from anxiety. He then spent his life in one place and demonstrated for all a new way of teaching. He first realized God, then opened to others the store of wisdom that he had gathered for distribution. Immediately, many seekers of God began to turn up uninvited from who knows where. Not only were they blessed by his pure touch and divine grace, but they also spread his message wherever they went and made others blessed. This was so because wherever we go, we express the thoughts within us. As the Master used to say in his patois: "A man belches what he eats. If he eats cucumbers, he belches cucumbers; if he eats radishes, he belches radishes."

Meeting the Bhairavi Brahmani was a special event in the Master's life.

| 5. The Master's condition when he met the Brahmani. | From this point on he began making rapid progress in his sadhana, following the injunctions of the scriptures. At the same time his power as a guru began to |

manifest itself. However, it cannot be said that prior to this meeting he had no such power. As we described in previous chapters, the manifestation of this power was evident in him from his childhood onward to greater or lesser degrees. And this power even enabled his own gurus to rid themselves of any need, deficiency, or lassitude in their spiritual journey, thereby attaining perfection.

Before the Bhairavi's arrival, the Master's unprecedented passion for God and extreme longing were considered by those around him to be mental and physical illness, for which he was placed under treatment. When the Master went to be treated at the house of Dr. Gangaprasad Sen, another physician happened to be present. This doctor, from East Bengal, was also a spiritual aspirant. After observing the Master's physical symptoms, he concluded that his condition was a yogic disease and that the physical changes were the outcome of practising yoga. Nobody took his opinion seriously. Mathur and the others were convinced that the Master suffered from insanity associated with longing for God. It was the learned Brahmani, an adept in devotional scriptures, who first declared to all that the Master's physical changes were caused by corresponding changes in his mental state, originating in his extraordinary devotion to God and transforming his body into a divine body. She did not stop at merely giving her opinion. She cited devotional scriptures to show how extraordinary spiritual experiences had caused similar physical changes in the devout Radha of Vrindaban, in Lord Chaitanya, and in other great teachers and yogis of times past. The Brahmani proved her theory by comparing the Master's physical symptoms with descriptions given in passages from the scriptures. This delighted the Master; he was like a boy encouraged and given strength by his mother's assurance. At the same time, Mathur and others in the Kali temple were not a little surprised. Their wonder knew no bounds when the Bhairavi told Mathur: "Invite the best pandits, who are well versed in the scriptures. I am ready to prove my position to them."

> 6. What others understood about the Master's exalted state.

This was astonishing, no doubt. Who would be willing to trust the words and scholarship of an insignificant and obscure woman who lived on alms? Like the words of that East Bengal physician, the Brahmani's words would have entered one of Mathur's ears and gone out the other, but the Master's eager request changed the situation. The childlike Master importuned Mathur, saying, "Please bring the best pandits to evaluate the Brahmani's statement." The wealthy Mathur thought to himself: "I am already spending so much money on medicine and doctors for the young priest; I see nothing wrong in inviting the pandits. When they disprove the Brahmani's theory by quoting the scriptures — which they will definitely do — then at least one thing will be achieved: The simple-hearted young priest will believe the words of the pandits and become convinced that he has some kind of disease. He may then try to

> 7. To evaluate the Master's exalted state, the Brahmani suggests that reputable pandits be invited: Mathur agrees.

control his mind. A man becomes insane when he makes no effort to regulate his thoughts and control his mind, believing, 'What I do and understand is right, and what others understand and ask me to do is wrong.' This is the way someone becomes insane. If I do not invite the pandits, and just allow the young priest to believe what the Brahmani has said, his mental problem and associated physical illness will undoubtedly worsen." Partly out of curiosity and partly out of love for the Master, Mathur deliberated in this manner and then agreed to invite the pandits.

At that time Vaishnavcharan was well established among the community

8. Vaishnavcharan and Gauri of Indesh are invited.

of pandits in Calcutta. He had also achieved tremendous fame in other places by beautifully reciting the Bhagavata and explaining it to the general public, so the Master, Mathur, and the Brahmani all knew of him. Mathur decided to invite him. He also resolved to invite Pandit Gauri of Indesh, Bankura, upon hearing of his extraordinary power and erudition. Thus, both Vaishnavcharan and Gauri came to Dakshineswar. Now and again the Master told us many stories about them, which we shall now relate to the reader.

Vaishnavcharan was not only a scholar but was also known to be a sincere

9. Vaishnavcharan was then very famous.

spiritual aspirant. His devotion to God and keen philosophical insight, especially concerning devotional scriptures, made him a leader in the Vaishnava community of the time. That community respectfully invited him to religious festivals and public functions, where they offered him gifts and treated him as the guest of honour. Often, the Vaishnava community asked him to resolve religious disputes, always accepting his conclusions. Many aspirants went to him for proper guidance in their spiritual disciplines and then proceeded as he advised. So it is not strange that Mathur decided to bring Vaishnavcharan to ascertain whether excessive devotion or some physical disease was causing the Master's ecstasy.

In the meantime, the Brahmani was excited by her discovery of additional

10. The Brahmani's prescription for relieving the burning sensation in the Master's body.

evidence that her evaluation of the Master's condition was correct. Her discovery surprised others greatly. Sometime before the Brahmani's arrival, the Master suffered terribly from a burning sensation all over his body. He underwent various treatments to no effect. The Master told us that the burning would start at sunrise and increase steadily as the day advanced. By noon it would become so unbearable that he would immerse himself in the water of the Ganges for two or three hours with a wet towel over his head. Fearing that he might develop a cold or other difficulties because of this lengthy immersion, he would come out of the water unwillingly. Then he would go to Mathur's bungalow, wipe the marble floor in one of its rooms with a wet towel, close the doors and windows, and roll on the floor.

When the Brahmani learned of the Master's physical difficulty, she formed a novel opinion about it. She said that it was not a disease; it appeared as a result of the Master's spiritual awakening, or his intense love for God. Such physical signs had also appeared in Radha and Chaitanya, caused by their excessive longing for God-realization. The treatment for this condition was extraordinary: one was to wear a garland of fragrant flowers and cover the entire body with scented sandal paste.

Mathur and the others could not control their laughter when they heard the Brahmani's diagnosis of the disease. They did not believe her at all and thought to themselves: "The young priest has taken so many medicines and has used Madhyamnarayana, Vishnu, and other medicated oils, and his illness has still not abated. Now the Brahmani says that it is not a disease at all!" But no one raised any objection to the Master's receiving the simple treatment prescribed by the Brahmani. If there was no result after a couple of days, the patient would give it up himself. So according to the Brahmani's instructions, the Master's body was smeared with sandal paste, and a garland was placed around his neck. After three days the Master's burning sensation disappeared completely. Everyone was dumbfounded. But the doubt of the sceptical mind does not leave so easily. The sceptics commented: "This is nothing but coincidence. According to the physician, the Vishnu oil that the young priest used last time was genuine. That medicated oil was working, and after a couple of days he would have been free of the burning pain even without the Brahmani's sandal-paste treatment. Regardless of what the Brahmani says or prescribes, the young priest should continue to use the Vishnu oil."

Some days later, the Master developed another problem. The Master

11. The Brahmani's prescription for stopping the Master's insatiable hunger.

told us that this one also was cured within three days by following the Brahmani's simple instructions. The Master said: "I was seized with a ravenous appetite that no amount of food could satisfy. No sooner had I eaten something than I would feel hungry again. Day and night my mind was possessed by one thought alone: what to eat. I pondered, 'What kind of disease is this?' When I described it to the Brahmani, she replied: 'My son, don't worry. The scriptures explain that those who advance on the path of spirituality pass through such abnormal states. Wait, I shall cure it.' She asked Mathur to supply various kinds of food — from flattened rice and sugar-coated parched rice to sandesh, rasagolla, luchi, and other delicacies — and stack it all in a room. She then told me, 'My son, stay in this room day and night and eat whenever and whatever you like.' I remained in that room and walked around, touching different foods. Every now and then I would taste one item or another, according to my fancy. In this way three days passed, that strange hunger and desire for food left me, and I was relieved."

We have heard that such inordinate hunger appears before the mind of an aspirant has become absorbed and settled naturally in yoga or God, and sometimes after that. We ourselves were amazed when we witnessed this phenomenon in later days, though it took a slightly different form. Later in the Master's life, he did not suffer from the kind of continuous inordinate hunger that we just described. But we did see that when he was in an ecstatic mood he would eat four or more times his normal quantity of food without experiencing any stomach trouble. The reader will easily understand this if we relate a few incidents.

> 12. These things arise as the result of practising yoga. What we witnessed regarding the Master's inordinate hunger.

Perhaps the reader remembers that we mentioned an incident earlier (see III.1.32-33) regarding the Master's relationship with women. A few women devotees from Baghbazar bought a big piece of sar [a sweet] from Bhola's shop and went to Dakshineswar to visit the Master. They did not see him there, so with great difficulty they went to M.'s house, where they met the Master. While they were there, however, Prankrishna Mukhopadhyay suddenly arrived. Three of the women were shy and hid themselves under the cot where the Master was seated. We recorded that when the Master returned to Dakshineswar after supper that night, he felt terribly hungry again and ate almost all of the sar that those women had brought. Now we shall mention just a few similar events, because such things occurred almost daily in the Master's life and it is impossible to record all of them.

> 13. First example: The Master ate a big piece of sar.

Even now older people say that before the malaria epidemic that devastated many lives in the largest part of scenic Bengal, especially the western region, the climate of Hooghly, Burdwan, and other districts was not inferior to that of the northwestern part of India. They say that at that time people would go to Burdwan and other nearby places for a change of climate. Kamarpukur is situated about twenty-five miles from Burdwan, and the air in that place was also healthy. We mentioned earlier that the Master's strong body gradually became weaker, and he was sometimes attacked by serious illness. This was due to his performing prolonged and severe austerities for twelve years, and later staying in bhavamukha without caring for his body. Because of this, at the end of his sadhana, the Master spent July through October (*Chaturmasya*) in the Kamarpukur area nearly every year. Hriday, his nephew and faithful attendant, accompanied him. Mathur paid their travelling expenses and always sent along everything that the Master might need in that remote village.

> 14. Second example: At Kamarpukur he ate two pounds of sweets and some puffed rice.

When a daughter goes to her father-in-law's house after her wedding, her parents send with her even trifling things such as toothpicks, lamp wicks, and so on. Similarly, Mathur and his devoted wife, Jagadamba, sent everything needed to provide for the Master's household in Kamarpukur. They knew that the condition of the Master's household in his native village was as austere as that of Shiva. From the time of his ancestors, the Master's family had never made any provisions for the future. Holding strictly to the path of righteousness, they lived on whatever was available day by day, although they did have the rice produced annually from the half-acre of land endowed for the family deity, Raghuvir. The village grocery shop was the only storehouse for this pious family. If they received honorariums for performing rituals, they would buy from that shop the salt, oil, spices, vegetables, and other items they needed that day; otherwise, they would live happily on rice and the spinach that grew wild around the ponds. At all times and in every matter, they depended completely upon their living family deity, Raghuvir. Because Mathur was aware of the condition of the Master's family, he wanted to buy a few acres of rice fields in the name of Raghuvir. His awareness of their condition also prompted him to send the necessary articles along with the Master.

As we mentioned, the Master went to Kamarpukur almost every year. During one visit there was a malaria epidemic, and he suffered from a fever. He decided then not to visit his native village again, and he never did. He made that resolve eight or ten years before he passed away.

Before that event, however, he visited Kamarpukur as usual one year. The neighbours crowded together to see him and to hear him talk on spiritual matters. It was a mart of joy. The women of the household were happy to have the Master in their midst, and they served his visitors joyfully. They did not notice how their blissful days passed, one after another. Ramlal's mother, then the mistress of the house, her daughter Lakshmi, and the Holy Mother were all there.

At about 9:00 p.m., the visitors left for their homes. The Master had been having stomach trouble for a few days, so at night he was taking only sago water or barley water. That night he had milk and barley and went to bed. The women of the household then had their supper and were about to go to bed after finishing their other work.

Suddenly the Master opened his door and emerged in an ecstatic mood. Addressing Ramlal's mother and the others, he said: "Are you all going to bed? How can you go to bed without giving me any food?"

"My goodness!" Ramlal's mother replied. "What do you mean? You've just finished your meal!"

The Master said: "When did I eat? I've just come from Dakshineswar. When did you feed me?"

The women looked at one another in amazement. They realized that the Master's ecstasy was making him say this. What could they do now? There was no food in the house that they could serve him. Ramlal's mother could find no solution, and told him timidly: "Look, there is no cooked food at home except for some puffed rice. Why don't you eat that? It won't upset your stomach." She then brought a big plate of puffed rice and placed it in front of the Master. He turned his face away like a petulant boy and said, "I won't eat just puffed rice." She tried to persuade him, saying: "Your stomach isn't good, and you can't eat anything else. The shops are closed now, so it isn't possible for me to get sago and barley and fix it for you. Please eat this puffed rice tonight; as soon as I get up tomorrow morning I shall cook rice and soup for you." But who would listen to that? His childish insistence continued, "I won't eat just puffed rice."

At last Ramlal was sent to a sweets shop. He called loudly to wake up the shopkeeper, and bought two pounds of sweets. His mother served those sweets on a plate along with heaps of puffed rice — more than an ordinary person could consume. The Master then happily sat down to eat and finished everything. Everyone in the household was concerned and told themselves: "He has such a weak stomach that half of the month he lives on sago and barley. And now he has eaten such a huge quantity of food so late at night! Who knows what will happen tomorrow?" But amazingly the Master's health was fine the next day; he was not sick at all because of what he had eaten the night before.

Another time when the Master was staying in Kamarpukur, he paid a

15. Third example: At Jayrambati he ate three pounds of soaked rice and a tiny fish with gravy.

visit to his father-in-law's house in Jayrambati. The Master went to bed after supper, but shortly afterwards got up and said he was very hungry. The women of the household were worried because there was no food to offer him. On that day many people had come to the house to attend an annual ceremony, and there was nothing left except for some rice soaking in water. When the Holy Mother, with great hesitancy, told the Master that, he said, "Serve it to me." "But there are no vegetables," she told him.

The Master replied: "Why don't you look more carefully? Today you made a hot fish curry. See if any of that is left."

The Holy Mother went to the kitchen and found that a tiny *maurala* [a kind of smelt] with gravy was left at the bottom of a bowl. The Master was happy when she brought it to him. He ate three pounds of soaked rice with that fish and gravy and was satisfied.

Similar situations would sometimes occur in Dakshineswar. One mid-

16. Fourth example: In Dakshineswar he ate two pounds of farina pudding at midnight.

night the Master got up, called Ramlal, and said: "I'm very hungry. Find some food for me."

There were usually some fruits and sweets in the Master's room, but when Ramlal searched he found nothing. So he went to the nahabat and informed the Holy Mother and other women devotees. They hurriedly made a fire with hay and wood and cooked about two pounds of farina pudding. A woman devotee carried it to the Master in a big stone bowl. Entering the room, she saw a dim oil lamp flickering in the corner. The Master was pacing in an ecstatic mood, and Ramlal was seated nearby. In that calm and silent night, she was startled to see the Master's solemn and luminous face, and his unclothed god-intoxicated form. His large eyes — before which the whole universe merged into and emerged from samadhi at will — focussed inward. Her heart was filled with joy as she watched the Master pace majestically, moving blissfully and without motive, his mind one-pointed. It seemed to her that the Master's body had become much larger, as if he were not a person of this world! A god had taken human form, descending from heaven to this earth full of misery. Prompted by his compassionate heart, he had disguised himself and was pacing fearlessly in that dark night, intently considering ways to transform this death-stricken world into an abode of gods. This was not the same Master whom she saw all the time. She shivered with an indescribable awe as she drew near him.

Ramlal had already brought a seat for the Master, and the woman devotee put the bowl of farina in front of it. The Master sat down and, still in an ecstatic mood, gradually consumed all of it. Did the Master know what was in that woman's mind? Who can say? While eating, he noticed that she was silently watching him. He asked her, "Well, can you tell me who is eating — myself, or someone else?"

The woman devotee replied, "It seems to me that there is someone else inside you who is eating."

The Master was pleased to hear this and said with a smile, "You are right."

We could mention many such events. When the Master was in an ecstatic

| 17. The Master's intense spiritual moods affected his body. |

state, intense thought currents would change his body so much that he seemed to be a different person. His demeanour, how he ate and moved, and how he acted and conducted himself would change. But when the ecstasy ended, one would notice that his unusual conduct had not affected his health at all. The indwelling mind is always making, unmaking, and changing the gross body — this phenomenon is difficult to understand and hard to believe. But we actually witnessed the proof of these kinds of changes in the aforesaid events, which were common in the Master's astonishing life. But let us conclude this topic and resume the previous subject.

Some say that it was from the Bhairavi Brahmani that Mathur first came to

| 18. Vaishnavcharan attends the meeting of pandits at Dakshineswar. |

know about Vaishnavcharan. Mathur decided to invite him to ascertain whether the Master's spiritual experiences were associated with physical disease. Some days later, Vaishnavcharan arrived at Dakshineswar. We can assume that a small meeting of pandits was held on that day. Some aspirants and pandits must have accompanied Vaishnavcharan as usual, and the learned Brahmani and Mathur's party were also assembled to evaluate the Master's condition, so we can call this a meeting.

The discussion began. The Brahmani described everything that she had

19. The meeting's discussion about the Master's condition.

heard about the Master from others and that she had seen for herself. She then referred to the experiences of the great teachers of the devotional path in ancient times, which were recorded in the scriptures, and compared them with the Master's present condition. She concluded that his state was the same as theirs. Addressing Vaishnavcharan, she said, "If you hold a different opinion on this matter, please explain to me why you do so." As a mother stands heroically to protect her child, so the Brahmani came forward to defend the Master, as if she were endowed with some divine power. And what of the Master, the one for whom all this commotion was going on? We can picture him relaxed, seated in the midst of the scholars debating about him, smiling and enjoying the bliss of his own Self. Perhaps he took a few fennel seeds and cubebs from a nearby spice bag and put them into his mouth, listening to their conversation as if they were talking about someone else. Perhaps he touched Vaishnavcharan and described his condition, saying, "Look, this happens to me."

Some say that subtle insight developed from sadhana allowed Vaishnav-

20. Vaishnavcharan's conclusion regarding the Master's condition.

charan to recognize the Master as a great soul at first sight. In any case, the Master told us that Vaishnavcharan listened to the Brahmani and heartily approved what she said about the Master's condition. Not only that, the pandit also remarked with amazement that according to the devotional scriptures mahabhava consists of nineteen main spiritual moods, which so far had been manifested only in Radha and Chaitanya. Now all those signs were visible in the Master. If anyone were fortunate enough to get a glimpse of mahabhava, at most only two or three of those nineteen signs would appear in that person. In the past, no human body had been capable of withstanding the indomitable force of those nineteen moods; and this state of affairs would continue in the future, according to the scriptures. Mathur and the others were dumbfounded by Vaishnavcharan's comments. The childlike Master said to Mathur with joy and surprise: "Ah! What does he say? At any rate, I'm glad to hear that it's not a disease after all!"

Vaishnavcharan's comments regarding the Master's condition were not

21. The Master's opinion of the Kartabhaja sect.

superficial; from that time on his love and respect for the Master increased. He visited Dakshineswar frequently to enjoy the holy company of the Master, sought the Master's opinion regarding his own esoteric sadhanas, and sometimes brought the Master to visit his fellow spiritual aspirants who followed the same path, so that they could be acquainted with the Master and be blessed like he was. After associating with these aspirants and learning about their lives and their esoteric sadhanas, the ever-pure, divine-natured Master came to realize that if people practised rituals that the public might see as faulty and reprehensible, but did so as sadhana, whole-heartedly seeking God-realization, they would not go astray. Gradually, they would develop renunciation and self-control, make progress in spiritual life, and attain devotion for God. But the Master told us that when he first heard about those esoteric practices and saw some of them himself, this thought arose in his mind: "They talk big, but why do they perform such abominable acts?" However, the Master also told us that he finally changed his opinion when he saw that those aspirants among them who were truly simple and sincere indeed made spiritual progress. To eliminate our antipathy towards the followers of that esoteric path, the Master sometimes told us how he saw them: "Look, never harbour any hatred towards them. Know that theirs is also a path, although it is a dirty one. There are many doors to enter a house — the main gate, the back door, and the one for the sweeper to enter the house and clean the toilets. No matter which door people use to enter the house, they all reach the same destination. This doesn't mean you should follow their ways, or associate with them. But don't hate them."

Is it easy for the human mind, so full of worldly desires, to move towards

| 22. The type of religion sought by worldly people. | the path of renunciation? Can a person call on God without any motive and with sincerity proceed to attain Him? |

In the pursuit of a pure life, one willfully keeps some impure desires; even after renouncing lust and gold, a person loves to have a little taste of them. The books of worship enjoin worshipping the Divine Mother with austerity and purity of heart, but there are some people who prescribe singing a few lustful songs for Her satisfaction. One should not wonder at this or condemn it. It proves that weak human beings are strongly bound with the chain of lust and gold by the all-powerful Mahamaya, ruler of myriad universes. It is impossible for human beings to attain liberation if She is not merciful and removes that bondage. It is beyond human ability to comprehend how She helps each individual to move forward towards liberation along a particular path. When we closely study our inner lives and compare our own with the Master's mystical life, it becomes evident that he was a unique and divine Supreme Being. Prompted by his divine will, or perhaps by compassion for us, he lived in this sordid world apparently humbler than the humblest. But in the realm of wisdom he was a king of kings.

In the Vedic period, yoga and bhoga [enjoyment] were blended in the sacri-

| 23. The history of Tantra and its uniqueness. | ficial and ritualistic portion of the Vedas. The goal of human life was to enjoy sense objects legitimately through worship of the deities. |

By performing those Vedic rituals, the worshippers' minds would become desireless, to some extent, and they would become blessed as they worshipped God with pure devotion as recommended in the Upanishads. But this tradition took a different turn during the Buddhist period. The pure spiritual disciplines that were meant for desireless, forest-dwelling monastics were indiscriminately taught to worldly householders. The government supported the Buddhist monks in that effort. Consequently, Vedic rituals and sacrifices, which were meant to gradually direct people to renunciation through enjoyment, were suppressed. But those rituals reappeared surreptitiously in the forms of secret Tantric sadhanas, practised in the dead of night in lonely and frightening cremation grounds. According to Tantra, the great yogi Shiva noticed that the Vedic rituals were flagging, so He revitalized them and revealed them in a different form as the Tantras.

In fact, there is a great truth behind the belief that one can find the combination of yoga and bhoga in the Tantra, just as in the ritualistic portion of the Vedas. However, in the Vedas rituals are quite separate from the knowledge revealed in the Upanishads, but in the Tantra scriptures rituals are closely connected with nondual knowledge. For example, when you sit to perform Tantric worship, you must first rouse the kundalini to the sahasrara in the crown of the head and then think of yourself as being completely united with God. Then you must consider that you have become a jiva separate from God, and that the divine light has become condensed and manifest as a deity to be worshipped. Thus, you move the deity from within yourself to outside and start to worship Him or Her. This form of worship shows a wonderful method of becoming one with God in love, which is the goal of human life. Of course, perhaps only one advanced soul among a thousand can perform this worship properly. But when everyone makes an effort to do this, they certainly get some benefit and thus slowly make progress in spiritual life. Every Tantric ritual is connected with nondual knowledge, thus reminding the spiritual aspirants of their ultimate goal. Herein lies the uniqueness of Tantric rituals as distinguished from Vedic rituals; and for this reason, Tantric sadhana has had a tremendous impact on the masses of India.

Another innovation of Tantra is the preaching of the motherhood of Maha-

24. The history of virachara in Tantra.

maya, the cause of the universe, and simultaneously the promotion of a pure attitude towards all female forms. If you explore the Vedas and Puranas, you will not find these wonderful ideas — they belong exclusively to Tantra. The rudiments of worshipping the female body are found in the Samhita portion of the Vedas. For example, during the marriage ceremony there is a mantra describing the bride's genitals as *Prajapater-dvitiyam mukham* [the second mouth of the creator Prajapati]. There is also the prayer *Garbham dhehi Sinivali* [O Sinivali (Goddess Uma), conceive the embryo], so that the couple will have a beautiful and vigorous child (Rig-Veda Samhita 10:184:2). There are other Vedic prayers concerning the female sex organ that admonish one to look upon it as pure. But let no one think that the worship of the male and female organs was prevalent in India during the Vedic period. History has shown that this worship, in a gross form, was first popular in the Sumer sect in Babylon and in its Dravidian branch.

The Tantra system of India incorporated the ideas of karma-kanda [ritual portion] and jnana-kanda [knowledge portion] from the Vedas and combined them with its own rituals. Again, knowing that the worship of the female form might help a certain class of aspirants to easily make spiritual progress, the Tantra adopted to a great extent the Dravidian's gross method of worship of the female body and combined it with the high spiritual ideals of the Vedas. Thus, the Tantra developed a new ideal and absorbed it into its own system. It seems that the Tantric virachara [heroic mode] evolved in this manner. The teachers of Tantra realized that lustful human beings would in any case enjoy sense objects to some degree and that they should generate in those people genuine reverence for the objects of enjoyment. Even though they might enjoy those objects to their hearts' content, that intense reverence must soon engender self-control and other spiritual traits. Consequently those Tantric teachers preached that a woman's body is like a pure and holy place. Shun the idea that women are mere human beings; rather, think of them as goddesses. Always love and respect all female forms, considering them to be special manifestations of the Divine Mother. Dip a woman's toe in water and then sip that water with devotion. Never condemn or injure any woman, even inadvertently.

Here are some passages from the Tantric scriptures: "O Parvati, all holy places truly exist within a woman's body."[1] "O goddess of beautiful face, he who looks upon a woman as a human being, his repetition of the mantra does not bring perfection, but rather produces the opposite result."[2] "He who drinks with devotion the water that has been touched by a woman's toe, or eats a woman's leavings, attains uninterrupted success."[3] "Women are goddesses; they are holy; and they are the ornaments of society. One should not hate, condemn, or assault any woman."[4]

Regardless of all the high ideals regarding women, in the course of time a particular period arrived when Tantric aspirants focussed their minds on achieving occult powers instead of realizing God. During this period various bizarre sadhanas and the worship of ghosts and ghouls entered the system of Tantra and converted it to its present form. That is why one can discern two levels in each Tantra — good and bad, high and low. In addition, lower gross sadhanas were incorporated into the highest rituals of worship. People selected among them according to their natures.

25. Two levels in each Tantra: high and low.

1. *Purashcharanollasa Tantra,* chapter 14.
2. *Uttara Tantra,* chapter 2.
3. *Nigama Kalpadruma.*
4. *Mundamala Tantra,* chapter 5.

With the advent of Chaitanya, another change developed in Tantric
26. The new method of | sadhana. Chaitanya and the Vaishnava teachers who
worship introduced by | followed him believed that the dualistic approach
the Vaishnava sect of | towards God would be beneficial for most people, so
Bengal. | they propagated the Tantric mantras and the associ-
ated external worship, but they discarded to a great extent the nondualistic
practices from the Tantric sadhana. They also introduced a novel idea into
their worship and prayer, advising people to serve God as they wished to be
served themselves. According to the Tantric tradition, the deities purify
offered fruits and food by a mere glance. It was commonly believed that if an
aspirant ate such prasad, it would increase spiritual inclinations rather than
animal propensities such as lust, anger, and so on. According to the new
method of worship introduced by the Vaishnava teachers, the deities accept
the subtle parts of the offered food, and sometimes even the physical part,
depending on the devotees' eagerness and intensity of devotion. This belief
gained momentum. Thus, various changes in their methods of worship were
introduced by Vaishnava teachers. The main change was that they promoted
the Tantric pashu bhava, or bestial mode of worship, as much as possible
and favoured external purification. They preached that one should maintain
purity in eating, in conduct, and in every other respect; and that one should
repeat the name of God, knowing that the Name is Brahman. Thus, one
would attain perfection. They also quoted this proverb: *Japat siddhih japat
siddhih, japat siddhih na samshayah* [Without a doubt, repeating japa brings
success].

The early Vaishnava teachers tried to keep their traditional ideal high but
27. The doctrines of the | eventually it degenerated. Soon after these teachers
Kartabhaja and other | passed away, worldly minded people adopted
sects gradually came | impure practices and polluted the pure path that had
from the aforesaid | been introduced. Men shunned subtle ideas in
method: their effect. | favour of gross objects. Instead of adopting the atti-
tude of a woman's attraction for the paramour and superimposing that onto
God, they took mistresses themselves. Thus, men introduced sensual enjoyment into the chaste devotional path of the early teachers and shaped it to
some extent according to their own natures. But what else could they do?
Because they were incapable of leading such a pure life, they absorbed a
mixture of yoga and bhoga. They wanted to be spiritual and at the same time
keep a little desire to enjoy sensual objects. For that reason, various modes of
worship and secret esoteric practices evolved among the Kartabhajas, Auls,
Bauls, Darveshas, Sains, and other sects in the Vaishnava community. At the
root of all these practices, one could find the current of many ancient Vedic
rituals, the mixture of yoga and bhoga, and the incorporation of nondual
knowledge within each ritual that had been introduced by the hereditary
Tantric teachers.

The reader will easily understand this topic if we discuss how the Karta-

28. Spiritual instructions about the goal and the means according to the Kartabhaja and other sects.

bhaja and other Vaishnava sects conceive of God, liberation, self-control, renunciation, and love. The Master quite often told us various things about those sects. It will amaze the reader to learn how the teachings of these sects were recorded in simple language and in a verse form that helped the illiterate masses to understand them. Followers of those sects call God *Aleklata*. The word *Alek* derives from the Sanskrit word *alakshya*, the invisible. This Alek enters a pure mind and becomes manifest as a *Karta* [Master] or a guru. Such a teacher is given the title of *Sahaj*, one who has an innate awareness of God. Because this sect worships this genuine human guru, it is called *Kartabhaja*. Regarding the real nature of the Aleklata and Its descent on a pure soul, the Kartabhajas say: "It comes imperceptibly and goes imperceptibly, and no one can see the Alek. He who has known the Alek becomes the object of worship in the three worlds."

The sign of the male Sahaj is that he always remains "intact"; in other words, although he lives with women he does not allow lust to control him. They say in this regard, "He lives with women but does not indulge in sex."

In this world of lust and gold, an aspirant cannot make any progress in spiritual life if he or she does not remain detached. This is the advice of the Kartabhaja sect to aspirants: "Be a cook. Serve the curry, but do not touch the cooking pot. Make the frog dance in the mouth of the snake, but do not let the snake swallow it. Bathe in the ocean of nectar, but do not let your hair get wet."

Just as Tantric aspirants are classified into three categories — the bestial, the heroic, and the divine — so there is a saying about the gradation of aspirants among the Vaishnava sects: "Auls, Bauls, Darveshas, and Sains; there is no one above Sain." Only after attaining perfection does a person become a Sain.

The Master used to say that they all worship the formless aspect of God. Sometimes he would sing some songs from the Kartabhaja tradition to us. For example:

> Dive deep, O mind, dive deep in the Ocean of God's beauty;
> If you descend to the uttermost depths,
> There you will find the gem of Love.
> Go seek, O mind, go seek Vrindaban in your heart,
> Where with His loving devotees
> Sri Krishna sports eternally.
> Light up, O mind, light up true wisdom's shining lamp,
> And let it burn with steady flame
> Unceasingly within your heart.
> Who is it that steers your boat across the solid earth?
> It is your guru, says Kubir;
> Meditate on his holy feet.

The main sadhana of this sect is to worship the guru and to become absorbed in practising disciplines and singing together. Although they do not reject the forms of the gods and goddesses, they generally do not worship them. Guru worship is very ancient in India. It probably began in the age of the Upanishads. It is mentioned in the Taittiriya Upanishad (1:11:2): "Treat your teacher as God." It seems that at that time the worship of gods and goddesses had not yet begun. It is amazing how in the course of time, guru worship took various forms in India.

Kartabhaja aspirants also have to undergo various religious disciplines in order to purge their minds of dualistic concepts such as purity and impurity and good and evil. The Master said that these instructions were passed down from guru to disciple. Sometimes he would mention some of these instructions.

The Master would say quite often, "One should listen to the teachings of the Vedas and Puranas, but the sadhanas of the Tantras should be put into practice." Almost everywhere in India one can see that the followers of Smriti scriptures practise Tantric sadhana in some form or other. Even the pandits of Nyaya and Vedanta are Tantrics in practice. Within Vaishnava communities it can be seen that some great scholars of the Bhagavata and devotional scriptures practise the esoteric sadhanas of the Kartabhaja and other sects. Pandit Vaishnavcharan belonged to the Kartabhaja group. He was closely connected with this sect's Kachibagan centre, which was located a few miles north of Calcutta. Many men and women of this sect lived there and practised sadhana under his guidance. Vaishnavcharan took the Master there a few times. We heard that some women of that centre observed the Master and found him always unperturbed. When they saw that his love for God had put him into ecstasy, they attempted to test the Master to determine whether he had completely conquered lust. They then paid him their respect and declared him to be *Atut Sahaj*, a man of unbroken chastity and natural awareness of God. It was at Vaishnavcharan's request that the childlike Master visited that place. He was completely unaware that those women would test him in that manner. After this, he never visited that place again.

29. Vaishnavcharan took the Master to the Kachibagan centre to test him.

As he observed the Master's wonderful strength of character and purity and witnessed him in bhava samadhi, Vaishnavcharan's love for and faith in him increased day by day. Ultimately he did not hesitate to declare publicly that the Master was an incarnation of God.

30. Vaishnavcharan considered the Master to be an avatar.

Shortly after Vaishnavcharan began visiting the Master, Pandit Gauri of Indesh came to Dakshineswar. Pandit Gauri was a distinguished Tantric aspirant. The Master told us an interesting incident that took place when Gauri

31. The occult powers of Pandit Gauri, a Tantric adept.

entered the Dakshineswar Kali temple. The Master said that Gauri had an occult power that he had developed by means of his austerities. When he was invited to a scriptural debate, while entering a house or meeting place, he would loudly recite the following a few times: *Ha-re-re-re, Niralambo lambodara-janani kam yami sharanam* [Oh, I am helpless! To whom shall I go for shelter except to Thee, O Mother of Ganesha?].[5] The Master said that when people heard that thunderous, heroic voice exclaiming "Ha-re-re-re" and the line from Shankara's hymn on the Devi, their hearts shook with an indescribable fear. This served two purposes: First, that sound would fully awaken the power within Gauri; second, he would frighten and overwhelm his opponents with it and rob them of their strength. Gauri would then menacingly slap his left arm with the palm of his right hand like [Indian] wrestlers do, enter the meeting hall, and sit with his legs folded beneath him, his knees in front like courtiers in the court of a Muslim king. Thus, would he challenge his opponents. The Master said that it was then impossible for anyone to defeat him.

But at that time the Master did not know about Gauri's occult power. As soon as Gauri entered the Dakshineswar Kali temple and roared "Ha-re-re-re" a few times, immediately someone within the Master made him shout those syllables louder than Gauri. Amazed, Gauri yelled louder than the Master had. Excited, the Master again out-roared Gauri, "Ha-re-re-re!" With a smile the Master told us later that the noise the two of them made sounded like a whole band of robbers charging to the attack. When the temple guards heard the ruckus they ran to the spot, armed with sticks and clubs. All were panic-stricken. When Gauri could not utter those words louder than the Master, he became silent and dejectedly entered the Kali temple. When people realized that the Master and the visiting pandit had been making that loud noise, they laughed and returned to their places. The Master said: "The Mother then made me know that Gauri used his occult power to take away others' strength and remain invincible. When that power was defeated by this place (*himself*), he lost it. The Divine Mother drew his power into here (*pointing to himself*) for his good." In fact, every day Gauri was increasingly charmed by the Master's spirituality and ultimately completely surrendered to him.

Pandit Gauri was an outstanding Tantric aspirant. The Master told us that

| 32. Gauri worshipped his wife as a goddess. | every year during Durga Puja, Gauri would arrange everything needed for the worship, and then adorn his wife with a new cloth and ornaments, place her |

on a painted wooden altar, and worship her devoutly for three days as the Divine Mother. According to the Tantra, all female forms are the veritable forms of the Divine Mother, and Her powers of sustaining and delighting are

---

5. *Devi-aparadha-kshmapana-stotra* by Shankara, verse 5.

manifest in them to a great degree. So men should worship all women with purity of heart. When a man forgets that the Divine Mother is hidden in all women and lustfully looks at the female body as an object of enjoyment, he insults the Divine Mother and consequently does harm to himself. In the Chandi (11:6), while praising the Divine Mother, the gods also say this: "O Goddess, You are the embodiment of knowledge and You are manifest in all higher and lower forms of conceptual knowledge. You are embodied in every woman in the world. O Mother, You alone are present everywhere in this universe, pervading everything. You are incomparable and beyond expression. Who can describe Your infinite glories by singing hymns?"

Many of us in India recite this hymn daily. But alas! How many of us even for a moment strive to see a woman's body as the Divine Mother Herself, and by thus paying proper respect to Her become blessed with the experience of heartfelt and pure bliss? Now men view a woman, a special manifestation of the Divine Mother, with an impure mind and sinful eyes, insulting her a hundred times a day! O India, your present degradation is due to disrespecting women with your bestial attitude and forgetting to serve human beings as God. Only the Divine Mother knows when She, out of compassion, will remove your bestial attitude!

The Master told us of another of Pandit Gauri's amazing abilities. Eminent

33. Gauri's incredible method of homa fire.

Tantric aspirants generally perform a fire sacrifice every day at the end of the Divine Mother's worship. Gauri also used to perform this on many occasions, if not daily. But his method of homa fire was unconventional. People usually put clay or sand on the ground and make an altar. They then set wood on it, kindle the fire, and offer oblations. But Gauri's method was different. He would stretch out his left arm in the air and pile one *maund* [82 pounds] of wood upon it; then with his right hand he would light the wood and pour oblations into the fire. A fire sacrifice takes at least an hour. It seems impossible that a man could hold 82 pounds of wood on his extended arm for such a long time without support. In addition, how could he keep his mind calm, ignoring that terrible heat on his bare arm, and properly make his offerings with devotion? Many of us heard this story from the Master, but had trouble believing it. Observing our doubt, the Master said: "Look, I've seen him do this with my own eyes. It was one of his occult powers."

A few days after Gauri's arrival in Dakshineswar, Mathur convened a

34. The meeting held at Dakshineswar with Vaishnavcharan and Gauri; in an ecstatic mood the Master sits on Vaishnavcharan's shoulders, and the latter praises him with a hymn.

meeting with Vaishnavcharan and some scholarly aspirants. The purpose of the meeting was to debate with Gauri and determine the Master's spiritual condition through scriptural testimony as they had done before. The meeting was convened that morning in the natmandir facing the Kali temple. Because Vaishnavcharan was late in arriving from

Calcutta, the Master proceeded with Gauri to the meeting place. Before entering the natmandir, the Master first went inside the shrine of the Divine Mother Kali, bowed down, and devoutly worshipped Her feet. When he came out of the temple, he was staggering in ecstasy. At that very moment Vaishnavcharan arrived and bowed down at his feet. When he saw Vaishnavcharan, the Master became overwhelmed with love and went into samadhi. In that state, he sat on Vaishnavcharan's shoulders. Vaishnavcharan considered himself blessed. Impelled by joy, he spontaneously composed a hymn in Sanskrit that glorified the Master. Mathur and others stood motionless around them, observing intently and with heartfelt devotion the Master's gracious and luminous form in samadhi, and listening to Vaishnavcharan's joyous and melodious hymn. After a while, the Master descended from samadhi, and everyone slowly proceeded to the meeting place and sat down.

The conference began. At once Gauri said (*pointing to the Master*): "Since he has bestowed such grace upon Vaishnavcharan, I shall not debate with him today. If I do, I am sure to be defeated because he is endowed with divine power. Moreover, I find that Vaishnavcharan belongs to my school of thought, so his opinion about the Master must be the same as mine. In this case, debate is unnecessary." The meeting ended after a little conversation on other scriptural topics.

Gauri did not refrain from debate that day because he was intimidated by Vaishnavcharan's erudition. For a few days he had observed the Master's demeanour, conduct, behaviour, and other signs, and had come to the deep

35. Gauri's opinion of the Master.

realization that the Master was not an ordinary man but a great soul. This insight came to him by virtue of the austerities he had undergone. A few days later, the Master asked Gauri a question to test his understanding: "Hello, Vaishnavcharan calls this (*pointing to himself*) an avatar. How can it be? Tell me what you think about it."

Gauri gravely replied: "Does Vaishnavcharan call you an avatar? I consider that an understatement! I believe you are He by a fraction of Whose power the avatars come forth to this world in every age and accomplish their mission." The Master smiled and said: "Ah — so you outbid him! What do you find in me that leads you to entertain this idea?" Gauri replied: "I am saying this based on my deep personal experience and the testimony of the scriptures. I am ready to prove my contention to anyone who challenges me in the matter."

"Well, it is you who say so," the Master said, like a boy, "but I know nothing about it."

Gauri said: "That is as it should be. The scriptures agree on this point. Because you don't know yourself, how can others know you? Only one whom you have graciously allowed to know you can do so."

The Master smiled upon hearing Gauri's expression of faith. Gauri's

36. Gauri's association
with the Master leads
him to renunciation; he
leaves home to practise
austerities.

attraction for the Master grew day by day. With the Master's divine companionship, Gauri's knowledge of the scriptures and the effects of his sadhana reached fulfillment and became manifest as intense renunciation of the world. He gradually lost interest in erudition, name and fame, occult powers, and so on, and his mind started to become absorbed in God. Gauri lost his pride of scholarship and his pomposity, and his passion for debate was silenced. He now realized that he had spent so much of his time in vain without trying his utmost to realize God and that he should no longer misuse his time. He firmly resolved to renounce everything, completely depend on God with wholehearted devotion, and spend his remaining days calling on Him with intense longing. Thus, he hoped to achieve divine grace and the vision of God.

Gauri passed days and months in meditation and in the blessed company of the Master. Because he had been away from home for a long time, his wife, sons, and others repeatedly wrote letters asking him to return. They had heard that he was associating with a crazy monk of Dakshineswar and that his mind had been affected.

Gauri was quite worried. He deduced from those letters that members of his family might come to Dakshineswar and try to drag him back to worldly life. After long deliberation, he hit upon a plan. When he learned that an auspicious time for renouncing the world had come, Gauri went to the Master and bowed before him, tearfully asking his permission to leave. The Master asked: "What happened, Gauri? Why do you want to leave so suddenly? Where will you go?"

Gauri replied with folded hands: "Please bless me so that my desire will be fulfilled. I will never return home without realizing God." From then on, no one could locate Pandit Gauri, despite a great deal of searching.

On many occasions the Master related to us various episodes from the lives

37. The Master's advice,
quoting the words of
Vaishnavcharan and
Gauri: Have faith in the
divine play of God as a
human being.

of Vaishnavcharan and Gauri. Sometimes he would refer to their opinions while discussing a particular topic with us. We remember that while advising a devotee one day, the Master said: "Only when one develops the firm conviction that the Chosen Deity dwells in every person will one realize God. Vaishnavcharan used to say, 'One attains full knowledge when one believes that God plays as human beings.'"

Sometimes when the Master observed a devotee's bigoted sense of

38. Gauri's view
regarding the oneness of
Kali and Krishna.

distinction between Kali and Krishna, he would say: "Your mind is so mean and dogmatic! Know that your Chosen Deity has become Kali, Krishna, Gaur, and everything. This doesn't mean I am asking you to renounce your

Chosen Deity and worship Gaur, but you must give up your dogmatic idea. Hold on to the firm conviction that your Chosen Deity has become Krishna as well as Gaur. Look, when a bride goes to her father-in-law's house, she loves, respects, and serves her father-in-law, mother-in-law, sisters-in-law, and brothers-in-law accordingly, but only with her husband does she open her heart and share her bed. She knows that it is through her husband that her father-in-law, mother-in-law, and others are her own. Similarly, you must relate to your Chosen Deity as a woman relates to her husband, and realize that it is through your Chosen Deity that you are connected with His or Her other forms. You must love and respect them. Thus, you avoid any dogmatic ideas. Gauri used to say, 'Only when I experience Kali and Gauranga as one shall I consider that I have true knowledge.'"

When the Master came to know that a devotee's mind was agitated because of his attachment to someone in his family, he advised that devotee to love and serve the object of his affection as a form of God. We mentioned earlier (see III.1.27) that the Master advised a woman devotee who was very attached to her young nephew to love and serve that child as Gopala (child Krishna), and as a result, she soon began to experience bhava samadhi. Sometimes while speaking about how to love and respect one's object of love as God, the Master would refer to Vaishnavcharan's opinion: "Vaishnavcharan used to say, 'If anyone considers his object of love as his Chosen Deity, his mind gets absorbed in God quickly.'" He would explain it immediately, saying: "Vaishnavcharan would advise the women of his sect to practise that kind of sadhana. They incurred no blame for doing this because they had adopted the mood of having a paramour. They tried to superimpose upon God the attraction that they felt for their paramour." The Master said further that this sadhana should not be taught to the general public because it would promote adultery. However, we know that he did not disapprove if any woman devotee wanted to love and serve her husband, son, or any relative as a form of God, and he even taught some devotees who took refuge in him to practise that attitude.

On a little reflection, one can easily understand that the previously mentioned view is neither new nor unscriptural. The rishi of the Brihadaranyaka Upanishad (2:4:5), in the dialogue between Yajnavalkya and Maitreyi, taught: "Verily, not for the sake of the husband, my dear, is the husband loved, but he is loved for the sake of the Self. Verily, not for the sake of the wife, my dear, is the wife loved, but she is loved for the sake of the Self." Thus, all human beings, all wealth, and everything in this world prompt loving feelings and attract the mind because the loving, blissful Divine Being pervades them. The rishis of the Upanishads experienced this truth and from ancient times taught us to love all beings

Margin notes:

39. Vaishnavcharan's opinion on considering the object of one's love as a form of God.

40. The scriptures enjoin the aforesaid advice: the dialogue between Yajnavalkya and Maitreyi in the Upanishad.

and objects. It is evident that Narada and other teachers of the path of devotion followed in the footsteps of the Upanishadic rishis when they advised people to divert the forces of lust, anger, and so on towards God and call on Him by adopting attitudes such as sakhya, vatsalya, and madhura. So the Master's view on this matter obviously agrees with the scriptures.

It is well known that divine incarnations bring a new gospel to the reli-

41. Avatars always abide by the authority of the scriptures. The Master's advice to respect all religious paths.

gious world without contradicting the previous ones and always honour the authority of earlier scriptures. One sees this when studying the life of any avatar. In this book we are attempting to explain to the reader that we have found full evidence of this in the life of Sri Ramakrishna, the avatar of this modern age. But if we fail, let the reader know that it is due to the fault of our narrow-mindedness and is not a flaw of the Master, who marvelled humankind by unveiling for the first time in the spiritual world a unique truth: "As many faiths, so many paths." Generally, clever, worldly-minded Western people judge another person or a nation by one standard; but when judging themselves, they reverse it. If we followed that Western method, we would look down upon "the horrible Kartabhaja doctrine" with disgust. But the godman Sri Ramakrishna respectfully placed the doctrines of the Kartabhaja alongside the pure nondualistic Vedanta as different paths to God-realization, and advised people to practise a particular path according to their individual temperaments. Disgusted, many of us sometimes asked the Master: "Sir, how could the Brahmani, being an aspirant of high calibre, practise Tantra with five articles [wine, meat, fish, cereal, and sex]? And is it not wrong that the great and devout scholar Vaishnavcharan did not hesitate to keep a mistress as part of his sadhana?"

The Master invariably replied: "Look, that kind of act was not sinful for them. They wholeheartedly believed that it was their path to the realization of God. One should not condemn and criticize a method that someone genuinely believes in and sincerely practises for God-realization. One should not disturb another's faith because if anyone follows a particular spiritual attitude properly, he or she will reach God, the embodiment of all attitudes. Hold on to your own attitude and go on calling for God. And never criticize another's attitude, or try to adopt another's attitude as your own." Saying so, the ever-blissful Master would sing this song:

> Dwell, O mind, within yourself;
> Enter no other's home.
> If you but seek there, you will find
> All you are searching for.
> God, the true Philosopher's Stone,
> Who answers every prayer,
> Lies hidden deep within your heart,

The richest gem of all.
How many pearls and precious stones
Are scattered all about
The outer court that lies before
The chamber of your heart!
O mind, do not be restless to
Embark on painful journeys to holy places.
Why don't you cool yourself by bathing joyfully
In the confluence of three streams[6] at the muladhara?[7]
What do you see, O Kamalakanta?[8]
This world is a juggler's trick.
You have not recognized that juggler
Who dwells in this very body.

6. This confluence is called *Triveni,* the meeting place of Ida, Pingala, and Sushumna.
— *Translator*
7. This is the basic centre of the kundalini that lies at the bottom of the spine.
— *Translator*
8. Kamalakanta is a Bengali mystic and the composer of this song. — *Translator*

Chapter 2

Sri Ramakrishna as a Guru, and Sadhus of Various Orders

I am the origin of all; from Me all things evolve. The wise know this and worship Me with all their heart.

Solely out of compassion for them, I, dwelling in their hearts, dispel with the shining lamp of wisdom the darkness born of ignorance. — GITA 10:8,11

ONCE THE MASTER TOLD US: "After Keshab Sen came, a group of 'Young

| 1. How the Master met other monks. |

Bengal'[1] like yourselves began to come here. You don't know that before this many sadhus, ascetics, all-renouncing monks, and Vaishnava anchorites would visit this place. They stopped coming this way as much when the railroad was constructed. But prior to that, all the holy men would pass by as they travelled the road alongside the Ganges on their way to bathe in the Gangasagar or to visit the Lord Jagannath in Puri. They would invariably stop for a few days at Rasmani's temple garden, setting up their tents to rest. Some of them would stay longer. Do you know why? Monks do not set up camp in a place that lacks facilities for food and water, and is not close to a secluded jungle where they can answer the call of nature. Monks live on alms, so they set up their dwellings where alms are easily available.

---

1. The Master knew nearly a dozen English words, which he sometimes used during conversation. He meant here English-educated Bengali youths. — *Translator*

"When monks get tired while travelling, they will set up their tents for a couple of days, even if it is difficult to obtain alms there. But they never stay in a place where water is scarce and it's difficult to find a secluded jungle where they can answer the call of nature. Good monks do not relieve themselves in places where others do so or where they may be seen. They go far away to a secluded spot for that purpose. A monk told me the following story.

2. Monks rest where water is convenient and there is a secluded jungle for answering the call of nature.

"A man was looking for a monk of true renunciation. Someone told him that if he could find a monk answering the call of nature at a place far away from human habitation, this person would be a man of genuine renunciation. The man kept that in mind as he left the area. One day he saw a monk relieving himself far away from other people. From a distance he followed that monk and began to learn about him.

3. A story illustrating this.

"The princess of that country heard that a woman would have a good son if she married a true yogi, because the scriptures say that great souls are fathered by yogis. So this princess went to a monk's camp nearby to find a husband. She selected that particular monk, returned home, and informed her father that she would marry him. The king was very fond of his daughter, and because she insisted, the king went to the monk. He offered him half of his kingdom and tried to convince him to marry the princess. But the king's words could not sway the monk. He left the area that night, without informing anyone. As the man witnessed that monk's true renunciation, he realized that he had in fact met a knower of Brahman. He sought refuge in that monk, got spiritual instructions from him, and by his grace became blessed with devotion.

"Food was available in Rasmani's temple garden, and by the grace of Mother Ganges there was no scarcity of water. Furthermore, there was a secluded jungle nearby for answering the call of nature. So monks would set up their tents here. Word travelled from mouth to mouth. One monk would tell another about this place, and the latter would tell a subsequent monk who was coming in this direction. Thus, news that there was a nice resting place at Rasmani's temple garden was well circulated among the monks who went on pilgrimage to Gangasagar and Puri."

4. Monks came to the temple garden of Dakshineswar because of the availability of food and the secluded jungle.

The Master continued: "At particular times, certain types of monks would gather here in large numbers. Once the great paramahamsa sannyasins began to come. They were not like vagabond mendicants looking for food. This room (*pointing to his own*) was always crowded with sannyasins. Day and

5. Monks of different orders came at different times.

night they would talk about Vedanta — Brahman, the nature of maya, and *asti-bhati-priyam*."[2]

Referring to Existence-Knowledge-Bliss, the Master would explain to us:

6. The paramahamsas' Vedantic discussion: Existence-Knowledge-Bliss.

"Do you know what this is? It's the true nature of Brahman. Vedanta explains it this way: Whatever truly exists, manifests itself. This manifestation is the nature of knowledge. The thing that we know becomes manifest to us, and the thing that we do not know remains unmanifest. Isn't this true? So Vedanta says that whenever we are conscious of an object's existence, that object is simultaneously revealed along with our consciousness of it; in other words, we become conscious of its nature as knowledge. And forthwith we feel it as dear; that is, its blissful nature rouses a feeling of love within us and causes us to love it. Thus, wherever we are conscious of Existence, we are also conscious of Knowledge and Bliss. Therefore, what is Existence is also Knowledge and Bliss; what is Knowledge is also Existence and Bliss; and what is Bliss is also Existence and Knowledge. This world, the objects within it, and all beings, have their source in Brahman, and the true nature of that Brahman is asti-bhati-priyam, or Satchidananda. The Uttara Gita says that after illumination one realizes that the Paramatman dwells in the place, person, or thing to which one's mind is drawn: *Yatra yatra mano yati, tatra tatra param padam* (3:9). It is also said in the Vedas that because sense objects are permeated by Brahman, the human mind runs after them.

"Those sannyasins had heated discussions concerning these topics. I was then suffering terribly from dysentery. As I was having frequent movements, Hriday placed a commode in the corner of my room. Despite my stomach trouble, I would listen to their discussions on Vedanta. Whenever they could not find any answer to a knotty problem, the Divine Mother revealed a simple solution to me. As soon as I told it to them, their dispute would be resolved.

"Once a monk came who had a beautiful glow on his face. He often

7. The story of a monk's experience of the blissful Self.

remained seated in one place, just smiling. In the morning and evening he would come out of his room and look around. Seeing the trees, the bushes, the sky, and the Ganges, he would raise his arms and dance with joy. Sometimes he would roll on the ground laughing and exclaiming: *Bah, bah, keya maya — kaisa prapancha banaya!* [Bravo! What fun! How wonderful it is, this maya! What an illusion God has conjured up!] That was his way of worship. He had attained the bliss of God.

---

2. In Vedanta, the Absolute (Brahman) is described as *asti* (It is), *bhati* (It shines), and *priyam* (It is blissful), or Existence-Knowledge-Bliss. — *Translator*

"Another time a monk came who was drunk with divine knowledge. He

8. The Master sees a
monk drunk with divine
knowledge.

looked like a ghoul: He was naked, with dust covering his body and head, and with long hair and nails. On the upper part of his body he wore a tattered chadar; it looked as if he'd gotten it off some corpse on a cremation ground. He stood in front of the Kali temple, fixed his eyes on the image, and recited a hymn with such power that it seemed to me the whole temple shook, and Mother looked pleased and smiled. Then he went to the place where beggars were waiting for prasad. But they wouldn't let him sit near them because of his disgusting appearance, and they drove him away. Then I saw him sitting with the dogs in a dirty corner where they'd thrown away the leaf-plates. He had put one arm around a dog, and the two of them were sharing the remains of food on one of the leaves. The dog didn't bark or try to get away even though the man was a stranger. As I watched him, I felt afraid that I might end up like him and have to live like that, roaming around as he did.

"After I'd seen him, I said to Hriday: 'That is not ordinary madness; he is

9. When Brahman is
realized, Ganges water
and gutter water appear
the same. People regard
a paramahamsa as a
child, a ghoul, or a
madman.

mad with the highest God-consciousness.' When Hriday heard this, he ran out to get a look at the holy man. He found him already leaving the temple garden. Hriday followed him a long way and kept begging, 'Maharaj, please teach me how I can realize God.' He did not respond at first. But at last, when Hriday kept following him and wouldn't leave him alone, he pointed to the gutter by the roadside and said: 'When that water and the water of the Ganges seem to be the same and equally pure to you, then you'll realize God.' He said this much and nothing more. Hriday wanted to hear something more, and said, 'Maharaj, please make me your disciple and take me with you.' But he went on without replying. When he'd gone a great distance, he looked back and saw that Hriday was still following him. He made an angry face and picked up a brick, threatening to throw it at Hriday. When Hriday fled, he dropped the brick, left the road, and disappeared. After that, he was nowhere to be found. Such great monks go around like that so people won't bother them. This monk was a true paramahamsa.

"The scripture says that paramahamsas live in this world like boys, ghouls, or madmen. They allow little boys to play around them because they want to learn to be like them. Children are not attached to the things of the world, so paramahamsas try to imbibe that quality from them. Haven't you seen how happy a boy feels when his mother dresses him in a new piece of clothing? If you say, 'Please give it to me,' he'll answer, 'I won't — Mother gave it to me.' And he'll tighten his grip on the cloth with all his might, looking at you in fear lest you snatch it away from him. You'd think it was the treasure of his heart. But if in the next minute he sees a toy in your hand

— worth perhaps no more than half a penny — he'll most likely say, 'Give me that, and I'll give you my cloth.' And maybe a little later, he'll drop the toy and run to pick a flower. He's as little attached to the toy as he was to the cloth. And that's the way it is with the knowers of Brahman.

"Many days passed. Gradually, the visits of the paramahamsa monks

| 10. Ramait monks arrive at Dakshineswar. |

became fewer. The Ramait babajis then began to come in groups. They were wonderful monks — devout and full of renunciation. Ah, what devotion and faith they had! How steadfastly did they serve the Lord! It was from one of them that Ramlala[3] came to me. That is a long story.

"That babaji [Jatadhari] served the image of Ramlala for many years. He

| 11. The Master relates the story of Ramlala. |

carried his deity wherever he went. Whatever he got by begging he would cook and offer to him. Not only that, he actually saw Ramlala eating, or demanding something to eat, or wanting to go for a walk, or childishly asking for something, and so on. Jatadhari was absorbed in serving Ramlala and overwhelmed with joy. I also saw Ramlala acting like that. I stayed with Jatadhari for almost the whole day and watched Ramlala.

"As the days passed, I felt that Ramlala loved me more and more. As long as I remained with Jatadhari, Ramlala was happy and playful. But whenever I left and went to my own room, he followed me there at once. He wouldn't remain with Jatadhari, even though I ordered him not to come with me. I thought at first that this must be an illusion. For how could the deity whom Jatadhari had worshipped for so long with such devotion love me more than him? But it was not my imagination. I actually saw Ramlala as I see you — now dancing ahead of me, now following me. Sometimes he insisted on being taken on my lap. But then when I picked him up, he wouldn't want to stay there. He would run around in the sun, plucking flowers among the thorns, or splashing and swimming in the Ganges. I told him over and over again: 'Don't do that, my child. You'll get blisters on the soles of your feet if you run in the sun. You'll catch cold and fever if you stay in the water so long.' But he never listened to my words, however much I warned him. He'd go right on with his pranks. Sometimes he'd look at me sweetly with his beautiful eyes, or he'd pout and make faces at me. Then I'd get really angry and scold him. 'Just you wait, you rascal,' I'd tell him, 'I'll give you a big thrashing today. I'll pound your bones into powder.' I'd pull him out of the water or the sun and try to tempt him with some gift to stay and play inside the room. If he went on being naughty, I'd give him a couple of slaps. But

---

3. Ramlala is the form of Ramachandra as a boy. In the northwestern part of India, people affectionately call little boys *lal* or *lala*, and girls *lali*. That is why Jatadhari addressed the image of the boy Ramachandra, which was made of eight metals, as Ramlala. In the Bengali language the words *dulal* and *dulali* are used in the same sense.

Image of Ramlala, the child form of Ramachandra, who played with Ramakrishna.

Chandni ghat at Dakshineswar, where Ramakrishna bathed.

when I did that he'd pout and look at me with tears in his eyes, and I'd feel such pain that I'd take him on my lap and comfort him. All these things actually happened.

"One day, when I was going to bathe in the Ganges, he insisted on coming with me. What could I do? I had to let him. But then he wouldn't come out of the water. I begged him to, but he wouldn't listen. At last I got angry and I dunked him, saying, 'All right — stay in as long as you like!' While I was doing this, I actually saw him gasping and struggling for breath! 'What am I doing?' I thought to myself in dismay. I pulled him out of the water and took him in my arms.

"I can't describe how greatly another incident pained me and how bitterly I wept because of it. On that day Ramlala kept asking me for something to eat, and all I had to give him was some coarse parched rice that wasn't properly husked. As he was eating it, the husks scratched his delicate, tender tongue. I felt so sorry! I took him on my lap and exclaimed: 'Your mother Kausalya used to feed you cream and butter with the greatest care, and I've been so thoughtless, giving you this coarse food!'" While recounting this incident to us much later, the Master became overwhelmed with the same feeling and began to cry so intensely that tears came from our eyes, although we did not have the slightest understanding of his loving relationship with Ramlala.

We were dumbfounded when we heard these stories about Ramlala. We

| 12. What we thought when the Master told us about Ramlala. |

would look timidly at the image of Ramlala, hoping to see his living presence — but we did not, because we were ignorant bound souls. How could we see him as living? We did not have the Master's devotion to Ramlala. Our love for Ramachandra was not intense enough; we had not developed the spiritual insight that the Master had, so we could not see the living Ramlala. We saw only a small image, and thought: "Could what the Master said really have happened? Is it possible?" We encounter this kind of doubt in every aspect of our lives, and we are satisfied with our basketful of disbelief. Look, the omniscient rishis say, *Sarvam khalvidam Brahma, neha nanasti kanchana* [All this is Brahman. There is no diversity in It].[4] So everything and everyone we see around us does not actually exist. "That could be," we think.

But when we look at the world, we do not see even a little trace of Brahman, the One without a second. We see only wood, earth, houses, doors, people, cows, and objects of various colours. Or at most we see the vast blue sky spangled with stars and the white snow-capped peaks of the yellow-green mountain arrogantly attempting to touch it. Or we see the murmuring streams flowing downwards and teaching humility to the mountains, reprimanding them by saying, "It is not good to be so arrogant!" Or we see the

4. Chandogya Upanishad 3:14:1 and Brihadaranyaka Upanishad 4:4:19.

vast tempest-tossed ocean rushing to swallow everything with its mighty waves but unable to cross the shore despite a thousand efforts. And finally we conclude that those rishis must have made such statements under the influence of intoxicants. The rishis may tell us: "Look, we are not drug addicts. You will understand what we say if you can make your minds one-pointed and calm by practising self-control and purity in body, mind, and speech. You will see that this world is a manifestation of your intensely held ideas. There is diversity inside you, so you see diversity outside."

We may respond to the rishis: "Revered sirs, we do not have enough time to think about all those things; we are busy earning our livelihoods and we are tormented by our senses." Or we may say: "Sirs, if you gave us a list of things to be done to realize Brahman, it would not be possible to accomplish them within a few days, months, or years. It is even doubtful that we could achieve them in one lifetime. If we listen to your advice and engage ourselves but do not have the vision of Brahman, we shall believe that the attainment of infinite bliss is an illusion. We shall fall between two stools: Neither shall we be able to enjoy the sweet pleasures of the world — momentary though they may be — nor your infinite bliss. What will happen then? No, revered sirs! It is all right that you have tasted infinite bliss; you enjoy it happily along with your succession of disciples. Let us have the pleasures that we can easily obtain from sense objects. Please don't spoil our enjoyment with arguments and reasoning, tricks and plots."

The scientist tells us: "I can use my instruments to show you that an

13. We are attracted to modern material science because it provides more pleasure.

all-pervading energy exists uniformly in brick and wood, gold and silver, trees and plants, people and cattle, and is manifesting itself variously." We also witness the vibration of energy in everything and in every being. To this we say: "Bravo! Your intellectual range is wide, indeed! But what can be achieved with that knowledge? Long ago the rishis, who authored the scriptures, told us that.[5] It is wonderful that you have demonstrated it. Can you tell us that it will add to our pleasure? Only then will we appreciate it." The scientist says: "What do you mean? It will definitely enhance sense pleasures. Just see how the invention of electricity has made it convenient for you to get news of different countries, and how steam power presents suitable opportunities to earn money, the source of all your enjoyment, through trade and commerce carried on by railways, ships, mills, and workshops. What a great advantage you have to destroy your enemies — who hinder your enjoyment of pleasures — by using your knowledge of explosives to invent guns and cannons. Because science has made you aware

5. *Antahsanjna bhavantyete sukhaduhkha-samanvitah* [Consciousness exists even in insentient things like trees and stones and they experience happiness and misery also].
— *Manu Samhita* 1:49

of this all-pervading energy, you will surely enjoy some advantages from it in the future." We reply: "Well, that may be so. But can you use your newly discovered power to quickly create a device that will give us more enjoyment? Only then will we appreciate your intelligence and believe that you are not talking under the influence of intoxicants like those rishis, the teachers of the Vedas and Puranas." To this, the scientist realizes our trend of thought and says, "So be it."

But the rishis, teachers of the path of knowledge, could not encourage

14. The result of the Kapalikas' preaching *sakama-dharma* at the end of the Buddhist period; the impossibility of yoga and bhoga coexisting.

worldly enjoyment by saying, "So be it," so a tremendous commotion ensued in the religious world. The rishis were forced to live in the forest with a few all-renouncing followers, far from the bustle of the world. Of course, in the field of religion the compromising "so be it" attitude does have precedents in Indian religion. Remember that in the latter part of the Buddhist age, the Tantric Kapalikas taught how to use magical rites to subdue, distract, torture, or kill others. At that time relieving and curing physical and mental illnesses by performing various propitiatory rites and exorcising evil spirits became very popular. Remember the belief held in that period: You were not considered a religious teacher if you could not produce a miracle through occult powers gained from your austerities, or if you did not pretend that you were able to control destiny so your disciples would enjoy undisturbed pleasure in this world. At that time the religious world focussed on preaching hidden spiritual truths that would assist people in fulfilling their worldly desires. But how can light and darkness coexist? It was not long before the Kapalikas forgot yoga and descended into the realm of enjoyment. In the name of religion, they secretly began advocating a variety of elaborate sensual practices. Then the truly religious people of the country came to realize that yoga and bhoga [enjoyment] contradict each other and can by no means coexist. They therefore favoured the path of knowledge that had been established by the rishis and began to practise it in their own lives.

How is it possible for us to advocate enjoyment, saying "so be it," like

15. The Master's phenomenal renunciation and its propagation alarmed worldly people.

worldly people? We have started to tell the story of a Master so otherworldly that the spirit of renunciation was embedded deeply in his mind. If he touched metal even in deep sleep, his hand would contract and become numb, his breathing would falter, and he would suffer excruciating pain. He considered any woman he saw to be the veritable manifestation of the Divine Mother, and no one could eradicate that attitude by any means. When the devoted Mathur offered him ownership of an estate worth thousands of rupees, it caused him such terrible pain that he angrily chased Mathur, trying to beat him. Later on, he would sometimes relate this story excitedly: "When I heard that Mathur and Laxminarayan

Marwari had plotted to give me money and an estate, I felt so much pain — it was as if someone were sawing through my head." His mind continuously experienced the transcendental bliss that arises from samadhi, and it was never tarnished by the sensual attractions of the world.

O worldly human beings, we knew beforehand that when we discussed this unusual Master we would have to endure criticism and reproach. And we know that you will not hesitate to slander his divine character if a simple-hearted soul among your friends and family becomes attracted to this unique person because of our words and tries to renounce home and worldly enjoyment. But what can we do? We have undertaken this project, and we cannot discontinue it or try to hide the truth even partially. We must narrate what we know to be the truth, or we will have no peace. It is as if someone were forcing us to speak out. O reader, let us narrate, as far as we know, the story of this extraordinary godman; you may accept as much as you can digest. If you prefer, "omit the head and the tail." Or if you wish, you may throw this book away — thinking that a hemp smoker has written some cock-and-bull stories — and run after sweet pleasures, constantly seeking new objects of enjoyment. But if you later fall into the terrible whirlpool of this world and become disgusted with the sweet pleasures that lust brings — such a situation may arise because of your bad luck (or good fortune) — then read the life story of this wonderful man. You will definitely find peace and come to appreciate our Master.

When the Master described the marvellous behaviour of Ramlala, he said: "On some days Jatadhari would cook food to offer Ramlala, but couldn't find him. Then he would come running in distress to my room, and there would be Ramlala playing on the floor. Jatadhari's feelings were terribly hurt. He'd scold Ramlala, saying: 'I took so much trouble to cook food for you. I looked all over the place — and here you were, all the time! You don't care about me. You have forgotten everything. And that's how you always are. You do just as you please. You have no kindness or affection. You left your parents and went into the forest. Your poor father died of a broken heart, and you never even came back to show yourself to him on his deathbed!' Talking like this, Jatadhari would drag Ramlala back to his own room and feed him. Thus, the days rolled on. Jatadhari stayed on at Dakshineswar for a long time, because Ramlala didn't want to go away and leave me. And Jatadhari couldn't bear to leave Ramlala behind, having loved him for so long.

16. How Ramlala stayed with the Master permanently.

"Then one day Jatadhari came to me, crying with joy, and said: 'Ramlala has revealed himself to me in a way that I have never known before but have always longed for. Now the desire of my life is fulfilled. Ramlala says he won't go away from here; he doesn't want to leave you. But I'm not sad about it anymore. He lives happily with you and plays joyfully, and I am full of bliss when I see him this way. I have learned now to be happy simply in his happiness, so I can now leave him with you and go away. I will enjoy knowing that he is happy with you.' Then Jatadhari gave me the image of Ramlala and said good-bye. And Ramlala has been here ever since."

Truly it was due to the divine companionship of the Master that Jatadhari

| 17. Jatadhari experienced unselfish love in the Master's holy company. | got a taste of unselfish and pure love, and subsequently realized that there could be no fear of separation from the beloved. He became convinced |

that his Chosen Deity, the embodiment of pure love, was always with him and that he could see him whenever he wanted. Undoubtedly, Jatadhari received that assurance so he could leave his beloved Ramlala behind.

The Master told us: "On a different occasion another Ramait monk came.

| 18. A monk's faith in Rama's name. | This man had overwhelming faith in God's name. He carried nothing with him but a water pot and a book. The book was his treasure. Every day he would |

worship it with flowers and from time to time would open it carefully. After I got to know him, I begged him to let me have a look at it. But when I opened the book I found that on every page the same two words were written in bold red letters: *Om Rama*. He said to me: 'What's the use of reading many books? God is the origin of the Vedas, the Puranas, and other scriptures, and there is no difference between Him and His Name. Therefore, whatever is written in the four Vedas, eighteen Puranas, and other scriptures is contained in His Name alone. So I am satisfied with that.' That monk had such faith in God's name!"

The Master told us many stories about various Ramait monks. Sometimes

| 19. Devotional songs and couplets of the Ramait monks. | he would sing bhajans to us that he had learned from those holy men. Here are some of the songs: |

> O mind, you have not recognized my Rama.
> What then have you recognized?
> What then have you known?
> He is a sadhu who tastes the bliss of Rama's name.
> But what is he who tastes pleasures of the senses?
> He who delivers his dynasty from maya is a true son.
> What good are other sons?

Another song:

> Sing the glory of Ramachandra, Lord of Sita,
> Chief of the Raghus and Prince of Ayodhya.
> There is no one else like him.
> Sweet are his smile and words; sweet, his playful step.
> Beautiful are his face and large eyes; beautiful, his nose,
> His arched eyebrows, the mark on his forehead.
> His forehead, adorned with saffron, shines like the morning sun;

And with his dazzling earrings, he seems to be the God of Love.
The pearls in his necklace glitter like stars on his broad chest;
They shine like the Ganges flowing down from the mountains.
The hero of the Raghu dynasty is walking
With his friends on the banks of the Saraju River.
Tulasidas looks at him with great joy
And craves the dust of his feet.

The Master used to sing these two songs, but unfortunately we have forgotten the rest of the lines:

"In this world one who worships Rama truly lives; One truly lives who adores him."

"No one but Rama can save me."

Sometimes the Master recited Hindi couplets that he had learned from the Ramait monks. He said, "The monks always counselled that one should protect oneself from these three sins: theft, adultery, and falsehood." Again, he said: "Listen to what Tulasidas has said in these couplets:

'Tulasidas stands as surety that God is realized by truthfulness, obedience, and absence of covetousness.

'Call Tulasidas a liar if God is not attained by practising truthfulness and obedience, and maintaining a filial attitude towards women.'"

The Master continued: "Do you know what obedience is? It is humility. When one develops true humility, the ego is destroyed and one realizes God. A similar idea can be found in one of Kabir's songs: 'The Lord Rama is easily attained through service, worship, and humility. Brother, cling joyfully to God.'"

On another occasion the Master said: "Once a desire arose in my mind to supply aspirants of all sects with whatever they needed for their sadhanas. If all their needs were met, they could then practise sadhana without anxiety, and I would watch them joyfully. When I told this to Mathur, he said: 'That's no problem, Father. I'll arrange everything right now. You distribute everything as you wish.' Arrangements had already been made to give rice, lentils, flour, and so on to mendicants regularly from the temple store. Now Mathur made additional provisions for water pots, blankets, seats for meditation, and even marijuana and hemp for those who used them and wine for Tantric aspirants.

20. The Master wishes to supply the necessities for sadhana to all kinds of aspirants: the story of Rajkumar (Achalananda).

"At that time many Tantric aspirants who came would arrange a Chakra, a holy circle in which they would perform rituals as a group. I supplied them with peeled ginger, onion, puffed rice, and fried gram — ingredients used in their rituals — and observed how they used these articles in their worship and prayers to the Divine Mother. On many occasions they made me join their holy circle, and sometimes invited me to lead the group. They would always ask me to drink the consecrated wine, but when they found that I was incapable of taking it because I got intoxicated while merely chanting the Mother's name, they did not ask me anymore. However, because it was the custom to drink wine in the holy circle, I'd put a drop on my finger and mark my forehead with it, or smell it, or at the most sprinkle a drop on my tongue, then pour the wine in their glasses. I noticed that after drinking wine, some of them would concentrate on the Divine Mother and call on Her passionately. Some of them, however, would drink greedily and become drunk instead of calling on the Divine Mother. One day I saw them become excessively drunk, so I stopped supplying wine to them. I consistently noticed that Rajkumar[6] would become absorbed in japa immediately after drinking the consecrated wine. Sometime later on, however, he had a desire to attain name and fame. But this was natural: He had a wife and children at home, so he needed to pay attention to making money to satisfy their financial needs. Nevertheless, Rajkumar would use wine only as an aid to sadhana. I never saw him drinking greedily and losing control."

So many thoughts arise in our minds in connection with the Master's

21. The Master became inebriated with divine ecstasy merely by uttering the words *siddhi* or *karan*; he even went into samadhi when saying obscene words or singing scurrilous songs.

inability to drink wine. On many occasions in the course of conversation, we saw him become overwhelmingly intoxicated, and even go into samadhi, when uttering the words *siddhi* [marijuana], or *karan* [wine]. Again we saw our wonderful Master go into samadhi while merely uttering the word *yoni* [a woman's sex organ]. In spite of our pretensions to high culture, that word stimulates horrible lust in our roguish minds. And those among us who consider themselves to be righteous run away as soon as they hear that obscene word, seeking to protect themselves from the bad thoughts in their own minds. But as for the Master, we saw that when he came down a little from samadhi and regained a semiconscious state, he began to speak in reference to this topic: "Mother, You are the embodiment of fifty letters.[7] Those letters of Yours that constitute the Vedas and Vedanta also compose filthy words and obscene songs. The *ka* and *kha*[8] of Your Vedas and Vedanta are no different from those of the obscene songs. Mother, You are verily the Vedas and Vedanta as well as obscene words and songs." With that the Master would again enter into samadhi.

Alas, how can we describe or explain this phenomenon? Who can understand how all the things of the world — good and bad — were visible to this extraordinary godman, by means of an indescribable light that is beyond our minds and intellects? Who else can have the divine eyes needed to see the

6. Rajkumar lived mostly in Kalighat [South Calcutta] and became known as Achalananda Nath. He left behind some disciples, who had their own disciples. When he died his disciples buried him with great pomp in a village near Kalighat.
7. The Sanskrit alphabet consists of fifty letters. — *Translator*
8. Ka and kha are the first two consonants in the Sanskrit alphabet. — *Translator*

world as he did? O reader, pay attention and take the Master's words seriously. Consider how deep and unfathomable was the mental purity of this wonderful Master!

After attaining the vision of the Divine Mother, the mystic Ramprasad sang:

> I drink no ordinary wine, but the Wine of Everlasting Bliss,
> As I repeat my Mother Kali's name;
> It so intoxicates my mind that people take me to be drunk!

Before we met the Master, we could not have imagined that a person could be in a drunken state by virtue of divine bliss alone, without using any intoxicants. We vividly remember a time when we considered an author superstitious and foolish because he wrote that Chaitanya would lose outer consciousness while uttering the name of Lord Hari. At that time a current of scepticism flowed in the minds of the young generation in Calcutta, who tended to doubt everything. When we happened to meet this unique Master sometime afterwards, we carefully observed him day and night. We saw for ourselves how he would frequently lose outer consciousness while dancing and singing kirtan. If a coin touched his body, he would lose consciousness. As soon as he uttered the words *siddhi* or *karan*, he would become completely intoxicated with divine bliss. In addition to uttering the name of God and His avatars, he would become overwhelmed with pure transcendental bliss, even when saying the word *yoni*, which reminds ordinary men of sensual pleasure. This word, however, would bring to his mind the blissful Divine Mother, who is the *Brahmayoni*, the source of the universe. Reader, is it necessary to explain further why our eyes were permanently dazzled by seeing the extraordinary qualities of this godman and why we placed him in our hearts as an incarnation of God?

The Master would often visit the house of his great devotee, Ram

22. First example: at Ram Datta's house.

Chandra Datta, at Simla, Calcutta. Other devotees would also join that joyful gathering. One day he talked about God with the devotees there and then got ready to return to Dakshineswar. Ram's home was on Madhu Roy's lane, which was so narrow that carriages could not reach the house. One had to leave a carriage on one of the main streets, on either the east or the west side, and walk up to the house. On that day a carriage was waiting for the Master on the main street to the west. The Master walked in that direction, followed by the devotees. He was so overwhelmed with divine ecstasy that he was staggering; he could not walk that short distance without help. Two devotees held onto his arms and helped him to slowly move forward. A few people were standing at the end of the lane. Not understanding the Master's condition, they said amongst themselves: "Oh, look! That man is dead drunk." We heard their remark although they spoke in low tones. We couldn't help but laugh and say to ourselves, "Dead drunk indeed!"

At Dakshineswar, one day the Master asked the Holy Mother to prepare a

few betel rolls and clean his bed and room while he went to bow down to the Divine Mother in the Kali temple. She hurried through her work and had almost finished when the Master returned from the temple. When he entered the room he seemed completely intoxicated: His eyes were red, his steps were terribly unsteady, and his speech was indistinct and incoherent. He staggered to where the Holy Mother was attentively tending to her duties, unaware that the Master had arrived in that drunken condition. Suddenly touching her, the Master asked, "Hello, have I drunk wine?" Immediately the Holy Mother looked around and was amazed to see the Master in that ecstatic state.

She said, "No, no, why should you drink wine?"

"Why then am I staggering?" asked the Master. "Why can't I speak? Am I drunk?"

The Holy Mother replied: "No, no, you haven't drunk wine. You've drunk the divine nectar of Mother Kali!"

The Master joyfully responded, "You're right!"

Since the devotees had begun to visit the Master and received his grace,

almost once or twice a week the Master visited one or two of the Calcutta devotees in their homes. If a devotee could not visit him on a regular basis, or if he could get no news about that person through someone else, the gracious Master would rush to see him. And even if someone visited him regularly, he would still become restless to see that particular devotee within a few days and would immediately go to see him. Invariably, however, his auspicious visit was to benefit that devotee; it was not in the slightest motivated by self-interest.

Beni Saha of Baranagore had some good hackney carriages. Because the Master frequently visited Calcutta, it was arranged with Beni that he would send a carriage to Dakshineswar as soon as he heard from the Master. He would raise no objection if the carriage returned from Calcutta late at night; he was paid for this extra time at his regular rate. At first, payment of carriage fare was covered by Mathur, then by Mani Sen of Panihati, Shambhu Mallick, and Jaygopal Sen of Sinduriapati, Calcutta. But when the Master visited the house of a particular devotee, that person would pay the fare if it was within his means.

One day the Master decided to visit Jadu Mallick's house in Calcutta to see his mother, who was very devoted to the Master. The Master had not heard any news about the family for a long time. A carriage arrived after the Master had finished his lunch. Meanwhile, our friend A. had come to Dakshineswar by boat to see the Master. The Master inquired about A.'s welfare, then said: "It is nice that you've come. I'm going to Jadu's house today. On the way I shall stop at your house and see G., whose work has kept him from coming here for many days. Let us go together." A. agreed. He was then newly acquainted with the Master and had seen him at only a few places. He did not yet know that the wonderful Master could experience bhava samadhi at any time, at any place, even at the sight of trivial, contemptible, or untouchable things or persons.

The Master got into the carriage. The young devotee Latu, now known as Swami Adbhutananda, took the Master's towel, spice bag, and other necessities and followed him into the carriage. A. also climbed in. The Master sat on one side and Latu and A. occupied the other. The carriage started and after crossing through the market at Baranagore it passed by Mati Lake. Nothing eventful happened. As the childlike Master saw the various sights along the way, he asked questions of Latu and A., or made jokes on different topics as he normally did.

There was a small market to the south of Mati Lake. To the south of that market was a tavern, a dispensary, a few rice warehouses with tiled roofs, and a stable. At this point, the same road went straight towards Calcutta, but another wide road extended right up to the Ganges, and one could take it to the well-known Sarvamangala and Chitreswari temples.

In the tavern some drunkards were drinking and laughing noisily. Some of them were singing out of joy and some were dancing and gesticulating. The owner of the tavern, having engaged his bartender in serving his customers, was standing absent-mindedly at the door of the shop. There was a large vermilion mark on his forehead. The Master's carriage passed in front of the tavern just then. Perhaps the owner knew the Master; when he saw him in the carriage, he saluted him with both hands.

The noise in the tavern attracted the Master's attention and he perceived the merry mood of the drinkers. The bliss of God arose in the Master's mind as he observed their intoxicated delight. But in addition to this bliss, he also experienced the state of drunkenness: He became deeply intoxicated and his speech became slurred. Suddenly he stood up, leaned out of the carriage, and stood with one foot on the footboard. Like a drunkard, he expressed his joy at seeing their pleasure, and waving his hand, addressed them loudly: "Wonderful! Have fun! Bravo! Bravo!"

A. said: "We had no warning that the Master would suddenly be in that ecstatic state. He'd been talking like a normal person. But his mood changed so abruptly when he saw those drunkards! I was scared to death. I was about to grab him and pull him back inside the carriage, but immediately Latu intervened, saying: 'You don't have to do anything. He'll control himself and won't fall.' So I kept quiet, but my heart was palpitating. I thought that I had made a mistake by travelling in the same carriage with this mad Master. I told myself I would never do so again. Of course, describing these events takes more time than the events themselves. The carriage continued past the tavern, and the Master returned to his seat. When the Master saw the Sarvamangala temple, he said: 'That goddess Sarvamangala is a living deity. Bow down to Her.' Saying so, he himself bowed down and we followed his example. When I looked at the Master then, I found him to be as usual, smiling gently. But my heart did not stop palpitating for a long time, as I kept remembering what a bloody accident could have happened if he had fallen from the carriage.

"When the carriage reached our house, the Master said to me, 'Go and find out whether G. is at home.' I went, came back, and reported, 'No, G. is not at home.' He then said: 'Well, I missed G. I thought I'd ask him to pay today's extra carriage fare. However, I'm now acquainted with you. Could you pay one rupee today? You see, Jadu Mallick is a miserly man. He will not pay more than the fixed fare of two rupees and four annas. But after I've visited several devotees, who knows how late I shall return to Dakshineswar tonight? If it becomes too late, the driver pesters me to return. So it has been arranged with Beni that however late it may be, the driver will not disturb me if he is paid three rupees and four annas. I am asking you because Jadu will pay two rupees and four annas, and if you pay one rupee then there will be no problem for today's fare.' I gave one rupee to Latu and bowed down to the Master, who then left to see Jadu Mallick."

Such an apparently intoxicated state could come over the Master on any day at any time. It is not possible to record all such events for the reader.

The Master told stories about the travelling monks who visited

25. Monks of all orders who came to Dakshineswar received spiritual help from the Master.

Rasmani's Kali temple, not only to us, but to many others also. There are still many alive to testify to this. At that time we were studying in St. Xavier's College, which was closed on Thursdays and Sundays. This allowed us to visit the Master on Thursdays, while many devotees visited the Master on Saturdays and Sundays. Thus, we had the opportunity to hear various stories of his life. With the exception of the Bhairavi Brahmani, Tota Puri, Sufi Govinda, the monk who came providentially to the Kali temple to protect the Master's body by forcibly feeding him during the six months of his nirvikalpa state, and one or two others like that, it is evident that each of the monks and aspirants of various denominations who arrived before we did came to enrich their respective spiritual lives with the help of the Master's wonderful life. After thus attaining fulfillment in their lives, they then had the opportunity to demonstrate to the spiritual aspirants of their respective sects how to realize God through their own paths. They came to learn — and when they had done so, they returned to their own places. Although the Bhairavi Brahmani, Tota Puri, and some others had the great fortune to help the Master in his spiritual life, they were also blessed by the power of the Master's divine life, and experienced precious spiritual truths that they had not been able to achieve despite their long sadhanas.

The chronology of those monks' and aspirants' arrival at Dakshineswar illustrates another truth. For the convenience of studying this chronology, in this chapter we have told the reader as far as possible the words of the Master as we heard them. We understood from what the Master told us that whenever he practised and realized the goal of a particular mode of worship and sadhana, true aspirants of that religious sect would come to him in groups for some time, and he would discuss that particular sadhana with them day and night. As soon as he attained perfection in repeating the name of Rama, Ramait monks began to come to him in groups. When he attained perfection in each of the attitudes of the Vainshnava Tantra of Bengal — such as shanta and dasya — aspirants of that particular attitude would appear. When he completed the practice of the sixty-four sadhanas of Tantra, with the help of the Bhairavi Brahmani, or when he attained perfection in Shakti sadhana, the prominent Tantric aspirants of Bengal started to arrive. When he practised Advaita sadhana with the help of Tota Puri, and subsequently experienced Brahman, the monks of the Paramahamsa Order came in groups.

> 26. When the Master attained perfection in a particular religious path, monks of that path came to him.

There is clearly a hidden significance in the fact that aspirants of different sects enjoyed the Master's divine company at different times. This has always happened with the auspicious advent of avatars in the past and so will happen in the future. According to a hidden law of the spiritual world, avatars are born to avert the degradation of religion as a whole or to revive a dying religion. But when we study their lives, we find differences in the manifestation of powers within them. This clearly indicates that some of them came to meet the needs of a particular country or a few religious communities, whereas others came to revive spirituality throughout the whole world. But while they promulgated their own revelations and beliefs, at the same time they fully supported the spiritual truths that were discovered and preached by the sages, seers, and avatars who preceded them. Avatars do not seek to destroy what has come before because their divine yogic power reveals a sequence to the previous spiritual truths and relationships among them. The history of the spiritual realm and the connections between faiths always remain hidden to us because our minds are obscured by worldliness. But avatars see previous religions as strung "like a strand of pearls," and each adds another precious pearl to it from his own spiritual experience, then quietly departs.

> 27. Power is not equally manifest in all avatars because some come to teach religion to a particular nation and some to all of humanity.

We shall understand this subject thoroughly by studying the history of foreign religions. For example, Jesus promulgated the truths that he experienced without disturbing those truths preached by the Jewish prophets. A few centuries later, Muhammad preached his own religion without destroying the religious views of Jesus — and moreover, one can realize God as Muhammad did by following the path that he preached. From this it does not follow that the religious ideals preached by the Jewish prophets and by Jesus are incomplete, or that one cannot realize God as they did by following their respective paths. Surely one can. This is the law everywhere in the spiritual world, and it applies to the religious paths of India as well. One can realize any particular aspect of God preached by the sages of the Vedas, Puranas, or the great teachers of Tantra if one sincerely follows the methods prescribed by them. The Master experienced this wonderful truth by practising the sadhanas of various religious sects one after another, and taught us that truth.

28. The manifestation of the Master's spiritual power compared to the avatars who established Hinduism, Judaism, Christianity, and Islam.

"When flowers bloom, bees come of their own accord" — this is also a spiritual law, as the Master told us repeatedly. According to this law, when the great avatars attain perfection and experience the truths of the spiritual world, seekers of spirituality become attracted to them in order to know and learn the truth. This is evident everywhere. Aspirants of all religious denominations came to the Master, not only those belonging to a single sect, because he had practised the disciplines of all those paths and had realized God accordingly, and he could give specific instructions about each path. But not all of those aspirants attained perfection in their respective paths and recognized the Master as an avatar of the age; only those who were foremost amongst them understood the Master's divinity. However, each of them truly made progress in their respective path by virtue of the Master's divine company. And they were fully convinced that eventually they would realize God by following their respective paths. When people lose faith in their own religious paths, religion declines and aspirants become unable to experience the truth in their own lives.

29. Why monks and spiritual aspirants of all sects came to the Master.

Nowadays [in the 1910s], some people say that the Master learned the means for attaining God-realization from visiting monks, practised severe austerities, and as a result became completely mad for a period of time. According to these people, his brain was deranged and he developed a permanent disease that caused him to lose consciousness when under the influence of any excessive emotion. O God, we are such a herd of learned fools! The rishis of India demonstrated in their own lives, and explained through the Vedas, Puranas, Tantras, and other scriptures that normal consciousness disappears as soon

30. It is not true that the monks who came to Dakshineswar awakened the Master's spiritual tendencies.

as a person ascends to samadhi by means of full concentration of the mind. These sages bequeathed to us a complete explanation of the mystery of samadhi that is unique to India. These great souls — who were considered avatars and received the heartfelt respect of people in all countries — experienced samadhi in their own lives and declared that losing consciousness in this manner was inevitable along the spiritual path. They unveiled this mystery to us again and again. If we spread the idea that this loss of consciousness is a disease and listen to others propound it, is there any hope for us? O reader, if you wish, you may respectfully listen to those worthless words. May all good attend you and the people who say those things! But we beg you to allow us to remain at the feet of this wonderful god-intoxicated man — this is our fervent request to you. But before you come to any firm conclusion, please give the matter careful consideration so that you may not fall into the condition that was described by the rishi in the Katha Upanishad (1:2:5): "Fools dwelling in darkness, but thinking themselves wise and erudite, go round and round by various tortuous paths, like the blind led by the blind."

The claim that the Master's bhava samadhi is a kind of disease is not new. Some of his Western-educated followers also said that, even during his lifetime. As time passed, however, the crazy prophesies of this divine madman were fulfilled, his unprecedented messages were eagerly accepted by people all over the world, and the remarks of those critics lost their force. Their efforts became as futile as throwing dust at the moon. People realized that those statements were false and rested in the satisfaction of knowing that the Master's teachings were true. This will continue to happen in the future. As a blazing fire cannot be covered by a cloth, neither can the truth be obscured. It is therefore unnecessary for us to discuss this subject any further. We shall stop after quoting a couple of the Master's statements on this topic.

Reverend Shivanath Shastri, a preacher of the Sadharan Brahmo Samaj,

31. The Master's loss of consciousness during samadhi was not a disease. Proof: a conversation between the Master and Shivanath.

sometimes told us that the Master's bhava samadhi was a medical condition like hysteria or epilepsy, brought about by a nervous disorder. He added that the Master's periodic loss of consciousness was like that suffered by people who are afflicted by those diseases. The Master eventually came to know of his belief. Shivanath had been visiting the Master off and on for a long time. One day when he was at Dakshineswar, the Master raised the topic and said: "Well, Shivanath, I hear that you call my samadhi a disease and say that I become unconscious at that time. You think day and night of bricks, wood, earth, money, and all sorts of material things and yet consider yourself to be of sound mind, while I — who meditate day and night on God, whose consciousness makes the whole universe conscious — you consider to be ignorant and unconscious. A fine piece of reasoning! What sort of intellect do you have?" Shivanath was speechless.

Ishwar Chandra Vidyasagar
(1820-1891)

Shivanath Shastri (1847-1919),
a leader of the Brahmo
Samaj movement.

While speaking to us, the Master quite often used the phrases "divine

32. Why the Master behaved like a madman during sadhana.

madness" and "drunk with divine knowledge." He said openly that for twelve years a powerful tempest of divine passion had blown over his life. He said: "Ah, all things look alike when dust is stirred up by a storm. When that happens one cannot differentiate between a mango tree and a jackfruit tree — one cannot even see them. A similar event happened to me, keeping me from differentiating between good and bad, praise and blame, pure and impure. I had only one thought, one intent: how could I realize God? This one idea continually dwelt in my mind. People said that I had become mad!"

Some of the scholarly aspirants who came to the Master in those early

33. Some spiritual aspirants who came to Dakshineswar received initiation from the Master. Example: Narayan Shastri.

days yielded to their exuberant devotion and took initiation and even sannyasa from the Master. Pandit Narayan Shastri was among them. The Master told us that Narayan Shastri had lived with his gurus like a devout brahmacharin of ancient times and had studied the scriptures for twenty-five years without pause. He cherished a strong desire to acquire equal knowledge of and mastery over the six types of philosophy.[9] He completed five of them while living with different gurus in Varanasi and other places in northwestern India. But it was impossible to become a famous logician without studying Nyaya philosophy under the great logicians of Navadwip in Bengal. For that reason he came to Bengal eight years before he met the Master in Dakshineswar, completing his study of Nyaya philosophy in seven years while living in Navadwip. It was now time for him to return home. It was doubtful that he would return to this part of the country, so he visited Calcutta and nearby Dakshineswar, where he met the Master.

Narayan Shastri was known in his area as a pandit before he came to

34. Narayan Shastri's background.

Bengal to study Nyaya. The Master told us that once the Maharaja of Jaipur respectfully invited Narayan Shastri to become his court pandit and offered him a high salary. But Narayan Shastri's thirst for knowledge had not yet been satisfied, and he had not fulfilled his intense desire to master the six schools of philosophy. So he was compelled to decline the Maharaja's cordial offer. We believe that Shastri came from some place in or near Rajputana.

Narayan Shastri was not like ordinary pandits. Along with his knowledge

35. Shastri met the Master after finishing his studies.

of the scriptures, he was gradually developing detachment. He understood clearly that one could not gain mastery over Vedanta and other scriptures

9. Sankhya, Yoga, Nyaya, Vaisheshika, Purva Mimamsa, and Uttara Mimamsa or Vedanta. — *Translator*

merely by study without practice. Before he had finished his studies he would sometimes worry that he was not gaining true knowledge; he should practise sadhana for several days to try to experience what the scriptures were telling him. But then he feared that if he involved himself in sadhana, giving up his studies midway, he might lose both; so he suppressed his desire for sadhana and concentrated on his studies. Finally, his long-cherished desire was fulfilled: He had attained the wisdom of the six philosophical schools. He decided to do some sadhana after returning home. At this time he met the Master, and from that moment on he felt drawn to him in a mysterious way.

As we mentioned earlier, the Dakshineswar Kali temple at that time had excellent arrangements for boarding and lodging guests, ascetics, sadhus, sannyasins, and brahmin pandits. Shastri was a brahmin brahmacharin from a distant region, and moreover, a great pandit, so it was not surprising that he was honoured by being allowed to stay at Dakshineswar as long as he wished. It was a charming place with all the necessary facilities for food and other things — in addition to the company of such a godman! So Shastri decided to stay at Dakshineswar for some time. What else could he do? The more he got to know the Master, the more his love and respect for him grew. As the days passed, he developed an intense desire to see the Master and to know him intimately. For the Master's part, he was extremely happy to have the simple-hearted and great-souled Narayan Shastri with him, and he spent much time with him in conversation about God.

Shastri had read about the seven planes of consciousness according to

36. Shastri's resolve after experiencing the holy company of the Master.

Vedanta. The scriptures told him that as one's mind rises from the lower to the higher planes of consciousness, different experiences and visions take place simultaneously, and finally one arrives at nirvikalpa samadhi. In that state one becomes immersed in the experience of Brahman, the indivisible Existence-Knowledge-Bliss Absolute, immediately dissolving the worldly delusion that has accumulated throughout the succession of lives. Now Shastri saw that the Master experienced for himself everything that he had memorized from the scriptures. Shastri also realized that he merely uttered the words *samadhi, aparokshanubhuti* [direct knowledge], and so on, whereas the Master actually attained samadhi many times, day and night, while talking about God. Shastri thought: "Ah, how wonderful! Where shall I find another person like him who can teach me and explain the hidden meaning of the scriptures? I must not miss this opportunity. I must learn from him the means of immediate knowledge of Brahman at any cost. Life is uncertain. Who knows when I shall die? Shall I die without attaining true knowledge? No, it cannot be. At the least I will try my utmost to realize God. Let my return home be postponed."

As the days passed, Shastri's renunciation and longing for God became

| 37. Shastri's renunciation. | more intense under the Master's divine influence. Desires such as "I shall charm people with my erudition; I shall achieve the greatest name, fame, and |

position by becoming Mahamahopadhyay"[10] became trifling and distasteful and completely disappeared from his mind. Like a humble disciple, Shastri stayed with the Master and attentively listened to his nectar-like teachings. He resolved not to put his mind on anything other than God. There was no way to ascertain when his body would die, but he still had time, so he resolved to make a sincere effort to realize God. As he watched the Master, he pondered: "Ah, the Master has known what is to be known in this human life. How calm and carefree he is! He has even defeated death. It can no longer torment him with the frightening form of the Mother Kali as it does ordinary people. Well, the rishis of the Upanishads say that whatever a great soul resolves becomes true. If one truly receives the grace of such a person, one becomes free from worldly desires and attains the knowledge of Brahman. Why then should I not hold fast to him and take refuge in him?" Thus, Shastri's thoughts continued in this vein, and he stayed with the Master at Dakshineswar. But he was hesitant to say anything to the Master, lest he refuse to accept him, considering him to be unfit. Thus, time rolled on.

The following event proves that, day by day, Shastri's mind was being

| 38. Shastri was disgusted when he spoke to Michael Madhusudan Datta. | filled with intense renunciation of the world. At that time Michael Madhusudan Datta, the glorious poet of Bengal, was practising law and had undertaken a lawsuit on behalf of Rani Rasmani's estate. To learn |

the details of the case, he had come to the Dakshineswar Kali temple with one of Rasmani's relatives.[11] After being briefed on the case, he learned that the Master was there and asked to see him. When word was sent to the Master, he first sent Narayan Shastri to talk to Madhusudan and then went a little later himself. While talking to Madhusudan, Shastri asked why he had given up his own religion and embraced Christianity. Madhusudan replied that he was compelled by poverty to do so. We don't know if he gave that answer because he was reluctant to disclose his life story to a stranger, but the Master and others felt that he was speaking from his heart; he was not being ironic to conceal the truth about himself. When Shastri heard that answer he became very annoyed. He said: "What? You have given up your religion for the sake of a livelihood in this transitory world! What disgraceful low-mindedness! Everyone will die one day. You should have died rather than changed your religion." Shastri thought: "People consider him a great man and read his books with eagerness!" He so

10. A title meaning the most learned scholar. — *Translator*
11. Dwaraka Nath Biswas, Mathur's son. — *Translator*

abhorred this thought that he refused to continue the conversation with Madhusudan.

Madhusudan then asked the Master to give him some spiritual advice.

39. The conversation between the Master and Michael.

The Master told us later: "It was as if someone were pressing my mouth closed and not allowing me to speak." Hriday and some others said that after a while that mood left the Master, and he charmed Madhusudan by singing a few devotional songs of Ramprasad, Kamalakanta, and other mystics in his sweet voice. In that context, he also told Madhusudan that devotion to God was the essential thing in this world.

Even after Madhusudan left, Shastri continued to express his disgust at

40. Shastri wrote his opinion on the wall.

the reason Madhusudan had abandoned his religion. Shastri, using a piece of charcoal, then wrote in big letters on the wall of the eastern veranda leading to the Master's room: "It is very disgraceful to give up one's religion for the sake of one's livelihood." When we later saw Shastri's opinion written on the wall in large and distinct Bengali letters, we became curious. One day we inquired about it and learned the whole story. As Shastri lived in Bengal for a long time, he had learned Bengali very well.

Here is the last story concerning Narayan Shastri. One day when Shastri

41. Shastri took sannyasa and left to practise austerities.

found the Master alone, he took the opportunity to express his heart's desire, insisting that the Master initiate him into sannyasa. Seeing his eagerness, the Master agreed and initiated him into sannyasa on an auspicious day. Shastri did not remain in the Kali temple after taking the vows of sannyasa. He told the Master that he had resolved to go to Vashishtha Ashrama [in Assam] and practise strenuous sadhana until he succeeded in realizing Brahman. With tearful eyes, he begged the Master to bless him, bowed down, and left Dakshineswar forever. Thenceforth, there was no definite news about Narayan Shastri. Some said that he became ill and died while practising severe austerities in Vashishtha Ashrama.

Whenever the Master heard that genuine monks, spiritual aspirants, or

42. The Master loved to visit monks and spiritual aspirants.

devotees of various religious communities were living nearby, he wished to visit them. When such a desire arose, he would visit one of them uninvited and spend some time talking about God. He was not at all concerned whether the person would like or dislike his visit, whether an aspirant he did not know would be pleased or displeased, or whether he himself would be properly honoured or not. He would somehow make his way there and try to determine the spiritual attitude of that particular aspirant, evaluate how much progress he had made, and so on. He would not stop until he had reached a firm conclusion. The Master followed the same procedure when he visited scholarly spiritual aspirants who were well versed in the scriptures. The Master visited Pandit Padmalochan, Swami Dayananda Saraswati, and others, and sometimes he would tell us their stories. Now we shall tell the reader about Pandit Padmalochan.

Before the Master's advent, the study of Vedanta was rare in Bengal.

43. Why Nyaya philosophy was prevalent in Bengal. Although many centuries ago Shankara defeated the Tantric theologians of Bengal in debate, he was not able to establish his Vedanta philosophy among the masses. As a result, the Tantrikas accepted the basic truths of Vedanta and incorporated some of them in their prayer and meditation, but they continued to preach their traditional rituals to the public. The Bengali pandits expended all the energy of their fertile brains in studying Nyaya philosophy, creating Navya-Nyaya [a new school of logic], and bringing about an epoch-making revolution in the realm of Nyaya philosophy. Perhaps the study of logic became greatly prevalent among Bengalis because Shankara had defeated and humiliated them in debate — who can say? The world has often witnessed that when one nation is defeated by another in a certain field, the defeated and humiliated people strive to surpass their conquerors in the same endeavour.

Although the study of Vedanta was then rare in Bengal, the playground of

44. Padmalochan, a Vedantic pandit. Tantra and Nyaya, it was not as if no one was attracted to the liberal conclusions of Vedanta. Pandit Padmalochan, for example, was such a one. After attaining mastery of Nyaya, or logic, he had a desire to study Vedanta. He went to Varanasi, lived with a guru, and studied Vedanta philosophy for a long time. After some years he became known as a great scholar of Vedanta. When Padmalochan returned home, he accepted the position of court pandit for the Maharaja of Burdwan. As the Maharaja became acquainted with Padmalochan's wonderful abilities, he gradually promoted him to chief court pandit. Padmalochan's fame spread throughout Bengal.

It will not be out of place to relate a story of Pandit Padmalochan's

45. An example of Padmalochan's genius. extraordinary talent. One-sided and narrow views in spiritual matters develop from a lack of intelligence. In this context the Master would sometimes refer to the pandit. As we mentioned earlier, the Master was extremely truthful. Whenever he heard a catholic view or opinion that he liked, he would store it in his memory. When he later quoted it in the course of conversation, he always mentioned the source.

The Master said that once there was a great argument among the pandits in

46. Who is greater — Shiva or Vishnu? the royal court of Burdwan on the subject of whether Shiva or Vishnu is greater? Pandit Padmalochan was not present at the time. The other pandits created a terrible uproar as they debated, some insisting on Shiva and some Vishnu, according to their knowledge of the scriptures or perhaps influenced by their temperamental preferences. The dispute continued between the Shaivas and the Vaishnavas, and no solution could be found. At last the chief court pandit was called to settle the problem. Pandit Padmalochan arrived at the royal court and after listening to the question, he remarked: "None of my ancestors for fourteen generations has seen Shiva or Vishnu, so how can I say who is superior or inferior? But if you want to know what the scriptures say, it can be stated that the Shaiva scriptures glorify Shiva, and the Vaishnava scriptures, Vishnu. Therefore, a devotee's own Chosen Deity is greater to that person than any other deities." Padmalochan then quoted as evidence verses indicating the magnificence of both Shiva and Vishnu compared to other gods, and concluded that both were equally great. This conclusion settled the dispute, and everyone applauded him. We get a glimpse of his genius from his humility, outspokenness, and clear understanding of the scriptures, and we understand the reason for his widespread popularity.

Padmalochan's reputation did not depend solely on the fact that he had

| 47. Padmalochan's love for God. | gained his wisdom by travelling widely in the dense forest of the scriptures. Even in his daily life, people saw his good conduct, nobility, austerity, detach- |

ment, steadfast devotion to God, and other fine qualities, and ascertained that he was a remarkable spiritual aspirant and a lover of God. The coexistence of true erudition and deep devotion to God is rare indeed in this world, so people are attracted to anyone who has both. It was therefore not surprising that when the Master heard of Padmalochan's greatness, he wished to see him. At that time the pandit had been adorning the royal court of Burdwan for a long time and was past middle age.

Whenever the Master wished to do anything, he was as anxious as a boy

| 48. The Master's mental condition. Padmalochan arrives in Calcutta. | to do it immediately. From his childhood onward the Master held this attitude: "Life is short; therefore, do quickly whatever should be done." As a result, it was |

in his nature to accomplish every task intensely and speedily. It is easily understood that the mind develops that habit through practising steadfastness and concentration.

When Mathur saw the Master's eagerness, he contemplated whether to send him to Burdwan. In the meantime, news arrived that Pandit Padmalochan had been ill for a long time and was currently staying in a garden house in Ariadaha on the bank of the Ganges for a change of climate. He was feeling better after enjoying the fresh pure air of the Ganges. Hriday was sent to verify this.

Hriday returned, having confirmed this information. Moreover, when the pandit heard about the Master, he expressed his eagerness to meet him, and cordially received Hriday when he learned that he was a relative of the Master. A date was then fixed, and the Master went to visit the pandit, accompanied by Hriday.

Hriday said that at their first meeting the Master and Padmalochan were pleased to see each other. The Master recognized Padmalochan as a modest, openhearted, and profound scholar, as well as a spiritual aspirant; the pandit for his part realized that the Master was a great soul and had reached a very lofty spiritual plane. When the Master sang some songs of the Divine Mother in his sweet voice, the pandit could not control his tears. He was also dumbfounded as he witnessed the Master frequently lose outer consciousness in samadhi and on hearing of his experiences while in that state. We understand that the pandit, who was well versed in the scriptures, tried to compare the Master's spiritual condition with those recorded in the scriptures. While trying to do so that day, however, he could not arrive at any definite conclusion and became perplexed. As he searched the scriptures he could find no parallels to the Master's ultimate experiences, so he could not ascertain which was true — the scriptures or the Master's realizations. Because of this the discriminating mind of the pandit, which was accustomed to arriving at a firm conclusion on spiritual matters by means of his scriptural knowledge and keen intellect, felt a sort of restlessness in the midst of joy like a dark shadow falling across light.

> 49. Padmalochan's first meeting with the Master.

The Master and Padmalochan met a few more times, compelled by the love and attraction that had developed on their first meeting. Moreover, the pandit developed a deep understanding regarding the Master's spiritual states. The Master later told us the reason for the pandit's firm conviction.

> 50. Why the pandit's love and respect for the Master increased.

Pandit Padmalochan had for a long time been practising the sadhanas prescribed by Tantra along with the disciplines of Vedanta, and he had experienced some of their results. The Master said that the Divine Mother made known to him at that time a secret of the power that had originated from the pandit's sadhana. The Master learned that the Divine Mother, the pandit's Chosen Deity, was pleased with his sadhana and gave him a boon that allowed him to remain invincible in innumerable conferences of scholars, and thereby maintain his supremacy. The pandit always kept beside him a jug of water and a towel. Before proceeding to solve any critical problem, it was his long-standing custom to leave the meeting room and wash his face with his water and towel. When he returned he would give the matter his consideration. So far no one had become curious about the pandit's unusual habit, and no one ever imagined that there was a hidden reason for it. In truth, however, he acted that way at the direction of his Chosen Deity. And whenever he did so, immediately scriptural knowledge, intelligence, and presence of mind awakened in him by Providence, making him invincible in debate. The pandit never disclosed this profound secret to anyone, not even his wife. The Divine Mother had secretly instructed him to perform this act, and he obeyed without question, experiencing its result without anyone's knowledge.

The Master said that he learned of the pandit's secret power by the grace

51. The Master knew of the pandit's occult power.

of the Divine Mother, and one day managed to remove the pandit's water pot and towel without his knowledge. Meanwhile, the pandit faced a question that required immediate resolution, and he was desperately looking for the missing items. Later, he was extremely surprised to learn that the Master had hidden them. Tears came to his eyes when he realized that the Master had done it because he knew his secret, and he effusively praised the Master with hymns, considering him to be his Chosen Deity. From then on the pandit thought of the Master as an incarnation of God and offered his devotion accordingly. The Master said: "Padmalochan was such a great pandit, but he still had so much faith in and devotion for me! He said: 'As soon as I recover, I shall have all the pandits summoned to a meeting where I shall declare you to be an avatar. I'll see who can refute my pronouncement.'

"On the occasion of a festival, Mathur was planning to convene a meeting of pandits at Dakshineswar. Padmalochan was an orthodox brahmin, free from greed, and would not accept gifts from men of low caste. Mathur was afraid that the pandit would refuse him, so he asked me to invite the pandit to come to the meeting. Accordingly I asked him, 'Hello, will you come to Dakshineswar?' He replied: 'Why not? With you I can go and dine even at a scavenger's house. Attending a meeting in a lower-caste home is a small matter!'"

Padmalochan could not attend the meeting that Mathur convened. His

52. Padmalochan passed away in Varanasi.

illness worsened before the meeting started, and with tearful eyes he took his leave of the Master and left for Varanasi. It is said that he passed away shortly afterwards.

When the Master's Calcutta devotees took refuge in him, long after the pandit's death, some of them were prompted by exuberant devotion to publicly proclaim that the Master was an avatar. When the Master heard this he sent someone to forbid them to do so. But in spite of that, they kept declaring their opinion about him. When the Master heard of this some days later, he was indignant and told us: "One is a doctor and the other is the manager of a theatre — and they come here and call me an avatar! They think by doing that they add to my prestige and make me appear great in the eyes of the world. But do they understand what it means to be an avatar? Long before they came here and called me an avatar, many persons like Padmalochan — who spent their whole lives in the study of this subject, some of them pandits in six philosophical systems, and some in three — came here and declared me an avatar. I am sick of this idea of calling me an avatar. What will they add to me by addressing me so?"

In addition to Padmalochan, the Master met some other well-known pandits. Sometimes, in the course of conversation, he described to us the noble qualities that he found in them. It will not be out of place to briefly mention some stories about them here.

Once Swami Dayananda Saraswati, the founder of the Arya Samaj,

| 53. The Master on Dayananda Saraswati. |

visited Bengal and stayed at a gentleman's garden house at Sinthi in Baranagore, a northern suburb of Calcutta. Although Dayananda was then a renowned pandit, he had not yet preached his doctrine and established his organization. When the Master heard about him, he paid him a visit. One day, during a conversation about Dayananda, the Master told us: "I went to see him [Dayananda] in a garden house at Sinthi. I noticed that he had developed a little spiritual power and that his chest was always red. He was in a *vaikhari* [articulative] state — discussing the scriptures day and night. However, he used his knowledge of Sanskrit grammar to distort the meaning of many passages in the scriptures. He was ambitious: He wanted to do something original and start a new sect."

Referring to Pandit Jaynarayan, the Master said: "He was a great pandit

| 54. Pandit Jaynarayan. |

but had no trace of ego. He knew beforehand about his own death and prophesied that he would give up his body in Varanasi. That actually came to pass."

The Master quite often spoke of Krishnakishore Bhattacharya of

| 55. Krishnakishore, a devotee of Rama. |

Ariadaha, who had great devotion to Ramachandra. The Master visited his house frequently, and Krishnakishore's pious wife was deeply devoted to the Master. The Master said that in addition to being devoted to the name of Rama, Krishnakishore was devoted to the word *Mara* and considered it to be a great mantra. According to the Puranas, the sage Narada gave this mantra to Valmiki, a highway robber. Valmiki was such a sinner that he could not utter the word *Rama*, so he repeated its reverse form, *Mara*, with great devotion. As a result, the divine play of Ramachandra was revealed to him and he became a great poet and the author of the great epic Ramayana. Krishnakishore suffered much grief and misery when his two grown sons died. The Master said that although Krishnakishore was a supreme devotee, even he was so overwhelmed with grief in the beginning that he could not control himself.

In addition to the spiritual aspirants mentioned earlier, the Master visited Maharshi Devendra Nath Tagore, Pandit Ishwar Chandra Vidyasagar, and others. Sometimes he told us about the Maharshi's all-encompassing devotion and Ishwar Chandra's zeal for karma yoga.

Chapter 3

Pilgrimage of the Master as a Guru and His Association with Holy Men

Whatever glorious or beautiful or mighty being exists anywhere, know that it has sprung from but a spark of My splendour. — GITA 10:41

IT IS NOT POSSIBLE TO RECORD EVERYTHING ABOUT HOW the Master, inspired as a guru and established in bhavamukha, enacted his divine play in so many places among so many people and in so many ways. We have already presented some incidents to the reader, but we will now relate how he also went on pilgrimages in the role of a guru.

As far as we have seen, no action of the Master was without purpose or

| 1. Compared with the lives of other great teachers, the Master's life is remarkable and unique. | meaning. When we study the most ordinary daily activities of his life, they appear to be endowed with deep significance — so what can we say of special events? In this modern age we have not seen another |

life in the spiritual world so filled with unusual events. Even after a lifetime of austerity and effort it is almost impossible for a person to fully realize only one of the innumerable aspects of God. The Master, however, saw and experienced God in many ways, discovered that all religious paths are true by practising the sadhana of each one, and helped the aspirants of each faith to move forward to their respective goals. Has anyone ever seen or even heard of another such person in the spiritual world?

In ancient times, Vedic rishis or great avatars realized God by adopting a particular spiritual attitude. They then proclaimed that their attitude was the only means to God-realization. They did not try to discover whether one could realize God by means of other attitudes. Or they themselves may have experienced that truth to some degree, but did not publicly proclaim it for fear it might undermine people's steadfast devotion to their Chosen Ideal and might harm their spiritual realization. But whatever their motive, history bears testimony to the fact that they used their authority as gurus to preach narrow religious doctrines. In the course of time, that caused tremendous hatred and jealousy in the minds of people, creating endless conflict and even bloodshed on many occasions.

Various contradictory doctrines evolved from the preaching of those

<table>
<tr><td>2. What the Master's life proves, and how his catholic view will spread in the future.</td><td>stereotyped and narrow religious views. This made the path of God-realization so complicated that it appeared to be impossible for the human intellect to disentangle the intricacies and see God. Shortly before</td></tr>
</table>

the advent of the Master, worldly and hedonistic Western materialism found an opportunity to enter the educational system of India with irresistible force, polluting the minds of immature boys and young men and flooding the country with atheism, foreign ideas, and the craving for sense pleasures. Who can say how far this degradation would have gone if religion had not been reestablished by the wonderful Master, a glowing example of purity, renunciation, and love of God? The Master himself demonstrated that every way in which the ancient rishis, teachers, avatars, and great souls of India and abroad had realized God and in whatever way they preached doctrines to attain God in the spiritual world — all of the methods were true. Even now a sincere aspirant can be blessed with a vision of God by following any of those paths.

The Master showed that Hinduism and Islam are equally valid even though their social rules, manners, and customs contradict each other and mountain-high differences exist between them. Aspirants of each religion worship the same God, though in different ways and following diverse paths; but in the course of time all become one in love with the God of love. The Master taught that, based on this truth, they should embrace each other and attain peace by putting aside their ongoing quarrels. He preached that eventually the worldly West would realize that peace comes through detachment and would experience the truth that the religions preached by the rishis and avatars of India and other countries are equally as valid as Christianity, finally becoming blessed by reconciling the active and the contemplative life. The more we study the life of this wonderful Master, the more we shall see that he does not belong to any particular country, nation, sect, or religion. One day all the nations of the world will have to take refuge in him to attain peace. The Master, who is established in bhavamukha, will enter peoples' minds as liberal ideas, breaking all narrow barriers, putting people in his new mould, and binding them together with a unique cord of unity.

The following example is proof of what was said before: The Master
attracted aspirants from the major religious denomi-

3. The evidence for this
view.

nations of India, who were antagonistic and hostile to
each other. They found in him the perfect ideal of
their respective faiths and considered him to be a fellow traveller along their
own paths. The spiritual ministry of the Master as a world teacher, which
began in India and brought harmony to her religious communities, will not
stop at resolving India's religious conflicts. His ministry will slowly dispel
the religious conflicts of Asia, as well as the impiety and religious animosity
of Europe, bringing an unprecedented kingdom of peace to the entire world.
Do you not see how this work has rapidly progressed since the Master's
passing away? Do you not see how the Master's message has entered the
United States and Europe by means of the devout Swami Vivekananda and
has brought a revolution in thought throughout the world within a short
time? As time rolls on, the infallible spiritual ideas of the Master will spread
their influence to all nations, all religions, and all societies, bringing about a
new age. Who can resist this progress? Who can go beyond the pure, sattvic,
illuminating ideas that originated from the Master's unprecedented austerities? The disciples who are now spreading that message will disappear;
perhaps as time passes people will not be able to determine, or understand,
the source of that message. But it is certain that one day people of the world
will accept in their hearts the Master's infinite, glorious, illuminating, loving,
and exhilarating ideas and be blessed by living their lives accordingly.

O reader, we have shown you how aspirants of various religious
denominations of India came to the Master, were

4. How the Master's
ideas spread.

blessed, and achieved true spirituality. Please do not
take these stories lightly. First try to understand as
far as possible the divine ideas of the wonderful Master, who was established in bhavamukha. Then reflect deeply on his messages. How did
these ideas first begin to spread? How did they develop and begin to
spread their influence among older orthodox people and then among the
younger generation that was endowed with a modern education? Finally,
how did these ideas spread across India and move abroad, bringing about
a revolution in the realm of ideas?

The Master's spiritual ideas were first spread by aspirants of the different
religious denominations of India. We have already

5. The Master's spiritual
ideas first disseminate
among the monks of
different orders who
visit Dakshineswar and
who meet him in holy
places.

narrated that whenever the Master was perfected in a
particular spiritual attitude, the aspirants of that attitude came to him spontaneously, saw in him their
supreme ideal, received spiritual help from him, and
left. In addition, at the request of Mathur and his
devout wife, Jagadamba, the Master made a pilgrimage to Vrindaban. There
is no scarcity of monks and devotees in holy places like Varanasi and

Vrindaban. In those places some well-known spiritual aspirants met the Master and were blessed by him in his aspect as a guru. We have not imagined this. The Master himself told us some stories in this connection that need to be recorded here.

The Master told us: "A game piece travels through all the squares before it reaches home. Similarly, it's only when one experiences all conditions — from that of a sweeper to that of an emperor — and is convinced of their worthlessness by seeing, hearing, and enjoying them for oneself, that one can reach the state of paramahamsa and become a true knower of Brahman." This is how an aspirant can reach Ultimate Reality. Regarding what is needed to become a world teacher, the Master said, "To kill others (to conquer enemies) one needs a sword and a shield, but to kill oneself a nail-parer suffices." If one wants to be a true teacher, one has to gain knowledge by undergoing all kinds of experiences, thus becoming more powerful than ordinary people. The Master told us repeatedly, "Avatars, perfected souls, and ordinary souls differ only in the amount of shakti, or power, that they possess." Look, in the practical world of politics, geniuses like Otto von Bismarck and William Ewart Gladstone must keep in mind the entire history of their countries, past and present, and in addition develop the power to see the future more clearly than ordinary people can. As a result, such men can understand how, after fifty years or more, the present state of affairs will take shape and harm the people of their countries. To prevent negative consequences from the very beginning, they set in motion counter forces to prevent present events from taking terrible forms and causing harmful effects far into the future. The same abilities are needed in the spiritual world also.

Avatars and true teachers must know the following: How did the rishis of previous ages introduce various spiritual movements, and how have these movements taken shape after all this time? How much good have these movements done in the past, and what good are they now doing for people? And now that they have been distorted, how much harm have they caused so far, and what harm will they bring in the future? How did they become corrupted? How will the current religious movements in their countries degenerate over a number of centuries, and what forms will they eventually take? And how much will they harm people? Once they have in-depth answers to these questions, avatars and world teachers need to found new movements. If they do not have a clear understanding of these issues, how will they comprehend the present condition of their people? If one cannot properly diagnose the disease, how can one prescribe the medicine? In addition to practising severe austerities, thus acquiring the power necessary to prescribe that medicine, the great teachers must encounter different situations in the world and gain more experience than ordinary people.

---

6. The Master develops a wonderful teaching ability after experiencing various high and low conditions.

Consider the various situations that the Master faced in his life: Born into a poor family, he had to struggle against dire poverty during his childhood. In his youth he accepted the job of priest in the Kali temple and suffered the dishonour of serving a rich person. When he lost control of himself during his sadhana, he had to endure his relatives' scoldings, humiliating words, and laments, as well as the indifference and pity of people who considered him mad. When Mathur, inspired by his love and respect for the Master, began to honour him and provide him with luxurious comforts, he had to absorb that too. He was not puffed up with pride in his divine power when various religious leaders considered him to be an avatar and offered him their heartfelt devotion. Thus, the Master experienced diverse conditions, remained unperturbed in all circumstances, and passed every severe test. On one hand, his supreme devotion drove him to perform extraordinary austerities for God-realization and awoke his transcendental and subtle yogic vision. On the other, his varied experiences in the world gave him perfect understanding of the mental conditions of all types of people. He also learned how to deal with people tactfully and how to empathize with both their happiness and their misery. It is evident that the Master's authority as a guru developed by means of those internal and external situations, becoming more apparent every day.

Pilgrimage undoubtedly caused the Master's power as a guru to manifest

7. What the Master learns from pilgrimage. Divine and human moods coexist in the Master.

itself. It was necessary for the Master, the spiritual teacher of the age, to be acquainted with the spiritual condition of the country's masses. This purpose was fulfilled to a great extent when he went with Mathur on a pilgrimage. Piercing the veil of maya, the Master's eye of wisdom was capable of seeing and experiencing the manifestation of the indivisible Satchidananda, One without a second. However, when he came in contact with worldly people, the same eye of wisdom made him adept in learning people's inner feelings from casual conversation and understanding the conditions of society and the country as a whole by observing a few events. Of course, the reader should understand that we are describing this in reference to the Master's normal state. When the Master used his yogic power to ascend to a higher plane, he could see and comprehend individual, social, or national problems by means of his divine sight, and ascertain specific solutions to them. In that state he went beyond the process of ordinary learning — which includes seeing, hearing, and comparative study — and he did not need to ascertain the truth in the usual manner. We saw the godman Sri Ramakrishna evaluate the truth of all things through both types of perception: ordinary external vision and extraordinary yogic insight. If we do not present both the divine and human aspects of the Master, the reader will get only a partial picture of this divine character. For that reason we are trying to thoroughly study both aspects of this godman.

There is another reason why the Master went on pilgrimages: The scriptures say that perfected, illumined souls visit places
of pilgrimage in order to intensify the sanctity and
spiritual atmosphere of those places. Because these
perfected beings go to those places with longing
hearts, seeking a more vivid vision of God, God becomes manifest there in a
special form, or the presence of God becomes more palpable than before.
Then, when others visit that holy place, they experience this divinity more
easily. The scriptures have said this regarding perfected souls; how much
more powerful must be the influence of avatars like the Master! When
mentioning holy places, the Master told us many times in his simple
language: "Look, know for certain that there is a special manifestation of
God where for a long time many people have practised austerities, concentration, meditation, japa, prayer, and worship in order to attain His vision.
Their devotion has caused a spiritual atmosphere to solidify in that place, so
one can easily become spiritually awakened and have a vision of God there.
Throughout the ages many monks, devotees, and perfected souls have
visited sacred places to see God and call on Him wholeheartedly, shunning
all other desires. That's why there is a special manifestation of God in those
places. However, God exists everywhere equally. If one digs deeply enough,
one can find water in any place. But one doesn't need to dig for water where
there is a well, a pool, a pond, or a lake. One can get water there at any time. It
is like that."

> 8. What the scriptures say about why godmen like the Master go on pilgrimages.

The Master taught us how to "chew the cud" after visiting places that are
endowed with a special manifestation of God. He
said: "As cows eat their fill of fodder mixed with
oil-cake and water, then sit and happily chew the
cud, likewise, after visiting temples and holy places,
one should sit in a secluded spot to ruminate and become absorbed in the
godly thoughts that arose in the mind there. After visiting sacred places, one
shouldn't immediately put one's mind on worldly things and drive holy
thoughts away. If that happens, those godly thoughts cannot leave permanent impressions on the mind."

> 9. The Master's advice to "chew the cud" after visiting temples and holy places.

Once some of us went with the Master to visit the Divine Mother in
Kalighat. The special manifestation in that ancient Devi temple and the
living presence of the Divine Mother in the Master produced immense joy in
the devotees' hearts. On the way back, a devotee was persuaded to go to his
father-in-law's house and to pass the night there. When he returned to the
Master the next day, the latter asked him where he had stayed the night
before. When the Master learned that he had been at his father-in-law's
house, he said: "What! You saw the Divine Mother. You were supposed to
ruminate on thoughts of Her and of your visit to Her, but instead you passed
the night at your father-in-law's like a worldly man! After visiting a temple

or a sacred place, one should be absorbed in holy thoughts and contemplation. How can divine feelings settle in the heart otherwise?"

The Master told us many times that unless one first devoutly cultivates

<table>
<tr><td>10. Only when one feels devotion in the heart should one go on a pilgrimage.</td><td>divine feelings in the heart, one cannot get any special benefit from a pilgrimage. During his lifetime, many of us occasionally expressed to him our desire to visit holy places. He sometimes told us in</td></tr>
</table>

response, "Look, one who has it here [in the heart], has it there; one who has
it not here, has it not there either."[1] He said further: "For one who is endowed
with devotion, devotion increases with the influence of holy places. And as
for one who does not have that, what can be derived? Sometimes we hear
that someone's son has fled to Varanasi or somewhere else; then the news
comes that he has gotten a job there and that he has sent some money home
with a letter. Some people go to live in holy places and then open shops and
set up business there. When I visited the northwestern parts of India, I saw
the same things there as here: the same mango trees, tamarind trees, and
bamboo groves were there as here. Seeing that, I told Hriday: 'O Hriday,
what have I then come to see? What is there is here too. Only when I observe
the excreta in the meadows, it seems that the digestive power of these people
is greater than that of people in other places.'"[2]

We mentioned earlier that the devotees first took the Master to a rented

<table>
<tr><td>11. How the Master advises a devotee who is anxious to visit Bodh Gaya after Swami Vivekananda has gone there.</td><td>house at Shyampukur in Calcutta and then to the Cossipore garden house, a little north of the city, for cancer treatment. A few days [actually, four months] after arriving at Cossipore, without informing anyone, Swami Vivekananda left for Bodh Gaya with two brother disciples. During that period, day and</td></tr>
</table>

night, we had been discussing the wonderful life of Buddha and his great
departure from home, his renunciation, and his austerities. We stayed in a
small room on the southern side of the lower floor in the garden house. We
wrote on its wall a verse from the *Lalita Vistara* (9:57) that proclaims the firm
resolution of Buddha: *Ihasane sushyatu me shariram tvag-asthi-mamsam
pralayanca yatu, Aprapya bodhim bahukalpa-durlabham naivasanat kayamatash-
calishyate.* [Let my body wither away on this seat; let my skin, flesh, and
bones disintegrate. But I will not let my body move from this seat until I
attain enlightenment, which is rare and difficult to achieve over many ages.]
Day and night those words were in front of our eyes, reminding us that we
would have to lay down our lives for God-realization in the same way.

---

1. Avatars quite often teach people in the same way. Once Jesus said to his disciples, "To him
who hath more, more shall be given and from him who hath little, that little shall be taken
away." — Matthew 13:12
2. The Master made this last remark in different words.

While thus talking about Buddha's renunciation, Swamiji suddenly left for Bodh Gaya. He did not let us know where he was going or when he would return. We thought that perhaps he would never come back and that we would never see him again. Later, we heard that he had donned the ochre cloth and gone to Bodh Gaya. Our minds were so attached to Swamiji that it was painful for us to live without him even for a moment. Many of us therefore became restless and felt a constant desire to join him. Gradually the Master came to know all about this. One day Swami Brahmananda learned of a disciple's intention in this regard and informed the Master.

The Master told that disciple: "Why are you anxious? Where will Naren go? How long will he stay away? Just wait. He will be back soon." Then he said with a smile: "Travel in all four directions. You will not find anything (true spirituality) anywhere. Whatever exists is here (*pointing to his body*)." The Master used the word *here* in two senses perhaps: first, meaning that at present one would not find a greater manifestation of spirituality or divinity anywhere than in him; and second, that God dwells in every human being. If one cannot kindle love and devotion for God within oneself, one cannot achieve any benefit by travelling to various places. One thus finds two or more meanings in many of the Master's statements. But why the Master alone? This is true of all avatars born in different ages. People understand the meaning of their words according to their own inclinations and habits. But as for the person to whom the Master spoke those words, he understood them according to the first meaning given above. He was firmly convinced that such a manifestation of divinity could not be found anywhere except in the Master, and thus reassured, he stayed with him. Swami Vivekananda did in fact return to Cossipore a few days later.

Sometime before the Master passed away, a pious woman devotee went to him and expressed her desire to go to Vrindaban and practise austerities. The Master discouraged her with a movement of his hand and said: "Why will you go? What will you do there? One who has it here, has it there; and one who does not have it here, does not have it there." Because of her longing, the woman devotee could not accept the Master's words and so left for Vrindaban. But she later told us that she did not derive much benefit from the pilgrimage on that occasion. Moreover, she never saw the Master again because he passed away shortly after she left.

12. "One who has it here, has it there."

The Master told us many times that he visited each holy place with a specific spiritual mood in mind. He said: "I expected to find everyone in Varanasi absorbed in samadhi, meditating on Shiva twenty-four hours a day, and everyone in Vrindaban wild with ecstatic joy in the company of Krishna. But when I went to those places, I found them to be different." The Master's extraordinary and simple mind accepted and believed everything like a

13. What the Master's simple mind expects to see at the holy places.

five-year-old boy. Since childhood, we have learned to look upon people and things with critical eyes. How can our crooked minds have that kind of faith? When we find people who believe anything without question, we consider them foolish and dull-witted. We heard from the Master for the first time: "Look, people become guileless and open-minded as a result of many austerities and various sadhanas. One cannot attain God without simplicity. He reveals His true nature to a person who is simple and believing." Again, lest one think that one must be stupid in order to become honest and believing, the Master said: "Be a devotee. But does that mean you should be a fool?" He also said: "Always discriminate between what is real and what is unreal, what is eternal and what is transient. Shun the transitory and fix your mind on the eternal."

Unable to reconcile these two statements, some of us were scolded by the Master many times. Swami Yogananda had not then renounced his home. His household needed an iron pot, so he went to Barabazar to buy one. After reminding the shopkeeper of the evil consequences of dishonesty, he said, "Look here, take a fair price for the article, and please make sure that there is no crack or leak in it." "Of course, sir, I shall do that," replied the shopkeeper. He then selected a pot and gave it to Yogananda. Trusting the shopkeeper, he took the pot and brought it home without examining it. But after returning to Dakshineswar he found a crack in it. When the Master heard of this, he reproached him: "What? You bought a pot and didn't examine it first? The shopkeeper was there to do business, not to practise religion. Why did you believe him and get cheated? Just because you're a devotee, that's no reason to be a fool. Should you be deceived by people? Henceforth, when you go shopping, first examine the thing thoroughly and then pay. Don't accept the article without confirming that it is the right weight. And don't fail to demand the little extras that are customary." We could give many such examples, but this is not the place to do so. We shall continue our topic now, after having referred to the Master's extraordinary simplicity along with his wonderful power of discrimination.

14. The Master's advice to Swami Yogananda: "Be a devotee. But does that mean you should be a fool?"

The Master told us that Mathur spent more than 100,000 rupees on their pilgrimage to Varanasi. After arriving at Varanasi, Mathur arranged a feast for the local brahmin pandits; another day he invited their entire families, fed them sumptuously, and gave a cloth and a rupee to each one of them. When Mathur's party returned to Varanasi after visiting Vrindaban, at the Master's command Mathur acted like a "wish-fulfilling tree" and freely distributed utensils, clothes, blankets, shoes, and other articles to people according to their needs. On the first day of the feast, the Master

15. Observing the worldly attachment of the people in Varanasi, the Master cries, "Mother, why did you bring me here?"

was extremely displeased to see the brahmin pandits quarrelling, shouting, and even fighting among themselves. He was disappointed when he noticed that even in a sacred place like Varanasi people were as attached to lust and gold as they were elsewhere. With tears in his eyes, he said to the Divine Mother: "Mother, why did you bring me here? I was much happier in Dakshineswar."

Although the Master was distressed when he saw that even in Varanasi

| 16. The Master's vision of "Golden Varanasi." |

people were attached to worldly things, he nonetheless had wonderful visions and experiences there that convinced him of the greatness of Shiva and the glory of Varanasi. As his boat crossed the Ganges and approached Varanasi, he saw in a vision that the city of Shiva was truly made of gold: There was no clay or stone in Varanasi. The subtle form of the city had been made golden by the priceless love and faith of innumerable monastics and devotees throughout the ages. The real Varanasi is luminous and full of spirituality while the external one is but its shadow.

It is not difficult to understand why this city is called "Golden Varanasi."

| 17. Why Varanasi is regarded as being made of gold. |

Varanasi is a city of innumerable temples and mansions; it has a two-mile-long embankment on the Ganges consisting of many bathing ghats with wide steps; its roads are decorated with beautiful stone gates; it has a good drainage system and a good supply of water from ponds, lakes, and wells; it has monasteries and garden houses; and above all, its many alms houses provide food to brahmin pandits, students, monks, and poor people. After seeing all this, who would deny that this magnificent city of Shiva was constructed in ancient times by people from all parts of India, who spent their fortunes on it. Who would not be astounded by the thought that this holy city came into existence by the unified devotion of 300 million Indian people throughout the ages? Who would not be impressed when encountering the tremendous current of spirituality in this city, and be overwhelmed when trying to trace its origin? And who would not be wonderstruck and affirm with heartfelt devotion and humility that this holy city of Varanasi is indeed incomparable. Truly, it was not built by humankind: It came into existence through the infinite compassion of Lord Vishwanath, refuge of the helpless poor and deliverer of the afflicted. The Divine Mother Annapurna, the shakti of Shiva, dwells here eternally. She provides food to nourish people's physical and vital sheaths, and spirituality to nourish their mental, intellectual, and blissful sheaths. Thus, She speedily brings liberation, the knowledge of oneness with Lord Vishwanath, to individual souls. It is no wonder that after arriving in Varanasi, the Master, established in bhavamukha, saw a divine and luminous spiritual current pervading the entire city of Shiva, and he also experienced its solid gross form as Golden Varanasi.

In the eyes of Hindus, all luminous things originate from sattva guna and

18. After seeing Golden Varanasi, the Master is afraid to defile it by answering the call of nature there.

are therefore pure. As all objects are illuminated by light, so light or luminosity is holy to us. We understand from the scriptures that one should keep a vigil lamp lit in front of a deity and one should not extinguish lights in the presence of deities. It is perhaps for this reason that custom dictates one should look upon luminous things like gold as pure, and one should not wear gold ornaments on the lower part of the body. Always seeing Varanasi as golden, the childlike Master was initially concerned that he would defile the sacred ground by answering the call of nature there. The Master told us that for some days Mathur arranged for a palanquin to carry the Master across the stream Asi [which is beyond Varanasi] to answer the call of nature. When that particular mood later came to an end, he did not need to do that anymore.

The Master told us about another of his extraordinary visions in Varanasi.

19. The Master's vision at Manikarnika regarding the liberation of jivas who die in Varanasi.

Many people take a boat trip to visit five holy spots in Varanasi, Manikarnika, and other places nearby that lie along the banks of the Ganges. One day Mathur took the Master on this boat trip. The main cremation ground of Varanasi is near Manikarnika. When Mathur's boat approached the Manikarnika ghat, the air of the cremation ground was full of smoke because many bodies were being cremated on the funeral pyres. The Master's face expressed ecstatic joy at the sight, and the hairs of his body stiffened. He emerged from the covered part of the boat and walked over to the bow, where he went into samadhi. Mathur's guide and the boatmen all ran to catch him, lest he fall into the water. But they did not need to do anything. The Master remained standing, calm and motionless, with a wonderful smile on his face. The whole place appeared to be serene and holy. Mathur and Hriday stood protectively nearby but did not touch the Master. In astonishment, the boatmen gazed at this extraordinary figure. When the Master's ecstasy came to an end sometime later, everyone disembarked at the Manikarnika ghat, had their baths, performed rituals, and then returned to the boat to continue their journey.

The Master then described his vision to Mathur and the others: "I saw a tall white figure with tawny matted hair steadily approach each funeral pyre in turn, carefully raise each individual soul from its cast-off body, and whisper into its ear the particular name of Brahman that liberates a soul. Seated on the opposite side of the pyre, the all-powerful Divine Mother Kali untied the gross, subtle, and causal knots of bondage created by each individual soul, thus sending the soul to the Absolute by opening the gate of liberation. Lord Vishwanath was blessing those souls by bestowing in an instant the experience of nondual, infinite bliss that people can attain only after ages of concentration and austerity."

Trailanga Swami (d. 1887),
a revered but reclusive
saint of Varanasi.

Manikarnika cremation ground at Varanasi.

The pandits who were with Mathur verified this vision from their knowledge of the scriptures. They said to the Master: "The *Kashikhanda*[3] mentions that Shiva confers nirvana on those who die at Varanasi, but does not explicitly state how. Your vision clearly elucidates how this is accomplished. Your visions and experiences have surpassed even the scriptural records."

During his stay in Varanasi the Master visited Trailanga Swami and other

20. The Master meets Trailanga Swami.

famous holy men. He was pleased with Trailanga Swami and told us many stories about him. He said: "I found in him the living manifestation of Vishwanath. Varanasi was sanctified and made vibrant by his presence. He was in an exalted state of knowledge. He had no body-consciousness: The sand there gets so hot in the sun that no one can walk on it, but he lay on it comfortably. I cooked rice pudding and brought it with me to feed him. At that time he couldn't speak to me because he had taken a vow of silence. So I asked him by signs whether God was one or many. He replied in the same manner, indicating that God is known to be one when a person enters into the state of samadhi; but as long as there is any consciousness of I, you, jiva, and the world, God is perceived as many. I pointed to him and told Hriday, 'In him you see the condition of a true knower of Brahman.'"

After staying for some days in Varanasi, the Master accompanied Mathur

21. The Master's ecstasy on seeing Vraja and the image of Bankabihari in Vrindaban.

to Vrindaban. We heard that when he saw the image of Bankabihari [Krishna] he was so overwhelmed with ecstasy that he ran to embrace him. In the evening when he saw the cowherd boys crossing the Jamuna to return from the pastures with their cows, he beheld among them the cowherd Krishna, dark like a rain cloud, with a peacock feather in his hair. He was then beside himself with feelings of devotion. The Master visited Nidhuban, Govardhan, and some of the important places in Vraja, which he liked better than Vrindaban. He experienced intense love in these places and enjoyed visions of Krishna and Radha, the queen of Vraja. We heard that while they were visiting Govardhan and other places, Mathur arranged a palanquin for the Master. On one side within it he spread a cloth and covered it with heaps of rupees and coins so that the Master could give them away to the poor and make donations to the temples. But during the journey he was so overwhelmed with love and devotion that he could not touch the money to distribute it. Having no alternative, the Master pulled back a corner of the cloth and scattered the coins among the poor in those places.

In Vraja the Master saw many Vaishnava monks absorbed in japa and

22. The Master's special affection for Vraja.

meditation in their small thatched huts, with their backs to the door lest they see the people and things outside. The Master's mind was very attracted by the

3. A section of the Skanda Purana. — *Translator*

Temple images of Radha and her companions in Nidhuban.

Nidhuban (Vrindaban), where Krishna played with the gopis.

natural beauty of Vraja. He was charmed by Govardhan Hill covered with fruits and flowers, by the deer and peacocks who moved freely and fearlessly in the forest, by the monks and hermits who passed their days in constant contemplation of God, and by the simple inhabitants of Vraja, who were guileless and respectful. Moreover, the Master was moved when he visited Gangamata, an elderly woman hermit and a perfected soul; he decided that he would not leave Vraja but would rather spend the rest of his life there.

Gangamata was then about sixty years old. After observing her exuberant love for Radha and Krishna over a long period of

23. Gangamata of the Nidhuban. The Master's desire to live in Vraja. His concern about taking care of his aged mother makes him return to Calcutta.

time, the local people had come to regard her as a reincarnation of Lalita, the main female confidante of Radha, who had descended to earth to teach people divine love. The Master told us that when Gangamata first saw him, she recognized the same manifestation of mahabhava in him that she saw in Radha. She understood him to be a reincarnation of Radha herself, and she addressed him as "Dulali," darling friend. Gangamata considered herself blessed to have met Dulali without any effort of her own, and realized that her lifelong service of and love for the Lord had been fulfilled. The Master also felt that she was a longtime friend, and he stayed at her ashrama for some days, forgetting all else. We heard that they were so charmed with each other's devotion that Mathur became concerned that the Master might not return to Dakshineswar with him. We can easily imagine how anxious the devout Mathur was about the whole situation. However, the Master's love for his mother at last triumphed over his resolve to stay in Vraja permanently. The Master told us: "I forgot everything when I went to Vraja. I thought that I would never return to Dakshineswar. But after a few days I remembered my mother, and I realized that she would suffer and grieve for me. Who would look after her and serve her in her advanced age? When this thought arose in my mind, I could no longer stay there."

The more we reflect, the more this godman's words and actions amaze us,

24. Contradictory ideas and qualities are wonderfully harmonized in the Master's life. Although a sannyasin, he serves his mother.

and the more we are fascinated to see how apparently contradictory qualities were perfectly harmonized in him. Consider how the Master offered his body, his mind, and everything else to the Divine Mother, but could not offer truthfulness to Her. Although he relinquished all earthly human relationships, he did not forget his love for and duty towards his mother. He had no physical relationship with his wife at any time, but he always maintained a loving relationship with her as a guru. We can cite many such examples of his extraordinary behaviour. Can anyone find such harmony among such a collection of contradictions in the lives of great teachers or avatars of the past? Who will not admit that such a person is unprecedented? It does not matter whether people acknowledge the Master as an avatar, but who can deny that there is no one else like him in the spiritual world?

The Master told us many times that when his aged mother lived with him at Dakshineswar for the last few years of her life, he considered himself blessed to personally serve her every day. Again, when his beloved mother died, the grief-stricken Master was extremely distressed and shed tears more profusely than most people do in this world. Although he grieved at his mother's death, he never forgot that he was a sannyasin, even for a moment. According to the scriptures a sannyasin does not have the right to perform funeral and shrāddha ceremonies for his parents, so the Master had them done by his nephew Ramlal. In solitude he cried for his mother and thus tried his utmost to pay his debt to her. Regarding this, the Master told us many times: "Look, my children, parents are the greatest gurus in this world. As long as they are alive, one should serve them to one's utmost ability; when they die, one should perform the shrāddha ceremony as far as one is able. One who is poor and has no means to perform the shrāddha ceremony for parents should go to the forest and weep for their memory, thus repaying the debt to them. One may disobey one's parents without incurring any sin only for the sake of God. Although his father forbade it, Prahlada did not stop repeating the name of Krishna. Dhruva disobeyed his mother and went into the forest to practise austerities. But in performing these actions, neither of them incurred any sin." Thus, we have been blessed by seeing the Master's power as a guru manifest itself through his devotion to his mother.

Reluctantly the Master took his leave of Gangamata and returned to Varanasi with Mathur. We heard that after staying there for some days he visited the golden image of Mother Annapurna on the occasion of Dipavali and was overwhelmed with love and ecstasy.

Mathur wanted to leave Varanasi and visit Gaya, but he had to give up that plan because the Master refused to go there. The Master told us that while his father was in Gaya, he had a dream in which he was told that the Master would be born as his son. That is why the Master was named Gadadhar [Lord Vishnu in the temple at Gaya]. The Master sometimes told us that he refused to go to Gaya with Mathur because he believed that if he saw the lotus feet of Gadadhar there, he would be overwhelmed with devotion, forget that he existed independently from Gadadhar, and become united with Him forever. The Master was firmly convinced that He who was born in previous ages as Ramachandra, Krishna, Gauranga, and others had descended to the world in his own body. We observed that an indescribable feeling would come upon him whenever there was any talk about a possible visit to Gaya, which he knew

25. The Master refuses to visit Gaya, knowing it will cause his life to end in samadhi: the reason.

from his father's dream as the place of his origin, or whenever he heard about other sites where avatars had ended their divine play. The Master declared that if he were to go to any of those places, his body would not last; he would become absorbed in such deep samadhi that his mind would never come back to this world.

At another time he expressed a similar notion at the proposal of visiting Puri, where the divine play of Gauranga ended. In addition to this caution regarding himself, if his yogic vision revealed that any of his devotees were a part of or had risen from a particular deity, he would express a similar concern to the devotee and forbid him to visit the holy place that was associated with that deity. It is difficult to explain to the reader this idea of the Master. It would not be appropriate to describe it as fear because even when ordinary people experience samadhi, they see while still living how the soul departs from the body during death, and they become fearless, understanding death to be a transition just as childhood, youth, and so on are different stages in human development.

It is therefore not surprising that avatars who can enter samadhi at will, become completely fearless and conquer death. We cannot call the Master's concern an eagerness to preserve the body or to live like others do. Ordinary people zealously protect their bodies for the purposes of self-gratification or enjoyment; such a motivation cannot be ascribed to one whose mind has been washed clean of selfishness. How then can we understand that conviction of the Master? Our dictionaries provide only those words which express and explain ideas that arise in our minds. Can any words express the exalted and divine ideas of great souls like the Master? Therefore, O reader, we have no alternative but to give up vain arguments and accept with faith what the Master said about his experiences, trying to use our imaginations to imprint them in our minds.

The Master said that a divine manifestation originating from a place, an

26. The effect dissolves into the cause — this is the law.

object, or a person, will dissolve into its source when it intimately identifies with it. Many examples of this are found in the scriptures. A jiva [soul] originates from Brahman; when knowledge brings it close to Brahman, it merges into its source. Our little individual minds are manifestations of the Cosmic Mind; when that little mind of ours becomes more and more detached, and develops more and more compassion, purity, and other noble qualities, it becomes similar to the Cosmic Mind and then merges into It. The same law acts in the gross world. The earth emerged from the sun; if the earth by some force or other comes close to the sun, it will dissolve into it. So it is to be understood that behind the Master's conviction, there is a particular substance unknown to us. And in fact if there were any such Person or Thing as Lord Gadadhar, and if the Master's body and mind somehow originated from Him, then if those two entities drew near to one another they would be attracted to one another and become united. This conclusion is very rational.

No reasoning is necessary to explain that avatars are not like ordinary

27. The doctrine of karma cannot explain the mystery of avatars' lives: the reason.

human beings. Sensing an inconceivable and incredible power in them, people humbly offer their heartfelt worship and take refuge in them. The great sage Kapila and the talented philosophers of India tried their utmost to solve the mystery of the lives of those extraordinary, powerful beings. While attempting to discover why there was a greater manifestation of power in them than in ordinary people, those philosophers first observed that the common law of karma was quite insufficient to explain the mystery. Good and bad actions performed by ordinary people are done in the service of self-gratification, but actions done by avatars are completely without selfish motives. The desire to remove the suffering of others generates an indomitable enthusiasm that forces them to work, and they sacrifice their personal enjoyment for that noble desire. In addition, that desire is not grounded in the urge to achieve name and fame in this world. They invariably renounce the desire for heavenly abodes as well as for earthly name and fame, which are like the droppings of crows to them.

Following are some examples of this: Nara and Narayana, two ancient rishis, practised austerities for ages in the Himalayas at the Badarika Ashrama for the purpose of learning how to benefit humanity. Ramachandra banished his beloved Sita in order to satisfy his subjects. Every one of Krishna's actions was performed for the purpose of establishing truth and religion. Buddha renounced his kingdom and his wealth to rescue people from the sufferings of birth, disease, and death. Jesus sacrificed his life to establish the kingdom of an all-loving God on this earth full of grief and misery. Muhammad took up the sword against unrighteousness. Shankara expended all of his energy to make people understand that real peace comes only through the nondual experience. Chaitanya realized that in God's name resides all the power needed to benefit humanity, so he gave up all worldly enjoyments and dedicated his life to preaching God's name with full enthusiasm. What motive drove these great teachers to perform such actions? And what pleasure did they enjoy by enduring so much hardship?

The philosophers also saw clearly in these avatars all the physical signs

28. Philosophers' conclusions after seeing the signs of a free soul in an avatar's life from childhood. Sankhya says that avatars belong to the class of beings described as prakriti-lina [absorbed in prakriti].

that the scriptures describe as manifest in liberated beings as a result of their extraordinary inner spiritual experiences. They were therefore compelled to assign these avatars to a new class. Kapila, the founder of Sankhya philosophy, said that these great beings had a noble desire to do good to humanity. Although the austerities they had performed in previous lives gave them liberation, they did not dwell in the realm of nirvana. They remained absorbed in prakriti and lived for a cycle with the knowledge that all the powers of prakriti belonged to them. He among them who possessed that power in a particular cycle appeared as Ishwara [Personal God] to the people in that period. Because He experienced the powers that existed in prakriti as His own, He could implement and withdraw that power as He wished. We can use the limited powers of prakriti that exist in our own bodies and minds because we feel them to be ours; similarly, those great beings consider all powers of prakriti as belonging to them, and therefore they use them at will. Thus, although Kapila did not admit the existence of an eternal Ishwara, he acknowledged the existence of all-powerful beings that live for a cycle and called them *prakriti-lina*, "absorbed in prakriti."

The authors of Vedanta admitted the eternal existence of Ishwara, who has become manifest as all beings and the entire world. Those special, powerful beings are therefore part of Ishwara, who is eternal, pure, illumined, and free by nature. Apart from that, these extraordinary individuals are born, when needed, for a special purpose for the good of humanity. Because they are endowed with a particular power suitable to their task, they are called *adhikarikas*, which means that these persons are equipped with the authority to perform a particular action, and have been entrusted to accomplish it. The authors of Vedanta observed greater and lesser degrees of power in these adhikarikas and noticed that some of these beings performed actions that were of permanent benefit to all people of the world, while others affected the people of one country or a part of it only. So the Vedantins recognized some of these adhikarikas as avatars, incarnations of God, and others as ever-free ishwarakotis, godlike souls endowed with lesser authority. Building on this theory, the authors of the Puranas tried to use their imaginations to ascertain the degrees to which avatars manifest their power; but these writers went beyond the limit of their understanding. The author of the Bhagavata made this statement : "All these are the manifestations of an aspect or part of the Supreme One, but Krishna is God Himself" (1:3:28).

29. Vedanta philosophy calls these great beings *adhikarikas,* and this group is divided into two categories: avatars and ever-free ishwarakotis.

We have already explained to the reader (see III.3.22-28) that in truth the power of the guru belongs to God. Finding jivas to be deluded by ignorance and unable to overcome this by their own efforts, God, in His infinite mercy, becomes eager to deliver them. This divine, compassionate eagerness and God's will to help become manifest as the guru and the power of the guru. From time immemorial that power has become manifest now and then in some special individuals who are charged with enlightening people suffering in ignorance. These great persons are worshipped as avatars, so it is understood that the avatars are humanity's true gurus.

The bodies and minds of adhikarikas are composed of elements that

30. Adhikarikas' bodies and minds are made differently from those of ordinary people, so their intentions and actions are amazing and unique.

allow them to absorb and digest divine ecstasy and love as well as a high degree of spiritual power. When jivas attain a little spiritual power and are honoured for it, they are elated and become puffed up with ego; but though adhikarikas achieve a thousand times more spiritual power than jivas, they remain unperturbed, balanced, and free from egotism. And once a jiva becomes free from bondage and experiences the supreme bliss of the Atman in samadhi, that person does not want to return to this world for any reason whatsoever. When adhikarikas attain that bliss, however, they think of ways to share it with others. After realizing God, the jiva is released from karma and all duty. But when adhikarikas realize God, they understand the specific purpose for their human birth and set out on their missions. As a rule, until their specific tasks are completed, adhikarikas are eager to live in this world. They do not share the feeling of ordinary liberated beings that "it does not matter if the body dies at this moment." But the will to live of divine incarnations and that of ordinary beings is as different as heaven and earth. Adhikarikas immediately realize when their missions are accomplished; then they joyfully give up their bodies in samadhi without pausing for a moment. Far from giving up the body at will in samadhi, ordinary beings never feel that their work has been accomplished, but rather feel that many of their desires remain unfulfilled. Similar differences exist in other respects as well. For that reason, we fall into terrible error when we try to evaluate the lives and missions of avatars or adhikarikas by our own standards.

It is only in the context of the above scriptural discussions that the reader will understand to some extent these statements of the Master: "This body will not last if I go to Gaya"; "An eternal samadhi will ensue if I visit Jagannath in Puri." That is why we have briefly but clearly discussed this subject here. The reader will understand from the above analysis that no idea of the Master was contrary to the scriptures.

We mentioned earlier that the Master refused to go to Gaya with Mathur, so no one could visit that holy place during the trip. Everyone returned to Calcutta by way of Vaidyanath. During his first visit to Deoghar, the Master was overwhelmed with compassion at seeing the poverty-stricken people in a nearby village. He persuaded Mathur to feed them sumptuously and to distribute a piece of cloth to each person. We have narrated this story in detail in another place (see III.7.38).

In addition to visiting Varanasi, Vrindaban, and other holy places, the

31. The Master's visit to Navadwip.

Master once went to Navadwip, the birthplace of Chaitanya. Mathur accompanied him on this trip as well. We understand from what the Master once said about Chaitanya that even avatars cannot hold all truths in their minds at all times. But if they want to know any truth of the spiritual world, it comes to them very easily.

Many among us were sceptical about Chaitanya's being an avatar, and some even believed that the word Vaishnava stood for "lower-class people." To remove this doubt, some of us asked the Master about it. In reply, he said: "Previously I also thought that way. Chaitanya is not even alluded to in the Bhagavata and other Puranas, so how could he be an avatar? I thought the shaven-headed Vaishnavas had set him up as an avatar. At any rate, I did not believe it. Then I went to Navadwip with Mathur. I thought that if Chaitanya were an avatar, there must be some signs of his manifestation, and that I would recognize them. I looked around with a view to seeing his divine manifestation and visited the deities in the houses of Senior Gosain and Junior Gosain, but found nothing. Everywhere I saw wooden images of Chaitanya standing with raised arms. I felt dejected and wondered why I had come. When I was about to board the boat to return, I had a wonderful vision of two beautiful teenaged boys.[4] I had never seen such beauty before. Their complexions were as bright as molten gold and they had halos round their heads. Smiling, they rushed towards me through the air, their arms raised. Immediately I cried out: 'Here they come! Here they come!' No sooner had I uttered those words than they came near and entered here (*pointing to his body*), and I fell down, unconscious. I would have fallen into the water, but Hriday was nearby and caught hold of me. Thus, I was shown many such things and became convinced that Chaitanya was a true avatar, a manifestation of divine power." The Master used the words "was shown many such things" because he had previously told us about his vision of Chaitanya singing in the streets of the city. We have described this elsewhere (see II.Appendix.26 and IV.7.2).

32. The Master's former opinion about Chaitanya: a vision at Navadwip changes his view.

In addition to visiting the holy places already mentioned, the Master once went to Kalna with Mathur. Many Bengali villages on the banks of the Ganges have become places of pilgrimage because they were touched by the holy feet of Chaitanya. Kalna is among these. Every visitor can feel this place to be full of grandeur because the royal dynasty of Burdwan established 108 Shiva temples and many monuments there. But at that time the Master had a different reason for visiting Kalna: He intended to meet Bhagavandas Babaji, a noted Vaishnava monk.

33. The Master's visit to Kalna.

Bhagavandas Babaji was then probably more than eighty years old. We do not know where he was born, nor do we have any information about his family. But everyone in Bengal had heard about his renunciation, self-surrender, and

34. Bhagavandas Babaji's renunciation, devotion, and power.

4. Chaitanya and Nityananda. — *Translator*

Bhagavandas Babaji's Ashrama at Kalna, which Ramakrishna visited in 1870.

devotion to God. Towards the end of his life, his feet were numb and paralyzed because of the austerities, japa, and meditation he had practised day and night, sitting motionless in one place. Despite his old age, illness, and near-inability to walk, Babaji's enthusiasm for chanting Hari's name, and the profuse tears he shed for love of God, did not decrease but rather increased day by day. The Vaishnava community of Kalna was rejuvenated by his presence, and many Vaishnava monks had an opportunity to pattern their lives on his vibrant example and to follow his spiritual instructions. Anyone who visited Babaji at that time deeply felt the accumulated effects of his lifelong austerities, renunciation, purity, and devotion, and returned home with the experience of wonderful bliss. People accepted as infallible truth whatever Babaji said about Chaitanya's religion of love and tried to translate his opinions into action.

So the perfected Babaji was not only busy with his own sadhana but also spent much time in spiritual discussions about how to improve the Vaishnava community, how Vaishnava ascetics could be blessed by implicitly practising the ideal of renunciation, and how ordinary householders could attain peace under the shelter of Chaitanya's religion of love. People would report to Babaji whatever happened in the Vaishnava communities — the good or bad conduct of the monks, and so on. He would listen to them and after reflection instruct them accordingly. Those who live a life of renunciation, austerity, and love always bind people with their invisible, spiritual power. People therefore obeyed Babaji's instructions without question and rushed to implement them immediately. Although he did not use spies, Babaji nonetheless observed all the activities within the Vaishnava communities, and everyone felt his influence. Under his spiritual influence, the faith and longing of simple folk increased day by day; and hypocrites, who were afraid in his presence, had an opportunity to reform themselves.

During the twelve years when the Master was practising severe austeri-

| 35. Religious movements in India during the Master's sadhana. |

ties, driven by intense longing for God, and the power of the guru was wonderfully manifest in him, various religious movements started in many parts of India. We have mentioned these elsewhere (see IV.5.11). The Harisabha and Brahmo Samaj movements started in Calcutta and its surrounding areas; Swami Dayananda began to propagate his own brand of Vedic religion, which turned into the Arya Samaj, in the Punjab and northwest India; the pure Vedanta movement, the Kartabhaja sect, and the Radha-Swami sect emerged in Bengal; and the Narayana-Swami order evolved in Gujarat. These religious movements originated and spread shortly before or after this period. It is not our intention to discuss these movements in detail here. We shall only narrate an event that took place in connection with the Master at a Harisabha service in Colootola, Calcutta.

One day the Master was invited to attend a Harisabha service at

36. The Master's visit to the Harisabha at Coolootola.

Coolootola. Hriday accompanied him. Some say that Pandit Vaishnavcharan, whom we mentioned earlier, was engaged in reading and expounding upon the Bhagavata there on that day and that the Master went there to listen to him. But we do not remember hearing from the Master that he went to listen to Vaishnavcharan. Be that as it may, when the Master arrived, someone was reading the Bhagavata, and others were listening attentively. The Master joined the audience and listened to the reading.

The members of the Harisabha considered themselves to be ardent

37. Recitation of the Bhagavata at the Harisabha gathering.

followers of Chaitanya. To remember this constantly, they put an *asana* [seat] on the altar and envisioned Chaitanya's presence there. They performed their worship, reading, and other congregational functions in front of that seat, which they called "Sri Chaitanya's Seat." Everyone bowed down to the seat with devotion, and no one was allowed to sit upon it. On this day, like any other, the reading was performed in front of the seat, which had been decorated with flowers and garlands. The reader was reading with devotion, believing himself to be reciting the glory of Hari to Chaitanya himself; and the devotees were excited to be drinking the nectar of the Lord's words while in Chaitanya's divine presence. The joy and devotion of the reader and the audience were enhanced a hundredfold by the Master's arrival.

While listening to the nectar-like words of the Bhagavata, the Master

38. The Master occupies Sri Chaitanya's Seat.

became overwhelmed and suddenly ran towards Sri Chaitanya's Seat. He stood upon it and went into such deep samadhi that there was not even the slightest sign of life in him. As they beheld the Master's wonderful and sweet smile, luminous face, and raised arms with fingers held up as seen in the common images of Chaitanya, the prominent devotees were convinced that the Master had become completely identified with Chaitanya in bhavamukha. Although there were external differences between his body and mind and those of Chaitanya with respect to time, place, and circumstance, the Master did not perceive these differences at all as he ascended to the plane of bhavamukha. The reader stopped and looked at the Master in wonder. Although most in the audience did not understand the Master's ecstasy, they were overpowered by indescribable awe and wonder and remained calm. No one could say anything, positive or negative. As they experienced indescribable bliss, all felt as if they had been carried away to an unknown realm by the powerful spiritual current caused by the Master. At first they were nonplussed but then were compelled by that indescribable phenomenon to burst forth loudly with "Haribol!" and to begin singing kirtan.

While discussing the nature of samadhi earlier (see III.7.6), we pointed out that when the mind goes into samadhi while experiencing the infinite divine mood connected with a particular name of God, it returns to the external world by means of that same name. We witnessed this phenomenon daily while living with the Master. The same thing happened here. When the Master heard the name of Hari sung in kirtan, he regained some body-consciousness. Filled with love and devotion, he then joined the kirtan party and began to dance gracefully in ecstasy, at times becoming calm and motionless in samadhi as he experienced overflowing spiritual emotion. The Master's participation enhanced the enthusiasm of the audience a hundred-fold and they became wild in kirtan. Who could then judge whether it was right or wrong for the Master to occupy Sri Chaitanya's Seat? After a long time spent in ecstatic dancing and singing the glories of Hari and Chaitanya, the crowd ended that day's exalted performance amid joyous shouts of the Lord's name. After a while the Master returned to Dakshineswar.

Rising to a higher plane of spirituality through the divine influence of the Master's singing and dancing, the members of the congregation stopped their fault-finding for the time being. But when the Master left, they reverted to their usual state. In fact, this is a defect in those religions that teach the path of God-realization only through emotion and devotion rather than through knowledge and discrimination. The aspirants of this devotional path may rise easily to a higher blissful plane of spirituality while dancing and singing the name of Hari, but the next moment they return to a lower plane. They are not to be blamed because it is the nature of the body and mind, which exist within prakriti, to become depressed after being excited. It is a law of nature that a wave rises and falls, and after elation comes depression. When the exalted spiritual emotion ended, the members of the Harisabha, influenced by their previous nature and habits, began to criticize the Master's behaviour. One group was in favour of the Master's occupying Sri Chaitanya's Seat while in bhavamukha; the other group vehemently opposed it. As a result, an acrimonious debate ensued between the parties and there was no solution.

39. This creates a commotion in the Vaishnava community.

Gradually, the news spread throughout the Vaishnava communities by word of mouth. Bhagavandas Babaji also heard about it, but the matter did not end there. Some members of the Harisabha community thought that this kind of situation might happen again in the future, and some shrewd hypocrite who desired name and fame might feign devotion and occupy the holy seat for selfish reasons. So they went to Babaji to ask how that seat could be protected.

The perfected Babaji was terribly annoyed when he heard that the seat of his Chosen Deity had been desecrated by a stranger named Ramakrishna. He was so enraged that he did not hesitate to bitterly reproach the Master and call him a hypocrite. Babaji's annoyance and anger

40. Bhagavandas is annoyed when he hears that Sri Chaitanya's Seat is occupied.

doubled when he saw the members of Harisabha, and he scolded them for the offence of allowing this sacrilegious act to take place in front of them. Later, when his anger abated, he instructed them to take all precautionary measures so that no one could do this in the future. But the person who was the target of this commotion knew nothing of it at all.

Some days after the incident, the Master went to Kalna of his own accord with Hriday and Mathur. After their boat arrived at the Kalna ghat in the morning, Mathur busied himself finding food and lodging for the party. Meanwhile, the Master went to see the town with Hriday; after obtaining Bhagavandas Babaji's address, they visited his ashrama.

41. The Master's visit to Bhagavandas' ashrama.

Whenever the childlike Master visited someone he did not know, he always felt an indescribable fear and bashfulness at first. We noticed this trait quite often. He had the same reaction when he visited Babaji. Asking Hriday to go on ahead, he covered himself from head to foot with a piece of cloth and then entered the ashrama behind Hriday. Hriday reached Babaji and after bowing down to him, said: "My uncle loses himself in the name of God. He's been doing it for a long time now. He has come to pay a visit to you."

42. Hriday tells Babaji about the Master.

Hriday said that as soon as he approached Babaji, he found evidence of the power that had evolved from his sadhana. Before Hriday could speak, he heard Babaji say, "It seems to me that some great soul has come to the ashrama." After this, Babaji looked around and found no newcomer except Hriday. He then continued talking to the visitors before him about a certain Vaishnava sadhu who had done something wrong and what action should be taken against him. Babaji exclaimed indignantly that he would personally confiscate the sadhu's rosary and expel him from the Vaishnava community. At that moment the Master arrived, and after bowing to Babaji he humbly joined the visitors seated there. As his body was wrapped in a cloth, no one could see his face clearly. When the Master sat down, Hriday introduced him to Babaji as described above. Babaji then broke off his denunciation of the erring sadhu, saluted the Master, and asked politely where he and Hriday had come from.

43. Babaji is annoyed at a monk's misdeed.

Hriday noticed that Babaji was telling his beads when he was not speaking, so he asked: "Sir, why do you tell your beads, now that you have attained enlightenment? You no longer need to." We do not know whether Hriday asked that question on behalf of the Master or on his own initiative. Probably he did it on his own. Because Hriday was always engaged in the service of the Master and therefore associated with many people that he knew, of high and low degree, Hriday had developed the presence of mind and ability to speak and raise questions appropriate to the time and

44. Babaji keeps his ego to teach people.

circumstances. In response to Hriday's question, Babaji first expressed his humility and then said: "It is true that I don't need to practise such disciplines for myself. But I must tell my beads to set an example for others. It is extremely important. Otherwise they might go astray in trying to imitate me."

Like a child, the Master always depended solely on the Divine Mother in

| 45. Noticing Babaji's annoyance and egotism, the Master, while in ecstasy, protests. |

every respect, so his reliance on Her became effortless, natural, and inherent in him. As a result he could not do anything to save his ego, and it pained him to see or hear anyone speaking or acting out of egotism. He would use the word "I" very seldom when speaking as a servant of God; but other than those few instances he could not utter that word as we do. Those who knew the Master even for a short while were amazed and moved by his wonderful nature. And when they saw how annoyed the Master became when someone expressed his ego by saying "I shall do it," they wondered what wrong the person had done to irritate the Master so.

The first thing the Master heard when he came to Bhagavandas was that he would confiscate a sadhu's rosary and expel him from the community. A little later, he heard that it was in order to teach others that Babaji had continued telling his beads and wearing marks on his body. Thus, when Babaji said repeatedly, "*I* will expel that sadhu; *I* will teach people; *I* have not given up telling beads and wearing marks," the simple-hearted Master could suppress his annoyance no more. He could no longer remain seated like a courteous and gentle guest. He rose to his feet, demanding: "Is that how you think of yourself even now? You think *you* teach people? You think *you* will expel this man from your community? You think *you* can decide to give up telling your beads or not? Who made *you* a teacher? Do you think *you* can teach the world unless the Lord who made it allows you to?" The Master's cloth had fallen from his shoulders to the ground as had the cloth from around his loins. A wonderful radiance shone from his face. He was in such ecstasy that he was not aware of what he was saying and to whom he was speaking. After those few words he became overwhelmed with emotion and went into samadhi.

To this point everyone had shown love and respect for the perfected

| 46. Babaji humbly accepts the words of the Master. |

Babaji, and no one had been capable of protesting his words or pointing out his shortcomings — or bold enough to do so. The Master's conduct surprised him at first. Under such circumstances ordinary human beings would become angry and try to take revenge, but Babaji did not react that way. The simplicity that had developed in him from his austerities helped him to realize the true meaning of Sri Ramakrishna's words. He sincerely believed that there was no doer other than God in this world. An egotistical man may think that he is doing everything, but truly he is nothing but a slave of circumstances; he can understand and accomplish only what he has been permitted to. Let worldly people do whatever they like, but devotees and spiritual aspirants should not forget even for a moment that God is the doer. If they do, they will deviate from the right path and fall. Those powerful words of the Master awakened Babaji's insight intensely, and he recognized his own shortcomings and became humble and modest. Moreover, the extraordinary manifestation of a spiritual mood in Sri Ramakrishna convinced Babaji that the Master was not an ordinary person.

We can easily infer that their spiritual conversation caused a wonderful current of divine bliss to flow there. Babaji was moved by seeing Sri Ramakrishna's repeated ecstasies and overflowing bliss during their discussion. Furthermore, he saw in Sri Ramakrishna the vivid manifestation of mahabhava that he had been struggling to understand for a long time by studying the scriptures, so he felt a deep love and respect for Sri Ramakrishna. When he heard that this was the paramahamsa of Dakshineswar who out of ecstasy had occupied Sri Chaitanya's Seat at the Harisabha congregation at Coolootola, there was no limit to his sorrow and repentance for the bitter reproaches he had used against the Master. Humbly, he bowed down to Sri Ramakrishna and begged his forgiveness. Thus, the spiritual meeting between the Master and Bhagavandas Babaji ended that day.

47. The loving conversation between the Master and Bhagavandas. Mathur's service to the monks of the ashrama.

After a while, the Master and Hriday returned to Mathur and told him the whole story, praising the advanced spiritual state of Babaji. After this, Mathur also went to visit Babaji. He made arrangements for a worship service of the deity in the ashrama and a special festival with a daylong feast.

Chapter 4

The Master as a Guru:
Conclusion

Though I am unborn and eternal by nature, and though I am the Lord of all beings, yet, subjugating My prakriti, I accept birth through my own maya.

Whenever there is a decline of dharma, O Bharata, and a rise of adharma, I incarnate Myself. For the protection of the good, for the destruction of the wicked, and for the establishment of dharma, I am born in every age. — GITA 4:6-8

THE VEDAS AND OTHER SCRIPTURES SAY THAT THE KNOWERS of Brahman are omniscient.

1. The Vedas declare that a knower of Brahman is omniscient: We argue about this without understanding.	No false thoughts arise in their minds as they do in the minds of ordinary human beings. Whenever they want to know or understand anything, it immediately becomes visible to their inner vision and they become aware of its essential nature.

When we used to listen to the scriptures without understanding them, we took an opposite view and argued in vain. We said: "If it were true that knowers of Brahman are omniscient, then why were the ancient knowers of Brahman in India so ignorant of the physical sciences? Did they know that water is made of a combination of hydrogen and oxygen? Why did they not tell us that we could get news from the United States with the help of electric power within four or five hours [via telegraph in 1911] that otherwise takes several months to reach us [by boat]? Or why did they not know that people would fly like birds with the help of aeroplanes?"

After listening to the Master, we realized that we would fail if we tried to understand the scriptures in that manner. Yet that passage would surely appear to be true if studied according to its context. The Master explained it by using a couple of rural examples. He said: "When rice is boiling in a pot, if you take one grain and press it between your fingers, you instantly know whether all the grains in the pot are soft. Why is this? You haven't pressed all the grains one by one. How then do you come to this conclusion? Similarly, by examining two or three things in the world, one can know whether the world is eternal or transient, real or unreal. A man is born, lives for some time, and then dies. The same is true of a cow and a tree. After thus observing one thing after another, you come to the conclusion that whatever has name and form follows the same law. The earth, the sun, the moon, and so on have names and forms: they are therefore subject to the same law. Thus, you become aware that everything in this universe is of a similar nature. Don't you then know the nature of everything in this world? When you thus realize that this world is transient and unreal, you can't love it anymore; you will remove it from your mind and will be without desire. As soon as you give up desire for the world, you will see God, the source of the world. So when a man has the vision of God, tell me: Is he omniscient or not?"

2. The Master explains the truth of this: "By pressing one grain of rice from the pot, one can verify whether all the grains are soft."

When the Master explained it in those words, we understood: "This is true indeed. A knower of Brahman becomes omniscient in a way. When we know the origin, the middle, and the end of a particular thing, we say we have knowledge of that thing. If one knows the world in the same way, that too is knowledge. That understanding is equally true of everything in the world. So one should consider it knowledge of all objects of the world. One who is endowed with that knowledge is indeed omniscient. Therefore, what the scriptures say is quite true."

3. Omniscience about an object means understanding it from its origin to its end; one attains omniscience about the world after God-realization.

We can get a rough understanding of the scriptural passage, "All the desires of a knower of Brahman come to pass and are fulfilled." We realize from everyday experience that we can attain knowledge of a particular object by studying it with complete concentration. It is therefore not surprising that when knowers of Brahman, who have completely mastered and controlled their minds, focus all of their mental powers on understanding a particular thing, they can very easily achieve knowledge of that thing. But there is something to be considered here: Can one who is fully convinced that the world and the objects in it are transient, and has realized through love the all-powerful God, the source of

4. It is true that the desire of a knower of Brahman is always fulfilled. This can be understood in light of the Master's life: "I couldn't bring the mind back to this cage of flesh and bone."

the world, ever have the desire to drive a train or build a factory to manufacture destructive weapons? If it is impossible for such desires to arise in the mind of such a person, that person cannot build those machines or factories. We have witnessed the truth of this in the Master's divine company. It actually becomes impossible to bring up those worldly propensities in such a mind.

At this time in Cossipore the Master was suffering terribly from cancer. Swami Vivekananda and some of us tearfully implored the Master to apply his mental powers to freeing himself from disease for our sakes, but he could not make such an effort. He said that although he tried to do this, he could not create a strong resolve in his mind at all. He told us: "I could by no means bring this mind back from Satchidananda and put it in this cage of flesh and bone. I've always considered this body to be trifling and contemptible, and have offered my mind to the Divine Mother forever. Now, my children, how can I bring it back from Her and put it on the body?"

It will be easier for the reader to understand this subject if we mention

5. Another example from the Master's life: "The mind is in a high state; I cannot bring it down."

another incident. One morning at about 10:00 the Master went to Balaram Basu's house at Baghbazar. This visit was prearranged, so Narendra and other young devotees met the Master there. At times they talked with the Master, and at times discussed various topics among themselves. While discussing how to see subtle things beyond the senses, someone mentioned the microscope. There are many subtle things that cannot be seen with the naked eye but can be seen with a microscope. A very tiny hair looks like a stick when seen through this instrument, and every hair of the body looks like the hollow stem of a papaya leaf. The Master expressed a boyish eagerness to see a couple of things through a microscope, so the devotees decided that they would borrow one and show it to the Master that afternoon.

On inquiry the devotees learned that their dear friend Dr. Bipinbehari Ghosh, a cousin of Swami Premananda, had recently received a microscope from the Calcutta Medical College as a reward for passing a medical examination with honours. A man was sent to ask him to bring that instrument so the Master could see it. Bipin got the message and arrived with the instrument at about 4:00 p.m. He set it up and invited the Master to look through it.

The Master got up and went to the microscope but returned without looking through it. When he was asked why, he said, "The mind is now in such a high plane that I can by no means bring it down to a lower plane to see things." We waited quite a while to see if the Master's mind would come down. But that day the Master's mind did not return from that exalted spiritual plane, so he could not see anything through the microscope. Bipin showed it to some of us and finally left with the instrument.

When the Master's mind transcended body-consciousness and travelled

6. The Master saw every-
thing in two different
ways from two different
planes of consciousness
— the nondual and the
dual. From the first, he
saw with supersensuous
vision and from the sec-
ond, sense perception.

into higher and higher spiritual states, he had extraordinary divine visions. When he reached the highest
nondualistic plane, having completely risen beyond
the body, his heart and his senses stopped functioning
for a time. His body lay like a corpse on the floor, all
functions of the mind became completely still, and he
remained fully identified with the indivisible Satchidananda. As the Master gradually descended to the
lower planes from that high state, he would again feel "this is my body" like
other people, and again his eyes could see, ears hear, skin feel, and mind think.

An eminent philosopher of the West had a glimpse of the mind ascending

7. Ordinary people
perceive everything in
the second way.

to and descending from samadhi, and then
expressed his belief that within the human body
consciousness is not always present in the same
degree.[1] This reasonable view was also held by the ancient rishis of India. In
fact human beings' true home lies in the highest nondual plane, but ordinary
people have completely forgotten this and have a firm conviction that
knowledge can be acquired only through the senses. Satisfied with this, they
have anchored their boats to this world without attempting to cross the
ocean of maya. World teachers, adhikarikas, and celebrated avatars like the
Master are born in every age to remove this delusion by demonstrating
another way in their own lives and transcending the world of the senses.
Such is the teaching of the Vedas and of other scriptures.

It is now clear that the Master was not limited to seeing people and things of

8. The Master cites two
kinds of vision.

the world from a single perspective, as we are. As he
ascended to higher and higher planes, his view of
people and things changed accordingly. It was there-
fore impossible for him to harbour the one-sided beliefs and narrow attitudes
that we have. That is why we could not understand his words or his thoughts,
although ours were clear to him. We know a man as a man, a cow as a cow, and
a mountain as a mountain. He saw a man, a cow, and a mountain as they truly
are, and at the same time he saw the indivisible Satchidananda, the cause of
the world, shining through them. The only differences between a man, a cow,
and a mountain are the greater and lesser degrees to which Satchidananda is
visible through the veil of ignorance that covers each of them to varying extents.

The Master told us: "I see all things — trees, plants, people, cows, grass,

9. The Master narrates
his vision: "The Divine
Mother peeps through
different disguises. She
has even become the
prostitute Ramani."

water — as if they are covered with different sheaths,
like pillow cases. Haven't you seen them? Some are
made of coarse cloth dyed red, some of finely
patterned cloth, and others of different kinds of cloth;
some are quadrangles and some round. Everything in

1. Ralph Waldo Emerson: "Consciousness ever moves along a graded plane."

the universe is just like that. Just as there is only one substance — cotton — stuffed into all those pillow cases, so the same indivisible Satchidananda exists within the sheaths of people, cows, grass, water, mountains, and everything else. Look, I see clearly that the Divine Mother has covered Herself with different wrappers — She has assumed various forms and is peeping through them. For a time I experienced a state in which I saw everything like that all the time. Without understanding my condition, people tried to correct and pacify me. Ramlal's mother and others began to cry out in grief and to weep. When I looked at them, I saw that it was the same Mother (*pointing to the Kali temple*) who had assumed those forms and was doing all that. Watching their behaviour, I rolled with laughter and exclaimed, 'Mother, you are acting well!'

"One day when I was meditating, seated in the Kali temple, I could not bring the Mother's form to my mind at all. Then I saw that She had appeared in the form of Ramani, a prostitute who came to bathe at the Dakshineswar ghat, and was peeping from behind the water pot before the image. I laughed and said: 'O Mother, you have a desire to become Ramani today! All right. Accept my worship today in this form.' Thus, She made me understand: 'I am also the prostitute. There is none other than Me.' Another day while passing through Mechuabazar Street by carriage, I saw Her in the form of a prostitute. She was dressed nicely, wore jewellery and a small ornament on her forehead, and her hair was braided. Standing on a veranda, She was smoking tobacco from a gold-plated hubble-bubble and enticing passers-by with her charms. Surprised, I exclaimed: 'Mother, here You are in this form!' Saying so, I bowed down to Her." We have forgotten to see people and things from a higher plane of consciousness. How is it then possible for us to understand the Master's experiences?

When the Master remained in the normal plane of body-consciousness that we occupy, his intellect and powers of observation could thoroughly grasp many more things than ours could because his mind did not contain even the slightest desire for selfish enjoyment. The intense desire for sense objects that we all have causes objects of desire to appear shining in front of us at all times, whether we are eating, resting, seeing, hearing,

10. The Master's senses, mind, and intellect were keener than those of ordinary people because of his detachment from sense pleasures. A comparison between the actions of an attached mind and a detached mind.

walking, sleeping, or talking with others. For that reason our minds disregard unpleasant objects and people and are more attracted to pleasant ones. So we have no opportunity to know the nature of objects and people that we ignore. Thus, we spend our entire lives making or attempting to make particular things and persons our own. That is why we see in ordinary people such a range in ability to learn. Although we all have eyes, ears, and other sense organs, can we apply them equally to all objects and thereby acquire knowledge? Those among us who have less selfishness and desire for enjoyment are capable of achieving knowledge of all subjects more easily than others.

It will not be out of place here to cite a couple of examples that illustrate

11. Examples of the keenness of the Master's mind.

how sharp the Master's power of observation was, even in the normal plane. The Master's amazingly keen powers of observation were evident in the examples, metaphors, and similies he used to explain difficult spiritual truths. With them he would create vivid pictures and convince his audience of the solutions to particularly intricate problems.

For example, one day we were discussing Sankhya philosophy.

(1) He easily explains the Sankhya philosophy: "The master and mistress of a house during a wedding."

Describing the origin of the universe from Purusha and Prakriti, the Master told us: "According to Sankhya, Purusha is not the doer: It is static. Prakriti does everything; Purusha is a witness to those actions. But Prakriti cannot do anything by herself — she needs the help of Purusha." The Master's audience included office clerks, accountants, doctors, lawyers, deputy magistrates, and schoolboys and college students — none of them were scholars. When they heard the Master say this, they stared at one another. The Master understood their confusion and said: "Hello, haven't you seen what happens in the house during a wedding ceremony? After issuing orders, the master sits and smokes tobacco from a hubble-bubble. The mistress runs around the house and supervises all the activities. Her sari is stained with turmeric and she welcomes the ladies. With hand gestures and animated face she reports to her husband from time to time: 'This has been done this way, and that, that way. This is to be done, and the other not to be done.' While smoking, the master listens and nodding his head, he assents to everything, saying, 'Yes, yes.' It is just like that." All laughed after listening to the Master's explanation of the Sankhya philosophy, but they understood it.

Another topic arose: "According to Vedanta, Brahman and Its power —

(2) He explains Brahman and maya: "The same snake is sometimes in motion and sometimes motionless."

Purusha and Prakriti — are identical; that is, they are not two different entities. The same substance appears sometimes as Purusha and sometimes as Prakriti." When he saw that we did not understand this, the Master said: "Do you know how it is? It's like a snake — sometimes it moves, and sometimes it remains motionless. When it's still, it represents the nature of Purusha. Prakriti is then united with Purusha and they have become one. When the snake moves, Prakriti is then working, as it were, separating herself from Purusha." As we visualized this, we asked ourselves: "Why could we not understand this simple thing before?"

Someone once raised a question: "Maya is God's power and dwells in

(3) God is not bound by maya: "A snake has poison in its fangs, but it does not die."

God. Is God then bound by maya as we are?" The Master replied: "No, not at all. Although maya belongs to God and dwells always with God, He is never bound by maya. Look, whoever is bitten by a snake dies. But there is always poison in the fangs of the snake, and the snake eats and gulps saliva through its mouth, but the snake does not die. It is just like that." Everyone present realized that this was indeed possible.

It is clear from these examples that when the Master dwelt in the normal plane of consciousness, nothing could hide its true nature from his keen sight. Changes in external nature could not hide themselves from his sight, much less changes in human nature. Of course, we are not referring to those changes in external nature that can be detected and understood only through instruments. Another amazing fact is that extraordinary changes and unusual manifestations in external nature that are not generally noticed by people were invariably seen immediately by the Master when he was in the normal plane of consciousness. It is by the will of God that all kinds of objects are manifested within creation; He directly controls the destinies of everything and everyone in the world. It seems it was to impress this idea into the Master's mind that the Divine Mother presented him with exceptional manifestations of nature that are beyond the general laws. From the visions he had since his childhood, we get the clear meaning of his words, "If He so desires, He who made the law can replace it with another law." It will not be out of place here to mention a few examples.

> 12. Observing extraordinary changes in nature, the Master is convinced that God changes His laws.

In college we were amazed when we read about some modern scientific inventions relating to electricity. One day out of boyish mischievousness, we raised that topic in the Master's presence and began to discuss it with one another. Hearing the word *electricity* repeatedly, the Master was as curious as a boy and asked us: "Hello, what are you talking about? What do you mean by *electictic*?"[2] We laughed when we heard his childish pronunciation of the English word that was strange to him. We then described to him the general laws of electricity and also the uses for the lightning conductor: Because lightning always strikes the highest point, the lightning rod should be a little higher than the house, and so on.

> 13. Referring to the lightning rod, the Master relates what he himself has seen: "Lightning struck a thatched hut adjacent to a three-storeyed building."

The Master listened to us attentively and then said: "But I once saw that wretched lightning strike a thatched hut instead of the three-storeyed building next to it. How do you explain that? Can these things be said precisely? All laws came into existence by the will of God, and they can change as He wills." While trying to explain natural laws to the Master we, like Mathur, could not find a suitable answer to the Master's question. We told him that lightning gravitated towards the three-storeyed house, but some unknown event caused it to suddenly change its course and strike the hut. We explained that there might be one or two exceptions to this law, but otherwise it is as we

---

2. Sri Ramakrishna knew only a few words of the English language. — *Translator*

said — lightning has struck the highest point in thousands of other places. We pointed out various examples, but the Master would not accept that natural events take place according to inviolable laws. He said: "You say that the lightning conductor is effective in thousands of places. Well, let it be. But there are a few exceptions, proving that laws change."

Botanists have recorded some exceptions to the rule that plants that

| 14. He saw a white hibiscus on a red hibiscus tree. |

generally produce either white or red flowers must do so exclusively. However, these exceptions are so rare that it is no exaggeration to say that ordinary people have never seen it. But look at what happened to the Master: Once there was a controversy between the Master and Mathur about the inviolability of the laws of nature. The Master held that these laws could change by God's will. At that time he found an example [a white bloom on a red hibiscus tree] and he showed it to Mathur (see III.6.8).

The Master saw a stone become conscious.[3] He saw a man's tailbone elon-

| 15. As the Master observes uncommon events in nature, he is convinced that the whole universe is the playground of the Divine Mother. |

gate a little like an animal's tail and later shrink to its natural length (see II.8.8). He saw a male body function to some extent like a female body when under the influence of a feminine spiritual attitude, and then return to normal when that mood subsided (see II.14.16). He also saw ghosts and celestial beings. We have heard about many such events in the Master's life. Imitating the West, we consider Nature — the creative force of the world — to be insentient and completely devoid of intelligence. So we remain at ease, saying that those uncommon events in nature are natural aberrations, and we think that we understand all the laws by which nature is regulated. But the Master had a different attitude. He saw the whole of nature — external and internal — as nothing but the sport of the living Divine Mother and considered those uncommon events as emanating from Her particular will. It was evident that this conviction gave the Master more peace and joy than we enjoy, if nothing else. We have already mentioned a few such instances in the Master's life and will mention some more later.

It was only after observing each thing and each person from two stand-

| 16. From a higher plane of consciousness, the Master could determine the degree of spirituality in a particular place. |

points, as mentioned before, that the Master would come to a definite conclusion. He did not form any opinions based on observations made from the ordinary plane of consciousness, as we do. So it is certain that he made his evaluations from both perspectives whenever he went on pilgrimage and met holy people. When the Master was in the higher plane of consciousness, he could see and feel the degree to

3. After a vision of the Divine Mother, Sri Ramakrishna said, "If this vision of mine is true, let this rock [which was in front of the nahabat] jump three times." The rock actually jumped. — *Translator*

which spirituality was concentrated in a particular sacred place, or how much power that place had to raise the human mind to a higher plane. The Master's divine and pure mind was free from attachment to sense objects, so it was a wonderful instrument for detecting those subtle things. When he entered holy places or temples, his mind would immediately rise to the higher plane of consciousness and reveal to him the divine presence in those places. It was when the Master's mind had ascended to the higher plane of consciousness that he saw Golden Varanasi and realized how a jiva became free from bondage after dying there. He also experienced the tangible divine presence in Vrindaban, and he clearly perceived that Chaitanya's subtle manifestation exists in Navadwip even now.

It is said that Chaitanya was the first to experience a manifestation of the divine presence in Vrindaban. Long before his advent, the holy spots of Vraja were almost forgotten. When Chaitanya travelled in those places, he ascended to the higher plane of consciousness and experienced whatever Krishna's lila [divine play] had occurred there. In fact, Bhagavan Krishna enacted the same lila long before in the same place. His disciples — Rupa, Sanatan, and others — were the first to accept these revelations, and later all Indians believed what the disciples told them. We could not have understood how Chaitanya discovered Vrindaban in that way, nor would we have entertained the possibility of such a thing, had we not seen the Master's power of accurately detecting and understanding things and persons from a higher plane of consciousness. Now we believe it to some extent. The reader will understand what we mean if we relate examples of this from the Master's life.

17. It is well known how Chaitanya discovered the places of Krishna's *lila* in Vrindaban.

Hriday's home was in Sihar, not far from Kamarpukur. We have already told the reader that the Master sometimes spent time there when he visited Kamarpukur. Once during a visit to Sihar, Rajaram [Hriday's youngest brother] had a dispute with a villager concerning a business affair. The argument gradually developed into a physical assault and Rajaram hit his opponent's head with a hubble-bubble that was at hand. The wounded man filed a criminal lawsuit. The incident took place in front of the Master, so the man called the Master as a witness because he knew the Master to be a truthful and holy man. So the Master had to go to Vana-Vishnupur to give testimony. After the incident, the Master severely scolded Rajaram for becoming blind with rage. When they arrived in Vana-Vishnupur, he told Rajaram: "Look, you somehow settle with the plaintiff by giving him money; otherwise the case will go against you. I can by no means lie. When asked, I will tell what I have seen and what I know." Frightened, Rajaram settled the case amicably. The Master took that opportunity to visit the town of Vana-Vishnupur.

18. A similar incident happens in the Master's life: While in ecstasy he sees the original image of the goddess Mrinmayi in Vana-Vishnupur.

That Vishnupur was once a very prosperous place is evident by its large

19. The condition of
Vishnupur.

population and the existence of Lalbandh, Krishna-bandh, and other large lakes, many beautiful temples, and the ruins of many old temples. The town has clean, wide, paved roads, and a big bazar with many shops. There is a constant flow of people in connection with business. In times past the rulers of Vishnupur were extremely powerful, virtuous, and fond of learning. Vishnupur was also once noted for its music school.

Shortly after Rupa, Sanatan, and other companions of Chaitanya had

20. Madanmohan.

passed away, the royal dynasty of Vishnupur converted to Vaishnavism. The image of Madan-mohan Krishna that is installed at Baghbazar in Calcutta previously belonged to this royal family. It is said that Gokul Chandra Mitra of Baghbazar once lent a huge amount of money to a ruler of Vishnupur. He was so charmed by the image of Madanmohan that when the time for repayment came, he asked for that image instead of the money.

In addition to the image of Madanmohan, the rulers of Vishnupur also

21. Mrinmayi.

installed an ancient image of a goddess named Mrin-mayi. People said that the goddess Mrinmayi was a living presence. After the royal dynasty declined, a madwoman destroyed the image. Some family members reinstalled a new statue similar to the old one.

After he had visited various temples in Vishnupur, the Master was on his way to see the goddess Mrinmayi when he went into ecstasy and saw Her face. When he entered the temple and saw the newly installed image, he noticed that it was not the same image he had seen in his ecstatic vision. He could not understand the reason for this. Later, upon inquiry it was learned that the new image was not exactly like the old one. To display his skill, the sculptor of the new image had made the face look different. The broken head of the old image had been carefully preserved by a brahmin who kept it in his house. Shortly afterwards, that devout brahmin engaged a sculptor to make a new image using the old head. The brahmin installed this image in a beautiful spot near the shore of Lalbandh and worshiped Her daily.

It would be good to relate here a few examples of the Master's ability to

22. The Master's ability
to detect a person's
mood and intentions:
first example.

detect the moods and intentions of people who visited him. We mentioned earlier that the Master loved Swami Brahmananda as if he were his own son. One day Brahmananda and the Master were discussing various things, standing on the northern side of the long veranda to the east of the Master's room. As they were talking, they observed a coach drawn by two horses enter the gate of the temple garden and come towards them. A few gentlemen were seated in the phaeton. The Master immediately knew that the coach belonged to a wealthy man who was famous in

Calcutta. At that time many people from Calcutta came to see the Master, so he and Swami Brahmananda were not surprised by the visit.

As soon as the Master saw that phaeton, however, he was horrified and hurriedly retreated to his room. Swami Brahmananda was surprised by his reaction and followed him. The Master told him: "Go to them. If they want to come here, tell them that they can't see me now." When Brahmananda returned to the veranda as instructed, the visitors approached him and asked, "Does not a sadhu live here?" Swami Brahmananda said: "Sri Ramakrishna? Yes, he lives here. May I know the purpose of your visit?" One of the visitors replied: "One of our relatives is seriously ill, and his disease is not abating at all. We have come here because this holy man may be kind enough to give us some medicine." Swami Brahmananda replied: "You have been misinformed. He [Sri Ramakrishna] never gives medicine to anyone. Perhaps you have heard about Durgananda Brahmachari. He indeed gives medicine. He lives in a hut at the Panchavati. Please go there and you will see him."

When the visitors left, the Master told Swami Brahmananda: "I saw such horrible tamas in them that I couldn't look at them. How could I talk to such people? So fear drove me away."

We saw the Master regularly ascend to a higher plane of consciousness, where he could see greater or lesser manifestations of spirituality in a particular place, thing, or person. Whatever spirituality the Master perceived did in fact exist in them. We verified this repeatedly and ever afterwards trusted his words. We shall mention a second and a third example regarding his perception from the higher plane. We will then describe for the reader what the Master experienced from the normal plane of consciousness in holy places.

From his childhood, the large-hearted Swami Vivekananda would

23. Second example: Swami Vivekananda takes his classmates to Dakshineswar.

become heartsick at the misery of others. Whenever he benefited by some action, he would encourage his relatives and friends to do the same thing; and when someone helped him in a particular matter, he would ask his benefactor to help others he knew. This was Swamiji's nature in matters of education, religion, and everything else. We find evidence of this in Swamiji's actions when he was a youth. In college, he organized meetings and associations with his classmates to practise meditation and prayer at different places on a regular basis. When he became acquainted with Maharshi Devendra Nath Tagore and Keshab Chandra Sen, the leaders of the Brahmo Samaj, he took some of his classmates to see them.

After meeting the Master and seeing his extraordinary purity, renunciation, and love of God, it became a sort of religious vow for Swamiji to bring his intimate classmates to meet the Master. Let no one conclude from our statement that Swamiji took his casual acquaintances to the Master. He brought to Dakshineswar only those whom he had known for a long time and considered to be of good character and religiously inclined.

Swamiji thus introduced many of his friends to the Master. But the Master,
with his divine insight, looked within them and some-
times arrived at a different assessment than Swamiji's,
as we heard from time to time from both the Master
and Swamiji. Swamiji said: "After accepting me, the Master bestowed his
grace by giving me spiritual instructions. But he did not do the same for my
friends, and I insisted that he do so. Because I was young, I would sometimes
argue with him on this point. I said: 'Sir, God is not partial; He does not bestow
grace on one person and withhold it from another. Why will you not then
accept them as you did me? Just as everyone can become a learned pandit by
willpower and self-effort, similarly, all can definitely cultivate spirituality and
attain God.' To this, the Master replied: 'What can I do, my child? The Divine
Mother is showing me that they have bestial tendencies, like bulls. They won't
attain spirituality in this life. What can I do? What do you say? Can any man
become what he wishes to be by mere will and effort?' But who then had the
patience to listen to the Master? I responded: 'What do you mean, sir? Can't one
become as one wishes to be if one wills it and makes an effort? Surely one can. I
cannot accept your words on this.' The Master reiterated: 'Whether you believe
it or not, the Mother is showing me that.' At that time I did not believe what he
said. As time passed, however, and I gained more experience, I understood
more and more that what the Master had said was right and I was wrong."

Swamiji said that it was through testing and evaluating the Master that he
gradually believed in his words. It will not be out of
place here to narrate another incident that Swamiji
told us in regard to his testing of the Master's words
and conduct. After hearing from Swamiji about
Pandit Shashadhar Tarkachudamani, the Master went to see him on the day
of the Chariot Festival in 1885 (see IV.5.12-13,15-16). The Master told the
pandit that only those who had received a command directly from the
Divine Mother were truly entitled to preach religion and that the grand words
of other famous so-called preachers were in vain. He then asked for a glass of
water to drink. We are not sure whether the Master asked for that water to
quench his thirst or if he had some other purpose: He once told us that it was
inauspicious for a householder if a sadhu, a sannyasin, a guest, or a fakir left
that person's house without eating or drinking anything. So whenever the
Master visited anyone's home, he always asked for something to eat or drink
if that person forgot to offer anything.

As soon as the Master asked for water, a man wearing religious marks and
a rosary respectfully brought a glass to him. The Master tried to drink it but
could not. Another person saw that and brought him a new glass of water,
removing the other one. The Master drank a little from the new glass, then
took his leave of the pandit. Everyone thought that the Master could not
drink the first glass of water because there was something in it.

24. "Even with effort one cannot become what one wishes."

25. Third example: While visiting Pandit Shashadhar, the Master asks for water to drink.

Swamiji said that he was seated very close to the Master at that time and saw clearly that there was nothing in the water, yet the Master had refused to drink it. While investigating the cause of this, Swamiji hypothesized that the water had been polluted by coming in contact with an impure person. He had previously heard the Master say that it was impossible for him to accept food or drink from people who were worldly-minded; who had dishonestly earned money by cheating, robbery, or doing harm to others; or who wore religious marks in order to deceive others and enjoy lust and gold. The Master's hands might move to accept the offered food or drink, but invariably they would contract and he would immediately become aware of that person's true nature.

Swamiji further said that when that thought arose in his mind he decided to ascertain the truth of the matter. When the Master asked Swamiji to accompany him, he said, "I have urgent business, so I can't come." He escorted the Master to his carriage and then left. The younger brother of that man who wore religious marks was known to Swamiji, so he called on him privately and asked him about his elder brother's character. When asked, the brother hesitated, then replied, "How can I speak about my elder brother's shortcomings?" Swamiji confided to us: "I understood the truth from that. Later, I asked another person whom I knew in that household and learned everything from him. I was then fully convinced of this matter and wondered how the Master could see into people's minds."

If we want to know how the Master could detect or understand the inherent good or bad qualities of all things while dwelling on the normal plane of consciousness, we must first understand his mental constitution. Then we must learn how he developed a fixed standard by which he could judge all things and arrive at correct conclusions about them. We have already given the reader some hints regarding this in different places throughout this book, so now it will suffice to make brief mention of it.

26. The nature of the Master's mental constitution, and how he evaluated every thing and every being.

We noticed that the Master's mind was not attached to any worldly object, so whenever he decided to accept or reject anything, his mind would immediately unite with or separate from that thing. Once it was separated, he never again looked at that object in all his life. The Master's unique steadfastness, powerful discrimination, and one-pointed concentration gave him full control over his mind. As a result, he could focus it firmly on any particular thing for any particular length of time and at any particular place according to his will. He never allowed his mind even for a moment to think of or imagine anything else. Whenever he accepted or rejected anything, part of his mind would immediately ask, "Why are you doing this?" And if it got a correct and reasonable answer to this question, it would say: "All right. So be it." As soon as it reached that conclusion, another part of the mind would say: "Then stick to it firmly. You must not act otherwise — even when you are eating or resting, sleeping or dreaming." His entire mind thus worked in harmony to accept that thing and act accordingly. His steadfastness acted as a guard and always observed the mind's actions so carefully that if the Master by accident tried to do something contrary to its resolve, he would distinctly feel as if someone from within had tied down his senses and would not allow him to do it. We will understand this if we study the Master's conduct throughout his life with every thing and every being.

After Gadadhar had gone to school for only a few days, the boy said: "I

27. First example: "I don't want a bread-winning education."

don't care for an education that teaches how 'to pack rice and plantain.' I don't want a bread-winning education." Ramkumar thought that his younger brother was going astray, so he brought him to his own school in Calcutta and tried to educate the boy himself; but he failed to change Gadadhar's childhood resolve regarding a money-making education. The Master was fully aware that his elder brother was a devout pandit: He had opened a school and was teaching his students sincerely. But he could not meet the financial needs of the family. So because he had no alternative, Ramkumar accepted the position of priest in the temple of Rani Rasmani. The Master approved of his elder brother's decision, considering it better to earn money this way than by flattering wealthy people [like other pandits].

During the Master's sadhana, when he sat for meditation he felt all the

28. Second example: While sitting in meditation the Master experiences someone locking all the joints of his body; his vision of a person with a trident in hand.

joints of his body lock, making the sound "khat khat." It was as if someone within himself were locking those joints with a key to keep him in that sitting position for a long time. And until that inner being unlocked them, he could not move from the spot despite his efforts, or change his position, or use his limbs as he wished, as we can. Sometimes he would see a person seated near him with a trident in hand, saying, "If you think about anything other than God, I will stab your chest with this trident."

The scriptures say that one should identify oneself with the Divine Mother

29. Third example: The validity of the Vedic scriptures is proven by the spiritual experiences of the unlettered Master. While attempting to offer a flower at the feet of the Mother, the Master placed it on his own head instead; and while trying to perform rites for his departed ancestors, he failed.

during worship. The Master's mind acted accordingly: While trying to offer bel leaves and a hibiscus at the feet of the Divine Mother, it was as if someone took his hand and directed it towards his own head.

In addition, when the Master was initiated into sannyasa, his mind began to perceive the one nondual Brahman in all beings continuously. After that, when he tried to perform tarpana [a water offering] to his departed ancestors as part of a regular practice, his hands became numb and he could not cup his palms to lift water in them. He then realized that having accepted sannyasa, he could no longer perform rituals.

We can cite so many examples that clearly prove how renunciation, discrimination, concentration, and steadfastness were easy for the Master and natural to his mind. Moreover, these experiences of the Master are the same as those recorded in the scriptures — so what is written in the scriptures is true. "It was for this reason," said Swami Vivekananda, "that the Master came this time as an unlettered person. He demonstrated that the spiritual states recorded in the Vedas and in Vedanta — as well as in the scriptures of other faiths — are true, and that all human beings can indeed achieve those states by treading the path of any religion."

As we discuss the nature of the Master's mind, it becomes evident that human life reaches its culmination when one ascends to the nirvikalpa plane and realizes God as One without a second. Regarding the spiritual experiences in that plane, the Master said, "All jackals howl alike there." In other words, as all jackals make the same noises, so those who have ascended to the nirvikalpa plane and experienced God, the cause of the universe, all describe Him in a similar way. The Master said of Chaitanya, the incarnation of love: "As the elephant's external tusks are meant for attacking enemies and its inner teeth are for masticating food, so Chaitanya's dualistic mood and nondualistic mood were external and internal attitudes." It is clear that the Master judged everything by the standard of unchanging nondual knowledge. Any thought or action that made people and societies advance towards the nondual plane he would consider to be higher than others.

> 30. The goal of human life is to attain nondual knowledge. Then one experiences that "All jackals howl alike." Chaitanya's devotion was like the tusks of an elephant, and his nondual knowledge was like its inner teeth. The Master determined the high or low status of an individual or of an entire society according to the manifestation of nondual knowledge.

When we study the Master's visions originating from his spiritual moods, we find that some of them were *sva-samvedya* [experienced by himself] and some were *para-samvedya* [experienced by others]. In other words, when his thoughts and steadfast spiritual practices took a concrete form, some visions would be manifest within the Master and only he could see them. Other visions took place when he had ascended to higher and higher planes and had come near the nirvikalpa state or when he dwelled in bhavamukha. At such times he could see what was happening at present and what would happen in the future, although this was unknown to others. When he told others about those visions, people would discover later that what he had seen actually came to pass. To verify the authenticity of visions in the first group, one had to be endowed with the Master's faith, sincerity, and steadfastness and ascend to the same state in which he had those visions. To understand the second group of visions, one needed neither faith nor sadhana; witnessing the result, people were compelled to believe that those visions were true.

> 31. Two kinds of visions: *sva-samvedya* and *para-samvedya*.

From what we have said earlier about the nature of the Master's mind and

32. The Master's mind could not rest until it arrived at a definite conclusion about the condition of objects and persons.

what we say now, it is clear that such a mind could not remain idle, even in the normal plane of consciousness. If it focussed even for a moment on a particular thing or person, it could not stop until it reached a definite conclusion about it by studying its nature and behaviour. In boyhood his mind discerned that scholars studied the scriptures to earn money, so he did not learn the type of education that taught how "to pack rice and plantain." We will now discuss how, as the Master grew older, his mind came in contact with various people in different places and arrived at different conclusions about them.

It is well known that after Chaitanya passed away, an ongoing antago-

33. On the normal plane of consciousness, the Master saw antagonism between the Shaktas and Vaishnavas.

nism arose between the Shaktas and Vaishnavas in Bengal. Ramprasad and a few Shakti worshippers realized through sadhana that Kali and Krishna are the same and proclaimed that the antagonism was misguided, but the masses paid no heed to their words and became carried away by the current of conflict. This is evident from their jokes, songs, and stories, which ridicule each other's deities. From his boyhood onward, the Master was well acquainted with this situation. The Master attained perfection after practising the sadhanas prescribed by both the Shakta and Vaishnava scriptures and realized that each path was equally valid. It then became evident to him that the antagonism between the Shaktas and the Vaishnavas had been caused by vanity and egotism springing from a lack of spirituality.

The Master's father worshipped Ramachandra; Providence had given

34. To remove antagonism from the minds of family members, he had them all initiated into a Shakti mantra.

him the stone emblem of Raghuvir Ramachandra, and he installed it in his house. Although the Master was born into a Vaishnava family, from his childhood onward he had equal devotion for Shiva and Vishnu. Even now his neighbours point out a place where, during his boyhood, he went into samadhi for a few hours while performing the role of Shiva. We can mention another incident as evidence of his catholic view. The Master had each member of his family initiated into both Vishnu and Shakti mantras. We think that the Master did this in order to remove any antagonism from their minds.

It is now well known that in ancient times the virtuous king Ashoka was

35. How it became the custom for monks to dispense medicine. Gradually it undermined their spiritual lives.

determined to spread Buddhism and education for the good of humankind. He established hospitals throughout India to treat the ailments of human beings and of animals; he also arranged to collect medicinal plants, cultivate them, and make them easily available to the public. He sent Buddhist monks to various parts of the country and abroad to dispense those medicines and medicinal plants and also to preach the message of Buddha. It seems that from that time on monks began to collect and carry medicines; but this custom became more prevalent in the Tantric age. In the era that followed, the authors of the Smriti scriptures noticed that the monks' spirituality was declining because of this custom, and they raised a strong objection to it. But even now that custom has not been uprooted in conservative India. It is evident to us that while the Master was living in Dakshineswar and travelling to holy places, he noticed a lack of spirituality among the sadhus. They had gained a reputation by dispensing medicines and had fallen from their ideals forever, entrapped by enjoyment. The Master told us many times: "Never believe sadhus who give out medicines; who exorcise evil spirits by uttering charms and incantations; who receive money; who adorn themselves excessively with ashes and religious marks; or who wear wooden sandals to advertise their austerity, and thus give others the impression that they are great sadhus."

Let no one conclude from the above statement that the Master, after

| 36. The Master's opinion about hypocritical monks. |

observing hypocritical and fallen monks, would consider abolishing the monastic orders as some Westerners advocate. Regarding this, the Master told us from time to time: "An ordinary monk in religious garb, who lives on alms, must be regarded as greater than a good householder. If that monk maintains a good character and spends his life depending only on alms, even if he does not practise yoga or perform austerities, he has proceeded farther on the path of renunciation than has an ordinary householder." This statement illustrates the Master's conviction that renouncing everything for God is the standard by which a person's character and conduct are to be judged.

We have shown many times how a genuine and saintly devotee or a jnani

| 37. The lives of true monks bring the scriptures to life. |

sadhu commanded special respect from the Master regardless of which religious order he or she belonged to. The Sanatana Dharma [eternal religion] of India still exists because of the spiritual experiences of such sadhus. The authority of the Vedas and other scriptures is confirmed by those amongst them who have realized God and freed themselves from the bondage of maya. That the truths of the Vedas are revealed to aptas [illumined souls] has been unanimously affirmed by all philosophers of India — including rationalists like the Vaisheshikas. So it is not surprising that the deeply insightful Master understood their greatness and accorded them respect.

Although the Master had a particular affection for those monks who had

| 38. The Master discerned narrow-mindedness even among genuine monks. |

advanced along their respective paths, and he always greatly enjoyed their company, he would at times become extremely sorrowful when he saw that one thing was lacking in them: While he could mix with monks from all sects with equal love, they could not do likewise. He noticed this bigoted attitude even among sannyasins advanced on the nondual path — not to speak of aspirants following the path of devotion. Long before they attained the liberal equality of the nondual plane, some self-absorbed sannyasins considered aspirants of other sects inferior and looked on them with contempt or at best with pity. The broad-minded Master was pained when he saw aspirants who were moving towards the same goal harbouring antagonism towards one another. And he clearly understood that their narrowness originated from a lack of true spirituality.

While the Master lived in the Kali temple of Dakshineswar, every day he observed a lack of spirituality and a narrowness among both householders and monks. When he visited holy places, he found these evils to be even more prevalent there. In Varanasi, he watched as brahmin pandits argued amongst themselves while

| 39. The Master sensed a lack of spirituality in holy places. The difference between our observations and the Master's. |

receiving gifts from Mathur. When some Tantric aspirants invited him to attend their ritual, he noticed that they paid only cursory attention to the ritual, then drank to excess and lost control of themselves. He saw Dandi Swamis striving their utmost to establish name and fame for themselves. In Vrindaban, he met some Vaishnava Babajis who were living with women under the pretext of sadhana. All these events revealed their true form to the Master's keen sight and helped him understand the real condition of society and the country. Of course, he would not have been helped by observing these things if he had not had a deep experience of nondual Reality. As he had already experienced the Truth, he developed a firm conviction regarding the ultimate goal of the individual and social lives of people, and it became easier for him to understand other things by comparing them with that Truth. He knew with certainty how true progress, civilization, religion, knowledge, devotion, steadfastness, yoga, karma, and other guiding forces were leading human beings, in which direction they were going, and where they would ultimately arrive. As a result, when the Master was on the normal plane of consciousness, this knowledge helped him to ascertain the truth of all things by observing and discussing everyday events in individual lives and in society.

How could he have evaluated the progress of a particular sadhu if he had not known what true saintliness is? How could the truthful Master strongly encourage people to go on pilgrimage and worship the deities in holy places if he had not seen for himself that the prayer and meditation of many people had caused intense manifestations of spirituality to appear in holy places and in the images of deities? Or how could he have understood that the bigotry evident in all religions is reprehensible, if he had not known the direction they were taking and their ultimate goal? We often see holy people, sacred places, and images of gods and goddesses. The endless roar of religious and scriptural debate deafens our ears. As we listen to clever arguments and intellectual artistry, we sometimes consider one particular view to be right and sometimes another. After studying life's day-to-day events, we sometimes think that the goal of life should be this and sometimes that; we constantly oscillate between opinions without coming to a definite conclusion on any matter. Sometimes we consider ourselves atheists and are satisfied that the goal of life is worldly enjoyment. Do we derive any benefit from these observations and oscillating conclusions? It is certain that without the help of the great world teachers, our pleasure-loving minds would never, even in a hundred lives, understand what the Master detected and understood at first sight by virtue of the wonderful structure and nature of his mind. Although all minds may appear to be similar, there is a gulf of difference between the Master's mind and ours that is apparent in every one of our actions. For that reason, devotional scriptures have said that the mind of an avatar is made of different material than that of ordinary people — it is made with pure sattva, devoid of rajas and tamas.

From both the divine and ordinary planes of consciousness, the Master

40. The Master understood that his liberal view was unique.

observed the present degradation of religion in India and the narrow-mindedness of existing religious faiths. He saw that previous teachers were ignorant of the fact that all religious paths are equally true and that people, according to their different natures, follow different paths but finally reach the same goal; he also saw that the preaching of previous teachers was inappropriate because they did not take into consideration place, time, and person. The Master realized these great and novel truths especially when he travelled to holy places. He also learned that his attitude, which was completely free from bigotry and antagonism, was utterly unique. This was his personal discovery, and he would have to give it to the world.

Many of us have now come to know that many people were charmed

41. The Master realizes that he is the first person in the world to experience that "all religions are true — as many faiths, so many paths."

upon hearing for the first time this great liberal message from the Master: "All religions are true — as many faiths, so many paths." Some may object, saying that at least a partial version of this liberal message can be found among the rishis and religious teachers of the past. But if one scrutinizes this matter thoroughly, one finds that those teachers used their intellects to reject some parts of each religious faith, extract the essence of each, and then somehow try to show a harmony among them. The Master, however, practised the sadhana of each faith, without rejecting any part of it and with equal affection for each one, and thereby reached their respective goals. Thus, he experienced a harmony of religious faiths that had never been experienced by any teacher in the past. But we do not intend to discuss this subject in detail here. We merely want to tell the reader this much: We find indications of this liberal attitude in the Master's life from his childhood onward. But it was only after finishing his pilgrimage that the Master was able to under-stand the truth that he was the only person who had perceived such liberality in the spiritual world. Although in the past, rishis, teachers, and avatars had taught people how to reach the goal by following a particular path, none of them had ever preached the message that one could reach the same goal through all the different spiritual paths. During his sadhana, the Master wholeheartedly offered all his desires at the feet of the Divine Mother and firmly resolved that he would never return to the realm of maya. He wanted to stay on the plane of nondual consciousness, but the Divine Mother did not allow that. She preserved his body in mysterious ways for one purpose: to eradicate as far as possible religious narrowness from this world. The world was eager to receive this eternally beneficial message. We shall now try to tell the reader how we arrived at this conclusion.

The Master had been convinced from his childhood onward that spiritual experience was realized through practice rather than verbal expression. Sometimes during his sadhana, and often after he had attained God-realization, the Master had experiences that made him realize that the spirituality he had accumulated by long practice could actually be transmitted to others. We have already indicated this in other places (see III.6.11-12, 7.17-20). Many times in his life, the Master saw evidence that the Divine Mother had made him an instrument of Her grace by storing spiritual power abundantly in him and sometimes using it on behalf of Mathur and some other special persons. Before he experienced this himself, he understood that the Divine Mother would use his body and mind as instruments to bestow Her grace on a few fortunate people, but he did not know how and when She would do it. Like a child, the Master depended completely on the Mother, so he did not try to understand this. It never occurred to him, even in his dreams, that he would have to spread spirituality in India and flood the world with a spiritual tidal wave.

42. The Master realized that the Divine Mother had given him immense power to impart religion to the world.

After the pilgrimage, the Master began to feel deeply that the Divine Mother had started a new lila [divine play] and was working through his body and mind. But although he had that feeling, he had no idea what the Divine Mother would have him do, how She would direct him, and where She would ultimately take him. He truly became the Divine Mother's child forever as he knew only this: "The Mother is mine and I am Mother's." No desire other than the Mother's arose in his mind. Sometimes, however, one desire would arise in his mind: to know the Mother in various forms and by means of different spiritual paths. The Mother had made him understand clearly that it was She who had put that desire into his mind on many occa-sions. Now having had this experience, the Divine Mother's child joyfully looked forward to Her guidance, and She continued to play with him as before.

After he had visited holy places, the Master became aware of his spiritual

43. The Master did not assume the position of a teacher motivated by ego, as we do.

mission to the world. But he did not assume the position of a teacher to feed his ego, as we do. This is clear from his intention to spend the rest of his life in Vrindaban with the great devotional ascetic Gangamata, but the Mother's will prevailed. "Mother does Her own work. Who am I to work for the world and teach all of humanity?" We cannot even imagine how deeply this attitude was rooted in the Master's mind throughout his life.

The Master's self-abnegation made him a true instrument for Mother's work. It kept him in the state of bhavamukha without interruption, caused the power of the guru to become manifest in him, and developed this power in his mind so intensely that he became a wonderful teacher. As long as the Master was possessed by that power, he lost control of himself, and he came to know what happened through his body and mind only after the work had been accomplished. Eventually, his body and mind learned how to absorb and manifest that power constantly, and this became easy and natural to him. And this power, contrary to his expectation, established him as a true teacher. Previously, the natural state of the Master's mind had been that of a humble aspirant or a child. That attitude remained for a long time, and the power of the guru displayed itself in him for short periods of time. But now the states were reversed: He was staying in the mood of a guru for longer periods and reverting to the attitude of a humble aspirant or of a child for shorter periods.

It was completely impossible for the Master to assume the role of a teacher

44. Evidence thereof: During ecstasy the Master quarrelled with the Divine Mother.

to serve his ego, as we learned by witnessing his many boyish quarrels with the Divine Mother during ecstasy. As bees swarm to a full-blown hundred-petalled lotus, attracted by its fragrance, so a large crowd began to visit Dakshineswar, drawn there by the Master's spirituality. When we arrived one day, we heard the Master saying to the Divine Mother in ecstasy: "What are You doing? Why are You bringing such large crowds here? I have no time to bathe or eat. (*Pointing to his own body*) This is nothing but a broken drum. (*The Master had recently developed throat cancer.*) If it's beaten too much, it will be perforated. What will You do then?"

One day in October 1884, we were seated with the Master at Dakshi-

45. Second example.

neswar. Some days previously we had been present when we learned about the illness of Pratap Hazra's mother, and the Master persuaded Pratap to go home to serve her. On this day news reached us that Pratap had gone to Vaidyanath instead of going home. The Master was a little annoyed by this. After a brief conversation, the Master asked us to sing a song, and a little later he went into ecstasy. While he was in ecstasy, the Master began to quarrel with the Mother like a little boy. He said: "Why do You bring such hopeless people here? (*After a brief silence*) I can't do so much. Let one seer of milk be diluted with a quarter-seer of water, but here you have five seers of water and one seer of milk! I'm pushing firewood into the oven to boil this milk; now my eyes are burning with smoke. If You want them to have it, You give them spirituality. I can't push enough fuel into the fire. Don't bring that type of person here anymore." Overwhelmed with awe and wonder, we sat there quietly and wondered whom the Master was talking about to the Divine Mother and how unfortunate that person was. Quite often he would quarrel with the Mother in this manner. This proves that the Master considered the honourable position of a teacher — which others so coveted — to be trivial, and repeatedly asked the Mother to relieve him of it.

In Her inscrutable lila, the Divine Mother gave the Master wonderful and unprecedented spiritual experiences throughout his life. She also infused into him universal and liberal religious ideas that She had never inspired in any other great teacher of the world. The Divine Mother made the Master understand this and simultaneously revealed to him the amount of spiritual power that She had instilled in him and the fact that She had made him a wonderful instrument to transmit this power to others. The Master was amazed when he realized the dearth of spirituality in the world and how the Mother's grace had given him a stockpile of extraordinary spiritual power to be used in removing that want.

> 46. The Master's experience: "Wherever there is any trouble in the Divine Mother's empire, I shall have to rush there to stop it, like a government officer."

He soon realized that the Divine Mother had once more descended to the battlefield to kill the invincible Raktabija,[4] the demon of delusion sprung from ignorance! The people of the world would again be blessed by bearing witness to the Mother's overflowing compassion and would lack the words necessary to glorify Her infinite divine qualities and Her sovereignty over millions of universes! As excessive heat generates clouds, as waxing is followed by waning, and as prosperity arises after adversity, so when innumerable people feel a long-accumulated spiritual emptiness, the infinite compassion of the Divine Mother takes form and appears as a living and moving manifestation of the power of the guru. Out of grace, the Divine Mother made the Master understand this and showed him that She had enacted Her lila through him many times in previous ages and would continue to do so many times in the future. The Master could not enjoy liberation like ordinary human beings. It is clear that from this time on, the Master experienced this: "Wherever there is any trouble in the Divine Mother's empire, I shall have to rush there to stop it, like a government officer."

4. It is mentioned in the Chandi that Raktabija, a terrible demon, was killed by the Divine Mother Durga. — *Translator*

The Master realized that out of Her grace, the Divine Mother had for the benefit of humanity developed in him this catholic view, "As many faiths, so many paths." It is evident that at that time his discriminating mind began investigating another matter. He became extremely eager to know those fortunate ones who would accept this new and liberal attitude directly from the Mother who was residing in him and would mould their lives accordingly. Who would be empowered by the Mother to be his helper in the divine play of this age and assist in propagating the liberal view among others? Whom had the Mother marked to carry out that great mission? When we discussed Mathur's relationship with the Master, we mentioned that he had a vision about the devotees who would come to him (see III.7.33). It was due to the inscrutable lila of the Divine Mother that the Master, who to this point had been completely unattached to worldly affairs, now saw in his mind, brightly and vividly, the faces of those whom he had seen in his vision. Then the mind of this wonderful sannyasin began to churn with various thoughts: How many people would come? When would the Mother bring them to him? What work would the Mother do through each one? Would the Mother make them sannyasins like him or keep them as householders? So far, only a few people had understood a little of the Mother's wonderful lila as it manifested itself through him; would any of the newcomers understand the Mother's lila completely and accurately or would they all be left with only a partial understanding?

The Master later described to us his mental anguish: "In those days there was no limit to my yearning to see you all. My heart was wrung like a wet towel, and I was restless with pain. I wanted to weep loudly, but I couldn't cry in public or people would misunderstand me. I could just manage to keep my grief under control during the daytime. But when evening came and the vesper music resounded from the temples of the Mother and of Vishnu, I could master my feelings no longer; I was overcome by the thought that another day had gone and still you were not here. I would climb onto the roof of the kuthi and cry out at the top of my voice: 'Come to me, my boys! Where are you? I can't bear to live without you!' I thought that I would go mad. Then after some days, you began to come one after another, and I calmed down. As I had seen you all earlier in my vision, I immediately recognized you when you came, one by one. After Purna came, the Mother said: 'You had visions about those who were to come. It is now complete with Purna's arrival. No others belonging to this class of devotee will come in the future.' The Mother showed you all to me and said, 'These devotees are your inner circle.'" What a wonderful vision and wonderful fulfillment! How much of the Master's words can we understand? We have quoted the Master's own words to convince the reader that we have not invented anything in our description of the Master's condition.

While determining who would realize and accept his liberal religious view, the Master had another conviction that he often shared with us. He said: "One who is living his last birth will come here. A person who has sincerely called on God, even once, will definitely come here."

48. The Master's conviction: "One who is living his last birth will come here. A person who has sincerely called on God, even once, will definitely come here."

So many people had different reactions to these words; it is hard to record all of them. Some concluded that this statement was absolutely unreasonable. Some thought that these were incoherent words caused by the Master's devotion and faith. Some found in this statement mental illness or egotism. Some thought that although they could not understand it, it must be true because the Master said so. These people therefore stopped analyzing it and arguing about it, considering such doubt to be detrimental to their faith. Some others concluded that they could understand if the Master allowed them to; so setting aside any firm belief or disbelief, they listened calmly to others' opinions for or against it. But it would not take long to understand those words if we could make the reader realize that the Master was simple, natural, and devoid of ego, and that the Divine Mother made him realize Her liberal religious view and established him as a true teacher. That is not all. If the reader examines those words thoroughly, he or she will understand that the statement is an important proof that the Master attained a high spiritual state in an easy and natural way.

As a child of the Divine Mother, the Master saw within himself a stockpile of extraordinary spiritual power and the ability to transmit that power. Because he had completely surrendered to Her, it never occurred to his mind even for a moment that he had achieved this through his own effort.

49. This conviction of the Master arose because of his complete dependence on the Divine Mother.

He saw in it the inscrutable and playful Mother's lila and was amazed and astounded. What great sport has the Divine Mother — who makes the impossible possible — set into motion with the unlettered Master! People are overwhelmed and sing the Mother's glories when they see what She has done — making the mute become eloquent, the lame scale mountains, and so on — but Her present lila has surpassed previous records a thousand times over. This present divine play of the Mother has proven the Vedas, the Bible, the Koran, the Puranas, and other scriptures to be true; has established all religions; and has fulfilled the crying need of the world [religious harmony], which no one had achieved in the ages past. All glory to the Divine Mother! All glory to the sportive power of Brahman! These thoughts arose when the Master had the vision described above. Because of his complete faith in the Mother's words, in Her infinite grace, and in Her inscrutable power, the Master took that vision to be absolutely true. He then questioned Her: How far would that lila spread? Who would assist in its propagation? What kind of people would receive this

Mother's power? In answer to these questions, he was given a vision of his inner circle of devotees and the conviction that those among them who were living their last birth and who had sincerely called on God even once were competent to receive this wonderful new liberal doctrine of the Mother. It is therefore evident that this conclusion entered his mind as a result of his absolute faith in the Mother. Because the Master depended on Her completely, like a child, he had no alternative than to accept that conclusion, and consequently not the slightest trace of egotism cropped up in his mind.

"One who is living his last birth will come here. A person who has sincerely called on God, even once, will definitely come here." If we take the word "here" to mean "the Mother's new and liberal doctrine" then this statement will not seem unreasonable or objectionable to others. If this meaning is admitted, then another question arises: Will people come on their own to accept the Divine Mother's liberal message "As many faiths, so many paths," or will they accept it through that person who became the instrument of the Mother and brought that message to the world? The answer to this question, as we understand it, must be determined by the questioner after seeing the result of the full realization of this doctrine either within themselves or in others. Until that realization dawns, silence is the best answer. But if the reader asks what we believe, we say that along with an authentic experience of this liberal attitude, one must have a vision of that person whom the Divine Mother, for the first time, sent to embody that doctrine for the good of the world. And one must pour out heartfelt love and respect for him who was free from ego and delusion. The Master will not demand this; no one else will prompt it; love for the Divine Mother will drive one to do it spontaneously. Here we end this topic.

50. The meaning of the Master's words "last birth."

The authors of the Tantras have repeatedly said that if the power of the guru develops even a little in any person by the grace of the Divine Mother, that person's actions, deportment, behaviour, and selfless compassion for others will take wonderful forms beyond the range of human intelligence. According to the Tantras, the manifestation of that power is called *divya bhava*, the divine state. These scriptures further state that teachers who are established in divya bhava teach and give initiation in a mysterious way: They are not limited by the injunctions of the scriptures. Their compassion can prompt them to awaken the power of spirituality in others and instantly put them in samadhi by merely willing it, or by touch. Or these teachers can partially awaken that power in aspirants, so that it can manifest itself completely in them in this very life, eventually enabling them to attain true God-realization. According to the Tantras, when the power of the guru is slightly intensified, the teacher is able to give *Shakti* initiation to the disciple; and in

51. According to Tantra, divya bhava is the state in which the power of the guru is concentrated. How do the gurus established in this state initiate disciples?

its highly intense state, the teacher can give the *Shambhavi* initiation. Ordinary gurus are enjoined by the Tantras to give their disciples *Mantri* or *Anavi* initiation.

Regarding Shakti and Shambhavi initiation, the *Rudrayamala*, the *Shadanwaya Maharatna*, the *Vayaviya Samhita*, the *Sarada*, the *Vishwasara*, and other Tantras have said the same thing. We quote here from the *Vayaviya Samhita*:

In the *Agama* scripture, the Supreme Lord Shiva has taught three kinds of initiation — the Shambhavi, the Shakti, and the Mantri. When a disciple attains knowledge instantly by merely seeing, touching, or saluting the guru, it is called *Shambhavi* initiation. When an illumined guru transmits his divine power into the disciple's heart and awakens spirituality, it is called *Shakti* initiation. In the Mantri initiation, the guru draws a diagram, installs a water pot, performs worship of the deity, and then utters a mantra into the ear of the disciple.

> 52. When a disciple attains knowledge by merely seeing, touching, or saluting the guru, it is called *Shambhavi* initiation; when the guru's power enters the disciple and awakens knowledge, it is called *Shakti* initiation.

According to the *Rudrayamala*, Shakti and Shambhavi initiations bring about instant liberation. When without any external means perfected souls generate divine knowledge in their disciples through their spiritual powers only, it is called Shakti initiation. In Shambhavi initiation, there is no previous resolve to impart or to receive initiation in the minds of the guru or the disciple respectively. As soon as they see each other, compassion dawns in the guru's heart, and he or she feels a desire to bestow grace on the disciple. Thus, the knowledge of the nondual Reality arises in the disciple and that person accepts discipleship.

According to the *Purascharanollasa Tantra*, one does not need to be concerned about proper or improper times for such initiation: "O playful-eyed Parvati, it is unnecessary to discriminate between auspicious and inauspicious times when one receives initiation from a guru endowed with the heroic or the divine moods. If one meets an illumined guru who is motivated by mercy to invite a disciple to be initiated, the latter should receive it without calculating the auspiciousness of the moment."

> 53. It is not necessary to discriminate between the proper and improper time for such initiation.

The scriptures have prescribed informal rules in the case of ordinary gurus endowed with the divine mood. How can we then determine the method of teaching and transmitting spiritual power to others employed by this divine, compassionate Master, who remained an instrument in the hands of the Divine Mother? Out of grace, the Divine Mother used the Master to enact divya bhava according to Tantra. At the same time, for the good of humanity, She began to manifest in the Master the great liberal message "As many faiths, so many paths," which had never

> 54. The Master was foremost among gurus of the divine mood: the reason.

before been practised and experienced by other teachers established in the divine mood. This is why we say that here a new chapter began in the Master's life.

A devout reader may comment sarcastically on this conclusion, asking:

55. All of the powers do not always manifest in the great avatars: proof of this.

"How can you say such a thing? If you consider Sri Ramakrishna to be an incarnation of God, you can never say that divya bhava, or the manifestation of that divine power, did not exist before." To this, we reply: "Brother, we say this based on the words of the Master. When God becomes incarnate in a human form, all of the divine qualities and powers do not always appear in each incarnation. Only the particular power needed becomes manifest. At the Cossipore garden house, when the Master's body was reduced to skin and bone by his long fight with cancer, he noticed his mental attitude and the manifestation of power within himself and said to us: 'The Divine Mother is showing that such power has come into this (*pointing to his own body*) that I need not touch people anymore. I'll ask you to touch them, and as you do, they will attain illumination. If the Divine Mother cures the body this time, you won't be able to push the crowds away from the door. You will face so many people and work so hard that you will have to take medicine to relieve your aching bodies.'"

The Master's own words make it clear that he was experiencing the manifestation of a particular power that he had not encountered before. Many such examples can be cited.

The Master could not rest after the divine mood had compelled him to call

56. The Master's meeting with Keshab Chandra Sen; shortly after, his own devotees began to arrive.

out for his devotees, as we described above. The Divine Mother told him to go to the place where all his devotees would learn about his stay at Dakshineswar. She took him to the garden retreat at Belgharia and introduced him to Keshab Chandra Sen. Shortly after this the Master's intimate devotees, whom he had seen while in ecstasy (Swamis Vivekananda, Brahmananda, and others) began to come, one after another. If the Master wills, we shall try to describe his divine play with them on some other occasion. During the Chariot Festival in 1885, the Master spent several days with his devotees while under the influence of that extraordinary divine mood. We shall now narrate that story and conclude this part of the book.

Chapter 5

Sri Ramakrishna in the Company of Devotees: The *N*ine-Day Festival in 1885

[Even the most sinful man, if he worships Me with unswerving devotion,] he soon becomes righteous and attains eternal peace. Proclaim it boldly, O son of Kunti, that my devotee never perishes. — GITA 9:31

TO UNDERSTAND A LITTLE OF THE WONDERFUL CHARACTER of Sri Ramakrishna, one must see him in the company of his devotees. One will get a glimpse of his divine play if one observes — and understands thoroughly — how and in what ways the Master lived every day, how he talked and joked with various kinds of devotees and at the same time remained in a divine mood and in samadhi. We shall now present to the reader the story of the Master's divine play with devotees for a few days.

As far as we have seen, even the trifling acts and efforts of this extraordi-

| 1. The harmony of divine and human natures in the Master. |

nary and great soul were not without purpose or meaning. It is rare to find such a coexistence of divine and human natures in one person. I have not met another such person while travelling throughout the world for the last twenty-five years. A Bengali proverb states: "One does not understand the value of teeth until they are gone." This is exactly what happened for many of us regarding the Master. When the devotees brought the Master to Shyampukur, Calcutta, for his cancer treatment, Vijay Krishna Goswami came to see him one day and told us the following story.

Sometime before this visit Vijay was in Dhaka. As he sat in meditation one

| 2. Vijay Krishna Goswami's vision. |

day, he had a vision of Sri Ramakrishna. The door of the room he was in was locked. To determine whether this vision was a trick of his mind, he felt the body and the limbs of the form visible before him for a long time. He told this story to the Master and to us when he visited Shyampukur.

Vijay: "I have travelled to various parts of this country and across the mountains, and have met many sadhus and great souls, but I have never seen anyone like him (*pointing to the Master*). Here I see one hundred percent spirituality. Elsewhere I have seen twelve percent, sometimes six, sometimes two, and sometimes one percent, but I have never found even twenty-five percent in any other soul."

The Master (*with a smile to us*): "What does he say?"

Vijay (*to the Master*): "The other day I saw you in Dhaka in such a way that if you say 'no' now, I'll pay no heed to your words. By being too accessible, you confuse us. Dakshineswar is adjacent to Calcutta; we can visit you whenever we want. It is not difficult to get here — there are plenty of boats and carriages. We do not understand your worth because you are so near to our homes and easily available. We would appreciate your value if you were seated on top of a mountain and we had to climb on foot to reach you, holding onto tree roots and going without food. We think that if such a great spiritual personality is here close to home, there must be many even greater souls in far-off places; so we leave you to run around hither and thither and suffer because of this."

This is true, indeed. The compassionate Master embraced almost everyone

| 3. How the devotees felt about the Master's extraordinary behaviour with them. | who came to him. And once he had accepted them as his own, he would not let them go, even if they wanted to. He first destroyed the impressions they had accumulated over past lives — sometimes dras- |

tically and sometimes gently — and then cast their current lives into his new, extraordinary, and everlasting mould, and thus led them to eternal peace. There will be no doubt about this if the devotees tell their own life stories.

Narendra was tormented with worldly suffering while he was living at home. He felt that he had been surrendering himself to God for such a long time, yet was not fortunate enough to have His vision, and he also thought that the Master had not helped him. His feelings wounded, he secretly planned to renounce the world — but the Master intervened. Through his divine power the Master learned of Narendra's intention and persuaded him to come to Dakshineswar. When Narendra arrived, the Master touched his hand and began to sing, in ecstasy:

> I am afraid to speak,
> I am afraid not to speak,
> For the fear rises in my mind
> That I shall lose you.

The Master thus talked to Narendra in many ways and convinced him to cancel his plans and remain with him.

Although the Master had blessed Girish by taking on his "power of attorney," still Girish was sceptical and fearful as he remembered the influence of his former bad habits. The Master reassured him: "Rascal, do you think you have been seized by a poisonless water snake? You have been bitten by a real cobra. Even if you run to your home, you will die there. Have you not seen that when water snakes seize bullfrogs, the frogs croak a thousand times before they die, and some may even escape. But when bullfrogs are seized by venomous cobras, they are silenced after three croaks at the most. And if a bullfrog by chance escapes, it dies in its hole. Know this place (*pointing to himself*) to be like that."

At that time, however, who understood the significance of the Master's words and conduct? As the Master went about fulfilling people's importunate demands, visiting devotees' homes unasked, and distributing boons and freedom from fear, everyone thought that perhaps people like him existed everywhere. Under the affectionate protection of the compassionate Master, how strong the devotees felt, how insistent they were to have their demands satisfied, and how easily their feelings were wounded! Almost all of them believed that religious practice was a very easy thing. They were quite certain that whenever they wished to enjoy spiritual ecstasy or have a vision, they would get it immediately. The only thing they needed to do was press the Master a little eagerly, and he would give it to them with a touch, a word, or merely by wishing it.

Baburam (Swami Premananda) wanted to have bhava samadhi. With tearful eyes he implored the Master, saying, "Please help me to have samadhi." The Master consoled him, saying: "All right, I shall ask the Divine Mother about it. Does anything happen by my will, my child?" But who would listen to him? Baburam kept on, saying, "Please let me have that experience." A few days after this request, Baburam had to go to his country home at Antpur on some business. It was 1884. The Master was extremely anxious about how Baburam could have samadhi. He expressed his concern to others: "You see, Baburam wept much and asked for samadhi before he left. What will happen? If he doesn't have it, he will have no regard for the words of this place (*meaning himself*)." He then prayed to the Mother: "Mother, please grant that Baburam may have a little ecstasy or some other spiritual experience." The Mother replied, "He will not have ecstasy, but he will have knowledge." Even with the Mother's assurance, the Master remained anxious. He told some of us: "Well, I prayed to the Mother for Baburam, but She said, 'He will not have ecstasy; he will have knowledge.' At any rate, let him have something at least so that he can have peace. I'm anxious for him. He wept bitterly before he left." Ah, how anxious the Master was that Baburam might have some kind of spiritual experience! Expressing his concern, he repeated, "If he doesn't have a spiritual

4. Swami Premananda implores the Master for bhava samadhi: the Master's anxiety and vision.

experience, he won't respect me anymore." It was as if the Master's life and all depended on Baburam's regard or disregard!

Sometimes the Master asked his visitors: "Well, can you tell me why I

5. The Master explains why he is anxious for the devotees. Hazra forbids the Master to be apprehensive: the Master's vision and response.

think so much about these young boys? Why am I so concerned about their successes and failures? They are all schoolboys. They are penniless. They don't have any means to support me — not even to buy for me one pice worth of sugarplum. Still I think of them. Why? If one of them doesn't come here for a couple of days, I feel terribly restless and become eager to get news of him. Why is this?" The boy he asked replied: "I don't know why, sir. Perhaps it's for their good that you think of them."

"Let me tell you," the Master responded, "these boys are pure souls. They are still untouched by lust and gold. If they give their minds to God, they can easily realize Him. This is the reason I think of them. My nature is like that of a hemp smoker. A hemp smoker isn't satisfied to smoke alone. He draws one puff and then hands the pipe to another smoker, and thus he enjoys intoxication. My nature is like that. But despite my concern for all these boys, I don't have feelings as intense for the others as I had for Narendra in the early days. If he was late in coming for two days, I'd feel a pain in my heart as if it were being wrung like a wet towel. To avoid public criticism, I'd go to the pine grove[1] and cry loudly. Once Hazra[2] told me: 'What are you doing? You are a paramahamsa. You are supposed to be always united with God in samadhi. Why do you think of such things as why Narendra has not come? Or what will happen to Bhavanath?' I thought that Hazra was right and resolved not to do it again. Later, as I was returning from the pine grove, the Divine Mother displayed the whole of Calcutta in front of me. I saw that, day and night, people were drowning in lust and gold and suffering terribly. I felt compassion while watching this. I decided that if I had to suffer a million times, I'd do good for them and help them to attain liberation. I returned to Hazra and said: 'I did right in thinking about them. What is that to you, rascal?'

"Narendra once said to me: 'Why do you think of Narendra so much? As

6. Swami Vivekananda cautions the Master not to be anxious: the Master's vision and response.

King Bharata thought of his deer and became a deer in his next life, so if you keep on thinking of Narendra, you will have to become like Narendra.' I have tremendous faith in Narendra's words, you see, so I was scared. I went to the temple and reported this to the Mother. She said: 'He is a mere boy. Why do you listen to him? You are attracted to him because you see Narayana in him.' I returned to Narendra

---

1. The pine grove is on the northern side of Rani Rasmani's temple garden. People went to that solitary place only to answer the call of nature.
2. Pratap Chandra Hazra.

and said: 'You rascal, I won't listen to you anymore. Mother says that I love you because I see Narayana in you. The day I no longer see Him in you, I won't be able to bear even the sight of you.'" So there was deep significance in each of the Master's unusual actions. He would explain his behaviour to us lest we misunderstand and come to harm.

We observed that the Master always appreciated the talent of the gifted

| 7. The Master honoured those who were respected and talented: the reason. |

and paid respect to those worthy of it. He said: "Look, God is displeased if one doesn't pay respect to an honourable person. They have become great by His power. It is He who has made them great, so by neglecting them, one neglects God." We therefore understand why whenever the Master heard of any noble person in a particular place, he was immediately eager to meet that person by any means. He was delighted if that great one came to him; otherwise, he would visit that person uninvited to pay his respects and to converse with him or her. Thus, he visited Padmalochan, the court pandit of the Raja of Burdwan; Pandit Ishwar Chandra Vidyasagar; Mahesh, the renowned vina player of Varanasi; Gangamata, the well-known female ascetic of Vrindaban; Keshab Chandra Sen, the famous Brahmo leader, and many more. The Master heard of their noble qualities, and then on his own initiative sought such people out and arrived at their doors.

It is not surprising that the Master appeared at someone's door uninvited,

| 8. The Master's efforts to be free from egoism. |

because this thought never occurred to him: "I am a great man. If I were to visit someone in this manner, I would cheapen myself and lose my prestige." He had completely burnt his ego and vanity to ashes and consigned them forever to the Ganges. When beggars were fed in the Kali temple, he carried their dirty leaf-plates on his head, dumped them outside, and cleaned the place where they had eaten. Once he even ate the food left by those beggars, considering them to be Narayana. He washed the outhouse that the servants and workers of the Kali temple used. While wiping that place with his hair,[3] he prayed, "Mother, may I never feel that I am superior to them." So we are not surprised at all when we see the Master's amazing humility; but when we find even a little humility in others, we exclaim, "How wonderful!" Indeed, the Master was not a man of this world!

The Master was once walking in the temple garden with one end of his

| 9. Examples of the Master's lack of ego: events concerning Dr. Kailash and Trailokya Biswas. |

wearing cloth on his shoulder. A gentleman [Dr. Kailash Basu] thought he was an ordinary gardener and called out to him, "Hello, pick those flowers for me." The Master immediately obeyed him without saying anything and left. Once Trailokya, Mathur's son, was annoyed with Hriday and ordered him to leave the temple. In his

---

3. During sadhana the Master was indifferent to his body and his hair grew long and was matted with dust and moisture.

rage Trailokya told others that the Master was no longer needed in the Kali temple. As soon as that news reached the Master, he immediately put his towel on his shoulder and left his room with a smile. When the Master reached the front gate, Trailokya — afraid that evil might befall him — rushed to him and asked him to return, saying: "I have not asked you to go. Why are you leaving, sir?" The Master came back, smiling as before, and sat in his room as if nothing had happened.

Many such events can be narrated. We may not be surprised by such

| 10. Worldly people act in a different manner. | actions of the Master, but if another man behaves in a similar way we applaud him highly. Whether we express it or not, we have mentally calculated that if |

we want to live in the world we must look after our self-interest; we must clear our path by forcibly removing the weak; we must glorify ourselves by beating drums all around; and as far as possible we must hide our weaknesses from others. We believe ourselves to be useless if we sincerely and completely trust in God and in each other. Ah, this is the world! We find the same beliefs in the field of international politics, national politics, society, and religion. Those who have eaten the *Delhi-ka-Laddu*[4] of the world lament, and those who have not eaten it also lament.

It was 1885 and the Master had become widely known. Every day many

| 11. When the Master's divinity had become fully manifest, various religious movements began: the reason. | new people were attracted to Dakshineswar and were blessed by seeing him. Everyone in Calcutta, young and old, had heard of the Paramahamsa of Dakshineswar, and many had met him. An invisible religious current was flowing constantly in the minds |

of those who lived in Calcutta. The Harisabha, the Brahmo Samaj, and other religious organizations were scattered throughout the city, and people busied themselves with kirtan and expounding the scriptures. Although others might not understand the cause of this religious upheaval, the Master knew, and he explained it clearly to us as well as to his devotees, both men and women. In this connection, one day the Master told a female devotee: "Hello, all of these religious organizations that you see around — the Harisabhas and others — are due to this place (*pointing to himself*). Did they exist before? Society was chaotic with materialism. After the advent of this (*again pointing to himself*) all these changes took place. A current of religion is flowing inside the people."

On another occasion the Master told us: "Did the 'Young Bengal' whom you see here care for devotion? Did they respect others? They didn't even know how to bow down properly. Because I started to bow, bending my head down, they gradually learned how to bow. I went to see Keshab in his house. He was sitting in a chair and writing something. I bowed to him by

---

4. This is a Hindi figure of speech: A fancy sweet with a beautiful appearance but no substance. — *Translator*

bending down my head, but he just acknowledged me with a nod. When I left him I bowed down by putting my head on the floor, and he then folded his hands and touched them to his head. But the more he visited and listened to me and I continued to bow by bending my head down, the more he began to lower his head. Did they previously know how to show reverence and humility to others or believe in the importance of these things?"

Through its contact with the Master, the Navavidhan Brahmo Samaj [the

| 12. At that time Pandit Shashadhar arrived in Calcutta and began to expound on religion. | New Dispensation founded by Keshab Chandra Sen] was flourishing. At that time Pandit Shashadhar arrived in Calcutta to expound the Hindu religion. He was trying to explain the daily religious duties of |

the Hindus from the scientific viewpoint of the West. The saying "As many sages, so many opinions" is true in all matters. The pandit's scientific interpretation of religion was no exception. He attracted a large audience that included students from schools and colleges, and office clerks and workers on their way home. Albert Hall, where he lectured on orthodox Hinduism, was so packed that those in the audience had to stand very close to one another. Everyone was calm and eager to hear something of the pandit's wonderful exposition of religion. We remember one day when we also stood there and heard a few words. We somehow pushed our heads through that dense crowd to get a glimpse of the middle-aged pandit's beautiful face. His beard was black and his chest was bedecked with ochre rudraksha beads. Pandit Shashadhar's religious exposition was then the talk of Calcutta.

There is a saying, "Words travel by ears." It did not take long for news of

| 13. The Master's desire to meet Shashadhar. | the great soul of Dakshineswar to reach the pandit and for word of the pandit's greatness to reach the Master. Some devotees reported to the Master: "He is |

a great pandit and a wonderful speaker. The other day he interpreted the Hari mantra that consists of thirty-two letters from the perspective of the Devi, and the audience praised him highly." To this, the Master said: "Is that so? I want to hear him." Thus, the Master expressed to the devotees his desire to meet the pandit.

Any desire that arose in the Master's pure mind was fulfilled somehow or

| 14. Desires arising in the Master's pure mind are always fulfilled. | other. It was as if someone cleared the path to its fulfillment by quietly removing the obstacles. We had heard that one reaches such a state by continu- |

ously practising purity and truthfulness in body, mind, and words. And once one is in this state, despite all efforts one cannot entertain a falsehood. Any thought that arises in such a person's mind is fulfilled. But we never thought that this could actually happen to such an extent in a human being. We were gradually convinced of this when we repeatedly saw how the Master's desires were unexpectedly fulfilled. But in spite of this, did we have full faith in the Master while he was alive?

The Master told us: "In Keshab and Vijay I saw the light of knowledge burning like a candle flame, but in Narendra it blazes like the sun. Keshab has stirred up the world with one power, whereas Narendra is endowed with eighteen such powers." These words burst forth not from his imagination but from knowledge born in ecstasy. But did we then have complete faith in his words? Sometimes we pondered: "It may be true that the Master can see what is inside a person. There must be a hidden mystery in what he says." Sometimes we wondered: "Keshab Chandra Sen is a world-famous orator, and Narendra is an insignificant schoolboy! How can the Master's statement be true?" When we had such doubts about the truth of what the Master experienced, how can we say that we had no doubts about the fulfillment of his desires when he said, "I wish for this"?

*   *   *

The Chariot Festival of Jagannath [Krishna] began a few days after the Master had told us about Pandit Shashadhar. Because the Chariot Festival continues for nine days, it is called *Navayatra,* the Nine-Day Festival. We can think of many events concerning the Master that took place during the Navayatra of 1885. On the morning of the festival's first day, the Master went to the house of Ishan Chandra Mukhopadhyay of Thanthania, Calcutta, for lunch, and from there he went to visit Pandit Shashadhar in the afternoon. In the evening he attended the Chariot Festival at Balaram's house in Baghbazar, spent the night there, and the next morning left for Dakshineswar by boat with some devotees. A few days later, Pandit Shashadhar gave a lecture on religion in Alambazar or North Baranagore, and from there he visited the Master at the Dakshineswar Kali temple. On the morning of the return chariot festival, the Master went to Balaram's house at Baghbazar and joyfully passed that day and the next with the devotees. On the morning of the third day, he returned to Dakshineswar by boat with Gopal-ma and other devotees. On the day of the return chariot festival, Pandit Shashadhar came to Balaram's house and prayed to the Master with folded hands and tearful eyes: "Sir, philosophy has dried up my heart. Please bestow upon me a drop of devotion." The Master went into ecstasy and touched the pandit's heart on that day. It will not be out of place to give the reader details of these stories.

15. The places the Master visited during the Nine-Day Festival in 1885.

On the first day of the Chariot Festival, the Master went to Ishan's house at Thanthania in Calcutta with Jogin, Hazra, and a few other devotees. Seldom does one meet a devotee like Ishan, so kind and generous, with such faith in God. He had eight sons, all of them well educated. His third son, Satish, was a classmate of Narendra and an expert *pakhoaj* [drum] player. Narendra visited him quite often and would sing with his sweet voice while Satish accompanied him on his drum. Swami Vivekananda [Narendra] once told

16. Ishan Chandra Mukhopadhyay.

us that Ishan's kindness was not less than that of Pandit Ishwar Chandra Vidyasagar. On many occasions Swamiji himself saw Ishan give away his entire meal to beggars and practically go without food himself because there was no cooked food at home. He also told us that many times he saw Ishan weeping when he found that he could not mitigate the suffering of others. Ishan was very kind and also devoted to practising japa. On a regular basis he would practise japa at Dakshineswar from sunrise to sunset. His steadfast devotion made him very dear to and a favourite of the Master. We remember that one evening after finishing his japa Ishan bowed down at the Master's feet, and the Master, in ecstasy, touched Ishan's head with his feet. When the Master later regained normal consciousness, he told Ishan emphatically: "O brahmin, dive deep, dive deep!" (In other words, become absorbed in the name of God instead of superficially repeating a mantra.) At that time Ishan was performing worship and japa from morning till four in the afternoon. After a light meal, he would talk to people or listen to devotional songs; later in the evening he would resume practising japa for several hours. His sons took responsibility for his worldly affairs. The Master visited Ishan's house now and then, and when Ishan was in Calcutta, he would go to see the Master in Dakshineswar. Otherwise, he passed his days practising austerities in holy temples or places of pilgrimage.

On the day of the Chariot Festival in 1885, the Master went to Ishan's house and had spiritual discussions with some brahmin scholars from Bhatpara. The Master heard from Swami Vivekananda that Pandit Shashadhar was staying nearby, so he went to see him that day. Swamiji knew of the pandit's arrival in Calcutta from the people who had cordially invited the pandit to speak on religion. Swamiji had been acquainted with these people for some time and often visited their house on College Street. Swamiji felt that the pandit's symbolic exposition of religion was full of errors, so he frequently went to that house to reason with the pandit on various points. Swami Brahmananda told us that Swamiji thus learned many things about the pandit, which he reported to the Master. Swamiji took the Master to meet the pandit, and on that day the Master gave the pandit some valuable instructions. During this first visit the Master told the pandit that if one tries to teach religion without a "command," or authority from the Divine Mother, one's efforts will be totally fruitless. Sometimes the attempt inflates a preacher's pride and egoism, leading that person down the path of destruction. After listening to these great fiery and powerful words of the Master, the pandit stopped preaching and went to Kamakhya to practise austerities.

In the evening, after taking his leave of the pandit, the Master went with

| 17. Swami Yogananda's [Jogin's] rigidness in his religious practices. | Jogin to Balaram's house at Baghbazar. At that time Jogin was strictly observing caste rules regarding food; he would not even drink water in anyone else's |

house. That day he ate a little breakfast at home in the morning before he left

Dakshineswar with the Master. The Master usually did not ask Jogin to eat anything because he knew of his strictness concerning food. But after observing Balaram's devotion and faith in the Master, Jogin would accept fruit, milk, and sweets at his house. The Master knew that. Shortly after arriving at Balaram's, the Master said to him: "Hello, he (*pointing to Jogin*) has not eaten anything since morning. Please give him some food." Balaram immediately took Jogin to the dining hall and fed him sumptuously. We mention this incident as an example of how the Master, even though he was often absorbed in ecstasy, still paid attention to the physical and mental needs of his devotees.

During the Chariot Festival at Balaram's a current of bliss flowed among those in the company of the Master. Shortly after sunset, the image of Jagannath was adorned with garlands and sandal paste and brought from the inner family shrine to the front part of the house. The image was then placed in a small chariot that was decorated with cloth and flags. Fakir, Balaram's family priest and also a devotee of the Master, performed the worship.

18. The Chariot Festival at Balaram Basu's house in Calcutta.

While Fakir was living at Balaram's house, he went to school and tutored Balaram's only son, Ramakrishna. Fakir was a sincere and devout person, and he became dedicated to the Master at their first meeting. The Master was fond of listening to him sing hymns, and one day taught him how to slowly and distinctly recite every word of Shankara's hymn on Kali. That evening the Master took Fakir to the northern veranda of the room he was staying in, touched him while in ecstasy, and asked him to meditate. As a result Fakir had wonderful visions and experiences.

Now the devotees began to sing kirtan and pull the chariot. The Master also took hold of the chariot rope and pulled briefly. While in ecstasy he began to dance rhythmically. Charmed with that ecstatic dance and the loud roar of spiritual excitement, the devotees were overwhelmed with devotion as they pulled the chariot around the rectangular upper veranda at the front of the house, singing and dancing. The kirtan finally ended by glorifying the names of Jagannath, Govinda, Radha, and Chaitanya and his companions and devotees. Afterwards, the image of Jagannath was taken from the chariot and transferred to an attic room on the third floor where it would remain for seven days. This was meant to symbolize that Jagannath had gone to a different place, and after seven days would return in His chariot. After installing Jagannath in the attic room, the priest offered food to Him. The prasad was distributed first to the Master and then to the devotees. The Master and Jogin spent that night at Balaram's, but the devotees returned to their homes.

At 8:00 or 9:00 the next morning, a boat was obtained for the Master's return to Dakshineswar. The Master went to the inner chambers of the house to bow down to Jagannath in the shrine. He received salutations from the

19. The women devotees' devotion for the Master.

family members, then walked towards the front of the house. The women devotees followed the Master up to the front roof of the kitchen on the eastern side of the inner chambers, then sadly returned. Who wanted to be separated from such a wonderful living God? After one crossed the roof, there were three or four steps up, then a door that opened upon the rectangular veranda in the front part of the house. Most of the women stopped where the roof ended, but one of them was so overwhelmed with devotion that she was not aware of her surroundings. She followed the Master to the rectangular veranda and appeared before the unfamiliar men assembled there [which was contrary to the social norm].

After he took his leave of the women devotees, the Master was walking in such an abstracted mood that he was not at all aware that the women devotees had followed him and then returned, and that one of them was still following him. Only those who have seen the Master walk in that manner will understand how extraordinary it was. It is difficult to explain it to others. As a result of practising concentration for twelve years, nay for his whole life, the Master's mind had become so one-pointed that whatever action he set it to, it remained there, oblivious to distractions. His body and senses were so well controlled that they expressed whatever mood was in his mind, without wavering. They could not play pranks on him. It is hard to explain this because when we look at our own minds, it seems as if all the contending thoughts reign there simultaneously, and the thoughts that are comparatively strong by habit run of their own accord, disobeying the body and the senses. What a difference between the constitution of the Master's mind and that of ours!

20. The Master walks in an abstracted mood, and a woman devotee follows him.

Many more events can be mentioned here as examples of the Master's abstracted mood. When the Master left his room at Dakshineswar to visit Mother Kali in the temple he would go to the eastern veranda of his room, descend the steps to the courtyard, and then walk straight to the Kali temple, even though the Radha-Govinda temple was on the way. He could have bowed down first to the deities in this temple and then gone to the Kali temple, but he was unable to do that. He always went directly to the Kali temple and bowed down to the Mother, and then on his way back to his room he would visit the Radha-Govinda temple. We thought that the Master did this because he loved the Mother more, but one day he told us: "Well, can you tell me why this is? When I intend to see Mother Kali, I have to go directly to Her temple. I have no choice other than to go there; I can't wander elsewhere or visit the Radha-Govinda temple. It's as if someone drags my feet straight to the Kali temple and doesn't let me turn this way or that. After seeing Mother Kali, I can then go other places. Can you tell me why this is?"

21. More examples of how the Master would walk in an abstracted mood: the reason.

We replied, "We don't know, sir." We thought to ourselves: "Why is this not possible? If he wishes, he can easily visit the Radha-Govinda temple first. Perhaps his desire to see Mother Kali is greater." But we could not express our thoughts to him just then. Sometimes the Master would answer his own question: "You see, whenever I decide to do something, I have to do it immediately. I can't wait for a moment." Who knew then that a one-pointed mind was constrained to moving and functioning in that way? Who knew then that the Master's whole mind was one-pointed throughout his life and that when a particular thought arose no contrary thought could override it? Sometimes the Master said: "Look, when I reach the nirvikalpa state, there is no more I or you, no more seeing or hearing, no more speaking or reasoning. Everything disappears. When the mind comes down two or three steps, a divine intoxication persists and I cannot interact with various people or things. If at that time I sit down to take my meal and fifty dishes are served to me, my hand will not move towards all of them; it will take food from one bowl only. When I am in that state, I have to mix rice, lentils, vegetables, rice pudding, and other foods together before I can eat."

We were dumbfounded when we heard about this state, which was two or three steps below the Absolute. The Master also said: "Sometimes I'm in such a state that I can't touch anyone. If any one of them (*pointing to the devotees*) touches me, I cry out in pain." Who among us could understand these words of the Master? At that time pure sattva was so prevalent in the Master's mind that he could not bear the touch of anyone who had even the slightest impurity! He said: "During ecstasy I reach another state, and then I can touch only him (*pointing to Baburam*). If he holds[5] me at that time, I don't suffer from pain. If he feeds me, I can eat." Now let us continue our topic.

While walking in that abstracted mood, the Master reached the outer
22. The Master invites a woman devotee to come to Dakshineswar.
veranda where the chariot had been pulled the night before. Suddenly he looked back and saw that a woman devotee was following him. The Master stopped and saluted her repeatedly, saying, "Blissful Mother! Blissful Mother!" She bowed down to the Master. When she got up, the Master looked at her and said, "Why don't you come, O Mother, why don't you come with me?" The Master asked her in such a way that she felt compelled to follow him to the ferry ghat on foot without any reservations. (She was

5. As the Master had no body-consciousness during ecstasy, his limbs (hands, head, and neck) would become limp, and sometimes his whole body leaned to one side and was in danger of falling. The devotees nearby would catch hold of him so that he might not fall and would slowly set his limbs in their proper positions. They repeated the name of that particular deity under whose influence the Master had entered samadhi, such as, Kali, Kali; Rama, Rama; Om, Om; Om Tat Sat, and so on. After listening to the name of the deity for some time, the Master would slowly regain normal consciousness. He felt terrible pain if the name of a deity other than the one that had put him into that ecstatic state was uttered to him.

then thirty and had never gone anywhere without a palanquin or carriage.) She rushed back inside the house and told Balaram's wife, "I am going to Dakshineswar with the Master." When another woman devotee heard this, she also gave up her household work and joined her. After the Master asked that woman to come with him, he did not look back; he went in that ecstatic mood straight to the boat with Jogin and Junior Naren. The two women ran to the boat and seated themselves on the deck outside the awning just before it embarked.

During the journey the first woman devotee said to the Master: "I want to call on God more and put my mind wholly on Him, but it is hard to control. What shall I do?"

> 23. On the boat the Master answers one woman's question: "Be like a fallen leaf in a gale."

The Master responded: "Why don't you surrender to Him? Be like a leaf in a gale. Do you know what that is like? A fallen leaf lies on the ground and moves about as the wind carries it. Similarly, one should depend on God. Let the mind move as the power of divine consciousness moves it. That is all."

While they were talking, the boat reached the Kali temple ghat. The Master got out of the boat and went into the Kali temple. The women devotees went to the Holy Mother at the nahabat,[6] and after bowing down to her they visited the Kali temple.

The Master bowed down to the Mother. Then, in an ecstatic mood, he walked with his boy devotees to the natmandir. He sat down and began to sing in his sweet voice:

O Mother, Consort of Shiva, You have deluded this world.
You entertain Yourself by playing the vina in the great lotus of the
  muladhara.
Your music vibrates through the great mantra in three scales, taking the
  form of the three gunas.
Your music strikes the three cords — sushumna, ida, and pingala — of
  that musical instrument, the body.
You play with melody, rhythm, and tempo at the six centres of kundalini:
  Bhairava-raga in muladhara, Sri-raga in swadhisthana, Mallara-raga
  in manipura, Vasanta-raga in anahata, Hindola-raga in vishuddha,
  and Karnataka-raga in ajna.
Again, O Mother, You transcend all sound by crossing the three octaves.
O Mother, Sri Nandakumar[7] says that one cannot realize the Supreme
  Truth unless You remove the veil of Your three gunas, which covers
  the face of Brahman.

6. Holy Mother used to sleep on the lower floor of the nahabat [the concert tower], where she kept all the household goods. She would cook in the front veranda of her room. Sometimes at daytime she would stay in the upper room of the nahabat and, if there were a number of women devotees from Calcutta, she would arrange for them to stay in the upper room.
7. The composer. — *Translator*

The Master was singing while seated in the northern part of the natmandir facing the Divine Mother. The devotees — some sitting and some standing — were overwhelmed as they listened to the song. While singing, the Master suddenly stood up and went into ecstasy. The singing stopped. His divine smile flooded the entire place with bliss. The devotees remained motionless

24. Reaching Dakshineswar, the Master goes into ecstasy; the devotees see proof that a person with a sore should not touch a deity.

as they gazed upon the beautiful form of the Master. Seeing the Master's body leaning a little, Junior Naren reached out to hold him and keep him from falling. But as soon as he was touched, the Master cried out in pain. Junior Naren withdrew himself when he realized that the Master did not want to be touched. From inside the temple Ramlal heard the Master cry out and hurried to take hold of him. The Master remained in that state for some time and only gradually regained his normal consciousness after hearing the name of God. But he could still not stand in a normal way because of that divine intoxication. His legs were wobbling excessively.

In this condition the Master crawled down the steps of the northern side of the natmandir to the temple courtyard. He was then speaking like a little child, saying: "Mother, I will not fall. Will I fall?" In truth, when watching the Master at that time one felt that he was a boy of three or four years. He was saying those words as he gazed at the Mother, depending on Her as he confidently made his way down the steps. Shall we ever see anywhere else such wonderful reliance on God, even in such small matters?

After crossing the courtyard, the Master reached his own room and went

25. The Master sees kundalini while in ecstasy; what he says about it.

to the western semicircular veranda to sit. He was still in ecstasy; the mood possessed him. Sometimes it lessened a little, but would increase again and he would almost lose consciousness. After being in this

condition for some time, the Master — still in that condition — said to the devotees: "Have you seen the Snake? It is giving me so much trouble!" Forgetting the devotees, he addressed the snake-like kundalini (for he was then experiencing the Serpent Power): "Please go now. Madam, move away. I shall smoke tobacco and wash my mouth. I have not yet brushed my teeth." Thus, he spoke with the devotees at times and sometimes addressed the divine form seen in ecstasy. Gradually he returned to the normal plane of consciousness.

When the Master returned to the normal state, he was concerned about

26. When his ecstasy is over, the Master is concerned about the devotees' food; he sends the women to the market.

the devotees. He sent someone to the Holy Mother to ask whether she had any vegetables in her store and received word that she had nothing. The Master was anxious, wondering who would go to the market. If vegetables were not bought from the market, how would the devotees from Calcutta have their meal?

After thinking awhile, the Master asked the women devotees who had come with him, "Can you go to the market and buy some vegetables?" "Yes, we can," they replied. They went to the market and bought two large eggplants, some potatoes, and some spinach, which the Holy Mother cooked. Meanwhile, someone brought a plate full of prasad from the Kali temple for the Master, as usual. When he had finished his meal, the devotees had some of the prasad.

Later, the reason for the Master's pain when Junior Naren touched him during ecstasy came to light. Junior Naren had a tumour on his left temple that was growing day by day. Doctors had performed surgery on his tumour and applied medicine to reduce the pain, but the wound had not yet healed. We had heard that one with a wound on the body should not touch a divine form, and that statement was unexpectedly proven to be true in front of us. The Master had undoubtedly suffered pain. However, we were unable to understand the inner power that caused him to recoil automatically from that unpleasant touch when he was absorbed in a divine mood and had lost consciousness of his surroundings. We knew that the Master had a high opinion of Junior Naren's purity of character. And when the Master was in a normal state, he touched Junior Naren as he did others, despite his wound, allowing him to touch his feet and mix freely with him. How then could Junior Naren have known that the Master could not bear his touch during ecstasy? But after that, until his wound was completely healed, Junior Naren did not again touch the Master during ecstasy.

The whole day thus passed in spiritual discussion in the company of the Master. In the evening the devotees left for their respective homes, and the two women took leave of the Master and the Holy Mother and returned to Calcutta on foot.

*   *   *

Two or three days elapsed after the incidents described above. Then one

27. The childlike Master became as frightened as a boy.

afternoon Pandit Shashadhar was scheduled to visit the Master at the Dakshineswar Kali temple. Sometimes the childlike Master was as nervous as a boy, especially when he heard that a famous person was coming to see him. He was nervous because he had no education. Moreover, there was no way to predict when he would go into ecstasy. When he did, he had no body-consciousness — not to speak of wearing clothes! And if his clothes dropped off, how would the visitor react? The Master taught again and again: "People are like worms. One cannot realize God as long as one has these three: shame, hatred, and fear." Was the Master then a beggar of name and fame? When we tested him we invariably found that his attitude was that of a little boy who shrinks in fear and shyness upon meeting a strange man. But as soon as he became a little familiar with that person, he jumped on his shoulder, pulled his hair, and freely indulged in various sweet pranks with him. If the Master had possessed even the slightest desire for name and fame, he could not have spoken so freely and bluntly to Maharaja Jatindra Mohan Tagore and the great national leader Krishnadas Pal.[8]

Sometimes one noticed that the Master was very apprehensive about his visitors' welfare. Although he did not care whether his visitors understood his actions and the way he conducted himself, he knew that it would be inauspicious for them if they criticized him because they did not understand, so he was concerned for them. Once Girish spoke harshly to the Master because his feelings were wounded. He also made importunate demands. At this, the Master said: "Look, let him say whatever he likes about me. But I hope he didn't speak ill of my Mother."

The Master became quite fearful when he heard that Pandit Shashadhar

| 28. Pandit Shashadhar's second visit to the Master. |

was coming to visit. He said to Jogin, Junior Naren, and others, "Look, be here when the pandit comes." What the Master meant was this: He was an unlettered man and might not speak to the pandit properly, so we should be present to converse with the pandit and to protect the Master from his own lapses. Ah, it is hard to explain that boyish insecurity to others! But when Pandit Shashadhar arrived, the Master became a different person. Smiling, he looked at the pandit steadily, then went into a semiecstatic state. Addressing the pandit, the Master said: "Hello, you are a pandit. Please say something."

Shashadhar replied: "Sir, my heart is dried up with too much philosophy, so I have come to you for a little sweet devotion. Let me listen to what you say."

"What can I say?" responded the Master. "No one can describe the true nature of Brahman. It first manifested Itself as a twin principle, half man and half woman. Why? To show that It was both Purusha and Prakriti. Descending a step lower, It separated into Purusha and Prakriti as distinct entities."

As he spoke about the hidden truths of spirituality, the Master became excited and stood up. He then said to Shashadhar: "As long as one's mind is not absorbed in Satchidananda, one can both call on Him and perform household duties. Afterwards, when the mind merges in Him, there is no more need to perform any duties. For example, consider this line of the kirtan: *Nitai amar mata hati* [Nitai is my mad elephant].[9] When a musician

8. During their first meeting, the Master said to Maharaja Jatindra Mohan Tagore: "My dear sir, I cannot address you as 'Raja.' How can I tell a lie?" Again, when Jatindra Mohan compared himself with the virtuous King Yudhisthira, the Master criticized his attitude with disgust. When Krishnadas Pal argued with the Master that there was no religion other than doing good to the world, the Master with great annoyance pointed out the flaw in his understanding.

9. While singing kirtan, Nitai (Nityananda, the main disciple of Chaitanya) became so intoxicated that he would jump about like a mad elephant. — *Translator*

starts singing, he is very careful about the words of the song — its tone, measure, rhythm, and tempo. When his mind becomes absorbed in the theme of the song, he sings only, 'Mata hati, mata hati.' Later, when his mind is more absorbed, he repeats only, 'Hati, hati.' And finally when his mind is submerged in the spiritual mood, he cannot say even 'Hati,' only 'Ha —'" (he remains silent with mouth agape).

Thus, saying "Ha —," the Master became speechless and motionless in ecstasy and remained in that state for about fifteen minutes. His face was serene and bright, and he had no outer consciousness. When his ecstasy ended, he told Shashadhar: "O pandit, I have seen everything about you.[10] You are a good person. After cooking food and feeding everyone, a housewife places her towel on her shoulder and goes to the pond to bathe and to wash her clothes. She doesn't return to the kitchen. Similarly, when you're done telling people about God, you will depart, never to return."

Pandit Shashadhar responded by saying, "It is all your grace." He then took the dust of the Master's feet again and again. As he listened to the Master's words, the pandit was dumbfounded and began to shed tears at the thought that he had not yet realized God.

One of our close friends went to the Master the day following Shasha-

29. The Master describes this incident to a devotee.

dhar's visit to Dakshineswar. We shall now narrate how the Master described that incident to him:

"Look, there is no book-learning here. I'm an unlettered man. I was terribly afraid when I heard that the pandit was coming to see me. You see, I'm not even aware of my clothing. I was extremely nervous that I might say something improper. I prayed to the Divine Mother: 'Look after me, Mother. I don't know any scriptures except You. Please protect me.' I told some people around me: 'You all be present when the pandit arrives. I shall feel confident if I see you near me.' When the pandit arrived, I was not entirely rid of my nervousness; I kept looking at him and listening to his words. Suddenly, the Mother revealed Shashadhar's inner self to me. I saw that scriptural erudition was of no avail without discrimination and renunciation. Then I felt a current rush towards my head, and the last trace of fear vanished from my mind. I was completely overwhelmed. My face turned upward and out of my mouth came an incessant torrent of words. The more I talked, the more I felt that a fresh supply was coming from within, just as when a man in Kamarpukur measures paddy, another person pushes forward a fresh supply. I was entirely unaware of what I was saying. When I regained a little consciousness I found the pandit in tears, completely overwhelmed.

"Occasionally, I have this experience. One day Keshab sent word that he would take me for a boat trip on the Ganges and bring with him a Westerner

10. The Master meant that he went to the higher realm through samadhi and saw all of the pandit's past impressions.

(*Reverend Joseph Cook, who was visiting India*). I was nervous that day also, and had to go to the pine grove again and again to answer the call of nature. When they arrived and I got into the boat, I had the same experience that I did when the pandit came. I said many things unconsciously. Later, they (*pointing to us*) said, 'You gave much wonderful advice.' But you see, I was completely unaware of it."

How can we understand these wonderful experiences of our glorious

| 30. Observing the superhuman actions of the Master, one understands that similar stories about other avatars are true. | Master? An extraordinary Power enacted Its divine play through his body and mind, inexplicably attracting any person It liked to Dakshineswar and giving that person the ability to reach a higher realm of spirituality. We witnessed this but could not comprehend it. But because we saw the results, we |

realized that those events actually did take place. Many times we saw a malicious man come to the Master with hostile intentions, but when the Master touched that person while in ecstasy and overwhelmed him with that divine power, his inner nature began to change. From then on that man would be blessed with a new life.

Jesus transformed the life of Mary [Magdalene], a courtesan, with a mere touch. When Chaitanya, in ecstasy, sat on a man's shoulders, the man's doubt, disbelief, and other heretical feelings were quelled and he attained devotion to God. On reading about similar events in the lives of previous avatars, we used to think that those stories had been concocted by generations of their disciples to develop fanaticism and attract a large following. We believed these stories to be stumbling blocks on the path to true spirituality. We remember that when we read in the *Bhakti-Chaitanya-Chandrika*, published by the New Dispensation, about Chaitanya losing outer consciousness when he chanted Hari's name, we thought that the author had lost his mind. How narrow-minded we were then! What misfortune would have befallen us if we had not met the Master! But after knowing the Master, we are now in the position described by this saying: "We don't know how to thatch, but we know the right kind of straw." Now we are at least protected from accepting anything and everything as religion, be it from charlatans or from our own roguish doubting minds. Now that we know that one can directly impart devotion, faith, and other spiritual qualities to others as though they were tangible objects, we are waiting with confidence to attain immortality by the grace of the infinitely merciful Master.

Chapter 6

Sri Ramakrishna in the Company of Devotees: The Story of Gopal-ma, First Part

I worship Krishna in the form of the child Gopala, the son of a gopi. His complexion is as dark as a rain cloud, his eyes are like the petals of a blue lotus, and his curly dark hair is tied up on his head with a peacock feather.... I bow to Gopala who is like a bee sipping honey from the lips of the gopis. — GOPALA STOTRA 1,2,6

Whatever may be the form a devotee seeks to worship with faith — in that form alone I make his faith unwavering. — GITA 7:21

And whoso shall receive one such little child in my name receiveth me.
— MATTHEW 18:5

WE CANNOT SAY EXACTLY WHEN GOPAL-MA[1] FIRST MET the Master. We first saw her with the Master at Dakshineswar sometime in March or April of 1885. At that point, she had been visiting the Master for six months and had enjoyed a wonderful lila with him as Gopala, the child Krishna. We still remember that day. Gopal-ma was seated near the large jar of Ganges water in the northwest

---

1. We have seen how the Master, established in bhavamukha, enacted his divine play with certain special aspirants and devotees. As an example, we present to the reader the wonderful spiritual visions and experiences of Gopal-ma, a devotee of Sri Ramakrishna. To those who think that we have exaggerated her story, we want to say that we have not embellished it nor have we even changed the language. We have presented her story almost exactly as we collected it from the Master's female devotees. We have gathered the information from people who always try to speak the whole truth and lament if they fail. They were not flatterers of the "Brahmani of Kamarhati" at all; rather, at times they vehemently criticized some of her actions and conduct to us.

corner of the Master's room, facing southeast towards the Master. Although she was about sixty years old at the time, her face was beaming like that of a young girl. When we were introduced, she said: "You are G——'s son? Then you belong to us. Ah! G——'s son has become a devotee! This time Gopala will attract everyone, one after another — with no exceptions. Very well. Until now I was related to you from a worldly standpoint, but now we are related spiritually, and this relationship is much closer."

Gopal-ma's first visit was sometime in the fall of 1884. The sky was clear

| 1. Gopal-ma's first visit to the Master. |

and bright. We remember that it was a little cold in the middle of October that year; Gopal-ma probably met Sri Ramakrishna for the first time during this period. They came to visit the Master by boat, embarking at the temple garden on the bank of the Ganges at Kamarhati, which belonged to Govinda Chandra Datta of Pataldanga, Calcutta. We say "they" because Gopal-ma was not alone that day. She was accompanied by the widow of Govinda Chandra Datta and her distant relative, Kamini. Sri Ramakrishna was then well known in Calcutta, and when the two ladies heard about this extraordinary holy man they became eager to see him. A special worship service honouring Krishna was performed every year between mid-October and mid-November, and Govinda's widow (the landlady) would come and live in the temple garden to supervise the service. The distance between Kamarhati and Dakshineswar is two or three miles, so the ladies took the opportunity to visit the Kali temple of Rani Rasmani.

When they arrived that day, the Master cordially received them in his room, gave them many instructions in devotion, sang devotional songs to them, and bade them good-bye, asking them to come again. The landlady invited Sri Ramakrishna to visit her at the Kamarhati temple. The Master promised to go there when it was convenient for him. The Master spoke highly of the landlady and Gopal-ma that day. He said: "Ah! What beautiful expressions on their faces! They are floating in the ocean of bliss and devotion. Their eyes are soaked with divine love. Even the *tilak* [holy mark] on their noses is beautiful!" In other words, they were not ostentatious: Their devout nature appeared in their manners and in the way they dressed with no special effort on their part.

Govinda Chandra Datta of Pataldanga had been an agent for a European

| 2. Govinda Chandra Datta of Pataldanga. |

firm well known in Calcutta. His efficiency and reliability made him very wealthy. Later in life, he was paralyzed and incapacitated by a stroke. Prior to this, his only son had died. His two daughters, Bhuto and Naran,[2] had children. Govinda's property was considerable, so he was able to spend his time in spiritual discussions and religious activities. He arranged for discourses on

---

2. Yajneswari and Narayani.

Aghoremani Devi (1822-1906), known as Gopal-ma.

Gopal-ma's thirty-year sadhana was spent in this room at the Kamarhati temple garden.

the Ramayana and the Mahabharata to be held in his house, and also for the entire Bhagavata to be recited. He installed images of Radha and Krishna with great pomp in the garden at Kamarhati, and to brahmins and the poor he made a generous gift of valuables equal to the weight of himself and his wife. Moreover, the temple celebrated many festivals all year round in connection with worship of the deities, and the prasad of Radha and Krishna was distributed among guests and visitors, as well as among the poor and downtrodden.

After Govinda's death, for a long time his virtuous and devoted wife

3. His devoted wife.

continued the worship services in a grand way. Later, however, the greater part of the property was lost for various reasons, so to ensure that the worship service would not be neglected, the landlady lived in the temple garden and supervised all the activities. She was an old-fashioned woman. She underwent many sorrows and suffered much grief in her life, so she had a deep realization that peace comes only through the practice of religion. But horrible maya does not leave a person so easily: she had to care for her daughters and sons-in-law, and take into account society, status, honour, and other worldly concerns. After her husband's death, she strictly observed the vows of brahmacharya. She slept on the floor, bathed three times daily, and ate only one meal a day. She spent her time observing religious rules and rites, fasting, serving the deities, practising japa and meditation, and performing charity and other philanthropic activities.

Govinda's family priest lived very near the Kamarhati temple. Nilmadhav

4. Aghoremani belonged to the family of Govinda's priest.

Bandyopadhyay, the priest, was well respected; his sister, Aghoremani Devi, was known as Gopal-ma. She had been widowed when she was young and lived with her father's family. Because she closely associated with the landlady, Aghoremani spent much of her time serving the deities in the [Kamarhati] temple. As her devotion gradually increased, she felt a strong desire to live in the temple garden on the Ganges. With permission from the landlady, she moved into one of the rooms in the women's quarters there, but she visited her family briefly once or twice a day.

Aghoremani and the landlady shared a passion for practising austerities and brahmacharya, so there was a similarity of thought and feeling between them. As a wealthy woman, the landlady outwardly had to maintain her social status, but Aghoremani was free from those burdensome obligations because she owned almost nothing and had no children. Aghoremani had sold her jewellery and her husband's property and had received six or seven hundred rupees, which she had invested in securities and left in the landlady's care. Aghoremani lived on the interest from her savings. Sometimes in dire need she was forced to draw on her capital a little. The landlady helped her and her brother's family in every possible way.

Aghoremani was a child-widow and knew nothing about the joys of a

5. Aghoremani's rigid observance of religious practices.

husband's company. Women say, "Child-widows are so fastidious that they wash even their salt before using it." Aghoremani was like that as she grew up.
She was extreme in her religious customs and practices. For example, one day while she was serving rice from a pot onto Sri Ramakrishna's plate, the Master's hand somehow touched the wooden spoon she was using. Aghoremani could not eat the rice left in the pot, and she even threw that wooden spoon into the Ganges. This happened during one of her early visits to the Master.

There were two or three clay ovens in the nahabat at Dakshineswar. The food offering to the Mother Kali was invariably late; sometimes it would not be completed until 1:30 p.m. Sri Ramakrishna quite often suffered from stomach trouble. So before noon, the Holy Mother would start cooking rice and soup for him using those ovens. She also prepared lentils and chapati for the devotees who occasionally spent the night with the Master. When women devotees from Calcutta and other places came to visit the Master, they stayed in the nahabat with the Holy Mother during the day and sometimes spent the night there as well. The Holy Mother cooked for them using the same ovens. But on days when Aghoremani — or the Brahmani of Kamarhati, or Bamni, as the Master called her in the beginning — visited the Master, the Holy Mother would cook rice and soup for the Master first and then would purify the earthen oven with three layers of cow dung and some Ganges water. Afterwards, Aghoremani would start her own cooking. It is amazing how strictly she observed her rules and customs!

From her childhood onward, Aghoremani was very sensitive. She could

6. Aghoremani lived in the temple garden of Govinda and practised austerities there.

not bear anyone's criticism, and she could not ask anyone for financial help. In addition, if she discovered any improprieties, she did not hesitate to speak out bluntly. So very few people got along with her.
The room her landlady gave to her was at the southern part of the [Kamarhati] garden. One could see the Ganges through three southern windows, and there were two doors — one on the north side and the other on the west. Aghoremani sat in her room watching the Ganges and repeating her mantra day and night. Thus, she passed thirty years in that room through happiness and misery before she met Sri Ramakrishna.

It is possible that the family of Aghoremani's father was Shakta; we do not know the religious tradition of her husband's family. However, Aghoremani was devoted to Vishnu and had received the Gopala mantra from her guru. Perhaps her close relation with the landlady helped her to develop that attitude. Govinda's family guru belonged to the Goswami dynasty of Malpara, and a couple of Goswami priests had quite often stayed at the Kamarhati temple garden from the time it was dedicated. It is hard to understand how she developed such an intense maternal attitude towards God and worshipped Him as her son in the form of Gopala without having had any experience of a mother's affection towards a child. Some will say that this was due to her previous birth and the impressions accumulated through past lives. Be that as it may, this story actually came to pass.

The women of England and the United States become interested in reli-

| 7. Women of the East and the West practise religion differently. | gion when they encounter suffering in the world, or for some other reason. This urge then manifests itself in charitable works, philanthropic activities, and |

service to the poor and the sick. Their goal becomes to help others all the time. In India it is the opposite. The inclination towards religion appears here in the form of brahmacharya, austerities, religious rules and rites, japa, and so on. Gradually the practitioner becomes more and more introspective and eventually seeks to renounce the world. The attitude that the goal of human life is to attain God, and therein lies real peace, pervades the atmosphere of this country and has penetrated into the very marrow of its men and women. So Aghoremani's solitary life and austerities might seem unusual to readers from other countries, but they are natural in India.

*   *   *

Aghoremani felt drawn to Sri Ramakrishna upon their first meeting, but she did not know why or how far-reaching this attraction would be. As she experienced this indescribable fascination, she thought: "He is a wonderful holy man and a true devotee. As soon as I have time, I shall come back to see him." The landlady felt the same way, but it is doubtful that she ever returned. She may have felt that she would be criticized, and in addition she had to spend much time with her daughters and sons-in-law at her home in Pataldanga. Dakshineswar is quite a distance from that place, and before visiting the Master, she would have had to tell everyone and make special arrangements. So most probably she never returned to Dakshineswar.

Aghoremani had no such difficulties. While practising japa a few days

| 8. Aghoremani's second visit to the Master. | after her first visit, she had a desire to visit the Master again. She left for Dakshineswar immediately with two or three pice worth of stale sandesh [a sweet]. |

When the Master saw her, he exclaimed: "Oh, you've come! Please give me what you brought for me." Gopal-ma later said: "I was terribly embarrassed. How could I give him that stale sandesh? So many people brought so many fancy dishes to feed him. But as soon as I arrived, he asked for that bad sandesh." She was speechless with fear and shame, but she reluctantly handed those stale sweets to him. The Master immediately started to eat them with great relish and said to her: "Why do you spend money on sweets? Prepare some sweet coconut balls, and when you visit this place bring one or two of them with you. Or you may bring a little of the ordinary dishes that you cook yourself — a hodge-podge curry with pumpkin leaves or a preparation with potatoes, eggplants, drumsticks, and little balls of mashed legumes. I want to eat your cooking." Gopal-ma later related: "There was no talk about God or religion. He went on speaking about this dish and that. I thought: 'What a strange monk I've come to see! He talks only about food. I'm a poor widow. Where shall I get so many delicacies for him? Enough! I won't come back again.' But as soon as I passed through the gate of the Dakshineswar garden, I felt as if he were pulling me back. I couldn't proceed further. I had a hard time persuading my mind to leave, but at last I returned to Kamarhati." A few days later, Aghoremani again walked the three miles to see Sri Ramakrishna, this time carrying a hodge-podge curry for him. As soon as she arrived, the Master demanded food as before and after relishing it said: "What a delicacy! It's like nectar." Tears rolled down Aghoremani's cheeks as she saw the Master's joy. She thought that the Master had appreciated her humble offering only because she was poor.

Over the next three or four months, Aghoremani visited Dakshineswar often. Whenever she cooked a dish that she particularly liked, she would take it to the Master on her next visit. The Master relished that immensely and would ask her to bring more new dishes, such as a soup of watercress or a curry with *kalmi* spinach. As she listened to the Master's requests — "bring this dish or that" — she sometimes thought in disgust: "O Gopala, is this how you have answered my prayers? You have brought me to a holy man who only asks for food. I shall not come again." But as soon as she returned to Kamarhati, she would feel that irresistible pull, and could think only of how soon she could visit the Master again.

Sri Ramakrishna paid a visit to Govinda's temple garden at Kamarhati

9. The Master's visit to Govinda's temple garden.

and greatly enjoyed the worship service of Radha and Krishna. On that occasion he sang many devotional songs in front of the deities and had prasad there before returning to Dakshineswar. The landlady and others were very impressed by the Master's wonderful ecstasy during kirtan. It is hard to say whether the Goswami priests feared that they might lose control over the landlady and felt some jealousy and hatred towards the Master, but we heard that this was so.

        *   *   *

It was Aghoremani's long-standing routine to get up at 2:00 a.m., tend to personal hygiene, and then start performing japa at 3:00 a.m., finishing at 8:00 or 9:00 a.m. She then took her bath, visited Radha and Krishna in the temple, and performed service to the deities as best she could. She started her own cooking at noon, when the food offering to the deities was over. After lunch she would rest a little, then resume her japa. She interrupted her japa to attend the vesper service, then went back to it until late evening. When she was finished, she drank a little milk and slept for a few hours.

She slept little because wind was the predominant humour of her body. Sometimes she had heart palpitations and difficulty breathing. When the Master learned of this, he told her: "The pressure built up by the spiritual energy generated during your meditation on Hari has caused this. How will you pass your time if you remove the cause? When you feel too much pain, please eat something."

The winter of 1884 passed, and the pleasant spring of 1885 arrived. The whole world was alive with birdsong, and plants and trees were adorned with new leaves and blossoms. In the external awakening of the natural world, there is no distinction between good and bad, except the tendencies of human beings. Nature manifests itself to people according to their good and bad habits and past impressions. The holy are awake to the spiritual side of nature and the unholy to worldly matters. That is the difference.

10. Aghoremani's condition after she sees the divine form of the child Krishna.

It was 3:00 one spring morning when Aghoremani started to practise her japa. After finishing, she began pranayama and was about to offer the result of her practices to her Chosen Deity when she noticed Sri Ramakrishna seated at her left, his right fist clenched. She saw the Master vividly — as alive as she saw him in Dakshineswar. She wondered: "What is this? How did he get here at such an odd hour?" Gopal-ma later described it thus: "I looked at him in amazement and thought, 'How did he get here?' Meanwhile, Gopala (*as she called Sri Ramakrishna*) kept smiling sweetly. I gathered my courage and grasped his left hand — and Sri Ramakrishna's form disappeared. In its place appeared the real Gopala — a large baby of ten months old. His beauty and appearance beggars description! He crawled towards me and, raising one hand, said, 'Mother, give me butter.' I was overwhelmed and bewildered by this amazing experience! I cried out so loudly that if there had been men around the house they would have rushed there. With tearful eyes, I said: 'My son, I am a poor, helpless widow. What shall I feed you? Where shall I get butter and cream, my child?' But that wonderful Gopala did not listen to me. 'Give me something to eat,' he kept saying. What could I do? Sobbing, I got up and took some dry coconut balls from a hanging basket. Placing them in his hand, I said, 'Gopala, my darling, I offer you these wretched things; but please don't give me such poor food in return.'

"I could not perform japa at all. Gopala sat on my lap, snatched away my rosary, jumped on my shoulders, and crawled around the room. At daybreak, I rushed to Dakshineswar on foot like a crazy woman. Gopala accompanied me. I held his buttocks with one hand and his back with the other while his head rested on my shoulder. I distinctly saw Gopala's two tiny, rosy feet dangling over my bosom."

11. In that ecstatic mood she goes to the Master in Dakshineswar.

When the intoxicated Aghoremani walked from the Kamarhati temple garden to the Master in Dakshineswar that morning — still enjoying the vision of her Chosen Deity — one of the women devotees we know was present. Here is what she told us: "It was seven or half past seven in the morning. I was cleaning the Master's room when I heard a familiar voice calling, 'Gopala, Gopala!' I looked outside and saw Gopal-ma coming towards the Master's room. She entered through the eastern door like one intoxicated, her hair dishevelled, her eyes staring, and the end of her cloth trailing on the ground. She was completely oblivious to her surroundings. Sri Ramakrishna was seated on his small cot.

"I was dumbfounded when I saw Gopal-ma in that condition. The Master immediately entered into an ecstatic mood. Gopal-ma sat beside him, and he sat on her lap like a child. Tears were flowing profusely from her eyes. She fed the Master with cream, butter, and sweets that she had brought with her. I was astounded, for never before had I seen the Master touch a woman while he was in a state of ecstasy, although I had heard that the Master once sat on the lap of Bhairavi Brahmani, his guru, when he was in the mood of Gopala and she was in the mood of Yashoda [Krishna's foster mother]. However, I was stupefied witnessing Gopal-ma's condition and the Master's ecstasy. After some time the Master regained his normal consciousness and went back to his cot. But Gopal-ma could not control her exuberant emotion. In rapture, she began dancing around the room, repeating, 'Brahma is dancing and Vishnu is dancing.' As he watched her ecstasy, the Master told me with a smile: 'Look, she is engulfed in bliss. Her mind is now in the abode of Gopala.' Gopal-ma did indeed have such visions while in ecstasy, and she became a different person because of them.

"On another occasion, while Gopal-ma was eating her meal, she became overwhelmed by ecstasy and fed all of us by hand, considering us to be her Gopala. She disliked me a little because I had not married my daughter into a family of equal rank, but on that day she humbly apologized, saying: 'Did I know that you have so much faith and devotion? Gopala [Sri Ramakrishna] can touch almost no one when he is in ecstasy, but today he sat on your shoulders while in bhava samadhi. You are not an ordinary person.'" It is true that on that day the Master suddenly became absorbed in the mood of Gopala after seeing Gopal-ma, and sat on the shoulders of this woman devotee, then on Gopal-ma's lap for a short time.

After arriving at Dakshineswar that spring day, Aghoremani, gripped by that exuberant spiritual mood, shed tears and said many things to Sri Rama-krishna: "Here is Gopala in my arms. . . . Now he enters into you (*pointing to Sri Ramakrishna*). . . . There, he comes out again. . . . Come, my child, come to your wretched mother." While talking in this manner, she saw the naughty Gopala vanish into the Master's body and reappear before her in the form of a luminous boy. His extraordinary play and childish pranks overwhelmed her, making her forget the strict rules, rites, and routines of the external world. Who could control oneself after being caught by that mighty spiritual tidal wave?

On that day Aghoremani became Gopal-ma, and the Master began to call

12. The Master praises her rare state and calms her down.

her by that name. Sri Ramakrishna expressed great delight as he observed her wonderful ecstasy. To calm her, he stroked her chest and fed her with delicacies from his room. Even as she ate, Gopal-ma remained in ecstasy, saying: "Gopala, my darling, your wretched mother has led a life of dire poverty. She has to make her living by spinning and selling sacred thread. Is that why you are taking special care of her today?"

The Master kept her at Dakshineswar that day. She took her bath and meals there. In the evening, when she had calmed a little, the Master sent her back to Kamarhati. The Gopala of her vision went with her, nestled in her arms. When she reached her room, she started to tell her beads as usual; but it became impossible. Her Chosen Deity, for whom she had practised japa and meditation all her life, was now pestering her, demanding this and that as he played in front of her. When Gopal-ma got up and went to bed, Gopala was at her side. She had a hard bed without a pillow, and Gopala began to grumble. Even in bed she had no rest. At last she cradled his head on her left arm and tried to console him, saying: "My child, sleep in this way tonight. Tomorrow I shall go to Calcutta and ask Bhuto [the landlady's eldest daughter] to make a soft pillow for you and to remove all the seeds from the cotton."

As we mentioned earlier, Gopal-ma usually cooked her own food and ate it as prasad after offering it to Gopala. The next morning she went to the garden to collect dry wood for cooking so that she could feed Gopala as early as possible. She saw Gopala collecting wood alongside her and piling it in the kitchen. Thus, the mother and the child collected wood. When she began to cook, the naughty Gopala sat near her or rode around on her back, watching her as she worked. He went on prattling and making many demands. She tried to control him, sometimes with sweet words and sometimes with scolding.

A few days after this event Gopal-ma went to Dakshineswar. After seeing

13. The Master tells Gopal-ma, "You have attained everything."

the Master she went to the nahabat, where the Holy Mother lived, and sat down to practise japa. She told her beads as usual and then bowed down to her Chosen Deity. At that moment the Master arrived from the Panchavati. Seeing Gopal-ma, the Master said: "Why do you practise so much japa now? You have plenty of visions."

"Shall I not practise japa anymore?" Gopal-ma asked "Have I attained everything?"

The Master responded, "Yes, you have attained everything."

"Everything?" asked Gopal-ma.

"Yes, everything," said the Master.

"What are you saying?" asked Gopal-ma. "Have I accomplished everything?"

The Master said: "Yes, you have. It is no longer necessary for you to practise japa and austerity for yourself. But you may continue these disciplines for the welfare of this body (*pointing to himself*)."

Gopal-ma agreed: "All right. Whatever I do henceforth will be for you — you — you."

Gopal-ma referred to this incident later, telling us: "When I heard those words from Gopala [Sri Ramakrishna] I threw my rosary and its little bag into the Ganges that day. I decided to repeat japa on my fingers for his welfare. Long after, I procured another rosary. At that time I thought: 'I must do something. How can I pass twenty-four hours without doing anything?' So I tell my beads for his welfare."

From that point on Gopal-ma's japa and austerities for herself came to an end, but her visits to the Master in Dakshineswar became more frequent. Her previously strict observance of rules concerning food, cleanliness, and routine began to dissipate gradually in that great spiritual current. Gopala now occupied her mind and heart completely; there was no limit to the things that he taught her. How could she maintain her orthodox habits now? Gopala demanded food now and then, and sometimes he put part of his food into her mouth as he ate. How could she refuse it? When she did so, Gopala wept. Buffeted by that spiritual tidal wave, Gopal-ma realized that it was all Sri Ramakrishna's play and that it was he who was her Krishna in the form of Gopala, "dark like a rain cloud, with eyes like the petals of a blue lotus." So she cooked for him, fed him, and no longer hesitated to eat his prasad.

Gopal-ma lived in this manner and carried Krishna in the form of Gopala for two months continuously. It is possible only for a most fortunate one to live for such a long period in the high spiritual realm and to experience and see the Divine Name, the Divine Abode, and the Divine Lord as Pure Consciousness. In the first place, motherly love towards God is rare: It is impossible to have that love if even the slightest awareness of God's power remains in the mind. Moreover, one can easily surmise how much more rare it is to have such a vision of God through motherly love, solidified by steadfast devotion. There is a saying: *Kalau jagarti Gopala, kalau jagarti Kalika* [Gopala is awake in the Kaliyuga, and Mother Kali is awake in the Kaliyuga]. So it seems even now that people sometimes have the vivid experience of those two forms of God.

Sri Ramakrishna told Gopal-ma: "You have achieved enough spiritual experiences. In this Kaliyuga, if one has such visions continuously, one's body cannot last long." Perhaps it was the Master's will that the pure body of this poor woman should be spared some years more for the good of humanity, as a glowing example of motherly love for God. After two months, Gopal-ma's visions and experiences subsided to a great degree. However, she was able to regain the vision as before when she sat quietly and meditated on Gopala.

Chapter 7

Sri Ramakrishna in the Company of Devotees: The Return Chariot Festival in 1885 and the Story of *G*opal-ma, Last Part

Those persons who worship Me, meditating on their identity with Me and ever devoted to Me — to them I carry what they lack and for them I preserve what they already have. — GITA 9:22

SOMETIME AFTER GOPAL-MA SAW GOD IN THE FORM of Gopala, the Master and his devo-

1. The Return Chariot Festival at Balaram Basu's house.	tees went to Balaram's house in Calcutta on the occasion of the Chariot Festival. Balaram was extremely happy and cordially received the devotees.

He was a staunch devotee and belonged to a family that had been dedicated to God for generations. The Master bestowed his unbounded grace on Balaram and on his family.

The Master told us that once he had wished to see Chaitanya singing kirtan

2. The Master's desire to see Chaitanya in his Sankirtan party and his vision. He saw Balaram in that group.	through the streets of the town. His desire was later fulfilled when he was in ecstasy, and it was a marvellous sight: A limitless crowd dancing and singing Hari's name in unrestrained madness! And in the midst of that wave of overwhelming devotion was the

intoxicated Chaitanya, enthralling all with his irresistible charm. The vast crowd had gathered at the Panchavati in Dakshineswar and had slowly made its way past the Master's room, moving towards the gate. The Master said that among all those faces in the crowd, a few had become imprinted on his mind forever; Balaram's serene face, luminous with devotion, was among them. On

Balaram's first visit to the Master in Dakshineswar, the Master immediately recognized him as one of those he had seen in the crowd.

At Kothar in Orissa, Balaram had an estate and a shrine to Krishna where

3. Balaram supervised worship services in various places: All of his food was pure.

worship was conducted regularly. Moreover, he had a shrine to Shyamsundar [Krishna] in Vrindaban and one to Jagannath in his Calcutta residence.[1] He made arrangements for worship of the deity in all of these shrines. The Master used to say: "Balaram's food is very pure. The members of his family have been devotees for generations and have long been hospitable to monks and to the poor. His father is living a retired life at Vrindaban, where he passes his time calling upon the Lord. Not only can I eat Balaram's food, but I take it with pleasure." We noticed that the Master truly enjoyed Balaram's food more than that of any other devotee. Whenever he went to Calcutta in the morning, he invariably took his noon meal at Balaram's home. Although the Master had some reservations about accepting food from others, he had no such qualms when offered the prasad of Narayana or of any other deities.

One can always find something novel and extraordinary in the activities

4. The Master's four suppliers of provisions. Balaram also had the privilege of serving the Master.

of superhuman great souls, be they everyday or occasional events. Those who associated with Sri Ramakrishna, even for a day, will certainly understand what we mean. If one probes a little regarding the Master's acceptance of Balaram's food, the matter will be quite clear. During his sadhana, the Master prayed to the Divine Mother, "Mother, don't make me a dry monk; allow me to enjoy the fun in life." The Divine Mother showed him that she had sent to the world four persons who would provide for his needs. The Master mentioned that the first of these four suppliers was Mathur, a son-in-law of Rani Rasmani. The second was Shambhu Mallick. Surendra Nath Mitra of Simla (whom the Master called "Surendar" or sometimes "Suresh") was a "half supplier." We did not have the good fortune to witness Mathur's and Shambhu's loving service to the Master because we came to the Master long after their passing away. But the Master told us that their service was remarkable. We do not remember whether the Master ever mentioned that Balaram was one of his suppliers. But we were amazed by the way Balaram served the Master; his service was not inferior in any respect to that of other suppliers, except Mathur's. We shall try to describe these things at another time. But this much we can say: Balaram supplied all the food that the Master needed — rice, rock candy, farina, sago, barley, vermicelli, tapioca, and so on — from the day he first met the Master at Dakshineswar until the latter passed away. And as for Surendra, shortly after his first visit, he made arrangements for food and

---

1. Later, this image was transferred to Kothar.

bedding for those devotees who spent the night in Dakshineswar in order to serve the Master.

Who can describe the mysterious relationships that these people had with the Master? And who can explain how they earned such a great privilege? We understand only this much: They were extremely fortunate people to have been thus marked by the Divine Mother! They could not otherwise have been born with the privilege of being helpers in the divine play of Sri Ramakrishna. Their faces could not otherwise have been imprinted on the free, pure, and awakened mind of Sri Ramakrishna, so that he could recognize them at first sight and remark: "They belong to this place [*to him*]. They are born with this special privilege [*of serving him*]."

Because there was not the slightest trace of I-consciousness in the

| 5. The Master always used the words "here" and "of this place" instead of "I" and "mine": the reason. | pure mind of Sri Ramakrishna, he would say, "They belong to this place," instead of "They are mine." It was extremely difficult for him to use the words "I" and "mine." Why say it was difficult? He could not utter either of those words at all. When it was abso- |

lutely necessary, he used those words in this manner: "I am the servant or the child of the Divine Mother." And he could say this only if his mind was full of that sentiment beforehand. If he needed to say "mine" during a conversation, he would say "this place" and point to his body, and the devotees understood him. For example, when the Master said, "That person does not belong to this place," or "That is not the attitude of this place" we knew that he meant, "That person is not my devotee," or "That is not my attitude."

Let us now discuss those who supplied the Master's provisions. Mathur

| 6. How and when the suppliers served the Master. | was the first supplier. He served the Master for four- teen years beginning with the Master's arrival in Dakshineswar and continuing until sometime after |

the end of his sadhana. Shambhu was the second supplier. Shortly after Mathur passed away, Shambhu served the Master until the arrival of Keshab and the Calcutta devotees. Surendra was a half supplier. He served the Master for six or seven years before the Master passed away, then served the monastic disciples for another four or five years. It was Surendra's eagerness and financial support that facilitated the founding of Baranagore Monastery (which later became Belur Math) sometime between mid-September and mid-October 1886 at Munshi's old and dilapidated house. Now one and a half suppliers are yet to be accounted for. Who are they? Are Balaram and Mrs. Sara C. Bull (an American woman who helped Swami Vivekananda build Belur Math) the remaining suppliers? As Sri Ramakrishna and Swami Vivekananda are no longer physically among us, who will settle this question?

*   *   *

After Balaram began to visit Dakshineswar, every year he invited the

7. "All members of Balaram's family are tuned to the same pitch."

Master to visit his house for the Chariot Festival. He lived at 57 Ramkanta Bose Street in Baghbazar, in a house that was owned by his cousin, Harivallabh Basu, a famous lawyer in Cuttack. The Master visited this house countless times. Who can determine how many people were blessed by seeing the Master there? Sometimes the Master jokingly referred to the Kali temple of Dakshineswar as "Mother Kali's Fort," so it would not be an exaggeration to call Balaram's house Her second fort. The Master used to say, "All the members of Balaram's family are tuned to the same pitch." Everyone in the house, from the master and mistress to the little children, was a devotee of God. No member of that family took anything — not even water — without first chanting His name. All had an equal passion for worship, study of the scriptures, service to monks, and charity in noble causes. In some families, one or two persons are religious and others are completely different. But not in Balaram's family: All were of a similar nature. Only a few unselfish and spiritual families can be found in this world. It is even more rare to find a family in which all the members are devoted to the same religious ideal and who help one another to achieve their common goal. So it is not surprising that Balaram's household was the Master's second fort and that it delighted him to be there.

As we mentioned earlier, there was a regular worship service for Lord

8. The Chariot Festival at Balaram's house was unostentatious and performed with devotion.

Jagannath in Balaram's house, and in addition, devotees would gather there to pull the chariot during the Chariot Festival of Jagannath. This ceremony was performed with great devotion: There were no external trappings such as decorating the house, or music, or the noisy frolicking of strangers, or any other tumult or noise. Devotees pulled a small chariot around the upper rectangular veranda in the front part of the house. A kirtan party sang as the chariot was being pulled, and the Master and his devotees joined in the singing. Where else could one find such bliss, such exuberant devotion, and such an intoxicating spiritual mood, and also see the sweet and rhythmic dance of the Master? It was as if Lord Jagannath, pleased with the pure devotion of that sattvic family, had appeared in the image within the chariot and also in Sri Ramakrishna. Where else could one see such a wonderful scene? If a godless man were to fall into the current of that pure devotion, his tears would flow and melt his heart — what can we say of the devotees?

After a few hours of such kirtan, cooked food was offered to Jagannath, and after the Master had eaten, the devotees partook of the prasad. Late at night the mart of joy would come to an end, and all but a few of the devotees would leave for their homes. The author enjoyed this blissful festival only once in his life, during the Return Chariot Festival in 1885 when Gopal-ma

Balaram Basu (1848-1890)

Residence of Balaram Basu in Baghbazar, Calcutta.
Ramakrishna came here 100 times.

was invited to Balaram's house at the Master's request. On that occasion the Master stayed with Balaram's family for two days and nights. He returned to Dakshineswar by boat at 8:00 or 9:00 a.m. of the third day.

*   *   *

The Master arrived at Balaram's in the morning [during the Return Chariot Festival in 1885]. He sat for a while in the front living room and then was taken into the inner apartment for refreshment. Gradually quite a few devotees assembled in the front living room, and his women devotees came to the inner apartment from neighbouring houses. Most of them were either Balaram's relatives or known to him. Whenever the Master came to his house, Balaram would invite the women to visit. And when he went to see Sri Ramakrishna in Dakshineswar, Balaram invited them to accompany him there. Many women devotees — Lady Bhavini, Asim's mother, Ganu's mother [Yogin-ma] and grandmother, and someone's aunt, or sister-in-law, neighbour, or others — came to Balaram's home that festival day.

It is difficult to describe the wonderful relationship that the ever-pure Master had with these pure-hearted, virtuous, and devoted women. Many of them considered the Master to be their Chosen Deity and harboured that faith in him. Some fortunate ones, like Gopal-ma, had even had visions concerning this. So they knew the Master as their very own and were not shy or apprehensive in his presence. Whenever they prepared a delicacy at home, they would send the first portion of it to the Master — or take it to him themselves — before serving it to their husbands and children. During the Master's lifetime, these ladies walked back and forth between their Calcutta residences and Dakshineswar innumerable times. Some days they returned home from Dakshineswar in the evening, sometimes at 10:00 p.m., and sometimes as late as midnight after attending a kirtan or festival. The Master, like a boy, eagerly consulted some of them regarding medicine for his stomach troubles. If anyone laughed, amused by this, the Master would say: "What do you know? She is the wife of a famous physician! She must at least know a couple of medicines." When the Master saw how affectionate and devoted one woman was, he remarked, "She is a gopi made perfect by God's grace." As he enjoyed another's delicious food, he remarked, "She is a cook of Vaikuntha [heaven]; she is an expert in making bitter squash curry."

9. The Master's wonderful relationship with the women devotees.

On the day we are discussing, the Master told the women about Gopal-ma's good fortune as he had his refreshment. He said: "You see, that brahmin woman who comes from Kamarhati loves God as her Gopala. She has had many visions. She said that Gopala extended his hand to her and demanded to be fed. After she had that vision, she came to Dakshineswar one day, overwhelmed with ecstasy and devotion. She calmed down a little after

10. The Master tells the women devotees about Gopal-ma's visions: He sends for her.

eating some food. I asked her to stay that night, but she refused. When she was ready to return to Kamarhati, she again entered that intoxicated state. Her upper cloth was dragging on the ground, but she was not aware of this. I put the cloth back on her shoulder and gently stroked her head. She has tremendous faith and devotion! Well, why don't you send for her?"

As soon as Balaram heard this, he sent someone to fetch Gopal-ma. There was sufficient time for her to arrive as the Master was staying at his house that day and the next.

When the Master had finished his refreshments, he returned to the front living room and began to talk to the devotees about spiritual matters.

At noon the Master ate his lunch and the devotees had prasad. After resting for a little while, the Master went to the outer hall and began talking to the devotees. Shortly before evening the Master went into ecstasy. We have seen the metal image of Gopala in a crawling posture: Its knees and left hand are on the ground, and it is looking joyfully and wistfully upward and asking for something with its right hand raised, palm up. The Master went into ecstasy and assumed that posture, except that his eyes remained half-closed, as if focussed on something within. Shortly after the Master's ecstasy had begun, Gopal-ma's carriage arrived at Balaram's gate. She went upstairs and found the Master in the posture of her Chosen Deity. The devotees present understood that it was Gopal-ma's intense devotion that had brought about this sudden manifestation of Gopala in the Master. They appreciated Gopal-ma and adored her, considering her to be most fortunate. They remarked: "What wonderful devotion! The Master assumed the form of Gopala because of her intense devotion." But Gopal-ma said: "Truly speaking, I don't care for this stiff posture in ecstasy. My Gopala should laugh and play, walk and run. But what is this? He has become stiff like a log. I don't like to see this sort of Gopala!" In fact, when the Master visited Kamarhati for the first time, Gopal-ma had been frightened when she saw him lose outer consciousness in samadhi. She nudged the Master's body, exclaiming, "My child, why have you become like this?"

When we first met the Master, he was about forty-nine years old — or perhaps five or six months short of that. Gopal-ma was there when we visited. Before we became acquainted with the Master, we thought that although people love to see children dance and make gestures, it disgusts them or seems ludicrous if a robust man acts that way. Swami Vivekananda used to say, "Does anyone enjoy watching a rhinoceros dance like a dancing girl?" When we came to the Master, we had to change our views. Although the Master was advanced in age, when he danced, sang, and made gestures — they were so sweet and beautiful! Girish once

11. In the afternoon the Master suddenly becomes absorbed in the mood of Gopala. Just then Gopal-ma arrives.

12. Whatever the Master did during ecstasy was beautiful: the reason.

remarked: "I never dreamt that an old fellow could look so beautiful when he danced!" And it was remarkably beautiful when he assumed the posture of Gopala while in ecstasy that day at Balaram's home. We did not understand why it looked so beautiful; we only felt it to be so. Now we know that the Master completely identified with any mood that came over him. There was not a trace of any other mood in him, nor any insincerity or pretension. He was so inspired and absorbed in that mood that he would become dissolved in it. At that time no one could perceive that an older man was acting like a boy or a woman. The current of his spiritual mood would burst forth from within and completely transform his body.

*   *   *

The Master spent a joyful two days and nights at Balaram's home with the

13. After the festival, the Master returns to Dakshineswar.

devotees. On the third day at 8:00 or 9:00 a.m. he was ready to return to Dakshineswar. The boat was waiting at the Baghbazar ghat. It was arranged that Gopal-ma and a woman devotee named Golap-ma would go with the Master; in addition, a few young boy devotees who had come to serve the Master would accompany them. Kali (Swami Abhedananda) was probably one of them.

The Master went to the inner apartment of Balaram's house and bowed down to Jagannath in the shrine. The members of Balaram's family saluted the Master. He then went to the boat, followed by Gopal-ma and the others. Some members of Balaram's family presented Gopal-ma with clothes, a ladle, cooking utensils, and some other articles, knowing that she needed them. A big bundle containing these things was sent to the boat, which then departed.

As their boat headed back to Dakshineswar, the Master noticed the bundle.

14. The Master is annoyed when he sees Gopal-ma's bundle on the boat. He loved the devotees but disciplined them strictly.

Upon inquiry he learned that it contained some articles that Balaram's family had given to Gopal-ma. He immediately became grave. He said nothing to Gopal-ma but instead began to talk to Golap-ma about renunciation: "Only one who is endowed with renunciation realizes God. One who is satisfied simply with another devotee's hospitality and leaves empty-handed — that person sits very close to God." During the journey he did not say a single word to Gopal-ma, but he kept looking at her bundle. Gopal-ma noticed the Master's mood and was stung with remorse. She thought of throwing the bundle into the Ganges.

Although the Master would laugh, joke, and play with his devotees like a five-year-old boy, he was a strict disciplinarian. He would not tolerate improper conduct, and he took note of even the smallest things. If anyone performed the slightest impropriety, his keen eye would fall on that person and he would make every effort to correct that devotee. But this did not require any extraordinary effort on his part. He would simply make his face stern and stop talking to that devotee for a while. Immediately that person would become uncomfortable and repent of his or her fault. For those who refused to rectify their mistakes, a little scolding was enough to change their minds. Thus, the wonderful Master behaved with and taught each devotee in his unique way. He would first conquer their hearts with his superhuman love, then explain to them in a few words whatever he had to say.

As soon as she reached Dakshineswar, Gopal-ma went to the nahabat to

| 15. The Master's annoyance pains Gopal-ma; the Holy Mother consoles her. | see the Holy Mother and said anxiously: "O my child, Gopala [Sri Ramakrishna] is annoyed by seeing this bundle of things. What shall I do? Should I distribute them here instead of taking them home?" |

Seeing her in such distress, the compassionate Holy Mother consoled her, saying: "Don't worry, Mother. Let the Master say what he wants. You have no one in the world to help you. You accepted these things because you need them."

Nevertheless, Gopal-ma took a cloth and a few other things from the bundle and gave them away. Frightened, she cooked a couple of curries for the Master and carried the food to him. The omniscient Master saw that she was repentant and said nothing to her of the matter. He smiled at Gopal-ma and began to talk with her and behave in his usual manner. She was greatly relieved. After feeding the Master, she returned to Kamarhati that afternoon.

As we mentioned earlier, two months after her first vision Gopal-ma no longer saw Gopala's living form continuously. But let no one think that she seldom had any visions of Gopala. In fact, she saw Gopala several times a day. Whenever she was anxious to see Gopala, she saw him. If she needed to learn anything, Gopala suddenly appeared before her, teaching her through a sign, or words, or demonstration, and inducing her to do as he did. By merging himself into the Master again and again, Gopala convinced Gopal-ma that he and Sri Ramakrishna were one. Gopala taught her how to serve him by asking her for special foods to eat and things to lie upon. By showing Gopal-ma how he associated with some special devotees of Sri Ramakrishna and how he behaved with them, Gopala showed his mother that there was no difference between them and himself: the devotees and God were one. Thus, her unwillingness to eat food that devotees had touched gradually disappeared.

Gopal-ma had fewer visions of Gopala once she became convinced

| 16. Gopal-ma's experience after she becomes firmly convinced that the Master is her Chosen Deity. | that Sri Ramakrishna was her Chosen Deity. She saw the form of Sri Ramakrishna instead, and through that form Lord Gopala would instruct her as necessary. At first she was anxious because she no longer saw the form of Gopala. One day she went to |

Sri Ramakrishna in tears and asked: "Gopala, what have you done to me? Did I do anything wrong? Why don't I see you in the form of Gopala as before?" Sri Ramakrishna consoled her, saying: "In this Kaliyuga the body does not last long if one has such visions continuously. It survives only twenty-one days and then drops off like a dry leaf." After her first vision, Gopal-ma had been intoxicated by this spiritual mood for two months. She had performed her daily activities — cooking, bathing, eating, doing japa and meditation, and so on — only because of her long-standing habits and duties. At that time her body went through her routine automatically somehow or other by sheer force of habit. But how long could her body last while she was continuously absorbed in this highly intoxicating spiritual mood? It is a wonder that it survived two months! After that time the divine intoxication gradually diminished to a great extent. But because she could not see Gopala as before, an intense longing took hold of her. The humour of wind then increased in her body and she began to experience terrible chest pains. She said to Sri Ramakrishna, "The strong humour of wind makes me feel as if someone is sawing into my heart." The Master consoled her, saying: "That is caused by your *Hari-bai*, an excess of spiritual energy. How will you pass your time if the cause is removed? It's good that you have it. When you feel too much pain, please eat something." As he said that, he fed her with various delicacies.

*   *   *

Just as a number of [Bengali] men and women devotees from Calcutta would visit the Master, many men and women from the Marwari community also came to see him from time to time. After arriving at the Dakshineswar temple garden by carriage, they would bathe in the Ganges, pick flowers, worship Shiva, and then assemble in the Panchavati. They would set up an earthen hearth there and prepare lentils, bread, sweets, and other dishes. After offering that food to God, they took a share of the prasad to the Master, and then distributed the rest among themselves. Many of them would also present the Master with nuts, raisins, pistachios, dates, rock candy, grapes, pomegranates, guavas, betel leaves, and so on, and bow down to him. They were not like most of us: They all knew that one should not visit monasteries or temples empty-handed, so they invariably brought something with them.

17. Marwari devotees visit the Master.

Sri Ramakrishna, however, could not accept those gifts from the Marwaris, with one or two exceptions. He told us: "If they offer one betel roll, they connect with it sixteen desires: 'May I win the law-suit,' 'May I be cured from disease,' 'May I make a profit in my business,' and so on." The Master did not eat those things himself, nor did he allow the devotees to eat them. But sometimes he took a little of the cooked food that they had offered to the deity as prasad and would give that to us to eat. The only person who was

18. The Master could not accept anything that had desires attached to it; he would not even give such things to the devotees to eat.

able to eat the Marwaris' fruits and rock candy was Narendra (Swami Vivekananda). The Master said: "Narendra has the sword of knowledge. It is ever unsheathed, dazzling like a blazing fire. If he eats their food, it will not do him any harm, nor will his mind be contaminated."

Whenever a devotee was available, the Master would send the Marwaris'

| 19. The Master sends the food given by the Marwaris to Narendra. | offerings to Narendra in Calcutta; otherwise he sent them through Ramlal, his nephew who was the priest of the Kali temple. Ramlal told us that the |

Master was concerned that he would be irritated by these regular requests to bring food to Narendra. One day after lunch the Master asked him, "Well, Ramlal, do you need anything in Calcutta?"

Ramlal replied: "Uncle, I don't need anything right now, but if you want me to go, I will."

"I was thinking that you haven't visited Calcutta for a long time," said the Master, "so if you wish, why don't you go for a little outing? If you go, please take some coins from that tin trunk to pay for the shared carriage from Baranagore. Otherwise, you may fall ill from the scorching sun. Please carry that rock candy and the nuts to Narendra and bring me news of him. He has not visited me for a long time and my mind is anxious to hear about him."

Ramlal later told us, "Ah, what hesitation, lest I get annoyed by doing this errand for him!" At any rate, Ramlal always took the opportunity to go to Calcutta and bring joy to the devotees there by talking about the Master.

*   *   *

One day many Marwari devotees visited Dakshineswar, and a large

| 20. The Master gives Gopal-ma rock candy that had been given by the Marwaris. | quantity of fruits and rock candy accumulated in the Master's room. Gopal-ma and some other women devotees came to see the Master. When the Master saw Gopal-ma, he went to her and took her hand like |

a little child. Pointing to her, he announced to those present: "Ah, there is nothing inside this body but God. He fills it through and through." Gopal-ma stood there motionless. She was not even embarrassed when the Master touched her feet. The Master then gathered the delicacies he had in his room and began to feed them to Gopal-ma. The Master always fed Gopal-ma whenever she visited Dakshineswar. One day she asked Sri Ramakrishna, "Gopala, why are you so fond of feeding me?"

Sri Ramakrishna replied, "You've fed me with so many things in the past."

"In the past?" Gopal-ma asked. "When did I feed you?"

Sri Ramakrishna said, "In your previous life."

On this day, when in the evening Gopal-ma came to take her leave before returning to Kamarhati, the Master gave her the entire amount of rock candy that the Marwaris had given him and asked her to take it with her. Gopal-ma asked, "Why are you giving me so much rock candy?"

Sri Ramakrishna replied (*affectionately touching her chin*): "Well, you were molasses before, then became sugar, and afterwards rock candy. Because you have now become rock candy, eat this rock candy and rejoice!"

All were surprised when the Master gave Gopal-ma the rock candy left by the Marwaris. They understood that by the Master's grace henceforth Gopal-ma's mind would never become contaminated. She finally took the rock candy at Sri Ramakrishna's insistence; she had no choice. Moreover, one needs all sorts of things in day-to-day life. As Gopal-ma sometimes told us: "As long as you have a body, you need everything, even cumin and fenugreek. It is indeed amazing!"

*   *   *

From their first meeting on, Gopal-ma told the Master whatever she saw or experienced during her japa and meditation. One day the Master told her, "One shouldn't disclose one's visions to others, because it stops further visions." Gopal-ma asked: "Why? Those visions are connected with you. Can't I even tell you about them?" The Master replied, "No, you're not supposed to tell me about your visions, even if they pertain to me." Gopal-ma said, "All right." From then on she rarely discussed her visions with anyone. The sincere and simple-hearted Gopal-ma firmly believed whatever the Master said. But what about doubting souls like us? We spent our lives testing the Master's words; and we could not make our lives joyful by translating those words into practice.

21. One should not divulge one's visions to others.

One day during this period, Gopal-ma and Narendra (Swami Vivekananda) were at Dakshineswar. Narendra was then very inclined to the formless aspect of God as prescribed by the Brahmo Samaj. He had a terrible aversion for idolatry — deities, images, and so on. However, he did understand that people could eventually reach the formless God dwelling in all beings by worshipping images. The Master had a wonderful sense of humour. On one hand, here was Narendra, learned, intelligent, rational, and a devotee endowed with all good qualities; and on the other, here was Gopal-ma, poor, simple-hearted, uneducated, entirely lacking scriptural knowledge, who strove for grace and the vision of God by chanting His name. Having them both present on that day, the Master playfully arranged an encounter between them. He asked Gopal-ma to tell Narendra about her visions of God as Gopala and how Gopala had been playing with her ever since.

22. The Master introduces Gopal-ma to Swami Vivekananda.

At this, Gopal-ma said, "But will there be harm in telling him?" After being assured by the Master that it would be all right, she began to describe, in a voice choked with tears, how she had first seen Gopala. She then narrated in detail the divine play of Gopala over the next two months: how she had carried Gopala in her arms from Kamarhati to Dakshineswar, placing his head on her shoulder; how she had clearly seen his two red feet dangling over her chest; how Gopala had entered and come out of the Master's body from time to time; how Gopala had complained when he did not get a pillow to sleep on; how Gopala collected firewood for cooking and behaved mischievously to get food. As she described these events, she became overwhelmed with devotion and again began to see God in the form of Gopala.

Although Narendra had a strong rationalistic veneer, his heart was filled with love and devotion. He could not control his tears when he was faced with Gopal-ma's ecstatic state and heard about her visions. The elderly lady now and then interrupted her story to say: "My son, you are learned and intelligent, and I am a poor, illiterate widow. I don't understand anything. Please tell me, are these visions true?" Narendra repeatedly assured her, "Yes, Mother, whatever you have seen is all true." Gopal-ma anxiously questioned Narendra about this because it seemed that she was not having as many visions of Gopala as before.

On another day the Master went to visit Gopal-ma with Rakhal (Swami Brahmananda). They reached Kamarhati at about 10:00 a.m. Gopal-ma had a great desire to cook some delicacies for the Master. She was beside herself with joy at having the Master in her home. She served them whatever she could procure as refreshment and arranged a bed in the owner's parlour for their rest. After settling them there she went off to cook with great enthusiasm. She had collected some nice ingredients from others, which she cooked for the Master. At noon she fed the Master with various delicacies to her heart's content. She then made a bed with her quilt and put a clean sheet over it in the southern room on the first floor of the house. The Master lay down to rest with Rakhal nearby, as the Master considered him to be his spiritual son.

23. Invited by Gopal-ma, the Master goes to Kamarhati; he sees ghosts there.

The Master saw something strange while they were in that room. It is because the Master himself told us this story that we dare to narrate it — otherwise we would leave it out. The Master slept very little either during the day or at night. He was just lying down, and Rakhal had already fallen asleep. The Master said: "Suddenly a foul odour permeated the room. I then saw two hideous ghosts in the corner. Their entrails hung from their bellies and their faces, hands, and feet were exactly like the human skeletons that I once saw in the Medical College. They humbly said to me: 'Why are you here? Please leave this place. The sight of you causes us unbearable pain.'" Probably the Master's divine presence reminded them of their pitiable condition. "On one side of me, they were thus imploring me, and on the other, Rakhal was sleeping. Seeing how they suffered, I got up and was about to leave with my spice bag and towel when Rakhal wakened and asked, 'Master, where are you going?' Saying, 'I'll explain later,' I took his hand and we went downstairs. I took leave of the old woman, who had just finished her lunch, and went to the boat. I then told Rakhal: 'Two ghosts live there. The Jute Mill of Kamarhati is adjacent to the garden. After meals, the European officers of that mill throw away the leftover bones, and the ghosts sniff them — because for them sniffing is eating. They live in that room. I said nothing of this to the old woman because she has to live in that house alone; otherwise she would be frightened.'"

*   *   *

Mati Lake is situated in front of the garden of Mati Sil, a wealthy man of Calcutta. This lake is next to a road that has been extended northward from Calcutta to the Baranagore Market over the Baghbazar Bridge running parallel to the Ganges. The garden house of Gopal Chandra Ghosh, the son-in-law of Rani Katyayani and Lala Babu, is situated on the eastern side of the road along the northern shore of Mati Lake. Sri Ramakrishna lived in this garden house for eight months (from mid-December 1885 to mid-August 1886) before he passed away. This garden is known to the devotees as the Cossipore garden house, and it raises in their memories as much joy as grief. One may ask: "At that time the Master was sick in bed. How was joy possible?"

> 24. At the Cossipore garden the Master feeds Gopal-ma pudding and says, "Gopala eats through her mouth."

The Master did indeed seem to be bedridden; but with the disease manifesting in his divine body, he classified the devotees into various groups and united them with a wonderful bond of love. At Cossipore it became clear who among the devotees belonged to the inner or outer circle, who was a monk, a householder, a jnani, or a devotee; and it was here that the conviction that all of them belonged to one family was firmly established. Innumerable people came to the Master and were blessed by experiencing the light of spirituality. It was at Cossipore that Narendra experienced nirvikalpa samadhi through sadhana, and twelve [actually eleven] boy disciples received ochre robes from the Master. And it was here — on 1 January 1886 between 3:00 and 4:00 p.m. — that the Master walked for one last time on the garden path. Upon seeing the devotees, he went into an extraordinary ecstatic mood and exclaimed: "What more need I tell you? May you all be illumined!" Saying this, he touched their chests one by one with the palm of his hand and transmitted spiritual power to them instantly.

Every day a crowd of men and women devotees assembled here, as they had in Dakshineswar. The Holy Mother would prepare food for the Master and perform the regular work of the household. Gopal-ma and other women devotees helped her serve the Master and his devotees, and some of them spent a night or two there. As we reflect on the wonderful assemblage of devotees at Cossipore, we think that the Divine Mother created the disease in the Master's divine body to fulfil a great purpose. As many of the longtime devotees daily witnessed the Master's ever-changing divine play, the arrival of new devotees, and the Master's blissful form, as well as the manifestation of his wonderful power, they thought that he was feigning this illness for the benefit of humanity, and that he would rid himself of this disease when he wished and would then become normal as before.

*   *   *

At the Cossipore garden house the Master lived on a soft diet of barley, vermicelli, and farina. One day the Master expressed a desire to eat *palo* pudding[2] because hosts in Calcutta sometimes served it to invited guests. No one objected to this; he had been eating farina or barley cooked in milk, so there was little chance of aggravating his disease by having some palo pudding. The doctors also approved. It was decided that Jogin (Swami Yogananda) would go to Calcutta the next morning to buy that pudding.

Jogin left for Calcutta on time. But on the way he reflected: "Palo pudding from the market might be adulterated with other things that could aggravate the Master's illness." All of the devotees looked upon the Master as the life of their lives, so from the beginning of his illness they had constantly thought of the Master's welfare. It was for that reason that this thought arose in Jogin's mind. He again considered: "I did not consult with the Master about this before I left. If I have a devotee make the pudding, will he be annoyed?" Thinking of these things, Jogin arrived at Balaram's house in Baghbazar. When asked the reason for his visit, he told the whole story. The women devotees told him: "Why market pudding? We will make it. But you cannot have it before noon because it takes time to make. You have your lunch here; the pudding will be ready when you are finished. You can take it back at three in the afternoon." Jogin followed their suggestion and returned to Cossipore with the pudding at about 4:00 p.m.

The Master had wanted to eat his pudding at noon. He waited for a long time but had finally eaten his regular meal. When Jogin arrived later, he told the Master everything. The Master was annoyed and told Jogin: "I wanted to eat the pudding from the market, and you were told to buy it. Why did you go to a devotee's house and give them trouble over it? Moreover, this pudding is very rich and difficult to digest. I shall not eat it." In fact, he did not touch it. He asked Holy Mother to feed the pudding to Gopal-ma. He explained: "This is given by devotees. Gopala dwells in her heart, so if she eats it, it will be the same as my eating it."

*   *   *

When the Master passed away, Gopal-ma's grief knew no bounds. For a
25. Gopal-ma had the cosmic vision of God.
long time she did not leave Kamarhati to go anywhere. She lived alone in seclusion. After a while, when she began to have visions of the Master as

---

2. A custard made from the zedoary root. — *Translator*

before, her grief came to an end. We heard many stories of the visions that Gopal-ma had after the Master passed away. Once she attended the Chariot Festival at Mahesh, across the Ganges, and was overwhelmed with joy as she saw Gopala in all living beings and in everything else. She said that she saw her beloved Gopala in the chariot, in the image of the Lord Jagannath in the chariot, in those who were pulling the chariot, and in the vast crowd — her beloved Gopala had become manifest in different forms. She was beside herself with joy at this cosmic vision of God and lost outer consciousness of her surroundings in ecstasy. Gopal-ma described this vision to a woman friend, saying: "I was not myself. I danced and laughed and created quite a commotion."

Whenever Gopal-ma felt despondent, she would visit the Master's monastic disciples at the Baranagore monastery to find peace. On such occasions the monks asked her to cook a few dishes and offer them to the Master.

26. Gopal-ma at the Baranagore monastery.

Gopal-ma was always delighted to prepare vegetable curries and offer them to the Master. When the monastery was moved to Alambazar, and then to Nilambar Babu's house across the Ganges at Belur, Gopal-ma visited those places as well. She was happy in the company of the Master's disciples and sometimes spent a day or two with them.

After Swami Vivekananda returned from the West [in 1897], Sara (Mrs. Sara C. Bull), Jaya (Miss Josephine MacLeod), and Nivedita (Miss Margaret Noble) came to India. One day they went to visit Gopal-ma in Kamarhati and were highly pleased with her conversation and hospitality. On that day, Gopal-ma saw her Gopala in them and affectionately kissed them, touching their chins. She cordially asked them to sit on her bed and served them puffed rice, sweet coconut balls, and whatever else she had in her room. She narrated some of her visions to them when asked, and they were overwhelmed. They enjoyed her simple refreshments and asked her for some puffed rice to take back to America.

27. Gopal-ma with the Western women.

*　　　　　　*　　　　　　*

In 1904 when Gopal-ma was very ill and incapacitated, she was brought to Balaram's house at Baghbazar. When Sister Nivedita heard the wonderful life story of Gopal-ma, she was so impressed that she expressed a keen desire to take Gopal-ma into her own home at Baghbazar (17 Bosepara Lane). Observing her eagerness, Gopal-ma agreed to move to her place. As we mentioned earlier, Gopala had slowly removed every vestige of her old orthodox behaviour. We relate the following event as an example: One day at Dakshineswar, when the Master was alive, Narendra ate a bowl of goat meat that had been offered to Mother Kali. When he left the room to wash his hands, the Master asked a woman devotee to clean the place where he had

28. Gopal-ma at Sister Nivedita's residence.

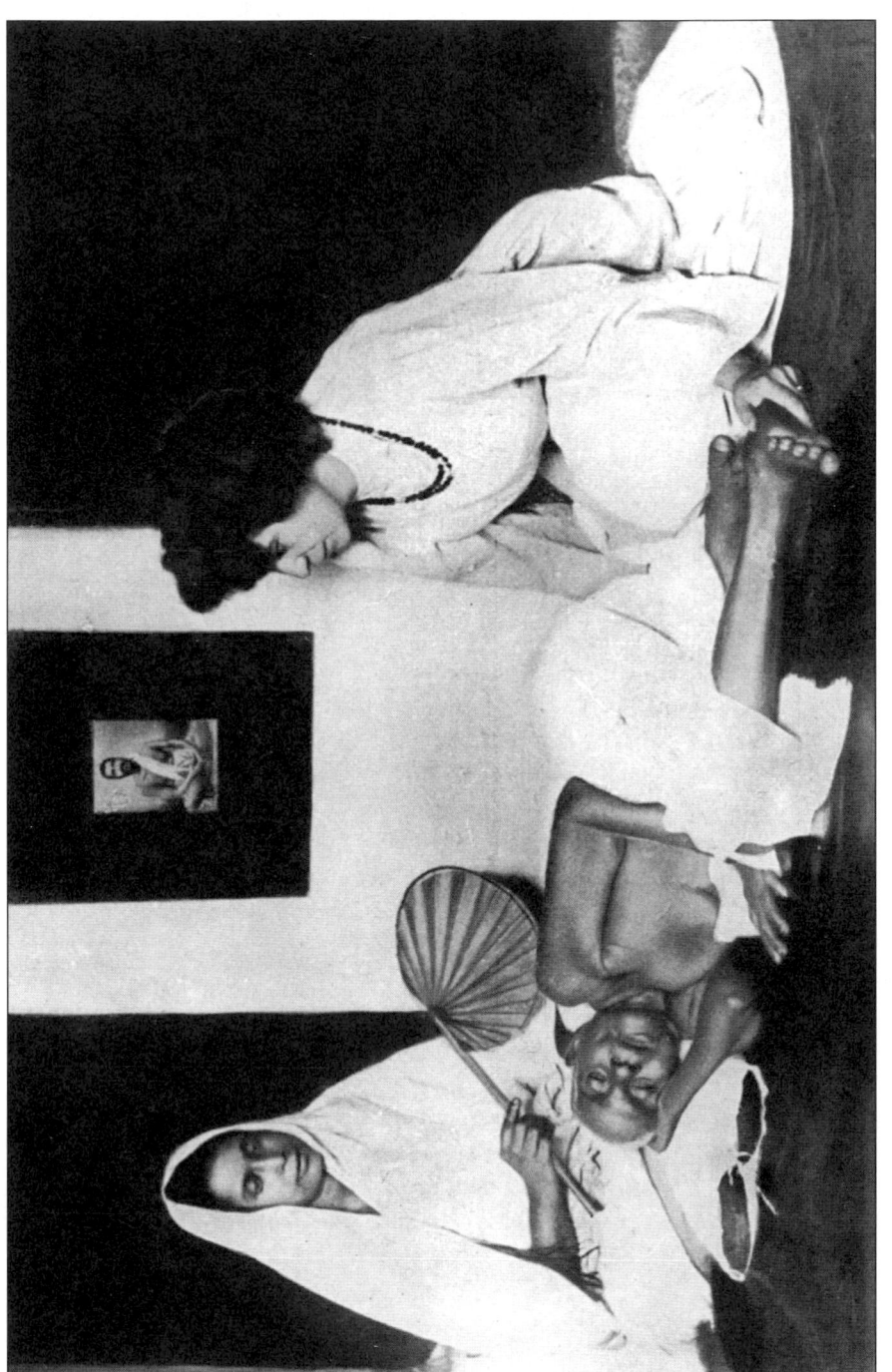

Gopal-ma towards the end of her life. Kusumkumari, a disciple of Gopal-ma at left and Nivedita, the Irish disciple of Swami Vivekananda, is seated at right. Photo taken in June 1906.

eaten. Gopal-ma was present, and as soon as she heard the Master's words, she immediately removed Narendra's leavings and cleaned the area. Seeing this, the Master joyfully expressed to the other woman devotee, "See how liberal she is becoming day by day!"

Gopal-ma then lived at Sister Nivedita's residence, where Nivedita, Swamiji's spiritual daughter, served Gopal-ma just as she would her own mother. Gopal-ma's food was prepared by a nearby brahmin family. She would go there to have her lunch, and at night one of the family members would bring a few luchis [fried bread] and other things to her room. Gopal-ma lived like this for two years. When she was on her deathbed, she was taken to a room on the bank of the Ganges. Nivedita decorated her bed beautifully with flowers, sandal paste, and garlands. She invited a kirtan party to sing devotional songs and joined the procession to the Ganges barefooted and with tearful eyes. She stayed with Gopal-ma during her last two days in this world.

29. The passing away of Gopal-ma.

On 8 July 1906 as the rising sun painted the eastern horizon with a reddish hue, a few dim stars in the blue sky were still twinkling as they looked downward towards the earth. When the high tide of the Ganges, the daughter of the Himalayas, flooded both banks with white waves and the river flowed with a gentle and sweet murmur, Gopal-ma's body was immersed halfway into that holy water. The five vital forces of her pure life merged into the Divine and she attained the eternal abode of fearlessness.

Because none of her relatives was available, a brahmin brahmacharin from Belur Math performed the funeral rite for Gopal-ma and observed the customary rites for twelve days according to the scriptures.

At the end of the twelve days, the grief-stricken Sister Nivedita invited to her school building some local women whom Gopal-ma had known and arranged for kirtan, worship, and a feast.

30. The conclusion of Gopal-ma's story.

Gopal-ma left the picture of Sri Ramakrishna that she had worshipped for such a long time to the shrine of Belur Math[3] and bequeathed two hundred rupees for service of the Master.

During the last ten or twelve years of her life, Gopal-ma considered herself to be a sannyasini and wore the ochre cloth.

---

3. Now that picture is in the Holy Mother's temple of Belur Math. — *Translator*

Appendix

The *H*uman Aspect of the Master[1]

MANY PEOPLE SPEAK OF THE DIVINE NATURE OF Sri Ramakrishna. If one looks for the

| 1. Common people venerated Sri Ramakrishna because of his yogic powers. |

reason most people revered him, had faith in him, and relied upon him, one will find that it lay in his superhuman yogic powers. When asked why they respect him, people generally answered: "While sitting in the temple at Dakshineswar, Sri Ramakrishna could see events happening in distant places. He sometimes cured severe physical diseases with merely a touch. He was in constant communication with gods and goddesses. His words were infallible: If he said anything that seemed to be impossible, the external world would change to conform to his words. For example, a man was sentenced to death by the court, but through the Master's grace and blessing his life was saved and later he was honoured instead. On another occasion a white flower blossomed on a red hibiscus tree."

Others said that Sri Ramakrishna could read minds. His keen insight penetrated the coverings of peoples' physical bodies, allowing him to see their thoughts, propensities, and mental constitutions. His gentle touch could instantly impart visions of Chosen Deities or deep meditation to even restless devotees, and open the gate of nirvikalpa samadhi to a few competent aspirants.

Still others said: "We do not know why we respect Sri Ramakrishna. But we saw in him wonderful knowledge and perfect devotion, the likes of

---

1. An article read by the author at a meeting in Belur Math on the occasion of the seventy-second birth anniversary [1908] of Sri Ramakrishna.

703

which we have not found in the great world teachers mentioned in the Vedas and Puranas, much less in living human beings! Compared with the Master, those world teachers are dim in our eyes. We cannot tell if we are deluded, but our eyes are dazzled by his brilliant splendour and our minds are permanently merged into his love. Despite our efforts, we cannot withdraw our minds, nor can we make them analyze the situation. It is as if knowledge, logic, and reasoning have drifted away. We can only say:

> I am Your servant, birth after birth, O Ocean of Mercy!
> Your ways are unknown to me, as are my own — but who cares to know?
> It was at Your command that I cast from my mind
> Delight, liberation, devotion, discrimination,
> Japa, austerities, and spiritual disciplines.
> But still I desire to know You, O Lord —
> Take me beyond that longing as well.[2]"

So it is evident that, except for a few people of the last sort, all others who came in contact with the Master were devoted to him, had faith in him, and relied upon him either because of how his powers manifested themselves or because of his mental abilities. Materialistic people believed that if they paid honour to him they would be cured of disease or that events would unfold in their favour during times of danger or difficulty. One can easily see that a current of selfishness was flowing in their minds, though they might not have admitted it.

We are aware of many instances of Sri Ramakrishna's divine powers; and we have no doubt that even if people offer devotion to him in order to fulfill their desires, they still receive immense benefit thereby. We do not intend to discuss this topic here. Rather, our aim is to depict Sri Ramakrishna's human traits.

Sakam bhakti — devotion with the purpose of fulfilling one's desires — does not allow a devotee to ascend to the highest level of Truth. Selfishness begets fear, and that fear makes a person gradually become weaker. Serving one's self-interest also engenders egotism and sometimes increases laziness. It obstructs peoples' vision, rendering them incapable of seeing things as they really are. For that reason, Sri Ramakrishna watched his devotees closely to ensure that this defect would not surface in them. If the Master learned that a devotee had developed clairvoyance or any supernatural power by practising meditation, he forbade that person to meditate for some time lest egotism develop and divert the devotee from the goal of God-realization. We have witnessed this many times. We heard him say repeatedly that developing supernatural

2. Although *sakam bhakti* is fruitful, we will not discuss it because it is detrimental to spiritual progress.

2. A stanza from a Bengali poem, "Gai Git Shunate Tomai" (A Song I Sing to Thee) by Swami Vivekananda.

powers is not the goal of human life. But ignorant human beings do not do anything or obey anyone without calculating their own profit and loss. Instead of learning renunciation from Sri Ramakrishna, who was a glowing example of that quality, they take recourse in his noble life in order to fulfill their personal desires. They believe that Sri Ramakrishna's superhuman austerities, his extraordinary passion for truth, his simplicity and childlike reliance were all intended to provide them with enjoyment. This attitude is caused by lack of strength. It would therefore be immensely beneficial for us to discuss the human aspect of Sri Ramakrishna.

When devotion is sincerely practised even a little, it makes a devotee

> 3. True devotion makes the worshipper akin to the worshipped.

resemble his or her object of worship. The scriptures of all world religions describe this phenomenon. Examples of this follow: Blood issued from the hands and feet of a devotee whose mind was fully absorbed in the form of Jesus on the cross. When Chaitanya identified with Radha, who experienced intense pain when separated from Krishna, he felt a terrible burning sensation in his body and sometimes fell as motionless as a corpse. Some Buddhist devotees meditate for very long periods of time, remaining absolutely still in front of the image of Buddha in meditation. We have seen that when a lover's passion is completely focussed on the beloved, it slowly and unconsciously causes the lover to become similar to the beloved; the lover's gestures, movements, deportment, and even his or her way of thinking change radically to resemble those of the beloved. Similarly, if our devotion to Sri Ramakrishna does not change our lives day by day, making us even a little similar to him, then we should understand that our love and devotion are not worthy of the name.

One may ask: "Is it possible for each of us to become Ramakrishna Paramahamsa? Has anyone in this world ever become completely identical to another?" We say in reply that one may not become exactly similar to another, but surely one can become as like another as things cast in the same mould. The lives of the great religious teachers are like different moulds. Having cast themselves in those moulds, successive generations of disciples preserve the original moulds. Human beings are weak. Even lifelong effort is not enough to allow a person to become exactly the same as one of those prototypes. If someone does become very similar to one of those original models, we respect that person as a perfected soul. Such a one's demeanour, speech, thoughts, and other physical and mental traits have become similar to those of the particular great teacher who established that model. The body and mind of the perfected soul are then appropriate instruments for storing and transmitting to others a little of the tremendous spiritual power that first appeared in the life of the great teacher and enchanted the whole world. Thus, from time immemorial different religious traditions have preserved the spiritual powers transmitted by their great teachers.

In the spiritual world, those great teachers who have modelled extraordi-

4. One can learn many extraordinary things by studying the life of an avatar.

nary and entirely new ways of living are worshipped by people as avatars, incarnations of God. Avatars discover new doctrines and new paths in the religious world, and they transmit spiritual powers by a mere touch. Their minds are never attracted to the glamour of lust and gold in this transitory world. As we study their lives, we understand that they were born to show others the way. Neither personal enjoyment nor liberation is the goal of their lives. Their intense sympathy and love for suffering humanity induce them to work and discover ways to remove misery.

Before we witnessed the divine life of Sri Ramakrishna, we were incapable of understanding the lives and messages of the avatars, such as Krishna, Buddha, Jesus, Shankara, Chaitanya, and others. We considered the extraordinary events of their lives to be exciting stories invented by successive generations of disciples to lure more members to their groups. We thought that avatars were mysterious and imaginary beings removed from the rational civilized world. Or when we did acknowledge that it could be possible for God to be born as avatars, we could not believe that these beings would possess human traits as we do. It was inconceivable to us that avatars' bodies could be subject to the diseases that we suffer, that avatars could experience happiness and misery as we do, or that they would have to struggle with the divine and demonic tendencies that contend within us. But now, due to the holy company of Sri Ramakrishna, we have a correct understanding of these things.

We had read and heard that divine and human traits coexist wonderfully in an avatar's body. But before we met Sri Ramakrishna we could not imagine how childlike simplicity and strong masculinity could coexist harmoniously in a man. Many say that they were attracted by the Master's childlike nature — he was like a five-year-old boy. An innocent child always inspires affection and protective instincts in all. Such feelings arose in people who met Sri Ramakrishna, overwhelming them and drawing them to him, even though he was an adult at the time. This is true to some extent, but it was not only the Master's pure and childlike nature that attracted people. As people approached the Master with love and joy, feelings of reverence and devotion would rise in their minds simultaneously, indicating that the cause of that attraction was his inner adamantine masculinity covered by his tender childlike simplicity. Describing the superhuman character of Ramachandra, the king of Ayodhya, the famous poet Bhavabhuti wrote: "Who can comprehend the minds of superhuman souls, which are stronger than a thunderbolt and softer than a flower?" This remark is equally applicable to Sri Ramakrishna.

Sri Ramakrishna's childlike nature was an unprecedented phenomenon. Although his mind was characterized by unbounded simplicity, unlimited faith, and unending passion for truth, worldly-minded people found him to be foolish and lacking in worldly wisdom. The Master sincerely believed what anyone told him, especially those who wore religious marks. The prevalent ideas and customs of India and of his own village greatly contributed to this childlike nature.

Kamarpukur is surrounded by vast stretches of land covered with green paddy fields. Before harvest, the fields look like an

> 5. Kamarpukur Village, the birthplace of Sri Ramakrishna.

ocean of green; after the harvest, the bare soil resembles an ocean of grey. The village itself is like a cluster of beautiful islands, each one covered with bamboo groves and banyan, peepul, date palm, mango, and other trees, with the peasants' clean mud-built thatched huts nestled among them. The area has many large lakes and ponds, such as Haldar Pond, which are surrounded and shaded by tall palm trees. Humming bees hover over lotuses in the lakes. In the village are many small temples of brick and stone; among them is the famous temple to the "Old Shiva." The ruins of Fort Mandaran are close to the village, and in the outskirts lie two ancient cremation grounds. Kamarpukur has pastureland covered with green grass, a dense mango grove, and a small zigzag canal called Bhuti's Canal. More than half of the village is encircled by a long public road from Burdwan to Puri, which is thronged by pilgrims. This is Kamarpukur, the birthplace of Sri Ramakrishna.

The Vaishnava religion, founded by Chaitanya and his disciples, is prevalent in Kamarpukur. The peasants relieve their fatigue

> 6. Amazing events in Sri Ramakrishna's early life.

by joyfully singing devotional songs of the Vaishnava poets while they plough and in the evening after work. This religion is based upon a simple and poetic faith that pervades the hearts of these remote villagers, who live far from the rough waves of the struggle for existence. A child's heart is fertile ground for such faith and religion. Even so, the childlike nature of the young Ramakrishna was regarded as unusual in this village. Although people did not understand many of his actions, they were amazed at seeing the depth and one-pointedness of purpose that he brought to his actions.

When the boy [Ramakrishna] heard a narrator of the Puranas say "a person becomes pure by chanting the name of Rama," he wondered, "Why then does the narrator still need ablution?" After hearing a theatrical performance only once, the boy could memorize the entire script and would reenact it in the mango grove with his friends. Passersby who saw their wonderful performance and heard their music were so overwhelmed that they forgot to continue to their destinations. Ramakrishna's talent was manifest in several areas — making images, painting pictures of deities, mimicry, music and sankirtan, learning by heart the passages of the Ramayana, the Mahabharata, the Bhagavata, and other scriptures after hearing them only once, and in deeply experiencing the beauty of nature. The Master told us that he first experienced samadhi at the age of six or seven when he saw a flock of white cranes flying against a black cloud heavy with rain.

A special characteristic of this boy's mind was that he would become completely absorbed in any mood that came upon him. The villagers even now point to the courtyard of a merchant and tell this story: One day the actor who was supposed to perform the role of Shiva in the drama *Hara-Parvati Sambad* [Conversation of Shiva and Parvati] suddenly became ill. People asked Ramakrishna to take that role, and they dressed him as Shiva. But when he entered the stage in that courtyard as Shiva, he became motionless and lost outer consciousness for a long time. These events make it clear that although he was a child, boyish restlessness could not seize him. Whenever he saw or heard anything that attracted him, its image so deeply imprinted itself in his mind that he could not stop until he had attained complete mastery over it and had expressed it in a new form.

Although the young Ramakrishna did not study any books, his senses 7. His search for truth. and mind developed quickly by encountering the external world. The guiding principle of his life was: "I shall accept nothing until I have determined it to be true after thorough scrutiny. I shall implement in action whatever I learn. I shall not look down upon anything in this world unless I find it to be false." During his boyhood, the wonderfully talented Ramakrishna was sent to the village school, but his inquisitive childlike nature did not wane. He asked himself: "What is the purpose of studying until late at night and ruminating over the glosses of commentators? Will this help me to attain the truth?" Thinking of the school's teacher, who had successfully completed that kind of education, he said to himself: "You will become as adept as he is in interpreting simple words in a complicated way. You will make your living as he does by flattering wealthy people and collecting honorariums. You will study and teach the truths recorded in the scriptures but you will not be able to experience them in your life, like an ass who carries sandalwood but cannot enjoy its fragrance." His discriminating intellect decided: "You do not need this bread-winning education. Learn the supreme knowledge that will help you realize the complete truth that unveils the hidden mystery of human life."

Ramakrishna therefore gave up his studies to concentrate on worshipping the blissful image of the Divine Mother. But even this gave him no peace. Again his mind questioned: "Is She truly the living blissful form of the Divine Mother or merely a stone image? Does She truly accept the flowers, fruits, and sweets that I offer with devotion? Does a person by Her gracious glance truly become free from all bondage and see Her? Or is this nothing but a long-accumulated superstition of the human mind, given form by a strong imagination? Have human beings been thus deceived from time immemorial?" He was anxious to resolve these doubts. At the same time, the seed of intense renunciation was beginning to sprout in his mind. He grew up and married, but it became impossible for him to enjoy the world without answering these questions. Every day his mind became absorbed in various solutions to these problems. Marriage, family, planning for worldly life, earning money, enjoyment, and even food and other physical necessities receded into useless memories.

Sri Ramakrishna's childlike nature was an object of ridicule for the worldly minded in Kamarpukur. When this same childlike nature came to full fruition in the temple garden of Dakshineswar, worldly people there considered him mad, which was much more contemptible. But was there any incoherence or aimlessness in this madness? Its main characteristic was: "I will achieve direct knowledge of the Reality beyond the senses. I will touch It and experience It fully." That firm determination, indomitable perseverance, sincerity, and single-mindedness had conferred a unique beauty on the childlike nature of the boy in Kamarpukur, and those qualities now created an unprecedented phenomenon in the apparent insanity of the god-intoxicated Ramakrishna in Dakshineswar.

A violent storm raged in Sri Ramakrishna's mind over a period of twelve years, and his lifeboat was imperiled by the dreadful waves of doubt and disbelief churned up by that terrible inner struggle. But his heroic heart was not shaken even in the face of imminent death, and he did not deviate from the course towards his goal. Endowed with faith in and passion for God, he methodically and steadily proceeded ahead. He left far behind him the worldly tumult of lust and gold, and what public opinion calls good and bad, merit and demerit, virtue and vice. The tidal wave of spiritual longing carried him speedily forward against the worldly current. Sri Ramakrishna's severe austerities and endless, overflowing spiritual moods shattered his strong body and mind, shaping them into new forms and giving them a new beauty. Thus was made a perfect instrument to hold and transmit great truth, great spirituality, and great power.

O reader, can you comprehend this wonderful and heroic story of Sri

8. The result of his
search for truth.

Ramakrishna? From a materialistic point of view, you determine the weight and worth of a thing by weighing it or by counting it. How can you fathom a subtle power that completely uproots selfishness and egotism, making it impossible for one's body and mind to indulge in even a little self-aggrandizement? If Sri Ramakrishna touched any metal — whether consciously or unconsciously — his hand would become numb and incapable of holding that object. If he tried to return to his place with even a flower, a leaf, or another trifling thing without its owner's permission — whether or not he was aware of it — he would invariably lose his way and walk in the opposite direction. If someone tied a knot in his cloth, he could not breathe, no matter how hard he tried, as long as the knot remained. If a worldly woman touched him, his sex organ would shrink into his body just as the limbs of a tortoise withdraw into its shell. These physical phenomena are external manifestations of his pure mental state. Is it possible for ordinary human beings, who are self-motivated from their very birth, to believe these things? Can we extend our imagination far enough to enter into the purest realm of spirituality?

We have learned from birth how to be hypocritical, "to steal in the chamber of the heart." Many of us would not hesitate to gain wealth by cheating others or to become famous by concealing the truth. And what about courage? Although many of us may not be bold enough to return ten blows for one or to throw ourselves in front of cannon fire to fulfill our selfish desires, we are excited when we listen to such stories. Are we capable of feeling a little bit of the courage that allowed Sri Ramakrishna to renounce earthly and heavenly enjoyment and risk even his body and mind for a thing beyond the senses, unfamiliar and unknown to the world? If you can feel this kind of courage, O heroic reader, you have attained immortality and we will all adore you.

Even Sri Ramakrishna's trifling words and small actions were so full of deep significance that no one could understand them unless he explained their meaning. One day he explained the mystery hidden behind a habit of his: After coming down from samadhi, he would sometimes mention the names of some familiar objects or persons and would touch them, or express a desire to eat or drink particular things. He told us: "The minds of ordinary people dwell in the subtle nerve centres near the anus, the sex organ, and the navel. When a person's mind is purified to some extent, it sometimes rises to the heart centre, has a vision of light or of luminous divine forms, and experiences a little bliss. When the mind is accustomed to remaining in this place, it ascends to the throat centre. At that time, it's almost impossible for that person to talk about anything other than the ideal on which the mind has been concentrated. Although it has reached this height, the mind can descend to the lower centres and completely forget that high ideal. But if through steadfast devotion the mind transcends the throat centre and reaches the centre between the eyebrows, that person experiences supreme bliss in samadhi. Compared to that state, the enjoyment of sense objects in the lower centres seems insipid. There is no fear of falling from this centre. Here the light of the Supreme Self is visible behind a thin veil. Although a little separation from the Supreme Self remains, one gets clear glimpses of nondual knowledge when the mind reaches that point. No sooner does the mind pass beyond this centre than the knowledge of difference and sameness vanishes and that person becomes established in complete nondual knowledge.

> 9. The profound meaning of Sri Ramakrishna's simple words.

"My mind descends to the throat centre so that I can teach all of you, but it's a struggle to keep it down there. Because I dwelt continually in the realm of complete nondual knowledge for a period of six months, my mind is natu-rally inclined in that direction. It is difficult for me to bring my mind down without nurturing some trifling desires such as, 'I shall do this,' 'I shall eat that,' 'I shall see this person,' 'I shall go there,' and so on. And if my mind doesn't come down, it is impossible for me to perform functions such as talking, moving, eating, protecting the body, and the like. So when I merge into samadhi, I entertain a small desire such as 'I shall smoke tobacco,' or 'I shall go there'; but even then I've to express that desire again and again so my mind will come down a little."

In one place, the author of the *Panchadashi* mentions: "In whatever state a man lived before samadhi, he does not wish to return to that state after samadhi, even if he was endowed with considerable power at that time. All objects and conditions, except Brahman, appear to be insignificant

10. One can get an indication of the Master's way of life from his daily activities.

to him." However, to get a glimpse of how Sri Ramakrishna led his life before he had that intense longing for God, we can examine some of his routine activities in Dakshineswar. It will not be out of place to mention a few here.

It was his habit to keep his body, clothes, bedding, and other things very clean. He always kept things in their proper places and loved to teach others to do so as well. He was annoyed if someone did otherwise. When he went anywhere, he would inquire whether his towel, spice bag, and other necessi-ties had been packed; and when he returned, he would remind the disciple who attended him to put those things back where they belonged, without mistake. If the Master said he would do a thing at a certain time, he was anxious to do it as planned. If he said he would accept something from a particular person, he would receive it from none other than that person rather than be guilty of falsehood. Even if this caused great inconvenience to himself, he endured it rather than break his word.

If he saw a man with a worn-out cloth, umbrella, or shoes, Sri Rama-krishna advised him to buy new ones if he was able to; if he was not, the Master would sometimes buy the item for him. He used to say, "Fortune abandons the man who uses such worn-out things, and he loses grace." Words indicating pride or egoism could never pass through his lips. When he had to convey his own idea or opinion, he would point to his body and use words such as, "the idea of this place," or "the opinion of this place." He minutely observed his disciples' hands, feet, eyes, faces, and the formation of their limbs, as well as their demeanour and the way they ate, walked, slept, and performed other activities. From such observations he could accurately assess the trend of their mental propensities, how strong a particular propen-sity was, and so on. We never found any of his conclusions to be incorrect.

Everyone who went to Sri Ramakrishna felt that the Master loved him or her above all others. It seems to us that the cause of that feeling was his intense understanding of the weal and woe of each person. Although sympathy and love are two different things, the external signs of the latter are not much different from those of the former. So it was no wonder that people considered his sympathy to be love. It was the very nature of his mind to be absorbed in whatever he chose to think about. Because of this characteristic, he could accurately ascertain the mental condition of each disciple, and he could correctly prescribe whatever was necessary to improve that mind. In our description of Sri Ramakrishna's childlike nature, we have tried to show the intensity with which he learned to focus his eyes and other sense organs, from his childhood onward. This power of observation undoubtedly helped him later in training his disciples and in shaping human character. He tried his utmost to develop this quality in his disciples so that they could learn to apply it in all situations. He constantly advised them to use their discrimination when performing every action. We heard him say again and again that reasoning reveals the benefits and drawbacks of things and makes the mind advance towards true renunciation.

He was not very fond of anyone who was narrow-minded or dull-witted. We all heard him say: "You should be a devotee of God, but does that mean you should be a fool?" Or "Don't be bigoted and narrow-minded; that is not the attitude of this place. The attitude of this place is, 'I shall enjoy food prepared in various ways — in a plain soup, a hot dish, or a sour dish.'" He considered a bigoted intellect to be monotonous and hackneyed. If a disciple could not enjoy a particular attitude of God, he scolded him or her, saying, "You are too narrow-minded." He expressed those words in such a way that the disciple had to hide his or her face in shame. Undoubtedly motivated by this liberal and universal attitude, Sri Ramakrishna practised the modes of sadhana in all faiths and discovered this great truth: "As many faiths, so many paths."

The flower blossomed and the bees came flying from countries far and near to taste the intoxicating honey. As the sun's touch makes the lotus open its petals and allows bees to sip honey, so spiritual illumination revealed the spiritual honey in Sri Ramakrishna's heart, allowing him to share it with devotees without reservation, satisfying them completely. Sri Ramakrishna's life was built on the so-called superstitious religious tradition of India, with no influence from Western education. But as for the spiritual honey that he distributed to the world in this modern age, has anyone ever tasted its equal? Has the world ever before witnessed the play of great spiritual power that Sri Ramakrishna accumulated and transmitted to his disciples? Has the world ever before witnessed how, with the help of this overwhelming power, people are experiencing religion as an object of immediate knowledge and realizing that there is an unchanging, living, eternal spiritual current in all religious faiths — even in the scientific age of the twentieth century?

11. How and to what extent Sri Ramakrishna preached religion, and what will happen in the future.

As the wind blows from one flower to another, so human beings travel from truth to truth. Gradually and steadily they are moving towards the unchanging nondual Truth; surely one day they will attain perfection by realizing the infinite, boundless Truth beyond mind and speech. Has such a gospel of fearlessness and hope ever before been proclaimed in this world? Krishna, Buddha, Shankara, Ramanuja, and Chaitanya of India, and Jesus, Muhammad, as well as religious leaders of other countries could not eradicate sectarianism in the world of religion. But in his own life this unlettered brahmin boy completely destroyed that attitude and was able to accomplish the most difficult task of bringing true harmony to the apparently contradictory doctrines of various religions. Has anyone ever seen this before?

O reader, if you are capable of ascertaining how high Sri Ramakrishna ascended in the spiritual world, please tell us. We dare not attempt it. Only this much we can say: With the advent of Sri Ramakrishna, a lifeless India became awakened and greatly sanctified, and has assumed a place of glory and hope in this world. By assuming a human form, he has become venerated even by divine beings. The world has seen the great power awakened by Sri Ramakrishna in the form of Swami Vivekananda, but even this wonderful manifestation is only the beginning.

A painting of Ramakrishna by Frank Dvorak.

THE MASTER'S DIVINE MOOD
AND NARENDRANATH

VOLUME FIVE

Preface to Volume Five

The fifth volume of *Sri Ramakrishna and His Divine Play* is now published. In this volume we have recorded the events of the Master's life as much as possible from the time of his first meeting with the Brahmo devotees to his stay at Shyampukur, Calcutta, when he went there to undergo treatment for his throat cancer. During this period, the Master was continuously in a divine mood. He dealt with people and performed every action in accordance with that mood. And from this period until the end of his life, he was so closely connected with Narendra (Swami Vivekananda) that when we narrate the Master's life, Narendra's story shares prominence. This is why we titled this volume "The Master's Divine Mood and Narendranath."

When we first started writing of the divine play of the Master, we never imagined that we would proceed so far. It was possible only by his inconceivable grace. We bow down to the Master again and again and offer this volume to the reader.

The Author [Swami Saradananda]
Second day of the bright fortnight
[*Sri Ramakrishna's birthday*]
20 Phalgun 1325 B.E. [March 1919]

Prologue

We mentioned earlier that Sri Ramakrishna completed his sadhana after

1. Ascertaining the period during which the divine mood was especially manifest in the Master's life.

performing the worship of Shodashi in 1873. So it would not be inappropriate to say that from that point on everything he did in his life was inspired by the divine mood. The Master was then thirty-eight years old. So from the age of thirty-nine, he remained in the divine mood until the end of his life, a little more than twelve years later. During this period all of his actions were transformed into new and extraordinary events by the will of the Divine Mother. Driven by Her will, he concentrated on imparting spirituality to modern Western-educated people. It is therefore evident that after practising austerities for twelve full years [1856–1868], the Master spent six years becoming familiar with his own power and with the spiritual condition of the masses. He devoted the next twelve years to halting the decline of religion in India, which had been brought about by the tremendous influence of worldly Western ideas and ideals, and to reestablishing the eternal religion. When his work was over, he departed from this world. We shall now describe as best we can how he accomplished his mission.

The reader may think from our earlier statement that the Master remained

2. Why it is said that the divine mood was especially prevalent during the last twelve years of his life.

a spiritual aspirant until his thirty-ninth year. This is not so. We tried to explain earlier in "Sri Ramakrishna as a Guru," the third part of this book, that in those who have received the world's enduring adoration for benefitting humanity as gurus, prophets, or founders of religions, we see the manifestation of divine qualities from childhood onward. We find the qualities of a guru in the Master's life as early as his childhood. We know that in his youth he did many spectacular things during his sadhana, inspired by the divine mood. When he had completed his sadhana at the age of thirty-two, he went on a pilgrimage

717

with Mathur. We see that the Master continued to perform most of his actions as directed by the same mood during that pilgrimage and afterwards. We have pointed out that the divine mood became completely manifest in the Master in 1875, when he began to propagate his spiritual mission. At that time, Western materialism, science, and civilization were having a profound influence on the Indian people, making them extremely materialistic and diverting them from the path of the eternal religion. So from this point on, the Master was constantly driven by the divine mood to take a stand against the Western influence and to instill spirituality among English-educated Indians. He thus blessed the lives of many people.

It was extremely important for the Master to act as he did at that time. If the Master's divine life, fortified with an extraordinary spiritual power, had not by the grace of God held back the forces of Western materialism, it is likely that India's national character and the eternal religion would have disappeared forever. In fact, it is

3. The Master, through his divine mood, has freed India of the degradation caused by Western materialism.

evident that the Master did immense good to people in all countries by practising most of the world religions and discovering this great truth: "As many faiths, so many paths." For twelve years he demonstrated an ideal life to Western-educated people and tried to infuse them with spirituality, thus checking the current of Western materialism and enabling India to avoid a terrible crisis. The first mission of the Master's life was to unite the prevalent religious paths with the eternal religion and to prove that they are all of equal importance, even though each one appeals to individuals of different temperaments and tendencies. His second mission was to prevent India from sinking into the terrible current of Western materialism. In the same year that English education was officially introduced to India [1836] the Master was born. The Master's power mitigated the negative aspects of Western education while absorbing the positive aspects and simultaneously helped India maintain her own character. It is amazing that these two forces appeared in India simultaneously by Providence.

The full manifestation of the divine mood, the pinnacle of spiritual realization, is rarely seen in human life. When an individual becomes free from the fetters of karma by God's grace, he or she can taste a little of that divine

4. When the divine mood arises in a human life.

mood. When a person's control over the mind and external senses becomes as effortless and natural as breathing, when the little I-consciousness loses itself in love of the Supreme Self and merges forever into the ocean of the indivisible Satchidananda, when the mind and intellect are purified in nirvikalpa samadhi and assume completely pure sattvic forms, when the unending flow of desires is completely dried up by the blazing fire of knowledge and is incapable of producing any new tendencies and actions — it is only then that this divine mood appears and the individual's life becomes blessed. Rarely can one find a person in whom the divine mood has manifested itself completely, bringing everlasting contentment. And because such a person's actions are not prompted by desire, they appear to be without any motivation. That person then becomes incomprehensible to ordinary people. Only one who is established in the divine mood can comprehend the true nature of that state. It is not possible for ordinary minds and intellects like ours to understand even partially the extraordinary activities performed at the prompting of that mood, unless we study them with deep faith and reverence.

Only avatars possess the most complete manifestation of the divine mood,

| 5. Divinity is manifest extraordinarily in the lives of avatars, making their characters inscrutable and mysterious. |

as the religious history of the world testifies. This is why the character of an avatar is always mysterious to us. We can imagine only an incomplete picture of the state of the knowledge of Brahman which is devoid of maya. But we cannot understand how the knowers of Brahman dwell in that state effortlessly and naturally, or how and why their actions are sometimes like ours and sometimes like those of all-powerful gods. Both our imagination and reason are completely defeated by this mystery. So it is not possible to completely describe Sri Ramakrishna's activities during this period. We can only give the reader a chronology of his activities and describe how we guessed at the motive behind each of his actions by observing the results. We can thus measure the greatness of the cause by evaluating the importance of the effect. It will not take long to understand the extent to which the divine mood manifested in the Master's heart if we reflect upon the extraordinary nature of his activities during this period.

Although the activities of Sri Ramakrishna, who was then established in the

| 6. Seven major categories of actions that the Master performed under the influence of the divine mood. |

divine mood, were performed only for the sake of establishing the eternal religion, they can be classified into seven major groups:

1) He moulded the spiritual life of his immaculate and virtuous wife, Sri Sarada Devi, in a remarkable way and made of her a powerful dynamo capable of transmitting spirituality to others.

2) With his spiritual power he sought to perfect the lives of those religious leaders in Calcutta who were already guided by high ideals.

3) He shared his spirituality with seekers of all religious paths who came to Dakshineswar, thus quenching their thirst.

4) He classified his marked disciples, whom he had previously seen in visions, according to their capacities, and he worked to develop their spiritual lives.

5) He initiated some of his disciples in the vow of renunciation so that they would realize God, and made them conduits for disseminating his unique, universal religious views to the world.

6) He frequently visited the homes of his devotees in Calcutta and inspired their families and friends with his spiritual talks and devotional singing.

7) He firmly tied his devotees with a wonderful cord of love and created a remarkable unity among them; as a result they became very close to one another and eventually formed an inclusive religious organization.

The Master started the first of these seven types of activity in 1874, as we described in the last portion of the second volume of this book. In the appendix of the same volume we discussed how he began the second type in 1875 when he visited Keshab Chandra Sen, leader of the Indian Brahmo Samaj. We presented to the reader the third, fourth, and sixth types of activity in a general way in the fifth, sixth, and seventh chapters of volume four of this book. Now we shall describe when and how the Master undertook the remaining fifth and seventh types.

Chapter 1

Section 1

The *J*nfluence of the Master on the Brahmo Samaj

THE PUBLIC OF CALCUTTA LEARNED OF THE MASTER after he met Keshab Chandra

> 1. The love and respect of Keshab Sen and other Brahmos for the Master.

Sen, leader of the Indian Brahmo Samaj. We mentioned earlier that Keshab, who appreciated good qualities in others, was very attracted to the Master from their first meeting. Although he was influenced by Western ideas, Keshab's heart was full of true devotion for God, and it was impossible for him to keep the nectar of divine love to himself. The more he found new light in his own life from visiting the Master and listening to his sweet, immortal message, the more he freely disseminated this light to the public and enthusiastically invited others [to meet the Master] so that they could share in the peace and joy that he had found. Thus, we see the Master's pure life story, his words of wisdom, and his religious views extensively discussed in the *Sulabh Samachar, Sunday Mirror, Theistic Quarterly Review,* and in other English and Bengali magazines published by the Brahmo Samaj. While addressing the congregation from their pulpits at the end of their services and prayers, Keshab and other Brahmo leaders quite often repeated the Master's messages. Whenever they had the opportunity they visited Dakshineswar — sometimes with only a few members of their inner circle and sometimes with the whole party — and spent some time in spiritual conversation with the Master.

The Master was delighted to observe the Brahmo leaders' thirst for

> 2. The Master's loving relationship with the Brahmos.

spirituality and love of God, and he made special efforts to show them how to dive deep into the ocean of sadhana and obtain the precious pearl of

God-realization. He so enjoyed talking about God and singing of His glory with them that he occasionally visited Keshab's house uninvited. Thus he gradually became acquainted with many spiritual seekers of the Brahmo Samaj. Sometimes he even visited the houses of Brahmos other than Keshab, thus increasing their joy. For example, during their festivals and on other special occasions he visited the houses of Manimohan Mallick of Sinduriapati, Jaygopal Sen of Mathaghasa Lane, Benimadhav Pal of Sinthi in Baranagore, Kashiswar Mitra of Nandan Bagan, and others. Sometimes it happened that while Keshab was giving instructions from his pulpit he would see the Master enter the temple unannounced. Keshab would interrupt his sermon to come down from the pulpit and receive him cordially. He would then conclude the service by listening to the Master's words and singing devotional songs with him.

People of the same faith can associate freely with one another and share

3. The reason the Brahmos felt that the Master belonged to their faith.

their joy without any hesitation. So it is not surprising that because they saw the Master mixing freely with them and enjoying their company, the Brahmo leaders believed that he shared their religious faith, and they considered him to be a member of their group. People of the Shakta, Vaishnava, and other Hindu sects also felt this way because they saw him join them and rejoice with them. Who understood at the time that the Master could behave naturally with those of all sects and faiths because he was established in bhavamukha, the source of all ideas and the common ground of all faiths? But the people of the Brahmo Samaj did not have the slightest doubt that the Master was experiencing more bliss than they when they sang kirtan and held their group meditation on the formless Brahman with attributes. Furthermore, they saw darkness when their eyes were closed in meditation, and they knew that the Master saw a wonderful light. They also understood that it was not possible to have that kind of vision and enjoy that bliss without surrendering completely to God and becoming as absorbed as the Master was.

When the Master saw that some members of the Brahmo Samaj possessed

4. The Master helped the Brahmo devotees make progress in sadhana.

a love for truth, detachment, thirst for spirituality, and other good qualities, he tried to help them make progress in their chosen religious path. He always considered all devotees of God to be his close relatives, regardless of what community they belonged to, and he would help them without reservation so that they could attain perfection by following their respective paths. The Master always said that all true devotees of God belonged to a distinct class, and he never hesitated to eat and drink with them. The Master therefore looked with great affection upon Keshab and his followers, who included Vijay Krishna Goswami, Pratap Chandra Majumdar, Chiranjiv Sharma, Shivanath Shastri, Amritalal Basu, and others. The

Master helped them in their spiritual quest and despite his orthodoxy was always willing to eat or drink with them. It did not take long for him to realize that the influence of Western education and ideas was leading them away from the national religious ideal, and that they sometimes considered social reform to be the goal of their religious practice. That is why the Master worked to infuse in them a passion for real sadhana and tried to make them adopt God-realization as the only goal of life — whether their organization came along with them or not.

As a result, Keshab and his disciples made good progress along the path that the Master showed them: They began to address God by the sweet name of the Divine Mother and introduced the worship of God as Mother into their organization. The Master's ideas entered into the literature and music of the Brahmo Samaj and influenced many of its customs, thus enlivening the organization. In addition to this, the light of the Master's life revealed to the Brahmo leaders that the Hindu religion had much to teach them, and that many of its practices were worthy of consideration — even though the Brahmos had previously considered them to be erroneous and superstitious, a belief that had led them to separate their organization from the Hindu religion.

The Master had known from the beginning that because Keshab and his

5. Why the Master told the Brahmos they could accept his words, leaving off the "head and tail."

followers had drunk deeply of Western ideas, they would not be able to properly understand all of his ideas and teachings. They might understand some of what he said but they might not want to accept all of it fully. Keeping this in mind, after giving them instructions, the Master would often tell them: "I have said whatever came into my head. Take as much of it as you wish. You may leave off the head and the tail." He also realized that many Brahmo Samaj members had as their goals achieving social reform and enjoying the things of this world. Sometimes he addressed this humourously.

He said: "I went to Keshab's place and watched their prayer service. After

6. The Master taught through humour.

speaking at length about the glories of God, Keshab announced, 'Let us now meditate on God.' I wondered how long they would meditate. But, oh dear, they'd scarcely shut their eyes for two minutes before it was all over! How can one know God by meditating like that? While they were meditating, I was watching their faces. Afterwards I said to Keshab: 'I've seen a lot of you meditate, and do you know what it reminded me of? Troops of monkeys sometimes sit quietly under the pine trees at Dakshineswar, just as if they were perfect gentlemen, quite innocent. But they aren't. As they sit there, they're thinking about all the gourds and pumpkins that householders train to grow over their roofs, and about all the gardens full of plantains and eggplants. After a little while, they'll jump up with a yell and rush away to the gardens to stuff their stomachs. I saw many of you meditating like that.' And when the Brahmos heard that, they laughed."

Sometimes the Master would also use humour to teach us. We remember one day when Swami Vivekananda was singing a devotional song. At that time Swamiji was visiting the Brahmo Samaj regularly and practising prayer and meditation in the morning and evening, according to the Brahmo tradition. Absorbed, Swamiji began to passionately sing this song on Brahman, "Concentrate your mind on that One, ancient, and stainless Purusha." There is a line in that song, "Pray to and meditate on God continuously." To imprint those words deeply in Swamiji's mind, the Master said suddenly: "No, no, don't say that. You'd better say, 'Pray to and meditate on God twice a day.' Why vainly repeat something that you don't actually intend to do?" All laughed loudly, and Swamiji was a little embarrassed.

On another occasion the Master talked to Keshab and other Brahmos about their prayer service, saying: "Why do you talk so much about the various powers of God? Does a child, sitting in front of his father, keep thinking about how many horses, cows, houses, and estates his father has? Isn't he simply happy knowing how much he loves his father and how much his father loves him? Is it any wonder that the father feeds and clothes his child? We are all God's children. Is it so extraordinary that He looks after us? Instead of dwelling on that, a real devotee makes God his very own by loving Him. He begs importunately, demanding that his prayer be answered and that God reveal Himself to him. If you dwell too much on God's powers, you can't think of Him as your nearest and dearest, and you can't feel free to demand things of Him. Thinking about His greatness makes Him seem distant from us. Think of Him as your very own. That's the only way to realize Him."

> 7. The Master taught the Brahmos that one could not make God one's own simply by thinking of His powers.

In addition to learning about the absolute necessity of practising spiritual disciplines and giving up worldly desires to realize God, Keshab and other Brahmos learned another thing from the Master. Western missionaries and English literature had taught them that God is formless and that it is a great sin to believe that God can be present in an image, and to pray to and worship Him in that form. But then they heard the Master's remarks on image worship: "As formless water freezes and becomes ice, so the formless Satchidananda is frozen by devotion and given form." Or, "As an imitation custard apple reminds one of the real fruit, so one can experience the true nature of God by worshipping an image that represents Him." The Brahmo devotees realized that there was much to say and think about the practice of "idolatry" that they had for so long held in contempt and considered extremely irrational. They undoubtedly saw image worship in a new light when the Master proved to Keshab and the Brahmos that "As fire and its

> 8. One cannot limit the infinite nature of God.

power to burn are identical, so Brahman and Its power — which manifests Itself as the universe — are identical."

These devotees came to realize that the description of God as formless but with attributes indicated only part of His true nature. They understood that it was as erroneous to insist that God's true nature is with form as to insist only that He is formless but has attributes. Although God is manifest as the world, which has various forms, God also controls the world as the formless Saguna Brahman with attributes. God is beyond all attributes and exists as the eternal substratum that underlies everything that has name and form — persons and things, the Personal God, the jiva, and the universe. Keshab and his followers were amazed to discover the profound meaning that lay within this ordinary saying of the Master: "One should never set limits to God's nature. He is with form and also formless. In addition, who can know and say what else He is?"

Keshab first met Sri Ramakrishna in March 1875. For a little over three years after their meeting, the Indian Brahmo Samaj under Keshab's leadership began to take new shape, freeing itself from infatuation with Western ideas. The Brahmos' passion for sadhana drew the attention of the public. On 6 March 1878, Keshab married his daughter to the Maharaja of Coochbehar. At that time his daughter was a little younger than the marriageable age that had been set for girls by the Brahmo Samaj. This caused a tremendous uproar in the Brahmo Samaj, which had established its customs based on social reform according to the West. The organization finally split into two groups: the Indian Brahmo Samaj and the Sadharan Brahmo Samaj. The Master's influence on the Brahmo Samaj was not affected by this incident. He treated both parties cordially and impartially, and the spiritual seekers from both continued to come to him for spiritual help.

9. The change in the Indian Brahmo Samaj.

After this schism, Keshab, leader of the Indian Brahmo Samaj, made rapid progress in his sadhana; and with the Master's grace, his spiritual life developed to a great extent. He deeply believed that the human mind could ascend to more subtle and higher strata of the spiritual realm with the help of external rituals such as performing fire sacrifices, taking ceremonial baths, shaving one's head, wearing ochre robes, and so on, and he adopted them all to greater or lesser degrees. He felt that Buddha, Gauranga, Jesus, and other great teachers were ever-present in their subtle bodies and that each one of them existed in the spiritual realm as a perennial spring expressing a particular mood. So, with the intention of realizing the spiritual moods that they embodied, he would from time to time meditate deeply on one or another of them. It is evident that Keshab followed these methods because he had heard that when the Master practised the sadhanas of various faiths he took initiation into each one, adopting

10. Keshab forms and preaches the "New Dispensation," which incorporates some of the Master's ideas.

its methods fully. After Keshab had practised some of these sadhanas, he began preaching to the public what he understood about the Master's newly discovered truth, "As many faiths, so many paths," calling it the *Navavidhan*, or the "New Dispensation." This took place two years after the Coochbehar marriage. We cannot describe the depth of Keshab's faith in and devotion to the Master; we can say only that he knew that the Master was the embodiment of the New Dispensation. When Keshab came to see the Master at Dakshineswar, many of us saw him take the dust of the Master's feet while loudly repeating, "Victory to the New Dispensation! Victory to the New Dispensation!" Who can say how deep his spiritual life would have become had he not passed away about four years after he started preaching the New Dispensation?

The Master considered Keshab to be so closely related to him that upon

| 11. The extent to which the Master considered Keshab to be his own. | hearing of his illness he promised to offer green coconuts and sugar to the Divine Mother for his recovery. When the Master went to see Keshab during his |

illness, he could not hold back his tears when he saw Keshab's emaciated body. He told Keshab: "A gardener sometimes prunes the Basra rose plant and excavates the ground around it to expose its roots to the sun and dew so that it will flourish and produce big flowers. The Gardener (*God*) has brought your body to this condition for that purpose." And when in January 1884 the Master heard that Keshab had passed away, he was so overwhelmed with grief that for three days he remained in bed and would not talk to anyone. Later he remarked, "When I heard the news of Keshab's passing away, I felt as if one of my limbs had been paralyzed." The men and women in Keshab's family were very devoted to the Master. Sometimes they invited the Master to their Lily Cottage in Calcutta, and sometimes they went to Dakshineswar to hear his spiritual instructions. During Keshab's lifetime it was an indispensable part of the *Maghotsava* [Winter Festival] of the New Dispensation to spend a day with the Master talking about God and singing kirtan. Keshab and his followers would go to Dakshineswar by steamer and pick up the Master; while travelling on the Ganges, they celebrated their festival in talking of spiritual matters and singing kirtan with the Master.

When the Brahmo Samaj was divided over the controversy of the

| 12. Under the Master's influence Vijay Krishna Goswami changed his beliefs and left the Brahmo Samaj. | Coochbehar marriage, Vijay Krishna Goswami and Shivanath Shastri became leaders of the Sadharan Brahmo Samaj. Vijay had been dear to Keshab because of his truthfulness and his passion for sadhana. Like Keshab, Vijay's passion for sadhana |

increased greatly after he met the Master. Following his spiritual path, Vijay had many new visions within a short period and developed faith in God with form. A reliable source told us that when Vijay was studying at the Sanskrit College in Calcutta before joining the Brahmo Samaj, he had a long

tuft of hair on his head and wore the sacred thread and amulets of an orthodox brahmin. But one day he gave up all of these for the sake of accepting the
ideal of the Brahmo Samaj, which he believed to be true, and he joined that
organization. After the Coochbehar marriage, he shunned Keshab — who
was like his guru — because he believed it to be the right thing to do. Again,
prompted by his love of truth, he was compelled to separate himself from the
Brahmo Samaj because he could not bring himself to hide his faith in God
with form. He lost his job because of this and underwent terrible financial
difficulties for some time, but he was not depressed at all.

On many occasions Vijay told us how the Master gave him spiritual help.
He also said that he sometimes had a vision of the Master in a mysterious
way. We do not know if he loved and respected the Master as a secondary
guru or in some other way. He also told us that while he was at Akashganga
Hill in Gaya, a monk used his yogic power to put him into samadhi in an
instant, thus becoming his guru. There is no doubt, however, that Vijay had a
very high opinion of the Master, and elsewhere in this book (see IV.5.14) we
have recorded what the Master told us about him.

In the days after his separation from the Brahmo Samaj, Vijay's spiritual

13. The progress that Vijay made in sadhana after separation.

life deepened more and more. People were charmed
by his unrestrained, ecstatic dance during kirtan and
by his frequent samadhi. The Master told us about
Vijay's advanced spiritual state: "Vijay has reached the room just next to the
innermost chamber, where one attains fulfillment of sadhana, and now he is
knocking at its door." After he had achieved such spiritual depths, Vijay
initiated many people with mantras. He died in Puri about fourteen years
after the Master passed away.

After the Coochbehar marriage, a terrible discord developed between the

14. The Master's story of "the fight between Shiva and Rama" removed ill feelings between Keshab and Vijay.

members of the Indian Brahmo Samaj and the Sadharan Brahmo Samaj; they were not even on speaking
terms with each other. However, as we mentioned
earlier, the spiritual seekers of both parties continued
to visit Dakshineswar as usual.

One day Keshab and Vijay both came to visit the
Master with their close followers. Each party was of course unaware of the
other's visit, and there was much tension between them as they remembered
their disagreement. Observing the uneasiness in Keshab and Vijay that day,
the Master told them this story to relieve the discord: "Once there was a
quarrel between Shiva and Ramachandra. A terrible war broke out. It is well
known that Shiva's guru is Rama and Rama's guru is Shiva. So it didn't take
long for them to make up again after the war ended. But there was no recon-
ciliation between the followers — Shiva's ghosts and Rama's monkeys. The
fight between the ghosts and the monkeys continued. (*Addressing Keshab and
Vijay:*) Whatever was to happen has happened. You shouldn't harbour this

mutual ill will anymore; let it remain with the ghosts and monkeys." From then on Keshab and Vijay at least began to speak to each other again.

Because of his direct spiritual experiences, Vijay did not want to be bound by responsibility for any organization. When he left the Sadharan Brahmo Samaj some of the members who had absolute faith in him also left. Membership in the Sadharan Brahmo Samaj then decreased considerably. Its new leader, Shivanath Shastri, sought to protect what remained of the Sadharan Brahmo Samaj. Shivanath had previously visited the Master many times and had great love and respect for him, and the Master had much affection for Shivanath. But Shivanath was in deep trouble when Vijay left. He knew that Sri Ramakrishna's advice had influenced Vijay's religious views, leading him to withdraw from the Brahmo Samaj. Shivanath therefore stopped visiting the Master. A short time before this, Swami Vivekananda had joined the Sadharan Brahmo Samaj and become a favourite of Shivanath and other Brahmos. Even though he had joined this group, Swamiji also continued to visit Keshab from time to time, as well as the Master at Dakshineswar. Swamiji told us that one day he asked Shivanath why he had stopped visiting the Master, and he replied, "If I visit Dakshineswar frequently, other members of the Sadharan Brahmo Samaj will follow me, and the Brahmo Samaj will then fall apart." Swamiji also said that, based on this belief, Shivanath had advised him to stop going to Dakshineswar. Shivanath told him: "The Master's spiritual ecstasy and samadhi are the result of a nervous debility, and his brain has been deranged by his excessive practice of physical austerities." We have mentioned elsewhere what the Master said when he heard about this (see IV.2.30-32).

Be that as it may, it was due to the Master's influence that a passion for sadhana had entered the Brahmo Samaj, and the spiritual seekers from both the Navavidhan and the Sadharan Brahmo Samaj tried to form their lives so that they could realize God. Pratap Chandra Majumdar, a preacher of the New Dispensation, came to Dakshineswar once. When we asked him how and to what extent spiritual ideas had developed in the Brahmo Samaj after it came in contact with the Master, he replied: "Did we understand what true religion was before we met him? We had merely rebelled against orthodox Hinduism. But after we met him, we realized what true spiritual life is." On this occasion Chiranjiv Sharma (Trailokya Nath Sanyal) was present with Pratap.

The Master's influence on the New Dispensation was quite evident, but it was by no means insignificant on the Sadharan Brahmo Samaj while Vijay was its leader. This influence on the Sadharan Brahmo Samaj diminished when

15. Shivanath Shastri stopped visiting Dakshineswar, lest the Brahmo Samaj fall apart under the Master's influence.

16. Pratap Majumdar's comment on the Master's influence on the Brahmo Samaj.

17. The Master's influence on the Sadharan Brahmo Samaj.

Vijay and a large number of spiritual seekers left the group. Consequently this Samaj became less spiritual, engaging itself mainly in social reforms, philanthropic activities, and so on. The Master's influence on this Samaj may have diminished, but it did not disappear completely. For example, one finds that some members of this Samaj practised yoga, studied Vedanta, and became involved in spiritualism. We know that some members of the Sadharan Brahmo Samaj practised Vedic rituals as followed by the highest class of the Kartabhaja sect. They also attempted to use meditation to cure physical ailments.

It is well known that Chiranjiv Sharma of the New Dispensation played a large role in developing the musical tradition of the Brahmo Samaj. But if one traces the source of the songs used, one finds that Chiranjiv composed his

18. The Master's influence on Brahmo songs.

most inspiring songs after becoming acquainted with the Master's visions, ecstatic moods, and samadhi. We quote below the first line of a few songs:

1) In dense darkness, O Mother, Thy formless beauty shines.
2) The deep ocean of samadhi is endless and boundless.
3) In Wisdom's firmament the moon of Love is rising full.
4) Upon the Sea of Blissful Awareness waves of ecstatic love arise.
5) O Mother, make me mad with Thy love.

The poet Chiranjiv Sharma undoubtedly deserves the gratitude of the people of Bengal and also of the spiritual aspirants in that area for composing those wonderful songs. But there is no doubt that he was able to compose them only after witnessing the Master's samadhi. Chiranjiv had a sweet voice, and on many occasions we saw the Master go into samadhi while listening to him sing.

Thus was the Brahmo Samaj inspired by the wonderful spiritual influence of the Master. The Brahmo Samaj preached the worship of the formless aspect of God, which the Master sometimes described as an immature method (see III.2.54-57). But we heard him say many times that an

19. The Master declares the Brahmo religion to be a path to God-realization.

aspirant who worships in that manner with sincere faith will realize God. When the Master bowed down to God and His devotees of all sects after kirtan, he never forgot to bow down to the Brahmos, saying, "Salutations to the modern Brahmajnanis." It is evident that the Master truly believed that the Brahmo religion was one of the faiths or paths to God-realization preached to the world according to God's will. The Master made a sincere effort to help the Brahmos become free from the influence of the West and follow the true spiritual path. He told them that although social reforms and philanthropic activities might be praiseworthy — and indeed obligatory — they should not be represented as the main goal of life by their organization. Spiritual practices for God-realization should not be neglected.

The Brahmo Samaj was the first organization to study the extraordinary spiritual life of the Master and the first to draw the attention of the Calcutta public to Dakshineswar. Everyone who was blessed by the Master with spiritual power and peace is eternally indebted to the New Dispensation and to the Sadharan Brahmo Samaj. The present author himself is greatly indebted to both of them because in his youth they helped him to mould the beginning of his spiritual life by setting a high ideal before him. We therefore bow down again and again with love and gratitude to the Holy Trinity — Brahman, the Brahmo religion, and the Brahmo devotees — considering them to be one in essence. Now we shall present to the reader two accounts of the Master's joyous meetings with Brahmo devotees, which we were fortunate enough to witness.

Chapter 1

Section 2

The Brahmo *Festival* at Manimohan Mallick's House

WE REMEMBER VIVIDLY THAT IT WAS THE FALL SEASON. After enduring the torments

| 1. The date of the event. | of a hot summer, Nature was enjoying bathing in the rains and adorning herself with the beauties of |

autumn, and was now pulling her veil her as the chill of winter drew near. It was the last quarter of the season. Balaram Basu, a great devotee of the Master and our esteemed friend, was present on this occasion. He marked the day in his almanac, as was his habit, and from that record we know that the exact date was Monday, 26 November 1883.

We were then studying at St. Xavier's College in Calcutta and had had the

| 2. Acquaintance with Vaikuntha Nath Sanyal. | privilege of meeting the Master only two or three times. The college was closed that day, so we decided |

to visit the Master that afternoon.[1] We remember that on the boat to Dakshineswar we learned that one of our fellow passengers was also going to visit the Master. His name was Vaikuntha Nath Sanyal, and he too had met the Master only recently. We also remember that another passenger overheard the Master's name during our conversation and made a sarcastic remark and that Vaikuntha silenced the man with a scornful retort. When we reached Dakshineswar, it was about 2:00 or 2:30 in the afternoon.

---

1. The party included Barada Sundar Pal of Comilla, Hari Prasanna Chattopadhyay of Belgharia (later Swami Vijnanananda), and the author.

As soon as we entered the Master's room and bowed down to him, he said: "Ah, you've come today! Had you come a little later, you would have missed me. I'm going to Calcutta to attend a Brahmo festival, and a carriage has been called for. But it's nice that you could see me. Please sit down. How disappointing it would have been for you to return home without seeing me."

We sat on a mat spread on the floor of his room and asked the Master, "Sir,

3. First acquaintance with Baburam.

would we be allowed at the Brahmo festival that you are going to?" The Master replied: "Why not? You are free to go there if you like. It is at the house of Mani Mallick of Sinduriapati." A slender, fair young man wearing a red cloth entered the room, and the Master asked him, "Could you tell these boys the address of Mani Mallick's house?" The young man replied humbly, "81 Chitpore Road, Sinduriapati." Because of his modest behaviour and sattvic nature we thought he was the son of a temple priest. A couple of months later, we saw him as he was leaving the examination hall at school. When we spoke to him, we realized that our previous impression had been incorrect. We learned that his name was Baburam and that he was from Antpur near Tarakeswar. He was living in a rented house at Kambuliatola in Calcutta, and he occasionally stayed with the Master. He is now known in the Ramakrishna Order as Swami Premananda.

The carriage pulled up shortly after we arrived. The Master asked Baburam to carry his towel, some warm clothes, and a small spice bag. Then he bowed down to the Mother and entered the carriage. Baburam took the Master's things and sat on the other side of the carriage. A third person, who we later learned was Pratap Chandra Hazra, went to Calcutta with the Master.

As soon as the Master left, we fortunately found a passenger boat to take us to Barabazar in Calcutta. We thought that the festival would start in the evening, so we waited for a while at a friend's house. Our new acquaintance, Vaikuntha, left to take care of some business, assuring us that he would see us at the festival at the appropriate time.

We arrived at Mani Mallick's house about 4:00 p.m. When we inquired about the Master, a man showed us to the parlour upstairs. The room was beautifully decorated with flowers and leaves for the festival, and some devotees were there, talking with one another. They told us that the noon service and music were over and that the Master had gone to the inner apartment at the request of the women devotees. In the evening there would be another service and kirtan.

When we heard that it would be some time before the evening service

4. The wonderful kirtan in Mani Mallick's parlour.

began, we went out for a while. In the evening we returned to the festival. While we were in the street in front of the house, we heard sweet music and the loud sound of a *mridanga* [a drum]. We hurried into the house and up to the

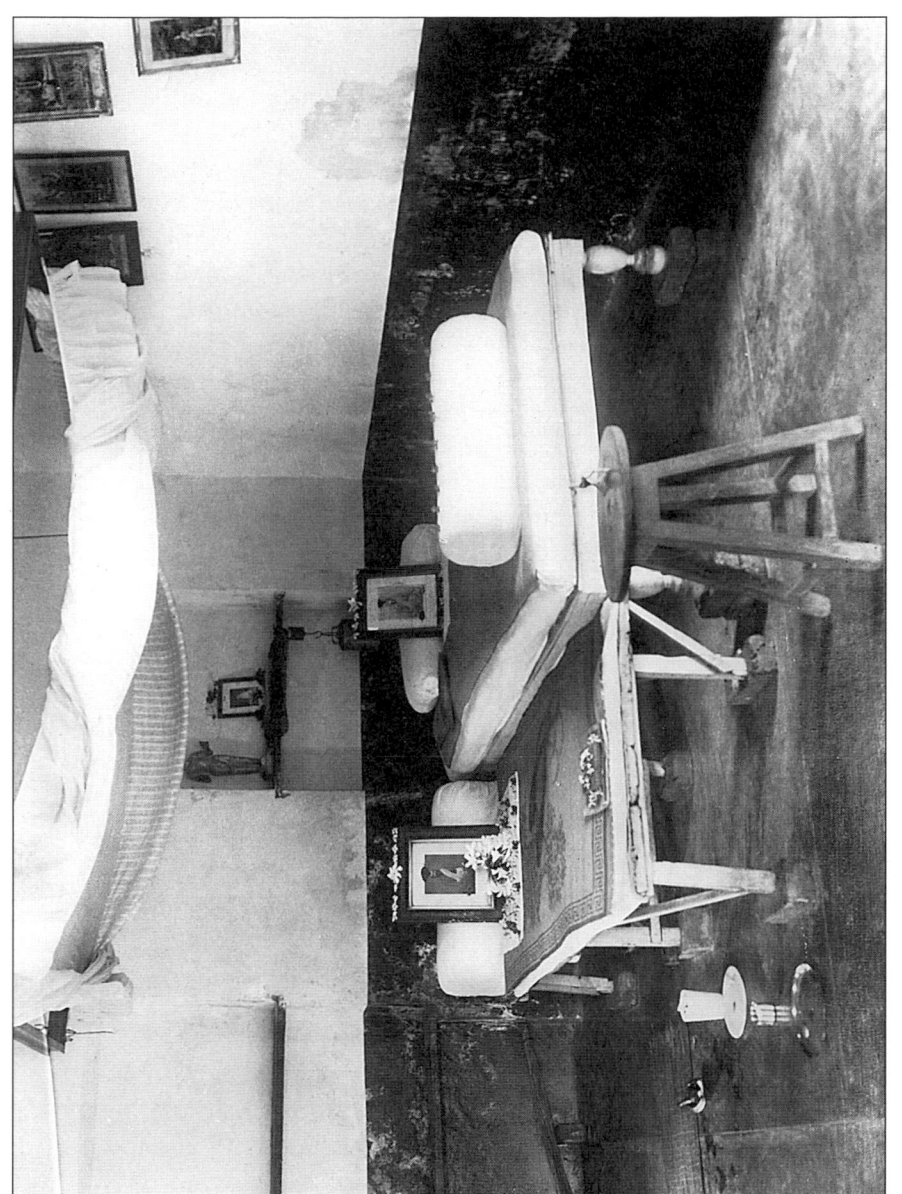

Ramakrishna's room at the northwest corner of the temple complex of Dakshineswar, where he lived for fourteen years.

parlour, knowing that the kirtan had begun. What we saw there defies description! Inside the hall was a thick crowd that spilled outside. So many people were standing in every doorway and on the western roof that it was almost impossible to push through the crowd into the room. The devotees were all craning their necks and intently watching what was happening inside the hall. Full of devotion, they were completely unaware of their surroundings. When we saw that it would be impossible to enter the room through the front door, we went around the house, crossed the western roof, and approached the northern door of the hall. The crowd there was somewhat thinner, so we were able to thrust our heads into the room. We saw a wonderful scene.

High waves of heavenly bliss seemed to be flowing in the room. Everyone there was laughing, crying, and dancing — they had become completely lost in the kirtan. Some people fell on the ground, unable to control themselves.

5. The Master's fascinating dance.

Others were overwhelmed with emotion and acted like lunatics. The Master was dancing in the centre of that god-intoxicated group, rapidly moving forward and backward with rhythmic steps. In whatever direction he moved the crowd made room for him, as if enchanted.

An extraordinary combination of tenderness, sweetness, and leonine strength was visible in every one of the Master's limbs. His face shone with a divine smile. What a superb dance! There was no artificiality or affectation in it — no jumping, no unnatural gestures or acrobatics. Nor was any absence of control apparent. Rather, one saw in the Master's dancing a rhythm of natural gestures and movements that sprang from his overwhelming bliss, sweetness, and zeal. His phenomenal dance was like that of a big fish that swims freely and joyfully throughout a vast clear lake, sometimes slowly and sometimes quickly. Absorbed in the ocean of blissful Brahman, the Master used his body to express his inner feelings. At times he lost consciousness of his surroundings as he danced, and sometimes his cloth fell from his body. When that happened, someone fastened it tightly around his waist. And if he saw anyone become overwhelmed with spiritual emotions and lose consciousness, he touched that man's chest, bringing him back to a normal state.

A current of divine bliss emanated from the Master and spread in all directions, allowing the devotees to see God face to face. Those of a lukewarm temperament found their fervour intensified; those with idle minds began to enthusiastically progress in the realm of spirituality; and those who were attached to the world became, for a while, free from their attachment. Among those who experienced ecstasy and lost outer consciousness from time to time were Vijay Krishna Goswami (the leader of the Sadharan Brahmo Samaj) and even some of the Brahmo devotees. Chiranjiv Sharma, accompanied by a one-stringed instrument, sang in his sweet voice, "Dance,

O children of the Blissful Mother, round and round." He also was beside himself. The kirtan continued for more than two hours in this manner, closing with this song:

> Who has brought this sweet name of Hari to the world?
> Has Nitai brought this name?
> Or was it brought by Gaur, or Advaita of Shantipur?

Finally, everyone present praised and bowed down to all religious denominations and spiritual teachers, and the wonderful kirtan came to an end.

We remember that when all were seated after the kirtan, the Master asked Nagendra Nath Chattopadhyay, a Brahmo teacher, to sing the following song. In an ecstatic mood, he repeated it a couple of times, bringing happiness to those present.

> Be drunk, O mind, be drunk with the Wine of Heavenly Bliss!
> Roll on the ground and weep, chanting Hari's sweet name!
> Fill the arching heavens with your deep lion roar
> Singing Hari's sweet name! With your arms upraised,
> Dance in the name of Hari and give His name to all.
> Swim by day and by night in the bliss of Hari's love;
> Slay desire with His name, and blessed be your life!

Afterwards, the Master told those assembled that one attains supreme bliss when one lifts the mind above sense objects and directs it towards God. The women devotees, who were seated behind a screen in the eastern part of the parlour, also asked him various questions on spiritual matters and enjoyed his inspiring replies. As he answered the questions put to him, the Master now and then sang a few songs composed by Ramprasad and Kamalakanta in praise of the Divine Mother to impress the subject deeply into his listeners' minds. We distinctly remember hearing him sing these songs:

1) The black bee of my mind is drawn in sheer delight
   To the blue lotus of Mother Shyama's feet.
2) High in the heaven of the Mother's feet, my mind was soaring like a kite.
3) All creation is the sport of my mad Mother Kali.
4) What is the fault of the poor mind?
   Why do you blame it falsely?
5) Mother, this is the grief that sorely grieves my heart,
   That even with Thee for Mother and though I am wide awake,
   There should be robbery in my house.

While the Master was singing the Mother's name, Vijay went to another room with a few devotees and began to expound on the Ramayana by Tulasidas. When it was the time for the evening service, Vijay returned to the parlour to

6. The Master teases Vijay Goswami.

Vijay Krishna Goswami (1841-1899), a Brahmo leader.

bow down to the Master before beginning the prayer service. When the Master saw Vijay, he said jokingly: "Nowadays Vijay takes great delight in kirtan. But I'm frightened when he dances, for the whole roof may collapse!" Everyone laughed. "Yes, such a thing actually happened in our part of the country, where people build two-storeyed houses out of wood and mud. A Vaishnava teacher went to a disciple's house and began kirtan on the upper floor. When the singing reached the right mood, people began to dance. Now that teacher was a little plump, like you (*addressing Vijay*). After he danced for a while, the floor collapsed, and he fell through to the ground floor! That is why I'm afraid — your dancing might repeat that scene!" All laughed.

Noticing Vijay's ochre clothes, the Master said: "Nowadays Vijay is very fond of the ochre colour. Generally people dye their clothes and chadars ochre, but Vijay even dyes his shirt and shoes. That is good: A state comes when one wishes to do so, and one no longer wears clothes of any other colour. Ochre is indeed the mark of renunciation. It reminds the aspirant that he has renounced everything for God." Vijay then bowed down to the Master, who blessed him heartily, saying: "Peace! Peace! Peace be unto you."

When the Master was singing the Mother's name, something occurred

7. The Master's love for the devotees.

that shows how keen was his power of observation, though he always remained in an introspective state. While he was singing, the Master looked at Baburam and immediately realized that he was hungry and thirsty. The Master knew that Baburam would not eat before he did, so he asked for some sweets and water for himself. He took a little, but he gave a large portion to Baburam and shared whatever remained with the devotees.

Vijay began his evening prayers downstairs, and shortly thereafter the Master was taken to the inner apartment for supper. It was 9:00 p.m. When we came downstairs to attend Vijay's service, we saw that the Brahmo devotees had assembled in the courtyard for prayer while Vijay sat on a dais in the northern veranda of the house. Recollecting the glory of Brahman, he began the prayer in chorus with the Brahmo devotees: *Satyam jnanam anantam Brahma* [Brahman is Truth, Knowledge, and Infinity]. Thus the prayer service continued. After a while, the Master came into the room and joined them, sitting there calmly for fifteen minutes. At about 10:00 p.m. the Master asked for a carriage so he could return to Dakshineswar. He put on his socks, coat, and a cap that covered his ears to protect himself from the cold. He slowly got into the carriage with Baburam and others. Vijay then began to give instructions to the Brahmos from the dais, and we left for home.

On that day we saw how the Master rejoiced in the company of the

8. The devoted family of Mani Mallick.

Brahmo devotees. We do not know whether Mani Mallick was a formal member of the Brahmo Samaj. But we know with certainty that the members of his family followed the Brahmo religion and practised daily prayer and meditation according to that faith. When the Master heard that a woman of this family could not concentrate during meditation, he asked her affectionately, "Tell me, whom do you think of at that time?" The woman was then raising her young nephew and thoughts of him were continually arising in her mind. When the Master heard this, he advised her to serve that boy as a form of the child Krishna. The woman practised his advice and experienced bhava samadhi within a short time. We narrated this story in detail elsewhere (see III.1.27). On another occasion, we saw the Master rejoicing with some Brahmo devotees in another place. We shall now describe that event to the reader.

Chapter 1

Section 3

The Master at *J*aygopal Sen's House

WE WERE DEEPLY MOVED WHEN WE SAW THE MASTER'S ecstasy and his joy during kirtan at Mani Mallick's house in Sinduriapati. We had found an extraordinary new light in the spiritual realm. Our friend Barada Sundar felt this so intensely that he began to make inquiries concerning when the Master would attend a similar function and where it would be held. It did not take long for his wish to be fulfilled. His efforts bore fruit two days later, on Wednesday morning, 28 November 1883. As soon as we met him that day, he said: "This afternoon Sri Ramakrishna is coming to see Keshab at Lily Cottage, and in the evening he is going to Jaygopal Sen's house at Mathaghasa Lane. Do you want to go?" We knew that Keshab was very ill. Considering that we were strangers and that our presence at Lily Cottage might be inconvenient, we decided to visit the Master at Jaygopal's place.

We knew that Mathaghasa Lane was in the Barabazar area, so we went
1. Jaygopal Sen's house. | there first that evening and, after inquiring, we
located Jaygopal's house. It rained that afternoon, as it had on the day of the festival at Mani Mallick's, for we distinctly remember wading through the muddy road to get to our destination. We also remember that Jaygopal's house faced west, like Mani Mallick's, and that we turned eastward to enter the house. Upon our arrival, we asked a man there whether the Master had come. He received us cordially and asked us to take the staircase on the right and proceed upstairs to the large parlour on the east side of the house. When we entered the spacious hall, which extended from

north to south, we observed that it was neat, clean, and well furnished. For seating there was a large cushion on the floor; the Master sat on one part of it surrounded by some Brahmo devotees. We remember that Chiranjiv Sharma and Amritalal Basu, two teachers of the New Dispensation, were there, as well as Jaygopal and his brother, a few of Jaygopal's neighbours, and one or two of the Master's devotees. It seems on that day we saw Junior Gopal, a young devotee whom the Master called "Hutko" [he who appears and disappears suddenly]. Thus seeing only a dozen people with the Master, we realized that this day's function was not open to the public and that it was improper for us to be there. We decided to leave before all were called to have food.

We bowed down to the Master upon entering the room. When he asked how we came to be there, we replied, "Sir, we got the news that you were coming here today, so we have come to see you." The Master seemed pleased with our answer and asked us to sit down. Reassured, we joined the group and began to watch people and listen to the Master's illuminating talk.

Although we had enjoyed the good fortune of meeting the Master only

| 2. The Master's method of teaching. |

recently, from the beginning we felt an irresistible attraction to his words of nectar. At the time we did not understand why, but we now know that it was his unique method of teaching that drew us to him: In it there was no show of scholarship, no glamourous logic, no skilful use of bombastic words, no effort to use pompous language to make a small idea appear great, nor any effort to condense great ideas into a few words like an aphoristic philosopher. We cannot say whether the Master, who embodied the spiritual ideas he taught, carefully considered his words when he spoke. But whoever listened to him even once must have noticed how he presented to them picture after picture drawn from familiar objects and events from their daily life to instill what he was feeling into the hearts of his listeners. When the Master spoke, the audience visualized what he was talking about, as though it were taking place in front of them, and thus their doubts were settled and they were fully satisfied as to the truth of his words. When we reflect on how these images instantly came to his mind, we suggest that the cause lay in his extraordinary memory, prodigious intelligence, keen insight, and unique presence of mind. But the Master always made clear that the Divine Mother's grace was behind everything he said. He told us: "In a man who depends on the Mother completely, She sits in his heart and makes him say whatever he must by showing it to him through unmistakable signs. Because the Divine Mother does that, his store of knowledge is never empty. The Mother keeps his heart full by continuously supplying a storehouse of knowledge. He may spend as much as he can, but his supply of wisdom never runs out." While explaining this one day, he related to us the following incident:

There is a government magazine to the north of the Kali temple at Dakshineswar that used to be constantly guarded by Sikh soldiers who were extremely devoted to the Master. Sometimes they would bring him to their quarters to settle their doubts on spiritual matters. The Master said: "One day they asked, 'How should a man live in this world so that he will realize God?' Immediately the image of a husking machine appeared before me. One woman kicks the end of the wooden beam, and another woman cautiously turns the paddy in a mortar dug into the earth. She is always alert lest the pestle of the machine fall on her hand. As soon as I saw this I realized that the Mother was explaining to me that one should live in this world as carefully as that. One should keep the mind fixed on God while performing every action in this world. If one isn't attached to external objects and worldly duties, one can escape the entanglement of maya and avoid suffering and destruction. As soon as I saw the husking machine, the Mother raised this idea in my mind. When I told it to them they were very pleased with that analogy. Such images appear to me when I talk to people."

The Master never confused the minds of his audience by using unneces-

3. Another characteristic of his teaching method.

sary words. He quickly grasped the subject and purpose of an inquirer's question and answered it with a few decisive words, and then to convince that person he would illustrate his answer with an analogy, as we have described earlier. We call this characteristic of his teaching method "the conclusive statement" because he said only what he himself had experienced to be true. Although he never said that there was only one answer to any question, his deep-rooted conviction was firmly imprinted on the minds of those listening. If anyone in the audience, due to education and past experiences, was unable to accept the Master's conclusions — even though they sprang from his sadhana — and argued with him, he would generally finish his discussion of the topic by saying: "I've said whatever came into my head. Take as much of it as you want. You may leave out the head and the tail." He never tried to destroy anyone's beliefs by stifling one's freedom to think for oneself. Perhaps he desisted because he thought that the listener would be unable to recognize the true solution to the question until he or she had reached a higher spiritual state, by God's will. The Master did not stop at making his audience understand his conclusions by using analogies and imagery as we have described. He substantiated his statements by mentioning similar sayings of other well-known mystics, by singing the songs that they had composed, and by referring to examples taken from the scriptures. This would remove all doubt from the inquirer's mind regarding that subject. Firmly convinced that the instruction was valid, he or she would try to carry it out in daily life.

It is necessary to mention another thing here. The Master often told us that

| 4. The Master's disgust with flowery speech that is not based on experience. |

at the end of their paths, spiritual aspirants of both devotion and knowledge become established in nondual knowledge and experience their identity with their respective Chosen Deities. As proof of this, we can quote some of his statements: "Pure love and pure devotion are the same (thing)" and "In that ultimate state, all jackals howl in the same way" (that is, all illumined souls express the same truth in a similar way). Although he referred to nondual knowledge as the ultimate goal, to worldly people busy with sense objects he generally gave instruction in the truths of qualified nondualism, and sometimes he taught them how to love God in a dualistic way. He was disgusted with people who supported their arguments by quoting from the lofty philosophical truths of nondualism and qualified nondualism when they lacked devotion and had no high spiritual experiences. He did not hesitate to use harsh words when condemning their actions. One day he asked our friend Vaikuntha Nath Sanyal, "Hello, have you read *Panchadashi*?" Vaikuntha replied: "What is that, sir? I don't know of any such thing." To this, the Master said: "I'm relieved that you didn't know it. Some impudent boys come here after reading all sorts of books. They won't practise anything; they just pester me with all sorts of questions."

We mentioned this to introduce the following: At Jaygopal's house a man once asked the question, "How can we receive God's grace while living in this world?" The Master's answer was based on the philosophy of qualified nondualism. To emphasize this he sang three or four songs on the Divine Mother. We present the essence of what he said below.

As long as a person considers the world as "mine" and acts accordingly, that

| 5. The Master's advice about practising spiritual disciplines when living a householder's life. |

person becomes entangled in the world of maya, even though he or she knows it is impermanent. Such a person suffers terribly and cannot find a way out of this predicament. After saying this, the Master sang a song:

> When such delusion veils the world, through Mahamaya's spell,
> That Brahma is bereft of sense
> And Vishnu loses consciousness,
> What hope is left for humans?

One should therefore mentally associate everything in this transitory world with God and perform every action accordingly. Hold God with one hand and work with the other. One should always remember that all beings and everything in this world belong to God, not to any human being. One who maintains this attitude will not suffer from a deluded attachment to the world. One who believes that whatever one does is the Lord's work will move towards God. To imprint this idea on the minds of his audience, the Master sang this song:

> O mind, you do not know how to farm!
> Fallow lies the field of your life.
> If you had only worked it well,
> How rich a harvest you might have reaped!

When the song was over, the Master continued: "When one takes refuge in God, even while performing household duties, one gradually realizes that everything and every being in this world are manifestations of God. One will then serve one's father and mother as veritable manifestations of God and the Divine Mother, see the child Gopala and the Divine Mother in a son and daughter, and consider others to be representations of God and treat them with love and respect. A person who lives in the world with this attitude is an ideal householder from whose mind the fear of death has completely disappeared. Such a person is rare indeed, but not altogether nonexistent." The Master then outlined the means needed to reach that ideal: "One should perform all duties with discrimination, leave the bustle of the world and go into solitude from time to time, and engage oneself in spiritual practices to realize God. Only then can one build an ideal spiritual life."[1] Then the Master sang this song of Ramprasad:

> Come, O mind, let us go for a walk to Kali, the Wish-fulfilling Tree,
> And there beneath It gather the four fruits of life.

He explained the word *discrimination* as follows: With the help of a discriminating intellect, an aspirant accepts God as eternal and real and rejects the sense objects of the world as transitory and insubstantial. After realizing the eternal God, that very intellect makes the aspirant understand that He who is the Absolute has become the diverse universe and all living beings in the relative plane. Ultimately the aspirant is blessed to experience both the absolute and relative aspects of God.

Chiranjiv Sharma then began to sing, accompanied by his one-stringed instrument. He sang this song: "O Mother, make me mad with Thy love." All sang in chorus after him. The Master stood up in ecstasy as the kirtan began. When that song was over, Chiranjiv began the next: "In Wisdom's firmament the moon of Love is rising full." The song continued for a long time, and everyone danced. They then bowed down to God and His devotees and ended the kirtan. Before they sat down they also bowed to the Master. On this occasion the Master danced gracefully, but he did not have the kind of long and intense ecstasy that we had witnessed at Mani Mallick's house. After kirtan, the Master sat down and told Chiranjiv, "When I first heard you sing this song

6. The joy of kirtan.

---

1. We are indebted to M., the recorder of *The Gospel of Sri Ramakrishna*, for part of the Master's conversation on this day.

— 'In Wisdom's firmament the moon of Love is rising full'[2] — I immediately went into ecstasy and saw the bright full moon rising!"

Jaygopal and Chiranjiv then discussed Keshab's illness with each other. We remember that the Master told someone on that day that Rakhal (later, Swami Brahmananda) was also unwell. We are not sure if Jaygopal was a formal member of the Brahmo Samaj, but undoubtedly he respected and was devoted to Keshab and had a special love for the Brahmo organization. Sometimes Keshab and his followers went to Jaygopal's garden house at Belgharia near Calcutta and spent time there practising spiritual disciplines. It was there that Keshab had first met the Master. From that point on, his spirituality had gradually deepened, eventually leading to the founding of the New Dispensation with its beautiful message. On that day Jaygopal also became very devoted to the Master; sometimes he went to see the Master in Dakshineswar and sometimes he invited him to his house to enjoy his spiritual conversation. We heard that for a certain period Jaygopal bore a great part of the carriage fare for the Master's Calcutta trips. His family was also extremely devoted to the Master.

As the night drew on, we took leave of the Master and left for home.

2. In Wisdom's firmament the moon of Love is rising full,
And Love's flood tide, in surging waves, is flowing everywhere.
O Lord, how full of bliss Thou art! Victory unto Thee!
On every side shine devotees, like stars around the moon;
Their Friend, the Lord All-merciful, joyously plays with them.
Behold! The gates of paradise today are open wide.
The soft spring wind of the New Day raises fresh waves of joy;
Gently it carries to the earth the fragrance of God's love,
Till all the yogis, drunk with bliss, are lost in ecstasy.
Upon the sea of the world unfolds the lotus of the New Day,
And there the Mother sits enshrined in blissful majesty.
See how the bees are mad with joy, sipping the nectar there!
Behold the Mother's radiant face, which so enchants the heart
And captivates the universe! About Her lotus feet
Bands of ecstatic holy men are dancing in delight.
What matchless loveliness is Hers! What infinite content
Pervades the heart when She appears! O brothers, says Premdas,
I humbly beg you, one and all, to sing the Mother's praise!

Chapter 2

Devotees Foreseen in the Master's Visions Begin to Come

WE HAVE ALREADY TOLD THE READER HOW Keshab, Vijay, Pratap, Shivanath, Chiran-

1. The Master learns from the Brahmo Samaj.

jiv, Amrita, Gaur-Govinda, and other leaders of the Indian Brahmo Samaj greatly benefited from their contact with the Master, learning steadfast devotion to their own faith and the greatness of renouncing everything for God. Now the question is: Did the Master, who was a knower of Brahman and established in bhavamukha, learn anything from his contact with Keshab and the other Brahmos? Many devotees of Sri Ramakrishna would immediately answer "no" to this. But the law of give and take is a constant in the world. When we teach a totally inexperienced and immature boy, we learn which method of instruction helps his intellect to grasp the subject quickly, how what he has learned in the past is useful or a barrier to his comprehension of that subject, how to remove the obstacles, and so on. It is therefore unreasonable to say that the Master did not learn anything from his contact with the Brahmo Samaj, which was founded on Western ideas and education. Our impression is quite different: We say that the Master learned many things from the Brahmo Samaj while sharing his extraordinary ideas and spiritual experiences with its members. Thus, it is proper to discuss here what he learned from them.

Before the Master came in contact with Keshab and other Brahmos, he

2. The Master learns the extent to which Western ideas were changing the lives of Indians.

was leading a life far from the influence of the West. Up to that time he had seen that, except for Mathur, all those who came to him were striving to focus their life on either the path of worldly prosperity or the eternal path of renunciation to attain immortality. Although the Master observed that Mathur's temperament was a little different from the others, and he knew that Mathur had been educated in the Western manner, he had not yet experienced how the lives of all Indians who were thus Westernized had been influenced in complex ways. Mathur's nature had changed shortly after meeting the Master and enjoying his holy company, so the Master felt no need to consider the issue further. When he came in contact with the Brahmos, however, he noticed that although they were striving for spirituality, they had deviated from the ancient ideal of renunciation. His mind then began to investigate the cause of this and discovered for the first time how the Western system of education and its ideas were bringing an alien influence into the lives of modern Indians.

At first the Master probably thought that when Keshab and other

3. Westernized Indians refused to accept the experiences of Indian sages without comparing them with the teachings of Western savants.	Brahmos were introduced to the spiritual truths that he had realized, they would accept them completely in a short time. But as the days went by, despite their close association with him, they could not transcend the influence of their Western education to fully believe the Master's spiritual experiences. The Master

then realized how deeply rooted the Western influence was in their minds. He then understood that Western savants permanently occupied the position of the guru in their hearts, and that they would never accept the experiences of India's illumined rishis without comparing them with the words and ideas of those savants. That is why after instructing the Brahmos, the Master would say: "I have said whatever came into my head. Take as much of it as you want. You may leave out the head and the tail." The Master gave them freedom without contradicting their views, allowing them to accept his teachings and experiences as best they could.

The Master embodied the collective spiritual ideas of the Indian rishis; he

4. The Master remained undisturbed, knowing that this happened by the Divine Mother's will.	was not at all perturbed by the Brahmos' attitude. He realized deep in his heart that everything happens in this world through the Divine Mother's will, and he conditioned himself to be guided in every respect by

Her command. As a result, nothing in this world upset him. The Divine Mother, who makes the impossible possible, revealed and explained Her true nature to him and endowed him with an unwavering and abiding peace. He fully realized that it was the Divine Mother's will that Western ideas and ideals had penetrated India, and that it was Her will that the Brahmos and other educated communities had become puppets in the hands of Western influences. So how could he express annoyance at their weaknesses, or deprive them of his infinite love and affection? He therefore remained content with this thought: "Let them absorb the spiritual truths of the sages as much as they can; in time, the Divine Mother will bring to me those who can accept those truths completely."

Even though he realized that the Brahmos were incapable of accepting all

5. What the Master does when he realizes the Brahmos could not comprehend the full knowledge of Brahman.

of his teachings, when guiding them he shared not only his personal spiritual experiences, but also did not hesitate to tell them the hidden truths of the spiritual world: "One cannot have the vision of God unless one renounces everything for Him." "As many faiths, so many paths." "At the end of each spiritual path, the worshipper becomes identified with the worshipped." "Real sadhana requires uniting thoughts and speech." "One should have full faith in and reliance on God, discriminate between the real and the unreal, and perform one's duties without seeking the results of one's actions. Only then can one move forward towards God."

He helped Keshab and some others to understand that it is impossible to cut one's attachment to the body and to attain the highest spiritual experiences without practising chastity in body, mind, and speech. He also engaged them in practising this. When he found that many of them could not grasp his ideas despite repeated instruction, he realized that once past impressions become deep-seated in the mind, it is almost impossible to take in new ideas. He remarked: "One invariably fails if one tries to teach a mature parrot to repeat the name 'Radha-Krishna' once the ring of colour has appeared around its neck."[1] He understood that those who had firmly rooted desires for sense enjoyment — either due to the influence of Western materialism or for some other reason — could not completely incorporate the eternal ideal of renunciation into their lives. That is why this earnest prayer burst forth from his mind at that time: "O Mother, please bring all-renouncing devotees with whom I can rejoice and talk open-heartedly about You." It is not unreasonable to say that from that point on the Master was firmly convinced that only young boys with pure minds would be able to accept his ideas completely, understand his message, and come forward to experience these truths without any hesitation.

It did not take long for the public of Calcutta to observe that Keshab and

6. People of Calcutta become attracted to the Master through the Brahmos: Ram and Manomohan arrive and take refuge in the Master.

other Brahmo leaders had adopted the Master's unique spiritual ideas and had consequently undergone a great change. When Keshab and his associates began to publish some of the Master's extraordinary religious views and inspiring teachings in Brahmo newspapers and journals, the people of Calcutta became interested and started to visit Dakshineswar to see him. In this way the Master's chosen devotees gradually came to the Dakshineswar Kali temple. We heard that towards the end of 1879, four years after the Master's first meeting with Keshab, Ramchandra Datta and Manomohan Mitra read

---

1. A ring of colour around the neck marks maturity in parrots. — *Translator*

Ramchandra Datta
(1851-1899)

Manomohan Mitra
(1851-1903)

about the Master in Keshab's magazine and came to him. The lives of those householders were transformed after meeting the Master. Ramchandra has written about this in his Bengali book *Sri Sri Ramakrishna Paramahamsadever Jivanvrittanta*, so there is no need to discuss it here.

It is enough to mention briefly that although they could not completely accept the Master's ideal of renouncing lust and gold for the realization of God, they were blessed to make good progress on the path of renunciation through their devotion to and faith in the Master. One can ascertain a householder's degree of faith and devotion by observing how freely he spends his hard-earned money for charitable activities. Ram first placed the Master in his life as a guru and then as his Chosen Ideal. He invited the Master and his devotees to his house in Simla, Calcutta, many times. He spent money lavishly on festivals, proving how much faith he had in the Master and how devoted to him he had become. The Master sometimes said about Ram: "See how generous Ram is now? I can't describe how miserly he was when he first came to me. I once asked him to bring some cardamom. He brought one pice worth of cheap dry cardamom, put it before me, and bowed down. Now you see how much Ram's nature has changed."

When the Master accepted Ram and Manomohan as his own, sheltering

7. The Master's wonderful vision, and Rakhal's arrival.

them forever with his protection, they felt themselves blessed by his unconditional grace. Such refuge in this world was beyond their imagination. It is therefore not surprising that they tried to bring their relatives and friends to the shelter of the Master. Within a year of their first meeting, they brought their family members to see him. Thus the Master's all-renouncing disciples and companions arrived one after another beginning in 1881. We heard that Swami Brahmananda was the first among them to come to the Master.[2] His premonastic name was Rakhal, and he was married to Manomohan's sister. He heard about the Master from his wife's family shortly after his wedding and went to see him. Sri Ramakrishna later said: "Just a few days before Rakhal came, I saw Mother put a child on my lap and say, 'This is your son.' I shuddered at the thought and asked Her in surprise: 'What do You mean? I too have a son?' Then She explained with a smile, 'He is not a son in the ordinary worldly sense but an all-renouncing spiritual son.' I was reassured. Rakhal came shortly after this vision, and I recognized him at once as the boy presented by the Divine Mother.

"In those days, Rakhal had the nature of a child of three or four. He treated

8. Rakhal's boyish nature.

me just like a mother. He kept running to me and sitting on my lap. He wouldn't move a step from this place. He never thought of going home. I forced him to, from time to time, lest his father forbid his coming here altogether. His father was a landowner

2. Rakhal was actually among the first group of chosen disciples to come. — *Translator*

and immensely rich, but he was a miser. At first he tried in various ways to keep his son from coming here. But when he came here once and saw how many wealthy and famous people visit this place, he didn't object anymore. After that, he would come now and then to visit Rakhal. I was most respectful and attentive to him. He liked that.

"As for the family of Rakhal's wife, they raised no objection. Mano-

9. Rakhal's wife.

mohan's mother, wife, and sisters used to come here very often. Soon after Rakhal first came here, his mother-in-law brought Vishweswari, his wife. I wanted to see if she would stand in the way of Rakhal's devotion to God. I carefully examined her physical features and saw that there was no cause for fear. She represented an auspicious aspect of the divine Shakti and wouldn't be an obstacle to her husband's spiritual journey. I sent word to the nahabat [i.e. to Sarada Devi] to give Vishweswari a rupee and unveil her face.[3]

"The very sight of me used to evoke in Rakhal a childlike feeling that

10. Loss of Rakhal's boyish nature.

cannot be described. It impressed everyone who saw him. While in ecstasy I would feed him with butter and sweets and play with him as a mother plays with her child. I often carried him around on my shoulders. But none of this created any hesitation in his mind. At that time I said that Rakhal's childlike nature would disappear when he grew up and began living with his wife.

"When Rakhal did anything wrong, I scolded him. One day he was

11. The Master disciplines Rakhal.

hungry, so he took butter from the temple prasad and ate it without waiting for me. 'How greedy you are,' I said. 'From being here you ought to have learned how to control yourself! Instead, you've taken the butter and eaten it without asking me.' He shrank with fear and never did that again.

"Rakhal was also as jealous as a child. He simply couldn't bear it if I loved

12. Rakhal's jealousy and the Master's apprehension.

anyone but him. His heart would feel wounded. I was afraid that he would harm himself from the jealousy he felt towards the people the Divine Mother brought to this place.

"Three years after Rakhal first came to Dakshineswar, he fell ill and went

13. Rakhal leaves for Vrindaban.

to Vrindaban with Balaram [for a change of climate]. Shortly before that, I saw in a vision that the Divine Mother was removing him from here. I sincerely prayed: 'Mother, Rakhal is a mere boy. He is ignorant, so he sometimes becomes piqued. For the sake of Your work, if You want to remove him from

3. According to Bengali custom, a mother-in-law welcomes her daughter-in-law in the following manner. When the daughter-in-law arrives, she is wearing a veil. The mother-in-law gives her a present, removes her veil, and kisses her. Since Rakhal was to be the spiritual son of Sri Ramakrishna and Sarada Devi, Vishweswari became their daughter-in-law. — Translator

here for a short time, please keep him in a good place and in a blissful mood.' Shortly after that he had to go to Vrindaban.

"I can't express how anxious I became when I heard of Rakhal's illness in

| 14. Rakhal's illness worries the Master. |

Vrindaban. The Divine Mother had shown me that Rakhal had truly been one of the cowherd companions of Krishna. Generally when a great soul was previously born in a sacred place and then in a following incarnation returns to that place and remembers his divine identity, he leaves his present body. So I was afraid that Rakhal would give up his body in Vrindaban. I prayed intently to the Mother, and She comforted me with an assurance. The Mother has revealed many things to me about Rakhal. I am forbidden to tell some of them."[4]

The Master said many things about this boy devotee, who was one of the

| 15. Rakhal's future. |

first chosen disciples. Whatever the Divine Mother revealed to the Master about Rakhal was later proven to be completely true. As he grew up, this boy became a steady and serious spiritual aspirant. He eventually renounced everything for God and occupied the highest position in the Ramakrishna Order.

Swami Vivekananda came to the Master three or four months after Swami

| 16. Narendra's arrival. |

Brahmananda's first visit to Dakshineswar. We shall now narrate the story of Vivekananda.

---

4. The Master did not make all the above statements about Rakhal at one time, but we have arranged them here chronologically for the reader's convenience.

Chapter 3

Narendra's Early Life and His First Visit to Dakshineswar

THE VEDAS AND OTHER SCRIPTURES DECLARE THAT a knower of Brahman is omni-

<table>
<tr><td>1. A discussion on the Master's mental state in the divine mood.</td></tr>
</table>

scient. We find this scriptural testimony to be absolutely true when we observe the behaviour of the Master, who was firmly established in the knowledge of Brahman. He was then [at the time of Narendra's first visit] fully acquainted with the Saguna and Nirguna aspects of Brahman; with his knowledge of the mystery of maya, which is the power of Brahman, he transcended all doubts and impurities; and he dwelt in an ever-blissful state. In addition, because he remained constantly in the state of bhavamukha, he could immediately understand any mystery hidden in the realm of maya whenever he wished. Maya could no longer conceal her nature from his penetrating insight. This should be the case because both the state of bhavamukha and the Cosmic Mind of God, the Lord of maya — in which all ideas of the universe are formed, and in which they exist in both manifest and potential forms — are the same substance. To one who has transcended the limitations of the small individual "I" and become identified with the Cosmic "I" all the thoughts of the Cosmic Mind become apparent.

The Master had reached that state, and he knew the events in the previous lives of his devotees before they came to him. He also knew the purpose of his present incarnation, in which he would manifest a particular lila of the Cosmic Mind. He knew that some great souls were born to help him fulfill that lila. He knew who, among those sent by the will of God, would be

Narendranath Datta (1863-1902), later Swami Vivekananda.
Photo taken in London in 1896.

Surendra Nath Mitra
(1850-1890), a businessman
who generously provided for
Ramakrishna's needs.

Rakhal (1863-1922),
later Swami
Brahmananda.
Photo taken in 1903
at Varanasi.

playing greater and lesser roles in that lila, and who would be blessed by merely enjoying its results. He knew that those devotees would arrive soon, and he eagerly awaited them. So it is clear that one who knew all those hidden mysteries while living in the realm of maya must be considered omniscient.

Established in the divine state, the Master knew when his chosen devo-

| 2. The Master and Narendra meet for the first time at Surendra's house. | tees would arrive. The eagerness he felt during this period can be fully understood by considering the first time he met Swami Vivekananda. Swami |

Brahmananda said that Surendra Nath Mitra of Simla, Calcutta, first visited the Master in Dakshineswar at almost the same time as himself. From their first meeting, Surendra was very attracted to the Master. He soon became close to him, invited the Master to his home, and arranged a festival. Because Surendra could not find a professional singer for that day, he cordially invited Narendra, the son of his neighbour Vishwanath Datta, to sing devotional songs for the Master. Thus the first meeting between the Master and Swami Vivekananda, the chief companion in his divine play, took place. It was November 1881. Narendra was eighteen years old and was preparing for his F.A. [First of Arts] examination at Calcutta University.

Swami Brahmananda said that the Master was very attracted to Narendra

| 3. The Master invites Narendra to Dakshineswar. | at first sight. To learn everything he could about that wonderful young singer, he first called Surendra to him, then Ramchandra. He also asked them to bring |

Narendra to Dakshineswar one day. When the singing was over, he approached Narendra and carefully examined his features. The Master then talked with him a little and invited him to visit Dakshineswar soon.

The F.A. examination of Calcutta University concluded a few weeks after

| 4. Narendra refuses to marry. His first visit to Dakshineswar. | this event. At the request of a respected gentleman in Calcutta, Vishwanath was arranging his son's marriage with the man's daughter. Some say that |

because the bride had a dark complexion, her father agreed to pay a dowry of ten thousand rupees. Vishwanath persuaded Ramchandra Datta and other relatives to try their utmost to convince Narendra to agree to this marriage. But Narendra vehemently refused, so the matter ended. Ramchandra was a distant relative of Narendra and had been raised in Vishwanath's household. He eventually became a physician. Ram knew that Narendra had spiritual reasons for refusing to marry, so he told him: "If you have a real desire to realize God, then come to see the Master in Dakshineswar instead of visiting the Brahmo Samaj and other such places." One day during this time Surendra invited Narendra to accompany him to Dakshineswar in his carriage. Narendra agreed and went to Dakshineswar with Surendra, bringing two or three of his friends as well.

Later on, in the course of conversation, the Master told us briefly what he
had thought when he saw Narendra on that occasion:

5. The Master's impression of Narendra.

"Narendra entered the room by the western door, the one that faces the Ganges. I noticed that he was not concerned about his appearance; his hair and his clothes weren't tidy at all. Unlike his companions, he seemed completely detached, as if nothing external appealed to him. His eyes showed that the greater part of his mind was turned inward all of the time. When I saw this, I marvelled to myself, 'How is it possible that such a great spiritual aspirant can live in Calcutta, home to such materialistic people?'

"There was a mat spread out on the floor. I asked him to be seated, and he sat down near the jar of Ganges water. A few of his friends were with him that day. I saw that their nature was that of ordinary worldly people, just the opposite of his. They were thinking only of their pleasure.

"I asked him about his singing and found that he knew only two or three

6. Narendra sings.

songs in Bengali. I asked him to sing them. He began singing this Brahmo song: 'Let us return once more, O mind, to your own abode!'[1]

"He sang that song with his whole soul, as though he were deep in meditation. When I heard it, I couldn't control myself. I went into ecstasy.

"After Narendra left I felt a constant and agonizing desire to see him. At

7. The Master yearns to see Narendra.

times the pain was so excruciating that I felt as if my heart were being squeezed like a wet towel. When I could no longer control myself, I would run to the

1. Let us go back once more, O mind, to your own abode!
Here in this foreign land of earth
Why should we wander aimlessly in stranger's guise?
These living beings round about and the five elements
Are strangers to you, all of them; none is your own.
Why do you thus forget yourself
In love with strangers, O my mind?
Why do you thus forget your own?
Ascend the path of Truth, O mind! Unflaggingly climb
With Love as the lamp to light your way.
As your provision for the journey, bring with you
The virtues, carefully concealed; for, like two highwaymen,
Greed and delusion wait to rob you of your wealth.
And keep beside you constantly,
As guards to shelter you from harm,
Calmness of mind and self-control.
Companionship with holy men will be for you
A welcome rest-house by the road;
There rest your weary limbs awhile, asking your way,
If ever you should be in doubt, of him who watches there.
If anything along the path should frighten you,
Then loudly shout the name of the Lord;
For He is Ruler of that road,
And even Death must bow to Him.

pine grove on the northern side of the garden where people seldom go and cry at the top of my voice: 'O my child, come to me! I can't live without seeing you!' After crying this way for a while, I was able to control myself again. This state continued for six months. There were other boys who also came here. I felt greatly drawn to some of them, but nothing like the way I was attracted to Narendra."

Afterwards a reliable source told us that the Master was very hesitant to speak of the wonderful spiritual feelings that arose in his mind when he saw Narendra at Dakshineswar for the first time. Later on, when we were talking with Narendra, he gave us his account of that day:

"As soon as I finished the song, the Master stood up, took me by the hand,

8. Narendra describes the Master's behaviour and what he said on that occasion.

and led me out to the northern veranda. It was winter, so the open spaces between the pillars were covered with screens of matting to keep out the north wind. This meant that anyone standing on the veranda was completely hidden when the door of the room was closed. The Master closed the door as soon as we were on the veranda. I thought he was going to give me some private instructions. But what he said and did next was something I could never have believed possible. He suddenly caught hold of my hand and began shedding profuse tears of joy. He said to me affectionately, as to an intimate friend: 'You've come so late! Was that right? Didn't you guess how I've been waiting for you? My ears have nearly burned off from listening to the talk of these worldly people. I thought I would burst without anyone to tell how I really feel!' He went on like that — raving and weeping. Then he suddenly stood up with his palms folded together and began addressing me as if I were some divine being: 'I know who you are, my Lord. You are Nara, the ancient sage, the incarnation of Narayana. You have come to earth to take away the suffering and sorrow of human beings.'

"I was absolutely dumbfounded by his conduct. I said to myself: 'What

9. Narendra promises to return.

kind of a man is this? He must be raving mad! How can he talk like this to me, a nobody — the son of Vishwanath Datta?' But I didn't answer him, and I let this wonderful madman go on talking as he wished. Presently he asked me to stay there on the veranda, and he went back into the room. When he returned he brought butter, rock candy, and a few pieces of sandesh, and then he began to feed me with his own hands. I kept asking him to give me the sweets so I could share them with my friends, but he wouldn't. 'They'll get some later,' he said. 'You take these for yourself.' And he wasn't satisfied until I'd eaten all of them. Then he took my hand and said, 'Promise that you'll come back soon, alone.' His request was made so earnestly that I couldn't refuse. I had to say, 'I will.' Then I went back into the room with him and sat down with my friends.

"I watched him closely. I observed nothing abnormal in his words, movements, or behaviour towards others. On the contrary: His words and ecstatic states showed him to be a man of true renunciation who had given up everything for God. He practises what he preaches. He said: 'God can be seen and spoken to, just as I'm seeing you and speaking to you. But who wants to see and speak to God? For wife, children, money, and property people grieve and shed jugs of tears — but who weeps for the vision of God? And yet, if anyone really wants to see God and calls upon Him, God will certainly reveal Himself to that person.'

10. Narendra's impression of the Master on this first visit: he is a monomaniac, but one who has genuinely renounced everything for God.

"When I heard these words, I became more and more convinced that he wasn't like any of the other religious teachers I had met, so full of poetry and fine figures of speech. He spoke only of what he himself had actually realized by giving up everything and calling on God wholeheartedly. As I tried to reconcile his words with his strange behaviour towards me, I recalled the descriptions of monomaniacs mentioned in books by Abercrombie and other English philosophers, and I concluded that he must be a monomaniac. Yet I could not help acknowledging the magnitude of his renunciation. I thought: 'Well, he may be mad — but this is indeed a rare soul who can undertake such renunciation. Yes, he is mad. But how pure! And what renunciation! He is truly worthy of the reverence, love, and adoration of humankind.' Thinking this, I bowed down at his feet, took my leave of him, and returned to Calcutta that day."

Naturally the reader will be curious about the early life of Narendra, the sight of whom awakened in the Master such a wonderful, spiritual emotion. We shall now briefly relate Narendra's story.

11. Narendra's spiritual practices at this time.

When he first met the Master, Narendra was not only spending his time on his education and study of music, but he was also practising strict brahmacharya and austerities, driven by an intense spiritual impulse. He was a vegetarian, and he slept on the bare floor or on a blanket there. His grandmother had rented a house near his ancestral home. After his Entrance examination, he mainly lived in a front room on the upper floor of that house. When it was inconvenient to stay there for any reason, he rented a room nearby and lived alone, away from his family and relatives, keeping himself busy in pursuit of his spiritual goal. His noble father and other family members thought that he was living alone because he could not study amid the bustle of their extended family.

During this time, Narendra was visiting the Brahmo Samaj and spending long hours in meditation. He believed in the formless Brahman with attributes, as taught by the Brahmo faith. Unlike others, he was not satisfied with basing

12. Narendra's visits to the Brahmo Samaj.

his faith in the formless God on reasoning alone. Driven by the good tendencies of his past lives, he constantly thought to himself: "If God truly exists, He will not conceal His own nature from the human heart that prays sincerely. He certainly must have laid down the path to reach Him. It is meaningless to lead life for any purpose other than to realize God." We remember that he once told us the following:

"From the time I reached my youth, every night when I went to bed two

| 13. Narendra has two strong ideals. |

ideal lives appeared before me. One of them was a man of great wealth, surrounded by servants and dependents, enjoying high rank and immense power. I saw myself as foremost among the great men of the world, and I was certain that I had the necessary ability to fulfill that ambition. But the very next moment I'd picture myself as having renounced everything in the world. I was wearing nothing but a loincloth, without anxiety, eating whatever food came my way, sleeping under a tree, and living in complete reliance on God's will. I knew that it was within me to lead the life of the rishis and ascetics if I should choose to do so. These images of the two directions that I could take in life kept appearing before me, but I always ended by choosing the latter. I knew that this was the only path by which a man could achieve true happiness, and I resolved to follow it and not the other. As I dwelt on the happiness of such a life, my mind would become absorbed in God, and I'd fall asleep. Surprisingly, this phenomenon continued every day for a long time."

From a very young age, Narendra was convinced that meditation was the

| 14. Narendra's natural inclination for meditation. |

best way to realize God. It is clear that this knowledge came to him from experiences in his past lives. When he was four or five years old, he bought clay images of Sita, Rama, Shiva, and other deities at the market, set them on an altar, and decorated them with flowers. He would sit in front of them with eyes closed, pretending to meditate. As he sat there, motionless, he sometimes opened his eyes to see whether his hair had become matted and grown long enough to plunge into the earth like the roots of a banyan tree: The elderly ladies in his household had told him that the rishis would meditate for such a long time that their matted hair grew into the ground. His mother said that during this period Narendra once entered a secluded attic room without anyone's knowledge and practised his pretend meditation for a long time with a neighbour boy named Hari. Narendra's family began looking for him everywhere, thinking that he had become lost and could not find his way home. When someone later discovered that the attic room was locked from the inside, he broke open the door to find Narendra seated there motionless. Although this was just a child's fancy, it indicates the remarkable spiritual tendencies that Narendra had from his birth.

At the time of which we are now speaking [young adulthood], most of Narendra's relatives did not know that he was meditating every day. He would lock his door and sit for meditation when everyone went to bed. Sometimes he would become so absorbed in meditation that he was unaware of anything else until the entire night had passed.

Shortly before this period, the following incident greatly increased

15. Maharshi Devendra Nath Tagore's advice strengthens his inclination.

Narendra's desire for meditation. One day he went with his friends to see Maharshi Devendra Nath Tagore, the leader of the Adi Brahmo Samaj. On that occasion the Maharshi cordially received them, gave them much good advice, and asked them to meditate on God every day. Addressing Narendra, he said: "The signs of a yogi are visible in you. If you practise meditation, you will soon experience the results recorded in the yoga scriptures." Narendra had a deep reverence for the Maharshi because of his pure and noble character. His advice undoubtedly induced Narendra to intensify his meditation.

From his childhood onward, Narendra's many-faceted talents manifested

16. Narendra's diverse talents.

themselves in various fields. Before he reached the age of five, he could recite all the aphorisms of Sanskrit grammar in the *Mugdhabodha*. Every evening an elderly relative taught him the names of his ancestors, hymns of gods and goddesses, and those Sanskrit aphorisms. When he was six, he memorized an entire musical composition on the Ramayana and he attended all nearby performances. Once, near his house, a singer performing the Ramayana could not recall part of the composition. Narendra immediately prompted him and was rewarded with some sweets and the singer's appreciation. As he listened to the Ramayana, the boy Narendra would sometimes look around to see whether Mahavir Hanuman, Ramachandra's servant, was there to fulfil his vow to be present wherever the glory of Rama was sung. Narendra developed a memory as prodigious as that of a *shrutidhar* [one who can remember a person's exact words merely by hearing them]. He mastered any subject after hearing about it only once, and that knowledge never left his memory. For that reason, the way in which he learned was not like that of other boys. When he was admitted to school, a tutor was appointed to help him with his studies every day. Narendra later recalled: "When the tutor arrived, I'd bring my English and Bengali books to him, show him each section that was to be studied that day, and then sit or lie down quietly. The teacher repeated the spelling, pronunciation, and meaning of the words from the sections of those books, as if he was learning them himself, then went away. That was enough for me to learn the lessons."

As he grew older, he would begin studying his textbooks two or three months before the final examinations, and for the rest of his time would read anything he chose. For example, before his Entrance examination he read nearly all of the major books in English and Bengali literature and many history books as well. As a result, he sometimes had to work hard on the eve of a final examination. We remember that one day he told us: "Just two or three days before the Entrance examination, I found I hardly knew anything about geometry. So I began to study the subject, staying awake the entire night, and in twenty-four hours I'd mastered the four books of geometry." He could do this because, by the grace of God, he had a strong body and a wonderful memory.

Just because Narendra spent much of his time reading, let no one think

17. Narendra's propensity for study.

that he wasted his time with novels and plays. At a particular time he would have a tremendous desire to study a certain subject, and would then collect whatever books were available on it and master them. For example, in 1879, the year of his Entrance examination, he felt an urge to study Indian history as written by Marshman, Elphinstone, and other Western historians, so he read them all. While studying for his F.A. he mastered all of the important English books on logic written by Whitley, Jevons, Mill, and others. And while studying for his B.A. he had a great desire to study ancient and modern histories of England and all of Europe, as well as books on Western philosophy.

As a result of reading many books, by the time of his Entrance examina-

18. His ability to read quickly.

tion Narendra had developed a special talent for reading quickly. He said: "It so happened that I could understand an author without reading his book line by line. I could read the first and the last lines of a paragraph and grasp its meaning. As this power developed, I found it unnecessary to read even the paragraphs. I could understand the subject matter by reading only the first and last lines of a page. Later, I could follow the whole trend of a writer's argument merely by reading a few lines in the beginning even when the author continued his reasoning on the subject for another five or more pages."

Narendra's vast study and deep thinking led him to a fondness for argu-

19. Narendra's strength in debate.

mentation. He did not care for sophistry; he always argued for what he knew to be true deep within his heart. If anyone expressed to him any idea or opinion contrary to what he knew to be true, he could not listen passively. He would silence his opponents by refuting their arguments with his formidable reasoning and solid evidence. Rare was the person who would not yield when confronted by Narendra's reasoning. And those whom he defeated did not look on him kindly. During a debate he would listen to a few of his opponent's words to understand the essence of that person's defense and then mentally prepare his reply. When asked how he could spontaneously craft such penetrating arguments to defeat his opponent, he replied: "How many new thoughts are there in this world? If one knows and has mastered those few thoughts together with the reasons for and against them, one need not think too much in order to reply. Any reason the opponent might adduce to support his position must fall within those few thoughts. Rare are those who bring to the world new ideas on any subject."

From his childhood onward, Narendra was as interested in all types of

| 20. Narendra's interest in physical exercise. |

physical activity as he was in acquiring knowledge. When he was a child his father bought him a pony, and he became expert in riding as he grew up. In addition, he became more or less proficient in gymnastics, wrestling, exercising with clubs, fighting with sticks, fencing, swimming, and other sports that use force to develop physical strength and skill. At that time, competitions in all of these sports were held at the Hindu Fair established by Navagopal Mitra. The winners were awarded prizes. We heard that Narendra sometimes competed there.

From his childhood onward, Narendra had love for his friends as well as

| 21. His love for friends and his courage. |

indomitable courage. These two wonderful qualities helped him to take a leadership role when he was a student and later when he became head of the Ramakrishna Order. When he was seven or eight years old, he went with his friends to visit the Zoological Gardens of Wazid Ali, the former Nawab of Lucknow, at Metiaburuz, which is to the south of Calcutta. The boys collected the funds needed from among themselves and hired a boat for the round trip at the Chandpal ghat. During their return trip one of the boys became sick and threw up in the boat, annoying the Muslim boatman. After anchoring his boat at Chandpal, he said that he would not allow anyone to leave until the boat was cleaned up. The boys offered to pay to have someone else clean it, but the boatman did not agree to this. The argument threatened to become physical as other nearby boatmen joined the Muslim and prepared to assault the boys. The boys did not know what to do.

Narendra was the youngest among them, and while the quarrelling was going on, he stepped aside and got out of the boat. Because he was a little boy the boatmen did not stop him. As he stood on the shore, he saw that the situation was becoming serious. While he was thinking about how he could protect his friends, he saw two English soldiers walking along the street. Narendra rushed over, greeted them, and caught hold of their hands. Despite his deficiency in English, he tried to make them understand the situation with signs and a few broken words, thus bringing them to the scene. Those soldiers were charmed by the behaviour of this handsome boy. Coming near the boat, they immediately understood the situation, and raising their canes, ordered the boatmen to release the boys. Terrified at the sight of British soldiers, the boatmen returned to their boats, and Narendra's friends were released. The soldiers were so pleased with Narendra's fearlessness that they invited him to accompany them to the theatre. But Narendra thanked them and declined, taking his leave.

Other events in Narendra's early life also exemplify his indomitable

22. He ingeniously obtains a permit to visit the warship *Syrapis*.

courage, and it will not be out of place to mention a couple of them. Narendra was eleven or twelve years old when the emperor, Edward VII, visited India as the prince of Wales. At that time the *Syrapis*, a gigantic British warship, was docked at the port of Calcutta. Many people had passes to take tours of it. Narendra and his friends wanted to see the ship, so he filled out an application for a group pass and took it to the office on Chowringhee Road [now Jawharlal Nehru Road]. He noticed that the gatekeeper was allowing only a few distinguished people to enter. As he stood near the door he watched the people leaving with passes and thought of how he could meet the English officer who was distributing them. He saw that people were going to the veranda on the second floor of the office building, so he knew that the officer was issuing passes from there. While searching for another way into the building, he found a spiral staircase at the rear leading to the back room of that veranda. He knew that the stairs were used only by the officer's servants and that he would be humiliated if someone discovered him, but he gathered his courage and took those stairs to the second floor. He entered the veranda through the officer's room. Applicants were crowded around the officer, who was bent over his desk signing applications. Narendra stood at the end of the line. When he had his group pass signed, he saluted the officer and left the building through the front staircase along with the others.

At that time there was a gymnasium on Cornwallis Street [now Bidhan

23. An accident occurs while setting up a trapeze in the gymnasium.

Sarani] for the physical training of boys in the Simla area. Navagopal Mitra, founder of the Hindu Fair, had established it. As it was close to Narendra's home, he exercised there every day with his friends. Nava-

gopal knew those boys, and he left the management of the gymnasium in their hands. One day the boys were trying their utmost to lift and set up a heavy wooden trapeze frame in the gymnasium, but they kept failing. A crowd gathered to watch, but no one came forward to help them. Seeing a stout English sailor in the crowd, Narendra asked for his help. He gladly agreed to join them. The boys tied a rope to the top of the trapeze and began to pull it up as the sailor tried to set its legs into two sockets. When the frame was almost up, the rope suddenly gave way and the heavy trapeze fell to the ground. One of the legs came out of its socket and hit the sailor's forehead. He fell down unconscious, bleeding profusely from his wound. Seeing the English sailor unconscious, everyone thought that he was dead.

Almost all of the boys ran away for fear of the police. But Narendra and a couple of his close friends stayed behind to try to find a solution to the crisis. Narendra tore a piece from his cloth, soaked it in water, and bandaged the sailor's wound. He then tried to bring him around by splashing water on his face and fanning him. When the sailor regained consciousness, they carried him to a room in the Training Academy, a school nearby, and then sent a message to Navagopal, asking him to come immediately with a doctor. When the doctor came to examine the sailor, he told them: "The wound is not serious. He needs a week of rest and nursing, and he will be fine." Narendra tended the sailor, giving him medicine and a good diet, and he recovered. Narendra then collected money from distinguished local people, gave it to the sailor, and bade him good-bye. We have heard many such stories of Narendra's early life that show how he remained unperturbed in the midst of dangers and difficulties.

From his childhood onward, Narendra was intently devoted to truth. This

24. Narendra's love for truth.

steadfast honesty increased tremendously when he reached young adulthood. He later recalled: "I never frightened children by telling them stories of hobgoblins because I was afraid of uttering a falsehood. If I saw anyone in our house doing that, I would scold that person severely. As a result of my English education and frequent visits to the Brahmo Samaj, I developed a tremendous passion for speaking the truth."

Narendra was always joyful because he had been born with a strong body,

25. His fondness for harmless fun and amusements.

a keen intellect, a wonderful memory, and a pure heart. He was carefree in every respect and participated in physical exercise, instrumental music, singing, dancing, harmless fun and amusements with his friends, and so on. Those who did not know him and did not understand the reason for his cheerfulness often doubted his character. But the spirited Narendra paid no heed to others' praise or criticism. His proud heart never stooped to refute slander.

Compassion for the poor was ingrained in Narendra's nature. While still a

26. Narendra's compassion for the poor.

child he gave beggars whatever they asked for — clothing, utensils, and other things. When his family became aware of this, they scolded him and bought the articles back from the beggars. Because this happened several times, his mother locked him in a room upstairs one day. But when a beggar in the street began calling loudly for alms, Narendra threw some of his mother's expensive clothes through the window to him.

Narendra's mother said: "From his childhood onward, Narendra had a

27. Narendra's anger.

terrible weakness. If he became angry for any reason, he completely lost control and destroyed furniture and other things in the house. I had prayed and made a special offering to the Lord Vireswara of Varanasi for a son, but perhaps He sent me one of His demons instead. Otherwise, why should he behave like a demon when angry?" She, however, discovered a wonderful remedy for Narendra's anger. When she could not control him by any other means, she would think of Vireswara Shiva and then pour a couple of pitchers of cold water on

Narendra's head. This subdued the boy's anger immediately. After meeting the Master at Dakshineswar, Narendra told us: "Spiritual life has at least given me control over my anger, by God's grace. Previously, when I was angry I could not control myself, and later I would be torn by guilt. But now even if someone beats me without cause or does me great harm, I don't become angry as before."

Rarely in this world do we see a person whose head and heart are equally well developed. Those who are endowed with this quality become prominent in society in their respective fields. And those who establish their uniqueness in the spiritual world are found to have developed their intellects, emotional capacities, and imaginations from childhood onward. This is evident when we study Narendra's life. The reader will easily understand this from the following example.

28. Narendra's head and heart were equally developed.

Narendra's father lived for some time at Raipur in Madhya Pradesh [in central India] while conducting some business there. Because he found that he needed to stay there longer than he expected, he sent for his family shortly after he arrived. Narendra was entrusted to take them there. He was then fourteen or fifteen years old. At that time there was no railroad in Madhya Pradesh, so to get to Raipur, people had to travel by bullock cart from the nearest railway station for over a fortnight through a dense forest infested with ferocious animals. Narendra said that although the journey was full of physical hardship, he did not feel it because of the awe-inspiring beauty of the forest. He was overwhelmed by the infinite power and boundless love of God who had adorned the earth with such incomparable beauty.

29. Narendra's first deep meditation on the way to Raipur.

He said: "What I saw and felt as we passed through that forest has remained imprinted in my memory, particularly a certain event that occurred on the day we skirted the lofty range of the Vindhya mountains. The peaks on either side of the road rose very high into the sky. The slopes were covered with beautiful trees and creepers that were wonderfully heavy with fruit and flowers. Birds of all colours were flying from grove to grove or swooping to the ground in search of food, filling the gorge with sweet cries. I felt an extraordinary peace of mind as I watched this. The slow-moving procession of bullock carts reached a place where two great rocks had come together in a lover's embrace over the narrow forest trail. As I carefully observed the area below the point where they met on one side of the trail, I saw a very deep cleft from the top to the bottom of the rock. Inside that cleft hung an enormous honeycomb, the result of bees' labour throughout many years. Filled with wonder, I thought about the kingdom of the bees — how it had begun and how it had ended — and my mind became so deeply absorbed in thoughts of the infinite power of God, ruler of the three worlds, that I lost all consciousness of my surroundings for some time. I don't know how long I

lay in the bullock cart in that condition. When I regained external consciousness, I found that we had passed that place and were already far away. As I
was alone in the cart, no one ever knew what happened to me." This was
perhaps the first time that Narendra became completely absorbed in meditation with the help of his intense imagination.

We shall conclude this chapter by giving a brief account of Narendra's
ancestry. The Datta family with all its various
branches was one of the ancient dynasties of Calcutta.
Among the middle-class *kayastha* caste, this family
was foremost in wealth, learning, and social status. Rammohan Datta,
Narendra's great-grandfather, was a lawyer. He made a great deal of money
and led a dignified life with his big family at Gaur Mohan Mukherjee Street
in Simla. His son Durgacharan inherited great wealth from his father, but he
developed a dispassion for the world at an early age and became a monk
later in life. It is said that from his boyhood onward he was very devoted to
monks and holy people. When he reached his youth, his monastic tendency
kept him engaged in studying the scriptures and soon made him a scholar.
Although he married, Durgacharan was not attached to his family. He spent
much of his time in his own garden with holy company. Narendra said that
his grandfather left home forever shortly after a son was born, thus fulfilling
the injunction of the scriptures. Although he left home, Durgacharan twice
saw his wife and relatives briefly by the will of Providence. When his son,
Vishwanath, was two or three years old, Durgacharan's wife and relatives
went to Varanasi — perhaps in search of him — and stayed there for some
time. There was no railroad in those days, so wealthy people went on
pilgrimage to Varanasi by boat, and Durgacharan's wife joined a group of
pilgrims. On the way, Vishwanath fell into the Ganges. When his mother saw
this, she jumped into the river to save him, although she could not swim.
After a great effort, both were rescued. People saw that the unconscious
mother still had a firm hold on her son's hand. Thus Vishwanath's life was
saved by the limitless love of his mother.

After arriving in Varanasi, Durgacharan's wife visited the Vishwanath
temple every day. One day it was raining and the street was slippery, and she
fell in front of the temple. A monk passing by saw this and rushed to her. He
carefully lifted her up, made her sit on the step of the temple, and began to
examine her to see if she was seriously injured. The moment their eyes met,
Durgacharan and his wife recognized each other. The all-renouncing monk
Durgacharan fled without looking at her for a second time.

The scriptures say that after embracing the monastic life for twelve years,
a monk should visit his birthplace, which is "superior even to heaven." So
Durgacharan returned to Calcutta after twelve years and stayed at the house
of a former friend. He fervently asked him not to tell his relatives that he had
come. Durgacharan's worldly friend disregarded this request and secretly

---

30. Narendra's
grandfather was a monk.

sent word to his relatives. The entire family came immediately and forced him to return home, where he was confined to one room. He remained seated silently in a corner of that room like a log, his eyes closed. It is said that he remained in that position continuously for three days and nights. His relatives became fearful that he might fast unto death, so they unlocked the door. The next day they realized that Durgacharan had slipped away from the house unnoticed.

As Vishwanath grew up, he became well versed in Persian and English,

31. Narendra's father, Vishwanath.

and ultimately became an attorney of the Calcutta High Court. He was extremely generous and affectionate with his friends. Although he earned a good deal of money, he was unable to save any of it. Vishwanath had inherited his father's character and could not save money or spend wisely. In many respects, Vishwanath's nature was not like that of ordinary householders: He never worried about the future; he helped anyone without considering whether they were worthy of it; and although he was affectionate, he was also dispassionate. Even when he was far from home for a long time, he was not anxious to hear from his family. Many things like this can be said about him.

Vishwanath was intelligent and gifted. He loved music and the fine arts.

32. Vishwanath's love for music.

Narendra later said that his father had a sweet voice and that he could sing Nidhu Babu's *Tappa* [light song] beautifully even though he had no formal training. Vishwanath considered music to be a harmless amusement, so he arranged for his eldest son, Narendra, to learn music along with his regular studies. His wife, Bhuvaneswari, was able to master devotional songs — including their tune, measure, and tempo — after hearing them sung only once by Vaishnava minstrels and beggars.

Vishwanath was fond of reading the Bible and also of reciting the couplets

33. The influence of Muslim manners and customs on Vishwanath.

of the Persian mystic poet Hafiz. Every day, he read one or two chapters of Jesus's holy life from the Bible. Sometimes he would read to his wife and sons stories about Jesus and the mystical love poems of Hafiz. Because his work as an attorney often took him to Lucknow, Lahore, and other places in northwestern India, where people were mainly Muslim, he became fond of some of their manners and customs. Perhaps for this reason the custom of serving pilaf at the dining table every day was introduced in the Datta family.

Vishwanath was calm and serious, but also witty and humourous. If any

34. Vishwanath's sense of humour.

of his sons and daughters misbehaved, he did not discipline them with harsh language, but instead let their friends know what they had done in such a way that his children were ashamed and never did it again. For example, one day in the course of an argument with his mother, Narendra used rude words to her. When Vishwanath heard about this, he did not scold his son directly. Instead, he wrote with charcoal in large letters above the door of the room where Narendra received his friends: "Today Naren Babu spoke to his mother as follows —" adding the words that he had used. Whenever Narendra and his friends entered that room, their eyes fell on those words. For a long time afterwards, Narendra felt terribly embarrassed by his rudeness.

Vishwanath maintained a large family that included many distant rela-

35. Vishwanath's generosity.

tives, lavishly spending money on food and other necessities. Some of those relatives wasted their lives in laziness, and others indulged in drugs and alcohol. When Narendra grew older, he reproached his father for supporting those worthless people. Vishwanath replied: "How can you now understand the great misery of human life? When you feel the depth of their suffering, you will sympathize with the unfortunate ones who are trying to forget their sorrows even for a moment by using intoxicants."

Vishwanath had several sons and daughters, all of them endowed with

36. Vishwanath's death.

noble qualities. Most of his daughters died young. Narendra was born after three or four daughters, so he was very dear to his parents. In the winter of 1883, as Narendra was preparing for his B.A. examination, his father had a heart attack and died.[2] Vishwanath's sudden death plunged his wife and children into dire poverty.

We have heard many things about the greatness of Bhuvaneswari,

37. Narendra's mother.

Narendra's mother. Not only was she extremely beautiful and deeply devout, but she was also very intelligent and efficient in running the household. She shouldered all of the responsibility for her husband's large family. She managed the household so easily and effectively that she had spare time to sew, sing, and enjoy other pursuits. Although her education was very limited — she had not gone any further than reading the Ramayana and the Mahabharata — she learned many things by listening to her husband and children. When one conversed with her, one felt that she was an educated woman. She had a prodigious memory and great power of understanding. She could repeat anything after hearing it only once; and she remembered everything that she had heard of or experienced long ago as though it had taken place the day before.

When she was in deep poverty after her husband's death, she developed patience, perseverance, courage, and other noble qualities. Before her husband's death, she had one thousand rupees a month with which to manage the household; now she had to maintain herself and her children on thirty rupees a month. Despite this predicament, she was never disheartened. She managed her little family with that meagre income so efficiently that

2. Narendra's father actually died on 23 February 1884, when Narendra was waiting for the result of his B.A. examination. — *Translator*

people assumed her monthly allotment to be much higher than it was. One feels terrible when one considers the pitiable condition that Bhuvaneswari found herself in after her husband's death. She had no guaranteed income with which to maintain the family, but she nonetheless had to support her mother and children who had been brought up in opulence, and she had to meet the children's educational expenses. Instead of helping her, the relatives who had been making good money with her husband's assistance now took the opportunity to attempt to deprive her of her legitimate right to her property and possessions. Although her eldest son, Narendra, had many good qualities, he could not find a job despite his best efforts. Moreover, he had become disgusted with the world and was slowly trying to renounce it forever. One cannot help but appreciate and respect Bhuvaneswari as one considers how she performed her duties calmly and steadily in that terrible situation. When we discuss the Master's relationship with Narendra, we shall tell the reader more about his family's distressing circumstances. Instead of elaborating on this topic here, we shall now tell the reader about Narendra's second and third visits to Dakshineswar.

Chapter 4

Narendra's Second and Third Visits to the Master

WHEN INDIVIDUALS ENDOWED WITH SELF-RELIANCE AND steadfast goals see great-

1. The reason Narendra delayed his second visit to the Master, even though he considered him to be a true lover of God.

ness in others, they acknowledge it without hesitation and rejoice in their hearts. And if they meet a great soul who possesses an overwhelming majesty, they consider this deeply and their minds become amazed and enchanted for a time. But this cannot distract them from their goal and induce them to imitate that great soul. The followers of such a one do not show the effects of their teacher's influence immediately; for that to happen, a long association, intimate companionship, and a bond of love are required. Narendra was in that situation after his first meeting with Sri Ramakrishna at Dakshineswar.

Although Narendra was fascinated by and attracted to the Master's wonderful renunciation and saw that his thoughts and speech were in complete harmony, he was not ready to accept the Master as his life's ideal. When he returned home after his first visit to Dakshineswar, he frequently thought about the Master's unique character and behaviour, but he indefinitely put off fulfilling his promise to visit again and concentrated on his regular activities. The reason for this postponement was probably that the influence of his Western education had led him to believe that the Master was a monomaniac. In addition, he was busy with his meditation practice and college studies, as well as his daily music lessons and physical exercises. Apart from all this, Narendra was following the ideal of the Brahmo Samaj and was forming study and prayer groups in different neighbourhoods of Calcutta for the mental and spiritual improvement of his friends. So it is not surprising that Narendra's numerous activities buried all thought of visiting Dakshineswar in his mind for a few weeks. But although he was preoccupied with his studies and his busy daily schedule, his memory and devotion to truth would urge him from time to time to keep his promise to visit Dakshineswar by himself. So one day about a month after his first visit, Narendra returned to Dakshineswar, alone and on foot. He later described this second visit to Dakshineswar to us. We shall now share it with the reader.

Narendra said: "I had no idea that the Dakshineswar temple was so far

2. Narendra's second visit; his wonderful experience through the Master's power.

from Calcutta because I had been there only once before, and that was by carriage. I used to visit Dasharathi Sanyal, Satkari Lahiri, and other friends at Baranagore and thought that Rasmani's temple garden was somewhere near their houses. But this time it seemed as if the journey would never end, however far I walked. After asking many people the way, I arrived at Dakshineswar at last and went straight to the Master's room. I found him sitting, deep in meditation, on the smaller bed that stands beside the bigger one. There was no one with him. When he saw me, he joyfully called me to him and made me sit down on one end of the bed. He was in an ecstatic mood. He muttered something to himself that I couldn't understand, looked hard at me, and then arose and approached me. I thought we were about to have another crazy scene. Scarcely had that thought passed through my mind when he placed his right foot on my body. Immediately I had a wonderful experience. My eyes were wide open, and I saw that everything in the room, including the walls themselves, was rapidly whirling around me and receding. At the same time, it seemed to me that my consciousness of self, together with the entire universe, was about to vanish into a vast, all-devouring void. This destruction of my self-consciousness seemed to me the same thing as death. Terrified, I felt death right before me, very close. Unable to control myself, I cried out loudly: 'Ah, what are you doing to me? Don't you know I have parents at home?' When the Master heard this, he gave a loud laugh. Then he touched my chest with his hand and said: 'All right, let it stop now. It needn't be done all at once. It will happen in its own good time.' To my amazement, the extraordinary vision vanished as suddenly as it had come. I returned to my normal state and saw things inside and outside the room standing as still as before.

"Although it has taken so long to describe all this, it actually happened in

3. Narendra's resolve to know the cause of that experience and not be overwhelmed again in the future.

only a few moments. And yet it changed my whole way of thinking. I was bewildered and kept trying to analyze what had happened. I saw how this experience had begun and ended in obedience to the will of this extraordinary man. I had read about mesmerism and hypnotism in books, and I wondered if this was something like that. But my heart refused to believe that it was, for even people of great willpower can create such conditions only in weak minds. And my mind was by no means weak. In fact, up to then I had been proud of my intelligence and will-power. Ordinary people are overwhelmed and become puppets under the influence of a great personality, but this man hadn't bewitched me or reduced me to that condition. On the contrary, when I first met him, I had decided that he was mad. Why then should I have suddenly found myself in this state? I couldn't come to any conclusion. It seemed an utter mystery to me. Then I remembered the words of a great poet, 'There are more things in heaven and earth than are dreamt of in your philosophy.' I thought that this might be one of those things. After much reflection, I concluded that this mystery could not be solved. I determined to be on my guard lest he exert more influence over me in the future.

"The next moment I thought: How can I consider this person mad when

4. Narendra's speculations about the Master and his determination to understand him.

he was able to destroy the strong structure of my mind at will — a mind that is endowed with tremen-dous willpower — and reshape it as if it were a lump of clay, making it think as he wished? But during my first visit he took me aside and said so many strange things; how can I believe them to be true, or to be anything other than an eccentric outburst? Because I couldn't determine the cause of the wonderful experience I've just described, I could come to no firm resolution about this person, who was as pure and simple as a child. From my boyhood I have always used observation, investigation, reasoning, and argumentation to form an opinion about a person or a thing, but on that day my character was dealt a terrible blow, which distressed my heart. Consequently, a fierce deter-mination arose in my mind to truly understand the nature and power of this wonderful man by any possible means.

"Thus was my mind occupied with various thoughts and resolutions

5. The Master treated Narendra as if he had known him for a long time.

throughout the day. After this last incident, the Master became quite a different person. He began to feed me lovingly as he had during my first visit, and he treated me as cordially as if he had known me for a long time. He behaved with me exactly like a man who meets an old friend or relative after a long separation. But feeding and entertaining me, talking to me and making jokes with me, didn't seem to satisfy him. His affectionate behaviour created a good deal of anxiety in me. As the day was coming to a close, I asked leave to go. This seemed to make him unhappy, and as on the previous occasion he demanded a promise: 'Say that you will come back soon.' So on that day I promised as before, and then I returned home."

We do not know how long it was before Narendra returned. After encoun-

6. Narendra's third visit.

tering the Master's miraculous power, Narendra had an intense desire to know him, so it seems it must not have been long before he came back to Dakshineswar. His eagerness must have brought him back to the Master as soon as he was able. Because he was attending college, the third visit probably took place on a weekend. When Narendra wanted to investigate something, he lost all interest in food, sleep, or relaxation; he would take no rest until he had mastered the situation. So, quite naturally he was extremely anxious to understand the Master. It is certain that during the third visit Narendra was extremely cautious and very much on his guard lest he fall under a hypnotic spell as before. But what happened was inconceivable. We shall now present what the Master and Narendra told us about it.

On that day the Master invited Narendra for a walk in Jadu Mallick's

| 7. Narendra loses outer consciousness at the Master's touch. | garden, just south of the Dakshineswar compound, either because the temple complex was crowded with devotees or for some other reason. Jadu and his |

mother were very devoted to the Master, and they had left a standing order with the manager that if the Master wished to walk in the garden when they were absent, the parlour facing the Ganges should be kept open for him. On that day the Master walked with Narendra in the garden on the bank of the Ganges. As the Master and Narendra talked about various things, they eventually came to the parlour, where the Master sat down and soon went into samadhi. Narendra sat nearby, closely watching the Master's condition, when the Master suddenly touched him, just as he had on the previous occasion. Although Narendra was on his guard, he was completely overwhelmed by that powerful touch. This time he became completely unconscious, not partially as before. When he regained his normal consciousness after some time, he saw the Master passing his hand over his chest and smiling at him, sweetly and gently.

Narendra did not tell us anything about what he experienced when he lost his outer consciousness. We thought that he did not tell us about it because it was a secret. But one day in the course of conversation the Master told us what had happened during that incident and we realized that Narendra had no memory of it.

The Master told us: "That day, after Narendra lost consciousness of his

| 8. The Master asks Narendra various questions while he is in that state. | current incarnation, I asked him many questions, such as who he really was, where he had come from, why he had come [been born], how long he would stay in this world, and so forth. He entered his inner- |

most being and found the correct answers to my questions. These answers confirmed what I'd already learned about him in visions. It's forbidden to reveal those things, but I can tell you this: On the day he knows who he really is, he will no longer remain in this world. With a strong effort of will, he will immediately give up his body through the power of yoga. Narendra is a great soul, perfect in meditation."

Later the Master described to us one of his earlier visions concerning Narendra. We shall mention it here for the reader's convenience, but when the Master told us about it, it seemed that he had this vision before Narendra first visited Dakshineswar.

The Master said: "One day I found that my mind was soaring high in

9. The Master's wonderful vision concerning Narendra.

samadhi along a luminous path. It soon transcended the stellar universe and entered the subtle realm of ideas. As it ascended higher and higher, I found the path lined with ideal forms of gods and goddesses on both sides. My mind then reached the outer limits of that region, where a luminous barrier separates the sphere of relative existence from that of the Absolute. My mind crossed that barrier to enter the transcendental realm, where no corporeal being was visible. Even the gods dare not enter that sublime realm and are content to keep their seats far below. But the next moment I saw seven venerable rishis seated there in samadhi. It occurred to me that these rishis must have surpassed not only humans but even the gods in knowledge and holiness, in renunciation and love. Lost in admiration, I was reflecting on their greatness when I saw a portion of that undifferentiated luminous region condense into the form of a divine child. The child came to one of the rishis, tenderly clasped his neck with his lovely arms and, addressing him in a sweet voice, tried to drag his mind down from the state of samadhi. That magic touch roused the rishi from the superconscious state, and he fixed his half-opened eyes upon the wonderful child. His beaming countenance showed that the child was the treasure of his heart. In great joy the divine child spoke to him: 'I am going down. You must go with me.' The rishi remained mute but his tender look expressed his assent. As he gazed at the child, he again became immersed in samadhi. I was surprised to see a fragment of his body and mind then descending to earth in the form of a bright light. No sooner had I seen Narendra than I recognized him to be that rishi."[1]

Narendra was completely dumbfounded when the influence of the

10. Narendra's conviction about the Master as a result of his direct experience.

Master's divine power put him under the same hypnotic spell for a second time. He deeply felt the insignificance of his mental and intellectual power compared to this unsurpassable divine power. His former belief that the Master was a monomaniac was changed. But we cannot say that this encounter brought him to understand the meaning and significance of what the Master had told him privately during his first visit to Dakshineswar. He felt that the Master must be an extraordinarily great soul

1. The Master described this vision to us in his unique, simple language. It is not possible for us to reproduce that language exactly. Having no alternative, we have briefly described this vision keeping his language as far as possible. When at another time we asked him about the divine child in the vision, we learned that the Master himself had assumed the form of that child.

endowed with divine power, and that he could at will drive the mind of a person like him to a higher path. He also understood that because the Master's will was completely identified with that of God, he would not have the desire to raise everyone's mind to a higher realm [because a person must work through his or her own karma]. Narendra was therefore fortunate to receive such unsolicited grace from this great soul.

Narendra was forced to come to this conclusion, and he had to adapt

| 11. Consequently, Narendra's conception of the guru changes. | many of his former ideas accordingly. Previously he had been strongly against accepting a man — who like himself was weak and shortsighted — as a guru, |

or a guide to the spiritual world, and carrying out all his instructions without question. This attitude had been strengthened considerably when he joined the Brahmo Samaj. But the last two incidents dealt terrible blows to his beliefs. He realized that on rare occasions some great souls are born in this world whose extraordinary renunciation, austerities, love, and purity surpass what the limited minds of ordinary people conceive of as God. And ordinary people would benefit greatly if they accepted those great souls as gurus. Narendra did in fact agree to accept the Master as his guru, but at that time declined to accept all of his words indiscriminately.

Because of his experiences in past lives, Narendra had a strong belief from

| 12. In the Master's company Narendra's spirit of renunciation increases. | his boyhood onward that one cannot realize God without renunciation. For that reason, although he was a member of the Brahmo Samaj, he had no desire to attend its meetings concerning marriage reform. |

Narendra's inclination towards renunciation now increased tremendously as he observed the all-renouncing Master and realized how extraordinary was the power he wielded.

At this time only one thing greatly concerned Narendra: Upon coming in

| 13. Narendra resolves not to accept any of the Master's words without testing them. | contact with such a powerful and great soul, one usually either believes that person's words without evaluating them fully, or indeed without testing them at all. He resolved to protect himself from that |

by any means. For that reason, although the last two meetings had awakened in Narendra a love and respect for the Master, he decided not to accept anything that the Master said about his visions and experiences without experiencing them himself and examining them carefully, even if this incurred the Master's displeasure. So on one hand, he earnestly kept his mind open to receive the novel and hitherto unknown truths of the spiritual world, and on the other, he engaged himself from then on in subjecting the Master's visions and his behaviour to rigorous testing.

Narendra's keen intellect revealed to him that the words spoken by the

| 14. Narendra's next step. | Master during his first visit — which had led him to consider the Master a monomaniac — could only be |

understood as meaningful if he believed that the Master was an avatar. But how could his truth-seeking and rational mind admit this so quickly? He decided that if God ever gave him the ability to understand those words of the Master, he would consider them at that time. So, without forming any further opinion, he devoted himself to learning from the Master and discussing with him how to be blessed with God-realization.

When a powerful mind replaces an old idea with a new one, it faces strong

15. Narendra's mental condition at this time.

resistance from within. Narendra now encountered this situation. Although he realized the wonderful power of the Master, Narendra could not accept him completely; and although he was attracted to the Master, he tried to stay away from him. We shall find out later what happened as a result of these efforts.

Chapter 5

The Master's Selfless *L*ove and Narendra

WE HAVE ALREADY MENTIONED THAT NARENDRA was born with wonderful spiritual

> 1. Extraordinary experiences in Narendra's early life. He saw a light while falling asleep.

tendencies. For that reason, the spiritual experiences that he had before he met the Master were unique. The reader will understand this if we cite a few examples here. Narendra said: "As far back as I can remember, I'd see a marvellous point of light between my eyebrows as soon as I shut my eyes to go to sleep. I watched it and paid great attention as it went through various changes. To see it better, I would lie on my bed like one prostrating before a deity, with forehead touching the ground. That marvellous point of light would change colours and grow bigger and bigger until it took the form of a ball, finally bursting and covering my body from head to foot with a white liquid light. As soon as that happened I lost outer consciousness and fell asleep. I used to believe this was how everybody went to sleep, and I was under that impression for a long time. When I grew older and began to practise meditation, that point of light would appear to me as soon as I closed my eyes, and I'd concentrate upon it. At that time I was practising meditation with a few friends, following the instructions of Devendra Nath Tagore. We told each other about our visions and experiences, and I discovered that none of them had ever seen that point of light or had gone to sleep as I did.

"From my very childhood, whenever I came in contact with a particular

> 2. Memories of past lives awaken when he sees a particular place, person, or thing.

object, person, or place, it would sometimes seem as if I were already acquainted with it. I'd try to recall when, but couldn't bring it to mind. Nonetheless, I was not convinced that I had never seen it before. This

777

happened quite often. Perhaps I would be discussing various topics with my friends at a particular place. Someone would say something, and immediately the thought would flash in my mind that sometime past, in this very house, I'd had the same discussion with these friends, and on that occasion this person had said the same thing. After long deliberation I couldn't ascertain when I'd had such a discussion with them. When I became aware of the doctrine of reincarnation, I thought that perhaps I might have been familiar with those places and people in a previous life and that partial memories concerning them sometimes surfaced in my mind. Later, I realized that such a conclusion wasn't reasonable. It now seems to me that before I was born I must have somehow seen, as in motion pictures, the people and things I would come in contact with in this life.[1] Those memories now arise in my mind from time to time."

Narendra visited the Master after various people told him about the Master's pure life and his samadhi.[2] He had not even dreamt that seeing the Master would cause him to undergo any mental change or have any extraordinary experience. But the situation turned out contrary to what he expected. Narendra's previous visions and experiences seemed dull and trifling compared to the extraordinary experiences he had during his second and third visits to the Master at Dakshineswar. His exceptional intellect was baffled by this mystery, so he faced a very difficult problem when he tried to understand the Master's personality. He could find no reason to doubt that those extraordinary experiences had been brought on by the Master's inscrutable divine power. The more Narendra thought about this, the more he became lost in wonder.

3. Witnessing the Master's divine power, Narendra's awe and speculations.

One is truly amazed when thinking about the wonderful experience that Narendra had during his second visit to the Master. According to the scriptures, an ordinary aspirant with a limited amount of power attains that rare

4. The extent to which Narendra was a spiritual aspirant.

---

1. Narendra described this wonderful experience to us shortly after we became acquainted, and he told us the cause of the phenomenon towards the end of his life.

2. We have already said that when he first went to Dakshineswar, Narendra was preparing for the F.A. examination at the General Assembly's Institution in Calcutta. Mr. Hastie, a liberal-minded scholar, was the principal of the college. Narendra had a special love and respect for this Englishman because of his manifold talents, his pure life, and his simple and loving behaviour towards the students. One day the professor of literature suddenly fell ill, and Mr. Hastie taught the class on literature to the F.A. students. While discussing the poems of Wordsworth, he mentioned that the poet had experienced ecstasy while enjoying the beauty of nature. When the students did not understand the mystery of samadhi, he tried to explain as much as he could and then finally said: "The state of samadhi originates from a pure mind and its concentration on a particular object. Rarely does one find a person who has achieved that state. At present I have seen only Ramakrishna Paramahamsa of Dakshineswar in the state of samadhi. You will understand this subject if you go there and see him in that state." Thus Narendra first heard about the Master from Mr. Hastie. He met the Master for the first time at Surendra Mitra's house. But as he was visiting the Brahmo Samaj, it seems that he might have also heard about the Master there.

type of experience by practising austerities and renunciation over a long period of time. And once it happens, the aspirant becomes overwhelmed by the manifestation of God in the guru and surrenders to the guru completely. It is surprising that Narendra did not do that. His reaction is evidence that he occupied a high position in the spiritual world. He was not overwhelmed by that event because he had such a great capacity for spiritual power. Instead, he was able to maintain self-control and proceed to engage himself in examining and evaluating the Master's divine character and behaviour for a long time. However, although he was not overwhelmed and did not surrender to the Master completely, from that point on he was undoubtedly greatly attracted to him.

For his part, the Master felt an attraction to Narendra from their first

| 5. The degree to which the Master was attracted to Narendra. | meeting. Endowed with the knowledge of Brahman, the large-hearted guru became intensely anxious to transmit his life experience to the worthy disciple as |

soon as he met him. The magnitude of that eagerness cannot be measured; that kind of unselfish and unmotivated impatience arises only in the hearts of self-controlled and self-contented gurus, prompted by divine inspiration. When the great teachers of the world see worthy disciples, this inspiration drives them to share the knowledge of Brahman and make those disciples perfect and free from worldly desires.[3]

The Master was undoubtedly greatly inclined to use samadhi to impart

| 6. The Master's attempt to impart the knowledge of Brahman to Narendra on the first day. | the knowledge of Brahman to Narendra on the day he went to Dakshineswar alone. When Narendra fully surrendered to the Master three or four years later and was imploring him again and again for |

nirvikalpa samadhi, the Master would refer to this incident and ask him in front of us: "Why are you pestering me? Didn't you tell me that you have parents at home and needed to serve them?" At other times the Master would say: "Look, once a man died and became a ghost. He was alone for a long time, so he felt terribly lonely and began to look everywhere for a companion. Whenever he heard that someone had died in a particular place, he would rush there, thinking that he might finally have a companion. But when he saw that the dead person's soul had become liberated by the touch of Ganges water, or by some other means, he would be disappointed and return to his own place to lead his lonely existence. That poor ghost never had a companion. My condition was similar to his. When I met you, I thought that I'd finally found a companion, but you cried out that you had parents. So I couldn't have a companion." Thus, the Master teased Narendra about that incident.

---

3. The scriptures call this Shambhavi initiation (see IV.4.52).

We have already mentioned that [during Narendra's second visit] when

7. The difference between Narendra's experiences during his first and second visits.

the Master saw him panic-stricken on the verge of entering samadhi, he stopped transmitting it. Because of how this incident turned out, it is no wonder that the Master had some doubt about his earlier visions and experiences regarding Narendra. We think that is why, when Narendra came to Dakshineswar for the third time, the Master overwhelmed him with his power and extracted from him many secrets regarding his life; he was relieved when he found that Narendra's answers confirmed his visions. If our assumption is correct, it is proof that Narendra did not have the same kind of samadhi on his second and third visits, but had two different kinds of experience.

After questioning Narendra, the Master was relieved of anxiety about

8. The Master's apprehension about Narendra.

him to some extent, but not completely. He knew that a man could achieve extraordinary fame and influence if he had but one or two supernatural powers or qualities, but Narendra displayed eighteen such powers, and those to their full extent. If Narendra failed to direct these powers through a spiritual channel and use them to realize the ultimate truth about God, humanity, and the world, the result would be undesirable. The Master said that if that happened, Narendra would found a new religion or a sect as other religious leaders had and would become famous throughout the world. But to fulfill the need of the present age, it was necessary to realize and propagate liberal spiritual truths; if Narendra failed to realize this and was unable to help in this pursuit, it would not be possible for him to do real good in the world. So from that point on, the Master was very eager that Narendra should of his own will and without reservation follow him and experience the spiritual truths just as he had.

The Master used to say: "As watercress and some weeds grow in ponds and small pools where there is no current, so religious cults and narrow-minded sects develop in a religious world where people are satisfied with a partial truth that they think is the whole truth." It is really amazing to consider the many ways in which the Master tried to give Narendra the experience of the whole truth, lest he — who was endowed with extraordinary intelligence and mental qualities — go astray and form a sect of his own.

It is evident that from the very beginning the Master's attraction to Naren-

9. The reason for the Master's attraction to Narendra.

dra was based on many factors. This feeling of his did not easily assume a more normal form until he was convinced that it would be impossible for Narendra to go astray as we have just described. As we consider the reasons [underlying the Master's concern] we find that some of them originated from his wonderful visions about Narendra, and the rest arose from fear that

Narendra would yield to the influence of the modern age and willingly accept the bondage of desire for a wife, wealth, or fame, and thereby fail to even partially fulfill the ultimate purpose of his great life.

Due to his long practice of renunciation and austerity, the concept of the

| 10. This attraction was natural and predestined. | little "I and mine" had disappeared from the Master's mind completely. He was eternally identified with God, the source of the universe, and he constantly felt |

that the Lord's work of doing good to humanity was his own duty. He was convinced that it was the will of the Cosmic Being that his body and mind would be the instruments by which the decline of religion in this present age would be halted. The experience we described earlier assured him that Narendra was not born merely to enjoy a few selfish pleasures, but that he had come down to earth because of his intense love for God, and to help the Master in his mission to benefit humanity. So it is not surprising that the Master considered the selfless and ever-free Narendra to be his very own, and that he was attracted to him. The Master's attraction to Narendra may seem surprising, but with a little reflection one will understand that it was natural and inevitable.

It is almost impossible for us to describe the extent to which the Master

| 11. The Master's love for Narendra was not of a worldly type. | considered Narendra to be his own and how deeply he loved him from their first meeting. The reasons that prompt worldly people to offer their love to |

others and consider them as their own were totally absent in this situation. Nowhere else have we seen the anxiety that the Master felt when separated from Narendra, or the joy that he experienced upon seeing him. We had never thought that one could selflessly love another so intensely. We saw how this could be possible only after witnessing the Master's incredible love for Narendra, and we now believe that eventually the day will come when people will experience the manifestation of God in each other and will truly be blessed by pouring selfless love into one another.

Swami Premananda went to Dakshineswar for the first time shortly after

| 12. Swami Premananda's testimony. | Narendra's arrival. Because Narendra could not visit Dakshineswar for a week or more [after his third visit], the Master was extremely anxious about him. |

Premananda was amazed by the Master's deep concern for Narendra, as he later related to us.

Swami Premananda recalled: "Swami Brahmananda and I went to

| 13. Swami Premananda's first visit to Dakshineswar; he notices the Master's concern for Narendra. | Hathkhola ghat in West Calcutta to take a boat to Dakshineswar. We met Ramdayal there. When we learned that he was also going to see Sri Rama- krishna, we got into a boat together. It was almost dusk when we reached Rani Rasmani's Kali temple. |

We went to the Master's room and were told that he'd gone to the temple to pay obeisance to the Divine Mother. Swami Brahmananda asked us to wait there and went to the Mother's temple to find the Master. Soon I saw them coming. Swami Brahmananda was holding onto the Master very carefully and guiding him, saying: 'Steps. Go up here, down here.' I'd already heard that the Master often became overwhelmed with ecstasy and lost outer consciousness of his surroundings, so I knew that he was in an ecstatic mood when I saw him coming, reeling like a drunken man. He entered his room in this state and sat on a small bedstead. Shortly afterwards he came to normal consciousness and asked me a few questions about myself and my relatives. He then began to examine my face, hands, feet, and so on. For some time he held my forearm in his hand to feel its weight, and then he said, 'Good.' He alone knew what he meant by that. Afterwards, he asked Ramdayal about Narendra's health. Hearing that he was all right, the Master said: 'It's been a long time since he came here. I want to see him. Please ask him to come sometime.'

"We spent a few delightful hours in spiritual talk, then took our supper at 10:00 p.m. and lay down in the southeast veranda of the Master's room. Beds were arranged for the Master and for Swami Brahmananda in the room. Scarcely an hour had passed when the Master emerged from his room, with his cloth under one arm like a boy, and came to our bedside. Addressing Ramdayal, he asked affectionately, 'Are you sleeping?' Both of us quickly sat up in our beds and replied, 'No, sir.' The Master said: 'Look, I haven't seen Narendra for a long time, and I feel as if my whole heart were being wrung forcibly like a wet towel. Please ask him to come at once to see me. He is a person of pure sattva qualities. He is Narayana himself. I cannot have peace of mind unless I see him now and then.'

14. Premananda's conclusion after observing the Master's anxiety.

"Ramdayal had been visiting Dakshineswar for some time, so the childlike nature of the Master was familiar to him. When he saw that childlike behaviour, he knew that the Master was in ecstasy. He tried to console the Master by promising that he would see Narendra first thing in the morning and ask him to come to Dakshineswar. But that night the Master's longing could not be appeased. Knowing that we were getting no rest, he would return to his bed for a time now and then, but after a while he would forget and come back to us to begin speaking of Narendra's good qualities, pathetically expressing his terrible anguish because of Narendra's long absence. As I observed his agony, I thought to myself: 'How marvellous is the Master's love! And how hardhearted is that person for whom the Master is in such distress!' We spent the night that way. In the morning we went to pay our obeisance to the Divine Mother in the temple, and then bowed down to the Master and took leave of him before returning to Calcutta."

One day in 1883, Vaikuntha Nath Sanyal went to Dakshineswar and

15. Vaikuntha describes the Master's love for Narendra.

found the Master anxious because Narendra had not come for a long time. He later described the Master's condition: "That day the Master's mind was fully absorbed in thoughts of Narendra. He spoke of nothing else but what praise he had for him. The Master addressed me, saying: 'Look, Narendra is a man of pure sattva qualities. I saw in my vision that Narendra was one among the four[4] in the indivisible realm and also one of the seven rishis.[5] There is no limit to his good qualities.' After saying that, the Master became restless to see Narendra and began shedding tears profusely like a mother separated from her child. He thought that we might misunderstand him when he could no longer control himself, so he hurried to the northern veranda. We heard him cry in a choked voice, praying, 'Mother dear, I can't live without seeing him,' and so on.

"After a while he controlled himself somehow, returned to his room, and sat near us. He then said plaintively: 'I weep so much, but Narendra does not come. My desire to see him causes a pain as if my heart were being wrung like a wet towel. He doesn't understand my spiritual attraction to him.' Saying so, he again became restless and left the room. He returned shortly and said: 'Just see, I'm an old man pining and weeping for Narendra. What will people think of me? You are my own, so I'm not ashamed to express my feelings in your presence. But how will others react? I'm sorry, but I can't control myself.' We were amazed by the Master's love for Narendra. We thought that Narendra must be a godlike person, or why would the Master be so drawn to him? To console him, we said: 'Sir, it is indeed wrong of Narendra. He knows that you feel pain when you can't see him and still he doesn't come.'

"Sometime after this event the Master introduced me to Narendra. I saw that the Master was as anxious when he was separated from Narendra as he was delighted when Narendra visited. Sometime later we went to Dakshineswar to celebrate the Master's birth anniversary. The devotees had adorned him beautifully with a new cloth, a garland, sandal paste, and so on. Kirtan was arranged in the northeastern veranda of his room. Surrounded by his devotees, the Master listened to the kirtan. Sometimes he was in ecstasy, and sometimes he made the kirtan more interesting by improvising a line or two in his sweet voice. But his joy was not complete because of Narendra's absence. Now and then he would look around and say, 'Well, Narendra has not come!' Narendra arrived about noon and bowed down to the Master. As soon as the Master saw him, he jumped up, sat on his shoulders, and went into ecstasy. When he regained his normal state afterwards,

4. Sanaka, Sanandana, Sanatana, and Sanatkumara. — *Translator*
5. Marichi, Atri, Angira, Pulaha, Pulastya, Kratu, and Vashishtha. — *Translator*

he became busy with talking to Narendra and feeding him. He could not listen to kirtan anymore that day."

The rare divine love that Narendra received from associating with the Master is truly amazing. Narendra, however, remained unperturbed by this and proceeded to test the Master at every step to realize the truth, proving how much passion he had for truth. The Master was not at all offended by Narendra's conduct. On the contrary, he submitted to all kinds of tests for the benefit of his disciple and gladly came forward to help Narendra realize spiritual truths. One is awestruck at the Master's humility and magnanimity. The more we discuss the relationship between Narendra and the Master, the more we shall marvel at the eagerness of the former to test everything before accepting it and the willingness of the latter to submit to all manner of ordeal so that his disciple could experience the highest spiritual truths. Furthermore, we shall understand how a true guru teaches a highly qualified disciple without disturbing his spiritual attitude, and how the guru consequently occupies a place of love and respect in the heart of that disciple.

16. Narendra remained poised while being the focus of the Master's special affection, which indicates his high competency as a spiritual aspirant.

Chapter 6

Section 1

The Master and Narendra's
*D*ivine Relationship

NARENDRA WAS BLESSED WITH THE HOLY COMPANY of the Master for a period of five

| 1. How long Narendra had the Master's holy company. |

long years. The reader might assume that Narendra lived with the Master at Dakshineswar continuously during these years, but that was not so. During this time he visited the Master from his home as other Calcutta devotees did. But it is true that from the beginning Narendra was very dear to the Master, so his visits to Dakshineswar were frequent. It gradually became one of Narendra's most important duties to visit Dakshineswar once or twice a week, and to stay there for at least three or four days when he had some free time. Sometimes there were interruptions in this routine, but the Master was so very fond of Narendra from the beginning that he did not often allow him to break this routine. If for any reason Narendra could not come to Dakshineswar for a week, the Master became anxious to see him. He would then send a messenger to bring Narendra to Dakshineswar, or he would go to Calcutta and spend a few hours with him there. As far as we know, Narendra visited Dakshineswar regularly without interruption for the first two years after he became acquainted with the Master. After Narendra's B.A. examination in early 1884, complete responsibility for his family fell on his shoulders when his father passed away suddenly, and he was forced to break his earlier routine.

The Master's dealings with Narendra during those five years can be

| 2. During this period the Master dealt with Narendra in five ways. |

divided into five main categories:

1) At their first meeting the Master's unique insight made him understand that students like Narendra,

who was a spiritual aspirant of the highest order, were very rare. Narendra was born to assist in the mission that the Divine Mother had entrusted to him: to establish the eternal religion as required by the need of the age by alleviating the degradation that had taken place for so long.

2) He tied Narendra to him permanently with his infinite love and trust.

3) By subjecting Narendra to various tests, the Master confirmed that his insights about Narendra's greatness and life's goal were valid.

4) He trained Narendra in many ways, making him a suitable instrument to fulfill the great mission of his life.

5) When his training was complete, Narendra achieved the knowledge of Brahman. The Master then taught Narendra how to establish the religion for this age, relieving himself of responsibility by handing over to Narendra his mission and his religious order.

We mentioned earlier that shortly before Narendra's arrival the Master had

3. The Master's faith in and love for Narendra arose from his extraordinary visions.

a few extraordinary visions about Narendra's greatness. Influenced by those visions, the Master loved Narendra and placed unbounded faith in him from the very beginning. That trust and affection flowed from his heart without pause throughout the rest of his life, binding Narendra to him with a cord of love. So it is evident that it was based on this faith and love that the Master began training Narendra and sometimes testing him as well.

One may question why the Master tested Narendra even though his yogic

4. His reason for testing Narendra.

vision had assured him of Narendra's greatness and of the goal of his life. The answer is that when human beings assume bodies and enter the realm of maya even godmen like the Master have their vision limited to greater or lesser degrees — not to speak of ordinary people. There is therefore a possibility of falling into error regarding what is seen. It is for that reason that such trials are sometimes necessary. The Master explained this to us, saying, "One cannot make jewellery without an alloy." In other words, just as one cannot make jewellery with pure gold that has not been mixed with base metals, so the bodies and minds of avatars cannot be produced out of enlightened and pure sattva guna that has no admixture of rajas and tamas. While we were discussing the Master's sadhana, we mentioned that although by the Divine Mother's grace the Master had many spiritual visions as a wonderful knowledge awakened within him, he doubted those visions many times and was able to accept them with ease only when they were later tested and found to be true. So it is not surprising that he decided to test any extraordinary visions he had about Narendra before believing them.

Of the Master's five modes of conduct towards Narendra that were

5. How the Master looked upon Narendra.

mentioned earlier, three among them — faith and love, testing, and teaching — began simultaneously. We have already briefly described the first one: the

Master's unbounded faith in and love for Narendra. We shall have more to say about it later. From their first meeting, the Master's life was more connected with Narendra's life than with that of any other devotee. It is said that when Jesus first met one of his main disciples [Simon Peter], he proclaimed, "Upon this immovable rock I shall build my church." By Providence such a feeling also arose in the Master's mind when he met Narendra. The Master had a vision that Narendra was his child, his friend who was born to carry on his mission, and that their lives were bound eternally with an unbreakable cord of love from previous lives. But this love is an exalted spiritual love in which the lover gives full freedom to the beloved, yet keeps the other as his or her own from age to age. In this love, the lover and the beloved do not seek anything in return from one another and are satisfied instead by offering everything to each other. It is doubtful that people have ever seen a love as selfless as that we saw between the Master and Narendra. We are not capable of telling the reader the story of that divine love. But for the sake of truth, we shall try to provide a little glimpse of it and then will discuss the Master's dealings with Narendra in detail.

From their first meeting, just as Narendra was attracted to the Master

6. The erroneous impressions that ordinary people had about Narendra.

upon seeing his one-pointed devotion, purity, and renunciation, so the Master observed Narendra's indomitable self-confidence, courage, and passion for truth, and was moved to make Narendra his own. Leaving aside the Master's yogic vision about Narendra's greatness and bright future, if we try to uncover the reason for their reciprocal attraction, we find it in our previous statement.

Some people who lacked insight considered Narendra's wonderful self-confidence to be pride, his indomitable vigour to be arrogance, and his uncompromising love of truth to be either feigned or a sign of an immature intellect. They undoubtedly came to that conclusion from seeing his complete indifference to praise, his outspokenness, and his free and forthright behaviour in all matters. Above all, they saw that he had no fear of what others thought of him, and never kept anything he did secret. We remember that before we met Narendra, one of his neighbours told us about him: "There's a boy in that house — I've never known anyone so hopelessly spoilt. Since he got his B.A. degree, he's so vain; he thinks that nothing in the whole world matters but him. When his father and other older people are present, he'll quite rudely start singing and beating his drum without any respect. He walks through the street smoking cigars in the presence of respected elder neighbours. He is heedless in every respect."

Shortly after this, during our second or third visit to Dakshineswar, the

7. The author hears the Master praise Narendra.

Master praised Narendra's noble qualities. While talking to Ratan, the manager of Jadu Mallick's garden house, the Master pointed to us and said:

"These boys are good. They are polite and gentle, and they have one-and-a-half degrees. (We were then preparing for our final F.A. examination.) But I have never seen another boy like Narendra. He's as proficient in vocal and instrumental music as he is in studies, in conversation, and in religious matters. He meditates the entire night and is completely unaware when morning comes. Narendra isn't like a fake coin; if you test him as a money-changer checks a coin [by tapping it], you will hear the right sound. I see other boys pass two or three examinations somehow by working as hard as they can, and there it ends, as if they used up all their energy in accomplishing this. But Narendra isn't like that. He does everything with ease and joy, and passing an examination is a trifling thing for him. He also goes to the Brahmo Samaj and sings devotional songs there. But he isn't like the other Brahmos; he is a true knower of Brahman. He sees a light when he sits for meditation. Is it for nothing that I love Narendra so much?" This made us long to meet him and we asked the Master, "Sir, where does Narendra live?" He replied, "Narendra is a son of Vishwanath Datta of Simla, Calcutta." When we later returned to Calcutta, we learned that the Master's highly-praised Narendra was the same young man whom his neighbour had harshly criticized earlier. We were amazed by this and thought about how we sometimes misjudge a person based on his or her behaviour.

It will not be out of place to mention another incident in connection with this topic. A few months before we heard the Master praise Narendra, we had an opportunity to meet him at a friend's house. We saw him that day but did not try to talk to him because of our mistaken ideas about him. However, what he said on that occasion was so deeply imprinted on our memory that even after so much time has passed it seems as though we heard it just yesterday. It is necessary to explain to the reader the circumstances in which we heard Narendra's conversation, or it will not be clear how we developed a wrong impression of him on that day.

8. The author's mistaken impression of Narendra when they first met.

We met Narendra that day at a house that our friend had rented. It was a two-storeyed building on Gaur Mohan Mukherjee Street, Simla, in front of Narendra's house. We had been classmates with this friend for four or five years. A couple of years before the Entrance examination, our friend decided to go to England and travelled as far as Bombay but could go no further. He became a newspaper editor and was preparing some books of collected articles and poems that he had written in Bengali. He had married sometime prior to this incident, and some people told us that he was leading a wayward life and earning money by unscrupulous means. To ascertain the truth, we went to his house that day without warning.

9. The author meets Narendra for the first time at a friend's house.

We sent word of our arrival through a servant and waited in the living

10. Narendra's behaviour at that time.

room. In the meantime, a young man suddenly entered the room as if he were known to the owner of the house. Without any hesitation, he reclined on a bolster and began to softly sing a Hindi song. As far as we remember, that song was connected with Krishna, as we distinctly heard two words *Kanai* [Krishna], and *Bansari* [flute]. The young man was well dressed and his hair was nicely combed, although he was not foppish. Because he was absent-mindedly singing a love song about Krishna and was closely associated with our wayward friend, we could not come to a favorable opinion of him. He simply ignored our presence. As we observed his carefree manner and watched him smoking tobacco, we concluded that he was a true companion of our wayward friend, who had gone astray by associating with this kind of person. At any rate, although he knew we were present he remained aloof, absorbed in his own thoughts, so we did not try to talk to him.

After a while, our friend came into the living room. Although it had been

11. Narendra's discussion with our friend on literature.

a long time since we last met, he greeted us with only a few words, then turned joyfully to talk to that young man on various topics. We did not like his indifference, but we felt that it would be discourteous to leave abruptly, so we began listening to the conversation between our literary friend and this young man. The subject was English and Bengali literature. Although both agreed to a great extent that classical literature must correctly express human sentiments, they had a difference of opinion about whether every expression of human sentiments should be considered as literature. As far as we can remember, our friend took the stand that all kinds of writing that express human feelings should be considered as literature, but the young man refuted this. He tried to convince our friend that while literature might correctly express good or bad sentiments, it could not be considered classical unless it was written with good taste or it set a high ideal. In support of his position, the young man mentioned the books of famous English and Bengali writers, beginning with Chaucer, and showed how each of them had achieved immortality in the literary world by following that principle.

In conclusion, the young man said: "Although people experience both positive and negative feelings, they always try to hold to a particular ideal within themselves. The differences that exist among people are based on how completely they realize and manifest their particular ideals. Ordinary people consider the enjoyment of sense objects to be permanent and real, and they are satisfied with achieving those pleasures as the goal of life. *They idealize what is apparently real.* There's little difference between these people and animals. Writers such as they could never create classical literature. Moreover, there's another kind of human being who isn't satisfied with the enjoyment of pleasures that appear to be real. These people hold the highest ideal within themselves and strive to fit everything they encounter into that mould. *They want to realize the ideal.* Only people such as they can create true literature. Among these, there are people who are eager to translate the very highest ideal into their lives; they generally have to renounce worldly life. I've seen only Sri Ramakrishna Paramahamsa of Dakshineswar who fully embodies the highest ideal in his life, and that's why I revere him."

Although we were moved by the young man's profound ideas and by his

| 12. The author subsequently learns of Narendra's greatness from the Master. |

scholarship on that day, we were nonetheless disappointed at seeing his close relationship with our wayward friend, believing his words and actions to be incongruous. We took leave of our friend. A few months after this incident, we were impressed by the praise that the Master had for Narendra, and we visited him at his home. We were dumbfounded when we saw that the Master's highly-praised Narendra was the young man whom we had seen at our friend's house.

Ordinary worldly people who saw how Narendra behaved often found

| 13. The Master recognizes Narendra at their first meeting. |

him to be proud, arrogant, and ill behaved. The Master, however, never fell into that error about him. He understood at their first meeting that Narendra's apparent arrogance and vanity originated from his tremendous self-confidence, which arose from his inherent and extraordinary mental power. His bold and carefree behaviour was nothing but a sign of his natural self-control. His indifference to name and fame sprang from the self-satisfaction inherent in his pure character. The Master knew that in time Narendra's extraordinary character would bloom like a thousand-petalled lotus and become established in its own unparalleled glory and greatness. He knew that when Narendra's life encountered the afflicted world, his arrogance and vanity would melt into infinite compassion, his unique self-confidence would serve to reestablish faith in the broken-hearted, and his carefree conduct, which always remained under his control, would demonstrate to others that self-control was the only way to attain freedom.

So, from their first meeting, the Master praised Narendra extravagantly to

| 14. Knowing him to be a great soul, the Master publicly praises Narendra. |

one and all. Although he knew that praise inflates a weak man's ego and ruins his life, the Master made an exception regarding Narendra because he was convinced that Narendra's mind dwelt high above that kind of weakness. The reader will understand this if we cite a few examples here.

One day Keshab Chandra Sen, Vijay Krishna Goswami, and other cele-

| 15. The Master mentions Narendra's innate powers. |

brated Brahmo leaders were seated with the Master. Young Narendra was also present. In an exalted mood, the Master looked on Keshab and Vijay with a kind gaze. Then his eyes fell on Narendra, and a bright picture of the young man's future life suddenly appeared in his mind. The Master compared the advanced lives of Keshab and others with what he had seen of Narendra's future, keeping his affectionate gaze on Narendra. When Keshab and Vijay had left after the meeting, the Master said: "Keshab possesses one power, which has made him world-famous, but Narendra is endowed with eighteen such powers. I have seen the divine light in Keshab and Vijay burning like a candle flame, but in Narendra it shines with the radiance of the sun, dispelling the last vestiges of ignorance and delusion."

If a weak man devoid of insight had received such praise from the Master, he would have been overwhelmed and filled with pride. But Narendra was different. His wonderfully intuitive mind dived within and began to impartially compare the innumerable good qualities of Keshab and of Vijay with his own mental condition at that time. Considering himself to be unworthy of such praise, he vehemently protested, saying to the Master: "Sir, why do you say such things? People will think you're mad if you talk like that! Keshab is famous all over the world. Vijay is a saint. I'm an insignificant schoolboy. How can you speak of us in the same breath? Please, I beg of you, never say such things again!" Pleased, the Master responded: "But what can I do about it, my child? You don't suppose I'd say such things of my own accord? It was Mother who showed me the truth about you, and so I had to tell it. Mother has never lied to me."

The Master could not always convince Narendra by saying that the 16. Narendra's protest. | Divine Mother had revealed something to him or had made him speak. The outspoken and fearless Narendra sometimes doubted the truth of the Master's visions and said: "How do you know it was Mother who told you? All this may be your imagination. If I were in your position, I would consider such visions to be mere fancies. Western science and philosophy have proven that our senses often deceive us, and that the chances of deception are much greater if our minds hold a constant desire to see a particular thing. You are fond of me and always want to see me become great — this may be why you have such visions."

In this manner Narendra would talk to the Master, trying to explain with 17. Overwhelmed by Narendra's arguments, the Master questions the Divine Mother. | various apt illustrations how physical science had investigated and verified such visions, which are subjective, and had proven them to be erroneous. When the Master's mind dwelt in a high spiritual plane, he considered Narendra's guileless explanations to be a sign of his love for truth, which made him still more pleased with Narendra. But when he was in the normal plane, Narendra's sharp argumentation would overwhelm the Master's childlike and simple mind, sometimes upsetting him. He would think: "Well, Narendra is completely devoted to truth; he isn't one to tell a lie. Also, the scriptures say that no falsehood appears in the mind of a truthful person like him. Could there then be any possibility of error in my visions?" Again, he thought: "I've tested my visions in various ways and have found that the Divine Mother has never revealed anything false to me. I've also received repeated assurances from Her. So why does the honest Narendra say that my visions are caused by my imagination? Why doesn't he believe them to be true as I describe them?"

Worried, the Master at last asked the Divine Mother for an answer. He was reassured when he heard Her voice say: "Why do you listen to Narendra? He will accept the truth before long." The reader will understand what we have said if we describe an incident that illustrates the subject.

At this time the Brahmos had split into two groups because of the

18. An example: The Master goes to the Sadharan Brahmo Samaj to see Narendra.

controversial marriage between the Maharaja of Coochbehar and Keshab's daughter (see II.Appendix.21). The Sadharan Brahmo Samaj had been formed a few years before the event we describe here. Although Narendra visited Keshab from time to time, he also went regularly to the Sadharan Brahmo Samaj and would sing devotional songs at their Sunday prayer meetings. Around this time, Narendra had not been able to visit the Master at Dakshineswar for a couple of weeks. Every day the Master waited for him to come. Disappointed, at last he decided to go to Calcutta and see Narendra.

It was a Sunday. The Master worried that Narendra might go somewhere to visit friends and he might miss seeing Narendra even if he went to Calcutta. The Master finally concluded that Narendra would certainly sing at the evening service of the Sadharan Brahmo Samaj, so he could see him there. He then worried that if he went there uninvited, the Brahmo devotees might be displeased. But the next moment he reasoned to himself: "Well, I visited Keshab's Brahmo Samaj a few times without any invitation, and they were invariably pleased to see me. Moreover, Vijay, Shivanath, and other leaders of the Sadharan Brahmo Samaj have visited Dakshineswar many times." While trying to decide what to do, however, the simple Master forgot an important fact: It did not occur to him even for a moment that Shivanath and other Brahmos of the Sadharan Samaj had gradually stopped visiting him when they observed that Keshab and Vijay had changed their religious views under the influence of the Master. This oversight is quite understandable. Throughout his life, the Master had realized the truth that as human beings ascended to higher spiritual planes, driven by an intense longing for God, thus receiving His grace, their religious views evolved accordingly. How could the Master understand that the [Sadharan] Brahmos, who were lovers of truth and ardent fighters for its cause, had now taken a new course and set limits on their spiritual realizations?

It was evening. Hundreds of Brahmo devotees were ardently repeating

<table>
<tr><td>19. The result of his visit.</td><td>the mantra, satyam jnanam anantam Brahma [Brahman is Truth, Knowledge, and Infinity], directing their heartfelt devotion to God.</td></tr>
</table>

Prayer and meditation came to an end, and the preacher began to speak to the congregation from the pulpit on the love of and longing for God. At that moment, the Master entered the Brahmo temple in a semiconscious state and moved forward towards the pulpit. Many in the audience had seen him before, so it did not take long for news of the Master's sudden arrival to spread throughout the congregation. Those who had not seen him before stood up, some even standing on the benches to get a better look at him. The noise and disorder in the congregation forced the preacher to interrupt his sermon. Narendra was seated in the choir area. When he realized that the Master was there he immediately rushed to him. But the preacher and other prominent Brahmos did not come forward to receive the Master. They neglected to show him even common courtesy, because they considered him to be responsible for creating dissension among certain Brahmos such as Vijay and others.

Without glancing to the left or to the right, the Master advanced towards

<table>
<tr><td>20. The gaslights are turned off in an effort to disperse the crowd.</td><td>the pulpit, where he went into samadhi. The congregation, excited to see the Master in that state, made more of a commotion than before.</td></tr>
</table>

The ushers, finding that they could not restore order, turned out all the gaslights to force people to leave the building. This caused even more confusion among the crowd as people tried to leave the dark hall.

Narendra was terribly hurt when he saw that no one in the Sadharan

<table>
<tr><td>21. Narendra manages to get the Master out of the building and escorts him to Dakshineswar.</td><td>Brahmo Samaj received the Master. Now he was deeply concerned about getting the Master out of the darkened temple. As soon as the Master's samadhi came to an end, Narendra found a way to lead him</td></tr>
</table>

out through a back door. He got him into a carriage and rode with him to Dakshineswar. Narendra later said: "It's impossible to describe the pain I felt that night when I saw the Master being humiliated like that, and all on my account! How I scolded him for what he'd done! But he didn't care one bit about my scolding or his humiliation.

"I know that the Master gave no thought to himself because of his love for

<table>
<tr><td>22. Narendra scolds the Master for his love for him; the Master is consoled after hearing the words of the Divine Mother.</td><td>me, so I didn't hesitate to use harsh words with him on occasion. I said: 'It's written in the Puranas that King Bharata thought so much of his favourite deer that he himself became a deer in his next life. If that's true, you should beware of thinking too much about me!'</td></tr>
</table>

The Master was as simple as a young boy. He took what I said literally and replied in great distress: 'You're right. So what is going to happen to me, since I can't bear not seeing you?' Then he anxiously went off to consult the Divine Mother. After a while he came back beaming with delight and exclaimed: 'Leave me in peace, you rascal! I'll never listen to anything you tell me again! Mother said to me: "You love him so much because you regard him as Narayana [Vishnu] Himself. If the day ever comes when you don't see Narayana in him, then you won't spare him a single glance!"' With this short but emphatic statement, he dismissed once and for all everything I'd ever said to him on that subject."

Chapter 6

Section 2

The Master and Narendra's *D*ivine Relationship

FROM THE OUTSET, THE MASTER'S KEEN INSIGHT OBSERVED that Narendra's pure

| 1. The Master's remarks about Narendra's greatness. |

mind and heart were always motivated by high ideals. So the Master's everyday behaviour with Narendra was different from his treatment of other disciples. The Master himself observed strict rules regarding food, sleep, japa, meditation, and so on, and always encouraged his devotees to cultivate devotion by following his example. However, he did not hesitate to say again and again in front of all that Narendra would come to no harm if he disregarded those rules. The Master said: "Narendra is *nitya-siddha,* eternally perfect"; "Narendra is *dhyana-siddha,* perfect in meditation"; "The fire of knowledge that burns all impurities caused by food is always ablaze in Narendra. That's why his mind will never be distracted or polluted, no matter where or what he eats"; "Narendra is constantly cutting the bonds of maya into pieces with the sword of knowledge, so Mahamaya is incapable of bringing him under Her control." We were overwhelmed when we heard the Master make so many wonderful remarks about Narendra every day.

When the Marwari devotees visited the Master, they presented him with

| 2. Food brought by the Marwari devotees is given to Narendra. |

nuts, pistachios, raisins, rock candy, and various sweets. But the Master would not eat any of these things, nor would he give them to the devotees around him. He said: "They don't know how to make gifts without wanting something in return. If they give one roll of betel to a holy man, they attach to

795

it prayers for the fulfillment of sixteen desires. If one eats food from such a materialistic person, one loses devotion." So there was the question of what should be done with their gifts. The Master said: "Take those things to Narendra. If he eats them, no harm will befall him."

One day Narendra ate his meal in a hotel. He then went to the Master and

| 3. Narendra's devotion is not affected by eating forbidden food.

said, "Sir, I've been in a hotel and have eaten food that others consider to be forbidden." The Master knew that Narendra was not speaking in a spirit of bravado but was warning him so that he would not touch Narendra or allow him to use the utensils in his room if he had any reservations. The Master promptly replied: "It won't do you any harm. If a man keeps his mind on God, eating pork and beef is equivalent to eating the purest *havishyanna* made of boiled vegetables, rice, and ghee. Likewise, if a man is engrossed in worldly desires, eating spinach and vegetables is by no means better than eating pork and beef. I don't mind at all that you've eaten some forbidden food; but if any one of them (*pointing to others*) came and told me that, I couldn't touch him."

It is almost impossible to describe to the reader the extent of the love,

| 4. The Master's unselfish love helps Narendra's spiritual progress, and the latter surrenders to him.

praise, and freedom in every respect that the Master gave to Narendra from the beginning. If one examines the lives of the great teachers, it is doubtful that one will find any situation in which they treated their great disciples with as much respect for their inherent power. The Master could find no rest until he had divulged all of his innermost thoughts to Narendra. He consulted Narendra's opinion in every matter, and to evaluate his visitors' intelligence and intensity of faith he would ask Narendra to engage them in debate. The Master never asked Narendra to accept anything as true without having fully tested it. This way of dealing with Narendra enhanced his self-confidence, self-effort, passion for truth, love, and faith a hundredfold within a short time. The Master's infinite trust and love created an invincible wall around Narendra that protected him from all types of temptation and mean conduct at all times and in all situations, without his knowledge, allowing him to safely enjoy his beloved freedom.

Within a year of their first meeting, Narendra had dedicated himself to the Master forever. Did he understand at the time how the Master's selfless love was slowly carrying him forward towards the goal of his life? Perhaps not. It seems that his heart was constantly full, satisfied with a pure bliss that he had never felt before, a bliss that had its origin in the Master's heavenly love. At this point he had not yet come in contact with the selfish and cruel world, so he had nothing to compare this to and thus did not understand that such love was extremely rare, indeed coveted even by the gods. It will not be out of place to cite a few examples to make this clear to the reader.

M., the recorder of *The Gospel of Sri Ramakrishna*, met the Master in

5. The Master arranges a debate between M. and Narendra.

Dakshineswar in February 1882, a few months after Narendra's arrival. In that book M. records how he had the opportunity of visiting the Master for a few days consecutively while staying at Baranagore, and how a few of the Master's enlightening and ironic remarks removed his pride in learning and made him a humble disciple forever. Narendra told us: "During that period I spent a night with the Master at Dakshineswar. I'd been seated quietly in the Panchavati for a while when the Master suddenly appeared. He took my hand and said, smiling: 'Your learning and intelligence will be tested today. You have only two-and-a-half degrees. Today a schoolteacher [M., Mahendra Nath Gupta] who possesses three-and-a-half degrees is here.[1] Come, I want to hear you talk to him.' Like it or not, I had to go with the Master. Reaching his room, I was introduced to M. and we began to discuss various topics. In that manner the Master got us involved in conversation, then remained quietly seated. He continued listening to what we said and observing us. When M. left, the Master said: 'He might have more degrees, but he's effete. He's too shy. He's not a spirited conversationalist.' In this way the Master enjoyed himself by engaging me in debate with others."

Kedarnath Chattopadhyay was one of the Master's householder devo-

6. Kedarnath Chattopadhyay, a devotee.

tees. We think that he started visiting the Master sometime before Narendra came to Dakshineswar. He worked at Dhaka in Bangladesh, so he could visit the Master only during Durga Puja and on other holidays. Kedar was a spiritual aspirant who practised sadhana according to the spiritual attitude of the Vaishnava Tantra, and tears trickled from his eyes when he listened to devotional songs and kirtan. For these reasons the Master praised him before others. Many people of Dhaka saw Kedar's love of God and treated him with love and respect accordingly. Again, many patterned their spiritual lives on his instructions. It is said that when a large number of people began to come to the Master, he grew tired of talking about God to all of them. Once while in ecstasy, he prayed to the Divine Mother: "Mother, I cannot talk so much anymore. Give a little power to Kedar, Ram, Girish, and Vijay,[2] so that people can go to them first, learn a little, and finally come here (*to me*) to have their spirituality awakened with a word or two." But this he said much later.

Kedar once took an extended leave from his work so he could go to Cal-

7. Kedar's power of reasoning and his first meeting with Narendra.

cutta and have the opportunity to visit the Master from time to time. The Master was delighted to discuss spiritual matters with this wonderful aspirant,

---

1. The Master meant that Narendra was then studying for the B.A., while M. had passed the B.A. and was studying law (B.L.).
2. Kedarnath Chattopadhyay, Ramchandra Datta, Girish Chandra Ghosh, and Vijay Krishna Goswami.

and he introduced the other devotees to him. One day during that time Narendra came to see the Master, and he met Kedar in his room. As he sang devotional songs, he observed Kedar's overflowing emotion. Later, the Master initiated a brief debate between Narendra and Kedar. Kedar was very good at repartee, and he sometimes used sarcasm to point out an opponent's poor logic. On another occasion, the Master was charmed when Kedar used a particular statement to silence his opponent. If anyone later asked that question of the Master, he responded with Kedar's answer. Kedar's opponent had asked this question: "If God is truly compassionate, why did He create so much pain and suffering, injustice and oppression? Why from time to time do thousands of people suffer from poor harvests and die of starvation during famines?" Kedar answered: "Well, I wasn't invited to the meeting on the day when God, although He is merciful, decided to keep pain, suffering, unnatural death, and so on in His creation. So how can I tell you the reason?" However, on that day Narendra's sharp reasoning silenced Kedar in front of everybody.

When Kedar left, the Master asked Narendra: "Well, what did you think

8. Asked by the Master, Narendra expresses his opinion of Kedar.

of him? Did you notice his great devotion, and how he burst into tears when repeating God's name? It is a sign that a man is jivanmukta, liberated-in-life, if tears flow from his eyes during the chanting of Hari's name. Kedar is really wonderful! Don't you think so?" The pure-hearted and vigorous Narendra cherished a deep hatred of men who displayed feminine emotions, be it for religion or for any other reason. He considered it an insult to manliness when a man resorted to tears to attain God, instead of using firm resolution and perseverance. He believed that while a man might completely surrender himself to God, he must always behave like a man and surrender to Him in a masculine way.

Narendra was therefore unable to agree wholeheartedly with the Master, and he replied: "Sir, how should I know? You understand human nature, so only you can say. It's difficult to determine whether a man is good or bad simply by watching him weep and wail. If a man looks at a point for some time without blinking, tears will pour from his eyes. Those who cry when listening to the kirtan of Radha's separation from Krishna undoubtedly do so because they are thinking of their own separation from their wives, or perhaps they force that mood on themselves. Men like me, who are unfamiliar with that condition, may hear the *Mathur-kirtan*[3] and not feel any inclination to cry as others do." Thus if asked, Narendra would always fearlessly express to the Master whatever he felt to be true. The Master was pleased with that rather than angry, because the intuitive Master knew well

3. The Mathur-kirtan was composed to express the intense pang of separation felt by the gopis of Vrindaban when Krishna left for Mathura. — *Translator*

that there was no theft [hypocrisy] in the chamber of the truthful Narendra's heart.

Narendra had joined the Brahmo Samaj shortly before he met the Master. When he did so, he signed the pledge of the Brahmo Samaj to believe in the formless, nondual God and to worship and meditate on Him alone. However, it never occurred to him that he would have to follow the social rules and conduct introduced by the Brahmo Samaj. Rakhal had been acquainted with Narendra before this, and they spent time together. It is not surprising that Rakhal, dependent and soft-natured like a child, was moved by Narendra's affectionate behaviour and allowed himself to be guided in all matters by his strong willpower. So Rakhal followed Narendra's advice and also signed the pledge of the Brahmo Samaj. Rakhal met the Master shortly after this event. After receiving instruction from him, the love of worshipping God with form, which had lain dormant in Rakhal's heart, reawakened.

9. Narendra scolds Rakhal for worshipping God with form, and Rakhal is afraid. The Master reestablishes their friendship.

A few months later, Narendra began to visit the Master. He was very pleased to see Rakhal there. However, after a few days, Narendra saw Rakhal visiting the temples with the Master and bowing down to the deities there. This upset the truth-loving Narendra, and he rebuked Rakhal, reminding him of his pledge. He said: "You're guilty of hypocritical conduct. You bowed down to the deity in the temple even though you signed the pledge of the Brahmo Samaj." The gentle-natured Rakhal remained silent at his friend's blunt remark, and for some time thereafter he was afraid of Narendra and hesitant in his presence. When the Master learned of Rakhal's predicament, he said sweetly to Narendra: "Please don't say anything more to Rakhal. When he sees you, he is stupefied with fright. Now he believes that God has form. What can he do? Look, can everyone conceive of a formless God in the very beginning?" From that point on, Narendra stopped blaming Rakhal.

The Master knew that Narendra was an aspirant of the highest order, so from the outset he tried to instill in him the truths of nondualism. When Narendra first started coming to Dakshineswar, the Master would give him the *Ashtavakra Samhita* and other nondualistic books to read. But because Narendra was then practising a dualistic mode of worship that had as its object the formless Brahman with attributes, he found fault with the nondualistic treatises and considered them to be atheistic. He would read a little at the Master's request, but would then ask bluntly: "What is the difference between this Advaita philosophy and atheism? Should the created jiva think of itself as the Creator? Is there any greater sin than this? I am God; you are God; and everything that is born and dies is God — what could be more absurd? The *munis* and rishis, the authors of these

10. The Master attempts to make Narendra believe in nondualism, and Narendra's protest.

books, must have been mad — how could they have written such stuff otherwise?" The Master would smile at Narendra's bluntness, and then say mildly, so as not to hurt his feelings: "You may not be able to accept these truths at present, but is that any reason to condemn the great sages who taught them? Why do you try to limit God's nature? Keep calling on Him. He is Truth itself. In whatever way He reveals Himself to you, believe that to be His true nature." But at that time Narendra paid no heed to the Master's words. He considered as false anything that had not been verified by reason, and it was his nature to stand against all falsehood. He therefore did not hesitate to attack nondualism with various arguments; sometimes he even made sarcastic remarks against it to the Master and many others.

At this time a man named Pratap Chandra Hazra was living in the Dakshi-

11. Pratap Chandra Hazra.

neswar temple garden. His financial condition had deteriorated, so although he made efforts to be religious, his desire to make money occupied his mind most of the time. Worldly prosperity was the main goal of his spiritual practices. He did not want to let anyone know this, however, so he always sought praise from others by speaking of high philosophy and selfless worship of the Lord. Not only that, it was his nature to calculate profit and loss at every step — even as he practised religion. He probably had the idea that through japa and austerities he could fulfill his desire for money by achieving some occult powers. From the outset the Master understood Hazra's frame of mind and advised him to shun all worldly desires and call on God without ulterior motives. However, not only was the weak-minded Hazra unwilling to accept the Master's advice, but also — driven by his misguided beliefs, pride, and self-interest — whenever he found an opportunity, he would announce to the Master's visitors that he himself was not an ordinary holy man. In spite of all this, it seems that he did have a sincere but limited desire to be good. We think this because although the Master always knew what Hazra was up to, and sometimes scolded him severely for it, he did not drive Hazra away from Dakshineswar. He just cautioned some of us not to mix with him too much. He said: "That rascal Hazra has a very calculating mind. Don't listen to him."

In addition to Hazra's positive and negative qualities, he had a sceptical

12. Narendra is pleased with Hazra's intelligence.

temperament. And compared to others who had as little education as himself, he was quite intelligent. He could understand some of the discussions on the doctrines of Western agnostic philosophers that were carried on by English-educated people like Narendra. The intelligent Narendra was pleased with him for this reason and when he visited Dakshineswar, he would spend a couple of hours conversing with Hazra if it was convenient. Hazra was always humble in the presence of Narendra because of the latter's brilliant intellect. He listened with great attention to what Narendra said and occasionally prepared a smoke for him. Observing Narendra's gracious attitude towards Hazra, we said jokingly, "Hazra is Narendra's 'fe – rend'"(friend).

When Narendra came to Dakshineswar, the Master quite often went into

| 13. The Master's behaviour during Narendra's visits to Dakshineswar. |

ecstasy at the very sight of him. When he later regained some consciousness, he would have long spiritual talks with Narendra. At such times the Master would joyfully try to transmit the highest spiritual experiences to Narendra through words and other means. Sometimes the Master wished to listen to devotional songs, and as soon as he heard the sweet melodious voice of Narendra, he would go into samadhi. But this did not interrupt Narendra's singing. Absorbed, he would continue to sing one song after another for hours. When the Master again regained partial consciousness, he would request Narendra to sing a particular song. He would not be completely satisfied until he had heard Narendra sing "All that exists art Thou."[4] After that they would spend some time discussing the various mysteries of Advaita Vedanta, such as the difference between the jiva and Ishwara, the real nature of the jiva and of Brahman, and so on. Narendra's presence thus created a wave of bliss in Dakshineswar.

One day the Master told Narendra various things regarding the oneness

| 14. Narendra joins Hazra in criticizing nondualistic philosophy; in ecstasy, the Master touches Narendra. |

of jiva and Brahman according to nondualistic philosophy. Although he listened attentively, Narendra did not understand. When the Master finished speaking, Narendra went to see Hazra. While smoking and discussing that topic again, Narendra said, "Can it ever be possible that the water pot is God, that the cup is God, that everything we see and all of us are God?" Hazra joined Narendra in ridiculing the idea, and they both burst into laughter. The Master was in an ecstatic mood, and when he heard Narendra laughing he came out of his room, holding his cloth under his arm like a boy. "What are you talking about?" he asked them. Smiling, he touched Narendra and went into samadhi.

---

4. I have joined my heart to Thee: all that exists art Thou;
Thee only have I found, for Thou art all that exists.
O Lord, Beloved of my heart! Thou art the Home of all;
Where indeed is the heart in which Thou dost not dwell?
Thou hast entered every heart: all that exists art Thou.
Whether sage or fool, whether Hindu or Mussalman,
Thou makest them as Thou wilt: all that exists art Thou.
Thy presence is everywhere, whether in heaven or in Kaaba;
Before Thee all must bow, for Thou art all that exists.
From earth below to the highest heaven, from heaven to deepest earth,
I see Thee wherever I look: all that exists art Thou.
Pondering, I have understood; I have seen it beyond a doubt;
I find not a single thing that may be compared to Thee.
To Jafar [the composer] it has been revealed that Thou art all that exists. — *Translator*

Narendra later related this to us: "That day my mind underwent a

15. Narendra's extraordinary experience as a result of the Master's touch.

complete revolution at the marvellous touch of the Master. I was aghast to realize that there really was nothing whatsoever in the entire universe but God. I remained silent, wondering how long this state of mind would continue. It didn't pass away all day. I got back home, and I felt just the same there: Everything I saw was God. I sat down to eat, and I saw that everything — the plate, the food, my mother who was serving it, and I myself — everything was God and nothing but God. I swallowed a couple of mouthfuls and then sat still without speaking. My mother lovingly asked me: 'Why are you so quiet? Why don't you eat?' That brought me back to everyday consciousness and I began eating again. But from then on I kept having the same experience, no matter what I was doing — eating, sitting, lying down, or going to college. It was a kind of intoxication that I can't describe. If I were crossing a street and saw a carriage coming towards me, I didn't have the urge to get out of its way for fear of being run over, as I would ordinarily. I said to myself: 'I am that carriage. There's no difference between it and me.' During that time, I had no sensation in my hands or my feet. When I ate food, I felt no satisfaction from it; it was as if someone else were eating. Sometimes I would lie down in the middle of a meal and then get up again after a few minutes and go on eating. Thus, it happened on those days that I would eat far more than usual, but this never upset me. My mother became alarmed. She thought I was suffering from some terrible disease. 'He won't live long,' she would say.

"When that first intoxication lost some of its power, I began to see the world as though I were dreaming. When I went for a walk around Hedua, or Cornwallis Square [now Azadhind Bagh], I would knock my head against the iron railings to see if they were dream-railings or real ones. The loss of feeling in my hands and feet made me afraid that I was becoming paralyzed. That overwhelming intoxication didn't leave me for some time. When I did at last return to normal consciousness, I was convinced that the state I'd been in was a revelation of nondualistic experience. And then I knew that what is written in the scriptures about this experience is all true. From that time on, I had no doubts about the truth of nonduality."

On another occasion Narendra described a wonderful incident to us. He

16. The author has an eventful day with Narendra.

told us about it in the winter of 1884, when we were well acquainted. We believe that the incident must have taken place during this period, so we are relating it to the reader here. We remember going to Narendra's house at Gaur Mohan Mukherjee Street in Simla on that day a little before noon and staying till eleven at night. Swami Ramakrishnananda was with us. Since our first meeting, we had felt a divine attraction to Narendra, and this feeling was intensified a thousandfold that day. Before this we understood the

Master to be a knower of God or a perfected soul. But on that day Narendra's inspired talks brought a new light to our hearts. We realized that the extraordinary events recorded in the lives of Jesus, Chaitanya, and other great teachers of the world, which we had studied but disbelieved, had parallels in the Master's daily life. With merely a touch, or his desire that it be so, the Master released from bondage those who had taken refuge in him and granted them devotion. He granted them samadhi, thus endowing them with divine bliss. Or he diverted the course of their lives into a spiritual channel so strong that they attained a vision of God immediately and were blessed forever. We remember that in the evening Narendra took us for a walk in Cornwallis Square. On the way he told us of divine experiences that he had experienced by the grace of the Master. He was absorbed within himself for a while and then finally expressed his inner bliss with his heavenly voice:

> Gora[5] bestows the Nectar of love;
> Jar after jar he pours it out,
> And still there is no end!
> Sweetest Nitai[6] is summoning all;
> Beloved Gora bids them come;
> Shantipur[7] is almost drowned,
> And Nadia is flooded with love!

When he had finished singing, Narendra gently soliloquized: "He is actually distributing love. Love, devotion, knowledge, liberation, and whatever one desires — Gora [Sri Ramakrishna] is bestowing upon us whatever he wishes. What wonderful power!" He was silent for a while and then continued. "One night, I was lying on my bed with the door bolted. Suddenly he attracted me — or rather the soul that lives in this body — and drew me to Dakshineswar. He talked with me about various topics, gave me advice, and finally allowed me to return home. He can do anything — this Gora of Dakshineswar can do anything!"

17. Narendra relates an amazing story.

The evening shadows melted into a darkness so deep that we could not see each other. But it was not necessary to do so: Narendra's fiery spiritual feelings penetrated our hearts, creating a divine intoxication that left us reeling. We felt as though the real world that we had perceived for so long had disappeared into a dream. We then realized the truth of what worldly people believe to be nothing but a fabrication: the beginningless, infinite God had become manifest as a finite human being out of His unconditional grace and was destroying the bondage of jivas and setting in motion the

18. Narendra's unusual experience at the author's house.

---

5. Gora is the nickname of Gauranga, or Chaitanya. — *Translator*
6. Nitai is the main disciple of Chaitanya. — *Translator*
7. Shantipur and Nadia are places associated with Chaitanya. — *Translator*

wheel of dharma. We did not notice how the time passed, but suddenly we heard the bell strike nine. Reluctantly, we prepared to take leave of Narendra, but he said, "Let us go — I'll accompany you for a short distance."

As we walked we began discussing a similar topic, which absorbed us until we reached our home in Champatala. We realized that it was not right for us to have let Narendra come such a long distance. We brought him inside, gave him some refreshment, accompanied him to his home, and then returned home once more. We vividly remember another incident: When Narendra entered our house, he suddenly stood still, exclaiming: "I have seen this house before! It's amazing! I'm familiar with its corridors, rooms, and everything!" Elsewhere we have told the reader that Narendra some-times had such experiences and what he said was their cause, so we will not repeat that here (see V.5.2).

Chapter 7

The Master's *M*ethods of Testing, and Narendra

WE HAVE ALREADY EXPLAINED HOW, FROM THEIR FIRST meeting, the Master saw extraordinary signs in Narendra and ascertained that he was an aspirant of the highest calibre. He then bound Narendra to him with a cord of selfless love, tested him at times, and began to teach him various aspects of spiritual life.

When the Brahmo Samaj was on the verge of splitting over the difference of opinion regarding the Coochbehar marriage, the Master told Keshab: "You've taken anybody and everybody without testing them, merely to increase your society's numbers. So is it any wonder that your group is dissolving? I never accept anyone without testing them." It is truly amazing how the Master tested his devotees in various ways, with or without their knowledge. How did he who presented himself to society as an illiterate person master unseen and unheard-of methods for gauging human character? Was it due to a reemergence of knowledge acquired in his past lives? Did this ability arise from the extrasensory vision and omniscience that he had attained through sadhana as the rishis had? Or did that wisdom become manifest by virtue of his being an incarnation of God, as he declared himself to his intimate devotees? Although ideas such as these come to mind, we shall not discuss them at present. We shall describe events as accurately as possible and leave the reader to form his or her own conclusion.

> 1. The Master's distinctive way of testing human character.

The reader will understand the uniqueness of the means that the Master used to evaluate human character if we mention some relevant events. But before we begin, we should explain certain things regarding those methods. When a man

> 2. The Master's general method of examination.

first came to the Master, he observed him very closely. If he felt attracted to the visitor, he talked about spiritual matters with him and asked him to visit occasionally. As the days passed and the visits continued, unknown to the visitor, the Master would examine the formation of his body and his limbs, the nature of his thoughts, the degree of his attachment to lust and gold, the magnitude of his worldly desires, and the extent to which the visitor's mind was being drawn towards him. After the Master had collected these data by keenly observing the man's movements, actions, and conversations, he arrived at a firm conclusion about the visitor's latent spirituality. Thus, the Master became convinced of a man's character after having seen him a few times. If the Master felt that he needed to know hidden facts about the man's inner nature, he would then use his subtle yogic vision to learn about them. He once told us about this: "When I'm alone in the early hours of the morning, I think of your spiritual welfare. The Divine Mother then shows me how far one devotee has advanced on the spiritual path, why another cannot make progress, and so on." From this, however, do not conclude that his yogic power was active only at that time. Other conversations indicated that he could ascend to high states of spiritual consciousness and obtain similar visions at will. He told us, "Just as by merely looking at a glass case one can see all of its contents, so I can know the inmost thoughts and tendencies — indeed everything about someone — merely by looking at that person."

Although the Master adopted the general method described above to judge human character, he modified it to some extent for special devotees and applied other methods also. We have seen that he met his special devotees for the first time while inspired by the divine and in a high spiritual state. Elsewhere we have mentioned in this book (see III.3.3, 22-26) that the Master's body and mind had become wonderful instruments to hold and transmit subtle spiritual power by virtue of his extraordinary sadhana. This was literally true. We noticed that when the Master met a devotee who was imbued with a particular spiritual mood, suddenly the Master's mind would be divinely inspired to assume the same mood. And when he found that devotees who came to him had already ascended to a spiritual plane by virtue of their own efforts and of good tendencies from past lives, the Master's mind would go to those realms as soon as such devotees arrived in order to ascertain the facts of those devotees' inner lives. The reader will understand what we mean by recalling our earlier narration of the Master's experiences during Narendra's first visit to him.

3. The Master's ecstasy when he first meets advanced souls.

The Master did not exempt his intimate devotees from the methods that he usually used to evaluate human character. When he was present in the normal plane, he applied the same methods equally and observed those devotees' movements, conduct, and conversations. He was not satisfied until he had tested Narendra in this

4. Four kinds of tests.

way. So it is extremely important that the reader understand the Master's methods of evaluation. These tests can be divided into four main categories. We have introduced this subject earlier (see V.7.2); now we shall explain those four categories and provide examples.

The Master ascertained newcomers' predominant tendencies by

| 5. (1) Using physiog-nomy to determine inner tendencies. | observing their physiognomy and other physical characteristics. |

Every thought when it is acted upon, leaves an impression on the brain and affects particular parts of the body. Modern physiology and psychology have proven this fact to a great extent, substantiating this belief that the Vedas and other scriptures have always affirmed. Hindu philosophical and religious books unanimously agree that "the mind builds the body" and that one's physical form changes according to one's good or evil thoughts and propensities. Many common proverbs therefore concern ascertaining a person's character by examining the body and limbs. That is why during ceremonies such as marriage or initiation, it is considered necessary to examine the hands, feet, and other body parts of the bride or disciple.

It is not surprising that the Master, believing as he did in the scriptures,

| 6. The Master's unique knowledge in this respect. | should have examined the shape of the body and the limbs of his disciples. Sometimes in the course of |

conversation he told us so many facts on this subject that we were dumbfounded, and we wondered where he had obtained so much information. We thought that perhaps in ancient times there was a tome on that, and that he had learned these things by reading that book or hearing it recited. This thought, however, is groundless: We have neither seen nor heard of such a book. Amazed, we listened to his descriptions of how the formation of each limb and sense organ of men and women resembled everyday objects, and how each resemblance had a meaning. For example, the Master said about human eyes: "Some people have eyes like lotus petals, some like a bull's eyes, and some possess the eyes of a yogi or of a god. Those who have eyes like lotus petals are endowed with good and spiritual tendencies. Those whose eyes are like a bull's have a strong sex drive. A yogi's eyes have an upward look and a reddish tinge. Divine eyes are not very large but are long and stretch nearly to the ears. Those who glance to the side or look from the corner of their eyes while talking are more intelligent than the average person."

He also spoke of the general formation of the body: "Those who have a devotional temperament have a naturally soft body, and the joints of their hands and feet are flexible. And if their bodies are lean, their muscles and tendons are so shaped that they do not appear angular." To ascertain whether a person's mind was inclined towards good or evil, he would weigh the person's hand and forearm, from the fingers to the elbow, in his own hand. If he found the weight to be less than usual, he concluded that the person's mind had positive tendencies. We have already mentioned that when Swami Premananda first went to Dakshineswar, the Master weighed his forearm (see V.5.13). Because at that time he did not say why he did so, we could not mention anything about it at that point. But we now know that the Master used this method to determine whether a person had good or evil tendencies, which we learned another day from the following incident.

When the Master was living in the Cossipore garden house and suffering

7. Ascertaining good and evil tendencies by testing the weight of one's forearm.

from cancer, the author's younger brother, Charu-chandra Chakrabarty, came to visit him one day. The Master was very pleased to see him. He made him sit nearby, questioned him about various things, and gave him many spiritual instructions. When the author came in, the Master asked him, "Is this your younger brother?" When the author admitted that he was, the Master said: "He's a fine boy. He's more intelligent than you are. Let me see if he has good or bad tendencies." Saying so, the Master held the boy's forearm with his own hands and weighing it, said, "Yes, he has good tendencies." He then asked the author, while pointing to his brother: "Shall I draw him?" He meant, should he draw his mind away from the world and turn it towards God. "What do you say?" The author replied: "It would be nice, sir. Please do so." The Master thought for a while and then said: "No, no more. I've already taken one. If I take another, your parents, especially your mother, will be very grieved. I have displeased many a Shakti[1] in my life. No more now." The Master then gave further instructions to the author's brother, offered him some refreshments, and bade him good-bye.

The Master used to say: "Like the formation of the limbs, physiological

8. Differences in daily bodily functions indicate different tendencies.

functions such as sleep, evacuation, and other ordi-nary actions, differ according to people's particular mental tendencies. Experienced observers can find indications of human character in those things. For example, people don't all breathe the same way while sleeping. A worldly person breathes one way, a person of renunciation another. While answering the call of nature, the former's urine slants to the left while flowing and the latter's to the right. Pigs will not touch a yogi's faeces."

The Master told us an incident to illustrate this subject. During Mathur's

9. Hanuman Singh, a gatekeeper.

time, a man named Hanuman Singh was hired as a temple guard at Dakshineswar. He commanded great respect among the other guards not only because he was a famous wrestler but also because he was a steadfast devotee of Mahavir Hanuman. Once another wrestler came to Dakshineswar to chal-lenge him to a wrestling match; the winner would assume Singh's position.

---

1. Women, who embody the creating and sustaining powers of the Divine Mother.

Although Hanuman Singh could see his opponent's gigantic body and his physical strength, he did not shy away from the competition. A day was fixed. Mathur and some others were to judge the match.

A week before the day of the competition, the challenger began to eat huge quantities of nutritious food and to practise various physical exercises. Hanuman Singh, however, followed his usual routine: He bathed early in the morning, repeated the mantra of his Chosen Deity throughout the day, and ate his only meal in the evening. People thought that Hanuman Singh was frightened and had given up hope for a victory. The Master was very fond of Singh, so the day before the competition, he said to him: "You haven't made your body fit by exercising and eating nutritious food. How will you compete with the new wrestler?" Hanuman Singh bowed down respectfully and replied: "Master, if you bestow your grace on me, I'll definitely win. One can't gain strength merely by eating a huge quantity of food; one must digest it. I secretly checked the faeces of the new wrestler and found that he has been eating food beyond his digestive power." The Master later told us that Hanuman Singh defeated his opponent.

The Master also told us various things about the formation of a woman's

| 10. Ascertaining *vidya* or *avidya shakti* by observing a woman's physical form and behaviour. |

limbs, similar to what he said about the shape of a man's body. Observing these, the Master indicated that some women had *vidya shakti*, or a divine nature, and some had *avidya shakti*, or a demoniacal nature. He said: "Those with a divine nature eat and sleep little. Their desire for sense enjoyment is also less. Their hearts are filled with joy when they hear about God and when they talk about Him with their husbands. They protect their husbands from base tendencies and sinful acts by giving them spiritual inspiration. They help their husbands in every way so that they may eventually be blessed by realizing God.

"The character and behaviour of women with a demoniacal nature are the opposite. They eat and sleep more, and their appetite for physical comfort and enjoyment is greater. Their chief aim is to prevent their husbands from focussing on anything other than giving them happiness. If their husbands talk about spiritual subjects to them, they become angry rather than pleased." The Master sometimes mentioned that the external shape of a woman's organ of procreation indicates her desire for sense pleasures. These organs take different shapes, some of which indicate less animal instinct. In addition, he said that the animal instinct is extremely strong in the minds of women whose posteriors are prominent like those of ants.

Thus, the Master told us numerous ways to determine human character

| 11. The Master's comment on Narendra's physical characteristics. |

by observing physiognomical signs. He considered physiognomy to be one of the means for determining human character, and he tested Narendra and all other devotees with this method to greater or lesser degrees. After examining

Narendra, he was pleased and one day told him: "You have all the good marks on your body; the only defect is that you breathe heavily when sleeping. Yogis say that this indicates a short life."

The Master's second and third means of learning about human character were by observing people's ordinary behaviour, and thereby evaluating their mental tendencies and their degree of attachment to lust and gold. When a new-comer came to Dakshineswar, the Master would use those techniques as he silently observed that person for a while. When he later decided to accept that man into his inner circle, he would give him various instructions and, if necessary, some sweet scolding to correct his defects. But before accepting anyone into his inner circle, the Master would decide whether to mould that person's life as a monk or as a householder devotee. That is why he first inquired of newcomers whether they were married or single, whether their family lacked any bare necessities, and whether a close relative could maintain the family if they renounced their home.

> 12. The Master ascertained the inner tendencies of people (2) by watching their trivial actions and (3) by evaluating what those actions revealed about their attachment to lust and gold.

The Master was always very fond of students. He said: "Their minds aren't yet distracted by wife and children, name and fame. If they are properly trained, they can easily focus their minds exclusively on God." This is why he made special efforts to impart spiritual ideas to them. He expressed this view through various sayings: "The mind is like a packet of mustard seeds: Once scattered, it's almost impossible to gather them up." "Once the coloured ring appears around a parrot's neck, it's difficult to teach it to say 'Radha-Krishna.'" "A cow's hoofprints on unbaked tiles can easily be smoothed over, but once the tiles are baked, the prints cannot be removed." He therefore carefully questioned students who were inexperienced in worldly life to learn whether they tended towards worldly enjoyment or renunciation. He trained them for renunciation if he found them fit for it.

> 13. The Master's opinion regarding young students.

The Master did not stop at questioning a disciple to ascertain his tendencies. He also thoroughly investigated the disciple to determine how simple and truthful he was, whether he really practised what he professed, whether he used discrimination in all his actions, and how well he understood the Master's instructions. The reader will understand this subject from the following examples.

> 14. The Master observed every one of his disciple's actions.

After one young student had visited Dakshineswar a few times, the Master asked him, "Why don't you marry?" The student replied: "Sir, my mind isn't yet under my control. If I marry now, I shall become attached to my wife and lose discrimination between right and wrong. If I ever conquer lust, I shall marry." The Master

> 15. Examples.

understood that although the boy had a strong attraction to sense enjoyment, his mind was tending towards the path of renunciation. Laughing, the Master responded, "When you have conquered lust, you won't need to marry at all."

While talking to another boy at Dakshineswar, the Master said: "Can you explain this? I can't always keep my cloth around my waist. Sometimes it comes loose and drops off without my knowledge. I'm an old man and I walk around naked, yet I'm not ashamed. I've never cared whether people saw me naked. But now I notice that some people feel embarrassed, so I keep my cloth in my lap. Can you move around naked in front of people as I do?" The boy replied: "Sir, I'm not sure. But if you ask me, I can take off my cloth." The Master said: "Try it. Take off your cloth, wrap it around your head, and walk around the temple courtyard." The boy replied: "No, sir, I can't. I can do it only in front of you." The Master then said: "Yes, others say the same thing. They say, 'We aren't ashamed to take the cloth off in front of you, but we can't do so before others.'"

We remember another incident in this connection which occurred on a

| 16. The Ganges' flood tide. |

moonlit night perhaps a couple of nights after the full moon. Shortly after we had gone to bed, the flood tide came to the Ganges. The Master left his bed and ran towards the embankment, calling to us, "Come, come and see the incoming flood tide!" As he watched the formerly calm and white water of the Ganges rising in huge foamy waves, moving upward with tremendous force, and splashing against the embankment, the Master began to dance joyfully like a boy. We had been sleeping when the Master called us, so it took a little while for us to follow him, as we had to get up and fasten our cloths properly. The flood tide had passed by the time we arrived at the embankment. Some got a little glimpse of its beauty and some did not see it at all. The Master was absorbed in his own joy. When the flood tide had passed, he turned to us and asked, "Well, how did you enjoy the flood tide?" Hearing that it had moved away while we were dressing, he said: "You fools! Did you think that the tide would wait for you to dress? Why didn't you leave your clothes behind as I did?"

Sometimes the Master asked his young disciples: "Do you have any

| 17. Perform all actions knowing that the goal of life is to realize God. |

desire to marry? Will you take a job?" Some of us would reply, "Sir, I have no desire for marriage, but I will have to take a job to support myself." This answer was unreasonable to the Master because he was a great lover of freedom. He said: "If you won't marry and perform family duties, why should you be a slave to someone else all your life?" His view was: "Give your entire heart to God and worship Him. Once one is born in this world, there is no greater duty than that. If it isn't possible [to remain single], then marry, but make the realization of God your highest goal and always maintain yourself through honest means." The Master felt terribly hurt if he heard that any of the disciples whom he considered moderately or highly gifted spiritual aspirants had married, or had taken a job for pay like ordinary people without any specific need to do so, or were working to achieve name and fame, wasting their energy. When he heard that one of his young disciples (Swami Niranjanananda) had accepted a job, the Master told him: "It's all right that you've taken a job to support your elderly mother; if it were otherwise I couldn't have looked at you again." When another young devotee (Junior Naren) came to see him at the Cossipore garden house after his marriage, the Master grieved as if he had lost a son. He wept bitterly, throwing his arms around the boy's neck and telling him repeatedly, "Try not to forget God and sink into the world completely."

Some of the devotees misunderstood the saying "One cannot make progress without faith," and in their exuberant devotion, they began to believe everything and everyone. As soon as the Master noticed this, he understood the disciples' mistakes and cautioned them. In fact, he advised all of his devotees to tread the spiritual path with faith and never to give up discrimination between the real and the unreal. We think that he meant that one should first exercise discrimination, then continue along the spiritual path. One should never try to perform worldly duties without discriminating between right and wrong.

18. Simple faith in God and simple-mindedness are not the same; one should discriminate between the real and the unreal.

Once one of his disciples (Swami Yogananda) went to the market and bought an iron pan. But instead of examining it before paying, he merely appealed to the shopkeeper's religious sensibility. After returning home he found that the pan was cracked. When the Master heard about this, he reproved the disciple: "Should you be a fool just because you're a devotee of God? Do you think a shopkeeper sets up business to practise religion and that you must trust his words? Why didn't you examine the pan before purchasing it? Never act so foolishly again. When you go shopping, first determine the usual price of the item by going around to several shops. Then thoroughly examine the thing you want to buy. And don't fail to demand the little extras where allowed."

Some people who enter spiritual life develop so much compassion that it eventually becomes a burden on them and even drags them down from the path of spirituality. This happens very often with men and women who have a soft nature. The Master always instructed such people to be firm and those with the opposite nature to be gentle. One of our friends (Swami Yogananda) was very mild. We never saw him get angry or abuse anyone even when there was just cause. Even though it was quite against his nature and inclination, he married merely because he could not stand to see his mother cry. Because he fell victim to his

19. The Master advises people to be compassionate or stern according to their individual natures.

Niranjan (1862-1904), later
Swami Niranjanananda.
Photo taken at Alambazar
Math in 1896.

Jogin (1861-1899),
later Swami Yogananda.
Photo taken at Alambazar
Math in 1896.

own karma, the Master's grace and reassurance saved him from his terrible despair and repentance on that occasion. The Master watched over him closely, helping him to control his excessive mildness and compassion and to perform every action with proper discrimination. How the Master trained him even in trivial matters will be clear if we cite a couple of incidents.

One day a cockroach was found in a trunk in which the Master's clothes and other belongings were kept. The Master said to Yogananda, "Catch the cockroach, take it out, and kill it." But Swami Yogananda did not kill it. Instead, he took it outside the room and let it go. When he returned, the Master asked, "Did you kill it?" Embarrassed, Yogananda replied, "No, sir; I let it go." Then the Master scolded him, saying: "I told you to kill the cockroach, but you let it go! Always do exactly as I tell you. Otherwise, in more important matters later on you will also follow your own whims and come to grief."

One day Swami Yogananda was returning from Calcutta to Dakshi-

20. His advice to Swami Yogananda.

neswar by boat. When a passenger asked, he said that he was going to Rani Rasmani's Kali temple to see Sri Ramakrishna. At this, the passenger began criticizing the Master for no reason. He said: "Ramakrishna only pretends to be holy. He eats good food, sleeps on a cozy bed, and turns the heads of schoolboys under the pretext of religion." Yogananda was terribly hurt as he listened to this slander. At first he thought that he should rebuke the man, but his gentle nature prevailed as he thought: "Well, people don't know Sri Ramakrishna, so they have strange ideas about him and criticize him. What can I do?" So he remained silent, leaving the man's baseless remarks unchallenged.

When he arrived at Dakshineswar, Yogananda told the Master what had happened. He expected that the humble Master would simply laugh at it, since he was indifferent to praise and blame and that the matter would end there. But he met with a grave response. The Master did not see the incident as Yogananda had expected, and told him: "That man spoke ill of me without any cause, and you sat in silence and did nothing! Do you know what the scriptures say? A disciple should cut off the head of anyone who speaks ill of his guru, or he should leave the place at once. You didn't protest against these false accusations?"

The following incident, which is similar to the last one, will help the reader

21. In a similar situation the Master has different advice for Niranjan.

understand how the Master taught according to an individual's nature. Niranjan had a violent temper. Once on a boat trip to Dakshineswar he overheard some passengers speaking ill of Sri Ramakrishna for no reason. At first he protested vehemently, but the speakers ignored him. Enraged, Niranjan jumped to his feet and began to rock the boat, threatening to capsize it in midstream. Niranjan was very strong and an expert swimmer. Seeing his fury, the passengers became frightened and they begged to be forgiven. Only then did he calm down.

When the Master heard about this incident, he scolded Niranjan, saying: "Anger is a deadly sin. You ought never to let it carry you away. The anger of a good man is like a mark made on water — it vanishes instantly. Mean people say many things. If you want to fight with them, you'll spend your whole life quarrelling. In such cases, think of those people as being no more than insects. Be indifferent to what they say. See what a great crime you were about to commit under the influence of anger! Think of the boatmen — you were ready to drown them too, and they had done nothing!"

The advice that the Master gave to women devotees was similar to what

22. An example of the Master's similar advice to a woman devotee.

he told men. We remember that he once cautioned an extremely soft-hearted woman in this way: "Suppose a man you know takes great pains to help you on every occasion. However, you feel that this is because he's enchanted by your beauty and is too weak to break the spell. In that case would you be gentle to him? Wouldn't you instead give him a hard kick and stay away from him forever? So you see, you can't always treat everyone kindly under all conditions. There is a limit to showing kindness; one should consider time, place, and person."

We remember another incident in this connection. Harish was a strong

23. The story of Harish.

young man. He had a beautiful wife, a young son, and sufficient means to support his family. But after he had visited the Master in Dakshineswar a few times, he developed a strong antipathy to worldly life. The Master was pleased by his steadfast devotion and his simple, gentle nature and allowed him to stay in Dakshineswar. Harish began to spend most of his time there serving the Master and practising japa and meditation. Nothing could dissuade him from his purpose: His guardians began to pressure him; his father-in-law cordially invited him to return home; and his wife wept bitterly. He paid no attention to these entreaties or threats. Instead, he remained silent and went on in his own way. Sometimes the Master would draw our attention to Harish's calm and steadfast nature, saying, "Real men should be dead [to worldly affairs] while living, like Harish."

One day the news arrived at Dakshineswar that Harish's family was very

24. "This is no time to show kindness."

upset because he had given up all of his responsibilities and was engaging himself in spiritual disciplines. His wife was so grief-stricken at being separated from him for so long that she refused to eat and drink. Upon hearing this, Harish remained silent as before. To test him, the Master spoke to him privately and said: "Your wife is very anxious to see you. Why don't you go to see her once? She has almost no one to look after her.[2] What's the harm in showing her a little kindness?" Harish replied humbly: "Sir, this is no time to

2. Perhaps the Master said this because Harish's mother was not then alive.

show kindness. If I try to be kind to my wife, I'll be overwhelmed with maya and attachment, and I might forget the main purpose of life. Pray, don't ask me to do that." This reply greatly pleased the Master, and he often repeated Harish's words to us, praising his spirit of renunciation.

We can mention many instances in which the Master observed our daily routines and thereby understood the good and bad qualities of our minds. When he saw Niranjan eating too much ghee, he said: "My goodness, you take so much ghee! Will you one day abduct someone's daughter or daughter-in-law?" When one of us slept too much, the Master was displeased with him for some time. When one of the boys got deeply involved in studying medicine, despite his disapproval, the Master said to him: "You are supposed to renounce your desires, but you are increasing them instead! How will you make any spiritual progress?" We have cited many other examples in connection with other topics, so we will add no more here.

> 25. The Master's advice to different people after observing their daily routines.

The Master did not stop at merely ascertaining his disciples' characters through the methods described earlier and by gradually correcting their defects; he often inquired how those instructions were being carried out. In addition, he adopted another means for ascertaining the spiritual progress of a particular person. This is the fourth method.

> 26. (4) The Master observed the extent of a person's spiritual progress by determining if that person recognized the highest manifestation of spirituality in him.

When a disciple first started coming to him, the Master would inquire whether the disciple's faith and devotion were increasing. To ascertain this, he would sometimes ask that disciple how he understood the Master's spiritual state and manner. Or the Master would observe the disciple to see if he had complete faith in his words. He might also introduce this person to some intimate disciples with a similar character, so that by close association, the newcomer would develop a deep spirituality. The Master was not certain of a disciple's spiritual future until he had accepted the Master — intuitively and of his own accord — as the embodiment of the highest spiritual ideal of the world.

The foregoing statement will undoubtedly surprise the reader. But a little thought makes it clear that while there is some reason to be surprised at the idea, it was nonetheless reasonable and natural for the Master to act that way. Because the Master realized absolutely that he embodied a unique manifestation of spirituality, he had no alternative than to behave accordingly. We have tried to explain this elsewhere in this book. The Master had endured long and superhuman austerities and meditation, and he had attained samadhi, thus destroying any trace of egoism and eliminating any chance of delusion or error. He was

> 27. Why it was natural for the Master to evaluate someone's spiritual progress using this method.

then granted an uninterrupted memory of his past incarnations, as well as infinite knowledge, and he realized in the depths of his heart that the new spiritual ideal that was manifesting through his mind and body had never before been witnessed. So naturally he had to believe that those who truly understood this and tried to mould their lives in the light of the ideal he presented would find their spiritual progress to be easy and smooth. For this reason, it is not surprising that he carefully inquired whether his disciples realized that he embodied the highest spiritual ideal and whether they were committed to building their lives in accordance with it.

The Master expressed this conviction to us in various ways. He would say: "The currency during the reign of a *Nawab* [a Muslim governor] cannot be legal tender during the reign of a *Badsha* [a Muslim emperor]." "If you follow my instructions, you will reach the goal directly." "Those who have reached their last birth —who have finished the repeated cycle of birth and death in this world — will come here and accept the spiritual ideas and ideals of this place" (see IV.4.48-50). "Your Chosen Deity is within this (*pointing to himself*). If you meditate on this, you meditate on your Chosen Deity."

The reader will understand this if we mention a few examples of how the Master discovered whether the above ideal was gradually gaining ground in his disciples' hearts.

Those who had the great fortune of meeting the Master and receiving his grace knew that sometimes he would suddenly ask them privately, or in front of a few other devotees, "Well, what do you think of me?" He generally asked that question after a devotee had visited Dakshineswar a few times and was somewhat acquainted with him. Sometimes he would ask the question during the first meeting and sometimes a short while thereafter. We know that he asked this question during the very first meeting with those devotees whom he had seen through his yogic vision long before their arrival. Each of his disciples answered differently when asked. Someone said, "You are a real sadhu." Others said: "A true devotee of God"; "A Mahapurusha — a great soul"; "A Siddhapurusha — a perfect soul"; "An incarnation of God"; "Sri Chaitanya himself"; "Lord Shiva himself"; "You are God," and so on. Some who belonged to the Brahmo Samaj and did not believe in divine incarnations, said, "You are a lover of God, of the same rank as Krishna, Buddha, Jesus, and Chaitanya." A Christian named Williams[3] expressed this opinion: "You are Jesus Christ, the Son of God, the embodiment of Eternal Consciousness." We cannot say how far these people really

> 28. Each devotee had a different answer to the Master's question, "What do you think of me?"

---

3. We are reliably informed that Williams, after he had seen the Master a few times, became convinced that he was a divine incarnation. He gave up the world at the Master's advice, went to the Himalayas to the north of the Punjab, and passed away there after practising hard austerities.

understood the Master, but their answers indicate what they thought of him and what their conception of God was. The Master evidently understood the answers in that light. He behaved with and instructed these disciples according to their spiritual outlook and temperament. As the embodiment of all spiritual moods, the Master did not disturb anyone's belief. Instead, he helped the disciples to grow in their own ways so that they might eventually realize God, the Highest Truth beyond space and time. But he always carefully observed whether the disciple answered his question from sincere conviction or merely copied others.

When Purna first came to the Master, he was a mere boy, just a little over

29. First example: Purnachandra and "the kidnapping teacher."

thirteen years old. Mahendra Nath Gupta, a great devotee of the Master, was then headmaster of the Shyambazar School established by Ishwar Chandra Vidyasagar. Whenever he saw that any of his young students were devoted to God, he would take them to the Master at Dakshineswar. Tejachandra, Narayan, Haripada, Binod, Junior Naren, Pramatha (Paltu), and other boys from the Baghbazar area came to the Master in this manner. For this reason, some of us humourously called Mahendra "the kidnapping teacher." When the Master heard this, he laughed and said, "That is an appropriate name." Once while Mahendra was teaching a class of eighth-grade students, he was impressed with Purna's fine nature and sweet talk; shortly afterwards he arranged to introduce Purna to the Master. This arrangement was made secretly because Purna's guardians were very strict and of a harsh temperament. If by chance the visit became known to them, both teacher and student would be humiliated. Purna therefore came to school at the usual time, went to Dakshineswar in a hired carriage, returned to school before it closed, and then went home as usual.

The Master was highly pleased to meet Purna that day. He very affection-

30. The Master is pleased to meet Purna and talks about Purna's high spiritual state.

ately gave him some spiritual instructions and light refreshments. As Purna was leaving, the Master told him: "Come here whenever you find an opportunity. Take a carriage. You can get your carriage fare from here." Later, the Master told us: "Purna is a part of Narayana and a spiritual aspirant endowed with a high degree of sattva. In this respect he may be said to occupy a place just below Narendra (Swami Vivekananda). Long ago I saw in a vision those who would be coming to attain spirituality. Purna's arrival completes that class of devotees. No one else of this calibre will come in the future."

On that day Purna's spiritual mood was awakened. Memories of his past

31. The Master is very affectionate towards Purna.

relationship with the Master were revived, and he became completely calm and indrawn, with tears of joy rolling down his cheeks. Fearing his guardians, he controlled himself with great effort and returned home. From then on, the

Mahendra Nath Gupta
(1854-1932), known as M.,
who recorded *The Gospel of
Sri Ramakrishna*.

Purna Chandra Ghosh
(1871-1913)

Master was extremely eager to see Purna and to feed him. Whenever he found an opportunity, he sent various kinds of food to him through a devotee. He would instruct that person to give the food to Purna privately, for if his guardians found out, he could be punished.

We sometimes saw the Master profusely shedding tears in his eagerness

| 32. The Master's eagerness to see Purna. He asks Purna during their second meeting, "What do you think of me?" |

to see Purna. When he saw that his behaviour surprised us, he said: "You're amazed by my attraction to Purna. I wonder what you would have thought if you'd seen how I longed for Narendra in the beginning and how restless for him I was." From that point on, whenever the Master was eager to see Purna, he would come to Calcutta at noon and wait at Balaram's or someone else's house near Purna's school. He would then send someone to bring Purna to him. Thus, Purna met the Master for a second time in one of those places [Balaram's house] and was completely overwhelmed. On that occasion the Master fed him with his own hand like a loving mother and asked him: "Tell me, what do you think of me?" Overcome by exuberant devotion, Purna replied without hesitation, "You are God Himself, incarnated in flesh and blood!"

The Master was filled with wonder and joy when he knew that the young

| 33. The Master was delighted by Purna's answer, and he gave him spiritual instructions. |

Purna had accepted him as the highest spiritual ideal. He blessed Purna wholeheartedly, initiated him with a mantra, and gave him some spiritual instructions in secret. After he had returned to Dakshineswar, the Master told us: "Well, Purna is a mere boy and his intellect hasn't yet matured. How did he recognize me as an incarnation of God? Under the influence of a divine nature, some others have also answered that question as he did. It must be due to impressions accumulated over past lives that the truth in its entirety is naturally revealed in their pure sattvic minds."

It so happened that circumstances forced Purna to marry and lead a

| 34. Purna's greatness, although he was a householder. |

family life. But those who were close to him unanimously described his unique faith, dependence on God, love for sadhana, humility, and self-sacrifice in all situations.

We shall mention an example of the Master's asking this question of

| 35. Second example: The Master asks Vaikuntha the same question; his answer. |

another devotee. In the Master's room there was a picture of Chaitanya and his devotees singing kirtan. One day he pointed that picture out to one of our friends,[4] shortly after his first visit, and asked, "Do you see how absorbed they are in the divine mood?"

Vaikuntha: "Sir, they are low-class people."

The Master: "What are you saying? You shouldn't say that!"

___

4. Vaikuntha Nath Sanyal. — *Translator*

Vaikuntha: "Yes, sir. I come from Nadia,[5] and I know that only low-class people become Vaishnavas."

The Master: "Oh, your home is in Nadia? Then I salute you a second time.[6] Well, Ram and others say that this (*pointing to himself*) is an avatar. What do you think?"

Vaikuntha: "They estimate you very poorly, sir."

The Master: "What? They call me an incarnation of God and you think that is a poor estimation?"

Vaikuntha: "Yes, sir. An avatar is a part of God, but I look upon you as Shiva Himself."

The Master: "Indeed!"

Vaikuntha: "So indeed do I think of you. I can't help it. You asked me to meditate on Shiva. But though I try every day, I can't do so. Whenever I sit for meditation, your loving and blissful face appears before me in a luminous form. I can't replace it with the form of Shiva, nor do I want to. So I regard you as Shiva Himself."

The Master (*smiling*): "Is that so? But I know I'm as insignificant as a hair on your head. (*Both laughed.*) I've been anxious about you, but today I'm relieved."

We do not know whether Vaikuntha understood at that time why the Master made that last statement. Under similar circumstances our hearts were filled with joy, knowing that the Master was pleased, and we had no desire to know what his words meant. But now we understand that the Master said those words to Vaikuntha because he had accepted the Master as the highest spiritual ideal.

The Master made special efforts to ensure that his devotees would care-

36. Never trust a person whose words and actions do not agree.

fully observe every one of his actions and the manner in which he conducted himself, and accept him as the highest spiritual ideal only after they had understood him properly. He often told us, "Watch a sadhu [holy man] by day and by night, and then put your faith in him." The Master always encouraged us to discover whether a sadhu practised what he taught; he told us never to trust a man whose actions did not tally with his words and whose mind was not one with his speech. He told us the following story in this connection.

A man's young son continuously suffered from indigestion. The father

37. The Master's story about a physician and a sick boy.

took his boy to a famous physician in a remote village for treatment. The physician examined the boy and diagnosed his condition, but instead of prescribing any medicine, he asked them to return the next day.

5. Nadia is the birthplace of Chaitanya and of Bengal Vaishnavism. — *Translator*
6. It was the custom of the Master to salute a person as soon as he met him. That is why he said "a second time."

When the father went with his son on the following day, the physician told the boy: "Stop eating molasses and you will be cured. You don't need any other medicine." When the boy left the room, the father said to the doctor, "Sir, you could have easily said that yesterday and saved us the trouble of coming here again today." The physician replied: "I had a reason. You might have noticed yesterday that there were some jars of molasses in my room. If I had asked the boy to give up molasses then, he would have thought me a peculiar man indeed: 'This doctor enjoys molasses himself, and is now forbidding me to eat it.' If he had this thought in mind he would have had no faith in my words, and would have paid no heed to them. So I didn't give that instruction to the boy until I had removed the molasses from my room."

Thus encouraged by the Master, we carefully observed his conduct. Some of us did not hesitate to test him. He gladly put up with our excessive demands and unreasonable behaviour, understanding that we were sincerely trying to increase our faith and devotion. The reader will understand this clearly from the following example.

38. The devotees tested the Master.

We have already told the reader some stories about Swami Yogananda. The following incident concerned him, and he later told us about it. We shall first provide the reader with a brief biography of Yogananda, then narrate the story. Jogindra Nath Roy Chaudhury, who became Yogananda as a monk, was born into the family of the famous Savarna Chaudhury. His father, Navinchandra, was once a wealthy landowner; his family had lived in Dakshineswar for generations. Before Jogindra, or Jogin, was born, and when he was young, their house reverberated with the sounds of worship, kirtan, and recitals of the Mahabharata and the Bhagavata. The Master said that during his sadhana he visited Jogin's home many times to listen to discourses on Hari and was acquainted with some of his family members. Before Jogin had left his boyhood, however, the Chaudhury dynasty lost most of its property owing partly to a family dispute and partly to other reasons. The family eventually became poor.

39. An example: the story of Swami Yogananda.

From his childhood, Jogin was calm and humble, and had a sweet nature. He was born with extraordinarily noble qualities. As a boy developing self-awareness, he always thought that he was not of this world and that this was not his home: His real home was somewhere far-off among the stars and his true companions were still there. In later life, we never saw him angry. Swami Vivekananda said, "If any one of us has completely conquered lust, it is Jogin." Sometimes the Master scolded Jogin for his tendency to naïvely believe everyone, but Jogin was not foolish. He was always calmly occupied with his own duties, yet his discriminating mind was constantly observing the activities of others. Whatever opinion he formed about other people

40. Jogindra's good tendencies and intelligence.

invariably proved to be true. He therefore seemed to be a little proud of his intelligence.

As Jogin's home was in Dakshineswar, he was blessed to meet the Master when he was very young. When Jogin first arrived [at the Kali temple] and introduced himself, the Master was very pleased to see him. He was convinced that Jogin was one of those whom the Divine Mother had long ago shown him would come to him to attain spirituality. Moreover, he was one of the six ishwarakotis [godlike souls] whom the Divine Mother had later graciously revealed to him.

> 41. The Master recognizes Jogindra as an ishwarakoti.

We have stated elsewhere (see V.7.19) that Jogin precipitously married against his will, because of his mother's insistence and pathetic tears. Jogin told us: "As soon as I married, I thought that any hope for God-realization was now a mockery. Why should I go to the Master anymore? His first teaching was to renounce lust and gold. I thought that I'd ruined my life because of my tender heart. This decision couldn't be reversed. The sooner I died the better. I used to visit the Master daily, but after the wedding I stopped going to him altogether and spent my days in utter despair and repentance. But the Master didn't forsake me. He repeatedly sent messengers and called for me. When I disregarded his requests, he hit upon an unusual plan.

> 42. Jogindra marries, regrets it, and stops visiting the Master. The Master devises a means to bring him to the Kali temple, then reassures him.

"Before I married, a man from the Kali temple had given me a few rupees to buy something for him, and there were a few annas left. I sent the article to the man through a friend with a message that I would return the balance soon. When he heard of this the Master feigned anger and sent this message to me: 'What sort of man are you? A man gave you money to buy a certain article, and you haven't returned the balance or even sent word when you will return it!' These words wounded my heart. I thought: 'The Master considers me a cheat though he has known me for so long! Well, I'll go there today and somehow put an end to the quarrel. Afterwards, I'll never turn my steps towards the Kali temple.' Tormented with despair, repentance, wounded pride, and humiliation, I went to the Kali temple that afternoon.

"From a distance I could see the Master standing outside his room, as if in ecstasy, holding his cloth under his arm. As soon as he saw me, he quickly came forward and said: 'What if you are married? What is there to be afraid of? If you have the grace of this place [*meaning himself*], even a hundred thousand marriages are powerless to affect you. If you want to live a family life and realize God at the same time, bring your wife here once. I'll make both of you fit for that. And if you want to renounce worldly life and attain God, I'll make that possible for you as well.' The Master was in a semiecstatic state. His words penetrated my heart and the shadows of despair dissipated. With tearful eyes I bowed down to the Master. He affectionately caught hold of my hand and took me into his room. When I tried to raise the issue of settling accounts, he wouldn't listen to me at all."

Jogin was born with the attitude of an all-renouncing monk, and this did not change even when he married. He continued to serve the Master as before and to live under his protection. Jogin's parents began to complain when they saw their son's indifference to household duties and to earning money. Jogin said: "One day my mother complained, 'If you didn't want to earn money, why did you marry?' I replied: 'Didn't I tell you again and again that I had no intention of marrying? But I gave in to your tears.' My mother angrily retorted: 'What do you mean? How could you have married unless you wanted to do so?' Her words shocked me, but I remained speechless. I thought: 'O Lord, I was ready to forsake You to please my mother and now she talks like this? Forget it! The Master is the only person I've met in this world whose word and thought are in perfect accord.' From that day on, I was completely disgusted with the world. After this incident, I began to spend some nights with the Master."

Jogin once spent the day with the Master. That evening he watched as all

43. Jogindra stays at Dakshineswar overnight.

the devotees took their leave and left for their homes. Jogin set aside the idea of returning home that night so he could serve the Master if he needed anything. This pleased the Master. They talked about God till 10:00 p.m.; then the Master had a light supper and Jogin ate his dinner. The Master asked Jogin to make a bed in his room, and he went to his own bed. Sometime after midnight, the Master awoke and needed to answer the call of nature, but found that Jogin was in a deep sleep. The Master did not want to trouble him, so he walked alone towards the Panchavati and then to the pine grove.

Jogin had been a light sleeper throughout his life. Shortly after the Master

44. Jogin doubts the Master.

left, Jogin woke up to find the door open and the Master gone. Curious as to where the Master had gone this late at night, he checked the water pot that the Master used for washing and found it in its proper place. Then he thought that he might be walking outside. He came out of the room and found no one out in the moonlit night. Suddenly a terrible suspicion gripped him: "Has the Master gone to the nahabat to be with his wife? Can it be possible that his actions are contrary to his teachings?"

Jogin said: "As soon as the above thought arose in my mind, I became

45. His doubt is dispelled.

completely overwhelmed with suspicion, fear, and other unpleasant feelings. I then decided that although it might be terribly harsh and unpleasant, I must learn the truth. I stationed myself near the nahabat and watched its door. After a while, I heard the slapping sounds of the Master's slippers coming from the direction of the Panchavati. Soon the Master himself was before me. He saw me and asked, 'Hello, why are you standing here?' Embarrassed, I hung my head in shame and fear for having doubted the Master. I couldn't utter a single word. He understood everything from the expression on my face, and instead of taking offence, he assured me: 'Well, you're quite right. You must examine a sadhu by day and by night before believing in him.' With that, the Master asked me to follow him and proceeded towards his room. I could sleep no more that night thinking about the great offence that my suspicious nature had led me to."

Swami Yogananda completely atoned for his offence, first by surrendering

| 46. Jogindra surrenders to his guru. |

himself completely to his guru and serving him, and then by devoting his life to the service of the Holy Mother when the Master passed away. In the Ramakrishna Order it is rare to find a yogi and a man of samadhi so endowed with intense renunciation, knowledge, and devotion. He passed away in the beginning of 1899, merging into the Divine.

We have described earlier the way in which the Master had scrutinized

| 47. The Master's impression of Narendra after observing his actions. |

every one of Narendra's actions from the time he first came to Dakshineswar. He found Narendra's mind to be ablaze with spiritual hunger, self-control, courage, strength, self-sacrifice for a noble cause, and other good qualities. The Master further understood that Narendra's mind was so strongly endowed with good tendencies that it was not possible for him to behave meanly, as others do, even when tempted by adverse circumstances. Narendra's passion for truth was phenomenal. The Master was aware of Narendra's strict adherence to truth and not only trusted him completely, but was also convinced that Narendra would soon reach such a state when he would be unable to utter a falsehood, even accidentally. Furthermore the resolutions arising in his mind would always be fulfilled. For that reason, the Master always encouraged him in this, saying: "Whoever holds to truth in word, thought, and action is blessed by the vision of God, who is Truth Itself" and "One who observes truth in thought, word, and deed for twelve years reaches a state in which whatever he resolves comes to pass."

We remember an amusing incident concerning the Master's firm belief in

| 48. An amusing incident: Narendra mistakes a bat for a chataka bird. |

Narendra's truthfulness. Once in conversation the Master explained that the nature of a devotee is like a chataka bird. He said: "As the chataka bird drinks only rainwater, it is always looking to the clouds to quench its thirst. It depends completely on them. Similarly, devotees depend on God alone to appease their spiritual thirst and to fulfill other needs as well." Narendra said suddenly: "Sir, although it's a common belief that the chataka bird drinks only rainwater, it isn't true. I've seen these birds drink water from rivers and ponds like the others." The Master said: "What? Does the chataka bird drink water like other birds? Then this longstanding conviction of mine is proven false. But because you've seen this, I have no doubt about it." The childlike Master became anxious, thinking: "If this conviction of mine happens to be false, others may be the same." This made him very sad. After a few days Narendra called to the Master and said: "Sir, look! A chataka bird is drinking Ganges water." The Master rushed out of the room and asked, "Where?" But where Narendra was pointing the Master saw a small bat drinking water. He laughed and said: "That's a bat. You rascal! You mistook a bat for a chataka and made me anxious. I won't believe everything you say anymore."

It is often seen that when men come into the presence of women, they
| 49. Narendra's self-control. | become more gentle than can be accounted for by a mere sense of politeness, respect, and an appreciation of beauty. According to the scriptures, this is due to a |

kind of sensibility hidden deep in the heart. Such softness was almost entirely absent from Narendra's mind. When he realized this, the Master was convinced that Narendra would never lose his self-control under the spell of feminine beauty. The Master once compared Narendra with a devotee[7] whom we respected highly for his frequent ecstasies. The Master said: "That man loses himself in the loving care of women, but Narendra never does. I've watched him carefully. Though he doesn't say so, I find that he seems rather uncomfortable in their presence. It seems as if by turning his head away, he is asking, 'Why are they here?'"

The Master told us many times that although Narendra possessed knowl-
| 50. The Master evaluates Narendra's devotion by observing his physical signs. | edge and masculine qualities to a great degree, he did not lack tenderness and devotion. The Master came to this conclusion by observing how Narendra's attitudes revealed themselves in small actions as well |

as in his physical characteristics. We remember that one day he examined Narendra's face and remarked: "Could one who is a dry jnani have such eyes? Knowledge and feminine devotion are blended in you. And those who have only masculine qualities don't have black circles around their nipples. The great hero Arjuna didn't have those marks."

In addition to the four methods described earlier, the Master used other
| 51. Narendra's response to the Master's indifference. | means to test Narendra, some of which we know about. We shall now describe a couple of these. Earlier we mentioned that when Narendra visited |

Dakshineswar, the Master would pay much attention to him. The Master's heart would swell with divine love whenever he saw Narendra, even from a distance. Many times we saw the Master merge into samadhi, saying, "There's Na; there's Na." After many such visits to Dakshineswar, however, there came a day when the Master treated Narendra with utter indifference.

---

7. Nrityagopal, who later became Swami Jnanananda.

Narendra came, saluted the Master, sat before him, and waited for some time. The Master neither greeted him nor asked about his welfare. He glanced at Narendra as one would a stranger, and then remained absorbed within himself. Narendra thought that perhaps the Master was in an ecstatic mood. After a while Narendra left the room and began to smoke and chat with Hazra. When he heard that the Master was talking with others, Narendra returned to him. Even then the Master did not speak to Narendra; instead, he lay down on his bed, turning his face away from him. Thus the whole day passed, and even in the evening the Master's mood did not change. At last Narendra bowed down to the Master and returned to Calcutta.

A week later Narendra went to Dakshineswar again and found the Master in the same mood. Narendra spent the day talking to Hazra and the other devotees and returned home at nightfall. Narendra came to Dakshineswar a third and fourth time, but found no change in the Master's mood. However, this did not perturb him or make him resentful, and he continued to visit the Master as usual. When Narendra was at home, the Master would sometimes send someone to inquire about his welfare, but now he maintained an indifference when Narendra was present. This continued for more than a month. The Master noticed that Narendra did not stop coming to Dakshineswar, so one day he called him to his side and asked, "Why do you keep coming here when I don't say a single word to you?" Narendra replied: "Do you think I come here just to talk with you? I love you. I come because I want to see you." Delighted, the Master said: "I was testing you to see if you'd stop coming when you didn't receive love and attention. Only a spiritual aspirant of your calibre could have put up with such neglect and indifference. Anyone else would have left me long ago and would never have returned."

We shall conclude this topic by narrating an incident that makes clear the

52. Narendra rejects occult powers in favour of God-realization.

intensity of Narendra's longing for God-realization. Once the Master called him into the Panchavati and said: "Look, as a result of practising austerities, I have long since possessed all the supernatural powers. But what would a person like me do with such powers? I can't even keep a wearing-cloth tied around my own waist! So I'm thinking of asking Mother to transfer them all to you. She has told me that you will have to do much work for Her. So if these powers are transmitted to you, you can use them when necessary. What do you say?"

Narendra had seen various divine powers in the Master since their first meeting, so he had no reason to doubt him. But his deeply rooted love of God did not allow him to accept those powers without careful consideration. After serious thought, Narendra asked, "Sir, will they help me to realize God?" The Master replied: "No, they won't help you to do that. But they might be very useful once you have realized God and have started doing His work." To this, Narendra said: "Sir, I don't need them. Let me realize God first; after that, there will be time enough to decide whether I need them. If I get these marvellous powers now, I might forget the whole purpose of my life and use them to gratify worldly desires. Then they would only become my ruin." We cannot say whether the Master was actually ready to transmit those powers to Narendra or was simply testing him. But we do know that the Master was extremely pleased when Narendra refused his offer.

Chapter 8

Section 1

Narendra's Education in the World and from the Master

SOMETIMES THE MASTER COMPARED HIS OWN NATURE with Narendra's and told us,

> 1. The Master identifies a manifestation of the female nature in himself and of the male nature in Narendra: the meaning of this.

"The Person who exists within this (*himself*) has the nature of a woman, and the Person who dwells within Narendra has the nature of a man." It is difficult to determine what the Master meant when he said that. But we can come to a reasonable understanding if we study the paths that the Master and Narendra followed and the means they adopted to reach God, the ultimate Truth. The Master learned from his gurus all of the spiritual disciplines prescribed by the scriptures for God-realization and then practised them with complete faith. Narendra's behaviour was just the opposite: He first used his intellect to ascertain whether there was any error in the words of the guru or in the scriptures, and then followed them only when they withstood the test of his reason. As a result of deep-rooted tendencies from previous lives, Narendra had a firm belief in God, but all throughout his life he cherished this thought: Human beings are subject to superstition and error; so why should one indiscriminately accept what they say? Whatever the outcome or origin of reasoning, nowadays people consider it manly to proceed in the spiritual realm, and in all other matters, by keeping faith and devotion under the control of the intellect.

Environment plays an important part in human life. Not only does it play

> 2. Narendra's education, freethinking, scepticism, and rejection of the doctrine of the guru.

a vital role, it also always guides human life towards its goal. So it is not surprising that Narendra's life was marked by the power and influence of his environment. Before he met the Master, Narendra had become well versed in English poetry, literature, history, and logic through his extraordinary intellect. He was therefore greatly influenced by Western ideas, and indoctrinated with the fundamental Western principle that one should investigate every subject independently with the help of reason alone. So at that time he naturally doubted the scriptures and considered some of what they said to be false. He was also reluctant to accept any man as a guru, except in the sense of an experienced teacher.

The lifestyle of Narendra's guardians and the contemporary social condi-

3. His father's life and social conditions supported Narendra's education.

tions in Calcutta supported his way of thinking. Although Narendra's grandfather, who became a monk, had great faith in the Hindu scriptures throughout his life; his son, Narendra's father, fell under the influence of Western education and the doctrine of freethinking, and lost that faith. He believed that the culmination of spirituality could be found in the mystical poems of the Persian poet Hafiz and the teachings of Jesus as recorded in the Bible. Narendra's father was drawn to those books to satisfy his spiritual appetite because his ignorance of Sanskrit kept him from studying the Bhagavad Gita and other Hindu scriptures. We heard that once when Narendra's father saw him studying religious books, he presented Narendra with a Bible and told him, "If there is any religion to be found, it is in this book only." And although Narendra's father praised the Bible and the poems of Hafiz, his life was not regulated by the spiritual ideas in those books. Narendra's father, it seems, felt no need to practise religion, other than to read those books and derive some momentary pleasure from them. The ultimate goals of his life were to earn money, to enjoy himself, and to make others happy by being as charitable as possible. One can easily extrapolate from this attitude and from the man's daily life how inadequate his faith was regarding God, the Atman, and the hereafter.

Western materialism, which is based on the idea that earthly life is everything, had created a terrible scepticism — and sometimes even atheism — in the minds of people like Narendra's father. Those who propagated this materialism constantly tried to prove that there was nothing to be gained from our ancient rishis and scriptures except for weak-mindedness and superstition. As a result, many people lost their faith in religion and lost their moral strength. They harboured one idea inwardly but behaved differently and thus became selfish and hypocritical. For a short time, the Brahmo Samaj, established by Raja Rammohan Roy,[1] tried to hold back the tide of materialism that swept the country, but due to Western influence and conflicts within the group, it split into two and was weakened. There is also some evidence that the members of both factions also succumbed somewhat to that materialism.

1. Rammohan Roy (1774-1833) was a noted social reformer who worked to abolish child marriage, the immolation of widows, and *Purdah* (seclusion of women). — *Translator*

Narendra became well acquainted with Western science and philosophy after his F.A. examination in 1881. He had already mastered the doctrines of John Stuart Mill and of other Western logicians. Now he had great enthusiasm for attaining the truth by studying the doctrines of Western philosophers: Rene Descartes'

4. Narendra has no peace because he does not experience Truth, despite his knowledge of Western logic, science, and philosophy.

doctrine of I [*cogito, ergo sum* — I think, therefore I am], the atheism of David Hume and of Jeremy Bentham, the pantheism of Baruch Spinoza, the doctrine of evolution according to Charles Robert Darwin, the positivism of Auguste Comte, and the agnosticism of Herbert Spencer. When Narendra heard of the greatness of German philosophers, he studied the history of philosophy and tried to understand the views of Immanuel Kant, Johann Gottlieb Fichte, Georg Wilhelm Friedrich Hegel, Arthur Schopenhauer, and others. To learn the formation and function of the nervous system and the brain, he sometimes went to the Calcutta Medical College with his friends to study that subject and to listen to lectures on physiology. He had therefore amassed much knowledge of Western philosophy by the time he passed his B.A. examination in 1884. But this knowledge gave him no peace because it could not offer a definite method of knowing God, the Absolute Truth that is beyond the limit of the human mind and intellect. When Narendra realized that his learning was utterly inadequate to reveal the Truth, the current of restlessness flowed more strongly in his mind.

Western philosophy and science had taught Narendra that stimuli from the senses and the brain are constantly creating various reactions in the mind, producing pleasure and pain. Our experience of those reactions is mediated by space and time, and we are therefore ignorant of the real nature of the external world and the objects

5. Narendra's dilemma: whether to adopt Eastern or Western methods in his pursuit of Truth.

within it that create those stimuli and the subsequent responses. This situation is similar to the internal world and the real nature of human beings, where it is evident that an Unknown Entity is generating I-consciousness and other thoughts in the mind, but we cannot understand that Entity because Its real nature is beyond space and time. Whether people try to explore the Ultimate Truth, either internally or externally, they are thus obstructed by the impregnable wall of space and time and are rendered completely helpless. Thus, Narendra learned the futility of trying to unveil the mystery of this universe using the five sense organs, the mind, and the intellect because those instruments are completely inadequate to reveal the Ultimate Cause of the universe. He realized that people busy themselves in building arguments and drawing conclusions based on sense perceptions, which are full of errors and misunderstandings. He became aware that Western savants had utterly failed to discover whether the Self existed separately from the body. For that reason, the Western philosophers' final conclusions regarding spiritual truth did not appear reasonable to Narendra. So he began to question which path he should take: Would it be better to follow the Western ideal and build philosophical truths based on the perceptions of those who were attached to material objects? Or should one search for philosophical truth by following Eastern philosophy, founded upon the realizations of Buddha and other great souls, which are extraordinary even though they are contrary to what ordinary people perceive?

Although Narendra considered most of Western philosophy's spiritual

6. Narendra resolves to realize God, the Ultimate Truth, and accepts only the positive aspects of the Western system.

conclusions to be illogical, he had high regard for the inventions of material science and the Western method of analysis, and he always resorted to scientific methods in his experiments with the truths of psychology and spirituality. From then on [between his F.A. and B.A. examinations] he invariably tried to understand the Master's extraordinary realizations by analyzing them using scientific methods, accepting as true only those that withstood the test. These he practised fearlessly. Although he was anxious to experience the truth, it was against his nature to practise any discipline without first understanding it, or to respect anyone out of fear. If atheism was to be the outcome of using his discrimination, then so be it: He would not mind being an atheist. Narendra was ready to pursue truth and unveil the mystery of life even at the cost of his life, not to speak of worldly pleasures. During this period he was completely focussed on his search for the Ultimate Truth and kept himself engaged in studying the rational and positive aspects of Western thought. This Western influence, however, led him away from the straightforward path of faith and devotion, leaving him at times oppressed and bewildered by doubt. But his extraordinary perseverance and intellectual strength ultimately prevailed, and he was successful in his pursuit of truth. At that time people thought that Narendra would indiscriminately accept any opinion that was published in the books of the West. His bias for Western ideas was so well known among his friends that when he read the Gita one day and enthusiastically praised it to them, they were amazed and reported it to the Master. The Master remarked, "I hope he didn't say that because some Western scholars expressed the same opinion of the Gita."

When Narendra came under the influence of Western thought, he had

7. Narendra's faith in God is sustained at this time by his wonderful visions and his guru's grace.

already met the Master and was having some extraordinary spiritual experiences. We have already described them to the reader. It seems that these experiences were of great help in maintaining Narendra's faith in God. If he had not had these experiences it would have been difficult to say how far he would have been carried by Western ideas and philosophies that sought to prove that God, the Cause of the universe, is unknowable. Although Narendra's deep-rooted spiritual tendencies would have kept his faith in God from being completely destroyed, it could have been greatly disturbed by the influence of the West. But this was not to be, because Narendra's life was protected by God for the purpose of accomplishing a special mission in this world. By God's grace he had found Sri Ramakrishna, a true guru, and had taken refuge in him. His guru told him repeatedly: "God always listens to the sincere prayers of human beings. I swear that one can see God and talk with Him as clearly as you see me and talk with me. One can hear His words and feel His touch." The Master said further: "You may not believe that God takes different forms or subscribe to common ideas about Him; you may consider such ideas to be the products of human imagination; but if you believe in an Ultimate Reality that is the regulator of the universe, you can pray to It this way: 'O God, I do not know You. Be gracious and reveal Your real nature to me.' He will certainly listen to you and grant you grace if your prayer is sincere." The Master's words were immensely reassuring to Narendra, and he practised sadhana with even greater intensity.

William Hamilton, a Western philosopher, says at the end of his book on
8. Narendra's sadhana. | philosophy that the human intellect stops at the point of indicating the truth that there is a God Who controls the universe. The intellect is incapable of revealing the true nature of God, so philosophy ends there. He concludes, "Where philosophy ends, there religion begins." Narendra was very fond of Hamilton's saying and sometimes referred to it in conversation. Although Narendra concentrated on sadhana, he did not give up his study of philosophy. He spent most of his time on meditation, study, and music.

From now on [after his B.A. examination] Narendra adopted a new
9. Narendra meditates throughout the night after adopting a new method. | method of meditation. Earlier we said that whether we imagine God as having form or as being formless, we have no alternative but to think of God anthropomorphically. Previously when Narendra meditated on God he followed the Brahmo belief, thinking of God as formless but endowed with attributes. But now he considered the Brahmo concept of God to be flawed by human imagination, and he gave up that method. Instead, he prayed wholeheartedly, "O God, please make me fit to see Your true nature." He then banished all thoughts and practised keeping his mind as motionless as the unflickering flame of a lamp in a windless place. After a short while, Narendra's controlled mind would become so absorbed that he sometimes transcended body-consciousness and the concept of time. He sat for meditation in his room when members of his family went to sleep, often meditating through the whole night.

As a result of this meditation, Narendra had a divine vision that he
described to us later in the course of conversation. He
said: "When I removed all objects from my mind and
kept it calm, a current of serene bliss flowed within
me. Under its influence I felt a sort of intoxication that

10. That form of
meditation leads to a
wonderful vision of
Buddha.

would continue even after meditation ended, so I had no inclination to leave
my seat immediately. One day when I was still seated after meditation, the
room filled with a divine effulgence and the striking figure of a monk
suddenly appeared, standing before me at a little distance. He wore an ochre
cloth and held a *kamandalu* [water pot] in his hand. His face was calm, serene,
and indifferent to the world, and its contemplative expression captivated
me. He walked towards me slowly, fixing his gaze on me as if he wanted to
say something. But I was so seized with fear that I couldn't keep still. I got
up, opened the door, and quickly stepped out of the room. The next moment
I thought, 'Why should I be afraid?' I boldly returned to my room to hear
what the monk had to say, but he wasn't there, though I waited for him a
long time. I sadly asked myself, 'Why did I foolishly run away without
listening to him?' I've seen many monks but never have I seen such an
extraordinary expression on any other face. That face was imprinted on my
heart forever. I may be wrong, but quite often I think that I was blessed on
that day with a vision of Buddha."

Chapter 8

Section 2

Narendra's Education in the World and from the Master

NARENDRA BEGAN SPENDING HIS TIME IN SECLUSION, studying, practising austerities, and visiting Dakshineswar. To ensure Narendra's future as a lawyer, his father, Vishwanath, apprenticed him to Nimai Charan Basu, a well-known attorney in Calcutta. At the same time Vishwanath tried to find a suitable bride for Narendra, to establish him in a worldly life. But his effort was frustrated because Narendra objected strongly to marriage, and because a suitable bride could not be found.

1. Narendra apprentices to an attorney.

The Master sometimes visited Narendra in his study on Ramtanu Basu Lane and gave him various instructions concerning spiritual disciplines. He always encouraged Narendra to practise brahmacharya and cautioned him to ignore his parents' pleas to tie himself permanently to another in matrimony. The Master told Narendra: "If a man maintains absolute chastity for twelve years, he develops retentive power; his intellect is then able to penetrate the subtlest things and understand them. Only with the help of such an intellect can one realize God. He reveals Himself to an aspirant who is endowed with a pure intellect."

2. The Master advises Narendra to practise unbroken chastity.

The ladies in Narendra's household believed that his close association with the Master lay behind his refusal to marry. Narendra later told us: "One day when the Master came to my study and instructed me to practise strict brahmacharya, my grandmother overheard

3. Narendra's family fears that he will become a monk because he associates with monks.

835

everything and informed my parents. From that day on, they made a great effort to get me married lest I become a monk through my association with sannyasins. But to what avail? All of their efforts failed when faced with the strong will of the Master. Even when they had settled everything, the marriage negotiations broke off due to trifling differences between the two parties."

Although the members of Narendra's household did not like his frequent

4. Narendra continues to visit the Master regularly.

visits to the Master in Dakshineswar, no one dared to say anything to him because Narendra was very dear to his parents, and because from his childhood onward he had paid no heed to anyone who tried to restrict him in any way. During his youth he enjoyed complete freedom regarding what he ate, where he went, and so on. Narendra's family knew that if they tried to control the intelligent young man as one would attempt to restrain a boy or a fickle youth, he would most likely do exactly the opposite of what they wanted. Narendra therefore continued to visit the Master in Dakshineswar as before.

Narendra later cherished the sweet memory of those blessed days with

5. Narendra describes his days with the Master in Dakshineswar.

the Master in Dakshineswar; they filled his heart with joy throughout his life. Narendra recalled: "It's extremely difficult to describe to others how joyful were the days we spent with the Master. We still wonder at how the Master was constantly training us through play, merriment, and trivial daily activities, thus forming our spiritual lives without our knowledge. When a powerful wrestler trains a boy to wrestle, he controls himself and makes his student appear to be as strong as he is. He awakens his student's self-confidence by feigning to overpower him only with great effort and sometimes allowing himself to be defeated. The Master adopted this method with us. He always saw 'the whole ocean in a drop of water' [in other words, he saw infinite God in each individual]. Because he dwelt in the state of bhava-mukha, he knew how each person's latent spiritual power would manifest itself in the fullness of time. Keeping that bright picture in mind, he would speak highly of us and encourage us. Lest we miss the highest goal of life by becoming entangled in worldly desires, he carefully observed every action of ours and kept us under control with his instructions. But we had no idea that he was watching us so closely and had such control over us. This was his unique technique of training his disciples and moulding our lives.

"Once I felt that although my mind was concentrated to some extent during meditation, it wasn't going any deeper. I asked him what I should do. He told me what he'd done in similar circumstances and gave me additional instructions. I remember that when I meditated in Dakshineswar late at night the whistle of the nearby Alambazar Jute Mill would disturb me and distract my mind. When I reported this to the Master, he advised me to concentrate on the sound of the whistle. I followed his advice and derived much benefit from it.

"On another occasion I found it difficult to forget my body completely during meditation and concentrate my mind wholly on the Ideal. When I told him of my problem, he mentioned how Tota Puri had told him to concentrate between the eyebrows while practising samadhi according to Vedanta. He sharply pressed a fingernail into a spot between my eyebrows and said, 'Now concentrate on this painful sensation.' I found that I could easily concentrate on that sensation as long as I liked, and that during that period I completely lost awareness of the other parts of my body, which then caused me no distraction.

"The isolated Panchavati, where the Master had performed his sadhana, was the most suitable place for meditation. But in addition to our spiritual practices, we spent a good deal of time there in sheer fun and merrymaking. The Master sometimes joined us, intensifying our joy. There we used to run, climb trees, swing from the rope-like madhavi vines, and sometimes have a picnic. During our first picnic, the Master noticed that I'd cooked the food, but he partook of it nonetheless. I knew that he couldn't eat food unless it was cooked by brahmins, so I was planning to obtain prasad from the Kali temple for him. But he prevented me, saying, 'There's no harm in my taking cooked food from a pure and sattvic person like you.' He ignored my repeated objections and ate the food I'd cooked that day."

Bhavanath Chattopadhyay, a handsome and devout youth, stayed with the Master in Dakshineswar for a while. During that time he became acquainted with Narendra and a close friendship developed between them. Bhavanath was very dear to the Master because of his humility, modesty, simplicity, faith, and devotion. Observing his soft feminine nature and his affection for Narendra, the Master sometimes teased him, saying, "Perhaps you were Narendra's life-companion in a previous incarnation." Bhavanath lived at Baranagore, and whenever he had an opportunity he took Narendra to his home and fed him. Satkari Lahiri and Dasarathi Sanyal were Bhavanath's neighbours. Both of them were close friends of Narendra, and Dasarathi was a classmate as well. They all spent days and nights together whenever Narendra was available. Narendra would thus spend a few hours or a day or two with his friends at Baranagore when he visited Dakshineswar, or sometimes when he was specifically invited.

6. Bhavanath and Narendra's friends from Baranagore.

In the early part of 1884, sometime before he had received the result of his B.A. examination, a significant change took place in Narendra's life. Due to overwork Vishwanath's body had been exhausted for some time. One night at about 10:00, he suffered a heart attack and died. That day Narendra's friends had invited him to Baranagore. He arrived in the afternoon and sang

7. While at Baranagore, Narendra receives news of his father's death.

devotional songs until 11:00 p.m. After dinner they all lay in the same room and talked late into the night. Narendra's friend Hemali arrived at about 2:00 a.m. to give him the terrible news. Immediately they returned to Calcutta together.

After returning home, Narendra performed the customary rites for his

| 8. The tragic change in the situation of Narendra's family. | father. When the time came to look into his father's financial affairs, he found them to be in an extremely wretched condition. His father had been spending |

more than he earned and had left nothing but debt. Narendra's relatives, who had benefitted from his father's generosity, became hostile and even tried to evict his family from their home. Although his family had no income, and its six or seven members had to be supported. Narendra, who had been brought up in comfort, was now completely at a loss. Desperately he began searching for a job, but he met with disappointment everywhere. When times become bad, a person can achieve nothing even after a hundred attempts.

Three or four months after the death of his father there was no end to his distress and no relief from his poverty. Narendra did not see even the slightest ray of hope in his life. It is doubtful that he ever had been so engulfed by darkness. He sometimes described this period to us.

Narendra related: "Even before the prescribed period of mourning had

| 9. Narendra describes his difficulties: he struggles to find a job and his rich friends scorn him. | passed, I began running hither and thither in search of a job. Dizzy from lack of food, I went from office to office barefoot in the blazing sun, carrying my application papers. Some days one or two close friends accompanied me out of sympathy; other days I went |

alone. But everywhere I met with rejection. That early experience taught me that unselfish sympathy is rare in this world; there is no place here for the poor or the weak. Even those who only a short time ago would have regarded themselves fortunate to do me a favour, now made wry faces and were reluctant to help me, though they could easily have done so had they wished. When faced by all this, the world sometimes seemed to be the handiwork of the devil. I remember that one day when I was walking around in the sun, the soles of my feet became blistered. I was completely exhausted and had to sit down in the shade of the Ochterloney Monument [now Sahid Minar] on the Maidan. A couple of friends were with me, or perhaps they met me there. To console me, one of them sang:

> Here blows the wind, the breath of Brahman —
> It is His grace we feel.

When I heard that song I felt as if someone were violently beating me on the head. Thinking of my mother and brothers' helpless condition, I was filled with resentment and despair. 'Be quiet!' I told him. 'That fanciful nonsense is all right for people living in luxury — people who have no idea what hunger is — people whose nearest and dearest aren't wearing rags and starving. Previously this song sounded true and beautiful to me. But now I've seen what life is really like, and that song is nothing but a relentless mockery.'

"I dare say that my friend was terribly hurt by my words. How could he understand the grinding poverty that had made me utter them? Some mornings I'd get up to find that there wasn't enough food for all of us, so I'd tell my mother, 'A friend has invited me to lunch,' and leave home. On such days I had nothing to eat, for I had no money in my pocket. I was too proud to tell anyone about this. Sometimes my wealthy friends would invite me to their houses and pleasure gardens to sing at their parties as before. Unable to avoid them, I sometimes went and tried to entertain them. I had no inclination to tell them how I felt, and they did not try to find out how I was getting along. Rarely would a very few ask, 'Why do you look so pale and sad today?' But only one friend ever found out — and not from me — how things really were. He used to send money to my mother anonymously from time to time. I'm eternally indebted to him.

10. Crushed by poverty.

"Some of my boyhood friends, whose characters had become dissipated in their youth and who had resorted to unscrupulous means to earn money, now became aware of my poverty and tried to drag me into their company. I noticed that those among them who had suddenly fallen into difficult circumstances as I had, and were forced to adopt an ignoble path for their livelihood, actually had empathy for me. Mahamaya, the great enchantress, took advantage of my circumstances and tried to snare me with various temptations. A wealthy woman had been infatuated with me for a long time. When she found an opportunity, she sent a message inviting me to end my poverty by accepting her along with her wealth. Disgusted, I sternly rejected her offer. When another woman approached me with a similar proposal, I told her: 'Look, you've wasted your life seeking the pleasures of your worthless body. Now death is in front of you. Have you done anything to prepare yourself? Shun these filthy desires and call on God.'

11. Temptation from women.

"In spite of all these sufferings, I neither lost faith in the existence of God, nor did I doubt the truth of the saying 'God is merciful.' Every morning I repeated the Lord's name as I got out of bed, and then resumed my search for a job. One day as I was getting out of bed my mother overheard my prayer from the next room. She said bitterly: 'Keep quiet, boy! You've been repeating the Lord's name since you were a child. What has He done for you?' These words hurt me terribly. Stunned, I asked myself: 'Does God really exist? And if He does, does He listen to our fervent prayers? Why do I

12. His mother scolds him for chanting God's name.

pray so much and get no answer? Why is there so much woe in His benign kingdom? How could He be merciful when His creation is so full of evil?' Afflicted with the sufferings of others, Ishwar Chandra Vidyasagar once remarked, 'If God is compassionate and gracious, why then did millions of people die for want of a morsel of food during the terrible famine?' This harsh and taunting remark reverberated in my ears. My heart was filled with wounded feelings towards God, and at this opportune moment doubt occupied my mind.

"It was against my nature to do anything secretly. Even as a child, I was never able to conceal even the most trivial thought or action from fear or for any other reason. So it wasn't surprising that I now began aggressively to tell people that God did not exist, and that even if He did exist, it was of no use calling on Him because it produced no results. Of course, the rumour soon spread that I'd become an atheist and that I was drinking, mixing with people of bad character, and visiting houses of ill repute. Those lies made me all the more rebellious and aggressive. I began telling everyone — even those who didn't ask my opinion — that I had no objection to any man's drinking wine or going to a brothel if it would help him to forget his hard lot in this world of pain. And I added that I would do these things myself, without the least regard for public opinion, if I believed that they would make me happy even for a single moment.

13. His feelings wounded, Narendra adopts an atheistic outlook.

"Such news travels fast. It didn't take long for a completely distorted version of my words to reach the Master and his devotees in Calcutta. When some of them came to visit me to learn the truth, they made it obvious that they believed at least part of what they had heard, if not all. I was bitterly wounded when I realized that they could think so little of me. I told them that it was cowardice to believe in God merely from fear of hell. Quoting Hume, Mill, Bain, Comte, and other Western philosophers, I fiercely argued that there is no evidence for the existence of God. And so they went away, convinced more than ever of my downfall, as I afterwards learned. In my defiant mood, this actually pleased me. Then it occurred to me that perhaps they would tell the Master about this and that he would believe them. I felt terrible pain at the thought. But then I said to myself: 'Let him believe it. If he does, I can't help it. Others' good or bad opinions are worth nothing.' I later discovered that the Master *had* heard all these lies about me. He made no comment at first. But when Bhavanath tearfully said to him, 'Sir, we never dreamed that Narendra would sink so low!' the Master cried out excitedly: 'Silence, you scoundrel! Mother has told me that he could never do such things. If you talk like this anymore, I won't allow you in my presence again!'

14. The devotees believe Narendra has fallen, but the Master does not.

"But what was this atheism of mine? Nothing but egotism and pride. The experiences I'd had since childhood and, more important, since meeting the Master, rose vividly into my mind in bright colours. I said to myself: 'God certainly does exist and there is definitely a way to attain Him. Otherwise, what is life for? What is it worth? The path to God has to be found, no matter how great the struggle.' Days passed, and my mind continued to vacillate between doubt and certainty. Thus I had no respite from my emotional turmoil and financial woes.

15. Narendra's terrible anguish.

"Summer passed, and the rainy season began. I continued looking for work as before. One night as I returned home I was drenched with rain. I hadn't eaten all day, my legs were tired, and my mind was even more exhausted than my body. At length, I grew so exhausted that I couldn't go a single step farther, and I lay down motionless on the open veranda of a neighbour's house. Perhaps I lost external consciousness for a while. I remember that all kinds of thoughts and pictures went through my mind, and I had no power to ignore or concentrate upon any of them. Then I suddenly felt that Providence was lifting up screen after screen in my mind and that all the problems that had been tormenting me — where is the harmony between God's justice and His mercy, why does evil exist within a benign creation — all were resolved. I was beside myself with joy. When I later continued my walk home, I found that there was not a bit of fatigue in my body and that my mind was filled with infinite peace and strength. The day was just breaking.

16. Narendra finds peace in a wonderful vision.

"I now became absolutely indifferent to the praise or blame of the world. I was firmly convinced that I wasn't born to earn money, support a family, or seek worldly enjoyment like others. I was secretly preparing to renounce the world as my grandfather had done. When the day arrived on which I had decided to start life as a wandering monk, I heard that the Master was coming to a devotee's house in Calcutta. I thought this was very fortunate: I should see my guru before I left home forever. But when I met the Master, he told me imperiously, 'You must come with me to Dakshineswar today.' I offered various excuses, but he wouldn't accept any of them. I had to return with him. We didn't speak much in the carriage. When we got to Dakshineswar, I sat in his room for some time with other devotees. Then the Master went into a state of ecstasy. Suddenly he came over to me, took my hand in his, and sang, with tears pouring down his face:

17. Narendra resolves to become a monk. The Master's mysterious treatment of him at Dakshineswar.

> I am afraid to speak,
> I am afraid not to speak,
> For the fear rises in my mind
> That I shall lose you.

"All this time, I'd fought back the strong emotion I was feeling. I could do so no longer, and my tears poured down like his. I felt sure that the Master knew all about my plans. The others were astonished to see us behaving in this way. After the Master had returned to normal consciousness, one of the devotees asked him what was the matter. He smiled and answered, 'It's just something between the two of us.' That night he sent the others away. Calling me to him, he said in a voice choked with emotion: 'I know you've come to the world to do Mother's work; you can never lead a worldly life. But, for my sake, stay with your family as long as I'm alive.' As he said this, he began to cry again.

18. At the Master's request, Narendra cancels his plan to renounce home.

"I took leave of him the next day and returned home. A thousand concerns for my family occupied my mind, and with renewed energy I set myself to finding employment. I got a temporary job in an attorney's office translating some books, which brought just enough income to live on. I couldn't find a permanent job, so I had no fixed income with which to maintain my mother and brothers. It occurred to me that God grants the Master's prayers, so I should ask him to pray on my behalf that my family's financial crisis would be overcome. I was sure that he wouldn't refuse, for my sake. I rushed to Dakshineswar and importuned him, saying, 'Sir, you must speak to the Divine Mother so that my family's financial problems can be solved.' The Master replied: 'I can't make such demands. Why don't you go and ask the Mother yourself? You don't accept the Mother — that is why you have all these troubles.' I replied: 'I don't know the Mother. Please tell the Mother for me. You have to, or I won't let you go.' The Master said affectionately: 'My boy, I've prayed many times to the Mother to remove your suffering. But She doesn't listen to my prayers because you don't care for Her. All right, today is Tuesday, a day especially sacred to Mother. Go to the temple tonight and pray. Mother will grant whatever you ask for, I promise you that. My Mother is the embodiment of Pure Consciousness, the Power of Brahman, and She has produced this universe by mere will. What can She not do, if She wishes?'

19. Narendra resorts to divine intervention to end his poverty and implores the Master for help. The Master advises him to go to the Kali temple and pray.

"When the Master said that, I was fully convinced that all my suffering would cease as soon as I prayed to Her. I waited impatiently for night. At 9:00 p.m. the Master told me to go to the temple. On my way, I was possessed by a kind of drunkenness and began to stagger. I firmly believed that I would see the Mother and hear Her voice. I forgot everything else and became absorbed in that thought alone. When I entered the temple, I saw that the Mother was actually conscious and living, the fountainhead of infinite love and beauty. Overwhelmed with love and devotion, I bowed

20. Narendra has a vision of the Divine Mother and forgets the world.

down to Her again and again, praying, 'Mother — grant me discrimination, grant me detachment, grant me divine knowledge and devotion, grant that I may see You without obstruction, always!' My heart was filled with peace. The universe disappeared from my mind and the Mother alone occupied it completely.

"As soon as I returned to the Master, he asked, 'Hello, did you pray to the Mother to relieve your family's needs?' I was taken aback and replied: 'No, sir, I forgot. What shall I do now?' He said, 'Go — go again, and say that prayer.'

21. Thrice he goes to the Kali temple to pray for financial help, and thrice he fails.

Again I went to the temple. But when I stood before the Mother, I was again overwhelmed and forgot my intention. I repeatedly bowed down to Her and prayed for knowledge and devotion. When I returned to the Master, he smiled and asked, 'Well, have you prayed for your need this time?' Startled, I said: 'No, sir, I couldn't. As soon as I saw the Mother, I was overwhelmed by a divine power and forgot everything — I asked only for knowledge and devotion. What's to be done now?' The Master said: 'Silly boy! Couldn't you control yourself a little, and remember your prayer? Go back again and tell Mother what you want — be quick!' I went a third time, but as soon as I entered the temple I felt a sense of deep shame. I thought: 'What a trifling thing I am asking of the Mother! As the Master says, "It's like being graciously received by a king and then asking for gourds and pumpkins." It's that kind of stupidity! Am I so small-minded?' In shame and remorse I bowed down to Her again and again and said: 'Mother, I want nothing but knowledge and devotion.'

"When I came out of the temple, I thought that the Master must have played a trick on me: I'd gone to the Mother thrice but hadn't been able to ask for what I needed. I went to the Master and insisted: 'It was certainly you who made me intoxicated and forgetful. Now you must at least say a prayer that my mother and brothers will never lack for food and clothing.' He said: 'My child, you know I could never offer a prayer like that for anyone; the words wouldn't leave my mouth. I told you that you'd get whatever you asked Mother for; but you couldn't do that, either. You aren't destined to have worldly happiness. What am I to do about that?' I said firmly: 'No, sir, I won't let you go. You must say the prayer for my sake. I'm certain my family will be freed from want if only you say they will.' Thus I went on importuning him until at last he said, 'All right — they will never lack for plain food and clothing.'"

This acceptance of God with form was of course a most significant event in Narendra's life. Until then, he had not understood the hidden meaning behind worshipping God as Mother or [the meaning] of using symbols and images. Previously he had disregarded the images of gods and goddesses and had never visited their

22. Narendra gains faith in the worship of God through symbols and images, making the Master happy.

temples with love and respect. From now on, his heart saw clearly the true mystery of this worship, and his spiritual life became more full and expansive. This made the Master jubilant. Vaikuntha Nath Sanyal, a friend of ours, visited Dakshineswar the day after this incident. We shall now present his eyewitness account to give the reader a complete picture.

"I became acquainted with a person named Tarapada Ghosh, who worked

| 23. Vaikuntha Nath Sanyal describes the Master's happiness. | with me in the same office," said Vaikuntha. "Tarapada was a close friend of Narendra. I'd seen Narendra with Tarapada a few times in our office. Tarapada |

had told me that Sri Ramakrishna was very fond of Narendra. However, I never tried to get acquainted with him.

"On that day I went to Dakshineswar at noon. The Master was seated alone in his room and Narendra was sleeping on the veranda outside. The Master was beaming with joy. As soon as I bowed down to him, he pointed to Narendra and said: 'Look at that boy — that boy is very good. His name is Narendra. He wouldn't accept the Divine Mother before, but last night he did. He was in need of money, so I advised him to ask Mother for it. But he couldn't; he said he felt ashamed. When he came back from the temple, he asked me to teach him a song in praise of Mother. So I taught him, "Mother, Thou art our sole Redeemer,"[1] and he sang it all night long. That's why he's sleeping now.' And then the Master smiled with joy and said: 'Narendra has accepted Mother Kali. That's very good, isn't it?' Seeing that he was as happy as a child about this, I answered, 'Yes, sir, it is very good.' A little later he smiled and said again: 'Narendra has accepted the Mother. It's very good. What do you say?' And he kept smiling and saying that, over and over.

"When Narendra awoke at 4:00 p.m., he came and sat near the Master,

| 24. An example of how the Master regarded Narendra as his own. | appearing about to take leave of him and return to Calcutta. But the Master went into ecstasy and moved closer to Narendra. He said: 'What I see is that |

I'm this body (*his own body*) and that body (*Narendra's body*) also. It's true — I

---

1. Mother, Thou art our sole Redeemer,
Thou the support of the three gunas,
Higher than the most high.
Thou art compassionate, I know,
Who takest away our bitter grief.
Thou art in earth, in water Thou;
Thou liest at the root of all.
In me, in every creature,
Thou hast Thy home; though clothed with form,
Yet art Thou formless Reality.
Sandhya art Thou, and Gayatri;
Thou dost sustain this universe.
Mother, the Help art Thou
Of those who have no help but Thee,
O Eternal Beloved of Shiva!

see no difference. If you lay a stick on the surface of the Ganges, the water seems to be divided into two parts, but it's really all one; there's no division. The same thing is true here. Can you understand that? What else exists but Mother? Isn't that true?'

"Then he said suddenly, 'I'll smoke.' I hastily prepared the water pipe and gave it to him. After taking a few puffs, he said, 'No, I'll smoke straight from the bowl,' and he took the tobacco bowl in both hands. He puffed again, then held it to Narendra's mouth and said, 'Take a puff or two from my hands.' Narendra hesitated. The Master said: 'What ignorance! Are you and I different? This is I and that is also I.' Saying this, he put his hands to Narendra's mouth and forced him to smoke. Narendra took a couple of puffs and then stopped. Seeing that he had stopped, the Master was about to start smoking again when Narendra said quickly, 'Sir, wash your hands before you smoke!' But the Master wouldn't do so. 'You wretch,' he told Narendra, 'You're too conscious of differences!' Then he continued to smoke through his hands although Narendra's lips had touched them. He uttered many spiritual truths from his state of ecstasy. Normally the Master couldn't partake of anything that had been tasted by another — to him it was like refuse. I was amazed when I saw him behave that way with Narendra that day and realized the closeness between them.

"Our conversation continued till 8:00 p.m. When we saw that the Master's ecstasy had come to an end, Narendra and I took leave of him and returned to Calcutta on foot. Later, Narendra told us many times: 'Ever since our first meeting, it was the Master alone who always had faith in me — no one else, not even my own mother and brothers. That faith and that love of his have bound me to him forever. The Master was the only one who knew how to love and who really loved. Worldly people only feign love to gratify their own self-interest.'"

25. Vaikuntha returns to Calcutta with Narendra.

Chapter 9

The *D*evotees of the Master, and Narendra

We mentioned earlier that the devotees whom the Master had seen in his

---
1. The Master's marked devotees arrive by 1884.

---

yogic vision came to Dakshineswar before the end of 1884, with the exception of Purna, who arrived in the beginning of 1885. When the Master blessed Purna, he remarked: "In a vision I saw the class of devotees who were supposed to come here, and with Purna's arrival it is complete. No one else of this class will come here."

Most of these devotees came to the Master between the middle of 1883

---
2. The Master's behaviour with this group of devotees.

---

and the middle of 1884. At that time Narendra was struggling with his financial problems, and Rakhal was staying in Vrindaban for a while. Sometimes when the Master spoke to his audience he would predict the arrival of a chosen devotee, pointing to a particular direction and saying, "Today a devotee of this place is coming from this direction." As soon as a marked devotee arrived, the Master received him as cordially as an old acquaintance, saying, "You belong to this place." Once he had met such a fortunate man, the Master was eager to see him again, feed him, and speak with him privately about spiritual matters. After the Master had observed the character and habits of a new devotee, he would introduce him to a longtime devotee of a similar nature, so that they could spend time together and talk about God. Again, sometimes he visited the houses of his young devotees of his own accord and pleased their guardians with inspired talks, thus removing any obstacles to their occasional visits to him.

As soon as those marked devotees arrived, or a short while thereafter,

3. Absorbed in a divine mood, the Master touches or gives a mantra to the devotees according to their capacity: the result.

the Master took them aside and asked them to meditate. While in ecstasy, he then touched their chests or tongues. This powerful touch forced their minds inward, withdrawing them partially or completely from sense objects, awakening their accumulated spiritual tendencies, and engaging them in the effort to realize God. At that touch, some devotees had visions of divine light or of the luminous forms of gods and goddesses; some plunged into deep meditation and experienced an indescribable bliss; some felt an immediate release of the knots in their hearts and felt an intense longing for God; some became ecstatic and experienced savikalpa samadhi; and some rare souls had a foretaste of nirvikalpa samadhi. Thus, many people who came to him had visions of luminous divine forms and other experiences. The Master told us that his touch created in Tarak a tremendous longing and cry for God, awakening his heart suddenly. His touch also caused Junior Naren to become absorbed in meditation on the formless God. But there was evidence that only Narendra had a foretaste of nirvikalpa samadhi from that touch.

In addition to touching them, the Master initiated some of his devotees with mantras. When he initiated devotees, the Master did not consult their horoscopes or perform any ritual like other gurus. He used his yogic vision to see the tendencies they had inherited from past lives, then would tell them, "This is your mantra." This is how he initiated Niranjan, Tejachandra, Vaikuntha, and a few others, as they told us later. He did not initiate people with Shakti or Vishnu mantras just because they had been born into Shakta or Vaishnava families. After observing their inner tendencies, he sometimes initiated a Shakta with a Vishnu mantra and a Vaishnava with a Shakti mantra. It is evident that the Master always instructed each individual according to that person's tendencies.

The scriptures tell us that great souls can direct the minds of others to a

4. What the Master's divine touch proves.

higher realm by imparting their spiritual powers through a touch or merely by willing it to be so. These beings use that power to change the lives of their close disciples and even to affect the lives of prostitutes and profligates. The manifestation of that power is visible in varying degrees in the lives of Krishna, Buddha, Jesus, Chaitanya, and others who are adored even now as incarnations of God. Although the activities of great souls are recorded in the scriptures, people have had no direct contact with such divine activities for a long time and have lost faith in their power. Nowadays many people consider faith in God to be a kind of mental weakness deriving from superstition, and think even less of faith in a divine incarnation. It was an absolute necessity in this modern age for an extraordinary person like the Master to be born for the purpose of removing doubt from people's minds and making them spiritual. Now that we have seen the manifestation of that power in the Master, we can believe in the similar power of great souls in the past. Some may not believe the Master to be an incarnation of God, but seeing his power they cannot deny that he was superhuman like Krishna, Buddha, Jesus, Chaitanya, and other great souls.

The devotees seen by the Master in his yogic vision were people of different ages, classes, and religious backgrounds — young and old, householders and monks, worshippers of God with form and of a formless God, Shakta and Vaishnava, and so on. Despite their differences, however, they had one thing in common: They had sincere faith in and steadfast devotion to their respective paths and were prepared to make great sacrifices to realize God. The Master affectionately bound them together, and he supported their respective spiritual beliefs in his dealings with them. As a result, each devotee believed that although the Master was adept in all religious paths, he had greater love and more sympathy for his or her own path. Under this impression, each showed tremendous love and devotion for the Master. When the Master's noble qualities and training gradually influenced those devotees to cross the barriers of sectarianism and become liberal, they were amazed at the fullness of their liberality. As an example we shall mention an event here.

5. Devotees consider the Master to be a follower of their respective paths, and the Master behaves accordingly.

Balaram Basu, who was firmly devoted to Vishnu, was born in a Vaishnava family from Baghbazar in Calcutta. He was a householder but was not attached to the world; he had plenty of wealth but no pride. Even before he came to the Master he spent four or five hours every morning in spiritual disciplines and study. He was so careful in his practice of nonviolence that he never hurt anything for any reason, not even an insect. When the Master first met him, he received him as cordially as he would an old acquaintance. He said: "Balaram was one of the companions of Chaitanya. He belongs to this place. Once while in ecstasy I watched as Chaitanya inspired a large crowd with a flood of divine love, singing kirtan with Advaita, Nityananda, and others. Balaram was in that wonderful kirtan party."

6. As their open-mindedness increases, the devotees understand the Master better: the example of Balaram Basu.

After Balaram met the Master, his mind underwent a great change and he progressed rapidly in spiritual life. He surpassed the limits of external worship and other such preparatory devotions, and was soon able to live in the world depending completely on God and discriminating between the real and the unreal. His life eventually became completely focussed on following the Vaishnava ideal: He dedicated his wife, son, relatives, wealth, and everything he owned to God, living as His

7. Balaram's spiritual progress and way of life after meeting the Master.

servant, and he tried to spend most of his time in the Master's holy company. Balaram was not satisfied with enjoying for himself the peace that the grace of the Master brought him; he made all the appropriate arrangements for his relatives and friends to visit the Master and taste the divine bliss. Thus, because of Balaram, many people were blessed by becoming devotees of the Master.

As Balaram's view of external worship began to change, so did his obser-

8. Balaram's doubt about changing his views on nonviolence.

vance of nonviolence. Previously he could not kill mosquitoes even if they bit him while he was meditating and distracted him, let alone at other times. He considered killing them to be a sin. One day he realized that true religion requires concentrating the scattered mind on God, not dwelling on protecting mosquitoes and other insects. It could not be irreligious to kill a few mosquitoes if it kept the mind focussed on God even for a short while; it must be beneficial instead. Balaram told us: "My long practice of nonviolence was thus challenged by that thought, but my mind was not completely free from doubt. So I went to Dakshineswar to consult with the Master on this matter. On my way I was trying to remember if I'd ever seen the Master kill mosquitoes as others did. I thought not. As far as my memory went, the Master was far more careful in his practice of nonviolence than myself. I remembered that one day when the Master saw someone walk across a field of newly grown grass, he had felt excruciating pain in his chest because he vividly and intensely experienced the life force and consciousness of the grass. I thought it wasn't necessary to ask him this question. My mind was playing tricks on me. Nevertheless, I resolved to go and see him; it would purify my mind.

"When I reached the door of the Master's room at Dakshineswar, I was

9. His doubt is dispelled as he witnesses the Master's unusual behaviour.

dumbfounded by what I saw as I entered: The Master was removing bedbugs from his pillow and killing them. When I approached and bowed down to him, he said: 'There are many bedbugs breeding in the pillow. They bite me day and night, distracting my mind and keeping me from sleeping, so I'm killing them.' I no longer had any questions. All doubt was dispelled from my mind by the Master's words and actions. Amazed, I pondered: 'For the last two or three years I've been visiting the Master unannounced at all hours. Sometimes I come in the morning and return home in the evening, and sometimes come in the evening and leave at midnight. I've been visiting him three or four times a week, but had never seen him doing such a thing. Why did he do this today?' I found the answer within: If I'd seen him behaving in this manner previously, my belief in nonviolence would have been violated, and I would have lost faith in him. This is why the compassionate Master had never acted this way before me."

In addition to the devotees whom the Master had seen in visions before they arrived, many men and women devotees came to Dakshineswar to see the Master in search of peace.

10. The Master's circle of devotees and his young devotees.

He received them affectionately, blessing some of them with advice and some with a divine touch. As time went on, a large group of devotees gathered around the Master. The Master took special care in developing the spiritual life of the boys and unmarried young men who came to him. Many times he mentioned the following reason for this: "One can't have a vision of God unless one puts the entirety of one's mind on Him. The boys' whole minds are available to them: Their attention isn't scattered among wife and children, money and property, name and fame, and other worldly objects. If they try to focus their whole minds on God now, they will be blessed to see Him. That's why I'm extremely eager to guide them on the spiritual path." Whenever he had the opportunity, the Master took them one by one to a secluded place, instructed them in the practice of yoga and meditation, and advised them to observe unbroken brahmacharya and avoid getting entangled by marriage. He selected for each of them a different Chosen Deity according to aptitude and taught each one how to establish a relationship with the deity according to that devotee's spiritual disposition, so that the devotee could easily make progress in his own path.

After reading the description above, one should not conclude that the Master preferred to teach his young male disciples and had little grace and compassion for his householder devotees. The Master knew that many of those men and women had neither the ability nor the

11. How the Master advises householder devotees and the general public.

time to practise the most advanced spiritual disciplines, so he did not instruct them in the same manner as he did the young men. Rather, he taught householders to slowly reduce their desires for lust and gold, and he constantly guided them on the path of devotion so that they might eventually attain God. He first advised them to live unattached in God's world and to carry out their respective duties like servants in the house of a wealthy person. He encouraged them to practise chastity as much as possible. He told them, "After having one or two children, a husband and wife should live like brother and sister, keeping their minds focussed on God." He also directed them to follow the path of truth, to deal with people in a straightforward way, and to be content with simple food and clothing, shunning luxury. He told them to establish their minds in God; to practise meditation, japa, and worship every morning and evening; and to sing kirtan. If he realized that some of these householder devotees were incapable of doing that, he would advise them to go into solitude and chant Hari's name while clapping their hands, or to sing kirtan with their relatives and friends.

Many times we heard him say the following to groups of men and women: "The way to realize God in the Kaliyuga is the path of bhakti as prescribed by Narada. People will be liberated merely by singing the name and glories of God. In the Kaliyuga, human beings depend entirely on food to live. It's because they are weak and short-lived that this easy path to realizing God has been prescribed in this age." So as not to discourage them, as he talked about yoga, meditation, and difficult spiritual practices, he would say: "One who has renounced the world is supposed to call on God. It's for this reason that such a person has given up all worldly duties. Is there anything very remarkable or extraordinary about this? But if a man who carries the heavy responsibility of caring for his father, mother, wife, and children thinks of God even once, God is extremely pleased and thinks: 'It is not an insignificant feat for this man, who carries such a heavy load, to call upon Me even a little! This man is a real hero.'"

Words are inadequate to describe the exalted position that the Master

| 12. The Master gives Narendra the highest position among the devotees. |

gave to Narendra among the devotees whom he had seen in his vision, not to speak of the new devotees who came afterwards. Pointing to some of his special devotees, the Master said, "They are ishwarakotis — they have been born to accomplish a special mission for God." One day he compared Narendra to those select devotees: "Narendra is like a thousand-petalled lotus. The other few ishwarakotis are also like lotuses, but some have ten petals, some fifteen, and at most some have twenty." On another occasion he said, "So many devotees have come here, but there isn't another one like Narendra." In truth, no one but Narendra could understand and properly express the extraordinary actions and words of the wonderful Master. Narendra's interpretations of the Master's sayings sometimes amazed us, and we would think: "Well, we also heard the Master say those things, but we did not realize that they had such deep meanings." We shall mention an incident that illustrates this:

Sometime in 1884, a friend of ours went to Dakshineswar and found the

| 13. Narendra understands better than others the Master's message: "Serve all human beings as God." |

Master seated in his room surrounded by devotees. Narendra was present. Various spiritual discussions went on, relieved by wit and humour. When the topic of the Vaishnava religion arose during the conversation, the Master briefly explained the quintessence of that doctrine, saying: "This religion advises its followers to practise these three salient disciplines sincerely: love of God's name, compassion for all living beings, and service of devotees.[1] God and His name are identical. Knowing the Name and the possessor of the Name to be the same, the

---

1. *Jive daya name ruchi vaishnav sevan, Iha vina dharma nai shuna Sanatan.* (Listen, O Sanatan, there is no other dharma than practising compassion for all living beings, love of God's name, and service of devotees.) This is Chaitanya's instruction to his disciple Sanatan. — *Translator*

devotee should always chant His name with love. Knowing God and His devotees, Krishna and the Vaishnavas, to be the same, one should respect, worship, and pay obeisance to monks and devotees. Understanding that this world belongs to Krishna, one should show compassion for all beings." As he said, "compassion for all beings," he suddenly went into samadhi. After a while he came down to a semiecstatic state and said: "Compassion for all beings? How foolish to speak of compassion! Human beings are as insignificant as worms crawling on the earth — and they are to show compassion to others? That's absurd. It must not be compassion, but service to all. Recognize all as manifestations of God and serve them as such."

Everyone heard the Master's words, but no one except Narendra understood their significance. When the Master came to the normal plane of consciousness, Narendra left the room and said to some of his friends: "What a wonderful light I saw today in those words of the Master! How beautifully did he reconcile the simple, sweet, and refreshing ideal of devotion with the knowledge of Vedanta, which people believe to be dry, difficult, and heartless! For so long we've heard that anyone who wants to attain nondual knowledge must retire to the forest, shunning family and friends completely and forcibly uprooting love, devotion, and other sweet sentiments from the heart, driving them away forever. If aspirants who strive to attain that knowledge consider this world and all people within it to be impediments to their spiritual path, they will develop hatred towards them and go astray. But what the Master said today in his ecstatic mood is clear: One can bring Vedanta from the forest to the home and practise it in daily life. Let people continue with whatever they are doing; there's no harm in this. People must first believe and understand that God has manifested Himself before them as the world and its creatures. Whomever people come in contact with in every moment of their lives, whomever they treat with love, respect, and compassion — they all are parts of God, God Himself. If people consider every human being to be God, how can they consider themselves to be superior to others and harbour anger, hatred, and arrogance — or even compassion — towards them? Their minds will become pure as they serve all beings as God, and soon they will experience themselves as parts of the blissful God — by nature pure, illumined, and free.

"The Master's words also shed a special light on the path of devotion. As long as an aspirant can't see God in every being, it isn't possible to attain true and supreme devotion. When true devotees serve human beings as Shiva or Narayana, they see God in others and are soon blessed with supreme devotion. The followers of karma yoga and raja yoga will also find great light in the Master's words. Embodied beings cannot remain without activity for even a moment, so their duty is to perform every action as service to God within human beings; thus they will soon reach the goal. If it's the will of

14. Narendra sees a wonderful light in these words of the Master and explains their meaning.

God, I shall proclaim to the world at large the noble truth that I've heard today. I shall preach this wonderful message to all — the wise and the ignorant, the rich and the poor, the brahmin and the pariah."

When he entered the realm of samadhi, the extraordinary Master constantly shed a wonderful light on the paths of knowledge, devotion, yoga, and karma, and illumined the ways of human life. Unfortunately, we could not understand his words at the time. Only the talented Narendra understood his divine messages to a great extent and sometimes amazed us with his explanations of them.

Chapter 10

The Great Festival at
Panihati

WE HAVE ALREADY DESCRIBED HOW NARENDRA finally took refuge in the Master

1. Narendra accepts a teaching job.

and was blessed, thus ensuring that his family would never suffer from want of plain food and simple clothing. His family's financial condition gradually improved thereafter, and although they were not affluent, they were not poverty-stricken as before. Shortly after this incident, Ishwar Chandra Vidyasagar established a branch of the Metropolitan Institution in the Champatala district of Calcutta and appointed Narendra to be headmaster of that school. Narendra began teaching there probably in May 1885; he worked there for three or four months.

Although his financial condition had improved to some extent, at this

2. The enmity of Narendra's relatives, the Master's cancer, and Narendra's resignation from his job.

time Narendra was extremely disturbed by the enmity of his relatives, who had somehow found an opportunity to occupy the best rooms of his family's ancestral home. As a result he had to move out of his home temporarily and settle in his grandmother's house at Ramtanu Basu Lane. He was forced to file a lawsuit against his relatives in the Calcutta High Court. Nimai Charan Basu, an attorney and a friend of his father, was of great help to him with this case. In August 1885, Narendra had to resign from his teaching position to devote more time to the lawsuit and also to prepare for his final B.L. examination. He had another important reason: At this time the Master developed cancer, and it was gradually worsening. Narendra felt that he needed to spend more time with the Master to supervise his medical treatment and nursing.

In 1885, the Master suffered greatly from heat, so his devotees asked him

| 3. The Master falls ill after eating too much ice. |

to eat some ice. Seeing that ice chips relieved the Master, many devotees began to bring ice to Dakshineswar. The Master always added ice to his drinking water and sherbet and was as happy as a boy. Within a month or two, however, his throat began to hurt. It was probably April when he first felt pain.

A month passed and still the Master's pain did not lessen. In May the

| 4. His disease becomes worse due to excessive talking and repeated samadhi. |

disease took a new turn, worsening if he talked too much or if he went into samadhi. His condition was first diagnosed as an inflammation of the pharynx due to a cold, and an ointment was prescribed. When no result was seen after applying it for a few days, a devotee called in Dr. Rakhal Chandra Haldar of Bowbazar who was known to specialize in this kind of illness. The doctor diagnosed the disease and prescribed a medicine to be taken internally and an ointment to be applied externally to the throat. He also advised us to prevent the Master from talking too much or going into samadhi too frequently.

The thirteenth day of the bright fortnight of Jaishtha [mid-May to mid-

| 5. The history of the great festival at Panihati. |

June] drew near. On this day every year a special festival of the Vaishnava sect is held in the village of Panihati on the Ganges, a few miles north of Calcutta. The story of the austerity and burning renunciation of Raghunath Das Goswami, one of Chaitanya's main disciples, is well known in Bengal. Raghunath was the only son of an extremely wealthy man. When he first came to take refuge in Chaitanya at Shantipur, having renounced a beautiful wife and immense wealth, Chaitanya advised him to stay at home for a while to ensure that his renunciation was not superficial. Raghunath obeyed Chaitanya's command and returned home, but his intense desire to renounce the world lay hidden in his heart as he continued to help his father and uncle by performing his worldly duties as they did. Although he stayed at home, with his father's permission he would occasionally visit the disciples of Chaitanya, live a few days in their holy company, and then return home. The days thus rolled on as Raghunath waited for the right moment to renounce the world. Eventually, Chaitanya took his monastic vows and moved to Puri, leaving Nityananda to preach the Vaishnava religion. Nityananda made the village of Khardaha on the Ganges his headquarters and began to travel throughout Bengal, initiating many people into his faith, singing, and preaching God's name.

Once when Nityananda was preaching in Panihati along with his followers, Raghunath came to see him. Nityananda asked him to make an offering to the Lord of flattened rice, curd, milk, sugar, and banana mixed together, and to feed the huge circle of devotees. Raghunath gladly obeyed this order, then arranged a wonderful feast for the hundreds of people who had come to see Nityananda that day. After the festivities, Raghunath bowed down to Nityananda and wanted to take his leave, but the latter went into ecstasy and embraced him, saying: "Your time of waiting is over. If you renounce the world now and go to see Chaitanya in Puri, he will accept you. He will entrust you to Sanatan Goswami for training so that you can attain perfection in spiritual life." Raghunath's joy knew no bounds when he heard Nityananda's words. Soon after returning home, he left his family forever and went to Puri. Raghunath left Panihati, but every year from then on the Panihati Vaishnava devotees have observed that day in commemoration of him, arranging a feast to honour Chaitanya and Nityananda so that they can have God's grace as Raghunath did. In the course of time, it became known to devotees as the Festival of Flattened Rice of Panihati.

We have mentioned elsewhere (see II.8.22) that the Master had attended

6. The Master decides to attend the festival.

the great festival of Panihati many times. But for many reasons he had not gone there for several years, not since the arrival of his English-educated devotees. He expressed a desire to attend the festival this year [1885] with his devotees, telling us: "Many kirtan singers come there on that day and open a fair of bliss — a mart of Hari's name. You belong to the group of Young Bengal; you have never seen such an affair. Let us go and see the festival." Ramchandra Datta and some devotees were excited by the Master's proposal, but others were concerned about the Master's painful throat and tried to discourage him. To pacify them, he said: "I shall eat a little lunch early and will stay at the fair only a couple of hours. It won't do much harm. Excessive bhava samadhi may increase the pain in my throat, but I shall try to control myself in that respect." With these words he eliminated all objections, and the devotees began to arrange for his trip to Panihati.

At 9:00 a.m. on the thirteenth day of the bright fortnight, the day of the

7. Arrangements before the departure.

Panihati festival, about twenty-five Calcutta devotees rented two boats and came to Dakshineswar; some other devotees came on foot. A separate boat had been rented for the Master and was anchored at the ghat. Some women devotees came early in the morning to help the Holy Mother prepare a meal for the Master and the devotees. Everyone finished eating by 10:00 a.m. and prepared to leave.

When the Master had eaten, the Holy Mother requested a woman devotee

8. The Holy Mother decides not to go.

to ask him if she should accompany them. The Master told her: "Well, you're all going. She may go if she wishes." When the Holy Mother heard this, she said: "Many devotees are going with the Master. It will be overcrowded and it will be difficult for me to get off the boat and to visit the festival. I shall not go." Giving up the idea of accompanying them, the Holy Mother fed two or three women devotees who were to accompany the Master and asked them to go in the same boat with him.

Mani Sen's shrine at Panihati.

Festival ground at Panihati.
Ramakrishna attended the Vaishnava festival here several times.

After reaching Panihati about noon, we saw that many people were

9. The scene at the festival.

gathered around a pipal tree on the Ganges. The Vaishnava devotees were enjoying kirtan in different places, but it seemed to us that most of them were not truly absorbed in the glory of God's name. Something was missing, and the atmosphere seemed lifeless. Before we left Dakshineswar, and after arriving at Panihati, Narendra, Balaram, Girish, Ramchandra, Mahendra, and the other main devotees had implored the Master not to join any kirtan party and not to get overexcited. If he became deeply involved in kirtan, he would definitely go into ecstasy — and that would make his throat more painful.

After disembarking, the Master went straight to Mani Sen's house. All the

10. Mani Sen's house.

members of Mani's household were delighted to have the Master in their home. They bowed down to him and took him to their parlour. The room was decorated in the English fashion with tables, chairs, sofas, and carpets. The Master rested there for ten or fifteen minutes and then went with the devotees to pay obeisance to Lord Radhakanta in Mani Sen's family temple.

The parlour was very close to the temple. We went through a side door to

11. Mani Sen's family temple.

the natmandir adjacent to the temple to see the beautiful images of Radha and Krishna. After gazing upon the deities for a while the Master went into a semiecstatic state and bowed down. Six or seven steps down from the natmandir is the quadrangular temple courtyard, which has suites of rooms surrounding it. The location of the main gate to the household is situated in such a way that as soon as one enters, one sees the deities. As the Master was bowing down, a kirtan party entered the courtyard through the gate and began singing. It seemed that all kirtan parties first sang in front of the deities at this temple, then proceeded to the fairground on the bank of the Ganges. A tall, fat, middle-aged man entered the courtyard, counting beads in a pouch. The man had a fair complexion, wore a sacred thread, had a tuft of hair on his head, and was adorned with holy Vaishnava marks all over his body. He had a chadar thrown over his shoulder, wore an elegant borderless cloth (Rally's 49) that was folded neatly, and carried a bunch of coins in the fold of his waistcloth. He appeared to be a distinguished goswami who had adorned himself and come to the fair to make some money. He immediately joined the kirtan party and began to dance and shout in an apparently ecstatic state, attempting to excite the party and perhaps charm the audience with his greatness.

After paying obeisance to the deities, the Master stood to one side of the

12. The Master dances in ecstasy.

natmandir listening to the kirtan. Seeing the goswami's fancy and fastidious dress and his pretense of ecstasy, the Master smiled a little and whispered to Narendra and the nearby devotees, "Look, what a fake!" His light-hearted remark made the others smile as well and reassured them that he had his ecstatic mood under perfect control. But the very next moment, before any of them could react, he swiftly bounded down into the midst of the kirtan party and lost external consciousness in samadhi. The devotees hurriedly got down from the natmandir and encircled the Master. He regained partial consciousness and began to dance as powerfully as a lion, and again lost outer consciousness and stood still. He went in and out of samadhi like this for some time. As he danced his ecstatic dance, he moved rapidly and rhythmically forward and backward, as if he were a fish joyfully swimming and moving in a sea of bliss.

It is impossible to describe how this emotion manifested itself in every limb of his body, revealing strength blended with an extraordinary softness and sweetness, and an unbounded bliss. We have seen many men and women dance enchantingly with various gestures, but we have never seen before such beauty mixed with gentleness and strength as was manifested in the Master when he danced exuberantly, lost in ecstasy. Overflowing with ecstatic bliss, his body would swing and move as though it were not made of any hard stuff such as bones; rather, it was as if a tidal wave had arisen from the ocean of bliss and were vigorously sweeping away everything before it, and would again become liquid and disappear from sight. Everyone present realized the difference between the genuine ecstasy and the pretense. Without another glance at the Goswami, the kirtan party encircled the Master and began to sing, its zeal and joy magnified a hundredfold.

After about half an hour the Master began to come back to himself and the

13. On the way to Pandit Raghav's house.

devotees tried to remove him from the kirtan party. Before returning to our boats, we decided to visit the nearby house of Pandit Raghav, a disciple of Chaitanya who had daily worshipped the images of Radha and Krishna, and the shalagrama [the stone image of Vishnu]. The Master agreed to this plan and left Mani Sen's temple with the devotees. But the kirtan party would not give up the Master's company so easily; they followed him, enthusiastically singing of God's glory. The Master took a few steps and then became still in ecstasy. When he regained partial consciousness, the devotees asked him to move forward. He took another few steps and again went into samadhi. This happened repeatedly, and their progress was very slow.

We do not remember ever having seen the Master display such a lumi-

14. The Master's extraordinary beauty in ecstasy.

nous beauty in samadhi as he did that day. It is beyond human power to properly describe the extraordinary beauty of his divine form. We never could have imagined a human body changing in a moment of ecstasy. We saw the Master's tall figure every day, but on that day it appeared to grow even taller and become weightless, like a body seen in a dream. His slightly dark complexion became brighter and turned golden; the divine mood shone on his face and illumined everything around him. When people saw his incomparable smile — a combination of grace, compassion, peace, and joy — they forgot everything and followed him, spellbound. The beautiful colour of his skin blended with the bright ochre colour of his silk wearing-cloth so that it seemed as if he were enveloped in flames.

As soon as the Master came to the street from Mani Sen's temple, the

15. Seeing the Master, the kirtan party becomes joyful and enthusiastic.

kirtan party saw his divine beauty, captivating dance, and repeated ecstasy. Endowed with fresh energy, they sang:

> Who sings the name of Hari on the bank of the Ganges?
> It seems that our Nitai,[1] the love-giver, is here!
> Who calls out the name of Hari
> And who sings of Radha's glory?
> It seems that our Nitai, the love-giver, is here!
> Here comes our Nitai, bringing divine love!
> Without him, how can our heart's longing be appeased?
> Here is our Nitai, the love-giver!

Again and again they sang, "Here is our love-giver," pointing to the

16. People's attraction to the Master.

Master and dancing joyfully. The enthusiastic kirtan party drew the attention of the crowd at the festival ground and attracted them to the Master. Those who saw him were at once overwhelmed; they either joined the kirtan joyfully or were dazed by an inexpressible divine feeling in their hearts and silently followed the Master, looking at him with a steadfast gaze. Gradually, this enthusiasm spread like a contagious disease. A few more kirtan parties joined the first, forming a vast crowd that encircled the ecstatic Master and slowly moved towards the house of Pandit Raghav.

Some women devotees had taken a few earthen bowls of sweets to a spot

17. A bowl of prasad.

under the pipal tree on the Ganges, offered them to Chaitanya and Nityananda, and were bringing them to the Master. But before they arrived at the house of Pandit Raghav, an ugly babaji in Vaishnava garb and marks appeared suddenly and snatched a bowl of prasad from one of the women. Feigning divine emotion, the babaji put a little prasad into the mouth of the Master, who was then standing still in samadhi. As soon as the babaji touched him, the Master's entire body shuddered and his samadhi broke. He spat out the food immediately and washed his mouth. Onlookers realized that the babaji must be either unclean in some way or a hypocrite; they looked at him scornfully and he slunk away, humiliated. The Master then took a little prasad from a devotee and distributed the rest among the others.

---

1. The nickname of Nityananda, the main disciple of Chaitanya. — *Translator*

The group finally reached Pandit Raghav's house, after taking almost

18. The Master returns to the boat and bestows grace on Navachaitanya.

three hours to cross the distance [of half a mile]. The Master entered the temple and bowed down, touching the deities, then rested for a while. He spent half an hour there. The large crowd gradually dispersed, and the devotees escorted the Master to the boat. But here another wonderful incident took place. Navachaitanya Mitra of Konnagar had heard about the Master's presence at the festival and had been desperately searching for him. He finally found the Master in the boat, which was about to leave. He ran in wild haste and, throwing himself at the Master's feet, wept and begged, "Bestow your grace on me." When the Master saw Navachaitanya's longing and devotion, he went into ecstasy and touched him. We know nothing about the vision that the Master's touch produced in Navachaitanya, but his piteous cry turned in a moment to exuberant jubilation. He forgot where he was and began dancing excitedly on the boat, singing hymns praising the Master, and bowing down to him again and again.

After a while, the Master stroked Navachaitanya's back, calmed him down, and gave him some advice. Although Navachaitanya had visited the Master many times before, he had never before received the grace he was blessed with on that day. When he returned home, he turned his family responsibilities over to his son and moved to a thatched hut in his village on the bank of the Ganges, where he spent the rest of his life as a hermit, practising spiritual disciplines and chanting the Master's name. From that point on the elderly Navachaitanya experienced ecstasy during kirtan, and many people who saw his devout and blissful figure loved and respected him. By the Master's grace, in the last years of his life Navachaitanya enkindled devotion for God in the hearts of many people.

After Navachaitanya took his leave, the Master asked that the boat take

19. The Master arrives in Dakshineswar; what he says to a disciple who is about to leave.

off. We had not gone very far when dusk descended, and we reached the Dakshineswar temple garden at about 8:30 p.m. The Master sat in his room, and his devotees bowed down and took their leave of him

before returning to Calcutta. As everyone was boarding the boat, a young disciple remembered that he had forgotten his shoes, so he ran back to the Master's room to get them. When the Master saw him and learned why he had returned, he said jokingly: "It's fortunate that you remembered your shoes before the boat took off. Otherwise the fun and joy of today's festival would have been spoiled." The young disciple smiled at his comment, bowed down to him again, and was about to leave when the Master asked: "How did you enjoy the day? It was a veritable fair of Hari's name, wasn't it?" The disciple agreed. The Master then mentioned the names of those devotees who had had spiritual experiences at the festival, and praised Junior Naren, remarking: "That dark-complexioned boy has been visiting this place for a short time, but already he's having ecstasies. The other day his ecstasy was hard to stop — he had no outer consciousness of his surroundings for more than an hour! He says that nowadays his mind merges into the formless God. He's a good boy, isn't he? Please go to his house one day and talk to him. Will you?"

The young disciple agreed at first, but then he said, "But, sir, I like no one as well as I do Senior Naren [Vivekananda], so I don't feel like visiting Junior Naren." The Master scolded him, saying: "You brat! You're very one-sided! This is a sign of small-mindedness. Just as a tray of flowers offered to the Lord contains various kinds of blooms, so He has all kinds of devotees. It's a sign of narrowness when one can't enjoy mixing with everyone. You must visit Junior Naren one day. Won't you?" The disciple promised to visit him and left after saluting the Master. The boat reached Calcutta at about 10:00 p.m. This young disciple followed the Master's advice and a few days later went to visit Junior Naren. As they talked, the young disciple was blessed with the answer to a serious and complicated problem in his life.

That night the women devotees stayed with the Holy Mother. They

20. During supper the Master speaks to a woman devotee about the Holy Mother.

knew that the next day there would be a great celebration at the Kali temple and decided to return to Calcutta after seeing it. The celebration was held every year on Snanayatra, in connection with the installation ceremony of the Divine Mother. While having his supper that night, the Master told one of these women about the Panihati festival: "What a crowd! And everyone was watching me because of my bhava samadhi. She [the Holy Mother] made the correct decision not to go with us. If people had seen her with me, they would have remarked, 'A pair of swans has come.'[2] She is extremely intelligent." He continued commenting on the Holy Mother's extraordinary intelligence: "When a Marwari devotee offered me ten thousand rupees, I felt as if someone had taken a saw to my head. I prayed, 'Mother, after such a long time You tempt me again?' In order to test her [the Holy Mother's] mind, I called her in and said: 'Look, this devotee wants to give me this money. As I refused to accept it, he wants to give it to you. Why don't you take it?' She immediately replied: 'How could this be possible? No, the money shouldn't be accepted. My acceptance would be as good as yours. If I took it, I'd certainly spend it to serve you and buy things you need. You would therefore be the virtual owner of it. People love and respect you for your renunciation. For that reason, this money can by no means be accepted.' I heaved a sigh of relief at her words."

2. Sri Ramakrishna used the term *hamsa-hamsi,* which means male and female swans. Hamsa also means a soul. Sri Ramakrishna was known as paramahamsa, a great soul, an all-renouncing monk. — *Translator*

When the Master finished his supper, the women devotees returned to the
nahabat and reported to the Holy Mother what he
had said about her. The Holy Mother said: "From the
way he gave me permission this morning, I immedi-
ately realized that he wasn't giving it wholeheartedly. If he were, he would
have said, 'Yes, of course she may go.' Instead, he left the matter for me to
decide by saying, 'She may go if she wishes.' I then decided that I'd better
give up the idea of going."

21. What the Holy
Mother said on the
subject.

That night the Master could not sleep due to a burning sensation in his
body. It probably happened because different types
of people had touched his divine body at the festival.
Quite often he suffered from a burning sensation
whenever impure persons took the dust of his feet in
order to rid themselves of disease or to fulfill their
worldly desires.

22. Some worldly people
disturb the Master's
spiritual mood on the
Snanayatra festival day,
irritating him.

The Snanayatra celebration was held the day after the Panihati festival. We
were not present at Dakshineswar on that occasion, but the women devotees
told us that many men and women visited the Master that day. A.'s mother
was among them. She pestered the Master to solve a problem involving her
wealth and her estate, disturbing his blissful mood. As he ate lunch at noon
that day, the Master saw her seated nearby; he was so disgusted that he did not
talk and could not eat as well as he usually did. When he went to wash his
mouth after lunch, one of the women devotees we knew carried water for
him. He told her privately: "People come here to get love and devotion for
God. Please tell me, how can I settle that woman's worldly affairs? To fulfill
her desires the woman brought expensive mangoes and various sweets, and I
couldn't put even a bit of it into my mouth. Today is Snanayatra. On this day in
years past I've had bhava samadhi so often that its intoxication continued for
two or three days, but today I've experienced nothing. That high spiritual
mood couldn't come because of the vibrations of these worldly people."

As A.'s mother stayed at Dakshineswar that night, the Master's irritation
continued throughout the night. During supper he told a woman devotee: "It
is not good that so many women are crowded here. Trailokya, Mathur's son, is
here. What will he think of this? It's all right if one or two come occasionally
and stay a day or two, but now there's a crowd of women. I can't abide such a
rush of women." The women devotees thought that they had caused the
Master's annoyance, so at daybreak they sadly returned to Calcutta. The
Snanayatra festival was celebrated with great pomp in the Kali temple with
special worship and a performance of drama, but those women devotees
could not enjoy it for the reasons given above. From this event, the reader will
understand to some extent how watchful the Master was regarding
day-to-day affairs and how he admonished and guided his devotees for their
welfare, even though he lived on a higher plane of consciousness at all times.

Chapter 11

The Master Moves to Calcutta

AFTER THE MASTER TOOK PART IN THE PANIHATI FESTIVAL, his throat pain increased.

1. The Master's throat pain increases after the Panihati trip: the childlike Master's response.

On the day of the festival there had been intermittent showers. The doctors blamed his devotees for this escalation of the disease, because they had allowed the Master to become soaked by rain and remain in samadhi for a long time while standing barefoot on the wet ground. They warned the Master's devotees that if he underwent such a strain again, his case would become more serious. The Master's devotees decided to be more careful in the future. The childlike Master shifted the entire responsibility for the strain to Ramchandra and a few other senior devotees. He said, "Could I have gone to Panihati if they'd forbidden me a little more emphatically?" Although Ram did not practise medicine, he had studied at Campbell Medical School and obtained a diploma in medicine. Because of his love for the Vaishnava faith, Ram had encouraged the Master to attend the Panihati festival. He was therefore mainly to blame for the situation.

One day during this period a friend of ours went to Dakshineswar and found the Master seated silently on the small cot in his room, applying ointment to his throat. Our friend told us: "I saw that the Master's face was as sullen as that of a boy who had been punished by confinement to one place and forbidden to do anything. I bowed down to him and asked, 'What has happened?' Pointing to the ointment on his throat, he replied in low voice, 'Look, the pain has increased, and the doctor has forbidden me to speak much.' I said: 'Sir, I heard that you went to Panihati the other day. That may be the reason for the aggravation.' As piqued as a child, he said: 'Yes, it's true. Look, it was a rainy day and the road was muddy — there was water above and water below. Ram took me there and made me dance the entire day. He's a doctor with a degree. Would I have gone there if he'd strongly forbidden me?' I said: 'Indeed, sir, Ram was quite wrong. Anyway, what's done is done. Now be careful for a few days and you will be cured.' Pleased, he said: 'But is it possible to remain completely silent? Look, you've come from such a distance! Is it possible for me not to say a few words to you?' I replied: 'I get joy from seeing you. It's all right if you don't talk. We won't mind at all. Please get well; then we shall hear many things from you.' But who listens to me? Forgetting the doctor's advice and his own pain, he began to talk to me as usual."

The month of *Ashad* [mid-June to mid-July] passed. The Master had been

2. Despite his sore throat, the Master disobeys the doctor and continues to instruct people.

under treatment for over a month, but his throat pain was not going away. He had moderate pain all the time, but his pain increased during the days of the full moon, the new moon, and *ekadashi* [the eleventh day of each fortnight]. At those times it was almost impossible for him to swallow any solid food or vegetables. So on those days he ate only milk and rice, or farina pudding. The doctors who examined him diagnosed his condition as "Clergyman's sore throat," meaning that the cause of his pain was excessive use of his vocal cords caused by giving spiritual advice to people day and night. Such a disease affecting preachers has been recorded in medical journals. After they had diagnosed the disease, his doctors prescribed medicine and diet and gave other instructions. The Master followed their injunctions faithfully, except on two points: He was unable to control his samadhi because of his intense love for God, and he could not curtail his speaking because of his limitless compassion for suffering human beings. Whenever there was any talk of God, he would lose body-consciousness and go into samadhi as he always did. And when ignorant and grief-stricken people came to him for spiritual guidance and peace, he was overwhelmed with compassion and blessed them with spiritual advice as usual.

Many spiritual seekers visited the Master at this time. In addition to his

3. The Master's illness is due to his excessive exertion in instructing many people, his lack of sleep in mahabhava, and so on.

regular devotees, six or seven new people or even more were coming to the Master each day for spiritual instruction. This had happened every day since shortly after Keshab arrived at Dakshineswar in 1875. The Master's regular hours for bathing, eating, and resting were greatly interrupted throughout the last eleven years that he taught people. In addition, his mahabhava allowed him very little sleep. Whenever we stayed at Dakshineswar, we saw how he would go to bed at 11:00 p.m. but get up after a short while to pace in his room in ecstasy. Sometimes he would open the western or the northern door and go out; at other times he would quietly lie in bed, wide-awake. And although he got up three or four times at night, he would arise promptly at 4:00 a.m. to meditate and chant God's name. At dawn he would call us to get up. So it is not surprising that his body was exhausted because of sleeplessness at night and excessive labour in instructing many people during the day.

Although the Master did not tell us directly that his body was gradually

deteriorating because of overwork, there were hints of this in his loving quarrels with the Divine Mother, which we overheard but could not fully understand. A short time before he became ill, one of us went to Dakshineswar and saw the Master seated on his small cot in an ecstatic mood. He was addressing someone, saying: "Why do You bring all these worthless people here? They are like milk diluted with water five times over. My eyes are burning from smoke as I continually blow on the wet fuel to evaporate the water. I'm reduced to a skeleton. It's beyond my strength; do it Yourself if You want it done. Bring some good people here who can become spiritually awakened with one or two words." Another day he told his devotees: "Today I prayed to the Mother: 'Please give a little power to Vijay, Girish, Kedar, Ram, and Master [M.], so that they can prepare new-comers to a certain extent before they come to me.'" In regard to providing people with spiritual direction, he once said to a woman devotee, "You pour water and let me knead the mud." A few days after his throat began to hurt he noticed that the crowd of spiritual aspirants at Dakshineswar was growing daily. In an ecstatic mood, he told the Divine Mother: "Why do You bring so many people here? You've created a heavy crowd! I've no time even to bathe and to eat. This (*pointing to his own body*) is a perforated drum. How long will it last if You go on beating it day in and day out?"

By the end of 1884, the Master's unique spirituality, devotion, samadhi,

and immortal message had spread so far by word of mouth throughout Calcutta that a large number of people began to come to Dakshineswar to see him every day. Those who came once were so charmed that they visited him again and again. It is difficult to determine how many people came to him before his throat disease developed in July 1885, because they never had the opportunity to meet in one place on the same day. This was good in a way: For a long time the intimate devotees of the Master had experienced joy as they noticed that the number of his devotees was increasing, because their object of worship and love was becoming an object of worship and love for all. However, if they saw that large crowd in one place, their joy would have turned to sorrow and fear, for the Master had told them repeatedly, "When many people regard this (*me*) as God, and love and respect me as such, it (*this body*) will soon disappear."

The Master gave us many hints about the time of his passing away. But we

were then so overwhelmed by his love that we paid no heed to his words, although we heard them; and although we understood them intellectually, we did not truly comprehend their meaning. Our only goals at that time were to be blessed by his divine grace and to help all our relatives and friends attain a similar grace and peace. So the subject of his departure did not cross our minds. Four or five years before his throat disease appeared, he said to the Holy Mother: "When you find me accepting food from anyone and everyone, spending nights in Calcutta, and feeding a portion of food first to someone else and afterwards eating what is left — then you will know that the day is near when I will leave this body." Such things began to happen sometime before the Master fell ill. He accepted invitations from various people in Calcutta to visit their homes, where he ate all sorts of food that anyone offered him, except cooked rice. The Master had also stayed some nights at Balaram's house in Calcutta. Before the Master's illness Narendra had been suffering from dyspepsia and did not visit Dakshineswar for many days, thinking that his special diet would not be available there. So early one morning the Master had Narendra brought to Dakshineswar and fed him some of the rice and soup that had been cooked for himself and then ate what was left over. The Holy Mother objected to this and wanted to cook fresh food for him, but the Master said: "My mind didn't hesitate when I offered the first portion of the food to Narendra. It won't do any harm. You don't need to cook again." The Holy Mother later said, "Although the Master tried to reassure me, I was broken-hearted as I remembered his prediction."

Although the Master's body became exhausted from the strain involved

7. The Master serves human beings as God.

in teaching, his enthusiasm for this did not waver. Whenever a competent spiritual aspirant arrived, he knew this deep in his heart. Immediately overwhelmed with divine power, he would give instructions to the aspirant and with a touch start him or her on the spiritual path. The newcomer's spiritual mood would call forth a similar mood in the Master, subduing his other moods for a while. The Master could then use his divine vision to see how far that aspirant had proceeded on the path towards perfection, and why that person could go no further. Next the Master removed all obstacles and established the aspirant in a higher spiritual realm. Until the last moment of his life, the Master served all human beings as God, initiated them into the divine knowledge of the Fearless One, and fulfilled the spiritual longings that had been driving them birth after birth. This, according to the scriptures, is the greatest gift to humankind.

We always saw vividly in the Master a power to detect people's hidden

8. The Master's ability to detect people's hidden thoughts and impressions.

thoughts and impressions. This ability of his is excellent evidence that his mind was never affected by the condition of his body, be it in ill or good health. Although he knew everything that was hidden in the minds of others, he never divulged this in order to display his divine power.

He told only what was good for an individual and pointed out the higher path. Sometimes he would reveal his divine power to the heart of a fortunate individual to strengthen that person's faith and reliance on him. Here is a commonplace example to help the reader easily understand this.

In August 1885, hearing that the Master's throat pain had increased, a

9. An example.

woman devotee whom we knew well was preparing to visit him in Dakshineswar. When a neighbour heard of this, she asked: "Today I have nothing at home but milk to offer to the Master. Will you kindly take this small jar of milk to him?" The devotee refused, saying: "There is no lack of good milk in Dakshineswar, and I know that milk is allotted for him there [by the temple] also. It's difficult to carry milk, and I don't think it is necessary."

When she reached Dakshineswar she found that, due to his throat pain, the Master was unable to eat solid dishes such as rice with vegetables. He could eat rice with milk only. The Holy Mother was very anxious because that day the milkwoman had not been able to supply the allotted milk to the Master. The woman devotee regretted that she had not brought that milk from Calcutta. She asked if milk were available in the village of Dakshineswar and was told that near the temple garden, Mrs. Pande, a non-Bengali woman, had a cow and was selling milk. The woman devotee went to her house and learned that the milkwoman had sold almost all her milk; only a cup was left, and she had boiled the milk to preserve it. The milkwoman sold it to her because she knew it was badly needed. The woman devotee brought the milk, and the Master had his meal of milk mixed with rice. When the Master went out to wash his mouth after the meal, the woman devotee poured water for him.

Later, the Master privately called the woman devotee to him and said: "Look, my throat is very painful. You know a mantra to cure the disease. Please repeat it and pass your hand over the affected area." The woman was dumbfounded at first, then did just as the Master requested and passed her hand over his throat. Later she went to the Holy Mother and asked: "How did the Master learn that I know that mantra? I learned it long ago from a woman of the Ghoshpara sect because I knew that it would be very useful to me in accomplishing some worldly goals. But eventually I realized that the goal of life is to call on God without motive, so I renounced it. When I told my life story to the Master I didn't disclose that I had received a Kartabhaja mantra. I hid that part from him because I thought he might not like it. How could he know about it?" Smiling, the Holy Mother replied: "Look, he knows everyone's thoughts and actions. He doesn't hate anyone for doing something sincerely, with good intentions. Don't be afraid. I also was initiated into that mantra before I came here. When I told him about it he said, 'There's no harm in your having that mantra, but now you must offer it to your Chosen Deity.'"

In the last part of August the Master's throat pain kept increasing, and the devotees could find no solution to the situation. During that time an incident took place that clearly showed them that they needed to make a decision. One day a woman devotee from Baghbazar invited the devotees to her house for supper. She wanted to

10. The Master's throat hemorrhages as his disease worsens; the devotees discuss taking the Master to Calcutta.

have the Master at her home as well, but had all but given up that hope because the Master was not well. Nevertheless, she sent a devotee to Dakshineswar, hoping that the Master could visit her house even for a short time. By 9:00 p.m. that devotee had still not returned, so without further delay she prepared to serve the devotees she had invited. Just then, however, that devotee returned with news: Today the Master's throat has hemorrhaged, so he cannot come. Narendra, Ram, Girish, Devendra, Mahendra, and the other devotees became extremely anxious. After some consultation they decided that they should rent a house in Calcutta where the Master could be brought for immediate treatment. Seeing that Narendra was very sad during supper, a young disciple asked him why. He replied: "He who has made us all so happy may be leaving us. I've been reading medical books and questioning my doctor friends. They all say that this kind of throat ailment can develop into cancer. This bleeding makes me even more afraid that it is cancer. If so, there's no known cure for it."

The next day a few senior devotees visited Dakshineswar to ask that the Master move to Calcutta for treatment. He agreed. These devotees had rented a small house on Durgacharan Mukherjee Street in Baghbazar because one could see the Ganges from its roof. Soon they

11. The Master moves to Calcutta for treatment and stays at Balaram's house.

brought the Master to Calcutta. The Master had been accustomed to living in the spacious temple garden of Dakshineswar on the Ganges, and when he entered this tiny house he declined to stay there; he immediately walked to Balaram's house on Ramkanta Basu Street. Balaram cordially received him and invited him to stay there until a suitable house could be found. The Master agreed.

The devotees began to search for a suitable house. Meanwhile, considering it improper to waste any more time, the devotees had invited some prominent Calcutta physicians to give their opinions regarding the Master's disease. Gangaprasad, Gopimohan, Dwarikanath, Navagopal,

12. Prominent physicians are called in and the disease is diagnosed. A house is rented at Shyampukur.

and other Ayurvedic doctors examined the Master and determined that he had contracted *rohini*, an incurable disease. When a devotee asked Gangaprasad privately, he said: "Rohini is what the medical doctors call cancer. Although a treatment has been mentioned in the medical books, this disease is considered incurable." Receiving no hope from the Ayurvedic doctors and knowing that too much medication did

Group of Ramakrishna's devotees.
Front row: Tarak Datta, Akshay Sen, Girish Ghosh, Swami Adbhutananda (Latu), Mahendra Nath Gupta (M).
Middle row: Kalipada Ghosh, Devendra Majumdar, Swami Advaitananda (Senior Gopal).
Back row: Devendra Chakrabarty, unknown, unknown, Abinash Mukhopadhyay, Mahendra Kaviraj, Vijay Majumdar.

not suit the Master's system, the devotees thought it reasonable to have him treated with homeopathy. Within a week, they rented Gokulchandra Bhattacharya's house on Shyampukur Street for the Master and agreed to put him under the care of Dr. Mahendralal Sarkar, a famous Calcutta doctor.

News of the Master's move to Calcutta for treatment spread from person

13. People flock to see the Master at Balaram's house.

to person throughout the city. Crowds of people, both friends and strangers, continually invaded Balaram's home to see the Master, making the house as joyful as a festival ground. Although the Master remained silent from time to time in deference to the doctor's advice and his devotees' fervent requests, he got involved in spiritual discussions with such enthusiasm that it seemed he had come there for that sole purpose. It was as if he had come to the doors of those who were unable to go to Dakshineswar in order to impart spiritual knowledge. He was available to them every day from early morning till night, with a break of only two hours for his midday meal and rest. During that week he solved complicated personal problems for many people, attracted many others to the spiritual path by talking about God, and flooded the hearts of spiritual seekers with bliss and peace by entering into deep samadhi after listening to devotional songs. None of us was fortunate enough to be present there all the time, and even Balaram had to go out on errands and was busy making all the necessary arrangements for the Master and the devotees. So it is almost impossible to give a detailed account of that week. We shall present the following incident to show the reader how the Master spent those days at Balaram's house.

We were in college at that time, so we could visit the Master only once or

14. An event at Balaram's house.

twice a week. One afternoon we went to Balaram's house and found the hall of the upper floor packed with people. Girish and Kalipada were singing with great zeal:

> O Nitai, hold me![1]
> Today my heart feels unusual.

Entering the room with great difficulty, we saw that the Master was in samadhi, seated at the western end of the room facing east. His face was adorned with an expression of graciousness and a wonderful smile. His right foot was lifted and extended, and a man in front of him was carefully holding it to his chest with great love, his eyes closed and tears trickling over his cheeks and down his chest. The room was quiet and a divine atmosphere vibrated throughout. The song continued:

---

1. Chaitanya. — *Translator*

Today my heart feels unusual,
O Nitai, hold me!
O Nitai, the wave that arose in the river of love —
The wave that brings Hari's name to all beings —
I am being carried away by that wave.
O Nitai, I have written the bond with my own hand,
And eight female confidantes [of Radha] have witnessed it.
Now how shall I repay my debt to the Creditor of Love?[2]
All my accumulated wealth has run out,
And still the debt remains unpaid.
Now I will sell myself to pay that debt of love.

When the singing ended, the Master regained partial consciousness. He said to the person before him, "Say 'Sri Krishna Chaitanya! Sri Krishna Chaitanya! Sri Krishna Chaitanya!'" He thus made him utter that name three times, and after a while the Master returned to his normal state and began to talk with others. On inquiry, we learned later that the man was Nrityagopal Goswami, a college professor in Dhaka, who had come to see the Master when he heard of his illness. Nrityagopal was a handsome and devout man.

2. Radha, the spiritual consort of Krishna. — *Translator*

Chapter 12

Section 1

The Master's Stay at *S*hyampukur

THE HOUSE RENTED FOR THE MASTER IS ON THE NORTH side of Shyampukur Street,

1. A description of the Shyampukur house.

which runs from east to west. When one enters the house one finds a vestibule with a narrow passage extending to one's right and left. A few steps ahead lies a courtyard, and to one's right is a staircase to the upper floor. On the eastern side of the courtyard are two or three rooms. After ascending the staircase, one sees to the right a long room extending from north to south, which was used for receiving visitors, and to one's left there is a corridor leading to rooms that extend from east to west. The first door on this corridor leads to a spacious room called the parlour, where the Master lived. To the north and south of the parlour are two verandas, the northern one larger than the southern. To the west of the parlour are two small rooms — one used by devotees who stayed overnight, and the other by the Holy Mother for sleeping. The visitors' room has a narrow veranda to the west. A staircase to the roof is at the eastern end of the corridor leading to the Master's room. At the top of those stairs, near the door to the roof, is a covered terrace of about six feet by six feet in size. The Holy Mother spent her days on that terrace, and there she cooked the special diet needed by the Master. The Master moved to this house from Balaram's in the early part of September 1885. He stayed there a little over three months and then moved to the Cossipore garden house towards the middle of December [11 December 1885].

The house in the Shyampukur district of Calcutta where Ramakrishna stayed for the first three months of his cancer treatment in 1885.

Ramakrishna's room at Shyampukur, Calcutta.

A few days after the Master moved to the Shyampukur house, his devo-

2. Dr. Mahendralal
Sarkar takes
responsibility for the
Master's treatment.
tees called in Dr. Mahendralal Sarkar to treat him as had been previously decided. When Mathur was alive Dr. Sarkar had visited Dakshineswar a few times to treat Mathur's family and had become somewhat acquainted with the Master. But that had been long ago, and it would have been quite natural for a famous doctor to forget those meetings. The devotees called him in without telling him the patient's name, but he recognized the Master as soon as he saw him. He carefully examined the Master, diagnosed his disease, and prescribed medicine and an appropriate diet. Afterwards, he spent a little time discussing spiritual matters and talking about the Kali temple of Dakshineswar before finally taking his leave. We remember that on that day the doctor told the devotees to inform him of the Master's condition every morning. He accepted his usual fee from them as he left that day. During his second visit to the Master, Dr. Sarkar learned that the devotees had brought him to Calcutta for treatment and were bearing all of his expenses. Pleased by their devotion to their guru, he declined to accept any additional fees. He said: "I shall treat him to the best of my ability, and to help you in your noble cause I won't accept any payment."

Although they now had the help of an experienced doctor, the devotees

3. Discussion about his
diet and care at night.
were not free from anxiety. Within a few days they realized that the Master's diet needed to be prepared carefully, and that attendants would be required in order to care for him day and night. Money alone could not properly satisfy these needs; so they decided to resolve the first by bringing the Holy Mother from Dakshineswar, and the second by asking the boy devotees to help. But there were serious obstacles to handling these two problems. The house had no inner apartment for women, so they could not figure out how the Holy Mother could live there. They also realized that the guardians of the young devotees would be very displeased if they regularly spent sleepless nights in serving the Master, as they were all schoolboys or college students.

Many devotees doubted that the Holy Mother would agree to come to

4. An example of the
Holy Mother's shyness.
Shyampukur; she was extraordinarily shy and modest. Although she had lived in the northern nahabat of the Dakshineswar garden and served the Master every day, no one except for two or three young devotees whom the Master introduced to her himself ever saw her or heard her voice. She spent her entire day in her tiny room, preparing food for the Master and the devotees twice a day, and no one knew that someone was performing those duties from there. Every morning she arose shortly after 3:00 a.m., long before anyone else. After washing herself and bathing in the Ganges, she entered the nahabat and never left it for the entire day. Calmly and silently she performed all her duties quickly and then kept herself busy with worship,

japa, and meditation. Once in the early morning before dawn she went to bathe in the Ganges. As she descended the steps of the Bakultala ghat near the nahabat, she almost stepped on a crocodile lying there. The crocodile jumped into the water at the sound of her footsteps. From then on she always carried a lantern when she went to the ghat in the early morning.

The devotees could not imagine how the Holy Mother, who had lived in

5. The proposal to bring the Holy Mother to Shyampukur.

the nahabat for such a long period of time, unseen by anyone, could suddenly give up her modesty and shyness to live at Shyampukur, surrounded constantly by male devotees. They could find no alternative, however, so they asked the Master about bringing her to Shyampukur. The Master reminded them of her bashful nature and said: "Could she live here? You'd better ask her about it. If she's willing to come after knowing all the facts, let her do so." A messenger was sent to the Holy Mother at Dakshineswar.

The Master used to say, "Adjust yourself according to time, place, and

6. The Holy Mother's ability to act according to time, place, and person.

person." If one cannot adjust and perform all duties in this world according to time, place, and person, one cannot attain peace and reach the goal one desires. Although the Holy Mother lived behind an impregnable veil of modesty and shyness, she had received this teaching from the Master and had learned to apply it to her life. If necessary, she could cast off the veil of her habits and customs in order to deal with any situation appropriately and fearlessly. The reader will understand this clearly by recalling her first visit to Dakshineswar (see II.20) and from the following incident.

In those days the Holy Mother usually travelled from Jayrambati and

7. The route from Kamarpukur to Dakshineswar.

Kamarpukur to Dakshineswar on foot because she had no money, or little of it, or for some other reason. People travelled from the Jayrambati-Kamarpukur area to Jahanabad (Arambag) and then crossed a ten-mile-wide field near Telo and Bhelo to reach Tarakeswar. From there they had to traverse a similar field, Kaikala, to reach Vaidyabati, and finally cross the Ganges by boat to Dakshineswar. Those two vast fields were inhabited by highwaymen. Even now people say that many travellers lose their lives at the robbers' hands in the morning, at noon, and in the evening. Telo and Bhelo are two small villages situated almost side by side. In a field a couple of miles away from these villages is a temple with a fierce and dreadful form of Kali, known as the Robbers' Kali of Telo-Bhelo. People say that robbers worship this Kali before proceeding to rob and murder travellers. In those days people travelled in groups to traverse those two fields in order to protect themselves from robbers.

Once the Holy Mother was walking from Kamarpukur to Dakshineswar

8. An incident on the Holy Mother's journey to Tarakeswar on foot.

with the daughter and youngest son of Rameswar and a few other men and women. After reaching Arambag, her companions thought they had enough

Kali of Telo-Bhelo, known as the robber's Kali.

The field of Telo-Bhelo, where Sarada Devi encountered a highwayman in 1878.

time to cross the field of Telo-Bhelo before dusk, so they were unwilling to pass the night there. Although the Holy Mother was exhausted from the journey, she said nothing and walked on with the party. But they had scarcely walked four miles when she found she could not keep up with them and began to lag behind. They waited for her for a while, then asked her to walk faster and moved on. When they reached the middle of the field, they noticed that she was then quite far behind and was walking slowly. They waited for her again and when she caught up they said: "If we walk this slowly, we shall not cross the field before 9:00 p.m., and we may be attacked by robbers." The Holy Mother knew that she had inconvenienced the others and caused them alarm, so she asked them not to wait for her. She said: "You go on to the inn at Tarakeswar and rest there. I shall meet you as soon as possible." Seeing the approach of sunset and taking her at her word, without further delay they began to walk faster and were soon out of sight.

The Holy Mother then continued along as fast as she could, but she was

9. The field of Telo-Bhelo.

terribly exhausted. After a while the sun sank below the horizon of the field. Extremely anxious, she wondered what to do. Just then she saw a tall, dark, horrible-looking man with a staff on his shoulder rapidly approaching her. Another person, probably his partner, was behind him. She realized that it was useless to run away or to shout, so she stood still and awaited their arrival with great fear.

Within a few moments the man reached her and asked harshly: "Who are

10. The Bagdi highwayman and his wife.

you, standing here alone at this hour of the evening?" To placate him, the Holy Mother surrendered to him completely, addressing him as "father": "Father, my companions have left me behind, and it seems I have lost my way. Kindly accompany me to where they are. Your son-in-law lives at the Kali temple in Dakshineswar. I am going to him. If you accompany me there, he will certainly appreciate your kindness and show you proper courtesy." No sooner had she said this than his companion arrived. The Holy Mother noticed that it was not a man but a woman, his wife. When the Holy Mother saw her, she was greatly reassured. The Holy Mother then took her hand and addressed her as "mother," saying: "Mother, I am your daughter Sarada. My companions have left me behind and I was in great danger. It is sheer luck that you and Father have come; I do not know what I would have done otherwise."

The Holy Mother's unhesitating and simple behaviour, her complete

11. Her overnight stay at Telo-Bhelo under the care of the robber and his wife.

trust, and her sweet words melted the hearts of the Bagdi robber and his wife. Forgetting social customs and caste, they accepted her as their own daughter and consoled her. Aware of her physical exhaustion, they would not allow her to go farther that night, but they took her to a small shop near the villages of Telo and Bhelo and arranged for her to stay the night. The woman made a bed for the Holy Mother with some of her own clothes and other things, and the man bought puffed rice and sweetened parched rice for her to eat. Thus with parental love and care they let her sleep, guarding her throughout the night. They woke her the next morning and accompanied her to Tarakeswar about an hour after sunrise. There they took shelter at an inn and asked her to rest. The woman told her husband: "My daughter practically fasted last night. Finish your worship at the Shiva temple quickly and buy some fish and vegetables. I would like to feed her well."

While the man was carrying out his errands, the Holy Mother's compan-

12. After reaching Tarakeswar, the Holy Mother regretfully says good-bye to the Bagdi couple.

ions came to the inn in search of her and were delighted to see that she had arrived safely. When the man returned, the Holy Mother introduced her adopted parents to her companions, saying, "I don't know what I would have done last night if they hadn't taken me under their protection." Everyone performed worship in the Shiva temple, cooked and ate together, and had a little rest. When the party prepared for their journey to Vaidyabati, the Holy Mother expressed her gratitude to the Bagdi couple and took her leave of them. The Holy Mother told us later: "In one night we had become so close that when we parted we began to weep profusely. I repeatedly invited them to visit me at Dakshineswar when they could, but even when they agreed, I parted from them with great difficulty. They accompanied us for a considerable distance. The woman picked some green peas from a nearby field, tearfully tied them in a corner of my cloth, and said plaintively, 'Sarada, my child, when you eat puffed rice tonight, please have these peas with it.' They kept their promise and visited me a few times at Dakshineswar, bringing sweets and other gifts. I told the Master the whole story, and he received them warmly, treating them as kindly as if they were his own relatives. Although my robber-father is simple and well behaved now, I believe he used to commit robbery before we met."

When the Holy Mother heard that a competent person was needed to

13. How the Holy Mother lives in the Shyampukur house.

prepare the Master's diet according to the doctor's advice, without which his illness might worsen, she set aside all consideration for her own comfort and gladly moved into the Shyampukur house to undertake the task. It is truly amazing how for three months she performed her duties, forgetting all personal inconveniences, while living in that single-family house surrounded by men whom she did not know. As there was only one bathroom for all, she would get up before 3:00 a.m., finish her bathroom activities, and then silently go to the terrace on the second floor, without anyone knowing. She would spend the whole day there. When the Master's meals were ready, at

regular times she would send word downstairs through Swami Advaitananda or Swami Adbhutananda. At those times the people were asked to
leave so she could bring the food and feed the Master, or we [the young disci-
ples] would carry his meals to him if that was more convenient. At noon the
Holy Mother would eat and rest on the terrace. At 11:00 p.m., when everyone
else was asleep, she would leave that room and sleep in her bedroom on the
first floor until 2:00 a.m. Fortified by the expectation of the Master's recovery,
she spent day after day in that way. She lived there so silently and invisibly
that many of the regular visitors did not know that she was staying there and
carrying responsibility for the most important service to the Master.

When they had solved the problem of preparing the Master's diet, his

14. The young disciples
take charge of nursing
the Master.

devotees focussed on the issue of who would care for
the Master at night. Narendra took that responsibility
upon himself and began to spend his nights at
Shyampukur. He inspired Junior Gopal, Kali, Shashi, and some active young
devotees by his example, prompting them to do the same. Narendra's
immense self-sacrifice for the Master, his inspired spiritual talks, and his
holy association induced other young disciples to disregard their own
self-interest and to make a firm resolve to serve their guru and to dedicate
their lives to realizing God. As long as their guardians were unaware of the
boys' true intentions, they had no objection to their going to the house on
Shyampukur to serve the Master. But when the Master's illness grew worse,
the young disciples began spending all of their time in serving him wholeheartedly. They then abandoned their studies at college and even stopped
going home for meals. Their guardians were at first concerned by this and
then became fearful and tried by various means — both appropriate and
inappropriate — to get them to come home. Without Narendra's example,
inspiration, and encouragement, the boys would not have been able to overcome these obstacles and remain firm in their highest duty. Four or five
young disciples thus dedicated themselves and undertook a vow of service
in the Shyampukur house, and the number of attendants who dedicated
themselves to that vow of service had increased almost fourfold by the time
it reached its completion in the Cossipore garden house.

Chapter 12
Section 2

The Master's Stay at Shyampukur

ONE CANNOT SAY THAT THE DEVOTEES WERE RELIEVED after they had made

1. The householder devotees take financial responsibility for the Master and see a unique spiritual manifestation in him.

arrangements for the Master's medicine, diet, and around-the-clock care. After consulting with the best doctors in Calcutta, they clearly understood that the Master's cancer might be difficult to treat, though it was not completely incurable, and that his recovery would require a long period of time. Their main concern now was finding the funds needed to continue his care as long as it was necessary. This was a reasonable concern because Balaram, Surendra, Ram, Girish, Mahendra, and the others who had brought the Master to Calcutta and taken responsibility for his care were not wealthy. None of them had the means to support the Master along with his attendants and still meet the expenses of his own family. The Master's extraordinary divinity engendered in their hearts a current of hope, light, bliss, and peace that inspired them to undertake the responsibility without considering the future. But it would be quite unreasonable to expect that the spiritual current would flow without ceasing, and the thoughts of the future would not interrupt it during the ebb tide. In truth, the current did not flow without interruption. Amazingly, when interruptions came, the devotees experienced a unique spiritual manifestation in the Master that relieved their anxiety and filled their hearts with renewed enthusiasm and strength.

It seemed as though that overflowing current of bliss carried them to a realm beyond reason where a divine light revealed to them that the One they had accepted as their ideal was not only superhuman but also the refuge of the spiritual world, the supreme goal of all beings, a godman, Narayana Himself! His very birth, every action, the austerities he performed, how he ate and moved about — and even the suffering he underwent during his physical illness — everything was for the benefit of humanity. How could the Supreme Being be affected by physical illness? Everything such a One resolved would come to pass, and that Person was beyond the miseries of birth, death, old age, and disease. The Supreme Being was playing the role of a sick person in order to bless them by offering them the opportunity to serve. To enkindle spiritual wisdom in the hearts of those who did not have the time or the possibility of seeing him in Dakshineswar, he had now moved to Calcutta to be closer to them. Materialistic people who possess a Western education and scientific knowledge think themselves safe and practically omniscient. They make the enjoyment of sensual pleasure their life's goal. But the Master demonstrated to them the futility of their ways through the exalted light of his spiritual wisdom. He was therefore merely pretending to be sick to introduce them to the path of detachment. The devotees reasoned further: Why should they have any fear or anxiety about their lack of money? He who had given them the privilege of service would provide them with the means to fulfill their duty.

Let not the reader think that we are embellishing our statements in an emotional outburst. We have recorded them because we saw those devotees regularly and knew that they experienced and discussed things that resulted from their holy association with the Master. We saw for ourselves that when they gathered to discuss their concerns over possible interruptions in the Master's service for want of money, they were inspired by the thoughts we have described above and would return home reassured and relieved. One of them told us: "The Master himself will gather the things he needs. If he doesn't, what does it matter? What anxiety is there, as long as my house is standing." He pointed to his house and continued, "I will mortgage my house to continue the Master's service." Another said: "I will manage the Master's service just as I would meet the expenses of my children's marriages or illnesses. I'm not anxious as long as my wife has some jewellery left." Others might not express themselves in those ways, but they demonstrated their feelings by reducing their household expenses and spending generously on the Master's behalf. Surendra was inspired to undertake responsibility for the rent; and Balaram, Ram, Mahendra, Girish, and others together supplied whatever else the Master and his attendants needed.

2. The sacrifices that the householder devotees make for the Master.

Thus, the divine bliss that the devotees experienced in their hearts,

3. The purpose of the Master's disease is the formation of a community of devotees.

which was a great factor in their attraction to and sympathy for each other, centred upon the Master. Although the Ramakrishna Community had begun in Dakshineswar, it took form and grew so rapidly in Shyampukur and later in Cossipore that many devotees believed that one of the main purposes of the Master's illness was to bring about this coalescence.

As the days went on, the devotees began to develop different ideas about

4. Classification of the devotees' concepts of the Master: avatar of the age, guru and super-human, or godman.

the reasons for the Master's illness, when he would be cured, and so on, thus creating a few groups among themselves. It is evident that the devotees came to their conclusions by studying the extraordinary events of the Master's early life. One group believed this sentiment and publicly proclaimed it: "The Master is the avatar of this age. His physical illness is not real but merely feigned. He has intentionally assumed this disease in order to accomplish a specific task. Whenever he wishes, he will appear to us as he was before." Girish, who had a powerful imagination and great faith, was the leader of this group. The second group said: "The Master has always lived according to the will of the Divine Mother and has performed all actions as an instrument of Her will. She has given him this illness temporarily to fulfill some mysterious purpose of Her own for the well-being of humanity. The Master himself may be unable to fathom that mystery. However, when Her mission is fulfilled, the Master will come round again." The third group said: "Birth, death, old age, and disease are inherent in the human body and appear as long as one has a body. The Master's physical illness is the result of such natural laws. So what is the point of expending so much effort in speculation to seek a hidden mystery in it? We shall accept nothing about the Master without thoroughly analyzing it through reasoning and directly experiencing it ourselves. We shall wholeheartedly work for his recovery; we shall try our utmost to follow the great example of human life that he has set before us; and we shall continue to practise spiritual disciplines." Narendra, who represented the Master's young disciples, espoused this view.

The Master's disciples had different temperaments and cherished different

5. The mutual respect among the devotees.

attitudes towards and opinions about the Master. But they unanimously believed that they would derive great benefit if they followed his great liberal teachings in their lives and if they attained his grace by serving him unreservedly. For that reason, although one group considered him to be the avatar of the age, another group regarded him as a guru and superhuman, and yet another group believed him to be a godman — they never lacked love and respect for one another.

The devotees witnessed different manifestations of spirituality in the

6. Examples of the Master's spiritual manifestation seen by the devotees.

Master every day. We shall explain this phenomenon to the reader by describing some incidents that we ourselves saw. These incidents were also witnessed by people who were not the Master's devotees but who were visiting him when they happened.

We have already mentioned that Dr. Mahendralal Sarkar undertook

7. Dr. Sarkar's attraction for and attitude towards the Master: their conversation.

responsibility for the Master's treatment and was trying his best to cure him. He examined the Master for a few consecutive days, in the morning, at noon, and in the afternoon, and prescribed medicine and diet accordingly. After finishing his medical duties, the doctor spent some time with the Master discussing spiritual topics. After this, the doctor became greatly attracted to the Master's open-minded spirituality, and whenever he had time he would spend two or three hours with the Master. One day the Master started to thank him for spending so much of his precious time there, but the doctor interrupted him, saying: "Well, do you think that I spend my time here for your sake alone? I have a personal interest in it. I derive great joy from talking with you. Although I first met you long ago, I didn't then have the opportunity of knowing you so intimately. At that time I was busy with many things. You see, I like you for your unflinching devotion to truth. Whatever you consider to be true you never deviate from even slightly. I see other people saying one thing and doing another — I can't bear that at all. Don't think that I'm flattering you. I'm not that kind of person. I'm a disobedient son! If my father does anything wrong, I speak out to him plainly. That's why I'm known as a 'sharp-tongued' person."

The Master said with a smile: "Yes, I've heard that. But you've been coming here for a pretty long time and I have as yet no indication of it."

The doctor also smiled, then replied: "There is good fortune in this for

8. Dr. Sarkar's actions are motivated by his love of truth.

both of us. If anything isn't right, Mahendra Sarkar isn't a person to keep his mouth shut. Don't think that I have no love for truth. Whatever I consider to be true, I've tried to follow throughout my life. For that reason, I started practising homeopathy; I founded the Association for the Cultivation of Science; and so also with all my other works."

We remember that one of the disciples then insinuated that while the

9. The attainment of *para-vidya* through *apara-vidya*.

doctor might love truth, he had a passion for discovering only *apara-vidya* [relative truths], whereas the Master was devoted to *para-vidya* [the Ultimate Truth].

The doctor became excited and exclaimed: "That is your hackneyed belief! How can you divide knowledge into para and apara? It is knowledge itself that makes the truth manifest. So how can knowledge as such be higher or

Dr. Mahendralal Sarkar (1833-1904), a homeopathic physician of Calcutta who treated Ramakrishna.

lower? At any rate, even if you insist upon making an imaginary distinction, you must admit that one attains para-vidya by means of apara-vidya. We can clearly understand God, the primeval cause of the universe, through the truths that we experience by studying science. I'm not referring to those fellows, the atheistic scientists! I don't understand what they say. Although they have eyes, they're all blind. Anyone who claims to have understood the whole of God — One without beginning and without end — is a liar and a cheat; such a person should be sent to a lunatic asylum."

The Master looked at the doctor graciously and said with a smile: "You're

10. Trying to limit God is small-mindedness.

quite right. Those who try to set limits on God are small-minded. I can't bear their foolish babble."

The Master then asked one of the devotees to sing the song by the great

11. The mind understands but the heart does not.

devotee Ramprasad that begins with "Who is there that can understand what Mother Kali is? Even the six philosophies are powerless to reveal Her."[1] While

listening to the song, from time to time the Master explained the gist of it to the doctor in a low voice. When the singer sang the last line as, "But while my heart has understood, alas! my mind has not," the Master interrupted him, saying: "That is incorrect; please reverse the words. It ought to be, 'But while my mind has understood, alas! my heart has not.' While trying to know Him, the mind easily understands that it cannot comprehend the beginningless and endless God. But the heart is reluctant to admit this; it constantly feels that it can realize God."

The doctor was impressed by this interpretation and said: "You are quite right. The mind, a petty fellow, despairs at the slightest difficulty. But the heart doesn't go along with this; that's why many truths have been discovered so far and more will be in the future."

While listening to the song, a couple of young devotees went into ecstasy

12. Dr. Sarkar checks the pulse of young devotees in ecstasy.

and lost outer consciousness. The doctor examined each one's pulse and said, "It seems they have no consciousness of external objects, like one who has

---

1. Who is there that can understand what Mother Kali is?
Even the six philosophies are powerless to reveal Her.
It is She, the scriptures say, who is the inner Self
Of the yogi, who in the Self discovers all his joy;
She that, of Her own sweet will, inhabits every living thing.
The macrocosm and microcosm rest in the Mother's womb;
Now do you see how vast it is? In the Muladhara
The yogi meditates on Her, and in the Sahasrara:
Who but Shiva has beheld Her as She really is?
Within the lotus wilderness She sports beside Her Mate, the Swan [Shiva].
When a man aspires to understand Her, Ramprasad must smile;
To think of knowing Her, he says, is quite as laughable
As to imagine one can swim across the boundless sea.
But while my mind has understood, alas! my heart has not;
Though but a dwarf, it still would strive to make a captive of the moon.

fainted." The Master ran his hand over their chests and uttered God's name in a low voice, bringing them back to a normal state. The doctor observed this and said to the Master, "It all seems to be your play!" The Master replied with a smile: "It's not my play, but His will. The minds of these young men have not been scattered by thoughts of a wife, children, wealth, name and fame, so they easily become absorbed in God upon hearing the glory of His name."

Some devotees, continuing the topic they had been discussing, told the doctor that although he might believe in God and not set limits on Him, there were some scientists who did not believe in the existence of God, and there were others who accepted that God exists but only according to their own concept of Him. These scientists proclaimed loudly that God is as they believe Him to be, and that His power is limited to their description of it. The doctor replied: "Yes, that's partly true. But do you know what that is? It's the pride in their learning, which is something like intellectual indigestion. Because they know a few things about God's creation, they think that they understand everything in the universe. Those who've studied and experienced a great deal don't have this problem. I've never thought that I know everything."

13. Pride is caused by knowledge.

The Master then told the doctor: "You're right. With the acquisition of knowledge, one develops the kind of ego that claims: 'I am a pandit. Only what I know and understand is true; all others are mistaken.' The vanity of learning is one of the fetters that binds human beings. It's God's grace that you've learned so much but still don't have that kind of egotism."

14. The vanity of scholarship.

Excited, the doctor said: "Egotism is worthless. It seems that whatever knowledge I've acquired is insignificant — almost nothing. There are so many things yet to learn. I believe, or rather I actually perceive, that everyone knows something that I don't. So I never feel humiliated when I learn from someone else. I think that I may have many things to learn even from these people (*pointing to us*). For that reason, I'm ready to take the dust of their feet."

15. Dr. Sarkar's humility.

The Master motioned towards us and said: "I tell them, 'Friends, as long as I live, so long do I learn.'" Indicating the doctor, the Master told us: "Have you seen how humble he is? There is substance in him. That's why he has such a wonderful understanding." The doctor then took his leave for the day.

16. "There is substance in him."

As Dr. Mahendralal Sarkar's love and respect for the Master grew, the Master earnestly tried to help the doctor advance on the spiritual path. In addition, the Master knew that talented people love to talk to their peers, so he often sent Mahendra [M., the author of *The Gospel of Sri Ramakrishna*], Girish, Narendra, and other prominent disciples to talk to the learned doctor. After becoming acquainted with Girish [a famous actor and

17. The Master's efforts to help the doctor advance on the spiritual path.

playwright], the doctor went to see a performance of Girish's *Buddha-charit* and lavishly praised its author. He also saw some other plays that Girish had written. In addition, the doctor was impressed when he talked with Narendra, and he invited him to dinner one day. When the doctor learned that Narendra was a talented singer, he asked him to sing devotional songs for him sometime. One afternoon a few days later, when the doctor came to visit the Master, Narendra sang for two or three hours to keep the promise he had made. The doctor was so happy that before he took his leave, he affectionately embraced Narendra and blessed him as he would his own son. Dr. Sarkar then told the Master: "I'm very glad that such a boy has devoted himself to the spiritual life. He is a jewel, and I'm sure he will shine in any sphere of life." Looking graciously upon Narendra, the Master replied: "It's said that the fiery appeal of Advaita Goswami brought Gauranga to Nadia. Similarly, everything that you see here [*meaning his own advent*] is on account of him [*Narendra*]." From then on, whenever the doctor visited the Master, he invariably listened to Narendra sing a few devotional songs if he was there.

It was autumn and the time for Durga Puja was at hand. The Master's

18. The doctor's anxiety and reaction when his medicine is not completely effective.

condition was fluctuating — his illness seemed worse on some days and better on others. The medicine was not producing the desired result. One day when the doctor came he saw that the disease had been aggravated, and he remarked: "There must be something wrong with your diet. Please tell me, what have you eaten today?"

The Master told him that he was eating soft foods only: rice gruel, soup, and milk for lunch; and barley or farina pudding and milk at suppertime. The doctor said: "Still, there must be some irregularity in your diet. Well, what vegetables were in the soup?" The Master replied: "It contained potatoes, unripe bananas, eggplant, and a few pieces of cauliflower."

The doctor exclaimed: "What! You've eaten cauliflower? This is definitely not a good food. Cauliflower produces gas and is hard to digest. How many pieces did you eat?"

The Master said: "I didn't eat a single piece, but I saw some in the soup."

The doctor answered: "It doesn't matter whether you ate the cauliflower or not; its juice was in the soup. Your condition is worse today because your digestion was disturbed."

The Master replied: "What are you saying? I haven't eaten cauliflower, nor is my stomach upset. It's hard to believe that my disease has been aggravated by a little cauliflower juice in the soup."

The doctor said: "You have no idea how much harm a minor irregularity

19. An example of how a minor transgression and irregularity in one's diet can be injurious.

in one's diet can do to the system. You'll understand this if I tell you what happened to me. My digestion has always been poor and I occasionally suffer from dyspepsia. I'm therefore extremely careful about what I eat and I always follow a strict rule: I don't eat any prepared food from the market. I even have ghee and oil made at home. In spite of these precautions, I once caught a bad cold that developed into chronic bronchitis. I concluded that there must be something wrong in my diet. I investigated but couldn't find any problems with my food. One day I saw the servant feeding kidney beans to the cow that produced the milk I used. I learned upon inquiry that a few maunds of kidney beans had been procured from a certain place. No one wanted to eat those beans for fear of falling ill, so they were given to the cow for some days. I determined that my cold had started when the cow began to eat those kidney beans. I then told my servant to stop feeding those beans to the cow, and my bronchitis then slowly started to subside. It took many days to recover completely, and I spent four or five thousand rupees for a change of climate and other measures."

The Master said with a laugh: "My goodness! That sounds like the man who passed below a tamarind tree and caught a cold." Everyone laughed. Although the doctor's notion seemed to be a little exaggerated, no one raised any objection because they saw that he was convinced it was true. The doctor's advice was followed from then on, and cauliflower was no longer added to the Master's soup.

The Master's affection, simplicity, and spirituality attracted the doctor,

| 20. The doctor's respect for the Master and love for the devotees increase. | whose words and actions during his visits revealed the respect that he was developing for the Master. The doctor then loved not only the Master but also |

his devotees, and he was convinced that they were not making any exaggerated claims about the Master. But it is hard to determine what he thought of the devotees' intense love and respect for the Master. The doctor seemed to think it was a little extreme. However, it is clear he understood that their attitude towards the Master was not mere pretense, nor was it driven by any selfish motive. This phenomenon amazed the doctor and was a mystery to him. Although he had engaged his keen intellect in understanding this mystery, and associated closely with the devotees, their attitude towards the Master remained an enigma to him. He believed in God, but the influence of Western education prevented him from understanding how one could worship or revere a man as a guru or an avatar even if one did see an extraordinary divine power within him; and for this reason, he was against this practice. The rationale behind his antagonism is this: Those who are now worshipped as avatars had some aspects of their lives exaggerated by generations of disciples who preached their glories in such a biased way that it is now almost impossible to discern their true nature.

In this connection, one day the doctor said openly in the Master's presence: "I can understand the importance of love for and devotion to God. But I'm confused when it's said that the infinite God has descended to earth as a man. It's difficult to understand how God could have been born as the son of Yashoda, Mary, or Shachi.[2] This pack of sons has ruined the country." Amused, the Master told us: "What is he saying? However, it's true that narrow-minded fanatics sometimes disturb the peace by giving undue prominence to their own beliefs."

On many occasions Girish and Narendra took issue with the doctor's opinion concerning avatars. When it was proven to the doctor that many reasonable arguments could be made against his view, he became more cautious about expressing his views on such extremely controversial issues so bluntly. But what could not be done by reason was accomplished by the Master's divine love and sweetness and by the extraordinary spirituality that sometimes became manifest in him and that the doctor saw for himself. The doctor's opinion about the avatar gradually underwent a great change.

21. The doctor's opinion about and objection to the doctrine of avatars. His amazement when seeing the Master in samadhi during Durga Puja.

That year during the Durga Puja, at the juncture of the ashtami and the navami, a divine power suddenly appeared in the Master. Dr. Sarkar was able to see and verify it (see II.8.27). Dr. Sarkar and one of his doctor friends were present that day. When the Master went into samadhi, the doctor examined his heart with a stethoscope and could find no heartbeat. His friend did not hesitate to touch the Master's open eyes with his finger to check if he would blink, but he got no reaction. Dumbfounded, they admitted that the Master seemed to be completely dead during samadhi, and that science could shed no light on his state. Western philosophers considered the state of samadhi to be unconsciousness. They abhorred it, thus expressing their ignorance and limiting themselves to the world of the senses. But so many things exist in God's creation; philosophy and science have not yet revealed their mysteries, and perhaps never will. Although the Master looked dead that day, whatever he saw and experienced during samadhi was verified by the devotees, who found it all to be true. We have told this story elsewhere (see II.8.26-27), so we need not repeat it here.

It was the month of November, and the auspicious day of Kali Puja [Friday, 6 November 1885] was approaching. There was still no visible improvement in the Master's condition. The results that had been achieved when his treatment began were dissipating and the disease was beginning to take a serious turn. At the same time, it appeared to the devotees that the Master's spiritual joy and his cheerfulness were increasing rather than decreasing. Dr. Sarkar visited the Master frequently as usual, but although he kept adjusting the medication, he did not get the results he expected. He thought that this was due to the change of season and that the Master's condition would improve when winter set in.

22. The Master's disease becomes worse.

2. Referring to Krishna, Jesus, and Chaitanya respectively. — *Translator*

As they had at Durga Puja, the devotees witnessed a wonderful manifestation of divinity in the Master during Kali Puja. Devendra wished to buy an image of Mother Kali and perform worship of Her. He thought that it would be an extremely joyful occasion if he could fulfill that desire in the presence of the Master and his devotees, so he asked if he could perform the worship at the Shyampukur house. The devotees advised him to abandon the idea because the excitement, enthusiasm, and commotion surrounding the ritual might exhaust the Master. Devendra considered the devotees' response reasonable, so he gave up the idea. But the day before Kali Puja, the Master told some of his devotees: "Collect everything that is needed for worship on a small scale. Tomorrow we shall have Kali Puja." Delighted, they began consulting with the others. Because they received no further instructions from the Master, they discussed among themselves various ways of accomplishing their task and could not come to any agreement on whether the worship would have sixteen items or five, whether they would offer cooked food, who would perform the worship, and so on. Finally they decided to procure sandal paste, flowers, oil lamps, incense, fruits, and sweets, and then await the Master's instructions. But the Master gave no further directions that day nor did he on the day of worship.

23. The Master's wonderful ecstasy on the night of Kali Puja.

Evening arrived with the sunset. At 7:00 p.m. the devotees found the Master seated silently on his bed, as on other days. He said nothing further about the worship. They cleared some space on his right and placed the worship articles there. Some devotees had seen the Master occasionally worship his own form with sandal paste and flowers when he lived in Dakshineswar. Today they had come to the conclusion that the Master intended to worship himself as a symbol of Universal Consciousness and the embodiment of Divine Power, or to perform the worship of his own Self as identified with the Divine Mother according to the scriptures. It is therefore not surprising that they placed the worship articles next to his bed. The Master watched them do that, but raised no objection.

24. Preparations for the worship.

When everything had been brought to his room, someone lit the lamps and burnt the incense, filling the whole room with light and fragrance. Seeing the Master still sitting quietly, the devotees sat near him. Some looked at him intently, awaiting his direction; some began to meditate on the Divine Mother. Time passed, and the Master remained silent. He neither came forward to perform the worship himself, nor did he ask any of us to do it.

25. The Master remains silent.

The young devotees were present, along with Mahendra, Ram, Devendra, Girish, and some senior devotees. The Master sometimes said that of his devotees Girish had "one hundred and twenty-five percent" faith. Most

26. Girish offers flowers at the Master's feet, and the Master goes into samadhi.

of the devotees were puzzled by the Master's silence about the worship. But because Girish had such abundant faith in the Master, he was suddenly struck by this idea: "The Master does not need to worship the Divine Mother for his own sake. If his pure love has inspired him to perform the worship, why would he sit there quietly, doing nothing? That does not seem right. Were these arrangements made for the devotees to worship the Divine Mother in the Master's living form and be blessed? It must be so." He was overwhelmed with joy at that thought and immediately took flowers and sandal paste from a tray and offered them at the feet of the Master, saying, "Victory to the Mother." A thrill passed through the Master's body, and he went into deep samadhi. His face became luminous and a divine smile played upon it. His hands assumed the gestures symbolizing fearlessness and the bestowal of boons that are seen in images of Kali, thus indicating that the Mother was revealing Herself within him. These events happened so quickly that the devotees seated nearby thought Girish had offered flowers after seeing the Master in samadhi. To those who were a little farther away it appeared as if a luminous form of the Devi had suddenly appeared before them, taking possession of the Master's body.

The devotees' joy knew no bounds. Each one took flowers and sandal paste from the tray, uttered a mantra according to his mood, and worshipped the Master's feet. The room was filled with joyous shouts. Some time passed in this way. When the Master slowly regained partial consciousness, the sweets and fruits gathered for worship were placed before him. He partook of some and blessed the devotees that they might attain the highest devotion and knowledge. They ate some of the Master's prasad, then sang devotional songs and hymns to the glory of the Divine Mother until midnight.

27. The devotees worship the Master while he is in samadhi.

Thus, the devotees worshipped the Divine Mother that year in a unique way and experienced an unprecedented bliss that remained forever vivid in their hearts. And whenever they later became oppressed by difficulties in their lives, that image of the Master appeared before them, his serene face illumined with a divine smile and his hands bestowing blessings and fearlessness, reminding them that they were under God's protection.

The devotees experienced the power and nature of the Master's divinity not only on special holy days while he was at Shyampukur, but they also had other opportunities to witness the manifestation of divinity within him, thus helping to establish their firm faith in him as a godman day by day. Not all of these events occurred in the presence of others like those we have just described, but the devotees who witnessed them came to believe in the Master's divinity, and those to

28. The devotees experience the Master's spiritual manifestation at times other than on holy days.

whom they later described these events also became convinced of this. The reader will understand if we present a few more incidents.

We have already told some stories about Balaram. He and his immediate

29. Balaram's respect and devotion for the Master displease his relatives.

family were devoted to the Master and had great respect for him, which displeased some of his relatives. They had sufficient reasons for their grievance. Balaram's relatives had been born into the Vaishnava tradition and were raised in that faith, so their religious views were dogmatic to some extent and firmly rooted in external practices and rituals. So neither did they understand the spiritual attitude of the Master, who had strong faith in the truth of all religions and shunned religious marks, nor did they feel that one should be sympathetic to such a person. Balaram was gradually becoming open-minded by his association with the Master and by the Master's grace. Balaram's relatives considered this to be a sign of impiety. In addition, those who have wealth, fame, aristocracy, and all other sorts of worldly prosperity, very often become vain and egotistic. Balaram's relatives could trace their lineage back to the celebrated Krishnaram Basu, and they considered themselves equally great. Balaram was disregarding the prestige of his dynasty and frequently visiting the Master at Dakshineswar for spirituality as if he were an ordinary person. He even took his wife and children there. When his relatives learned of all this, their sensibilities were wounded and they determined to dissuade him from seeing the Master.

When proud people cannot succeed through fair means, they adopt

30. Their efforts to stop Balaram from visiting the Master.

underhanded tactics. Some members of Balaram's family were arrogant enough to do this. They repeatedly reminded Balaram of their family prestige and eulogized the great faith and devotion of Bhagavandas Babaji of Kalna and of other Vaishnava saints. When this did not dissuade Balaram from visiting the Master, they became malicious and did not hesitate to slander the Master from time to time. They had a distorted impression of the Master because others had told them that he lacked steadfast devotion to a single deity, was careless about what he ate, did not follow the injunctions of the scriptures in his daily life, was against the use of Vaishnava marks, and so on. When even these efforts had no effect, they resorted to fabricating lies about the Master and Balaram and reporting them to Balaram's cousins, Nimai Charan Basu and Harivallabh Basu.

We have already mentioned that Balaram possessed compassion,

31. Balaram's early life.

detachment, and other noble qualities. He realized that managing an estate required the occasional use of ruthless means, so he entrusted his property to Nimai Charan Basu and received a certain amount of income from him every month. Although it was sometimes insufficient, he somehow managed his household.

In addition, ill health prevented him from managing his own estate. He had suffered from dyspepsia during his youth, and his health had deteriorated to such an extent that he had given up normal food for twelve years, living on milk and barley water. While recuperating, he had lived for a long time in Puri, where he spent his time visiting the temple of Lord Jagannath every day, worshipping, doing japa, listening to discourses on the Bhagavata, and keeping the company of holy people. During this time, he had become acquainted with the positive and negative aspects of the Vaishnava sect. We have mentioned earlier (see IV.7.2-4 and V.9.6-7) that he met the Master shortly after arriving in Calcutta for family business and how that holy association changed Balaram's life.

Balaram had to come to Calcutta for a few weeks for the marriage of his oldest daughter. Other than this event, his peaceful life had been undisturbed during his eleven years in Puri. Shortly after the wedding, Harivallabh Basu purchased a house at 57 Ramkanta Basu Street. Harivallabh secretly consulted with Balaram's father and his brothers, and then asked Balaram to live in that house. Balaram's family feared he would renounce home because of his association with the monks in Puri. Thus Balaram was now deprived of his daily visit to Lord Jagannath and of the holy company of the monks. Sadly he began his life in Calcutta. It seems that previously [before he met the Master] he had intended to return to Puri after staying in Calcutta for a short time. Once he had met the Master, however, he completely gave up that idea and decided to live in Calcutta permanently to be near the Master. From time to time he became anxious that Harivallabh would ask him to vacate the house or that Nimai would deprive him of the Master's holy company by asking him to manage his own estate, which would require him to move to Kothar [in Orissa].

32. Balaram arrives in Calcutta and visits the Master.

Anxious thoughts sometimes foretell future events, as Balaram experienced: What he feared came to pass. Secretly prompted by Balaram's relatives, both of his cousins wrote to him expressing their displeasure. Harivallabh also sent news that he would come to Calcutta very soon and stay with him for a few days to discuss an important matter. Although Balaram knew that he had done nothing wrong and was unconcerned on that account, the thought that the course of events could take him away from the Master worried him. After long deliberation he decided that even if his cousins made accusations against him based on what others were saying, he would not leave the Master during his illness. Meanwhile, Harivallabh arrived in Calcutta. Balaram had made all arrangements so that his cousin would not have any inconvenience or difficulty during his stay with him. He remained calm and firm in his resolve and continued to visit the Master openly every day.

33. Harivallabh arrives in Calcutta.

The face is the best mirror of the mind. On the very day that Harivallabh

34. Out of compassion for Balaram, the Master asks to see Harivallabh.

arrived in Calcutta, the Master saw Balaram's face and understood that some inner struggle was going on. He considered Balaram to be his own and felt empathy with him, so he called him aside and learned everything. He asked: "What sort of man is Harivallabh? Can you bring him here some day?" Balaram replied: "Sir, as a man he is good, learned, intelligent, magnanimous, benevolent, charitable, and devout, but he has one defect: He is somewhat gullible, as wealthy people can be. He has formed a mistaken impression of me on the basis of what others have told him and is displeased because I come here. I therefore doubt if he would come at my request." The Master said: "Then you need not ask him. Please call Girish here."

Girish gladly agreed to introduce Harivallabh to the Master. He said: "Harivallabh and I were classmates in our youth. I always see him whenever he comes to Calcutta, so it won't be difficult for me to bring him here. I'll see him today."

The next afternoon at 5:00 Girish arrived with Harivallabh and intro-

35. Girish brings Harivallabh to the Master, whose conduct changes Harivallabh's attitude.

duced him to the Master, saying: "This is Harivallabh Basu, my boyhood friend and a government lawyer in Cuttuck, Orissa. He has come to see you." The Master greeted him warmly, made him sit close by and said, "I heard about you from others and wanted to meet you, but I was a little apprehensive that you would be very shrewd and calculating." Then he said to Girish, pointing to Harivallabh: "But now I see that isn't the case. He's as simple as a boy. Have you seen his eyes? One can't have such eyes if one's heart is not full of devotion." He suddenly touched Harivallabh, then continued: "Look, that apprehension is gone! I feel that you are my very own." Harivallabh bowed down, took the dust of his feet, and said, "That is your grace, sir."

Girish then remarked: "He should be endowed with devotion; he was born into a family of famous devotees. Krishnaram Basu is renowned for his devotion, and his piety has brought glory to this part of the country. Who else would be devout if not those who were born into his family?"

After a while, the topic of devotion arose. The Master said that the main purpose of human life is to attain faith in God, devotion, and complete self-surrender. While talking in that vein, he went into samadhi. When he afterwards regained partial consciousness, he asked one of us to sing a devotional song. In a low voice he explained the meaning of the song to Harivallabh and again went into deep samadhi. When the song ended, two or three young devotees were also in ecstasy. Harivallabh was so moved by the loving appearance and inspiring words of the Master that tears welled up in his eyes. He took his leave of the Master shortly after sunset.

At Dakshineswar we sometimes observed that if a newcomer argued with

36. Why the Master touched people while talking to them, and its effect.

the Master, adopting a contrary view, or if a person came to him with a hostile attitude for some reason, the Master would tactfully touch that person during their conversation, and immediately the person would begin to accept what he said. Of course he did that only with visitors who pleased him. One day he volunteered the reason for this gesture, telling us, "People don't easily accept what others say, because they are influenced by egoism and have the attitude that they are in no way inferior to anyone else." Pointing to his body, he explained: "As soon as they feel the touch of the Being within this and feel the influence of His divine power, their egoism can no longer raise its head. When a hooded snake is touched by a particular herb, it immediately bends its head; my touch has the same effect on an inflated ego. That's why I discreetly touch them during conversation."

Those words of the Master arose in our minds when we saw how Hari-vallabh's attitude towards the Master changed completely and how he took leave of the Master with reverence in his heart. After that, Balaram's cousins never again thought that he was doing wrong in visiting the Master.

As the Master's illness worsened during his stay at Shyampukur, the

37. The number of devotees increases; the Master gives instruction on sadhana and demonstrates postures conducive to meditation on God with form and without form.

number of visitors who were blessed to see him and to receive his grace increased. Harish Chandra Mustafi, Sarada Prasanna Mitra[3] (who later joined the Ramakrishna Order and became Swami Trigu-natitananda), Manindra Krishna Gupta,[4] and other young devotees and householder devotees first met the Master here. Some might have visited the Master a couple of times in Dakshineswar, but it was at Shyampukur that they had the opportunity to become close to him. The Master observed the character and past impressions of these newcomers and guided them to the form of sadhana that was appropriate for them, either of pure devotion or of devotion combined with knowledge. Whenever the Master had an opportunity, he gave them private instructions and inspired them to move forward on their paths.

One day the Master showed a young disciple postures and gestures that are appropriate for meditation on God with form and without form. Seated in the lotus position, the Master placed the back of his right hand on the palm of his left and then raised both to chest level. With his eyes closed, he said, "This is the best posture for all kinds of meditation on God with form." Then, seated in the same position, he placed his right and left hands, palms

3. According to *The Gospel of Sri Ramakrishna,* Sarada Prasanna Mitra first met the Master on 27 December 1884. — *Translator*
4. Manindra Krishna Gupta had seen the Master some years previously in Dakshineswar with a group but had become acquainted with him in Shyampukur. — *Translator*

upward, on his right and left knees respectively, and brought the tips of the thumb and the index finger of each hand together, keeping the other fingers straight. Fixing his gaze between his eyebrows, he said, "This is an excellent posture for meditation on the formless God." As he said that, the Master went into samadhi. He soon forced his mind back to the normal plane of consciousness, and continued: "I couldn't show you more. As soon as I sit in that position, my mind is stimulated and becomes absorbed in samadhi, making an air current move upward and hit the wound in my throat. That's why the doctor advised me to avoid going into samadhi." The young disciple said humbly: "Sir, why did you show me those techniques? I didn't ask you to." The Master replied: "That's true. But it's hard for me to remain quiet and refrain from teaching and demonstrating some spiritual techniques to you all." The young disciple was touched by the Master's infinite compassion and amazed by his natural inclination towards samadhi.

Many newcomers were charmed upon seeing the grace and uniqueness in the Master's daily activities. For an example, we shall refer to an event that we heard from Atul Chandra Ghosh, Girish's younger brother. We shall try to record this event in his own language as much as possible:

| 38. People are drawn to the Master by the beauty and uniqueness of his actions. An example: Upendra, a judge. |

"Upendra,[5] a close friend, was a judge who lived away from Calcutta. After I'd become acquainted with the Master, I wrote to him, 'When you come here next, I shall show you someone wonderful.' He came during his Christmas vacation and reminded me of this. I told him: 'I thought of introducing you to Sri Ramakrishna Paramahamsa. But now he is ill and living at Shyampukur. Doctors have forbidden him to talk. Moreover, you are a newcomer. How can I take you there?' The day passed. On another day Upendra came to see my brother Girish. When the topic of the Master arose, Girish told him, 'Go with Atul and see him some day.' Upendra replied: 'Atul has been telling me for the last six months that he would take me there, but when I reminded him after coming here, he said that it wouldn't be possible now.' I told my brother, 'Even we aren't always allowed to see him now. How can I take a newcomer there?' Brother Girish said: 'Nonetheless, take him to the Master some day. If he's lucky, the Master will see him and treat him with love.'

"One afternoon later on, I took Upendra to the Master. The room was packed with people sitting on the two mats that were spread on the floor near his bed. They were discussing various ordinary topics such as painting (Annada Bagchi, a famous painter was present), the

| 39. Upendra comes to Shyampukur; he experiences the Master's affectionate behaviour. |

5. Upendra Nath Ghosh. He was related to the famous Bhupendra Nath Basu of Shyambazar, Calcutta.

story of melting gold in a goldsmith's shop,[6] and so on. We sat there for a long time, but no spiritual topic was discussed, just ordinary chitchat. I thought: 'Today I've brought a newcomer and all this idle talk is going on here! What impression will Upendra have of the Master?' This thought made my mouth dry and from time to time I glanced at Upendra anxiously. But whenever I looked at him, I noticed that he looked cheerful, as if he were enjoying the conversation. I signaled him to get up, but he motioned to me to wait a little longer. After I'd beckoned to him two or three more times, he got up and came to me. I asked him: 'What were you listening to for so long? What is there to hear in that idle conversation? That is why we call you *bangal* [a rustic fellow].' We used that nickname because he had a tattoo on his forehead. He replied: 'Well, I was listening to wonderful conversation. Previously I'd heard about universal love, but I'd never seen anyone display it. Today I experienced it in him [the Master] when he was making merry on trifling subjects with everybody. I must come here another day; I have three questions to ask him.'

6. Atul is referring to the amusing story that the Master sometimes told us of the skillful goldsmiths who stole gold and silver. A man went to a goldsmith's shop with a few friends to sell jewellery. He saw an old goldsmith with holy marks all over his body, a rosary in his hand, and a tuft of hair on his head. He was intently chanting Hari's name. His three or four assistants also had holy marks and wore beads around their necks. They were inside the shop making various types of jewellery. Seeing the sattvic marks and clothing of the old goldsmith and his assistants, the man and his friends thought that they were very pious and would not cheat them. They then placed the jewellery before the old goldsmith and asked him to appraise it precisely. The old man cordially offered them a seat and asked an assistant to prepare a smoke for them. He then tested the gold on a touchstone, told them what it was worth, and with their permission, handed it to an assistant inside the room to melt. The assistant began to melt it immediately and suddenly remembering God, cried out, "Keshava! Keshava!" Seemingly inspired by a divine mood, the old man uttered loudly, "Gopala! Gopala!" Another assistant then cried out from inside, "Hari! Hari! Hari!" Meanwhile, the assistant who had prepared the tobacco handed the pipe to the customers and said aloud as he entered the room, "Hara! Hara! Hara!" When he said that, the first assistant stealthily dropped some melted gold in the pot of water before him, stealing it.
[In Bengali these names of God have double meanings; the goldsmith and his assistants used the second meaning.] The man who said "Keshava!" really asked, "Who are they?" as in, "Are they intelligent or foolish?" The man who replied "Gopala!" conveyed the idea that they were as foolish as a herd of cows. The man who shouted "Hari!" was asking, "May I rob them?" He who replied "Hara!" meant, "Do rob them by all means." The customers did not grasp the second meaning of those words. Pleased with the goldsmiths' devotion and piety, the customers began to smoke without worry. They had the melted gold weighed, took what they were given for it, and returned home cheerfully.
Once the Master met Bankim Chandra Chattopadhyay, the famous Bengali novelist, at Adhar Chandra Sen's house in Calcutta. On that day [6 December 1884] Bankim took the position of an agnostic and asked some intricate questions of the Master. He answered those questions appropriately and then said to him jokingly, "You are *bankim* [crooked] in name and in deed." Pleased with the Master's answers to his questions, Bankim said: "Sir, you must come to our house in Kanthalpara some day. We have regular worship service there and we also chant Hari's name." The Master then replied in fun: "How do you chant Hari's name? Is it like those goldsmiths?" He then told Bankim the above story and there was a peal of laughter among the audience.

"I took Upendra to the Master another morning. At that time there weren't too many people there, only a couple of his attendants and Mr. Mallick, my brother-in-law. On our way there I told Upendra categorically: 'If you have any questions, ask him yourself — only then will you get a satisfying answer. Don't ask your questions through someone else.' But he was shy by nature, and he did just what I'd forbidden him to do. He asked his question through Mr. Mallick and the Master answered. As I watched Upendra's face I saw that the answer did not satisfy him. I whispered to him: 'It was bound to be so. I repeatedly told you that if you had any questions, ask him personally. Why don't you ask yourself? Why are you engaging a lawyer?'

"He then took courage and asked: 'Sir, does God have form, or is He formless? And if He is both, how can those two contradictory natures be in Him at the same time?' The Master replied, 'He is both with form and without form, like water and ice.' Upendra had studied a science course in college, so the Master's simile satisfied him. Upendra was so pleased with this explanation that he asked no further questions. After a while, he bowed down to the Master and took his leave. As we were leaving the house, I asked him: 'Upendra, you mentioned that you had three questions. Why did you leave after asking only one?' He replied: 'Don't you understand? That one answer has solved all three of my questions.'

40. God is both with form and without form, like ice and water.

"Perhaps you remember that quite often at that time Ramchandra Datta used to eat his meal early at home and then come to the Master carrying his office clothes in a bag. He would spend an hour or two there, then change his clothes to go to his office. When the Master was answering Upendra's question that day, Ram suddenly entered the room wearing his office clothes to hear the Master's response. As soon as we left, Ram said: 'Atul, bring Upendra to me. The Master's reply to his question is too complicated for him to understand. He must read this book I've written (Tattvaprakashika). Only then will he understand the Master's words.' I was annoyed at this and blurted out: 'Brother Ram, you met the Master seven years before we did and you have visited him often since then. You say that Upendra will not understand what the Master told us, and that your book will explain to him what the Master couldn't make clear himself. What sort of idea is this? If you want to present your book to Upendra to read, please do so; that is a different matter.' Brother Ram was a little embarrassed, but nonetheless he gave his book to Upendra."

41. Atul is irritated by Ram Datta's words.

Chapter 12

Section 3

The Master's Stay at Shyampukur

ONE DAY IN SHYAMPUKUR THE MASTER HAD AN incredible vision. He saw his subtle body come out of his gross body and move around the room. He noticed some wounds on the back of its throat and was wondering how those wounds came to be, when the Divine Mother explained it to him: People who had committed various sins had become pure by touching him, thereby transferring their sins to his body and causing those wounds. At Dakshineswar the Master had sometimes told us that he would not hesitate to be born millions of times and suffer for the good of humanity. So it is not surprising that instead of being perturbed by this vision, he narrated it to us joyfully. We were moved by thus remembering and discussing his infinite grace, and the devotees, especially the younger ones, made special efforts to ensure that no newcomers bowed down to the Master or touched his feet until he had recovered his health. Some devotees, remembering their previous wayward lives, resolved not to touch the Master's pure body again. Narendra and a few others heard of the Master's vision and found in it the truth of vicarious atonement [in which one voluntarily takes upon oneself the suffering caused by the sins of others], a fundamental doctrine of Christianity, Vaishnavism, and other faiths. They began to think about this and to explore its possibilities.

> 1. The Master sees wounds through his subtle body. The cause of his cancer is his taking on the sins of others: the effect of this.

When Girish saw how the devotees were attempting to prevent new-

> 2. The devotees put restrictions on newcomers.

comers from visiting the Master, he told them: "There isn't any harm in trying to do this, but your efforts will fail because he [the Master] has assumed a body for that very purpose." As a result, strangers were kept from touching the Master; but it was not possible to stop newcomers whom the devotees knew. Other rules then came into effect: Strangers would not be allowed to approach the Master. If the devotees knew the visitors, they would be allowed to bow down to the Master but not to touch his feet. However, sometimes these rules were broken when the devotees encountered a newcomer with intense longing.

An amusing incident took place related to the above rules. When the

> 3. An actress visits the Master with the help of Kalipada.

Master lived at Dakshineswar, he went one day to see a religious drama[1] in a theatre managed by Girish and praised the performance of the actress who played the lead role. At the end of the play, the actress had the good fortune to take the dust of the Master's feet when he was in ecstasy. From then on she considered the Master to be a living god. She cherished a heartfelt love and respect for him, and she was now looking for an opportunity to see him once more. When she heard of the Master's terminal illness, she was extremely eager to see him. As she knew Kalipada Ghosh, she fervently requested him to help her visit the Master.

Kalipada was a follower of Girish in every respect and considered the Master to be the avatar of this age. He did not believe that the Master's illness would grow worse if a repentant sinner touched his holy feet. He therefore felt no fear and did not hesitate to take the actress to the Master. One evening he secretly advised her to dress like a gentleman, with hat and coat, and took her to the Shyampukur house. He introduced her to us as his friend, took her to the Master, and told him who she really was. We were not then in the Master's room, so they faced no obstacles. When the fun-loving Master learned that the actress had dressed like that to hoodwink us, he laughed heartily. He was pleased by her faith and devotion and praised her courage and cunning. He advised her to cultivate faith in and reliance on God, gave her a few spiritual instructions, and then shortly bade her good-bye. With tearful eyes she bowed down to the Master, placing her head at his feet, then left with Kalipada. The Master told us this story later, and when we saw him laughing and joking about the trick that had been played on us, we could not be angry with Kalipada.

---

1. Sri Ramakrishna went to the Star Theatre to see the play *Chaitanya Lila* on 21 September 1884. In this play, Binodini portrayed Chaitanya, and the Master blessed her, saying, "Mother, be illumined." — *Translator*

Binodini (1863-1942), a famous actress blessed by Ramakrishna.

Kalipada Ghosh (1849-1905).

Due to their association with and service to the Master, faith and devotion

4. The reason for the upsurge of sentimentalism among the devotees.

increased day by day in the devotees' hearts. But a dangerous situation arose: They began to move away from true spirituality as they grew to prefer temporary emotional excitement over firm renunciation and austere self-control. They did not understand that although their momentary ecstasies might be inspired by religious feelings, if they were not based on renunciation and self-control, they could not give them the strength to vanquish lust, anger, and other invisible enemies.

There are several causes for this kind of outbreak of sentimentalism. First, it is human nature to adopt the easiest or most comfortable practices. That is why most people who practise religion try to follow both paths: God and the world, renunciation and enjoyment. Some fortunate ones can see that these two paths are as contrary in nature as light and darkness. They do not fall into that error because they understand that it is impossible to harmonize both without compromising the ideal of complete renunciation for God. Those who want to maintain both paths soon set limits on their journey towards ideal renunciation, and thus anchor their lives in the world forever. For that reason, whenever a newcomer came, the Master would put him through various tests to see whether he would be satisfied with limits on his spiritual journey. If this was the case, the Master would give only as much advice about the ideal of renunciation for God as the newcomer could assimilate.

Because the Master's teachings varied according to the competency of the individuals involved, his spiritual instruction to householder devotees was different from what he gave to his young disciples. While addressing the general public, he would say, "In this Kaliyuga the only way to cultivate spirituality is by chanting the Lord's name and following the path of devotion prescribed by Narada." Religious practice and study of the scriptures was then so rare that it was doubtful that one in a hundred understood what he meant by "Narada's way of devotion." Most people did not know that Narada taught that one should renounce everything out of love for God. So it is not surprising that the Master's inexperienced devotees, under the spell of their weak nature, sometimes fell into error by attempting to maintain both worldly life and spiritual life, and considering extreme emotionalism to be the pinnacle of religious experience.

Another reason the devotees fell into this error was that the Master had practised his severe austerities and self-control before their arrival, so they did not see the firm foundation on which his divine ecstasy had been established. The primary cause of this excessive sentimentalism was that when Girish took refuge in the Master and became firmly convinced that the Master was the avatar of this age, he began to declare it loudly in front of all with great jubilation and enthusiasm. Although many devotees had realized this about the Master, he had forbidden them to divulge it, so they kept silent. All along, the Master had told them that shortly before he passed away many people would recognize him as an avatar. But Girish was a different sort of person: He could keep nothing in his life secret, be it good or bad. Girish could therefore not obey the Master's prohibition. He forgot that it was his sharp intellect, his phenomenal life and various experiences, and his infinite zeal and faith that had made him understand the greatness of the Master's divine power and had helped him to surrender to him completely. So he loudly insisted that others must do what he had done himself.

As a result, they [those who listened to Girish] disregarded the need for self-effort, spiritual disciplines, renunciation, and austerities, and began to say glibly, "We have given him the power of attorney," and "We have surrendered ourselves to him," thus making their spiritual lives comfortable. Girish's infinite love for the Master could have prevented him from preaching that way, but his keen intelligence convinced him that the Master had assumed a body to establish a new wheel of dharma by stopping the decline of religion. Girish also believed that the Master was voluntarily undergoing the suffering of birth, old age, and disease in order to give shelter to afflicted humanity. Moreover, Girish believed the Master would not give up his body until his mission was fully accomplished. So Girish found nothing wrong in calling people to come and take shelter in the Master and achieve peace and divine bliss as he himself had.

Girish's keen intelligence and persuasive reasoning overpowered the crit-

5. Ram tries to intensify his spiritual mood by imitating Girish.

ical faculties of Ram and other senior devotees. We have mentioned earlier that Ram had been born into a Vaishnava family. It is therefore not surprising that as he saw the divine power become manifest in the Master, he believed that the Master was identical to Krishna and Gauranga. Before Girish began to preach that the Master was an avatar, Ram expressed his own belief to others in a very restrained way. But with Girish's support, the passion of his belief increased greatly, and he now not only proclaimed the Master to be an avatar but also busied himself with tracing the identity of the Master's devotees to those of Krishna and Gauranga. And those who exhibited physical changes, or sometimes lost outer consciousness in a momentary surge of emotion, occupied a high spiritual rank in his estimation.

When many devotees firmly believed that the Master was an avatar of

6. Vijay Krishna Goswami enflames the situation.

the age and were allowing themselves to be carried away by this sentiment, Vijay Krishna Goswami came from Dhaka to see the Master. In front of all, he declared that one day while he was meditating in his room in Dhaka, the Master had physically appeared before him, and Vijay had confirmed the Master's presence by touching his limbs (see IV.5.2). This added fuel to the fire, and various emotions arose among the devotees. At that time five or six devotees were experiencing some physical changes and losing partial consciousness when they heard devotional songs. Setting aside common sense and the royal path of discrimination, they now became accustomed to waiting eagerly and in suspense for another miraculous manifestation of the Master's divine power.

The astute Narendra, whom the Master had made foremost among his devotees, observed that the devotees had come to regard this excessive emotionalism as the culmination of religion and were considering renunciation, self-control, and steadfast devotion as insignificant. Narendra knew that this attitude, if indulged freely, could eventually lead them into great danger. He explained this to the devotees and made a special effort to protect them from any negative consequences.

7. Narendra tries to curb that excitement and increase renunciation and self-control among the devotees. Why the Master did not take action.

One may question why the Master remained aloof when he knew that some of his devotees were going astray. The answer is that he was not indifferent: He knew that genuine devotion was one of the paths to God-realization and that some of those devotees were truly fit for it. He was looking for the right time and opportunity to guide them along that path. We heard him say many times, "One doesn't attain success suddenly by a mere wish; it happens in the course of time" and "Success in a particular matter comes at the proper time." It may be that he had observed Narendra's determination to remove the devotees' error and was awaiting the result. It may also have been his intention to use Narendra as an instrument to accomplish that task.

Narendra thought that the young devotees, who had strong bodies and resolute minds, would understand him easily. So he repeatedly reasoned with them: "An upsurge of emotion that doesn't transform life permanently makes people eager to realize God at one moment, but doesn't give them the power to desist from seeking lust and gold in the next. There's no depth in it, and it's therefore of little value in life. Under its influence people may experience physical reactions — such as tears, goose bumps, and so on — or may temporarily lose partial outer consciousness, but I'm fully convinced that these things are caused by nervous debility. If people can't control themselves through force of mind, they should eat nutritious food and seek medical help."

8. Emotionalism has little value because it does not permanently transform one's life.

Narendra continued: "There is much artificiality in those physical displays and lapses of outer consciousness. The higher and stronger the dam of self-control, the deeper spiritual emotion becomes. In the lives of a few rare persons, intense spiritual moods take the form of a huge tidal wave, overflowing that dam of self-control and manifesting as physical

9. Sometimes tears, goose bumps, and other physical reactions are feigned.

reactions and a loss of outer consciousness. Foolish people do not understand this and form a mistaken impression. They think that deep spiritual feelings result from those physical displays and lapses of consciousness, so they strive to achieve those signs quickly. This effort of will gradually turns into habit and weakens their nerves day by day. Soon those physical effects appear in them at the slightest awakening of emotion. Consequently, they develop chronic diseases or even become insane by indulging freely in those sentiments. When people try to practise religion, eighty percent of them turn into cheats and about fifteen percent go mad. It's only the remaining five percent who get some direct knowledge of the Truth and become blessed. Therefore, beware!"

At first we did not completely believe Narendra's words. But we soon

| 10. We believed Narendra's words when we saw how some devotees behaved. | learned accidentally that a devotee was singing inspiring Vaishnava songs in solitude, practising to bring on the physical effects that this mood can produce. This devotee also practised dancing like |

another devotee who had danced beautifully when he was overwhelmed by emotion and had lost partial consciousness. Shortly after seeing the first devotee dance, a third devotee began to dance when absorbed in a religious mood. We then realized the truth of Narendra's words. When he saw a devotee having frequent emotional outbursts, Narendra talked to him privately and instructed him to control his emotions and to eat nutritious food. Taking this advice, within a fortnight the devotee became healthy and greatly improved his self-control. Many devotees then trusted Narendra's words and no longer considered themselves unfortunate for not experiencing physical transformations or loss of consciousness as others did when overwhelmed by emotion.

Narendra did not stop at preaching against this emotional exuberance

| 11. Narendra mocks excessive emotion: *dana* and *sakhi*. | using reasoning only; if he sensed the slightest artificiality in any devotee's religious mood, he would ridicule him and embarrass him in public. Narendra |

would also raise the topic of men imitating women and demonstrate how ridiculous was the Vaishnava practice of men practising the attitude of a female confidante of Krishna, thus raising peals of laughter amongst the devotees. He would ridicule any of us who had that kind of tendency by referring to him as a *sakhi*, or a female confidante of Krishna. Narendra was a true lion among men. He could not bear the attitude that a man who came forward to practise religion should give up his manliness, his virility, and his desire to search for truth, and confine himself to imitating a woman's mood and gestures, singing Vaishnava lyrics, and weeping. The Master's masculine devotees, who were endowed with knowledge tempered with devotion, Narendra humorously called *dana* or Shiva's demons, and he called those who had an opposite nature sakhi or female confidantes of Krishna.

Narendra was not satisfied with trying to break the barrier of sentimen-

12. Narendra's efforts to establish true renunciation and love for God instead of emotionalism.

talism with reasoning, jokes, and ridicule. He was fully aware of the fact that his preaching could not be completely effective until the old attitude was replaced by a new one, and he made special efforts to accomplish that. To keep purity, renunciation, and devotion burning in the young disciples' hearts, Narendra would gather them together during leisure times and lead them in songs describing the impermanency of the world and extolling renunciation and devotion to God. Narendra sang these songs and hymns:

> O heart, what will you gain by union with a dear one?
> Ultimately all this will return to dust.
>
> *   *   *
>
> O Ocean of nectar and Embodiment of consciousness and bliss,
> Life becomes sweet and joyful while singing Your name.
>
> *   *   *
>
> I am neither the mind, the intellect, the ego, nor the chitta [mind-stuff],
> Neither the ears, nor the tongue, nor the senses of smell and sight;
> Neither ether nor air, nor fire, nor water, nor earth:
> I am Eternal Bliss and Awareness — I am Shiva! I am Shiva!

When people came to see the Master and heard Narendra sing those songs and hymns in his sweet and melodious voice, they were so inspired with renunciation and love of God that they would shed tears on their way home.

Sometimes Narendra told the devotees wonderful stories of how the

13. If one loves the Master, one's life grows to resemble his.

Master's sadhana had originated from his deep passion for God, and he charmed them with descriptions of the Master's glory. Quoting from *The Imitation of Christ* [by Thomas à Kempis], Narendra said: "'The life of anybody who truly loves the Lord will be perfectly moulded in His pattern.' Therefore, whether we truly love the Master or not will be proven by this." He reminded the devotees of the Master's teaching: "First tie the knowledge of nonduality in a corner of your cloth, then do as you please." Narendra then explained to them that every one of the Master's ecstatic moods arose from that nondual knowledge; so they should strive to attain that knowledge first.

Narendra very often encouraged the Master's devotees to verify new

14. Narendra asks the devotees not to accept new ideas until they have verified them.

ideas before accepting them. We remember that he once heard that one could cure physical ailments by concentrating the mind. He then gathered us in a closed room and engaged us in using that technique to try in curing the Master's illness. However, he always tried to see that the devotees stayed away from practices that were not based on reason. We mention the following incident as an example of this.

Mahimacharan Chakrabarty's house was across from the place where

15. Mahim Chakrabarty's thirst for name and fame.

the south side of Mati Lake met Cossipore Road. Although Mr. Chakrabarty had many good qualities, he always yearned for name and fame. It seems that he was not above resorting to falsehood if it would bring him honour. He arranged every aspect of his life with the expectation that people would call him wealthy, learned, intelligent, virtuous, generous, and so on, which sometimes made him appear ridiculous to others. Once Mr. Chakrabarty founded a free school and called it "Prachya-Arya-Shiksha-Kanda-Parishat" [The Educational Branch of the Institute of the Oriental Aryans]. He named his only son "Mriganka-Mauli Putatundi" [One with a beautiful face and the moon on his head]. He gave his pet deer the name "Kapinjal" [the name of an anchorite]. He was fond of using pompous titles such as these because he felt it unbecoming to a scholar like himself to give short and simple names. He had a large collection of English and Sanskrit books. One day after we became acquainted with him, we went to his house with Narendra. We asked him, "Sir, have you read all these books?" With due humility he replied that he had. But the next moment Narendra picked up some books from his shelf and found that some of their pages were uncut. When asked the reason for this, Mahim Chakrabarty replied: "Look, Brother, people borrowed those books that I read, and they did not return them. So I bought those new copies to replace them. Now I no longer allow anyone to borrow my books." Narendra soon discovered that the pages of most of Mr. Chakrabarty's collection were uncut, which convinced him that Mr. Chakrabarty kept those books in his living room for decoration and to solicit respect and admiration from his visitors.

Once while we were discussing methods of sadhana, Mahim described

16. The tiger skin of Mahim, a self-proclaimed jnani.

himself to us as an aspirant of the path of knowledge. Many years before the Calcutta devotees went to the Master, Mahim had visited the Master at Dakshineswar. On some festival days, he put on an ochre cloth and rudraksha beads, held an ektara (a one-stringed musical instrument) in his hand, sat on his tiger skin under the Panchavati, and began his spiritual practices in great pomp. Before returning home, he would hang his tiger skin on a wall in a corner of the Master's room at Dakshineswar. The Master saw right through him with only a cursory examination. One day one of us asked the Master whom that tiger skin belonged to, and he replied: "Mahim Chakrabarty left it there. Do you know why? So people will see it and ask me to whom it belongs. When I mention his name, they'll think that Mahim Chakrabarty must be a great aspirant."

Regarding his initiation, Mahim sometimes said, "My guru's name is

17. Mahim's guru.

Agamacharya Damaruvallabha." But at other times he mentioned that he had taken initiation from

Paramahamsa Parivrajaka Tota Puri, as the Master had. He said: "While making pilgrimages in Western India, I happened to meet him and was initiated. Tota told Sri Ramakrishna to follow the path of devotion and advised me to stick to the path of knowledge and to stay in the world." How far these assertions were true was known only to him and to omniscient God.

Mahim's sadhana consisted of chanting *Pranava* (Om) in unison with the sound of his ektara, reciting one or two verses from the Uttara Gita and other scriptures, and sometimes shouting loudly. He said that this was the traditional sadhana of the path of knowledge and no other sadhana was needed if one practised it. This would awaken kundalini and one would see God. The image of the goddess Annapurna was installed in his house, and he performed Jagaddhatri worship every year. One can infer from this that he was born into a Shakta family. It seems that towards the end of his life he adopted the method of Shakti sadhana, because when he travelled in his small buggy, one sometimes heard his loud cry from the carriage, "Tara, Thou art That; Thou art That." Mahim managed his household with income from his small estate.

18. Mahim's sadhana.

Mahim visited the Master two or three times at Shyampukur. After inquiring about the Master's welfare, he would sit in the living room, where he then performed his mantra sadhana with his Ektara and at intervals talked with those present about spiritual life. Attracted by his handsome and robust figure clad in ochre cloth and by his glamourous eloquence, many people would ask him spiritual questions at that time. The Master sometimes told him: "You are a pandit. Give them (*pointing to the visitors*) some advice." The Master knew that Mahim had a strong desire to gather disciples and spread his name as a preacher.

19. Mahim at Shyampukur.

One day Mahim came to Shyampukur and spoke on various topics, attempting to establish that the sadhana he followed was the best and easiest, and that all other sadhanas were inferior. Narendra could not bear to see the Master's young disciples listening to him without protest. Narendra raised counter-arguments and proved that Mahim's position was untenable. He asked, "What proof is there that a person will see God by uttering a mantra while accompanied by an ektara as you are doing?" Mahim replied: "*Nada* [sound] is Brahman. God is bound to reveal Himself if the mantra is uttered simultaneously with that musical note. One need not practise anything else." Narendra said: "Has God drawn up such a written agreement with you? Will God appear stealthily before you, like a snake charmed by a mantra and an herb, when you raise the pitch of your voice and utter *hum-ham*?" Unfortunately, because of Narendra's arguments, Mahim's preaching did not gain a following that day, and he quickly took his leave.

20. A debate between Mahim and Narendra.

Narendra kept watch over the Master's devotees so that they would pay

21. Narendra's advice to show equal respect for all true spiritual aspirants.

due respect to genuine spiritual aspirants of other religious communities. He said: "Ordinary people love and respect only those spiritual aspirants of their own faith; they criticize those of other faiths. This attitude shows disrespect for the Master's view 'As many faiths, so many paths,' and therefore to the Master himself." We remember a related incident that occurred when the Master was in Shyampukur.

Prabhudayal Mishra, a Christian clergyman, came to see the Master. We

22. Prabhudayal Mishra, a Christian clergyman.

did not immediately recognize him as a Christian because he was wearing an ochre cloth. When he introduced himself to us, we asked him why he wore ochre cloth if he were a Christian. He replied: "I was born in a brahmin family. Must I give up the customs and practices of my forefathers because I have established faith in Christ and accepted him as my Chosen Deity? I believe in the yoga scriptures and practise yoga disciplines daily with Christ as my Chosen Deity. I don't believe in the caste system, but I do believe that it is injurious to the practice of yoga if one indiscriminately accepts food from anyone. So every day I eat vegetarian food that I've cooked for myself. Consequently, even though I'm a Christian, I've experienced the results of yoga, such as seeing a light and so on. The devout yogis of India have been wearing ochre cloth from ancient times, so this cloth is dearer to me than any other." Narendra put questions to him one after another and learned about his personal life. When he had determined him to be a yogi and a holy man, Narendra showed great respect for him and asked us to do the same. Many of us took the dust of his feet, and together we had the Master's prasad of sweets and fruits. He told us that he believed the Master was Jesus Christ himself.

As Narendra was busily guiding the devotees along the right path, the

23. The Master's illness worsens, and the devotees move him to the Cossipore garden house.

Master's illness grew steadily worse. Dr. Sarkar was concerned when he discovered that the medicines that had been producing some good results were no longer working. He became convinced that the polluted air of Calcutta was harming the Master, so he recommended that he be moved to a garden house outside the city. The first half of the month of *Agrahayan* [mid-November to mid-December] passed. The devotees knew that the Master would not change his dwelling during *Paush* [mid-December to mid-January] because it was inauspicious, so they desperately began to search for a garden house. They soon located and rented the garden house of Gopal Chandra Ghosh, a son-in-law of Rani Katyayani, at eighty rupees per month. This house is situated at the junction of the northern part of the Mati Lake in Cossipore and the eastern side of the main road leading to Baranagore Bazar. Surendra Nath

Mitra of Calcutta, a great devotee of the Master, promised to pay the entire rent.

After securing the house, the devotees fixed an auspicious date and made plans to move the Master's belongings from the Shyampukur house. Finally, the devotees took the Master himself from the Shyampukur house to the Cossipore garden house in the afternoon one day before the end of Agrahayan [11 December 1885]. The devotees were pleased to see that the Master was delighted with the garden bedecked with flowers and fruit trees, and with the fresh air and solitude.

Chapter 13

Section 1

The Cossipore Garden House[1]

THE COSSIPORE GARDEN HOUSE IS SITUATED ON the main road that begins in North

1. Cossipore.
Calcutta and connects Baghbazar with Baranagore, about three miles from the city.

On both sides of the road, from north of the Baghbazar bridge to the Cossipore crossroads a little south of the garden house, are the huts of poor labourers and small shops full of articles necessary for their daily lives. Among these dwellings one can see some brick buildings — a few jute warehouses, the iron factory of Das Company, the firm of Ralli Brothers Ltd., and a couple of gardens and homes. There is a police station and a fire station at the northwest corner of the Cossipore crossroads, and not far to the west is the famous Sarvamangala temple. The huts and buildings bear witness to the different living conditions of the poor and the rich. As the Sealdah railway station has been improved and extended, many tin-roofed warehouses have recently been built near that road, ruining the beauty of the area that existed just a few years before.

Although this ancient road may not be pleasing to the eye, it has some value to historians. It is said that Nawab Siraj[2] marched his army along this road to capture the British fort at Govindapur, and that the notorious traitor Nawab Mirzaffar[3] had his palace on this road, a little over half a mile north of

1. This chapter (13-1, 13-2, and 13–3), which comprises some events of the Cossipore garden house, was added to this volume in its fourth edition on 13 Ashwin 1342 B.E. (September 1935). It was first published by Swami Saradananda as three articles in *Udbodhan* magazine in the Shravan, Bhadra, and Ashwin issues of 1326 B.E. (1919). —*Translator*
2. Nawab Sirajud-daula, a great patriot and the last independent Nawab of Bengal, Bihar, and Orissa. — *Translator*
3. The commander-in-chief of Nawab Sirajud-daula. — *Translator*

Baghbazar. The section of the road from Baghbazar to the Cossipore cross-roads may not be scenic, but its extension up to Baranagore Bazar is not unattractive. A bit north from the crossroads, one reaches the southern part of Mati Lake, and opposite that, on the eastern side of the road, is the beautiful house of Mahimacharan Chakrabarty, whom we knew. The Railway Company recently [circa 1919] purchased a large part of the garden surrounding that house and extended a branch line up to the bank of the Ganges through it; this ruined the beauty of the house.

Proceeding a little farther north, one reaches the northern side of Mati Lake on the left. Opposite it, on the eastern side of the road, one can see the Cossipore garden house, with its high walls and iron gate. To the west of Mati Lake is a road on which there were some beautiful garden houses on the bank of the Ganges. Among these houses, Matilal Sil's garden was the largest and most beautiful. It is now occupied by the Calcutta Electric Company, and its serenity and beauty are gone, replaced by the hubbub of business and the noise of a power generating station. To the north of Mati Sil's garden, the Basak family had a dilapidated house on the bank of the Ganges. Rows of pine trees lined the path that led from the main road to that dilapidated house, and visitors enjoyed the beautiful scenery and the wonderful rustling sound of the gentle breeze in those trees.

While we were staying with the Master at the Cossipore garden house, we often used to walk through Mati Sil's garden to bathe in the Ganges. Near the bathing ghat were some *gulchi* [Plumeria] trees from which we would pick flowers to present to the Master, as he was fond of them. Sometimes we would walk through the pine trees to the Basaks' solitary and uninhabited garden and sit on the bank of the Ganges. A little north of this garden was Prananath Chaudhury's spacious bathing ghat, and north of that was the beautiful Gopala temple of Rani Katyayani, wife of the famous Lalababu. Sometimes we would go there to bathe in the Ganges and visit the Lord Gopala. Gopal Chandra Ghosh, a son-in-law of Rani Katyayani, owned the Cossipore garden house. The devotees rented it for the Master at eighty rupees per month for six months at first, and then leased it for three months more. Surendra Nath Mitra of Calcutta, a devotee of the Master, signed the lease and paid all of the rent.

The Cossipore garden house was not large, but it was very beautiful. The

2. The Cossipore garden house.

house was situated on a quadrangular piece of land about five acres in size, which was a little longer from east to west than north to south, and was surrounded on all sides by high walls. A small building of three or four rooms adjacent to the middle of the northern boundary wall was used for cooking and storage. There was a two-storeyed residence in front of that building and next to the garden path. This house had two rooms upstairs and four downstairs. The middle room downstairs was a spacious hall. To the north of it were two

914

Cossipore garden house where Ramakrishna spent his last days (11 December 1885 to 16 August 1886).

small rooms side by side. In the western room was a wooden staircase that led upstairs. The eastern room was occupied by the Holy Mother. The Master's attendants and devotees used the spacious hall, which extended from east to west, and the room just south of it for sitting and sleeping. There was a small veranda on the eastern side of that room. On the upper floor, above the hall, there was a room of equal dimensions in which the Master lived. To the south of this room was a small open terrace surrounded by parapet walls where the Master sometimes walked or sat. An open terrace was above the room with the staircase. Above the Holy Mother's room was another of equal size that was used for the Master's bathing and for one or two attendants to rest in at night.

At ground level, a few stairs led to the hall entrances, which were located on the east and west sides of the residence. The house was encircled by a brick garden path. In the southwest corner of the garden, joined to its western wall, was a small lean-to for the gatekeeper, and to the north of that was an iron gate. From this gate a broad semicircular carriage path had been extended to the northeast to connect the path that encircled the house. There was a small pool to the west of the house. Opposite the steps of the hall's western entrance and the western side of the garden path, steps led down to the pool. In the northeast corner of the garden was a pond, four or five times larger than the pool. Northwest of this pond was a one-storeyed building with two or three rooms. In addition, there was a stable in the northwest corner of the garden to the west of the pool, and midway on the southern boundary wall of the garden there were two dilapidated single-room brick cottages for the gardeners. Many fruit trees, including mango, jackfruit, lichee, and others, grew throughout the garden, and the garden path was lined with flowering trees. Various kinds of vegetables and spinach for daily use were grown around the pool and the pond. Between the large trees were green lawns that enhanced the beauty of the garden.

The Master moved into the Cossipore garden house on 11 December 1885

3. The Master spends his last eight months at Cossipore training his young disciples.

and spent the winter, spring, summer, and rainy seasons there. His disease grew steadily worse during those eight months. Although his tall and robust body broke down and became as emaciated as a skeleton, his self-controlled mind completely disregarded his pain and the severity of the disease. He engaged himself in completing the mission he had undertaken among his devotees, both individually and collectively, by teaching them what they needed to know. In addition, we regularly witnessed the fulfillment of the prophecies about himself that he had made to the devotees at Dakshineswar. On various occasions he had said: "Before I leave the world, I'll cast my whole secret to the winds." In other words, he would reveal himself publicly as a godman. "When many people know (*my divine glory*) and whisper about it, this case (*my body*) will cease to exist. It will fall to pieces according to the Mother's will." "At that time (*during my illness*) it will be determined who among the devotees belong to the inner circle and who to the outer circle."

Here [at Cossipore] we came to understand the truth of the Master's predictions about Narendra and other devotees. He said to Narendra: "The Divine Mother has brought you into the world by force to do Her work." "You must follow me. Where else would you go?" "These young boys are like the fledglings of the homa bird [mentioned in the Vedas]. It lives high up in the sky, and there it lays its eggs. As soon as the eggs are laid, they begin to fall speedily towards the earth, and it appears as though they will be dashed to pieces. But this doesn't happen. Before hitting the ground, the fledglings break through their shells and emerge, spreading their wings and shooting up towards the mother bird high in the sky. Similarly, these boys will renounce the world before they are caught up in it, and will move towards God." The Master moulded Narendra's life at Cossipore and assigned him responsibility for his devotees — particularly the young ones — and trained him in how to guide them. The activities performed by the Master at the Cossipore garden house were extremely significant indeed.

Naturally, people have an intense desire to preserve as a memorial this

| 4. The importance of preserving the garden house. | special place, where such significant activities in the Master's life took place. It will serve to keep alive for |

future generations those holy memories of the Master, which will give them bliss and inspiration. But alas, an awful obstacle has recently cropped up [in the 1920s]. We have heard that the Railway Company is trying to acquire the garden house. So this wonderful playground of the Master will very soon be transformed into jute warehouses or some other ugly structures.[4] But if it is the will of Providence, what can we helpless human beings do? Let us conclude this subject by saying, "What exists in the mind of Providence will come to pass."

---

4. Fortunately, the author's sincere desire was fulfilled and the Railway Company's plan failed. In 1946 the Cossipore garden house came into the possession of the Ramakrishna Order and the old buildings were restored without changing their original appearance. Thus the Order preserved the holy spot where Sri Ramakrishna enacted the last part of his divine play and became the Kalpataru [wish-fulfilling tree] on 1 January 1886. — *Translator*

Chapter 13

Section 2

The Vow of Service to the Master at Cossipore

WE MENTIONED EARLIER (SEE V.12.3.23) THAT BECAUSE it was inauspicious to travel

1. The Master is joyful at the beauty and spaciousness of the garden house.

during the month of Paush [mid-December to mid-January], the Master moved to the Cossipore garden house just before the last day of Agrahayan [mid-November to mid-December]. The garden house was more spacious and secluded than the Shyampukur house, which was situated near a crowded and noisy road in Calcutta. In whatever direction one might look from this garden house, one could see the evergreen leaves of the trees, the bright colours of flowers, and the tender green grass of the lawns. The beauty of the Cossipore garden might be insignificant compared to the wonderful, natural, and panoramic beauty of the Dakshineswar temple garden, but the Master found the place pleasant after spending a stretch of four months in Calcutta. He was delighted when he entered the garden and breathed its fresh air. He took in the view as he walked slowly towards the house. When he went upstairs to his spacious room, he immediately walked to the southern terrace connected to his room and enjoyed the garden's beauty for a while. The Holy Mother was also happy when she saw that she would not have to live here in confinement and suffer the inconveniences that she had in the Shyampukur house, and at the same time she would be able to continue to serve the Master.

Naturally, with both of them happy, the hearts of their attendants were filled with joy.

It took a few days for the Master's attendants to overcome the preliminary

2. Narendra supervises the Master's service and the lay devotees supply the money.

difficulties of settling into the Cossipore garden house. While thinking over their problems, Narendra quickly concluded that the attendants who volunteered to serve the Master must stay there, as the place was far away from the doctors who were treating the Master. This required more men and more money than before. If these two problems were not tackled in the beginning, the Master's service would suffer. As Balaram, Surendra, Ram, Girish, Mahendra, and others had been dealing with the financial matters so far, so they would find a solution for this aspect of the situation. Narendra knew that he would have to continue being responsible for gathering attendants. He decided to spend most of his time at the Cossipore garden, because if he did not set an example, the other young devotees would not be able to carry on the work when faced by opposition from their guardians, or by the neglect of their studies or office duties. When the Master was in Shyampukur, his young attendants went home for their meals and then came back to serve him, but that kind of arrangement was not possible in Cossipore because of the distance.

Narendra was preparing for his law examination (B.L.) that year.

3. Narendra decides to stay in Cossipore to serve the Master and to prepare for his law examination.

Although it was absolutely necessary that he stay in Calcutta because of his studies and the High Court legal battle against his deceitful relatives, who were attempting to partition his ancestral property, he completely banished those concerns from his mind to serve his guru. Narendra decided to bring his law books with him to the Cossipore garden house and to read them whenever he found time. Thus, Narendra resolved to serve his guru first and then appear for the law examination, if possible. Having no alternative but to support his family, he planned to pass the law examination, work for a few years to provide necessities for his mother and brothers, and then renounce the world and devote himself entirely to spiritual practices. Alas, many of us make such good resolutions — but how many succeed? We plan to go only so far in pursuit of worldly achievement and then exert our strength to turn ourselves to the path of God. We start work according to our plan, but how many of us eventually succeed and escape the whirlpool of the world? Although Narendra was foremost amongst the spiritual aspirants and had received the Master's boundless grace, when his good intentions eventually collided with the world, would they be destroyed as a result and take a different form? O reader, have patience. Eventually we shall see how and in what way the Master's infallible will helped Narendra to reach his goal.

Narendra (Swami Vivekananda) at Cossipore garden house in 1886.

Thus far we have described how the devotees were serving the Master.

| 4. The Master always depended on the Divine Mother and accepted the devotees' service for their own welfare. |

The following question now arises: While at Dakshineswar we saw that even while the Master was experiencing truths beyond the Vedas and Vedanta, he was still keeping his keen sight on trivial everyday affairs as well as the material and spiritual condition of his devotees. How is it possible that the Master could now become completely dependent on his devotees, giving no thought to himself? The answer is that the Master's entire focus throughout his life was on the Divine Mother. As he had completely depended on Her in the past, so he did in the present. He had known in advance that the type and amount of service he would receive from each devotee was intended by the Divine Mother and was for their welfare. The more we tell of the Master's life story, the more we shall understand his phenomenal reliance on the Divine Mother.

Whenever the Master did not like arrangements that the devotees had

| 5. The Master himself discreetly manages his service with the devotees. |

made, he would make adjustments either with their knowledge or without it if he felt their feelings would be hurt. Just before going to Calcutta for treatment, he told Balaram: "Look, people collect money for my daily food, but this isn't to my liking. I'm not used to it. If you ask how I'm living in the Kali temple of Dakshineswar at present, when many owners of the temple jointly conduct the worship service, I would respond that I don't receive my food from the money that they pledged. When Rani Rasmani was alive, it was arranged that I would permanently continue to draw my salary as a priest, which was seven rupees per month, and that I would receive prasad from the temple as long as I lived here. So in a sense I live here on a pension.[1] I therefore ask that you carry my expenses for food as long as I live away from Dakshineswar for my treatment."

When the Cossipore garden house was rented for him, he learned that it would cost eighty rupees per month to rent, and he was concerned about how his devotees, who had to maintain large families, could bear this expense. Finally, he called his great devotee Surendra, an agent of the Dost Company, and said: "Look, Surendra, these devotees are mostly poor clerks and have large families to maintain. How can they raise so much money to rent this garden house? Please bear the whole of it yourself." With folded hands, Surendra gladly assented, saying, "As you command." One day the Master told us that very soon his physical weakness would make it difficult for him to go outside to answer the call of nature. The young devotee Latu[2]

1. The Master pronounced the English word *pension* as "pencil."
2. He is now well known among the devotees of the Master as Swami Adbhutananda. He came from the Chapra district of Bihar. He could understand Bengali, but when he tried to speak that language he had a strong accent that sounded as sweet as the lisping of a child.

Latu (d. 1920), later Swami Adbhutananda. Photo taken at Alambazar Math in 1896.

Brother Gopal (1828-1909), later Swami Advaitananda.

was pained when he heard the Master say this. He forthwith responded humbly, with folded hands: "Sir, whatever you order me to do, I will do. I am your sweeper and always ready." Latu uttered those words in his own form of Bengali, which made the Master and us laugh even in that dismal situation. Thus did the Master make his own arrangements as appropriate, making it easier for the devotees to carry out their respective duties.

Gradually everything fell into a routine and the young devotees came to

| 6. The vow of service brings the young devotees together. | Cossipore one after another. When they were not busy caring for the Master, Narendra engaged them in meditation, devotional singing, study, discussion |

of the scriptures, and spiritual conversation. They were carried away in such a blissful current that they did not notice how the days slipped away. The tremendous attraction of the Master's pure and unselfish love on one hand, and Narendra's wonderful friendship and holy companionship on the other, joined them in such a sweet and strong bond that they truly felt closer to one another than to members of their own families. If someone went home on urgent business, he invariably returned that evening or the next morning at the latest. They lived at Cossipore until the Master passed away and then completed their vow of service by renouncing the world. Although the devotees never numbered more than twelve,[3] they were extremely devoted to their guru and remarkably efficient.

One day shortly after the Master arrived at Cossipore, he went downstairs

| 7. The Master's health improves slightly. | and walked on the garden path for a short time. The devotees were delighted to see this, and hoped that he would soon regain his strength and recover if he |

could take walks like this every day. However, the next day he felt weaker, having caught a cold from the chilly air outside or for some other reason, so he could not go outside again for many days. His cold subsided in two or three days, but the weakness continued. The doctors prescribed a special broth for him. After taking it for a few days, his weakness lessened to a great extent and he felt better and stronger. This improvement continued for about a fortnight. Dr. Sarkar came to visit and was delighted to find him in better health.

The young attendants had to go to Calcutta every day to give the doctor a

| 8. Narendra assigns duties to the young disciples. | report on the Master's health and to obtain the food he needed. At first both tasks were given to one person, but this arrangement created some inconvenience. |

---

3. To satisfy the reader's curiosity we list the names of those twelve below: Narendra, Rakhal, Baburam, Niranjan, Jogindra, Latu, Tarak, Brother Gopal (the only elderly man amongst the young devotees), Kali, Shashi, Sharat, and (Hutko) Gopal. [Regarding the other devotees] Sarada could stay only a day or two from time to time because of his father's strong opposition. Hari, Gangadhar, and Tulsi practised austerities at home and visited the Master occasionally. In addition, a couple of young ones joined Mahimacharan Chakrabarty shortly afterwards [after the Master passed away] and stayed in his house.

So it was decided that two people would go to Calcutta every day for those important errands. If anything else was needed in Calcutta, a third person was sent. In addition, the young devotees began to take turns performing all other duties, such as cleaning the house, shopping for groceries at the Baranagore bazar every day, and caring for the Master day and night. Narendra supervised their activities and managed other affairs that cropped up.

As before, the Holy Mother was in charge of preparing the Master's diet.

9. The Holy Mother takes responsibility for the diet as before.

If the doctor prescribed a special diet for the Master in addition to regular food, Brother Gopal or another devotee would learn how to prepare it, then teach the Holy Mother how to do so. The Holy Mother would converse freely only with Brother Gopal and one or two others. In addition to preparing the Master's meals, the Holy Mother would carry the food tray to him a little before noon and shortly after sunset and wait until he had finished eating. The Master's niece Lakshmi was brought to Cossipore to help the Holy Mother cook and perform other household duties as well as to keep her company. In addition, some of the women devotees who had regularly visited the Master in Dakshineswar began to come to Cossipore and stay with the Holy Mother for a few hours, or sometimes for one or two days. After a week, the whole arrangement worked smoothly.

The householder devotees were not free from anxiety during that period.

10. The lay devotees regularly discuss financial matters.

They would meet at Ram's or Girish's house, as was convenient, to decide how much time and money they could provide for the Master's service, then they would act accordingly. They knew that not everyone might be able to contribute an equal amount every month, so they met once or twice a month to make decisions beforehand.

Most of the young devotees did not visit their homes for even a short

11. Narendra inspires the young devotees to give up worldly desires and devote themselves to God-realization.

while until everything regarding the Master's service was in order. Those who had to go home to handle urgent matters returned within a few hours. They somehow made their guardians understand that they would not be able to visit regularly or live at home as before until the Master had recovered. Of course, no guardian was pleased to hear that, and none of them approved. But what could they do? They thought the boys had been brainwashed and that if they were not handled carefully, more harm than good would result. So the guardians decided to somehow tolerate the boys' behaviour for a time and began to devise some means for bringing them back.

When the householder devotees and the young disciples jointly undertook their vow of service and everything was orderly and running as smooth as a machine, Narendra was relieved to a great extent and had an opportunity to think about his own affairs. One night he told us that he planned to visit home for a day or two. He then went to bed, but he could not sleep. He soon got up, and finding Gopal and a couple of us awake, he said, "Come, let us have a smoke and walk in the garden." As we walked, he said: "The Master's disease is extremely serious. Who knows whether he has decided to lay down his body? Make your best effort to achieve spiritual enlightenment through service to him and prayer and meditation while there is yet time. If you do otherwise, there will be no end to your repentance after he passes away. We waste our time with the foolish thought that we shall pray to God after finishing this duty, or practise spiritual disciplines after doing that. Thus we entangle ourselves in a net of desires. Those terrible desires lead to destruction — death. Shun those desires! Uproot them!"

On this cold winter night in Paush [mid-December to mid-January] the silence pulsated. Above, the infinite blue sky watched the earth steadily with its millions of starry eyes. Below, the sun's scorching rays had dried the ground under the garden trees, and one could sit

12. The disciples mentally offer their desires into the dhuni fire.

there because the place had been recently cleaned up. Narendra's detached and meditative mind felt that external silence and began to absorb it within. He stopped walking and sat down under a tree. After a while, he saw a heap of dry straw, leaves, and broken tree branches nearby, and told us: "Set fire to it. This is the hour when monks light their dhuni fires under the trees. Let us also light a dhuni fire and burn up our desires." The fire was lighted and we collected more twigs and piled them around us. As we placed bits of wood on that fire, we pictured ourselves as offering our desires as oblations. We experienced a wonderful bliss and truly felt that our worldly desires were utterly destroyed, our minds were pure and serene, and we were becoming close to God. We thought: "Ah, why didn't we do this before? It has given us so much joy! Henceforth, we shall light a dhuni fire whenever we have the opportunity." After two or three hours we could find no more fuel, so we extinguished the fire and returned to our room to retire again. It was then 4:00 a.m. Those who did not participate in our dhuni ceremony heard the story in the morning and were sad that they had not been called. Narendra consoled them by saying: "We didn't plan to do it, and we didn't know that we would experience such bliss. Don't worry, from now on we shall light the dhuni fire together whenever we find time."

Narendra left for Calcutta in the morning as planned and returned to Cossipore the next day with a few law books.

Chapter 13

Section 3

The *M*aster
Bestows Fearlessness through
Self-Revelation

WE HAVE ALREADY TOLD THE READER HOW, shortly after arriving at Cossipore, the

> 1. The Master feels better under Dr. Rajendra Datta's care.

Master left his room and walked in the garden briefly. He felt weak after that walk, so he did not venture to go outdoors again for about a fortnight. During that period, his doctor was changed but the homeopathic treatment continued. Dr. Rajendralal Datta had been born into the famous and wealthy family of Akrur Datta of Bowbazar, Calcutta. He had worked hard and spent much money for the study and propagation of homeopathy in the city. It was by associating with him that Dr. Mahendralal Sarkar had realized the success and usefulness of homeopathy and had started to practise with that system of medicine. Rajendra learned of the Master's illness by word of mouth and thought that if he could cure the Master, the reputation of homeopathy would be established among many people. So after much thought and study, he selected a specific medicine for the Master's disease. He was acquainted with Atul, Girish's brother. So far as we remember, Dr. Datta met with Atul around this time and abruptly inquired about the Master's illness. He expressed his desire to treat the Master and said: "Please tell Mahendra that after careful consideration I have selected a medicine, and I expect a good result from it. If he agrees, I'm willing to try it." When Atul reported this to the devotees and Dr. Sarkar, no one objected. A few days later Dr. Rajendra Datta came to see the Master, and after listening to the whole history of his disease, he prescribed Lycopodium 200.

This produced good results in the Master for more than a fortnight. The devotees thought that the Master might soon be free from disease and as strong as before.

On 1 January 1886, the Master felt better and expressed a desire to walk in

2. 1 January 1886: an historical event.

the garden for a short while. Because it was a holiday, the householder devotees began arriving at the Cossipore garden after midday individually and in groups. The Master came down from upstairs at 3:00 p.m.; there were more than thirty people talking amongst themselves inside the house and sitting under the trees in the garden. They all stood up reverently and bowed down when they saw him. The Master went out through the western door of the hall, descended onto the garden path, and proceeded slowly southward to the gate. The devotees followed him at a little distance. When he reached the midpoint of the path between the house and the gate, the Master saw Girish, Ram, Atul, and a few others under a tree on the west side of the path. They bowed down to him and came to him joyfully.

Before anyone had spoken a word, the Master addressed Girish, asking

3. The Master blesses the devotees, saying, "Be illumined."

him: "Girish, what have you seen and understood (*about me*) that makes you say all these things (*that I am an avatar, and so on*) to everyone, wherever you go?" Unperturbed, Girish knelt down at the Master's feet, folded his hands before his raised face, and responded in a voice choked with emotion: "What more can I say of Him? Even the sages Vyasa and Valmiki could find no words to measure His glory!" Girish's sincere faith expressed in those words so moved the Master that he said to the devotees, while looking at Girish: "What more need I tell you? I bless you all. May you all be illumined!" He became overwhelmed by love and compassion for his devotees, and went into ecstasy after uttering those few words.

That selfless and profound blessing touched the devotees deep within

4. The spiritual awakening among the devotees.

their hearts and they became mad with joy. They forgot time and space; they forgot the Master's illness; they forgot that they had vowed not to touch the Master until his recovery. They saw that a wondrous divine being had come down to them from heaven and was calling to them affectionately; they also felt that their suffering grieved him and that he was carrying in his heart an infinite pain and compassion for them and offering them shelter as selflessly as a loving mother. They became anxious to bow down to him and take the dust of his feet. Their cries of "Victory to Ramakrishna" resounded in all directions as one by one they bowed down to him. As they touched his feet, the ocean of the Master's compassion burst through all bounds and created an astonishing phenomenon. Almost every day in Dakshineswar we had seen the Master become overwhelmed with compassion and grace and bless some devotees with his powerful divine touch. On this day, as he remained in a semiecstatic state, he began to touch each devotee present in a similar way, and their joy was boundless.

The devotees understood that from this day on, the Master would no longer conceal his divinity from them or from anyone else in the world. They had no doubt that from now on all sinners and sufferers — despite their shortcomings, lack of spirituality, and feelings of inadequacy — would find shelter at his blessed feet. Seeing the Master in that unique and exalted state, some became speechless and could only watch him as if bewitched. Some called out loudly to everyone inside the house to come and be blessed by the Master's grace. Others picked flowers from the garden and began to worship him, uttering mantras and showering him with flowers. When the Master's ecstasy came to an end after some time, the devotees calmed down. The Master finished his walk in the garden, then returned to the house and sat down in his room.

Ramchandra and some devotees have said that on that day the Master became the Kalpataru, the wish-fulfilling tree. But we think it is more reasonable to describe this event as a manifestation of the Master's fearless divine nature, or to say that he revealed himself on that day, granting fearlessness to all. It is said that the Kalpataru gives people whatever they ask for, good or bad. But the Master did not do that; by this event he let it be known clearly that he was a godman and that he offered shelter from fear to all without discrimination.

5. Did the Master become the Kalpataru or bestow fearlessness by revealing himself?

At any rate, Haran Chandra Das is worthy of being mentioned amongst those who were blessed with the Master's grace that day. As soon as Haran bowed down to the Master, the Master placed his foot on Haran's head. Seldom did the Master bestow his grace in this way.[1] Ramlal Chattopadhyay, a nephew of the Master, was also present on that occasion and received his grace. When asked about his experience, Ramlal said: "Before this, when I meditated I could see only part of my Chosen Deity with my mind's eye. When I saw His feet I couldn't see His face, and when I saw His form from His face to His waist, I couldn't see His feet. Moreover, whatever I saw never seemed to be alive. But no sooner had the Master touched me that day than the whole form of my Chosen Deity appeared in my heart as a living presence, benign and effulgent."

We remember nine or ten devotees who were present on that day: Girish, Atul, Ram, Navagopal, Haramohan, Vaikuntha, Kishori Roy, Haran, Ramlal, and Akshay. Mahendra Nath Gupta, the recorder of *The Gospel of*

6. The names of those present during that historic event.

---

1. Haran Chandra Das of Beliaghata, Calcutta, worked in the offices of Messrs. Finlay Mayor Company. At his house, every year he used to celebrate a festival to commemorate the grace he received from the Master.

Cossipore garden house. Ramakrishna became the Kalpataru (a wish-fulfilling tree) on 1 January 1886, near the curve of the mango tree.

At Cossipore, Ramakrishna wrote in Bengali: "Victory to Radha, love personified. Naren will teach loudly inside and outside [India]. Victory to Radha." It is assumed that the head represents Narendra and the peacock his large following (see *The Gospel of Sri Ramakrishna*, p. 831).

Sri Ramakrishna, may also have been present. But, amazingly, none of the Master's would-be monastic disciples were there at the time. The night before, Narendra and some other disciples had been engaged in sadhana, in addition to serving the Master, so they were tired and were sleeping in their room. Latu and Sharat [the author] were awake and saw the whole affair from the roof south of the Master's room but did not feel any urge to go there. As soon as the Master had left for his walk, they had taken the opportunity to clean the Master's room and put his mattress and pillow on the roof to be sunned. Because they did not want to inconvenience the Master by leaving their work unfinished, they felt no inclination to go there.

We interviewed several devotees who were present on that occasion

7. Vaikuntha strives to have a vision.

about their experiences. We shall conclude this subject by recording what Vaikuntha told us. Vaikuntha met the Master about the same time that we did. We have recorded some stories in this book about how the Master gave him instructions and formed his spiritual life. The Master initiated Vaikuntha with a mantra and blessed him, and from then on he practised sadhana and tried his utmost to have a vision of his Chosen Deity. He understood that he would not succeed without the Master's grace, so from time to time he fervently prayed to the Master. When the Master became ill and had to move to Calcutta and then to Cossipore for treatment, Vaikuntha had the opportunity to ask him two or three times to fulfill his heart's desire. The Master smiled graciously and reassured him, saying: "Wait a little. Let my disease be cured. Afterwards, I shall do everything for you."

Vaikuntha was present when the events of 1 January took place. After the

8. Vaikuntha's testimony.

Master had blessed two or three devotees with his powerful divine touch, Vaikuntha went before him, reverently bowed down to him, and implored, "Sir, please bestow your grace on me." The Master answered, "You've achieved everything." Vaikuntha said: "Sir, when you say that I've achieved everything, it must be so. Kindly help me so that I can understand it a little." The Master said, "All right," and gently touched his chest for a moment. Vaikuntha described it thus: "Consequently, a wonderful change came across my mind. I began to see the Master's gracious, smiling, and luminous form in the sky, the houses, the trees, all human beings, and in everything else I saw in all directions. I was overwhelmed with extreme bliss. At that time I saw you both [the author and Latu] on the roof and called to you loudly: 'O you all! Wherever you are, come here right now.' That spiritual mood and vision continued for some days, even in the waking state. I was amazed and spellbound by seeing the blessed Master in all things. This experience remained whether I went to the office or elsewhere on business.

"My work suffered because I couldn't concentrate on my regular duties.

9. Spiritual ecstasy cannot be retained without preparation.

When I realized this, I tried unsuccessfully to stop that vision for a while. I now understood a little why Arjuna was afraid when he had the vision of the cosmic form of Lord Krishna and why he prayed to Krishna to withdraw it. I remembered that the scriptures said liberated souls dwelt in the same exalted state of consciousness. I now got a little glimpse from this experience of how much desirelessness is necessary for a person to remain continuously in that state. Hardly had a few days passed when I was overwhelmed by this continuous vision and spiritual mood, and found it difficult to function. Sometimes I thought: 'Shall I lose my mind?' At last I prayed to the Master fearfully: 'O Lord, I'm not able to contain this spiritual fervour. Please release me from this state.' Woe to human weakness and stupidity! Now I think: 'Why did I pray that way? Why didn't I have faith in him and wait patiently to see what the ultimate result would be? I might have become mad, or my body might have dropped away.' Soon after that prayer, my vision and spiritual mood abruptly came to an end. I was fully convinced that my experience came to an end by the same person from whom I had received it. But perhaps because the complete cessation of that vision didn't arise in my mind as I prayed, he kindly kept a little of that experience in me: I could see that divine, effulgent, gracious form of the Master several times a day and was overwhelmed with joy and blessedness."

Ramakrishna passed away in this room at the Cossipore garden house on
16 August 1886 at 1:02 a.m.

Romain Rolland wrote: "The man [Ramakrishna] himself was no more. His spirit
had departed to travel along the path of collective life in the veins of humanity."

These two photographs were taken on 16 August 1886 at Cossipore garden house, before Ramakrishna's body was cremated.

Monument on the site of Ramakrishna's cremation. Belur Math can be seen on the opposite bank of the Ganges, where the disciples of Ramakrishna established their permanent monastery and the headquarters of the Order.

Marble statue of Ramakrishna at Belur Math.
On 9 December 1898, Vivekananda said to a disciple: "The Master once told me,
'I will go and live wherever it will be your pleasure to take me, carrying me
on your shoulders — be it under a tree or in the humblest cottage.'"

Swami Saradananda:
A Brief Biography

"In a vision I saw that Shashi and Sharat had been among the followers of Christ," said Sri Ramakrishna. Shashi and Sharat, who were cousins, later became swamis Ramakrishnananda and Saradananda in the Ramakrishna Order. One day at Dakshineswar the Master sat on Saradananda's lap in an ecstatic mood. He later explained to his curious devotees, "I was testing to see how much weight he could bear." Later, Saradananda indeed carried the heavy responsibility of the young Ramakrishna Movement for over thirty years.

Sharat Chandra Chakrabarty was born in Calcutta on Saturday, 23 December 1865. His parents were devout Hindu brahmins and quite well-to-do. He was very gentle, intelligent, loving, and unselfish. He was a good student and passed the Entrance examination in 1882. In 1883 he was admitted to St. Xavier's College, Calcutta. As a young boy he was greatly influenced by the Brahmo leader Keshab Chandra Sen and learned about Sri Ramakrishna in Keshab's magazine.

In October 1883, Sharat went to Dakshineswar to visit Sri Ramakrishna with some of his friends and was attracted to the Master. Not only did he visit Sri Ramakrishna regularly, but he also began to spend nights in Dakshineswar in order to practise spiritual disciplines under his guidance. The Master would awaken his young disciples at midnight and send them out to meditate in different spots of the temple garden. Once Sharat could not concentrate, and reported this to the Master. Immediately the Master pressed his index finger in between Sharat's eyebrows, and his mind became calm like the flame of a lamp in a windless place.

One day at Dakshineswar, Sri Ramakrishna fulfilled the wishes of his disciples like the Kalpataru (wish-fulfilling tree). Some asked for devotion, some knowledge, and some liberation. Seeing Sharat silent, the Master asked him: "How would you like to realize God? What divine vision would you prefer to see in meditation?" Sharat replied: "I do not want to see any particular form of God in meditation. I want to see Him in all beings. I do not like visions." The Master said with a smile: "That is the last word in spiritual attainment. You cannot have it all at once." "But I won't be satisfied with anything short of that," replied Sharat. "I shall strive my best until I am able to attain it." At last the Master blessed him, saying, "Yes, you will attain it."

In 1885, Sharat passed the First of Arts examination and his father wanted him to study medicine. But Providence changed Sharat's life. In September 1885, the Master developed throat cancer and was moved to Calcutta for treatment. Sharat gave up his study of medicine so that he could serve the Master wholeheartedly.

As the air of Calcutta is polluted, the doctors advised the devotees to take the Master to an open place in the countryside. On 11 December 1885, Sri Ramakrishna was moved to a garden house in Cossipore, a suburb of Calcutta close to the Ganges. Sharat and other young disciples of the Master also moved with him to take care of their guru.

Day and night in Cossipore, Sharat witnessed the final divine play of Sri Ramakrishna. On 1 January 1886, the Master went for his last walk in the garden and became the Kalpataru. He blessed many devotees, saying, "Be illumined." Sharat and Latu were then busy cleaning the Master's room, but they witnessed that historic event from the roof. Later when somebody asked Sharat why he did not go to the Master for blessings that day, he replied: "I did not feel any necessity for that. Why should I? Was not the Master dearer than the dearest to me? Then, what doubt was there that he would give me, of his own accord, anything that I needed?"

During his last days Sri Ramakrishna began to train his young disciples to be monks. He even gave them ochre cloths and asked them to beg for food from door to door like traditional monks. Later Sharat told an amusing incident. When he appeared in front of a house and asked for alms, an old woman came out and indignantly asked him: "You have such a strong body, why are you living on alms? Can you not get a job as a tram conductor?" Saying so, she slammed the door.

After Sri Ramakrishna's passing away on 16 August 1886, the disciples established the Ramakrishna Monastery at Baranagore. In January 1887, they took formal vows of sannyasa under the leadership of Narendra (Swami Vivekananda), who gave the name "Swami Saradananda" to Sharat. From 1887 to 1895 Saradananda travelled to various holy places of northern and western India as an itinerant monk.

On 12 April 1890, Saradananda, Turiyananda, and Vaikuntha left Rishikesh for Gangotri (the source of the Ganges), Kedar, and Badri — three important holy places located at high altitudes in the interior part of the Himalayas. Each swami carried two blankets, personal clothing, and a walking stick, but no money. They began their journey barefoot on the trail. At that time travelling in the Himalayas was not only very difficult but also dangerous. Some days they had to go without food and some days without shelter. However, this pilgrimage was full of thrilling experiences for them.

On the fourth day Saradananda developed a blister on one foot, and it became difficult for him to walk. He asked his companions to go ahead and reach the nearest village before evening, then try to get help for him. He would wait for them by the side of the road. When they had left, Saradananda began to crawl towards the village. In the meantime, the workers of Kalikamli Baba's ashrama, who provided free food to mendicants, were carrying food on their horses along that same road. They put Saradananda on a horse and dropped him off at the nearest village. Saradananda arrived just as Turiyananda and Vaikuntha were preparing to rescue him. All were happy and realized the grace of the Master. They stayed in the village temple for three days while Saradananda recovered. At last they reached Gangotri and spent three days at Kalikamli Baba's Ashrama.

In 1893, Vivekananda represented Hinduism at the Parliament of Religions in Chicago, and the news of his success reached the brothers at Alambazar. Saradananda again left for pilgrimage, this time to West India, where he visited Jaipur, Pushkar, Mount Abu, Dwaraka, Prabhas, Junagad, and Chittor. After returning from that pilgrimage, he nursed Abhedananda, who was seriously ill from a severe infection in his feet. Under Saradananda's care, Abhedananda recuperated after three months. Saradananda also took care of Yajneswar Bhattacharya, a householder devotee of the Master, who was dying from tuberculosis. Forgetting himself, Saradananda served everyone throughout his life like a loving mother.

In Europe and America

After spreading the message of Vedanta in America and England for several years, Vivekananda desperately needed an assistant to continue the momentum. He wrote to Saradananda in India and asked him to come to England. Saradananda was reluctant at first, but then he went to the Holy Mother and sought her advice. The Mother told him: "My son, don't be afraid. You should go to the West. The Master will protect you, and will be with you wherever you go."

In March 1896, Saradananda left for England and arrived there on 1 April. On the way, his ship was buffeted by a hurricane in the Mediterranean Sea. "All the passengers were in a great panic," the swami recalled. "Some were crying; some were running here and there in fear; some were shaking out of nervousness. The whole scene was frightening, but I was not afraid in the least. My mind was as steady and calm as the needle of a compass." When the ship stopped at Rome, he went to visit St. Peter's Cathedral. Standing in the front of the sanctuary, his mind became absorbed in his previous incarnation, and he lost outer consciousness for some time.

In London Saradananda was the guest of Mr. E.T. Sturdy, a student of Vedanta. Vivekananda arrived there at the end of April 1896. The two swamis had not seen each other for a long time; Saradananda told Vivekananda all the news of their brother disciples at the Alambazar Monastery and of their activities in India. It was a most happy occasion.

Beginning in May 1896, Vivekananda began a whirlwind of activity in London: five classes a week, jnana yoga lectures on Sundays, and meeting new people. Saradananda attended Swamiji's lectures and learned how to give talks to audiences in the West, as he had had no previous experience in public speaking. In London, at Swamiji's behest, he gave some classes on the Bhagavad Gita. One of his early tasks was to supply materials about the life of Sri Ramakrishna to Professor Max Müller, the famous German orientalist. Years later, Saradananda told some devotees:

> At the invitation of Max Müller, Swamiji went to Oxford and stayed in his home as a guest. Max Müller wrote an article in the *Nineteenth Century* on Sri Ramakrishna entitled "A Real Mahatman." He asked Swamiji to furnish him with enough material for a book so he could write about Sri Ramakrishna in greater detail. Swamiji agreed to help. When he returned, he asked me to undertake the job forthwith. I worked hard and gathered all the incidents in the life of the Master and the teachings of the Master and showed the manuscript to Swamiji. I thought Swamiji would edit it and make extensive corrections. He didn't do that. He simply changed a few words for fear of exaggeration and sent the whole manuscript to Professor Müller. As I remember, Professor Müller incorporated the complete manuscript in his book [*The Life and Sayings of Sri Ramakrishna*] and published it without making any alterations.

Vivekananda had established the Vedanta Society of New York in 1894. Towards the end of June 1896, he asked Saradananda to go to America with J.J. Goodwin, his English disciple and stenographer, to carry on the Vedanta work. Saradananda was nervous about lecturing, but Swamiji encouraged him, saying: "Look, I have already lectured there. You just teach them a little Gita and Upanishad, and answer their questions. That is all."

After arriving in New York, Saradananda was introduced by the president of the Vedanta Society and gave his first talk. While Saradananda was speaking, Goodwin sat in the back, laughing. This made the swami nervous, thinking that he was not lecturing well. When the lecture was over, he asked Goodwin why he was laughing. "You were speaking well," answered Goodwin, "that's why I was laughing."

Saradananda's sweet and gentle personality and his masterful exposition of Vedanta philosophy proved attractive at once. He was invited to be one of the speakers at the Green Acre Conference of Comparative Religions in

Maine, where he lectured on Vedanta and held classes on yoga. After the sessions closed, Saradananda lectured in Brooklyn, New York, and Boston. At the Brooklyn Ethical Association he lectured on "The Ethical Ideas of the Hindus." Everywhere Saradananda went he made friends and drew staunch followers of Vedanta. Finally, in January 1897 he settled down in New York to carry on the Vedanta work in an organized way.

One time in New York a woman sought the swami's help regarding some terrible psychic experiences: At night the furniture of her room moved around, the windows flew open, she felt an unknown presence, and some formless being lifted her body a few inches off the floor. After reflecting a few moments, Saradananda said: "I am glad you have come. But if you ask my opinion, I will say that these experiences are the result of a weakened state of mind. Please train your mind firmly to think thoughts that are wholesome, good, and beneficial. By invigorating thoughts alone, these occult phenomena and psychic experiences can be averted." The swami gave her some spiritual instructions and asked her to meditate daily and read inspiring books. This eventually solved her problems.

Saradananda used to hold classes regularly in Montclair, New Jersey, where he would stay at the home of Mr. and Mrs. Wheeler. Swami Atulananda, a Western monk, wrote in his book *With the Swamis in America*:

> An interesting incident took place when Swami Saradananda was living at this happy home. The swami had often spoken about Sri Ramakrishna and one day he produced his Master's photograph and showed it to the lady of the house. "Oh, swami," she exclaimed, "it is the same face!" "What do you mean?" said the swami. And then she told him that long ago, in her youth, before she was married, she had had a vision of a Hindu and that it was the same face that now she saw in the photograph. "It was Sri Ramakrishna," she said, "but I did not know it until now. I was so much impressed and charmed at the vision at the time, that I remember the face very distinctly, and I have been going about here and there ever since I had the vision, wherever I heard that a Hindu had come to America, but I was always disappointed, not finding the same face. And now at last I see that it was Ramakrishna."

Referring to this incident, Saradananda later recalled: "The Master chooses his own men and women. We are mere instruments in his hands. It is a privilege to work under his banner. In America he had already prepared the ground for me; I was not alone. He brought to me men and women of exalted character who helped me in our work and bore great love for our Master."

Just at this time, when Saradananda was at the height of his usefulness in America, Vivekananda recalled him to India to help him organize the Ramakrishna Mission at Belur. After having stayed two and a half years in America, he sailed for India with Mrs. Ole Bull and Miss Josephine MacLeod on 12 January 1898, handing over the responsibility of the Vedanta Society to Abhedananda. Saradananda reached London on 20 January and Paris on 21

January. The party left for India via Rome. They arrived in Calcutta on 8 February 1898; Swamiji and other monks went to Howrah Station to receive them.

Back to India

On 3 February 1898, the Ramakrishna Monastery was moved from Alambazar to Nilambar Mukhopadhyay's garden house in the village of Belur, and a nearby plot of land was purchased on the bank of the Ganges, where the permanent home of the Order could be built. Under Vivekananda's direction, the brother monks took responsibility for levelling the ground, then building living quarters and a shrine. Saradananda was entrusted with overseeing the office and supervising Western visitors. He also organized plague relief in Calcutta. During August and September he gave a series of lectures in Bengali at Albert Hall in Calcutta that was later published in *Gitatattwa*.

Vivekananda framed the rules and regulations of Belur Monastery, and asked Saradananda and other brother disciples to implement them and train the young monks accordingly. With the vision of a seer, Swamiji knew that Saradananda would play an important role in the life of the organization he had founded in order to fulfill the mission of their Master. Saradananda was endowed with remarkable devotion and steadiness, sound judgement and a tender heart, and also was acquainted with Western methods of organization. Swamiji made Brahmananda the president (spiritual head) and Saradananda the general secretary (executive head) of the Ramakrishna Math and Mission. For nearly three decades (1898–1927), Saradananda was the chief organizer of the Ramakrishna Order in its manifold activities.

Saradananda was a born leader. He always considered the youngest member of the Order his equal and was perfectly just and democratic in his dealings. Whenever there was a lack of servants in the monastery, he would offer to share responsibility for the menial and domestic chores along with younger members. He never judged anyone or anything without considering all sides. Hasty judgements or decisions were foreign to his nature. This of course stood him in good stead as the general secretary of the Order. Everyone was sure to get a hearing from him. He never listened to slander: He followed Swamiji's instruction "to allow slander to enter one ear, only to throw it out by the other."

In December 1899, Saradananda was invited to give some lectures in East Bengal (now Bangladesh) and he spoke on Vedanta, yoga, and various religious topics. One day some devotees asked him to talk about Sri Ramakrishna. Saradananda said with a smile:

> It is futile to try to understand the Master as long as one has a little bit of ego. The more I grow, the more I see that I could not understand the Master. Only Swamiji and Nag Mahashay understood him to some extent. We are his servants; we are just trying to obey his orders. I shall understand him when he

makes me understand out of his mercy. I get scared when I speak about the Master. Even Swamiji said, "Unknowingly trying to make the Master great, I may make him small." When a person like Swamiji speaks this way, what to speak of others! Meditate on the Master, and he will undoubtedly reveal himself unto you. Have faith. How little we have understood the Infinite Master!

Saying so, Saradananda's voice choked, his body became motionless, tears rolled from his half-closed eyes, his breathing stopped, and a divine beauty was reflected on his face. The audience was dumbfounded. After a while, saying "Ramakrishna, Ramakrishna," the swami came back to external consciousness. He returned to Belur Math on 13 January 1900.

Once Swamiji sent Saradananda to Calcutta on an errand. When he learned that it had not been done, he rebuked him with harsh language. Saradananda remained as motionless as a statue. When tea was served, he began to drink it as if nothing had happened. Disappointed, Swamiji commented: "Sharat's veins carry the blood of fish; it will never warm up." Observing that Saradananda was free from anger, Swamiji teased him at other times, saying, "Your veins carry frog's blood, or the blood of sand fish." Swamiji knew that this noble evenmindedness is necessary for the head of a monastic order.

Vivekananda passed away on 4 July 1902, and the responsibilities of organizing and managing the growing work of the Order fell on Saradananda. But Saradananda always consulted with Brahmananda, the president, when making any decision on serious matters. He also became the caretaker of the Holy Mother and bought a house for her in Calcutta that is now called "Udbodhan," or "Mother's House."

As a Writer

In 1909, Saradananda began to write his monumental work *Sri Sri Ramakrishna Lilaprasanga* in Bengali, which has been translated as *Sri Ramakrishna, the Great Master* (and now as *Sri Ramakrishna and His Divine Play*). It is not only an authentic, interpretive biography of the Master, but also a classic in Bengali literature. It consists of five volumes and took nearly ten years to complete. Saradananda gave three reasons for this great undertaking: First, he wrote it to repay the money that he had borrowed in order to build the Holy Mother's house in Calcutta and to publish *Udbodhan* (a Bengali magazine started by Vivekananda). Second, he wished to publish an accurate and complete account of the Master's life. As an editor of *Udbodhan*, he had to correct and rewrite many articles about Sri Ramakrishna that were full of misinformation. As an eyewitness to the Master's life, he could not bear that any untruth be told about the Master. Third, he tried to justify the philanthropic activities of the Ramakrishna Mission and also to remove the misunderstanding about Ramakrishna's teaching, "Serve human beings as God." M., the recorder of *The Gospel of Sri Ramakrishna*, had commented that the monastic disciples changed the focus of the Master's teaching, which according to M. was God-realization and not social service. Of course, M. later changed his mind in 1912, when the Holy Mother visited the Ramakrishna Mission Home of Service in Varanasi and said, "The Master is ever-present in this place, and Mother Lakshmi always casts Her benign glance upon it."

Once Girish Chandra Ghosh had asked Vivekananda to write a biography of Sri Ramakrishna. Swamiji had declined, expressing his inability, "Shall I make the image of a monkey while trying to make that of Shiva?" On another occasion Swamiji said, "Sharat will write." Later Girish asked Saradananda to write about Sri Ramakrishna's divine life, his sadhana, and his message. Girish feared that otherwise, in the future, some less adept people might present the Master in a narrow, incorrect way, which might eventually form a cult and defeat the purpose of his incarnation. There was cause for such apprehension: It was well known that Girish had given his "power of attorney" to the Master, who took complete responsibility for him. Some people began to imitate this and deceive themselves, because they did not understand the importance of self-surrender. Saradananda first wrote "Sri Ramakrishna as a Guru," the third and fourth volumes of *Lilaprasanga*, and then wrote the rest. At the beginning of the third volume, Saradananda explained the mystery of the "power of attorney" that the Master had accepted from Girish. Before publication, Saradananda read the chapter to Girish, who wholeheartedly approved it.

Once a monk asked Saradananda to write a biography of Sri Ramakrishna that would contain all the stories about him. The swami replied: "Is it so easy to write about the Master? One should not undertake such work without having his command. If I receive his command, I shall try." Some years later when the *Lilaprasanga* was published, the same monk asked Saradananda whether he had received the command before writing the book. He avoided the question, saying, "That is none of your business."

One day, Asitananda, an attendant of Saradananda, worked up the courage to ask the swami if he had experienced nirvikalpa samadhi. "Did I waste my time cutting grass [i.e., living meaninglessly] when I lived in the company of Sri Ramakrishna?" Saradananda replied. When the attendant pressed him for details, the swami said: "Read the chapter on samadhi in the *Lilaprasanga*. I have not written anything about samadhi without experiencing it myself."

Christopher Isherwood, the author of *Ramakrishna and His Disciples*, wrote:

> Although Saradananda did not begin his work until more than twenty years after Ramakrishna's death, there is no doubt of its authenticity. Many of those who had known Ramakrishna were then still alive, and Saradananda carefully compared his memories with theirs. *The Great Master* has also the value of having been written by a monastic disciple, who has actually shared the extraordinary experiences he describes. "Nothing beyond my spiritual

experience has been recorded in the book," Saradananda once told a questioner. This seemingly cautious answer is in fact a claim so tremendous that it silences all suspicion of boastfulness; a man like Saradananda could not have made it unless it was literally true.

Having the permission and blessing from the Holy Mother, Saradananda began to write *Sri Sri Ramakrishna Lilaprasanga*. He collected all information about Holy Mother for the book directly from her. Whenever the Mother was in Calcutta, Saradananda would read the manuscript to her, as it was then being published serially in *Udbodhan* magazine. When she was in Jayrambati, someone else would read it to her. She commented: "Everything has been written correctly in Sharat's book." Once a learned disciple of the Mother said, "Mother, what a wonderful book Sharat Maharaj has written!" The Mother replied, "Yes, it needs learning and intellect to understand Sharat's book."

In 1925, during the Chariot Festival in Puri, Saradananda talked about the adverse conditions in which he wrote the *Lilaprasanga* in the Udbodhan house:

Holy Mother was living upstairs with Radhu; I was surrounded by devotees and I had to keep the accounts also; the burden of the loan for the house was on me. I used to write the *Lilaprasanga* sitting in the small room downstairs. Then nobody dared to talk to me, as I had no time to chat for a long time. If anybody would ask anything, I would say, "Be quick," and finish the talk briefly. People would think that I was egotistic. I could not write much about the devotees [except Gopal-ma and Vivekananda], because there was so much material to write about the Master. When the mind was ready, only then could I write.

The Bhagavad Gita says, "He who finds action in inaction, and inaction in action, he is a perfect yogi" (4:18). Amidst the hectic surroundings and crowds, Saradananda continued his serious writing project. One day some young monks were talking loudly and laughing in the Udbodhan office, adjacent to the swami's room. Golap-ma, an attendant of the Holy Mother, scolded them: "Shame on you! Mother is upstairs and Sharat is doing serious work, and you boys are making such great noise!" Overhearing Golap-ma's loud voice, the swami said to her: "Well, Golap-ma, please don't give your ears to them. It is the nature of the boys to behave like that. I am so close to them, but I don't listen to what they are talking about. I have told my ears, 'Don't listen to anything that is unnecessary.' So my ears are not listening to them." Saradananda had total control over his senses.

Moreover, his life was extremely disciplined and he followed his routine strictly. After having his morning bath in the Ganges, Saradananda would go to the shrine and bow down to the Master and then to the Holy Mother. At 7:00 a.m., he would go downstairs and write for hours sitting in the same place. He had no time to stretch. As a result, in later years the circulation in

Swami Saradananda in 1920s at Udbodhan house, Calcutta. He wrote
Sri Sri Ramakrishna Lilaprasanga (*Sri Ramakrishna and His Divine Play*)
sitting in this room.

his legs was greatly impaired, and they would sometimes tremble. In between his writing sessions he would drink tea and smoke his hubble-bubble. He would have lunch at 1:30 p.m., and after that he would rest for an hour and a half on his office carpet. He would write again until evening, and then he would meet the devotees. Sometimes he would go to Belur Math and stay for a couple of days.

In his memoirs, Swami Nikhilananda wrote about an important incident:

Before we left for Varanasi [in 1925], Swami Shuddhananda asked Swami Saradananda in front of me to finish the Cossipore chapter of the *Lila-prasanga* [which would describe Sri Ramakrishna's last days]. He said that he had some notes but he was not well enough to write the article. Swami Shuddhananda then said: "You can dictate it and Nikhilananda will write it." He said he would see what could be done. I believe he took his notebook with him. He did not feel well in Varanasi, so nothing was done. When we were leaving for Puri, Swami Shuddhananda reminded him about the article and again asked him to dictate the whole thing to me. Then the swami made the following significant remark: "When the Holy Mother was alive I felt a great deal of inner strength and began to write the *Lilaprasanga*. She died and I felt as if all my powers were gone. Then I saw Swami Brahmananda and began to feel strong again. When he died I felt as if my brain was completely paralyzed. I simply cannot finish the book." Then he added: "When I began to write the *Lilaprasanga* I thought I understood the Master. But now I clearly see that the life of the Master is very deep. I was merely hovering over the top branches; the root is far beneath the ground."

Neither M. nor Saradananda recorded the last days of Sri Ramakrishna. Perhaps it was not the will of the Master. In 1925 when a disciple asked him to complete the Master's life, Saradananda said humbly: "Perhaps it will never be completed. I am not getting any inspiration from within. The Master made me write whatever he wanted. Now when I read the *Lilaprasanga*, I wonder, have I written all these things? I have no more inclination to do anything. It seems that the Master is doing everything."

An Ideal Karma Yogi

A real karma yogi is fearless and is not concerned about others' criticism. He works for God and depends on His will. As the karma yogi has no selfish motives, he cannot be affected by praise or blame. Krishna said in the Gita, "They are wretched who seek the results of their actions." Saradananda was a role model for leading a balanced life. His character was a perfect blend of the four yogas: he was a jnani (man of wisdom) and attained nirvikalpa samadhi; his devotion for the Master, the Mother, and Swami Vivekananda was profound; he was a perfect yogi — even a thousand problems could not perturb the equanimity of his mind; and he was an ideal worker who offered his body, mind, and soul to carry out Sri Ramakrishna's mission.

Once the Holy Mother said to one of her disciples: "Look at Sharat! He works so much, he faces so many problems, yet he remains calm and never complains. He is a *sadhu* [holy man]. Why does he undergo all these things? If he wishes he can remain absorbed in God day and night. It is only for your good that he is living on this earthly plane." Another time Swamiji commented, "The Master brought Sharat for his work."

Once Swami Pavitrananda talked to Saradananda about a conflict regarding work. He said, "Swami, I work but I don't feel that I am working for the Master." Saradananda calmly asked, "Don't you think that it is not your work?" "Yes, I do. It is not my work. I am just following your orders. I do whatever you have asked me to do." "That is enough," Saradananda replied.

Swami Nikhilananda recalled:

> I am active by nature. One day Swami Saradananda said to me: "It is good to be active but work depends on several factors. Your health must be good and you must be able to get along with fellow workers. But suppose you injure one of your limbs, then it will be difficult for you to work. Therefore, I request that you cultivate the habit of reading. Even that is not enough. Suppose you become blind. Therefore, it is good that you also practise meditation so that if you cannot read or work at least you can meditate."

The secrets of Saradananda's great success in his active life were his humility and his respect for the dignity of others. He knew human nature very well. Monks who were unbalanced or who had been rejected by other centres would take shelter in Udbodhan with the Holy Mother and Saradananda. The swami adopted three basic methods for making these monks work: He gave them freedom; he put his trust in them; and finally he poured his love and affection on them. He was *ajatashatru*, a person whose enemy has never been born. In 1919, the head of a centre had problems with his monastic workers. Saradananda wrote to him: "Each soul is eternally free, so each person desires to be free in every respect of his life. A real leader never obstructs others' freedom; rather, he teaches how one should enjoy freedom properly even in the field of action." In another letter he wrote: "The causes of friction and factions in the monastery are: anger, hatred, intolerance for others' mistakes, incompatibility between the mind and the speech [meaning, taking the course of untruth and duplicity], and above all, an effort to control the monks through tricks and politics instead of unselfish love."

Once Saradananda advised a devotee: "If you want to work, depend on God and stand on your own feet. Don't depend on any human being — even myself. If nobody comes forward to help your work, resolve to do it alone, even at the cost of your body. When you have such courage, strength, and dependence on God, only then are you eligible to do work."

"Service to man is service to God." This message of Vivekananda was exemplified in Saradananda's life. He acted as the mother of the Order. Whenever the Holy Mother or any of the direct disciples were sick, he was always present to look after their treatment. Once when Brahmananda was living in Belur Math he was suffering from an abscess and needed minor surgery. Saradananda accompanied Dr. Kanjilal (a devotee and disciple of the Holy Mother) from Calcutta, and they left for the monastery by boat. In the middle of the Ganges, a heavy storm arose and the boat began tossing violently. Saradananda was calmly smoking his hubble-bubble, but the panicky doctor could not control himself. Angrily he threw the hubble-bubble into the Ganges, and told Saradananda: "You are a strange man! The boat is about to sink, and you are enjoying your smoke!" The swami calmly said, "Is it wise to jump into the water before the boat sinks?" He then advised the boatman to put the sail down. Gradually the storm subsided and the boat safely reached the Belur ghat. This incident indicates that a knower of Brahman conquers the fear of death, and that nothing in this world can perturb him.

As a Spiritual Teacher

Only a jivanmukta (one who is liberated-in-life) can be a real teacher. He is free, so he can teach others how to be free. In the language of the Gita, Saradananda was *sthita-prajna*, a man of steady wisdom. To those who knew him intimately, he seemed almost perfect, with his deep spirituality, intellectual acumen, and above all, his wonderful, pure character. He was equally great in the graces of head, hand, and heart. This unique synthesis, apart from his intense spirituality, was the main quality that made him irresistibly attractive. Saradananda was the refuge of the sick, mentally disturbed, disobedient, rejected, dejected, and fallen. His love for them was not mere passive tolerance, but was silently active and positive in result. The secret was that, along with loving patience, his behaviour with all was actuated by his consciousness of the inner divinity of each person. Thus, like a good teacher, he helped forlorn people regain their self-confidence.

Doubt is a horrible disease of the human mind. An illumined teacher always tries to remove the doubts of his disciples. In 1925 two young scientists came to Calcutta to visit Saradananda at Udbodhan. One of them asked, "Does God exist?" "Yes," replied the swami.

Scientist: "What is the proof?"

Saradananda: "The words of the rishis. After experiencing God, they proclaimed that God exists."

Scientist: "There is a possibility of their making mistakes."

Saradananda: "Is it possible that all the sages have made mistakes?"

Scientist: "I won't believe without experiencing God myself."

Saradananda: "Very well. Is it possible that you will only believe after seeing everything yourself? Suppose you have never been in England. You will have to know about England from those who have visited it. Although you have not seen it, you can't deny the existence of England. Likewise, God exists; you will have to trust the judgement of those who have seen Him. After seeing God, Ramakrishna said to all: 'I have seen God. You can also see Him through spiritual disciplines and longing.' In this scientific age, the Master came to dispel the doubts of the people by demonstrating religion." The young scientists were convinced and accepted Saradananda's words.

Once a disciple asked Saradananda: "X. instructs his disciples not to practise japa without taking a bath, etc. Are such observances compulsory?"

Saradananda: "The Master came to make religion easy. People were being crushed under the weight of rules and regulations. To repeat the Lord's name or to worship Him, no special time or place is necessary. In whatever condition one may be, one can take His name. The Master never gave too much importance to these external observances. As to means, adopt whichever suits you best. If you like God with form, that will also lead you to the goal. If you like God without form, well and good; stick to it and you will progress. If you doubt His very existence, then better put the question to Him thus: 'I do not know whether You exist or not, whether You are formless or have form. Do please grant that I may know Your real nature.'"

Whenever there was an opportunity, young monks would ask questions of Saradananda either about their spiritual problems or about the Master's teachings. In January 1925, when Saradananda was visiting Varanasi, some monks asked him the following questions:

B.: "Swami, the Master has exhorted us to 'make thought tally with speech.' What does it mean?"

Saradananda: "That you must be sincere, that your inner life should tally with the outer."

B.: "It is naturally so. Whatever we speak we think in our mind."

Saradananda: "Do you think it is so easy? We chant the name of the Lord very superficially. We say, 'O Lord, I am Your servant and You are my Master; I have renounced everything for You; I call You, Lord, please grant me Your vision.' And at the same time we are harbouring bad thoughts in the mind. It does not work. As you speak, so you must think. In other words, while you take the name of the Lord think of Him alone."

S.: "The Master used to say, 'Having the knowledge of nonduality as your own, you can go wherever you like.' What does it mean?"

Saradananda: "Not 'go wherever you like,' but 'do whatever you like.' He meant evidently that after attaining Supreme Knowledge one cannot commit any evil deed. How can one who has realized God or attained knowledge through discrimination, renunciation, love, devotion, and purity, do mischief? Therefore, after attaining nondual knowledge, whatever a person does, it must be good."

K.: "Swami, we do not see God. How can we love Him without seeing Him? How can we love a Being who is unseen and whose very existence is doubtful?"

Saradananda: "Act according to the instructions of the guru. If you can strictly follow what the guru has prescribed for the realization of God, everything will be smooth at last. Meditation comes afterwards. If one fails to meditate, one should go on repeating the mantra very earnestly. . . . The repetition of the mantra in a proper spirit even once purifies the mind. Instantly, the mind fills with delight and becomes blissful."

Towards the End

Beginning in 1920 with the Holy Mother's passing away, Saradananda underwent several heavy bereavements. Before she left, Holy Mother said to one of her disciples, "My child, I am leaving Sharat behind."

In 1922, Swamis Brahmananda and Turiyananda passed away. Saradananda felt an emptiness and he became more indrawn. He told the monks: "Mother and Maharaj [Brahmananda] have left. Now you take the responsibility and get involved in the activities of the Order. I no longer have any enthusiasm or inclination to work." However, with Brahmananda's passing away, the position of president became open. According to the rules of the Order, an election was held and the monks cast their votes. There were two nominees: Swami Shivananda and Swami Saradananda. When the election was over, it was found that Saradananda had received ninety-five percent of the votes. When his name was announced as the president, he declined, saying: "Swamiji appointed me the secretary. I shall never give up that post." He himself had originally proposed Swami Shivananda's name as the president of the Order, and he remained as secretary until the end.

Saradananda was extremely conscientious. Although he felt that his work was almost finished, he thought about how to guide the Ramakrishna Math and Mission so that the activities and the spiritual current of the Order might flow in the right direction. In 1926, he convened the first convention of the Ramakrishna Math and Mission in Belur Math, which was attended by many monks and devotees from all over the world. The convention began on 1 April 1926 and continued till 8 April. Saradananda was the chairman, and he gave two important and inspiring speeches: "Ramakrishna Mission: Its Past, Present, and Future" (1 April) and "The Ideas, Ideals, and Activities of the Ramakrishna Mission" (3 April). Both of these precious speeches were published in *Ramakrishna Math and Mission Convention 1926*. Saradananda's speeches were considered to be the guidelines of the Ramakrishna Order.

The saying, "Absolute power corrupts absolutely," lost its meaning in the case of Swami Saradananda, the executive secretary of the Ramakrishna Math and Mission. On his last birthday, in 1927, Saradananda went to Belur Math, where the monks and devotees paid homage to him. When a devotee placed a beautiful garland around his neck, the swami smilingly said: "I am a doorkeeper of the Mother's house. You are decorating me with a garland? Does a doorkeeper deserve such an expensive garland?" All laughed, and at the same time got a glimpse of his humility.

During his last years Saradananda was in poor health. He suffered from diabetes, rheumatism, and high blood pressure. In spite of these physical ailments, he spent long hours in japa and meditation. His doctor, D.P. Ghosh, suggested that he reduce his meditation time, for otherwise it would damage his health. The swami remarked: "What am I to do in old age? Here I sit quietly and repeat the name of the Lord. Nobody will do anything. At least by seeing me they may be inclined to do something."

When one of his attendants asked him what need there was for a man like him to meditate so long, thus impairing his health, he said: "The call has come. I am preparing for the great journey. Now meditation is the food of my life, and chanting His name, the source of my delight."

In early August 1927, Saradananda went to Belur Math to attend a trustee meeting. He greeted the monks joyfully and had lunch with Shivananda. While leaving for Udbodhan he said to Shivananda, "Mahapurush, my body has deteriorated; it seems it will not last long."

On 6 August 1927, Saradananda followed his regular routine of taking his morning bath, meditating three hours in his room, and then going to the shrine to prostrate before the pictures of the Master and the Holy Mother. On that day he stayed in the shrine for half an hour; then came near the exit door and again returned to the shrine. He repeated this unusual behaviour a few times. Standing in front of the Holy Mother's picture he silently prayed, perhaps requesting her to take her tired son back. When he finally came out of the shrine, Saradananda's face was glowing with joy and serenity. It is said that during her last illness, Mother once remarked: "I am tired of this life. I shall now depart with Sharat in my arms and take him wherever I go."

After vespers, swamis Haripremananda and Aseshananda went to Saradananda's room and found him half reclining on his bed, struggling to get up but unable to do so. It was 8:30 p.m. He said to his attendants: "Don't tell anybody. Make no noise. I will go downstairs to meet the devotees soon." But he felt dizzy and laid down on the bed. His forehead began to perspire. He asked his attendant to rub his head with a little medicated oil and prepare an ayurvedic medicine. Very soon three doctors came, examined him, and declared that the swami had had a stroke. One doctor suggested that an icepack be put on Saradananda's head. Three kinds of medication — allopathic, homeopathic, and ayurvedic — were tried with no visible results.

The sad news spread. Monks and devotees came from all over India to visit him. Saradananda retained consciousness throughout, but his speech was impaired. A few days later the swami could only smile in response to Dr. Ghosh's question, "Swami, do you want to drink tea?" On another day he used his left hand to drink sanctified water from a spoon. Thus the swami passed thirteen days.

Saradananda's condition was rapidly deteriorating and he had a temperature of 105 degrees. The doctors lost all hope and indicated that the final moment was imminent. Friday, 19 August 1927, was the birth anniversary of Sri Krishna. About 1:00 a.m. the monks began to chant "Hari Om Ramakrishna." At 2:34 a.m. Swami Saradananda, the great yogi and beloved disciple of Sri Ramakrishna, breathed his last. At that very moment in Belur Math, Shivananda heard the familiar and sweet voice of Saradananda, "Tarak-da, I am going to Kashi [Varanasi]." At noon Saradananda's remains were taken from Calcutta to Belur Math and cremated there.

In his early days with Sri Ramakrishna, the young Sharat had asked a blessing that he might see God in every being. The Master blessed him, saying, "Yes, you will attain it." The following incident (related by Pravrajika Bharatiprana) indicates how that blessing was fulfilled towards the end of his life: "One of the devotees who was nurtured by Swami Saradananda's loving care one day remarked, 'Swami, why do you love us so much?' Swami Saradananda did not say anything. After a few days when that devotee came to Udbodhan, the swami said: 'A few days ago I went to Belur Math and prostrated before Sri Ramakrishna. The Master appeared before me and said, "You love all because you find me in all." That is the answer I would give today.'"

Sri Ramakrishna: A Chronology

1775   Birth of Kshudiram.

1791   Birth of Chandramani Devi.

1799   Marriage of Kshudiram and Chandramani Devi.

1805   Birth of Ramkumar.

1810   Birth of Katyayani.

1815   Kshudiram settles at Kamarpukur.

1821   Ramkumar marries; Katyayani marries.

1824   Kshudriram's pilgrimage to Rameswar.

1826   Birth of Rameswar.

1835   Kshudiram's pilgrimage to Gaya.

1836   Birth of Ramakrishna, 18 February, approx. 5:00 a.m.

1839   Birth of Sarvamangala.

1843   First ecstasy (*age six or seven*) seeing flock of cranes; death of Kshudiram in autumn.

1844   Dresses self as monk (*age eight*). Second ecstasy; loses consciousness on the way to worship Vishalakshi.

1845   Sacred Thread ceremony (*age nine*). First manifestation of guru: solves scriptural problem for pandits.

1848   Rameswar marries; Sarvamangala marries.

1849   Birth of Ramkumar's son, Akshay; death of Ramkumar's wife.

1850   Ramkumar opens school in Calcutta.

1852   Ramakrishna moves to Calcutta.

1853   Birth of Sarada Devi, 22 December.

1855   Dakshineswar Kali temple inaugurated 31 May. Hriday arrives at Dakshineswar. Ramakrishna is appointed priest of Radha-Govinda temple. Repairs broken image of Krishna. Is appointed to dress Kali. Is appointed priest of Kali temple. Initiation in Shakti mantra by Kenaram Bhattacharya.

1856   Death of Ramkumar. Realization of God and first god-intoxicated state. First four-year period of sadhana begins. First vision of Divine Mother, followed by divine madness. Normal schedule is no longer possible.

1857   Treatment under Dr. Gangaprasad Sen.

1858   Hriday temporarily serves as priest in Kali temple; then Haladhari is appointed. Ramakrishna goes to Kamarpukur.

1859   Marriage of Ramakrishna and Sarada Devi, the Holy Mother, in May.

1860   Return to Dakshineswar in autumn or December. Mathur's vision of Shiva and Kali in Ramakrishna. Second period of sadhana begins.

1861   Death of Rani Rasmani. Bhairavi Brahmani arrives at Dakshineswar. Tantra practice begins. Second period of divine madness.

1863   Completion of Tantra practice.

1864   Practice of vatsalya bhava under Jatadhari; receives Ramlala. Practice of madhura bhava. Chandramani Devi comes to live at Dakshineswar. Approximate period of conference of pandits to evaluate Ramakrishna. Initiation into Vedic sannyas by Tota Puri.

1865   Akshay replaces Haladhari as priest of Radha-Govinda temple. Tota Puri leaves Dakshineswar.

1866   In Advaita plane for six months. Illness. Instruction from the Sufi Govinda Roy, and practice of Islam.

1867   To Kamarpukur in spring. First meeting of Sarada and Ramakrishna since wedding. Receives command to remain in bhavamukha. Brahmani takes leave.

1868   Pilgrimage with Mathur. Meets Gangamata in Vrindaban.

1869   Death of Akshay.

1870   Tour with Mathur. Attends Coolootola Harisabha. Visits Kalna and Navadwip.

1871   Death of Mathur in July.

1872   The Holy Mother's first visit to Dakshineswar, in spring. Shodashi Puja. She returns to Kamarpukur in September.

1873   Death of Rameswar.

1874   Ramlal arrives in Dakshineswar. Practice of Christian path and vision of Christ. Conviction that all faiths are valid ways to reach God. The Holy Mother's second visit to Dakshineswar.

1875   First visit to Keshab Chandra Sen, in March. Last visit to Kamarpukur. The Holy Mother returns to Jayrambati ill; worships Simhavahini.

1876   Death of Chandramani Devi.

1877   The Holy Mother's third visit to Dakshineswar. Girish Chandra Ghosh meets the Master.

1879   Approximate arrival of Jogin; arrival of Ram Datta and Manomohan Mitra, November; approximate arrival of Latu.

1880   Arrival of Hari; arrival of Tarak in May or June.

1881   Arrival of Rakhal in summer and Narendra in November. The Holy Mother's fourth visit to Dakshineswar. Dismissal of Hriday.

1882   Visit to Pandit Vidyasagar. The Holy Mother's fifth visit to Dakshineswar. Arrival of Niranjan; arrival of Mahendra Nath Gupta (M.) in February; arrival of Baburam in April.

1883   Arrival of Gangadhar in May; Sharat and Shashi in October; Hari Prasanna in November. Brahmo festival at Manimohan Mallick's home, 26 November.

1884   Death of Keshab in January. Death of Narendra's father in February; acceptance by Narendra of God with form. Approximate arrival of Senior Gopal in April; arrival of Kali in June. Meeting with Pandit Shashadhar. Gopal-ma meets the Master in autumn. The Holy Mother comes to live at Dakshineswar. Arrival of Sarada Prasanna in December.

1885   Arrival of Purna in March. First signs of cancer in April. Attends Panihati Festival on 26 May; attends Chariot Festival at Balaram's in July. Arrival of Subodh in August. Is moved to Shyampukur in early September. Treatment by Dr. Mahendralal Sarkar. Is worshipped as Divine Mother by devotees. Is moved to Cossipore on 11 December.

1886   Treatment at Cossipore. Becomes Kalpataru on Friday, 1 January. Distribution of ochre cloths in January. Narendra's nirvikalpa samadhi. Organization of disciples. Final training of Narendra. Mahasamadhi on 16 August, 1:02 a.m.

Glossary

Abhedananda, Swami (Kali Prasad Chandra; 1866–1939): One of the sixteen monastic disciples of Ramakrishna; minister of Vedanta Society of New York, 1896–1910; founder, Ramakrishna Vedanta Math, Calcutta.

achintya-bheda-abheda: Lit., "incomprehensible dualistic monism," that is, an "inscrutable relation of difference and non-difference."

Adbhutananda, Swami (Latu; Rakhturam; d. 1920): One of the sixteen monastic disciples of Ramakrishna; referred to in the Ramakrishna Order as Latu Maharaj. He served as personal attendant to Ramakrishna during his final illness.

Adhyatma Ramayana: A spiritual interpretation of the life of Rama; a subordinate Ramayana, interpreting the epic in terms of nondualism and emphasizing the divine nature of Rama and his close associates. It is part of the Brahmanda Purana.

adhikari: A qualified aspirant after liberation; a competent student who has disciplined himself or herself according to the prescribed method.

Adhikarika purusha: An advanced seer or rishi, commissioned by God to benefit the world, who is capable of manifesting special spiritual powers. Though liberated-in-life, he is born again and again with full memory of his previous lives until he finishes his duty. Also referred to as prakriti-lina in Sankhya scriptures. Vedanta divides adhikarikas into avatars and ishwarakotis.

Advaita: *See* **nondualism**.

Advaitananda, Swami (Senior Gopal, Brother Gopal; 1828–1909): One of the sixteen monastic disciples of Ramakrishna.

agami karma: Actions performed in one's current life that will bear results in the future. *See* **prarabdha karma; sanchita karma**.

Aghoremani Devi: *See* **Gopal-ma**.

agni: The element fire. *See* **five elements**.

Agrahayana: Bengali month, mid-November to mid-December.

ahamkara: The part of the inner organ that functions as one's ego or I-consciousness. *See* **antahkarana**.

ajna: Centre of consciousness, or *chakra*, located between the eyebrows. *See* **kundalini; chakra**.

akasha: The element space or ether. *See* **five elements**.

Akhandananda, Swami: (Gangadhar Gangopadhyay; 1864–1937): One of the sixteen monastic disciples of Ramakrishna. He served as the third president of the Ramakrishna Order, from 1934 to 1937.

Akshay Chattopadhyay (1849–1869): The only son of Ramkumar Chattopadhyay. Served as priest of Radha-Govinda temple of Dakshineswar.

alankara shastra: The science of rhetoric.

Aleklata: Lit., "The Incomprehensible One." The word for God used by the Kartabhaja sect of the Vaishnavas. *See* **Kartabhaja**.

amalaki: A sacred tree planted in the Panchavati. Ramakrishna practised sadhana under an amalaki tree.

anahata: Centre of consciousness, or chakra, located at the heart. *See* **kundalini**; **chakra**.

anahata dhvani: Music of the spheres, heard by aspirants in deep meditation. *See* **Pranava**.

anandamayakosha: The blissful sheath covering the Atman. *See* **causal body**; **five sheaths**.

anganyasa: During worship, touching the heart, hair on the crest of the head, the arms, the eyes, and the palms while uttering proper mantras, the idea being that the presence of deities represented by those mantras is invoked and purifies those parts of the body. *See* **karanyasa**; **nyasa**.

anima: One of the eight occult powers that occur naturally in yogis, the power of becoming very small. The other powers are: laghima, becoming very light; prapti, obtaining anything at will; prakamya, having an irresistible will; mahima, increasing one's size at will; ishitwa, supremacy or lordship; vashitwa, firm control; and kamavasayita, supression of desires.

annamayakosha: The physical sheath covering the Atman. *See* **gross body**; **five sheaths**.

annameru-vrata: A ritual performed in which one offers a mound of food for distribution among the needy.

Annapurna: A name of the Divine Mother, as provider of food.

antahkarana: The inner organ, which consists of manas (mind); buddhi (intellect); chitta (mind-stuff, or seat of memory); and ahamkara (ego).

ap: The element water. *See* **five elements**.

apana: The vital force that goes downward and eliminates the residue of gross food products. *See* **five vital forces**.

apara-vidya: Relative truths or lower knowledge such as science, language, literature, mathematics. Opposite of para-vidya.

Aparokshanubhuti: True and direct knowledge of God, or Brahman.

apatya, apatya bhava: The attitude in which one feels God to be one's father or mother. *See* **vatsalya bhava**; **five attitudes**.

Apta: A realized soul; one who has realized his or her true nature, or Self.

Arjuna: A cousin and disciple of Krishna and the great hero of the Mahabharata. Krishna teaches him in the Bhagavad Gita.

artha: Wealth or prosperity. Refers to one of four traditional goals of life in Indian society. *See* **dharma**; **kama**; **moksha**.

Arya Samaj: A religious movement founded by Swami Dayananda Saraswati in the Punjab and northwest India in the nineteenth century.

asana: 1. Seat or mat for sitting for meditation. 2. Posture or position for sitting in meditation. 3. A hatha yoga posture.

Ashad: Bengali month, mid-June to mid-July.

ashoka: A sacred tree planted in the Panchavati.

Ashoka: The famous king of the Maurya dynasty in northern India who reigned 272–236 B.C. and who attempted to spread Buddhism and education for the welfare of humankind.

ashtami: The eighth day of the bright lunar fortnight. *See* **Durga Puja**.

Ashtavakra Samhita: A nondualistic treatise of Vedanta philosophy written by the sage Ashtavakra.

ashwatha: A kind of fig tree, also called *peepul*. Ramakrishna himself planted this sacred tree in the Panchavati.

Ashwin: Bengali month, mid-September to mid-October.

Asphanaka: A type of Buddhist meditation.

Atman: Self or Soul; denotes also the Supreme Brahman, which is one with the individual soul, according to Advaita Vedanta.

Aul: A Vaishnava sect.

avatar: An Incarnation of God. An avatar is born of free choice, not as a result of past actions; and throughout his life, he is conscious of his divine mission. An avatar's actions are of permanent benefit to humanity. Among those widely accepted as avatars are Rama, Krishna, Buddha, Christ, and Ramakrishna. *See* **adhikarika purusha; ishwarakoti**.

avidya shakti: The power of ignorance in a demoniacal nature.

avidya-maya: Maya, or illusion causing duality, has two aspects: avidya-maya and vidya-maya. Avidya-maya, or the maya of ignorance, consisting of anger, passion, and so on, entangles one in worldliness. Vidya-maya, or the maya of knowledge, consisting of kindness, purity, unselfishness, and so on, leads one to liberation. Both belong to the relative world. *See* **maya**.

Babu: A masculine courtesy title equivalent to Mr. or Esq. Used by itself, it conveys deep respect.

Baburam Ghosh: *See* **Premananda, Swami.**

Balaram Basu (1848–1890): A well-known devotee of Ramakrishna who hosted the Master and his devotees many times, and whose home in the Baghbazar section of Calcutta was later used as a residence by monks of the Ramakrishna Order. It is now a branch centre of the Order.

Balarama: Krishna's elder brother.

banalingam: A stone image of Shiva.

Bankabihari: A name of Krishna. The Bankabihari, or Bankubehari, temple in Vrindaban is very famous.

banyan: A sacred tree planted in the Panchavati.

Bauls: Lit., "god-intoxicated devotees." A Vaishnava sect of wandering minstrels.

B.E.: Bengali Era. It was instituted 594 years after the Gregorian calendar was begun. The Bengali new year is mid-April.

bel: A sacred tree, also known as Vilva. Its leaves are used to worship Lord Shiva.

Bhagavad Gita: Lit., "the Song of God." One of the most important scriptures of the Vedanta philosophy, the Bhagavad Gita, or Gita, consists of the teachings of Sri Krishna to Arjuna on how to realize God while carrying on the duties of life. The eighteen chapters of this work are part of the Indian epic, the Mahabharata. It is considered the practical scripture of Vedanta, containing the essence of the Upanishads.

Bhagavan: Lit., "One endowed with the six attributes": infinite treasures, strength, glory, splendour, knowledge, renunciation. An epithet of the godhead; also, Personal God of the devotee.

Bhagavata: A devotional scripture illustrating religious truths through the life story of Sri Krishna and stories of seers, saints, and kings of India. It is sacred to the Vaishnavas who worship Sri Krishna. Its authorship is ascribed to the sage Vyasa.

Bhairava: A form of Shiva, especially one of His eight frightening forms. Also, an aspirant of the Tantric sect.

Bhairavi: A wandering nun or sannyasini of a Tantric sect.

Bhairavi Brahmani: A nun who initiated Ramakrishna into Tantric disciplines. She was the first to declare him an avatar.

bhakta: A spiritual aspirant who follows the path of devotion.

bhakti yoga: The path of devotion.

bhava: Existence; feeling; emotion; idea; ecstasy; samadhi. Also denotes any one of the five attitudes or modes that a dualistic worshipper assumes towards God. *See* **five attitudes**.

bhava samadhi: Spiritual ecstasy in which the devotee retains his or her ego and enjoys communion with the Personal God.

bhavamukha: Exalted state in which aspirant keeps his or her mind on the border between the Absolute and the Relative. From this position one can contemplate the ineffable and attributeless Brahman and also participate in the activities of the relative world, seeing in it the manifestation of God alone.

bhoga: Enjoyment of sense objects.

Bhuh: Earth.

Bhuvah: Ethereal region

Bhuvaneswari Datta (d. July 1911): The mother of Narendranath Datta (later, Swami Vivekananda).

Bodh Gaya: The place in India where Buddha attained enlightenment.

Brahma: The Creator, the first god of the Hindu Trinity, the other two being Vishnu and Shiva.

brahma muhurta: An auspicious period lasting 48 minutes and ending at sunrise.

brahmachari: 1. A religious student devoted to the practice of spiritual disciplines. 2. A celibate belonging to the first stage of life. *See* **four stages of life**.

brahmacharya: 1. Continence in thought, word, and action. 2. Initiation into monastic life. 3. In the traditional Indian culture, the first stage of life is that of a student. *See* **four stages of life**.

Brahman: The Absolute; the Supreme Reality of the Vedanta philosophy. It is described as *Satchidananda*, Existence Absolute, Knowledge Absolute, Bliss Absolute. It is also described as *asti* (It is), *bhati* (It shines), and *priyam* (It is blissful).

Brahmananda, Swami (Rakhal Chandra Ghosh; 1863–1922): The spiritual son of Ramakrishna and one of his sixteen monastic disciples. He served as the first president of the Ramakrishna Order. In the Order, he is referred to as Maharaj. Ramakrishna declared him to be one of six ishwarakotis among his disciples.

Brahmani: *See* **Bhairavi Brahmani**.

brahmarandhra: Aperture in the crown of the head.

Brahma-vari: A liquid form of Brahman. Ramakrishna considered Ganges water to be Brahma-vari.

Brahmayoni: The source of creation.

brahmin: Highest caste in Hindu society.

Brahmo Samaj: A nineteenth-century Indian socio-religious reform movement devoted to the formless Brahman with attributes. This movement was founded by Rammohan Roy (1772–1833) and organized by Devendra Nath Tagore (1817–1905); *see* **Tagore, Maharshi Devendra Nath**. Membership was open to all, irrespective of caste, race, or nationality. In 1857 Keshab Chandra Sen became the third leader of the movement. There was a schism in 1878 resulting in the Indian Brahmo Samaj, led by Keshab, and the Sadharan Brahmo Samaj, led by Vijay Krishna Goswami and Shivanath Shastri. *See* **New Dispensation**.

buddhi: The intellectual function of the inner organ which makes decisions. *See* **antahkarana**.

causal body: The blissful sheath (anandamaya kosha) covering the Atman. *See* **gross body; subtle body; five sheaths**.

chadar: A shawl.

Chaitanya (1485–1533): Regarded by many as a divine incarnation, he popularized repetition of the Lord's name and the path of bhakti, or love of God. He is regarded as an incarnation of Krishna and Radha in one body, manifesting Radha's ideal transcendental love, or madhura bhava. Also referred to as Nimai, Gora, Gaur, Gauranga, and Krishna Chaitanya.

Chaitanya Bhagavata: Biography of Chaitanya written by Vrindaban Das.

Chaitanya Charitamrita: Biography of Chaitanya written by Krishnadas Kaviraj.

Chaitra: Bengali month, mid-March to mid-April.

chakra: A centre of consciousness within the body. Along the central spinal canal (sushumna) are six main chakras. These chakras, and a seventh centre in the cerebrum, are spiritual and parallel certain nerve plexuses. When kundalini awakens and travels upwards, it produces various mystical experiences. The centres are: muladhara (between base of sexual organ and anus); swadhisthana (at base of sexual organ); manipura (at navel), anahata (at heart), vishuddha (at base of throat), ajna (between eyebrows), sahasrara (crown of head). *See* p. 423, footnote 4; **sushumna**.

Chakra: A holy circle formed to perform group rituals.

chamara: A fan used in worship to cool the deity.

chandala: An "untouchable," one who belongs to the lowest rank in Hindu society.

Chandi: A Hindu scripture, part of the Markandeya Purana, in which the Divine Mother is described as the Ultimate Reality.

Chandika: A form of the Divine Mother in Her terrible aspect.

chandni: An open portico. In the Dakshineswar Kali temple complex, the chandni has steps leading to the Ganges, where Ramakrishna used to bathe.

Chandra Haldar: The family priest of Mathur Mohan Biswas. He became jealous of Ramakrishna.

Chandramani Chattopadhyay (Chandra; Chandradevi (1791–1876): The second wife of Kshudiram Chattopadyay; mother of Ramakrishna.

Chattopadhyay: Ramakrishna's family name. *See* by first name: Kshudiram; Chandramani, etc.

Chatu Babu (Asutosh De): The son of Ramdulal De and a wealthy import-export merchant in Calcutta who supported many philanthropic activities.

Chaturmasya: The four months (July to October) of the rainy season in India, when monks generally remain in one place, performing sadhana.

Chiranjiv Sharma (Trailokya Nath Sanyal): A member of the Brahmo Samaj who helped develop the musical tradition of the movement. Ramakrishna was very fond of his singing.

chit: Pure Consciousness; the Atman.

chitta: The mind-stuff of the inner organ. It functions as memory. *See* **antahkarana**.

Chosen Deity, Chosen Ideal: The aspirant's spiritual ideal; a manifestation of God.

Colootola Harisabha: An organization devoted to the worship of Chaitanya at Colootola in Calcutta.

Cook, Reverend Joseph (1838–1901): An American Protestant pastor. On 23 February 1882, while on a lecture tour in India, he met Ramakrishna with a group of Brahmo devotees. In 1893 he spoke at the Parliament of Religions held in Chicago.

Cosmic Consciousness: According to Vedanta philosophy, Hiranyagarbha is the first manifestation of Brahman in creation. He is the Cosmic Mind, the source of all other gods and living beings, and is the very stuff of knowledge.

Cosmic Mind: The indivisible consciousness of Brahman that pervades everything and every being.

Cossipore garden house: Ramakrishna spent his last eight months in this house, 11 December 1885 to 16 August 1886. It was owned by Gopal Chandra Ghosh, a son-in-law of Rani Katyayani. In 1946 the Ramakrishna Order acquired the house.

Dakshineswar: A village, four miles north of Calcutta; the location of the Kali temple complex, where Ramakrishna lived for 30 years (1855–1885).

dama: Restraining the senses from worldly objects.

dāna: Offering gifts to the beloved.

dānā: Shiva's demons.

Dandi Swamis: A sect of sannyasins who always carry a staff.

darshana: Lit., "to see." 1. Spiritual visions. 2. Philosophy.

Darvesha: 1. A Vaishnava sect. 2. A Muslim holy person.

Dashamahavidya: A temple devoted to ten forms of the Divine Mother: Kali, Tara, Shodashi, Bhuvaneswari, Bhairavi, Chinnamasta, Dhumavati, Vagala, Kamala, and Matangi.

dashami: The tenth day of the bright lunar fortnight. *See* **Durga Puja**.

Dasharatha: The father of Ramachandra.

dasya, or **dasya bhava:** Thinking of oneself as the servant of God. God is felt to be one's master. *See* **five attitudes**.

Dayananda Saraswati, Swami: A renowned pandit who founded the Arya Samaj in the Punjab and northwest India.

Dere (Derepur): The ancestral village of Kshudiram.

Deva/devi: A god/a goddess.

Devendra Nath Tagore, Maharshi: *See* **Tagore, Maharshi Devendra Nath.**

Deviloka: The celestial abode of the Divine Mother.

Dhani: A lower-caste village woman of Kamarpukur and a friend of Chandramani who tended her during Ramakrishna's birth. Gadadhar accepted alms from her after his sacred thread ceremony.

Dharma: Formerly one of the Buddhist Trinity. Dharma is worshipped by many names, according to region. *See* **Kurma.**

dharma: Lit., "that which holds together." 1. Righteous conduct. 2. The inmost constitution of a thing. The dharma of a person results from past actions, and determines conduct and sense of right and wrong. Also refers to one of four traditional goals of life in Indian society. *See* **artha; kama; moksha.**

Dharmadas Laha: The village landlord of Kamarpukur; a close friend of Kshudiram.

Dharmapatra: The leaf of impartiality; an Indian village method for ascertaining truth or right action in any matter. *See* p. 191, footnote 9.

dhauti: A hatha yoga cleansing technique. *See also* **neti-dhauti.**

dhoti: A long cloth worn by men to cover the body from the waist down.

dhuni: A sacred fire used by wandering monks, around which one meditates and sleeps.

diksha: *See* **initiation.**

Dipavali: An autumn festival of lights and fireworks held during the new moon. In Bengal it is associated with the worship of Kali and Lakshmi.

Divine Mother: Mother of the Universe and the Shakti (or power) of Brahman. This term refers to God, the cosmic consciousness whose power manifests Itself as the universe, pervades all sentient and insentient beings, and appears as diverse names and forms. The term Divine Mother refers to personal goddesses such as Kali, Durga, and others.

divya bhava (mode): A Tantric form of worship appropriate to a person with a divine nature. *See* **pashu bhava; vira bhava.** *See* p. 266, footnote 5.

divya bhava: An intensified state of the divine mood. One established in divya bhava can give initiation spontaneously and instantly through a mere glance or a touch, or by willing it.

Dol-yatra: The swing festival of Krishna, which is held in spring.

dualism (dvaita): A spiritual attitude in which one considers God to be separate from one's self; the Relative is considered to be real. *See also* **qualified nondualism; nondualism.**

Durga: One of the ten names of the Divine Mother.

Durga Puja: The preliminary ritual and invocation of Durga Puja starts on the sixth day of the bright lunar fortnight in autumn and continues for four days. Saptami puja is the first main worship, held on the seventh day of the bright fortnight. Then come the ashtami, navami, and dashami pujas. Sandhi-puja is a special worship held between the ashtami and navami pujas. *See* p. 240, footnote 3.

Durgacharan Datta: The paternal grandfather of Narendranath Datta (Swami Vivekananda). Though a householder with great wealth, he renounced the world and became a monk following the birth of his son, Vishwanath.

Dvaita: *See* **dualism.**

Dwaraka Biswas: Son of Mathur and Jagadamba Biswas.

ekadashi: The eleventh day after the new or full moon. It is observed by many as a day for fasting, worship, and meditation.

five attitudes: Five ways of relating to God. Shanta bhava, calm or serene attitude: Seeing God in every thing and in every being, one becomes calm. Dasya bhava, servant attitude: One thinks of God as one's master. Vatsalya bhava, affectionate attitude: One thinks of God as one's child. Sakhya bhava, friendly attitude: One thinks of God as one's friend. Madhura bhava, lover's attitude: One thinks of God as one's beloved. In addition, there is apatya bhava, the atttitude of a child: One thinks of God as one's father or mother.

five elements: In order of their evolution from Brahman: akasha, space or ether; vayu, air; agni, fire; ap, water; prithivi, earth. These subtle elements combine to create the gross elements. These five elements constitute all creation. Their properties are: akasha, sound; vayu, touch; agni, visibility; ap, taste; prithivi, fragrance. Each gross element contains its own property plus those of any preceding elements.

five sheaths (koshas): The five sheaths that cover the Atman: annamayakosha, physical sheath; pranamayakosha, vital sheath; manomayakosha, mental sheath; vijnanamayakosha, intellectual sheath; and anandamayakosha, blissful sheath.

five vital forces (pranas): prana, apana, vyana, udana, and samana. Prana manifests as motion, gravitation, magnetism, the vital principle that sustains physical life, thought force, and bodily action. Five modifications of prana are concerned with bodily functions: Prana is that vital force which goes upwards and has its seat at the tip of the nose; apana goes downward below the navel, and has its seat in the organs of excretion; vyana moves in all directions and pervades the body; udana helps the subtle body to leave the gross body at the time of death, and has its seat in the throat; samana assimilates food and drink and has its seat in the middle of the body.

four stages of life: In ancient India, life was divided into four twenty-five year periods: brahmacharya (student); garhasthya (householder); vana-prastha (when one practises spiritual disciplines in seclusion); and sannyasa (renunciation of the world).

Gadadhar: A name of Lord Vishnu, lit., "wielder of the mace." According to Ramakrishna's birth sign, his name was Shambhuchandra. But Ramakrishna's father called him Gadadhar in public in honour of his dream at Gaya about the boy's birth. In Gaya Lord Vishnu is worshipped as Gadadhar.

Gajan: A religious festival dedicated to Shiva.

Ganesha: The elephant-headed god, son of Shiva and Parvati, is chief among the luminous deities.

Gangadhar Gangopadhyay: *See* **Akhandananda, Swami**.

Gangamata: A holy woman devotee whom Ramakrishna met in Nidhuban during his pilgrimage to Vrindaban in 1868.

Gangaprasad Sen, Kaviraj: A prominent Calcutta physician who treated Ramakrishna during his early days at the Dakshineswar temple.

Gangasagar: Confluence of the Ganges and the Bay of Bengal.

garhasthya: Traditionally, the second stage of life, during which one works, marries, raises children, and manages a household. *See* **four stages of life**.

Garuda: A mythical bird, the carrier of Vishnu.

Gaur, or **Gauranga:** *See* **Chaitanya.**

Gauri Pandit (Gaurikanta Tarkabhushan): A Tantric pandit from Indesh who met the Master when he had completed his sadhanas, sometime between 1871 and 1873. He took part in a conference called to assess the authenticity of Ramakrishna's spiritual experiences.

Gaya: Holy city of Lord Vishnu, where Kshudiram received Vishnu's request to be born as his son.

Gayatri: A sacred Vedic mantra recited daily by Hindus of the three upper castes after they have been invested with the sacred thread; also, the presiding deity of the Gayatri.

ghat: A section of a river or a pond that is designated for either bathing or cleansing dishes or clothing, with adjacent steps leading onto the bank.

ghee: Butter clarified through boiling.

Girish Chandra Ghosh (1844–1912): Well-known dramatist and actor in Calcutta, and devotee of Ramakrishna.

Gita: Lit., "song." By itself, Gita refers to the Bhagavad Gita (the Song of God). Some other Gitas are the *Guru Gita*, *Gopi Gita*, *Rama Gita*, and *Uddhava Gita*. *See* **Bhagavad Gita**.

Gokul-vrata: A Vaishnava festival.

Golap-ma (Golap Sundari Devi; c. 1840–1924): A woman devotee of Ramakrishna and close companion of Sri Sarada Devi.

Gopal Chandra Ghosh: *See* **Advaitananda, Swami.**

Gopala: The child Krishna.

Gopal-ma (Aghoremani Devi; c. 1822–1906): A female devotee of Ramakrishna who regarded the child Krishna (Gopala) as her living companion and as God. She saw Gopala in Ramakrishna, whom she first met in the fall of 1884. She lived in a temple garden at Kamarhati. The Master referred to her as the Brahmani of Kamarhati or Bamni.

Gora: *See* **Chaitanya**.

***Gospel of Sri Ramakrishna, The*:** The conversations of Sri Ramakrishna were recorded by Mahendra Nath Gupta and published under the pen name M. They were originally written in Bengali in five volumes under the title *Sri Sri Ramakrishna Kathamrita* and published between 1902 and 1932. Swami Nikhilananda translated the *Kathamrita* into English and chronologically reorganized the various sections for publication in 1942 by the Ramakrishna-Vivekananda Centre (New York) under the title *The Gospel of Sri Ramakrishna*.

goswami: A Vaishnava priest.

Govardhan Hill: A holy place in Vraja that is associated with Krishna.

Govinda: A name of Krishna. The image of Govinda in the Radha-Govinda temple at Dakshineswar was repaired by Ramakrishna.

Govinda Chandra Datta: The wealthy owner of a temple garden in Kamarhati. When he died, his widow managed that temple garden.

Govinda Roy: A Sufi who initiated Ramakrishna into Islamic sadhana in 1866.

gross body: The physical sheath (annamayakosha) covering the Atman. *See* **causal body; subtle body; five sheaths**.

gunas: Lit., "qualities." According to Sankhya philosophy, the three gunas — sattva, rajas, and tamas — constitute prakriti, or nature. Everything in the universe, including both gross and subtle matter, is made up of the three gunas. When the gunas are in balance, no creation takes place. When they are disturbed, creation begins. In the physical world, sattva embodies what is pure and fine; rajas embodies activity; and tamas embodies solidity and resistance. In the human mind, sattva expresses itself as calmness and purity; rajas as activity, passion, and restlessness; tamas as laziness, inertia, and dullness. All beings are made up of the three gunas, with one predominant at various times.

guru: The spiritual teacher who initiates a disciple into spiritual practice. *See* **mantra**.

gutika-siddhi: An occult power that makes one very small.

Haladhari: *See* **Ramtarak Chattopadhyay**.

Hanuman: *See* **Mahavir Hanuman**.

Hari Prasanna Chattopadhyay: *See* **Vijnanananda, Swami**.

Hari-bai: An excess of spiritual energy that may cause pain in the chest area.

Harinath Chattopadhyay: *See* **Turiyananda, Swami.**

Harisabha: Religious congregation of the Vaishnavas where people listen to the reading of scriptures, sing kirtan, and dance.

Harish: A devotee of Ramakrishna.

hatha yoga: Physical exercises and postures, called *asanas*.

Hazra: *See* **Pratap Chandra Hazra**.

Hemangini Mukhopadhyay: The daughter of Ramakrishna's aunt, Ramshila.

heroic mode: A Tantric discipline in which the male aspirant practises sadhana with a female companion until he is established in the divine mood. *See also* vira bhava.

Holy Mother (Sri Sarada Devi; 1853–1920): Spiritual consort of Ramakrishna; she carried on his ministry from 1886 to 1920.

homa: A ceremony, dating from Vedic times, in which oblations are offered into a fire built according to scriptural injunctions. The fire is considered to be the visible manifestation of the deity being worshipped. The homa is a ritual of inner purification, at the end of which the devotee makes a mental offering to the deity of all thoughts, words, actions, and their results.

Hridayram Mukhopadhyay (1840–1899): Third son of Ramakrishna's cousin Hemangini; in Indian terms, a nephew of Ramakrishna; and in Western terms, a cousin. He served Ramakrishna from 1855 to 1881.

hubble-bubble: A water pipe used for smoking tobacco.

Ida: A channel within the spinal column that carries nerve impulses. *See* **sushumna**.

Indra: The king of the Hindu gods.

initiation (diksha): When a guru awakens the disciple's spirituality and imparts spiritual instruction. There are three types of initiation: Shakti initiation, during which the power of the guru is slightly intensified and he or she awakens knowledge in the disciple; Shambhavi initiation, during which the guru is in a highly intense state and the disciple attains knowledge instantly by merely seeing, touching, or saluting the guru; and Mantri or Anavi initiation, which is given by ordinary gurus through ritual and the imparting of a mantra. *See* **divya bhava**.

Inner organ: *See* **antahkarana.**

Ishta: One's Chosen Deity, or spiritual ideal.

Ishwar Chandra Vidyasagar (1820–1891): A great pandit, social reformer, and philanthropist whom Ramakrishna visited in 1882. Mahendra Nath Gupta was a headmaster at one of the boys' schools that he founded in Calcutta.

Ishwara: Saguna Brahman, or the Personal God; creator, preserver, and destroyer of the universe.

ishwarakoti: A godlike, ever-free soul, born with a special spiritual message for humanity. His actions are of benefit to a portion of humanity. Ramakrishna considered six of his disciples to be ishwarakotis: Narendra, Rakhal, Baburam, Jogin, Niranjan, and Purna. *See* **adhikarika purusha;** **avatar.**

iti iti: This, this.

jada: Gross matter.

jada samadhi: The same as nirvikalpa samadhi, from the yogic view.

Jadulal Mallick: A wealthy devotee of Ramakrishna. The Master had a vision of Christ in his garden house, which was adjacent to the Dakshineswar temple.

Jagadamba Das (1823–1881): The fourth and youngest daughter of Rani Rasmani; second wife of Mathur Mohan Biswas.

Jagannath: A name of Vishnu, meaning lord of the universe; the form of Krishna worshipped in the temple at Puri.

Jaina religion: The religion founded by Mahavira, a contemporary of Buddha.

Jaishtha: Bengali month, mid-May to mid-June.

Janaka: King of Mithila in ancient India; a great spiritual aspirant.

Janmashtami: The birth anniversary of Krishna.

japa: The practice of repeating one's spiritual mantra, as instructed by one's guru.

Jatadhari: A Ramait monk who initiated Ramakrishna in a Rama mantra appropriate for seeing God as one's child, and gave him the image of Ramlala, the child Rama. It is likely that he met the Master in 1864.

Jaygopal Sen: A member of the Brahmo Samaj and a devotee of Ramakrishna.

Jayrambati: A village three to four miles from Kamarpukur; the birthplace of Sarada Devi.

Jiva: As a little boy he met Chaitanya, and later became a Vaishnava teacher.

jiva: The embodied soul; a living being.

jivakoti: An ordinary liberated soul who does not return to a gross body to benefit humanity.

jivanmukta: Lit., "liberated-in-life." One who practises spiritual disciplines and is liberated while still living in the body.

Jnana yoga: Path of discrimination and knowledge.

jnana-kanda: 1. Knowledge portion of the Vedas. 2. The Upanishads. 3. Vedanta. *See* **karma-kanda.**

jnani: 1. A knower of Brahman. 2. One who follows the path of discrimination and knowledge.

Jogindra Nath Roy Chaudhury: *See* **Yogananda, Swami.**

Junior Gopal: A devotee of Ramakrishna whom the Master called Hutko.

Junior Naren: Narendranath Mitra, a young disciple of Ramakrishna.

kaivarta: Fisherman caste in Hindu society.

Kali: One of the ten names of the Divine Mother.

Kali Prasad Chandra: *See* Abhedananda, **Swami**.

Kali Puja: Annual worship of the goddess Kali, held in fall.

Kalipada Ghosh (1849–1905): A devotee of Ramakrishna. It was he who enabled the actress Binodini, disguised as a European gentleman, to visit Ramakrishna during his last illness.

Kaliyuga: The present age or cycle, in which people tend towards worldliness and achievement. *See* **yuga**.

Kalki: The last of ten incarnations of God, who, it is said, will come at the end of the Kaliyuga.

Kalna: A village of Bengal on the bank of the Ganges, famous for its 108 Shiva temples.

kalpa-niyamaka ishwara: A classification of prakriti-lina purushas that refers to those sages who were rulers of a cycle. *See also* **ishwarakoti**.

Kalpataru: Mythical wish-fulfilling tree. On Friday afternoon, 1 January 1886, at Cossipore garden house, Ramakrishna became the Kalpataru for many devotees, saying "Be illumined!"

kama: Legitimate desires. Refers to one of four traditional goals of life in Indian society. *See* **artha**; **dharma**; **moksha**.

Kamalakanta: A mystic poet of Bengal, composer of devotional songs mainly addressed to the Divine Mother.

Kamarpukur: A village sixty miles northwest of Calcutta; the birthplace of Ramakrishna.

kamini-kanchana, or **kama-kanchana:** Translated in this book as "lust and gold," which take the mind away from God. They have other connotations: woman and gold, lust and greed, sex and money. The root of the word *kamini* is *kama*, which means "lust" or "desire"; *kanchana* means "gold" or "money."

Kapalikas: A Tantric sect found in Hinduism and Buddhism.

Kapila: The founder of Sankhya philosophy.

karana: 1. Wine. 2. Cause.

karanyasa: Imagining the deity in the palms. In worship, the fingers and back of the hand are used to invoke deities in the forms of letters. *See* **anganyasa** and **nyasa**.

karma: 1. Action. 2. The results of past actions.

karma yoga: Path of unselfish action in which one offers the results of actions to the Lord.

karma-kanda: The portion of the Vedas that describes rituals and Vedic sacrifices and the results of practising them. *See* **jnana-kanda**.

Kartabhaja: An esoteric Vaishnava sect. *Karta* means "master" or "guru"; *bhaja* means "worship." Believing that God has entered the pure mind of the spiritual master, this sect worships the guru as God. *See* **Sahaj**.

Kartika: The son of Shiva and Parvati; younger brother of Ganesha.

Karunamayi Das (1817–1833): The third daughter of Rani Rasmani; first wife of Mathur Mohan Biswas.

Katyayani: The gopis begged this goddess to give them Krishna as their husband.

Katyayani Chattopadhyay: The first daughter of Kshudiram and Chandramani; elder sister of Ramakrishna.

kaupin: A loincloth worn by monks.

kavi: A versifier or composer of songs for competition.

Kenaram Bandyopadhyay: The husband of Ramakrishna's sister Katyayani. His sister married Ramakrishna's brother Ramkumar.

Kenaram Bhattacharya: He initiated Ramakrishna in a Shakti mantra.

Keshab Chandra Sen (1838–1884): The leader of the Brahmo Samaj and a devotee of Ramakrishna. Ramakrishna first visited him in 1875. Influenced by Ramakrishna, he founded *Navavidhan*, the New Dispensation. His writings helped make Ramakrishna known to the Calcutta public. *See* **Brahmo Samaj**; **New Dispensation**.

kirtan: Devotional singing by a group. When the group moves in procession around the street, it is called *nagar-kirtan*. When singing is in procession and accompanied by musical instruments, it is called *sankirtan*.

kosha: Sheath covering the Atman. *See* **five sheaths**.

Krishna: An incarnation of Vishnu or avatar; teacher of Arjuna in the Bhagavad Gita. Krishna is known by many names, including Jagannath, Govinda, and Gopala.

Kshatriya: The warrior caste in Hindu society.

Kshetranath Chattopadhyay: First priest of Radha-Govinda temple at Dakshineswar. He accidentally broke the leg of Krishna's image.

Kshudiram Chattopadhyay (1775–1843): The father of Ramakrishna.

Kumari Das (1811–1837): The second daughter of Rani Rasmani; wife of Pyari Chaudhuri.

kumbhaka: A practice of retaining or holding the breath in order to control the mind.

kundala: A necklace.

kundalini: The spiritual energy lying dormant in all individuals. Located in the tailbone, it is the dwelling place of the accumulated samskaras that force us towards good or bad actions. When this energy awakens in an aspirant and passes through the centres of consciousness in the central spinal canal, it manifests itself in mystic experiences and various degrees of illumination. *See* p. 423, footnote 4; **chakra**.

Kurma: The tortoise, the second of ten incarnations of Vishnu; this deity was formerly Dharma of the Buddhist Trinity.

kuthi: 1. A bungalow. 2. One of the original buildings in the Dakshineswar temple garden, in which Rani Rasmani and Mathur lived with their families. Ramakrishna spent fourteen years in one of its ground floor rooms facing the Ganges. In 1869, when Akshay died, Ramakrishna moved to the northwest corner room of the temple complex, where he lived until the fall of 1885.

Lakshmana: A brother of Rama.

Lakshmi: The goddess of fortune.

Lakshmi Chattopadhyay (1864–1926): The only daughter of Ramakrishna's brother Rameswar. She helped the Holy Mother in serving the Master during his last days.

Latu: *See* **Adbhutananada, Swami**.

leucoderma: A skin disease.

Liberation: Final liberation from karma and the cycle of birth, death, and rebirth through union with God or knowledge of the Ultimate Reality. It is the goal of spiritual practice. Also referred to as moksha or mukti.

lila: 1. Divine play. 2. The relative plane; opposite of nitya, or the Eternal.

loka: Abode or place.

luchi: Thin bread made of flour and fried in butter.

M.: *See* **Mahendra Nath Gupta**.

Madanmohan: A name of Krishna.

madhura, or **madhura bhava:** The attitude in which one thinks of God as one's beloved. *See* p. 512, footnote 3; **five attitudes**.

Mahabharata: Famous Hindu epic consisting of 100,000 verses, including the Bhagavad Gita. Composition is estimated at 5th century B.C. and is attributed to the sage Vyasa, whose purpose was to sing the glory of God. In 18 sections, it illustrates the truths of the Vedas through stories of King Bharata's descendants.

mahabhava: Nineteen spiritual emotions for God combine and manifest in the aspirant as intense love of God. Ramakrishna experienced mahabhava. *See* p. 291, footnote 4; p. 300, footnote 2.

Mahamaya: Lit., "the Great Enchantress."

mahavayu: Life force.

Mahavir Hanuman: A monkey who played a key role in the Ramayana; regarded as the greatest devotee of Rama. He is an exemplar of one having the servant attitude.

Mahendra Nath Gupta (M.; 1854–1932): A householder disciple of Sri Ramakrishna who later recorded the *Kathamrita*, translated as *The Gospel of Sri Ramakrishna*. Ramakrishna sometimes referred to him as "Master" because he was a schoolteacher.

Mahendralal Sarkar, Dr.: *See* **Sarkar, Dr. Mahendralal**.

Mahima Charan Chakrabarty: A spiritual aspirant who visited Ramakrishna and who had a desire for name and fame.

manas: Mind. The function of the inner organ that considers pros and cons. *See* **antahkarana**.

Manikarnika: A famous cremation ghat in Varanasi.

Manikram Chattopadhyay: The father of Kshudiram.

Manimohan Mallick: A member of the Brahmo Samaj and a devotee of Ramakrishna. When his son died, the Master removed his grief with a song. Ramakrishna attended a Brahmo festival at his home.

Manimohan Sen: A devotee who was considered one of the suppliers of Ramakrishna's needs. He was custodian of the Radha-Govinda temple at Panihati.

manipura: The centre of consciousness, or chakra, located at the navel. *See* **kundalini; chakra**.

manomayakosha: The mental sheath, or kosha, covering the Atman. *See* **subtle body; five sheaths**.

Manomohan Mitra (1851–1903): A disciple who met Ramakrishna in 1879. His sister's husband was **Rakhal Chandra Ghosh** (Swami Brahmananda). It was Manomohan who brought Rakhal to the Master.

mantra: A particular name of God, corresponding to an aspirant's Chosen Deity. The mantra is transmitted to a disciple by his or her guru, during initiation. *See* **japa**.

Manu: The author of *Manu Smriti*, an ancient Indian treatise on religious law and social obligation.

Mathur Mohan Biswas (1817–1871): A son-in-law of Rani Rasmani. He married her third daughter, Karunamayi, who died in 1833, then married the Rani's fourth daughter, Jagadamba. Mathur managed the Rani's estate as well as the temple at Dakshineswar. He served Ramakrishna for fourteen years as his foremost supplier of provisions.

Māthura: A cycle of songs expressing pangs of separation felt by gopis when Krishna left Vrindaban.

Max Müller: Oxford University professor and Sanskrit scholar who wrote an article on Ramakrishna entitled "A Real Mahatman," which was published in August 1896. His book *Ramakrishna: His Life and Sayings* was published in 1898. Vivekananda met him in 1896.

maya: 1. Ignorance or avidya. Maya covers Brahman and creates names and forms. It is because of maya that the One appears as many, the Absolute as the relative. 2. Attachment. The two aspects of maya are avidya-maya and vidya-maya.

Michael Madhusudan Datta: A famous Bengali poet and attorney, who practised Christianity.

Mishra, Prabhudayal: *See* **Prabhudayal Mishra**.

moksha: Final liberation from the cycle of birth and death through union with God. It is the highest of the four goals of human life. *See* **artha; dharma; kama**.

Mrinmayi: A goddess whose temple is in Vishnupur.

mukti: *See* **Liberation**.

muladhara: Centre of consciousness, or chakra, located between base of sexual organ and anus. *See* **kundalini; chakra**.

Naga: A sect of monks in India who wear no clothing, to symbolize absolute dependence on God and total renunciation of all worldly things.

nagar-kirtan: Devotional singing in a group, while moving in procession. *See also* **kirtan**.

nahabat: The music tower at Dakshineswar where Ramakrishna's mother and Sri Sarada Devi lived.

Nandotsava: The birthday festival of Krishna arranged by his foster father, Nanda.

Narada Pancharatra: A Vaishnava scripture.

Narayan Shastri: A respected scholar and pandit who became a disciple of Ramakrishna.

Narayana: A name of Vishnu.

Narendranath Datta: *See* **Vivekananda, Swami**.

Narendranath Mitra: *See* **Junior Naren**.

Natavar Goswami: A Vaishnava devotee who hosted Ramakrishna for seven days in his home in Phului-Shyambazar, sometime between 1879 and 1881.

natmandir: An open building located to the south of the Dakshineswar Kali temple that is used for musical festivals, dramas, and discourses. The scriptural debates organized by Mathur in 1861 were held here.

Navadwip: The birthplace of Chaitanya.

navami: The ninth day of the bright lunar fortnight. *See* **Durga Puja**.

Navarasik: A Vaishnava sect.

Navavidhan: *See* **New Dispensation**.

Navya-Nyaya: A new school of logic created in Bengal by pandits.

Nāyikas: Eight companion goddesses of the Divine Mother.

neti, neti: Lit., "not this, not this." The attitude of one who follows the path of knowledge, or jnana.

neti-dhauti: A hatha yoga practice for purifying the physical system. *See* p. 402, footnote 7.

New Dispensation (Navavidhan): The name of the group organized by Keshab Chandra Sen after his disagreement with the members of the Brahmo Samaj. It propagated a new type of outlook based on Ramakrishna's liberal religious views. Keshab considered Ramakrishna to be the embodiment of this New Dispensation and the newly discovered truth: "As many faiths, so many paths."

Nidhuban: A holy place in Vrindaban associated with Krishna.

Nihilist: A school of Buddhism that teaches that the world is void.

Niranjan Ghosh: *See* **Niranjanananda, Swami**.

Niranjanananda, Swami (Niranjan Ghosh; 1862–1904): One of the sixteen monastic disciples of Ramakrishna. He was considered by Ramakrishna to be one of six ishwarakotis among his disciples.

Nirguna: Lit., "without qualities." A term used to describe the Absolute.

Nirguna Brahman: Lit., "Brahman without attributes." A term used to describe the Absolute.

nirvana: Lit., "blowing out," as of a flame. Annihilation of desire, passion, and ego. Liberation, characterized by freedom and bliss.

nirvikalpa samadhi: The highest state of samadhi, in which the aspirant's mind is completely free of thought waves and in which one is completely absorbed in nondual consciousness. In this state there is no awareness of one's body or the world; no awareness of time, space, or causation.

nitya: The Eternal; opposite of lila.

nityamukta: An eternal and ever-free soul.

Nityananda: Lit., "God, the embodiment of eternal bliss." The main disciple of Chaitanya. Also referred to as Nitai.

nondualism (advaita): Complete identification with the Godhead; only the Absolute is considered to be real. *See also* **dualism** and **qualified nondualism**.

nyasa: During worship, the act of touching the different parts of the body with appropriate mantras and mentally identifying them with different parts of the deity being worshipped. *See* p. 352, footnote 5.

Nyaya: A philosophical system dealing with logic.

OM: The most sacred word of the Vedas; also written as *Aum*. A symbol of God, or Brahman. Also called the Nada-Brahman, the Sound-Brahman.

Padmalochan: The chief court pandit of the Maharaja of Burdwan. He was a Vedic pandit who met the Master in 1864 when he had become perfected in Tantra sadhana. He recognized Ramakrishna as an avatar.

Padmamani Das (1806–1878): The eldest daughter of Rani Rasmani; wife of Ramchandra Das.

Panchadasi: A Vedanta treatise of fifteen sections, written by Vidyaranya Muni.

panchamundi: A special seat constructed on or around skulls for the practice of Tantra sadhana. *See* p. 261, section 7 and footnote 2.

Panchavati: A grove made up of five trees: ashwatha, vilva, amalaki, banyan, and ashoka. They are planted according to a certain arrangement. *See* p. 229, footnote 2. The Panchavati at Dakshineswar was replanted by Ramakrishna himself.

pandit: One who is an authority on a particular scripture or ritual; a scholar.

papa-purusha: Evil, pleasure-loving spirit.

parakiya-prema: The Tantric practice of some rituals by a male with a mistress.

paramahamsa: Lit., "a great soul." 1. A monk who belongs to the highest order of sannyasins, a term often applied to Sri Ramakrishna. 2. A monk belonging to a particular sect of the Shankara Order.

Paramatman: The Supreme Atman; the Supreme Self.

para-samvedya: The thoughts and experiences that a person has that manifest to others. *See* **sva-samvedya**.

para-vidya: Ultimate Truth, or higher knowledge. The opposite of apara-vidya.

parinirvana: The cessation of individual existence. Natural end of life of those who realize nirvana in their present conscious existence.

Parvati: A form of the Divine Mother; a manifestation of Divine Energy, or Shakti. In the Puranas, she is the daughter of King Himalaya and the consort of Shiva.

pashu bhava: A Tantric form of worship appropriate to a person with animal or bestial nature. *See* **vira bhava**; **divya bhava**; p. 266, footnote 5.

Paush: Bengali month, mid-December to mid-January.

peepul: A sacred tree; also known as ashwatha.

Phalaharini Kali Puja: A special festival on the night of the new moon, during which Ramakrishna worshipped Sarada Devi as the goddess Shodashi.

Phalgu: A mythical subterranean river.

Phalgun: Bengali month, mid-February to mid-March.

pinda: Rice balls offered to a deity on behalf of departed ancestors.

pingala: A channel within the spinal column that carries nerve impulses. *See* **sushumna**.

Prabhudayal Mishra: A Christian minister who visited Ramakrishna at Shyampukur and who considered the Master to be Jesus Christ.

Prahlada: A famous devotee in the Puranas who remained steadfast in devotion to Vishnu, despite repeated torture and attempts on his life by his father.

Prakriti: Nature personified. The female principle; Purusha is the male principle. *See* **gunas**.

prakriti: Primordial nature. A term used in Sankhya philosphy that means the same as **maya**. It is the power of Brahman, used to create, preserve, and destroy.

prakriti-lina purusha: A free soul who, though capable of attaining full liberation, or nirvana, cherishes an intense desire to benefit humanity, and thereby becomes absorbed in prakriti, primordial nature, and experiences her powers as his. Referred to as adhikarika purusha in Vedanta.

prana: Vital force; breath. *See* **five vital forces**.

pranamayakosha: The vital sheath covering the Atman. *See* **subtle body**; **five sheaths**.

Pranava: The sound of OM heard by the aspirant in deep meditation. This sound combines all individual sounds in the universe; it arises spontaneously and unceasingly everywhere.

pranayama: Control of the breath to aid concentration and control of one's mind.

prarabdha karma: Actions performed in the past that bear results in the present. *See also* **sanchita karma**; **agami karma**.

prasad: Food or drink that has been offered to a deity, taken by devotees afterwards to purify the mind.

Pratap Chandra Hazra (1840–1905): A devotee who lived at the Dakshineswar temple garden and whose main goal was worldly prosperity and who also wanted to be regarded as a holy person.

Prayag: Another name for Allahabad, a holy place famous as the location of the confluence of the Ganges and the Yamuna rivers.

prayopavesana: One lies before the deity and remains there without taking food or drink, with a view to receiving a boon.

prema: Ecstatic, divine love of God, of the most intense kind.

Premananda, Swami: (Baburam Ghosh; 1861–1918): One of Ramakrishna's sixteen monastic disciples. When the Ramakrishna Order was established, he became the manager of the Belur monastery and trained the young monks. Ramakrishna stated that Baburam was one of six ishwarakotis among his disciples.

prithivi: The element earth. *See* **five elements**.

puja: Worship of a god or goddess.

Puranas: Eighteen epics composed by the sage Vyasa that elaborate and popularize religious truths by means of stories about divine incarnations, saints, kings, and devotees, both mythical and historical.

purashcharana: The practice of performing japa a certain number of times a day, then methodically increasing the amount daily, followed by a similar decrease.

purdah: A system of protection in Hindu society in which women were kept out of view of all men, except for family members.

Purna Chandra Ghosh (1871/1872–1913): A young devotee of Ramakrishna, considered by him to be an ishwarakoti.

Purnabhisheka: Full initiation into Tantric rites.

Purusha: According to Sankhya, the male principle; Prakriti is the female principle.

qualified nondualism (vishishtadvaita): The school of Vedanta that considers each being to be a part of God; both Absolute and Relative are considered real. *See also* **dualism**; **nondualism**.

Radha: The chief female confidante of Krishna. She is considered the ideal of true transcendental love.

raga: A musical term; also attachment.

raga bhakti: Spontaneous, supreme devotion that goes beyond all rules. *See* **vaidhi bhakti**.

Raghuvir: Lit., "the hero of Raghu dynasty"; a name of Ramachandra. The family deity of Ramakrishna's household.

raja yoga: The path of concentration and meditation.

rajas: Lit., "activity, desire." One of the three gunas.

Rajchandra Das (1783–1836): The husband of Rani Rasmani.

Rajendralal Datta, Dr.: A respected homeopathic physician who prescribed medicine for Ramakrishna as part of his cancer treatment.

Rajrajeswari: Another name for the goddess Shodashi.

Rakhal Chandra Ghosh: *See* **Brahmananda, Swami.**

Rakhal Chandra Haldar, Dr.: A Calcutta physician called in to treat Ramakrishna during the early stages of his cancer.

Ramachandra, or **Rama:** An incarnation of Vishnu; king of Ayodhya in ancient India; hero of the epic Ramayana. He is considered the ideal embodiment of Truth.

Ramait: A monk of the Vaishnava Order, devoted to Rama.

Ramakrishnananda, Swami (Shashi Bhusan Chakrabarty; 1863–1911): One of the sixteen monastic disciples of Ramakrishna. He established the system of worship in the Ramakrishna Order, and in 1897 he founded Sri Ramakrishna Math in Madras (now Chennai).

Ramananda Roy: The tyrannical landlord of Dere Village who caused Ramakrishna's father to leave his ancestral property and move to Kamarpukur.

Ramayana: The most ancient Sanskrit epic poem, written by the sage Valmiki. It describes the life of Ramachandra in 50,000 verses.

Ramchand Bandyopadhyay: The son of Ramakrishna's aunt, Ramshila; cousin of Ramakrishna.

Ramchandra Datta (1851–1899): A householder devotee of Ramakrishna who first came to the Master in 1879; he was a cousin of Narendranath Datta. A portion of Ramakrishna's ashes was buried at Ramchandra's garden house, Yogodhyan, Calcutta. The house is now a branch centre of the Ramakrishna Order.

Ramchandra Mukhopadhyay: The father of Sarada Devi, Ramakrishna's wife.

Rameswar Chattopadhyay (1826–1873): The second son of Kshudiram and Chandramani. He served as priest of the Radha-Govinda temple at Dakshineswar.

Ramkanai Ghosal: An advanced Shakti aspirant who advised Ramakrishna to wear an amulet of his Chosen Deity to rid himself of burning sensations; the father of Tarak Nath Ghosal (Swami Shivananda).

Ramkumar Chattopadhyay (1805–1856): The first son of Kshudiram and Chandramani.

Ramlal Chattopadhyay (1858–1933). First son of Ramakrishna's elder brother Rameswar; served Ramakrishna and was priest of the Kali temple of Dakshineswar.

Ramlala: The metallic image of child Rama that Jatadhari gave to Ramakrishna.

Rammohan Roy (1772–1833): The founder of the Brahmo Samaj movement.

Ramprasad: A mystic poet of Bengal and composer of devotional songs addressed to the Divine Mother.

Ramtarak Chattopadhyay: Also known as Haladhari. First son of Ramakrishna's uncle Kanairam Chattopadhyay. For one month he served as priest of the Kali temple, after Ramakrishna could no longer perform that service. He then served as priest of the Radha-Govinda temple at Dakshineswar.

rang: The worshipper chants this *rang* mantra while sprinkling water around the seat and imagining that the place is protected by a wall of fire.

Rani: Lit., "a queen."

Rani Rasmani (1793–1861): The wealthy founder of the Kali temple complex at Dakshineswar.

rāsa: The dance of Krishna and the gopis of Vrindaban.

rishi: A seer of truth or sage.

Rudra: A name of Shiva in His destroyer aspect.

rudraksha beads: A rosary of 108 kernels of the berry of the rudraksha tree, used to aid concentration when repeating the Lord's name.

sacred thread: At the time of initiation into the Gayatri mantra one is given a sacred thread to wear, crossed over one shoulder and around the torso.

sadhaka: A term of respect referring to an earnest spiritual aspirant.

sadhana: Spiritual disciplines.

sadhan-kutir: A meditation hut in the Dakshineswar temple garden.

sadhu: A holy person.

Saguna Brahman: Brahman with attributes; Ishwara, or the Personal God.

Sahaj: A spiritual teacher of the Kartabhaja sect who has an innate awareness of God. *Atut Sahaj* refers to a teacher of unbroken chastity who has natural awareness of God. *See* **Kartabhaja**.

sahasrara: Highest centre of consciousness, or chakra, located in the crown of the head. *See* **kundalini**; **chakra**.

sajina: Drumstick plant traditionally considered ordinary. Ramakrishna recognized this plant as sacred.

sakam bhakti: Devotion cultivated with the motive of having desires fulfilled.

Sakhi: A female confidante of Krishna.

sakhya bhava, or **sakhi bhava:** Attitude towards God as friend. *See* **five attitudes**.

samadhi: Ecstasy; communion with God; absorption in the godhead. *See* **bhava samadhi**; **jada samadhi**; **savikalpa samadhi**; **nirvikalpa samadhi**.

samana: Vital force or prana by which food and drink are assimilated. *See* **five vital forces**.

samskaras: Deep impressions made by past thoughts and actions; they are stored in the muladhara, retained in the subtle body, and carried from life to life.

Sanatana Dharma: The eternal religion.

sanchita karma: Actions accumulated in one's past lives. *See* **agami karma**; **prarabdha karma**.

sandhi-puja: A special worship that takes place between ashtami and navami pujas. *See* p. 240, footnote 4.

Sankhya: A philosophy founded by the rishi Kapila.

sankirtan: Devotional singing in a procession, also accompanied by musical instruments. *See also* **kirtan**.

Sannyasa: Renunciation. Traditionally, the fourth stage of life. *See* **four stages of life**.

sannyasin (*feminine* **sannyasini**): A monastic who has been given final vows of renunciation.

saptami: The seventh day of the bright lunar fortnight. *See* **Durga Puja**.

Sarada Mukhopadhyay (Sarada Devi): *See* **Holy Mother**.

Sarada Prasanna Mitra: *See* **Trigunatitananda, Swami**.

Saradananda, Swami (Sharat Chandra Chakrabarty; 1865–1927): One of the sixteen monastic disciples of Ramakrishna; the first General Secretary of the Ramakrishna Order; the author of *Sri Sri Ramakrishna Lilaprasanga*.

Sarkar, Dr. Mahendralal (1833–1904): Well-known physician of Calcutta who treated Ramakrishna during his final year.

Sarvamangala Chattopadhyay: Youngest child of Kshudiram and Chandramani; sister of Ramakrishna.

Satchidananda: Refers to Brahman as Sat (Existence Absolute), chid (Consciousness or Knowledge Absolute), ananda (Bliss Absolute).

sattva: Lit., "luminosity, calmness." One of the three gunas.

savikalpa samadhi: Communion with God in which the distinction between subject and object is retained. Although the aspirant has no awareness of the world in this state, the dualistic realm of ideas remains, and all ideas, attitudes, and emotions relate to one's Chosen Deity. The difference between savikalpa and nirvikalpa samadhi is that awareness of the meditator, meditation, and the object of meditation remains in the former state and not in the latter.

Shaktas: Worshippers of the Divine Mother.

Shakti: The power of Brahman, by which creation, preservation, and destruction take place. Shakti also refers to the feminine principle of this divine power, regarded as the Divine Mother of the Universe.

shalagrama: A natural stone emblem of Vishnu. It is oval and bears certain markings.

Shambhu Charan Mallick (d. 1877): A devotee who read the Bible to Ramakrishna; the second of four suppliers of provisions for the Master.

Shambhuchandra: Ramakrishna's actual birth name, given from his natal sign.

Shankara: Eighth-century exponent of Advaita (nondualism). He founded four monasteries and ten monastic orders in India, and he refuted all the great schools of Indian philosophy to prove Advaita to be the highest truth.

shanta, or **shanta bhava:** The attitude of peace and serenity towards God. Many Vaishnavas do not recognize shanta because it is not characterized by an intense love of God. *See* **five attitudes**.

Sharat Chandra Chakrabarty: *See* **Saradananda, Swami**.

Shashadhar Tarkachudamani, Pandit: A great Hindu evangelist who later became a devotee of Ramakrishna.

Shashi Bhusan Chakrabarty: *See* **Ramakrishnananda, Swami**.

shashthi: The sixth day of the bright lunar fortnight. *See* **Durga Puja.**

Shastra: Scripture.

Shitala: A goddess worshipped in Kshudiram's household.

Shiva: The destroyer, the third god of the Hindu Trinity, the other two being Brahma and Vishnu.

Shivananda, Swami (Taraknath Ghosal; 1854–1934): One of Ramakrishna's sixteen monastic disciples. From 1922 to 1934 he served as the second president of the Ramakrishna Order.

Shivanath Shastri (1847–1919): A preacher of the Sadharan Brahmo Samaj, and a devotee of Ramakrishna. With Vijay Krishna Goswami, he led the Sadharan Brahmo Samaj after a schism developed.

Shiva-ratri: The night of the fourteenth lunar day of the dark fortnight in the month of Phalgun when Shiva is worshipped. Shiva is worshipped every three hours, and fasting and vigil are kept throughout the night.

Shivaram Chattopadhyay: The second son of Ramakrishna's brother Rameswar.

Shodashi: The Divine Mother seen as a pure sixteen-year-old girl. Ramakrishna worshipped Sarada Devi as the goddess Shodashi.

Shrāddha: Obsequial rites for the deceased.

Shraddhā: The spiritual quality of having great faith and belief in a supreme goal.

Shravan: Bengali month, mid-July to mid-August.

shrutidhar: One who has the ability to remember whatever one has heard.

shudra: Labouring caste of Hindu society.

Shukadeva: A great illumined soul; son of Vyasa. The narrator of the Bhagavata.

Shyampukur: A neighbourhood in North Calcutta where Ramakrishna stayed from early September to 11 December 1885 for cancer treatment.

Shyamsundar: A name of Krishna.

siddhi: 1. Spiritual perfection. 2. Occult power. 3. Marijuana.

Sikhism: The religion founded by Guru Nanak (1469–1538).

Simhavahini: The name of a goddess in Jayrambati who is worshipped in order to cure disease.

Sita: The daughter of King Janaka and spiritual consort of Rama. She is considered an ideal model of purity and devotion.

Smriti: The law books, subsidiary to the Vedas, that guide Hindus' daily life and conduct.

Snanayatra: The bathing festival of Jagannath, or Krishna. The Kali temple at Dakshineswar was inaugurated on this day, 31 May 1855.

Subodh Chandra Ghosh: *See* **Subodhananda, Swami**.

Subodhananda, Swami (Subodh Chandra Ghosh; 1867–1932): One of the sixteen monastic disciples of Ramakrishna.

subtle body: The intellectual (vijnanamayakosha), mental (manomayakosha), and vital (pranamayakosha) sheaths covering the Atman. It is made up of 17 limbs: five organs of action, five organs of knowledge, five vital forces, mind, and intellect. The subtle body carries from one body to the next all impressions from actions, perceptions, thoughts, and words. It is destroyed only by Self-knowledge. *See* **gross body; causal body; five sheaths**.

Sukhlal Goswami: A good friend of Kshudiram Chattopadhyay who gave him land in Kamarpukur.

Surendra Nath Mitra (1850–1890): A devotee of Ramakrishna; also called Suresh. Ramakrishna considered him a "half supplier" for his needs. It was at his house that Narendranath Datta first met the Master in November 1881. Surendra also served the direct disciples of Ramakrishna during the first four years of their monastic lives, and he helped them to establish the first Ramakrishna monastery in Baranagore.

sushumna: The hollow canal that runs through the centre of the spinal cord in the human body. Western science calls it the *canal centralis*. It is flanked on the left by the ida and on the right by the pingala, the main channels through which nerve impulses travel to and from the brain. When awakened, kundalini travels upwards through the sushumna passing through the six centres of consciousness and reaching the sahasrara. *See* **kundalini; chakra**.

svagata-bheda: Lit., "the difference in itself." An example is a tree that has different parts within the whole: trunk, branches, leaves, flowers, and fruits.

Svah: Heaven.

sva-samvedya: Those thoughts and spiritual visions that are seen within one's own self, and which are known only by oneself. *See* **para-samvedya**.

swadhisthana: Centre of consciousness, or chakra, located at base of sexual organ. *See* **kundalini; chakra**.

Swaha: The mantra uttered when offering oblations to the gods.

Swami: A title of monks belonging to the Vedanta school.

Swamiji: In the Ramakrishna Order, this term refers specifically to Swami Vivekananda. In India this term is used when addressing male monastics.

Tagore, Maharshi Devendra Nath (1817–1905): A leader of the Adi Brahmo Samaj in the late nineteenth century and father of the great poet Rabindra Nath Tagore.

tamas: Lit., "dullness, lethargy." One of the three gunas.

Tantra: A Hindu scripture.

Tara: One of the ten names of the Divine Mother

Taraknath Ghosal, or **Tarak:** *See* **Shivananda, Swami.**

Tarkalankar: A title given to one who is learned in logic.

tarpana: The offering of oblations to the departed.

Thakur: God; Lord; Master; teacher. A respectful way by which the disciples of Ramakrishna referred to and addressed him.

Third eye: The eye of wisdom, located in the forehead between the eyebrows.

Tirthankaras: Founders of the Jaina religion.

titiksha: Forbearance; fortitude.

tol: A Sanskrit school.

Tota Puri: A monk of the Shankara Order who initiated Ramakrishna into Vedanta in 1864.

Trailokya Biswas: A son of Mathur Mohan Biswas.

Trailokya Nath Sanyal: *See* **Chiranjiv Sharma**.

Trigunatitananda, Swami (Sarada Prasanna Mitra; 1865–1915): One of the sixteen monastic disciples of Ramakrishna; head of the Vedanta Society in San Francisco, California, from 1903–1915.

Tripura-sundari: A name of the Divine Mother.

Tulasidas: A medieval Indian saint and composer of the Ramayana in Hindi.

tulsi: A plant sacred to Vishnu.

Turiyananda, Swami (Harinath Chattopadhyay; 1863–1922): One of the sixteen monastic disciples of Ramakrishna. He established Shanti Ashrama in California and taught Vedanta there from 1899 to 1902.

udana: The vital force or prana by which the subtle body leaves the gross body at the time of death. *See* **five vital forces**.

upa-guru: A subsidiary spiritual teacher, supplementary to the guru who has given initiation.

upanayana: The sacred thread ceremony, during which one receives initiation into the Gayatri mantra and takes vows of purity, truthfulness, and self-control. *See* **sacred thread**.

vaidhi bhakti: Preparatory devotion; certain practices, following prescribed rules, used to cultivate devotion. *See* **raga bhakti**.

Vaidyanath: A name of Shiva. Ramakrishna worshipped in the temple of Lord Vaidyanath at Deoghar, Bihar in 1868.

vairagya: Renunciation; dispassion; detachment.

Vaishakh: Bengali month, mid-April to mid-May.

Vaisheshika: One of the six systems of philosophy in India; it emphasizes rationality.

Vaishnava Tantra: Disciplines connected with the five kinds of relationship with God that one can practise. *See* **five attitudes.**

Vaishnavas: Devotees of Vishnu who focus on His incarnation as Ramachandra, Krishna.

Vaishnavcharan:A Vaishnava pandit of the Kartabhaja sect who first met Ramakrishna in 1858 at the Panihati festival. He first came to Dakshineswar in 1865 and visited Ramakrishna occasionally until 1873. He took part in a conference convened to decide on the authenticity of Ramakrishna's spiritual experiences. He declared Ramakrishna to be an incarnation of God.

Vaishya: The commercial and agricultural caste in Hindu society.

Vajrayana: A school of Buddhism that taught that one must shun physical pleasures in order to enjoy subtle sense pleasures uninterruptedly in the realm of ideas.

Valmiki: The author of the Ramayana.

Vamachara: The left-handed, or unorthodox, path of Tantra.

vana-prasthi, or **vana-prastha:** Lit., "forest dweller." Traditionally, the third stage of life. In this period householders are supposed to retire to secluded areas to practise spiritual disciplines. *See* **four stages of life.**

Varanasi: One of the ancient holy cities of India; the City of Shiva. Ramakrishna went on pilgrimage here in 1868.

vatsalya, or **vatsalya bhava:** The attitude in which one thinks of God as one's child. *See* **five attitudes.**

vayu: The element air. *See* **five elements.**

Vedanta: Lit., "the end of the Vedas." One of the six systems of orthodox Hindu philosophy, based mainly on the teachings of the Upanishads, the Brahma Sutras, and the Bhagavad Gita.

Vedas: The four scriptures of recorded experiences of the sages: Rig, Sama, Yajur, and Atharva. The concluding portion of each Veda consists of various Upanishads.

Vibhishana: A half-brother of Ravana, who tried to persuade Ravana to follow the path of dharma.

vidya shakti: 1. Spiritual power. 2. A woman of godly nature.

vidya-maya: The maya of knowledge; kindness, purity, renunciation and other qualities that lead one to liberation; opposite of **avidya-maya.** *See* **maya.**

Vidyasagar: *See* **Ishwar Chandra Vidyasagar.**

Vidyavagish: A title given to a Sanskrit scholar.

Vijay Krishna Goswami (1841–1899): A leader of the Brahmo Samaj and devotee of Ramakrishna. With Shivanath Shastri, he led the Sadharan Brahmo Samaj after a schism developed in the organization.

vijaya dashami: The final day of Durga worship, when the image of the deity is immersed in a body of water. *See* **Durga Puja.**

vijnanamayakosha: The intellectual sheath covering the Atman. *See* **subtle body; five sheaths.**

Vijnanananda, Swami (Hari Prasanna Chattopadhyay; 1868–1938): One of the sixteen monastic disciples of Ramakrishna. He was an engineer, and he supervised construction of the buildings and temples at Belur Math. He served as the fourth president of the Ramakrishna Order from 1937 to 1938.

vilva: A sacred tree planted in the Panchavati; also known as bel.

vina: A stringed musical instrument.

vira bhava, or **virachara:** A Tantric form of worship appropriate to a person with a heroic nature. *See* **divya bhava**; **pashu bhava**. *See* p. 266, footnote 5.

viraja homa: A special fire ceremony during which monks pour oblations while taking their final vows.

Vishalakshi: Lit., "One with large eyes." Deity of Anur, a village near Kamarpukur.

vishishtadvaita: *See* **qualified nondualism**.

Vishnu: The Preserver; the second god of the Hindu Trinity, the other two being Brahma and Shiva; the Personal God of the Vaishnavas.

vishuddha: Centre of consciousness, or chakra, located at the base of the throat. *See* **kundalini**; **chakra**.

Vishwanath: A name of Shiva; the deity of a temple in Varanasi.

Vishwanath Datta (d. 1884): The father of Narendranath Datta (Swami Vivekananda) and an attorney of the Calcutta High Court.

Vishwanath Upadhyay, Captain: An officer of the Nepalese government and a devotee of the Master. He helped supply materials to build the Holy Mother's cottage near the Dakshineswar temple complex.

Vishweswari Ghosh: Wife of Rakhal Ghosh (Swami Brahmananda) and sister of Manomohan Mitra, a householder disciple of Ramakrishna. Ramakrishna and Sarada Devi considered Rakhal their spiritual son and she their spiritual daughter-in-law.

Vivekachudamani: Lit., "the crest jewel of discrimination." A famous treatise on Vedanta by Shankara.

Vivekananda, Swami (Narendranath Datta; 1863–1902): The chief disciple of Ramakrishna and, later, organizer of the Ramakrishna Order of India. He first carried the message of Vedanta to the West in 1893 and founded the first two Vedanta Societies in the United States. Ramakrishna sometimes referred to Narendra as "Naren." Others sometimes referred to him as Senior Naren. In the Ramakrishna Order he is referred to as Swamiji. Ramakrishna indicated that Narendra was one of six ishwarakotis among his disciples.

Vraja: Vraja is a large area around Mathura where Krishna grew up among the cowherd boys. He was born in Mathura, raised by his foster parents in Gokul, and then spent his boyhood days in Vrindaban. Vrindaban is also called Vraja.

Vrindaban: A famous holy place on the bank of Yamuna, 80 miles from Delhi, associated with boy Krishna and the cowherd boys and girls.

vyana: The vital force by which upward and downward breaths are held together. *See* **five vital forces**.

Vyasa: The great sage who compiled the four Vedas. He also reputedly composed the Mahabharata and the Bhagavata.

Yashoda: The foster mother of Krishna.

yatra: A dramatic performance.

yoga: Union of the individual soul with the Universal Soul; also the method by which this union is achieved. There are many yogas. The main ones are bhakti yoga, jnana yoga, karma yoga, and raja yoga.

Yoga Sutras: Aphorisms on yoga, composed by Patanjali.

Yogamaya: A name of the Divine Mother, Shakti, or divine Power.

Yogananda, Swami (Jogindra Nath Roy Chaudhury; Jogin; 1861–1899): One of the sixteen monastic disciples of Ramakrishna. He was recognized by Ramakrishna as an ishwarakoti.

Yogin-ma (Yogindra Mohini Biswas; 1851-1924): A woman devotee of Ramakrishna, she was a close companion of Sri Sarada Devi and became one of her main attendants after Ramakrishna's passing away.

Yogeswari: *See* **Bhairavi Brahmani**.

yuga: A cosmic cycle or world period. According to Hindu mythology, the duration of the world is divided into four yugas: Satya, Treta, Dwapara, and Kali. In the first, also known as the Golden Age, there is a preponderance of virtue in humanity. With each succeeding yuga virtue diminishes and vice increases. In the Kaliyuga, our current age, there is a minimum of virtue and a great excess of vice.

*   *   *

Ramakrishna's sixteen monastic disciples:

Monastic name	*Given name*
Abhedananda	Kali Prasad Chandra
Adbhutananda	Rakhturam (Latu)
Advaitananda	Gopal Chandra Ghosh
Akhandananda	Gangadhar Gangopadhyay
Brahmananda	Rakhal Chandra Ghosh
Niranjanananda	Niranjan Ghosh
Premananda	Baburam Ghosh
Ramakrishnananda	Shashi Bhusan Chakrabarty
Saradananda	Sharat Chandra Chakrabarty
Shivananda	Taraknath Ghosal
Subodhananda	Subodh Chandra Ghosh
Trigunatitananda	Sarada Prasanna Mitra
Turiyananda	Harinath Chattopadhyay
Vijnanananda	Hari Prasanna Chattopadhyay
Vivekananda	Narendranath Datta
Yogananda	Jogindra Nath Roy Chaudhury

Index

*Rk =Ramakrishna. Page numbers followed by "n" indicate
a footnote. Page numbers for illustrations are in italics.*

Abhedananda, Swami (Kali): at Chariot festival, 692; Shiva-ratri incident, 148–9; vision of Vaikuntha, 435; and Vivekananda, 148–9

actress' (Binodini) blessing by Rk, 901

Adbhutananda, Swami (Latu): *921*; at Cossipore, 451, 929; Rk, service to, 585, 920; at Shyampukur, 880

adhikarika purushas, 412

adhikarikas: avatars, 618; described, 619; ever-free ishwarakotis, 618

Adhyatma Ramayana, 147, 234

Advaitananda, Swami (Brother Gopal): *921*, 923; at Shyampukur, 880; in Vrindaban, 405.

Aghoremani. *See* Gopal-ma

Akshay: birth, 97; to Dakshineswar, 306, 337, 338; genealogy, *196n*; life and death, 337–9, 370; marriage, 338; after mother's death, 134; Radha-Govinda temple, priest of, 306; Ramachandra, devotion to, 337; Ramkumar's son, 179; Rk, grace bestowed by, 927

amalaki tree, 207

annameru-vrata: feeding the needy, 271; Mathur's performance of, 363

Anur, 167

apatya bhava, 285n

Arjuna: divine sight, 392; in Gita, 457; guru, devotion to, 456; vision, fear of, 930

Arya Samaj, 622

"As many faiths, so many paths", Ramakrishna's declaration, 380, 568, 646, 712, 910

Ashoka, 643

ashtami, 240

Ashtavakra Samhita, 147

Atman, 69, 73, 103

Atul: Girish's brother, 897; Rk, grace bestowed by, 927; and Rk's doctor, 925

Avadhuta and gurus, 522

avatar: adhikarikas, 618; advent of, 73; birth, purpose of, 72–3; Buddha, Jesus, Shankara, Chaitanya, 102; described, 70–3; devotion, supreme, 219; disease, subject to, 706; human and divine, 159, 160, 164–5, 167, 484, 719; in Indian scriptures, 72–3; liberation, paths to, 151; as model, 706; omniscience, 166; power of, 509, 521, 587, 654; Prakriti, absorbed in, 617; previous births, memory of, 72; in Puranas, 72–3; renunciation of, 617; Rk as, 255–7, 316–8, 384, 562, 565; Rk embodiment of all, 380; samadhi, 414; sattvic mind, 646; self-control, 162; as spiritual aspirant, 160–72; superhuman actions, 672; teaching, method of, 388; Three friends, story of, 161; true guru, 618; unselfish motive, 617. *See also* incarnation

aversion, 263

avidya-maya, 450

avidya shakti, 809

Balaram Basu: Baghbazar, house in, *689*; 699; Brahmo festival, dating of, 731; Calcutta, arrival in, 894; Calcutta, Rk's host in, 630, 685–92, 867, 869; Chariot festival, host of, 662, 664; at Cossipore, 922; family described, 688; ill health, 894;

Books and Videos on Ramakrishna

Books

Apostles of Ramakrishna, The. Edited and compiled by Swami Gambhirananda. Calcutta: Advaita Ashrama, 1972.

God Lived with Them. Swami Chetanananda. St. Louis: Vedanta Society, 1997.

Gospel of Sri Ramakrishna, The. Original in Bengali by M. (Mahendranath Gupta). Translated and with introduction by Swami Nikhilananda. Foreword by Aldous Huxley. New York: Ramakrishna-Vivekananda Centre, 1942.

History of Ramakrishna Math and Ramakrishna Mission. Swami Gambhirananda. Foreword by Christopher Isherwood. Calcutta: Advaita Ashrama, 3rd edition, 1983.

Life of Ramakrishna, The. Foreword by Mahatma Gandhi. Calcutta: Advaita Ashrama, 13th Reprint, 1995.

Life of Ramakrishna, The. Romain Rolland. Translated from French by E. K. Malcolm-Smith. Calcutta: Advaita Ashrama, 1979.

My Master. Swami Vivekananda. Calcutta: Advaita Ashrama, 1978.

Portrait of Sri Ramakrishna, A. Edited by Amrita M. Salm, Satchidananda Dhar, and Prasun Kumar De. Calcutta: Ramakrishna Mission Institute of Culture, 1998.

Ramakrishna: A Biography in Pictures. Swamis Smaranananda and Chetanananda. Calcutta: Advaita Ashrama, 3rd edition, 1991.

Ramakrishna and His Disciples. Christopher Isherwood. Hollywood, California: Vedanta Press, 1965.

Ramakrishna and His Message. Swami Vivekananda. Calcutta: Advaita Ashrama, 1998.

Ramakrishna and His Mission. Swami Ramakrishnananda. Chennai: Sri Ramakrishna Math.

Ramakrishna and His Unique Message. Swami Ghanananda. Calcutta: Advaita Ashrama, 1987.

Ramakrishna and Spiritual Renaissance. Swami Nirvedananda. Calcutta: Ramakrishna Mission Institute of Culture, 1978.

(over)

(*Books continued*)

Ramakrishna as We Saw Him. Swami Chetanananda. St. Louis: Vedanta Society, 1990.

Ramakrishna: His Life and Sayings. Max Müller. Calcutta: Advaita Ashrama.

Ramakrishna's Dakshineswar. Pravrajika Atmaprana. Dakshineswar: Ramakrishna Sarada Mission, 1986.

Sayings of Sri Ramakrishna. Chennai: Sri Ramakrishna Math, 1960.

Sri Ramakrishna: A Prophet for the New Age. Richard Schiffman. New York: Paragon House, 1989.

Sri Ramakrishna's Life and Message in the Present Age. Swami Satprakashananda. St. Louis: Vedanta Society, 1976.

Tales and Parables of Sri Ramakrishna. Chennai: Sri Ramakrishna Math.

Teachings of Ramakrishna. Calcutta: Advaita Ashrama

They Lived with God. Swami Chetanananda. St. Louis: Vedanta Society, 2nd edition, 2004.

Visions of Ramakrishna. Swami Yogeshananda. Chennai: Sri Ramakrishna Math, 1996.

Words of the Master. Swami Brahmananda. Calcutta: Udbodhan Office.

Videos

Holy Footprints of Sri Ramakrishna, Vol I: Kamarpukur and Hooghly District (*video CD*). Ramakrishna Mission Saradapith, 2002.

Parables of Ramakrishna (*videotape*). Swami Chetanananda. St. Louis: Vedanta Society, 2003.

Ramakrishna: A Documentary (*videotape*). Swami Chetanananda. St. Louis: Vedanta Society, 1990.

World Thinkers on Ramakrishna

"THE STORY OF RAMAKRISHNA'S LIFE is a story of religion in practice. His life enables us to see God face to face. Ramakrishna was a living embodiment of godliness. His sayings are not those of a mere learned man but they are pages from the Book of Life. They are revelations of his own experiences. In this age of scepticism Ramakrishna presents an example of a bright and living faith which gives solace to thousands of men and women who would otherwise have remained without spiritual light."

Mahatma Gandhi, Indian nationalist leader and social reformer

"RELIGION IS NOT JUST A MATTER FOR STUDY; it is something that has to be experienced and to be lived, and this is the field in which Sri Ramakrishna manifested his uniqueness. He practised successively almost every form of Indian religion and philosophy, and he went on to practise Islam and Christianity as well.

"Sri Ramakrishna's testimony to the harmony of religions can make it possible for the human race to grow together into a single family — and, in the Atomic Age, this is the only alternative to destroying ourselves."

Arnold J. Toynbee, English historian

"THE GREATNESS OF THE TEACHING of Ramakrishna lies in the fact that he was able to appreciate and recognize the essential background and unity of all the different faiths and religions."

Sarvapelli Radhakrishnan, Indian philosopher and former President of India

"WHAT RAMAKRISHNA WAS OR WAS NOT the reader must decide for himself; but at least his decision can be based on words and deeds Ramakrishna indubitably spoke and did. I believe, or am at least strongly inclined to believe, that he was what his disciples declared that he was: an incarnation of God upon earth.

"I only ask you approach Ramakrishna with the same open-minded curiosity you might feel about any highly unusual human being: a Julius Caesar, a Catherine of Siena, a Leonardo da Vinci, an Arthur Rimbaud. Dismiss from your mind, as far as you are able, such categories as holy–unholy, sane–insane, wise–foolish, pure–impure, positive–negative, useful–useless. Just say to yourself as you read: this, too, is humanly possible."

Christopher Isherwood, English novelist and author of Ramakrishna and His Disciples

"RAMAKRISHNA PARAMAHAMSA OBVIOUSLY was completely outside the run of average humanity. He appears to be in the tradition of the great rishis of India, who have come from time to time to draw our attention to the higher things of life and of the spirit."

Jawaharlal Nehru, Indian leader and former Prime Minister of India

"I AM BRINGING TO EUROPE, as yet unaware of it, the fruit of a new autumn, a new message of the Soul, the symphony of India, bearing the name of Ramakrishna. The man whose image I here evoke was the consummation of two thousand years of the spiritual life of three hundred million people.

"He was no hero of action like Gandhi, no genius in art or thought like Goethe or Tagore. But his inner life embraced the whole multiplicity of men and gods."

> **Romain Rolland**, *French writer, winner of the Nobel prize (1915),*
> *and author of* The Life of Ramakrishna

"GREAT SOULS, LIKE RAMAKRISHNA, have a comprehensive vision of Truth."

> **Rabindra Nath Tagore**, *Indian poet, winner of the Nobel prize*
> *(1913)*

"WONDERFUL SAYINGS! Ramakrishna . . . a remarkable sage."

> **Leo Tolstoy**, *Russian novelist and social reformer*

"THIS ENORMOUSLY DETAILED ACCOUNT of the daily life and conversations of Sri Ramakrishna produced a book [*The Gospel of Sri Ramakrishna*] unique in the literature of hagiography."

> **Aldous Huxley**, *English novelist and essayist*

"RAMAKRISHNA PARAMAHAMSA WAS NOT ONLY a high–souled man, a real Mahatman, but a man of original thought. He was certainly thoroughly imbued with the spirit of Vedanta philosophy. His utterances which have been published breathe the spirit of that philosophy: 'As a lamp does not burn without oil, so a man cannot live without God.' 'God is in all men, but all men are not in God: that is the reason why they suffer.'

"From such sayings we learn that though the real presence of the Divine in nature and in the human soul was nowhere felt so strongly and so universally as in India, and though the fervent love of God, nay the sense of complete absorption in the Godhead, has nowhere found a stronger and more eloquent expression than in the utterances of Ramakrishna, yet he perfectly knew the barriers that separate divine and human nature.

"He was a wonderful mixture of God and man."

> **Max Müller**, *German Orientalist and author of* Ramakrishna:
> His Life and Sayings

"WHAT WAS RAMAKRISHNA? God manifest in a human being; but behind there is God in His infinite impersonality and His universal Personality. In him the spiritual experiences of the millions of saints who had gone before were renewed and united."

> **Sri Aurobindo**, *Indian religious leader and writer*